SOUTH

LOUISIANA

RECORDS

CHURCH AND CIVIL RECORDS OF LAFOURCHE — TERREBONNE PARISHES

VOLUME 10

(1896-1899)

Reprinted and for sale by
CLAITOR S PUBLISHING DIVISION
3165 S. Acadian at I-10, P.O. Box 261333
Baton Rouge, LA 70826-1333
Tel: 800-274-1403 (In LA 225-344-0476)
Fax: 225-344-0480
Internet address:
e mail: claitors@claitors.com
World Wide Web: http://www.claitors.com

SOUTH

LOUISIANA

RECORDS

CHURCH AND CIVIL RECORDS OF LAFOURCHE — TERREBONNE PARISHES

VOLUME 10

(1896-1899)

by

Rev. Donald J. Hebert

HEBERT PUBLICATIONS

Exclusive distributing agent:

CLAITOR'S PUBLISHING DIVISION
3165 S. Acadian at I-10, P.O. Box 3333
Baton Rouge, LA 70821

Reprinted 2008

Library of Congress Card Number 78-52481

PRINTED IN USA

(art by Jan Lewis)

Reprinted and for sale by
CLAITOR S PUBLISHING DIVISION
3165 S. Acadian at I-10, P.O. Box 261333
Baton Rouge, LA 70826-1333
Tel: 800-274-1403 (In LA 225-344-0476)
Fax: 225-344-0480
Internet address:
e mail: claitors@claitors.com
World Wide Web: http://www.claitors.com

CONTENTS

ABBREVIATIONS

account	Statements of debts, credits, or monetary transaction.
affranchi	freedman
affranchie	freedwoman
Articles of Agreement	Arrangement between two or more parties, similar to a treaty or contract.
Assemblies	Persons meeting together for a common purpose.
Assemblies of Minors	Gathering of children under 21 years of age, usually for appointment of tutors, etc.
b.	born
bt.	baptized
BRDA	Baton Rouge Diocesan Archives. (Refers to those church records belonging to Catholic Churches in the Baton Rouge Diocese. In 1962 work was begun to collect all parish records prior to 1870. These are housed at the Diocesan Archives; P. O. Box 2028; Baton Rouge, Louisiana 70821.
ca.	circa (About; approximately)
Ch.	Church (Refers to a record found in a Church archive.)
c.l.	couleur libre or free color
Ct.Hse.	Courthouse. (Refers to any record located in a civil courthouse archive.)
Chacahoula Ch.	St. Lawrence Catholic Church; P. O. Box 229; Gibson, Louisiana 70356. These records also include the St. Patrick Catholic Church records of Gibson, La. The Chacahoula records begin in 1858; the Gibson records begin in 1887.
Chackbay Ch.	Our Lady of Prompt Succor Catholic Church; Rt. 3, Box 625; Thibodaux, Louisiana 70301. These records begin in 1892.

d.	died (Usually refers to the date of burial and not necessarily to the date of death. Whenever it precedes a person's name it then indicates that the person is deceased.
Diocese of Houma-Thibodaux	1220 Aycock Street; P. O. Box 9077; Houma, Louisiana 70360.
Donation	Donations. The Book of Donations lists donations of slaves, land or property. This book sometimes includes marriage contracts.
esc.	esclave or slave
Estimation of Property	Approximate opinion of size, value, etc. of property; sometimes interchanged with Inventory.
Family meeting	Assembly of family members for the purpose of deciding tutorship, emancipations, etc.
f.d.c.l.	femme de couleur libre or free woman of color.
fdm	freedman
fdw	freedwoman
f.p.o.c.	free people of color
f.m.o.c.	free man of color
f.w.o.c.	free woman of color
g.d.c.l.	gens de couleur libre or free people of color
Gibson Ch.: Epis.Ch.:	St. Anne's Mission Episcopal Church. This church is served by the Pastor of St. Mathew's Episcopal Church; 243 Barrow Street; Houma, Louisiana 70360. These records begin in 1880 and are in the custody of Mr. Stanley Walther; P. O. Box 35; Gibson, La. 70357.
h.d.c.l.	homme de couleur libre or free man of color

ABBREVIATIONS

Houma Ch.	St. Francis de Sales Cathedral; P. O. Box 4014; Houma, Louisiana 70361. These records begin in 1848.
Houma Ch.: Epis.Ch.:	St. Matthew's Episcopal Church; 243 Barrow Street; Houma, La. 70360. These records begin in 1860.
Houma Ch.: First Presbyt.:	The Presbyterian Church; 414 Barrow Street; Houma, Louisiana 70360. It was founded in 1848; the records begin in 1861.
Houma Ct.Hse.	Terrebonne Parish Courthouse; Clerk of Court; P. O. Box 1569; Houma, La. 70361. Its records of Marriages (1814) and Successions (1807) are included in this volume
Houma Ct.Hse.: OA:	The Original Acts of Terrebonne Parish included here are taken from Volume 1 and 2 only. They cover the years 1809 - 1839.
Hypotheque	An old legal term for mortgage - property pledged remain in possession of debtor.
Inventory	Detailed listing of all goods or stock, and the values and descriptions of these, of a deceased person.
Inventory & Estimations	Same as an estimation.
Inventory of Property	Listing of value and description of property - land or items.
joined	Date a person joined or entered a church congregation.
Judgment	Final order or decision of a court or law- the document drawn up as the record of the order is also called a Judgment.
LSU Archives	Louisiana State University; Library Archives; Baton Rouge, Louisiana 70803. These archives house several documents and papers from various parishes. The Confederate Soldier Death Record from 1862 - 1865 are found here.

ABBREVIATIONS

Lafourche Interior	In 1807, the Parish of Lafourche was established - being divided as follows: the settlement nearest the River shall be Assumption Parish with one half of the population -- the other settlements in the lower part of LaFourche shall be called the Interior Parish; thus the term of LaFourche Interior or LaFourche Internal. In 1853, the designation "Interior" was dropped and it was henceforth known as Lafourche Parish.
Larose Ch.	Our Lady of the Rosary Catholic Church; P.O. Drawer 10; Larose, La. 70373. These records begin in 1873.
Lockport Ch.	Holy Savior Catholic Church; 612 Main Street; Lockport, Louisiana 70374. These records begin in 1850. Volume 1 of Baptisms is in extremely bad condition - many records are lost due to the deterioration of this volume.
m.	married (Indicates a marriage, marriage bond, or a license issued in order to get married.)
m.(1); m.(2)	marriage (Referring to a first or second marriage.)
Mainlevee	Literally - "lifted hand" - a cancellation of mortgage or other debt.
Mainlevee & Hypotheque	Cancellation and mortgage.
Mainlevee & Quittance	These mean the same - Release from debt obligation.
Mar.	Marriage (Usually used in reference to a Civil Marriage document ordinarily found in a courthouse Archive.)
MC Ch.	Sacred Heart Catholic Church; P. O. Box 632; Morgan City, Louisiana 70380. These records begin in 1861. None of the Morgan City records are included in this series. They are found in my SOUTHWEST LOUISIANA RECORDS since Morgan City is in St. Mary Parish.
Montegut Ch.	Sacred Heart Catholic Church; P. O. Box 2; Montegut, Louisiana 70377. These records begin in 1865.
Mortgage	A temporary or conditional transfer of property pledged as security for repayment of a loan.

ABBREVIATIONS

mths.	months
mul. lib.	mulatre libre or free mulatoe
neg. esc.	negre esclave or negre slave
neg. lib.	negre libre or free negro
Note Cancellation	Rendering a debt void.
OA	Original Acts (Refers to those Original Acts found in Civil Courthouse records. Sometimes marriages can be found there.)
p.	page
Petition for Family Meeting:	Application requesting a gathering of the family members to decide matters concerning them and their property.
Petition for Inventory:	A formal, written application requesting that goods or property be itemized and valued.
Petition for Tutelage And Inventory:	Application containing a request that goods or property be itemized and valued as well as a request that an adult be appointed as tutor to any minor child.
Petition for Tutorship:	A formal written application requesting that an adult be appointed as tutor to a minor child.
p.o.c.	people of color
Power	Legal permission to act.
Probate Sale	Sale through the Court - a probate court has the jurisdiction to settle accounts of estates.
Procuration	Power of attorney; a "proxy" function of an attorney - acting for someone else.
Public Auction	A sale. The price is determined by highest bidder.
Public Sale	A sale. The price is determined by highest bidder.

quart. lib.	quarteroon libre or free quarteroon
Quittance	Cancellation of a debt.
Raceland Ch.	St. Mary's Nativity Catholic Church; Rt. 2, Box 451; Raceland, Louisiana 70394. These records begin in 1850.
Receipt	Written acknowledgment of payment or delivery.
Release	Relinguishing of interest; surrendering interest in land or other property - one part usually releases interest to another.
Renunciation	Act of giving up by formal declaration; abandon.
Request for Partition of Property:	Formal, written application requesting that property held in joint ownership be divided.
Sale of Property	Sale of any kind of property at public sale or auction.
Sale of Slaves	Slaves sold as property at public sale or auction.
Succ.	Succession. (Refers to a record of Succession. It may sometimes refer to a probate record, a will, or an estate record.)
Theriot Ch.	St. Eloi Chatolic Church; Theriot, Louisiana 70397. These records begin in 1875.
Thib. Ch.	St. Joseph's Co-Cathedral Church; P. O. Box 966; Thibodaux, Louisiana 70301. These records begin in 1803; although the records begin with more regularity in 1820.
Thib. Ch.: Epis. Ch.:	St. John's Episcopal Church; P. O. Box 751; Thibodaux, Louisiana 70301. These Church records begin in 1845, the year of the Church's foundation.
Thib. Ch.: First Meth.:	First United Methodist Church; P. O. Box 1201; Thibodaux, Louisiana 70301. The Church was founded in about 1836. The Records begin in 1842.

ABBREVIATIONS

Thib. Ch.: First Presbyt. Ch.:	The Presbyterian Church; 522 Green Street; Thibodaux, Louisiana 70301. This Church was organized on 6 June 1847. The records begin in 1856.
Thib. Ct. Hse.	Lafourche Parish Courthouse located in Thibodaux, La. 70301. Its records of Marriages and Successions are found in this volume. The marriages begin in 1803 and the Successions in 1794. (Only one entry dates to 1765.) The earliest Successions here have no assigned number. So the year is given instead of an identifaction number.
Tutelage	Guardianship; care of a minor or anyone under age 21.
v.	volume
ve.	veuve or widow
veuf	widower
veuve	widow
Voluntary Inventory:	An inventory made by a living person of his goods - usually of a business; to settle accounts with partners.
Voluntary Sale & Auction of Possessions:	Sale by a living person of his own property.
wid.	widow
widr.	widower
Will Probated:	Legal proof of authenticity of a will or testament.
yr.	year
#	number
-----	Indicates that the spelling was uncertain or that a word was illegible or missing.

A

--------, Brigitte (Thubal & Brigitte FYGHT) b. 29 June 1898 (Lockport Ch.: v.2, p.281)

ABADIE (Sometimes: LABADIE)

ABADIE, Jean Baptiste Edouard (Edouard & Bella CHAMPAGNE) b. 13 Oct. 1896 (Lockport Ch.: v.3, #8)

ABADIE, Jean Baptiste Edouard (Edouard & Bella CHAMPAGNE) b. 13 Oct. 1896 (Lockport Ch.: v.3-A, #8)

ABBENE, Philippa (Miguele & Angella CACCIOPPA) b. 19 June 1897 (Thib. Ch.: v.7, p.452)

ABENE, Catherina (Gasbard & Antonia CEROTA) b. 29 March 1896 (Houma Ch.: v.5, p.147)

ABOUT, Amedee A. m. 10 Feb. 1896 Venolia WOODS (Houma Ct. Hse.: Mar. v.28, #441)

ABOUT, Amedee A. (Leon & Aline GESMAR) m. 17 Feb. 1896 Velonlia WOODS (Houma Ch.: v.6-a, p.171)

ABOUT, Leonard d. 18 Feb. 1898 at age 10 mths. (Houma Ch.: v.3, p.16)

ABOUT, Marie Leonore (Amedee & Vennola WOOD) b. 13 April 1896 (Houma Ch.: v.5, p.179)

ABRAHAM, John Michel (Cacia & Angelle CICONET) b. 29 Sept. 1898 (Houma Ch.: v.5, p.218)

ABRAHAM, Mary m. 16 March 1898 Elizah COLWELL (Houma Ct. Hse.: Mar. v.30 & 31, #336)

ABRIBAT (Sometimes: ABRILOT, ALIRIBAT)

ABRIBAT, Mathilde m. 21 Dec. 1898 Richard WILLIAM (Larose Ch.: v.3, p.11)

ABRIBAT, Mathilde widow of Theophile DUCOS m. 29 Oct. 1898 Richard WILLIAM (Thib. Ct. Hse.: Mar. v.38, #293)

ACHE (See: HACHE)

ACOST (Sometimes: ACOSTA, ACOSTE)

ACOST, Albert Callixte (Julien & Dorothee DEFELICE) b. 14 Oct. 1897 (Larose Ch.: v.3, p.13)

ACOST, Clotilde (Julien & Melina BERNARD) m. 21 Sept. 1899 Camille BADEAUX (Larose Ch.: v.4, p.124)

ACOST, Clotilde (Julien & Melina BERNARD) m. 21 Sept. 1899 Camille BADEAUX (Thib. Ct. Hse.: Mar. v.39, #233)

ACOST, Clotille (Julien & Melina BERNARD) m. 21 Sept. 1899 Camille BADEAUX (Larose Ch.: v.3, p.12)

ACOST, Guillare Julien (Julien & Mary FOLDE) b. 12 July 1897 (Thib. Ch.: v.7, p.458)

ACOST, Marie Anita (Andre & Melia ALEMAN) b. 17 Feb. 1899 (Larose Ch.: v.3, p.36)

ACOST, Marie Lina (Maximillian & Melia GONSALES) b. 2 April 1896 (Larose Ch.: v.2, p.188)
ACOST, Marie Nida (Joseph & Ayma GAUTREAUX) b. 10 May 1896 (Lockport Ch.: v.2, p.329)
ACOST, Mathilda m. 9 Jan. 1896 Joseph HEBERT (Larose Ch.: v.4, p.76)
ACOST, Mathilda m. 9 Jan. 1896 Joseph HEBERT (Larose Ch.: v.3, p.2)
ACOST, Mathilde m. 2 Jan. 1896 Joseph HEBERT (Thib. Ct. Hse.: Mar. v.35, #4)
ACOST, Mathilde (Julien & Melina BERNARD) m. 9 Jan. 1896 Joseph HEBERT (Larose Ch.: v.2, p.185)
ACOST, Narcisse Mathurin (Michel & Melia GONSALES) b. 9 Nov. 1897 (Larose Ch.: v.3, p.5)
ACOST, Unece Sole (Mac & Emilia COZALES) b. 6 Dec. 1899 (Larose Ch.: v.3, p.49)
ACOST, William Davis (Andre & Amelia ALEMAN) b. 10 Jan. 1897 (Larose Ch.: v.3, p.5)

ADAM (Sometimes: ADAMS)

ADAM, Adelard d. 30 Oct. 1898 at age 60 yrs. (Thib. Ch.: v.3, p.221)
ADAM, Aglae m. Onesime MOLAISON d. 15 July 1896 at age 52 yrs. (Thib. Ch.: v.3, p.184)
ADAM, Albert (Evariste & d.Marie RODRIGUE) m. 26 June 1899 Lea RODRIGUE (Chackbay Ch.: v.1, p.71)
ADAM, Albert (Evariste & Mary RODRIGUE) m. 26 June 1899 Lea RODRIGUE (Thib. Ct. Hse.: Mar. v.39, #179)
ADAM, Albert (Joseph & Manelite HEBERT) m. 21 Jan. 1897 Aimee BOYER (Thib. Ch.: v.14, p.113)
ADAM, Albert (Joseph & Marcelite HEBERT) m. 21 Jan. 1897 Aimee BOYER (Thib. Ct. Hse.: Mar. v.36, #1)
ADAM, Alceste (Theodule & Aymee GROS) m. 6 Feb. 1897 Emelie HOTARD (Thib. Ct. Hse.: Mar. v.36, #45)
ADAM, Alceste (Theodule & Aymee GROS) m. 6 Feb. 1897 Emelie HOTARD (Lockport Ch.: v.2, p.159)
ADAM, Alfrida m. Elphege MARTIN d. 13 Oct. 1897 at age 33 yrs. (Lockport Ch.: v.1, #20)
ADAM, Alice (Azeme & Oceana DAIGLE) m. 18 Sept. 1899 George HEBERT (Thib. Ch.: v.14, p.296)
ADAM, Alice (Ozeme & Ociana DAIGLE) m. 18 Sept. 1899 George HEBERT (Thib. Ct. Hse.: Mar. v.39, #217)
ADAM, Alidia d. 18 July 1897 at age 3 yrs. (Thib. Ch.: v.3, p.203)
ADAM, Aline (Joseph & Octavie ONCALE) b. 22 Aug. 1897 (Chackbay Ch.: v.1, p.93)
ADAM, Alphonse (Aubin & Elvire CHIASSON) b. 7 Oct. 1896 (Larose Ch.: v.2, p.183)
ADAM, Amelia m. 11 Jan. 1896 Joseph BOUVIER (Larose Ch.: v.4, p.70)

ADAM, Amelia m. 11 Jan. 1896 Joseph BOUVIER (Larose Ch.: v.3, p.2)

ADAM, Amelia m.2 Jan. 1896 Joseph BOUVIER (Thib. Ct. Hse.: Mar. v.35, #6)

ADAM, Amelia (Volcar & Clemence SAVOIE) m. 11 Jan. 1896 Joseph BOUVIER (Larose Ch.: v.2, p.186)

ADAM, Antoine Edward (Edgard & Adolphine VALENS) b. 5 Dec. 1897 (Larose Ch.: v.3, p.26)

ADAM, Armand (Medius & Camila LEBLANC) b. 18 March 1896; m. Jeanne Marcelle LEDET on 5 Sept. 1911. (Houma Ch.: Bapt. Bk., v.5, p.151)

ADAM, Armelize (Joseph & Adolfine GROS) m. 20 July 1896 Leonce CLEMENT (Thib. Ct. Hse.: Mar. v.36, #123)

ADAM, Armelize (Joseph & Adolphine GROS) m. 20 July 1896 Leonce CLEMENT (Chackbay Ch.: v.1, p.28)

ADAM, Arthur Charles (Mathurin & Josephine ADAM) b. 21 Sept. 1897 (Thib. Ch.: v.7, p.518)

ADAM, Bernadette (Marcellin & Eve BLANCHARD) m. 23? June 1898 Louis CANTRELLE (Lockport Ch.: v.2, p.190 & 191)

ADAM, Bernadette (Marcellin & Eve BLANCHARD) m. 23 June 1898 Louis CANTRELLE (Thib. Ct. Hse.: Mar. v.38, #205)

ADAM, Bertha Lucinda (Joseph & Mary June DEHART) m. 15 June 1896 Walker LOVELL (Houma Ct. Hse.: Mar. v.29 & 30, #89)

ADAM, Brigitte (Albert & Anne BOYER) b. 5 Dec. 1897 (Thib. Ch.: v.7, p.478)

ADAM, Camilla Lucie (Herman & Hermina A. ADAM) b. 13 Feb. 1899 (Larose Ch.: v.3, p.43)

ADAM, Camille (Alexandre & Zulema BOURGEOIS) b. 31 Aug. 1896 (Thib. Ch.: v.7, p.417)

ADAM, Denesse d. 23 June 1897 at age 15 yrs. (Thib. Ch.: v.3, p.201)

ADAM, Dora (Marcellin & Eve BLANCHARD) m. 25 June 1898 Fielden PIERCE (Thib. Ct. Hse.: Mar. v.38, #212)

ADAM, Dora (Marcellin & Eve BLANCHARD) m. 25 June 1898 Fielden PIERCE (Lockport Ch.: v.2, p.191)

ADAM, Edee Joseph (Onezippe & Zulma LEBLANC) b. 24 Feb. 1898 (Chacahoula Ch.: v.4, p.3)

ADAM, Edgard d. 18 Jan. 1896 at age 33 yrs. (Lockport Ch.: v.1, #1)

ADAM, Edna (Edmond & Amanda GUILLOT) b. 2 June 1898 (Thib. Ch.: v.7, p.504)

ADAM, Edna Marie (Onezippe & Zulma LEBLANC) b. 12 May 1899; m. Walter Nicholas THAYER on 16 Jan. 1952. (Chacahoula Ch.: Bapt. Bk., v.4, p.26)

ADAM, Elias (Joachim & Augustine CANTRELLE) m. 27 Jan. 1898 Elodia PIERCE (Lockport Ch.: v.2, p.180)

ADAM, Elias (Joachim & Augustine CANTRELLE) m. 27 Jan. 1898 Elodia PIERCE (Thib. Ct. Hse.: Mar. v.37, #31)

ADAM, Emery Francois (Alfred & Henriette FAUCHEUX) b. 21 March 1896 (Lockpaort Ch.: v.2, p.326)

ADAM, Ernest d. 3 March 1897 at age 57 yrs. (Thib. Ch.: v.3, p.198)

ADAM, Ernest (Francois & Adeline AUCOIN) m. 10 Nov. 1896 Alexina HOTARD (Lockport Ch.: v.2, p.155 & 156)

ADAM, Ernest (Francois & Adeline AUCOIN) m. 16 Nov. 1896 Alexina HOTARD (Thib. Ct. Hse.: Mar. v.36, #160)

ADAM, Eugene Theos (Adolphe & Armande DUET) b. 22 Dec. 1899 (Larose Ch.: v.3, p.61)

ADAM, Evariste Edde (Olsindore & Angela GUILLOT) b. 8 Oct. 1898 (Thib. Ch.: v.7, p.577)

ADAM, Eve (Theophile & Josephine RODRIGUE) m. 18 April 1898 Clemile BENOIT (Chackbay Ch.: v.1, p.60)

ADAM, Eve (Theophile & Josephine RODRIGUE) m. 18 April 1898 Clemile BENOIT (Thib. Ct. Hse.: Mar. v.37, #141)

ADAM, Felicien (Joseph & Adolphine GRAUS) m. 9 Oct. 1899 Alida TROSCLAIR (Thib. Ct. Hse.: Mar. v.39, #238)

ADAM, Felicien (Joseph & Adolphine GROS) m. 9 Oct. 1899 Alida TROSCLAIR (Chackbay Ch.: v.1, p.74)

ADAM, Felicien Rosemond (Taylor & Felicie BERGERON) b. 26 July 1899 (Larose Ch.: v.3, p.43)

ADAM, Hallen Joseph (Bitha & Clara WAULKER) b. 24 Jan. 1896 (Larose Ch.: v.2, p.180)

ADAM, Harris Arsene (Fabre & Louise CHICHIZOLA) b. 29 Dec. 1899 (Larose Ch.: v.3, p.58)

ADAM, Hector (Eugene & Felicia ROBICHAUX) b 5 April 1899; m. Marie Elisabeth LEDET on 2 Feb. 1925. (Raceland Ch.: Bapt. Bk., v.5, p.95)

ADAM, Henriette Julia (Joachim & Adelma ORDOGNE) b. 17 March 1899 (Thib. Ch.: v.7, p.604)

ADAM, Ida m. 20 Feb. 1897 Thomas SANTEE (Houma Ct. Hse.: Mar. v.29 & 30, #327)

ADAM, Inez Margarite (Andrew & Ida EGLE) b. 1 March 1898 (Chacahoula Ch.: Gibson Ch.: v.2, p.120)

ADAM, Inez Marguerite (Andre & Ida EGLE) b. 1 March 1898 (Chacahoula Ch.: Gibson Record: Mar. Bk., v.1, #30)

ADAM, Jean (Jean & Marie TAUZIN) m. 25 Sept. 1899 Zoe BENOIT (Thib. Ch.: v.14, p.297)

ADAM, Jean (Jean & Marie TAUZIN) m. 25 Sept. 1899 Zoe BENOIT (Thib. Ct. Hse.: Mar. v.39, #229)

ADAM, Jean Ernest (Edgard & Dorsina ORGERON) b. 15 March 1898 (Larose Ch.: v.3, p.17)

ADAM, Jean Felix (Volcar & Clemence SAVOIE) b. 30 May 1897 (Larose Ch.: v.3, p.5)

ADAM, Jewel Andre (Abel & Aurelia ESTEVE) b. 18 June 1897 (Thib. Ch.: v.7, p.507)

ADAM, Joseph Harry (Alexandre & Zulema BOURGEOIS) b. 17 Nov. 1898 (Thib. Ch.: v.7, p.531)

ADAM, Joseph Henri (Theophile & Valerie TROSCLAIR) b. 9 March 1898 (Chackbay Ch.: v.1, p.108)

ADAM, Joseph Mary (Valcours & Eucy STEPHEN) b. 7 Feb. 1897 (Houma Ch.: v.5, p.201)

ADAM, Joseph Wilson d. 31 May 1899 at age 10 mths. (Thib. Ch.: v.3, p.234)
ADAM, Joseph Wilson (Joacin & Adeline ORDOGNE) b. 27 Aug. 1898 (Thib. Ch.: v.7, p.534)
ADAM, Jules (Adolphe & Armance DUAY) b. 12 Dec. 1897 (Larose Ch.: v.3, p.32)
ADAM, Leandre Elfere (Edgard & Dolcena ORGERON) b. 13 Jan. 1896 (Larose Ch.: v.2, p.179)
ADAM, Lelia (Valcour & Clementine MELANCON) m. 16 Dec. 1899 Arthur BOUDREAUX (Houma Ct. Hse.: Mar. v.31 & 32, #188)
ADAM, Lilia m. 26 Feb. 1897 John MIRE (Thib. Ct. Hse.: Mar. v.36, #92)
ADAM, Lilia (Edmond & Amanda GUILLOTE) m. 26 Feb. 1897 Jean MIRE (Thib. Ch.: v.14, p.132)
ADAM, Lina (Elfege & Marie R. ORGERON) b. 26 July 1899 (Larose Ch.: v.3, p.44)
ADAM, Liza m. 17 Dec. 1898 David PITRE (Thib. Ct. Hse.: Mar. v.38, #317)
ADAM, Liza m. 17 Dec. 1899 David PITRE (Larose Ch.: v.4, p.31)
ADAM, Liza m. 19 Dec. 1899 David PITRE (Larose Ch.: v.3, p.13)
ADAM, Loetitia (Joachim & Dilia ADAM) m. 7 Jan. 1899 Becca FALGOUT (Lockport Ch.: v.2, p.198)
ADAM, Loetitia (Joachim & Odilia ADAM) m. 7 Jan. 1899 Becca FALGOUT (Thib. Ct. Hse.: Mar. v.38, #7)
ADAM, Lorinza m. 27 Dec. 1897 Jules HOTARD (Thib. Ct. Hse.: Mar. v.37, #267)
ADAM, Louis (Jean Baptiste & Regina LESELYDER) m. 4 Oct. 1898 Melodia RODRIGUE (Chackbay Ch.: v.1, p.66)
ADAM, Louis (Jean Baptiste & Regina SEXLYDER) m. 4 Oct. 1898 Melodia RODRIGUE (Thib. Ct. Hse.: Mar. v.38, #280)
ADAM, Louis Dominique (Celestin & Lesima DELATTES) b. 4 Nov. 1896 (Chackbay Ch.: v.1, p.85)
ADAM, Louise Melodie (Fabre & Louise CHICHIZOLA) b. 4 June 1897 (Larose Ch.: v.3, p.11)
ADAM, Lucile Agnes (Valmont & Euphrasie RICHOUX) b. 28 June 1897 (Larose Ch.: v.3, p.2)
ADAM, Lydia m. 14 April 1898 Rodolphe AYO (Thib. Ct. Hse.: Mar. v.38, #152)
ADAM, Margaret m. 8 March 1898 Jerry ARNOLD (Thib. Ct. Hse.: Mar. v.37, #121)
ADAM, Marie m. 15 Jan. 1897 Amadeo BREAUX (Larose Ch.: v.3, p.4)
ADAM, Marie m. 15 Jan. 1897 Amadeo BREAUX (Larose Ch.: v.4, p.119-B)
ADAM, Marie Alice (Hilaire & Elvire THIBODAUX) b. 26 May 1899 (Chackbay Ch.: v.1, p.141)
ADAM, Marie Alice (Joseph & Octavie ONCALE) bt. 8 March 1896 (Chackbay Ch.: v.1, p.62)

ADAM, Marie Bertha (Willie LOCKS & Clara ADAMS) b. 7 Sept. 1899 (Thib. Ch.: v.8, p.15)

ADAM, Marie Dolciana (Claymore & Elvire THIBODEAUX) b. 21 May 1897 (Chackbay Ch.: v.1, p.90)

ADAM, Marie Justine (Henri & Eve PLAISANCE) b. 26 Nov. 1896 (Lockport Ch.: v.3, #22)

ADAM, Marie Justine (Henri & Eve PLAISANCE) b. 26 Nov. 1896 (Lockport Ch.: v.3-A, #22)

ADAM, Marie Linda (Willie & Oliva DUROCHER) b. 16 Sept. 1898 (Chackbay Ch.: v.1, p.121)

ADAM, Marie Urlin Mabel (Narcisse & Julia BAYE) b. 2 Feb. 1899 (Thib. Ch.: v.7, p.532)

ADAM, Mary m. 5 Jan. 1897 Amadeo BREAUX (Thib. Ct. Hse.: Mar. v.36, #9)

ADAM, Mathurin d. 25 Nov. 1898 at age 38 yrs. (Thib. Ch.: v.3, p.222)

ADAM, Melia (Theophile & Josephine RODRIGUE) m. 4 Jan. 1896 Sylvaine CHIASSON (Thib. Ct. Hse.: Mar. v.36, #173)

ADAM, Melia (Theophile & Josephine RODRIGUE) m. 4 Jan. 1897 Sylvaire CHIASSON (Chackbay Ch.: v.1, p.34)

ADAM, Narcisse (Mathurin & Elvina DANTIN) m. 16 Feb. 1898 Julia BAYE (Thib. Ch.: v.14, p.190)

ADAM, Narcisse (Mathurin & Elvina DANTIN) m. 16 Feb. 1898 Julia BAYE (Thib. Ct. Hse.: Mar. v.37, #101)

ADAM, Nicolas (Ernest & Euphrosine LERAY) m. 16 Jan. 1899 Ella ESTEVE (Thib. Ct. Hse.: Mar. v.38, #8)

ADAM, Nicolas (Ernest & Eusekrosine LERAY) m. 16 Jan. 1899 Ella ESTEVE (Thib. Ch.: v.14, p.237)

ADAM, Noe Maxime (Adam & Odalie EUSTE) b. 21 Feb. 1896 (Lockport Ch.: v.2, p.323)

ADAM, Nora Camilla (Mathurin & Josephine ADAM) b. 22 July 1896 (Thib. Ch.: v.7, p.412)

ADAM, Onezippe (Cleophas & Melina BAYE) m. 7 Feb. 1896 Zulma LEBLANC (Thib. Ch.: v.14, p.75)

ADAM, Ovilia (Valcour & Clementine MELANCON) m. 4 Oct. 1897 Bernard CHICO (Houma Ct. Hse.: Mar. v.29 & 30, #107)

ADAM, Paul Irwin (Valcour & Esse ESTIVEN) b. 5 Sept. 1899 (Thib. Ch.: v.7, p.569)

ADAM, Pauline Eudorcia (Raoul & Emida TERREBONNE) b. 27 March 1897 (Larose Ch.: v.3, p.7)

ADAM, Philomene (Checo & Victoria MORVAN) m. 30 Jan. 1899 Oscar BOYER (Thib. Ct. Hse.: Mar. v.38, #52)

ADAM, Philomene (Theca & Victoria MORVAN) m. 30 Jan. 1899 Oscar BOYER (Thib. Ch.: v.14, p.247)

ADAM, Raph Wilfrid (Augustin & Louisiana BALLARD) b. 13 June 1896 (Houma Ch.: v.5, p.181)

ADAM, Sidney Guillace (Ozemee & Hollenda BOURGEOIS) b. 1 Sept. 1897 (Thib. Ch.: v.7, p.463)

ADAM, Sylvain Leandre (Aubin & Elvire CHIASSON) b. 30 Oct. 1898 (Larose Ch.: v.3, p.30)

ADAM, Theodore m. 2 Dec. 1898 Delphine MALBROUGH (Larose Ch.: v.3, p.10)
ADAM, Theodore m. 2 Dec. 1898 Delphine MALBOROUGH (Larose Ch.: v.4, p.108)
ADAM, Theophile m. 1 Feb. 1897 Valery TROSCLAIR (Thib. Ct. Hse.: Mar. v.36, #61)
ADAM, Theophile m. 22 Feb. 1897 Valerie TROSCLAIR (Larose Ch.: v.3, p.5)
ADAM, Theophile m. 22 March 1897 Valerie TROSCLAIR (Larose Ch.: v.4, p.104)
ADAM, Thomassin d. 5 Oct. 1896 at age 47 yrs. (Thib. Ch.: v.3, p.188)
ADAM, Unis Marie (Henri & Clara ST. AMAND) b. 7 Sept. 1896 (Larose Ch.: v.3, p.13)
ADAM, Willie (Celestin & Marie TABOR) m. 17 Dec. 1896 Eva DUROCHER (Thib. Ch.: v.14, p.104)
ADAM, Willy Eli (Valcour & Esse ESTIVAN) b. 21 July 1896 (Thib. Ch.: v.7, p.418)
ADAM, Zoe Sophie (Joseph & Amelia GUILLOTE) b. 17 Oct. 1897 (Thib. Ch.: v.7, p.472)
ADDO, Joseph m. 27 July 1898 Mary BUCKLEY (Thib. Ct. Hse.: Mar. v.38, #233)
ADLEMAN, Frederic Herman (Henry & Margarite BIGGLIER) b. 16 Nov. 1897; bt. 28 March 1898 (Chacahoula Ch.: Gibson Ch.: v.2, p.119)
ADLEMAN, Frederic Herman (Henry & Marguerite BIGLER) b. 16 Nov. 1897 (Chacahoula Ch.: Mar. Bk., v.1, #24)
ADON, Paul Clarence (Octave & Ernestine BOYER) b. 24 Jan. 1897 (Houma Ch.: v.5, p.207)
ADOUX, Albert Abel Blaise (Albert & Lea BERNARD) b. 19 Sept. 1896 (Chacahoula Ch.: v.4, p.4)
ADOUX, Bessie Lorena (Ulysse & Ellen Hart SINGLETON) b. 29 April 1896 (Houma Ch.: Epis. Ch.: v.1, p.112-B)
ADOUX, Coldon Jean Baptiste (Albert & Lea BERNARD) b. 12 April 1898 (Chacahoula Ch.: v.4, p.8)
ADOUX, Edith Leizzie (Ulysse & Ellen Hart SINGLETON) b. 12 July 1898 (Houma Ch.: Epis. Ch.: v.1, p.120)
ADOUX, Edna Cecilia (Octave & Ernestine BOYER) b. 24 Feb. 1896 (Houma Ch.: v.5, p.149)
ADOUX, Josephine d. 25 Jan. 1898 at age 42 yrs., 6 mths. & 14 days (Houma Ch.: v.3, p.15)

AGUILLARD (Sometimes: AGUILAR, AIGULAR)

AGUILLARD, Bernadette Anita (Ferdinand & Marie LEJEUNE) b. 23 May 1899 (Larose Ch.: v.3, p.41)
AGUILLARD, Ferdinand Ted (Ferdinand & Marie LEJEUNE) b. 21 July 1897 (Thib. Ch.: v.7, p.459)
AGUILLARD, Pauline Therese (Ferdinand & Marie LEJEUNE) b. 30 June 1896 (Thib. Ch.: v.7, p.407)

AILLOT (See: AYO)

AISENNE (Sometimes: AISEN, AYSAINE)

AISENNE, Rodolphe (Justilien & Julie GROS) m. 18 Jan. 1897 Lea PORTIER (Thib. Ct. Hse.: Mar. v.36, #8)

ALARIO, Joseph Trene (Joseph & Olivia DE PAIX) b. 15 Dec. 1899 (Larose Ch.: v.3, p.59)

ALBA, Maria Notsee Victoria (Luciano & Celestine BELIAMOUR) b. 12 Feb. 1896 (Montegut Ch.: v.6, p.38)

ALBA, Modeste Verselesa (Lucian & Celestine BELLEAMOUR) b. 22 July 1897 (Theriot Ch.: v.2, p.19)

ALBANO, Antonina (Pietro & Vincenza LARASA) b. 20 July 1896 (Houma Ch.: v.5, p.155)

ALBANO, Vincenzo Albam (Pietro & Vincenza FARRAZO) b. 21 April 1898 (Houma Ch.: v.5, p.208)

ALBERT, Emilia m. 11 Feb. 1896 Theodule THIBODAUX (Thib. Ct. Hse.: Mar. v.35, #43)

ALBERT, Juanita (Thomas & Cecilia GAUDIN) m. 22 Jan. 1896 Louis Raphael GAIENNIE (Thib. Ch.: v.14, p.68)

ALBERT, Justilia Philomene (Clodomir & Philomene AISEN) b. 18 Jan. 1896 (Thib. Ch.: v.7, p.390)

ALBERT, Philippe Margus (Marcilien & Louise LESAGE) b. 18 Nov. 1897 (Thib. Ch.: v.7, p.474)

ALBERT, Philomene (Audressy & Eugenie ARPENE) m. 27 Jan. 1898 Ernest BERTRAND (Thib. Ct. Hse.: Mar. v.37, #13)

ALBERTI (Sometimes: ALBERTE)

ALBERTI, Irene Marie (Arthur & Marie RIVIERE) b. 23 April 1898 (Thib. Ch.: v.7, p.496)

ALBERTI, Juanita widow of Pierre LORIO (Thomas & Cecilia GAUDIN) m. 22 Jan. 1896 Louis Raphael GAIENNE (Thib. Ct. Hse.: Mar. v.35, #26)

ALBERTI, Lucile Florence (Arthur & Marie RIVIERE) b. 13 Jan. 1897 (Thib. Ch.: v.7, p.435)

ALDRIDGE, Bertha m. 3 Dec. 1897 George HARRIS (Houma Ct. Hse.: Mar. v.29 & 30, #140)

ALDRIDGE, Carrie m. 8 Feb. 1898 Uriah SMITH (Houma Ct. Hse.: Mar. v.30 & 31, #282)

ALECK, Celestin Jr. m. 17 June 1897 Elizabeth BAPTISTE (Thib. Ct. Hse.: Mar. v.36, #174)

ALECK, Mary m. 3 Feb. 1898 Willy DUPLANTIS (Thib. Ct. Hse.: Mar. v.37, #79)

ALEXANDRE (Sometimes: ALEXANDER)

ALEXANDRE, Felicie d. 17 Nov. 1898 at age 25 yrs. (Raceland Ch.: v.1, p.21)

ALEXANDRE, Louisa m. 10 Sept. 1898 Walter THOMPSON (Thib. Ct. Hse.: Mar. v.38, #276)

ALEXANDRE, Lucinda m. 27 March 1896 Charles THOMAS (Houma Ct. Hse.: Mar. v.29 & 30, #20)

ALEXANDRE, Mitchell m. 14 April 1898 Mary PREVOST (Thib. Ct. Hse.: Mar. v.37, #118)

ALEXANDRE, Polly m. 21 Jan. 1897 Charles WATSON (Thib. Ct. Hse.: Mar. v.36, #47)

ALEXIS, Jean Thomas (St. Just & Marie BAPTISTE) b. 6 Sept. 1897 (Thib. Ch.: v.7, p.465)

ALEXIS, Philomena (Joseph & Philomena ALEXIS) m. 8 April 1896 John VERNON (Thib. Ct. Hse.: Mar. v.35, #65)

ALEXIS, Philomene (Joseph & Philomene ALEXIS) m. 8 April 1896 John VERNON (Thib. Ch.: v.14, p.82)

ALLAIN (Sometimes: ALLIN)

ALLAIN, Louis Aoula (John & Sarah WILSON) b. 9 Dec. 1896 (Thib. Ch.: v.7, p.435)

ALLAIN, Olivio d. 19 Jan. 1899 at age 45 yrs. (Thib. Ch.: v.3, p.225)

ALLEMAN (Sometimes: ALLEMAND, ALLEMANT, ALLEMOND)

ALLEMAN, A. Joseph Ove (Adam & Emma McEVERS) b. 3 June 1899 (Larose Ch.: v.3, p.40)

ALLEMAN, Adam (Alfred & Emelia ORGERON) m. 21 April 1898 Emma McEVERS (Thib. Ct. Hse.: Mar. v.38, #158)

ALLEMAN, Adam (Alfred & Emelia ORGERON) m. 21 April 1898 Emma McEVIST (Lockport Ch.: v.2, p.188)

ALLEMAN, Albert Wade (Luma & Adele GUIDRY) b. 9 Dec. 1899 (Larose Ch.: v.3, p.49)

ALLEMAN, Anidos Joseph (Numa & Adele GUIDRY) b. 23 June 1897 (Larose Ch.: v.3, p.5)

ALLEMAN, Daisy m. 10 June 1897 Joseph PLAISANCE (Larose Ch: v.3, p.6)

ALLEMAN, Daisy m. 10 June 1897 Joseph PLAISANCE (Larose Ch.: v.4, p.72-A)

ALLEMAN, Daisy m. 15 May 1897 Joseph PLAISANCE (Thib. Ct. Hse.: Mar. v.36, #144)

ALLEMAN, Ellis Noe (Miguel & Melia HYMEL) b. 1 April 1899 (Larose Ch.: v.3, p.38)

ALLEMAN, Ernest (Miguel & Estellina MCEVIRS) d. 10 Nov. 1897 at age 1½ mths. (Lockport Ch.: v.1, #26)

ALLEMAN, Estella Marie (Miguel & Melia HYMEL) b. 17 April 1897 (Larose Ch.: v.3, p.10)

ALLEMAN, Eugene (Joseph & Melasie SAVOIE) m. 24 June 1897 Azema LERILLE (Lockport Ch.: v.2, p.173)

ALLEMAN, Eugene (Joseph & Melasie SAVOIE) m. 24 June 1897 Azema LERILLE (Thib. Ct. Hse.: Mar. v.36, #167)

ALLEMAN, Georges Luc (Georges & Livie TROSCLAIR) d. 4 Aug. 1899 at age 13 mths. (Lockport Ch.: v.1, #32)

ALLEMAN, Jho d. 31 Dec. 1897 at age 50 yrs. (Lockport Ch.: v.1, #36)

ALLEMAN, Josephine m. 10 March 1897 Joseph LEBLANC (Larose Ch.: v.4, p.103)

ALLEMAN, Josephine m. 15 Feb. 1897 Joseph LEBLANC (Larose Ch.: v.3, p.5)

ALLEMAN, Josephine m. 2 Feb. 1897 Joseph LEBLANC (Thib. Ct. Hse.: Mar. v.36, #64)
ALLEMAN, Josephine Brigitte (Georges & Lavie TROSCLAIR) b. 19 March 1896 (Lockport Ch.: v.2, p.326)
ALLEMAN, Numa m. 3 July 1896 Adele GUIDRY (Thib. Ct. Hse.: Mar. v.36, #116)
ALLEMAN, Numa m. 8 July 1896 Adele GUIDRY (Larose Ch.: v.4, p.89)
ALLEMAN, Numa m. 8 July 1896 Adele GUIDRY (Larose Ch.: v.3, p.3)
ALLEMAN, Numa m. 8 July 1896 Adele GUIDRY (Larose Ch.: v.4, p.41)

ALLEN (Sometimes: ALLENS)
ALLEN, Elizabeth m. 13 April 1899 Sam BUTLER (Houma Ct. Hse.: Mar. v.31 & 32, #397)
ALLEN, Eward bt. 14 Oct. 1899 (Thib. Ch.: v.7, p.568)
ALLEN, Henry m. 12 March 1898 Mathilda JOSEPH (Thib. Ct. Hse.: Mar. v.37, #126)
ALLEN, Henry m. 18 April 1899 Susan NOBLE (Thib. Ct. Hse.: Mar. v.39, #148)
ALLEN, John m. 18 Feb. 1896 Anna WILLINSON (Thib. Ct. Hse.: Mar. v.35, #46)
ALLEN, Richard H. Children listed: Thomas H.; James Sedden; Eleanor Katherine; Jean Elizabeth. Letters of undertutorship: 2 June 1896. (Thib. Ct. Hse.: Succ. #1475)
ALLEN, Sarah m. 31 May 1897 Andrew GREEN (Houma Ct. Hse.: Mar. v.29 & 30, #434)
ALLEN, Thomas H. Jr. of Memphis, Tenn. Child listed: Richard H., Jr. Letters of undertutor: 2 Jan. 1896. (Thib. Ct. Hse.: Succ. #1476)
ALLEN, Thomas Sr. d. 1895 in Memphis, Tenn. Petition for administration and Inventory: 15 Jan. 1896. (Thib. Ct. Hse.: Succ. #1480)
ALLIENDE, Antonio (Joseph & Secunda MORVA) m. 2 Feb. 1898 Barbe Armentine SILVE (Larose Ch.: v.3, p.7)
ALLIENDE, Antonio (Joseph & Secunda MORWA) m. 16 Feb. 1898 Barbe Armentine SILVE (Larose Ch.: v.4, p.114)
ALLONCHE, Francis (Johanna & Josa GAUCHE) b. 3 June 1899 (Houma Ch.: v.5, p.247)
ALOE, Francisco (Vincenzo & Rosalia BELLA) b. 19 Dec. 1897 (Chacahoula Ch.: Gibson Ch.: Mar. Bk., v.1, #13)
ALOE, Francisco (Vincenzo & Rosalia BELLA) b. 19 Dec. 1897; bt. 20 Feb. 1898 (Chacahoula Ch.: Gibson Ch.: v.2, p.117)
AMBROCHE, Antonina d. 26 Dec. 1899 at age 20 yrs. (Houma Ch.: v.3, p.27)
ANCTIT, Laurent who married Sulvilia LEBOEUF d. 3 Oct. 1899 at age 38 yrs. (Theriot Ch.: v.1, p.2)

ANDERSON (Sometimes: ANNERSON)

ANDERSON, Alice m. 22 April 1897 Joseph TOUSSAINT (Thib. Ct. Hse.: Mar. v.36, #128)
ANDERSON, Carline m. 2 Jan. 1896 Charlie JOHNSON (Thib. Ct. Hse.: Mar. v.35, #7)
ANDERSON, Dolley m. 17 Aug. 1899 Henry TERRY (Thib. Ct. Hse.: Mar. v.39, #208)
ANDERSON, George m. 29 July 1897 Zora PRUDEN (Thib. Ct. Hse.: Mar. v.37, #202)
ANDERSON, Lizzie m. 17 July 1899 Simon BURSE (Houma Ct. Hse.: Mar. v.31 & 32, #77)
ANDERSON, Matilda m. 9 March 1896 James MADISON (Houma Ct. Hse.: Mar. v.29 & 30, #8)
ANDERSON, Rachel m. 8 May 1897 Gabe STEWART (Houma Ct. Hse.: Mar. v.29 & 30, #410)
ANDERSON, Samuel m. 24 Feb. 1896 Violet MOORE (Thib. Ct. Hse.: Mar. v.35, #49)
ANDERSON, Silas m. 11 Aug. 1898 Nancy FREEMAN (Thib. Ct. Hse.: Mar. v.38, #245)
ANDERSON, Virginia Agnes m. 26 May 1898 Louis GILES (Thib. Ct. Hse.: Mar. v.38, #191)
ANDERSON, Willie m. 13 April 1899 Laura THOMPSON (Houma Ct. Hse.: Mar. v.31 & 32, #400)
ANDONE, Theresa Josephine (Olive & Adolphine BOUDREAUX) b. 9 Nov. 1899 (Thib. Ch.: v.7, p.575)

ANDRAS (Sometimes: ANDRA)

ANDRAS, Angela Valerie (Ovile & Julia ADAM) b. 29 Aug. 1897 (Thib. Ch.: v.7, p.464)
ANDRAS, Eve (Arsemie & Elmire ADAM) m. 20 April 1897 Danice ORDOGNE (Thib. Ct. Hse.: Mar. v.36, #111)
ANDRAS, Eve (Osemee & Elmire ADAM) m. 20 April 1897 Danice ORDOGNE (Chackbay Ch.: v.1, p.43)
ANDREWS, William Jr. m. 21 Sept. 1898 Stella JOHNSON (Thib. Ct. Hse.: Mar. v.38, #281)
ANE, Ferdinand J. d. 1 June 1896 at age 62 yrs., 9 mths., 8 days (Houma Ch.: v.3, p.8)
ANELLO, Joseph (Vito & Catherina SAGONA) b. 9 Oct. 1897 (Houma Ch.: v.5, p.188)
ANGELA HANNA d. 8 Dec. 1896 at age 8 days (Thib. Ch.: v.3, p.191)
ANGELET, Lucien (Emile & Marie PERRIN) b. 13 Dec. 1897 (Larose Ch.: v.3, p.32)
ANGELETTE, Etienne Emile (Emile & Marie PERRIN) b. 18 July 1896 (Larose Ch.: v.2, p.187)
ANGELINO, Vincenzo (Andre & Rosina UTZA) b. 7 Oct. 1899 (Thib. Ch.: v.7, p.569)
ANITTO, Carmelite (Nicasia & Emilia BIANCHINI) b. 1 July 1897 (Raceland Ch.: v.5, p.60)

ANIXIOUS (See: EXNICIOS)

ANKRUM, Fortune m. 9 Feb. 1897 Mary Jane BOYD (Thib. Ct. Hse.: Mar. v.36, #74)
ANSELM, Peter Avena (William & Asperyee HENRY) b. 20 Jan. 1898 (Chacahoula Ch.: Gibson Record: Mar. Bk., v.1, #28)
ANSELME, Francesca (Leonardo & Antonina CAMARATO) b. 11 Sept. 1898 (Thib. Ch.: v.7, p.532)
ANSERV, Sebastianime (Alexandre & Louise MARTIN) b. 23 March 1897 (Larose Ch.: v.3, p.10)

ANTILL (Sometimes: ANTIL, ANTILLE)
ANTILL, Earl Joseph (Willie & Evela BARRILLAUX) b. 28 Feb. 1898 (Houma Ch.: v.5, p.206)
ANTILL, Wilfred (William & Cornelia BEAL) m. 7 Nov. 1899 Josephine GIROIR (Houma Ct. Hse.: Mar. v.31 & 32, #160)
ANTILL, Zella Annett (Willie & Evela BARRIAU) b. 16 Sept. 1896 (Houma Ch.: v.5, p.158)
ANTONI, Francesco (Nicolas & Felina CONZALES) b. 14 Jan. 1899 (Thib. Ch.: v.7, p.532)
ANTONIO, Joseph Adrien b. 6 July 1899 (Thib. Ch.: v.8, p.6)
ANZALONE, Martino m. 20 May 1899 Chiara GIANCOLA (Houma Ct. Hse.: Mar. v.31 & 32, #9)
ANZALONE, Martino of Terrebonne Parish m. 15 July 1899 Chiara GIANCOLA (Houma Ch.: v.6-B, p.4, #11 & p.3, #9)
ANZALONE, Rosario (Martino & Chiara GIANCOLA) b. 4 July 1899 (Houma Ch.: v.5, p.207-A)
ANZALONE, Rosario (Martino & Chiara GONGOLA) b. 4 July 1899; m. Vita SCIMECA on 6 Sept. 1925. (Houma Ch.: Bapt. Bk., v.5, p.248)
AOUN, Catharina (Abraham & Menna ZBAYLE) b. 3 Dec. 1897 (Houma Ch.: v.5, p.195)

ARABIE (Sometimes: ARABY)
ARABIE, Alceste (Jules & Angelina RODRIGUE) m. 29 Jan. 1898 Philomene MOLAISON (Lockport Ch.: v.2, p.181)
ARABIE, Alceste (Jules & Angelina RODRIGUE) m. 29 Jan. 1898 Eudolia MOLAISON (Thib. Ct. Hse.: Mar. v.37, #19)
ARABIE, Henriette d. 18 Aug. 1896 at age 1½ yr. (Raceland Ch.: v.1, p.9)
ARABIE, Marie Rita (Gratien & Ordalie BOURGEOIS) b. 15 June 1896 (Raceland Ch.: v.5, p.24)
ARABIE, Odilia (Jules & Angelina RODRIGUE) m. 25 Jan. 1896 Joseph GERVAIS (Thib. Ct. Hse.: Mar. v.35, #14)
ARABIE, Odilia (Julien & Angelina) m. 25 Jan. 1896 Joseph GERVAIS (Lockport Ch.: v.2, p.144)
ARABIE, Paul (Jules & Azelina RODRIGUE) m. 22 Jan. 1897 Anita CHAMPAGNE (Lockport Ch.: v.2, p.179)
ARABIE, Paul (Jules & Azelina RODRIGUE) m. 22 Jan. 1898 Anita CHAMPAGNE (Thib. Ct. Hse.: Mar. v.37, #7)
ARABIE, Paul Horace (Jules & Albertine GERVAIS) b. 11 Nov. 1896 (Lockport Ch.: v.3, #20)

ARABIE, Paul Horace (Jules & Albertine GERVAIS) b. 11 Nov. 1896 (Lockport Ch.: v.3-A, #20)
ARBISE, Johanna (Rosario & Francisco CIACCIA) b. 14 Nov. 1899 (Houma Ch.: v.5, p.261)
ARBISE, Salvatore (Rosario & Francisca CHIACCIO) bt. 18 Nov. 1899 (Houma Ch.: v.5, p.261)
ARBISI, Rosario m. 21 Jan. 1899 Frangesca CIACCIA (Houma Ct. Hse.: Mar. v.30 & 31, #277)
ARBISI, Rosario (Salvatore & Angela BUCURA) m. 4 Feb. 1899 Frangesca CIACCIO (Houma Ch.:v.6-a, p.273)

ARCENEAUX (Sometimes: ARCENAUX, ARCENEAU, ARSENAUD, ARSENAUX, ARSENEAU)
ARCENEAUX, Agnes Linda (Gustave & Julia WITNEY) b. 24 Feb. 1899 (Thib. Ch.: v.7, p.540)
ARCENEAUX, Angela m. 28 Aug. 1897 Florestan RODRIGUE (Thib. Ct. Hse.: Mar. v.37, #224)
ARCENEAUX, Angela m. 30 Aug. 1897 Florestan RODRIGUE (Larose Ch.: v.3, p.6)
ARCENEAUX, Angela m. 30 Aug. 1897 Florestan RODRIGUE (Larose Ch.: v.4, p.53)
ARCENEAUX, Bernadette of Lafourche Parish (Desire & Zeolide MELANCON) m. 27 Jan. 1898 Firmin GUIDROZ, of Lafourche Parish (Larose Ch.: v.3, p.7)
ARCENEAUX, Bernadette (Desire & Zeolide MELANCON) m. 27 Jan. 1898 Firmin GUITROZ (Larose Ch.: v.4, p.1)
ARCENEAUX, Bernadette (Desire & Zeolide MELANCON) m. 27 Jan. 1898 Firmin GUITROZ (Thib. Ct. Hse.: Mar. v.37, #39)
ARCENEAUX, Camil Desire (Desire & Mary GRIFFIN) b. 27 Sept. 1899 (Houma Ch.: v.5, p.262)
ARCENEAUX, Emile (Desire & Zeoline MELANCON) m. 20 Sept. 1898 Georgina LABAT (Thib. Ct. Hse.: Mar. v.38, #278)
ARCENEAUX, Emile (Desire & Zeoline MELANCON) m. 20 Sept. 1898 Georgina LABAT (Lockport Ch.: v.2, p.195)
ARCENEAUX, Evela Courine (Desire & Mary GRIFFIN) b. 30 March 1896 (Theriot Ch.: v.1-B, p.94)
ARCENEAUX, Gracieuse (Nicholas & Eugenie LASSEIGNE) m. 13 Jan. 1896 Alfred ROBICHAUX (Houma Ct. Hse.: Mar. v.28, #384)
ARCENEAUX, Gracieuse (Nicholas & Eugenie LASSEIGNE) m. 27 Jan. 1896 Alfred ROBICHAUD (Theriot Ch.: v.1, p.3)
ARCENEAUX, Gustave (Jules & Marie GAUTREAUX) m. 8 Jan. 1896 Julia WHITNEY (Thib. Ch.: v.13, p.92)
ARCENEAUX, Gustave (Jules & Marie GAUTREAUX) m. 8 Jan. 1896 Julia WHITNEY (Thib. Ct. Hse.: Mar. v.35, #195)
ARCENEAUX, Jean Oreste (Alfred & Marguerite CAMPEOUT) b. 21 Nov. 1897 (Thib. Ch.: v.7, p.525)
ARCENEAUX, Joseph d. 6 Feb. 1899 at age 5 days (Raceland Ch.: v.1, p.23)
ARCENEAUX, Joseph Alex. (Desire & Mary GRIFFIN) b. 18 Sept. 1898 (Theriot Ch.: v.2, p.29)

ARCENEAUX, Joseph Hamilton (Hamilton & Celina CANTRELLE) b. 3 May 1896 (Lockport Ch.: v.2, p.330)
ARCENEAUX, Joseph Sidney (Doniscar & Julia HUMPHRY) b. 24 Nov. 1899 (Thib. Ch.: v.7, p.575)
ARCENEAUX, Josephine m. Raymond BARRIOS d. 18 Nov. 1897 at age 74 yrs. (Lockport Ch.: v.1, #28)
ARCENEAUX, Laura Emilie (Alfred & Marguerite CAMPO) b. 10 Aug. 1899 (Thib. Ch.: v.8, p.4)
ARCENEAUX, Leopold d. 23 Dec. 1896 at age 18 mths. (Lockport Ch.: v.1, #27)
ARCENEAUX, Lizzie Berthilde (Alfred & Marguerite CAMSSAN) b. 5 Nov. 1896 (Thib. Ch.: v.7, p.424)
ARCENEAUX, Louise Bertha (Oscar & Julia HUMPHREY) b. 9 Sept. 1897 (Thib. Ch.: v.7, p.465)
ARCENEAUX, Lucie Valerie (Alcee & Rosalie DUBOIS) b. 27 Feb. 1898 (Larose Ch.: v.3, p.17)
ARCENEAUX, Lucina Marie (Alcee & Rosalie DUBOIS) b. 18 Feb. 1898 (Larose Ch.: v.3, p.17)
ARCENEAUX, Maria Agnes (Alcee & Rosalie DUBOIS) b. 1 April 1896 (Larose Ch.: v.2, p.188 & p.205, #64)
ARCENEAUX, Marie Agnes (Alcee & Rosalie DUBOIS) b. 1 April 1896 (Larose Ch.: v.2, p.185 & p.212, #91)
ARCENEAUX, Marie Eda (Zephirin & Victoria MATHERNE) b. 8 March 1897 (Lockport Ch.: v.3-A, #39)
ARCENEAUX, Marie Eda (Zephirin & Victoria MATHERNE) b. 8 March 1897 (Lockport Ch.: v.3, #39)
ARCENEAUX, Marie Ilda (Elphege & Emelia AUTIN) b. 20 Jan. 1897 (Raceland Ch.: v.5, p.40)
ARCENEAUX, Onesippe m. 10 Feb. 1899 Gracieuse LACOSTE (Thib. Ct. Hse.: Mar. v.39, #102)
ARCENEAUX, Pierre Klebert (Louis & Marcelline RODRIGUE) b. 30 Jan. 1896 (Lockport Ch.: v.3-A, #9)
ARCENEAUX, Pierre Klebert (Louis & Marcelline RODRIGUE) d. 8 Aug. 1897 at age 7 mths. (Lockport Ch.: v.1, #16)
ARCENEAUX, Zephirin d. 27 Oct. 1896 at age 7 yrs. (Lockport Ch.: v.1, #21)
ARDOIN, Raoul Joseph (Arthur & Adelina THIBODEAUX) b. 8 Nov. 1899 (Thib. Ch.: v.7, p.573)
ARGENCE, Louise Blanche (Antoine & Josephine BREAUX) b. 24 Oct. 1897 (Thib. Ch.: v.7, p.518)
ARGENCE, Stella Catherine (Antoine & Josephine BRAUX) b. 4 Oct. 1896 (Lockport Ch.: v.3, #5)
ARGENCE, Stella Catherine (Antoine & Josephine BRAUX) b. 4 Oct. 1896 (Lockport Ch.: v.3-A, #5)
ARGUS, Charley Joseph (Charles Livay & Emelie BREAUX) b. 6 April 1896 (Lockport Ch.: v.2, p.327)
ARINGTON, Cora m. 13 July 1898 Baptist WILLIAMS (Thib. Ct. Hse.: Mar. v.38, #225)
ARMATO, Antonina (Gissepa & Antonina SANSONA) b. 27 Sept. 1899 (Houma Ch.: v.5, p.258)

ARMATO, Salvator d. 27 Nov. 1896 at age 20 days (Thib. Ch.: v.3, p.191)
ARMATO, Salvatore (Grovanni & Francisca DEZE) b. 7 Nov. 1896 (Thib. Ch.: v.7, p.425)
ARNOLD, Jerry m. 8 March 1898 Margaret ADAMS (Thib. Ct. Hse.: Mar. v.37, #121)

ARSEMENT (Sometimes: ARCEMAN, ARCEMENT, ARSEMAN, ARSEMANT)

ARSEMENT, Agathe Mabel (Gustave & Julia WITHEY) b. 23 May 1896 (Thib. Ch.: v.7, p.454)
ARSEMENT, Azema m. 22 Jan. 1898 Alceste FORET (Thib. Ct. Hse.: Mar. v.37, #3)
ARSEMENT, Azema (Victorin & Euranie THERIOT) m. 22 Jan. 1898 Alceste FORET (Raceland Ch.: v.2, p.58)
ARSEMENT, Ella d. 4 Sept. 1898 at age 2 yrs. (Raceland Ch.: v.1, p.20)
ARSEMENT, Emma m. 7 July 1896 Alphonse MATHERNE (Thib. Ct. Hse.: Mar. v.36, #119)
ARSEMENT, Emma (Olesippe & Aspasie ROBICHAUX) m. 23 July 1896 Alphonse MATHERNE (Raceland Ch.: v.2, p.18)
ARSEMENT, Eve Ella (Oscar & Eve BOURGEOIS) b. 13 July 1896 (Raceland Ch.: v.5, p.25)
ARSEMENT, Homere d. 29 Nov. 1899 at age 23 yrs. (Raceland Ch.: v.1, p.29)
ARSEMENT, Justine m. Alidor ROBICHAUX d. 24 Jan. 1899 at age 48 yrs. (Thib. Ch.: v.3, p.226)
ARSEMENT, Leo d. 12 Dec. 1896 at age 9 yrs. (Raceland Ch.: v.1, p.11)
ARSEMENT, Leotia m. 30 Jan. 1896 Fernand GAUDEZ (Thib. Ct. Hse.: Mar. v.35, #32)
ARSEMENT, Leotia (Victorin & Uranie THERIOT) m. 30 Jan. 1896 Fernand GAUDET (Raceland Ch.: v.2, p.11)
ARSEMENT, Marie Eda (Oscar & Eve BOURGEOIS) b. 2 July 1898 (Raceland Ch.: v.5, p.74)
ARSEMENT, Oceanie (Jules & Marie GAUTHREAUX) m. 7 July 1896 Arthur LEONARD (Thib. Ct. Hse.: Mar. v.36, #114)
ARSEMENT, Onesippe (Ovile & Azéma BLANCHARD) m. 13 Feb. 1899 Gracieuse LACOSTE (Raceland Ch.: v.2, p.91)
ARSEMENT, Pierre Georges (Victorin & Euranie THERIOT) b. 19 June 1897 (Raceland Ch.: v.5, p.51)
ARSEMENT, Pierre Klebert (Louis & Marcelline RODRIGUE) b. 30 Jan. 1896 (Lockport Ch.: v.3, #9)
ARSEMENT, Zelide d. 3 Nov. 1896 at age 18 yrs. (Raceland Ch.: v.1, p.10)
ARTHUR, Willie m. 12 Jan. 1899 Eliza SPENCER (Houma Ct. Hse.: Mar. v.30 & 31, #219)

ARTIGUES (Sometimes: ARTIGUE, LARTIGUE, ORTIGUE)

ASCHLEY (Sometimes: ACHELEY)

ASHLEY, Joseph m. 20 Jan. 1899 Amelina WAGUESPACK (Thib. Ct. Hse.: Mar. v.38, #47)
ASHLEY, Joseph (Sostine & Philomene ELLIOT) m. 25 Jan. 1899 Emelina WAGUESPACK (Raceland Ch.: v.2, p.86)
ATES, James (John W. & Lizzie WILSON) m. 21 Dec. 1898 Nathalie LESTER (Houma Ct. Hse.: Mar. v.30 & 31, #154)
ATES, Johnny Williams (James & Nathalie LESTER) b. 18 Sept. 1899 (Houma Ch.: v.5, p.261)

ATKIN (Sometimes: AITKENS)
ATKIN, Myrille Eleanord (John K. & Clara CHAUVIN) b. 26 April 1896 (Houma Ch.: v.5, p.153)
ATKINSON, Birt d. 22 Feb. 1899 at age 2 mths. (Raceland Ch.: v.1, p.24)

AUBERT (Sometimes: HOBERT)
AUBERT, Bienvenu d. 16 Jan. 1898 at age 68 yrs. (Thib. Ch.: v.3, p.209)
AUBERT, Charles d. 23 Nov. 1897 at age 22 yrs. (Thib. Ch.: Epis. Ch.: v.1, p.394)
AUBERT, Charles Samuel d. 15 Feb. 1896 at age 39 yrs. (Thib. Ch.: Epis. Ch.: v.1, p.392)
AUBERT, Edouard Joseph (Joseph & Marie BROWN) b. 14 Sept. 1899 (Thib. Ch.: v.8, p.17)
AUBERT, Isma d. 11 Dec. 1896 at age 3 mths. (Thib. Ch.: v.3, p.193)
AUBERT, John Webster (John, Jr. & Rachel AITKENS) m. 16 Feb. 1899 Edie CAMPBELL (Houma Ct. Hse.: Mar. v.31 & 32, #337)
AUBERT, Lemuel C. Sr. Petition & order: 6 Feb. 1896. (Thib. Ct. Hse.: Succ. #1482)
AUBERT, Marie Zema (Tauesaint & Armantine AUBERT) b. 9 Sept. 1896 (Thib. Ch.: v.7, p.418)
AUBERT, Olive Odelia d. 14 June 1896 at age 5 2/3 mths. (Thib. Ch.: Epis. Ch.: v.1, p.394)
AUBERT, Rita (Shmpest & Armentine AUBERT) b. 14 Oct. 1899 (Thib. Ch.: v.7, p.569)
AUCOIN, Alice (Franklin & Leontine BOURQUE) m. 12 Jan. 1897 Charles NAQUIN (Thib. Ct. Hse.: Mar. v.36, #22)
AUCOIN, Alice (Franklin & Leontine BOURQUE) m. 12 Jan. 1897 Charles NAQUIN (Thib. Ch.: v.14, p.107)
AUCOIN, Alice (Narcisse & Arthemise BOURG) m. 20 Dec. 1899 Aldon BARRIOS (Thib. Ct. Hse.: Mar. v.39, #292)
AUCOIN, Alice (Narcisse & Arthemise BOURG) m. 30 Dec. 1899 Abdon BARRIOS (Lockport Ch.: v.2, p.212)
AUCOIN, Amadeo E. m. 28 Jan. 1899 Alice V. MAUFFRAY (Thib. Ct. Hse.: Mar. v.38, #78)
AUCOIN, Edmond Edouard (Henri & Aline BRAUD) b. 4 Sept. 1898 (Thib. Ch.: v.7, p.563)
AUCOIN, Eleonore (Armand & Felicite LAMOREAUX) m. 15 Nov. 1899 Auguste POCHE (Thib. Ch.: v.14, p.308)

AUCOIN, Eleonore (Armand & Felicite LAMOUREUX) m. 15 Nov. 1899 Auguste E. C. POCHE (Thib. Ct. Hse.: Mar. v.39, #262)
AUCOIN, Elizabeth (Ulisse & Estellina GUILLOTE) m. 18 April 1898 Arthur GUILLOTE (Thib. Ct. Hse.: Mar. v.37, #140)
AUCOIN, Elizabeth (Ursin & Estelle GUILLOTE) m. 18 April 1898 Arthur GUILLOT (Thib. Ch.: v.14, p.194)
AUCOIN, Francis Albert (Albert Leo & Mary L. CONNOLY) b. 30 Jan. 1897 (Houma Ch.: v.5, p.200)
AUCOIN, Henry m. 18 Jan. 1897 Aline GROS (Thib. Ct. Hse.: Mar. v.36, #41)
AUCOIN, Joseph (Ulysses & Estelina GUILLOT) m. 3 Feb. 1896 Alida MIRE (Thib. Ch.: v.14, p.71)
AUCOIN, Joseph Edouard (Mauville & Oena BASCLE) b. 31 Dec. 1897 (Montegut Ch.: v.6, p.63)
AUCOIN, Joseph Martin Wilson (Henri & Aline GROS) b. 11 Nov. 1897 (Thib. Ch.: v.7, p.472)
AUCOIN, Laura Eve (Joseph & Mary CHAMPAGNE) b. 28 July 1897 (Chacahoula Ch.: Gibson Ch.: Mar. Bk. 1, #77)
AUCOIN, Laura Eve (Joseph & Mary CHAMPAGNE) b. 28 July 1897; bt. 23 Nov. 1897 (Chacahoula Ch.: Gibson Ch.: v.2, p.113)
AUCOIN, Leontia (Armand & Felicite LOUIOUREUX) m. 2 May 1898 Martin SCHWARTZ (Thib. Ch.: v.14, p.202)
AUCOIN, Leontia (Armant & Felicite LAMOUREUX) m. 2 May 1898 Martin SCHWARTZ of New Orleans (Thib. Ct. Hse.: Mar. v.38, #174)
AUCOIN, Marie Anne (Movil & Marie Onea BASCLE) b. 1 Nov. 1896 (Montegut Ch.: v.6, p.47)
AUCOIN, Odressi Mrs. d. 4 April 1899 (Thib. Ch.: v.3, p.231)
AUCOIN, Orcie Albert (Joseph & Alida MIRE) b. 15 Oct. 1897 (Thib. Ch.: v.7, p.469)
AUCOIN, Peter Elbert (Movile & Oena BASCLE) b. 18 July 1899 (Montegut Ch.: v.6, p.90)
AUCOIN, Valsin d. 1 May 1898 at age 68 yrs. (Thib. Ch.: v.3, p.214)

AUGERON (See: OGERAN)

AUGUSTIN (Sometimes: AUGUSTINE)
AUGUSTIN, Anne Catherine (Celestin & Catherine HAVORS) b. 18 July 1899 (Thib. Ch.: v.7, p.555)
AUGUSTIN, George m. 6 Oct. 1898 Victoria LEBLANC (Thib. Ct. Hse.: Mar. v.38, #288)
AUGUSTIN, Isabella m. 9 Sept. 1897 Augustus HAWKINS (Houma Ct. Hse.: Mar. v.29 & 30, #88)
AUGUSTIN, Jeanne Augusta (Celestin & Catherine GRAVOIX) b. 21 Aug. 1897 (Thib. Ch.: v.7, p.463)
AUGUSTIN, Louis (Jean Baptiste & Odile BOURGEOIS) m. 25 Jan. 1899 Louisiane BREAUX (Thib. Ct. Hse.: Mar. v.38, #46)

AUGUSTIN, Marie Olive Albert (Albert & Therese THIBODAUX) b. 29 Nov. 1897 (Thib. Ch.: v.7, p.474)
AUGUSTIN, Virginia m. 14 Jan. 1897 Charles LEBLANC (Thib. Ct. Hse.: Mar. v.36, #31)
AUGUSTUS, Mary m. 12 Aug. 1897 Elias THOMPSON (Thib. Ct. Hse.: Mar. v.37, #212)

AUPIED (Sometimes: AUPIEDS, AUXPIEDS)
AUPIED, Agnes Anne (Ulysse & Ellina BOURGEOIS) b. 24 Nov. 1898 (Thib. Ch.: v.7, p.576)
AUPIED, Anette Lucie (Hilaire & Octavie LAINE) b. 5 Oct. 1897 (Thib. Ch.: v.7, p.467)
AUPIED, Clemence Marie (Aristide & Cecilia BOURGEOIS) b. 7 Jan. 1898 (Thib. Ch.: v.7, p.479)
AUPIED, Elma d. 10 Jan. 1899 at age 2 yrs. (Thib. Ch.: v.3, p.225)
AUPIED, Philomene (Jules & Marie FORD) m. 22 Oct. 1898 Omer BERTRAND (Thib. Ct. Hse.: Mar. v.38, #297)
AUPIED, Philomene (Jules & Marie FORD) m. 22 Oct. 1898 Omer BERTRAND (Thib. Ch.: v.14, p.228)
AUSLET, Pierre Earl (Paul & Marie ADAM) b. 21 Dec. 1898 (Thib. Ch.: v.7, p.525)
AUSLUM, Peter Avena (William & Aspergia HENRY) b. 20 Jan. 1898 (Chacahoula Ch.: Gibson Ch.: v.2, p.120)

AUTHEMENT (Sometimes: OTHEMENT, OTTEMAN)
AUTHEMENT, Adele m. 17 Oct. 1898 William Edward LEBLANC (Houma Ct. Hse.: Mar. v.30 & 31, #123)
AUTHEMENT, Adele (Apollinaire & Emma DUPLANTIS) m. 20 Oct. 1898 William Edward LEBLANC (Houma Ch.: v.6-a, p.256)
AUTHEMENT, Adele (Octave & Octavie CHAUVIN) m. 17 Jan. 1899 Aurestile BABIN (Houma Ct. Hse.: Mar. v.30 & 31, #244)
AUTHEMENT, Adele (Octave & Octavie CHAUVIN) m. 13 Feb. 1899 Auristile BABIN (Montegut Ch.: v.4, p.258)
AUTHEMENT, Alice (Oscar & Melisaire BREAUX) m. 18 April 1898 Eugene SAVOIE (Larose Ch.: v.4, p.10)
AUTHEMENT, Alice (Oscar & Melisaire BREAUX) m. 18 April 1898 Eugene J. SAVOIE (Thib. Ct. Hse.: Mar. v.37, #139)
AUTHEMENT, Alice of Lafourche Parish (Oscar & Melisaire BREAUX) m. 18 April 1898 Eugene SAVOIE, of Lafourche Parish (Larose Ch.: v.3, p.8)
AUTHEMENT, Berthilde (Emile & Ada BERGERON) b. 22 Sept. 1896 (Montegut Ch.: v.6, p.46)
AUTHEMENT, Celeste Florence (Andre & Audasie THERIOT) b. 21 April 1898 (Montegut Ch.: v.6, p.74)
AUTHEMENT, Clemance Mrs. widow of Miguel EXPOSITO (Silvere & Alzina RIVETS) m. 28 Sept. 1898 Albert MARCEL (Houma Ct. Hse.: Mar. v.30 & 31, #108)
AUTHEMENT, Eddie (Fetin & Elvire DE LA BRUGERE) d. 31 July 1898 at age 4½ yrs. (Montegut Ch.: v.2, p.19)

AUTHEMENT, Ernestine (Octave & Philomene RODRIGUE) m. 4 Feb. 1897 Michel MOLAISON (Thib. Ct. Hse.: Mar. v.36, #48)
AUTHEMENT, Ernestine (Octave & Philomene RODRIGUE) m. 4 Feb. 1897 Michel MOLAISON (Lockport Ch.: v.2, p.159)
AUTHEMENT, Eulalie d. 11 April 1899 at age 74 yrs. (Montegut Ch.: v.2, p.24)
AUTHEMENT, Exzelina (Gassin & Roselia BLANCHARD) m. 21 May 1897 Luma TRAHAN (Houma Ct. Hse.: Mar. v.29 & 30, #423)
AUTHEMENT, Jean Sidney (Leon & Eugenie BERGERON) b. 26 Aug. 1896; bt. 30 June 1900 (Houma Ch.: v.6, p.9)
AUTHEMENT, Joseph Alcee (Neuville & Cecilonia GUIDRY) b. 16 March 1899 (Theriot Ch.: v.2, p.36)
AUTHEMENT, Joseph Arthur (Leonce & Aimee NAQUIN) b. 25 March 1897 (Montegut Ch.: v.6, p.52)
AUTHEMENT, Joseph Elvey (Joseph & Amanda PELEGRIN) b. 24 April 1898 (Montegut Ch.: v.6, p.72)
AUTHEMENT, Joseph Fremonts (Myrtil & Brigitte BERGERON) b. 27 Oct. 1896 (Montegut Ch.: v.6, p.47)
AUTHEMENT, Joseph Gaspard (Ozemee & Celeste BOURGEOIS) b. 27 Feb. 1896 (Raceland Ch.: v.5, p.20)
AUTHEMENT, Joseph Lennis (Oscar & Eva AUTHEMENT) b. 22 April 1897 (Montegut Ch.: v.6, p.57)
AUTHEMENT, Joseph Maurice (Auristile & Judith BOUDREAUX) b. 19 Aug. 1898 (Montegut Ch.: v.6, p.81)
AUTHEMENT, Joseph Morgan (Octave & Octavie CHAUVIN) b. 24 Aug. 1897 (Montegut Ch.: v.6, p.61)
AUTHEMENT, Joseph Neuville (Eugene & Eulalie BOURG) m. 1 June 1898 Cedonia GUIDRY (Theriot Ch.: v.1-B, p.3)
AUTHEMENT, Joseph Neuville (Eugene & Eulalie BOURG) m. 16 May 1898 Cedonia GUIDRY (Houma Ct. Hse.:Mar. v.30 & 31, #444)
AUTHEMENT, Joseph Whitney (Augustin & Elvine LABRUYERE) b. 7 March 1897 (Montegut Ch.: v.6, p.54)
AUTHEMENT, Josephine Angelina (Oscar & Helene MATERNE) b. 3 Oct. 1896 (Houma Ch.: v.5, p.167)
AUTHEMENT, Laurent Andre (Andre & Odasie THERIOT) b. 10 Aug. 1896 (Montegut Ch.: v.6, p.46)
AUTHEMENT, Louis Joseph (Oscar & Eva AUTHEMENT) b. 7 Feb. 1896 (Montegut Ch.: v.6, p.36)
AUTHEMENT, Loulie (Andre & Ordazie THERIOT) m. 19 Jan. 1899 Altay BERGERON (Houma Ct. Hse.: Mar. v.30 & 31, #273)
AUTHEMENT, Loulie (Andre & Ordazie THERIOT) m. 2 Feb. 1899 Altee BERGERON (Montegut Ch.: v.4, p.254)
AUTHEMENT, Marie Allie Alzina (Joseph & Amanda PELEGRIN) b. 14 Sept. 1896 (Montegut Ch.: v.6, p.47)
AUTHEMENT, Marie Felicie (Worhies & Alice DUAY) b. 7 Jan. 1899 (Larose Ch.: v.3, p.34)
AUTHEMENT, Marie Geneva (Emile & Ida BERGERON) b. 28 Sept. 1898 (Montegut Ch.: v.6, p.78)

AUTHEMENT, Marie Lily Lilianne (Auristile & Judith BOUDREAUX) b. 20 Jan. 1896 (Montegut Ch.: v.6, p.34)
AUTHEMENT, Myrtil (d.Auguste & Adele FOREST) m. 15 Jan. 1896 Constance Brigitte BERGERON (Montegut Ch.: v.4, p.205)
AUTHEMENT, Odilia m. 5 April 1899 Albert HEBERT (Thib. Ct. Hse.: Mar. v.39, #131)
AUTHEMENT, Odilia (Octave & Celina RODRIGUE) m. 22 April 1899 Albert HEBERT (Lockport Ch.: v.2, p.206)
AUTHEMENT, Raphael Robert (Merthilde & Brigitte BERGERON) b. 16 June 1898 (Montegut Ch.: v.6, p.76)
AUTHEMENT, Raphael Simpson (Auristile & Ada BERGERON) b. 23 Sept. 1899 (Montegut Ch.: v.6, p.93)
AUTHEMENT, Sylvere d. 2 Aug. 1897 at age 2 mths. (Raceland Ch.: v.1, p.14)
AUTHEMENT, Ubert Alcide (Leon & Eugenie BERGERON) b. 4 June 1899 (Houma Ch.: v.6, p.10)
AUTHEMENT, Virginie Anne (Paul & Theoline DUPLANTIS) b. 4 Dec. 1898 (Montegut Ch.: v.6, p.83)
AUTHEMENT, Voohries m. 4 Jan. 1898 Alice DUET (Larose Ch.: v.3, p.6)
AUTHEMENT, Voorhies m. 4 Jan. 1898 Alice DUET (Larose Ch.: v.4, p.110)
AUTHEMENT, Voorhies m. 4 Jan. 1898 Alice DUET (Thib. Ct. Hse.: Mar. v.37, #269)

AUTIN (Sometimes: AUTAIN, AUTTIN, OTAIN, OTIN)
AUTIN, ----- Mr. d. 22 July 1897 (Larose Ch.: v.1, p.41)
AUTIN, Adele m. 25 July 1896 Alexandre P. PERTUIT (Thib. Ct. Hse.: Mar. v.36, #128)
AUTIN, Adele (Uselien & Alzina FORET) m. 8 Aug. 1896 Alexandre PERTUIS (Raceland Ch.: v.2, p.19)
AUTIN, Alceste m. 16 Oct. 1897 Meloe FORET (Thib. Ct. Hse.: Mar. v.37, #242)
AUTIN, Alceste (Adam & Velleda DIEZ) m. 16 Oct. 1897 Moloe FORET (Raceland Ch.: v.2, p.52)
AUTIN, Alcida m. 26 Jan. 1899 Wallace LANDRY (Thib. Ct. Hse.: Mar. v.38, #63)
AUTIN, Alcida (Adam & Velleda DIEZ) m. 2 Feb. 1899 Wallace LANDRY (Raceland Ch.: v.2, p.90)
AUTIN, Alcide m. 8 Sept. 1899 Matilde PRICE (Thib. Ct. Hse.: Mar. v.39, #228)
AUTIN, Alice m. 13 Aug. 1896 Pierre FOLSE (Thib. Ct. Hse.: Mar. v.36, #135)
AUTIN, Alice (Uzelien & Alzina FORET) m. 8 Aug. 1896 Pierre FOLSE (Raceland Ch.: v.2, p.20)
AUTIN, Benjamin d. 9 May 1896 at age 59 yrs. (Raceland Ch.: v.1, p.8)
AUTIN, Blanche Louise (Alexis & Leonie FOLSE) b. 25 July 1896 (Raceland Ch.: v.5, p.26)
AUTIN, Charles Deveson (Charles Lovinsie & Josephine CANTRELLE) b. 13 May 1896 (Larose Ch.: v.2, p.183)

AUTIN, Charles Joseph (Victorin & Adelina SANGE) b. 30 Jan. 1896 (Lockport Ch.: v.3, #15)
AUTIN, Charles Joseph (Victorin & Adelina SANGE) b. 30 Jan. 1896 (Lockport Ch.: v.3-A, #15)
AUTIN, Eliska d. 1 Jan. 1896 at age 1 yr. (Raceland Ch.: v.1, p.7)
AUTIN, Eugenie Olympe (Louis & Josephine ZERINGUE) b. 28 Dec. 1898 (Raceland Ch.: v.5, p.86)
AUTIN, Frances (Charles & Elizia VITO) m. 5 May 1896 John PITRE (Houma Ct. Hse.: Mar. v.29 & 30, #54)
AUTIN, Henry (Charles & Luzin VITO) m. 29 Dec. 1898 Felicie HENRY (Houma Ct. Hse.: Mar. v.30 & 31, #163)
AUTIN, Henry (Charley & Luzia VITEAU) m. 11 Feb. 1899 Felicia HENRI (Montegut Ch.: v.4, p.257)
AUTIN, Joseph Alcide (Ernest & Clarinda THIBODAUX) b. 11 April 1896; m. 10 April 1923 to Josephine CANDILORA [Philip & Christine D'ANTONIO] (Raceland Ch.: Bapt. Bk., v.5, p.22)
AUTIN, Joseph Nelson (Charles & Josephine CANTRELLE) b. 28 Aug. 1899 (Larose Ch.: v.3, p.49)
AUTIN, Joseph Samson (Alcesse & Meloe FORET) b. 7 July 1898 (Raceland Ch.: v.5, p.74)
AUTIN, Joseph Whitney (Charles & Odilia BOURGEOIS) b. 18 Feb. 1897 (Raceland Ch.: v.5, p.43)
AUTIN, Joseph Widley (Alexis & Leonise FOLSE) b. 14 Feb. 1898 (Raceland Ch.: v.5, p.66)
AUTIN, Julie (Pierre & Marguerite DANOS) m. 17 Feb. 1899 Leopold PITRE (Thib. Ct. Hse.: Mar. v.39, #291)
AUTIN, Laurder Edia (Ernest & Clerinda THIBODAUX) b. 13 July 1898 (Raceland Ch.: v.5, p.75)
AUTIN, Letitia widow of Auguste EROCHE m. 27 Aug. 1897 Clovis BOURGEOIS (Thib. Ct. Hse.: Mar. v.37, #220)
AUTIN, Lucien (Lucien & Emma LESTE) m. 9 May 1899 Eugene THIBODAUX (Lockport Ch.: v.2, p.209)
AUTIN, Marie Alcida (Onesippe & Aglae PITRE) b. 4 April 1899 (Larose Ch.: v.3, p.41)
AUTIN, Marie Elvire (Lovencie & Josephine CANTRELLE) b. 30 Jan. 1898 (Larose Ch.: v.3, p.17)
AUTIN, Marie Inez (Alexandre & Adoliska BOURGEOIS) b. 10 Sept. 1896 (Raceland Ch.: v.5, p.30)
AUTIN, Marie Sidonia (Louis & Josephine ZERINGUE) b. 18 April 1897 (Raceland Ch.: v.5, p.48)
AUTIN, Marie Unez (Alexandre & Adoliska BOURGEOIS) b. 19 Feb. 1899 (Raceland Ch.: v.5, p.90)
AUTIN, Marie Willia (Charles & Odilia BOURGEOIS) b. 7 Feb. 1899 (Raceland Ch.: v.5, p.91)
AUTIN, Odillia m. 19 June 1897 John BRUCE (Larose Ch.: v.3, p.6)
AUTIN, Pierre Benoit (Pierre & Rosa CHARPENTIER) b. 13 Feb. 1896 (Larose Ch.: v.2, p.187)

AUTIN, Thomas Hennesy (Onesime & Aglae PITRE) b. 22 Dec. 1896 (Larose Ch.: v.3, p.4)

AVERY, Coralie m. 15 Jan. 1898 Pete PIERO (Thib. Ct. Hse.: Mar. v.37, #40)

AVET (Sometimes: AVER)

AVET, Corcile Roseline (Philippe & Rosalie BRUNET) b. 13 Nov. 1896; m. August Ernest CLEMENT on 7 Feb. 1929. (Houma Ch.: Bapt. Bk., v.5, p.174)

AYCOCK (Sometimes: AICOCK, AYCOK)

AYCOCK, Elvire m. Numa BERGERON d. 2 July 1897 at age 39 yrs. (Chacahoula Ch.: v.2, p.24)

AYCOCK, Henry Albert (Albert Henry & Emily BERGERON) b. 15 Jan. 1899 (Houma Ch.: v.5, p.236)

AYCOCK, John Buell (Albert & Eda GAUTREAUX) b. 21 Oct. 1897 (Raceland Ch.: v.5, p.59)

AYCOCK, Laura Pauline (d.Onezime & Celeste LEONARD) m. 28 Sept. 1899 Numa Joseph BERGERON (Chacahoula Ch.: v.1, p.71 [91])

AYCOCK, Louise Marguerite (Felix A. & Adeline DELATTE) m. 12 Jan. 1899 Gilbert A. BOUDREAUX (Houma Ct. Hse: Mar. v.30 & 31, #225)

AYCOCK, Louise Marguerite (Felix A. & Helene DESLATES) m. 8 Feb. 1899 Guilbert A. BOUDREAUX (Montegut Ch.: v.4, p.257)

AYCOCK, Marguerite d. 9 April 1897 at age 2 yrs. (Houma Ch.: v.3, p.12)

AYCOCK, Nita Jeanne (Felix & Helene DESLATES) b. 26 Aug. 1896 (Montegut Ch.: v.6, p.45)

AYCOCK, Odelia (Felix & Helene DESLATES) m. 7 July 1896 Felicien Eugene BOUDREAUX (Montegut Ch.: v.4, p.212)

AYCOCK, Odilia (Felix A. & Helene DELATTE) m. 7 July 1896 Felicien E. BOUDREAUX (Houma Ct. Hse.: Mar. v.29 & 30, #107)

AYCOCK, Rita Helene (Felix & Helene DESLATES) b. 26 Aug. 1896 (Montegut Ch.: v.6, p.45)

AYMARD (See: EYMARD)

AYO (Sometimes: AILLOT, AYOS, AYOT)

AYO, ----- child (Philippe) d. 23 Feb. 1899 at age 3 mths. (Lockport Ch.: v.1, #9)

AYO, Albert Joseph m. Marie Odilia BOUDREAU d. 5 Sept. 1897 at age 33 yrs. (Lockport Ch.: v.1, #18)

AYO, Alcide m. 13 Jan. 1898 Mary BRICKLEY (Thib. Ct. Hse.: Mar. v.37, #26)

AYO, Alfredia Leontia (Clinton & Seraphine HYMEL) b. 2 May 1897 (Thib. Ch.: v.7, p.449)

AYO, Clairfait (Gustave & Philomene TROSCLAIR) m. 17 Sept. 1896 Marie KELLER (Thib. Ch.: v.14, p.98)

AYO, Clerfe (Gustave & Philomene TROSCLAIR) m. 17 Sept. 1896 Mary KELLER (Thib. Ct. Hse.: Mar. v.36, #138)

AYO, Edmond (Joseph & Donatilde OLIVIER) m. 17 Feb. 1898 Emma BOUDRAUX (Thib. Ch.: v.14, p.192)

AYO, Edmond (Joseph & Donatilde OLIVIER) m. 17 Feb. 1898 Emma BOUDREAUX (Thib. Ct. Hse.: Mar. v.37, #65)

AYO, Eunice Marie (Joseph & Emilie DUBOIS) b. 26 Jan. 1899 (Chacahoula Ch.: v.4, p.18)

AYO, James Hubert (Jackson Joseph & Marie Alida LEPINE) b. 19 Jan. 1896 (Raceland Ch.: v.5, p.18)

AYO, Joseph Benoit (Joseph & Lydia ELLIOT) b. 9 April 1896 (Lockport Ch.: v.2, p.327)

AYO, Joseph Leon Alic (Clarphe & Marie KELLER) b. 10 July 1897 (Thib. Ch.: v.7, p.457)

AYO, Joseph Sampson (Claiffier & Marie KELLER) b. 11 Nov. 1899 (Thib. Ch.: v.7, p.576)

AYO, Milson Hampton (Clinton & Seraphine HYMEL) b. 26 March 1899 (Thib. Ch.: v.7, p.544)

AYO, Neuville (Augustave & Emilie TROSCLAIR) m. 12 Sept. 1898 Elda BOUDREAUX (Thib. Ct. Hse.: Mar. v.38, #261)

AYO, Odile Magnolia (Prudent & Magnolia BOUDREAUX) b. 14 Dec. 1896 (Chacahoula Ch.: v.4, p.10)

AYO, Prudent m. 25 March 1899 Odelia WALKER (Houma Ct. Hse.: Mar. v.31 & 32, #373)

AYO, Prudent (Ermogene & Leontine ROUSSEL) m. 10 April 1899 Odilia WALKER (Chacahoula Ch.: v.1, p.68 [88])

AYO, Rodolphe m. 14 April 1898 Lydia ADAM (Thib. Ct. Hse.: Mar. v.38, #152)

AYO, Sydney Joseph (Joseph & Emilie DUBOIS) b. 8 Sept. 1897 (Chacahoula Ch.: v.4, p.24)

AYO, Ulysse m. 10 June 1899 Marie NAQUIN (Thib. Ct. Hse.: Mar. v.39, #177)

AYOUSS, MaKaien d. 21 March 1899 at age 1½ mths. (Thib. Ch.: v.3, p.230)

AYSENE, Marie m. 21 Jan. 1899 Auguste BABIN (Thib. Ct. Hse.: Mar. v.38, #48)

AYUP, Joseph Davis Michel (Salomon & Myrthe NASTA) b. 16 Jan. 1898 (Thib. Ch.: v.7, p.539)

AZEMA, Alma (Cyprien & Victoria KNOBLOCK) m. 7 Jan. 1896 Joseph O. NAQUIN (Thib. Ch.: v.13, p.93)

AZEMA, Alma (Cyprien & Victoria KNOBLOCK) m. 7 Jan. 1896 Joseph A. NAQUIN (Thib. Ct. Hse.: Mar. v.35, #11)

"B"

BABIN, ----- d. 13 April 1896 at age 6 days (Houma Ch.: v.3, p.7)
BABIN, Adam Albert m. 16 Sept. 1897 Aliska PITRE (Houma Ct. Hse.: Mar. v.29 & 30, #92)
BABIN, Adam Albert (Jacques & Marianne LABIT) m. 4 Oct. 1897 Aliska PITRE (Houma Ch.: v.6-a, p.217)
BABIN, Adam Sydney (Elphege & Azelie MARCEL) bt. 2 May 1897 (Thib. Ch.: v.7, p.448)
BABIN, Adela d. 16 July 1897 at age 59 yrs. (Thib. Ch.: v.3, p.203)
BABIN, Agathe Esther (Hippolyte & Alice MARTIN) b. 5 Feb. 1898 (Raceland Ch.: v.5, p.66)
BABIN, Agnes m. 9 March 1897 Robert BALLARD (Houma Ch.: v.6-a, p.196)
BABIN, Agnes Anita (Wuilliam & Josephine DUGAS) b. 22 Sept. 1896 (Lockport Ch.: v.3, #3)
BABIN, Agnes Anita (Wuilliam & Josephine DUGAS) b. 22 Sept. 1896 (Lockport Ch.: v.3-A, #3)
BABIN, Albert m. 1 Aug. 1898 Josephine LESTER (Houma Ch.: v.6-a, p.250)
BABIN, Albert m. 7 April 1898 Brigitte MARCEL (Houma Ct. Hse.: Mar. v.30 & 31, #385)
BABIN, Albert (James & Elvire CROCHET) m. 20 April 1898 Brigitte MARCEL (Houma Ch.: v.6-a, p.239)
BABIN, Albert (Marcelin, Jr. & Josephine BABIN) m. 21 June 1897 Josephine LESTER (Houma Ct. Hse.: Mar. v.29 & 30, #36)
BABIN, Albert (Marcellin & Eudocia MARCEL) m. 12 June 1899 Mary Lester WOLFF (Houma Ct. Hse.: Mar. v.31 & 32, #25)
BABIN, Albert Jessie (Joseph & Victoria USE) b. 23 Dec. 1898 (Thib. Ch.: v.7, p.529)
BABIN, Alcide (Alex. & Marguerite DANOS) b. 16 Oct. 1896 (Raceland Ch.: v.5, p.32)
BABIN, Alice m. 2 Oct. 1897 Gilles PELEGRIN (Houma Ct. Hse.: Mar. v.29 & 30, #103)
BABIN, Alice m. 24 Jan. 1896 Alfred JONES (Houma Ct. Hse.: Mar. v.28, #414)
BABIN, Alice (Marcelin & Josephine BABIN) m. 7 Oct. 1897 Gillis PELEGRIN (Houma Ch.: v.6-a, p.218)
BABIN, Amelina m. Clement BOURGEOIS d. 27 May 1899 at age 25 yrs. & 7 mths. (Thib. Ch.: v.3, p.234)
BABIN, Anastasia m. 12 Jan. 1899 Jules HEBERT (Thib. Ct. Hse.: Mar. v.38, #18)
BABIN, Anastasie (Donat & Seraphine THERIOT) m. 28 Jan. 1899 Jules HEBERT (Raceland Ch.: v.2, p.84)
BABIN, Andre d. 7 Dec. 1896 at age 7 mths. (Thib. Ch.: v.3, p.191)

BABIN, Andre Luc (Leon & Theolaine TOUPS) b. 22 April 1896 (Thib. Ch.: v.7, p.400)
BABIN, Annette m. 28 Jan. 1899 Clay BERNARD (Houma Ct. Hse.: Mar. v.30 & 31, #288)
BABIN, Annette (Frank & Theolane FANGUY) m. 28 Jan. 1899 Clay BERNARD (Houma Ch.: v.6-a, p.269)
BABIN, Antoine Harris (Adam & Lisca PITRE) b. 24 July 1898 (Houma Ch.: v.5, p.215)
BABIN, Antoine Hughes (Euselien & Alfrida ROSS) b. 14 Dec. 1896 (Houma Ch.: v.5, p.164)
BABIN, Aploda m. 2 Aug. 1899 Celina SMITH (Houma Ch.: v.6-B, p.4)
BABIN, Aploda m. 28 July 1899 Celina Louviere SMITH (Houma Ct. Hse.: Mar. v.31 & 32, #86)
BABIN, Arbra d. 16 May 1899 at age 10 mths., 16 days (Houma Ch.: v.3, p.23)
BABIN, Auguste m. 21 Jan. 1899 Marie AYSENE (Thib. Ct. Hse.: Mar. v.38, #48)
BABIN, Augustin Hebert (Valerie & Olympe BERTRAND) b. 2 July 1897 (Thib. Ch.: v.7, p.466)
BABIN, Aurelie d. 10 March 1899 at age 52 yrs. (Houma Ch.: v.3, p.21)
BABIN, Aurestile (Antoine & Alida LOUVIERE) m. 17 Jan. 1899 Adele AUTHEMENT (Houma Ct. Hse.: Mar. v.30 & 31, #244)
BABIN, Auristile (Antoine & d.Alida LOUVIERE) m. 13 Feb. 1899 Adele AUTHEMENT (Montegut Ch.: v.4, p.258)
BABIN, Caliste Octave (Octave & Evelina GROW) b. 18 Aug. 1898 (Houma Ch.: v.5, p.223)
BABIN, Celeste (Felix & Celeste THERIOT) m. 5 Feb. 1898 Gratien LUQUET (Lockport Ch.: v.2, p.183)
BABIN, Celeste (Felix & Celeste THERIOT) m. 5 Feb. 1898 Gratien LUQUET (Thib. Ct. Hse.: Mar. v.37, #25)
BABIN, Celina m. Wuilliam PIERCE d. 19 May - 16 June 1898 at age 48 yrs. (Lockport Ch.: v.1, #12)
BABIN, Darcio Joseph (John & Auedillia BOUDREAU) b. 17 April 1896 (Houma Ch.: v.5, p.151)
BABIN, David Eloi (Arthur & Clothilde LEBOEUF) b. 18 Feb. 1899 (Houma Ch.: v.5, p.239)
BABIN, Davis d. 9 Dec. 1898 at age 5 mths. (Thib. Ch.: v.3, p.223)
BABIN, Davis Andre (Theophile & Amanda BAYE) b. 7 June 1898 (Thib. Ch.: v.7, p.500)
BABIN, Dolton (Anatole & Josephine CHAUVIN) d. 17 Aug. 1897 at age 10 mths. (Montegut Ch.: v.2, p.11)
BABIN, Edith Maunich (Theophile & Amanda BAYE) b. 7 Nov. 1899 (Thib. Ch.: v.8, p.17)
BABIN, Elvire m. Omer LIRETTE d. 9 Feb. 1898 at age 50 yrs. (Houma Ch.: v.3, p.15)
BABIN, Ernestine (Frosin & Celemee DUFRESNE) b. 24 Aug. 1896 (Raceland Ch.: v.5, p.29)

BABIN, Eugenie (Eugene & Adele HEBERT) m. 21 June 1897 Joseph DUPRE (Thib. Ch.: v.14, p.148)
BABIN, Eugenie (Eugene & Adele HEBERT) m. 21 June 1897 Joseph DUPRE (Thib. Ct. Hse.: Mar. v.36, #177)
BABIN, Euphemie m. 29 July 1897 Oscar ROBICHAUX (Thib. Ct. Hse.: Mar. v.37, #199)
BABIN, Euphemie (Froizin & Josephine UZE) m. 29 July 1897 Oscar ROBICHAUX (Raceland Ch.: v.2, p.47)
BABIN, Eva Odela (Augustin & Cora LEBOEUF) b. 16 Dec. 1896 (Thib. Ch.: v.7, p.437)
BABIN, Eve d. 21 Sept. 1897 at age 3 yrs. (Houma Ch.: v.3, p.14)
BABIN, Eve Daisy (Telesphore & Felicite LAPEROUSE) b. 27 May 1899 (Houma Ch.: v.5, p.248)
BABIN, Eve Maria (Louis & Armantine ROBICHAUD) b. 29 Dec. 1896 (Raceland Ch.: v.5, p.39)
BABIN, Evela m. 15 July 1898 George A. LESTER (Houma Ct. Hse.: Mar. v.30 & 31, #59)
BABIN, Evela (Jacques & Marie Anne LABIT) m. 1 Aug. 1898 George A. LESTER (Houma Ch.: v.6-a, p.250)
BABIN, Francis A. (Victor & Magaret P. JOLET) m. 25 July 1898 Mary Mathilde ESHTE (Houma Ch.: v.6-a, p.247)
BABIN, Francis R. m. 25 July 1898 Mary Mathilde ESHTE (Houma Ct. Hse.: Mar. v.30 & 31, #65)
BABIN, Gibera Marie (Augustin & Eda LEBOEUF) b. 3 Sept. 1899 (Thib. Ch.: v.7, p.569)
BABIN, Helene Josephine (Marcelin & Marie BRAUD) m. 10 Aug. 1898 Felix J. GAUDE (Thib. Ch.: v.14, p.289)
BABIN, Helene Josephine (Marcelin & Marie BRAUD) m. 3 Aug. 1899 Felix J. GAUDE (Thib. Ct. Hse.: Mar. v.39, #205)
BABIN, Henri (Trasimond & Alvina BREAUX) m. 26 April 1899 Brigitte BERGERON (Thib. Ct. Hse.: Mar. v.39, #153)
BABIN, Henry (Trasimond & Alvina BREAUX) m. 26 April 1899 Brigite BERGERON (Thib. Ch.: v.14, p.277)
BABIN, Hudson d. 19 Feb. 1898 at age 20 yrs. (Thib. Ch.: v.3, p.211)
BABIN, Israel Dalton (Anatole & Josephine CHAUVIN) b. 22 Sept. 1896 (Montegut Ch.: v.6, p.45)
BABIN, Jacque d. 13 April 1898 at age 68 yrs. (Houma Ch.: v.3, p.16)
BABIN, James (Marcellin & Josephine BABIN) m. 5 Jan. 1899 Alice CROCHET (Houma Ct. Hse.: Mar. v.30 & 31, #184)
BABIN, James (Olezime & Elvire CROCHET) m. 13 July 1896 Felicia DARCE (Houma Ct. Hse.: Mar. v.28, #216)
BABIN, Jean Claud (Henry & Emelie BERGERON) b. 18 April 1899 (Houma Ch.: v.5, p.243)
BABIN, Jean Marigus (John & Eva GUIDRY) b. 21 July 1897 (Montegut Ch.: v.6, p.58)
BABIN, John Larence d. 20 Dec. 1896 at age 2 yrs., 8 mths., 5 days. (Houma Ch.: v.3, p.10)

BABIN, Joseph Abre Pierre (Theodule & Magnolia SAMONI) b. 29 June 1898 (Houma Ch.: v.5, p.213)
BABIN, Joseph Adam (Ernest & Marie TOUPS) d. 3 Sept. 1899 at age 7 days (Montegut Ch.: v.2, p.28)
BABIN, Joseph Adam (Ernest & Marie TOUPS) b. 27 Aug. 1899 (Montegut Ch.: v.6, p.91)
BABIN, Joseph Alcide (Louis & Armantine ROBICHAUX) b. 5 March 1899 (Raceland Ch.: v.5, p.92)
BABIN, Joseph Alphonse (Jimmy & Henriette BABIN) b. 3 Aug. 1897 (Houma Ch.: v.5, p.186)
BABIN, Joseph Ben (Frosin & Celemie DUFRESNE) b. 3 July 1898 (Raceland Ch.: v.5, p.74)
BABIN, Joseph Calvin (Auristil & Felicia LEBLANC) b. 6 Nov. 1898 (Houma Ch.: v.5, p.223)
BABIN, Joseph Chester (Frank & Elvine BELANGER) b. 13 Dec. 1899 (Houma Ch.: v.5, p.267)
BABIN, Joseph Chester (Frank & Elvire BELANGER) b. 13 Dec. 1899 (Houma Ch.: v.6, p.3)
BABIN, Joseph Clarence (Henry & Octavie USEE) b. 2 Feb. 1898 (Montegut Ch.: v.6, p.65)
BABIN, Joseph Emile (Adam & Exelina BERGERON) b. 4 Nov. 1898 (Houma Ch.: v.5, p.228)
BABIN, Joseph Ernest (Ernest & Adele PARR) b. 11 Oct. 1898 (Houma Ch.: v.5, p.223)
BABIN, Joseph Nikles (Clovis & Valentine ROBICHAUD) b. 5 May 1896 (Raceland Ch.: v.5, p.23)
BABIN, Joseph Nole (Auguste & Mathilde ESCHET) b. 11 Dec. 1899 (Houma Ch.: v.5, p.265)
BABIN, Joseph Thomas (Albert & Josephine LESTER) b. 14 Nov. 1899 (Houma Ch.: v.5, p.265)
BABIN, Josephine d. 20 Sept. 1896 at age 5 yrs. & 6 mths. (Houma Ch.: v.3, p.9)
BABIN, Laurence Auguste (Henry & Emilie BERGERON) b. 4 March 1897 (Houma Ch.: v.5, p.172)
BABIN, Lawrance d. 11 Oct. 1898 at age 1 yr. & 8 mths. (Houma Ch.: v.3, p.18)
BABIN, Leufroy m. 30 May 1898 Mary BERGERON (Houma Ct. Hse.: Mar. v.30 & 31, #456)
BABIN, Lorinne Marie m. Jean Louis HEBERT d. 13 Sept. 1897 at age 63 yrs. (Montegut Ch.: v.2, p.11)
BABIN, Louis Earl (Alexander N. & Alice GAUDIN) b. 1 March 1898 (Chacahoula Ch.: Gibson Record: Mar. Bk., v.1, #27)
BABIN, Louis Earl (Alexandre & Alice GAUDIN) b. 1 March 1898 (Chacahoula Ch.: Gibson Ch.: v.2, p.120)
BABIN, Louis Joseph (Theophile & Amanda BYE) b. 4 July 1896 (Thib. Ch.: v.7, p.407)
BABIN, Louisa (Euzelien & Odele BROUSSARD) m. 13 Feb. 1896 Joseph HEBERT (Houma Ch.: v.6-a, p.169)
BABIN, Louise m. 25 Jan. 1896 Joseph HEBERT (Houma Ct. Hse.: Mar. v.28, #420)

BABIN, Louise m. 8 Nov. 1899 Alfred LOVEJOY (Thib. Ct. Hse.: Mar. v.39, #261)
BABIN, Louise (Louis & Aimee BOUDREAUX) m. 18 Nov. 1899 Alfred LOVEJOY (Raceland Ch.: v.2, p.105)
BABIN, Lucien (Trasimond & Marie GAUBERT) b. 22 Jan. 1897 (Thib. Ch.: v.7, p.437)
BABIN, Lucile (Appollinaire & Olinda PERTUIT) b. 19 March 1896 (Raceland Ch.: v.5, p.22)
BABIN, Marguerite Burnisse (Theodule & Magnolia SAMANI) b. 6 Nov. 1899 (Houma Ch.: v.5, p.265)
BABIN, Marguerite Odile (Aristile & Felicia LEBLANC) b. 15 Nov. 1896 (Houma Ch.: v.5, p.162)
BABIN, Maria Honora (Appollinaire & Olinda PERTUIT) b. 29 July 1898 (Raceland Ch.: v.5, p.76)
BABIN, Marie m. 29 Feb. 1896 Trasimond HENRI (Houma Ct. Hse.: Mar. v.28, #470)
BABIN, Marie (Denis & Marie Estelle BABIN) m. 29 Feb. 1896 Trasimon HENRI (Houma Ch.: v.6-a, p.172)
BABIN, Marie (Elfege & Azelie MARCEL) b. 1 May 1898 (Thib. Ch.: v.7, p.550)
BABIN, Marie (Francois & Rosa PICOU) m. 25 Jan. 1898 Dominique PROSPERI (Montegut Ch.: v.4, p.232)
BABIN, Marie (Leo & Theoreme TOUPS) m. 26 Jan. 1898 Wilfried BERGERON (Thib. Ct. Hse.: Mar. v.37, #28)
BABIN, Marie (Leo & Thereine TOUPS) m. 26 Jan. 1898 Wilfried BERGERON (Thib. Ch.: v.14, p.176)
BABIN, Marie Anette Constance (Homer & Odilia BRAU) b. 12 Dec. 1896 (Thib. Ch.: v.7, p.430)
BABIN, Marie Angele (John & Eva GUIDRY) b. 6 July 1899 (Montegut Ch.: v.6, p.91)
BABIN, Marie Athee (Henry & Octavie USEE) b. 7 Jan. 1896 (Montegut Ch.: v.6, p.32)
BABIN, Marie Bessie (Valerie & Victoria THERIOT) b. 20 Nov. 1898 (Houma Ch.: v.5, p.221)
BABIN, Marie Elisabeth Josephine (Frank & Alice BUFORD) b. 27 Feb. 1898 (Houma Ch.: v.5, p.199)
BABIN, Marie J. d. 5 March 1898 at age 5 days (Houma Ch.: v.3, p.16)
BABIN, Marie Jeanne (Jimmy & Elicia DARCY) b. 28 Nov. 1896 (Houma Ch.: v.5, p.163)
BABIN, Marie Josephine (Luffroy & Marie BERGERON) b. 7 March 1899 (Houma Ch.: v.5, p.239)
BABIN, Marie Laure (Clovis & Florentine ROBICHAUX) b. 14 Jan. 1899 (Raceland Ch.: v.5, p.87)
BABIN, Marie Lucie (Edwin & Eda OLIVIER) b. 22 May 1896 (Thib. Ch.: v.7, p.410)
BABIN, Marie Olivia (Ernest & Marie TOUPS) b. 21 Aug. 1896 (Montegut Ch.: v.6, p.44)
BABIN, Marie Osea (Adam & Exelina BERGERON) b. 2 Jan. 1897 (Houma Ch.: v.5, p.176)

BABIN, Marie Theodosia (Uselin & Alfrida ROSS) b. 13 Aug. 1898 (Houma Ch.: v.5, p.218)
BABIN, Marigus (John & Eva GUIDRY) d. 12 Aug. 1898 at age 1 yr. & 3 days (Montegut Ch.: v.2, p.19)
BABIN, Mary (Edwin & Edda OLIVIER) d. 19 Aug. 1896 at age 3 mths. (Houma Ch.: v.3, p.8)
BABIN, Mary (Francois & Rosa PICOU) m. 5 Jan. 1898 Dominique PROSPERE (Houma Ct. Hse.: Mar. v.30 & 31, #176)
BABIN, Mary (Sylvain & Malvina BERGERON) m. 8 Nov. 1898 Herbert PITRE (Houma Ct. Hse.: Mar. v.30 & 31, #130)
BABIN, Mary Adele (Jamy & Felicia DARCE) b. 19 July 1899 (Houma Ch.: v.5, p.251)
BABIN, Mary Bertha (Edwin & Louisiane BABIN) b. 7 Feb. 1896; m.Calvin Paul BERGERON on 12 Jan. 1924. (Houma Ch.: Bapt. Bk., v.5, p.149)
BABIN, Mary Lelia (Albert & Josephine LESTER) b. 13 June 1898 (Houma Ch.: v.5, p.214)
BABIN, Octavie m. 20 Feb. 1898 Francois BERGERON (Houma Ch.: v.6-a, p.237)
BABIN, Octavie (Sylvain & Malvina BERGERON) m. 5 Jan. 1898 Francois BERGERON (Houma Ct. Hse.: Mar. v.30 & 31, #179)
BABIN, Octavie (Valentin & Alvenia HEBERT) m. 14 Dec. 1898 Jacques Joseph BONVILLAIN (Houma Ct. Hse.: Mar. v.30 & 31, #146)
BABIN, Onesime d. 1 Jan. 1896 at age 86 yrs. (Raceland Ch.: v.1, p.7)
BABIN, Paul Claude (Jamy & Amedilia BOUDREAU) b. 3 May 1898 (Houma Ch.: v.5, p.209)
BABIN, Paul Percy (Lineus & Nelsona THIBODAUX) b. 24 March 1898 (Thib. Ch.: v.7, p.548)
BABIN, Pearl Loretta (Telesphore & Felicie LAPEROUSE) b. 7 Feb. 1896 (Houma Ch.: v.5, p.146)
BABIN, Pierre (Alexandre & Marguerite DANOS) b. 23 Oct. 1898 (Raceland Ch.: v.5, p.81)
BABIN, Richard m. 30 Jan. 1899 Elvina MATHERNE (Thib. Ct. Hse.: Mar. v.38, #80)
BABIN, Richard (Justin & Alexina LANEUVILLE) m. 14 Feb. 1899 Elvina MATERNE (Raceland Ch.: v.2, p.92)
BABIN, Severine Lucie (Octave & Evelina GRO) b. 23 Nov. 1896 (Houma Ch.: v.5, p.162)
BABIN, Sidonie (Felix & Celeste THERIOT) m. 19 Jan. 1897 Taylor CHIASSON (Thib. Ct. Hse.: Mar. v.36, #32)
BABIN, Sidonie (Felix & Celeste THERIOT) m. 19 Jan. 1897 Tayleur CHIASSON (Lockport Ch.: v.2, p.157)
BABIN, Sylvanie d. 5 June 1898 at age 72 yrs. (Houma Ch.: v.3, p.16)
BABIN, Telesphore Adam d. 25 Jan. 1898 at age 2 mths. & 21 days (Houma Ch.: v.3, p.15)
BABIN, Telesphore Adam (Thelesphore & Felicie LAPEROUSE) b. 3 Nov. 1897 (Houma Ch.: v.5, p.191)

BABIN, Theotice d. 24 Aug. 1897 at age 81 yrs. (Houma Ch.: v.3, p.13)
BABIN, Thibodeux Solange Marie (Trasimon & Marie GOBARD) b. 27 Dec. 1898 (Thib. Ch.: v.7, p.528)
BABIN, Thomas Jean Baptiste (Ernest & Adele PARRE) b. 27 April 1896 (Houma Ch.: v.5, p.153)
BABIN, Valerie d. 10 Jan. 1899 at age 7 wks. (Houma Ch.: v.3, p.20)
BABIN, Valerie m. 13 Oct. 1898 Joseph LEBOEUF (Thib. Ct. Hse.: Mar. v.38, #294)
BABIN, Valerie m. 27 April 1899 Pierre ROBICHAUX (Thib. Ct. Hse.: Mar. v.39, #149)
BABIN, Valerie (Frosin & Josephine UZEY) m. 27 April 1899 Pierre ROBICHAUX (Raceland Ch.: v.2, p.96)
BABIN, Valerie (Louis & Aimee Marie BOUDREAUX) m. 22 Oct. 1898 Joseph LEBOEUF (Raceland Ch.: v.2, p.82)
BABIN, Valery m. 18 Jan. 1898 Victoria THERIOT (Houma Ct. Hse.: Mar. v.30 & 31, #226)
BABIN, Valery (Sylvain & Malvina BERGERON) m. 19 Jan. 1898 Victoria THERIOT (Houma Ch.: v.6-a, p.222)
BABIN, Willy Albert (Frank & Elvire BELANGER) b. 12 Sept. 1897 (Houma Ch.: v.5, p.186)
BABIN, Yvez Laurence (Philippe & Celeste THIBODAUX) b. 24 Jan. 1899 (Thib. Ch.: v.7, p.585)
BACCARA, Vincent (Antonio & Rosa RAS) m. 5 Sept. 1898 Josephine CALLON (Thib. Ct. Hse.: Mar. v.38, #258)
BACCARA, Vincent (Antonio & Rosa RAS) m. 5 Sept. 1898 Josephine CALLON (Larose Ch.: v.4, p.28)
BACCARA, Vincent of Lafourche Parish (Antonio & Rosa RAS) m. 1 Sept. 1898 Josephine CALLON of Lafourche Parish (Larose Ch.: v.3, p.10)
BACON, Agnes Lizzie (Ralph & Nina ROGER) b. 27 Oct. 1897 (Montegut Ch.: v.6, p.63)
BACON, Lelina Maria (Raph. & Nina ROGERS) b. 4 Nov. 1898 (Houma Ch.: v.5, p.232)

BADEAUX (Sometimes: BADAUX, BADEAU, BADOS, BADOUX)

BADEAUX, ----- child (Marcellin & Egypte ORGERON) d. 25 Dec. 1898 (Larose Ch.: v.1, p.45)
BADEAUX, Alcibiade of Lafourche Parish (Thomassin & Marie ADAM) m. 10 Feb. 1898 Doleina HEBERT, of Lafourche Parish (Larose Ch.: v.3, p.7)
BADEAUX, Alcibiade (Thomassin & Marie ADAM) m. 10 Feb. 1898 Dalcina HEBERT (Larose Ch.: v.4, p.5)
BADEAUX, Alcibiade (Thomassin & Marie ADAM) m. 10 Feb. 1898 Dolcina HEBERT (Thib. Ct. Hse.: Mar. v.37, #82)
BADEAUX, Camille (Tomassin & Mary ADAM) m. 21 Sept. 1899 Clotilde ACOSTA (Thib. Ct. Hse.: Mar. v.39, #233)
BADEAUX, Camille (Tomassin & Mary NOLAN) m. 21 Sept. 1899 Clotille ACOSTA (Larose Ch.: v.3, p.12)

BADEAUX, Camille (Tomissin & Mary AOLARE) m. 21 Sept. 1899 Clotilde ACOSTA (Larose Ch.: v.4, p.124)
BADEAUX, Charles Adam (Marcellin & Egypte ORGERON) b. 7 July 1899 (Larose Ch.: v.3, p.40)
BADEAUX, Charles Aloysius minor over 18 yrs., b. 19 Ag. 1878. (Thomas A. & Emma A. BADEAUX) Emancipation: 4 Jan. 1897. (Thib. Ct. Hse.: Succ. #1502)
BADEAUX, Cora Notilia (Marcellin & Egypte ORGERON) b. 8 Nov. 1896 (Larose Ch.: v.2, p.186)
BADEAUX, Edna (Telemaque J. & Valentine TRICHE) m. 12 Jan. 1898 John P. EXNICIOS (Lockport Ch.: v.2, p.178)
BADEAUX, Edna (Telemaque J. & Valentine TRICHE) m. 12 Jan. 1898 John P. EXNICIOS (Thib. Ct. Hse.: Mar. v.37, #5)
BADEAUX, Felix d. 18 Dec. 1896 at age 16 yrs. (Thib. Ch.: v.3, p.192)
BADEAUX, Francis - priest Ordained a Deacon: 1899. (Thib. Ch.: v.7, p.585)
BADEAUX, Lina Marie (Alcibiade & Dolcina HEBERT) b. 7 April 1899 (Larose Ch.: v.3, p.38)
BADEAUX, Lise Agnes (Joseph & Aglae BELLANGER) b. 27 Oct. 1896 (Larose Ch.: v.2, p.187)
BADEAUX, Lovinia Emilie (Joseph & Aglae BELLANGER) b. 16 Feb. 1899 (Larose Ch.: v.3, p.36)
BADEAUX, Marie Georgina (Louis & Adorestine ORGERON) b. 13 Jan. 1897 (Larose Ch.: v.3, p.3)
BAHALA, Antonina (Vincenzo & Josephine CALO) b. 9 Nov. 1899 (Larose Ch.: v.3, p.50)
BAILEY, Anderson m. 16 Jan. 1896 Susanna BAPTISTE (Houma Ct. Hse.: Mar. v.28, #397)

BAILLE (See: BAYE)

BAILLEAUX, Rosina (Henri & Aurore BLANCHARD) m. 26 June 1899 Merille CHIASSON (Thib. Ct. Hse.: Mar. v.39, #180)
BALDASSARE, Cicio m. 9 Sept. 1897 Rosalia TORTORICA (Houma Ct. Hse.: Mar. v.29 & 30, #63)
BALDASSARE, Cicio (Cicio & Francisca LACATALANCIE) m. 13 Sept. 1897 Rosalie TORTORICI (Houma Ch.: v.6-a, p.214)

BALLARD (Sometimes: BALARD)
BALLARD, Alice (James & Marie PITRE) m. 24 June 1897 Alexandre HEBERT (Thib. Ch.: v.14, p.149)
BALLARD, Alice (James & Marie PITRE) m. 24 June 1897 Alexandre HEBERT (Thib. Ct. Hse.: Mar. v.36, #160)
BALLARD, Ellen Mrs. m. 5 Jan. 1899 Timothy NIPLITT (Houma Ct. Hse.: Mar. v.30 & 31, #187)
BALLARD, Robert m. 9 March 1897 Agnes BABIN (Houma Ch.: v.6-a, p.196)
BALLARD, Robert Christi (Robert & Mary Agnes BABIN) b. 25 Dec. 1897 (Houma Ch.: v.5, p.198)

BALLS, Clara m. 4 Feb. 1897 James WILLIAMS (Houma Ct. Hse.: Mar. v.29 & 30, #289)
BALLY, Gerome Joseph (Frank & Melisaire AUTIN) b. 7 March 1898 (Larose Ch.: v.3, p.22)
BANKS, Laura M. m. 25 Aug. 1898 Richard HAMMOND (Thib. Ct. Hse.: Mar. v.38, #265)
BANKS, Mally m. 28 Dec. 1896 Joseph BROWN (Thib. Ct. Hse.: Mar. v.36, #172)
BANKS, Ozemie m. 25 March 1898 Mary FINNIGS (Thib. Ct. Hse.: Mar. v.37, #133)
BAPTISTE, Anatole d. 10 April 1898 at age 36 yrs. (Thib. Ch.: v.3, p.213)
BAPTISTE, Anatole m. 25 March 1898 Louisa ROBINSON (Thib. Ct. Hse: Mar. v.37, #132)
BAPTISTE, Andre d. 11 Dec. 1899 at age 6 yrs. & 4 mths. (Thib. Ch.: v.3, p.246)
BAPTISTE, Andrew m. 5 March 1898 Eliska CARTER (Thib. Ct. Hse.: Mar. v.37, #119)
BAPTISTE, Augustine Mrs. d. 25 Dec. 1898 at age 70 yrs. (Thib. Ch.: v.3, p.224)
BAPTISTE, Clementine m. 21 Dec. 1898 Horace JONES (Thib. Ct. Hse.: Mar. v.38, #321)
BAPTISTE, Daniel m. 3 Feb. 1898 Cecilia SCRUBB (Houma Ct. Hse.: Mar. v.30 & 31, #274)
BAPTISTE, Elizabeth m. 17 June 1897 Celestin ALECK, Jr. (Thib. Ct. Hse.: Mar. v.36, #174)
BAPTISTE, Eugee m. 27 Dec. 1897 Virginia McGEE (Houma Ct. Hse.: Mar. v.29 & 30, #160)
BAPTISTE, Ida Baptiste (Levaudais & Minerva BAPTISTE) b. 11 Oct. 1898 (Thib. Ch.: v.7, p.518)
BAPTISTE, Jean Baptiste d. 19 July 1897 at age 35 yrs. (Thib. Ch.: v.3, p.203)
BAPTISTE, John m. 5 May 1897 Matilda HENRY (Thib. Ct. Hse.: Mar. v.36, #137)
BAPTISTE, Joseph (Jean & Lena DEVORD) b. 8 Jan. 1898 (Thib. Ch.: v.7, p.547)
BAPTISTE, Joseph (Wilbert & Ophelia EDMOND) b. 22 Oct. 1899 (Thib. Ch.: v.7, p.583)
BAPTISTE, Marie Augustine (Ida) b. 8 Aug. 1896 (Thib. Ch.: v.7, p.414)
BAPTISTE, Marie Eva (Louisiane) b. 13 April 1896 (Thib. Ch.: v.7, p.401)
BAPTISTE, Marie Sephonia (Ozemee & Odilia AUGUSTIN) b. 30 May 1896 (Raceland Ch.: v.5, p.27)
BAPTISTE, Mary m. 23 Nov. 1899 Benjamin JAMES (Thib. Ct. Hse.: Mar. v.39, #269)
BAPTISTE, Susanna m. 16 Jan. 1896 Anderson BAILEY (Houma Ct. Hse.: Mar. v.28, #397)
BAPTISTE, Sylvestre m. 28 April 1898 Anna CHARLES (Thib. Ct. Hse.: Mar. v.38, #172)

BAPTISTE, Wilbert m. 24 Feb. 1897 Julia EDMOND (Thib. Ct. Hse.: Mar. v.36, #89)

BARANCO, Charles m. 22 June 1897 Ozea ROBICHAUX (Thib. Ct. Hse.: Mar. v.37, #182)

BARBARIA, Francesco d. 30 Oct. 1899 at age 19 yrs. (Thib. Ch.: v.3, p.242)

BARBER, Mahala m. 22 May 1899 George BRADLEY (Houma Ct. Hse.: Mar. v.31 & 32, #12)

BARBIER, Emma (Pierre & Madeleine GAUTREAUX) m. 14 Oct. 1899 Joseph BOURGEOIS (Lockport Ch.: v.2, p.210)

BARBIER, Emma (Pierre & Magdeleine GAUTREAUX) m. 14 Oct. 1899 Joseph BOURGEOIS (Thib. Ct. Hse.: Mar. v.39, #242)

BARBIER, Marie (Pierre & Magdeleine GAUTREAUX) m. 25 Jan. 1897 Clay MELANCON (Thib. Ct. Hse.: Mar. v.36, #27)

BARBIER, Marie (Pierre & Magdeline GAUTRAUX) m. 25 Jan. 1897 Clay MELANCON (Lockport Ch.: v.2, p.158)

BARELETTE, Joseph Gratien (Charles & Celestine PLAISANCE) b. 31 Jan. 1897 (Raceland Ch.: v.5, p.41)

BARELETTE, Marie Adoe (Charles & Celestine PLAISANCE) b. 17 Dec. 1898 (Raceland Ch.: v.5, p.86)

BARILLEAUX (Sometimes: BARILLAUX, BARILLEAU, BARILLO, BARRILLAU, BARRILLEAUX)

BARILLEAUX, Alice (Francois & Alice DAIGRE) m. 18 Jan. 1897 Edgard TOUPS (Thib. Ct. Hse.: Mar. v.36, #37)

BARILLEAUX, Alice (Francois & Alice DAIGRE) m. 18 Jan. 1897 Edgard TOUPS (Lockport Ch.: v.2, p.156)

BARILLEAUX, Antoine Emile (Theophile & Elvire MELANCON) b. 6 Jan. 1898 (Thib. Ch.: v.7, p.480)

BARILLEAUX, Emma (Francois & Alice DAIGUE) m. 22 Oct. 1896 Joseph BASCLE (Thib. Ct Hse.: Mar. v.36, #153)

BARILLEAUX, Paul Amand (Anathole & Melina PONTIFF) b. 30 Dec. 1898 (Houma Ch.: v.5, p.237)

BARILLEAUX, Rosina (Henri & Aurore BLANCHARD) m. 26 June 1899 Merille CHIASSON (Lockport Ch.: v.2, p.208)

BARILLEAUX, Seraphine m. Joseph GROS d. 21 Aug. 1897 at age 81 yrs. (Lockport Ch.: v.1, #17)

BARIOUX, Arthur (Anathol & Melina PONTIFF) b. 15 Feb. 1896 (Houma Ch.: v.5, p.170)

BARKER, Adolphe Rey (Thomas & Anna ROSSIGNOL) b. 10 July 1897 (Thib. Ch.: v.7, p.456)

BARKER, Helene Agnes (Thomas & Anna ROSSIGNOL) b. 2 Oct. 1898 (Thib. Ch.: v.7, p.515)

BARKER, Julia m. 8 April 1899 Thomas HENDERSON (Thib. Ct. Hse.: Mar. v.39, #138)

BARKER, May Ive (Thomas & Anna ROSSIGNOL) b. 5 Feb. 1896 (Thib. Ch.: v.7, p.392)

BARKER, Warren Samuel (Jhon & Octavie LEJEUNE) b. 5 Dec. 1896 (Lockport Ch.: v.3-A, #34)

BARKER, Warren Samuel (Jhon & Octavie LEPINE) b. 5 Dec. 1896 (Lockport Ch.: v.3, #34)

BARKUS, Bertha m. 11 Nov. 1897 Edward JACKSON (Houma Ct. Hse.: Mar. v.29 & 30, #136)
BARKUS, Josephine m. 9 Oct. 1897 Edward VERRET (Houma Ct. Hse.: Mar. v.29 & 30, #115)
BARR, N. Mrs. d. 26 Dec. 1899 at age 72 yrs. (Houma Ch.: v.3, p.27)
BARRAH, ----- Mrs. d. 14 Oct. 1899 (Houma Ch.: v.3, p.25)

BARRAS (Sometimes: BARRA)

BARRAS, Clementine (Alcee & Leonie BOUDREAUX) b. 6 Sept. 1898 (Chackbay Ch.: v.1, p.127)
BARRAS, Georgiana (Leufroy & Mary Ann PENNISON) m. 8 July 1897 Isaac DUPLANTIS (Houma Ch.: v.6-a, p.209)
BARRAS, Georgie m. 19 June 1897 Isaac DUPLANTIS (Houma Ct. Hse.: Mar. v.29 & 30, #34)
BARRAS, Sue m. 30 Dec. 1897 Richard SCRUGGS (Houma Ct. Hse.: Mar. v.29 & 30, #167)
BARRE, Marie Leska (George & Marie BABIN) b. 15 March 1896 (Houma Ch.: v.5, p.149)
BARRET, Lizzie m. 14 April 1898 Henry FRANCIS (Thib. Ct. Hse.: Mar. v.38, #153)
BARRILA, Katherina m. 21 March 1899 Salvatore TOTORICH (Houma Ct. Hse.: Mar. v.31 & 32, #370)
BARRILE, Katharina of Terrebonne Parish m. 10 April 1899 Salvatore PORTORICHE (Houma Ch.: v.6-B, p.3)
BARRILE, Maria of Terrebonne Parish m. 29 April 1899 Bernardo MANCUSO, of Terrebonne Parish (Houma Ch.: v.6-B, p.3)
BARRILLE, Maria m. 1 April 1899 Bernardo MANCUSO (Houma Ct. Hse.: Mar. v.31 & 32, #382)

BARRIOS (Sometimes: BAR, BARIOS, BARR, BARRUIS)

BARRIOS, ----- girl (Ulysse) d. 25 Dec. 1899 at age 3 days (Lockport Ch.: v.1, #49)
BARRIOS, Abdon (Louis & Nathalie PEREZ) m. 30 Dec. 1899 Alice AUCOIN (Lockport Ch.: v.2, p.212)
BARRIOS, Adam (Leo & Marguerite DUHE) m. 29 June 1897 Amelie LASSEIGNE (Thib. Ct. Hse.: Mar. v.37, #184)
BARRIOS, Aglae m. Alindor Euesthe DIT (Dondonne) d. 19 Feb. 1896 at age 32 yrs. (Lockport Ch.: v.1, #6)
BARRIOS, Aimee m. 25 Aug. 1897 Anderique DELAUNE (Lockport Ch.: v.2, p.171)
BARRIOS, Aimee m. 25 Aug. 1897 Auderique DELAUNE (Thib. Ct. Hse: Mar. v.37, #215)
BARRIOS, Aiva Josephine (Jho & Catherine DAVIS) b. 21 Nov. 1896 (Lockport Ch.: v.3-A, #19)
BARRIOS, Aiva Josephine (Jho & Celestine DAVIS) b. 21 Nov. 1896 (Lockport Ch.: v.3, #19)
BARRIOS, Aldon (Louis & Nathalie PEREZ) m. 20 Dec. 1899 Alice AUCOIN (Thib. Ct. Hse.: Mar. v.39, #292)
BARRIOS, Anna (Gustave & Emelie BERGERON) m. 12 April 1899 Octave V. LEBRUN (Thib. Ct. Hse.: Mar. v.39, #137)

BARRIOS, Anna (Gustave & Emelie BERGERON) m. 12 April 1899 Octave LEBRUN (Lockport Ch.: v.2, p.205)
BARRIOS, Annie Rose (Urbain & Odille RICHOUX) b. 30 Aug. 1899 (Larose Ch.: v.3, p.44)
BARRIOS, Berthe Marie (Joseph & Zeolie LEGENDRE) b. 16 Aug. 1896 (Thib. Ch.: v.7, p.412)
BARRIOS, Charles (Alces & Leonie BOUDREAU) b. 6 July 1896 (Thib. Ch.: v.7, p.408)
BARRIOS, Emmanuel d. 25 March 1896 Children listed: Edgar J.; Noah J.; Julia M.; Alice M.; Luke J.; d.Emanuel J. m. 22 Jan. 1878 Josephine TOUPS (Joseph O.); Maxime J.; Argentine M. Petition for inventory for recognition of natural tutrix: 9 April 1896. (Thib. Ct. Hse.: Succ. #1487)
BARRIOS, Emmanuel d. 26 March 1896 at age 38 yrs. (Lockport Ch.: v.1, #9)
BARRIOS, Felicien d. 3 Oct. 1897 at age 22 mths. (Thib. Ch.: v.3, p.206)
BARRIOS, G. H. (Gustave & Emelie BERGERON) m. 7 Oct. 1896 Camelia BOURG (Lockport Ch.: v.2, p.154)
BARRIOS, G. H. (Gustave & Emelie BERGERON) m. 7 Oct. 1896 Camilia BOURG (Thib. Ct. Hse.: Mar. v.36, #149)
BARRIOS, James Joseph (Theophile & Ezilda BENOIT) b. 9 June 1897 (Chacahoula Ch.: v.4, p.20)
BARRIOS, Joseph David (Jho & Rosa LOUP) b. 2 Feb. 1897 (Lockport Ch.: v.3-A, #11)
BARRIOS, Joseph David (Jho & Rosa LOUP) b. 2 Feb. 1897 (Lockport Ch.: v.3, #11)
BARRIOS, Joseph Robert (Odon & Olivia LOUP) b. 2 April 1897 (Lockport Ch.: v.3-A, #40)
BARRIOS, Joseph Robert (Odon & Olivia LOUP) b. 2 April 1897 (Lockport Ch.: v.3, #40)
BARRIOS, Joseph Ronald (Myrtile & Adolphina BERGERON) b. 8 Aug. 1897 (Chacahoula Ch.: v.4, p.23)
BARRIOS, Joseph Ulysse (Ulysse J. & Corine LEBLANC) b. 20 Jan. 1897 (Lockport Ch.: v.3-A, #5)
BARRIOS, Joseph Ulysse (Ulysse J. & Corine LEBLANC) b. 20 Jan. 1897 (Lockport Ch.: v.3, #5)
BARRIOS, Josephine d. 29 June 1899 at age 56 yrs. (Lockport Ch.: v.1, #24)
BARRIOS, Lea (Leo & Marguerite DUHE) m. 8 Sept. 1898 Nicholas BENOIT (Thib. Ct. Hse.: Mar. v.38, #251)
BARRIOS, Lea (Leo & Marguerite DUHE) m. 8 Sept. 1898 Nicholas BENOIT (Thib. Ch.: v.14, p.220)
BARRIOS, Louis Wuillace (Joseph & Zeolide LEGENDRE) b. 15 May 1899 (Thib. Ch.: v.7, p.549)
BARRIOS, Marguerite Aida (Joseph & Angele THIBODEAUX) b. 12 Jan. 1898 (Chacahoula Ch.: v.4, p.4)
BARRIOS, Marie Aline (Myrtile & Adolphina BERGERON) b. 13 Dec. 1898 (Chacahoula Ch.: v.4, p.16)

BARRIOS, Michael (Paul & Melissaire ARCENAUX) m. 4 July 1898 Phelonise ROGER (Thib. Ct. Hse.: Mar. v.38, #217)

BARRIOS, Michel (Paul & Melissaire ARSENAUX) m. 4 July 1898 Phelonize ROGER (Lockport Ch.: v.2, p.191 & 192)

BARRIOS, Numa d. 20 Dec. 1899 (Chacahoula Ch.: Gibson Ch.: v.2, p.183)

BARRIOS, Shalby Alma (Theophile & Ezilda BENOIT) b. 23 Nov. 1899 (Thib. Ch.: v.7, p.587)

BARRIOS, Ulysse (Ulysse) d. 22 Feb. 1899 at age 2 yrs. & 1 mth. (Lockport Ch.: v.1, #8)

BARRIOS, Urbain m. 26 Oct. 1898 Odille RICHOUX (Thib. Ct. Hse.: Mar. v.38, #302)

BARRIOS, Urbain of Lafourche Parish (Barthelemy & Carmelite RODRIGUEZ) m. 29 Oct. 1898 Odille RICHOUX, of Lafourche Parish (Larose Ch.: v.3, p.10)

BARROW, Henry m. 18 Jan. 1896 Ellen BECKTON (Houma Ct. Hse.: Mar. v.28, #403)

BARROW, Nellie m. 8 Jan. 1897, Oscar BROOKS (Thib. Ct. Hse: Mar. v.36, #15)

BARTELLO, Amelia m. 21 Sept. 1899 Alcide UZE (Houma Ch.: v.6-B, p.4)

BARTELLS, Camillia m. 2 Sept. 1899 Alcide UZIE (Houma Ct. Hse.: Mar. v.31 & 32, #115)

BARTLEY, Charles Jr. m. 10 May 1899 Louisa SAVAGE (Thib. Ct. Hse.: Mar. v.39, #163)

BARTLEY, Lawless (Charles & Sera ANDRE) m. 17 Feb. 1896 Mary SEVERE (Thib. Ct. He.: Mar. v.35, #42)

BARTLEY, Willie m. 7 Oct. 1897 Tema GUIDROZ (Thib. Ct. Hse.: Mar. v.37, #245)

BARTON, George m. 12 Oct. 1898 Lalia DAVIS (Thib. Ct. Hse.: Mar. v.38, #291)

BASCLE, Irene m. 2 July 1898 Albert R. VIGUERIE (Houma Ct. Hse.: Mar. v.30 & 31, #46)

BASCLE, Irene (Felix & Ada LESTER) m. 12 July 1898 Albert R. VIGUERIE (Houma Ch.: v.6-a, p.245)

BASCLE, Joseph (Abel & Luise BIRDSALL) m. 22 Oct. 1896 Emma BARRILLEAUX (Thib. Ct. Hse.: Mar. v.36, #153)

BASCLE, Marie Florence (Ira & Cora BELANGER) b. 30 Dec. 1899 (Montegut Ch.: v.6, p.97)

BASCLE, Marie May (Joseph & Emma BARILLEAUX) b. 8 Aug. 1897 (Montegut Ch.: v.6, p.59)

BASCLE, Marie Pearl (Harry & Cora BELANGER) b. 22 Dec. 1897 (Montegut Ch.: v.6, p.64)

BASCLE, Thomas Abbey (Frank & Emelia GUIDRY) b. 7 March 1899 (Montegut Ch.: v.6, p.86)

BASCLE, Tilden Peter (Emile L. & Alice BIRDSALL) m. 23 Dec. 1899 Josephine FALGOUT (Houma Ct. Hse.: Mar. v.31 & 32, #189)

BASETT, Randolphe Auguste (Ovide & Agil WARZLOW) b. 16 Jan. 1899 (Houma Ch.: v.5, p.235)

BASSET, Marie Iviane Mabel (Jules & Louisiane LEBLANC) b. 10 May 1898 (Thib. Ch.: v.7, p.490)
BATCHE, Cecile Argentine (John & Dulcina CANTRELLE) b. 5 Jan. 1897 (Larose Ch.: v.3, p.4)

BAUDOIN (Sometimes: BAUDIN, BEAUDOIN, BODOUIN)
BAUDOIN, Alcide (Joseph & Justilia BOUDREAUX) b. 9 May 1896 (Theriot Ch.: v.1-B, p.100)
BAUDOIN, Bernadette (Felix & Eveline FALGOUT) m. 27 Jan. 1899 Albert ROUSSEL (Lockport Ch.: v.2, p.213)
BAUDOIN, Derris d. 17 July 1897 (Raceland Ch.: v.1, p.14)
BAUDOIN, Elphege m. 27 Feb. 1897 Evellia CHAUVIN (Lockport Ch.: v.2, p.160)
BAUDOIN, Elphege (Aristile & Zelia RODRIGUE) m. 27 Feb. 1897 Evelline CHAUVIN (Thib. Ct. Hse.: Mar. v.38, #65)
BAUDOIN, Ena Eve (Damas & Evellie SOPIA) b. 8 Sept. 1896 (Lockport Ch.: v.2, p.335)
BAUDOIN, Ernest m. 7 Aug. 1896 Julia SAPIA (Thib. Ct. Hse.: Mar. v.36, #130)
BAUDOIN, Ernest (Louis & Felicie BABIN) m. 22 Aug. 1896 Julia SAPIE (Raceland Ch.: v.2, p.21)
BAUDOIN, Eusebe Harry (Ernest & Julia SAPIER) b. 14 Aug. 1897 (Raceland Ch.: v.5, p.53)
BAUDOIN, Felix d. 29 June 1897 at age 35 yrs. (Raceland Ch.: v.1, p.14)
BAUDOIN, Joseph m. 18 Sept. 1897 Olympe GERVAIS (Thib. Ct. Hse.: Mar. v.37, #229)
BAUDOIN, Joseph m. 18 Sept. 1897 Olympe GERVAIS (Lockport Ch.: v.2, p.174)
BAUDOIN, Joseph Ollivier (Sylvain & Maxime WAGUESPACK) b. 21 Aug. 1897 (Thib. Ch.: v.7, p.461)
BAUDOIN, Louis d. 10 May 1896 (Montegut Ch.: v.2, p.4)
BAUDOIN, Louis (Emile & Emelie BARIOS) b. 23 Oct. 1897 (Raceland Ch.: v.5, p.57)
BAUDOIN, Louis Adam (Louis & Felicie BABIN) b. 4 April 1897 (Raceland Ch.: v.5, p.46)
BAUDOIN, Marie Anny (Joseph & Justilia BOUDREAUX) b. 28 April 1899 (Houma Ch.: v.5, p.245)
BAUDOIN, Paul Lawrence (Oscar & Liza MICHEL) b. 23 Nov. 1898 (Houma Ch.: v.5, p.249)
BAUDOIN, Samson Augustin (Sylvestre & Brigitte FALGOU) b. 20 June 1898 (Raceland Ch.: v.5, p.74)

BAUVAIS (See: BEAUVAIS)

BAYE (Sometimes: BAILLE)
BAYE, Agnes Laura (Pierre & Elmire ORGERON) b. 5 Nov. 1899 (Thib. Ch.: v.7, p.572)
BAYE, Antoine Nessen (Luke & --- THIBODEAUX) b. 8 Jan. 1899 (Thib. Ch.: v.7, p.531)

BAYE, Bulah Geneva (Albert & Cecile DANTIN) b. 11 Nov. 1899 (Thib. Ch.: v.7, p.574)
BAYE, Clarence Justin Adrien Olivier (Raoul & Laure ROGER) b. 8 Aug. 1899 (Thib. Ch.: v.7, p.558)
BAYE, Corinne Marguerite (Leon & Emelie DUHE) b. 1 March 1897 (Thib. Ch.: v.7, p.443)
BAYE, Estella Celine (Albert & Cecile DANTIN) b. 6 Sept. 1897 (Thib. Ch.: v.7, p.463)
BAYE, Eve Louise (Paul & Scholastie MARTIN) b. 17 Aug. 1897 (Thib. Ch.: v.7, p.461)
BAYE, Fernand (Claiborne & Emile HEBERT) m. 9 Oct. 1899 Octavie MALBROUGH (Thib. Ct. Hse.: Mar. v.39, #243)
BAYE, Fernand (Claiborne & Emilie HEBERT) m. 9 Oct. 1899 Octavie MALBROUGH (Thib. Ch.: v.14, p.302)
BAYE, Freddie Claude (Wallace & Lylie HEBERT) b. 25 Feb. 1899 (Thib. Ch.: v.7, p.591)
BAYE, Joseph Samgues (Pierre & Elmire AUGERON) b. 30 Dec. 1897 (Thib. Ch.: v.7, p.478)
BAYE, Julia (Claiborne & Emelie HEBERT) m. 16 Feb. 1898 Narcisse ADAM (Thib. Ct. Hse.: Mar. v.37, #101)
BAYE, Julie (Claiborne & Emelie HEBERT) m. 16 Feb. 1898 Narcisse ADAM (Thib. Ch.: v.14, p.190)
BAYE, Legendre Zulman (Edgard & Odilia DAIGLE) b. 26 March 1897 (Thib. Ch.: v.7, p.446)
BAYE, Luc (Theodule & Irma BOUTERIE) m. 27 April 1898 Zephire THIBODAUX (Thib. Ct. Hse.: Mar. v.38, #164)
BAYE, Luc (Theodule & Irma BOUTERIE) m. 27 April 1898 Zephise THIBODAUX (Thib. Ch.: v.14, p.199)
BAYE, Marie Berthe (Edgar & Odile DAIGLE) b. 27 Nov. 1899 (Thib. Ch.: v.7, p.576)
BAYE, Marie Bulah (Oscar & Philomene ADAM) b. 21 Nov. 1899 (Thib. Ch.: v.7, p.576)
BAYE, Marie Gussie (Paul & Scholastique MARTIN) b. 31 Dec. 1898 (Thib. Ch.: v.7, p.530)
BAYE, Marie Virginie (Wilfrid & Agathe ADAM) b. 28 Jan. 1898 (Thib. Ch.: v.7, p.483)
BAYE, Pierre m. 2 Jan. 1897 Elmire ORGERON (Thib. Ct. Hse.: Mar. v.36, #5)
BAYE, Pierre m. 4 Jan. 1897 Elmire ORGERON (Larose Ch.: v.3, p.4)
BAYE, Pierre m. 4 Jan. 1897 Elmire ORGERON (Larose Ch.: v.4, p.67)
BAYE, Pierre m. 4? Jan. 1897 Elmire ORGERON (Larose Ch.: v.4, p.120)
BAYE, Raoul (Claiborne & Amelie ABERT) m. 26 Sept. 1898 Laura ROGER (Thib. Ch.: v.14, p.225)
BAYE, Raoul (Claiborne & Amelie ABERT) m.26 Sept. 1898 Laura ROGER (Thib. Ct. Hse.: Mar. v.38, #282)
BAYE, Wallace (John & Josephine -----) m. 9 Feb. 1899 Lily HEBERT (Thib. Ch.: v.14, p.262)

BAYE, Wallace (John & Josephine DANTIN) m. 9 Feb. 1899 Lily HEBERT (Thi. Ct. Hse.: Mar. v.38, #79)

BAYEUX, Camille Joseph (Henri & Marcelitte BADEAU) b. 12 Aug. 1899 (Larose Ch.: v.3, p.44)

BAYEUX, Marie Leona (Henry & Marcelitte BADEAUX) b. 6 Nov. 1896 (Larose Ch.: v.2, p.186)

BAZET, Ernestine Ray (Ovide & Agnes WURZLOW) b. 7 Feb. 1897 (Houma Ch.: v.5, p.168)

BAZET, Eva (Bernard F.) m. 1 March 1897 Randolph L. ZELENKA (Houma Ch.: v.6-a, p.195)

BAZET, Eve m. 27 Feb. 1897 Rudolph L. ZELENKA (Houma Ct. Hse.: Mar. v.29 & 30, #335)

BAZET, Hugh Maxwell Wallis (Theophile & Mary Helen WALLIS) b. 16 Oct. 1897 (Houma Ch.: Epis. Ch.: v.1, p.116)

BAZET, Ovid F. (Bernard F. & Mary Ernestine THERIOT) m. 24 Sept. 1896 Mary Agnes WURZLOW (Houma Ch.: v.6-a, p.181)

BAZET, Ovid F. (Bernard F. & Mary Ernestine THERIOT) m. 24 Sept. 1896 Mary Agnes WURZLOW (Houma Ct. Hse.: Mar. v.29 & 30, #152)

BAZET, Theophile F. m. 19 Nov. 1896 Helen Gertrude WALLIS (Houma Ct. Hse.: Mar. v.29 & 30, #188)

BAZET, Theophile F. (Bernard D. & Mary Ernestine THERIOT) m. 26 Nov. 1896 Helene Gertrude WALLIS (Houma Ch.: v.6-a, p.185)

BEADLE, Louise Angeline (Thomas & Olivia SUAREZ) b. 16 Jan. 1898 (Chacahoula Ch.: Gibson Records: Mar. Bk., v.1, #17)

BEADLE, Louise Angeline (Thomas & Olivia SUAREZ) b. 16 Jan. 1898 (Chacahoula Ch.: Gibson Ch.: v.2, p.118)

BEARD, Robert T. m. 20 Jan. 1897 Camillia MATHERNE (Thib. Ct. Hse.: Mar. v.36, #43)

BEAUFORT, Virginie m. William QUICK d. 12 Jan. 1897 at age 57 yrs. (Houma Ch.: v.3, p.11)

BEAULAIN, Joseph Valmo (Louis & Emma CROCHET) b. 1 Feb. 1899 (Houma Ch.: v.5, p.237)

BEAUVAIS (Sometimes: BAUVAIS, BOVAIS)

BEAUVAIS, Elisabeth (Ernest & Marie EVANS) m. 28 April 1897 Raoul JEANMARD (Thib. Ch.: v.14, p.140)

BEAUVAIS, Elizabeth (Ernest & Marie EVANS) m. 28 April 1897 Raoul JEANMARD (Thib. Ct. Hse.: Mar. v.36, #127)

BEAUVAIS, Henry E. m. 27 Sept. 1899 Maggie M. TUCKER (Thib. Ch.: v.14, p.299)

BEAUVAIS, Henry E. (Ernest & Mary EVANS) m. 27 Sept. 1899 Maggie May TUCKER (Thib. Ct. Hse.: Mar. v.39, #222)

BEAUVAIS, Marie Elizabeth (Ernest & Ernestine LEDET) b. 28 Sept. 1899 (Thib. Ch.: v.8, p.10)

BEAUVAIS, Marie Ophile (Ernest & Ernestine LEDET) b. 8 Jan. 1898 (Thib. Ch.: v.7, p.482)

BECKTON, Ellen m. 18 Jan. 1896 Henry BARROW (Houma Ct. Hse.: Mar. v.28, #403)
BECKTON, Minerva m. 21 Feb. 1898 Oville WILLIAMS (Houma Ct. Hse.: Mar. v.30 & 31, #315)
BECNEL, Felicie (Telesmar & Ezelda RODRIGUES) m. 9 Feb. 1899 Lucien LORIO (Houma Ct. Hse.: Mar. v.30 & 31, #239)
BECON, Marie Aijdebella (Raphael & Nina ROGERE) b. 16 Jan. 1896 (Houma Ch.: v.5, p.145)
BEHR, Lure (Samuel & Adile KAHN) m. 18 Aug. 1897 Louise O. GREEN (Houma Ch.: Epis. Ch.: v.1, p.342)
BEHR, Rosalie Adele (Leon & Louise Alberta GREEN) b. 28 July 1898 (Houma Ch.: Epis. Ch.: v.1, p.118)
BELASON, John m. 23 Sept. 1899 Margaret GINSMORE (Houma Ct. Hse.: Mar. v.31 & 32, #142)
BELATRE, Joseph Leonie (Felix & Henriette DAIGLE) b. 1 Aug. 1896 (Thib. Ch.: v.7, p.410)
BELE, Francois (Laurent & Barbe GRILLON) m. 15 Oct. 1897 Louise BOURGEOIS (Houma Ct. Hse.: Mar. v.29 & 30, #122)
BELISLE, Gilbert John (John & Julia DOMINGUE) b. 30 March 1899 (Theriot Ch.: v.2, p.37)
BELL, Eddie m. 31 Aug. 1899 Alice DAVIS (Thib. Ct. Hse.: Mar. v.39, #216)
BELL, Marguerite m. 27 April 1898 Edward JOHNSON (Thib. Ct. Hse.: Mar. v.38, #171)
BELL, Rosa m. 11 Feb. 1897 John PINCKNEY (Houma Ct. Hse.: Mar. v.29 & 30, #305)
BELLA, Emmanuel (Charles & Rosalie GAGLIANELLA) b. 6 Nov. 1897 (Chacahoula Ch.: Gibson Ch.: v.2, p.113)
BELLA, Emmanuel (Charley & Rosalia GAGLIANELLA) b. 6 Nov. 1897 (Chacahoula Ch.: Gibson Ch.: Mar. Bk., v.1, #79)
BELLAMORE, Emelia (Felix & Victoria RODRIGUEZ) m. 26 Dec. 1896 Victor BOURG (Houma Ct. Hse.: Mar. v.29 & 30, #208)
BELLAMORE, Felicia (Felix & Frances RODRIGUEZ) m. 26 Dec. 1896 Ernest CARRERE (Houma Ct. Hse.: Mar. v.29 & 30, #216)

BELLANGER (Sometimes: BELANGER, BELLENGER)

BELLANGER, Adam (d.Nicholas & Eulalie COMEAUX) m. 19 Dec. 1896 Armelia BOURG (Montegut Ch.: v.4, p.214)
BELLANGER, Adam (Nicholas & Eulalie COMEAUX) m. 23 Nov. 1896 Armelia BOURG (Houma Ct. Hse.: Mar. v.29 & 30, #192)
BELLANGER, Agnes (Ermogene & Liza KNIGHT) b. 24 Feb. 1896 (Raceland Ch.: v.5, p.19)
BELLANGER, Agnes Levie (Henri & Celemee HENRI) b. 20 April 1899 (Theriot Ch.: v.2, p.40)
BELLANGER, Aimee m. Edouard CHIASSON d. 27 June 1899 at age 49 yrs. (Montegut Ch.: v.2, p.27)
BELLANGER, Ather Agnes (Otto & Ida PORTIER) b. 18 Nov. 1897 (Montegut Ch.: v.6, p.62)

BELLANGER, Calvin Hobson (Clodio & Florence BELLANGER) b. 26 May 1898 (Houma Ch.: Epis. Ch.: v.1, p.118)
BELLANGER, Carrie m. 19 June 1899 Pierre HOTARD (Houma Ch.: v.6-B, p.3)
BELLANGER, Carrie m. 24 May 1899 Pierre HOTARD (Houma Ct. Hse.: Mar. v.31 & 32, #14)
BELLANGER, Charles d. 15 Aug. 1896 at age 2 yrs. (Raceland Ch.: v.1, p.9)
BELLANGER, Clay (Celestin & Adele CHAUVIN) m. 5 May 1898 Alzina PITRE (Montegut Ch.: v.4, p.244)
BELLANGER, Clay (Celestin & Adele CHAUVIN) m. 9 April 1898 Alzina PITRE (Houma Ct. Hse.: Mar. v.30 & 31, #392)
BELLANGER, Emelie Miss d. 8 Dec. 1898 at age 68 yrs. (Houma Ch.: v.3, p.19)
BELLANGER, Emeline (Robert & Malvina BUFORD) m. 30 April 1896 Ernest LIRETTE (Houma Ch.: v.6-a, p.174)
BELLANGER, Emeline E. m. 18 April 1896 Ernest P. LIRETTE (Houma Ct. Hse.: Mar. v.29 & 30, #42)
BELLANGER, Eva m. 5 July 1897 Henry TRAHAN (Houma Ct. Hse.: Mar. v.29 & 30, #48)
BELLANGER, Eva (Gustave & Mathilde HEBERT) m. 13 July 1897 Henry TRAHAN (Houma Ch.: v.6-a, p.210)
BELLANGER, Gertrude Efai (Hermogene & Francis JACKSON) b. 26 April 1898 (Thib. Ch.: v.7, p.503)
BELLANGER, Harris (Otto & Eda PORTIER) d. 2 Nov. 1897 at age 18 mths. (Montegut Ch.: v.2, p.12)
BELLANGER, Harry Richard (Ola Henry & Marie Eda PORTIER) b. 27 June 1896 (Montegut Ch.: v.6, p.42)
BELLANGER, Helene Eve (Jean Banan & Henriette GARIBOTTEE) b. 19 Jan. 1897 (Montegut Ch.: v.6, p.59)
BELLANGER, Henri d. 18 Sept. 1898 at age 67 yrs. (Theriot Ch.: v.1, p.6)
BELLANGER, James John (Ludger & Margueritte NAQUIN) b. 16 March 1898 (Larose Ch.: v.3, p.17)
BELLANGER, Jennie M. (Celestin & Adele CHAUVIN) m. 25 March 1899 William J. WALKER (Houma Ct. Hse.: Mar. v.31 & 32, #375)
BELLANGER, Jennie M. (Celestin & Adele CHAUVIN) m. 4 April 1899 William J. WALKER (Montegut Ch.: v.4, p.260)
BELLANGER, Joseph Adam (Banon & Henriette GALIPOTTE) b. 8 Nov. 1898; bt. 22 Oct. 1899 (Montegut Ch.: v.6, p.93)
BELLANGER, Joseph George (Ernest & Celeste LEONARD) b. 20 Jan. 1896 (Larose Ch.: v.2, p.180)
BELLANGER, Joseph Leon (Willy & Evela TOUPS) b. 30 Dec. 1898 (Theriot Ch.: v.2, p.32)
BELLANGER, Joseph Willy (Gustave & Mathilde HEBERT) d. 11 Dec. 1896 at age 19 yrs. (Houma Ch.: v.3, p.10)
BELLANGER, Klebert Benoit (Arthur & Pauline SEVIN) b. 13 Feb. 1896 (Lockport Ch.: v.2, p.322)
BELLANGER, Laurent Andre (Hubert & Emeline CUNNINGHAM) b. 10 Dec. 1897 (Montegut Ch.: v.6, p.66)

BELLANGER, Lois Elbertha (Clodio & Florence BELANGER) b. 19 Sept. 1896 (Houma Ch.: Epis. Ch.: v.1, p.114)
BELLANGER, Lorine Elizabeth (Celestin & Adele CHAUVIN) b. 2 May 1898 (Montegut Ch.: v.6, p.72)
BELLANGER, Marguerite Honorine (Agnes BELANGER) b. 16 Feb. 1896 (Montegut Ch.: v.6, p.41)
BELLANGER, Marguerite Mode (Willie & Evela TOUPS) b. 6 April 1896 (Theriot Ch.: v.1-B, p.94)
BELLANGER, Marie m. 4 Sept. 1896 Adam HENRI (Houma Ct. Hse.: Mar. v.29 & 30, #143)
BELLANGER, Marie (Sidney & Ernestine PITRE) b. 26 June 1899 (Houma Ch.: v.5, p.248)
BELLANGER, Marie Adele (Celestin & Adele CHAUVIN) b. 3 April 1896 (Montegut Ch.: v.6, p.37)
BELLANGER, Marie Adele (Celestin & Adele CHAUVIN) d. 2 Nov. 1896 at age 7 mths. (Montegut Ch.: v.2, p.7)
BELLANGER, Marie Agathe (Leo & Felicie LUQUET) b. 20 Aug. 1896 (Lockport Ch.: v.2, p.334)
BELLANGER, Marie Corinne (Ludger & Eveline HENRI) b. 26 Jan. 1896 (Montegut Ch.: v.6, p.36)
BELLANGER, Martha (Robert & Melvina BUFORD) m. 1 June 1897 Harry CHAUVIN (Montegut Ch.: v.4, p.221)
BELLANGER, Martha (Robert & Melvina BUFORD) m. 1 May 1897 Harry V. CHAUVIN (Houma Ct. Hse.: Mar. v.29 & 30, #397)
BELLANGER, Mary (Nicholas & Ordalie COMEAUX) m. 5 Sept. 1896 Adam HENRI (Houma Ch.: v.6-a, p.180)
BELLANGER, Mary Bernice (Clay & Azina PITRE) b. 24 Feb. 1899 (Montegut Ch.: v.6, p.84)
BELLANGER, Sidney Albert (Celestin & Adele CHAUVIN) m. 14 Feb. 1898 Ernestine PITRE (Montegut Ch.: v.4, p.236)
BELLANGER, Sidney Albert (Celestin & Adele CHAUVIN) m. 17 Jan. 1898 Ernestine PITRE (Houma Ct. Hse.: Mar. v.30 & 31, #224)
BELLANGER, Viola d. 29 Aug. 1897 at age 2½ yrs. (Theriot Ch.: v.1, p.1)
BELLAVIA, Carmelo (Calogero & Vincenzo PRIVATERA) m. 18 Jan. 1896 Angela PATTI (Thib. Ct. Hse.: Mar. v.35, #10)
BELLAVIA, Guiseppa Vigenza (Carmello & Angelina PATTE) b. 19 March 1897 (Thib. Ch.: v.7, p.444)
BELLE ILE, Joseph Julien (Jean & Julia DOMINGUE) b. 18 Aug. 1897 (Theriot Ch.: v.2, p.12)
BELLEAUMOUR, Sylvestre (Georges & Mathilde DUBOIS) b. 1 May 1897 (Theriot Ch.: v.2, p.4)
BELLMAN, William m. 6 Feb. 1897 Jane JONES (Houma Ct. Hse.: Mar. v.29 & 30, #298)
BELOPPE, Laura Rosa (Thomas & Julie BELOPPE) bt. 27 July 1896 (Thib. Ch.: v.7, p.409)
BELTCHAM, Mary Edna (Edmond & Mary ADAM) b. 12 Sept. 1898 (Thib. Ch.: v.7, p.515)

BELTEAU, Louise m. 22 Dec. 1899 Thomas J. NAQUIN (Thib. Ct. Hse.: Mar. v.39, #295)
BELTEAU, Louise (Louis & Emelia ROOS) m. 27 Dec. 1899 Thomas NAQUIN (Thib. Ch.: v.14, p.316)
BENANTE, Salvadore (Citro & Rosalia DE GIACOMO) b. 15 Oct. 1897 (Raceland Ch.: v.5, p.65)
BENDON, Charley m. 16 April 1896 Luminica HENDERSON (Thib. Ct. Hse.: Mar. v.35, #73)
BENEDETTO, Maria D. (Leonardo & Concetta SCHIFANI) b. 13 April 1899 (Thib. Ch.: v.7, p.603)
BENIGNO, Jeanne (Gerolonio & Angela BRUCCIA) b. 21 April 1899 (Thib. Ch.: v.7, p.548)
BENITTE, Virginie d. 27 Sept. 1898 at age 27 yrs. (Raceland Ch.: v.1, p.20)
BENNETT, Maria m. 15 March 1899 Jesse WEST (Houma Ct. Hse.: Mar. v.31 & 32, #367)

BENOIT (Sometimes: BENOIST)
BENOIT, Adam (Jack & Emelia AUCOIN) m. 14 Feb. 1898 Louisa BOURG (Houma Ct. Hse.: Mar. v.30 & 31, #295)
BENOIT, Adam (Jacques & Amelia AUCOIN) m. 9 April 1898 Louise BOURK (Theriot Ch.: v.1-B, p.3)
BENOIT, Adele (Ulysse & Odile NAQUIN) m. 14 Oct. 1897 Louis FORD (Thib. Ch.: v.14, p.164)
BENOIT, Adele (Ulysses & Odile NAQUIN) m. 14 Oct. 1897 Louis FORD (Thib. Ct. Hse.: Mar. v.37, #239)
BENOIT, Agathe Valerie (Paulin & Finne BOURGEOIS) b. 13 Dec. 1897 (Chackbay Ch.: v.1, p.99)
BENOIT, Aimee (Sylvain & Eulalie ONCALE) m. 18 Jan. 1897 Octave ONCALE (Chackbay Ch.: v.1, p.35)
BENOIT, Aimee (Sylvain & Eulalie ONCALE) m. 18 Jan. 1897 Octave ONCALE (Thib. Ct. Hse.: Mar. v.36, #12)
BENOIT, Albert Adam (Nicholas & Aurelia GRAUS) b. 27 Sept. 1899 (Chackbay Ch.: v.1, p.143)
BENOIT, Alexina Josephine (Arthur & Louisa ORDOGNE) b. 7 March 1899 (Thib. Ch.: v.7, p.602)
BENOIT, Amedee Adeol (Jean Marie & Emelile BLANCHARD) b. 11 June 1896 (Houma Ch.: v.5, p.183)
BENOIT, Amelia (Ulysse & Odile NAQUIN) m. 11 June 1896 Edgar GONZALES (Thib. Ct. Hse.: Mar. v.35, #99)
BENOIT, Amelie (Ulysse & Odile NAQUIN) m. 11 June 1896 Edgar GONZALES (Thib. Ch.: v.14, p.92)
BENOIT, Angelina d. 16 Dec. 1897 at age 12 yrs. (Thib. Ch.: v.3, p.208)
BENOIT, Arthur (Joe & Henriette BOUDREAU) m. 27 Aug. 1896 Lucia THEBE (Chackbay Ch.: v.1, p.30)
BENOIT, Arthur (Joseph & Henriette BOUDREAU) m. 27 Aug. 1896 Lucie TABOR (Thib. Ct. Hse.: Mar. v.36, #131)
BENOIT, Beatrice Eleonore Bernadette (Ernest & Justilia CHIASSON) b.2 March 1897 (Thib. Ch.: v.7, p.442)

BENOIT, Clemile (Joseph & Julienne CHIASSON) m. 18 April 1898 Eve ADAM (Chackbay Ch.: v.1, p.60)

BENOIT, Clemile (Joseph & Julienne CHIASSON) m. 18 April 1898 Eve ADAM (Thib. Ct. Hse.: Mar. v.37, #141)

BENOIT, Clevin Joacim (Arthur & Louisa ORDOGNE) b. 25 June 1898 (Thib. Ch.: v.7, p.517)

BENOIT, Denicia (Amede & Amelie VOISIN) b. 9 Oct. 1898 (Theriot Ch.: v.2, p.43)

BENOIT, Dolphine (Joseph & Felicia BERGERON) m. 5 Sept. 1898 Abel GROS (Thib. Ct. Hse.: Mar. v.38, #259)

BENOIT, Dolphine (Joseph & Felicia BERGERON) m.5 Sept. 1898 Abel GROS (Thib. Ch.: v.14, p.219)

BENOIT, Edward Edmond (Odressie & Faustine GONZALES) b. 1 Feb. 1898 (Thib. Ch.: v.7, p.485)

BENOIT, Elda m. 18 Dec. 1899 Joseph THIBODAUX (Thib. Ct. Hse.: Mar. v.39, #290)

BENOIT, Fanny d. 5 Dec. 1899 at age 7 yrs., 5 mths. (Thib. Ch.: v.3, p.245)

BENOIT, Felicien (Joseph & Felicia BERGERON) m. 25 Aug. 1898 Felicia TROSCLAIR (Thib. Ct. Hse.: Mar. v.38, #240)

BENOIT, Felicien (Joseph & Felicia BERGERON) m. 25 Aug. 1898 Felicia TROSCLAIR (Thib. Ch.: v.14, p.215)

BENOIT, Gabriel (Ernest & Justilia CHIASSION) b. 4 May 1899 (Thib. Ch.: v.7, p.607)

BENOIT, Henri Joseph (Felicien & Felicie TROSCLAIR) b. 18 Sept. 1899 (Thib. Ch.: v.7, p.566)

BENOIT, Henriette (Odressie & Faustine GONZALES) b. 17 July 1898 (Thib. Ch.: v.7, p.557)

BENOIT, Hubert Douglas (Jos. & Louisiane THIBODAUX) b. 13 Nov. 1898 (Houma Ch.: v.5, p.233)

BENOIT, Jean Baptiste Noely Acknil (Joseph & Engelia THIBODAUX) b. 29 Nov. 1897 (Thib. Ch.: v.7, p.473)

BENOIT, Jean Ferdinand (Arthur & Felicia THEBE) b. 6 Feb. 1899 (Chackbay Ch.: v.1, p.130)

BENOIT, Joachim (Osemee & Clara MORVAN) m. 22 Feb. 1897 Malvina RODRIGUE (Thib. Ct. Hse.: Mar. v.36, #85)

BENOIT, Joachim (Osemee & d.Clara MORVAN) m. 22 Feb. 1897 Malvina RODRIGUE (Chackbay Ch.: v.1, p.40)

BENOIT, Joseph (Charles & Amelia DARCE) m. 5 Feb. 1898 Louisiana THIBODAUX (Houma Ct. Hse.: Mar. v.30 & 31, #278)

BENOIT, Joseph (Joseph & Adolphine BORNE) b. 12 April 1897 (Chackbay Ch.: v.1, p.87)

BENOIT, Joseph (Madeo & Vina LOUVIERE) m. 26 July 1897 Engelie THIBODAUX (Thib. Ch.: v.14, p.154)

BENOIT, Joseph (Madeo & Vina LOUVIERE) m. 26 July 1897 Eugelie THIBODAUX (Thib. Ct. Hse.: Mar. v.37, #196)

BENOIT, Joseph (Willie & Valerie BOUDREAU) b. 13 June 1897 (Chackbay Ch.: v.1, p.91)

BENOIT, Joseph Eleonore (Amedie & Emelie VOISIN) b. 25 June 1896 (Theriot Ch.: v.1-B, p.104)

BENOIT, Joseph James (Adam & Justilia PINEL) b. 4 Feb. 1898 (Montegut Ch.: v.6, p.72)

BENOIT, Joseph Lucian (Adam & Louisa BOURQUE) b. 18 Jan. 1899 (Theriot Ch.: v.2, p.34)

BENOIT, Lena m. 16 Dec. 1899 John ENGOALL (Thib. Ct. Hse.: Mar. v.39, #286)

BENOIT, Louis Joseph (Joseph & Felicie BORNE) b. 31 July 1897 (Thib. Ch.: v.7, p.509)

BENOIT, Ludger (Adam & Henriette LAPEROUSE) m. 19 Oct. 1896 Julie BRUNET (Houma Ch.: v.6-a, p.183)

BENOIT, Ludger (Adam & Henriette LAPEROUSE) m. 15 Oct. 1896 Julie BRUNET (Houma Ct. Hse.: Mar. v.29 & 30, #169)

BENOIT, Marie (d.Felix & Myra RODRIGUE) m. 15 Feb. 1898 Arthur RODRIGUE (Chackbay Ch.: v.1, p.56)

BENOIT, Marie Cecile (Joseph & Marie BRUNUR) b. 6 Sept. 1897 (Houma Ch.:, v.5, p.193)

BENOIT, Marie Cecilia (Arthur & Louisa ORDOGNE) b. 9 Aug. 1896 (Chackbay Ch.: v.1, p.72)

BENOIT, Marie Ernest Mabel (Duglas & Amilia TABOR) b. 4 March 1898 (Thib. Ch.: v.7, p.496)

BENOIT, Marie Ludovine (Joseph & Leonie SHAUBUTT) b. 11 Nov. 1897 (Chackbay Ch.: v.1, p.106)

BENOIT, Marie Oceana (Arthur & Ulicia THEBE) b. 27 Aug. 1897 (Chackbay Ch.: v.1, p.96)

BENOIT, Marie Sophe (William & Valerie BOUDREAUX) b. 28 April 1898 (Thib. Ch.: v.7, p.550)

BENOIT, Marie Valerie (Ulysse & Lea TROSCLAIR) b. 26 Sept. 1897 (Chackbay Ch.: v.1, p.95)

BENOIT, Mary (Felix & Myrza RODRIGUE) m. 15 Feb. 1898 Arthur RODRIGUE (Thib. Ct. Hse.: Mar. v.37, #68)

BENOIT, Nicholas (Joseph & Adolphine BARA) m. 8 Sept. 1898 Lea BARRIOS (Thib. Ch.: v.14, p.220)

BENOIT, Nicholas (Joseph & Adolphine BORNE) m. 8 Sept. 1898 Lea BARRIOS (Thib. Ct. Hse.: Mar. v.38, #251)

BENOIT, Noe Helesse (Severe & Victoria MORVAN) b. 11 May 1899 (Chackbay Ch.: v.1, p.138)

BENOIT, Noemie Lotie (Wallace & Eugenie THIBODAUX) b. 18 July 1898 (Thib. Ch.: v.7, p.558)

BENOIT, Octave W. (Willie & Valerie BOUDREAU) b. 14 Feb. 1896 (Chackbay Ch.: v.1, p.63)

BENOIT, Odressy (Ulysses & Odile NAQUIN) m. 4 Oct. 1897 Faustine GONZALES (Thib. Ct. Hse.: Mar. v.37, #241)

BENOIT, Odressy (Uysses & Odile NAQUIN) m. 4 Oct. 1897 Faustine GONZALES (Thib. Ch.: v.14, p.161)

BENOIT, Ozeme Alcesse (Joachim & Malvina RODRIGUE) b. 29 March 1899 (Chackbay Ch.: v.1, p.131)

BENOIT, Pauline (Gregoire & Henriette BOUDREAU) m. 24 April 1897 Alces GOODMAN (Chackbay Ch.: v.1, p.43)

BENOIT, Pauline (Gregoire & Henriette BOUDREAU) m. 24 April 1897 Alies GOODMAN (Thib. Ct. Hse.: Mar. v.36, #113)

BENOIT, Pierre (Severe & Victoria MORVAN) b. 6 June 1897 (Chackbay Ch.: v.1, p.89)
BENOIT, Therese (Ernest & Justilia CHIASSON) b. 26 Aug. 1898 (Chackbay Ch.: v.1, p.117)
BENOIT, Therese Bernadette (Nicolas & Aurelia GROS) b. 14 Dec. 1897 (Thib. Ch.: v.7, p.481)
BENOIT, Ulysse (Joseph & Zulma CHIASSON) m. 13 April 1896 Olea TROSCLAIR (Thib. Ct. Hse.: Mar. v.35, #60)
BENOIT, Ulysse (Joseph & Zulma CHIASSON) m. 13 April 1896 Olea TROSCLAIR (Chackbay Ch.: v.1, p.26)
BENOIT, Ulyssia (Ulysses & ---- NAQUIN) m. 14 Jan. 1897 Leo NAQUIN (Thib. Ch.: v.14, p.108)
BENOIT, Ulyssia (Ulysses & Odile NAQUIN) m. 14 Jan. 1897 Leo NAQUIN (Thib. Ct. Hse.: Mar. v.36, #3)
BENOIT, Valcour d. 27 June 1898 at age 29 yrs., 6 mths. (Thib. Ch.: v.3, p.216)
BENOIT, Volgie (Madere & Elvina ROUVIERE or LOUVIERE) m. 21 Dec. 1899 Celestine TOUPS (Thib. Ct. Hse.: Mar. v.39, #288)
BENOIT, Volgie (Madere & Elvina ROUVIERE) m. 21 Dec. 1899 Celestine TOUPS (Thib. Ch.: v.14, p.314)
BENOIT, Wallace (Joseph & Felicia BERGERON) m. 17 Jan. 1897 Eugenia THIBODAUX (Thib. Ct. Hse.: Mar. v.36, #10)
BENOIT, Wallace (Joseph & Felicia BERGERON) m. 14 Jan. 1897 Eugelia THIBODAUX (Thib. Ch.: v.14, p.100)
BENOIT, Zoe (Ulysse & Odile NAQUIN) m. 25 Sept. 1899 Jean ADAM (Thib. Ch.: v.14, p.297)
BENOIT, Zoe (Ulysse & Odile NAQUIN) m. 25 Sept. 1899 Jean ADAM (Thib. Ct. Hse.: Mar. v.39, #229)
BENSBERG, Robert of New Orleans (Gerhard & Catherine WEYERS) m. 19 Jan. 1897 Maude Odette KNOBLOCK (Thib. Ch.: v.14, p.111)
BENSON, Claire Louise m. 15 Aug. 1899 Emile ROQUES (Thib. Ct. Hse.: Mar. v.39, #211)
BENSON, Robert m. 27 Dec. 1899 Leonie FRANK (Thib. Ct. Hse.: Mar. v.39, #300)
BENSON, Sidney m. 24 Oct. 1898 Laura E. SEEMAN (Thib. Ch.: Epis. Ch.: v.1, p.331)
BENSON, Sidney m. 24 Oct. 1898 Laura SEEMAN (Thib. Ct. Hse.: Mar. v.38, #300)
BERANGER, Hyacinthe Celeste (Henry & Mathilde DUPUIS) b. 26 Jan. 1896 (Houma Ch.: v.5, p.171)
BERANGER, Marie m. Leo LEBLANC d. 6 Sept. 1896 at age 48 yrs. & 5 mths. (Thib. Ch.: v.3, p.186)
BERD, Anna Nora (Robert C. & Camelia MARTIN) b. 28 March 1899 (Raceland Ch.: v.5, p.95)
BERDON, Henri m. 7 Dec. 1897 Helena FORET (Thib. Ct. Hse.: Mar. v.37, #216)
BERDOU, Henri (Jean & Josephine HYDEL) m. 7 Dec. 1897 Helena FORET (Raceland Ch.: v.2, p.55)

BERENGER, Marie m. Leo Andre LEBLANC, d. 5 Sept. 1896. Children listed: Louis; Leon; Ernest C.; Maggie; d.Augustin; Louise, 19; Xavier, 16; Laura, 14; Rosa, 12; Elizida, 10; Beatrice, 7. Petition for inventory & family meeting for tutorship: 21 Jan. 1899. (Thib. Ct. Hse.: Succ. #1558)

BERGER, Antoine Aimet (Theodore & Helene LAROSE) b. 31 Oct. 1896 (Raceland Ch.: v.5, p.33)

BERGER, Benjamin Beveley (Charles & Phoebe LEPINE) b. 27 Nov. 1899 (Raceland Ch.: v.5, p.109)

BERGER, Charles of Franklin m. 28 July 1897 Phoebie LEPINE, of St. Mary (Thib. Ct. Hse.: Mar. v.37, #200)

BERGER, Charles (Theodore & Edilee DARCE) m. 28 July 1897 Phelie LEPINE (Raceland Ch.: v.2, p.46)

BERGER, Henry Harris (Henry Philip & Martha Jane HARRIS) b. 27 June 1897 (Houma Ch.: First Presbyt. Ch.: v.1, p.1)

BERGER, Herman Peter (Herman & Lizzie BERGER) bt. 13 April 1898 (Thib. Ch.: First Presbyt. Ch.: v.1, p.176)

BERGER, James W. (Henry Philip & Martha Jane HARRIS) b. 5 June 1899 (Houma Ch.: First Presbyt. Ch.: v.1, p.1)

BERGER, Marie Madeleine (John Adam & Emelie HOCK) b. 24 Dec. 1898 (Houma Ch.: v.5, p.237)

BERGER, Martha Jane (Ch. W. & Nancy Ann DAVIS) b. 12 Dec. 1896 (Houma Ch.: Epis. Ch.: v.1, p.114)

BERGER, Rosa Magdelina (Charles W. & Nancy A. BERGER) b. 3 Dec. 1898 (Houma Ch.: First Presbyt. Ch.: v.1, p.262)

BERGER, Theodore m. 22 June 1896 Helene LAROSE (Thib. Ct. Hse.: Mar. v.35, #110)

BERGER, Theodore (Theodore & Edilia PIERCE) m. 22 June 1896 Helene LAROSE (Raceland Ch.: v.2, p.17)

BERGERON, ----- girl (Frank & Iliska LAGRASSI) d. 23 May 1896 at a couple of hours old. (Thib. Ch.: v.3, p.182)

BERGERON, Adele Marie (Gilbert & Cecile CROCHET) b. 31 Dec. 1898 (Houma Ch.: v.5, p.236)

BERGERON, Adeline Victoria (Uselien & Marie J. DUBOIS) b. 21 Oct. 1899 (Houma Ch.: v.5, p.264)

BERGERON, Aimee Pearly (Joseph & Angele BRUNET) b. 5 May 1897 (Houma Ch.: v.5, p.178)

BERGERON, Albert m. 3 July 1897 Cecilia CROCHET (Houma Ch.: v.6-a, p.208)

BERGERON, Alfred m. 17 Feb. 1897 Helene BRIEN (Houma Ct. Hse.: Mar. v.29 & 30, #314)

BERGERON, Alfred (Augustin & Esther BUFORD) m. 25 Feb. 1897 Helene BRIEN (Theriot Ch.: v.1, p.10)

BERGERON, Alice (Joseph & Marie BERGERON) m. 3 Feb. 1898 Leonard MARCEL (Houma Ct. Hse.: Mar. v.30 & 31, #271)

BERGERON, Alice (Maxin & Lydia NOEL) m. 24 April 1897 Armand ELLIOT (Lockport Ch.: v.2, p.161)

BERGERON, Alice (Narcisse & Lydia NOEL) m. 24 April 1897 Armand ELLIOT (Thib. Ct. Hse.: Mar. v.36, #110)

BERGERON, Alphonse (Franklin & Melasie ESTIVEN) m. 26 June 1899 Emilie BERGERON (Thib. Ct. Hse.: Mar. v.39, #186)

BERGERON, Alphonse (Franklin & Melasie ESTIVEN) m. 26 June 1899 Emilie BERGERON (Thib. Ch.: v.14, p.287)

BERGERON, Altay (Raphael & Bertile DUPLANTIS) m. 19 Jan. 1899 Loulie AUTHEMENT (Houma Ct Hse.: Mar. v.30 & 31, #273)

BERGERON, Altee (Raphael & Berthilde DUPLANTIS) m. 2 Feb. 1899 Loulie AUTHEMENT (Montegut Ch.: v.4, p.254)

BERGERON, Alvin Simplice (Evariste & Neilla BOURGEOIS) b. 2 March 1899 (Chacahoula Ch.: v.4, p.30)

BERGERON, Andre Eugene (Emile & Helena BREAUX) b. 25 May 1899 (Thib. Ch.: v.7, p.604)

BERGERON, Anne Rebecca Milda (Raphael) d. 7 June 1898 at age 19 yrs. & 1 mth. (Montegut Ch.: v.2, p.17)

BERGERON, Anny Josephine (Silvere & Ortense BERGERON) b. 13 March 1896 (Theriot Ch.: v.1-B, p.92)

BERGERON, Armantine m. 21 May 1896 Joada DOMINGUE, Jr. (Houma Ct. Hse.: Mar. v.29 & 30, #78)

BERGERON, Armont Paul (Henri & Livie FOREST) b. 28 July 1897 (Thib. Ch.: v.7, p.506)

BERGERON, Arthur m. 23 Jan. 1896 Albertine PRICE (Thib. Ct. Hse.: Mar. v.35, #5)

BERGERON, Arthur (Narcisse & Lydia NEWELL) m. 23 Jan. 1896 Albertine PRICE (Raceland Ch.: v.2, p.10)

BERGERON, Auguste (Auguste & Lorenza HEBERT) m. 2 Feb. 1899 Lovinia MARTIN (Raceland Ch.: v.2, p.88)

BERGERON, Azelie m. 11 June 1897 Prosper CHAUVIN (Larose Ch.: v.3, p.6)

BERGERON, Azelie m. 11 June 1897 Prosper CHAUVIN (Larose Ch.: v.4, p.74)

BERGERON, Azelie m. 25 May 1897 Prosper CHAUVIN (Thib. Ct. Hse.: Mar. v.36, #149)

BERGERON, Beatrice Bernadette (Onesime & Lydia TOUPS) b. 31 Dec. 1899 (Thib. Ch.: v.7, p.581)

BERGERON, Beverly Rufus (Lawson & Victorine BERGERON) b. 31 Jan. 1898 (Houma Ch.: v.5, p.201)

BERGERON, Blanche Agnes (Lason & Victoria BERGERON) b. 14 Dec. 1899 (Houma Ch.: v.6, p.3)

BERGERON, Blanche Agnes (Lawson & Victoria BERGERON) b. 14 Dec. 1899 (Houma Ch.: v.5, p.267)

BERGERON, Bornisa (Frank & Octavie GAUTHIER) b. 17 July 1897 (Houma Ch.: v.5, p.186)

BERGERON, Brigite (Auguste & Lorenza HEBERT) m. 26 April 1899 Henry BABIN (Thib. Ch.: v.14, p.277)

BERGERON, Brigitte (Auguste & Lorenza HEBERT) m. 26 April 1899 Henri BABIN (Thib. Ct. Hse.: Mar. v.39, #153)

BERGERON, Camille Milcar (Milcar & Josephine USE) b. 9 Aug. 1898 (Thib. Ch.: v.7, p.560)

BERGERON, Carlin (Wilfrid & Alesina HEBERT) b. 4 June 1896; m. Lilly Martin MARLBROUGH on 30 Aug. 1946. (Houma Ch.: Bapt. Bk., v.5, p.154)

BERGERON, Celeste (Trasimond & Philomene ROUSSEL) m. 14 April 1898 Charles LAJAUNIE (Chacahoula Ch.: v.1, p.61)
BERGERON, Celeste (Trasimond & Philomene ROUSSEL) m. 14 April 1898 Charles LAJAUNIE (Chacahoula Ch.: v.1, p.66 [86])
BERGERON, Celeste (Trasimond & Philomene ROUSSEL) m. 25 March 1898 Charles LAJAUNIE (Houma Ct. Hse.: Mar. v.30 & 31, #352)
BERGERON, Cezerie (Sylvere & Ida CLOSE) m. 12 Feb. 1898 Octave DUPRE (Montegut Ch.: v.4, p.235)
BERGERON, Charles m. 12 Jan. 1898 Camilla BOUDELOCHE (Houma Ct. Hse.: Mar. v.30 & 31, #194)
BERGERON, Charles m. 23 Jan. 1899 Lovinia MARTIN (Thib. Ct. Hse.: Mar. v.38, #53)
BERGERON, Charles (Octave & Leontine SOIGNE) m. 19 April 1897 Louise MORVAN (Thib. Ch.: v.14, p.136)
BERGERON, Charles (Wash & Elmire DION) m. 20 Jan. 1898 Camilla BOUDELOCHE (Houma Ch.: v.6-a, p.224)
BERGERON, Charles A. (Octave & Leontine SOIGNET) m. 19 April 1897 Louise MORVAN (Thib. Ct. Hse.: Mar. v.36, #119)
BERGERON, Clara b. 26 Sept. 1880 (Valfroid & Philomene GAUTHREAUX) Emancipation: 18 Oct. 1898. (Thib. Ct. Hse.: Succ. #1550)
BERGERON, Clara Helene (Joseph & Angele BRUNET) b. 21 July 1899 (Houma Ch.: v.5, p.252)
BERGERON, Clifford Willy (Aurelien & Lea BOUDELOCHE) b. 25 Oct. 1896 (Houma Ch.: v.5, p.163)
BERGERON, Constance Brigitte (Raphael & Berthilde DUPLANTIS) m. 15 Jan. 1896 Myrtil AUTHEMENT (Montegut Ch.: v.4, p.205)
BERGERON, Corinne Zeolide (Alberic & Celeste GUITREAU) b. 9 Nov. 1896 (Thib. Ch.: v.7, p.427)
BERGERON, Dewey Joseph (Sydney & Nobby ESTIVEN) b. 23 July 1898 (Thib. Ch.: v.7, p.512)
BERGERON, Drausin m. Mathilde MALBROUX Child listed: Augustine m. d.John BERGERON. Inventory: 5 June 1899. (Houma Ct. Hse.: Succ. #919)
BERGERON, Drosin Mrs. d. 13 April 1899 at age 61 yrs. (Chacahoula Ch.: v.2, p.29)
BERGERON, Eddy d. 4 Feb. 1899 at age 1 yr. & 1 mth. (Thib. Ch.: v.3, p.227)
BERGERON, Edgar (Evariste & Neela BOURGEOIS) m. 14 Aug. 1899 Floy EVANS (Houma Ct. Hse.: Mar. v.31 & 32, #98)
BERGERON, Edgard (Eusebe & Alida GERBAU) m. 13 May 1897 Alice BOUDREAUX (Thib. Ch.: v.14, p.145)
BERGERON, Edgard (Eusebe & Alida GERBAU) m. 13 May 1897 Alice BOUDREAUX (Thib. Ct. Hse.: Mar. v.36, #121)
BERGERON, Edna Annette (Clet & Sidonia SCHEXNAYDER) b. 30 Sept. 1899 (Thib. Ch.: v.8, p.10)
BERGERON, Edouard (Leo & Letitia DUPUIT) b. 4 Nov. 1896 (Raceland Ch.: v.5, p.37)

BERGERON, Elda Agnes (Raphael Joseph & Josephine GUIDRY) b. 14 Nov. 1897 (Chacahoula Ch.: Gibson Ch.: Mar. Bk., v.1, #1)

BERGERON, Elda Agnes (Raphael Joseph & Josephine GUIDRY) b. 14 Nov. 1897 (Chacahoula Ch.: Gibson Ch.: v.2, p.115)

BERGERON, Eleonore Nola (Alfred & Helena BRIEN) b. 29 Dec. 1897 (Theriot Ch.: v.2, p.16)

BERGERON, Elie (Jean Baptiste & Josephine PITRE) m. 22 Aug. 1896 Josephine BERGERON (Houma Ct. Hse.: Mar. v.29 & 30, #134)

BERGERON, Elisabeth (Norman & ----) m. 29 April 1897 Charles ELFERT (Thib. Ct. Hse.: Mar. v.36, #132)

BERGERON, Elisabeth (Norman) m. 29 April 1897 Charles ELFERT (Thib. Ch.: v.14, p.142)

BERGERON, Elisabeth Augustine d. 22 Feb. 1896 at age 2 mths. (Thib. Ch.: v.3, p.179)

BERGERON, Elize m. 14 Jan. 1899 Joseph CHETE (Houma Ct. Hse.: Mar. v.30 & 31, #233)

BERGERON, Elize (Hubert & Elize MARCEL) m. 14 Jan. 1899 Joseph ESHTE (Houma Ch.: v.6-a, p.265)

BERGERON, Elmer (Eusebe & Euselia DARCE) m. 24 Feb. 1897 Julia NAVARRE (Houma Ct. Hse.: Mar. v.29 & 30, #257)

BERGERON, Elmer (Eusebe & Euzelia DARCE) m. 24 Feb. 1897 Julia NAVARRE (Thib. Ch.: v.14, p.128)

BERGERON, Elodie Madeleine (Ernest & Alice DAIGLE) b. 27 April 1897 (Thib. Ch.: v.7, p.448)

BERGERON, Elphege (Ernest & Alice DAIGLE) b. 27 May 1899 (Houma Ch.: v.5, p.250)

BERGERON, Emilie (Drauzin & Eda GERBAUX) m. 26 June 1899 Alphonse BERGERON (Thib. Ct. Hse.: Mar. v.39, #186)

BERGERON, Emilie (Drauzin & Eda GERBAUX) m. 26 June 1899 Alphonse BERGERON (Thib. Ch.: v.14, p.287)

BERGERON, Emma (Drausin & Azema BOURG) m. 28 Dec. 1897 Nicholas MALBROUGH (Houma Ct. Hse.: Mar. v.29 & 30, #163)

BERGERON, Emma (Drozin & Azema BOURG) m. 15 Jan. 1898 Nickles MARLBOROUGH (Montegut Ch.: v.4, p.229)

BERGERON, Ernest (Eusebe & Euzelia DARCE) m.16 Feb. 1897 Elvire PONTIFF (Thib. Ch.: v.14, p.126)

BERGERON, Ernest (Eusebe & Euzelie DARCE) m. 16 Feb. 1897 Elvire PONTIFF (Houma Ct. Hse.: Mar. v.29 & 30, #255)

BERGERON, Estelle m. 7 Jan. 1898 William T. DILLON (Thib. Ct. Hse.: Mar. v.37, #9)

BERGERON, Estelle (Joachim & Estelle LAGARDE) m. 17 Jan. 1898 William Thomas DILLON, Jr. (Thib. Ch.: v.14, p.169)

BERGERON, Ethna Agnes (Arthur & Albertine PRICE) b. 25 Jan. 1897 (Lockport Ch.: v.3, #10)

BERGERON, Etna Agnes (Arthur & Albertine PRICE) b. 25 Jan. 1897 (Lockport Ch.: v.3-A, #10)

BERGERON, Eugene d. 25 June 1897 at age 61 yrs. (Thib. Ch.: v.3, p.201)

BERGERON, Euranie Marguerite (Emile & Camilia NAQUIN) b. 17 May 1897 (Thib. Ch.: v.7, p.455)
BERGERON, Eusebe Mrs. d. 1 Jan. 1899 at age 77 yrs. (Thib. Ch.: v.3, p.227)
BERGERON, Euselia (Aubert & Aurore MARCEL) m. 31 Jan. 1899 Oliva PELEGRIN (Montegut Ch.: v.4, p.253)
BERGERON, Euzalia (Hobert & Aurore MARCEL) m. 12 Jan. 1899 Oliva PELEGRIN (Houma Ct. Hse.: Mar. v.30 & 31, #216)
BERGERON, Eve d. 26 Jan. 1896 at age 12 yrs. (Lockport Ch.: v.1, #4)
BERGERON, Francois d. 9 Aug. 1898 at age 58 yrs. (Thib. Ch.: v.3, p.218)
BERGERON, Francois m. 20 Feb. 1898 Octavie BABIN (Houma Ch.: v.6-a, p.237)
BERGERON, Francois (Claiborne & Emelia ESHETE) m. 5 Jan. 1898 Octavie BABIN (Houma Ct. Hse.: Mar. v.30 & 31, #179)
BERGERON, Germain d. 24 Jan. 1896 at age 72 yrs., 3 mths., & 18 days (Montegut Ch.: v.2, p.3)
BERGERON, Harrison Paul (Adam & Alfrida BELANGER) b. 6 March 1898 (Houma Ch.: v.5, p.204)
BERGERON, Hector Joseph (Emile & Emerentia BOUDREAUX) b. 24 Feb. 1897 (Thib. Ch.: v.7, p.489)
BERGERON, Helene (Frank & Melanie ESTIVEN) m. 15 Feb. 1898 Gillis SAVOIE (Thib. Ch.: v.14, p.187)
BERGERON, Helene (Frank & Melanie ESTIVEN) m. 15 Feb. 1898 Gillis SAVOIE (Thib. Ct. Hse.:Mar. v.37, #88)
BERGERON, Henry b. 5 July 1879 (Valfroid & Philomene GAUTHREAUX) Emancipation: 18 Oct. 1898. (Thib. Ct. Hse.: Succ. #1551)
BERGERON, Henry (Octave & Leontine SOIGNET) m. 3 Feb. 1897 Livie FOREST (Thib. Ch.: v.14, p.119)
BERGERON, Henry (Octave & Leontine SOIGNET) m. 3 Feb. 1897 Livie FORET (Thib. Ct. Hse.: Mar. v.36, #63)
BERGERON, Henry Gilbert (Philippe C. & Laura BOUDREAUX) b. 29 Jan. 1899 (Chacahoula Ch.: v.4, p.19)
BERGERON, Hermina (Arsene & Marie GAUBERT) m. 2 Jan. 1898 Felix ORDONNEAU (Thib. Ct. Hse.: Mar. v.38, #325)
BERGERON, Hermina (Arsene & Marie GAUBERT) m. 2 Jan. 1899 Felix ORDONNEAU (Thib. Ch.: v.14, p.233)
BERGERON, Howard Paul (Ernest & Elvire PONTIFF) b. 15 July 1899 (Houma Ch.: v.5, p.250)
BERGERON, Ida Irby (Ursilien & Marie DUBOIS) b. 28 Aug. 1897 (Theriot Ch.: v.2, p.16)
BERGERON, Irma Felicie (Elma & Julia NAVARRE) b. 25 Nov. 1897 (Houma Ch.: v.5, p.195)
BERGERON, Jean Baptiste (Iberville & Eveline LIRETTE) b. 28 April 1897 (Montegut Ch.: v.6, p.56)
BERGERON, Jean Eddy (Walter & Cecilia LEDET) b. 11 Jan. 1898 (Thib. Ch.: v.7, p.481)
BERGERON, Jean Sydney (Orestile & Gracieuse GOBERT) b. 6 Jan. 1896 (Thib. Ch.: v.7, p.389)

BERGERON, Joachim d. 1 June 1899 (Houma Ch.: v.3, p.23)
BERGERON, John (Ulysse & Josephine GIROIR) m. 9 Jan. 1899 Cora CHIASSON (Houma Ct. Hse.: Mar. v.30 & 31, #197)
BERGERON, Joseph d. 27 July 1898 at age 4 yrs. (Houma Ch.: v.3, p.17)
BERGERON, Joseph of Houma m. 7 Dec. 1899 Flavie GUILLOT (Houma Ch.: v.6-B, p.5)
BERGERON, Joseph (Elie & Josephine BERGERON) b. 6 May 1898 (Houma Ch.: v.5, p.209)
BERGERON, Joseph (Frank & Jennie GUERIN) m. 7 Dec. 1899 Flavia GUILLOT (Houma Ct. Hse.: Mar. v.31 & 32, #174)
BERGERON, Joseph Adam (Aurilien & Marie BERGERON) b. 30 Oct. 1899 (Houma Ch.: v.5, p.263)
BERGERON, Joseph Addy (Belville & Eveline LIRETTE) b. 9 March 1899 (Houma Ch.: v.5, p.242)
BERGERON, Joseph Ambroise (Philippe & Myrthe HILL) b. 11 July 1897 (Thib. Ch.: v.7, p.465)
BERGERON, Joseph Druby (Joseph & Sucky CHAUVIN) b. 1 Sept. 1897 (Montegut Ch.: v.6, p.60)
BERGERON, Joseph E. (Joseph & Marie BERGERON) b. 18 March 1896 (Houma Ch.: v.5, p.176)
BERGERON, Joseph Edna (Laurant & Artilia PITRE) b. 15 Nov. 1897 (Houma Ch.: v.5, p.192)
BERGERON, Joseph Ellie (Aubert & Aurore MARCEL) b. 1 March 1899 (Montegut Ch.: v.6, p.83)
BERGERON, Joseph Hamilton (Aurele & Lena BOUTDELOCHE) b. 3 June 1898; m. Louisiana TAUZIN on 22 Oct. 1922. (Houma Ch.: Bapt. Bk., v.5, p.214)
BERGERON, Joseph Mauris (Wilfrid & Alexina HEBERT) b. 8 Nov. 1897; m. Mabel ESCHTE on 5 Feb. ---- (Houma Ch.: Bapt. Bk., v.5, p.193)
BERGERON, Joseph Simson (Sylvere & Octavie BERGERON) b. 3 Sept. 1898 (Houma Ch.: v.5, p.218)
BERGERON, Josephine d. 2 Sept. 1898 at age 35 yrs. (Houma Ch.: v.3, p.18)
BERGERON, Josephine (Lubin & Evelina BERGERON) m. 22 Aug. 1896 Elie BERGERON (Houma Ct. Hse.: Mar. v.29 & 30, #134)
BERGERON, Josephine (Theophile & Azelina PITRE) m. 17 Feb. 1898 Elie V. BOUDREAU (Houma Ch.: v.6-a, p.233)
BERGERON, Josephine Annette (Augustin & Bertille FORET) b. 11 July 1899 (Houma Ch.: v.5, p.249)
BERGERON, Kleber (Octave & Berthilde TOUPS) m. 25 Jan. 1897 Aimee CHAMPAGNE (Thib. Ch.: v.14, p.114)
BERGERON, Kleber (Octave & Berthilde TOUPS) m. 25 Jan. 1897 Aimee CHAMPAGNE (Thib. Ct. Hse.: Mar. v.36, #49)
BERGERON, Laurena Marie (Alfred & Helene BRIEN) b. 20 Oct. 1899 (Theriot Ch.: v.2, p.56)
BERGERON, Laurent m. 5 June 1897 Arfelia PITRE (Houma Ch.: v.6-a, p.206)

BERGERON, Laurent (Urbai & Evelina BERGERON) m. 1 Aug. 1896 Artelia PITRE (Houma Ct. Hse.: Mar. v.29 & 30, #122)
BERGERON, Lea (Wilson & Clara BERGERON) m. 16 Jan. 1899 Jefferson FINLEY (Houma Ct. Hse.: Mar. v.30 & 31, #242)
BERGERON, Lelia m. 25 Jan. 1897 Vital PELLEGRIN (Houma Ct. Hse.: v.29 & 30, #249-A)
BERGERON, Lelia (Amelien & Marie BERGERON) m. 25 Jan. 1897 Vital PELEGRIN (Houma Ch.: v.6-a, p.190)
BERGERON, Leona Gladies (Jamas & Elden MOOR) b. 22 Feb. 1897 (Houma Ch.: v.5, p.201)
BERGERON, Leonce Augustin (Emile & Helena BRAUD) b. 11 Oct. 1897 (Thib. Ch.: v.7, p.468)
BERGERON, Lilia Augustine (Ernest & Victoria BOUDREAUX) b. 27 April 1896 (Houma Ch.: v.5, p.154)
BERGERON, Louisa Priscilla (Ernest & Elvire PONTIFF) b. 1 Jan. 1898 (Houma Ch.: v.5, p.197)
BERGERON, Lucille (John & Augustine BERGERON) m. 14 May 1896 Charles CROCHET (Chacahoula Ch.: v.1, p.58)
BERGERON, Lucille (John & Augustine BERGERON) m. 14 May 1896 Charles CROCHET (Houma Ct. Hse.: Mar. v.29 & 30, #58)
BERGERON, Luvinia d. 18 Jan. 1898 at age 64 yrs. (Houma Ch.: v.3, p.15)
BERGERON, Lydia m. 7 May 1896 Orphie BREAUX (Thib. Ct. Hse.: Mar. v.35, #86)
BERGERON, Lydia (Frank & Josephine BENOIT) m. 3 Feb. 1898 Orphie BREAUX (Thib. Ch.: v.14, p.179)
BERGERON, Mac d. 30 Aug. 1899 at age 5½ yrs. (Thib. Ch.: v.3, p.240)
BERGERON, Marcelline d. 24 July 1899 at age 4 mths. & 23 days (Houma Ch.: v.3, p.24)
BERGERON, Marcelline Marie (Alexandre & Emelie BERGERON) b. 1 March 1899 (Houma Ch.: v.5, p.241)
BERGERON, Maria Angeline (Germain & Angela BOUDREAU) b. 25 March 1896 (Chackbay Ch.: v.1, p.65)
BERGERON, Maria Magdelena (Louis & Louise BOURGEOIS) b. 10 Nov. 1896 (Houma Ch.: v.5, p.170)
BERGERON, Marie d. 16 June 1899 at age 45 yrs. (Houma Ch.: v.3, p.23)
BERGERON, Marie m. Joseph BOUDREAU d. 17 July 1899 at age 38 yrs. (Montegut Ch.: v.2, p.27)
BERGERON, Marie Adele (Henry & Felicia TOUPS) b. 8 Feb. 1896 (Theriot Ch.: v.1-B, p.90)
BERGERON, Marie Adenise (Henrie & Felicia TOUPS) b. 11 March 1898 (Theriot Ch.: v.2, p.21)
BERGERON, Marie Alice (Henri & Cecilia GUILLOTE) b. 2 Feb. 1899 (Thib. Ch.: v.7, p.594)
BERGERON, Marie Amelie (Willy & Elisa TOUPS) b. 5 March 1898 (Theriot Ch.: v.2, p.23)
BERGERON, Marie Anna (Laurent & Altilia PIT) b. 12 July 1899 (Houma Ch.: v.5, p.250)

BERGERON, Marie Anne (Clay & Josephine CROCHET) b. 7 Nov. 1897 (Houma Ch.: v.5, p.192)
BERGERON, Marie Annie d. 23 Nov. 1899 at age 1 yr. & 1 mth. (Thib. Ch.: v.3, p.244)
BERGERON, Marie Annie (Wilfrid & Marie BABIN) b. 6 Nov. 1898 (Thib. Ch.: v.7, p.521)
BERGERON, Marie Augustine (Evariste & Melina BOURGEOIS) b. 12 Oct. 1897 (Chacahoula Ch.: v.4, p.17)
BERGERON, Marie Carrie (Adam & Emma BERGERON) b. 3 Aug. 1899 (Montegut Ch.: v.6, p.91)
BERGERON, Marie Eugenie (Henri & Cecilia GUILLOT) b. 4 July 1898 (Thib. Ch.: v.7, p.503)
BERGERON, Marie Exolide (Germain & Angela BOUDREAUX) b. 29 Oct. 1898 (Chackbay Ch.: v.1, p.123)
BERGERON, Marie Ida (Aubin & Louise COLIN) b. 8 April 1897 (Theriot Ch.: v.2, p.18)
BERGERON, Marie Jessy (Jean Baptiste & Marie LEGRAND) b. 11 Nov. 1896 (Houma Ch.: v.5, p.166)
BERGERON, Marie Lezida (Gilbert & Cecilia CROCHET) b. 21 April 1896 (Houma Ch.: v.5, p.181)
BERGERON, Marie Louise (Alcide & Eleda BOUDREAU) b. 16 Feb. 1898 (Theriot Ch.: v.2, p.19)
BERGERON, Marie Lucie (Jean & Caroline NOBLOCH) b. 16 Sept. 1896 (Thib. Ch.: v.7, p.418)
BERGERON, Marie Marcelina (Alexandre & Emily BERGERON) b. 1 March 1899 (Houma Ch.: v.5, p.236)
BERGERON, Marie Melanie (Walter & Cecile LEDET) b. 15 Sept. 1899 (Thib. Ch.: v.7, p.564)
BERGERON, Marie Olga (Aurelius & Octavie BERGERON) b. 29 Feb. 1896 (Houma Ch.: v.5, p.148)
BERGERON, Marie Rita (Henry & Cecilia GUILLOTE) b. 24 Dec. 1896 (Thib. Ch.: v.7, p.432)
BERGERON, Marie Rosalie (Adrien & Ernestine BOUDREAUX) b. 25 April 1898 (Thib. Ch.: v.7, p.496)
BERGERON, Marie Vernar (Klebert & Anne CHAMPANGE) b. 9 May 1898 (Thib. Ch.: v.7, p.497)
BERGERON, Marie Victorine (Charly & Marie BABIN) b. 22 March 1899 (Houma Ch.: v.5, p.245)
BERGERON, Marie Victorine (Edgar & Alice BOUDRAUX) b. 13 March 1898 (Thib. Ch.: v.7, p.496)
BERGERON, Marie Viola (Henry & Felicia TOUPS) b. 23 Oct. 1899 (Theriot Ch.: v.2, p.54)
BERGERON, Mary m. 30 May 1898 Leufroy BABIN (Houma Ct. Hse.: Mar. v.30 & 31, #456)
BERGERON, Mary Camile (Charly & Marie BABIN) b. 15 Sept. 1896; m. Laurence Paul LEVRON on 4 Feb. 1929. (Houma Ch.: Bapt. Bk., v.5, p.158)
BERGERON, Mary Louise d. 13 Oct. 1898 at age 9 yrs. (Houma Ch.: v.3, p.18)
BERGERON, Mary Louise (Louis & Mary CHATAGNIER) m. 27 Aug. 1896 John L. VIDAL (Houma Ct. Hse.: Mar. v.29 & 30, #138)

BERGERON, Mary Mable (Willie & Alida PITRE) b. 7 Nov. 1899 (Houma Ch.: v.5, p.262)
BERGERON, Mary Saidy (Sidnay & Nolie STEVENS) b. 4 Feb. 1897 (Houma Ch.: v.5, p.168)
BERGERON, Maud (Numa) d. 11 Jan. 1898 at age 12 yrs. & 11 days (Chacahoula Ch.: v.2, p.26)
BERGERON, Maud Louise (Arthur & Louise CHAPPUIS) b. 15 Dec. 1898 (Thib. Ch.: v.7, p.526)
BERGERON, Maurice Witcliff (Adam & Emma BERGERON) b. 14 June 1896 (Montegut Ch.: v.6, p.42)
BERGERON, Narcisse d. 29 Feb. 1897 at birth (Thib. Ch.: v.3, p.197)
BERGERON, Nellie Burnice (Henry & Levie FORET) b. 26 July 1899 (Thib. Ch.: v.8, p.2)
BERGERON, Numa Joseph (Valfroid & d.Philomene GAUTHREAUX) m. 28 Sept. 1899 Laura Pauline AYCOCK (Chacahoua Ch.: v.1, p.71 [91])
BERGERON, Oanita (Charles & Camila BOUDELOCHE) b. 4 March 1899 (Theriot Ch.: v.2, p.39)
BERGERON, Octave d. 12 April 1887; m. Leontine SOIGNET Children listed: Charles; Felix; Albert; Emile; Octavie Henry; Anna; Paul. Petition for inventory: 28 May 1898. (Thib. Ct. Hse.: Succ. #1535)
BERGERON, Olivier Joseph (Aristide & Marie TOUPS) b. 28 June 1898 (Thib. Ch.: v.7, p.505)
BERGERON, Onezime (Auguste & Laurenza HEBERT) m. 13 Feb. 1899 Lydia TOUPS (Thib. Ct. Hse.: Mar. v.38, #91)
BERGERON, Onezime (Auguste & Laurenza HEBERT) m. 13 Feb. 1899 Lydia HEBERT (Thib. Ch.: v.14, p.264-a)
BERGERON, Osciana (Napoleonville & Marcelie FOLTEMAN) m. 20 May 1899 Frank RUSSELL (Raceland Ch.: v.2, p.97)
BERGERON, Patrick (Ozeme & Marie BERGERON) b. 17 July 1897 (Raceland Ch.: v.5, p.52)
BERGERON, Paul d. 25 Aug. 1898 at age 21 yrs. (Theriot Ch.: v.1, p.1)
BERGERON, Paul Calvina (Ernest & Victoria BOUDREAU) b. 26 Nov. 1897; m. Bertha BABIN on 12 Jan. 1924. (Houma Ch.: Bapt. Bk., v.5, p.199)
BERGERON, Paul Ivy (Joseh & Sukey CHAUVIN) b. 6 Nov. 1899 (Montegut Ch.: v.6, p.96)
BERGERON, Paul Olivier (Cleophas & Sidonia SHEXNAYDER) b. 15 Nov. 1897 (Thib. Ch.: v.7, p.472)
BERGERON, Pauly Marie (Wilfred & Alexina HEBERT) b. 4 Feb. 1899 (Houma Ch.: v.5, p.237)
BERGERON, Philippe d. 23 June 1897 at age 18 yrs. (Thib. Ch.: v.3, p.201)
BERGERON, Philodia Marie (Frank & Josephine BENOIT) m. 11 Jan. 1897 Vincenzo TERRECINA (Thib. Ch.: v.14, p.106)
BERGERON, Philodion m. 8 May 1896 James TERRACHIM (Thib. Ct. Hse.: Mar. v.35, #87)

BERGERON, Pierre Celestin d. 30 June 1898 at age 3 days (Houma Ch.: v.3, p.17)
BERGERON, Polinaire d. 15 Nov. 1898 at age 45 yrs. (Thib. Ch.: v.3, p.222)
BERGERON, Robert Raoul (Philippe & Laura BOUDREAUX) b. 13 Aug. 1896 (Thib. Ch.: v.7, p.467)
BERGERON, Rosee Marie (Edgard & Alice BOUDREAUX) b. 4 April 1899 (Thib. Ch.: v.7, p.602)
BERGERON, Rosemond d. 11 Feb. 1899 at age 75 yrs. (Lockport Ch.: v.1, #5)
BERGERON, S. Marie d. 16 Jan. 1899 at age 8 yrs. (Houma Ch.: v.3, p.20)
BERGERON, Stanly Edward (Jamy & Elda MOORE) b. 26 April 1896; m. Edith Josephine TRAHAN on 23 Dec. 1920. (Houma Ch.: Bapt. Bk., v.5, p.151)
BERGERON, Valerie Aggie (Valere & Alida DUPLANTIS) b. 10 March 1898 (Montegut Ch.: v.6, p.68)
BERGERON, Valerie Lionesse (Octave & Berthile TOUPS) b. 18 June 1898 (Thib. Ch.: v.7, p.502)
BERGERON, Valfroid d. 19 June 1898; m. Philomene GAUTHREAUX Children listed: Simon; d.Malvina m. Charles T. HANAGRIFF; Numa; Louise m. d.Clay NAQUIN; Philip; Lucile m. Etienne THIBERVILLE; Marie m. Ozeme NAQUIN; Odile m. Henry C. CHOL; Cecile m. John B. TAYLOR; Henry, about 20 yrs.; Clara. Petition for inventory: 21 June 1898. (Thib. Ct. Hse.: Succ. #1537)
BERGERON, Valfroid d. 20 June 1898 at age 67 yrs., 6 mths. (Thib. Ch.: v.3, p.216)
BERGERON, Volcar (Drauzin & Elda GERBEAU) m. 8 Feb. 1898 Josephine UZE (Thib. Ch.: v.14, p.182)
BERGERON, Volcar (Drauzin & Elda GERBEAU) m. 8 Feb. 1898 Josepine UZE (Thib. Ct. Hse.: Mar. v.37, #42)
BERGERON, Walter (Octave & Berthet TOUPS) m. 3 Feb. 1897 Cecile LEDET (Thib. Ch.: v.14, p.121)
BERGERON, Walter (Octave & Berthet TOUPS) m. 3 Feb. 1897 Cecile LEDET (Thib. Ct. Hse.: Mar. v.36, #59)
BERGERON, Wilfried (Octave & Ber--- TOUPS) m. 26 Jan. 1898 Marie BABIN (Thib. Ch.: v.14, p.176)
BERGERON, Wilfried (Octave & Berthilde TOUPS) m. 26 Jan. 1898 Marie BABIN (Thib. Ct. Hse.: Mar. v.37, #28)
BERGERON, Willie d. 19 Nov. 1899 (Houma Ch.: v.3, p.26)
BERGERON, Willie m. 12 Aug. 1896 Francis CALBERT (Thib. Ct. Hse.: Mar. v.36, #134)
BERGERON, Willie (Ursin & Adele COMEAUX) m. 7 June 1897 Eliza TOUPS (Houma Ct. Hse.: Mar. v.29 & 30, #13)
BERGERON, Willy Claye Joseph (Adam & Alfrida BELANGER) b. 20 Oct. 1896 (Houma Ch.: v.5, p.170)
BERGERON, Zulma Marie Sintia (Elma & Julia NAVARRE) b. 7 April 1899 (Houma Ch.: v.5, p.244)
BERGNARD, Marie Emelie Isabelle (Joseph & Anna Angela BOURG) b. 10 Sept. 1898 (Thib. Ch.: v.7, p.511)

BERGNIARD, Marie Anna Earline (Joseph & Marie Anna Ella BOURG) b. 24 June 1897 (Thib. Ch.: v.7, p.453)
BERMUCHO, Catherine Sinclair (Peter & Mary BESSON) b. 7 Sept. 1899 in Bayou Boeuf (Thib. Ch.: Epis. Ch.: v.1, p.44)
BERNARD, ----- boy d. 10 July 1898 at age 6 mths. (Thib. Ch.: v.3, p.216)
BERNARD, Alice (John & Octavie KRAEMER) b. 22 Oct. 1898 (Chackbay Ch.: v.1, p.124)
BERNARD, Bernadette Ottie (Valcour & Velma GONZALES) b. 20 Dec. 1899 (Thib. Ch.: v.7, p.580)
BERNARD, Camille (Zenon & Azelie ROGER) m. 14 Feb. 1898 Henri HEBERT (Thib. Ch.: v.14, p.184)
BERNARD, Camille (Zenon & Azelie ROGER) m. 14 Feb. 1898 Henri HEBERT (Thib. Ct. Hse.: Mar. v.37, #102)
BERNARD, Cecile (Valan & Adrienne LEONARD) m. 13 Feb. 1899 Valcour NAVARRE (Thib. Ct. Hse.: Mar. v.38, #89)
BERNARD, Cecile (Volan & Adrienne LEONARD) m. 13 Feb. 1899 Valcour NAVARRE (Thib. Ch.: v.14, p.264)
BERNARD, Charles d. 15 April 1899 (Larose Ch.: v.1, p.53)
BERNARD, Clara (Elie & Lisa LEBOEUF) b. 29 May 1897; m. Matthieu PALMIERI on 6 July 1925. (Houma Ch.: Bapt. Bk., v.5, p.206)
BERNARD, Clay m. 28 Jan. 1899 Annette BABIN (Houma Ct. Hse.: Mar. v.30 & 31, #288)
BERNARD, Clay (Joseph & Julma BARRIOS) m. 28 Jan. 1899 Annette BABIN (Houma Ch.: v.6-a, p.269)
BERNARD, Degella Gratieuse (Louis & Suzanne REEPSTOCK) b. 15 Feb. 1898 (Larose Ch.: v.3, p.21)
BERNARD, Ellen (Theophile & Celina PITRE) m. 2 April 1898 Elles DUPRE (Houma Ch.: v.6-a, p.238)
BERNARD, Ellen Bergeron Mrs. m. 2 April 1898 Ellis DUPRE (Houma Ct. Hse.: Mar. v.30 & 31, #366)
BERNARD, Emilia m. 14 June 1898 Sylvain GALIANO (Thib. Ct. Hse.: Mar. v.38, #207)
BERNARD, Emilienne m. 10 Jan. 1896 Albert NAQUIN (Thib. Ct. Hse.: Mar. v.35, #17)
BERNARD, Emma (Volan & Adrienne LEONARD) b. 13 Aug. 1897 (Thib. Ch.: v.7, p.516)
BERNARD, Eugenie m. 19 March 1898 Samson MELANCON (Thib. Ct. Hse.: Mar. v.37, #128)
BERNARD, Eugenie (St. James & Dora ADAM) m. 23 Jan. 1899 Gustave PLAISANCE (Thib. Ct. Hse.: Mar. v.38, #36)
BERNARD, Eugenie (St. James & Dora ADAM) m. 23 Jan. 1899 Gustave PLAISANCE (Larose Ch.: v.4, p.32)
BERNARD, Eugenie (St. James & Dora ADAM) m. 23 Jan. 1899 Gustave PLAISANCE (Larose Ch.: v.3, p.11)
BERNARD, Eusebe Antoine (Samjest & Theodora ADAMS) b. 17 Jan. 1898 (Larose Ch.: v.3, p.16)
BERNARD, Helene d. 29 Dec. 1899 (Thib. Ch.: v.3, p.247)
BERNARD, Ignes Berthe Marie (Edgar & Malvina BENOIT) b. 23 Aug. 1896 (Thib. Ch.: v.7, p.415)

BERNARD, Irene Clara (Simeon & Oliva MIRE) b. 7 Nov. 1898 (Thib. Ch.: v.7, p.574)
BERNARD, Jean Baptiste d. 31 Dec. 1897; m. (1) first wife not listed Children of 1st marriage: Louis; Lea m. Albert ADOU. m.(2) Eliza RICHARD Children of 2nd marriage: Joseph; Victoria m. Wash WHITNEY. Petition to put heirs in possession: 7 Jan. 1898. (Houma Ct. Hse.: Succ. #894)
BERNARD, John (Andrew & Louisa JOHNSON) m. 19 Jan. 1898 Octavie KRAMER (Chackbay Ch.: v.1, p.51)
BERNARD, John (Andrew & Louisa JOHNSON) m. 16 Jan. 1898 Octavie KRAEMER (Thib. Ct. Hse.: Mar. v.37, #2)
BERNARD, Joseph (Jean & Pamelise LANDRY) m. 29 Sept. 1896 Annie O. BOURG (Thib. Ch.: v.14, p.100)
BERNARD, Joseph (Jean & Pamelise LANDRY) m. 29 Sept. 1896 Annie O. BOURG (Thib. Ct. Hse.: Mar. v.36, #147)
BERNARD, Joseph Delvis d. 15 Jan. 1899 at age 1 yr. (Thib. Ch.: v.3, p.225)
BERNARD, Joseph Edgard (Edgard & Telvina BENOIT) b. 27 Jan. 1899 (Thib. Ch.: v.7, p.591)
BERNARD, Joseph Elvis (Valcour & Velma GONZALES) b. 5 Jan. 1897 (Thib. Ch.: v.7, p.486)
BERNARD, Julia (Lubin & Jeanne THIBAULT) m. 4 Feb. 1896 Rodolphe SOIGNIER (Thib. Ct. Hse.: Mar. v.35, #29)
BERNARD, Julia (Lubin & Jeanne THIBAUT) m. 4 Feb. 1896 Rodolphe SOIGNIER (Thib. Ch.: v.14, p.73)
BERNARD, Leontia (Roselien & Josephine MIRE) m. 9 Oct. 1898 Joseph PONTIFF (Thib. Ch.: v.14, p.227)
BERNARD, Leontia (Roselius & Josephine MIRE) m. 9 Oct. 1898 Joseph PONTIFF (Thib. Ct. Hse.: Mar. v.38, #286)
BERNARD, Lubin d. 1 June 1892; m.(1) Odile GUILLOT Children listed: Taylor of West Baton Rouge; Adelia m. d.Gustave MIRE; Philomene m. Theophile CLEMENT; Willie; Odilia m. Aurelien Jack NAQUIN; Victoria m. Wilfrid CLEMENT; d.Clay m. Helene BERGERON. m.(2) Jeanne THIBAUT Children listed: Julia; Julian. Petition for inventory & administration: 12 Feb. 1896. (Thib. Ct. Hse.: Succ. #1483)
BERNARD, Manuella m. 12 Oct. 1896 Emilien PLAISANCE (Larose Ch.: v.4, p.47)
BERNARD, Manuella m. 12 Oct. 1896 Emilien PLAISANCE (Larose Ch.: v.3, p.4)
BERNARD, Manuella m. 7 Oct. 1896 Milien PLAISANCE (Thib. Ct. Hse.: Mar. v.36, #151)
BERNARD, Marguerite Adele (Elie & Felicia BUQUET) b. 2 Feb. 1896 (Houma Ch.: v.5, p.143)
BERNARD, Marie Agnes (Edgard & Telvina BENOIT) b. 7 Dec. 1898 (Thib. Ch.: v.7, p.525)
BERNARD, Marie Glader (Joseph D. & Gracieuse LEPINE) b. 2 Dec. 1898 (Raceland Ch.: v.5, p.84)
BERNARD, Marie Theodule m. Timothee LEDET d. 26 June 1897 at age 71 yrs. (Thib. Ch.: v.3, p.202)

BERNARD, Ophelia m. 2 Feb. 1898 Elles SAVOIE (Larose Ch.: v.4, p.115)

BERNARD, Ophelia m. 2 Feb. 1898 Elles SAVOIE (Larose Ch.: v.3, p.7)

BERNARD, Ophelia (Emilien & Daisie SAVOIE) m. 2 Feb. 1898 Elles SAVOIE (Thib. Ct. Hse.: Mar. v.37, #56)

BERNARD, Sydney Jules (Willie & Dolphina MIRE) b. 25 Sept. 1896 (Thib. Ch.: v.7, p.468)

BERNARD, Valcour (Valcourt & Adrienne LEONARD) m. 6 Aprl 1897 Velma GONZALES (Thib. Ct. Hse.: Mar. v.36, #107)

BERNARD, Valde d. 20 Nov. 1899 at age 4½ mths. (Thib. Ch.: v.3, p.243)

BERNO, Rudder m. 19 Jan. 1899 Alphonse PERRO (Houma Ct. Hse.: Mar. v.30 & 31, #257)

BERNUCHO, Thelma Lorraine (Pierce & Mary BESSON) b. 12 April 1898 (Houma Ch.: Epis. Ch.: v.1, p.118)

BERTEAU, Ambroise (Trasimond & d.Sydalis BABIN) m. 1 March 1897 Helene LAFOREST (Chackbay Ch.: v.1, p.40)

BERTEAU, Ambroise (Trasimond & Sydalis BABIN) m. 1 March 1897 Helen LAFOREST (Thib. Ct. Hse.: Mar. v.36, #88)

BERTEL, Marie Louise (Joseph & Theoline LEVRON) b. 2 July 1898 (Houma Ch.: v.5, p.212)

BERTHAUET, Frank Sydney (Ambroise & Helena FOREST) b. 13 Nov. 1898 (Thib. Ch.: v.7, p.574)

BERTHELOT (Sometimes: BERTHELOTTE)

BERTHELOT, Adam Insanity of: 11 Sept. 1898. (Thib. Ct. Hse.: Succ. #1549)

BERTHELOT, Claude Sylvin (Sylvin & Elizabeth DAIGLE) b. 14 Feb. 1898 (Thib. Ch.: v.7, p.488)

BERTHELOT, Marie Annette (Adam & Anita BREAUX) b. 23 April 1896 (Thib. Ch.: v.7, p.401)

BERTHELOT, Myrthil Denys (Gustave & Cecile NAQUIN) b. 8 April 1897 (Thib. Ch.: v.7, p.449)

BERTHELOT, Virginie Mathilde (Gustave & Cecile NAQUIN) b. 26 Aug. 1898 (Thib. Ch.: v.7, p.518)

BERTRAND, ----- boy d. 6 April 1898 at birth (Thib. Ch.: v.3, p.213)

BERTRAND, Agnes Valery (Homer & Lea LAINE) b. 3 Jan. 1897 (Thib. Ch.: v.7, p.434)

BERTRAND, Charles Persival d. 21 Aug. 1899 at age 2 yrs. (Thib. Ch.: v.3, p.239)

BERTRAND, Ella Josephine (Omer & Philomene AUBIN) b. 18 Aug. 1898 (Thib. Ch.: v.7, p.560)

BERTRAND, Emma (Desire & Celestine BOUDREAUX) m. 2 July 1898 Thomas L. BILLINGS (Houma Ct. Hse.: Mar. v.30 & 31, #42-A)

BERTRAND, Ernest (Hebert & Josephine COMEAUX) m. 27 Jan. 1898 Philomene ALBERT (Thib. Ct. Hse.: Mar. v.37, #13)

BERTRAND, Eugene Percival (Gustave & Celeste LEBLANC) bt. 3 Oct. 1897 (Thib. Ch.: v.7, p.466)

BERTRAND, Gustave Pierre (Gustave & Celeste LEBLANC) b. 7 Oct. 1899 (Thib. Ch.: v.8, p.18)
BERTRAND, Lea Laine d. 14 April 1898 at age 21 yrs. (Thib. Ch.: v.3, p.213)
BERTRAND, Lydia (Desire & Celestine BOUDREAUX) m. 13 Feb. 1896 Neuville CUNNINGHAM (Houma Ct. Hse.: Mar. v.28, #417)
BERTRAND, Lydia (Desire & Celestine BOUDREAUX) m. 13 Feb. 1896 Neuville CUNNINGHAM (Chacahoula Ch.: v.1, p.55)
BERTRAND, Marie (Euphemon & Elmire ROBICHAUX) m. 5 May 1898 Felix Alexandre LEPINE (Thib. Ct. Hse.: Mar. v.38, #168)
BERTRAND, Marie (Euphemon & Elmire ROBICHAUX) m. 5 May 1898 Felix Alexandre LEPINE (Thib. Ch.: v.14, p.203)
BERTRAND, Marie Emelie Viola (Olivier & Elmire LEBLANC) b. 15 Sept. 1896 (Thib. Ch.: v.7, p.417)
BERTRAND, Norma d. 23 Jan. 1899 at age 4 mths. (Thib. Ch.: v.3, p.226)
BERTRAND, Norma Louise (Gustave P. & Celeste LEBLANC) b. 29 Sept. 1898 (Thib. Ch.: v.7, p.519)
BERTRAND, Omer (Clement & Olivia GAUDIN) m. 22 Oct. 1898 Philomene AUPIED (Thib. Ct. Hse.: Mar. v.38, #297)
BERTRAND, Omer (Clement & Olivia GAUDIN) m. 22 Oct. 1898 Philomene AUPIED (Thib. Ch.: v.14, p.228)
BERWICK, Elizabeth (Horace M. & Mary R. HATCH) b. 2 Aug. 1897 (Houma Ch.: Epis. Ch.: v.1, p.116)
BESSON, Adrien (Adrien & Leonida SANTINI) b. 9 Nov. 1897 (Larose Ch.: v.3, p.12)
BESSON, Dellauson m. 13 July 1898 Laura DAIGLE (Houma Ct. Hse.: Mar. v.30 & 31, #54)
BESSON, Edwin Joseph (Emes & Marie BOUDREAUX) b. 2 Jan. 1899 (Thib. Ch.: v.7, p.529)
BESSON, Gustave Henry (Amos & Mary BOUDREAU) b. 1 Jan. 1897 (Thib. Ch.: v.7, p.433)
BESSON, Julia m. Edgard LEGENDRE d. 31 Aug. 1896 at age 28 yrs. (Thib. Ch.: v.3, p.186)
BETES, Joseph (Felix & Emilie Louise PELTIER) b. 13 Dec. 1896 (Thib. Ch.: v.7, p.429)

BETHANCOURT (Sometimes: BETANCOURT)

BETHANCOURT, Joseph Easton (Athos & Lucie BOUDREAUX) b. 2 April 1899 (Montegut Ch.: v.6, p.86)
BETHANCOURT, Marie Anne (Athas & Lucie BOUDREAUX) d. 23 Feb. 1898 at age 15 days (Montegut Ch.: v.2, p.15)
BETTAS, Aima (Felix & Louise PELTIER) b. 22 Jan. 1899 (Thib. Ch.: v.7, p.534)
BETTIS, Lily m. 8 June 1898 Joseph JONES (Houma Ct. Hse.: Mar. v.30 & 31, #6)
BIAZIO d. 28 June 1898 at age 6 days (Houma Ch.: v.3, p.17)
BIBA, Margarita (Guiseppe & Guiseppa GIARRAPUTO) m. 15 April 1896 Guiseppe PREUZENI (Houma Ch.: v.6-a, p.174)

BILA, Margerita m. 15 April 1896 Guiseppe PENZENI (Houma Ct. Hse.: Mar. v.29 & 30, #41)

BILINA, Girintonia of Terrebonne Parish m. 3 June 1899 Antonio CARNOVA (Houma Ch.: v.6-B, p.3)

BILLIMORE, Elizabeth m. 23 April 1897 Lucas YBANGELESTA (Houma Ct. Hse.: Mar. v.29 & 30, #391)

BILLINGS, Thomas L. (Thomas L. & Laurence MARTINEZ) m. 2 July 1898 Emma BERTRAND (Houma Ct. Hse.: Mar. v.30 & 31, #42-A)

BILLIOT, Armantine (Alcide & Elizabeth BILLIOT) m. 31 Dec. 1897 Bernard BILLIOT (Houma Ct. Hse.: Mar. v.30 & 31, #171)

BILLIOT, Aurelien m. 10 July 1897 Marguerite DARDARD (Thib. Ct. Hse.: Mar. v.37, #187)

BILLIOT, Bernard (Jean & Estelle BILLIOT) m. 31 Dec. 1897 Armantine BILLIOT (Houma Ct. Hse.: Mar. v.30 & 31, #171)

BILLIOT, Bertrand (Joseph & Henriette FITCH) m. 8 Feb. 1896 Ellen BILLIOT (Houma Ct. Hse.: Mar. v.28, #439)

BILLIOT, Bertrand (Joseph & Henriette FITCH) m. 17 Feb. 1896 Ellen BILLIOT (Theriot Ch.: v.1, p.4)

BILLIOT, Ellen (J. R. C. & Marie GARUSET) m. 17 Feb. 1896 Bertrand BILLIOT (Theriot Ch.: v.1, p.4)

BILLIOT, Ellen (Jean Baptiste & Marie GANIVET) m. 8 Feb. 1896 Bertrand BILLIOT (Houma Ct. Hse.: Mar. v.28, #439)

BILLIOT, Etienne d. 17 Oct. 1897 at age 81 yrs. (Theriot Ch.: v.1, p.1)

BILLIOT, Felicia (Michel & Lena LINER) b. 28 Feb. 1897 (Theriot Ch.: v.1-B, p.102)

BILLIOT, Gilbert (Chas Michel & Lizzie LIVER) b. 15 Nov. 1896 (Theriot Ch.: v.1-B, p.102)

BILLIOT, Jean (Jean & Rosalie LOVELL) b. 28 Oct. 1897 (Theriot Ch.: v.2, p.66)

BILLIOT, Joseph Corbet (Thelesphore & Laura LINA) b. 6 Oct. 1898 (Theriot Ch.: v.2, p.31)

BILLIOT, Joseph Healy (Leo & Julie BILLIOT) b. 26 Oct. 1897 (Theriot Ch.: v.2, p.16)

BILLIOT, Julie (Louis & Lonise FITCH) m. 24 Dec. 1896 Leo BILLIOT (Houma Ct. Hse.: Mar. v.29 & 30, #206)

BILLIOT, Julie (Louis & Louise FITCH) m. ----- 1897 Leo BILLIOT (Theriot Ch.: v.1, p.8)

BILLIOT, Julien (Jean Louis & Marie Louise FITCH) m. 26 Nov. 1898 Julienne CHIASSON (Houma Ct. Hse.: Mar. v.30 & 31, #133)

BILLIOT, Leo (Joseph & Henriette FITCH) m. 24 Dec. 1896 Julie BILLIOT (Houma Ct. Hse.: Mar. v.29 & 30, #206)

BILLIOT, Leo (Joseph & Henriette FITCH) m. ----- 1897 Julie BILLIOT (Theriot Ch.: v.1, p.8)

BILLIOT, Louis Mayfied (Tarcelle of Grand Caillou & Marie PARFAIT of Grand Caillou) b. 17 Nov. 1896 (Theriot Ch.: v.2, p.1)

BILLIOT, Lucie d. 6 Feb. 1898 at age 3½ yrs. (Theriot Ch.: v.1, p.1)
BILLIOT, Marie Alice (Bertrand & Helene BILLIOT) b. 7 April 1898 (Theriot Ch.: v.2, p.22)
BILLIOT, Pierre Victor (Jules & Celaira BILLIOT) b. 24 July 1898 (Theriot Ch.: v.2, p.41)
BILLIOT, Thelesphore (Victor & Josephine VERRET) m. 6 Nov. 1898 Laura LINA (Theriot Ch.: v.1-B, p.5)
BILLIOT, Willie (Severin & Roseline MOLINAIRE) m. 9 Dec. 1896 Anitas CHIASSON (Houma Ct. Hse.: Mar. v.29 & 30, #198)
BILLIU, Mary m. 11 Dec. 1899 A. H. DAVID (Thib. Ct. Hse.: Mar. v.39, #279)
BILLIU, Mary m. 11 Dec. 1899 Archie H. DAVIS (Thib. Ch.: Epis. Ch.: v.1, p.331)

BILLOT (Sometimes: BILLEAU, BILLIOT)
BILLOT, Agnes Angelina (Abel & Pauline CREPEL) b. 22 Aug. 1897 (Larose Ch.: v.3, p.14)
BILLOT, Agnes Laurentia (Jean & Adele DARDAR) b. 7 June 1896 (Larose Ch.: v.3, p.12)
BILLOT, Albert (Marcel & Marie PARFAIT) b. 14 Feb. 1899 (Montegut Ch.: v.6, p.96)
BILLOT, Alcide (Leon & Caroline ----) m. 6 Oct. 1897 Elizabeth BILLOT (Houma Ct. Hse.: Mar. v.29 & 30, #111)
BILLOT, Alcide (Leon & Caroline) m. 6 Oct. 1897 Elizabeth BILLOT (Montegut Ch.: v.4, p.224)
BILLOT, Alfred Augustin (Alfred & Evelide BILLOT) b. 23 Feb. 1896 (Montegut Ch.: v.6, p.40)
BILLOT, Alida Marie (Alidor & Lucia BILLOT) b. 1 Dec. 1898 (Larose Ch.: v.3, p.54)
BILLOT, Anatole Antoine (Guillaume & Azema Marguerite LOVERS) b. 2 Jan. 1899 (Larose Ch.: v.4, p.86)
BILLOT, Andre Victor (Bernard & Josephine DARDAR) b. 4 Feb. 1898 (Montegut Ch.: v.6, p.74)
BILLOT, Augustine Amelia (Alfred & Marie BILLOT) b. 30 March 1899 (Larose Ch.: v.3, p.54)
BILLOT, Charles Hyppolite (Neuville & Rosame DARDAR) b. 14 June 1897; bt. 10 March 1903 (Larose Ch.: v.4, p.29)
BILLOT, Donat Edouard (Bernard & Armantine BILLOT) b. 29 Oct. 1898 (Larose Ch.: v.3, p.60)
BILLOT, Elizabeth (Celestin & Melanie VERDUN) m. 6 Oct. 1897 Alcide BILLOT (Montegut Ch.: v.4, p.224)
BILLOT, Elizabeth (Celestin & Melanie VERDUN) m. 6 Oct. 1897 Alcide BILLOT (Houma Ct. Hse.: Mar. v.29 & 30, #111)
BILLOT, Emelia Scholastique (Lartigue & Adelaide BILLOT) b. 22 May 1896 (Montegut Ch.: v.6, p.40)
BILLOT, Georges Jefferson (Welly & Anita CHIASSON) b. 9 June 1898 (Montegut Ch.: v.6, p.75)
BILLOT, Homere m. 16 Oct. 1899 Marie GAUTRAU (Thib. Ct. Hse.: Mar. v.39, #237)

BILLOT, James Richmond (James & Mary McCULLOM) b. 31 March 1898 (Chacahoula Ch.: v.4, p.13)

BILLOT, Jean Edouard (Donquine & Brigitte THIBODEAUX) b. 22 March 1897 (Montegut Ch.: v.6, p.54)

BILLOT, Joseph Alvans (Edwin & Octavie PARFAIT) b. 4 April 1897 (Montegut Ch.: v.6, p.55)

BILLOT, Joseph Edwin (Joseph Severin & Rosaline Clemence MOLINAIRE) m. 17 Feb. 1896 Marie Octavie PARFAIT (Montegut Ch.: v.4, p.206)

BILLOT, Joseph Edwin (Joseph Severin & Rosalie Clemence MOLINAIRE) m. 13 Feb. 1896 Marie Octavie PARFAIT (Houma Ct. Hse.: Mar. v.28, #458)

BILLOT, Joseph Waley (Frank & Clotilde MOLINIERE) b. 9 Jan. 1896 (Montegut Ch.: v.6, p.34)

BILLOT, Joseph Walley (Frank & Clotilde MOLINIERE) d. 11 June 1896 (Montegut Ch.: v.2, p.5)

BILLOT, Joseph Wilson (Clodomir & Aureline CHIASSON) b. 4 March 1897 (Montegut Ch.: v.6, p.54)

BILLOT, Josephine m. Charles HOTARD d. 5 July 1898 at age 31 yrs. (Montegut Ch.: v.2, p.18)

BILLOT, Josephine (Edwin & Octave PARFAIT) d. 24 Jan. 1898 at age 2 hrs. (Montegut Ch.: v.2, p.15)

BILLOT, Julien (d.Jean Louis & Marie Louise FITCH) m. 26 Dec. 1898 Julienne CHIASSON (Montegut Ch.: v.4, p.250)

BILLOT, Louis Dewey (Julien & Julienne CHIASSON) b. 5 Nov. 1899 (Montegut Ch.: v.6, p.96)

BILLOT, Luc Alphonse (Aurelien & Marguerite DARDAR) b. 18 Oct. 1898 (Larose Ch.: v.3, p.57)

BILLOT, Madeleine Edna (Donquine & Brigitte THIBODAUX) b. 25 Aug. 1899 (Montegut Ch.: v.6, p.93)

BILLOT, Marie Agnes d. 6 March 1899 at age 24 yrs. (Raceland Ch.: v.1, p.24)

BILLOT, Marie Alcidie (Aubin & Bernadette BILLOT) b. 1 June 1899 (Montegut Ch.: v.6, p.94)

BILLOT, Marie Alfrida (Alfred & Marie BILLOT) b. 6 March 1898 (Larose Ch.: v.3, p.54)

BILLOT, Martilia Rosalie (Dominique & Marie VERDIN) b. 30 Jan. 1898; bt. 10 March 1903 (Larose Ch.: v.4, p.29)

BILLOT, Mathilde (Auguste & Heloise BILLOT) m. 12 July 1898 Etienne DION (Theriot Ch.: v.1-B, p.4)

BILLOT, Mathilde (Auguste & Heloise BILLOT) m. 2 July 1898 Etienne DION (Houma Ct. Hse.: Mar. v.30 & 31, #44)

BILLOT, Nacina Agnes (Arthemise BILLOT) b. 31 Dec. 1899; bt. 11 April 1902 (Larose Ch.: v.4, p.9)

BILLOT, Ortance m. Joseph COURTEAU d. 29 Sept. 1896 at age 60 yrs. old (Montegut Ch.: v.2, p.7)

BILLOT, Sidonia m. 9 Feb. 1899 Victor VERDIN (Houma Ct. Hse.: Mar. v.31 & 32, #331½)

BILLOT, Theophile Gilbert (Etienne Justilien & Marie BILLOT) b. 3 Nov. 1898; bt. 18 May 1900 (Larose Ch.:v.3, p.57)

BILLOT, Willie (Severin & Roseline MOLINAIRE) m. 28 Dec. 1896 Anitase CHIASSON (Montegut Ch.: v.4, p.215)
BILLUPS, Robert (Ebero & Louisa JACKSON) m. 30 Jan. 1896 Leontine CHARLES (Thib. Ch.: v.14, p.70)
BILLUPS, Robert (Herom & Louisa JACKSON) m. 30 Jan. 1896 Leontine CHARLES (Thib. Ct. Hse.: Mar. v.35, #35)
BILONA, Girintonia m. 22 May 1899 Antonio CANOVA (Houma Ct. Hse.: Mar. v.31, & 32, #13)
BINNINGS, S. Amanda d. 31 May 1898 at age 64½ yrs. (Thib. Ch.: Epis. Ch.: v.1, p.394)
BIOZ, Samuel Martial (Rene & Valentine ROUBION) b. 1 July 1898 (Raceland Ch.: v.5, p.74)
BIRD, Samuel m. 21 Sept. 1899 Hattie STREAMS (Thib. Ct. Hse.: Mar. v.39, #234)

BIRDSALL (Sometimes: BIRDSELL)
BIRDSALL, Joseph Clifton (Henry Clay & Emelie MATERNE) b. 4 Aug. 1899 (Raceland Ch.: v.5, p.100)
BIRDSALL, Joseph Edith (Edey & Mary BRICKLEY) b. 21 Feb. 1898 (Raceland Ch.: v.5, p.71)
BIRDSALL, Mabel m. 12 Dec. 1899 Mathews STATEM (Thib. Ct. Hse.: Mar. v.39, #281)
BIRDSALL, Marie (Edith & Marie BRIKLEY) b. 27 Feb. 1897 (Raceland Ch.: v.5, p.45)
BIRDSALL, Miriam Jeanne (Henri Clay & Emilia MATERNE) b. 24 June 1896 (Raceland Ch.: v.5, p.24)
BISLAND, Georgianna m. 19 Jan. 1899 George GRIFFIN (Houma Ct. Hse.: Mar. v.30 & 31, #254)
BISLAND, Henry m. 6 June 1899 Anna HICKMAN (Houma Ct. Hse.: Mar. v.31 & 32, #35)
BISSON, Ulysse d. 21 Oct. 1899 at age 24 yrs. (Raceland Ch.: v.1, p.28)
BLACK, Delilah m. Raphael BLACK Children: Samuel; Harrison; Ophelia. Inventory: 15 Sept. 1897. (Thib. Ct. Hse.: Succ. #1521)
BLACK, Elmire Edna (Abraam & Josephine JONES) b. 26 Aug. 1896 (Larose Ch.: v.2, p.183)
BLACK, Rosine Camelia (Abraham & Josephine JONES) b. 12 April 1898 (Larose Ch.: v.3, p.18)
BLACKLEDGE, Charles m. 18 Feb. 1897 Mary REED (Thib. Ct. Hse.: Mar. v.36, #82)
BLAKE, Bannon d. 6 Feb. 1899 (Eugene W. & Cecilia THIBODAUX) Judgment placing heir in possession: 4 March 1899. (Thib. Ct. Hse.: Succ. #1566)
BLAKE, Bannon Eugene d. 7 Feb. 1899 (Thib. Ch.: v.3, p.227)
BLAKE, Eugene William d. 17 Feb. 1898 at age 5 mths. (Thib. Ch.: v.3, p.210)
BLAKE, Eugene William (Bannon Thibodaux & Henriette Olympe THIBODAUX) b. 12 Sept. 1897 (Thib. Ch.: v.7, p.463)
BLANCHARD, Adelia m. 12 Dec. 1898 Howard Frank DARCE (Houma Ct. Hse.: Mar. v.30 & 31, #141)

BLANCHARD, Alice m. 24 April 1897 Adam COMEAUX (Houma Ct. Hse.: Mar. v.29 & 30, #392)
BLANCHARD, Alice (Ozemee & Emelie BONVILLAIN) m. 24 April 1897 Adam COMEAUX (Houma Ch.: v.6-a, p.200)
BLANCHARD, Antiliope (Theophile & Elidia PELLEGRIN) m. 30 Dec. 1897 Jules BOQUET (Houma Ct. Hse: Mar. v.30 & 31, #168)
BLANCHARD, Antiliope (Theophile & Elidia PELEGRIN) m. 18 Jan. 1898 Jules BOQUET (Montegut Ch.: v.4, p.229)
BLANCHARD, Baptiste (Joseph & Armentine EXBRESS) m. 31 Jan. 1899 Clotile GASPARD (Houma Ct. Hse.: Mar. v.30 & 31, #294)
BLANCHARD, Edna (Sylvain & Aspasie TOUPS) m. 21 Feb. 1898 Cestive THIBODEAU (Theriot Ch.: v.1-B, p.2)
BLANCHARD, Edna (Sylvain & Aspazie TOUPS) m. 1 Feb. 1898 Cestive THIBODAUX (Houma Ct. Hse.: Mar. v.30 & 31, #264)
BLANCHARD, Elvire (Adam & Euphrosine BABIN) b. 22 Jan. 1898 (Raceland Ch.: v.5, p.65)
BLANCHARD, Emma (Firmin & Erma DOMANGUE) m. 6 April 1899 Louis SOUDELIER (Houma Ct. Hse.: Mar. v.31 & 32, #387)
BLANCHARD, Felix Theophile (Felix & Eve CHARPENTIER) b. 9 Feb. 1897 (Montegut Ch.: v.6, p.50)
BLANCHARD, Firmin (d.Firmin & Irma DOMINGUE) m. 15 June 1896 Agnes PORTIER (Montegut Ch.: v.4, p.212)
BLANCHARD, Firmin (Firmin & Irma DOMINGUE) m. 15 May 1896 Agnes PORTIER (Houma Ct. Hse.: Mar. v.29 & 30, #71)
BLANCHARD, Hattie Zita (Sylvire & Josephine BERGERON) b. 26 Dec. 1899 (Theriot Ch.: v.2, p.58)
BLANCHARD, Joachim Algin (Clairville Pierre & Marie Noela MARTIN) b. 19 Aug. 1897 (Montegut Ch.: v.6, p.59)
BLANCHARD, Joseph Ernest (Alexis & Odilia DUBOIS) b. 14 Aug. 1896 (Houma Ch.: v.5, p.164)
BLANCHARD, Joseph Lincoln (Joseph & Ameline CHAMPAGNE) b. 2 June 1897 (Montegut Ch.: v.6, p.57)
BLANCHARD, Joseph William (Felix & Eve CHARPENTIER) b. 10 Jan. 1899 (Montegut Ch.: v.6, p.82)
BLANCHARD, Josephine Napoline (Joseph & Elselina BLANCHARD) b. 13 Jan. 1899 (Houma Ch.: v.5, p.239)
BLANCHARD, Justilia m. 31 Dec. 1898 Gustave PITRE (Houma Ct. Hse.: Mar. v.30 & 31, #168)
BLANCHARD, Justilia (Amedee & Pauline LEBLANC) m. 16 Jan. 1899 Gustave PITRE (Houma Ch.: v.6-a, p.264)
BLANCHARD, Louis (Simon & Antoinette PERES) m. 10 Feb. 1898 Delphine VEDROS (Thib. Ct. Hse.: Mar. v.37, #49)
BLANCHARD, Louis (Simon & Antoinette PERES) m. 10 Feb. 1898 Delphine VEDROS (Lockport Ch.: v.2, p.185)
BLANCHARD, Marcelle Pierre (Theophile & Lydia PELEGRIN) m. 17 Jan. 1898 Alzina DUPRE (Houma Ct. Hse.: Mar. v.30 & 31, #215)

BLANCHARD, Marie Celestine (Beloni & Angelina THIBODEAU) b. 16 Jan. 1897 (Theriot Ch.: v.1-B, p.104)
BLANCHARD, Marie Flocy (Sylver & Josephine BERGERON) b. 22 Aug. 1897 (Theriot Ch.: v.2, p.11)
BLANCHARD, Marie Irene (Joseph & Emeline CHAMPAGNE) b. 13 Nov. 1898 (Montegut Ch.: v.6, p.78)
BLANCHARD, Marie Lelia (Marcel & Azina DUPRE) b. 11 Dec. 1898 (Montegut Ch.: v.6, p.81)
BLANCHARD, Marie Nora Daisy (Firmin & Agnes PORTIER) b. 5 Feb. 1897 (Montegut Ch.: v.6, p.51)
BLANCHARD, Octavie m. Alidor GUIDRY d. 11 April 1897 at age 45 yrs. (Montegut Ch.: v.2, p.10)
BLANCHARD, Pierre Cyrille (Theles & Olympe HOTARD) b. 27 Dec. 1897 (Montegut Ch.: v.6, p.64)
BLANCHARD, Randolph (Neuville & Felicie SAVOIE) m. 4 Feb. 1896 Lillie M. GAUTREAUX (Houma Ct. Hse.: Mar. v.28, #435)
BLANCHARD, Randolphe (Neuville & Felicie SAVOIE) m. 4 Feb. 1896 Lillie M. GAUTREAUX (Thib. Ch.: v.14, p.72)
BLANCHARD, Raoul Joseph (Cleophat & Albertine CHAMPAGNE) b. 25 April 1897 (Montegut Ch.: v.6, p.56)
BLANCHARD, Sudonicus Joseph (Alex & Odilia DUBOIS) b. 25 Dec. 1898 (Theriot Ch.: v.2, p.33)
BLANCO, John Louis (Benjamin & Theresa MINI) b. 15 Dec. 1897; bt. 28 Jan. 1898 (Chacahoula Ch.: Gibson Ch.: v.2, p.116)
BLANCO, John Louis (Benjamin & Theresa NINI) b. 15 Dec. 1897 (Chacahoula Ch.: Gibson Ch.: Mar. Bk., v.1, #6)
BLANCOT, Sidonia Eve (Maurice & Mary HEBERT) b. 26 Dec. 1897 (Chacahoula Ch.: Gibson Ch.: Mar. Bk., v.1, #9)
BLANCOT, Sidonia Eve (Maurice & Mary HEBERT) b. 26 Dec. 1897; bt. 8 Feb. 1898 (Chacahoula Ch.: Gibson Ch.: v.2, p.116)
BLAND, Earle Jasper (William & Annette VIGUERIE) b. 7 Dec. 1897; m. Edith Evelyn EHRHARDT on 18 Oct. 1923 (Houma Ch.: Bapt. Bk., v.5, p.195)
BLOUIN, J. A. m. 27 June 1898 Ida THERIOT (Thib. Ct. Hse.: Mar. v.38, #214)
BLOUIN, Joseph Clarence (Louis Adolphe & Clara JOHNSON) b. 15 Sept. 1897 (Thib. Ch.: v.7, p.516)
BLOUIN, Marie Gertrude (Arthur & Aida THERIOT) b. 6 Aug. 1899 (Raceland Ch.: v.5, p.100)
BLUE, Mary m. 9 Aug. 1899 Isiah SHEDRICK (Houma Ct. Hse.: Mar. v.31 & 32, #90)
BLUE, Reuben m. 28 April 1898 Kitty HENDERSON (Houma Ct. Hse.: Mar. v.30 & 31, #423)
BLUE, Trooty m. 7 Jan. 1896 Polly JACKSON (Houma Ct. Hse.: Mar. v.28, #377)
BLUM, Leon m. 23 Jan. 1897 Irma LEVY (Thib. Ct. Hse.: Mar. v.36, #50)
BOBE, Alibie d. 26 Jan. 1899 at age 30 yrs. (Lockport Ch.: v.1, #2)

BOEHM, Carrie (Martin & Marianne BRUNNER) m. 6 April 1897 Marcelus CORTEZ (Thib. Ct Hse.: Mar. v.36, #104)
BOEHN, Carrie (d.Martin & Marianne BRUNNER) m. 6 April 1897 Marcellus CORTEZ (Chackbay Ch.: v.1, p.41)
BOCLAIR, Mary Lelia (Louis & Emma CROCHET) b. 29 April 1896 (Houma Ch.: v.5, p.151)
BODIN, Antoinette M. P. (Norbert & Melesie VERRETTE) b. 16 Oct. 1897 (Houma Ch.: v.5, p.190)
BOFFANIE, Maria Andrea (Francisco B. & Lucille CHERAMI) b. 6 Jan. 1896 (Larose Ch.: v.2, p.181)
BOFFANIE, Marie Andrea (Francisco & Lucille CHERAMI) b. 6 Jan. 1896 (Larose Ch.: v.2, p.183 & p.194, #26)
BOFFINGER, Alfred m. 10 Jan. 1899 Daisy PARSON (Thib. Ct. Hse.: Mar. v.38, #13)
BOLDEN, Amy m. 7 June 1897 Willie DANGERFIELD (Houma Ct. Hse.: Mar. v.29 & 30, #10)
BOLDEN, Mary m. 17 March 1898 Robert CARTER (Houma Ct. Hse.: Mar. v.30 & 31, #340)
BOLDEN, Mary m. 9 July 1896 Jake MITCHELL (Houma Ct. Hse.: Mar. v.29 & 30, #111-C)
BOLOTTE, Camelia m. 5 Jan. 1898 Andrew E. DOLESE (Thib. Ct. Hse.: Mar. v.37, #6)
BOMPHILIA, Thuride (John & Vencenza ONTZ) b. 4 Nov. 1899 (Thib. Ch.:v.7, p.574)
BONADONA, Anna (Pietro & Rosa REDESSI) b. 17 Sept. 1899 (Raceland Ch.: v.5, p.104)
BONADONA, Francisco (Petro & Rosa PERIN) b. 24 Sept. 1897 (Raceland Ch.: v.5, p.55)
BONADONNE, Georges (Petro & Rosa LEROS) b. 6 Jan. 1896 (Raceland Ch.: v.5, p.18)
BONAFORD, Salvador Jr. (Salvador, Sr. & Azelie AUTIN) d. Dec. 1899 at age 7 yrs. (Larose Ch.: v.1, p.54)

BONAMOUR (Sometimes:BONNAMOUR,BONNE AMOUR,BON-AMOUR)

BONAMOUR, Antoine (Antoine & Zelida SANDROS) m. 6 Jan. 1898 Leonide BOURGEOIS (Lockport Ch.: v.2, p.178)
BONAMOUR, Antoine Jr. (Antoine & Zelida ANDRA) m. 6 Jan. 1898 Leonide BOURGEOIS (Thib. Ct. Hse.: Mar. v.37, #268)
BONCHE, R. d. 9 Jan. 1897 at age 19 yrs. (Houma Ch.: v.3, p.10)
BOND, Francis J. m. 30 Nov. 1896 Mabel E. TUCKER (Houma Ct. Hse.: Mar. v.29 & 30, #196)
BOND, Francis J. (Welman N. & Helina ROUSSEAU) m. 8 Dec. 1896 Mabel E. TUCKER (Houma Ch.: v.6-a, p.186)
BOND, Howard Tucker (Francis J. & Mable TUCKER) b. 14 Sept. 1897; m. Frances Agnes ABADIE on 28 Feb. 1923. (Houma Ch.: Bapt. Bk., v.5, p.187)
BOND, Louisa W. d. 7 Sept. 1897 (Houma Ch.: Epis. Ch.: v.1, p.386)
BONFIGLIA, Maria (Francesco & Salvalice GENTUSSA) m. 12 Jan. 1899 Antonio GIMARVO (Thib. Ch.: v.14, p.236)

BONFIGLIO, Maria (Francesco & Salvatia GENTUSSA) m. 12 Jan. 1898 Antonino GIMARVO (Thib. Ct. Hse.: Mar. v.28, #316)
BONN, Armantine Elisabeth (Martin & Cazilda BOUDREAU) b. 4 Dec. 1898 (Larose Ch.: v.3, p.42)
BONNECARRERE, Gaston Ulysse (Baptiste & Victorine SCHANOFF) b. 27 June 1899 (Thib. Ch.: v.7, p.610)

BONNER (Sometimes: BONER)
BONNER, Virginia m. 19 Feb. 1896 Henry HARTMAN (Houma Ct. Hse.: Mar. v.28, #463)

BONVILLAIN (Sometimes: BONVILAIN, BOVILLON)
BONVILLAIN, Alphonse Mrs. d. 28 Jan. 1896 at age 54 yrs. (Houma Ch.: v.3, p.6)
BONVILLAIN, Camilia Cecilia (Eugene & Evela BONVILLAIN) b. 26 June 1897 (Houma Ch.: v.5, p.188)
BONVILLAIN, Doling Agnes (Madeo & Augustine TRAHAN) b. 9 March 1897 (Houma Ch.: v.5, p.204)
BONVILLAIN, Edna M. m. 12 June 1896 Paul D. DUPONT (Houma Ct. Hse.: Mar. v.29 & 30, #87)
BONVILLAIN, Edna M. (Arthur & Dorciana BODIN) m. 16 June 1896 Paul J. DUPONT (Houma Ch.: v.6-a, p.176)
BONVILLAIN, Jacques Joseph (Wash. & Emma BABIN) m. 14 Dec. 1898 Octavie BABIN (Houma Ct. Hse.: Mar. v.30 & 31, #146)
BONVILLAIN, James Laurence (Adam & Emelie GLAND) b. 31 Jan. 1896 (Houma Ch.: v.5, p.145)
BONVILLAIN, Joseph Buddy (George & Edda CROCHET) b. 22 March 1899; m. Mary Mabel BERGERON on 21 Nov. 1923. (Houma Ch.: Bapt. Bk., v.5, p.242)
BONVILLAIN, Josephine d. 21 May 1897 at age 47 yrs. (Houma Ch.: v.3, p.13)
BONVILLAIN, Laura (Mazuro & Zulema BABIN) m. 29 Dec. 1899 Frank SMITH (Houma Ct. Hse.: Mar. v.31 & 32, #213)
BONVILLAIN, Lea (Lovenski & Lavinia BONVILLAIN) m. 8 Sept. 1899 Lodi BOUDREAUX (Houma Ct. Hse.: Mar. v.31 & 32, #120-A)
BONVILLAIN, Lovinsky d. 1890; m. Luvinia BERGERON Children listed: Marcellin; Leo; Gustave; Joseph; Julia. Petition for administration: 24 Nov. 1896. (Houma Ct. Hse.: Succ. #879)
BONVILLAIN, Marie Fanny (Alcide & Marie BURGUIERES) b. 16 June 1899 (Houma Ch.: v.5, p.249)
BONVILLAIN, Mary d. 1 Oct. 1896 at age 5 days (Houma Ch.: v.3, p.9)
BONVILLAIN, Mary (Albert & Antonia BEAUDET) b. 17 July 1896 (Houma Ch.: v.5, p.183)
BONVILLAIN, Mary Virginia (Arthur & Dorsina BODAIN) b. 31 May 1899 (Houma Ch.: v.5, p.246)
BONVILLAIN, Minilla Clara (Adam & Emelie GLYNN) b. 2 June 1898 (Houma Ch.: v.5, p.212)

BONVILLAIN, Octavie d. 7 Aug. 1884 m. G. Shyler PORCHE Children listed: Henry Franklin; James Schyler; Edward Irving; George Evariste; Mary Rosa; John Arthur; William Mitchel, aged 20; Emma Magdaline, aged 18; Guy, aged 16. Petition for inventory: 25 Aug. 1898. (Houma Ct. Hse.: Succ. #907)
BONVILLAIN, Sophie m. 11 Feb. 1899 Joseph W. WATKINS (Houma Ct. Hse.: Mar. v.31 & 32, #333)
BONVILLAIN, Sophie (Clay & Emma HAMI) m.11 Feb. 1899 Joseph W. WATKIN (Houma Ch.: v.6-a, p.278)
BONVILLAIN, Terzile m. 20 Aug. 1898 Amedee LEONARD (Houma Ct. Hse.: Mar. v.30 & 31, #84)
BONVILLAIN, Terzile (Ozemee & Pilomene TRAHAN) m. 5 Sept. 1898 Amede LEONARD (Houma Ch.: v.6-a, p.252)
BONVILLAIN, Virginia d. 7 April 1899 at age 78 yrs. (Houma Ch.: v.3, p.22)
BONVILLAIN, Washington d. 23 Oct. 1898 at age 57 yrs. (Houma Ch.: v.3, p.19)
BONVILLAIN, William m. 6 Feb. 1899 Susie NIXON (Houma Ct. Hse.: Mar. v.31 & 32, #319)
BONVILLAIN, William Henry d. 11 Oct. 1898 at age 3 mths. & 10 days (Houma Ch.: v.3, p.18)
BONVILLAIN, William Henry (Alcide J. & Marie A. BURGUIERES) b. 29 June 1898 (Houma Ch.: v.5, p.215)
BONVILLAIN, William Lee (Clay & Frances ANTYLL) b. 6 Feb. 1898; m. Madge HEBERT on 3 March 1924. (Houma Ch.: Bapt. Bk., v.5, p.199)
BOOKER, John N. m. 8 Jan. 1898 Josephine EDWARDS (Thib. Ct. Hse.: Mar. v.37, #11)

BOQUET (See: BUQUET)
BOQUET, Albert Paul (Adam & Alfrida HEBERT) b. 7 April 1899 (Montegut Ch.: v.6, p.88)
BOQUET, Josephine Lorine (Adam & Alfrida HEBERT) b. 22 July 1897 (Montegut Ch.: v.6, p.60)
BOQUET, Jules (Joseph & Josephine PHILIPPE) m. 30 Dec. 1897 Antiliope BLANCHARD (Houma Ct. Hse.: Mar. v.30 & 31, #168)
BOQUET, Jules (Joseph & Josephine PHILIPPE) m. 18 Jan. 1898 Antiliope BLANCHARD (Montegut Ch.: v.4, p.229)
BOQUET, Marguerite Louise (Jules & Antilia BLANCHARD) b. 2 Feb. 1899 (Montegut Ch.: v.6, p.85)
BOQUET, Marie Nora (Joseph & Marie BLANCHARD) b. 31 Jan. 1896 (Montegut Ch.: v.6, p.33)
BORNE, Charles Leonce (Gratien & Leontine TRAIGLE) b. 4 Feb. 1898 (Chackbay Ch.: v.1, p.103)
BORNE, Eliza Eugenie (Leonidas & Marie TRAIGLE) b. 13 July 1898 (Thib. Ch.: v.7, p.506)
BORNE, Elvee Azoline Marie (Jean & Anna TREGLE) b. 11 July 1896 (Thib. Ch.: v.7, p.408)
BORNE, Flore Elisabeth (Anatole & Noemie NAQUIN) b. 19 Nov. 1898 (Thib. Ch.: v.7, p.578)

BORNE, Florence (Jean & Louise PELLETIER) m. 15 Sept. 1898 Cyprien CLEMENT (Chackbay Ch.: v.1, p.65)
BORNE, Florence (Jean & Louise PELLETIER) m. 15 Sept. 1898 Cyprien CLEMENT (Thib. Ct. Hse.: Mar. v.38, #275)
BORNE, Florence Valerie (Joseph & Josephine BENOIT) b. 18 Feb. 1896 (Thib. Ch.: v.7, p.393)
BORNE, Jean (Jean & Louise PELLETIER) b. 16 March 1897 (Chackbay Ch.: v.1, p.87)
BORNE, Jean Felicien (Anatole & Noemie NAQUIN) b. 19 July 1897 (Thib. Ch.: v.7, p.458)
BORNE, Joseph (Joseph & Josephine BENOIT) b. 1 Aug. 1898 (Thib. Ch.: v.7, p.508)
BORNE, Joseph (Louis & Philomene RODRIGUE) b. 5 May 1897 (Chackbay Ch.: v.1, p.89)
BORNE, Joseph Elphege (Henry & Virginie USE) b. 27 June 1899 (Chackbay Ch.: v.1, p.135)
BORNE, Joseph Richard (Leo & Helene FORD) b. 28 Nov. 1897 (Thib. Ch.: v.7, p.473)
BORNE, Josephine m. Benjamin THABOR d. 10 April 1896 at age 65 yrs. (Thib. Ch.: v.3, p.181)
BORNE, Jules G. (Joseph & Louisa LANDRY) m. 2 Dec. 1899 Mary TAUZIN (Thib. Ct. Hse.: Mar. v.39, #274)
BORNE, Jules G. (Joseph & Louisa LANDRY) m. 14 Dec. 1899 Marie TAUZIN (Thib. Ch.: v.14, p.309)
BORNE, Justine d. 24 July 1899 at age 74 yrs. (Thib. Ch.: v.3, p.238)
BORNE, Marie Helene (Leo & Marie Helene FORDE) b. 19 April 1899 (Thib. Ch.: v.7, p.600)
BORNE, Maurice (Gratien & Leontine TREIGLE) bt. 28 Jan. 1896 (Chackbay Ch.: v.1, p.59)
BORNE, Octavie m. 19 April 1896 Joseph MARTINEZ (Chackbay Ch.: v.1, p.27)
BORNE, Olympe (Ulger & Mathilde LEBLANC) m. 25 Oct. 1899 Philippe POCHE (Thib. Ct. Hse.: Mar. v.39, #252)
BORNE, Olympe (Ulger & Nathilde LEBLANC) m. 25 Oct. 1899 Philippe POCHE (Thib. Ch.: v.14, p.304)
BORNE, Philodia (Clayborne & Felicia BENOIT) m. 18 Jan. 1897 Laurent CHIASSON (Chackbay Ch.: v.1, p.34)
BORNE, Philodia (Clayborne & Felicie BENOIT) m. 18 Jan. 1896 Laurent CHIASSON (Thib. Ct. Hse.: Mar. v.36, #171)
BORNE, Philomene (Adelar & Elisa BOUDREAUX) m. 17 Jan. 1898 Joseph Enet BREAUX (Thib. Ch.: v.14, p.169)
BORNE, Philomene (Adelar & Elisa BOUDREAUX) m. 17 Jan. 1898 Joseph Enet BREAUX (Thib. Ct. Hse.: Mar. v.37, #34)
BORNE, Ursina Argence (Jean & Louise PELLETIER) b. 7 June 1899 (Chackbay Ch.: v.1, p.136)
BORNE, Volzi (Jos. & Louisa LANDRY) m. 23 Jan. 1899 Laura GROS (Thib. Ct. Hse.: Mar. v.38, #1)
BORNE, Volzi (Joseph & Louise LANDRY) m. 23 Jan. 1899 Laura GROS (Chackbay Ch.: v.1, p.67)

BOSEMAN, Emily m. 16 July 1896 Reuben HOWARD (Houma Ct. Hse.: Mar. v.29 & 30, #114)
BOSMAN, Henry m. 24 Dec. 1896 Mandy PIERRE (Thib. Ct. Hse.: Mar. v.36, #169)
BOSSUET, Aime m. 15 June 1897 Alcide MATHERNE (Thib. Ct. Hse.: Mar. v.36, #173)
BOTAGLIO, Salvatore (Joachim & Nimpha LIVERITA) b. 3 July 1898 (Raceland Ch.: v.5, p.89)

BOUDELOCHE (Sometimes: BOUDLOCHE)
BOUDELOCHE, ----- Mrs. d. 8 Jan. 1899 at age 64 yrs. (Houma Ch.: v.3, p.20)
BOUDELOCHE, Adam d. 12 Feb. 1896 at age 39 yrs. (Houma Ch.: v.3, p.6)
BOUDELOCHE, Adele m. Lucien LAJAUNIE d. 7 April 1896 at age around 53 yrs. (Chacahoula Ch.: v.2, p.23)
BOUDELOCHE, Alina Josephine (Adolphe & Euselia BABIN) b. 23 Jan. 1896 (Houma Ch.: v.5, p.172)
BOUDELOCHE, Camilla m. 12 Jan. 1898 Charles BERGERON (Houma Ct. Hse.: Mar. v.30 & 31, #194)
BOUDELOCHE, Camilla (Ozemee & Autema BONVILLAIN) m. 20 Jan. 1898 Charles BERGERON (Houma Ch.: v.6-a, p.224)
BOUDELOCHE, Clovis Jean (Adolphe & Us. BABIN) b. 9 Feb. 1899 (Houma Ch.: v.5, p.236)
BOUDELOCHE, Marcel m. 9 Jan. 1899 Josephine MATHERNE (Houma Ct. Hse.: Mar. v.30 & 31, #200)
BOUDELOCHE, Marcel (Ursin & Sylvanise MARCEL) m. 19 Jan. 1899 Josephine MATHERNE (Houma Ch.: v.6-a, p.266)
BOUDELOCHE, Marie (Odile) m. 29 Dec. 1898 Benjamin DUMESNIL (Houma Ch.: v.6-a, p.261)
BOUDELOCHE, Marie (Ozemee & Ultima BONVILLAIN) m. 24 Jan. 1896 Arthur HEBERT (Houma Ct. Hse.: Mar. v.28, #409)
BOUDELOCHE, Marie Alice (Oseme & Julienne ROSS) b. 29 May 1898 (Houma Ch.: v.5, p.215)
BOUDELOCHE, Marie Zoe d. 11 Feb. 1897 at age 9 mths. (Houma Ch.: v.3, p.11)
BOUDELOCHE, Marie Zoe (Uselien & Urselia BABIN) b. 21 April 1896 (Houma Ch.: v.5, p.152)
BOUDELOCHE, Mary m. 22 Dec. 1898 Benjamin DUMESNIL (Houma Ct. Hse.: Mar. v.30 & 31, #158)
BOUDELOCHE, Mary Fanny (Uselien & Ursule BABIN) b. 29 Oct. 1898 (Houma Ch.: v.5, p.226)

BOUDREAUX (Sometimes: BOUDRAU, BOUDRAUX, BOUDREAU)
BOUDREAUX, ----- child (Mrs. Elie) d. 19 Oct. 1899 (Houma Ch.: v.3, p.25)
BOUDREAUX, Abdon Bayhie (Numa & Anastasie MIRE) b. 10 Feb. 1899 (Thib. Ch.: v.7, p.540)
BOUDREAUX, Achline Cesar (Anatole & Marie MALBROUGH) b. 8 Feb. 1898 (Thib. Ch.: v.7, p.486)

BOUDREAUX, Adeline m. Joseph DESROCHES d. 15 Nov. 1898 at age 65 yrs. (Montegut Ch.: v.2, p.22)

BOUDREAUX, Adolphe (Adolphe & Melite PREJEAN) m. 6 June 1898 Telcide NAQUIN (Thib. Ct. Hse.: Mar. v.38, #184)

BOUDREAUX, Adolphe (Adolphe & Melite PREJEAN) m. 10 June 1898 Talcide NAQUIN (Thib. Ch.: v.14, p.205)

BOUDREAUX, Agathe (Arthur & Clotilde HEBERT) m. 25 Oct. 1899 Ernest BOURGEOIS (Thib. Ct. Hse.: Mar. v.39, #248)

BOUDREAUX, Agathe (Arthur & Clotilde HEBERT) m. 25 Oct. 1899 Ernest BOURGEOIS (Thib. Ch.: v.14, p.305)

BOUDREAUX, Aglae (Luke & Victoria FOREST) m. 6 Feb. 1899 Jean Marie LEBLANC (Houma Ch.: v.6-a, p.276)

BOUDREAUX, Agnes Nobby (Fernest & Lydie BERGERON) b. 23 Oct. 1898 (Thib. Ch.: v.7, p.519)

BOUDREAUX, Aimee (Augustin & d.Heloise WALKER) d. 31 Oct. 1899 at age 9 yrs. & 10 mths. in a shooting accident. (Chacahoula Ch.: v.2, p.29)

BOUDREAUX, Alexandre Anidas (Alphonse & Arseline HEBERT) b. 29 June 1898 (Thib. Ch.: v.7, p.513)

BOUDREAUX, Alexina d. 23 Aug. 1899 at age 8 yrs. (Thib. Ch.: v.3, p.239)

BOUDREAUX, Alfred d. 12 April 1896 at age 17 mths. (Thib. Ch.: v.3, p.182)

BOUDREAUX, Alfred d. 28 July 1898 at age 56 yrs. (Montegut Ch.: v.2, p.19)

BOUDREAUX, Alfred d. 28 July 1898; m. Louisiana FIELDS Children listed: Myrtile aged 25, m. Alphonse J. DUGAS; Angelle, aged 18; Albert, aged 23; Denis, aged 16; Annette, 14; Davis, 11; Laura, 9;, Annita, 7; Florence, 5; Lucille, 3. Tutorship: 6 Aug. 1898. (Houma Ct. Hse.: Succ. #904)

BOUDREAUX, Alfred (Victor & Ophelia RIGAULT) b. 6 Oct. 1898 (Larose Ch.: v.3, p.43)

BOUDREAUX, Alice m. Lovincy ESTIVEN d. 12 Oct. 1899 at age 25 yrs. & 6 mths., 3 days (Thib. Ch.: v.3, p.241)

BOUDREAUX, Alice m. 10 Feb. 1899 Lovincy ESTIVENS (Thib. Ct. Hse.: Mar. v.39, #103)

BOUDREAUX, Alice (Francois & Alfrida BOUDREAUX) m. 13 Feb. 1899 Lovincy ESTIVEN (Thib. Ch: v.14, p.265)

BOUDREAUX, Alice (Joseph & Elda GUILLOT) m. 5 April 1899 Eugene LEGENDRE (Thib. Ch.: v.14, p.269)

BOUDREAUX, Alice (Joseph & Elda GUILLOTE) m. 5 April 1899 Eugene LEGENDRE (Thib. Ct. Hse.: Mar. v.39, #123)

BOUDREAUX, Alice (Treville & Victoria ROGER) m. 13 May 1897 Edgard BERGERON (Thib. Ch.: v.14, p.145)

BOUDREAUX, Alice (Treville & Victoria ROGER) m. 13 May 1897 Edgard BERGERON (Thib. Ct. Hse.: Mar. v.36, #121)

BOUDREAUX, Alice Josephine (Alphonse & Marceline HEBERT) b. 31 Aug. 1899 (Thib. Ch.: v.8, p.17)

BOUDREAUX, Allain Patrick (Luc & Marie Anastasie TOUPS) b. 17 March 1899 (Thib. Ch.: v.7, p.543)

BOUDREAUX, Anastasia Liby (Edescar & Malvina WALKINS) b. 21 Feb. 1897 (Theriot Ch.: v.1-B, p.106)
BOUDREAUX, Anne Josephine (Felix & Theresa ALLEMAND) b. 5 Oct. 1896 (Lockport Ch.: v.3, #4)
BOUDREAUX, Anne Josephine (Felix & Theresa ALLEMAND) b. 5 Oct. 1896 (Lockport Ch.: v.3-A, #4)
BOUDREAUX, Anne Laure (Thomas & Seraphine GRAVOIS) b. 27 Aug. 1898 (Thib. Ch.: v.7, p.564)
BOUDREAUX, Antoine Jessey (---- & Mendey SMALL) b. 7 July 1898 (Theriot Ch.: v.2, p.26)
BOUDREAUX, Antoine Jessy d. 2 Aug. 1898 at age 1 mth. (Theriot Ch.: v.1, p.1)
BOUDREAUX, Antoine Raoul (Ernest & Elmire GAUTREAUX) b. 11 Aug. 1897 (Larose Ch.: v.3, p.4)
BOUDREAUX, Antony Byron (Oscar & Josephine WATKINS) b. 12 April 1899 (Houma Ch.: v.5, p.244)
BOUDREAUX, Arthur (Auguste & Marie HEBERT) m. 16 Dec. 1899 Lelia ADAM (Houma Ct. Hse.: Mar. v.31 & 32, #188)
BOUDREAUX, Arthur Joseph (Mathias & Josephine DUTU) b. 14 July 1897 (Houma Ch.: v.5, p.214)
BOUDREAUX, Ashly Adam (Alphonse Z. & Alzina TROSCLAIR) b. 26 Feb. 1896 (Houma Ch.: v.5, p.148)
BOUDREAUX, Azema Anastasie (Marcilien & Marie ROGER) b. 22 Nov. 1899 (Thib. Ch.: v.7, p.576)
BOUDREAUX, Berthe m. 2 Sept. 1899 Anidas GUILLOT (Thib. Ct. Hse.: Mar. v.39, #240)
BOUDREAUX, Bessie Josephine (Joseph Beauregard & Mary SINGLETON) b. 29 March 1899 (Chacahoula Ch.: v.4, p.29)
BOUDREAUX, Brigitte Alcida (Octave & Victoria ROGER) b. 8 Aug. 1896 (Thib. Ch.: v.7, p.418)
BOUDREAUX, Cecile Nella (Joseph & Viola HIDALGO) b. 15 Oct. 1897 (Thib. Ch.: v.7, p.470)
BOUDREAUX, Cecilia Adela (Charles & Georgina GAUBERT) b. 6 Oct. 1897 (Thib. Ch.: v.7, p.469)
BOUDREAUX, Celeste deceased (Joseph) m. Felix THIBODAUX (Orville) Children listed: Eddy, 16; Vienna, 14; Ezema, 12. Petition for Inventory: 27 Jan. 1899. (Houma Ct. Hse.: Succ. #914)
BOUDREAUX, Celeste (Desire & Luvina HEBERT) m. 3 Feb. 1896 Joseph MOLAISON (Chacahoula Ch.: v.1, p.56)
BOUDREAUX, Celeste (Desire & Survina HEBERT) m. 3 Feb. 1896 Joseph MOLAISON (Houma Ct. Hse.: Mar. v.28, #431)
BOUDREAUX, Charles Anatole (Anatole & Emelie DAIGLE) b. 2 May 1896 (Theriot Ch.: v.1-B, p.90)
BOUDREAUX, Charles Mirtil (Louis & Marie PARR) b. 11 Oct. 1897 (Houma Ch.: v.5, p.189)
BOUDREAUX, Charles Wilfred (Eugene & Emilienne HEBERT) b. 14 Dec. 1898 (Chacahoula Ch.: v.4, p.15)
BOUDREAUX, Clairtus d. 27 Dec. 1898 at age 46 yrs. (Houma Ch.: v.3, p.20)

BOUDREAUX, Clara m. 3 Feb. 1899 Felix BOURG (Thib. Ct. Hse.: Mar. v.38, #87)
BOUDREAUX, Clarence Elmer (Bourgard & Mary Isabel SINGLETON) b. 27 May 1897 (Houma Ch.: Epis. Ch.: v.1, p.114)
BOUDREAUX, Clay (Emile & Natalie RICHARD) m. 12 Jan. 1898 Bernadette MOLAIRE (Houma Ct. Hse.: Mar. v.29 & 30, #148)
BOUDREAUX, Clay (Emile & Natalie RICHARD) m. 12 Jan. 1898 Bernadette MOLAIRE (Chacahoula Ch.: v.1, p.64[84])
BOUDREAUX, Clet Charles (Prosperi & Leontine TOUPS) b. 12 March 1899 (Chackbay Ch.: v.1, p.134)
BOUDREAUX, Clotilde Ida (Theodule & Louise NAVARE) b. 19 Jan. 1898 (Chackbay Ch.: v.1, p.104)
BOUDREAUX, Corinne m. Whitney WEBRE d. 6 May 1897 at age 27 yrs. & 7 mths. (Thib. Ch.: v.3, p.199)
BOUDREAUX, Davis (Melize & Angele BARRIOS) bt. 2 Nov. 1896 (Lockport Ch.: v.3, #12)
BOUDREAUX, Davis Joseph (Melize & Angele BARRIOS) b. 1 Nov. 1896 (Lockport Ch.: v.3-A, #12)
BOUDREAUX, Delphine (Joseph & Elisa ANDRA) m. 9 Feb. 1899 Olivain ORDOGNE (Thib. Ct. Hse.: Mar. v.38, #74)
BOUDREAUX, Delphine (Joseph & Elisa ANDRA) m. 9 Feb. 1899 Olivain ORDOGNE (Thib. Ch.: v.14, p.262-a)
BOUDREAUX, Duncan m. 26 June 1896 Ophelia MICHEL (Houma Ct. Hse.: Mar. v.29 & 30, #99)
BOUDREAUX, Eddy Joseph (Anatole & Julia RICHARD) b. 6 March 1898 (Chacahoula Ch.: Gibson Records: Mar. Bk., v.1, #41)
BOUDREAUX, Eddy Joseph (Anatole & Julia RICHARD) b. 6 March 1898 (Chacahoula Ch.: Gibson Ch.: v.2, p.127)
BOUDREAUX, Elda (Clovis & Victoria TROSCLAIR) m. 12 Sept. 1898 Neuville AYO (Thib. Ct. Hse.: Mar. v.38, #261)
BOUDREAUX, Elie V. (Norbert & Azelina LIRETTE) m. 17 Feb. 1898 Josephine BERGERON (Houma Ch.: v.6-a, p.233)
BOUDREAUX, Elisabeth (Henry & Eva WITNEY) b. 28 April 1898 (Houma Ch.: v.5, p.209)
BOUDREAUX, Eliska m. 26 Dec. 1899 Nicholas HIMEL (Houma Ct. Hse.: Mar. v.31 & 32, #197)
BOUDREAUX, Elma Ida (Aurelien & Henriette MAYER) b. 22 Oct. 1896 (Thib. Ch.: v.7, p.477)
BOUDREAUX, Elve m. 16 April 1897 Edgar PORTIER (Thib. Ct. Hse.: Mar. v.36, #117)
BOUDREAUX, Emile d. 1898 at age 55 yrs. (Chacahoula Ch.: v.2, p.25)
BOUDREAUX, Emile Frozin (Fabien & Felicia ORDOGNE) b. 25 Feb. 1898 (Thib. Ch.: v.7, p.496)
BOUDREAUX, Emilien (Orestile & Mary GROSS) m. 21 Feb. 1898 Camilia LAGRANGE (Houma Ct. Hse.: Mar. v.30 & 31, #305)
BOUDREAUX, Emma (Treville & Marianne BOUDREAUX) m. 17 Feb. 1898 Edmond AYO (Thib. Ct. Hse.: Mar. v.37, #65)

BOUDREAUX, Emma (Treville & Marianne) m. 17 Feb. 1898 Edmond AYO (Thib. Ch.: v.14, p.192)
BOUDREAUX, Etienne d. 18 Dec. 1899 at age 67 yrs. (Thib. Ch.: v.3, p.246)
BOUDREAUX, Eugene Onesiphore (Henry & Marie MORVANT) b. 15 June 1899 (Chackbay Ch.: v.1, p.137)
BOUDREAUX, Eve Agnes (Ernest & Anne FORD) b. 23 Aug. 1899 (Thib. Ch.: v.7, p.565)
BOUDREAUX, Eveline m. 29 Jan. 1898 Alec CHATTAGNIER (Houma Ct. Hse.: Mar. v.30 & 31, #261)
BOUDREAUX, Eveline (Norbert & Evelina LIRETTE) m. 31 Jan. 1898 Abe CHATAIGNIER (Houma Ch.: v.6-a, p.227)
BOUDREAUX, Exelina Marie (Teler & Alice MARCEL) b. 19 June 1899 (Houma Ch.: v.5, p.247)
BOUDREAUX, Faustine m. 10 June 1899 Ellis MIRE (Thib. Ct. Hse.: Mar. v.39, #178)
BOUDREAUX, Felicie Helene (Felicien & Odilia AYCOCK) b. 16 Oct. 1896 (Chacahoula Ch.: v.4, p.7)
BOUDREAUX, Felicien E. (Eugene C. & Josephine MOLAISON) m. 7 July 1896 Odilia AYCOCK (Houma Ct. Hse.: Mar. v.29 & 30, #107)
BOUDREAUX, Felicien Eugene (Eugene C. & Josephine MOLAISON) m. 7 July 1896 Odelia AYCOCK (Montegut Ch.: v.4, p.212)
BOUDREAUX, Felix (Luc & Louise HENRI) d. 22 April 1898 at age 18 yrs. (Montegut Ch.: v.2, p.16)
BOUDREAUX, Felix Deweye (Alphonse & Alzina TROSCLAIR) b. 15 July 1898; m. Gracie BERGER on 8 Nov. 1922. (Houma Ch.: Bapt. Bk., v.5, p.216)
BOUDREAUX, Felix Joseph d. 22 April 1898 at age 17 yrs. (Theriot Ch.: v.1, p.1)
BOUDREAUX, Florentin Antoine (Thelar & Alice MARCEL) b. 14 Aug. 1896; m. Anita BOUDREAUX on 19 March 1920. (Houma Ch.: Bapt. Bk., v.5, p.157)
BOUDREAUX, Gaston (Gerasime & Marcelite BORNE) m. 1 March 1899 Lula Josephine HOCK (Thib. Ct. Hse.: Mar. v.39, #114)
BOUDREAUX, Gaston (Gerasime & Marcelite BORNE) m. 1 March 1899 Lula Josephine HOCK (Thib. Ch.: v.14, p.267)
BOUDREAUX, George Alexandre (Charles & Georgina GAUBERT) b. 24 July 1899 (Thib. Ch.: v.7, p.556)
BOUDREAUX, Gilbert A. (Alphonze Z. & Cynthia GUIDRY) m. 12 Jan. 1899 Louise Marguerite AYCOCK (Houma Ct. Hse.: Mar. v.30 & 31, #225)
BOUDREAUX, Guilbert A. (Alphonse Zacharie & Cynthia GUIDRY) m. 8 Feb. 1899 Louise Marguerite AYCOCK (Montegut Ch.: v.4, p.257)
BOUDREAUX, Henri (d.Onesiphore & Elia ONCALE) m. 24 Jan. 1898 Marie MORVANT (Chackbay Ch.: v.1, p.52)
BOUDREAUX, Henri (Onisephore & Elia ONCALE) m. 24 Jan. 1898 Mary MORVAN (Thib. Ct. Hse.: Mar. v.37, #22)

BOUDREAUX, Henry Clay (Joanis & Elisa BOUDREAU) m. 5 Sept. 1898 Annie Virginie QUICK (Theriot Ch.: v.1-B, p.5)
BOUDREAUX, Henry Clay (John P. & Elise BOUDREAUX) m. 17 Aug. 1898 Annie Elizabeth QUICK (Houma Ct. Hse.: Mar. v.30 & 31, #80)
BOUDREAUX, Ida (Clay & Josephine COMEAUX) m. 25 Oct. 1897 James A. FOLKES (Houma Ct. Hse.: Mar. v.29 & 30, #128)
BOUDREAUX, Jacques Denis d. 27 June 1896 at age 14 mths. (Thib. Ch.: v.3, p.184)
BOUDREAUX, Jean m. 15 Sept. 1896 Aurelia GUILLOT (Thib. Ct. Hse.: Mar. v.36, #143)
BOUDREAUX, Jean m. 6 Feb. 1897 Ezelia CHERAMI (Larose Ch.: v.4, p.117)
BOUDREAUX, Jean m. 6 Feb. 1897 Ezelia CHERAMI (Larose Ch.: v.4, p.5)
BOUDREAUX, Jean Baptiste (Taylor & Alice MARCEL) b. 25 Nov. 1897; m. Mary LOUVIERE on 16 April 1920. (Houma Ch.: Bapt. Bk., v.5, p.193)
BOUDREAUX, Jean Ives (Merthilde & Milisere DOMINGUE) b. 26 Dec. 1896 (Montegut Ch.: v.6, p.50)
BOUDREAUX, Jean Louis (Valerie & Julie THERIOT) b. 24 June 1897 (Theriot Ch.: v.2, p.8)
BOUDREAUX, Jeanne Catharina (Telero & Alice MARCEL) b. 19 June 1899 (Houma Ch.: v.5, p.246)
BOUDREAUX, Joeph Alfred Allan (Alfred & Louisianne FIELDS) b. 28 Jan. 1896 (Montegut Ch.: v.6, p.32)
BOUDREAUX, Johanne Catharina d. 25 Sept. 1899 at age 3 mths. (Houma Ch.: v.3, p.25)
BOUDREAUX, John m. 25 Jan. 1897 Ezelia CHERAMI (Thib. Ct. Hse.: Mar. v.36, #56)
BOUDREAUX, John Colbert (John A. & Camillia LAGRANGE) b. 11 March 1896 (Houma Ch.: v.5, p.153)
BOUDREAUX, John Henry (Henry Jean Baptiste & Eva WHITNY) b. 5 May 1896; m. Nita MUNSON on 7 April 1925. (Houma Ch.: Bapt. Bk., v.5, p.153)
BOUDREAUX, Joseph (Emile & Elizabeth DARCE) m. 9 Aug. 1899 Lodo HENRI (Chacahoula Ch.: v.1, p.72 [92])
BOUDREAUX, Joseph (Willy & Emma CHAMPAGNE) b. 7 Dec. 1897 (Houma Ch.: v.5, p.194)
BOUDREAUX, Joseph A. m. 1 Feb. 1899 Henriette FALGOUT (Thib. Ct. Hse.: Mar. v.38, #82)
BOUDREAUX, Joseph A. m. 13 Feb. 1899 Henriette FALGOUT (Larose Ch.: v.4, p.37)
BOUDREAUX, Joseph A. m. 13 Feb. 1899 Henriette FALGOUT (Larose Ch.: v.3, p.11)
BOUDREAUX, Joseph A. m. 29 July 1899 Loda HENRI (Houma Ct. Hse.: Mar. v.31 & 32, #87)
BOUDREAUX, Joseph Albert (Alfred & Louisiane FIELDS) m. 28 Dec. 1899 Brigitte ROGER (Houma Ct. Hse.: Mar. v.31 & 32, #211)

BOUDREAUX, Joseph Allen d. 29 Sept. 1896 at age 8 mths. (Montegut Ch.: v.2, p.7)
BOUDREAUX, Joseph Beauregard (Fabien & Felicia ORDOGNE) b. 8 June 1896 (Chackbay Ch.: v.1, p.72)
BOUDREAUX, Joseph Charles (Charles & Azalie DARDEN) bt. 21 May 1896 (Chackbay Ch.: v.1, p.66)
BOUDREAUX, Joseph Clarence (Augustin & Heloise WALKER) b. 3 April 1899 (Chacahoula Ch.: v.4, p.20)
BOUDREAUX, Joseph Claud (Duncan & Ophelia MICHEL) b. 6 Dec. 1898 (Houma Ch.: v.5, p.230)
BOUDREAUX, Joseph Claude (Leo Joseph & Victorine DAUNIS) b. 23 April 1898 (Thib. Ch.: v.7, p.495)
BOUDREAUX, Joseph Colden (Valerie & Helena THIBODAUX) b. 21 July 1898 (Thib. Ch.: v.7, p.508)
BOUDREAUX, Joseph Curby (Felicien & Marie LEJEUNE) b. 17 Sept. 1896 (Thib. Ch.: v.7, p.428)
BOUDREAUX, Joseph Denesse (Charles & Julie HEBERT) b. 7 June 1897 (Chackbay Ch.: v.1, p.89)
BOUDREAUX, Joseph Denis (Philocles & Emma BOURGEOIS) b. 29 March 1897 (Thib. Ch.: v.7, p.495)
BOUDREAUX, Joseph Earl (Felicien & Odilia AYCOCK) b. 16 July 1898 (Chacahoula Ch.: v.4, p.10)
BOUDREAUX, Joseph Emile (Nicholas & Josephine RICHARD) b. 6 Oct. 1898 (Thib. Ch.: v.7, p.516)
BOUDREAUX, Joseph Laurent (Joseph & Marie DUBOIS) b. 9 Aug. 1899 (Montegut Ch.: v.6, p.92)
BOUDREAUX, Joseph Nolan (Adam & Marie DELORETTE) b. 30 March 1896 (Thib. Ch.: v.7, p.399)
BOUDREAUX, Joseph Oscar (Theodule & Aglae GUIDRY) m. 11 March 1897 Josephine WATKINS (Houma Ct. Hse.: Mar. v.29 & 30, #344)
BOUDREAUX, Joseph Oscar (Theodule & Aglaee GUIDRY) m. 18 March 1897 Josephine WATKINS (Montegut Ch.: v.4, p.220)
BOUDREAUX, Joseph Sydney (Leon Zephyrin & Marie Lucina HAYDEL) b. 12 June 1899 (Thib. Ch.: v.7, p.552)
BOUDREAUX, Josephine (Victor & d.Celima DANTIN) m. 1 June 1897 Etienne PERRIN (Larose Ch.: v.4, p.97)
BOUDREAUX, Josephine (Victor & Celima DANTIN) m. 1 June 1897 Etienne PERRIN (Larose Ch.: v.3, p.5)
BOUDREAUX, Jules Wilson (Ludgere & Emilienne HEBERT) b. 28 Oct. 1896 (Chacahoula Ch.: v.4, p.8)
BOUDREAUX, Julie m. Landreau ANXICIOS d. 8 July 1896 at age 48 yrs. (Theriot Ch.: Mar. Bk., v.1, #1)
BOUDREAUX, Julie m. Landreau ANXICUIS d.8 July 1896 at age 48 yrs., 5 mths. (Theriot Ch.: v.1, p.101)
BOUDREAUX, Julie m. Trasimon HENRI Children listed: Willis; Caliste; Robert; Claude; Vital. Petition for tutorship: 29 June 1899. (Houma Ct. Hse.: Succ. #921)
BOUDREAUX, Klebert (Joseph & Elisa ANDRA) m. 7 Feb. 1899 Eve FORD (Thib. Ch.: v.14, p.257)

BOUDREAUX, Klebert (Joseph & Elisa ANDRA) m. 7 Feb. 1899 Eve FORD (Thib. Ct. Hse.: Mar. v.38, #57)

BOUDREAUX, Klebert Augustin (Klebert & Louise PREJEANT) b. 28 Aug. 1898 (Thib. Ch.: v.7, p.562)

BOUDREAUX, Laura d. 15 July 1898 at age 3 yrs. (Thib. Ch.: v.3, p.217)

BOUDREAUX, Laurenza d. 23 Feb. 1897 at age 72 yrs. (Houma Ch.: v.3, p.12)

BOUDREAUX, Leon Zephyrin (Leon Zephirin & Marie Ucina HAYDEL) b. 18 Oct. 1899 (Thib. Ch.: v.8, p.19)

BOUDREAUX, Leonard (Claybert & Louise PREJEAN) b. 15 May 1897 (Chackbay Ch.: v.1, p.90)

BOUDREAUX, Leonce P. (Forestal & Artemise BOURG) m. 16 Sept. 1899 Justine Mary CHAUVIN (Houma Ct. Hse.: Mar. v.31 & 32, #136)

BOUDREAUX, Leonce P. (Forestal & Artemise BOURG) m. 28 Sept. 1899 Justine Marie CHAUVIN (Montegut Ch.: v.4, p.270)

BOUDREAUX, Lezida who married Adam LEONARD d. 24 July 1899 at age 40 yrs. (Theriot Ch.: v.1, p.2)

BOUDREAUX, Liliane Marie (Emile & Felicia TOUPS) b. 18 May 1897 (Thib. Ch.: v.7, p.500)

BOUDREAUX, Lodi (Eugene & Mary JARBEAUX) m. 8 Sept. 1899 Lea BONVILLAIN (Houma Ct. Hse.: Mar. v.31 & 32, #120-A)

BOUDREAUX, Louis d. 21 Feb. 1899 at age 60 yrs. (Thib. Ch.: v.3, p.229)

BOUDREAUX, Louis (Tucker & Lovilia THIBODEAUX) b. 30 Jan. 1896 (Houma Ch.: v.5, p.145)

BOUDREAUX, Louis Don (Louis Don) d. 21 Nov. 1899 at age 13 yrs. (Theriot Ch.: v.1, p.2)

BOUDREAUX, Louis Vincent (Joseph & Marie DUBOIS) b. 28 Feb. 1897 (Montegut Ch.: v.6, p.52)

BOUDREAUX, Louise Agate (Louis G. & Marie PARR) b. 22 Sept. 1899 (Houma Ch.: v.5, p.254)

BOUDREAUX, Louise Josephine (Joseph & Rosalie B. MALBROUGH) m. 10 June 1899 Marcellin Paul BOUDREAUX (Houma Ct. Hse.: Mar. v.31 & 32, #24)

BOUDREAUX, Louise Josephine (Joseph & Rosalie MARLBOROUGH) m. 19 June 1899 Marcellin Paul BOUDREAUX (Montegut Ch.: v.4, p.266)

BOUDREAUX, Louisiane (Henry & Aimee ANDRAS) m. 4 Aug. 1896 Albert RODRIGUE (Thib. Ct. Hse.: Mar. v.36, #125)

BOUDREAUX, Louisiane (Henry & Aimee ANDRAS) m. 4 Aug. 1896 Albert RODRIGUE (Chackbay Ch.: v.1, p.28)

BOUDREAUX, Luc Eugene (Clovis & Victoria TROXCLAIR) b. 8 Sept. 1897 (Thib. Ch.: v.7, p.466)

BOUDREAUX, Ludovic Anne (Jean & Azelie CHERAMI) b. 26 July 1898 (Larose Ch.: v.3, p.42)

BOUDREAUX, Maggie (Prospere & Marie CAILLOUET) m. 28 April 1896 Sylvestre KRAMER (Thib. Ct. Hse.: Mar. v.35, #80)

BOUDREAUX, Maggy d. 13 March 1896 at age 3 mths. (Houma Ch.: v.3, p.7)

BOUDREAUX, Mai Celima (Lazare & Alzire COULON) b. 5 Dec. 1899 (Larose Ch.: v.3, p.59)
BOUDREAUX, Marcelien (Marcelien & Anastasie KELLER) m. 16 Aug. 1898 Marie ROGER (Thib. Ch.: v.14, p.214)
BOUDREAUX, Marcellin Paul (Forestal & Arthemise BOURG) m. 10 June 1899 Louise Josephine BOUDREAUX (Houma Ct. Hse.: Mar. v.31 & 32, #24)
BOUDREAUX, Marcellin Paul (Forestal & Arthemise BOURG) m. 19 June 1899 Louise Josephine BOUDREAUX (Montegut Ch.: v.4, p.266)
BOUDREAUX, Marcilien (Marcilien & Anastasie KELLER) m. 16 Aug. 1898 Marie ROGER (Thib. Ct. Hse.: Mar. v.38, #249)
BOUDREAUX, Marguerite (Prosperi & Marie CAILLOUET) m. 28 April 1896 Sylvestre KRAMER (Chackbay Ch.: v.1, p.27)
BOUDREAUX, Marguerite May (Clay & Bernadette MOLAIRE) b. 27 Dec. 1899 (Chacahoula Ch.: v.4, p.33)
BOUDREAUX, Maria Elma (Joseph & Viola IDARGO) b. 6 April 1898 (Thib. Ch.: v.7, p.545)
BOUDREAUX, Marie d. 21 Sept. 1896 at age 39 yrs. (Thib. Ch.: v.3, p.188)
BOUDREAUX, Marie m. 6 Feb. 1897 Ozemee MARCEL (Houma Ct. Hse.: Mar. v.29 & 30, #294)
BOUDREAUX, Marie (Alcide & Octavie SAVOIE) b. 15 July 1898 (Thib. Ch.: v.7, p.558)
BOUDREAUX, Marie (Cleb & Amelia GRAUS) m. 13 Feb. 1899 Thomassi LANDRY (Thib. Ct. Hse.: Mar. v.38, #40)
BOUDREAUX, Marie (d.Clet & Aurelia GROS) m. 13 Feb. 1899 Thomas LANDRY (Chackbay Ch.: v.1, p.69)
BOUDREAUX, Marie (Norbert & Exzelina LIRETTE) m. 25 Feb. 1897 Ozemee MARCEL (Houma Ch.: v.6-a, p.193)
BOUDREAUX, Marie Adele d. 16 Feb. 1899 at age 90 yrs. (Thib. Ch.: v.3, p.228)
BOUDREAUX, Marie Adele (Paul & Santy ROGER) b. 3 April 1896 (Montegut Ch.: v.6, p.37)
BOUDREAUX, Marie Alida (Ernest & d.Elmire PELEGRIN) d. 13 Feb. 1898 at age 7 yrs. & 8 mths. (Montegut Ch.: v.2, p.15)
BOUDREAUX, Marie Blanche (Luc & Alida DAIGLE) b. 4 Oct. 1896 (Chacahoula Ch.: v.4, p.6)
BOUDREAUX, Marie Boudreau (Elfege & Estelle LASSEIGNE) b. 22 Dec. 1896 (Chackbay Ch.: v.1, p.81)
BOUDREAUX, Marie Florence (Joseph & Elda GUYOT) b. 21 Nov. 1898 (Thib. Ch.: v.7, p.523)
BOUDREAUX, Marie Flossy Alta (Edescar & Marie Malvina WATKIN) b. 5 Oct. 1898 (Theriot Ch.: v.2, p.30)
BOUDREAUX, Marie Frida (Ernest & Elmire PELEGRIN) d. 23 June 1898 at age 4 yrs. (Montegut Ch.: v.2, p.18)
BOUDREAUX, Marie Joanne (Caliste & Maria GAUTHREAUX) b. 12 Jan. 1896 (Larose Ch.: v.2, p.179)
BOUDREAUX, Marie Josephine (Justilien & Exelina FANGUY) b. 18 March 1899 (Houma Ch.: v.5, p.245)

BOUDREAUX, Marie Lucile (Emile & Felicia TOUPS) b. 14 Jan. 1896 (Thib. Ch.: v.7, p.440)
BOUDREAUX, Marie Lucille (Luc & Alida DAIGLE) b. 4 May 1898 (Chacahoula Ch.: v.4, p.10)
BOUDREAUX, Marie Medora (Valerie & Julie THERIOT) b. 22 July 1899 (Theriot Ch.: v.2, p.49)
BOUDREAUX, Marie Rose d. 29 July 1898 at age 36 yrs. (Thib. Ch.: v.3, p.218)
BOUDREAUX, Marie Stanislas Elphege & Elphege & Estelle LASSEIGNE) b. 19 Nov. 1899 (Thib. Ch.: v.7, p.575)
BOUDREAUX, Mary E. m. A. J. BESSON d. 14 May 1899 at age 27 yrs., 10 mths., 21 days (Thib. Ch.: v.3, p.234)
BOUDREAUX, Mary Madeline (Rodolphe & Camila LEDET) b. 13 July 1897 (Houma Ch.: v.5, p.185)
BOUDREAUX, Mary Manilla (Tucker & Lovillia THIBODEAU) b. 18 June 1898 (Houma Ch.: v.5, p.228)
BOUDREAUX, Mathildia m. Justilien BOURGEOIS d. 30 Dec. 1899 at age 45 yrs. (Lockport Ch.: v.1, #49)
BOUDREAUX, Mathilia Emelie (Mititle & Melissa DOMINGUE) b. 13 May 1899 (Theriot Ch.: v.2, p.42)
BOUDREAUX, Maurice (Delmas & Flowelie ROGER) b. 25 Oct. 1897 (Thib. Ch.: v.7, p.470)
BOUDREAUX, May Alice (Albert & Alice RICHE) b. 23 May 1898 (Thib. Ch.: v.7, p.507)
BOUDREAUX, Mirtille m. 24 June 1899 Melissa DOMINGUE (Theriot Ch.: v.1-B, p.10)
BOUDREAUX, Myrthile m. 26 Jan. 1899 Felton THIBODAUX (Houma Ct. Hse.: Mar. v.30 & 31, #282)
BOUDREAUX, Myrtilde (Numa & Zolide BLANCHARD) m. 6 Feb. 1899 Felton THIBODAUX (Houma Ch.: v.6-a, p.275)
BOUDREAUX, Myrtilia M. (Alfred & Louisiane FIELDS) m. 14 May 1897 Alphonse J. DUGAS (Houma Ct. Hse.: Mar. v.29 & 30, #421)
BOUDREAUX, Myrtilia M. (Alfred & Louisianne FIELDS) m. 16 June 1897 Alphonse DUGAS (Montegut Ch.: v.4, p.223)
BOUDREAUX, Nicolas (Drausin & Ordalise STEVENS) m. 22 Jan. 1896 Josephine RICHARD (Thib. Ct. Hse.: Mar. v.35, #19)
BOUDREAUX, Nicolas (Drauzin & Ordalise STEVENSON) m. 22 Jan. 1896 Josephine RICHARD (Thib. Ch.: v.14, p.67)
BOUDREAUX, Noe Benoit (Camille & Rosalia ALBARES) b. 20 April 1896 (Lockport Ch.: v.2, p.328)
BOUDREAUX, Notilia Appoline (Joseph & Leontine HYMEL) b. 18 March 1897 (Thib. Ch.: v.7, p.492)
BOUDREAUX, Oceana (Victorin & Philomene CONSTANT) m. 6 Feb. 1899 Fernand DESLATTES (Thib. Ct. Hse.: Mar. v.38, #83)
BOUDREAUX, Oceana (Victorin & Philomene CONSTANT) m. 6 Feb. 1899 Fernand DELATTES (Thib. Ch.: v.14, p.256)
BOUDREAUX, Octave Joseph (Sylvin & Lea TROSCLAIR) b. 13 Jan. 1898 (Thib. Ch.: v.7, p.485)
BOUDREAUX, Odile Madeleine (Adam & Marie DE LORETTE) b. 10 Aug. 1898 (Thib. Ch.: v.7, p.510)

BOUDREAUX, Odilia Marie m. d.Albert J. AYO. Children: Hamilton Joseph; Robert; Albert; Faustine; Marie. Family meeting: 26 Oct. 1897. (Thib. Ct. Hse.: Succ. #1523)

BOUDREAUX, Paul Melton (Paul & Santie ROGER) b. 28 Oct. 1898 (Montegut Ch.: v.6, p.78)

BOUDREAUX, Paul Sidney (Faustin & Evelia DUPRE) b. 2 Sept. 1896 (Montegut Ch.: v.6, p.45)

BOUDREAUX, Pauline (Joeph & Eveline EXNICIOUS) m. 5 Nov. 1898 Joshua EXNICIOUS (Houma Ct. Hse.: Mar. v.30 & 31, #128)

BOUDREAUX, Pauline (Joseph & Evelline EXNICIOUS) m. 17 Nov. 1898 Joshua EXNICIOUS (Theriot Ch.: v.1-B, p.5)

BOUDREAUX, Pauline Mabel (Octave & Victoria ROGER) b. 5 April 1898 (Thib. Ch.: v.7, p.497)

BOUDREAUX, Philippe Oncile (Luc & Marie TOUPS) b. 11 June 1897 (Thib. Ch.: v.7, p.452)

BOUDREAUX, Pierre Lewis (Caliste & Marie GAUTREAUX) b. 6 Aug. 1896 (Larose Ch.: v.3, p.4)

BOUDREAUX, Raoul Maurice (Thomas & Seraphine GRAVOIS) b. 30 May 1897 (Thib. Ch.: v.7, p.451)

BOUDREAUX, Robert Jean Baptiste (Emile & Evelina TOUPS) b. 13 Aug. 1897 (Thib. Ch.: v.7, p.461)

BOUDREAUX, Robert Joseph (Ernest & Aimee FORD) b. 3 Dec. 1897 (Thib. Ch.: v.7, p.480)

BOUDREAUX, Sidney Joseph (Willy & Emma CHAMPAGNE) b. 12 Jan. 1896 (Houma Ch.: v.5, p.142)

BOUDREAUX, Sydonia (d.Onesiphore & Melia ONCALE) m. 2 Feb. 1899 Zephyr ONEAL (Chackbay Ch.: v.1, p.67 & 68)

BOUDREAUX, Sydonia (Onisiphore & Melia ONCALE) m. 2 Feb. 1899 Zephire ONCALE (Thib. Ct. Hse.: Mar. v.38, #27)

BOUDREAUX, Sylvain (d.Louis & d.Sylvanie SEVAIN) m. 26 Jan. 1897 Lea TROSCLAIR (Chackbay Ch.: v.1, p.37)

BOUDREAUX, Sylvain (Louis & Sylvanie SEVIN) m. 26 Jan. 1897 Lea TROSCLAIR (Thib. Ct. Hse.: Mar. v.36, #7)

BOUDREAUX, Theogene Urdan (Clebert & Cora LABAUVE) b. 20 Feb. 1896 (Larose Ch.: v.2, p.189)

BOUDREAUX, Therma Marie Ethel (Anatole & Marie MALBOROUGH) b. 4 Sept. 1899 (Thib. Ch.: v.8, p.11)

BOUDREAUX, Urbain Octave (Arthur & Adele DUGAS) b. 9 July 1897 (Thib. Ch.: v.7, p.455)

BOUDREAUX, Valerie (Louisdon & Medora BOUDREAUX) m. 1 Sept. 1896 Julie THERIOT (Theriot Ch.: v.1, p.7)

BOUDREAUX, Valerie (Louisdone & Medora BOUDREAUX) m. 23 Aug. 1896 Julie THERIOT (Houma Ct. Hse.: Mar. v.29 & 30, #132)

BOUDREAUX, Victoire d. 14 July 1897 at age 68 yrs. (Thib. Ch.: v.3, p.203)

BOUDREAUX, Victor of Jefferson Parish (Alfred & Adele FABRE) m. 6 Feb. 1898 Ophelia RIGAULT, of Jefferson Parish (Larose Ch.: v.3, p.7)

BOUDREAUX, Victor (Alfred & Adele FABRE) m. 6 Feb. 1898 Ophelia RIGAULT (Larose Ch.: v.4, p.3)
BOUFIGLIO, Maria (Francesco & Salvatia GENTUSSA) m. 12 Jan. 1898 Antonino GIMARVO (Thib. Ct. Hse.: Mar. v.38, #316)
BOULIGNY, Stella Amelie (Charles & Mary STUBBS) b. 6 Oct. 1898 (Houma Ch.: Epis. Ch.: v.1, p.122)

BOURG (Sometimes: BOURK, BOURQUE)

BOURG, Agnes Marie (Ricard & Edilia FIELDS) b. 6 May 1897 (Theriot Ch.: v.2, p.2)
BOURG, Aimee (Felix & Francoize DUBOIS) m. 1 Aug. 1898 Leonard VOISIN, Jr. (Houma Ct. Hse.: Mar. v.30 & 31, #72)
BOURG, Albert Gabriel (Aubert & Josephine NAQUIN) b. 14 March 1898 (Montegut Ch.: v.6, p.69)
BOURG, Alexis Salvador (Menace & Olympe GUIDRY) b. 1 April 1899 (Larose Ch.: v.3, p.39)
BOURG, Alida (Faustin & Josephine DUPRE) m. 2 May 1898 ----- LEBOEUF (Montegut Ch.: v.4, p.244)
BOURG, Alida (Faustin & Josephine DUPRE) m. 9 April 1898 Etienne LEBOEUF (Houma Ct. Hse.: Mar. v.30 & 31, #386)
BOURG, Anna Lilian (Delma & Malvina PONTIF) b. 15 Oct. 1897 (Theriot Ch.: v.2, p.12)
BOURG, Annette (Oscar & Amanda JUNEAU) m. 25 April 1899 Willie WEBRE (Thib. Ch.: v.14, p.275)
BOURG, Annette L. m. 13 April 1899 William W. WEBRE (Thib. Ct. Hse.: Mar. v.39, #143)
BOURG, Annie O. (James E. & Amela SIGUR) m. 29 Sept. 1896 Joseph BERNARD (Thib. Ch.: v.14, p.100)
BOURG, Annie O. (James E. & Aurela SIGURD) m. 29 Sept. 1896 Joseph BERNARD (Thib. Ct. Hse.: Mar. v.36, #147)
BOURG, Armelia (Telesfore & Malvina HEBERT) m. 23 Nov. 1896 Adam BELANGER (Houma Ct. Hse.: Mar. v.29 & 30, #192)
BOURG, Armelia (Telesphore & Malvina HEBERT) m. 19 Dec. 1896 Adam BELANGER (Montegut Ch.: v.4, p.214)
BOURG, Aubin d. 2 March 1898 at age 66 yrs. (Houma Ch.: v.3, p.16)
BOURG, Aubin d. 28 Feb. 1898; m. Elizabeth E. DUROY Children listed: Laura; Minnie m. Dr. J. J. DAIGRE; J. Charles; F. Xavier; Joseph; Nellie; Henry M.; J. Conrad; d.Marie Ina Louise m. Dr. F. A. SILVESTRE. Petition for inventory: 16 March 1898. (Houma Ct. Hse.: Succ. #900)
BOURG, Augustine m. 15 Sept. 1897 Oleus DESROCHES (Houma Ct. Hse.: Mar. v.29 & 30, #90)
BOURG, Augustine (Gilbert & Eulalie LEBOEUF) m. 7 Oct. 1897 Oleus DESROCHES (Montegut Ch.: v.4, p.225)
BOURG, Azema d. 28 Oct. 1898 at age 65 yrs. (Thib. Ch.: v.3, p.220)
BOURG, Camelia (Prudent & Julia RICHARD) m. 7 Oct. 1896 G. H. BARRIOS (Lockport Ch.: v.2, p.154)

BOURG, Camilia (Prudent & Julie RICHARD) m. 7 Oct. 1896 G. H. BARRIOS (Thib. Ct. Hse.: Mar. v.36, #149)
BOURG, Charles (Charles & Ordalie AUCOIN) m. 18 Sept. 1896 Emelie GUILLOT (Chacahoula Ch.: v.1, p.54)
BOURG, child (Augustin & Delia LAPEYROUSE) d. 10 Feb. 1897 at age 14 yrs. (Montegut Ch.: v.2, p.9)
BOURG, Clothilde Fannie (Gabriel & Malvina LEBOEUF) b. 13 Sept. 1898 (Montegut Ch.: v.6, p.78)
BOURG, Elda (Edgar & Ernestine MALBROUGH) b. 20 Jan. 1897 (Theriot Ch.: v.1-B, p.106)
BOURG, Elisabeth Elvire (Havier & Josephine VIGUERIE) b. 23 Sept. 1897 (Houma Ch.: v.5, p.189)
BOURG, Elizabeth Alina (Felicien & Berthilde THIBODAUX) b. 15 Sept. 1899 (Montegut Ch.: v.6, p.93)
BOURG, Elvie Cecile d. 24 May 1896 at age 4 yrs. & 5 mths. (Thib. Ch.: v.3, p.182)
BOURG, Esthel Genevieve (Nemour & Juliette WEBB) b. 28 May 1897 (Thib. Ch.: v.7, p.451)
BOURG, Ethel Juliette d. 28 May 1896 at age 4 mths. (Thib. Ch.: v.3, p.183)
BOURG, Eva (Telefort & Evalina HEBERT) m. 15 Jan. 1898 Justin PELEGRIN (Houma Ct. Hse.: Mar. v.30 & 31, #207)
BOURG, Eva (Telesphore & d.Evelina HEBERT) m. 24 Jan. 1898 Justin PELEGRIN (Montegut Ch.: v.4, p.232)
BOURG, Felicia (Faustin & Josephine DUPRE) m. 5 Feb. 1899 Joseph LEBLANC (Montegut Ch.: v.4, p.255)
BOURG, Felicia (Fautin & Josephine DUPRE) m. 12 Jan. 1899 Joseph LEBLANC (Houma Ct. Hse.: Mar. v.30 & 31, #213)
BOURG, Felicien (d.Paulin & Evaline DESROCHES) m. 11 April 1898 Berthilde THIBODAUX (Montegut Ch.: v.4, p.240)
BOURG, Felicien (Paulin & Eveline DEROCHE) m. 26 March 1898 Bertille THIBODAUX (Houma Ct. Hse.: Mar. v.30 & 31, #355)
BOURG, Felix m. 3 Feb. 1899 Clara BOUDREAUX (Thib. Ct. Hse.: Mar. v.38, #87)
BOURG, Francois (Delmas & Marie ABADIE) b. 22 March 1896 (Larose Ch.: v.2, p.192)
BOURG, Gabriel (Gilbert & Eulalie LEBOEUF) m. 17 July 1899 Philomene NAQUIN (Montegut Ch.: v.4, p.268)
BOURG, Gabrielle (Gilbert & Eulalie LEBOEUF) m. 29 June 1899 Philomene NAQUIN (Houma Ct. Hse.: Mar. v.31 & 32, #60)
BOURG, Guillaune (Meance & Olympe GUIDRY) b. 2 April 1897 (Larose Ch.: v.3, p.2)
BOURG, Ida (Delmas & Marie ABADIE) b. 12 March 1898 (Larose Ch.: v.3, p.19)
BOURG, Ida (Severin & Marie DESROCHES) d. 5 Feb. 1899 at age 3½ yrs. (Montegut Ch.: v.2, p.24)
BOURG, Ida M. (Silvere & Emelie MIRE) m. 3 May 1898 Elson A. DELAUNE (Thib. Ct. Hse.: Mar. v.38, #169)
BOURG, Ida M. (Silvere & Emelie MYRE) m. 3 May 1898 Elson O. DELAUNE (Lockport Ch.: v.2, p.189)

BOURG, John Albert (G. A. & Kate BASCLE) b. 13 March 1898 (Houma Ch.: v.5, p.203)
BOURG, Joseph Adam (Oscar & Irma DOMINGUE) b. 29 Dec. 1899 (Houma Ch.: v.5, p.268)
BOURG, Joseph Adam (Oscar & Irma DOMINGUE) b. 29 Dec. 1899 (Houma Ch.: v.6, p.4)
BOURG, Joseph Alfred (Marcellin & Erelina DUPRE) b. 27 April 1897 (Montegut Ch.: v.6, p.56)
BOURG, Joseph Alvin Aubin (Joseph Charles & Carrie Emilia BELANGER) b. 4 April 1896 (Houma Ch.: v.5, p.178)
BOURG, Joseph Fane Suthon (J. Charles & Carrie Emelia BELANGER) b. 21 Sept. 1899 (Houma Ch.: v.5, p.257)
BOURG, Joseph Felix (Victor & Emilia BELLEAMOUR) b. 30 Nov. 1897 (Theriot Ch.: v.2, p.20)
BOURG, Joseph Fredy (Edgard & Ernestine MALBROUGH) b. 24 Sept. 1898 (Theriot Ch.: v.2, p.32)
BOURG, Joseph Gilbert (Laurence & Odilia THIBODEAUX) b. 15 March 1899 (Montegut Ch.: v.6, p.85)
BOURG, Joseph Paul (Andre & Francoise RODRIGUE) b. 10 Feb. 1899 (Montegut Ch.: v.6, p.84)
BOURG, Julia Venelia (Onesippe & Aurelia DUPRE) b. 25 Feb. 1899 (Montegut Ch.: v.6, p.85)
BOURG, Lawrence (d.Paulin & Eveline DESROCHES) m. 2 June 1898 Odile THIBODAUX (Montegut Ch.: v.4, p.245)
BOURG, Lawrence (Paulin & Eveline DESROCHES) m. 3 May 1898 Odile THIBODAUX (Houma Ct. Hse.: Mar. v.30 & 31, #428)
BOURG, Louisa (Ricard & Caroline GAGNE) m. 14 Feb. 1898 Adam BENOIT (Houma Ct. Hse.: Mar. v.30 & 31, #295)
BOURG, Louise (Ricard & Edilia FIELDS) m. 9 April 1898 Adam BENOIT (Theriot Ch.: v.1-B, p.3)
BOURG, Lucie Izoline Eniola (Onesippe & Aurelia DUPRE) b. 13 Dec. 1896 (Montegut Ch.: v.6, p.49)
BOURG, Marie m. Oscar CARO d. 16 Feb. 1899 (Thib. Ch.: v.3, p.228)
BOURG, Marie (Joseph & Amelie BOUDELOCHE) m. 17 Feb. 1896 Joseph CROCHET (Montegut Ch.: v.4, p.207)
BOURG, Marie (Joseph & Emelie BOUDELOCHE) m. 24 Jan. 1896 Joseph CROCHET (Houma Ct. Hse.: Mar. v.28, #407)
BOURG, Marie Alexina (Munier & Leontine LEBOEUF) b. 6 Jan. 1897 (Houma Ch.: v.5, p.172)
BOURG, Marie Rosie Eve (Oscar & Emma DOMINGUE) b. 26 Sept. 1896 (Montegut Ch.: v.6, p.46)
BOURG, Nellie M. m. 14 Sept. 1899 Adolphe P. DELCOURT (Houma Ch.: v.6-B, p.4)
BOURG, Octavie (John & Marie DUBOIS) m. 25 Jan. 1897 Oscar LEVRON (Montegut Ch.: v.4, p.216)
BOURG, Octavie (John & Marie DUBOIS) m. 9 Jan. 1897 Oscar LEVRON (Houma Ct. Hse.: Mar. v.29 & 30, #226)
BOURG, Olympe m. 19 Oct. 1896 Amede LAROSE (Thib. Ct. Hse.: Mar. v.36, #157)

BOURG, Rose Alfrida (Victor & Melia BOUDREAUX) b. 22 March 1899 (Montegut Ch.: v.6, p.87)
BOURG, Roseline m. Oleus RICHARD d. 17 Feb. 1898 at age 63 yrs. (Lockport Ch.: v.1, #4)
BOURG, Rosemond d. 31 Jan. 1896 at age 86 yrs. (Lockport Ch.: v.1, #5)
BOURG, Silvere Joseph Paul (Joseph & Emelie FORET) b. 29 June 1896 (Lockport Ch.: v.2, p.331)
BOURG, Sylvere A. (Francois S. & Josephine BOURG) m. 26 Aug. 1896 Josephine NAQUIN (Montegut Ch.: v.4, p.213)
BOURG, Sylvestre (Sylvestre & Franklina GUILLOT) b. 13 Sept. 1898 (Thib. Ch.: v.7, p.563)
BOURG, Telesfor d. 22 March 1897 m. Malvina HEBERT Children listed: Amelia m. Adam BELANGER; Emma m. Justillien PELLEGRIN; Virginia, 18; Angele, 16; Homer, 14; Agnes, 12; Zenor, 10; Ferbus, 8; Francois, 6; Aline, 4. Petition for tutorship: 25 May 1899. (Houma Ct. Hse.: Succ. #920)
BOURG, Victor (Felix & Frances DUBOIS) m. 26 Dec. 1896 Emelia BELLAMORE (Houma Ct. Hse.: Mar. v.29 & 30, #208)

BOURGEOIS (Sometimes: BURGEOIS)
BOURGEOIS, ----- girl d. 27 Jan. 1897 at age 3 mths. (Thib. Ch.: v.3, p.195)
BOURGEOIS, Adam (Edmund & Dorestile ROBICHAUX) m. 3 Feb. 1898 Clothilde LANCON (Houma Ct. Hse.: Mar. v.30 & 31, #259)
BOURGEOIS, Adam Didier (Clement & Amelina BABIN) b. 23 May 1898 (Thib. Ch.: v.7, p.498)
BOURGEOIS, Agnes d. 16 Aug. 1896 at age 1 yr. (Raceland Ch.: v.1, p.9)
BOURGEOIS, Aimee Clara (Alfred & Rosa LAPEYROUSE) b. 12 Aug. 1897 (Thib. Ch.: v.7, p.511)
BOURGEOIS, Albert m. 3 Feb. 1898 Florestine CHAMPAGNE (Thib. Ct. Hse.: Mar. v.37, #63)
BOURGEOIS, Albert (Marcilien & Emma BROWN) m. 3 Feb. 1898 Florestine CHAMPAGNE (Raceland Ch.: v.2, p.63)
BOURGEOIS, Albert Damien (Albert & Victoria FOLSE) b. 27 Sept. 1896 (Raceland Ch.: v.5, p.31)
BOURGEOIS, Albertine m. 10 Feb. 1898 Albert BRAUD (Thib. Ct. Hse.: Mar. v.37, #71)
BOURGEOIS, Albertine (Augustin & Leontine CHIASSON) m. 27 April 1899 Alexandre BOURGEOIS (Thib. Ct. Hse.: Mar. v.39, #151)
BOURGEOIS, Albertine (Augustin & Leontine CHIASSON) m. 27 April 1899 Alexandre BOURGEOIS (Thib. Ch.: v.14, p.278)
BOURGEOIS, Albertine (Marcilien & Emma BROWN) m. 10 Feb. 1898 Albert BREAUX (Raceland Ch.: v.2, p.66)
BOURGEOIS, Alcide (Vasseur & Odilia GUILLOTE) m. 15 Feb. 1898 Juliette TOUPS (Thib. Ch.: v.14, p.189)

BOURGEOIS, Alcide (Vasseur & Odilia GUILLOTE) m. 15 Feb. 1898 Juliette TOUPS (Thib. Ct. Hse.: Mar. v.37, #90)
BOURGEOIS, Alexandre (Oscar & Mathilde TOUPS) m. 27 April 1899 Albertine BOURGEOIS (Thib. Ct. Hse.: Mar. v.39, #151)
BOURGEOIS, Alexandre (Oscar & Mathilde TOUPS) m. 27 April 1899 Albertine BOURGEOIS (Thib. Ch.: v.14, p.278)
BOURGEOIS, Alfred (Olivier & Josephine LARPENTER) m. 12 Feb. 1896 Rosa LAPEROUSE (Thib. Ch.: v.14, p.76)
BOURGEOIS, Alfred (Olivier & Josephine LARPENTER) m. 12 Feb. 1896 Rosa LAPEROUSE (Houma Ct. Hse.: Mar. v.28, #433)
BOURGEOIS, Alice (Jean Baptiste & Odile BOURGEOIS) m. 6 Feb. 1896 Duval WAGUESPACK (Thib. Ch.: v.14, p.74)
BOURGEOIS, Alice (Jean Baptiste & Odile BOURGEOIS) m. 6 Feb. 1896 Duval WAGUESPACK (Thib. Ct. Hse.: Mar. v.35, #33)
BOURGEOIS, Ambroise J. (Numa & Emilie BOURGEOIS) m. 19 Jan. 1899 Meloe TOUPS (Thib. Ct. Hse.: Mar. v.38, #21)
BOURGEOIS, Anatole d. 9 May 1898 at age 4 mths. (Raceland Ch.: v.1, p.18)
BOURGEOIS, Anatole Melaney (Argus & Eveleda BOURGEOIS) b. 14 Dec. 1897 (Raceland Ch.: v.5, p.63)
BOURGEOIS, Andre Clarence (Paul & Marie BABIN) b. 30 Nov. 1897 (Thib. Ch.: v.7, p.474)
BOURGEOIS, Angelina (Klebert & Judith BOUDREAUX) m. 20 July 1897 Edmond THIBODAUX (Thib. Ch.: v.14, p.153)
BOURGEOIS, Angelina (Klebert & Judith BOUDREAUX) m. 20 July 1897 Edmond THIBODAUX (Thib. Ct. Hse.: Mar. v.37, #194)
BOURGEOIS, Appollinaire d. 4 Feb. 1897 at age 69 yrs. (Lockport Ch.: v.1, #3)
BOURGEOIS, Aramis (Marcelin & Marguerite THIBODAUX) m. 7 Feb. 1898 Cecile PREJEAN (Thib. Ch.: v.14, p.180)
BOURGEOIS, Aramis (Marcilien & Marguerite THIBODAUX) m. 7 Feb. 1898 Cecile PREJEAN (Thib. Ct. Hse.: Mar. v.37, #89)
BOURGEOIS, Armantine m. 3 May 1897 Thomas EHRHART (Thib. Ct. Hse.: Mar. v.36, #136)
BOURGEOIS, Basilise m. Gaspard AUTHEMENT d. 24 Dec. 1898 at age 89 yrs. (Raceland Ch.: v.1, p.21)
BOURGEOIS, C. Arthur d. 28 July 1898 at age 42 yrs. & 10 mths. (Thib. Ch.: v.3, p.218)
BOURGEOIS, Camille d. 21 June 1897 at age 18½ yrs. (Thib. Ch.: v.3, p.201)
BOURGEOIS, Camille Sydney (Louis & Louisiane BREAUX) b. 29 Nov. 1898 (Thib. Ch.: v.7, p.576)
BOURGEOIS, Caroline (Norbert & Odelia GUILLOTE) m. 25 Jan. 1898 Thomas THIBODAUX (Thib. Ch.: v.14, p.175)
BOURGEOIS, Caroline (Norbert & Odilia GUILLOTE) m. 25 Jan. 1898 Thomas THIBODAUX (Thib. Ct. Hse.: Mar. v.37, #38)
BOURGEOIS, Cecile m. 9 Jan. 1899 Harry BRADFORD (Thib. Ct. Hse.: Mar. v.38, #10)

BOURGEOIS, Cecile (Adam & Cecile MELANCON) b. 16 Jan. 1899 (Raceland Ch.: v.5, p.88)
BOURGEOIS, Celestine m. 19 July 1899 Eugene LEBLANC (Thib. Ct. Hse.: Mar. v.39, #198)
BOURGEOIS, Celestine (Joseph & Hales ADAM) m. 19 July 1899 Eugene LEBLANC (Lockport Ch.: v.2, p.209)
BOURGEOIS, Charles (Justilien & Adelina BOUDREAUX) m. 2 Feb. 1899 Lydia TOUPS (Thib. Ct. Hse.: Mar. v.38, #69)
BOURGEOIS, Charles (Justilien & Adelina BOUDREAUX) m. 2 Feb. 1899 Lydia TOUPS (Thib. Ch.: v.14, p.254)
BOURGEOIS, Charles (Vasseur & Odile GUILLOTE) m. 17 May 1898 Elisabeth RICHARD (Thib. Ct. Hse.: Mar. v.38, #179)
BOURGEOIS, Charles (Vasseur & Odile GUILLOTE) m. 17 May 1898 Elisabeth RICHARD (Thib. Ch.: v.14, p.204)
BOURGEOIS, Charles Paul (Charles & Elisabeth RICHARD) b. 17 Feb. 1899 (Thib. Ch.: v.7, p.536)
BOURGEOIS, Clarence Joseph (William & Elisabeth RICHARD) b. 29 May 1899 (Thib. Ch.: v.7, p.605)
BOURGEOIS, Clement Arthur Dr. d. 27 July 1898; m. 23 Dec. 1881 Georgina BERGERON Petition for probate of will: 6 Aug. 1898. (Thib. Ct. Hse.: Succ. #1546)
BOURGEOIS, Clemile m. 20 Jan. 1898 Alice RODRIGUE (Thib. Ct. Hse.: Mar. v.37, #12)
BOURGEOIS, Clemile (Jackson & Cephise BAUDOIN) m. 20 Jan. 1898 Alice RODRIGUE (Raceland Ch.: v.2, p.57)
BOURGEOIS, Cleopha (Faustin & Emelie HEBERT) m. 4 Feb. 1899 Lucille PACKS (Lockport Ch.: v.2, p.201)
BOURGEOIS, Cleopha (Faustin & Emelie HOTARD) m. 4 Feb. 1899 Lucille PAQUES (Thib. Ct. Hse.: Mar. v.38, #70)
BOURGEOIS, Clovis m. 27 Aug. 1897 Letitia AUTIN, widow of Auguste EROCHE (Thib. Ct. Hse.: Mar. v.37, #220)
BOURGEOIS, Desire m. 8 June 1898 Marie LUQUETTE (Thib. Ct. Hse.: Mar. v.38, #200)
BOURGEOIS, Durand (Numa & Emilie BOURGEOIS) m. 19 Jan. 1899 Meloe TOUPS (Thib. Ch.: v.14, p.241)
BOURGEOIS, Edia Marie (Arthur & Amelia BERNARD) b. 20 Sept. 1896 (Raceland Ch.: v.5, p.31)
BOURGEOIS, Edmond B. m. 25 May 1898 Edna DEZAUCHE (Thib. Ct. Hse.: Mar. v.38, #188)
BOURGEOIS, Elda (Marcilien & Margurite THIBODEAUX) m. 7 June 1899 Theophile LEDET (Thib. Ch.: v.14, p.284)
BOURGEOIS, Eleonore (Justilien & Mathilda BOUDREAUX) m. 8 Feb. 1898 Albert FORET (Thib. Ct. Hse.: Mar. v.37, #45)
BOURGEOIS, Eleonore (Justilien & Mathilde BOUDREAUX) m. 5 Feb. 1898 Albert FORET (Lockport Ch.: v.2, p.184)
BOURGEOIS, Elina d. 17 May 1898 at age 1 yr. & 8 mths. (Thib. Ch.: v.3, p.214)
BOURGEOIS, Elizabeth (Sylvain & Mary FORET) m. 31 Aug. 1898 Wuilly MORILLON (Lockport Ch.: v.2, p.193)
BOURGEOIS, Elizabeth (Sylvain & Mary FORET) m. 31 Aug. 1898 William L. MORILLON (Thib. Ct. Hse.: Mar. v.38, #263)

BOURGEOIS, Emile Albert (Ursin & Marie HEAD) b. 24 Dec. 1896 (Larose Ch.: v.2, p.190)
BOURGEOIS, Ernest (Adam & Rosela POCHE) m. 25 Oct. 1899 Agathe BOUDREAUX (Thib. Ct. Hse.: Mar. v.39, #248)
BOURGEOIS, Ernest (Adam & Rosela POCHE) m. 25 Oct. 1899 Agathe BOUDREAUX (Thib. Ch.: v.14, p.305)
BOURGEOIS, Ernest Nelson (Philippe & Celeste LECHE) b. 12 Oct. 1899 (Thib. Ch.: v.8, p.17)
BOURGEOIS, Ernestine m. 26 Oct. 1897 Charles PLAISANCE (Lockport Ch.: v.2, p.177)
BOURGEOIS, Ernestine (Joseph & Alice ADAM) m. 26 Oct. 1897 Charles PLAISANCE (Thib. Ct. Hse.: Mar. v.37, #252)
BOURGEOIS, Estelle Aurelie (Walter & Marie BABIN) b. 2 Dec. 1897 (Raceland Ch.: v.5, p.59)
BOURGEOIS, Ethen m. 11 April 1896 Sidonie RICHOUX (Larose Ch.: v.4, p.45)
BOURGEOIS, Ethen m. 11 April 1896 Sidonie RICHOUX (Thib. Ct. Hse.: Mar. v.35, #67)
BOURGEOIS, Etienne m. 11 April 1896 Sidonie RICHOUX (Larose Ch.: v.3, p.2)
BOURGEOIS, Eugene (Eugene & Felicia ROBICHAUX) b. 19 Jan. 1898 (Raceland Ch.: v.5, p.64)
BOURGEOIS, Eugene Oliver (Augustin & Leontine CHIASSON) b. 19 Dec. 1899 (Thib. Ch.: v.8, p.21)
BOURGEOIS, Eva Valry (Adam & Cecile HYMEL) b. 2 Jan. 1897 (Larose Ch.: v.3, p.1)
BOURGEOIS, Eve Canilia (Albert & Victoria FOLSE) b. 28 Jan. 1899 (Raceland Ch.: v.5, p.90)
BOURGEOIS, Eve Notilia (Paul & Euphrasine THERIOT) b. 28 July 1896 (Raceland Ch.: v.5, p.27)
BOURGEOIS, Eveline m. Simon BOURGEOIS d. 27 Oct. 1898 at age 64 yrs. (Larose Ch.: v.1, p.44)
BOURGEOIS, Ferdinand m. 8 July 1897 Edna DARCE (Houma Ct. Hse.: Mar. v.29 & 30, #56)
BOURGEOIS, Ferdinand (Calixte & Philomene CALAHAN) m. 12 July 1897 Edna DARCE (Theriot Ch.: v.1-B, p.1)
BOURGEOIS, Fergus d. 2 Jan. 1898 at age 81 yrs. (Raceland Ch.: v.1, p.17)
BOURGEOIS, Fergus (Paul & Marguerite BOURGEOIS) m. 17 Feb. 1896 Elitia THIBODAUX (Raceland Ch.: v.2, p.13)
BOURGEOIS, Fergust m. 17 Feb. 1896 Elesia THIBODAUX (Thib. Ct. Hse.: Mar. v.35, #41)
BOURGEOIS, Fortune Joseph (Etienne & Sidonie RICHOU) b. 1 March 1897 (Lockport Ch.: v.3-A, #28)
BOURGEOIS, Fortune Joseph (Etienne & Sidonie RICHOU) b. 1 March 1897 (Lockport Ch.: v.3, #28)
BOURGEOIS, Francis Nettie (Calixte & Edna DARCE) b. 4 June 1898 (Theriot Ch.: v.2, p.25)
BOURGEOIS, Gaston Charles (Charles & Lydia TOUPS) b. 22 Nov. 1899 (Thib. Ch.: v.7, p.575)

BOURGEOIS, Georges (Pierre & Josephine ZERINGUE) b. 21 Feb. 1899 (Raceland Ch.: v.5, p.91)
BOURGEOIS, Hattie Celeste (Thomas & Mary Helena TEMPLE) b. 24 Nov. 1898 (Thib. Ch.: v.7, p.526)
BOURGEOIS, Helene (Vasseur & Marie GUILLOTE) m. 14 Sept. 1898 Raymond SAUCIER (Thib. Ct. Hse.: Mar. v.38, #270)
BOURGEOIS, Helene (Vasseur & Marie GUILLOTE) m. 14 Sept. 1898 Raymond SAUCIER (Thib. Ch.: v.14, p.223)
BOURGEOIS, Helene Anita (Wilfred & Cora BOURGEOIS) b. 7 Nov. 1896 (Thib. Ch.: v.7, p.424)
BOURGEOIS, Henriette Eugenie (Edgard & Eugenie GODET) b. 27 Nov. 1899 (Larose Ch.: v.3, p.48)
BOURGEOIS, Henriette Georgina (Georges & Palmyra) b. 15 July 1897 bt. 2 Aug. 1897 (Chacahoula Ch.: v.4, p.22)
BOURGEOIS, Hilda (Marcilien & Marguerite THIBODEAUX) m. 7 June 1899 Theophile LEDET (Thib. Ct. Hse.: Mar. v.39, #172)
BOURGEOIS, Honore (Oscar & Cordilia ONCALE) b. 31 Aug. 1899 (Thib. Ch.: v.8, p.6)
BOURGEOIS, Jacques Leonard (Oscar & Cordilia ONCALE) b. 21 Feb. 1897 (Thib. Ch.: v.7, p.439)
BOURGEOIS, James Louis (Alcide & Rosalie RODDY) b. 11 June 1898 (Chacahoula Ch.: v.4, p.11)
BOURGEOIS, Jean Andre (Edmond & Etna DEZANCHE) b. 9 Dec. 1899 (Thib. Ch.: v.8, p.22)
BOURGEOIS, Jean Eustache (Leon & Leontine GUIDROZ) b. 27 Jan. 1896 (Lockport Ch.: v.3, #7)
BOURGEOIS, Jean Eustache (Leon & Leontine GUIDROZ) b. 27 Jan. 1896 (Lockport Ch.: v.3-A, #7)
BOURGEOIS, John Max (Wilfrid & Cora BOURGEOIS) b. 18 June 1899 (Thib. Ch.: v.7, p.552)
BOURGEOIS, Joseph (Desire & Selima CANTRELLE) m. 14 Oct. 1899 Emma BARBIER (Lockport Ch.: v.2, p.210)
BOURGEOIS, Joseph (Desire & Selima CANTRELLE) m. 14 Oct. 1899 Emma BARBIER (Thib. Ct. Hse.: Mar. v.39, #242)
BOURGEOIS, Joseph (Frosin & Cora MATERNE) b. 25 April 1896 (Raceland Ch.: v.5, p.23)
BOURGEOIS, Joseph Avis (Joseph Napoleon & Elvire DELAUNE) b. 10 April 1896 (Lockport Ch.: v.2, p.328)
BOURGEOIS, Joseph David (Alcide & Juliette TOUPS) b. 8 Sept. 1898 (Thib. Ch.: v.7, p.561)
BOURGEOIS, Joseph Etienne (Louis & Marie RICHARD) b. 10 March 1896 (Thib. Ch.: v.7, p.395)
BOURGEOIS, Joseph Harry d. 3 Dec. 1898 at age 15 days (Raceland Ch.: v.1, p.21)
BOURGEOIS, Joseph Harry (Alain & Adelia FOURNIER) b. 17 Nov. 1898 (Raceland Ch.: v.5, p.83)
BOURGEOIS, Joseph Ives (Ede & Ophelia THERIOT) b. 19 May 1899 (Raceland Ch.: v.5, p.97)
BOURGEOIS, Joseph Maurice (Jules & Clemilia BRAUX) b. 16 Dec. 1898 (Thib. Ch.: v.7, p.525)

BOURGEOIS, Joseph Raymond (Frosin & Cora MATERNE) b. 25 April 1898 (Raceland Ch.: v.5, p.70)
BOURGEOIS, Joseph Wilson (Philippe & Celeste LECHE) b. 7 Nov. 1897 (Thib. Ch.: v.7, p.471)
BOURGEOIS, Josephine d. 11 Feb. 1898 at age 21 yrs. (Raceland Ch.: v.1 p.17)
BOURGEOIS, Julia (Adam & Julia PORCHE) m. 21 May 1897 Arthur RICHARD (Houma Ch.: v.6-a, p.203)
BOURGEOIS, Julie Ursule (Clement & Amelina BABIN) b. 21 Oct. 1896 (Thib. Ch.: v.7, p.422)
BOURGEOIS, Julien A. m. 22 April 1896 Blanche FORET (Thib. Ct. Hse.: Mar. v.35, #61)
BOURGEOIS, Julien A. (Justilien & Adelin BOURGEOIS) m. 22 April 1896 Blanche FORET (Raceland Ch.: v.2, p.15)
BOURGEOIS, Justilien (Aurelien & Julia MARTIN) m. 11 Nov. 1899 Seraphine BOURGEOIS (Thib. Ct. Hse.: Mar. v.39, #249)
BOURGEOIS, Justilien (Aurelien & Julia MARTIN) m. 11 Nov. 1899 Seraphine BOURGEOIS (Lockport Ch.: v.2, p.211)
BOURGEOIS, Justine (Norbert & Odile GUILLOT) m. 12 Oct. 1899 Joseph RICHARD (Thib. Ct. Hse.: Mar. v.39, #244)
BOURGEOIS, Justine (Norbert) m. 12 Oct. 1899 Joseph RICHARD (Thib. Ch.: v.14, p.303)
BOURGEOIS, Lena m. 6 April 1899 Edmond SAVOIE (Thib. Ct. Hse.: Mar. v.39, #134)
BOURGEOIS, Leonide (Justilien & Mathilde BOUDREAUX) m. 6 Jan. 1898 Antoine BONAMOUR (Lockport Ch.: v.2, p.178)
BOURGEOIS, Leonide (Justilien & Mathilde BOUDREAUX) m. 6 Jan. 1898 Antoine BONAMOUR, Jr. (Thib. Ct. Hse.: Mar. v.37, #268)
BOURGEOIS, Lina (Ursin & Annelie HEAD) m. 12 April 1899 Edmond SAVOIE (Larose Ch.: v.4, p.83)
BOURGEOIS, Lina (Ursin & Annelie HEAD) m. 12 March 1899 Edmond SAVOIE (Larose Ch.: v.4, p.107)
BOURGEOIS, Lina (Ursin & Aurelie HEAD) m. 12 April 1899 Edmond SAVOIE (Larose Ch.: v.3, p.11)
BOURGEOIS, Louis Augustin (Jean Baptiste & Odile BOURGEOIS) m. 25 Jan. 1899 Louisiane BREAUX (Thib. Ch.: v.14, p.245)
BOURGEOIS, Louis Thomas (Thomas & Nellie TEMPLE) b. 25 Sept. 1899 (Thib. Ch.: v.8, p.11)
BOURGEOIS, Louise (Louis & Myrtilia THIBODAUX) m. 15 Oct. 1897 Francois BELE (Houma Ct. Hse.: Mar. v.29 & 30, #122)
BOURGEOIS, Louise Anne d. 17 April 1899 at age 3 days (Thib. Ch.: v.3, p.231)
BOURGEOIS, Louise Anne (Adolphe & Heloise MORVAN) b. 15 April 1899 (Thib. Ch.: v.7, p.547)
BOURGEOIS, Louise Bussy (Denise & Augustine BERGERON) b. 16 May 1896 (Houma Ch.: v.5, p.181)
BOURGEOIS, Luc Eugene (Augustin & Leontine CHIASSON) b. 23 Feb. 1898 (Thib. Ch.: v.7, p.487)

BOURGEOIS, Maggie (Joseph N. & Marguerite LEBLANC) m. 29 July 1896 Elfert P. DELAUNE (Lockport Ch.: v.2, p.153)
BOURGEOIS, Maggie (Joseph N. & Marguerite LEBLANC) m. 29 July 1896 Elfert P. DELAUNE (Thib. Ct. Hse.: Mar. v.36, #127)
BOURGEOIS, Marguerite Dasee (Paul & Berthe DAIGLE) b. 1 Dec. 1899 (Houma Ch.: v.5, p.263)
BOURGEOIS, Marguerite Judith (Elsee & Alice LEBLANC) b. 20 Nov. 1898 (Houma Ch.: v.5, p.229)
BOURGEOIS, Marguerite Julie (Felix & Helene DAIGLE) b. 6 Jan. 1897 (Thib. Ch.: v.7, p.434)
BOURGEOIS, Marie d. 2 Sept. 1899 at age 8 mths. (Raceland Ch.: v.1, p.27)
BOURGEOIS, Marie m. Joseph DANTIN d. 29 Oct. 1899 at age 82 yrs. (Thib. Ch.: v.3, p.242)
BOURGEOIS, Marie Agathe (Philippe & Marie THIBODAUX) b. 2 Aug. 1899 (Thib. Ch.: v.7, p.557)
BOURGEOIS, Marie Agnes (Alphonse & Augustine BRAUD) b. 15 April 1899 (Thib. Ch.: v.7, p.545)
BOURGEOIS, Marie Aline (Alain & Adelia FOURNIER) b. 30 Dec. 1899 (Raceland Ch.: v.5, p.111)
BOURGEOIS, Marie Annette (Ede & Ophelia THERIOT) b. 27 March 1897 (Raceland Ch.: v.5, p.45)
BOURGEOIS, Marie Apolline (Paul & Berthe DAIGLE) b. 2 April 1896 (Thib. Ch.: v.7, p.398)
BOURGEOIS, Marie Canelia d. 4 May 1898 at age 6 mths. (Raceland Ch.: v.1, p.18)
BOURGEOIS, Marie Edith (Ferjus & Elitia THIBODAUX) b. 2 Sept. 1898 (Raceland Ch.: v.5, p.79)
BOURGEOIS, Marie Elina (Alphonse & Augustine BRAUD) b. 22 Oct. 1896 (Thib. Ch.: v.7, p.422)
BOURGEOIS, Marie Elina (Oscar & Emma POCHE) b. 8 Dec. 1899 (Thib. Ch.: v.7, p.582)
BOURGEOIS, Marie Helene (Robert & Germaine MORVANT) b. 18 Aug. 1899 (Thib. Ch.: v.7, p.560)
BOURGEOIS, Marie Lilia (Oscar & Emma POCHE) b. 11 Feb. 1897 (Thib. Ch.: v.7, p.490)
BOURGEOIS, Marie Liliane (Albert & Florestine CHAMPAGNE) b. 14 Feb. 1898 (Thib. Ch.: v.7, p.540)
BOURGEOIS, Marie Lina (Paul & Berthe DAIGLE) b. 7 Feb. 1898 (Houma Ch.: v.5, p.197)
BOURGEOIS, Marie Noelie (Paul & Marie BABIN) b. 25 Dec. 1899 (Thib. Ch.: v.8, p.21)
BOURGEOIS, Maximilien Mrs. d. 11 July 1899 at age 80 yrs. & 9 mths. (Thib. Ch.: v.3, p.236)
BOURGEOIS, May (Benjamin & Henriette CANTY) m. 22 June 1899 John SCHEXNAILDRE (Raceland Ch.: v.2, p.99)
BOURGEOIS, Modeste m. Onezime DAIGLE d. 8 March 1896 at age 67 yrs. (Larose Ch.: v.1, p.36)
BOURGEOIS, Myrthe m. 8 Feb. 1899 Nolsey PIERCE (Thib. Ct. Hse.: Mar. v.38, #97)

BOURGEOIS, Myrthe (Joseph & Eulalie HEBERT) m. 11 Feb. 1899 Volsey PIERCE (Larose Ch.: v.4, p.123)
BOURGEOIS, Myrthe (Joseph & Eulalie HEBERT) m. 11 Feb. 1899 Valsey PIERCE (Larose Ch.: v.4, p.36)
BOURGEOIS, Myrthe (Joseph & Eulalie HEBERT) m. 11 Feb. 1899 Volsey PIERCE (Larose Ch.: v.3, p.11)
BOURGEOIS, Nettie d. 14 Sept. 1899 at age 7 days (Raceland Ch.: v.1, p.27)
BOURGEOIS, Nettie Clement (Argus & Vellida BOURGEOIS) b. 7 Sept. 1898 (Thib. Ch.: v.7, p.561)
BOURGEOIS, Norbert (Eugene & Dulcina MELANCON) b. 2 Feb. 1897 (Larose Ch.: v.3, p.13)
BOURGEOIS, Oliva Remi (Louis & Myrtilia THIBODEAUX) b. 26 Feb. 1899 (Houma Ch.: v.5, p.240)
BOURGEOIS, Oscar m. 26 Feb. 1897 Emma PUNCH (Thib. Ct. Hse.: Mar. v.36, #91)
BOURGEOIS, Oscar (Paul & Marguerite BOURGEOIS) m. 1 March 1897 Emma PAUCH (Raceland Ch.: v.2, p.36)
BOURGEOIS, Oscar Achille (Oscar & Mathilde Codilia ONCALE) b. 11 June 1898 (Thib. Ch.: v.7, p.499)
BOURGEOIS, Paul d. 26 Dec. 1897 at age 38 yrs. (Raceland Ch.: v.1, p.16)
BOURGEOIS, Paul d. 26 Dec. 1897; m. Froizine THERIOT Children listed: Froizillie, 9 yrs.; Annie, 6 yrs.; Beauregard, 7 yrs.; Sidney, 4 yrs.; Notillia, 2 yrs. Petition for inventory: 29 June 1898. (Thib. Ct. Hse.: Succ. #1538)
BOURGEOIS, Paul (Louis & Nathalie THIBODEAUX) b. 27 June 1896 (Houma Ch.: v.5, p.154)
BOURGEOIS, Paul Laurens (Adolphe & Louise MORVAN) b. 8 Aug. 1897 (Thib. Ch.: v.7, p.461)
BOURGEOIS, Paul Octave (Calixte & Edna DARCE) b. 15 Sept. 1899 (Theriot Ch.: v.2, p.51)
BOURGEOIS, Paul Rene (Alain & Adelia FOURNIER) b. 12 May 1897 (Raceland Ch.: v.5, p.49)
BOURGEOIS, Philippe (Marcelien & Marguerite THIBODAUX) m. 24 Feb. 1897 Celeste LECHE (Thib. Ch.: v.14, p.130)
BOURGEOIS, Philippe (Marcilien & Marguerite THIBODAUX) m. 24 Feb. 1897 Celeste LECHE (Thib. Ct. Hse.: Mar. v.36, #78)
BOURGEOIS, Pierre J. m. 21 Feb. 1898 Josephine ZERINGUE (Thib. Ct. Hse.: Mar. v.37, #108)
BOURGEOIS, Pierre J. (Evelien & Froselie FORET) m. 21 Feb. 1898 Josephine ZERINGUE (Raceland Ch.: v.2, p.72)
BOURGEOIS, Ralph Antoine (Alcee & Alice LEBLANC) b. 3 Sept. 1896 (Thib. Ch.: v.7, p.422)
BOURGEOIS, Regina (Walter & Marie BABIN) b. 30 Oct. 1899; m. 10 Nov. 1925 Abel MATHERNE, widow of Henriette DANOS (Raceland Ch.: Bapt. Bk., v.5, p.105)
BOURGEOIS, Robert (Alfred & Evilia THIBODAUX) m. 27 Oct. 1898 Marie Germaine MORVANT (Thib. Ct. Hse.: Mar. v.38, #303)

BOURGEOIS, Robert (Alfred & Evilia THIBODAUX) m. 27 Oct. 1898 Marie Germaine MORVANT (Thib. Ch.: v.14, p.229)
BOURGEOIS, Seraphine (Justin & Victoria PERTUIS) m. 11 Nov. 1899 Justilien BOURGEOIS (Thib. Ct. Hse.: Mar. v.39, #249)
BOURGEOIS, Seraphine (Justin & Victoria PERTUIS) m. 11 Nov. 1899 Justilien BOURGEOIS (Lockport Ch.: v.2, p.211)
BOURGEOIS, Sidonie Philomene (Frank & Marie DUFRENE) b. 2 April 1897 (Lockport Ch.: v.3-A, #42)
BOURGEOIS, Sidonie Philomene (Frank & Marie DUFRENE) b. 2 April 1897 (Lockport Ch.: v.3, #42)
BOURGEOIS, Theophile Joseph (Willie & Marie BABIN) b. 24 Aug. 1896 (Thib. Ch.: v.7, p.414)
BOURGEOIS, Therese (Jean Baptiste & Odile BOURGEOIS) m. 9 Feb. 1898 Frank BREAUX (Thib. Ch.: v.14, p.183)
BOURGEOIS, Therese (Jean Baptiste & Odile BOURGEOIS) m. 9 Feb. 1898 Franck BREAUX (Thib. Ct. Hse.: Mar. v.37, #73)
BOURGEOIS, Thomas (Oscar & Celeste TOUPS) m. 14 Feb. 1898 Marie Eleonore TEMPLE (Thib. Ch.: v.14, p.187)
BOURGEOIS, Thomas (Oscar & Celeste TOUPS) m. 14 Feb. 1898 Marie Eleonore TEMPLE (Thib. Ct. Hse.: Mar. v.37, #98)
BOURGEOIS, Thomas Huet (Oliva & Josephine LARPENTEUR) b. 10 Aug. 1897 (Houma Ch.: v.5, p.187)
BOURGEOIS, Valerie d. 16 Dec. 1898 at age 6 days (Houma Ch.: v.3, p.19)
BOURGEOIS, Valmon d. 18 Oct. 1896 (Lockport Ch.: v.1, #20)
BOURGEOIS, Victoria (Eugene & Dulcina MELANCON) b. 23 Sept. 1898 (Larose Ch.: v.3, p.29)
BOURGEOIS, Victoria (Justin & Victoria PERTUIT) b. 25 Oct. 1897 (Raceland Ch.: v.5, p.57)
BOURGEOIS, Victorine Beatrice (Alfred & Rosa LAPEROUSE) b. 26 Nov. 1896 (Thib. Ch.: v.7, p.431)
BOURGEOIS, Walter (Leo & Camilia BOURGEOIS) b. 17 Sept. 1897 (Raceland Ch.: v.5, p.55)
BOURGEOIS, Whitney Joseph (Ferjus & Eletia THIBODAUX) b. 17 Nov. 1896 (Raceland Ch.: v.5, p.36)
BOURGEOIS, Willie (Cyprien & Elmire CHAMPAGNE) m. 16 Aug. 1897 Elisabeth RICHARD (Thib. Ct. Hse.: Mar. v.37, #207)
BOURGEOIS, Willie (Cyprien & Elmire CHAMPAGNE) m. 16 Aug. 1897 Elisabeth RICHARD (Thib. Ch.: v.14, p.157)
BOUSSOT, Aimee (Joseph & Oceana FREGAT) m. 10 July 1897 Alcide MATHERNE (Raceland Ch.: v.2, p.45)

BOUTARI (Sometimes: BOUTARIE, BOUTARY, BOUTIRI)

BOUTARI, Berenice Marie (Abel & Emilie BALLARD) b. 8 Nov. 1897 (Thib. Ch.: v.7, p.526)
BOUTARI, Celestin d. 26 June 1897 at age 74 yrs. (Thib. Ch.: v.3, p.202)
BOUTARI, Justilienne m. Leo BAYE d. 4 Jan. 1896 at age 30 yrs. (Thib. Ch.: v.3, p.177)

BOUTARI, Victor Joseph (Victorin & Cecilia HERNANDEZ) b. 20 Jan. 1898 (Chacahoula Ch.: Gibson Records: Mar. Bk., v.1, #16)
BOUTARI, Victor Joseph (Victorin & Cecilia HERNANDEZ) b. 20 Jan. 1898 (Chacahoula Ch.: Gibson Ch.: v.2, p.118)
BOUTIERRE, Xavier d. 16 Oct. 1899 at age 20 yrs. (Lockport Ch.: v.1, #39)

BOUVIER (Sometimes: BOVIER)
BOUVIER, ----- child (Joseph) d. 22 July 1897 (Larose Ch.: v.1, p.41)
BOUVIER, Alphonse Augustin (Joseph & Melia ADAM) b. 21 July 1898 (Larose Ch.: v.3, p.23)
BOUVIER, Dominique Ignace (Louis & Clemence RICHOUX) b. 3 Feb. 1897 (Larose Ch.: v.3, p.2)
BOUVIER, Elola Marie (Pierre & Augusta SAVOIE) b. 21 Sept. 1899 (Larose Ch.: v.3, p.45)
BOUVIER, Joseph m. 11 Jan. 1896 Amelia ADAMS (Larose Ch.: v.4, p.70)
BOUVIER, Joseph m. 11 Jan. 1896 Amelia ADAMS (Larose Ch.: v.3, p.2)
BOUVIER, Joseph m. 2 Jan. 1896 Amelia ADAM (Thib. Ct. Hse.: Mar. v.35, #6)
BOUVIER, Joseph (Martial & Julianne BOURGEOIS) m. 11 Jan. 1896 Amelia ADAM (Larose Ch.: v.2, p.186)
BOUVIER, Joseph Clovis (Joseph & Lelia ADAM) b. 5 Nov. 1896 (Larose Ch.: v.2, p.189)
BOUVIER, Joseph Harris (Louis & Clemence RICHOU) b. 22 Oct. 1899 (Larose Ch.: v.3, p.46)
BOUVIER, Marie Eleonore (Louis & Clemence RICHOUX) b. 15 July 1898 (Larose Ch.: v.3, p.23)
BOUVIER, Pierre of Lafourche Parish (Martial & Julienne BOURGEOIS) m. 25 June 1898 Augusta SAVOIE, of Lafourche Parish (Larose Ch.: v.3, p.9)
BOUVIER, Pierre (Martial & Julienne BOURGEOIS) m. 25 June 1898 Augusta SAVOIE (Thib. Ct. Hse.: Mar. v.38, #204)
BOUVIER, Pierre (Martial & Julienne BOURGEOIS) m. 25 June 1898 Augusta SAVOIE (Larose Ch.: v.4, p.18)
BOUZIGARD, Edgard of Jefferson Parish (Clement & Melanie TERREBONNE) m. 28 July 1898 Eve TERREBONNE, of Jefferson Parish (Larose Ch.: v.3, p.10)
BOUZIGARD, Edgard of Jefferson Parish (Clement & Melanie TERREBONNE) m. 28 July 1898 Eve TERREBONNE, of Jefferson Parish (Larose Ch.: v.4, p.24)
BOWIE, William m. 9 Aug. 1897 Amanda TILLMAN (Thib. Ct. Hse.: Mar. v.37, #209)
BOYCE, Henry (Harry & Minnie BOYCE) m. 5 April 1897 Mary PORTIER, widow of A. ESCASUT (Houma Ct. Hse.: Mar. v.29 & 30, #377)
BOYD, Mary Jane m. 9 Feb. 1897 Fortune ANKRUM (Thib. Ct. Hse.: Mar. v.36, #74)

BOYER, Aimee (Desire & Marie THABOR) m. 21 Jan. 1897 Albert ADAM (Thib. Ct. Hse.: Mar. v.36, #1)
-OYER, Aimee (Desire & Marie THABOR) m. 21 Jan. 1897 Albert ADAM (Thib. Ch.: v.14 p.113)
BOYER, Charles Noe (Hudson & Adelina ADAM) b. 9 Dec. 1897 (Thib. Ch.: v.7, p.481)
BOYER, Georges Allendey (Winfield & Victoria HEBERT) b. 8 Dec. 1896 (Houma Ch.: v.5, p.166)
BOYER, Josephine (Winfin & Victoria HEBERT) b. 3 Jan. 1899 (Houma Ch.: v.5, p.239)
BOYER, Lily Valerie (Sydney & Emma LEBLANC) b. 30 April 1899 (Thib. Ch.: v.7, p.607)
BOYER, Oscar (Hudson & Adelina ADAM) m. 30 Jan. 1899 Philomene ADAM (Thib. Ct. Hse.: Mar. v.38, #52)
BOYER, Oscar (Hudson & Adelina ADAM) m. 30 Jan. 1899 Philomene ADAM (Thib. Ch.: v.14, p.247)
BOYER, Paul Desire (William & Valerie PONTIFF) b. 5 Nov. 1897 (Thib. Ch.: v.7, p.484)
BOYER, Sidney J. m. 26 Jan. 1899 Irma LEBLANC (Houma Ct. Hse.: Mar. v.30 & 31, #287)
BOYER, Sidney J. (Desire & Mary TABOR) m. 13 Feb. 1899 Irma LEBLANC (Houma Ch.: v.6-a, p.280)
BOYER, Wilfrid (Desire & Mary TABOR) m. 13 Feb. 1896 Victoria HEBERT (Houma Ch.: v.6-a, p.170)
BOYER, Winifield m. 25 Jan. 1896 Victoria HEBERT (Houma Ct. Hse.: Mar. v.28, #419)
BOYKINS, Joseph m. 4 May 1897 Bertha MAHONEY (Houma Ct. Hse.: Mar. v.29 & 30, #403)
BOYNE, Anthony Howard (Johnny & Alice BELANGER) b. 8 Dec. 1899 (Montegut Ch.: v.6, p.99)
BOYNE, Mary Doris Bertha (Johnny Alexander & Marie Elise BELANGER) b. 24 Aug. 1897 (Montegut Ch.: v.6, p.63)
BOYNES, Mary m. 17 Jan. 1898 Daniel TURNER (Houma Ct. Hse.: Mar. v.30 & 31, #210)
BRADBERRY, Henry Theophile (Theophile & Marie N. VERDON) b. 22 Nov. 1897 (Larose Ch.: v.3, p.11)
BRADEY, Daniel d. 5 Aug. 1899 at age 66 yrs. (Houma Ch.: v.3, p.24)
BRADFORD, Harry m. 9 Jan. 1899 Cecile BOURGEOIS (Thib. Ct. Hse.: Mar. v.38, #10)
BRADFORD, Leonora B. (John R. BISLAND & Fannie A. BROWN, of Chicago) m. 17 Dec. 1896 Claiborne A. DUVAL, Jr. (Houma Ch.: Epis. Ch.: v.1, p.340)
BRADFORD, Leonora Bisland (John R. & Fannie Ashton BROWNSON) m. 11 Dec. 1896 Claiborne A. DUVAL, Jr. (Houma Ct. Hse.: Mar. v.29 & 30, #203)
BRADFORD, Ralph Ashton d. 25 June 1899 at age 8 yrs. (Houma Ch.: Epis. Ch.: v.1, p.388)
BRADLEY, Edward (Edgar & Julia LEE) b. 8 Nov. 1898 (Chackbay Ch.: v.1, p.133)

BRADLEY, Ella m. 6 Oct. 1898 Thomas MOSELY (Thib. Ct. Hse.: Mar. v.38, #289)
BRADLEY, George m. 22 May 1899 Mahala BARBER (Houma Ct. Hse.: Mar. v.31 & 32, #12)
BRADY, Laura J. d. 22 Jan. 1896 (Houma Ch.: Epis. Ch.: v.1, p.386)
BRADY, Timothy J. (Daniel & Ellen GLYNN) m. 9 March 1897 Carrie H. DAVIS (Houma Ct. Hse.: Mar. v.29 & 30, #342)
BRADY, Timothy Joseph (Paul & Ellen GLYNN) m. 11 March 1897 Carrie Hannah DAVIS (Houma Ch.: Epis. Ch.: v.1, p.342)
BRANSON, Rosaline m. 28 Oct. 1897 Jordan LAWTON (Thib. Ct. Hse.: Mar. v.37, #254)
BRASS, Mary d. 30 March 1896 at age 15 yrs., 22 days (Houma Ch.: v.3, p.7)

BREAUX (Sometimes: BRAU, BRAUD, BRAUS, BRAUX, BREAU)

BREAUX, ----- child (Edgard) d. 8 March 1899 at age 20 days (Lockport Ch.: v.1, #11)
BREAUX, ----- Mrs. d. 27 Jan. 1896 at age 53 yrs. (Houma Ch.: v.3, p.6)
BREAUX, Abasalon (Theodule & Odillia HEBERT) d. 13 April 1899 at age 4 yrs. (Larose Ch.: v.1, p.52)
BREAUX, Adam Etienne (Therance & Louisa DOMINIQUE) b. 8 Feb. 1896 (Lockport Ch.: v.2, p.322)
BREAUX, Adele (Emile) d. 25 Oct. 1899 at age 2 mths. (Theriot Ch.: v.1, p.2)
BREAUX, Adele Eucharis (Pierre & Camillia DUAY) b. 1 April 1896 (Larose Ch.: v.2, p.188)
BREAUX, Adeline d. 3 March 1899 at age 80 yrs. (Thib. Ch.: v.3, p.229)
BREAUX, Adolestin d. 6 Sept. 1898 at age 8 mths. & 11 days (Thib. Ch.: v.3, p.219)
BREAUX, Alaisa (Wilfrid & Joseph OTARD) b. 18 Sept. 1898 (Houma Ch.: v.5, p.230)
BREAUX, Albert m. 10 Feb. 1898 Albertine BOURGEOIS (Thib. Ct. Hse.: Mar. v.37, #71)
BREAUX, Albert (Alidor & Zulema CHAMPAGNE) m. 10 Feb. 1898 Albertine BOURGEOIS (Raceland Ch.: v.2, p.66)
BREAUX, Albert Joseph d. 1 Oct. 1899 at age 6 days (Raceland Ch.: v.1, p.28)
BREAUX, Alcida Althee (Olivain & Augustine LIRETTE) b. 6 Feb. 1898 (Thib. Ch.: v.7, p.483)
BREAUX, Alte d. 2 Jan. 1899 at age 11 mths. (Thib. Ch.: v.3, p.224)
BREAUX, Amadeo m. 15 Jan. 1897 Marie ADAM (Larose Ch.: v.4, p.119-B)
BREAUX, Amadeo m. 15 Jan. 1897 Marie ADAM (Larose Ch.: v.3, p.4)
BREAUX, Amadeo m. 5 Jan. 1897 Mary ADAM (Thib. Ct. Hse.: Mar. v.36, #9)

BREAUX, Anastasie (Froisin & Mathilde LEDET) m. 20 April 1897 Edouard SHEXNAYDER (Thib. Ct. Hse.: Mar. v.36, #112)
BREAUX, Anastasie (Froisin & Nathalie LEDET) m. 20 April 1897 Edouard SCHANYDER (Thib. Ch.: v.14, p.137)
BREAUX, Angele (Luffroy & Mathilde LEBLANC) m. 20 Oct. 1896 Elles LEDET (Thib. Ct. Hse.: Mar. v.36, #154)
BREAUX, Anitta Josephine (Camille & Marie Louise OCHMICHEN) b. 12 July 1898 (Thib. Ch.: v.7, p.505)
BREAUX, Anna (Ernest & Justine BROWN) b. 2 Dec. 1898 (Raceland Ch.: v.5, p.85)
BREAUX, Apoline Dela (Pierre & Camillia DUAY) b. 9 Feb. 1898 (Larose Ch.: v.3, p.16)
BREAUX, Arthur (Benjamin & Marie GAUBERT) m. 30 Aug. 1897 Adela GUILLOT (Thib. Ct. Hse.: Mar. v.37, #223)
BREAUX, Arthur (Benjamin & Marie GAUBERT) m. 30 Aug. 1897 Adela GUILLOTE (Thib. Ch.: v.14, p.159)
BREAUX, Arthur (Joseph & Aimee LAGRANGE) d. 14 Aug. 1896 at age 18 yrs. (Houma Ch.: v.3, p.8)
BREAUX, Augusta (Augustin & Marie LEBLANC) m. 16 Feb. 1898 Theophile GAUBERT (Thib. Ch.: v.14, p.191)
BREAUX, Augusta (Augustin & Marie LEBLANC) m. 16 Feb. 1898 Theophile GAUBERT (Thib. Ct. Hse.: Mar. v.37, #81)
BREAUX, Augusta (Clay & Euphemie MOREAU) m. 14 Oct. 1897 Andre TOUPS (Thib. Ch.: v.14, p.163)
BREAUX, Augusta (Clay & Euphemie MOREAU) m. 14 Oct. 1897 Andre TOUPS (Thib. Ct. Hse.: Mar. v.37, #247)
BREAUX, Augusta (Felicien & Louise BABIN) m. 18 Jan. 1896 Charles FALGOUT (Lockport Ch.: v.2, p.149)
BREAUX, Augusta (Felicien & Louise BABIN) m. 18 Jan. 1896 Charles FALGOUT (Thib. Ct. Hse.: Mar. v.35, #191)
BREAUX, Augustine (Felicien & Louise BABIN) m. 11 Feb. 1899 Albert F. GERVAIS (Thib. Ct. Hse.: Mar. v.38, #72)
BREAUX, Augustine (Felicien & Louise BABIN) m. 11 Feb. 1899 Albert GERVAIS (Lockport Ch.: v.2, p.203)
BREAUX, Benjamin Joseph (Eugene & Cecilia GAUBERT) b. 19 Dec. 1898 (Thib. Ch.: v.7, p.527)
BREAUX, Bernard d. 19 July 1896 at age about 55 yrs. (Houma Ch.: v.3, p.8)
BREAUX, Camilla Annie (Alfred & Camilla THIBODAUX) b. 3 Dec. 1899 (Thib. Ch.: v.7, p.578)
BREAUX, Cecilia minor over 18 Emancipation: 30 June 1898. (Thib. Ct. Hse.: Succ. #1517)
BREAUX, Cecilia (Aurelien & Ernestine ROGER) m. 31 Jan. 1899 Edgard HEBERT (Thib. Ct. Hse.: Mar. v.38, #30)
BREAUX, Cecilia (Aurelien & Ernestine ROGER) m. 31 Jan. 1899 Edgard HEBERT (Thib. Ch.: v.14, p.250)
BREAUX, Charles d. 16 Dec. 1896 at age 2 days (Thib. Ch.: v.3, p.192)
BREAUX, Charley d. 10 Sept. 1896 (Houma Ch.: v.3, p.9)
BREAUX, Clara (Gratien & Clara HEBERT) m. 15 Feb. 1897 Joseph UZE (Thib. Ch.: v.14, p.124)

BREAUX, Clara (Gratien & Clara HEBERT) m. 15 Feb. 1897 Joseph UZE (Thib. Ct. Hse.: Mar. v.36, #58)
BREAUX, Clinton Paul (Aurelien & Armance MARONGE) b. 1 Dec. 1898 (Thib. Ch.: v.7, p.524)
BREAUX, Clotilde (Donat & Camilia BARBIER) m. 25 April 1896 Oscar GERVAIS (Thib. Ct. Hse.: Mar. v.35, #72)
BREAUX, Clovis d. 4 April 1896 at age 37 yrs. (Lockport Ch.: v.1, #10)
BREAUX, Colastie m. David BABIN d. 21 July 1897 at age 74 yrs. (Lockport Ch.: v.1, #15)
BREAUX, Curtis Guilbert (Guilbert & Louise BONVILLAIN) b. 17 Nov. 1896 (Houma Ch.: v.5, p.167)
BREAUX, Dasas Jean (Albert & Celestine PLAISANCE) b. 22 Feb. 1897 (Larose Ch.: v.3, p.13)
BREAUX, Dora m. 8 May 1897 John KING (Houma Ct. Hse.: Mar. v.29 & 30, #407)
BREAUX, Dora (Frederick & Louise ESCHETE) m. 20 May 1897 John KING (Houma Ch.: v.6-a, p.202)
BREAUX, Early d. 8 Dec. 1899 at age 3 yrs. (Houma Ch.: v.3, p.26)
BREAUX, Edgar m. 3 Jan. 1898 Bernadette PICHOFF (Thib. Ct. Hse.: Mar. v.37, #270)
BREAUX, Edmond d. 24 Aug. 1898 at birth (Lockport Ch.: v.1, #17)
BREAUX, Edna Eve (Felicien & Irma DEGRIZE) b. 12 July 1897 (Thib. Ch.: v.7, p.458)
BREAUX, Edouard Paul (Henri & Olivier MORVAN) b. 13 July 1896 (Thib. Ch.: v.7, p.408)
BREAUX, Eliza m. Charles LEBLANC d. 1 Oct. 1896 at age 72 yrs. (Lockport Ch.: v.1, #18)
BREAUX, Elles (Joachim & Mathilde HEBERT) m. 29 Jan. 1898 Melia MATHERNE (Lockport Ch.: v.2, p.181)
BREAUX, Ellis (Joachim & Mathilde HEBERT) m. 27 Jan. 1898 Melia MATHERNE (Thib. Ct. Hse.: Mar. v.37, #37)
BREAUX, Elmire (Donat & Camillia BABIN) m. 20 Aug. 1898 Lovincy GERVAIS (Lockport Ch.: v.2, p.193)
BREAUX, Elmire (Donat & Camillia BARBIER) m. 20 Aug. 1898 Lovincy GERVAIS (Thib. Ct. Hse.: Mar. v.38, #235)
BREAUX, Ernest d. 5 Oct. 1898 at age 35 yrs. (Lockport Ch.: v.1, #18)
BREAUX, Ernestine m. 28 July 1897 Willie ROWNTREE (Thib. Ct. Hse.: Mar. v.37, #201)
BREAUX, Ernestine (Clay & Euphemie MOREAU) m. 6 Aug. 1897 Willie ROUNDTREE (Thib. Ch.: v.14, p.156)
BREAUX, Ethelyn Catherine (James M. & Ellida BERTRANT) b. 4 May 1899 (Theriot Ch.: v.2, p.41)
BREAUX, Euphrasine m. Theresile TOUPS d. 26 March 1896 at age 73 yrs. (Lockport Ch.: v.1, #8)
BREAUX, Euphroisine m. Jules SOIGNET d. 23 April 1899 at age 77 yrs. (Thib. Ch.: v.3, p.232)
BREAUX, Felicia (Marcel & Mathilde BABIN) m. 22 April 1896 Lovincy DUET (Thib. Ch.: v.14, p.85)

BREAUX, Felicia (Marcel & Mathilde BABIN) m. 22 April 1896 Lovincy DUET (Thib. Ct. Hse.: Mar. v.35, #63)
BREAUX, Felicien m. 28 Aug. 1897 Marie LOUPE (Thib. Ct. Hse.: Mar. v.37, #221)
BREAUX, Felicien (Pierre & Louisa BABIN) m. 28 Jan. 1897 Eliska ELLIOT (Lockport Ch.: v.2, p.158)
BREAUX, Felicien (Theogene & Mary LAROSE) m. 1 Sept. 1897 Marie LOUPE (Lockport Ch.: v.2, p.167)
BREAUX, Ferjus (Terence & Mathilde FORET) m. 4 Feb. 1899 Adolphine FORET (Lockport Ch.: v.2, p.200)
BREAUX, Ferjus (Terence & Mathilde FORET) m. 4 Feb. 1899 Adolphine FORET (Thib. Ct. Hse.: Mar. v.38, #71)
BREAUX, Franck m. 9 Feb. 1898 Therese BOURGEOIS (Thib. Ct. Hse.: Mar. v.37, #73)
BREAUX, Frank m. 9 Feb. 1898 Therese BOURGEOIS (Thib. Ch.: v.14, p.183)
BREAUX, Freddy d. 22 April 1899 at age 5 yrs. (Thib. Ch.: v.3, p.232)
BREAUX, Frederic Euray (Robert & Zivia LANCON) b. 27 April 1896 (Houma Ch.: v.5, p.177)
BREAUX, Gaston Louis (Joseph & Philomene BORNE) b. 9 Dec. 1898 (Thib. Ch.: v.7, p.524)
BREAUX, Georges Scuddy (Henri & Lovincia MIRE) b. 23 April 1896 (Thib. Ch.: v.7, p.450)
BREAUX, Gilbert Paul (Amadeo & Melie ADAM) b. 13 Feb. 1899 (Larose Ch.: v.3, p.36)
BREAUX, Helene Louise d. 14 Jan. 1897 at age 21 yrs. (Thib. Ch.: v.3, p.195)
BREAUX, Henri (Luffroy & Mathilde LEBLANC) m. 26 April 1897 Octavie DALFERES (Lockport Ch.: v.2, p.162)
BREAUX, Henri (Luffroy & Mathilde LEBLANC) m. 26 April 1897 Octavie DALFERES (Thib. Ct. Hse.: Mar. v.36, #122)
BREAUX, Henriette Vivian (Henri & Lovincia MIRE) b. 14 Oct. 1898 (Thib. Ch.: v.7, p.517)
BREAUX, Hippolyte d. 6 Feb. 1898 at age 42 yrs. (Raceland Ch.: v.1, p.17)
BREAUX, Jean Adolestin (Arthur & Adele GUILLOTE) b. 26 Dec. 1897 (Thib. Ch.: v.7, p.478)
BREAUX, Jean Isa (Jules & Aimee HEBERT) b. 24 June 1896 (Houma Ch.: v.5, p.183)
BREAUX, Jean Tressi (Theodule & Odillia HEBERT) b. 20 Oct. 1897 (Larose Ch.: v.3, p.14)
BREAUX, John Nolen (Orphee & Lylia BERGERON) b. 24 Nov. 1897 (Thib. Ch.: v.7, p.476)
BREAUX, Joseph (Paul & Lucinda MONTE) m. 16 Jan. 1896 Nirah CHIASSON (Lockport Ch.: v.2, p.148)
BREAUX, Joseph (Paul & Luncida MONTE) m. 16 January 1896 Novah CHIASSON (Thib. Ct. Hse.: Mar. Vol.35, #9)
BREAUX, Joseph Albert (Basile & Eve FIELDS) b. 8 April 1898 (Montegut Ch.: v.6, p.71)

BREAUX, Joseph Albert (Bazile & Eve FIELDS) d. 6 March 1899 at age 11 mths. (Montegut Ch.: v.2, p.24)
BREAUX, Joseph Alexandre (Felix & Marie GAUBERT) b. 18 April 1896 (Thib. Ch.: v.7, p.399)
BREAUX, Joseph Ellis (Basile & Eva FIELDS) d. 15 July 1896 at age 50 days (Montegut Ch.: v.2, p.5)
BREAUX, Joseph Ellis Neuville (Brazile & Eve FIELDS) b. 26 May 1896 (Montegut Ch.: v.6, p.41)
BREAUX, Joseph Enet (Froisin & Nathalie LEDET) m. 17 Jan. 1898 Philomene BORNE (Thib. Ch.: v.14, p.169)
BREAUX, Joseph Enet (Froisin & Nathalie LEDET) m. 17 Jan. 1898 Philomene BORNE (Thib. Ct. Hse.: Mar. v.37, #34)
BREAUX, Joseph Eucle Valery (Wuilfred & Josephine HOTARD) b. 4 May 1896 (Lockport Ch.: v.2, p.331)
BREAUX, Joseph Gaston (Alfred & Camilla THIBODAUX) b. 29 July 1897 (Thib. Ch.: v.7, p.459)
BREAUX, Joseph Jacques Alexis (Henri & Olivia MORVANT) b. 10 June 1899 (Thib. Ch.: v.7, p.606)
BREAUX, Joseph Lewis Osy (Eba & Josephine TRAHAN) b. 6 May 1899 (Thib. Ch.: v.7, p.604)
BREAUX, Joseph Marcel Adrien (Marcel & Armina GUEDRY) b. 28 Feb. 1897 (Thib. Ch.: v.7, p.442)
BREAUX, Joseph Roland (Anatole & Laura LAGARDE) b. 16 March 1896 (Thib. Ch.: v.7, p.396)
BREAUX, Joseph Wallace (Brazile & Eve FIELDS) b. 26 May 1896 (Montegut Ch.: v.6, p.41)
BREAUX, Josephine (Joachim & Mathilde HEBERT) m. 1 May 1897 Octave DUFRENE (Lockport Ch.: v.2, p.166)
BREAUX, Josephine (Joachim & Mathilde HEBERT) m. 1 Ma 1897 Octave DUFRENE (Thib. Ct. Hse.: Mar. v.36, #108)
BREAUX, Julien Fernand (Oscar & Olinda MOUTARDIER) b. 6 Dec. 1896 (Montegut Ch.: v.6, p.48)
BREAUX, Leo m. 11 Aug. 1897 Mary MATHERNE (Lockport Ch.: v.2, p.165)
BREAUX, Leo m. 11 Sept. 1897 Mary MATHERN (Thib. Ct. Hse.: Mar. v.37, #217)
BREAUX, Leonel Camille (Henri & Olivia MORVANT) b. 24 May 1897 (Thib. Ch.: v.7, p.499)
BREAUX, Leontine m. Ozemee NAQUIN Children: Edna Marie b. 16 April 1884; Agnes Aline b. 20 Jan. 1886; Pauline Therese b. 11 June 1889; Lucile Marie b. 18 Sept. 1891. Tutorship decree: 11 Jan. 1899. (Thib. Ct. Hse.: Succ. #1369)
BREAUX, Louis d. 14 Aug. 1899 at age 73 yrs. (Lockport Ch.: v.1, #34)
BREAUX, Louis Paul Francois (Jean & Augusta LIRETTE) b. 4 Oct. 1899 (Thib. Ch.: v.7, p.567)
BREAUX, Louisiane (Pierre & Julienne BABIN) m. 25 Jan. 1899 Louis AUGUSTIN (Thib. Ct. Hse.: Mar. v.38, #46)
BREAUX, Louisiane (Pierre & Julienne BABIN) m. 25 Jan. 1899 Louis Augustin BOURGEOIS (Thib. Ch.: v.14, p.245)

BREAUX, Luc of Lafourche Parish (Amadeo & Daisie BOUDREAUX) m. 1 Aug. 1898 Eugenie LEJEUNE of Lafourche Parish (Larose Ch.: v.3, p.10)

BREAUX, Luc (Amadeo & Daisie BOUDREAUX) m. 1 Aug. 1898 Eugenie LEJEUNE (Larose Ch.: v.4, p.27)

BREAUX, Luc Anidas (Wilfrid & Leotitia THIBODAUX) b. 18 Oct. 1897 (Thib. Ch.: v.7, p.469)

BREAUX, Luc Armand (Albert & Celestine PLAISANCE) b. 15 Jan. 1899 (Larose Ch.: v.3, p.35)

BREAUX, Luke (Amadeo & Daisie BOUDREAU) m. 1 Aug. 1898 Eugenie LEJEUNE (Thib. Ct. Hse.: Mar. v.38, #229)

BREAUX, Magdeleine Eunice (Arthur & Julia DETILLEAUX) b. 22 July 1898 (Thib. Ch.: v.7, p.556)

BREAUX, Marie m. Emile DOUCET d. 7 Nov. 1899 at age 61 yrs. (Thib. Ch.: v.3, p.243)

BREAUX, Marie (Hippolyte & Louisiane DANTIN) b. 18 Oct. 1896 (Raceland Ch.: v.5, p.34)

BREAUX, Marie Adelia (Emile & Rose BOUDREAUX) b. 22 Nov. 1896 (Houma Ch.: v.5, p.165)

BREAUX, Marie Anne Milisser (Pierre & Camilla DUET) b. 26 Nov. 1899 (Larose Ch.: v.3, p.48)

BREAUX, Marie Annette (Arthur & Adela GUILLOT) b. 15 Feb. 1898 (Thib. Ch.: v.7, p.538)

BREAUX, Marie Cesla (Joseph & Enora CHIASSON) b. 22 Oct. 1896 (Lockport Ch.: v.3-A, #10)

BREAUX, Marie Cesla (Joseph & Eurora CHIASSON) b. 22 Oct. 1896 (Lockport Ch.: v.3, #10)

BREAUX, Marie Ella (Felicien & Irma DUGREZE) b. 17 March 1896 (Thib. Ch.: v.7, p.400)

BREAUX, Marie Esilda (Ernest & Justine BROWN) b. 18 March 1897 (Raceland Ch.: v.5, p.47)

BREAUX, Marie Guerdi (Albert & Albertine BOURGEOIS) b. 10 Feb. 1899 (Thib. Ch.: v.7, p.536)

BREAUX, Marie Iselle Mable (James & Henriette HEBERT) b. 22 Oct. 1898 (Thib. Ch.: v.7, p.520)

BREAUX, Marie Lydia (Felicien & Irma DEGRAIZE) b. 9 Dec. 1898 (Thib. Ch.: v.7, p.527)

BREAUX, Marie May (Wilfred & Marie THIBODAUX) b. 7 May 1898 (Thib. Ch.: v.7, p.548)

BREAUX, Mary Beca (Mioni & Cecilia TRAHAN) b. 11 Jan. 1897 (Houma Ch.: v.5, p.169)

BREAUX, Mathilde m. 18 Jan. 1899 Alfred DUFRENE (Lockport Ch.: v.2, p.198)

BREAUX, Mathilde Aimee (Marcel & Hermina GUIDRY) b. 17 March 1899 (Thib. Ch.: v.7, p.541)

BREAUX, Matile m. 29 Nov. 1898 Alfred DUFRESNE (Thib. Ct. Hse.: Mar. v.38, #313)

BREAUX, Maurice Alcide (Anatole & Laura LAGARDE) b. 20 Aug. 1899 (Thib. Ch.: v.7, p.560)

BREAUX, Menarard (d.Joseph & Aimee LAGRANGE) d. 25 Aug. 1896 at age 16 yrs. (Houma Ch.: v.3, p.8)

BREAUX, Neville d. 2 June 1898 (Thib. Ch.: v.3, p.215)
BREAUX, Oleus (Emile & Rosema BOUDREAUX) b. 20 July 1898 (Houma Ch.: v.5, p.220)
BREAUX, Orphie m. 7 May 1896 Lydia BERGERON (Thib. Ct. Hse.: Mar. v.35, #86)
BREAUX, Orphie (Octave & Irma POTIER) m. 3 Feb. 1898 Lydia BERGERON (Thib. Ch.: v.14, p.179)
BREAUX, Oscar (Octave & Marie ARCEMENT) m. 15 Aug. 1898 Alice MATHERNE (Houma Ct. Hse.: Mar. v.30 & 31, #78)
BREAUX, Ozeme (Joachim & Mathilde HEBERT) m. 2 Jan. 1896 Sante PICOU (Lockport Ch.: v.2, p.143 & 144)
BREAUX, Ozeme (Joachim & Mathilde HEBERT) m. 22 Jan. 1896 Sante or Semte PICOU (Thib. Ct. Hse.: Mar. v.35, #27)
BREAUX, Pauline (Alfred & Camilla THIBODAUX) m. 1 Feb. 1899 Henri NAQUIN (Thib. Ct. Hse.: Mar. v.38, #50)
BREAUX, Pauline (Alfred & Camilla THIBODAU) m. 1 Feb. 1899 Henri NAQUIN (Thib. Ch.: v.14, p.253)
BREAUX, Peym Thomas (Paul & Augusta PARR) b. 5 June 1896 (Lockport Ch.: v.2, p.330)
BREAUX, Philippe Adam (Aurelien & Alexina LADOUCEUR) b. 8 Dec. 1897 (Thib. Ch.: v.7, p.486)
BREAUX, Pierre (Felicien & Loisa BABIN) m. 28 Jan. 1897 Eliska ELLIOT (Thib. Ct. Hse.: Mar. v.36, #28)
BREAUX, Pierre Voice (Prosper & Aymee LOUP) b. 23 Feb. 1896 (Lockport Ch.: v.2, p.324)
BREAUX, Raoul Felix (Felix & Louise AYCOCK) b. 26 Feb. 1899 (Chacahoula Ch.: v.4, p.21)
BREAUX, Rene Henry (Jules & Emma HEBERT) b. 7 Nov. 1898 (Houma Ch.: v.5, p.235)
BREAUX, Rene Joseph (Felicien & Irma DEGRUISE) b. 12 March 1899 (Thib. Ch.: v.7, p.599)
BREAUX, Rene Joseph (Felix & Louise AYCOCK) b. 2 March 1897; bt. 24 April 1897 (Chacahoula Ch.: v.4, p.19)
BREAUX, Robert d. 26 Oct. 1899 at age 38 yrs. (Theriot Ch.: v.1, p.2)
BREAUX, Roberta (Robert & Silvia LONSON) b. 1 Nov. 1898 (Houma Ch.: v.5, p.228)
BREAUX, Roger (Desire & Clemence ROBICHAUX) d. 9 Aug. 1897 at age 27 yrs., an accident at the Mill of Mr. Narcisse ROBICHAUX. (Montegut Ch.: v.2, p.11)
BREAUX, Rose Helene (Roger & Lucie CHAUVIN) b. 6 March 1898 (Montegut Ch.: v.6, p.66)
BREAUX, Sidney Evans (Auban & Ernestine LEONARD) b. 9 Dec. 1899 (Houma Ch.: v.5, p.239)
BREAUX, Snider Cecile (Wilfred & Josephine HOTARD) b. 18 Sept. 1897 (Houma Ch.: v.4, p.251)
BREAUX, Valerie Azelie (Felix & Heletia GAUBERT) b. 2 Nov. 1899 (Thib. Ch.: v.7, p.573)
BREAUX, Valery d. 26 Nov. 1896 at age 69 yrs. (Lockport Ch.: v.1, #23)

BREAUX, Viola Marie (Guilbert & Louise BONVILLAIN) b. 28 Oct. 1899 (Theriot Ch.: v.2, p.53)
BREAUX, W. Mrs. d. 7 Feb. 1897 at age 70 yrs. (Lockport Ch.: v.1, #5)
BREAUX, Wallace minor, over 18 Emancipation: 7 April 1899. (Thib. Ct. Hse.: Succ. #1572)
BREAUX, Welly d. 26 Nov. 1896 at age 30 yrs. (Thib. Ch.: v.3, p.190)
BREAUX, Wilfred d. 20 Jan. 1898 at age 34 yrs. (Lockport Ch.: v.1, #33)
BREAUX, Xavier Paul (Ernest & Mary Ann EDOUARD) b. 22 March 1896 (Houma Ch.: v.5, p.177)
BRENT, Tempy m. William BRENT Children listed: Bernett m. Alex WILLIAMS; Anthony m. Renette ADAMS; Celia Ann m. John STOBALL. Sworn testimony: 10 Nov. 1899. (Houma Ct. Hse.: Succ. #927)
BREUX, Paul Etienne (Octave & Marie ARSEMA) b. 2 Sept. 1896 (Thib. Ch.: v.7, p.421)
BREZILLAC, Michel (Michel & Antoinette JONEY) m. 24 June 1899 Berthilde HEBERT (Houma Ct. Hse.: Mar. v.31 & 32, #50-A)

BRIANT (Sometimes: BRIAN, BRIEN)

BRIANT, Claude Paul (Serguis & Aimee DORSEY) b. 13 May 1896 (Thib. Ch.: v.7, p.407)
BRIANT, Helena formerly married to WATKINS m. 18 Dec. 1896 Ulysse J. THERIOT (Houma Ct. Hse.: Mar. v.29 & 30, #205)
BRIANT, Helene m. 17 Feb. 1897 Alfred BERGERON (Houma Ct. Hse.: Mar. v.29 & 30, #314)
BRIANT, Helene (Amede & Adolphine LAJAUNIE) m. 25 Feb. 1897 Alfred BERGERON (Theriot Ch.: v.1, p.10)
BRIANT, John Charles (Paul E. & Angele HAYDEL) m. 23 Jan. 1897 Mary Loulie JONES (Houma Ct. Hse.: Mar. v.29 & 30, #253)
BRIANT, Joseph Alfred (Amedie & Adolphine LAJAUNIE) b. 28 Feb. 1896; m. 12 Oct. 1942 to Osey DAIGLE. (Theriot Ch.: Bapt. Bk., v.1-B, p.88)
BRIANT, Marie Julie (John & Louise BREAUX) b. 17 Dec. 1896 (Lockport Ch.: v.3, #36)
BRIANT, Marie Julie (John & Louise BREAUX) b. 17 Dec. 1896 (Lockport Ch.: v.3-A, #36)
BRIANT, William m. 18 Jan. 1899 Julia CARTER (Thib. Ct. Hse.: Mar. v.38, #33)
BRICKLEY, Joseph (Ralph & Susi BRICKLEY) b. 5 June 1898 (Raceland Ch.: v.5, p.73)
BRICKLEY, Mary m. 13 Jan. 1898 Alcide AYO (Thib. Ct. Hse.: Mar. v.37, #26)
BRIGANTE, Calaggiero (Vincenzo & Bernada DE PALMERO) m. 23 Jan. 1899 Guiseppa STELLONE (Thib. Ct. Hse.: Mar. v.38, #29)

BRIGANTE, Caloggino (Vincenzo & Bernada DI PALERMA) m. 23 Jan. 1899 Guiseppa STEELONE (Thib. Ch.: v.14, p.243)
BRIGGS, Kate Nelly (James & Virginie GRIMA) b. 14 Oct. 1898 (Thib. Ch.: v.7, p.571)
BRINKLEY, William (William & Lilly BURNS) b. 15 Feb. 1898 (Chacahoula Ch.: Gibson Ch.: v.2, p.121)
BRINKLEY, William (William & Lily BURNS) b. 15 Feb. 1898 (Chacahoula Ch.: Gibson Records: Mar. Bk., v.1, #34)
BRONI, Rosa (Dominique & Josephine MANNINE) b. 12 Nov. 1898 (Thib. Ch.: v.7, p.578)
BROOKS, Abraham m. 29 April 1896 Pinkey HARRIS (Houma Ct. Hse.: Mar. v.29 & 30, #46)
BROOKS, Bessie m. 16 Jan. 1896 A. John WILLIAMS (Houma Ct. Hse.: Mar. v.28, #398)
BROOKS, Indiana m. 5 Feb. 1898 Thomas MELANCON (Thib. Ct. Hse.: Mar. v.37, #75)
BROOKS, Martha m. 2 Nov. 1899 Ephraim DONALDSON (Houma Ct. Hse.: Mar v.31 & 32, #159)
BROOKS, Nathan m. 1 Oct. 1896 Delia DICKERSON (Thib. Ct. Hse.: Mar. v.36, #150)
BROOKS, Oscar m. 8 Jan. 1897 Nellie BARROW (Thib. Ct. Hse.: Mar. v.36, #15)
BROOKS, Rebecca m. 15 Dec. 1898 Eddie TURNER (Houma Ct. Hse.: Mar. v.30 & 31, #148)
BROOM, George m. 17 July 1897 Odelia CHARLES (Thib. Ct. Hse.: Mar. v.37, #195)
BROOMFIELD, Fred Jr. m. 6 July 1897 Laura TURNER (Houma Ct. Hse.: Mar. v.29 & 30, #51)
BROOMFIELD, Frederick m. 10 May 1898 Maria WATKINS (Houma Ct. Hse.: Mar. v.30 &31, #436)
BROUSSARD, Bernard Leon (Louis & Elfejar DARDAR) b. 11 April 1896 (Larose Ch.: v.2, p.195)
BROUSSARD, Dassas m. 27 Jan. 1897 Lucille HEBERT (Thib. Ct. Hse.: Mar. v.36, #57)
BROUSSARD, Louis m. 23 July 1896 Elfeijar DARDAR (Larose Ch.: v.4, p.69)
BROUSSARD, Louis m. 23 July 1896 Elfezas DARDAR (Larose Ch.: v.3, p.3)
BROUSSARD, Sylvanie Marie Julie (Louis & Elphega DARDAR) b. 9 Jan. 1898 (Larose Ch.: v.3, p.20)
BROUSSARD, Themir Josephine (Louis & Elpheja DARDA) b. 5 Oct. 1899 (Larose Ch.: v.3, p.48)
BROWN, Agathe d. 27 Jan. 1897 at age 5 yrs. (Thib. Ch.: v.3, p.195)
BROWN, Agathe (Albert & Evaina SAPIER) b. 12 Oct. 1899 (Raceland Ch.: v.5, p.103)
BROWN, Albert d. 8 Nov. 1899 at age 4 wks. (Raceland Ch.: v.1, p.28)
BROWN, Albert m. 29 May 1897 Petronille SAPIA (Thib. Ct. Hse.: Mar. v.36, #151)

BROWN, Albert (Robert & Clara BOURGEOIS) m. 12 June 1897 Petronille SAPIER (Raceland Ch.: v.2, p.42)
BROWN, Annie m. 4 Jan. 1899 Philip GRAY (Thib. Ct. Hse.: Mar. v.38, #4)
BROWN, Armogilde d. 25 Jan. 1897 at age 3 yrs. (Thib. Ch.: v.3, p.195)
BROWN, Bartley m. 1 June 1899 Lettie SANDERS (Thib. Ct. Hse.: Mar. v.39, #174)
BROWN, Benny m. 29 March 1897 Mary LANDRY (Thib. Ct. Hse.: Mar. v.36, #103)
BROWN, Clara m. 5 Dec. 1898 Frank JACKSON (Thib. Ct. Hse.: Mar. v.38, #315)
BROWN, Cora m. 9 Jan. 1899 Arthur DENNIS (Houma Ct. Hse.: Mar. v.30 & 31, #196)
BROWN, Edmund m. 10 March 1898 Geneva RAINEY (Houma Ct. Hse.: Mar. v.30 & 31, #333)
BROWN, Elizabeth m. 8 March 1897 Lazarus DUBOUE (Thib. Ct. Hse.: Mar. v.36, #95)
BROWN, Esther Lucretia (Gaspar & Lalie PADELIA) b. 14 Aug. 1896 (Larose Ch.: v.2, p.185)
BROWN, Eugene John (Joseph & Henriette GAUDEAU) b. 5 Aug. 1897 (Houma Ch.: v.5, p.180)
BROWN, Hannah m. 26 Dec. 1899 Thomas PERKINS (Houma Ct. Hse.: Mar. v.31 & 32, #200)
BROWN, Hattie m. 8 March 1899 John COLLINS (Thib. Ct. Hse.: Mar. v.39, #116)
BROWN, Helene (Joseph & Helene BARBIER) b. 15 April 1896 (Lockport Ch.: v.2, p.328)
BROWN, Jake m. 7 July 1898 Emma VERNON (Thib. Ct. Hse.: Mar. v.38, #222)
BROWN, Joachim (Nelson & Theresa JOACHIM) m. 20 May 1896 Emelie HENRY (Houma Ct. Hse.: Mar. v.29 & 30, #76)
BROWN, Joachim (Nelson & Theresa JOACHIM) m. 8 June 1896 Emelie HENRY (Montegut Ch.: v.4, p.211)
BROWN, Joseph m. 28 Dec. 1896 Mally BANKS (Thib. Ct. Hse.: Mar. v.36, #172)
BROWN, Joseph m. 4 Oct. 1898 Louvinia THIBODAUX (Thib. Ct. Hse.: Mar. v.38, #287)
BROWN, Joseph Clarance (Joachim & Emelie HENRI) b. 23 Oct. 1899 (Montegut Ch.: v.6, p.97)
BROWN, Joseph Gester (Joachim & Emelie HENRY) b. 26 Jan. 1897 (Montegut Ch.: v.6, p.55)
BROWN, Joseph Philippe (John & Julie UZE) b. 14 Nov. 1898 (Thib. Ch.: v.7, p.521)
BROWN, Lemuel m. 26 Jan. 1899 Mary JACKSON (Houma Ct. Hse.: Mar. v.30 & 31, #286)
BROWN, Lettie m. 5 Aug. 1899 Willie THRON (Thib. Ct. Hse.: Mar. v.39, #188)
BROWN, Louisa m. 3 March 1898 Richard MOORE (Houma Ct. Hse.: Mar. v.30 & 31, #327)

BROWN, Lulu m. 12 Oct. 1899 Charley COURTNEY (Houma Ct. Hse.: Mar. v.31 & 32, #148)
BROWN, Luther m. 22 Jan. 1898 Elizabeth WHEELER (Thib. Ct. Hse.: Mar. v.37, #43)
BROWN, Mable Brigitte (Charley & Marie TOUPS) b. 6 Feb. 1898 (Thib. Ch.: v.7, p.487)
BROWN, Marguerite Jeanette (Joseph & Henriette GOUDEAU) b. 1 May 1898 (Houma Ch.: v.5, p.244)
BROWN, Marie Alzina (Joachim & Amelie HENRY) b. 2 Feb. 1898 (Montegut Ch.: v.6, p.70)
BROWN, Marie Brigitte (Argus & Ophelia BOURGEOIS) b. 10 March 1897 (Raceland Ch.: v.5, p.43)
BROWN, Marie Josephine (John & Julie UZE) b. 12 Dec. 1896 (Thib. Ch.: v.7, p.430)
BROWN, Matoheogene (Charley & Marie TOUPS) b. 14 May 1896 (Thib. Ch.: v.7, p.402)
BROWN, Matthews m. 14 April 1898 Bella WILLIAMS (Thib. Ct. Hse.: Mar. v.38, #155)
BROWN, Nelson m. 25 April 1898 Julia CHARLES (Thib. Ct. Hse.: Mar. v.38, #167)
BROWN, Oliver m. 26 May 1897 Gertrude LEVRON (Thib. Ct. Hse.: Mar. v.36, #150)
BROWN, Rosa m. 3 March 1898 Rosa BROWN (Houma Ct. Hse.: Mar. v.30 & 31, #323)
BROWN, Simon d. 15 Aug. 1896 (Houma Ch.: Epis. Ch.: v.1, p.386)
BROWN, Timothy m. 2 Aug. 1897 Cora FRANCIS (Houma Ct. Hse.: Mar. v.29 & 30, #78)
BROWN, Wash. m. 15 Sept. 1897 Mary WINSLOW (Houma Ct. Hse.: Mar. v.29 & 30, #91)
BROWN, William m. 21 Feb. 1898 Loulie NOLAS (Houma Ct. Hse.: Mar. v.30 & 31, #317)
BROWN, William Henry m. 11 Oct. 1897 Frankie WHITE (Houma Ct. Hse.: Mar. v.29 & 30, #121)
BROWN, William Henry m. 23 Jan. 1899 Carrie E. WILLIAMS (Houma Ct. Hse.: Mar. v.30 & 31, #280)
BROWN, Willie m. 16 April 1898 James CLARK (Houma Ct. Hse.: Mar. v.30 & 31, #405)
BROWNLEE, Laurel A. (Alexandre & Mary P. PEARL) m. 3 Nov. 1896 Mary CLEMENT (Houma Ct. Hse.: Mar. v.29 & 30, #185)
BROWNLEE, Pearl Adeline (L. Augustin & Marie CLEMENT) b. 18 Sept. 1897 (Houma Ch.: v.5, p.204)
BROYL, Primas m. 1 June 1899 Ana HARRIET (Houma Ct. Hse.: Mar. v.31 & 32, #65)
BRUBACHER, Marie Amelie (Robert D. & Cecilia JOUCLAS) b. 5 Nov. 1899 (Raceland Ch.: v.5, p.106)

BRUCE (Sometimes: BRUSE, BRUZE)

BRUCE, Aglae m. Jules MELANCON d. 26 Oct. 1898 at age 72 yrs. (Larose Ch.: v.1, p.44)

BRUCE, Aglonie of Lafourche Parish (Adam & Eulalie PIERCE) m. 8 June 1898 Felix PITRE, of Lafourche Parish (Larose Ch.: v.3, p.9)
BRUCE, Aglonie (Adam & Eulalie PIERCE) m. 8 June 1898 Felix PITRE (Thib. Ct. Hse.: Mar. v. 38, #198)
BRUCE, Aglonie (Adam & Eulalie PIERCE) m. 8 June 1898 Felix PITRE (Larose Ch.: v.4, p.15)
BRUCE, Aimand (Adam & Eulalie PIERCE) m. 23 Jan. 1899 Alice CRETINI (Larose Ch.: v.4, p.33)
BRUCE, Albert m. 6 June 1896 Pauline DANOS (Larose Ch.: v.4, p.98)
BRUCE, Albert m. 6 June 1896 Pauline DANOS (Larose Ch.: v.3, p.3)
BRUCE, Albert (Adam & Eulalie PIERCE) m. 6 June 1896 Pauline DANOS (Thib. Ct. Hse.: Mar. v.35, #95)
BRUCE, Armand (Adam & Eulalie PIERCE) m. 23 Jan. 1899 Alice CRETINI (Thib. Ct. Hse.: Mar. v.38, #38)
BRUCE, Armand (Adam & Eulalie PIERCE) m. 23 Jan. 1899 Alice CRETINI (Larose Ch.: v.3, p.11)
BRUCE, David d. 22 Sept. 1899 at age 33 yrs. (Larose Ch.: v.1, p.54)
BRUCE, Elvire Jeanne (Alcindor & Julia SAVOIE) b. 10 Dec. 1898 (Larose Ch.: v.3, p.30)
BRUCE, Etienne Jules (Joachim & Emilia SAVOIE) b. 24 Dec. 1899 (Larose Ch.: v.3, p.51)
BRUCE, Evia Marie (David & Clementine PLAISANCE) b. 1 Nov. 1899 (Larose Ch.: v.3, p.48)
BRUCE, Jean m. 19 June 1897 Odillia DANTIN (Larose Ch.: v.4, p.63)
BRUCE, Jean m. 29 May 1897 Odillia DANTIN (Thib. Ct. Hse.: Mar. v.36, #154)
BRUCE, John m. 19 June 1897 Odillia HAUTIN (Larose Ch.: v.3, p.6)
BRUCE, Leon (Salomon & Flore PERILLO) m. 15 June 1898 Delfine MORVAN (Thib. Ct. Hse.: Mar. v.38, #199)
BRUCE, Lolitte of Lafourche Parish (Joachim & Pauline RAYMOND) m. 25 April 1898 Pierre TERREBONNE, of Lafourche Parish (Larose Ch.: v.3, p.9)
BRUCE, Lolitte (Joachim & Pauline RAYMOND) m. 25 April 1898 Pierre TERREBONNE (Thib. Ct. Hse.: Mar. v.38, #161)
BRUCE, Lolitte (Joachim & Pauline RAYMOND) m. 25 April 1898 Pierre TERREBONNE (Larose Ch.: v.4, p.13)
BRUCE, Maria Stella (Joachim & Melia SAVOIE) b. 1 Dec. 1897 (Larose Ch.: v.3, p.15)
BRUCE, Olestine Philomene (Jean & Odillia AUTIN) b. 15 June 1898 (Larose Ch.: v.3, p.22)
BRUCE, Ulgeline Genevieve (Albert & Pauline DANOS) b. 3 Jan. 1899 (Larose Ch.: v.3, p.35)
BRUCE, Vital Gaetan (Albert & Pauline DANOS) b. 7 Aug. 1897 (Larose Ch.: v.3, p.9)

BRUNET (Sometimes: BRUNE, BRUNEE)

BRUNET, Andre Albert (Elie Gaudet & Marie BLANCHARD) b. 11 May 1899 (Theriot Ch.: v.2, p.37)

BRUNET, Annette Eleonore (Lucien & Berthe DUPLANTIS) b. 12 Nov. 1897 (Theriot Ch.: v.2, p.13)

BRUNET, Augustin Ambroise (Felicien & Felecie PELEGRIN) b. 28 Aug. 1897 (Theriot Ch.: v.2, p.9)

BRUNET, Emilia (Armand & Constance LEDET) b. 17 Aug. 1897 (Larose Ch.: v.3, p.9)

BRUNET, Ermine (Armand & Constance LEDET) b. 18 Feb. 1899 (Larose Ch.: v.3, p.40)

BRUNET, Eugenie Olimpe (Lucien & Berthe DUPLANTIS) b. 31 Oct. 1899 (Theriot Ch.: v.2, p.54)

BRUNET, Eva (Theodule & Marie BOUDREAU) m. 13 Jan. 1896 Leo DUPRE (Theriot Ch.: v.1, p.6)

BRUNET, Felicia Bernadette (Cleophat & Evelina AUCOIN) b. 9 June 1896 (Montegut Ch.: v.6, p.41)

BRUNET, Gilbert Elie (Elie V. & Marie BLANCHARD) b. 24 April 1897 (Theriot Ch.: v.2, p.3)

BRUNET, Israel Adam (Felicien & Felicie PELEGRIN) b. 14 June 1896 (Theriot Ch.: v.1-B, p.98)

BRUNET, Ives Fortune (Theles & Josephine CANTRELLE) b. 12 Sept. 1898 (Larose Ch.: v.3, p.28)

BRUNET, Jean Francois Dennis (John & Georgiana DUMOUT) b. 16 April 1896 (Theriot Ch.: v.1-B, p.96)

BRUNET, Jean Rodolphe (Teles & Josephine CANTRELLE) b. 9 May 1896 (Larose Ch.: v.2, p.191 & p.200, #43)

BRUNET, Jean Rodolphe (Teles & Josephine CANTRELLE) b. 9 May 1896 (Larose Ch.: v.2, p.183 & p.223, #129)

BRUNET, Joseph (John) d. 16 Aug. 1896 at age 10 mths. (Theriot Ch.: Mar. Bk., v.1, #2)

BRUNET, Joseph (John) d. 16 Aug. 1896 at age 10 mths. (Theriot Ch.: v.1, p.101)

BRUNET, Joseph Adam (Jean & Georgiana DUMONT) b. 11 May 1897 (Theriot Ch.: v.2, p.4)

BRUNET, Joseph Clarence (Jimmy & Henriette HEBERT) b. 12 Sept. 1896 (Thib. Ch.: v.7, p.418)

BRUNET, Joseph Eleste (Cletus & Clotilde DUMONT) b. 31 July 1897 (Theriot Ch.: v.2, p.10)

BRUNET, Joseph Elie (Cleophat & Evelina AUCOIN) b. 25 Aug. 1898 (Montegut Ch.: v.6, p.76)

BRUNET, Julie (Theodule & Marie BOUDREAU) m. 19 Oct. 1896 Ludger BENOIT (Houma Ch.: v.6-a, p.183)

BRUNET, Julie (Theodule & Marie BOUDREAUX) m. 15 Oct. 1896 Ludger BENOIT (Houma Ct. Hse.: Mar. v.29 & 30, #169)

BRUNET, Marie Eve (Ulysse & Celestine MATHERNE) b. 30 July 1897 (Montegut Ch.: v.6, p.59)

BRUNET, Paul (Baptiste & Eliska LEBEUF) m. 21 Nov. 1896 Victoria PELEGRIN (Houma Ct. Hse: Mar. v.29 & 30, #189)

BRUNET, Theodore (Jean B. & Eliska LEBOEUF) m. 22 April 1899 Marie LEBOEUF (Houma Ct. Hse.: Mar. v.31 & 32, #412)

BRUNET, Theodore (Jean Baptiste & Eliska LEBOEUF) m. 15 May 1899 Marie LEBOEUF (Montegut Ch.: v.4, p.263)
BRUNET, Wilda d. 18 March 1898 at age 11 yrs. (Theriot Ch.: v.1, p.1)
BRUNO, Domenico (Trofrico & Rosalia CANGGIEMI) m. 3 Sept. 1898 Guiseppa MANINO (Thib. Ct. Hse.: Mar. v.38, #242)
BRUNO, Dominico (Inoffrico & Rosalia CAUGGIEMI) m. 3 Sept. 1898 Guiseppa MANINO (Thib. Ch.: v.14, p.217)
BRUNO, Dominique (Andrea & Rosalia ELEVAFI) b. 1 Jan. 1899 (Raceland Ch.: v.5, p.89)
BRUNO, Marie (Dominico & Francisca RECILA) b. 20 March 1899 (Raceland Ch.: v.5, p.94)
BRUPBACHER, Jean Joseph (Robert & Cecile JOUCLAN) b. 10 Feb. 1898 (Raceland Ch.: v.5, p.66)
BRYAN, Olivia m. 7 April 1898 Charles PARKER (Thib. Ct. Hse.: Mar. v.37, #144)
BUBSER, Joseph m. Evela OLIVIER, d. 24 June 1891. Children: Amelie, 7; Joseph, 6; Manuel, 5. Tutorship: 17 June 1896. (Houma Ct. Hse.: Succ. #848)
BUCHALA, Giovannino (Guiseppe & Antonia ALCUORE) b. 24 Oct. 1898 (Houma Ch.: v.5, p.232)
BUCKLEY, Mary m. 27 July 1898 Joseph ADDO (Thib. Ct. Hse.: Mar. v.38, #233)
BUD, Matthew m. 13 Jan. 1898 Louisiana DRUMGOULD (Thib. Ct. Hse.: Mar. v.37, #17)
BUFIGGERIO, Giovanino (Frank & Salvatora GANNOS) m. 10 Sept. 1898 Vincenza UZZO (Thib. Ct. Hse.: Mar. v.38, #257)
BUFIGGERIO, Giovanino (Frank & Salvatora IANNOS) m. 10 Sept. 1898 Vincenza UZZO (Thib. Ch.: v.14, p.222)

BUFORD (Sometimes: BUFFORD)

BUFORD, James D. (Joseph W. & Emily McEVERS) m. 15 April 1896 Catherine FANDALL (Houma Ct. Hse.: Mar. v.29 & 30, #11)
BUFORD, John Howard m. 10 June 1897 Mary FANDAL (Houma Ct. Hse.: Mar. v.29 & 30, #19)
BUMPHELIA, Salva Teresa (Antonia & Marianna GISEPFANIA) b. 15 Sept. 1899 (Thib. Ch.: v.7, p.566)
BUQUET, Albert (Andre & Josephine LAJAUNIE) m. 27 Jan. 1898 Julie LEBLANC (Thib. Ch.: v.14, p.177)
BUQUET, Albert (Andre & Josephine LAJAUNIE) m. 27 Jan. 1898 Julie LEBLANC (Thib. Ct. Hse.: Mar. v.37, #48)
BUQUET, Albert E. d. 4 Feb. 1899 at age 2 mths., 20 days (Houma Ch.: v.3, p.20)
BUQUET, Ceserine d. 2 July 1898 at age 46 yrs., 3 mths. & 3 days (Houma Ch.: v.3, p.17)
BUQUET, Helena widow WATKINS (Joseph & Adeline BABIN) m. 20 Dec. 1896 Ulysse J. THERIOT (Houma Ch.: v.6-a, p.187)
BUQUET, Joseph Andre (Ulisse & Mathilde BABIN) b. 11 Oct. 1897 (Houma Ch.: v.5, p.193)

BUQUET, Laurence m. 30 Dec. 1897 Evelina CLARK (Houma Ct. Hse.: Mar. v.30 & 31, #170)

BUQUET, Lawrence (Andre & Josephine LAJAUNIE) m. 17 Jan. 1898 Evelina CLARK (Houma Ch.: v.6-a, p.221)

BUQUET, Lawrence (Dargus & Exelina CLARK) b. 3 July 1896; m. Cecile HEBERT on 10 Oct. 1923 (Houma Ch.: Bapt. Bk., v.5, p.183)

BUQUET, Lina Marie (Alcide & Octavie SAVOIE) b. 28 June 1896 (Thib. Ch.: v.7, p.414)

BUQUET, Louis (Osemee & Justile LEBLANC) b. 22 Sept. 1897; m. Angelina Brigitte LIRETTE on 26 Nov. 1925. (Houma Ch.: Bapt. Bk., v.5, p.188)

BUQUET, Lucia Gertrude (---- & Exelina CLARK) b. 24 Jan. 1898 (Houma Ch.: v.5, p.232)

BUQUET, Marie Dora (Joseph & Marie BLANCHARD) b. 7 May 1898 (Montegut Ch.: v.6, p.73)

BUQUET, Noeline (Andre & Josephine LAJAUNIE) m. 20 Jan. 1898 Joseph Clifford BUTCHER (Thib. Ch.: v.14, p.171)

BUQUET, Noeline (Andre & Josephine LAJAUNIE) m. 20 Jan. 1898 Joseph Clifford BUTCHER (Houma Ct. Hse.: Mar. v.30 & 31, #188)

BURGUIERES, Camilla m. Alphonse BONVILLAIN Children listed: Arthur; Flavia m. Joseph L. DUHART; Elmira M.; Felix A.; Marshall J.; Alcide J. Petition to put heirs in possession: 28 Aug. 1896. (Houma Ct. Hse.: Succ. #821)

BURK, Georges Hamilton (Hamilton & Augustine SAIMPEY) b. 24 Aug. 1897 (Raceland Ch.: v.5, p.54)

BURKE, Peter E. m. 12 Sept. 1896 Mary A. PENISON (Houma Ct. Hse.: Mar. v.29 & 30, #144)

BURKS, Volumnia m. 23 April 1898 John SCOTT (Houma Ct. Hse.: Mar. v.30 & 31, #413)

BURKS, William m. 1 July 1899 Sarah LYONS (Houma Ct. Hse.: Mar. v.31 & 32, #70)

BURNES, John m. 19 Jan. 1899 Bertha COLEMAN (Houma Ct. Hse.: Mar. v.30 & 31, #270)

BURNS, Benjamin m. 4 Jan. 1896 Josephine EDWARDS (Houma Ct. Hse.: Mar. v.28, #373)

BURNS, Ezelida m. 21 Oct. 1899 Eize CHERAMI (Thib. Ct. Hse.: Mar. v.39, #250)

BURON, Victore d. 13 Feb. 1898 at age 65 yrs. (Houma Ch.: v.3, p.16)

BURREL, Sidney m. 29 June 1899 Louisa HOLMES (Thib. Ct. Hse.: Mar. v.39, #189)

BURRELL, Martha m. 16 Aug. 1898 Ben STEWART (Thib. Ct. Hse.: Mar. v.38, #253)

BURRIGHT, Francis D. A. (Cornelius & d.Jane COBB) m. 25 May 1899 Lorinne CHAUVIN (Montegut Ch.: v.4, p.264)

BURRIGHT, Francis D. A. (Cornelius & June COBB) m. 6 May 1899 Lorine CHAUVIN (Houma Ct. Hse.: Mar. v.31 & 32, #2)

BURSE, Simon m. 17 July 1899 Lizzie ANDERSON (Houma Ct. Hse.: Mar. v.31 & 32, #77)
BURTON, Clarence R. m. 21 June 1897 Helene E. STONE (Thib. Ct. Hse.: Mar. v.36, #178)
BURTON, Clarence R. m. 22 June 1897 Helen E. STONE (Thib. Ch.: Epis. Ch.: v.1, p.331)
BURTON, Thomas Harold (Clarence R. & Helen E. STONE) b. 1 July 1898 (Thib. Ch.: Epis. Ch.: v.1, p.44)
BUSH, Baptiste d. 20 Sept. 1897 at age 55 yrs. (Thib. Ch.: v.3, p.205)
BUSH, Baptiste m. 4 Sept. 1897 Virginia SIMMS (Houma Ct. Hse.: Mar. v.29 & 30, #83)
BUSIELLE, Suzanne Nolan (Eugene & Lusina LESCOT) b. 11 Aug. 1896 (Thib. Ch.: v.7, p.412)
BUTCHER, Charles (Cliford & Noalie BUQUET) b. 19 Oct. 1898 (Thib. Ch.: v.7, p.519)
BUTCHER, Cleontine (Charles & Rosa CHIASSON) m. 9 Jan. 1899 Arthur LEBOEUF (Houma Ct. Hse.: Mar. v.30 & 31, #177)
BUTCHER, Cleontine (Charles & Rosa CHIASSON) m. 9 Jan. 1899 Arthur LEBOEUF (Thib. Ch.: v.14, p.235)
BUTCHER, Joseph Clifford (Charles & Rose BUTCHER) m. 20 Jan. 1898 Noeline BUQUET (Thib. Ch.: v.14, p.171)
BUTCHER, Joseph Clifford (Charles & Rose BUTCHER) m. 20 Jan. 1898 Noeline BUQUET (Houma Ct. Hse.: Mar. v.30 & 31, #188)
BUTCHER, Joseph Roffin (Alix & Josephine WATKIN) b. 12 Nov. 1896; m. Jennie CHAUVIN on 3 Dec. 1917. (Houma Ch.: Bapt. Bk., v.5, p.169)
BUTCHER, Mary (Charles & Rosa CHIASSON) m. 17 Feb. 1897 John CLEMENT (Houma Ct. Hse.: Mar. v.29 & 30, #311)

BUTLER (Sometimes: BUTTLER)

BUTLER, Alexander m. 28 Sept. 1896 Elizabeth LOYER (Houma Ct. Hse.: Mar. v.29 & 30, #160)
BUTLER, Elizabeth Odilia (Loule & Mary SEVIN) b. 18 Sept. 1896 (Lockport Ch.: v.2, p.336)
BUTLER, Ernestine of Lockport (Charles & Sera ANDRE) m. 17 Feb. 1898 Munford or Melford REED, of Lafourche Crossing (Thib. Ct. Hse.: Mar. v.37, #84)
BUTLER, Ernestine (Charles & Sera ANDRE) m. 17 Feb. 1898 Munford REED (Lockport Ch.: v.2, p.186)
BUTLER, Josephine m. 6 Oct. 1898 H. C. SAULSBRY (Houma Ct. Hse.: Mar. v.30 & 31, #118)
BUTLER, Louisa m. 18 Jan. 1899 Richard SEALS (Houma Ct. Hse.: Mar. v.30 & 31, #251)
BUTLER, Marie Agnes (Charles & Sera ANDRE) b. 17 May 1896 (Lockport Ch.: v.2, p.330)
BUTLER, Martha m. 1 Aug. 1898 Joseph YOUNG (Thib. Ct. Hse.: Mar. v.38, #237)
BUTLER, Robt. Boner (Paul H. & Susan A. ROWLEY) m. 7 July 1898 Agnes HARTY (Houma Ch.: Epis. Ch.: v.1, p.342)

BUTLER, Sam m. 13 April 1899 Elizabeth ALLEN (Houma Ct. Hse.: Mar. v.31 & 32, #397)

BUTLER, William m. 20 Jan. 1897 Lucinda FELIX (Thib. Ct. Hse.: Mar. v.36, #44)

BYE, Marie Josephine (Paul & Scholastica MARTIN) b. 11 Feb. 1896 (Thib. Ch.: v.7, p.392)

BYRD, Cyrena m. 10 Aug. 1899 Munson DORSEY (Thib. Ct. Hse.: Mar. v.39, #209)

"C"

CABARIERE, Vancenzo (Dominique & Rose FERILLI) m. 11 Jan. 1897 Pamela VINET (Thib. Ch.: v.14, p.106)
CACCATORA, Angela of Terrebonne Parish m. 12 Dec. 1899 Hypolite GENNARA (Houma Ch.: v.6-B, p.5)
CAECATORA, Angela m. 6 Nov. 1899 Hypolite GENNARD (Houma Ct. Hse.: Mar. v.31 & 32, #165)
CACCIA, Seraphina (Guitrand & Rosa CITRUNA) b. 11 Dec. 1897 (Thib. Ch.: v.7, p.481)
CACCIATORE, Vitia (Antonio & Rosalia MOROSE) b. 23 March 1899 (Houma Ch.: v.5, p.238)
CACIEPPO, Paolo (Tonio & Philippa JAENDA??) m. 11 Jan. 1896 Gacoma LAPUMA (Houma Ch.: v.6-a, p.164)
CACIOPPO, Filippa (Paolo & Giacama LAPUMA) b. 1 April 1897 (Houma Ch.: v.5, p.173)
CADIERE, Eugene m. 4 March 1897 Celema GROS (Thib. Ct. Hse.: Mar. v.36, #94)
CADIERE, Eugene (Oleus & Clementine BABIN) m. 11 March 1897 Celema GROS (Houma Ct. Hse.: Mar. v.30 & 31, #291)
CADIERE, Eugene (Oleus & Clementine BABIN) m. 11 March 1897 Celema GROS (Thib. Ch.: v.14 p.131)
CADIERE, Louis Eugene (Eugene & Celima GROW) b. 15 Nov. 1898 (Houma Ch.: v.5, p.223)
CADIERE, Noel d. 12 Feb. 1897 at age 84 yrs. & 6 mths. (Thib. Ch.: v.3, p.196)
CADOSSO, Carmela (Vincenzo & Maria Antonia CANNINA) b. 26 Nov. 1899 (Thib. Ch.: v.8, p.20)
CAFFERY, Peter m. 8 April 1897 Francis DURNS (Thib. Ct. Hse.: Mar. v.36, #109)
CAGE, Carrie Bisland (Albert G. & Carrie BISLAND) b. 26 Jan. 1897 (Houma Ch.: Epis. Ch.: v.1, p.114)
CAGE, Thomas A. d. Dec. 1896 in New Orleans; m. (1) Clara PARKER; m.(2) Aurena L. WILLIAMS Children listed: (1) marriage: Agnes Rebecca; Carrie m. James HARVEY; (2) marriage: Julius C.; Harold W.; Walter R.; Inez M. Petition for inventory: 20 Jan. 1897. (Houma Ct. Hse.: Succ. #880)
CAGGIOPPE, Philippa (Guisepe & Anna MARGUISE) b. 9 Oct. 1898 (Houma Ch.: v.5, p.229)
CAGLIA, Angelina (Calogero & Rosa CIANGIMINO) b. 12 Sept. 1896 (Chacahoula Ch.: v.4, p.6)
CAGNINA, Charles (John & Maria CHIMON) b. 4 Feb. 1899 (Houma Ch.: v.5, p.234)

CAILLOUET (Sometimes: CAILHOUET, CAILLOUETTE, CALLOUET)

CAILLOUET, Berthe (Joseph & d.Zulma BRAUD) m. 2 Feb. 1897 Clay RODRIGUE (Chackbay Ch.: v.1, p.38)
CAILLOUET, Berthe (Joseph & Zulma BRAUD) m. 2 Feb. 1897 Clay RODRIGUE (Thib. Ct. Hse.: Mar. v.36, #52)

CAILLOUET, Carmelite (Edouard & Marie GUEDRY) m. 21 Nov. 1896 Joseph MARTINEZ, Jr. (Thib. Ct. Hse.: Mar. v.36, #161)
CAILLOUET, Carmelite (Edouard & Marie GUEDRY) m. 21 Nov. 1896 Joseph MARTINEZ (Chackbay Ch.: v.1, p.33)
CAILLOUET, Charles (Raoul & Lea BENOIT) bt. 19 Sept. 1896 (Chackbay Ch.: v.1, p.75)
CAILLOUET, Denis Alexandre (Felix & Anida LASSEIGNE) b. 17 Oct. 1896 (Thib. Ch.: v.7, p.423)
CAILLOUET, Florestine m. 29 April 1897 Anderson RILEY (Thib. Ct. Hse.: Mar. v.36, #133)
CAILLOUET, James Jr. (James) In the matter of the insanity of: 25 Jan. 1899. (Thib. Ct. Hse.: Succ. #1559)
CAILLOUET, Joseph (Raoul & Lea BENOIT) b. 21 Sept. 1898 (Chackbay Ch.: v.1, p.119)
CAILLOUET, Joseph Jean Baptiste (Emile & Philomene BERGERON) b. 19 March 1898 (Houma Ch.: v.5, p.203)
CAILLOUET, Josephine Nelly (Edouard & Marie GUEDRY) b. 20 Jan. 1899 (Chackbay Ch.: v.1, p.127)
CAILLOUET, Julia (Theophile & Cecile ROBICHAUX) m. 8 Feb. 1899 Valfroid M. TOUPS (Thib. Ct. Hse.: Mar. v.38, #88)
CAILLOUET, Julia (Theophile & Cecile ROBICHAUX) m. 8 Feb. 1899 Valfroid M. TOUPS (Lockport Ch.: v.2, p.202)
CAILLOUET, Louis m. 15 June 1898 Martha WALLER (Thib. Ct. Hse.: Mar. v.38, #209)
CAILLOUET, Mabel Marie (Norbert & Nathalie SINITIERE) b. 11 April 1898 (Houma Ch.: v.5, p.208)
CAILLOUET, Marie (Edmond & Marie GUEDRY) m. 4 Oct. 1897 Oscar CLEMENT (Chackbay Ch.: v.1, p.49 & 50)
CAILLOUET, Marie (Edouard & Marie GUEDRY) m. 4 Oct. 1897 Oscar CLEMENT (Thib. Ct. Hse.: Mar. v.37, #240)
CAILLOUET, Marie Eloise (Louis Philippe & Marie Adele LAGARDE) bt. 4 Aug. 1896 (Thib. Ch.: v.7, p.410)
CAILLOUET, Marie Ida Irvy (Anatole & Valerie LEBLANC) b. 26 Dec. 1899 (Thib. Ch.: v.7, p.581)
CAILLOUET, Marie Louie (Arnauld & Marie BENOIT) b. 27 July 1897 (Houma Ch.: v.5, p.185)
CAILLOUET, Marie Stella (Anatole & Valerie LEBLANC) b. 28 Feb. 1897 (Thib. Ch.: v.7, p.489)
CAILLOUET, Theogene d. 27 Feb. 1896 at age 80 yrs. (Thib. Ch.: v.3, p.179)
CAILLOUET, Theogene d. 27 Feb. 1896; m. Marguerite CAILLOUET Children listed: J. Norbert; Edward; Joseph T.; P. Felix; Mary m. Prosper BOUDREAUX; Eliza m. Clay CAILLOUET. Petition & order putting heirs in possession: 18 Aug. 1896. (Thib. Ct. Hse.: Succ. #1497)
CAILLOUET, Theresa d. 11 Oct. 1899 at age 24 yrs. (Houma Ch.: v.3, p.25)
CALABAS, Marie Cora (Derouin & Sylvai LOUIS) b. 11 Jan. 1896 (Lockport Ch.: v.2, p.319)

CALAHAN (Sometimes: CALAHEN, CALLAGHAN, CALLAHAN)

CALAHAN, Adele Marguerite (Silvain & Eugene DUGUET) b. 10 May 1896 (Theriot Ch.: v.1-B, p.96)

CALAHAN, Caliste m. 11 Feb. 1899 Emelia DUPLANTIS (Houma Ct. Hse.: Mar. v.31 & 32, #332)

CALAHAN, Coliste (Neuville & Emelie MARCEL) m. 13 Feb. 1899 Emelia DUPLANTIS (Houma Ch.: v.6-a, p.287)

CALAHAN, Emilia d. 14 Aug. 1899 at age 24 yrs. (Houma Ch.: v.3, p.24)

CALAHAN, Eveline Emma (Oleus & Emma PREJEAN) b. 30 Jan. 1897 (Thib. Ch.: v.7, p.488)

CALAHAN, Joseph Tresimon (Joseph & Marie GAUDET) b. 8 June 1896 (Larose Ch.: v.2, p.197)

CALAHAN, Laura Alice (Denis & Augusta PICHOFF) b. 13 Aug. 1897 (Larose Ch.: v.3, p.5)

CALAHAN, Laura Alice (Denis & Augusta PICHOFF) d. 3 May 1898 at age 1 yr. (Larose Ch.: v.1, p.42)

CALAHAN, Mary m. Raphael GAUDE Children listed: Malvina m. Francois PICOU; Mary Louise, 15 yrs.; Alcide, 13; Edgar, 10; Selima, 8. Petition for tutorship: 3 July 1896. (Thib. Ct. Hse.: Succ. #1494)

CALAHAN, Paul Toussaint (Sylvain & Virginie BUQUET) b. 1 Nov. 1898 (Theriot Ch.: v.2, p.31)

CALAIS (Sometimes: CAILLE)

CALAIS, Charles of Lafourche Parish (Mathurin & Helene COX) m. 2 July 1898 Louise GISCLAIR, of Lafourche Parish (Larose Ch.: v.3, p.10)

CALAIS, Charles (Mathurin & Helene COX) m. 2 July 1898 Louise GISCLAIR (Thib. Ct. Hse.: Mar. v.38, #201)

CALAIS, Charles (Mathurin & Helene COX) m. 2 July 1898 Louise GISCLAIR (Larose Ch.: v.4, p.22)

CALAIS, Edville Joseph (Felix & Marie VINET) b. 30 March 1898 (Larose Ch.: v.3, p.33)

CALAIS, Felicie m. 13 June 1896 Henry D. KELLEY (Thib. Ct. Hse.: Mar. v.35, #94)

CALAIS, Josephine m. 16 Sept. 1899 Julien CHERAMIE (Thib. Ct. Hse.: Mar. v.39, #224)

CALAIS, Julia Usevia (Paul & Malvina DANTIN) b. 7 June 1898 (Larose Ch.: v.3, p.32)

CALAIS, Julie Dorsillia (Paul & Malvina DANTIN) b. 7 June 1898 (Larose Ch.: v.3, p.32)

CALAIS, Malvina m. 15 Dec. 1898 Fernand FERADES (Thib. Ct. Hse.: Mar. v.38, #318)

CALAIS, Marie m. 1 Feb. 1897 John JANFRAU (Thib. Ct. Hse.: Mar. v.36, #60)

CALAIS, Martial Felicien (Euzilien & Mary AUGERON) m. 14 Dec. 1896 Julia Letitia LEE (Thib. Ct. Hse.: Mar. v.36, #167)

CALAIS, Mathilda m. 28 May 1896 Georges KELLEY (Thib. Ct. Hse.: Mar. v.35, #89)

CALAIS, Paul m. 7 July 1899 Irma GUIDRY (Thib. Ct. Hse.: Mar v.39, #196)
CALAIS, Paul (Mathurin & Helene COX) m. 8 July 1899 Irma GUIDRY (Larose Ch.: v.3, p.12)
CALAIS, Paúl (Mathurin & Helene COX) m. 8 July 1899 Irma GUIDRY (Larose Ch.: v.4, p.95)
CALANDRO, Rosalia m. 30 March 1897 Lorenzo RERIS (Thib. Ct. Hse.: Mar. v.36, #106)
CALANDRO, Rosalia (Salvatore & Francisca ROGGIERE) m. 19 April 1897 Lorenzo RERIS (Raceland Ch.: v.2, p.37)
CALBERT, Francis m. 12 Aug. 1896 Willie BERGERON (Thib. Ct. Hse.: Mar. v.36, #134)
CALCAGNA, Anna (Zerolamo & Francesca VITALE) m. 21 Aug. 1899 Andrea PINTO (Raceland Ch.: v.2, p.102)
CALCAGNIO, Georges (Georges & Rosa CANNOVA) b. 7 Dec. 1898 (Houma Ch.: v.5, p.231)
CALDWELL, Liddy m. 21 March 1898 Abner HILL (Thib. Ct. Hse.: Mar. v.37, #130)
CALET, Dorsillia Nillia Marie (Charles & Rosalie LEE) b. 17 Feb. 1898 (Larose Ch.: v.3, p.21)
CALET, Eulalie (Mathurin & Helene COCKE) m. 16 April 1898 Ovide CHERAMI (Larose Ch.: v.3, p.8)
CALET, Evelina m. 25 June 1896 Ernest CHERAMI (Larose Ch.: v.4, p.88)
CALET, Evelina m. 25 June 1896 Ernest CHERAMI (Larose Ch.: v.3, p.3)
CALET, Henderson Xavier (Martial & Julia LEE) b. 3 Jan. 1898 (Larose Ch.: v.3, p.21)
CALET, Louis Hubert (Joseph & Louise TERREBONNE) b. 28 Nov. 1897 (Larose Ch.: v.3, p.20)
CALET, Octave Alexandre (Paul & Malvina DANTIN) b. 28 Jan. 1896 (Larose Ch.: v.2, p.191)
CALI, Catarina (Salvatore & Victoria GUADAGUINA) m. 16 Feb. 1899 Telice ZILIO, Jr. (Thib Ch.: v.14, p.255)
CALI, Cattarina (Salvatore & Victoria GUADOGNINA) m. 6 Feb. 1899 Felice ZILIO of New Orleans (Thib. Ct. Hse.: Mar. v.38, #45)
CALI, Maria Concietta (Salvatore & Vittoria GUADAGUERIA) m. 9 Oct. 1897 Guisto MERANTE (Thib. Ch.: v.14, p.162)
CALI, Maria Madelena (Rosario & Francesca BONVIOVANNI) b. 26 May 1899 (Thib. Ch.: v.7, p.605)
CALI, Marie Concietta (Salvatore & Vittoria GUADAGUINA) m. 9 Oct. 1897 GUisto MERCANTE (Thib. Ct. Hse.: Mar. v.37, #232)
CALLAWAY, Frank m. 31 Aug. 1896 Mariah OWENS (Houma Ct. Hse.: Mar. v.29 & 30, #141)
CALLAWAY, Pricilla m. 9 June 1898 William KNIGHT, Jr. (Houma Ct. Hse.: Mar. v.30 & 31, #1)
CALLAWAY, Sam m. 1 Aug. 1898 Mary SHIELDS (Thib. Ct. Hse.: Mar. v.38, #236)

CALLIA, Calogero (Calogero & Rosa CANGIAMINO) b. 27 March 1899 (Chacahoula Ch.: v.4, p.21)
CALLON, Josephine of Lafourche Parish (Isidore & Francoise VINET) m. 1 Sept. 1898 Vincent BACCARA, of Lafourche Parish (Larose Ch.: v.3, p.10)
CALLON, Josephine (Isidore & Francoise VINET) m. 5 Sept. 1898 Vincent BACCARA (Thib. Ct. Hse.: Mar. v.38, #258)
CALLON, Josephine (Isidore & Francoise VINET) m. 5 Sept. 1898 Vincent BACCARA (Larose Ch. v.4, p.28)
CALLOUSE, Frank (Felix & Leonal SPINELLA) b. 25 July 1898 (Houma Ch.: v.5, p.213)
CALLOVA, Leoluca (Salvatore & Mancisca GAZZANA) m. 4 Feb. 1899 Corcilia ZITA (Houma Ch.: v.6-a, p.271)
CALLURA, Leoluca m. 21 Jan. 1899 Cecilia ZITA (Houma Ct. Hse.: Mar. v.30 & 31, #278)
CAMARATA, Rosalia (Rosolino & Maranna LANZA) b. 10 Jan. 1898 (Thib. Ch.: v.7, p.535)

CAMARDELLE (Sometimes: CAMARDEL, CAMARDELL, CAMORDEL)
CAMARDELLE, Meranthe d. 28 Nov. 1896 (Lockport Ch.: v.1, #24)
CAMARDELLE, Theophile d. 17 June 1899 at age 18 mths. (Lockport Ch.: v.1, #23)
CAMBECHE, Rosalie m. 18 Oct. 1898 Antonio MAVRICHA (Houma Ct. Hse.: Mar. v.30 & 31, #124)
CAMBECHE, Rosalie (Miguel & Angele VEREDO) m. 29 Oct. 1898 Antonio MAURICHA (Houma Ch.: v.6-a, p.257)
CAMBO, Sebastiano (Joseppo & Maria CENTURA) b. 12 April 1899 (Thib. Ch.: v.7, p.603)
CAMPAGNA, Mariano (Andrea & Maria Antonia MOLONI) b. 6 March 1897 (Thib. Ch.: v.7, p.519)

CAMPBELL (Sometime: CAMBELL)
CAMPBELL, Alice Gertrude (Walther & Alice FALGOUT) b. 30 March 1898 (Thib. Ch.: v.7, p.547)
CAMPBELL, Charles Watkins (Levy Watkins & Amanda Claire LANDRY) m. 1 March 1897 Aline FALGOUT (Thib. Ch.: v.14, p.133)
CAMPBELL, Edie (John & Rose WHITE) m. 16 Feb. 1899 John Webster AUBERT (Houma Ct. Hse.: Mar. v.31 & 32, #337)
CAMPBELL, James Green (John Pascy & Henriette W. BELANGER) b. 24 April 1896 (Houma Ch.: v.5, p.152)
CAMPBELL, Robert m. 13 Aug. 1896 Nellie JOHNSON (Houma Ct. Hse.: Mar. v.29 & 30, #130)
CAMPBELL, Sydney Moise Louis (John C. & Henriette BELANGER) b. 9 Oct. 1899 (Houma Ch.: v.5, p.261)
CAMPBELL, Thomas Blak d. 8 May 1899 at age 1 yr., 1 mth. (Houma Ch.: v.3, p.22)
CAMPBELL, Thomas Blake (John Pasey & Henriette BELANGER) b. 7 April 1898 (Houma Ch.: v.5, p.210)

CAMPO (Sometimes: CAMPOS)

CAMPO, Guiseppe (Sebastiano & Guiseppa GALLIANA) m. 30 July 1898 Marguerita FERRANTELLE (Thib. Ct. Hse.: Mar. v.38, #220)

CAMPO, Guiseppe (Sebastien & Guiseppa GALLIANO) m. 30 July 1898 Marguerite FERRANTELLE (Thib. Ch.: v.14, p.212)

CAMUS, Marie Elisa m. Simon HESSE d. 4 Nov. 1898 at age 81 yrs. (Thib. Ch.: v.3, p.221)

CAMUS, Marie Elisa m. 30 Aug. 1898 Simon HESSE (Thib. Ch.: v.14, p.214-a)

CAMUS, Marie Eliza d. 4 Nov. 1898; m.(1) Antoine RUFFET; m.(2) Simon HESSE. Petition to be placed in possession: 30 Nov. 1898. (Thib. Ct. Hse.: Succ. #1553)

CANCIENNE, Avie Wilfrid (Oscar & Odilia BOURGEOIS) b. 5 Feb. 1898 (Thib.Ch.: v.7, p.483)

CANCIENNE, Germaine (Cyprien & Octavie TOUPS) b. 15 July 1896 (Thib. Ch.: v.7, p.408)

CANCIENNE, Jeanne Edith (Cyprien Albert & Marie Octavie TOUPS) b. 14 July 1898 (Thib. Ch.: v.7, p.504)

CANCILLA, Giuseppa (Antonio & Guiseppa PIDDACAMBISA) m. 16 Sept. 1899 Giovanni TORTORICI (Thib. Ct. Hse.: Mar. v.39, #207)

CANCILLA, Guiseppa (Antonio & Guiseppa PIDDAEAMBISA) m. 16 Sept. 1899 Giovanni TORTORICI (Thib. Ch.: v.14, p.294)

CANDIEZ, Philippe Ferdinand (Benjamin & Morelise MATERNE) b. 23 Aug. 1899 (Raceland Ch.: v.5, p.125)

CANNOVA, Anita (Felice & Maria Adenzia CANNOVA) b. 10 Dec. 1898; bt. 7 Jan. 1899; confirmed at St. Cecilia's Church on 16 March 1954. (Houma Ch.: Bapt. Bk., v.5, p.227)

CANNOVA, Ludovica (Felici & Maria AUDENGIA) b. 10 March 1896 (Houma Ch.: Bapt. Bk., v.5, p.173)

CANNOVA, Marguerite (Guiseppe & Rosalia MONZOUGUE) b. 6 Oct. 1897; m. Joseph GENOVESE on 18 June 1932. (Houma Ch.: Bapt. Bk., v.5, p.187)

CANOVA, Antonio m. 22 May 1899 Girintonia BILONA (Houma Ct. Hse.: Mar. v.31 & 32, #13)

CANOVA, Luigia (Vincenza & Maria BARDISSA) b. 16 May 1899 (Raceland Ch.: v.5, p.97)

CANTONE, Josephina (Tone & Angelina FAUCHE) b. 4 Dec. 1897 (Thib. Ch.: v.7, p.400)

CANTRELLE (Sometimes: CANTREL)

CANTRELLE, Amanda m. 15 June 1898 Seraphin GAUTREAUX (Houma Ct. Hse.: Mar. v.30 & 31, #18)

CANTRELLE, Amanda (Casimir & Marcelline PECHOT) m. 3 June 1898 Serafin GAUTHREAUX (Chacahoula Ch.: v.1, p.62)

CANTRELLE, Anasthasie Eleonore (Joseph & Lucie SAVOIE) b. 1 Nov. 1899 (Larose Ch.: v.3, p.47)

CANTRELLE, Arthur (Washington & Pelagie BAYEAUX) b. 13 March 1897 (Larose Ch.: v.3, p.10)

CANTRELLE, Casimir Jean (----ssin & Julia PLAISANCE) b. 15 July 1896 (Larose Ch.: v.2, p.194)
CANTRELLE, Charles (William & Julienne LEDET) d. 13 Sept. 1897 at age 15 days (Larose Ch.: v.1, p.41)
CANTRELLE, Charles Herman d. 30 March 1898 at age 6 yrs. (Theriot Ch.: v.1, p.1)
CANTRELLE, Emile (Casimir & Marie ALLEMAND) m. 6 Nov. 1899 Coralie GUIDROZ (Thib. Ct. Hse.: Mar. v.39, #259)
CANTRELLE, Emile (Casimir & Marie ALLEMAND) m. 6 Nov. 1899 Coralie GUIDROZ (Lockport Ch.: v.2, p.210)
CANTRELLE, Emilie of Lafourche Parish (Hermogene & Laurenza BADEAU) m. 18 April 1898 William COOPER, of Lafourche Parish (Larose Ch.: v.3, p.8)
CANTRELLE, Emilie (Hermogene & Laurenza BADEAU) m. 18 April 1898 William COOPER (Larose Ch.: v.4, p.9)
CANTRELLE, Emilie (Hermogene & Laurenza BADEAU) m. 18 April 1898 William COOPER (Thib. Ct. Hse.: Mar. v.37, #145)
CANTRELLE, Ernest m. 7 July 1899 Vina PITRE (Thib. Ct. Hse.: Mar. v.39, #193)
CANTRELLE, Herman m. 20 Dec. 1898 Mary LEBLANC (Thib. Ct. Hse.: Mar. v.38, #319)
CANTRELLE, Jean Augustin (Paul & Bernadette ORGERON) b. 5 Dec. 1898 (Larose Ch.: v.3, p.31)
CANTRELLE, Jean Hermann (Ernest & Georgiana BROUCE) b. 25 April 1897 (Theriot Ch.: v.2, p.5)
CANTRELLE, John (Paul & Bernadette ORGERON) d. 15 Sept. 1899 at age 9 mths. (Larose Ch.: v.1, p.53)
CANTRELLE, Josephine Eve (Daniel & Felicie CHERAMIE) b. 12 May 1896 (Lockport Ch.: v.2, p.329)
CANTRELLE, Jules Joseph (William & Julienne LEDET) b. 23 July 1898 (Raceland Ch.: v.5, p.75)
CANTRELLE, Louis (Wuach & Pelagie BAYEUX) m. 23? June 1898 Bernadette ADAM (Lockport Ch.: v.2, p.190 & 191)
CANTRELLE, Louis (Wuach & Pelagie BAYEUX) m. 23 June 1898 Bernadette ADAM (Thib. Ct. Hse.: Mar. v.38, #205)
CANTRELLE, Marie Claudia (Paul & Bernadette ORGERON) b. 17 Sept. 1896 (Larose Ch.: v.2, p.185)
CANTRELLE, Marie Emilie (Joseph & Lucie SAVOIE) b. 6 Dec. 1896 (Larose Ch.: v.3, p.5)
CANTRELLE, Marie Marguerite (Daniel & Felicie CHERAMI) b. 3 Sept. 1898 (Larose Ch.: v.3, p.28)
CANTRELLE, Marie Viola (Hermogene & Laurenza BADEAU) b. 13 Feb. 1896 (Larose Ch.: v.2, p.185)
CANTRELLE, Noemia d. 16 July 1898 at age 56 yrs. (Theriot Ch.: v.1, p.1)
CANTRELLE, Pierre Allain (Tommassin & Julia PLAISANCE) b. 21 Sept. 1898 (Larose Ch.: v.3, p.29)
CANTRELLE, Thomassin d. 15 March 1897 at age 56 yrs. (Larose Ch.: v.1, p.39)
CANTRELLE, Timon (L. & Amelie VALES) d. 22 July 1899 at age 19 yrs. (Lockport Ch.: v.1, #28)

CANTRELLE, Zoemie d. 21 July 1899 at age 14 yrs. (Lockport Ch.: v.1, #27)
CAONTON, Alodius d. 1 Dec. 1896 at age 11 mths. (Houma Ch.: v.3, p.9)
CARA, Elda (James & Sarah DAVIS) b. 5 Feb. 1896 (Chackbay Ch.: v.1, p.64)
CARANELLA, Franck (Georgio & Carmella SPITALLERA) b. 9 Nov. 1898 (Thib. Ch.: v.7, p.520)
CARANELLA, Ida (Giorgio & Carmella SPITALLERA) b. 9 Nov. 1898 (Thib. Ch.: v.7, p.520)
CARAWAY, Jarret m. 11 Nov. 1899 Bertha COLLINS, widow of Jessie DABNEY (Thib. Ct. Hse.: Mar. v.39, #264)
CARBARIERE, Vincenzo (Dominique & Rose FERILLI) m. 11 Jan. 1897 Pamela VINET (Thib. Ct. Hse.: Mar. v.36, #18)
CARCAGUE, George (Joseph & Anna MAJOR) b. 27 Aug. 1899; m. Frances SANTAGNELO on 15 June 1924. (Houma Ch.: Bapt. Bk.: v.5, p.251)
CARDARELLA, Dominico (Calogera & Gratia SCIORTINA) b. 6 Sept. 1896 (Thib. Ch.: v.7, p.419)
CARDY, George (Steven G. & Martha NASSAR) b. 28 May 1897 (Houma Ch.: v.5, p.180)
CARENZO, Rosario (Lodovica & Corrina VISCONTE) m. 8 Feb. 1897 Gilorma LIBERTA (Thib. Ct. Hse.: Mar. v.36, #71)
CARENZO, Rosario (Ludovic & Tonina VISCONTE) m. 8 Jan. 1897 Gilorma LIBERTA (Thib. Ch.: v.14, p.122)
CARIN, Eleonore (Bernard & Alcina VOISIN) b. 22 May 1896 (Theriot Ch.: v.2, p.2)
CARIN, Laurent (Bernard & Alcina VOISIN) b. 12 Feb. 1898 (Theriot Ch.: v.2, p.20)
CARLIN, Marguerita Ilda (Ursin & Victoria COULONG) b. 16 March 1899 (Theriot Ch.: v.2, p.35)
CARLIN, Marie Viola (Ursin J. & Victoria COLOMB) b. 23 Dec. 1897 (Theriot Ch.: v.2, p.14)
CARLIN, Ursin (Desire & Celestin FALGOUT) m. 22 Aug. 1898 Victoria COLOMB (Theriot Ch.: v.1-B, p.4)
CARLIN, Ursin J. (Desire & Celestine FALGOUT) m. 2 Feb. 1897 Victoria E. COLOMB (Houma Ct. Hse.: Mar. v.29 & 30, #272)
CARLOS, Alma Christiana (Louis & ---- KETNOID) b. 10 Feb. 1897 (Theriot Ch.: v.1-B, p.106)
CARLOS, Cecilia (Jacob & Marie CARET) b. 28 Jan. 1898 (Theriot Ch.: v.2, p.23)
CARLOS, Charles m. 7 Jan. 1899 Lucie MATHERNE (Houma Ct. Hse.: Mar. v.30 & 31, #193)
CARLOS, Charles (Salvador & Elvire LAGRASE) m. 23 Jan. 1899 Lucie MATHERNE (Houma Ch.: v.6-a, p.268)
CARLOS, Eugenie (Eugene & Marguerite CENAC) b. 11 March 1896 (Theriot Ch.: v.1-B, p.94)
CARLOS, Joseph Corbet (James & Marie CARERE) b. 12 Jan. 1896 (Theriot Ch.: v.1-B, p.92)

CARLOS, Joseph Pierre Eloi (Eugene & Marguerite CENACLE) b. 8 Oct. 1897 (Theriot Ch.: v.2, p.13)
CARLOS, Lawrence (Salvador & Elvire LA GRAVE) m. 6 Nov. 1899 Loula OZIO (Houma Ct. Hse.: Mar. v.31 & 32, #162)
CARLOS, Lawrence (Salvator & Elvire LAGROSE) m. 20 Nov. 1899 Lulu OZIO (Theriot Ch.: v.1-B, p.7)
CARLOS, Louise Victorine (Eugene & Marguerite SENACLE) b. 10 May 1899; m. Emile CHAUVIN on 12 Nov. 1925. (Houma Ch.: Bapt. Bk., v.5, p.247)
CARLOS, Salvador d. 20 Dec. 1897 at age 77 yrs. (Theriot Ch.: v.1, p.1)
CARLOS, Salvador d. 20 Dec. 1899. Inventory: 2 Feb. 1898. (Houma Ct. Hse.: Succ. #895)
CARLOS, Salvador m. 19 July 1897 Celestine DUBOIS (Theriot Ch.: v.1-B, p.1)
CARLOS, Unice Emilie (Louis & Ella Emilia GATEWOOD) b. 28 July 1899 (Theriot Ch.: v.2, p.44)
CARLSON, Mary Ruth (Carles & Chora THIBODEAUX) b. 5 April 1899 (Houma Ch.: v.5, p.245)
CARMOUCHE, Joseph Cleveland (Hypolite & Virginie BERGNARD) b. 17 July 1897 (Thib. Ch.: v.7, p.457)
CARNOVA, Antonio of Terrebonne Parish m. 3 June 1899 Girintonia BILINA (Houma Ch.: v.6-B, p.3)
CARO, ----- Mrs. d. 20 Jan. 1898 (Thib. Ch.: v.3, p.209)
CARO, Etienne m. 2 May 1896 Nathalie CROCHET (Houma Ct. Hse.: Mar. v.29 & 30, #47)
CARO, Etienne (Jean & Adele ORDONNEAU) m. 2 May 1896 Nathalie CROCHET (Houma Ch.: v.6-a, p.175)
CARO, Eugene m. 12 Jan. 1899 Inezida HOTARD (Houma Ct. Hse.: Mar. v.30 & 31, #222)
CARO, Eugene (Jean & Odele ARDONEAUX) m. 30 Jan. 1899 Inezeda HOTARD (Houma Ch.: v.6-a, p.270)
CARO, Eugenie d. 28 July 1899 at age 20 yrs. (Houma Ch.: v.3, p.23)
CARO, Eugenie Catherine (Eugene & Inesida HOTARD) b. 9 Dec. 1899 (Houma Ch.: v.5, p.268)
CARO, Eugenie Catherine (Eugene & Inesida HOTARD) b. 9 Dec. 1899 (Houma Ch.: v.6, p.4)
CARO, Jeames McAllister d. 25 May 1896 at age 2 yrs. 4 mths. (Thib. Ch.: v.3, p.182)
CARO, Jeanne d. 22 Sept. 1898 at age 2 mths. (Houma Ch.: v.3, p.18)
CARO, Jeanne Marguerite (John & Justine PITT) b. 8 July 1898 (Thib. Ch.: v.7, p.513)
CARO, Joseph Rolland (Oscar Leon & Marie Adeline BOURG) b. 14 Dec. 1896 (Thib. Ch.: v.7, p.429)
CARO, Mary Jenny (Etienne & Nathalie CROCHET) b. 10 July 1898 (Houma Ch.: v.5, p.216)
CARO, Mimie d. 9 May 1897 at age 37 yrs. (Houma Ch.: v.3, p.13)
CARO, Philomene (Alice) b. 8 April 1898 (Thib. Ch.: v.7, p.494)

CARRANE, John d. 8 Oct. 1898 (Houma Ch.: v.3, p.18)

CARRERE, Ernest d. 8 Sept. 1899 (Montegut Ch.: v.2, p.28)

CARRERE, Ernest (Dominique & Pauline RODRIGUEZ) m. 26 Dec. 1896 Felicia BELLAMORE (Houma Ct. Hse.: Mar. v.29 & 30, #216)

CARRERE, Eve (Dominique & Pauline RODRIGUE) m. 20 April 1899 Lawrence VOISIN (Houma Ct. Hse.: Mar. v.31 & 32, #407)

CARRERE, Jean Pierre (Pierre & Victorine CENACLE) b. 12 July 1899 (Theriot Ch.: v.2, p.50)

CARRERE, Josephine (Pierre & Victorine CENACLE) b. 27 Feb. 1897 (Theriot Ch.: v.2, p.3)

CARRERE, Marie (Bernard & Louisiane PITRE) m. 12 April 1897 Louis LINER (Houma Ct. Hse.: Mar. v.29 & 30, #381)

CARRICK, Ellen d. 5 Dec. 1895; m.(1) Patrick TYRREL; m. (2) William BURKE Child listed: James. Opposition of James TYRREL: 11 Aug. 1896. (Thib. Ct. Hse.: Succ. #1473)

CARRINGTON, Kate d. 8 Feb. 1896 at age 30 yrs. (Thib. Ch.: Epis. Ch.: v.1, p.392)

CARROLL, Howard m. 8 Feb. 1899 Annie RANDALL (Thib. Ct. Hse.: Mar. v.38, #98)

CARROUSSO, Maria (Felice & Leonarda SPENELLA) b. 3 Jan. 1896 (Houma Ch.: v.5, p.139)

CARTER, Charles m. 8 July 1897 Sarah Jane DENNIS (Houma Ct. Hse.: Mar. v.29 & 30, #59)

CARTER, Eliska m. 5 March 1898 Andrew BAPTISTE (Thib. Ct. Hse.: Mar. v.37, #119)

CARTER, Emilie widow of WELTON m. 9 June 1897 Dave PARKER (Thib. Ct Hse.: Mar. v.36, #165)

CARTER, Josephine m. 10 Feb. 1898 Sam MOLTON (Thib. Ct. Hse.: Mar. v.37, #97)

CARTER, Julia m. 18 Jan. 1899 William BRYANT (Thib. Ct. Hse.: Mar. v.38, #33)

CARTER, Lavinia m. 15 Jan. 1896 Adam KANE (Houma Ct. Hse.: Mar. v.28, #391)

CARTER, Leon m. 10 Oct. 1898 Lulilia MASON (Thib. Ct. Hse.: Mar. v.38, #290)

CARTER, Robert m. 17 March 1898 Mary BOLDEN (Houma Ct. Hse.: Mar. v.30 & 31, #340)

CARTER, Susan m. 7 May 1896 George MAGIOR (Thib. Ct. Hse.: Mar. v.35, #84)

CARUSO, Guiseppe (Vincenzo & Maria Antonia CANINA) b. 1 Sept. 1899 (Raceland Ch.: v.5, p.102)

CARVER, Earline m. 8 June 1897 Thomas D. KENT (Thib. Ct. Hse.: Mar. v.36, #163)

CARY, William m. 31 May 1897 Almeady HEARD (Thib. Ct. Hse.: Mar. v.36, #157)

CASALANOBBE, Vincenza (Archangelo & Vincenza VERSARA) b. 15 June 1896 (Thib. Ch.: v.7, p.406)

CASCARO, Philippe (Jacob & Lucie DONATO) b. 23 July 1898 (Thib. Ch.: v.7, p.558)

CASEY, Henry m. 4 Sept. 1899 Jane WILLIAMS (Houma Ct. Hse.: Mar. v.31 & 32, #118)

CASLIO, Josina (Joseph & Rosa CITRAUX) b. 13 April 1899 (Thib. Ch.: v.7, p.601)

CASPISA, Salvatore Jr. (Salvatore, Sr.) m. 12 Jan. 1899 Rozia INGNAFFIA (Houma Ch.: v.6a, p.262)

CASTANZA, Guiseppa (d.Guiseppe & Rosaria TANTILLO) b. 21 April 1899 (Thib. Ch.: v.7, p.602)

CASTLE, Dave m. 13 Jan. 1898 Louisa ROBINSON (Houma Ct. Hse.: Mar. v.30 & 31, #202)

CASTON, Samuel Butler m. 22 Aug. 1899 Waltrene GRAY (Houma Ct. Hse.: Mar. v.31 & 32, #105)

CASTON, Samuel Butler (Samuel N. & Virginia E. GAYLE) m. 23 Aug. 1899 Waltrene S. GRAY (Houma Ch.: Epis. Ch.: v.1, p.344)

CASTROGIOVANNE, Antonia (Guiseppe & Pietra SINAGRA) b. 6 Feb. 1898 (Thib. Ch.: v.7, p.535)

CASTROGIOVANNE, Nina d. 26 Feb. 1899 at age 1 mth. (Thib. Ch.: v.3, p.229)

CASTROGIOVANNI, Maria (Gaspere & Calogira GIORDANO) m. 3 Feb. 1898 Carmelo INZINGA (Thib. Ch.: v.14, p.179)

CASTROGIOVANNI, Maria (Gaspere & Calogira GIORDANO) m. 3 Feb. 1898 Carmelo INZINGA (Thib. Ct. Hse.: Mar. v.37, #54)

CATALANELLO, Guiseppe (Calagero & Guiseppo CAPARA) m. 12 Feb. 1898 Rosario CIACCIO (Houma Ch.: v.6-a, p.229)

CATALENELLO, Giuseppe m. 26 Jan. 1898 Rosario CIACCIO (Houma Ct. Hse.: Mar. v.30 & 31, #250)

CATANONIA, Angelina (Geneppa & Maria COME) b. 18 Oct. 1899 (Houma Ch.: v.6, p.4)

CATANONIA, Angelina (Guiseppa & Maria CAMES) b. 18 Oct. 1899 (Houma Ch.: v.5, p.268)

CAVALIER, Francois m. Pierre Rosemond DUFRENE d. 24 Nov. 1898 at age 63 yrs. (Lockport Ch.: v.1, #22)

CEASAR, Adam m. 22 Nov. 1899 Ruberda DUNBY (Thib. Ct. Hse.: Mar. v.39, #266)

CEASAR, Thomas m. 5 Aug. 1897 Priscilla RIGGINS (Thib. Ct. Hse.: Mar. v.37, #205)

CECALA, Antonino m. 11 Sept. 1899 Josephine SOLOMONE (Houma Ct. Hse.: Mar. v.31 & 32, #125)

CELESTIN, Arthemise m. 23 July 1896 Osborne RINGGOLD, Jr. (Houma Ct. Hse.: Mar. v.29 & 30, #117)

CELESTIN, Dewey Susie (Charles Amidee & Martha HANAGRIFF) b. 12 Feb. 1898 (Houma Ch.: Epis. Ch.: v.1, p.118)

CELESTIN, Felicien d. 7 July 1899 at age 62 yrs. (Thib. Ch.: v.3, p.236)

CELESTIN, Felicien d. 8 Oct. 1898 at age 28 yrs., 11 mths., 5 days (Houma Ch.: v.3, p.18)

CELESTIN, Felix d. 7 Dec. 1897 at age 26 yrs. (Thib. Ch.: v.3, p.208)

CELESTIN, Laura m. 13 March 1897 Cornelius WILLIAMS (Houma Ct. Hse.: Mar. v.29 & 30, #354)
CELESTIN, Louis J. d. 14 March 1896 at age 20 yrs. (Thib. Ch.: v.3, p.180)
CELESTIN, Marie Adele (Felix & Berthe BRAUD) b. 7 Sept. 1898 (Thib. Ch.: v.7, p.562)
CELESTIN, May Virginia (C. Amebee & Margaret HANAGRIFF) b. 10 Feb. 1896 (Houma Ch.: Epis. Ch.: v.1, p.112-B)
CELESTIN, Rita d. 16 July 1898 at age 3 yrs., 9 mths. & 15 days (Thib. Ch.: v.3, p.217)
CELESTIN, Robert Joseph (Felix & Berthe BRAUD) b. 8 Oct 1896 (Thib. Ch.: v.7, p.422)
CELESTIN, Roberta Lee (Matt. L. Hannagriff & Virginia WATKINS) m. 19 Dec. 1898 Stewart A. WILKINS (Houma Ch.: Epis. Ch.: v.1, p.342)

CENAC (See: SENAC)

CENACLE, Jimmy Willy (Baptiste & Fanny GATEWOOD) b. 4 Aug. 1897 (Theriot Ch.: v.2, p.13)
CENACLE, Josephine d. 3 May 1898 at age 18 yrs. (Theriot Ch.: v.1, p.1)
CENACLE, Lydia (Albert & Adelphine AINCHELLE) b. 8 Feb. 1897 (Theriot Ch.: v.2, p.3)
CENACLE, Ursule (Albert & Adelphine MICHEL) b. 31 Jan. 1898 (Theriot Ch.: v.2, p.18)
CERNIGLIA, Maria (Joseph & Rosalia GERRACCI) b. 16 Oct. 1897 (Thib. Ch.: v.7, p.480)

CEVIN (See: SEVIN)

CHABERT, Antoinette Laurenza (Louis & ----) b. 19 Jan. 1897 (Larose Ch.: v.3, p.2)
CHABERT, Felicie of Lafourche Parish (Louis & Ernestine LEFORT) m. 25 June 1898 Rodolphe TERREBONNE, of Lafourche Parish (Larose Ch.: v.3, p.9)
CHABERT, Felicie (Louis & Ernestine LEFORT) m. 25 June 1898 Rodolphe TERREBONNE (Thib. Ct. Hse.: Mar. v.38, #203)
CHABERT, Felicie (Louis & Ernestine LEFORT) m. 25 June 1898 Rodolphe TERREBONNE (Larose Ch.: v.4, p.19)
CHAMPAGNE, Adele (Alcide & Marie CHAMPAGNE) b. 17 Sept. 1896 (Theriot Ch.: v.1-B, p.102)
CHAMPAGNE, Aimee (Onesime & Louisa BOURGEOIS) m. 25 Jan. 1897 Kleber BERGERON (Thib. Ct. Hse.: Mar. v.36, #49)
CHAMPAGNE, Aimee (Onesime & Louise BOURGEOIS) m. 25 Jan. 1897 Kleber BERGERON (Thib. Ch.: v.14, p.114)
CHAMPAGNE, Anita (Pierre & Marie BOURGEOIS) m. 22 Jan. 1897 Paul ARABI (Lockport Ch.: v.2, p.179)
CHAMPAGNE, Anita (Pierre & Marie BOURGEOIS) m. 22 Jan. 1898 Paul ARABIE (Thib. Ct. Hse.: Mar. v.37, #7)

CHAMPAGNE, Anne May (Jimmy & Marie DOMINGUE) b. 30 March 1898 (Montegut Ch.: v.6, p.69)
CHAMPAGNE, Balden (Joseph & Julianne THIBODAUX) m. 13 Feb. 1899 Josephine CHAMPAGNE (Theriot Ch.: v.1-B, p.6)
CHAMPAGNE, Beldon m. 4 Feb. 1899 Josephine CHAMPAGNE (Houma Ct. Hse.: Mar. v.30 & 31, #309)
CHAMPAGNE, Camille Augustin (Raphael & Augustine FORET) b. 1 April 1896 (Raceland Ch.: v.5, p.23)
CHAMPAGNE, Charles d. 4 Aug. 1898 at age 38 yrs. (Thib. Ch.: v.3, p.218)
CHAMPAGNE, Charles Hugh Raoul (Walter & Lucile DUCOTE) b. 2 Aug. 1897 (Thib. Ch.: v.7, p.511)
CHAMPAGNE, Clement Israel (Alte & Eva BOUDREAUX) b. 30 Jan. 1896; m. 3 June 1920 to Lucille BRUNET (Theriot Ch.: Bapt. Bk., v.1-B, p.88)
CHAMPAGNE, Clotildia (Septime & Elmire PERTUIT) b. 30 Sept. 1899 (Raceland Ch.: v.5, p.104)
CHAMPAGNE, Dalmas m. 5 Feb. 1897 Josephine TOUPS (Thib. Ct. Hse.: Mar. v.36, #70)
CHAMPAGNE, Delmas (Florestan & Marie ZERINGUE) m. 16 Feb. 1897 Josephine TOUPS (Raceland Ch.: v.2, p.34)
CHAMPAGNE, Edwin Philippe (Arthur & Elitia BROWN) b. 27 Aug. 1898 (Raceland Ch.: v.5, p.79)
CHAMPAGNE, Elia m. 15 Jan. 1897 Elie THERIOT (Houma Ct. Hse.: Mar. v.29 & 30, #238)
CHAMPAGNE, Elia (Faustin & Marguerite CHAMPAGNE) m. 19 Jan. 1897 Elie THERIOT (Theriot Ch.: v.1, p.8)
CHAMPAGNE, Elizabeth (Leo & Helena CHAMPAGNE) b. 24 May 1899 (Theriot Ch.: v.2, p.44)
CHAMPAGNE, Elizabeth Alice (Francois & Ela CHAMPAGNE) b. 11 Sept. 1898 (Theriot Ch.: v.2, p.30)
CHAMPAGNE, Ella m. Noebert CHIASSON d. 22 Feb. 1899 at age 24 yrs. (Thib. Ch.: v.3, p.228)
CHAMPAGNE, Ernest d. 16 Aug. 1897 at age 22 yrs. (Theriot Ch.: v.1, p.1)
CHAMPAGNE, Eugenie (Charles J. & Cecilia GUIDRY) m. 17 Feb. 1896 Emile DOMINGUE (Montegut Ch.: v.4, p.207)
CHAMPAGNE, Eugenie (Charles J. & Cecilia GUIDRY) m. 25 Jan. 1896 Emile DOMINGUE (Houma Ct. Hse.: Mar. v.28, #415)
CHAMPAGNE, Eve d. 27 April 1899 at age 8 yrs. (Thib. Ch.: v.3, p.232)
CHAMPAGNE, Faustin m. 8 Jan. 1897 Leontine WAGENSPACK (Thib. Ct. Hse.: Mar. v.36, #14)
CHAMPAGNE, Faustin (Florestan & Marie ZERINGUE) m. 13 Jan. 1897 Leontine WAGUESPACK (Raceland Ch.: v.2, p.26)
CHAMPAGNE, Flora m. 9 Feb. 1899 David DANKS, Jr. (Houma Ct. Hse.: Mar. v.31 & 32, #328)
CHAMPAGNE, Florestan Sr. m. Adele BERGERON Children listed: Florestan, Jr.; Florestal; Mathilde m. Ad. KNOBLOCH; Charles; Taylor; Josephine m. Gabriel ZERINGUE; Sevillien; Fortin; Delia; Amadeo; Theodore. Petition

for administration: 6 Jan. 1896. (Thib. Ct. Hse.: Succ. #1503)

CHAMPAGNE, Florestine m. 3 Feb. 1898 Albert BOURGEOIS (Thib. Ct. Hse.: Mar. v.37, #63)

CHAMPAGNE, Florestine (Florestan & Marie ZERINGUE) m. 3 Feb. 1898 Albert BOURGEOIS (Raceland Ch.: v.2, p.63)

CHAMPAGNE, Francois (Francois & Ella CHAMPAGNE) b. 19 Aug. 1896 (Theriot Ch.: v.1-B, p.100)

CHAMPAGNE, Helena Laurina (Wiltz & Flauristive CHAMPAGNE) b. 18 Feb. 1899 (Theriot Ch.: v.2, p.37)

CHAMPAGNE, Honore d. 3 Oct. 1899 at age 65 yrs, 11 mths., 27 days (Thib. Ch.: v.3, p.241)

CHAMPAGNE, Ida d. 15 April 1898 at age 20 yrs. (Raceland Ch.: v.1, p.18)

CHAMPAGNE, Ida m. 2 Sept. 1897 Taylor FOLSE (Thib. Ct. Hse.: Mar. v.37, #219)

CHAMPAGNE, Ida (Jean Baptiste & Mathilde BOURGEOIS) m. 2 Sept. 1897 Taylor FOLSE (Raceland Ch.: v.2, p.49)

CHAMPAGNE, Irma (Oscar & Elema CHAUVIN) m. 10 May 1897 Olivier ESCHETE (Houma Ch.: v.6-a, p.201)

CHAMPAGNE, James Hayes (James & Marie DOMINGUE) b. 23 Nov. 1899 (Montegut Ch.: v.6, p.96)

CHAMPAGNE, Jean Baptiste d. 10 Oct. 1899 at age 68 yrs. (Raceland Ch.: v.1, p.28)

CHAMPAGNE, Jean Joseph (Damas & Josephine TOUPS) b. 19 Aug. 1898 (Thib. Ch.: v.7, p.560)

CHAMPAGNE, John Carl (Geo. & Mary Christine COOK) b. 20 June 1896 (Houma Ch.: Epis. Ch.: v.1, p.112-B)

CHAMPAGNE, Joseph Adam (Prosper & Elisa PERTUIT) b. 22 June 1897 (Raceland Ch.: v.5, p.50)

CHAMPAGNE, Joseph Alvin (William & Justine FOLSE) b. 9 June 1899 (Theriot Ch.: v.2, p.41)

CHAMPAGNE, Joseph Augustin (Camille & Esilia BAUDOUIN) b. 10 Nov. 1897 (Raceland Ch.: v.5, p.57)

CHAMPAGNE, Joseph Florestan d. 30 Dec. 1896 at age 79 yrs. (Thib. Ch.: v.3, p.192)

CHAMPAGNE, Joseph Fulbert (Alcide & Aimie CHAMPAGNE) b. 10 April 1899 (Theriot Ch.: v.2, p.39)

CHAMPAGNE, Joseph Heroad (Jean Baptiste & Ernestine HIMEL) b. 11 Dec. 1896 (Thib. Ch.: v.7, p.433)

CHAMPAGNE, Joseph O'Neil (Joseph & Annette FOLSE) b. 22 May 1898 (Raceland Ch.: v.5, p.71)

CHAMPAGNE, Joseph Oreste (Oscar & Mathilde BAYE) b. 2 May 1898 (Thib. Ch.: v.7, p.550)

CHAMPAGNE, Joseph Orestile (Orestile & Marie CHAMPAGNE) b. 20 Sept. 1896 (Thib. Ch.: v.7, p.416)

CHAMPAGNE, Joseph Ridley (Arthur & Elitia BROWN) b. 11 Dec. 1896 (Raceland Ch.: v.5, p.39)

CHAMPAGNE, Josephine m. 4 Feb. 1899 Beldon CHAMPAGNE (Houma Ct. Hse.: Mar. v.30 & 31, #309)

CHAMPAGNE, Josephine (Carol & Louisa CHAMPAGNE) m. 13 Feb. 1899 Balden CHAMPAGNE (Theriot Ch.: v.1-B, p.6)
CHAMPAGNE, Justin (Septime & Elmire PERTUIT) b. 17 Jan. 1897 (Raceland Ch.: v.5, p.41)
CHAMPAGNE, Latitia m. Jules SAUCIER d. 4 July 1897 at age 22 yrs. (Thib. Ch.: v.3, p.202)
CHAMPAGNE, Lawless Michel (Marie Letitia) b. 29 Sept. 1896 (Raceland Ch.: v.5, p.32)
CHAMPAGNE, Letitia m. 28 Aug. 1896 Jules SAUCIER (Thib. Ct. Hse.: Mar. v.36, #137)
CHAMPAGNE, Loetitia (Jean Baptiste & Mathilde BOURGEOIS) m. 10 Sept. 1896 Jules SAUCIER (Raceland Ch.: v.2, p.22)
CHAMPAGNE, Louise m. 17 Feb. 1897 Joseph HARDEN (Houma Ct. Hse.: Mar. v.29 & 30, #317)
CHAMPAGNE, Louise Marie Mathilde (Walter & Lucile DUCOTE) b. 9 Aug. 1896 (Thib. Ch.: v.7, p.413)
CHAMPAGNE, Maria (Camille & Esilia BAUDOUIN) b. 10 Jan. 1896 (Raceland Ch.: v.5, p.17)
CHAMPAGNE, Marie d. 10 Oct. 1896 at age 9 mths. (Raceland Ch.: v.1, p.10)
CHAMPAGNE, Marie Edna (Edouard & Elmire BRAUD) b. 28 July 1896 (Raceland Ch.: v.5, p.27)
CHAMPAGNE, Marie Louise (Althe & Eva BOUDREAU) b. 12 Nov. 1898 (Theriot Ch.: v.2, p.31)
CHAMPAGNE, Marie Melasie (Nelville & Mathilde FALGOUST) b. 27 May 1896 (Thib. Ch.: v.7, p.451)
CHAMPAGNE, Marie Melazie d. 11 July 1897 at age 2 mths. (Thib. Ch.: v.3, p.202)
CHAMPAGNE, Natty Rita (Jean Baptiste & Ernestine HYMEL) b. 21 Aug. 1898 (Thib. Ch.: v.7, p.512)
CHAMPAGNE, Noelie Bertille (Thomas & Marie ZERINGUE) b. 5 Nov. 1898 (Raceland Ch.: v.5, p.83)
CHAMPAGNE, Paul Dederick (Abel & Justilia Eva MALBROOK) b. 16 Oct. 1896 (Theriot Ch.: v.1-B, p.100)
CHAMPAGNE, Paul Faustin (Faustin & Marguerite CHAMPAGNE) b. 2 Nov. 1899 (Theriot Ch.: v.2, p.55)
CHAMPAGNE, Paul Willis (Willis & Florestine CHAMPAGNE) b. 18 June 1896 (Theriot Ch.: v.1-B, p.98)
CHAMPAGNE, Philip (Charles & Louisa CHAMPAGNE) m. 12 Jan. 1899 Felicia FANGUY (Houma Ct. Hse.: Mar. v.30 & 31, #223)
CHAMPAGNE, Philippe (Charles & Louisa CHAMPAGNE) m. 23 Jan. 1899 Felicia FANGUY (Theriot Ch.: v.1-B, p.5)
CHAMPAGNE, Philomene Beatrice (Faustin & Leontine WAGESPACK) b. 21 Nov. 1898 (Thib. Ch.: v.7, p.523)
CHAMPAGNE, Pierre Gester (Jimmy & Marie DOMINGUE) b. 19 Oct. 1896 (Montegut Ch.: v.6, p.47)
CHAMPAGNE, Pierre Olesie (Camille & Eselia BAUDOUIN) b. 17 Nov. 1899 (Raceland Ch.: v.5, p.107)
CHAMPAGNE, Pierre Vital (Sevilien & Celestine CHAMPAGNE) b. 23 Feb. 1899 (Raceland Ch.: v.5, p.91)

CHAMPAGNE, Sylvestre Clifford (William & Justine FAULS) b. 19 Sept. 1896 (Houma Ch.: v.5, p.160)
CHAMPAGNE, Thomas (Jean Baptiste & Mathilde BOURGEOIS) m. 17 Jan. 1898 Marie ZERINGUE (Lockport Ch.: v.2, p.179)
CHAMPAGNE, Thomas (Jean Baptiste & Mathilde BOURGEOIS) m. 17 Jan. 1898 Marie ZERINQUE (Thib. Ct. Hse.: Mar. v.37, #18)
CHAMPAGNE, Willoie Benoit (Faustin & Marguerite CHAMPAGNE) b. 7 Jan. 1896 (Theriot Ch.: v.1-B, p.88)
CHAMPION, Wallace m. 28 Dec. 1899 Josephine WHITE (Thib. Ct. Hse.: Mar. v.39, #304)
CHAPPUIS, Emilie (Alphonse & Oceana DANTIN) m. 7 July 1897 William D. McDONALD (Thib. Ct. Hse.: Mar. v.37, #186)
CHAPPUIS, Emily (Alphonse & Oceano DANTIN) m. 7 July 1897 William D. McDONALD (Thib. Ch.: v.14, p.152)
CHARLES, Anna m. 28 April 1898 Sylvestre BAPTISTE (Thib. Ct. Hse.: Mar. v.38, #172)
CHARLES, Cora (Anatole & Merraya CHARLES) b. 30 May 1898 (Thib. Ch.: v.7, p.504)
CHARLES, Julia m. 25 April 1898 Nelson BROWN (Thib. Ct. Hse.: Mar. v.38, #167)
CHARLES, Leontine (Anatole & Alice HANCOCK) m. 30 Jan. 1896 Robert BILLUPS (Thib. Ch.: v.14, p.70)
CHARLES, Leontine (Anatole & Alice HANCOCK) m. 30 Jan. 1896 Robert BILLUPS (Thib. Ct. Hse.: Mar. v.35, #35)
CHARLES, Marie Ange d. 4 Aug. 1897 at age 108 yrs. (Thib. Ch.: v.3, p.204)
CHARLES, Odelia m. 17 July 1897 George BROOM (Thib. Ct. Hse.: Mar. v.37, #195)
CHARLEY, Irving Carlos (Carlos & Lucie MARTIN) b. 7 Nov. 1899 (Theriot Ch.: v.2, p.52)

CHARPENTIER (Sometimes: CHARPENTEUR)

CHARPENTIER, Abel (Elizogone & Felicie BLANCHARD) m. 25 Sept. 1896 Bernadette FANGUY (Houma Ct. Hse.: Mar. v.29 & 30, #153)
CHARPENTIER, Adam (Elizogone & Felicie BLANCHARD) m. 8 Oct. 1896 Bernadette FANGUY (Montegut Ch.: v.4, p.214)
CHARPENTIER, Adam Laurent (Elisee & Aurelie FANGUY) b. 10 Feb. 1896 (Montegut Ch.: v.6, p.35)
CHARPENTIER, Albert Luc (Etienne & Eve ALEMAND) b. 4 Aug. 1896 (Larose Ch.: v.2, p.182)
CHARPENTIER, Alexina (Alexis & Armelise CHATAIGNIER) d. 3 Dec. 1899 at age 27 yrs. (Montegut Ch.: v.2, p.31)
CHARPENTIER, Elie Claude (Adam & Agnes LEBLANC) b. 24 Nov. 1898 (Montegut Ch.: v.6, p.80)
CHARPENTIER, Eve Leonise (Abel & Bernadette FANGUY) b. 18 April 1899 (Montegut Ch.: v.6, p.86)
CHARPENTIER, Felix Rosemond (----ge & Anastasia CHOUESS) b. 18 May 1896 (Larose Ch.: v.2, p.192)

CHARPENTIER, Ives Jean (Etienne & Eve ALEMAN) b. 14 March 1899 (Larose Ch.: v.3, p.38)
CHARPENTIER, Joseph Celestin (Elisee & Aurelie FANGUY) b. 17 Feb. 1898 (Montegut Ch.: v.6, p.68)
CHARPENTIER, Luc Albert (Etienne & Eve ALLEMAND) b. 4 Aug. 1896 (Larose Ch.: v.2, p.196)
CHARPENTIER, Marie Anceda (Abel & Bernadette FANGUY) b. 8 July 1897 (Montegut Ch.: v.6, p.59)
CHARPENTIER, Marie Felicia (Adam & Agnes LEBLANC) b. 8 Dec. 1896 (Montegut Ch.: v.6, p.49)
CHARPENTIER, Marie Seraphine m. d.Jean Baptiste DUPLANTIS; d. 1 Nov. 1898 at age 86 yrs. (Montegut Ch.: v.2, p.21)
CHARPENTIER, Palmiere (Elizigone & Felicie BLANCHARD) m. 14 July 1896 Frank ROBICHAUX (Houma Ct. Hse.: Mar. v.29 & 30, #112)
CHARPENTIER, Palmiree (Elizigone & Felicie BLANCHARD) m. 6 Aug. 1896 Frank ROBICHAUX (Montegut Ch.: v.4, p.213)
CHARPENTIER, Seraphine d. 1 Nov. 1898; m. John Baptiste DUPLANTIS Children: Joseph O.; Aglae m. Justin MARTIN; Felicien; Armelie m. J. A. GAIDRY; Elizogone; Seraphine m. Voltaire PELLEGRIN; Justin; Terrance; Leufroy Aived; Eugenie m. J. Augustin DUPLANTIS. Petition for appt. of Adm.: 5 Dec. 1898. (Houma Ct. Hse.: Succ. #909)
CHARPENTIER, Uzeline m. 23 April 1896 Florestal GUIDRY (Thib. Ct. Hse.: Mar. v.35, #77)

CHATAIGNIER (Sometimes: CHATAIGNE, CHATANIER)

CHATAIGNIER, Abe (George & Azelie BELANGER) m. 31 Jan. 1898 Eveline BOUDREAU (Houma Ch.: v.6-a, p.227)
CHATAIGNIER, Albert Elene (Elere & Eveline BOUDREAUX) b. 14 March 1899 (Houma Ch.: v.5, p.244)
CHATAIGNIER, Alec m. 29 Jan. 1898 Eveline BOUDREAUX (Houma Ct. Hse.: Mar. v.30 & 31, #261)
CHATAIGNIER, Clara (Eugene & Eve BERGERON) m. 17 March 1898 Wilfred PONTIFF (Houma Ct. Hse.: Mar. v.30 & 31, #344)
CHATAIGNIER, Francois d. 8 Feb. 1897 at age 42 yrs. (Houma Ch.: v.3, p.11)
CHATAIGNIER, James (Marcel & Louisiane STOUFFLET) d. 25 Dec. 1899 at age 21 yrs. (Montegut Ch.: v.2, p.32)
CHATAIGNIER, Joseph William (Ernest & Marie Rose LEDET) b. 19 March 1896 (Montegut Ch.: v.6, p.36)
CHATAIGNIER, Joseph Willis (Ernest & Marie Rose LEDET) b. 29 May 1899 (Montegut Ch.: v.6, p.88)
CHATAIGNIER, Marie d. 17 Oct. 1896 at age 2 mths. (Houma Ch.: v.3, p.9)
CHATAIGNIER, Victoria d. 30 Nov. 1899 at age 14 mths. (Houma Ch.: v.3, p.26)
CHATAIGNIER, Victoria (Seraphin & Josephine BERGERON) b. 23 Aug. 1898 (Houma Ch.: v.5, p.226)

CHATAIGNIER, Welsy d. 14 Nov. 1896 at age 9 yrs. (Houma Ch.: v.3, p.9)
CHAUFF, Laura Louise d. 23 Oct. 1898 at age 2 mths. (Houma Ch.: v.3, p.19)
CHAUFF, Laura Louise (Achil & Melissa CHAUVIN) b. 22 Aug. 1898 (Houma Ch.: v.5, p.217)

CHAUVIN (Sometimes: CHAUVET)
CHAUVIN, Albertine (Theogene & Louisa TOUPS) m. 4 Jan. 1896 Augustave THERIOT (Houma Ct. Hse.: Mar. v.28, #369)
CHAUVIN, Albertine (Theogene & Louise TOUPS) m. 21 Jan. 1896 Augustave THERIOT (Theriot Ch.: v.1, p.3)
CHAUVIN, Alfred m. 11 Dec. 1896 Denise SEVIN (Thib. Ct. Hse.: Mar. v.36, #166)
CHAUVIN, Alfred (Theodule & Emelie LALANNE) m. 16 Dec. 1896 Denise SEVIN (Raceland Ch.: v.2, p.23)
CHAUVIN, Alice J. (L. Stival & Elexiola BERTHEAUD) m. 25 Oct. 1897 George S. WHIPPLE (Montegut Ch.: v.4, p.227)
CHAUVIN, Alice J. (L. Stival & Elezida GAUTREAUX) m. 22 Oct. 1897 George S. WHIPPLE (Houma Ct. Hse.: Mar. v.29 & 30, #125)
CHAUVIN, Anne Pearl (Arthur & Virginie BERGERON) b. 18 Oct. 1897 (Montegut Ch.: v.6, p.62)
CHAUVIN, Arthee m. 14 Feb. 1899 Octavie PERRES (Thib. Ct. Hse.: Mar. v.39, #106)
CHAUVIN, Ather Mary (Henry & Suzanne PICOU) b. 27 Oct. 1897 (Montegut Ch.: v.6, p.62)
CHAUVIN, Audrey Clotilda (Camille & Emma LYALL) b. 18 Oct. 1899 (Raceland Ch.: v.5, p.106)
CHAUVIN, Aurelia Marie (Steve & Zulema DUPLANTIS) b. 5 March 1897 (Houma Ch.: v.5, p.175)
CHAUVIN, Cestive (Cestive & Lucette DUPLANTIS) m. 15 Feb. 1896 Zulema DUPLANTIS (Houma Ch.: v.6-a, p.170)
CHAUVIN, Cestive Jr. m. 15 Feb. 1896 Zulema DUPLANTIS (Houma Ct. Hse.: Mar. v.28, #460)
CHAUVIN, Charles Leon (Taylor & Victoria MOUTARDIER) b. 21 April 1897 (Montegut Ch.: v.6, p.53)
CHAUVIN, Charles Walter (Noe & Marie TOUPS) b. 16 Sept. 1898 (Theriot Ch.: v.2, p.30)
CHAUVIN, Cinthia (Emile & Bertile BERGERON) m. 26 Dec. 1899 Albert Joseph FOREST (Houma Ct. Hse.: Mar. v.31 & 32, #195)
CHAUVIN, Claude Zacharie (Aramis & Mathilde CHAUVIN) d. 22 May 1899 at age 7 yrs. (Montegut Ch.: v.2, p.26)
CHAUVIN, Clay (Adolphe & Celestine HEBERT) m. 12 Sept. 1899 Aglae MARTIN (Houma Ct. Hse.: Mar. v.31 & 32, #126)
CHAUVIN, Clay (d.Adolphe & d.Celestine HEBERT) m. 5 Oct. 1899 Aglaee MARTIN (Montegut Ch.: v.4, p.271)
CHAUVIN, David Claude (Ernest & Austin CHAUVIN) b. 27 July 1898 (Houma Ch.: v.5, p.217)

CHAUVIN, Edmond Leon (Theobert & Ulalie THERRIOT) b. 8 Jan. 1896 (Larose Ch.: v.2, p.179)
CHAUVIN, Edouard Joseph (Arthur & Virginie BERGERON) b. 3 March 1896 (Montegut Ch.: v.6, p.36)
CHAUVIN, Eleonore widow of Robert TASTET m. 23 Jan. 1897 Alexandre PERTUIT (Thib. Ct. Hse.: Mar. v.36, #51)
CHAUVIN, Eleonore (Zenon & Mathilde BAUDOIN) m. 25 Jan. 1897 Alexandre PERTUIS (Raceland Ch.: v.2, p.28)
CHAUVIN, Eli J. m. 26 Nov. 1897 Jesse M. YOUNG (Houma Ct. Hse.: Mar. v.29 & 30, #137)
CHAUVIN, Elie (Paupelus & Severine PELEGRIN) m. 28 Nov. 1897 Jessie M. YOUNG (Houma Ch.: v.6-a, p.220)
CHAUVIN, Elizabeth (Emile & Josephine PARR) m. 29 Nov. 1898 Philippe TOUPS (Thib. Ct. Hse.: Mar. v.38, #310)
CHAUVIN, Elizabeth (Emile & Josephine PARR) m. 29 Nov. 1898 Philippe TOUPS (Lockport Ch.: v.2, p.197)
CHAUVIN, Eloi Philippe (Miles &Amelie DUMEZ) b. 13 Oct. 1899 (Montegut Ch.: v.6, p.93)
CHAUVIN, Emelina (Theober & Eulalie THERIOT) m. 1 Feb. 1896 Joseph GUIDRY (Lockport Ch.: v.2, p.145 & 146)
CHAUVIN, Emelina (Theober & Eulalie THERIOT) m. 1 Feb. 1896 Joseph GUIDRY (Thib. Ct. Hse.: Mar. v.35, #23)
CHAUVIN, Emma (Octave & Camilla BABIN) m. 26 Dec. 1899 Orestile PELEGRIN (Houma Ct. Hse.: Mar. v.31 & 32, #204)
CHAUVIN, Eugene Joseph (Miles Joseph & Amelie DUMES) b. 20 Jan. 1896 (Montegut Ch.: v.6, p.32)
CHAUVIN, Eva (Valcour & Berthilde FOREST) m. 22 July 1899 Luke DUPLANTIS (Houma Ct. Hse.: Mar. v.31 & 32, #96)
CHAUVIN, Eva (Valcour & Berthilde FOREST) m. 7 Aug. 1899 Luc DUPLANTIS (Montegut Ch.: v.4, p.268)
CHAUVIN, Evellia m. 27 Feb. 1897 Elphege BAUDOIN (Lockport Ch.: v.2, p.160)
CHAUVIN, Evelline (Silvestre & Rosalie BLANCHARD) m. 27 Feb. 1897 Elphege BAUDOIN (Thib. Ct. Hse.: Mar. v.38, #65)
CHAUVIN, Felix Albert (Zenon & Laura ROUSSEL) b. 7 Aug. 1899 (Lockport Ch.: v.3-A, #3)
CHAUVIN, Felix Albert (Zenon & Laura ROUSSEL) b. 7 Aug. 1899 (Lockport Ch.: v.3, #3)
CHAUVIN, Freddie (Wilz & Agnes STOUFFLET) d. 13 Jan. 1899 at age 44 yrs. (Montegut Ch.: v.2, p.23)
CHAUVIN, Grace (Eloie & Olinda FALGOUT) m. 25 Sept. 1897 Farquard P. GUIDRY (Houma Ct. Hse.: Mar. v.29 & 30, #96)
CHAUVIN, Grace (Elvie & d.Olinda FALGOUT) m. 12 Oct. 1897 Farguard P. GUIDRY (Montegut Ch.: v.4, p.226)
CHAUVIN, Harold Leo (Camille & Emma LYALL) b. 21 June 1898 (Raceland Ch.: v.5, p.73)
CHAUVIN, Harry (L. Stival & Elexida BERTHEAUX) m. 1 June 1897 Martha BELANGER (Montegut Ch.: v.4, p.221)
CHAUVIN, Harry Leo d. 25 Sept. 1898 at age 3 mths. (Raceland Ch.: v.1, p.20)

CHAUVIN, Harry V. (L. Stival & Elezida BERTHEAUD) m. 1 May 1897 Martha BELANGER (Houma Ct. Hse.: Mar. v.29 & 30, #397)
CHAUVIN, Helene Bernice (Volcar & Euphrasie STOUFFLET) b. 3 Oct. 1898 (Montegut Ch.: v.6, p.79)
CHAUVIN, James Ars (Oleus & Frasalie DUPLANTIS) b. 1 April 1896 (Houma Ch.: v.5, p.151)
CHAUVIN, James Hase (Oleus & Froselie DUPLANTIS) b. 1 April 1896 (Houma Ch.: v.5, p.150)
CHAUVIN, John Adolphe (Stevan & Julia DUPLANTIS) b. 23 March 1899 (Houma Ch.: v.5, p.241)
CHAUVIN, Joseph (Franklin & Ida GUIDRY) d. 3 Dec. 1896 (Montegut Ch.: v.2, p.8)
CHAUVIN, Joseph Columbus (Albert & Josephine STOUFFLET) b. 15 May 1898 (Montegut Ch.: v.6, p.73)
CHAUVIN, Joseph Dewey (Anathole & Ophelia THERIOT) b. 27 July 1899 (Theriot Ch.: v.2, p.46)
CHAUVIN, Joseph Dewey (Henry & Suzanne PICOU) b. 18 Sept. 1899 (Montegut Ch.: v.6, p.92)
CHAUVIN, Joseph Evans Vanny (Emile & Berthilde BERGERON) b. 31 May 1897 (Montegut Ch.: v.6, p.57)
CHAUVIN, Joseph Laurent (Franklin & Ida GUIDRY) b. 12 Jan. 1898 (Montegut Ch.: v.6, p.64)
CHAUVIN, Joseph Lawrence (Harry & Martha BELANGER) b. 26 Oct. 1899 (Montegut Ch.: v.6, p.95)
CHAUVIN, Joseph Onesippe (Albert & Josephine STOUFFLET) d. 2 Sept. 1899 at age 9 yrs. (Montegut Ch.: v.2, p.28)
CHAUVIN, Joseph Roy (Albert & Anastasie BERGERON) b. 15 April 1898 (Houma Ch.: v.5, p.205)
CHAUVIN, Joseph Sidney Lafaillet (Sidny & Eveline WATKIN) b. 23 Jan. 1896 (Houma Ch.: v.5, p.144)
CHAUVIN, Joseph Villiard (Albert & Louise STOUFFLET) b. 25 Jan. 1896 (Montegut Ch.: v.6, p.34)
CHAUVIN, Josephine Mabel (Hudson & Emelie AYO) b. 25 March 1896 (Houma Ch.: v.5, p.176)
CHAUVIN, Jules (Leufroy & Melina BLANCHARD) m. 17 Jan. 1898 Louise PELEGRIN (Houma Ct. Hse.: Mar. v.30 & 31, #222)
CHAUVIN, Jules (Lufroy & Melina BLANCHARD) m. 7 Feb. 1898 Louise PELEGRIN (Theriot Ch.: v.1-B, p.2)
CHAUVIN, Justine Marie (Justin & d.Eulodie THIBODAUX) m. 28 Sept. 1899 Leonce P. BOUDREAUX (Montegut Ch.: v.4, p.270)
CHAUVIN, Justine Mary (Justin & Elodi THIBODAUX) m. 16 Sept. 1899 Leonce P. BOUDREAUX (Houma Ct. Hse.: Mar. v.31 & 32, #136)
CHAUVIN, Leodile m.28 March 1896 Nickless LECOMPTE (Houma Ct. Hse.: Mar. v.29 & 30, #26)
CHAUVIN, Leodile (Aramise & Mathilde CHAUVIN) m. 30 April 1896 Nickless LECOMPTE (Montegut Ch.: v.4, p.209)
CHAUVIN, Lorina m. Theophile BABIN d. 26 March 1898 at age 28 yrs. (Montegut Ch.: v.2, p.16)

CHAUVIN, Lorine (L. Stival & Elizida BERTHAUD) m. 6 May 1899 Francis D. A. BURRIGHT (Houma Ct. Hse.: Mar. v.31 & 32, #2)

CHAUVIN, Lorinne (L. Stival & Elezida BERTHEAUD) m. 25 May 1899 Francis D. A. BURRIGHT (Montegut Ch.: v.4, p.264)

CHAUVIN, Louis (Taylor & Victoria MOUTARDIER) m. 11 March 1899 Elmire DUPLANTIS (Houma Ct. Hse.: Mar. v.31 & 32, #363)

CHAUVIN, Louis (Taylor & Victoria MOUTARDIER) m. 3 April 1899 Elmire DUPLANTIS (Montegut Ch.: v.4, p.259)

CHAUVIN, Louis Hobson (Joseph Miles & Amelie DUMEZ) b. 6 June 1898 (Montegut Ch.: v.6, p.72)

CHAUVIN, Louis Ignes (Alies & Julia PELEGRIN) b. 23 Sept. 1896 (Montegut Ch.: v.6, p.47)

CHAUVIN, Lucile Brigitte (Argus & Amelina TOUPS) b. 8 Oct. 1897 (Raceland Ch.: v.5, p.56)

CHAUVIN, Lum d. 20 Feb. 1897 at age 38 yrs. (Houma Ch.: v.3, p.11)

CHAUVIN, Marguerite Florence (Albert & Alouisa JONES) b. 6 Jan. 1896 (Montegut Ch.: v.6, p.31)

CHAUVIN, Maria Myrtha (Joseph & Aurelia TOUPS) b. 22 Jan. 1899 (Theriot Ch.: v.2, p.33)

CHAUVIN, Marie (Arthur & Virginie BERGERON) d. 3 Sept. 1899 at age 3 days (Montegut Ch.: v.2, p.28)

CHAUVIN, Marie Lena (Henis & Cecilia CHAMPAGNE) b. 21 Dec. 1897 (Theriot Ch.: v.2, p.14)

CHAUVIN, Marie Leola (Wilz & Agnes STOUFFLET) b. 17 Sept. 1898 (Montegut Ch.: v.6, p.77)

CHAUVIN, Marie Louise (Oleus & Jenevieve Frosilia DUPLANTIS) b. 8 Oct. 1899 (Houma Ch.: v.5, p.258)

CHAUVIN, Marie Louise (Wills & Agnes STOUFFLET) b. 5 May 1896 (Montegut Ch.: v.6, p.41)

CHAUVIN, Marie Lydie (Merille & Lea FALGOUT) b. 1 May 1897 (Theriot Ch.: v.1-B, p.106)

CHAUVIN, Marie Rosa (Jules & Louise PELEGRIN) b. 14 Dec. 1898 (Theriot Ch.: v.2, p.40)

CHAUVIN, Marie Viola (Harry & Martha BELANGER) b. 24 March 1898 (Montegut Ch.: v.6, p.68)

CHAUVIN, Mary Bessie (Ernest & Aristine CHAUVIN) b. 25 Sept. 1896 (Houma Ch.: v.5, p.162)

CHAUVIN, Mary Rosa (Clay & Rosa JANSSEN) b. 21 Feb. 1899 (Houma Ch.: v.5, p.238)

CHAUVIN, Mirtee Mrs. d. 10 March 1896 at age 78 yrs. (Houma Ch.: v.3, p.7)

CHAUVIN, Mirtile d. 6 June 1898 at age 19 yrs. (Raceland Ch.: v.1, p.19)

CHAUVIN, Myrthilia (Silvestre & Rosela BLANCHARD) m. 5 Nov. 1898 Armand GERVAIS (Thib. Ct. Hse.: Mar. v.38, #301)

CHAUVIN, Myrthilia (Silvestre & Rosela BLANCHARD) m. 5 Nov. 1898 Armand GERVAIS (Lockport Ch.: v.2, p.196)

CHAUVIN, Octave d. 2 Jan. 1897 at age 60 yrs. (Montegut Ch.: v.2, p.9)
CHAUVIN, Octave John (Sidney & Eveline WATKINS) b. 23 Aug. 1898 (Houma Ch.: v.5, p.216)
CHAUVIN, Octavie m. Octave AUTHEMENT d. 29 May 1899 at age 40 yrs. (Montegut Ch.: v.2, p.26)
CHAUVIN, Odressie m. 12 June 1897 Ella PARKS (Thib. Ct. Hse.: Mar. v.36, #168)
CHAUVIN, Olum Otto (Henry Clay & Rosa Mary JANSON) b. 9 Jan. 1896 (Houma Ch.: v.5, p.170)
CHAUVIN, Oscar d. 29 Nov. 1899 (Houma Ch.: v.3, p.26)
CHAUVIN, Oswald Toussaint (Joseph & Carolie TOOPS) b. 1 Nov. 1896 (Theriot Ch.: v.1-B, p.102)
CHAUVIN, Philomene Elizabeth (Lygnes & Elvire BERGERON) b. 26 March 1897 (Montegut Ch.: v.6, p.55)
CHAUVIN, Pierre Paul (Anatole & Ophelia THERIOT) b. 29 June 1897 (Theriot Ch.: v.2, p.7)
CHAUVIN, Pompelus (Hyppolite) d. 20 March 1896 at age 45 yrs. (Montegut Ch.: v.2, p.3)
CHAUVIN, Prosper m. 11 June 1897 Azelie BERGERON (Larose Ch.: v.3, p.6)
CHAUVIN, Prosper m. 11 June 1897 Azelie BERGERON (Larose Ch.: v.4, p.74)
CHAUVIN, Prosper m. 25 May 1897 Azelie BERGERON (Thib. Ct. Hse.: Mar. v.36, #149)
CHAUVIN, Rosa (Jules) d. 4 Oct. 1899 at age 10 mths. (Theriot Ch.: v.1, p.2)
CHAUVIN, Rosa Mary d. 11 May 1899 at age 2 mths., 15 days (Houma Ch.: v.3, p.22)
CHAUVIN, Valerie Unisa (Sestive & Edda FALGOUT) b. 20 Nov. 1897 (Houma Ch.: v.5, p.193)
CHENET, Aexandre (Louis & Oinza LEBOURGEOIS) m. 3 Aug. 1897 Julia THIBODAUX (Thib. Ch.: v.14, p.155)
CHENET, Alexandre (Louis & Aima LEBOURGEOIS) m. 3 Aug. 1897 Julia THIBODAUX (Thib. Ct. Hse.: Mar. v.37, #203)
CHENET, Theophile Thibodaux (Alexandre & Julia Josephine THIBODAUX) b. 3 Sept. 1898 (Thib. Ch.: v.7, p.512)

CHERAMI (Sometimes: CHERAMIE)

CHERAMI or VEGA, Celeste Lucie (Raphael & Celestine HAUTIN) b. 10 April 1897 (Larose Ch.: v.3, p.8)
CHERAMI, Adam Dolte (Ozeme & Marie THERIOT) b. 22 Oct. 1898 (Larose Ch.: v.3, p.57)
CHERAMI, Adolsine (Gratien & Edilie CHERAMIE) m. 9 Dec. 1899 Cledomire LAFONT (Larose Ch.: v.4, p.130)
CHERAMI, Adolsine (Gratien & Edilie CHERAMIE) m. 28 Nov. 1899 cleodomire LAFONT (Thib. Ct. Hse.: Mar. v.39, #271)
CHERAMI, Adolsine (Gratien & Eolilie CHERAMIE) m. 9 Dec. 1899 Cledoniere LAFONT (Larose Ch.: v.3, p.13)
CHERAMI, Alcida Marguerite (Lovinci & Julia PLAISANCE) b. 10 Nov. 1899 (Larose Ch.: v.3, p.48)

CHERAMI, Angele (Lucien & Blanche PITRE) b. 27 Aug. 1897 (Larose Ch.: v.3, p.18)

CHERAMI, Antoine Camelet (Pierre & Clorinda GUEDRY) b. 1 March 1899 (Larose Ch.: v.3, p.39)

CHERAMI, Aramis Crespin (Rodolphe & Alexina DUAY) b. 25 Oct. 1897 (Larose Ch.: v.3, p.27)

CHERAMI, Armance m. 19 Feb. 1898 Andre TERREBONNE (Larose Ch.: v.3, p.8)

CHERAMI, Armance m. 19 Feb. 1898 Andre TERREBONNE (Larose Ch.: v.4, p.75)

CHERAMI, Armance (Orestile CHERAMIE) m. 29 Feb. 1898 Andre TERREBONNE (Thib. Ct. Hse.: Mar. v.37, #105)

CHERAMI, Arminta Josephine (Emmanuel & Rosema PITRE) b. 20 July 1899 (Larose ch.: v.3, p.47)

CHERAMI, Carlogica (Frank & Carmela SPERA) b. 25 Oct. 1899 (Thib. Ch.: v.7, p.584)

CHERAMI, Eize m. 21 Oct. 1899 Ezelida BURNS (Thib. Ct. Hse.: Mar. v.39, #250)

CHERAMI, Emanuel m. 18 May 1898 Rose PITRE (Thib. Ct. Hse.: Mar. v.38, #181)

CHERAMI, Emilienne Cleonise (Julien & Julie CHERAMI) b. 9 June 1897 (Larose Ch.: v.3, p.6)

CHERAMI, Ernest m. 25 June 1896 Evelina CALET (Larose Ch.: v.4, p.88)

CHERAMI, Ernest m. 25 June 1896 Evelina CALET (Larose Ch.: v.3, p.3)

CHERAMI, Ernest (Ernest & Evelina CALET) b. 6 or 8 May 1896 (Larose Ch.: v.2, p.193)

CHERAMI, Ernestine Margueritte (Ernest & Evelina COLET) b. 17 May 1898 (Larose Ch.: v.3, p.20)

CHERAMI, Ezelia m. 6 Feb. 1897 Jean BOUDREAU (Larose Ch.: v.4, p.5)

CHERAMI, Ezelia m. 6 Feb. 1897 Jean BOUDREAUX (Larose Ch.: v.4, p.117)

CHERAMI, Ezelia m.25 Jan. 1897 John BOUDREAUX (Thib. Ct. Hse.: Mar. v.36, #56)

CHERAMI, Felix Ese (Felix & Laurentia VEGAS) b. 3 Feb. 1897 (Larose Ch.: v.3, p.4)

CHERAMI, Francois Edward (Laurent & Elmire PITRE) b. 30 Jan. 1898 (Larose Ch.: v.3, p.22)

CHERAMI, Hubert Auson (Gratien & Odillia CHERAMIE) b. 13 April 1896 (Larose Ch.: v.2, p.192)

CHERAMI, Jackson Benoit (Julien & Julie CHERAMI) b. 13 Feb. 1899 (Larose Ch.: v.3, p.42)

CHERAMI, Jean Maurice (Ovide & Eulalie CALET) b. 8 Feb. 1898 (Larose Ch.: v.3, p.25)

CHERAMI, Julia (Lucien & Blanche PITRE) b. 1 Aug. 1899 (Larose Ch.: v.3, p.49)

CHERAMI, Julie (Rodolphe & Alexina DUET) m. 9 May 1896 Julien CHERAMI (Thib. Ct. Hse.: Mar. v.35, #79)

CHERAMI, Julien m. 16 Sept. 1899 Josephine CALLAIS (Thib. Ct. Hse.: Mar. v.39, #224)

CHERAMI, Julien (Aglee HEBERT) m. 9 May 1896 Julie CHERAMIE (Thib. Ct. Hse.: Mar. v.35, #79)

CHERAMI, Laurens m. 31 Jan. 1898 Emilie DANOS (Larose Ch.: v.3, p.7)

CHERAMI, Laurens m. 31 Jan. 1898 Emilie DANOS (Larose Ch.: v.4, p.113)

CHERAMI, Laurens (Andre & Melisaire AUTIN) m. 31 Jan. 1898 Emily DANOS (Thib. Ct. Hse.: Mar. v.37, #55)

CHERAMI, Lovincie m. 19 June 1897 Julia PLAISANCE (Larose Ch.: v.3, p.6)

CHERAMI, Lovincie m. 19 June 1897 Julia PLAISANCE (Larose Ch.: v.4, p.66)

CHERAMI, Lovincie m. 29 May 1897 Julia PLAISANCE (Thib. Ct. Hse.: Mar. v.36, #153)

CHERAMI, Marie m. 24 May 1898 Joseph DANOS (Thib. Ct. Hse.: Mar. v.38, #187)

CHERAMI, Marie Adela (Aramis & Josephine SAVOIE) b. 6 July 1899 (Larose Ch.: v.3, p.40)

CHERAMI, Marie Divienne (Cressin & Rosalie DOUCET) b. 14 Aug. 1897 (Larose Ch.: v.3, p.5)

CHERAMI, Marie Ernestine (Theophile & Lovinia CANTRELLE) b. 4 Dec. 1897 (Larose Ch.: v.3, p.25)

CHERAMI, Marie Eunitia (Pierre & Clorida GUEDRY) b. 16 May 1897 (Larose Ch.: v.3, p.9)

CHERAMI, Marie Eve (Jacqueline & Evelide DANTIN or AUTIN) b. 5 Nov. 1898 (Larose Ch.: v.3, p.41)

CHERAMI, Mathilde m. 17 July 1897 Hypolitte EYMARD (Larose Ch.: v.3, p.6)

CHERAMI, Mathilde m. 17 July 1897 Hyppolitte AYMARD (Larose Ch.: v.4, p.93-B)

CHERAMI, Mathilde m. 17 July 1897 Hyppolitte EYMARD (Larose Ch.: v.4, p.116)

CHERAMI, Matilde m. 1 July 1897 Hypolite EYMARD (Thib. Ct. Hse.: Mar. v.37, #188)

CHERAMI, Meline m. d.David PITRE d. 18 Jan. 1897 at age 84 yrs. (Larose Ch.: v.1, p.39)

CHERAMI, Olucien m. 2 July 1896 Blanche PITRE (Thib. Ct. Hse.: Mar. v.36, #115)

CHERAMI, Olucien (Olucien & Aglae HEBERT) m. 16 April 1898 Blanche PITRE (Larose Ch.: v.3, p.8)

CHERAMI, Olucien (Olucien & Aglae HEBERT) m. 16 April 1898 Blanche PITRE (Larose Ch.: v.4, p.80)

CHERAMI, Ovide (Olucien & Aglae HEBERT) m. 16 April 1898 Eulalie CALET (Larose Ch.: v.3, p.8)

CHERAMI, Ovide (Olucien & Aglae HEBERT) m. 7 April 1898 Eulalie COLET (Larose Ch.: v.4, p.82)

CHERAMI, Paul (Joseph & Marceline SEVIN) m. 8 Nov. 1899 Alvina TERREBONNE of Lacheniere (Larose Ch.: v.3, p.12)

CHERAMI, Paul (Joseph & Marceline SEVIN) m. 8 Nov. 1899 Almina TERREBONNE Civil marriage: 19 June 1897. (Larose Ch.: v.4, p.126)
CHERAMI, Paul Adam (Paul & Almina TERREBONNE) b. 5 Oct. 1899 (Larose Ch.: v.3, p.48)
CHERAMI, Pierre m. 29 June 1896 Clorinda GUIDRY (Thib. Ct. Hse.: Mar. v.36, #113)
CHERAMI, Pierre William (Theophile & Lovinia CANTRELLE) b. 5 Sept. 1897 (Larose Ch.: v.3, p.7)
CHERAMI, Placide Berthol (Ozeme & Marie THERIOT) b. 5 Oct. 1897 (Larose Ch.: v.3, p.8)
CHERAMI, William Albert (Oramis & Josephine SAVOIE) b. 11 Nov. 1896 (Larose Ch.: v.2, p.187)
CHERAULT, James (Felix & ---- BERCHERAN) m. 17 Feb. 1896 Mary COULAN (Thib. Ch.: v.14, p.81)
CHERAULT, James (Felix & Salome BOUCHERAU) m. 17 Feb. 1896 Mary COULON (Thib. Ct. Hse.: Mar. v.35, #45)
CHERAULT, Sarah Kathleen (James & Mary CONLAN) b. 9 Dec. 1898 (Thib. Ch.: v.7, p.530)
CHEST, Alida m. Emile MARLBOROUGH d. 26 July 1899 at age 44 yrs. (Montegut Ch.: v.2, p.27)
CHESTER, Ernest Joseph (Ernest & Nelly JOSEPH) b. 2 Jan. 1898 (Thib. Ch.: v.7, p.539)

CHETE (Sometimes: ACHETE, ECHETE, ECHTE, ESHETE, ESTHE)

CHETE, Alsane (Dalmas & Alida BOUDREAUX) m. 24 May 1899 Dominique CUNEO (Houma Ct. Hse.: Mar. v.31 & 32, #15)
CHETE, Angela m. 7 June 1897 Columbus Sidney RODDY (Houma Ch.: v.6-a, p.206)
CHETE, Angela m. 7 June 1897 Columbus Sidney RODDY (Houma Ct. Hse.: Mar. v.29 & 30, #11)
CHETE, Arsene (Delmas & Alida BOUDREAUX) m. 24 June 1899 Domingue CUNEO (Montegut Ch.: v.4, p.266)
CHETE, Arthur (Cadet & Sarah ROBINSON) m. 1 July 1897 Odelia MALBROUGH (Houma Ct. Hse.: Mar. v.29 & 30, #45)
CHETE, Asene Marie (Marcel & Eveline WATKIN) b. 19 April 1896 (Houma Ch.: v.5, p.154)
CHETE, Clothilde Aurelia (Justilien & Alicia MARTIN) b. 13 Dec. 1897 (Montegut Ch.: v.6, p.66)
CHETE, Jean Baptiste d. 6 March 1896 at age 21 yrs., 8 mths., 10 days (Houma Ch.: v.3, p.6)
CHETE, Jean Baptiste Ernest (Ollivan & Irma CHAMPAGNE) b. 2 Aug. 1898 (Houma Ch.: v.5, p.217)
CHETE, Jeanne d. 9 Sept. 1897 at age 6 days (Houma Ch.: v.3, p.14)
CHETE, John (Trazile & Zulema BOUDREAUX) m. 6 June 1899 Celestine MARCEL (Houma Ct. Hse.: Mar. v.31 & 32, #29)
CHETE, John Wilkinson (Joseph & Helene CUNIO) b. 22 May 1898 (Montegut Ch.: v.6, p.72)
CHETE, Joseph d. 25 Oct. 1898 at age 55 yrs. (Houma Ch.: v.3, p.19)

CHETE, Joseph m. 14 Jan. 1899 Elize BERGERON (Houma Ct. Hse.: Mar. v.30 & 31, #233)
CHETE, Joseph (Adam & Jane OLIVIER) m. 14 Jan. 1899 Elize BERGERON (Houma Ch.: v.6-a, p.265)
CHETE, Joseph (Dalmas & Alida BOUDREAUX) m. 4 May 1896 Ellen CUNEO (Houma Ct. Hse.: Mar. v.29 & 30, #48)
CHETE, Joseph (Delmas & Alida BOUDREAUX) m. 1 June 1896 Helene CUNEO (Montegut Ch.: v.4, p.210)
CHETE, Joseph Frederic (Alcindor & Aglae BARRIOS) b. 13 Feb. 1896 (Lockport Ch.: v.2, p.322)
CHETE, Joseph Hase (Joseph & Lilie COLWART) b. 5 June 1896 (Houma Ch.: v.5, p.184)
CHETE, Joseph Laurent (Ellis & Elvire PITT) b. 23 Sept. 1896 (Montegut Ch.: v.6, p.46)
CHETE, Josephine Inez (Charles & Julienne CROCHET) b. 9 Jan. 1899 (Houma Ch.: v.5, p.236)
CHETE, Julian m. 25 Nov. 1899 Louise DUET (Thib. Ct. Hse.: Mar. v.39, #267)
CHETE, Julien minor, over 18 (Louis & Azema OGERON) Emancipation: 2 Jan. 1897. (Thib. Ct. Hse.: Succ. #1501)
CHETE, Julien (Louis & Azèma ORGERON) m. 25 Nov. 1899 Louise DUET (Larose Ch.: v.3, p.13)
CHETE, Julien (Louis & Azeme ORGERON) m. 25 Nov. 1899 Louise DUET (Larose Ch.: v.4, p.127)
CHETE, Julien Cletus (Charly & Julienne CROCHET) b. 25 Aug. 1896; m. Cedy Victoria SAVOIE on 23 Feb. 1925. (Houma Ch.: Bapt. Bk., v.5, p.157)
CHETE, Malesie Antoinette (Dalmas & Alida BOUDREAUX) b. 28 March 1896 (Montegut Ch.: v.6, p.37)
CHETE, Marie Lidia (Arthur & Odilia MARLBROUGH) b. 12 Oct. 1898 (Houma Ch.: v.5, p.221)
CHETE, Marie Medonia (Ellis & Elvire PITRE) b. 11 April 1899 (Montegut Ch.: v.6, p.90)
CHETE, Mary Mathilde m. 25 July 1898 Francis R. BABIN (Houma Ct. Hse.: Mar. v.30 & 31, #65)
CHETE, Mary Mathilde (Trazil & Zulema BOUDREAUX) m. 25 July 1898 Francis A. BABIN (Houma Ch.: v.6-a, p.247)
CHETE, Olivier (Adam & Sarah Jane OLIVIER) m. 10 May 1897 Irma CHAMPAGNE (Houma Ch.: v.6-a, p.201)
CHETE, Oris Paul (Joseph & Helene QUINO) b. 7 May 1897 (Montegut Ch.: v.6, p.55)
CHETE, Paul Trazile (Louis & Aurina MARTIN) b. 4 Dec. 1897 (Montegut Ch.: v.6, p.66)
CHETE, Paula Emma (Marcel & Eveline WATKINS) b. 14 June 1898; m. Adam Euzelien MARCEL on 10 March 1926. (Houma Ch.: Bapt. Bk., v.5, p.216)
CHETE, Pierre Evariste (Louis & Oina MARTIN) b. 17 Jan. 1896 (Montegut Ch.: v.6, p.34)
CHETE, Trazile d. 20 Oct. 1899 at age 72 yrs. (Montegut Ch.: v.2, p.30)

CHETE, Wilsy Victor (Aubin & Julie BUQUET) b. 21 Aug. 1898 (Houma Ch.: v.5, p.218)

CHIASSON (Sometimes: CHAISSON)

CHIASSON, ----- boy d. 15 June 1898 at birth (Thib. Ch.: v.3, p.215)

CHIASSON, Ada of Terrebonne Parish m. 11 Dec. 1899 Masse THERIOT (Houma Ch.: v.6-B, p.5)

CHIASSON, Ada (Placide & Alexina BELANGER) m. 2 Dec. 1899 Nicesse THERIOT (Houma Ct. Hse.: Mar. v.31 & 32, #172)

CHIASSON, Aline Florance (Albert & Adolphine DUROCHER) bt. 27 June 1896 (Chackbay Ch.: v.1, p.68)

CHIASSON, Andre Davis (Arthur & Helene DUPRE) b. 5 Jan. 1898 (Montegut Ch.: v.6, p.70)

CHIASSON, Anitas (Odressi & Evelina BILLIOT) m. 9 Dec. 1896 Willie BILLIOT (Houma Ct. Hse.: Mar. v.29 & 30, #198)

CHIASSON, Anitase (Odressee & Evelina BILLOT) m. 28 Dec. 1896 Willie BILLOT (Montegut Ch.: v.4, p.215)

CHIASSON, Anne Azelina (Alcide & Arthemise BOURG) b. 27 July 1896 (Lockport Ch.: v.2, p.333)

CHIASSON, Annette Osea (Florentin & Philomene COURTEAU) b. 27 Sept. 1898 (Montegut Ch.: v.6, p.79)

CHIASSON, Aura Antoinette (Joachim & Arnetia CLEMENT) b. 11 Aug. 1897 (Thib. Ch.: v.7, p.462)

CHIASSON, Beatrice Nora (Justilien & Marie GRAUS) b. 12 Feb. 1898 (Chackbay Ch.: v.1, p.106)

CHIASSON, Brigitte Marie (Willy & Anna OCAR) b. 28 June 1897 (Thib. Ch.: v.7, p.458)

CHIASSON, Clementine d. 1 Feb. 1898 at age 19 yrs. (Houma Ch.: v.3, p.15)

CHIASSON, Clementine (Richard & Melazie LEBOEUF) m. 28 Sept. 1896 Felix THIBODAUX (Houma Ct. Hse.: Mar. v.29 & 30, #155)

CHIASSON, Colomb (Clemile & Glome ORGERON) m. 3 Sept. 1896 Marcelline ORGERON (Thib. Ct. Hse.: Mar. v.36, #133)

CHIASSON, Colomb (Clemile & Glomi ORGERON) m. 3 Sept. 1896 Marcelline ORGERON (Lockport Ch.: v.2, p.153)

CHIASSON, Cora (Edwin & Lucie GAUTIER) m. 9 Jan. 1899 John BERGERON (Houma Ct. Hse.: Mar. v.30 & 31, #197)

CHIASSON, Desiree (Evariste & Pauline HEBERT) m. 11 Nov. 1899 Armand RODRIGUE (Thib. Ct. Hse.: Mar. v.39, #255)

CHIASSON, Desiree (Evariste & Pauline HEBERT) m. 11 Nov. 1899 Armand RODRIGUE (Chackbay Ch.: v.1, p.76)

CHIASSON, Edgard Andressi (Clesmy & Aglonie ORGERON) b. 8 Sept. 1896 (Lockport Ch.: v.2, p.335)

CHIASSON, Edmond d. 22 Nov. 1896 at age 62 yrs. (Thib. Ch.: v.3, p.190)

CHIASSON, Edna (Survile & Melodia BOUDREAU) b. 25 Dec. 1898 (Chackbay Ch.: v.1, p.123)

CHIASSON, Edouard Armand (Edouard & Adela CHIASSON) b. 31 Dec. 1898 (Chackbay Ch.: v.1, p.127)

CHIASSON, Elfrida (Bernard & Eliza AUCOIN) m. 6 June 1898 Joseph FREMIN (Theriot Ch.: v.1-B, p.4)
CHIASSON, Elfrida (Bernard & Eliza AUCOIN) m. 19 May 1898 Joseph FREMIN (Houma Ct. Hse.: Mar. v.30 & 31, #446)
CHIASSON, Emile (Clemile & Aglome ORGERON) m. 14 June 1897 Marie RICHARD (Thib. Ct. Hse.: Mar. v.36, #170)
CHIASSON, Ernest (Edouard & Aimee BELANGER) m. 1 Feb. 1897 Camilla FOREST (Montegut Ch.: v.4, p.217)
CHIASSON, Ernest (Edouard & Aimee BELANGER) m. 13 Jan. 1897 Camilla FOREST (Houma Ct. Hse.: Mar. v.29 & 30, #236)
CHIASSON, Ernestine m. 31 Aug. 1897 Arthur RICHARD (Thib. Ct. Hse.: Mar. v.37, #218)
CHIASSON, Ernestine (Adrien & Estelle THIBODEAUX) m. 31 Aug. 1897 Arthur RICHARD (Lockport Ch.: v.2, p.172)
CHIASSON, Eugenie Marie (Ernest & Celestine BABIN) b. 30 Nov. 1896 (Larose Ch.: v.2, p.190)
CHIASSON, Euphrosine (Ulysse & Julie GUILLOT) m. 22 March 1897 Edgard KELLER (Thib. Ct. Hse.: Mar. v.36, #98)
CHIASSON, Euphrosine (Ulysse & Julie GUILLOT) m. 22 March 1897 Edgard KELLER (Thib. Ch.: v.14, p.135)
CHIASSON, Felicia (Onesippe & Celeste ADAM) m. 25 Jan. 1897 Theophile DUET (Chackbay Ch.: v.1, p.36)
CHIASSON, Felicia (Onesippe & Celeste ADAM) m. 25 Jan. 1897 Theophile DUET (Thib. Ct. Hse.: Mar. v.36, #11)
CHIASSON, Jean Faustin d. 19 Feb. 1898 at age 70 yrs. (Thib. Ch.: v.3, p.211)
CHIASSON, Joseph (Andre & Evelina BILLOT) d. 4 May 1896 at age 8 days (Montegut Ch.: v.2, p.4)
CHIASSON, Joseph Clarence Leonce (Ulysse & Marie TROSCLAIR) b. 7 May 1897 (Thib. Ch.: v.7, p.449)
CHIASSON, Joseph Claude (Wilfred & Victoria ONCALE) b. 8 Sept. 1896 (Chackbay Ch.: v.1, p.76)
CHIASSON, Joseph Edison (Florentin & Philomine COURTEAU) b. 19 Jan. 1896 (Montegut Ch.: v.6, p.35)
CHIASSON, Joseph Ernest (Ernest & Josephine PIL) b. 30 Oct. 1896 (Thib. Ch.: v.7, p.424)
CHIASSON, Joseph Harris (Joseph & Julie BARRIOS) d. 30 Oct. 1899 at age 2 mths. (Lockport Ch.: v.1, #40)
CHIASSON, Joseph Martial Robert (Silvere & Emelia ADAM) b. 11 April 1898 (Thib. Ch.: v.7, p.494)
CHIASSON, Joseph Octave (Camire & Suzane BERGERON) b. 16 June 1896 (Chackbay Ch.: v.1, p.69)
CHIASSON, Joseph Theophile (Jules & Julia CORTEZ) b. 8 Feb. 1898 (Chackbay Ch.: v.1, p.109)
CHIASSON, Joseph Veday (Ernest & Camilia FOREST) b. 2 Oct. 1897 (Montegut Ch.: v.6, p.61)
CHIASSON, Joseph Wilnesse Theophile (Camile & Felicia CLEMENT) b. 8 June 1898 (Chackbay Ch.: v.1, p.113)
CHIASSON, Josephine Berthe (Norbert & Ella CHAMPAGNE) b. 23 Feb. 1896 (Chackbay Ch.: v.1, p.63)

CHIASSON, Joseph Teday (Ernest & Camilia FOREST) d. 19 Oct. 1897 at age 17 days (Montegut Ch.: v.2, p.12)
CHIASSON, Julienne (Florentin & Philomene GOURTE) m. 26 Dec. 1898 Julien BILLOT (Montegut Ch.: v.4, p.250)
CHIASSON, Julienne (Florentin & Philomene COURTO) m. 26 Nov. 1898 Julien BILLIOT (Houma Ct. Hse.: Mar. v.30 & 31, #133)
CHIASSON, Laurent (Onesippe & Celeste ADAM) m. 18 Jan. 1896 Philodia BORNE (Thib. Ct. Hse.: Mar. v.36, #171)
CHIASSON, Laurent (Onesippe & Celeste ADAM) m. 18 Jan. 1897 Philodia BORNE (Chackbay Ch.: v.1, p.34)
CHIASSON, Laurentie (Georges & Doralise HIMEL) m. 5 Oct. 1896 Aurelia NAVARRE (Thib. Ct. Hse.: Mar. v.36, #144)
CHIASSON, Marguerite Henriette (Sally & Emma ANCOR) b. 16 June 1896 (Thib. Ch.: v.7, p.410)
CHIASSON, Marguerite Henriette (Willy & Emma ANCOR) b. 16 June 1896 (Thib. Ch.: v.7, p.414)
CHIASSON, Maria Eunice (Eleste & Exelina HEBERT) b. 26 Jan. 1898 (Theriot Ch.: v.2, p.22)
CHIASSON, Marie (Alfred & Marie DARDAR) d. 22 June 1898 at age 1 day (Montegut Ch.: v.2, p.17)
CHIASSON, Marie (Arthur & Henriette ANDRA) b. 2 April 1896 (Chackbay Ch.: v.1, p.86)
CHIASSON, Marie (Laurence & Philodia BORNE) b. 11 Sept. 1898 (Chackbay Ch.: v.1, p.119)
CHIASSON, Marie (Ulysse & Marie TROSCLAIR) b. 8 July 1899 (Theriot Ch.: v.2, p.45)
CHIASSON, Marie Brigitte d. 31 May 1898 at age 11 mths. (Thib. Ch.: v.3, p.215)
CHIASSON, Marie Celina (Adam & Severine GUIDRY) b. 18 Jan. 1897 (Houma Ch.: v.5, p.206)
CHIASSON, Marie Clara (Augustin & Delphine BENOIT) b. 15 July 1897 (Thib. Ch.: v.7, p.517)
CHIASSON, Marie Ernetia Leontia (Camire & Suzanne BERGERON) b. 26 Sept. 1899; m. Arnold MIRE on 23 Nov. 1957. (Chackbay Ch.: Bapt. Bk., v.1, p.142)
CHIASSON, Marie Eve (Alfred & Marie DARDAR) b. 10 Sept. 1899 (Montegut Ch.: v.7, p.1)
CHIASSON, Marie Felicia m. Leo DOMINIQUE d. 30 May 1898 at age 22 yrs.; buried 31 May 1898. (Montegut Ch.: v.2, p.16)
CHIASSON, Marie Flora (Joachim & Cecilia SHUBUTT) b. 16 April 1896 (Chackbay Ch.: v.1, p.72)
CHIASSON, Marie Laura (John & Nellie AYO) b. 6 Oct. 1898 (Larose Ch.: v.3, p.29)
CHIASSON, Marie Louise (Norbert & Evelia TRAHAN) b. 12 Nov. 1899 (Theriot Ch.: v.2, p.55)
CHIASSON, Marie Octavie (Octave & Rosalie GALLET) b. 4 March 1899 (Montegut Ch.: v.6, p.82)
CHIASSON, Marie Otasie (Albert & Adolphina DEROCHES) b. 11 April 1898 (Thib. Ch.: v.7, p.546)

CHIASSON, Marie Phrosine (Armogene & Evelina BELANGER) b. 3 April 1899 (Montegut Ch.: v.6, p.88)

CHIASSON, Marie Sidie (Edwin & Lucindy GAUTHIER) b. 30 Nov. 1896; m. Albert PREVOST on 29 April 1925. (Houma Ch.: Bapt. Bk., v.5, p.168)

CHIASSON, Marie Valerie (Loventie & Amelia NAVARE) b. 30 March 1898 (Chackbay Ch.: v.1, p.110)

CHIASSON, Merille (Adrien & Estelle THIBODAUX) m. 26 June 1899 Rosina BAILLEAUX (Thib. Ct. Hse.: Mar. v.39, #180)

CHIASSON, Merille (Adrien & Estelle THIBODAUX) m. 26 June 1899 Rosina BARILLEUX (Lockport Ch.: v.2, p.208)

CHIASSON, Niroh (Adrien & Esthel THIBODAUX) m. 16 Jan. 1896 Joseph BRAUX (Lockport Ch.: v.2, p.148)

CHIASSON, Novah (Adrien & Esthel THIBODAUX) m. 16 Jan. 1896 Joseph BRAUX (Thib. Ct. Hse.: Mar. Vol.35, #9)

CHIASSON, Noe (Arthur & Henriette ANDRAS) b. 25 May 1899 (Chackbay Ch.: v.1, p.135)

CHIASSON, Norbert (Bernard & Eliza AUCOIN) m. 7 June 1898 Evelia TRAHAN (Theriot Ch.: v.1-B, p.4)

CHIASSON, Norbert (Bernard & Eliza AUCOIN) m. 19 May 1898 Evelia TRAHAN (Houma Ct. Hse.: Mar. v.30 & 31, #448)

CHIASSON, Nore Joseph (Camire & Suzanne BERGERON) b. 7 Dec. 1897 (Chackbay Ch.: v.1, p.99)

CHIASSON, Octave (Andressy & Evelina BILLOT) m. 21 Feb. 1898 Roselia GALLET (Montegut Ch.: v.4, p.237)

CHIASSON, Octave (Audressy & Evelina BILLIOT) m. 24 Jan. 1898 Roselia GALLET (Houma Ct. Hse.: Mar. v.30 & 31, #245)

CHIASSON, Olivier (Joachim & Cecile SHAUBAUTH) b. 30 March 1898 (Chackbay Ch.: v.1, p.112)

CHIASSON, Paul Nolton (Edwin & Loucindy Rosa GAUTHIER) b. 11 Sept. 1899 (Houma Ch.: v.5, p.255)

CHIASSON, Pierre Arthur (Joseph & Julia BARRIOS) b. 18 Feb. 1896 (Lockport Ch.: v.2, p.323)

CHIASSON, Roselite (Augustin & Delfine BENOIT) bt. 30 March 1896 (Chackbay Ch.: v.1, p.63)

CHIASSON, Sylvaine (Lorentie & Angelina HEBERT) m. 4 Jan. 1896 Melia ADAM (Thib. Ct. Hse.: Mar. v.36, #173)

CHIASSON, Sylvaire (Loventie & Angelina HEBERT) m. 4 Jan. 1897 Melia ADAM (Chackbay Ch.: v.1, p.34)

CHIASSON, Symphorien (Oscar & Lima ORGERON) b. 22 Aug. 1898 (Larose Ch.: v.3, p.27)

CHIASSON, Taffy (George & Hettie CHISOM) b. 16 July 1898 Jane LYONS (Houma Ct. Hse.: Mar. v.30 & 31, #61)

CHIASSON, Tayleur (Adrien & Esthel THIBODAUX) m. 19 Jan. 1897 Sidonie BABIN (Lockport Ch.: v.2, p.157)

CHIASSON, Taylor (Adrien & Esthel THIBODAUX) m. 19 Jan. 1897 Sidonie BABIN (Thib. Ct. Hse.: Mar. v.36, #32)

CHIASSON, Uges Emile (Oscar & Selima ORGERON) b. 2 April 1897 (Larose Ch.: v.3, p.2)

CHIASSON, Vaures Augustin (Albert & Agalie HEBERT) b. 11 March 1896 (Larose Ch.: v.2, p.182)

CHIASSON, Victor Andrew (Ellis & Elzelima HEBERT) b. 21 July 1896 (Theriot Ch.: v.1-B, p.98)
CHIASSON, Welnesse Henri (Camille & Helecia CLEMENT) b. 25 June 1896 (Chackbay Ch.: v.1, p.69)
CHIASSON, Willie of Terrebonne Parish m. 25 July 1899 Philomene NAVARRE (Houma Ch.: v.6-B, p.4)
CHIASSON, Willis m. 13 July 1899 Philomene NAVARRE (Houma Ct. Hse.: Mar. v.31 & 32, #74)
CHIASSON, Willy m. 6 April 1896 Emma ONCAL (Thib. Ct. Hse.: Mar. v.35, #62)
CHICHIZOLA, Gaston of Jefferson Parish (Louis & Anastasie BARTHELEME) m. 30 July 1898 Josephine TERREBONNE, of Jefferson Parish (Larose Ch.: v.3, p.10)
CHICHIZOLA, Gaston of Jefferson Parish (Louis & Anastasie BARTHELEME) m. 30 July 1898 Josephine TERREBONNE, of Jefferson Parish (Larose Ch.: v.4, p.26)
CHICHIZOLA, Marie Miarza (Gaston & Josephine TERREBONNE) b. 29 April 1899 (Larose Ch.: v.3, p.47)
CHICHIZOLA, Marix Gaston (Georges & Rosa TERREBONNE) b. 26 March 1898 (Larose Ch.: v.3, p.26)
CHICHIZOLA, Thelemie of Jefferson Parish (Placide & Genevieve NERDON) m. 6 Feb. 1898 Mack TERREBONNE, of Jefferson Parish (Larose Ch.: v.3, p.7)
CHICHIZOLA, Thetenie (Placide & Genevieve VERDON) m. 6 Feb. 1898 Mack TERREBONNE (Larose Ch.: v.4, p.4)
CHICO, Bernard (Jean & Dominiche MOURE) m. 4 Oct. 1897 Ovilia ADAM (Houma Ct. Hse.: Mar. v.29 & 30, #107)
CHICOT, Marie (Bernard & Velia ADAM) b. 16 July 1898 (Chacahoula Ch.: v.4, p.11)
CHIERSON, Bernadette (Willis & Emma ENCOL) b. 11 Sept. 1899 (Thib. Ch.: v.7, p.565)
CHIERSON, Octave Louis (Ernest & Josephine PITRE) b. 6 Nov. 1899 (Thib. Ch.: v.7, p.573)
CHINN, Amelia m. 21 Dec. 1897 Arthur E. HAWTHORN (Thib. Ct. Hse.: Mar. v.37, #264)

CHIVERS (Sometimes: CHEEVERS)

CHOISTRE (Sometimes: CHOISTE, CHOUESTE, CHOUESTRE, SCHWEITZER)
CHOISTRE, Carmelite m. 3 March 1898 Leonce GUIDRY (Larose Ch.: v.3, p.8)
CHOISTRE, Cecilia (Leopold & Pauline DUFRESNE) m. 9 Aug. 1897 William FALGOUT (Thib. Ct. Hse.: Mar. v.37, #198)
CHOISTRE, Cecilia (Leopold & Pauline DUFRESNE) m. 16 Aug. 1897 William FALGOUT (Lockport Ch.: v.2, p.164)
CHOISTRE, Charmelitte m. 3 March 1898 Leonce GUIDRY (Larose Ch.: v.4, p.79)
CHOISTRE, Clovis Joseph (Joseph & Ernestine GALLIANO) b. 7 Feb. 1899 (Larose Ch.: v.3, p.37)

CHOISTRE, Gibson Richard (Augustin & Azeline DANOS) b. 16 April 1898 (Larose Ch.: v.3, p.26)
CHOISTRE, Joseph Edy (Pierre & Josephine GUIDRY) b. 10 Jan. 1896 (Larose Ch.: v.2, p.182)
CHOISTRE, Leonise Clothilde (Pierre & Josephine GUIDRY) b. 3 June 1898 (Larose Ch.: v.3, p.33)
CHOISTRE, Robert of Lafourche Parish (Joseph & Carmelite PLAISANCE) m. 6 March 1898 Mary GUIDRY of Lafourche Parish (Larose Ch.: v.3, p.8)
CHOISTRE, Robert (Joseph & Carmelitte PLAISANCE) m. 6 March 1898 Mary GUIDRY (Larose Ch.: v.4, p.7)
CHOISTRE, Suzanne Leona (Robert & Marie GUIDRY) b. 11 Aug. 1897 (Larose Ch.: v.3, p.7)
CHOISTRE, Tranquille Myer Joseph (Jean & Eulalie Valerie GALLIANEAU) b. 6 July 1897 (Larose Ch.: v.3, p.9)
CHOISTRE, Wilson m. 27 Sept. 1897 Melanie FALGOUT (Thib. Ct. Hse.: Mar. v.37, #230)
CHOISTRE, Wilson m. 27 Sept. 1897 Melanie FALGOUT (Lockport Ch.: v.2, p.176)
CHOL, Edouard Joseph (Charles H. & Odile BERGERON) b. 20 June 1897 (Thib. Ch.: v.7, p.453)
CHOL, Francis Xavier d. 6 June 1899 at age 5 mths. (Thib. Ch.: v.3, p.235)
CHOL, Francois Xavier (Henri & Odile BERGERON) b. 3 Dec. 1898 (Thib. Ch.: v.7, p.527)
CHONES, Mathieu Alces (Wuilson & Melanie FALGOUT) b. 12 Jan. 1899 (Lockport Ch.: v.3-A, #3)
CHONES, Mathieu Alces (Wuilson & Melanie FALGOUT) b. 12 Jan. 1899 (Lockport Ch.: v.3, #3)
CHRISTIAN, Sarah m. 6 Jan. 1898 Taylor STEWART (Thib. Ct. Hse.: Mar. v.37, #8)
CIACCIO, Antonia m. 3 Feb. 1898 Giovanne ROIA (Houma Ct. Hse.: Mar. v.30 & 31, #273)
CIACCIO, Antonino (Alberto & Vita MAGGIO) m. 19 Feb. 1898 Giovanni RAIA (Houma Ch.: v.6-a, p.234)
CIACCIO, Francesca m. 10 May 1898 Guiesseppe PLONGIOSSI (Houma Ct. Hse.: Mar. v.30 & 31, #433)
CIACIA, Francisca (Antonino & Cancitta SOHERS) b. 6 Sept. 1899 (Houma Ch.: v.5, p.252)
CIACCIA, Frangesca m. 21 Jan. 1899 Rosario ARBISI (Houma Ct. Hse.: Mar. v.30 & 31, #277)
CIACCIO, Frangesca (Coloquers & Gratia LATALANELLA) m. 4 Feb. 1899 Rosario ARBISI (Houma Ch.: v.6-a, p.273)
CIACCIO, Nunzia (Alberto & Vita MAGGIO) m. 2 July 1898 Antonino MANGIARACINA (Houma Ct. Hse.: Mar. v.30 & 31, #48)
CIACCIO, Nuzia (Alberto & Vita MAGGIA) m. 30 July 1898 Antonino MAUGIRACINO (Houma Ch.: v.6-a, p.249)
CIACCIO, Rosario m. 26 Jan. 1898 Giuseppe CATALENELLO (Houma Ct. Hse.: Mar. v.30 & 31, #250)
CIACCIO, Rosario (Calagero & Grifzia CATALANELLO) m. 12 Feb. 1898 Guiseppe CATALANELLO (Houma Ch.: v.6-a, p.229)

CIACCIO, Soccorso (Salvatore & Maria LAURO) b. 15 Nov. 1899 (Thib. Ch.: v.8, p.21)
CICIA, Vita m. 11 April 1899 Antonina GOGONO (Houma Ct. Hse.: Mar. v.31 & 32, #394)
CICIA, Vita of Terrebonne Parish m. 24 April 1899 Antonia ZAGONA (Houma Ch.: v.6-B, p.3)
CICIO, Rosa (Poollo & Francesca CICIO) b. 1 Jan. 1898 (Houma Ch.: v.5, p.195)
CIRNIGLIA, Guiseppe of Lascari, Sicile d. 26 Jan. 1897 at age 26 yrs. (Thib. Ch.: v.3, p.195)
CITIZEN, James m. 29 Dec. 1898 Patience JACKSON (Houma Ct. Hse.: Mar. v.30 & 31, #165)
CITRANO, Francesca (Patro & Francesca FAVA) m. 28 Aug. 1899 Rosario GLORIASO (Thib. Ch.: v.14, p.292)
CITRANO, Francisca (Pietro & Francisca FAVA) m. 28 Aug. 1898 Rosario GLORISO (Thib. Ct. Hse.: Mar. v.38, #285)
CITRANO, Pietro (Guiseppe & Concietta FLARDO) b. 6 Nov. 1897 (Thib. Ch.: v.7, p.473)

CLARK (Sometimes: CLARCK, CLARKE)
CLARK, Alice Marie (Rial & Sally SCYRUS) m. 26 Oct. 1896 Zachary Delaversary SCOTT (Houma Ct. Hse.: Mar. v.29 & 30, #179)
CLARK, Dina m. 11 May 1898 Wheeler DIGGS (Houma Ct. Hse.: Mar. v.30 & 31, #439)
CLARK, Emma m. 11 March 1897 Willie WILLIAMS (Houma Ct. Hse.: Mar. v.29 & 30, #351)
CLARK, Evelina m. 30 Dec. 1897 Laurence BUQUET (Houma Ct. Hse.: Mar. v.30 & 31, #170)
CLARK, Evelina (James & Eveline LEBOEUF) m. 17 Jan. 1898 Lawrence BUQUET (Houma Ch.: v.6-a, p.221)
CLARK, Hester m. 3 June 1899 Dan JONES (Houma Ct. Hse.: Mar. v.31 & 32, #27)
CLARK, Isabella d. 9 April 1899 at age 35 yrs., 3 mths. & 4 days (Houma Ch.: v.3, p.22)
CLARK, James m. 16 April 1898 Willie BROWN (Houma Ct. Hse.: Mar. v.30 & 31, #405)
CLARK, Lovinia m. 10 Aug. 1897 Franklin WHITE (Thib. Ct. Hse.: Mar. v.37, #211)
CLARK, Lucy m. 28 Jan. 1897 Duncan RILEY (Houma Ct. Hse.: Mar. v.29 & 30, #261)
CLARK, Marguerite m. Martial HEBERT d. 29 April 1896 at age 68 yrs. (Montegut Ch.: v.2, p.4)
CLAUDET, Joseph (Joseph & Agnes MEYER) b. 26 Aug. 1898 (Thib. Ch.: v.7, p.562)
CLAY, Henry Jr. m. 5 Sept. 1898 Fannie DEDRICK (Houma Ct. Hse.: Mar. v.30 & 31, #87)
CLAY, Nora m. 2 Sept. 1896 Joseph COULON (Thib. Ct. Hse.: Mar. v.36, #140)
CLAYTON, Bessie m. 8 July 1897 Peter QUILLER (Houma Ct. Hse.: Mar. v.29 & 30, #62)

CLEMENT, Amedee (Paul & Albertine PIRON) b. 8 Feb. 1898 (Larose Ch.: v.3, p.24)
CLEMENT, Anita Clara (Joseph & Octavie LEONARD) b. 1 May 1898 (Thib. Ch.: v.7, p.497)
CLEMENT, Anna (Joseph & Octavie LEONARD) b. 5 Feb. 1897 (Chackbay Ch.: v.1, p.84)
CLEMENT, Antoine Albon (Emile & Josephine BRAUD) b. 27 June 1898 (Thib. Ch.: v.7, p.554)
CLEMENT, Bernard m. 15 April 1899 Jeanne MIRE (Thib. Ct. Hse.: Mar. v.39, #144)
CLEMENT, Bernard (Theophile & Philomene BERNARD) m. 19 April 1899 Jeanne MIRE (Thib. Ch.: v.14, p.271)
CLEMENT, Cecile (Felix & Victorine DESROCHERS) m. 20 Dec. 1899 Louis THERAND (Thib. Ct. Hse.: Mar. v.39, #289)
CLEMENT, Cecile (Felix & Victorine DESROCHES) m. 20 Dec. 1899 Louis THERAND (Chackbay Ch.: v.1, p.77)
CLEMENT, Charles Robert (Joachim & Philomene ONCALE) b. 11 July 1898 (Thib. Ch.: v.7, p.555)
CLEMENT, Clay Leopold (Theophile & Philomene BERNARD) b. 18 Aug. 1896 (Thib. Ch.: v.7, p.414)
CLEMENT, Clemence (Joseph & Marie TRAHAN) m. 1 June 1896 Ernest HEBERT (Thib. Ch.: v.14, p.89)
CLEMENT, Clemence (Joseph & Marie TRAHAN) m. 1 June 1896 Ernest HEBERT (Thib. Ct. Hse.: Mar. v.35, #90)
CLEMENT, Clerfe Clarence Ovile (Andre & Aimee PANVELLE) b. 28 Nov. 1897 (Chackbay Ch.: v.1, p.99)
CLEMENT, Clotilde (Oscar & Marie CAILLONET) b. 3 Dec. 1898 (Chackbay Ch.: v.1, p.122)
CLEMENT, Cyprien (Joseph & Marie BOUDREAU) m. 15 Sept. 1898 Florence BORNE (Chackbay Ch.: v.1, p.65)
CLEMENT, Cyprien (Joseph & Marie BOUDREAU) m. 15 Sept. 1898 Florence BORNE (Thib. Ct. Hse.: Mar. v.38, #275)
CLEMENT, Elda Bernadit (Philippe & Marie DUPRE) b. 16 June 1898 (Houma Ch.: v.5, p.211)
CLEMENT, Elda Valerie (Claybert & Aurelie LANDRY) bt. 22 Sept. 1896 (Chackbay Ch.: v.1, p.75)
CLEMENT, Elfege J. (Theophile & Philomene BERNARD) m. 6 June 1899 Emma MIRE (Thib. Ch.: v.14, p.283)
CLEMENT, Ella (Leonce & Armelize ADAM) b. 24 Feb. 1897 (Chackbay Ch.: v.1, p.84)
CLEMENT, Elphege J. m. 2 June 1899 Emma MIRE (Thib. Ct. Hse.: Mar. v.39, #175)
CLEMENT, Elvina Sophie (Bernard & Jeannette MIRE) b. 11 April 1899 (Thib. Ch.: v.7, p.600)
CLEMENT, Emma Laurita (Klebert & Aurelia LANDRY) b. 15 Sept. 1897 (Thib. Ch.: v.7, p.515)
CLEMENT, Ermetia (Anatole & Ernestine CHIASSON) b. 21 Oct. 1897 (Chackbay Ch.: v.1, p.97)
CLEMENT, Ernest Adam (Ulysse & Elodie BENOIT) bt. 23 May 1896 (Chackbay Ch.: v.1, p.67)

CLEMENT, Euselien d. 12 Jan. 1899 at age 88 yrs. (Montegut Ch.: v.2, p.23)
CLEMENT, Eustache Adrian (Paul & Alice PIRON) b. 28 March 1896 (Larose Ch.: v.2, p.194)
CLEMENT, Felix (Ursain & Ázema SEVAIN) m. 3 Sept. 1896 Clara MAYER (Chackbay Ch.: v.1, p.30 & 31)
CLEMENT, Felix (Ursain & Azema SEVIN) m. 3 Sept. 1896 Clara MAYER (Thib. Ct. Hse.: Mar. v.36, #136)
CLEMENT, Francois Xavier (Emile & Josephine BRAUX) b. 14 Feb. 1897 (Thib. Ch.: v.7, p.439)
CLEMENT, George Samuel (Silvere & Marie HEBERT) b. 29 Oct. 1899 (Thib. Ch.: v.7, p.581)
CLEMENT, Georges Leonard (Libert & Estellina HEBERT) b. 28 Feb. 1897 (Thib. Ch.: v.7, p.491)
CLEMENT, Henri (Ovide & Aimee PAMVERT) d. 9 June 1896 at age 15 yrs. (Thib. Ch.: v.3, p.183)
CLEMENT, Hilaire d. 21 Feb. 1899 at age 71 yrs. (Thib. Ch.: v.3, p.228)
CLEMENT, Jean Norbert (Joachim & Philomene ONCALE) b. 11 July 1898 (Thib. Ch.: v.7, p.555)
CLEMENT, John (Cordelius & Leocadie HEBERT) m. 28 June 1898 Marie SHULENBERG (Thib. Ct. Hse: Mar. v.38, #213)
CLEMENT, John (Cordelius & Leocadie HEBERT) m. 28 June 1898 Marie SHULENBERG (Thib. Ch.: v.14, p.208)
CLEMENT, John (Joseph & Rosalie TRAHAN) m. 17 Feb. 1897 Mary BUTCHER (Houma Ct. Hse.: Mar. v.29 & 30, #311)
CLEMENT, John Henri d. 8 March 1898 at age 8 yrs. (Houma Ch.: v.3, p.16)
CLEMENT, Joseph d. 27 April 1897 at age 64 yrs. (Houma Ch.: v.3, p.12)
CLEMENT, Joseph (Marie) b. 28 June 1897 (Thib. Ch.: v.7, p.454)
CLEMENT, Joseph Charles (Arthur & Tanilia MORVAN) b. 30 Sept. 1896 (Chackbay Ch.: v.1, p.77)
CLEMENT, Joseph Clarence d. 13 Aug. 1897 at age 1½ mths. (Thib. Ch.: v.3, p.204)
CLEMENT, Joseph Cletus Sylvestre (Ulysse & Elodie BENOIT) b. 19 June 1898 (Chackbay Ch.: v.1, p.114)
CLEMENT, Joseph Odressy (Auresmile & Aurelie GRAUS) b. 1 Aug. 1897 (Chackbay Ch.: v.1, p.92)
CLEMENT, Laure Ovilia (Joseph & Octavie LEONARD) b. 11 May 1899 (Chackbay Ch.: v.1, p.134)
CLEMENT, Leonce (Auguste & Josephine BOUDREAU) m. 20 July 1896 Armelize ADAM (Thib. Ct. Hse.: Mar. v.36, #123)
CLEMENT, Leonce (Auguste & Josephine BOUDREAUX) m. 20 July 1896 Armelize ADAM (Chackbay Ch.: v.1, p.28)
CLEMENT, Leontia (Clesilia & Zulme DUROCHER) m. 23 Jan. 1899 Sylvestre DUROCHER (Thib. Ct. Hse.: Mar. v.38, #2)
CLEMENT, Leontia (Clesilia & Zulme DUROCHER) m. 23 Jan. 1899 Sylvestre DUROCHER (Thib. Ch.: v.14, p.244)

CLEMENT, Lionel Viole (Ernest & Sydonie ONCALE) b. 13 June 1897 (Chackbay Ch.: v.1, p.88)
CLEMENT, Louise (Evariste & Elisia BOUDREAUX) m. 21 Feb. 1899 Placide HEBERT (Houma Ct. Hse.: Mar. v.31 & 32, #345)
CLEMENT, Maggie m. 25 July 1898 Alcide T. DASPIT (Houma Ct. Hse.: Mar. v.30 & 31, #66)
CLEMENT, Maggie (Joseph & Rosalie TRAHAN) m. 28 July 1898 Alcide T. DASPIT (Houma Ch.: v.6-a, p.248)
CLEMENT, Malvina (Clezia & Zulmee DUROCHER) m. 19 Feb. 1898 Emile GUILLOT (Chackbay Ch.: v.1, p.57)
CLEMENT, Malvina (Clezia & Zulmee DUROCHER) m. 19 Feb. 1898 Emile GUILLOT (Thib. Ct. Hse.: Mar. v.37, #80)
CLEMENT, Marie d. 8 Dec. 1899 at age 77 yrs. (Houma Ch.: v.3, p.27)
CLEMENT, Marie Alida (Joachim & Philomene ONCALE) bt. 30 Aug. 1896 (Chackbay Ch.: v.1, p.73)
CLEMENT, Marie Armance (Arthur & Tanilia MORVAN) b. 1 July 1899 (Chackbay Ch.: v.1, p.135)
CLEMENT, Marie Bondella (John & Marie BUTCHER) b. 28 Feb. 1898 (Thib. Ch.: v.7, p.494)
CLEMENT, Marie Clotilde Emelina (Alfred & Azelie BERNARD) b. 28 Dec. 1898 (Thib. Ch.: v.7, p.529)
CLEMENT, Marie Philomene (Marie Edmonia) b. 18 Sept. 1898 (Thib. Ch.: v.7, p.513)
CLEMENT, Mary (Edward & Adeline BONVILLAIN) m. 3 Nov. 1896 Laurel A. BROWNLEE (Houma Ct. Hse.: Mar. v.29 & 30, #185)
CLEMENT, Mary Rosa Belle (Augustin & Justilia LEBOEUF) b. 7 March 1899 (Houma Ch.: v.5, p.245)
CLEMENT, Mathilde Miola (Augustin & Justilia LEBOEUF) b. 16 Oct. 1896 (Houma Ch.: v.5, p.169)
CLEMENT, Myrthe Odile (Antole & Angela GUILLOTE) b. 21 Dec. 1896 (Thib. Ch.: v.7, p.434)
CLEMENT, Norbert Clet (Leonce & Armelise ADAM) b. 10 Oct. 1898 (Chackbay Ch.: v.1, p.120)
CLEMENT, Oscar (Felix & Victorine DUROCHER) m. 4 Oct. 1897 Marie CAILLOUET (Chackbay Ch.: v.1, p.49 & 50)
CLEMENT, Oscar (Felix & Victorine DUROCHER) m. 4 Oct. 1897 Marie CAILLOUET (Thib. Ct. Hse.: Mar. v.37, #240)
CLEMENT, Paul (Ulysse & Angela CHIASSON) b. 1 July 1897 (Chackbay Ch.: v.1, p.90)
CLEMENT, Philip m. 16 March 1897 Marie DUPRE (Houma Ct. Hse.: Mar. v.29 & 30, #355)
CLEMENT, Philip (Peter & Mirza DAUNE) m. 22 March 1897 Marie DUPRE (Houma Ch.: v.6-a, p.197)
CLEMENT, Philomene Pauline Leonie (Teler & Oceana FAUCHER) b. 28 April 1896 (Houma Ch.: v.5, p.153)
CLEMENT, Rene Joseph (Alfred & Azelie BERNARD) b. 11 Aug. 1896 (Thib. Ch.: v.7, p.412)
CLEMENT, Rose (Cornelius & Leocadie HEBERT) b. 20 July 1896 (Thib. Ch.: v.7, p.414)

CLEMENT, Rose Clemence (Anatole & Angela GUILLOTE) b. 28 Oct. 1897 (Thib. Ch.: v.7, p.522)
CLEMENT, Samuel Willis Antoine (Willis & Sarah ECHETE) b. 3 April 1898 (Houma Ch.: v.5, p.210)
CLEMENT, Sidney Fernand (Leonce & Armelise ADAM) b. 15 Nov. 1899 (Chackbay Ch.: v.1, p.145)
CLEMENT, Thomas Claude (Cyprien & Florence BORNE) b. 19 July 1899 (Chackbay Ch.: v.1, p.139)
CLEMENT, Valrie Ernest (Beauregard & Valerie DONOHUE) b. 3 Jan. 1898 (Thib. Ch.: v.7, p.508)
CLENNON, Frank m. 15 Jan. 1896 Martha ROSS (Houma Ct. Hse.: Mar. v.28, #388)
CLOATRE, Marguerite Sarrazine m. d.Furcy GAUTREAUX; d. 14 Dec. 1898 at age 82 yrs. (Montegut Ch.: v.2, p.22)
CLOUNY, Sarah m. Peter SCALLY d. 25 Oct. 1896 at age 96 yrs. (Thib. Ch.: v.3, p.189)
CLULEE, Alice m. 26 Aug. 1898 Augustin HEBERT (Thib. Ct. Hse.: Mar. v.38, #267)
CLULEY, Alice (William & Marie CORDET) m. 3 Sept. 1898 Augustin HEBERT (Raceland Ch.: v.2, p.79)
COACH, Rebeca m. 19 March 1896 Wash SCOTT (Thib. Ct. Hse.: Mar. v.35, #54)

COALMANN (See Perhaps: COLEMAN)

COCKE, Mary Ringgold Wingfield (Ringgold Wingfield & Mary D. BUFFORD) b. 21 Nov. 1896 (Chacahoula Ch.: v.4, p.15)
COLBERT, Robert m. 7 Feb. 1898 Rebecca WASHINGTON (Thib. Ct. Hse.: Mar. v.37, #92)

COLEMAN (Sometimes: COLEMEN, COLLMEN, COLMAN)

COLEMAN, Bertha m. 19 Jan. 1899 John BURNES (Houma Ct. Hse.: Mar. v.30 & 31, #270)
COLEMAN, James m. 5 Aug. 1899 Harriet JONES (Thib. Ct. Hse.: Mar. v.39, #204)
COLEMAN, Johna Jr. m. 20 Feb. 1899 Victora FORD (Thib. Ct. Hse: Mar. v.39, #109)
COLEMAN, Joseph Everett (Annie) b. 15 Nov. 1897 (Thib. Ch.: v.7, p.497)
COLEMAN, Lorenza m. 7 March 1898 Fillis HENDERSON (Houma Ct. Hse.: Mar. v.30 & 31, #330)
COLEMAN, Nancy Elizabeth m. 11 Feb. 1897 Moses HITE (Houma Ct. Hse.: Mar. v.29 & 30, #304)
COLEMAN, Rosella m. 11 Feb. 1897 Thomas HILLS (Thib. Ct. Hse.: Mar. v.36, #77)
COLEMAN, Willie m. 4 July 1898 Easter MITCHELL (Thib. Ct. Hse.: Mar. v.38, #219)
COLET, Eulalie (Mathurin & Helene COOKE) m. 7 April 1898 Ovide CHERAMI (Larose Ch.: v.4, p.82)
COLIN, Corine (Pierre & Roseline VIZIER) b. 5 April 1898 (Larose Ch.: v.3, p.18)

COLLINS (Sometimes: COLIN, COLLIN)

COLLINS, Adeline m. 23 Sept. 1896 Dan HOGAN (Houma Ct. Hse.: Mar. v.29 & 30, #151)

COLLINS, Bertha widow of Jessie DABNEY m. 11 Nov. 1899 Jarret CARAWAY (Thib. Ct. Hse.: Mar. v.39, #264)

COLLINS, Bertile (Jacques & Felide TERREBONNE) b. 29 Nov. 1898 (Larose Ch.: v.3, p.41)

COLLINS, Charles Summer m. 20 July 1899 Bridget L. THIBODAUX (Houma Ct. Hse.: Mar. v.31 & 32, #80)

COLLINS, Clara m. 7 Jan. 1896 Belden LYONS (Houma Ct. Hse.: Mar. v.28, #378)

COLLINS, Denis Connonly (Eugene & Velina LOOK) b. 28 April 1897 (Theriot Ch.: v.2, p.6)

COLLINS, Edgar Silvain (Laurent & Nathelie HENRI) b. 24 March 1896 (Theriot Ch.: v.1-B, p.94)

COLLINS, Eugenie Agnes (Eugene & Evelina LOOK) b. 26 June 1899 (Theriot Ch.: v.2, p.46)

COLLINS, Georgiana m. 28 April 1898 Richardson DOUGLASS (Houma Ct. Hse.: Mar. v.30 & 31, #424)

COLLINS, Jacques (Philosat & Eveline PERRIN) b. 13 Dec. 1897 (Larose Ch.: v.3, p.32)

COLLINS, John m. 2 Jan. 1899 Louisa DAVIS (Houma Ct. Hse.: Mar. v.30 & 31, #169)

COLLINS, John m. 8 March 1899 Hattie BROWN (Thib. Ct. Hse.: Mar. v.39, #116)

COLLINS, Laurina (Laurent & Nathalie HENRI) b. 11 Dec. 1899 (Theriot Ch.: v.2, p.64)

COLLINS, Lawrence (Lawrence & Nathalie HENRI) b. 8 April 1897 (Theriot Ch.: v.2, p.2)

COLLINS, Lucy m. 20 Sept. 1898 Anderson WILKINS (Houma Ct. Hse.: Mar. v.30 & 31, #103)

COLLINS, Maggie m. 26 Sept. 1898 Thomas WILEY (Thib. Ct. Hse.: Mar. v.38, #284)

COLLINS, Marie (Jacques & Marie TERREBONNE) b. 4 July 1896 (Larose Ch.: v.2, p.190)

COLLINS, Merryman m. 16 Feb. 1898 Sarah Ann DURDEN (Houma Ct. Hse.: Mar. v.30 & 31, #300)

COLLINS, Monroe m. 8 March 1899 Louisa WILLIAMS (Houma Ct. Hse.: Mar. v.31 & 32, #357)

COLLINS, Nettie m. 14 Dec. 1899 James H. JOHNSON (Houma Ct. Hse.: Mar. v.31 & 32, #184)

COLLINS, Nick m. 9 March 1899 Ellen MORBLEY (Houma Ct. Hse.: Mar. v.31 & 32, #360)

COLLINS, Odile m. 6 Aug. 1898 Eugene MARTIN (Thib. Ct. Hse.: Mar. v.38, #241)

COLLINS, Pierre m. 24 June 1899 Elocadie TERREBONNE (Thib. Ct. Hse.: Mar. v.39, #181)

COLLINS, Randolphe Rameau (Fredric & Elusia TERREBONNE) b. 3 April 1898 (Larose Ch.: v.3, p.27)

COLLINS, Sarah m. 29 Jan. 1897 Denis McCLENNAN (Houma Ct. Hse.: Mar. v.29 & 30, #267)
COLLINS, Secriana m. 29 April 1899 Henry Hamilet YOUNG (Houma Ct. Hse.: Mar. v.31 & 32, #428)
COLLINS, Thomas m. 12 Feb. 1896 Lilly LEE (Houma Ct. Hse.: Mar. v.28, #453)
COLOMB, James m. 16 Dec. 1897 Rebecca G. MINOR (Houma Ct. Hse.: Mar. v.29 & 30, #145)
COLOMB, Victoria (Pierre & Sophie SMITH) m. 22 Aug. 1898 Ursin CARLIN (Theriot Ch.: v.1-B, p.4)
COLOMB, Victoria E. (Pierre & Sophie SMITH) m. 2 Feb. 1897 Ursin J. CARLIN (Houma Ct. Hse.: Mar. v.29 & 30, #272)
COLORA, Francisca Paola (Luca & Anna SALEMI) m. 3 July 1897 Guiseppe PROVENZANO (Thib. Ct. Hse.: Mar. v.36, #175)
COLORA, Francisca Pasla (Luca & Anna SALEMI) m. 3 July 1897 Guiseppe PROVENZANO (Thib. Ch.: v.14, p.150)
COLOTTA, Anna (Vitale & Salvatore FAZIA) b. 4 Jan. 1899 (Houma Ch.: v.5, p.233)
COLWELL, Elizah m. 16 March 1898 Mary ABRAHAM (Houma Ct. Hse.: Mar. v.30 & 31, #336)

COMEAUX (Sometimes: COMEAU, COMMAUX, COMMEAUX)

COMEAUX, Adam m. 24 April 1897 Alice BLANCHARD (Houma Ct. Hse.: Mar. v.29 & 30, #392)
COMEAUX, Adam (Eustache & Adelaide THIBODAUX) m. 24 April 1897 Alice BLANCHARD (Houma Ch.: v.6-a, p.200)
COMEAUX, Agnes Anna (Trasimon & Eva CROCHET) b. 15 Dec. 1899 (Houma Ch.: v.5, p.268)
COMEAUX, Agnes Anna (Trasimon & Eva CROCHET) b. 15 Dec. 1899 (Houma Ch.: v.6, p.4)
COMEAUX, Aline m. 14 July 1898 John PARR (Houma Ct. Hse.: Mar. v.30 & 31, #58)
COMEAUX, Aline (Desire & Alida DAIGLE) m. 14 July 1898 Joseph PARR (Houma Ch.: v.6-a, p.246)
COMEAUX, Elsie m. 31 May 1897 Lelia NAQUIN (Thib. Ct. Hse.: Mar. v.36, #156)
COMEAUX, Elvie m. 1 June 1897 Lelia NAQUIN (Houma Ch.: v.6-a, p.205)
COMEAUX, Eva (Alexis & Celisca GIROUARD) b. 13 Aug. 1896 (Houma Ch.: v.5, p.156)
COMEAUX, Georges (Alexis & Telesia GIROUARD) b. 17 Sept. 1897 (Houma Ch.: v.5, p.189)
COMEAUX, Hubert J. B. (Alexis & Felicie GIROIR) b. ----; bt. 26 Feb. 1899 (Houma Ch.: v.5, p.235)
COMEAUX, Joseph Stanly (Trasimond & Eva CROCHET) b. 3 April 1898 (Houma Ch.: v.5, p.209)
COMEAUX, Marguerite Louise Marie (Desire & Lida DAIGLE) b. 23 Nov. 1898 (Houma Ch.: v.5, p.226)
COMEAUX, Maria Celina (Edgar & Leda VERRET) b. 18 Sept. 1897 (Chacahoula Ch.: Gibson Ch.: Mar. Bk., v.1, #38)

COMEAUX, Maria Celina (Edgar & Leda VERRET) b. 18 Sept. 1897; bt. 13 May 1898 (Chacahoula Ch.: Gibson Ch.: v.2, p.122)
COMEAUX, Mary Rita (Alcee & Lilia NAQUIN) b. 11 June 1899 (Houma Ch.: v.5, p.248)
COMEAUX, Normand (Adam & Alice BLANCHARD) b. 27 Aug. 1898 (Houma Ch.: v.5, p.220)
COMEAUX, Trasimond m. 18 Jan. 1897 Eva CROCHET (Houma Ct. Hse.: Mar. v.29 & 30, #240)
COMEAUX, Trasimond (Eustache & Adelaide THIBODEAUX) m. 4 Feb. 1897 Eva CROCHET (Houma Ch.: v.6-a, p.191)
COMMODORE, Thomas m. 29 June 1899 Susanna JONES (Houma Ct. Hse.: Mar. v.31 & 32, #59)
CONDON, Florence Ordelia (Edward & Mary E. FIELDS) b. 11 April 1896 (Houma Ch.: v.5, p.150)
CONGELOSI, Marie Marguerite (Salvatore & Josephine BOURGEOIS) b. 13 Feb. 1897 (Thib. Ch.: v.7, p.438)
CONIGLIO, Guiseppe (Vincenzo & Rosalie STENOVA) m. 10 June 1899 Domenica MACALUSA (Raceland Ch.: v.2, p.98)
CONIGLIO, Josephina (Biaggio & Christina FASSINO) b. 5 Feb. 1898 (Chacahoula Ch.: Gibson Records: Mar. Bk., v.1, #12)
CONIGLIO, Josephine (Biaggio & Christina FASSINO) b. 5 Feb. 1898 (Chacahoula Ch.: Gibson Ch.: v.2, p.117)
CONNELY, Flora Bowdoin (Arthur W. & Clara HIMEL) b. 3 July 1898 (Houma Ch.: Epis. Ch.: v.1, p.118)
CONNELY, William Alexander (Arthur W. & Clara HIMEL) b. 2 April 1896 (Houma Ch.: Epis. Ch.: v.1, p.112)
CONNER, Thomas m. 4 Feb. 1899 Mary Rose PRESTENBACK (Thib. Ct. Hse.: Mar. v.38, #90)
CONNORS, George Wilmer (Thomas & Rosa PRESTENBACK) b. 1 Jan. 1899 (Thib. Ch.: v.7, p.591)
CONSTANT, Adrien Valcourt (John & Fernie GUILLOT) b. 8 Aug. 1897 (Thib. Ch.: v.7, p.460)
CONSTANT, Carmelite (Denys & Elodee TORES) b. 13 Nov. 1898 (Chackbay Ch.: v.1, p.125)
CONSTANT, Jean (Aurelien & Olympia TORES) bt. 14 April 1899 (Chackbay Ch.: v.1, p.134)
CONSTANT, Raoul Thomas (Jean & Euphemelia GUILLOTTE) b. 8 May 1899 (Thib. Ch.: v.7, p.603)
CONSTANT, Theodore (Denis & Elodie TORRES) b. 4 Nov. 1896 (Chackbay Ch.: v.1, p.78)
CONSTANT, Walace (Albert & Eugenie WALKER) b. 20 Oct. 1898 (Chackbay Ch.: v.1, p.120)
CONSTANTIN, Eugene Joseph Silvere (Eugene & Alice BOURG) b. 22 Feb. 1896 (Lockport Ch.: v.2, p.323)
CONSTANZA, Guiseppe d. 10 Aug. 1899 at age 36 yrs. (Thib. Ch.: v.3, p.238)
CONSTANZO, Tardeo (Guiseppe & Antonina POLLAUE) b. 8 Oct. 1898 (Thib. Ch.: v.7, p.570)
CONSTRINGEST, Marie Gracieuse (Nicol & Josephine LEE) b. 29 Jan. 1899 (Larose Ch.: v.3, p.42)

COOK (Sometimes: COOKE, COOKS)

COOK, ----- child d. 16 Feb. 1899 at age 3 days (Houma Ch.: v.3, p.21)

COOK, Arthur m. 14 Dec. 1899 Emma DICKERSON (Thib. Ct. Hse.: Mar. v.39, #282)

COOK, Catherine (Thomas W. & Phamantha Jane BROWN) m. 20 April 1898 George Washington WATKINS (Houma Ct. Hse.: Mar. v.30 & 31, #408)

COOK, Charles m. 21 Jan. 1897 Rosella WHITE (Houma Ct. Hse.: Mar. v.29 & 30, #246)

COOK, Ella m. 5 April 1897 William WILLIAMS (Houma Ct. Hse.: Mar. v.29 & 30, #372)

COOK, Gladys Anna (Leroy & Etha LEBLANC) b. 23 July 1897 (Theriot Ch.: v.2, p.9)

COOK, Minerva (Thomas W. & Samantha J. BROWN) m. 22 June 1897 Frederick LEBLANC (Houma Ct. Hse.: Mar. v.29 & 30, #38)

COOK, Minerva (Thomas W. & Samatha J. BROWN) m. 28 June 1897 Frederick LEBLANC (Houma Ch.: Epis. Ch.: v.1, p.342)

COOK, Moses m. 26 May 1898 Eleonora ROBERTSON (Thib. Ct. Hse.: Mar. v.38, #190)

COOK, Robert m. 15 Oct. 1896 Charlotte DEIGG (Thib. Ct. Hse.: Mar. v.36, #156)

COOPER, Enos m. 12 June 1899 Georgiana WHITE (Houma Ct. Hse.: Mar. v.31 & 32, #38)

COOPER, William of Lafourche Parish (John &Josephine FREKY) m. 18 April 1898 Emilie CANTRELLE, of Lafourche Parish (Larose Ch.: v.3, p.8)

COOPER, William (John & Joephine FREKY) m. 18 April 1898 Emilie CANTRELLE (Thib. Ct. Hse.: Mar. v.37, #145)

COOPER, William (John & Josephine FREKY) m. 18 April 1898 Emilie CANTRELLE (Larose Ch.: v.4, p.9)

COOPER, William Louis (William & Emilie CANTRELLE) b. 15 Feb. 1899 (Larose Ch.: v.3, p.36)

COPELLA (Sometimes: COPELA)

CORE, Lisa d. 22 Aug. 1899 at age 66 yrs. (Raceland Ch.: v.1, p.27)

CORNEY, ----- Mrs. d. 26 July 1899 at age 60 yrs. (Raceland Ch.: v.1, p.26)

CORSO, Caleocere (Antonino & Concetta MARIA) b. 3 Jan. 1899 (Chacahoula Ch.: v.4, p.17)

CORTERELLO, Josaria (Antonino & Maria SHARTINA) b. 25 Dec. 1899 (Thib. Ch.: v.7, p.580)

CORTEZ (Sometimes: CORTES)

CORTEZ, Alce (Froisin & Evilie LAROUSSE) bt. 7 March 1896 (Chackbay Ch.: v.1, p.62)

CORTEZ, Azelienia (Emilien & Emilia GRAMER) m. 22 July 1899 Joseph LOUPE (Chackbay Ch.: v.1, p.71)

CORTEZ, Azelima (Emilien & Emelia GRANIER) m. 15 July 1899 Joseph LOUPE (Thib. Ct. Hse.: Mar. v.39, #200)

CORTEZ, Desiree (Emilien & Emilia GRAMER) m. 18 Sept. 1897 Paul LOUP (Chackbay Ch.: v.1, p.49)

CORTEZ, Desiree (Emilien & Emilia GRANIER) m. 18 Sept. 1897 Paul LOUP (Thib. Ct. Hse.: Mar. v.37, #228)

CORTEZ, Edouard (Marcelus & Carrie BOHEN) b. 25 Jan. 1898; m. Dorestile GRABERT on 16 Oct. 1919. (Chackbay Ch.: Bapt. Bk., v.1, p.107)

CORTEZ, Froisine (Frozin & Evelie LAROUSSE) b. 28 June 1898 (Chackbay Ch.: v.1, p.116)

CORTEZ, Joseph Gueless (Jules & Emelie DANTIN) b. 14 Sept. 1898 (Raceland Ch.: v.5, p.80)

CORTEZ, Jules m. 14 June 1897 Emelie DANTIN (Thib. Ct. Hse.: Mar. v.36, #171)

CORTEZ, Jules (Jules & Antoinette CRAMER) m. 26 June 1897 Emelie DANTIN (Raceland Ch.: v.2, p.44)

CORTEZ, Marcellus (Emilien & Amelia GRAMER) m. 6 April 1897 Carrie BOCHN (Chackbay Ch.: v.1, p.41)

CORTEZ, Marcelus (Emilien & Amelia GRANIER) m. 6 April 1897 Carrie BOEHM (Thib. Ct. Hse.: Mar. v.36, #104)

CORTEZ, Maria Eloncia (Optimee & Victoire HEBERT) b. 20 Sept. 1898 (Chackbay Ch.: v.1, p.120)

CORTEZ, Marie Leonise (Joseph & Helene USE) b. 3 Oct. 1899 (Chackbay Ch.: v.1, p.141)

CORTEZ, Orestil m. 27 Jan. 1898 Lucia SAVOIE (Thib. Ct. Hse.: Mar. v.37, #29)

CORTEZ, Orestile (Joseph & Anaise CRAMER) m. 27 Jan. 1898 Lucia SAVOIE (Raceland Ch.: v.2, p.61)

CORTEZ, Otimen (Jos. & Marie KRAEMER) m. 7 June 1897 Victoire HEBERT (Thib. Ct. Hse.: Mar. v.36, #161)

CORTEZ, Ottimen (Joseph & Marie KRAMER) m. 28 June 1897 Victoria HEBERT (Chackbay Ch.: v.1, p.45)

CORTEZ, Virginie (Emilien & Emilia GRAMER) m. 2 Sept. 1899 Justilien GRABERT (Chackbay Ch.: v.1, p.72)

CORTEZ, Virginie (Emilien & Emilia GRANIER) m. 2 Sept. 1899 Justilien GRABERT (Thib. Ct. Hse.: Mar. v.39, #214)

CORTISSE, Francesca (Carlo & Giuseppa UZZO) b. 23 Nov. 1899 (Thib. Ch.: v.8, p.20)

COSENZA, Guiseppe (Salvatore & Domia CALLI) m. 13 April 1899 Caterina MOLLE (Thib. Ch.: v.14, p.270)

COSENZA, Guiseppe (Salvatore & Donina CALLI) m. 13 April 1899 Caterina MOLLE (Thib. Ct. Hse.: Mar. v.39, #141)

COTAIA, Cira (Antonino & Domenica DELUCA) b. 14 April 1898 (Thib. Ch.: v.7, p.547)

COTTON (Sometimes: COTON)

COTTON, Ernestine Effie (John & Elizabeth BILLOT) b. 15 Nov. 1897 (Montegut Ch.: v.6, p.71)

COTTON, Jean Denis (John & Elizabeth BILLOT) b. 28 March 1899 (Montegut Ch.: v.6, p.90)

COTTON, Leroy m. 29 Dec. 1898 Mary TAYLOR (Thib. Ct. Hse.: Mar. v.38, #326)
COTTON, Marie Ernestine (Ernest & Alexina VERDUN) b. 10 Jan. 1896 (Theriot Ch.: v.1-B, p.94)
COTTON, Phoebe m. 16 Aug. 1898 Richard DIXIE (Thib. Ct. Hse.: Mar. v.38, #252)
COUDERT, Adelaide d. Dec. 1896; m. Pierre ANGELLOZ Children listed: Marie m. Camille LAROQUE; Emile; Oscar; Arthur. Notice to newspaper of administration: 1 July 1896. (Thib. Ct. Hse.: Succ. #1493)
COULOMB, Esther Camille (Horace & Ludowiska COULOMB) b. 9 Aug. 1899 (Larose Ch.: v.3, p.47)

COULON (Sometimes: COULAN, COULAND)
COULON, Cecile m. 8 Sept. 1896 Herman NACCARI (Larose Ch.: v.4, p.49)
COULON, Cecile m. 8 Sept. 1896 Herman NACCARI (Larose Ch.: v.3, p.4)
COULON, Joseph m. 2 Sept. 1896 Nora CLAY (Thib. Ct. Hse.: Mar. v.36, #140)
COULON, Mary (Omer & Anna COGAN) m. 17 Feb. 1896 James CHERAULT (Thib. Ch.: v.14, p.81)
COULON, Mary (Omer & Annie -----) m. 17 Feb. 1896 James CHERAULT (Thib. Ct. Hse.: Mar. v.35, #45)
COULON, Octave Jr. (Octave & Zulma ADAM) m. 5 May 1898 Carie KEEFFE Both residents of Jefferson Parish. (Larose Ch.: v.4, p.14)
COULON, Octave Jr. of Jefferson Parish (Octave & Zulma ADAM) m. 5 May 1898 Carie KEEFE (Larose Ch.: v.3, p.9)
COULON, Onesiphore m. 8 Sept. 1896 Theresa RIGAULT (Larose Ch.: v.4, p.81)
COULON, Onesiphore m. 8 Sept. 1896 Theresa RIGAULT (Larose Ch.: v.3, p.4)
COULON, Sam m. 9 Feb. 1898 Ethel FLETCHER (Thib. Ct. Hse.: Mar. v.37, #95)

COURTEAU (Sometimes: COURTAUD, COURTAUX, COURTEAUX)
COURTEAU, Joseph Emile (Wallis & Odilia BILLOT) b. 28 Jan. 1897 (Montegut Ch.: v.6, p.50)
COURTEAU, Marie d. 10 Oct. 1898 at age 23 yrs. (Thib. Ch.: v.3, p.220)
COURTEAU, Marie Alice (Jules & Justilia BILLOT) b. 23 March 1899 (Montegut Ch.: v.6, p.87)
COURTEAU, Marie Overiste (Marcilare & Rosina VERDUN) b. 25 Jan. 1897 (Montegut Ch.: v.6, p.52)
COURTNEY, Charley m. 12 Oct. 1899 Lulu BROWN (Houma Ct. Hse.: Mar. v.31 & 32, #148)
COX, Aphonse Henri (William & Louise AUBERT) b. 11 April 1898 (Thib. Ch.: v.7, p.495)
COX, Joseph m. 13 April 1899 Effie A. WILLIAMS (Thib. Ct. Hse.: Mar. v.39, #142)

CRAM, Robert James (Harvey & Evelina HUTCHINSON) b. 4 Feb. 1898 (Chacahoula Ch.: Gibson Record: Mar. Bk., v.1, #18)
CRAM, Robert James (Harvey & Evelina HUTCHISON) b. 4 Feb. 1898 (Chacahoula Ch.: Gibson Ch.: v.2, p.118)

CRAMER Sometimes: KRAMER)

CRAPEL (See: CREPEL)

CRAWFORD, Joseph m. 19 Jan. 1899 Sarah WARNER (Thib. Ct. Hse.: Mar. v.38, #41)
CREECY, Beatrice m. 8 Feb. 1899 Lewis WHITE (Houma Ct. Hse.: Mar. v.31 & 32, #325)

CREPEL (Sometimes: CRAPEL, KREPEL)
CREPEL, Antoine Aurelien (Faustin Antoine & Lea Celestin WILLIAM) b. 13 Sept. 1898 (Larose Ch.: v.3, p.57)
CREPEL, Charles Prudent (Adam & Eloise DARDAR) b. 20 Aug. 1898 (Larose Ch.: v.3, p.19)
CREPEL, Dora Augustine (Augustin & Leonie WILLIAM) b. 6 Feb. 1898 (Larose Ch.: v.3, p.25)
CREPEL, Ida Maria (Antoine & Lea WILLIAM) b. 3 June 1896 (Larose Ch.: v.3, p.11)
CREPEL, Joseph Denise (Jacques & Evelina GRIFFIN) b. 9 Oct. 1897 (Larose Ch.: v.3, p.27)
CREPEL, Lawrence (Alex & Eve VERRET) d. 7 Oct. 1899 at age 21 yrs. (Theriot Ch.: v.1, p.2)
CREPEL, Melodia Lucile (Alexandre & Marie Eve VERRET) b. 30 Nov. 1898 (Theriot Ch.: v.2, p.56)
CREPEL, Philoces Augustin (Adam & Aloise DARDA) b. 17 May 1899 (Larose Ch.: v.3, p.58)
CRESCIONI, Noelie Philomene (Cleophas & Rosalie SANDRAE) b. 24 Dec. 1898 (Raceland Ch.: v.5, p.86)
CRESCIONI, Noemie d. 23 April 1899 at age 4 mths. (Raceland Ch.: v.1, p.24)
CRESSIONI, Marie Regina (Clay & Rosalie SANDRA) b. 28 July 1896 (Raceland Ch.: v.5, p.26)
CRETINI, Alice (Eugene & Anais DANOS) m. 23 Jan. 1899 Armand BRUCE (Thib. Ct. Hse.: Mar. v.38, #38)
CRETINI, Alice (Eugene & Anais DANOS) m. 23 Jan. 1899 Armand BRUCE (Larose Ch.: v.4, p.33)
CRETINI, Alice (Eugene & Anais DANOS) m. 23 Jan. 1899 Armand BRUCE (Larose Ch.: v.3, p.11)
CRETINI, Eugenie m. 23 April 1898 Henri PITRE (Larose Ch.: v.4, p.12)
CRETINI, Eugenie of Lafourche Parish m. 23 April 1898 Henri PITRE, of Lafourche Parish (Larose Ch.: v.3, p.9)
CRETINI, Eugenie (Eugene & Anais DANOS) m. 23 April 1898 Henry PITRE (Thib. Ct. Hse.: Mar. v.38, #154)
CRETINI, Paul Urbin (Paul & Celeste GUIDRY) b. 25 May 1896 (Larose Ch.: v.2, p.192)

CROCHET, ----- child (Alfred) d. 8 Dec. 1899 at age 1 yr. & 2 mths. (Houma Ch.: v.3, p.26)
CROCHET, Adam Joseph (Alfred & Malvina LEBLANC) b. 7 Oct. 1898 (Houma Ch.: v.5, p.234)
CROCHET, Agathe Eva (Orestide & Aurelia LEONARD) b. 11 Oct. 1897 (Houma Ch.: v.5, p.192)
CROCHET, Alfred m. 25 March 1899 Elvire HEBERT (Houma Ct. Hse.: Mar. v.31 & 32, #374)
CROCHET, Alfred of Terrebonne Parish m. 6 April 1899 Elvire HEBERT of Terrebonne Parish (Houma Ch.: v.6-B, p.3)
CROCHET, Alice (Clay & Elizada DARCE) m. 5 Jan. 1899 James BABIN (Houma Ct. Hse.: Mar. v.30 & 31, #184)
CROCHET, Alida (Clay & Elesida DARCE) m. 17 Jan. 1898 Willie THIBODAUX (Houma Ct. Hse.: Mar. v.30 & 31, #212)
CROCHET, Arthur (Prosper & Susanne LEDET) m. 29 May 1896 Mary LARPENTER (Houma Ct. Hse.: Mar. v.29 & 30, #80)
CROCHET, Catherine Mary Teresa (Alfred & Clarisse KELLER) b. 22 July 1898 (Chacahoula Ch.: v.4, p.11)
CROCHET, Cecilia m. 3 July 1897 Albert BERGERON (Houma Ch.: v.6-a, p.208)
CROCHET, Celeste Antoinette (Donis & Adoliska NAQUIN) b. 5 Jan. 1898 (Chacahoula Ch.: v.4, p.2)
CROCHET, Charles (Dannis & Eveline HEBERT) m. 14 May 1896 Lucille BERGERON (Chacahoula Ch.: v.1, p.58)
CROCHET, Charles (Dannis & Eveline HEBERT) m. 14 May 1896 Lucille BERGERON (Houma Ct. Hse.: Mar. v.29 & 30, #58)
CROCHET, Clarence Joseph (Charley & Lucide BERGERON) b. 30 June 1897 (Chacahoula Ch.: v.4, p.21)
CROCHET, Clay d. 27 April 1894; m. (2) Julia BERGERON Children listed: Cecilia m. Gilbert BERGERON; Eda m. George BERGERON; Alida m. Willie THIBODAUX; Alice; Henry Clay; Clovis. Petition for family meeting: 15 April 1898. (Houma Ct. Hse.: Succ. #845)
CROCHET, Dannis d. 21 May 1899 at age 51 yrs. (Houma Ch.: v.3, p.23)
CROCHET, Ernest (Alfred & Marie ROBICHAUX) m. 15 Jan. 1898 Clothilde LANDRY (Houma Ct. Hse.: Mar. v.30 & 31, #205)
CROCHET, Ernest (d.Alfred & Marie ROBICHAUD) m. 3 Feb. 1898 Clothilde LANDRY (Montegut Ch.: v.4, p.234)
CROCHET, Etienne Evans (Leo & Marie FIELDS) b. 3 Aug. 1897 (Montegut Ch.: v.6, p.59)
CROCHET, Eva m. 14 June 1897 Thomas MOORE (Houma Ch.: v.6-a, p.207)
CROCHET, Eva m. 18 Jan. 1897 Trasimond COMEAUX (Houma Ct. Hse.: Mar. v.29 & 30, #240)
CROCHET, Eva m. 5 June 1897 Thomas MOORE (Houma Ct. Hse.: Mar. v.29 & 30, #4)
CROCHET, Eva (John & Alvina BABIN) m. 4 Feb. 1897 Trasimond COMEAUX (Houma Ch.: v.6-a, p.191)
CROCHET, Henri d. 30 Sept. 1897 at age 63 yrs. (Montegut Ch.: v.2, p.12)

CROCHET, Jean Edgar (Ernest & Clothilde LANDRY) b. 23 Dec. 1899 (Montegut Ch.: v.6, p.97)
CROCHET, Jean Randolphe (Rodolphe & Eda NAQUIN) b. 27 Jan. 1897 (Chacahoula Ch.: v.4, p.12)
CROCHET, Joseph (Alfred & Marie ROBICHAUX) m. 24 Jan. 1896 Marie BOURG (Houma Ct. se.: Mar. v.28, #407)
CROCHET, Joseph (d.Alfred & Marie ROBICHAUX) m. 17 Feb. 1896 Marie BOURG (Montegut Ch.: v.4, p.207)
CROCHET, Joseph Alfred (Joseph & Marie BOURG) b. 29 March 1897 (Montegut Ch.: v.6, p.53)
CROCHET, Joseph Edwin (Joseph & Gertrude LEBLANC) d. 7 May 1899 at age 1 yrs. & 6 mths. (Montegut Ch.: v.2, p.25)
CROCHET, Joseph Elwood (Joseph & Gertrude LEBLANC) b. 12 Jan. 1898 (Houma Ch.: v.5, p.200)
CROCHET, Joseph Exavier (Arthur & Mary LORENTER) b. 21 Sept. 1897 (Houma Ch.: v.5, p.188)
CROCHET, Jules d. 14 Jan. 1899 at age 72 yrs. (Houma Ch.: v.3, p.20)
CROCHET, Laurence Joseph (Alfred & Clarisse KELLER) b. 6 July 1896 (Chacahoula Ch.: v.4, p.2)
CROCHET, Leopold m. 4 April 1896 Mary FIELDS (Houma Ct. Hse.: Mar. v.29 & 30, #29)
CROCHET, Leopold (Henri & Augustine ROBICHAUX) m. 30 April 1896 Marie FIELDS (Montegut Ch.: v.4, p.210)
CROCHET, Madeleine d. 9 Aug. 1899 at age 41 yrs. (Houma Ch.: v.3, p.24)
CROCHET, Marguerite Josephine (Albert & Augusta SAVOIE) b. 2 Oct. 1899 (Thib. Ch.: v.8, p.14)
CROCHET, Marie Aida Hattie (Rodolphe & Ada NAQUIN) b. 3 June 1899 (Chacahoula Ch.: v.4, p.28)
CROCHET, Marie Aline (Ernest & Clothilde LANDRY) b. 21 Nov. 1898 (Montegut Ch.: v.6, p.79)
CROCHET, Marie Eveline (Albert & Augusta SAVOIE) b. 23 April 1896 (Houma Ch.: v.5, p.176)
CROCHET, Marie Lucille (Leo & Marie FIELDS) b. 9 Sept. 1899 (Montegut Ch.: v.6, p.93)
CROCHET, Marie Malvina (Albert & Gusta SAVOIE) b. 27 Aug. 1898 (Houma Ch.: v.5, p.218)
CROCHET, Mary Onesia (John & Alvina BABIN) b. 2 April 1896 (Houma Ch.: v.5, p.149)
CROCHET, Nathalie m. 2 May 1896 Etienne CARO (Houma Ct. Hse.: Mar. v.29 & 30, #47)
CROCHET, Nathalie (Joseph & Marie MARCEL) m. 2 May 1896 Etienne CARRO (Houma Ch.: v.6-a, p.175)
CROCHET, Nettie m. 18 Sept. 1899 Charles MOORE (Houma Ct. Hse.: Mar. v.31 & 32, #138)
CROCHET, Nettie m. 18 Sept. 1899 Charles MOORE (Houma Ch.: v.6-B, p.4)
CROCHET, Prosper d. 21 July 1899 at age 55 yrs. (Houma Ch.: v.3, p.23)

CROCHET, Rodolphe (Denis & Evelina HEBERT) m. 6 April 1896 Ida NAQUIN (Chacahoula Ch.: v.1, p.57)
CROCHET, Rodolphe (Donis & Eveline HEBERT) m. 6 April 1896 Ada NAQUIN (Houma Ct. Hse.: Mar. v.29 & 30, #1)
CROCHET, Ruby Burthy (Richard & Ella EDWARDS) b. 30 Jan. 1898 (Houma Ch.: v.5, p.205)
CROCHET, Therese (Theophile & Rosina LABIT) m. 13 Jan. 1896 Joseph DUGAS (Montegut Ch.: v.4, p.205)
CROCHET, Thereze (Theophile & Rosina LABIT) m. 2 Jan. 1896 Joseph DUGAS (Houma Ct. Hse.: Mar. v.28, #367)
CROCHET, Willie Earl (Charles & Lucille BERGERON) b. 22 Nov. 1898 (Chacahoula Ch.: v.4, p.15)

CROSBY (Sometimes: CROASBE, CROSBE, KROSBE)
CROSBY, Andre m. 21 April 1898 Emma GRIFFIN (Thib. Ct. Hse.: Mar. v.38, #162)
CROSBY, Andre Angelina (Andrea & Emma GRIFFIN) b. 5 Aug. 1899 (Larose Ch.: v.3, p.46)
CROSBY, Athanaise Marie (Theodore & Adelaide INCLADE) b. 26 Dec. 1896 (Larose Ch.: v.3, p.10)
CROSBY, Dorothee Clarisse (Alexis & Emilia TERREBONNE) b. 6 Feb. 1896 (Larose Ch.: v.2, p.188)
CROSBY, Eselima m. 5 Feb. 1898 Etienne HEBERT (Thib. Ct. Hse.: Mar. v.37, #66)
CROSBY, Eselima (Louis & Emelie BAUDOIN) m. 5 Feb. 1898 Etienne HEBERT (Raceland Ch.: v.2, p.65)
CROSBY, Eustache Aramis (Eusebe & Elisa LEFORT) b. 20 Sept. 1899 (Larose Ch.: v.3, p.45)
CROSBY, Evelina m. 19 Feb. 1898 Joseph RODRIGUE (Thib. Ct. Hse.: Mar. v.37, #91)
CROSBY, Evelina (Louis & Emelie BAUDOIN) m. 19 Feb. 1898 Joseph RODRIGUE (Raceland Ch.: v.2, p.71)
CROSBY, Ida (Richard & Melia LEETHROP) b. 24 April 1899 (Larose Ch.: v.3, p.42)
CROSBY, Paul Sampson (Theodore & Adelaide INCALADE) b. 7 Aug. 1898 (Larose Ch.: v.3, p.31)
CROSIER, Alfred m. 19 Jan. 1899 Laura SMITH (Thib. Ct. Hse.: Mar. v.38, #42)
CROSIER, Alfred Clifford (Alfred & Severine VERETTE) b. 22 Aug. 1898 (Thib. Ch.: v.7, p.520)
CROSIER, Clifford Afred d. 20 Nov. 1899 at age 1 yr. & 5 mths. (Thib. Ch.: v.3, p.244)
CROSIER, Cora m. 21 Dec. 1898 Sidney EVANS (Houma Ct. Hse.: Mar. v.30 & 31, #156)
CROSIER, Joseph Christopher (Alfred O. & Laura SMITH) b. 25 Aug. 1899 (Thib. Ch.: v.7, p.590)
CROSIER, Maggie m. 8 July 1899 Philip GUEDRY (Thib. Ct. Hse.: Mar. v.39, #197)
CROSIER, Maggie (Oscar & Maggie HUVAL) m. 10 July 1899 Philippe GABRIEL (Thib. Ch.: v.14, p.288)

CROWLEY, Eve Edna (William & Lucienne RODRIGUE) b. 1 Oct. 1897 (Raceland Ch.: v.5, p.56)
CRUMP, Patsy m. 9 Feb. 1899 Henry DICKSON (Houma Ct. Hse.: Mar. v.31 & 32, #331)
CUBIT, Emerline m. 31 Aug. 1899 Edmond DAVIS (Thib. Ct. Hse.: Mar. v.39, #215)
CUNEO, Domingue (Joseph & Constance PIERRON) m. 24 June 1899 Arsene ESCHTE (Montegut Ch.: v.4, p.266)
CUNEO, Dominique (Joseph & Constance PIERRON) m. 24 May 1899 Alsane ESHTE (Houma Ct. Hse.: Mar. v.31 & 32, #15)
CUNEO, Ellen (Joseph & Constance PIERRON) m. 4 May 1896 Joseph ESHTE (Houma Ct. Hse.: Mar. v.29 & 30, #48)
CUNEO, Helene (Joseph & Constance PIERRON) m. 1 June 1896 Joseph ECHETE (Montegut Ch.: v.4, p.210)
CUNEO, Johanna (Joseph & Constance PIERRON) m. 10 June 1899 Aubin LECOMPTE (Montegut Ch.: v.4, p.265)
CUNIO, Johanna (Joseph & Constance PIERRON) m. 18 May 1899 Aubin LECOMPTE (Houma Ct. Hse.: Mar. v.31 & 32, #7)

CUNNINGHAM (Sometimes: CUNAGHAM, CUNENGHAM, CUNNAGHAM, CONINGHAM)

CUNNINGHAM, Celestin m. 14 Sept. 1899 Ophilia DOIRON (Houma Ch.: v.6-B, p.4)
CUNNINGHAM, Celestin m. 5 Sept. 1899 Ophelia DOIRON (Houma Ct. Hse.: Mar. v.31 & 32, #119)
CUNNINGHAM, Charles (Michel & Amanda BURKETT) m. 25 Nov. 1896 Zulema NAQUIN (Houma Ct. Hse.: Mar. v.29 & 30, #195)
CUNNINGHAM, Clarence (Marcel & d.Marguerite BELANGER) m. 1 March 1897 Flavie LANDRY (Montegut Ch.: v.4, p.219)
CUNNINGHAM, Clarence (Marcel & Marguerite BELANGER) m. 20 Feb. 1897 Flavie LANDRY (Houma Ct. Hse.: Mar. v.29 & 30, #323)
CUNNINGHAM, Ivy Joseph (Neville & Lydia BERTRAND) b. 24 Jan. 1898 (Chacahoula Ch.: v.4, p.1)
CUNNINGHAM, Joseph Edouard (Nelson & Josephine PECHAUD) b. 16 Sept. 1899 (Chacahoula Ch.: v.4, p.31)
CUNNINGHAM, Joseph Laurent (Clarance & Flavie LANDRY) b. 7 Feb. 1898 (Montegut Ch.: v.6, p.65)
CUNNINGHAM, Joseph Laurent (Clarance & Flavie LANDRY) d. 4 Oct. 1899 at age 1 yr. & 8 mths. (Montegut Ch.: v.2, p.30)
CUNNINGHAM, Joseph Louis (Beloni & Julie GUIDRY) b. 7 Oct. 1896 (Montegut Ch.: v.6, p.52)
CUNNINGHAM, Joseph Stelly (Bernard & Eve HEBERT) b. 17 Oct. 1899 (Montegut Ch.: v.6, p.98)
CUNNINGHAM, Josephine (Clarence & Flavie LANDRY) d. 20 Nov. 1899 at age 4 hours (Montegut Ch.: v.2, p.31)
CUNNINGHAM, Marie Annelia (Bernard & Eva HEBERT) b. 17 Sept. 1897 (Montegut Ch.: v.6, p.61)

CUNNINGHAM, Marie Elmire (Emile & Julienne GUIDRY) b. 6 March 1896 (Montegut Ch.: v.6, p.39)
CUNNINGHAM, Marie Emelia (Emile & Julienne GUIDRY) d. 25 Sept. 1899 at age 1 mth. (Montegut Ch.: v.2, p.29)
CUNNINGHAM, Marie Julienne (Martin & Corinne CHAUVIN) b. 16 Feb. 1896 (Montegut Ch.: v.6, p.33)
CUNNINGHAM, Marie Rose (Robert & Marie HEBERT) b. 5 Feb. 1898 (Montegut Ch.: v.6, p.66)
CUNNINGHAM, Nelson (Jean Louis & Leonie GUIDRY) m. 11 Aug. 1896 Ada MATHERNE (Houma Ct. Hse.: Mar. v.29 & 30, #127)
CUNNINGHAM, Neuville (Michel & Amanda BURKETT) m. 13 Feb. 1896 Lydia BERTRAND (Houma Ct. Hse.: Mar. v.28, #417)
CUNNINGHAM, Neuville (Michel & Amanda BURKETT) m. 13 Feb. 1896 Lydia BERTRAND (Chacahoula Ch.: v.1, p.55)
CUNNINGHAM, Pierre Edwin (Belonie & Julie GUIDRY) b. 9 March 1899 (Montegut Ch.: v.6, p.88)
CUPLANTIS, Cynthia m. 26 Sept. 1898 Omer DUPLANTIS (Houma Ct. Hse.: Mar. v.30 & 31, #105)

CUROL (Sometimes: CUROLE)

CUROL, Annelie Marie (Joseph & Alice PLAISANCE) b. 3 Aug. 1899 (Larose Ch.: v.3, p.44)
CUROL, Clotilde Pauline (Pierre & Adelina BONAMOUR) b. 24 Jan. 1897 (Larose Ch.: v.3, p.5)
CUROL, Marie Mazeppa (Etienne & Julienne PITRE) b. 24 May 1898 (Larose Ch.: v.3, p.22)
CUROL, Ursule Eleonore (Etienne & Julienne PEET) b. 21 Feb. 1896 (Larose Ch.: v.2, p.181)
CUROL, Ursule Leonel (Nicolas & Celina GASPAR) b. 15 Jan. 1898 (Larose Ch.: v.3, p.15)
CUROL, Victor Rene (Nicolas & Helene RICHARD) b. 27 Nov. 1896 (Lockport Ch.: v.3,-A, #26)
CURTZ, Walter H. d. 26 Nov. 1899 at age 26 yrs. (Raceland Ch.: v.1, p.29)
CUSTAIA, Antonio d. 26 Nov. 1899 at age 45 yrs. (Thib. Ch.: v.3, p.245)
CUTAIA, Antonina (d.Antonino & Maria SALERNA) b. 4 Nov. 1899 (Thib. Ch.: v.7, p.575)
CUTAIA, Maria Gati (Antonino & Marie SALERNA) b. 13 Jan. 1897 (Thib. Ch.: v.7, p.490)
CUTAYA, Lucia (Antonina & Dominica DELUCA) b. 13 June 1897 (Thib. Ch.: v.7, p.456)
CUTTOM, Marie Rosetta (Ernest & Alexina VERDUN) b. 14 Feb. 1898 (Theriot Ch.: v.2, p.21)

"D"

DA SYLVA (Sometimes: DA SILVA)

DABNEY, Julia m. 9 June 1897 Coleman WILLIAMS, Jr. (Houma Ct. Hse.: Mar. v.29 & 30, #17)
DABNEY, Peyton m. 2 Feb. 1898 Julia JOHNSON (Thib. Ct. Hse.: Mar. v.37, #67)
DAGATTE, Laurenzo (Vincenzo & Gurerce FRANCESCA) b. 1 March 1898 (Thib. Ch.: v.7, p.550)
DAICEY, Mary (Louisdane & Louisa DAIGLE) b. 21 Oct. 1896 (Thib. Ch.: v.7, p.428)

DAIGLE (Sometimes: DAIGRE, DAYGLE, DEGLE, DEGUES, DIGUES)
DAIGLE, Alexina Marguerite (Adam & Odillia THIBODAUX) b. 14 Jan. 1897 (Larose Ch.: v.3, p.3)
DAIGLE, Alfred m. 14 Nov. 1898 Lydia ROUNDTREE, widow of William CALLOWAY (Thib. Ct. Hse.: Mar. v.38, #308)
DAIGLE, Alfred (Treville & Malvina BOUDREAUX) m. 24 Nov. 1898 Lydia ROUNDTREE (Thib. Ch.: v.14, p.230)
DAIGLE, Alice Modeste (Eugene & Suzanne DANOS) b. 20 March 1898 (Larose Ch.: v.3, p.25)
DAIGLE, Bob d. 15 March 1899 at age 2 mths., 12 days (Houma Ch.: v.3, p.21)
DAIGLE, Boddy d. 25 June 1899 at age 27 yrs. (Houma Ch.: v.3, p.23)
DAIGLE, Brigette Marie Olivia (Tellin & Octavie BOUDRAUX) b. 2 Oct. 1898 (Thib. Ch.: v.7, p.530)
DAIGLE, Brigitte Marie (Treville & Malvina BOUDREAU) b. 21 July 1897 (Thib. Ch.: v.7, p.460)
DAIGLE, Buddy m. 19 Feb. 1898 Mary LEBLANC (Houma Ct. Hse.: Mar. v.30 & 31, #313)
DAIGLE, Buddy (Talma & Celestine BABIN) m. 21 Feb. 1898 Mary LEBLANC (Houma Ch.: v.6-a, p.236)
DAIGLE, Clara (Sylvain & Julie LOUVIERE) m. 5 July 1897 Albert LEONARD (Thib. Ch.: v.14, p.151)
DAIGLE, Clara (Sylvain & Julie LOUVIERE) m. 5 July 1897 Albert LEONARD (Thib. Ct. Hse.: Mar. v.36, #176)
DAIGLE, Elise m. 25 Sept. 1899 Nicholas LIRETTE (Houma Ct. Hse.: Mar. v.31 & 32, #143)
DAIGLE, Elise of Terrebonne Parish m. 25 Sept. 1899 Nicholas LIRETTE (Houma Ch.: v.6-B, p.4)
DAIGLE, Emile Jr. m. 17 April 1897 Edna J. TUCKER (Houma Ct. Hse.: Mar. v.29 & 30, #384)
DAIGLE, Emile Jr. (Emile & Annette PORCHE) m. 20 April 1897 Edna J. TUCKER (Houma Ch.: v.6-a, p.199)
DAIGLE, Emma m. Octave ADAM d. 15 March 1896 at age 46 yrs. (Thib. Ch.: v.3, p.180)
DAIGLE, Eugene (Jean Baptiste & Celina RAYMOND) b. 21 March 1896 (Lockport Ch.: v.2, p.326)

DAIGLE, Euphrosie d. 7 Aug. 1897 at age 70 yrs. (Houma Ch.: v.3, p.13)

DAIGLE, Flavia (Alfred & Lelia LANDRY) b. 7 Oct. 1899 (Thib. Ch.: v.7, p.570)

DAIGLE, Frank d. 26 May 1895 (Joseph, d.12 Oct. 1899 & Marceline BUQUET, d. 24 Dec. 1891) m. Alice KING Children listed: Aubin, 18; Ernest, 15; Joseph F., 12; Thomas, 10; Ephie, 8; Robert, 6. Petition for tutorship: 20 Oct. 1899. (Houma Ct. Hse.: Succ. #926)

DAIGLE, Frank m. 7 Oct. 1897 Mathilde MIDDLETON or MILTON (Thib. Ct. Hse.: Mar. v.37, #246)

DAIGLE, Harris Travis (Allens & Octavie BONAREAU) b. 3 Sept. 1896 (Houma Ch.: v.5, p.158)

DAIGLE, James (Treville & Malvina BOUDREAUX) m. 31 Jan. 1899 Marie ROUNDTREE (Thib. Ct. Hse.: Mar. v.38, #23)

DAIGLE, James (Treville & Malvina BOUDREAUX) m. 31 Jan. 1899 Marie ROUNDTREE (Thib. Ch.: v.14, p.248)

DAIGLE, Jean Lucas (Alfred & Armina BERGERON) b. 27 May 1896 (Thib. Ch.: v.7, p.409)

DAIGLE, Joseph d. 12 Oct. 1899 at age 65 yrs. (Houma Ch.: v.3, p.25)

DAIGLE, Joseph d. 12 Oct. 1899; m. Marceline BUQUET d. 24 Dec. 1891. Children listed: Talma; d.Edmond; d.Frank m. Alice KING. Petition for administration: 20 Oct. 1899. (Houma Ct. Hse.: Succ. #925)

DAIGLE, Joseph Chelby (Elvege & Malais PITRE) b. 19 Jan. 1897 (Thib. Ch.: v.7, p.444)

DAIGLE, Joseph Eugene (Adam & Delia THIBODEAUX) b. 5 Dec. 1898 (Larose Ch.: v.3, p.35)

DAIGLE, Joseph Robett (Alfred & Ermina BERGERON) b. 19 Dec. 1898 (Thib. Ch.: v.7, p.533)

DAIGLE, Joseph Wilson (Edgard & Marie DELAUNETTE) b. 21 March 1897 (Thib. Ch.: v.7, p.447)

DAIGLE, Josephine Celima (Eugene & Suzanne DANOS) b. 19 Oct. 1896 (Larose Ch.: v.2, p.195)

DAIGLE, Josephine Malvina (Treville & Malvina BOUDREAUX) b. 27 Oct. 1899 (Thib. Ch.: v.7, p.574)

DAIGLE, Laura m. 13 July 1898 Dellauson BESSON (Houma Ct. Hse.: Mar. v.30 & 31, #54)

DAIGLE, Lucie Louise (Eugene & Suzanne DANOS) b. 19 Oct. 1896 (Larose Ch.: v.2, p.195)

DAIGLE, Lydia d. 1 Sept. 1896 at age 13 mths. (Thib. Ch.: v.3, p.188)

DAIGLE, Marguerite Agnes (Albert & Lilia MARTINA) b. 21 Jan. 1898 (Thib. Ch.: v.7, p.538)

DAIGLE, Marie d. 22 Jan. 1898 at age 2 yrs. (Thib. Ch.: v.3, p.210)

DAIGLE, Marie Elesida (Octave & Zoe BENOIT) b. 11 Sept. 1896 (Chacahoula Ch.: v.4, p.8)

DAIGLE, Marjorie Marie (Emile & Edna J. TUCKER) b. 20 May 1899 (Houma Ch.: v.5, p.247)

DAIGLE, Mary Bella (Boddy & Marie LEBLANC) b. 23 Dec. 1898 (Houma Ch.: v.5, p.234)
DAIGLE, Mary Hazel (Albert & Lilia MANTENA) b. 1 May 1896 (Thib. Ch.: v.7, p.403)
DAIGLE, Octave George (Neuville & Emilie ROUNDTREE) b. 22 April 1898 (Thib. Ch.: v.7, p.497)
DAIGLE, Odile d. 25 Nov. 1898 at age 68 yrs. (Houma Ch.: v.3, p.19)
DAIGLE, Paul Charles (Elphege & Mollie PITRE) b. 24 July 1898 (Thib. Ch.: v.7, p.564)
DAIGLE, Paul Francis (Edgar & Lude-Marie DEBOISE) b. 22 July 1898 (Thib. Ch.: v.7, p.557)
DAIGLE, Paulin (Octave & Alexina DAIGLE) m. 10 Dec. 1898 Celeste STEVENS (Houma Ct. Hse.: Mar. v.30 & 31, #138)
DAIGLE, Paulin (Octave & Alexina DAIGLE) m. 9 Jan. 1899 Celeste ESTIVEN (Thib. Ch.: v.14, p.234)
DAIGLE, Pauline d. 19 Dec. 1899 at age 8 hours (Thib. Ch.: v.3, p.246)
DAIGLE, Pauline Virginie (Orville & Ermire BAYLE) b. 8 July 1896 (Thib. Ch.: v.7, p.409)
DAIGLE, Pierre Mrs. d. 9 May 1896 at age 69 yrs. (Chacahoula Ch.: Gibson Ch.: v.2, p.181)
DAIGLE, Sadie Elizabeth (Octave & Zoe BENOIT) b. 9 Oct. 1898 (Chacahoula Ch.: v.4, p.16)
DAIGLE, Sidney Joseph (Alcee & Mary HOLLAND) b. 7 Oct. 1896 (Chacahoula Ch.: v.4, p.5)
DAIGLE, Sidonie Margueritte (Desire & Anais THIBODEAUX) b. 1 July 1898 (Larose Ch.: v.3, p.23)
DAIGLE, Valerie Emy (Albert & Lylia GUIDRY) b. 27 July 1897 (Thib. Ch.: v.7, p.460)
DAIGNAULT, Pierre Walter (Hercule & Cecile LALANDE) b. 28 Sept. 1897 (Raceland Ch.: v.5, p.56)
DAKEL, Anna Amelia (Abraham & Eva SIMON) b. 19 Dec. 1898 (Houma Ch.: v.5, p.228)
DALFERES, Octavie (Frank & Argentine BARRIOS) m. 26 April 1897 Henri BREAUX (Lockport Ch.: v.2, p.162)
DALFERES, Octavie (Frenck & Argentine BARRIOS) m. 26 April 1897 Henri BREAUX (Thib. Ct. Hse.: Mar. v.36, #122)
DANA, ----- girl (Mr. Dana) d. 9 Sept. 1899 at age 13 hours (Houma Ch.: v.3, p.25)
DANA, Andrew J. m. 29 Oct. 1898 Mary J. PLASENCIA (Houma Ct. Hse.: Mar. v.30 & 31, #127)
DANA, Andrew J. (J. J. & Amanda DANA) m. 30 Oct. 1898 Mary J. PLASENCIA (Houma Ch.: v.6-a, p.258)
DANEL, Agnes Ida (Andresi & Alexina SAPIER) b. 18 June 1898 (Raceland Ch.: v.5, p.73)
DANGERFIELD, Willie m. 7 June 1897 Amy BOLDEN (Houma Ct. Hse.: Mar. v.29 & 30, #10)
DANIEL, Morris (Julia) b.12 Jan. 1896 (Raceland Ch.: v.5, p.19)

DANKS, David Jr. m. 9 Feb. 1899 Flora CHAMPAGNE (Houma Ct. Hse.: Mar. v.31 & 32, #328)
DANKS, William m. 15 April 1896 Rose WILLIAMS (Houma Ct. Hse.: Mar. v.29 & 30, #40)

DANNIS (See: DAUNIS)
DANNIS, Odile Ophelia (Marcelus & Marguerite ESTIVEN) b. 12 July 1897 (Thib. Ch.: v.7, p.464)

DANOS (Sometimes: DAMOS, DANNOS, DANOCE,DANOE,DANOSSE, DANOZ)
DANOS, Albert m. 7 July 1896 Melina GISCLAR (Larose Ch.: v.4, p.71)
DANOS, Albert m. 7 July 1896 Melina GISCLAIR (Larose Ch.: v.3, p.3)
DANOS, Albert W. (Albert & Melina GISCLAR) b. 17 May 1896 (Larose Ch.: v.2, p.193)
DANOS, Alcide (Jhonson & Leodile FORET) b. 21 Jan. 1898 (Raceland Ch.: v.5, p.65)
DANOS, Alexis m. 13 Jan. 1897 Pauline VEGAS (Thib. Ct. Hse.: Mar. v.36, #23)
DANOS, Alexis m. 25 Jan. 1897 Pauline VEGAS (Larose Ch.: v.4, p.118)
DANOS, Alexis m. 25 Jan. 1897 Pauline VEGAS (Larose Ch.: v.3, p.5)
DANOS, Clotilde (Toussaint & Helene BOURGEOIS) b. 9 April 1896 (Raceland Ch.: v.5, p.23)
DANOS, Emilie m. 31 Jan. 1898 Laurens CHERAMI (Larose Ch.: v.4, p.113)
DANOS, Emilie m. 31 Jan. 1898 Laurens CHERAMI (Larose Ch.: v.3, p.7)
DANOS, Emily (Adrien & Eugenie CRETINI) m. 31 Jan. 1898 Laurens CHERAMIE (Thib. Ct. Hse.: Mar. v.37, #55)
DANOS, Ernest Jean (Jean & Mary GUITROZ) b. 14 Nov. 1896 (Larose Ch.: v.2, p.187)
DANOS, Henrie (Toussaint & Helene BOURGEOIS) b. 7 April 1899 (Raceland Ch.: v.5, p.94)
DANOS, Jean Baptiste (Voltaire & Anastasie AUTIN) b. 24 June 1897 (Larose Ch.: v.3, p.3)
DANOS, Jean Onisse (Donatien & Marie FORET) b. 25 Aug. 1898 (Raceland Ch.: v.5, p.77)
DANOS, Joseph m. 24 May 1898 Marie CHERAMIE (Thib. Ct. Hse.: Mar. v.38, #187)
DANOS, Joseph Luc (Alexis & Pauline VEGAS) b. 22 March 1899 (Larose Ch.: v.3, p.39)
DANOS, Jules of Lafourche Parish (Jean Baptiste & Azina MELANCON) m. 21 Jan. 1898 Mezida TERREBONNE, of Lafourche Parish (Larose Ch.: v.3, p.7)
DANOS, Jules (Jean Baptiste & Azima MELANCON) m. 21 Jan. 1899 Mezida TERREBONNE (Thib. Ct. Hse.: Mar. v.38, #37)

DANOS, Jules (Jean Baptiste & Azina MELANCON) m. 21 Jan. 1898 Mezida TERREBONNE (Larose Ch.: v.4, p.2)
DANOS, Junius Toussaint (Gustave & Eugenie BABIN) b. 5 July 1899 (Chackbay Ch.: v.1, p.137)
DANOS, Laurentia Marie (Marcel & Alexina VEGAS) b. 13 Feb. 1897 (Larose Ch.: v.3, p.12)
DANOS, Louis (Felicien & Felicie BABIN) b. 15 Nov. 1896 (Raceland Ch.: v.5, p.35)
DANOS, Luc Clemile (Felicien & Felicie BABIN) b. 18 Oct. 1898 (Raceland Ch.: v.5, p.81)
DANOS, Ludovie Jean (Jules & Messida TERREBONNE) b. 29 Dec. 1899 (Larose Ch.: v.3, p.50)
DANOS, Marcel m. 27 April 1896 Alexina NEGUE (Larose Ch.: v.3, p.3)
DANOS, Marcel m. 27 April 1896 Alexina VEGUE (Larose Ch.: v.4, p.92)
DANOS, Marcel m. 27 April 1896 Alexina VEGAS (Thib. Ct. Hse.: Mar. v.35, #76)
DANOS, Marie Augusta (Gustave & Louise GUEDRY) b. 13 Feb. 1897 (Larose Ch.: v.3, p.1)
DANOS, Marie Lydie (Augustin & Marie ZERINGUE) b. 26 Nov. 1896 (Raceland Ch.: v.5, p.36)
DANOS, Marie Odilia (Gustave & Louise GUIDRY) b. 14 Dec. 1898 (Larose Ch.: v.3, p.34)
DANOS, Mathilda Suzanne (Adrien & Eugenie CRETINI) b. 11 Aug. 1896 (Larose Ch.: v.2, p.187)
DANOS, Medard Urbain (Urbain & Emilie GUEDRY) b. 8 June 1897 (Larose Ch.: v.3, p.10)
DANOS, Odressie (Albert & Melina GISCLAR) b. 30 March 1898 (Larose Ch.: v.3, p.19)
DANOS, Pauline m. 6 June 1896 Albert BRUCE (Larose Ch.: v.4, p.98)
DANOS, Pauline m. 6 June 1896 Albert BRUCE (Larose Ch.: v.3, p.3)
DANOS, Pauline (Adrien & Eugenie CRETINI) m. 6 June 1896 Albert BRUCE (Thib. Ct. Hse.: Mar. v.35, #95)
DANOS, Pierre Euclide (Donatien & Marie FORET) b. 24 Oct. 1896 (Raceland Ch.: v.5, p.33)
DANOS, Rose Lydia (Toussaint & Helene BOURGEOIS) b. 12 Nov. 1897 (Raceland Ch.: v.5, p.58)
DANOS, West Paul (Marcel & Alexina VEGAS) b. 30 Oct. 1898 (Larose Ch.: v.3, p.32)

DANSEREAU (Sometimes: DANCERAUX, DANSERAN, DANCEROT, DANCEROUX)

DANTIN (Sometimes: DAUTIN)
DANTIN, Alfrida m. 20 April 1896 Iba WALKER (Thib. Ct. Hse.: Mar. v.35, #71)
DANTIN, Alfrida (Alfred & Frosine WEBER) m. 20 April 1896 Iba WALKER (Raceland Ch.: v.2, p.14)

DANTIN, Anatole Ludovic (Octave & Adele MARTIN) b. 2 June 1897 (Larose Ch.: v.3, p.8)
DANTIN, Arcade Irma (Edgard & Emma FORET) b. 12 Jan. 1896 (Raceland Ch.: v.5, p.18)
DANTIN, Bernard T. (Aurestine & Angele ESPONGE) b. 20 May 1896 (Larose Ch.: v.2, p.194)
DANTIN, Blanche Nique (Gerasime & Victoire MARTIN) b. 4 April 1899 (Larose Ch.: v.3, p.41)
DANTIN, Catherine d. 16 April 1899 at age 10 mths. (Thib. Ch.: v.3, p.231)
DANTIN, Catherine Dillaid (Gustave Aubin & Catherine Aveline DILLARD) b. 2 June 1897 (Thib. Ch.: v.7, p.456)
DANTIN, Charles Dillard (Aubin & Catharine DILLARD) b. 30 Oct. 1899 (Thib. Ch.: v.7, p.588)
DANTIN, Daniel (Dudley & Martha URSIL) b. 22 March 1899 (Thib. Ch.: v.7, p.604)
DANTIN, Dora Josephine (Willie & Josephine WALKER) b. 21 Oct. 1899 (Raceland Ch.: v.5, p.105)
DANTIN, Dorcina m. 6 Sept. 1896 Isah PITRE (Larose Ch.: v.3, p.4)
DANTIN, Dorcina Mrs. a widow m. 6 Sept. 1896 Isah PITRE (Larose Ch.: v.4, p.68)
DANTIN, Dudley Joseph (Joseph & Helene DANTIN) m. 19 Jan. 1899 Mirtilia URSIN (Thib. Ct. Hse.: Mar. v.38, #22)
DANTIN, Dudley Joseph (Joseph & Helene DANTIN) m. 19 Jan. 1899 Mirtilia URSIN (Thib. Ch.: v.14, p.240)
DANTIN, Edouard (Omer & Marcella BERGERON) m. 13 June 1898 Josephine DANTIN (Thib. Ch.: v.14, p.206)
DANTIN, Edouard (Omer & Marcelline BERGERON) m. 13 June 1898 Josephine DANTIN (Thib. Ct. Hse.: Mar. v.38, #206)
DANTIN, Elles m. 8 Jan. 1897 Augusta HERNANDEZ (Thib. Ct. Hse.: Mar. v.36, #17)
DANTIN, Ellis (Jules & Rosema BROWN) m. 16 Jan. 1897 Auguste HERNANDEZ (Raceland Ch.: v.2, p.27)
DANTIN, Emelie d. 17 June 1899 at age 80 yrs. (Thib. Ch.: v.3, p.235)
DANTIN, Emelie m. 14 June 1897 Jules CORTEZ (Thib. Ct. Hse.: Mar. v.36, #171)
DANTIN, Emelie (Alfred & Euphrosine WEBER) m. 26 June 1897 Jules CORTEZ (Raceland Ch.: v.2, p.44)
DANTIN, Emesilda m. Louis DELACRETAZ d. 11 April 1898 at age 72 yrs. (Thib. Ch.: v.3, p.213)
DANTIN, Jean Baptiste Claude (Horace & Adrienne PITRE) b. 7 Sept. 1899 (Larose Ch.: v.3, p.45)
DANTIN, Jean Nelson (Edgard & Emma FORET) b. 20 June 1898 (Raceland Ch.: v.5, p.73)
DANTIN, Joseph Elesse (Elesse & Augusta HERNANDEZ) b. 28 Oct. 1897 (Raceland Ch.: v.5, p.56)
DANTIN, Josephine m. 6 Aug. 1898 Xavier MALGORME (Thib. Ct. Hse.: Mar. v.38, #239)

DANTIN, Josephine (Livaudais & Elizabeth GUILLOIS) m. 13 June 1898 Edouard DANTIN (Thib. Ch.: v.14, p.206)

DANTIN, Josephine (Livaudais & Elisabeth GUILLOI) m. 13 June 1898 Edouard DANTIN (Thib. Ct. Hse.: Mar. v.38, #206)

DANTIN, Julia m. 18 May 1898 Charles PITRE (Thib. Ct. Hse.: Mar. v.38, #183)

DANTIN, Julia (Jules & Rosema BROWN) m. 14 June 1898 Charles PITT (Raceland Ch.: v.2, p.75)

DANTIN, Marie Charlotte (Clotilde) b. 20 Sept. 1897 (Thib. Ch.: v.7, p.465)

DANTIN, Marie Mabel (Wilfred & Celemee MATERNE) b. 25 Nov. 1899 (Raceland Ch.: v.5, p.109)

DANTIN, Marie Oceana (Joseph & Carmelite BOURGEOIS) m. 12 Sept. 1899 Charles Arthur GAUDE (Thib. Ct. Hse.: Mar. v.39, #227)

DANTIN, Marie Oceana Mrs. (Joseph & Carmelite BOURGEOIS) m. 12 Sept. 1899 Charles Arthur GAUDE (Thib. Ch.: v.14, p.293)

DANTIN, Nora Marie (Willie & Josephine WALKER) b. 15 Aug. 1898 (Raceland Ch.: v.5, p.77)

DANTIN, Odillia m. 19 June 1897 Jean BRUCE (Larose Ch.: v.4, p.63)

DANTIN, Odillia m. 29 May 1897 Jean BRUCE (Thib. Ct. Hse.: Mar. v.36, #154)

DANTIN, Philippe d. 23 Feb. 1897 at age 34 yrs. (Thib. Ch.: v.3, p.197)

DANTIN, Pierre Samson (Edgard & Emma FORET) b. 20 June 1898 (Raceland Ch.: v.5, p.73)

DANTIN, Sampson d. 20 June 1899 at age 1 yr. (Raceland Ch.: v.1, p.25)

DANTIN, Thomas minor over 18 (d.Joseph P. & d.Alice LE-BLANC) Emancipation: 17 Jan. 1896. (Thib. Ct. Hse.: Succ. #1481)

DANTIN, Valery Gerasisa (Orestille & Angele ESPONGE) b. 12 Dec. 1898 (Larose Ch.: v.3, p.43)

DANTIN, Wilfred m. 25 Jan. 1899 Seleme MATHERNE (Thib. Ct. Hse.: Mar. v.38, #58)

DANTIN, Wilfrid (Jules & Rosema BROWN) m. 2 Feb. 1899 Semelie MAYERNE (Raceland Ch.: v.2, p.89)

DANTIN, William m. 27 Sept. 1897 Josephine WALKER (Thib. Ct. Hse.: Mar. v.37, #234)

DANTIN, William (Alfred & Euphrosine VEVE) m. 27 Sept. 1897 Josephine WALKER (Raceland Ch.: v.2, p.50)

DANTONE, Francesca (Nicolas & Paulina CONSALE) b. 7 April 1896 (Thib. Ch.: v.7, p.398)

DANTONE, Francisco d. 15 Feb. 1899 at age 1 mth. (Thib. Ch.: v.3, p.228)

DARBAN, Rene Willie (Rene & Emma DANTIN) b. 2 Aug. 1898 (Raceland Ch.: v.5, p.76)

DARBONNE, Catherine Euphronise (Rene & Emma DANTIN) b. 14 Aug. 1896 (Raceland Ch.: v.5, p.28)

DARCE (Sometimes: DARCY)

DARCE, Augustin (Camille & Andrellie MARONGE) b. 5 Sept. 1898 (Thib. Ch.: v.7, p.519)

DARCE, Cecile (Joseph & Mary ROBESON) m. 14 April 1896 George MARCELLE (Thib. Ch.: v.14, p.84)

DARCE, Cecile (Joseph & Mary ROBESON) m. 17 April 1896 George MARCELLE (Thib. Ct. Hse.: Mar. v.35, #69)

DARCE, Charles Joseph (Felix & Lylia LEBLANC) b. 30 March 1898 (Thib. Ch.: v.7, p.496)

DARCE, Edna m. 8 July 1897 Ferdinand BOURGEOIS (Houma Ct. Hse.: Mar. v.29 & 30, #56)

DARCE, Edna (Thomas & Laura GUIDRY) m. 12 July 1897 Ferdinand BOURGEOIS (Theriot Ch.: v.1-B, p.1)

DARCE, Ella m. 14 Dec. 1899 Jack WASHINGTON (Thib. Ct. Hse.: Mar. v.39, #283)

DARCE, Ernest (Leon & Zulma PORCHE) m. 23 June 1898 Ovilia LEBOEUF (Houma Ct. Hse.: Mar. v.30 & 31, #29)

DARCE, Felicia (Henry & Magdeleine CROCHET) m. 13 July 1896 James BABIN (Houma Ct. Hse.: Mar. v.28, #216)

DARCE, Felix (Lem & Mary ROBESON) m. 13 Feb. 1896 Lelia LEBLANC (Thib. Ct. Hse.: Mar. v.35, #38)

DARCE, Felix (Leus & Mary ROBESON) m. 13 Feb. 1896 Lelia LEBLANC (Thib. Ch.: v.14, p.77)

DARCE, Helena Veronique (Pierre & Oceana PIERCE) b. 10 May 1896 (Thib. Ch.: v.7, p.404)

DARCE, Henry Felix (Wallace & Louise AUBERT) b. 6 Dec. 1898 (Houma Ch.: v.5, p.233)

DARCE, Howard Frank m. 12 Dec. 1898 Adelia BLANCHARD (Houma Ct. Hse.: Mar. v.30 & 31, #141)

DARCE, Joseph Irvin (Emile & Adele AYO) b. 28 Dec. 1897 (Thib. Ch.: v.7, p.487)

DARCE, Joseph Nolan (Franclan & Emma BOUDREAU) b. 30 Aug. 1896 (Houma Ch.: v.5, p.158)

DARCE, Joseph Scuddy (Ernest & Eva PITT) b. 22 Jan. 1898 (Thib. Ch.: v.7, p.486)

DARCE, Joseph Steavens (Steven & Marie GARIBOTI) b. 27 Feb. 1896 (Houma Ch.: v.5, p.172)

DARCE, Joseph Ulysse (Porche & Faustine BOUDREAUX) b. 17 Nov. 1897 (Thib. Ch.: v.7, p.524)

DARCE, Lum (Leander & Rachael THIBODAUX) m. 14 July 1898 Clara MOORE (Houma Ct. Hse.: Mar. v.30 & 31, #55)

DARCE, Marguerite Louisiane (Felix & Lylia LEBLANC) b. 2 Sept. 1899 (Thib. Ch.: v.8, p.10)

DARCE, Marie Ella (Aristile & Angele MARLBROUGH) b. 19 Nov. 1896 (Houma Ch.: v.5, p.160)

DARCE, Marie Ledi (Andressi & Augustilia BERGERON) b. 21 Sept. 1896 (Houma Ch.: v.5, p.166)

DARCE, Mary m. 22 June 1898 Louis J. RODDY (Houma Ct. Hse.: Mar. v.30 & 31, #28)

DARCE, Mary (Guilbert & Marie BONVILLAIN) m. 22 June 1898 Louis J. RODDY (Houma Ch.: v.6-a, p.243)

DARCE, Nores Paul (Franklin & Emma BOUTRAUX) b. 12 Jan. 1898 (Thib. Ch.: v.7, p.541)
DARCE, Olympe Lucile (Wallace & Louise HEBERT) b. 19 Dec. 1896 (Chacahoula Ch.: v.4, p.18)
DARCE, Paul Abel (Henri & Madeleine CROCHET) b. 21 Sept. 1897 (Thib. Ch.: v.7, p.471)
DARCE, Pierre Andre (Felix & Lylia LEBLANC) b. 2 Dec. 1896 (Thib. Ch.: v.7, p.436)
DARCE, Samsson Joseph d. 13 July 1898 at age 6 days (Thib. Ch.: v.3, p.216)
DARCE, Sylvia m. 13 Feb. 1896 Sim LEDET (Houma Ct. Hse.: Mar. v.28, #457)
DARCE, Sylvia (Joseph & Mary ROBSON) m. 18 Feb. 1896 Simms LEDET (Houma Ch.: v.6-a, p.172)
DARCE, Thomas Victory Suster (Howard & Adelia BLANCHARD) b. 11 Dec. 1899 (Houma Ch.: v.6, p.5)
DARCE, Wills d. 24 Oct. 1898 at age 9 days (Theriot Ch.: v.1, p.1)
DARDA, Cleophas Appolinaire (---- & Ernestine DARDA) b. 23 July 1899 (Larose Ch.: v.3, p.57)
DARDARD, Marguerite m. 10 July 1897 Aurelien BILLIOT (Thib. Ct. Hse.: Mar. v.37, #187)

DARDARE (Sometimes: DARDAR, DARDARD, DARDERE)
DARDARE, Drosin (d.Marcellin & Henriette GUITREAU) m. 12 July 1898 Marie Lorinne NAQUIN (Montegut Ch.: v.4, p.247)
DARDARE, Drozin (Marcellin & Henriette GUITREAU) m. 8 July 1898 Marie Lorinne NAQUIN (Houma Ct. Hse.: Mar. v.30 & 31, #50)
DARDARE, Elfeijar m. 23 July 1896 Louis BROUSSARD (Larose Ch.: v.4, p.69)
DARDARE, Elfezas m. 23 July 1896 Louis BROUSSARD (Larose Ch.: v.3, p.3)
DARDARE, Emelia Odilia (Victor & Marguerite BILLOT) b. 18 April 1896 (Montegut Ch.: v.6, p.40)
DARDARE, Felicien Orestile (Privot & Dorestine CREPEL) b. 16 April 1899; bt. 20 April 1905 (Larose Ch.: v.4, p.85)
DARDARE, Joseph m. 22 April 1899 Lovinia ROBERT (Thib. Ct. Hse.: Mar. v.39, #155)
DARDARE, Joseph Leonce (Privat & Dorestine CREPEL) b. 10 April 1896 (Montegut Ch.: v.6, p.40)
DARDARE, Joseph Lucien (Emile Joachim & Evelina Augusta BILLOT) b. 20 Feb. 1898 (Larose Ch.: v.3, p.57)
DARDARE, Lelia Seraphine (Narcisse & Arthemise BILLOT) b. 28 Jan. 1897 (Montegut Ch.: v.6, p.74)
DARDARE, Myrthe Victoria (Privot & Dorestine CREPEL) b. 16 April 1899; bt. 20 April 1905 (Larose Ch.: v.4, p.85)
DARDARE, Omer Moise (Apolenaire & Victorine VERDIN) b. 8 Sept. 1897 (Larose Ch.: v.3, p.7)
DARDARE, Pierre Emile (Clement & Augustine VERDON) b. 5 Jan. 1898 (Larose Ch.: v.3, p.28)

DARDARE, Simon Thomas (Etienne & Marie NAQUIN) b. 12 Feb. 1899; bt. 10 March 1903 (Larose Ch.: v.4, p.28)

DARDARE, Ursule Licia (Gervais & Marguerite CHIASSON) b. 5 June 1897 (Montegut Ch.: v.6, p.64)

DARDARE, Victoria Lenis (Paulin & Victoria VERDIN) b. 8 Oct. 1899 (Larose Ch.: v.3, p.51)

DARDEAU, Alexandrine (Edouard & -----) d. 27 July 1899 at age 90 yrs. (Montegut Ch.: v.2, p.27)

DARDEN, Alida (John & Josephine ADAM) m. 21 April 1898 Bernard ONCALE (Chackbay Ch.: v.1, p.60)

DARDEN, Alida (John & Josephine ADAM) m. 21 April 1898 Bernard ONCALE (Thib. Ct. Hse.: Mar. v.37, #147)

DARSEY, Thomas Victory Suster (Howard & Adelia BLANCHARD) b. 11 Dec. 1899 (Houma Ch.: v.5, p.270)

DASPIT, ----- d. 24 Oct. 1896 (Houma Ch.: Epis. Ch.: v.1, p.386)

DASPIT, Alcide T. m. 25 July 1898 Maggie CLEMENT (Houma Ct. Hse.: Mar. v.30 & 31, #66)

DASPIT, Alcide T. (Claiborne & Aglae BONVILLAIN) m. 28 July 1898 Maggie CLEMENT (Houma Ch.: v.6-a, p.248)

DASPIT, Charles M. d. 24 March 1891; m. Elizabeth BERGER Children listed: Robert; V. Agnes; Mamie; Arthur J.; Charles M.; Lizzie. Tutorship: 23 March 1896. (Houma Ct. Hse.: Succ. #877)

DASPIT, Clay Peter m. 31 Jan. 1898 Agathe HEBERT (Houma Ct. Hse.: Mar. v.30 & 31, #262)

DASPIT, Clay Peter (Henry Claiborne & Galacta BONVILLAIN) m. 14 Feb. 1898 Agatha HEBERT (Houma Ch.: v.6-a, p.232)

DASPIT, Elvire (Myrthe DASPIT) d. 16 Feb. 1896; m. d.Joseph AYCOCK Application of heirs to be put in possession: 2 March 1896. (Houma Ct. Hse.: Succ. #875)

DASPIT, Felix m. Caroline WAGNER, d. 17 Sept. 1896. Children listed: Madeleine; Felix; Gabriel; Felide. Petition for tutorship: 11 March 1899. (Houma Ct. Hse.: Succ. #917)

DASPIT, Georges Divey (Isaac & Martha SWARTWORT) b. 10 March 1897 (Houma Ch.: v.5, p.207)

DASPIT, Helene Lelianne (Alfred G. & Josehine CHAUVIN) b. 2 July 1898 (Houma Ch.: v.5, p.221)

DASPIT, John (Clay Peter & Agatha HEBERT) b. 28 Dec. 1898 (Houma Ch.: v.5, p.235)

DASPIT, Joseph Octave (Alfred & Josephine CHAUVIN) b. 22 Oct. 1899 (Houma Ch.: v.5, p.268)

DASPIT, Joseph Octave (Octave Alf. & Josephine CHAUVIN) b. 22 Oct. 1899 (Houma Ch.: v.6, p.3)

DASPIT, Lilianne (Alfred & Josephine CHAUVIN) d. 6 June 1899 at age 11 mths. (Montegut Ch.: v.2, p.26)

DASPIT, Mary Avy Rose (Noe & Amanda BERGERON) b. 11 March 1896 (Houma Ch.: v.5, p.149)

DASPIT, Myrthe Chauvin d. 9 March 1896; m. d.Robert DASPIT Children listed: Oscar B.; Harry; Joseph R.; Victoria m. Sylvanus MUNSON; d.Charles M. Petition to put heirs

in possession: 3 March 1896. (Houma Ct. Hse.: Succ. #874)
DASPIT, Myrtle Laura Gaidry (J. C. & Annie M. DASPIT) b. 6 Dec. 1896 (Houma Ch.: First Presbyt. Ch.: v.1, p.262)
DASPIT, Noe Justin (Noe & Amanda BERGERON) b. 3 July 1899 (Houma Ch.: v.5, p.250)
DATHER, Marie Julie (Jules & Licia BABIN) b. 4 June 1896 (Houma Ch.: v.5, p.154)

DAUNAUD (Sometimes: DONNAUD)
DAUNAUD, Abel S. (Adolphe & Esilda FALGOUT) m. 16 June 1897 Emily GUIDRY (Thib. Ct. Hse.: Mar. v.36, #164)
DAUNAUD, Charles Emile (Abel Solet & Celeste Emilie GUIDRY) b. 27 March 1898 (Thib. Ch.: v.7, p.493)
DAUNAUD, Marie Ella d. 29 July 1898 at age 2 mths. (Raceland Ch.: v.1, p.19)
DAUNAUD, Marie Ella (Louis Albert & Elzida HEBERT) b. 18 May 1898 (Thib. Ch.: v.7, p.498)
DAUNAUD, Marie Stella (Louis Albert & Elzida HEBERT) b. 18 May 1898 (Thib. Ch.: v.7, p.498)
DAUNIO, Lufroid of Lafourche Parish m. 19 April 1899 Louise LEVRON (Houma Ch.: v.6-B, p.3)

DAUNIS (Sometimes: DANNIS, DONNIS)
DAUNIS, David Mason d. 4 Sept. 1897 at age 51 yrs. (Thib. Ch.: v.3, p.205)
DAUNIS, Ida m. 31 Jan. 1896 Abel S. PREJEANT (Houma Ct. Hse.: Mar. v.28, #430)
DAUNIS, Ida (Mason & Marthe Alice LEUDDY) m. 17 Feb. 1896 Abel L. PREJEAN (Thib. Ch.: v.14, p.78)
DAUNIS, Leufroid V. m. 8 April 1899 Louise LEVRON (Thib. Ct. Hse.: Mar. v.39, #139)
DAUNIS, Louise m. 2 Sept. 1898 Henry PREJEANT (Houma Ct. Hse.: Mar. v.30 & 31, #86)
DAUNIS, Louise (D. Mason & Lelia LEVRON) m. 12 Sept. 1898 Henry PREJEANT (Houma Ch.: v.6-a, p.253)
DAUNIS, Marcellus H. (D. Mason & Lelia M. SCUDDY) m. 26 Oct. 1896 Margaret M. STEVENS (Houma Ct. Hse.: Mar. v.29 & 30, #177)

DAUTEMENT (See: AUTHEMENT)

DAUTIN (See: DANTIN)

DAVE, Philip m. 4 Sept. 1899 Ella SWEETWINE (Thib. Ct. Hse.: Mar. v.39, #219)

DAVENPORT (Sometimes: DEVENPART)
DAVID, Jean Casimir (Jean Louis & Georgina AUTIN) b. 3 Nov. 1898 (Raceland Ch.: v.5, p.81)

DAVIDSON, Marguerite (William A. & Odalie LEBLANC) b. 22 Oct. 1898 (Houma Ch.: v.5, p.222)
DAVIDSON, William Gale (William & Audalie LEBLANC) b. 1 Jan. 1896 (Houma Ch.: v.5. p.173)

DAVIS (Sometimes: DAVIES)
DAVIS, A. H. m. 11 Dec. 1899 Mary BILLIU (Thib. Ct. Hse.: Mar. v.39, #279)
DAVIS, Alice m. 31 Aug. 1899 Eddie BELL (Thib. Ct. Hse.: Mar. v.39, #216)
DAVIS, Andrew m. 2 Feb. 1899 Louisa THOMAS (Thib. Ct. Hse.: Mar. v.38, #84)
DAVIS, Anna m. 1 July 1896 Aaron JOHNSON (Houma Ct. Hse.: Mar. v.29 & 30, #100)
DAVIS, Archie H. m. 11 Dec. 1899 Mary BILLIU (Thib. Ch.: Epis. Ch.: v.1, p.331)
DAVIS, Betsy m. 28 May 1896 Peter MILLER (Thib. Ct. Hse.: Mar. v.35, #92)
DAVIS, Carrie H. (James H. & Laura WRIGHT) m. 9 March 1897 Timothy J. BRADY (Houma Ct. Hse.: Mar. v.29 & 30, #342)
DAVIS, Carrie Hannah (Joseph A. & Laura J. WRIGHT) m. 11 March 1897 Timothy Joseph BRADY (Houma Ch.: Epis. Ch.: v.1, p.342)
DAVIS, Creacy m. 2 Oct. 1897 Isaac JOHNSON (Thib. Ct. Hse.: Mar. v.37, #238)
DAVIS, Edmond m. 31 Aug. 1899 Emerline CUBIT (Thib. Ct. Hse.: Mar. v.39, #215)
DAVIS, Eliza m. 13 May 1899 Joshua WILLIAMS (Thib. Ct. Hse.: Mar. v.39, #165)
DAVIS, Fanny m. 16 Sept. 1899 John HENRI (Thib. Ct. Hse.: Mar. v.39, #231)
DAVIS, Godfrey m. 26 June 1897 Mary MOORE (Houma Ct. Hse.: Mar. v.29 & 30, #43)
DAVIS, Guesley d. 15 Dec. 1899 at age 17 yrs. (Raceland Ch.: v.1, p.29)
DAVIS, Handy m. 2 June 1898 Elicia WILSON (Thib. Ct. Hse.: Mar. v.38, #192)
DAVIS, Henry W. d. 9 Nov. 1897 m. Mary Jane DAVIS Children listed: John C., 18; Horace Davis, 13; Henry H., 28; Sarah B., 29; Louisa, 22. Tutorship: 11 Nov. 1897. (Houma Ct. Hse.: Succ. #890)
DAVIS, Jean Casimir d. 10 Aug. 1899 at age 8 mths. (Raceland Ch.: v.1, p.26)
DAVIS, John m. 15 Jan. 1897 Nellie THORNTON (Thib. Ct. Hse.: Mar. v.36, #35)
DAVIS, Josephine d. 14 Jan. 1899 at age 4 yrs. (Houma Ch.: v.3, p.20)
DAVIS, Lalia m. 12 Oct. 1898 George BARTON (Thib. Ct. Hse.: Mar. v.38, #291)
DAVIS, Louisa m. 2 Jan. 1899 John COLLINS (Houma Ct. Hse.: Mar. v.30 & 31, #169)

DAVIS, Mary Eliza m. 20 July 1899 Mitchell WILLIAMS (Thib. Ct. Hse.: Mar. v.39, #202)

DAVIS, Mary Marguerite (James & Bertha BETHANCOURT) b. 7 Oct. 1898; m. 17 Dec. 1922 to Kenneth B. ANDERSON (Houma Ch.: Bapt. Bk., v.5, p.220)

DAVIS, Ophelia m. 6 March 1897 Oscar FLUENCE (Houma Ct. Hse.: Mar. v.29 & 30, #338)

DAVIS, Philippe d. 24 Aug. 1897 at age 80 yrs. (Thib. Ch.: v.3, p.205)

DAVIS, Philippe (Bob & Edne DAVIS) b. 5 Oct. 1899 (Thib. Ch.: v.7, p.570)

DAVIS, Rebecca m. 20 Jan. 1898 Joseph GREEN (Thib. Ct. Hse.: Mar. v.37, #46)

DAVIS, Rosa m. 26 Jan. 1899 Thomas HULING (Thib. Ct. Hse.: Mar. v.38, #64)

DAVIS, Sarah m. 21 Jan. 1899 Louis WILLIAMS (Thib. Ct. Hse.: Mar. v.38, #49)

DAVIS, Thom d. 21 Feb. 1899 at age 67 yrs. (Lockport Ch.: v.1, #7)

DAVIS, Thomas B. m. 20 Feb. 1899 Lucinda JACKSON (Houma Ct. Hse.: Mar. v.31 & 32, #344)

DAVIS, Vincent m. 3 Feb. 1897 Ida HAYES (Houma Ct. Hse.: Mar. v.29 & 30, #276)

<u>DE FONSECA (See FONSECA)</u>

DE GEORGIO, Concetta (Guiseppe & Vincensa NOTTO) b. 9 Dec. 1899 (Thib. Ch.: v.7, p.577)

DE GIOVANNE, Giapica (Georggi & Caloggera CACIPPO) b. 24 March 1896 (Houma Ch.: v.5, p.173)

DE LA BRETONNE, Florence Odette (Henri Victor & Elizabeth Celina ERNEST) b. 10 Nov. 1899 (Montegut Ch.: v.6, p.96)

DE LA BRETONNE, Henry O. m. 2 Feb. 1899 Elizabeth C. ERNEST (Houma Ct. Hse.: Mar. v.30 & 31, #298)

DE LA BRETONNE, Henry V. (Charles & Honora KISSANE) m. 11 - 13 Feb. 1899 Elizabeth ERNEST (Houma Ch.: v.6-a, p.279)

DE LA BRETONNE, Valentine (Charles & Honora CASHMAN) d. 22 July 1896 at age 38 yrs. (Houma Ch.: v.3, p.8)

<u>DE LA GARDE (See: LA GARDE)</u>

<u>DE LEPOLY (Sometimes: DE LIPOLI, DE LOPOLY)</u>

DECARLO, Francesca (Lucas & Anna Maria SALVAGIO) b. 6 Nov. 1897 (Thib. Ch.: v.7, p.480)

DEDRICK, Fannie m. 5 Sept. 1898 Henry CLAY, Jr. (Houma Ct. Hse.: Mar. v.30 & 31, #87)

DEFELICE, Augustine Bernadette (Estep & Georgina LENON) b. 8 March 1898 (Larose Ch.: v.3, p.17)

DEFELICE, Ignace Joseph (Elphege & Georgina LENON) b. 6 May 1896 (Larose Ch.: v.2, p.192)
DEFIGLIO, Carmela (Guiseppe & Madelena PANDANO) m. 3 Sept. 1898 Maria PANDANO (Thib. Ch.: v.14, p.218)
DEFIGLIO, Carmelo (Guiseppe & Madelena PANTANO) m. 3 Sept. 1898 Maria PANTANO (Thib. Ct. Hse.: Mar. v.38, #248)

DEGLE (See: DAIGLE)

DEGREER, Honorine (Augustave & Dalvina CHAMPAGNE) b. 24 Oct. 1899 (Raceland Ch.: v.5, p.105)

DEGRUISE (Sometimes: DEGRUIZE, DEGRUYS)
DEGRUISE, Bernadette d. 20 Aug. 1897 at age 11 mths. (Thib. Ch.: v.3, p.205)
DEGRUISE, Etienne Simon (Victorin & Armantine FOREST) b. 27 Oct. 1897 (Thib. Ch.: v.7, p.470)
DEGRUISE, Marie Olivia (Augustin & Darvina CHAMPAGNE) b. 16 June 1898 (Thib. Ch.: v.7, p.502)
DEHART, Henriette m. 12 Aug. 1899 Louis LINER (Houma Ct. Hse.: Mar. v.31 & 32, #93)
DEIGG, Charlotte m. 15 Oct. 1896 Robert COOK (Thib. Ct. Hse.: Mar. v.36, #156)
DEIGNAULT, Marie Zulme (Hercule & Cecile LOLAND) b. 7 July 1896 (Raceland Ch.: v.5, p.25)
DELARNO, Maria Concheda (Joseph & Marianne LAROSE) b. 23 Jan. 1897 (Montegut Ch.: v.6, p.58)
DELARNO, Vincentio d. 30 June 1898 at age 66 yrs. (Montegut Ch.: v.2, p.18)
DELASSE, Jeanne Marie (Raoul & Eugenie CHOL) b. 9 April 1896 (Thib. Ch.: v.7, p.399)

DELAUNE (Sometimes: DELANUE, DELONG)
DELAUNE, ----- child (Odgric) d. 2 Aug. 1898 at a couple of hours old (Lockport Ch.: v.1, #16)
DELAUNE, Adam alias Adam LANDREAU. Commission for inventory: 6 July 1899. (Thib. Ct. Hse.: Succ. #1581)
DELAUNE, Adela Bioula (Elma & Alice PARR) b. 16 Dec. 1896 (Lockport Ch.: v.3-A, #16)
DELAUNE, Adele Bioula (Elma & Alice PARR) b. 16 Dec. 1896 (Lockport Ch.: v.3, #16-a)
DELAUNE, Alice Odile (Orestile & Amanda SAVOIE) b. 24 April 1896 (Lockport Ch.: v.2, p.329)
DELAUNE, Anderique m. 25 Aug. 1897 Aimee BARRIOS (Lockport Ch.: v.2, p.171)
DELAUNE, Aristile d. 7 Nov. 1896 at age 50 yrs. (Lockport Ch.: v.1, #22)
DELAUNE, Auderique m. 25 Aug. 1897 Aimee BARRIOS (Thib. Ct. Hse.: Mar. v.37, #215)
DELAUNE, Elfert P. (Maxilien & Armantine BERGERON) m. 29 July 1896 Maggie BOURGEOIS (Lockport Ch.: v.2, p.153)

DELAUNE, Elfert P. (Maxillien & Armantine BERGERON) m. 29 July 1896 Maggie BOURGEOIS (Thib. Ct. Hse.: Mar. v.36, #127)
DELAUNE, Elson A. (Marcellin & Armantine BERGERON) m. 3 May 1898 Ida M. BOURG (Thib. Ct. Hse.: Mar. v.38, #169)
DELAUNE, Elson O. (Maxillien & Armantine BERGERON) m. 3 May 1898 Ida M. BOURG (Lockport Ch.: v.2, p.189)
DELAUNE, Louis m. 28 March 1898 Mary RANDOLPH (Thib. Ct. Hse.: Mar. v.37, #136)
DELAUNE, Marie Millie (Etienne & Gaelfe BRAUX) b. 27 Nov. 1896 (Lockport Ch.: v.3, #33)
DELAUNE, Marie Nellie (Etienne & Guelfe BRAUX) b. 27 Nov. 1896 (Lockport Ch.: v.3-A, #33)
DELAUNE, Zelien d. 8 March 1898 at age 50 yrs. (Houma Ch.: v.3, p.16)
DELCOURT, Adolphe P. m. 14 Sept. 1899 Nellie M. BOURG (Houma Ch.: v.6-B, p.4)
DELCOURT, Edward Henri Frances (Adolphe Joseph & Louise DESJUIN) b. 17 July 1899 (Houma Ch.: v.5, p.252)
DELERNO, Joseph deceased m. Mary Ann LAROSE Children listed: Angelina; Necent; Frank; Con Cliettie. App. for tutorship: 2 Dec. 1899. (Houma Ct. Hse.: Succ. #930)
DELERNO, Vincent d. 2 July 1898; m. Angelana MESTRAPASEIA, d. 1878 in Italy. Child: Joseph. Decree placing heir in possession: 5 Dec. 1898. (Houma Ct. Hse.: Succ. #908)
DEMATTIO, Titanna (Guiseppe & Angela TORTORECCI) b. 26 Dec. 1897 (Thib. Ch.: v.7, p.480)
DEMPSTER, Maria Palmire (Benoit & Julia CHENIER) bt. 25 July 1896 (Chackbay Ch.: v.1, p.70)
DEMPSTER, Marie (Michel & Eve LOUP) b. 22 Dec. 1897 (Chackbay Ch.: v.1, p.107)
DENNIS, Arthur m. 9 Jan. 1899 Cora BROWN (Houma Ct. Hse.: Mar. v.30 & 31, #196)
DENNIS, Fanny m. 26 May 1899 Henry NASH (Houma Ct. Hse.: Mar. v.31 & 32, #19)
DENNIS, Sarah Jane m. 8 July 1897 Charles CARTER (Houma Ct. Hse.: Mar. v.29 & 30, #59)
DEOARDI, Froncisca (Filippo & Angela DIMARCO) b. 18 Nov. 1899 (Thib. Ch.: v.8, p.21)
DERAMEE, Francois m. 29 Nov. 1899 Rose DUET (Thib. Ct. Hse.: Mar. v.39, #272)
DERAMEE, Francois Emile m. 2 Dec. 1899 Rosina DUET (Larose Ch.: v.4, p.128)
DERANIEE, Francois Emile m. 2 Dec. 1899 Rosina DUET (Larose Ch.: v.3, p.13)
DERCE, Clay Adam (Lousdon & Louisa DAIGLE) b. 1 Feb. 1898 (Thib. Ch.: v.7, p.542)
DERCE, Emile Joseph (Lousdon & Louisa DAIGLE) b. 1 Feb. 1898 (Thib. Ch.: v.7, p.542)
DERCEY, Marie Riza (Alphonse & Elda BAIE) b. 24 Feb. 1897 (Raceland Ch.: v.5, p.43)

DESAUCHE (Sometimes: DEZAUCHE)

DESAUCHE, Alice d. 25 Sept. 1898 at age 38 yrs. (Thib. Ch.: v.3, p.220)

DESAUCHE, Edna m. 25 May 1898 Edmond B. BOURGEOIS (Thib. Ct. Hse.: Mar. v.38, #188)

DESLATTES (Sometimes: DELAS, DELAT, DELATE, DELATTE, DESLATTE, DESLOTTES)

DESLATTES, Andrew m. 22 Feb. 1899 Margueritte SARGEANT (Thib. Ct. Hse.: Mar. v.39, #110)

DESLATTES, Emmanuel Chol (Raoul & Eugenie CHOL) b. 26 Jan. 1897 (Thib. Ch.: v.7, p.483)

DESLATTES, Felicien Antoine Erie (Felix & Florestine FOLSE) b. 17 May 1898 (Thib. Ch.: v.7, p.550)

DESLATTES, Felix m. 6 Oct. 1897 Florestine FOLSE (Thib. Ct. Hse.: Mar. v.37, #243)

DESLATTES, Fernand (Wilfried & Doralise MORVANT) m. 6 Feb. 1899 Oceana BOUDREAUX (Thib. Ct. Hse.: Mar. v.38, #83)

DESLATTES, Fernand (Wilfried & Doralise MORVAN) m. 6 Feb. 1899 Oceana BOUDREAUX (Thib. Ch.: v.14, p.256)

DESLATTES, Jean Olivier (Felix & Henriette DAIGLE) b. 29 Aug. 1897 (Thib. Ch.: v.7, p.462)

DESLATTES, Joseph Clerfe (Albert & Laura SANCHEZ) b. 16 Sept. 1897 (Chackbay Ch.: v.1, p.96)

DESLATTES, Leontine (Leonce & d.Theresa MOLEUR) m. 24 Sept. 1898 Alidore MARTINEZ (Chackbay Ch.: v.1, p.65)

DESLATTES, Leontine (Leonce & Theresa MOLEUR) m. 24 Sept. 1898 Alidore MARTINEZ (Thib. Ct. Hse.: Mar. v.38, #271)

DESLATTES, Lucien Levy (Fernand & Otianna BOUDREAUX) b. 9 Jan. 1899 (Thib. Ch.: v.7, p.583)

DESLATTES, Marie (Leo & Adelia SANCHEZ) b. 19 Oct. 1897 (Chackbay Ch.: v.1, p.101)

DESLATTES, Marie Clara (Albert & Laura SANCHEZ) b. 9 Dec. 1898 (Chackbay Ch.: v.1, p.130)

DESLATTES, Paul Henri (Felix & Henriette DAIGLE) b. 22 Aug. 1899 (Thib. Ch.: v.8, p.5)

DESROCHES (Sometimes: DEROCHE)

DESROCHES, Canilia Virginie (Prosper & Palmyra LEDET) b. 8 July 1897 (Montegut Ch.: v.6, p.58)

DESROCHES, Ernestine (Eusebe & Celestine DAZET) d. 27 Sept. 1899 at age 16 yrs. (Montegut Ch.: v.2, p.29)

DESROCHES, Gilbert Maurice (Henri & Alice BOURG) b. 3 Aug. 1898 (Montegut Ch.: v.6, p.76)

DESROCHES, Jean Colbert (Olaus & Augustine BOURG) b. 27 June 1898 (Montegut Ch.: v.6, p.75)

DESROCHES, Johnny Albert (Eusebe & Celestine DAZET) d. 12 May 1896 (Montegut Ch.: v.2, p.4)

DESROCHES, Joseph Albert (Olaus & Augustine BOURG) b. 16 Oct. 1899 (Montegut Ch.: v.6, p.95)

DESROCHES, Joseph Francois Deme (Henry & Alice BOURG) b. 28 April 1896 (Montegut Ch.: v.6, p.38)
DESROCHES, Joseph Nicles (Ozemee & Helena LEDET) b. 1 March 1897 (Montegut Ch.: v.6, p.53)
DESROCHES, Joseph Pierre (Ozemee & Helena LEDET) b. 13 May 1899 (Montegut Ch.: v.6, p.88)
DESROCHES, Marie Adeline (Prosper & Palmyra LEDET) b. 15 May 1899 (Montegut Ch.: v.6, p.88)
DESROCHES, Marie Anesia (Theodule & Eulodie BOQUET) bt. 4 Jan. 1896 (Montegut Ch.: v.6, p.31)
DESROCHES, Marie Bernise (Theodule & Eulodie BOQUET) b. 13 July 1897 (Montegut Ch.: v.6, p.58)
DESROCHES, Marie Josephine (Eusebe & Celestine DAZET) b. 6 Oct. 1896 (Montegut Ch.: v.6, p.46)
DESROCHES, Oleus m. 15 Sept. 1897 Augustine BOURG (Houma Ct. Hse.: Mar. v.29 & 30, #90)
DESROCHES, Oleus (Joseph & Adeline BOUDREAUX) m. 7 Oct. 1897 Augustine BOURG (Montegut Ch.: v.4, p.225)
DESROCHES, Vincent Laurent (Eusebe & Celestine DAZET) b. 5 April 1899 (Montegut Ch.: v.6, p.95)
DESTELANO, Marie (Vincente & Maria Antonia VINTEMILIA) b. 17 Dec. 1899 (Raceland Ch.: v.5, p.111)

DESTIVAUX (Sometimes: D'ESTIVAUX, DETIVAUX)
DESTIVAUX, Anne Beatrice (Ernest & Armelise PITRE) b. 13 Sept. 1899 (Montegut Ch.: v.6, p.92)
DESTIVAUX, Benny (Henri & Bazelise BRUNET) m. 5 Oct. 1897 Domatile DUPRE (Houma Ct. Hse.: Mar. v.29 & 30, #109)
DESTIVAUX, Jean Dewey (Martial & Celima SAVOIE) b. 28 June 1898 (Montegut Ch.: v.6, p.75)
DESTIVAUX, Joseph Georges (Benjamin & Domitilde DUPRE) b. 4 May 1899 (Montegut Ch.: v.7, p.18)
DESTIVAUX, William Adam (Martial & Celima SAVOIE) b. 14 April 1896 (Montegut Ch.: v.6, p.38)

DEVILLARD (Sometimes: DEVILLARS)

DHUET (See: DUET)

DI GIORGIO, Concetti d. 10 Dec. 1899 at age 4 hours (Thib. Ch.: v.3, p.246)
DIAN, Marie Lucie Anita (Etienne & Mathilde BILLOT) b. 12 Oct. 1899 (Montegut Ch.: v.6, p.101)

DIAS (Sometimes: DIAZ, DIES)
DIAS, Augustin O'Neil (Augustin Raphael & Sylvanie TOUPS) b. 23 April 1898 (Thib. Ch.: v.7, p.544)
DIAS, Catherine Lucile (Raphael & Sylvanie TOUPS) b. 29 March 1896 (Raceland Ch.: v.5, p.22)
DIAS, Cecilia m. 23 April 1898 Oscar LANDRY (Thib. Ct. Hse.: Mar. v.37, #149)

DIAS, Cęcilia (Theodule & Felicienne PLAISANCE) m. 23 April 1898 Oscar LANDRY (Raceland Ch.: v.2, p.73)
DIAS, Ernest (Augustin & Pamela CHAMPAGNE) m. 27 April 1898 Carmelite TOUPS (Thib. Ct. Hse.: Mar. v.38, #166)
DIAS, Ernest (Augustin & Pamela CHAMPAGNE) m. 27 April 1898 Carmelite TOUPS (Thib. Ch.: v.14, p.198)
DIAS, Etolaine m. 6 Feb. 1897 Eugene FORET (Thib. Ct. Hse.: Mar. v.36, #72)
DIAS, Etolene (Theodule & Felicie PLAISANCE) m. 8 Feb. 1897 Eugene FORET (Raceland Ch.: v.2, p.32)
DIAS, Joseph Vener (Gustave & Delia TOUPS) b. 3 Nov. 1899 (Raceland Ch.: v.5, p.105)
DIAS, Louis Beldom (Gustave & Delia TOUPS) b. 14 Dec. 1897 (Raceland Ch.: v.5, p.60)
DIAS, Odile Honorine (Raphael & Celonie TOUPS) b. 14 Dec. 1897 (Raceland Ch.: v.5, p.60)
DIAS, Paul Alain (Edgar & Emelie TOUPS) b. 26 March 1897 (Raceland Ch.: v.5, p.45)
DICKENS, Alouisia (Joseph & Lea DICKENS) b. 1 Feb. 1897 (Thib. Ch.: v.7, p.441)
DICKERSON, Cora m. 10 Aug. 1898 John M. SMITH (Thib. Ct. Hse.: Mar. v.38, #243)
DICKERSON, Delia m. 1 Oct. 1896 Nathan BROOKS (Thib. Ct. Hse.: Mar. v.36, #150)
DICKERSON, Emma m. 14 Dec. 1899 Arthur COOK (Thib. Ct. Hse.: Mar. v.39, #282)
DICKERSON, Lea m. 13 Jan. 1897 Joseph DYER (Thib. Ct. Hse.: Mar. v.36, #26)
DICKSON, Alfred m. 15 Oct. 1896 Sarah HARRISON (Thib. Ct. Hse.: Mar. v.36, #155)
DICKSON, Caldonia m. 19 May 1898 Lavery PROSPER (Thib. Ct. Hse.: Mar. v.38, #185)
DICKSON, Henry m. 9 Feb. 1899 Patsy CRUMP (Houma Ct. Hse.: Mar. v.31 & 32, #331)
DIFIGLIA, Calogeria d. 6 March 1899 at age 27 yrs. (Thib. Ch.: v.3, p.229)
DIGGS, John m. 7 May 1896 Celestine DOMINIQUE (Houma Ct. Hse.: Mar. v.29 & 30, #57)
DIGGS, Wheeler m. 11 May 1898 Dina CLARK (Houma Ct. Hse.: Mar. v.30 & 31, #439)
DILL, Gertrude (William & Serima HANAGRIFF) m. 23 March 1898 William L. KOHMANN (Houma Ct. Hse.: Mar. v.30 & 31, #348)
DILL, Gertrude M. (William & Jummina HANAGRIFFE) m. 23 March 1898 William L. KOHMANN (Houma Ch.: Epis. Ch.: v.1, p.342)
DILL, Louise Florence (James & Lydie MORVAN) b. 24 Sept. 1897 (Thib. Ch.: v.7, p.523)
DILL, Maud Emilie (James & Lydie MORVAN) b. 29 Aug. 1899 (Thib. Ch.: v.8, p.10)

DILL, Richard d. 28 June 1896 at age 11 mths. (Thib. Ch.: v.3, p.184)
DILL, Roger Armand (James & Lydia MORVAN) b. 9 Jan. 1896 (Thib. Ch.: v.7, p.440)
DILLARD, Elec Lee (Georges & Josephine BROWN) b. 11 Aug. 1898 (Houma Ch.: v.5, p.231)
DILLARD, John m. 27 Sept. 1899 Edna DYER (Houma Ct. Hse.: Mar. v.31 & 32, #146)
DILLON, William T. m. 7 Jan. 1898 Estelle BERGERON (Thib. Ct. Hse.: Mar. v.37, #9)
DILLON, William Thomas Jr. (William Thomas Sr. & Sarah ----) m. 17 Jan. 1898 Estelle BERGERON (Thib. Ch.: v.14, p.169)
DIMARCO, Maria (Antonino & Rosa CASTROGIOVANNI) m. 16 July 1898 Vincenzo RANDAZZO (Thib. Ct. Hse.: Mar. v.38, #196)
DIMECO, Maria (Lauriggi & Angela DENNIA) m. 13 Feb. 1897 Michale GUGGARDO (Houma Ch.: v.6-a, p.192)
DIMICO, Maria m. 11 Feb. 1897 Michele GUGGARDO (Houma Ct. Hse.: Mar. v.29 & 30, #301)
DINARCA, Maria (Antonino & Rosa CASTROGIOVANNI) m. 16 July 1898 Vicenzo RANDAZZO (Thib. Ch.: v.14, p.210)
DIOGUARDE, Maria Gratia (Philippo & Angela DEMARCO) b. 6 Aug. 1896 (Thib. Ch.: v.7, p.467)
DIOGUARDI, Philippa (Nicolo & Guiseppa CARAVELLO) b. 22 Sept. 1898 (Thib. Ch.: v.7, p.567)
DION, Etienne (Thomas & Azelie VERDIN) m. 2 July 1898 Mathilde BILLOT (Houma Ct. Hse.: Mar. v.30 & 31, #44)
DION, Etienne (Thomas & Zelie VERDUN) m. 12 July 1898 Mathilde BILLOT (Theriot Ch.: v.1-B, p.4)
DION, Gabriel (Etienne & Mathilde BILLIOT) b. 11 Sept. 1897 (Theriot Ch.: v.2, p.24)
DION, Georges m. 15 July 1898 Laura GAUTREAUX (Houma Ct. Hse.: Mar. v.30 & 31, #60)
DION, Georges (Georges & Eugenie VICNAIR) m. 7 Sept. 1898 Laura GAUTHREAUX (Chacahoula Ch.: v.1, p.67 [87])
DION, Marie Agnes (Placide & Marie BILLIOT) bt. 22 Feb. 1897 (Theriot Ch.: v.1-B, p.104)
DION, Marie Elvina (Joseph & Marie GREGOIRE) b. 4 Dec. 1896 (Theriot Ch.: v.2, p.7)

DIONNE (Sometimes: DION, DIONE, DIORNE)

DIRDEN, Simuel m. 13 Feb. 1896 Epsie MEADOWS (Houma Ct. Hse.: Mar. v.28, #455)
DISPENSA, Maria (Santa & Rosalia CUTAIA) m. 3 April 1899 Nicolo SCIORTINO (Thib. Ch.: v.14, p.268)
DISPENSA, Maria (Santo & Rosalia CUTAIA) m. 3 April 1899 Nicolo SCIORTINO (Thib. Ct. Hse.: Mar. v.39, #121)
DITU, Maria Carina (Joseph & Carmelita DARDARD) b. 15 Oct. 1898 (Theriot Ch.: v.2, p.35)

DIVARCA, Andrea m. 23 Oct. 1899 Mariana OLIVEA (Thib. Ct. Hse.: Mar. v.39, #253)
DIVARCA, Andrea (Placido & Margherite CUTAIA) m. 16 Dec. 1899 Marianne OLIVEA (Thib. Ch.: v.14, p.310)
DIXIE, Richard m. 16 Aug. 1898 Phoebe COTTON (Thib. Ct. Hse.: Mar. v.38, #252)
DIXL, James Joseph Deo (Robert & Eda POCHE) b. 8 June 1897 (Montegut Ch.: v.6, p.99)
DIXL, Valerie Jessie (Robert & Eda POCHE) b. 28 July 1899 (Montegut Ch.: v.6, p.99)
DOBERTY, Joseph m. 27 April 1899 Lucy JOSEPH (Thib. Ct. Hse.: Mar. v.39, #157)

DOHERTY (Sometimes: DOHARTY, DOHORTY)
DOIRON, Azelie m. ----- AUCOIN d. 6 Feb. 1899 (Chacahoula Ch.: Gibson Ch.: v.2, p.182)
DOIRON, Leonce Aloysious (Cleophas & Elvire LANCON) b. 9 Aug. 1897 (Houma Ch.: v.5, p.184)
DOIRON, Ophelia m. 5 Sept. 1899 Celestin CUNNINGHAM (Houma Ct. Hse.: Mar. v.31 & 32, #119)
DOIRON, Ophilia m. 14 Sept. 1899 Celestin CUNNINGHAM (Houma Ch.: v.6-B, p.4)
DOKERTY, Edouard d. 4 Feb. 1898 at age 64 yrs. (Thib. Ch.: v.3, p.210)
DOLAND, Alice d. 17 Sept. 1896 at age 26 yrs. (Thib. Ch.: v.3, p.187)
DOLESE, Andrew E. m. 5 Jan. 1898 Camelia BOLOTTE (Thib. Ct. Hse.: Mar. v.37, #6)
DOLEZE, George Lory (Natili & Esilda RAGAS) b. 23 April 1898 (Thib. Ch.: v.7, p.548)
DOMAGUE, Easton Jean (Adam & Malvina BLANCHARD) b. 10 March 1897; m. Lillian Marie FANGUI on 21 Feb. 1924. (Houma Ch.: Bapt. Bk., v.5, p.207)
DOMINGO, ----- girl d. 29 Dec. 1898 (Thib. Ch.: v.3, p.224)

DOMINGUE (Sometimes: DOMINGUEZ)
DOMINGUE, Albert (Edwin & Ozea TOUPS) m. 10 April 1899 Bertha HEBERT (Montegut Ch.: v.4, p.261)
DOMINGUE, Augustin (Leo & Octavie LAMBAS) m. 12 Feb. 1898 Effie PICOU (Montegut Ch.: v.4, p.236)
DOMINGUE, Augustin (Leo & Octavie LOMBAS) m. 25 Jan. 1898 Effie PICOU (Houma Ct. Hse.: Mar. v.30 & 31, #252)
DOMINGUE, Cecile Doris (Emile & Eugenie CHAMPAGNE) b. 13 June 1899 (Montegut Ch.: v.6, p.89)
DOMINGUE, Cecilia (Eusebe & Josephine LABAT) m. 24 Aug. 1898 Joseph MARY (Montegut Ch.: v.4, p.248)
DOMINGUE, Cecilia (Eusebe & osephine LABAT) m. 10 Aug. 1898 Joseph MARY (Houma Ct. Hse.: Mar. v.30 & 31, #75)
DOMINGUE, Celestine m. 16 March 1898 Willie RHODES (Houma Ct. Hse.: Mar. v.30 & 31, #339)

DOMINGUE, Celestine (Olezime & Elzina FOREST) m. 11 April 1898 Willie RHODES (Montegut Ch.: v.4, p.239)
DOMINGUE, Emile (d.Michel & d.Philomene LOUVIERE) m. 17 Feb. 1896 Eugenie CHAMPAGNE (Montegut Ch.: v.4, p.207)
DOMINGUE, Emile (Michel & Philomene LOUVIERE) m. 25 Jan. 1896 Eugenie CHAMPAGNE (Houma Ct. Hse.: Mar. v.28, #415)
DOMINGUE, Emma (Olezime & Elezima FOREST) m. 23 Dec. 1899 Estive RHODES (Houma Ct. Hse.: Mar. v.31 & 32, #191)
DOMINGUE, Jean Perly (Jean & Theo HACQ) b. 7 April 1897 (Thib. Ch.: v.7, p.450)
DOMINGUE, Joada Jr. m. 21 May 1896 Armantine BERGERON (Houma Ct. Hse.: Mar. v.29 & 30, #78)
DOMINGUE, Joseph Abbey (Joadda & Armantine BERGERON) b. 10 Aug. 1897 (Houma Ch.: v.5, p.185)
DOMINGUE, Joseph Beb. (Beb. & Emma BLANCHARD) b. 5 Jan. 1898 (Montegut Ch.: v.6, p.67)
DOMINGUE, Joseph Eddy (Joroda & Marguerite BEAUDOIN) b. 12 July 1897 (Theriot Ch.: v.2, p.8)
DOMINGUE, Joseph Wilson (Emmanuel & Marie SAVOIE) b. 1 Aug. 1899 (Theriot Ch.: v.2, p.47)
DOMINGUE, Josephine m. d.Eugene TOUPS d. 14 Jan. 1899 at age 90 yrs. (Montegut Ch.: v.2, p.23)
DOMINGUE, Julien (Joada & Marguerite BAUDOIN) m. 6 June 1899 Julienne DOMINGUE (Houma Ct. Hse.: Mar. v.31 & 32, #31)
DOMINGUE, Julienne (Leo & Octave LOMBAS) m. 6 June 1899 Julien DOMINGUE (Houma Ct. Hse.: Mar. v.31 & 32, #31)
DOMINGUE, Leo Jr. (Leo & Octavie LOMBARD) m. 8 Dec. 1899 Domatile NAVARRE (Houma Ct. Hse.: Mar. v.31 & 32, #176)
DOMINGUE, Leontine (Michel & Philomene LOUVIERE) m. 29 July 1896 Wallace LEBLANC (Thib. Ch.: v.14, p.95)
DOMINGUE, Leontine (Michel & Philomene LOUVIERE) m. 24 June 1896 Wallace LEBLANC (Thib. Ct. Hse.: Mar. v.36, #111)
DOMINGUE, Louise Iola (Emile & Eugenie CHAMPAGNE) b. 4 Dec. 1897 (Montegut Ch.: v.6, p.64)
DOMINGUE, Manuel d. 23 Aug. 1898 at age 82 yrs. (Montegut Ch.: v.2, p.20)
DOMINGUE, Manuel (Leo & Octavie LOMBAS) m. 28 Sept. 1898 Marie SAVOIE (Houma Ct. Hse.: Mar. v.30 & 31, #109)
DOMINGUE, Marceleste Aspasie (Adam & Malvina BLANCHARD) b. 19 Dec. 1899 (Theriot Ch.: v.2, p.59)
DOMINGUE, Marie Irine (Leo & Donatile BLANCHARD) b. 13 Aug. 1899 (Houma Ch.: v.5, p.257)
DOMINGUE, Marie Laura (Adam & Malvina BLANCHARD) b. 26 Jan. 1897 (Theriot Ch.: v.1-B, p.106)
DOMINGUE, Marie Mathilde (Augustin & Ephee PICOU) b. 31 Oct. 1899 (Montegut Ch.: v.6, p.96)
DOMINGUE, Marie Noelia (Jean & Celestine GUIDRY) b. 15 May 1898; bt. 12 May 1900 (Montegut Ch.: v.7, p.2)
DOMINGUE, Marie Olive (Joadam & Ermantine BERGERON) b. 2 Nov. 1899 (Theriot Ch.: v.2, p.54)

DOMINGUE, Marie Violette (Emile & Eugenie CHAMPAGNE) b. 30 Dec. 1896 (Montegut Ch.: v.6, p.50)
DOMINGUE, Melissa m. 24 June 1899 Mirtille BOUDREAUX (Theriot Ch.: v.1-B, p.10)
DOMINGUE, Raymond Sidney (Leo & Felicia CHIASSON) b. 23 Jan. 1897 (Montegut Ch.: v.6, p.51)
DOMINGUE, Valerie Nola Flevia (Jean & Theolene HOCQ) b. 31 May 1899 (Thib. Ch.: v.7, p.554)

DOMINGUEZ (See Perhaps: DOMINGUE)

DOMINIQUE, Albert (Edwin & Ozea TOUPS) m. 18 March 1899 Bertha HEBERT (Houma Ct. Hse.: Mar. v.31 & 32, #368)
DOMINIQUE, Celestine m. 7 May 1896 John DIGGS (Houma Ct. Hse.: Mar. v.29 & 30, #57)
DOMINIQUE, Ida Marie (Antoine & Julienne PLAISANCE) b. 29 Feb. 1896 (Lockport Ch.: v.2, p.325)
DOMMAY, Marie Bessy (Cleophas & Francisse CHIASSON) b. 28 May 1896 (Houma Ch.: v.5, p.181)
DONALDSON, Creecy m. 12 Jan. 1898 John KELLY or KELLER (Houma Ct. Hse.: Mar. v.30 & 31, #195)
DONALDSON, Ephraim m. 2 Nov. 1899 Martha BROOKS (Houma Ct. Hse.: Mar. v.31 & 32, #159)
DONAT, Abel Stephen (Abel & Celeste Emelie GUIDRY) b. 8 May 1898 (Thib. Ch.: v.7, p.547)
DONNAUD, Abel (Adolphe & Erilda FALGOUT) m. 16 June 1897 Emelie GUIDRY (Thib. Ch.: v.14, p.147)
DONNET, James d. 18 April 1899 at age 2 mths. (Thib. Ch.: v.3, p.232)
DONOHUE, Hartage (Thomas) d. 14 Aug. 1898 at age 9 mths. (Thib. Ch.: v.3, p.219)
DORCEY, Macdella m. 2 Nov. 1897 Jessie SMITH (Thib. Ct. Hse.: Mar. v.37, #255)
DORIO, Victorine Insanity: 2 June 1899. (Thib. Ct. Hse.: Succ. #1576)
DORSA, Guiseppe (Joanne & Maria Rita NUCCIA) m. March 1898 Maria Guiseppa MACALUSA (Thib. Ch.: v.14, p.193)
DORSA, Guiseppe (Joanne & Marie Rita NUCCIA) m. 19 March 1898 Marie Giuseppa MACALUSA (Thib. Ct. Hse.: Mar. v.37, #120)
DORSA, Vincenzo (Guiseppe & Guiseppa MAGALUSA) b. 9 Jan. 1898 (Thib. Ch.: v.7, p.533)
DORSEY, Munson m. 10 Aug. 1899 Cyrena BYRD (Thib. Ct. Hse.: Mar. v.39, #209)
DORSEY, Oliva (Gilbert & Eleonore CHALAHOUE) b. 13 May 1897 (Houma Ch.: v.5, p.186)
DOTTRY, Joseph m. 27 April 1899 Lucy JOSEPH (Thib. Ct. Hse.: Mar. v.39, #157)

DOUCET (Sometimes: DOUCE)

DOUCET, Alexina Marie (Francois & Adelina GUIDRY) b. 12 Nov. 1899 (Larose Ch.: v.3, p.49)

DOUCET, Alvana d. 16 May 1897 at age 40 yrs. (Thib. Ch.: v.3, p.200)

DOUCET, Aurelien d. 10 Jan. 1897 at age 61 yrs. (Thib. Ch.: v.3, p.195)

DOUCET, Aurelien Walter (Philippe & Clara BABIN) b. 2 Sept. 1898 (Thib. Ch.: v.7, p.511)

DOUCET, Edward Leopold (Augustin & Adele KNOBLOCK) b. 16 Dec. 1896 (Larose Ch.: v.3, p.8)

DOUCET, Francois (Francois & Marguerite ORGERON) m. 10 Jan. 1898 Adelina GUIDRY (Larose Ch.: v.3, p.6)

DOUCET, Francois (Francois & Margueritte ORGERON) m. 10 Jan. 1898 Adelina GUIDRY (Larose Ch.: v.4, p.109)

DOUCET, Francois L. m. 22 Dec. 1896 Adelina GUIDRY (Thib. Ct. Hse.: Mar. v.36, #168)

DOUCET, Motila m. 1 May 1899 Oscar TERREBONNE (Thib. Ct. Hse.: Mar. v.39, #161)

DOUCET, Notilia (Francois & Marguerite ORGERON) m. 13 May 1899 Oscar TERREBONNE (Larose Ch.: v.3, p.12)

DOUCET, Notilia (Francois & Margueritte ORGERON) m. 13 May 1899 Oscar TERREBONNE (Larose Ch.: v.4, p.85)

DOUCET, Notilia (Francois & Margueritte ORGERON) m. 13 May 1899 Oscar TERREBONNE (Larose Ch.: v.4, p.105)

DOUCET, Zilda (d.Adam & Linda GUIDRY) m. 1 Sept. 1896 Adolphe GUIDRY (Thib. Ct. Hse.: Mar. v.36, #139)

DOUDET, Joseph d. 30 March 1898; m. d.Marie GABASSE, d. 1885 Children listed: Paul. Sworn testimony: 15 Aug. 1898 (Houma Ct. Hse.: Succ. #906)

DOUGHINE, Maria m. 5 Aug. 1899 Filogene VIZIER (Thib. Ct. Hse.: Mar. v.39, #203)

DOUGLAS (Sometimes: DOGLES)

DOUGLAS, Bertha m. 27 May 1897 Andrew ROBINSON (Houma Ct. Hse.: Mar. v.29 & 30, #428)

DOUGLAS, Eveline m. 14 May 1896 Roden HARRIS (Houma Ct. Hse.: Mar. v.29 & 30, #68)

DOUGLAS, Richardson m. 28 April 1898 Georgiana COLLINS (Houma Ct. Hse.: Mar. v.30 & 31, #424)

DOVER, Joseph m. 5 May 1896 Eva TOUPS (Houma Ct. Hse.: Mar. v.29 & 30, #50)

DOVER, Joseph Stanley (Jos & Eve TOUPS) b. 7 March 1898 (Theriot Ch.: v.2, p.26)

DROUET, Louis (Azier & Felicie ALEXANDRE) b. 21 Oct. 1898 (Raceland Ch.: v.5, p.86)

DRUMGOULD, Louisiana m. 13 Jan. 1898 Matthew BUD (Thib. Ct. Hse.: Mar. v.37, #17)

DUAY (See: DUET)

DUAY, Stella Josephine (Adam & Eugenia HUNTER) b. 19 March 1896 (Larose Ch.: v.2, p.191)

DUBOIS, Anita Valerie (Alidor & Adolphine ORGERON) b. 3 Oct. 1898 (Larose Ch.: v.3, p.29)

DUBOIS, Annette d. 17 March 1898 at age 15 mths. (Chacahoula Ch.: v.2, p.25)

DUBOIS, Celestine m. 19 July 1897 Salvador CARLOS (Theriot Ch.: v.1-B, p.1)

DUBOIS, Ernest Thomas Wilfred (Aladin & Emelie BOUDREAUX) b. 21 Dec. 1896 (Chacahoula Ch.: v.4, p.11)

DUBOIS, Jean Baptiste (Adam & Marceline AUTEMENT) b. 24 June 1896 (Houma Ch.: v.5, p.182)

DUBOIS, Joseph Alcide (Joseph & Marguerite BLANCHARD) b. 2 Dec. 1896 (Theriot Ch.: v.1-B, p.104)

DUBOIS, Mathilde Annette (Romain & Marie BOUDREAUX) b. 4 Dec. 1896 (Chacahoula Ch.: v.4, p.9)

DUBOIS, Philomene m. 9 Sept. 1897 Edgard RICHARD (Thib. Ct. Hse.: Mar. v.37, #227)

DUBOIS, Philomene m. 9 Sept. 1897 Edgard RICHARD (Lockport Ch.: v.2, p.175)

DUBOIS, Regina Josephine (Silvere & Eulasie BARRIOS) b. 19 Sept. 1896 (Lockport Ch.: v.2, p.336)

DUBOIS, Romain d. 1898 (Chacahoula Ch.: v.2, p.25)

DUBOIS, Unetia (Alidor & Dolphine ORGERON) m. 30 Dec. 1899 Richard ORGERON (Thib. Ct. Hse.: Mar. v.39, #308)

DUBOUE, Lazarus m. 8 March 1897 Elizabeth BROWN (Thib. Ct. Hse.: Mar. v.36, #95)

DUCKER, Lily m. 23 Nov. 1898 Numa GOODMAN (Thib. Ct. Hse.: Mar. v.38, #312)

DUCOS, Celeste m. Francois DERAMEE d. 11 Feb. 1899 (Larose Ch.: v.1, p.51)

DUET (Sometimes: DHUET, DUE)

DUET, Abel d. 22 July 1896 at age 6 mths. (Thib. Ch.: v.3, p.185)

DUET, Abel Joseph (Lovincy & Felicia BRAUX) b. 23 July 1898 (Thib. Ch.: v.7, p.507)

DUET, Adele Adelphine (Felix & Alida GRAUS) b. 24 Dec. 1898 (Chackbay Ch.: v.1, p.124)

DUET, Albert Davis (Joseph & Eugenie MARTIN) b. 27 June 1898 (Chackbay Ch.: v.1, p.115)

DUET, Alcide Louis (Leo & Eulalie CHERAMI) b. 16 Jan. 1897 (Larose Ch.: v.3, p.8)

DUET, Alexandre d. 11 April 1899 at age 3 yrs. (Thib. Ch.: v.3, p.231)

DUET, Alice m. 4 Jan. 1898 Voohries AUTHEMENT (Larose Ch.: v.3, p.6)

DUET, Alice m. 4 Jan. 1898 Voorhies AUTHEMENT (Larose Ch.: v.4, p.110)

DUET, Alice m. 4 Jan. 1898 Voorhies AUTHEMENT (Thib. Ct. Hse.: Mar. v.37, #269)
DUET, Bula Violet (Zephirin & Adelina PISANI) b. 3 March 1898 (Chacahoula Ch.: Gibson Record: Mar. Bk., v.1, #22)
DUET, Bula Violet (Zephirin & Adelina PISANI) b. 3 March 1898 (Chacahoula Ch.: Gibson Ch.: v.2, p.119)
DUET, Camile (Felix & d.Marie HEBERT) m. 9 Aug. 1897 Amelia THIBODAUX (Chackbay Ch.: v.1, p.46)
DUET, Clarice Albertine (Laura) b. 18 Dec. 1897 (Thib. Ch.: v.7, p.484)
DUET, Claudia Josephine (---- & Clemence DUET) b. 12 Sept. 1896 (Larose Ch.: v.2, p.183)
DUET, Clemille m. 20 July 1897 Amelia THIBODAUX (Thib. Ct. Hse.: Mar. v.37, #197)
DUET, Eddy Joseph d. 25 Sept. 1897 at age 7 mths. (Thib. Ch.: v.3, p.206)
DUET, Eliza m. 1 July 1899 Charles WILLIAMS (Thib. Ct. Hse.: Mar. v.39, #184)
DUET, Elmire Laetitia (Auguste & Louise BRUCE) b. 16 June 1896 (Larose Ch.: v.2, p.184)
DUET, Felicien m. 18 April 1898 Louise GUIDRY (Thib. Ct. Hse.: Mar. v.38, #160)
DUET, Felicien Paul (Felicien & Louise GUIDRY) b. 31 March 1899 (Larose Ch.: v.3, p.39)
DUET, Francois Joseph (Joseph & Julie USAY) b. 3 Dec. 1898 (Larose Ch.: v.3, p.30)
DUET, Georgina (Armand & Marie ROUX) b. 30 March 1897 (Larose Ch.: v.3, p.3)
DUET, Helen Rita (Auguste & Louise BRUCE) b. 14 May 1898 (Larose Ch.: v.3, p.20)
DUET, Jean Absalon (Enock & Julie BRUCE) b. 27 Dec. 1897 (Larose Ch.: v.3, p.15)
DUET, Joseph Eddy (Joseph & Eugenie MARTIN) b. 9 Feb. 1897 (Thib. Ch.: v.7, p.441)
DUET, Joseph Lignes (Alceste & Christina ROSS) b. 26 March 1898 (Chacahoula Ch.: Gibson Records: Mar. Bk., v.1, #40)
DUET, Joseph Lucien (Donatien & Felonise SOURITA) b. 20 July 1898 (Larose Ch.: v.3, p.31)
DUET, Joseph Signes (Alceste & Christine ROSS) b. 26 March 1898 (Chacahoula Ch.: Gibson Ch.: v.2, p.127)
DUET, Joseph Vilfried d. 26 Sept. 1896 at age 8 mths. (Thib. Ch.: v.3, p.187)
DUET, Josephine Augusta (Lovincy & Felicia BREAUX) b. 3 April 1897 (Thib. Ch.: v.7, p.449)
DUET, Josephine Gabrielle (Robert & Velma MORVAN) b. 18 March 1898 (Thib. Ch.: v.7, p.491)
DUET, Justine Melanie (Felix & Alida GROS) b. 21 Aug. 1896 (Thib. Ch.: v.7, p.419)
DUET, Lea m. 7 June 1896 Peet MALCOMBE (Larose Ch.: v.4, p.99)

DUET, Lea m. 7 May 1896 Pete MALCOMBE (Thib. Ct. Hse.: Mar. v.35, #82)

DUET, Lea m. 7 May 1896 Pitre MALCOMBE (Larose Ch.: v.3, p.3)

DUET, Louis d. 3 March 1897 at age 76 yrs. (Lockport Ch.: v.1, #8)

DUET, Louis Aurelien (Etienne & Marie NAQUIN) b. 3 May 1899 (Chackbay Ch.: v.1, p.134)

DUET, Louis Joseph (Joseph & Eugenie MARTIN) b. 11 Feb. 1896 (Thib. Ch.: v.7, p.392)

DUET, Louise d. 15 April 1899 at age 64 yrs. (Larose Ch.: v.1, p.52)

DUET, Louise m. 25 Nov. 1899 Julian CHETE (Thib. Ct. Hse.: Mar. v.39, #267)

DUET, Louise (Adam & Testise LAUDRIE) m. 25 Nov. 1899 Julien ESCHETE (Larose Ch.: v.4, p.127)

DUET, Louise (Nolan & Testise LANDRIE) m. 25 Nov. 1899 Julien ESCHETE (Larose Ch.: v.3, p.13)

DUET, Lovincy (Adam & Mathilde HEBERT) m. 22 April 1896 Felicia BREAUX (Thib. Ch.: v.14, p.85)

DUET, Lovincy (Adam & Mathilde HEBERT) m. 22 April 1896 Felicia BREAUX (Thib. Ct. Hse.: Mar. v.35, #63)

DUET, Marie (Theophile & Felicia CHIASSON) b. 12 Nov. 1897 (Chackbay Ch.: v.1, p.98)

DUET, Marie Ceres (Ernest & Angelina CANTRELLE) b. 1 Jan. 1898 (Larose Ch.: v.3, p.25)

DUET, Marie Zulmee (Theophile & Felicia CHIASSON) b. 21 July 1899 (Chackbay Ch.: v.1, p.138)

DUET, Philippe Francois (Joseph & Eugenie MARTIN) b. 9 May 1899 (Thib. Ch.: v.7, p.605)

DUET, Reine Alice (Etienne & Marie NAQUIN) bt. 23 Sept. 1896 (Chackbay Ch.: v.1, p.76)

DUET, Robert (Felix & Mary HEBERT) m. 14 Jan. 1897 Eveline MORVANT (Thib. Ct. Hse.: Mar. v.36, #4)

DUET, Romela m. Alexis PITRE d. 11 May 1898 (Larose Ch.: v.1, p.42)

DUET, Rose (Eugene & d.Felicie PIERCE) m. 29 Nov. 1899 Francois DERAMEE (Thib. Ct. Hse.: Mar. v.39, #272)

DUET, Rosina (Eugene & Felicie PIERCE) m. 2 Dec. 1899 Francois Emile DERAMEE (Larose Ch.: v.4, p.128)

DUET, Rosina (Eugene & Felicie PIERCE) m. 2 Dec. 1899 Francois Emile DERANIEE (Larose Ch.: v.3, p.13)

DUET, Silvestre Perini (Joseph & Julie USAY) b. 12 Feb. 1896 (Larose Ch.: v.2, p.181)

DUET, Theobert (Felix & Marie HEBERT) m. 14 Jan. 1897 Eveline MORVAN (Thib. Ch.: v.14, p.110)

DUET, Theophile (Felix & d.Marie HEBERT) m. 25 Jan. 1897 Felicia CHIASSON (Chackbay Ch.: v.1, p.36)

DUET, Theophile (Felix & Mary HEBERT) m. 25 Jan. 1897 Felicia CHIASSON (Thib. Ct. Hse.: Mar. v.36, #11)

DUET, Victor Constant (Enoch & Julie BRUCE) b. 5 Oct. 1899 (Larose Ch.: v.3, p.45)
DUET, Wilson (Leo & Lelia BOUDREAU) b. 29 June 1898 (Chackbay Ch.: v.1, p.114)
DUFFY, Alice (Nicolas & Adolphine DUFFY) m. 16 Dec. 1899 Antoine FEDERINE (Thib. Ct. Hse.: Mar. v.39, #287)
DUFFY, Alice (Nicolas & Adolphine DUFFY) m. 18 Dec. 1899 Antoine FEDERINE (Thib. Ch.: v.14, p.311)
DUFOUR, Joseph Leopold (Louis & Emma GUEDRY) b. 3 March 1896 (Larose Ch.: v.2, p.181)
DUFOUR, Louis Odom (Louis & Emma GUIDRY) b. 18 Feb. 1898 (Larose Ch.: v.3, p.17)

DUFRENE (Sometimes: DUFRENEY, DUFRESNE)
DUFRENE, ----- child (Noel) d. 12 May 1899 at age 1 yr. & 6 mths. (Lockport Ch.: v.1, #19)
DUFRENE, Adelina m. Antoine MATHERNE d. 23 Nov. 1898 at age 75 yrs. (Lockport Ch.: v.1, #21)
DUFRENE, Agnes Bayola (Arthur & Cecilia PINTO) b. 21 Jan. 1899 (Lockport Ch.: v.3-A, #1)
DUFRENE, Agnes Bayola (Arthur & Cecilia PINTO) b. 21 Jan. 1899 (Lockport Ch.: v.3, #1)
DUFRENE, Alain (Joseph & Adele BOURGEOIS) m. 14 Feb. 1898 Helene GRABERT (Raceland Ch.: v.2, p.81)
DUFRENE, Albertine (Valcour & Zilda CAMARDELLE) m. 28 Jan. 1899 Wallace LEGENDRE (Thib. Ct. Hse.: Mar. v.38, #34)
DUFRENE, Albertine (Vasseur & Zilda CAMORDELLE) m. 28 Jan. 1899 Wallace LEGENDRE (Lockport Ch.: v.2, p.198)
DUFRENE, Alfred m. 18 Jan. 1899 Mathilde BRAUX (Lockport Ch.: v.2, p.198)
DUFRENE, Alfred m. 29 Nov. 1898 Matile BREAUX (Thib. Ct. Hse.: Mar. v.38, #313)
DUFRENE, Allain m. 7 Sept. 1898 Helene GRABERT (Thib. Ct. Hse.: Mar. v.38, #273)
DUFRENE, Anita d. 26 June 1896 at age 4½ yrs. (Raceland Ch.: v.1, p.8)
DUFRENE, Aymee Ayda (Wuille & Josephine ST. PIERRE) b. 29 May 1899 (Lockport Ch.: v.3, #1)
DUFRENE, Aymee Ayda (Wuillie & Josephine ST. PIERRE) b. 29 May 1899 (Lockport Ch.: v.3-A, #1)
DUFRENE, Baptiste (Aristile & Agnes BARRIOS) b. 13 March 1897 (Lockport Ch.: v.3-A, #47)
DUFRENE, Baptiste Alcide (Aristide & Agnes BARRIOS) b. 13 March 1897 (Lockport Ch.: v.3, #47)
DUFRENE, Charles Wilfred (Joseph & Pauline PLAISANCE) b. 9 Sept. 1896 (Lockport Ch.: v.2, p.336)
DUFRENE, Delmas d. 8 July 1897 at age 16 yrs. (Lockport Ch.: v.1, #13)
DUFRENE, Edouard Nicles (Alex & Clemantine RODRIGUE) b. 8 Nov. 1896 (Lockport Ch.: v.3, #22)

DUFRENE, Edouard Nicles (Alex & Clemantine RODRIGUE) b. 8 Nov. 1896 (Lockport Ch.: v.3-A, #22)

DUFRENE, Emilie Eleonore (Toussaint & Catherine TOUCHARD) b. 23 Feb. 1898 (Larose Ch.: v.3, p.19)

DUFRENE, Euphrasie m. 23 Oct. 1897 Pierre RIVET (Lockport Ch.: v.2, p.176)

DUFRENE, Euphrasie (Octave & Anais CHOUESSE) m. 23 Oct. 1897 Pierre RIVET, Jr. (Thib. Ct. Hse.: Mar. v.37, #251)

DUFRENE, Georgina d. 2 Jan. 1897 at age 40 days (Lockport Ch.: v.1, #1)

DUFRENE, Joseph d. 31 Oct. 1899 at age 4 days (Raceland Ch.: v.1, p.28)

DUFRENE, Joseph m. 10 July 1897 Helene PLAISANCE (Thib. Ct. Hse.: Mar. v.37, #183)

DUFRENE, Joseph m. 10 July 1897 Helene PLAISANCE (Lockport Ch.: v.2, p.169)

DUFRENE, Joseph (Alain & Helene GRABERT) bt. 29 Oct. 1899 at age 5 days (Raceland Ch.: v.5, p.104)

DUFRENE, Josephine (Valcour & Zeline CAMARDEL) m. 18 Jan. 1896 Philippe FABIONI (Lockport Ch.: v.2, p.149)

DUFRENE, Josephine (Valcour & Zeline COMARDEL) m. 18 Jan. 1896 Philippe FABIANI, of Smirne, Asia Minor (Thib. Ct. Hse.: Mar. v.35, #12)

DUFRENE, Justilia (Andre & Armogina GUIDRY) m. 25 July 1896 Gustave SAVOIE (Thib. Ct. Hse.: Mar. v.36, #120)

DUFRENE, Marguerite Mercedes (Wuill & Josephine ST. PIERRE) b. 31 Jan. 1896 (Lockport Ch.: v.3, #31)

DUFRENE, Marguerite Mercedes (Wuills & Josephine ST. PIERRE) b. 31 Jan. 1897 (Lockport Ch.: v.3-A, #31)

DUFRENE, Maria Elisabeth (Louis & Elisabeth TOUCHARD) b. 9 July 1898 (Larose Ch.: v.3, p.24)

DUFRENE, Marie m. ---- CHOVES d. 10 Dec. 1898 at age 93 yrs. (Lockport Ch.: v.1, #20)

DUFRENE, Mary (Valcour & Zilda CAMARDEL) m. 20 Aug. 1898 Oscar GERVAIS (Thib. Ct. Hse.: Mar. v.38, #247)

DUFRENE, Mary (Valcour & Zilda CAMORDEL) m. 20 Aug. 1898 Oscar GERVAIS (Lockport Ch.: v.2, p.193)

DUFRENE, Mathilde m. 4 Dec. 1899 Silvere RIVET (Thib. Ct. Hse.: Mar. v.39, #276)

DUFRENE, Mathilde (Alexandre & Florentine RODRIGUE) m. 16 Dec. 1899 Sylvere RIVET (Lockport Ch.: v.2, p.212)

DUFRENE, Melanny Lucie (Jean & Mary CORRINDAN) b. 7 Jan. 1897 (Lockport Ch.: v.3, #41)

DUFRENE, Melauny Lucin & Jean & Mary CORRINDAN) b. 7 Jan. 1897 (Lockport Ch.: v.3-A, #41)

DUFRENE, Melodia Josephine (Felix & Leontine BRAUX) b. 2 Oct. 1899 (Lockport Ch.: v.3-A, #8)

DUFRENE, Melodia Josephine (Felix & Leontine BREAUX) b. 2 Oct. 1899 (Lockport Ch.: v.3, #8)

DUFRENE, Octave (Andre & Marguerite GUEDRY) m. 1 May 1897 Josephine BRAUX (Lockport Ch.: v.2, p.166)

DUFRENE, Octave (Andre & Margueritte GUEDRY) m. 1 May 1897 Josephine BRAUX (Thib. Ct. Hse.: Mar. v.36, #108)
DUFRENE, Onesippe m. 17 Aug. 1898 Alida ROBICHAUX (Thib. Ct. Hse.: Mar. v.38, #256)
DUFRENE, Onesippe (Joseph & Adele BOURGEOIS) m. 29 Aug. 1898 Alida ROBICHAUX (Raceland Ch.: v.2, p.78)
DUFRENE, Paul m. 22 June 1897 Josephine PICHOFF (Thib. Ct. Hse.: Mar. v.36, #179)
DUFRENE, Pierre d. 27 July 1899 at age 14 mths. (Lockport Ch.: v.1, #29)
DUFRENE, Sidonie Agnes (Alfred & Mathilde BRAUX) b. 23 Aug. 1899 (Lockport Ch.: v.3-A, #4)
DUFRENE, Sidonie Agnes (Alfred & Mathilde BREAUX) b. 23 Aug. 1899 (Lockport Ch.: v.3, #4)
DUFRENE, Ulysse (Orestile & Leontine SAINT PIERRE) m. 29 April 1899 Augustine HARTMAN (Thib. Ct. Hse.: Mar. v.39, #130)
DUFRENE, Ulysse (Orestile & Leontine SAINT PIERRE) m. 29 April 1899 Augustine HARTMAN (Lockport Ch.: v.2, p.207)
DUFRENE, Valside Jony (Onezyppe & Marie DUFRENE) b. 5 Oct. 1899 (Lockport Ch.: v.3-A, #10)
DUFRENE, Valside Jony (Onezyppe & Marie DUFRENE) b. 5 Oct. 1899 (Lockport Ch.: v.3, #10)
DUFRENE, Vitellus Fabien (Valcourt & Zilda CAMARDEL) b. 20 Feb. 1896 (Lockport Ch.: v.2, p.325)
DUFRENE, Wuilliam (Alex & Florentine RODRIGUE) m. 1 Feb. 1896 Josephine ST. PIERRE (Lockport Ch.: v.2, p.145)
DUFRENE, Wuilliam (Alex & Florentine RODRIGUE) m. 1 Feb. 1896 Josephine ST. PIERRE (Thib. Ct. Hse.: Mar. v.35, #22)

DUGAS (Sometimes: DUGAST)

DUGAS, ----- boy (Bertrand) d. 5 April 1899 at age 4 mths. (Thib. Ch.: v.3, p.230)
DUGAS, Alice d. 30 April 1899 at age 5 mths. (Thib. Ch.: v.3, p.233)
DUGAS, Alice (Adam & Marie BOUDREAUX) b. 18 Oct. 1897 (Houma Ch.: v.5, p.194)
DUGAS, Alphonse (J. Lovincy & Rosa AYCOCK) m. 16 June 1897 Myrtilia M. BOUDREAUX (Montegut Ch.: v.4, p.223)
DUGAS, Alphonse J. (J. Lovincy & Rosa AYCOCK) m. 14 May 1897 Myrtilia M. BOUDREAUX (Houma Ct. Hse.: Mar. v.29 & 30, #421)
DUGAS, Amelia (Amedee & Ophelia JOLIBOIS) m. 14 Feb. 1898 Francis FALCON (Thib. Ch.: v.14, p.185)
DUGAS, Aurelia (Amedee & Ophelia JOLIBOIS) m. 14 Feb. 1898 Francis FALCON (Thib. Ct. Hse.: Mar. v.37, #96)
DUGAS, Aureline Agnes (Willie & Aureline BOUDREAUX) b. 25 Oct. 1898 (Theriot Ch.: v.2, p.38)
DUGAS, Elesida d. 5 Sept. 1896 at age 67 yrs., 8 mths. & 26 days (Houma Ch.: v.3, p.9)

DUGAS, Emilia Cecilia (Octave & Irma GUEDRY) b. 13 Jan. 1898 (Raceland Ch.: v.5, p.64)
DUGAS, Emilie Marie Anne (Emile & Laura MARONGE) b. 14 April 1896 (Thib. Ch.: v.7, p.400)
DUGAS, Florestal d. 2 Feb. 1899 at age 75 yrs. (Thib. Ch.: v.3, p.227)
DUGAS, Joseph d. 10 March 1896 at age 48 yrs. (Thib. Ch.: v.3, p.180)
DUGAS, Joseph (Octave & Marianne PICOU) m. 13 Jan. 1896 Therese CROCHET (Montegut Ch.: v.4, p.205)
DUGAS, Joseph (Octave & Marianne PICOU) m. 2 Jan. 1896 Thereze CROCHET (Houma Ct. Hse.: Mar. v.28, #367)
DUGAS, Joseph Harris (Joseph & Therese CROCHET) b. 25 April 1899 (Montegut Ch.: v.6, p.87)
DUGAS, Joseph Hector (Octave & Irma GUEDRY) b. 7 Oct. 1899; m. Althea BREAUX on 16 Aug. 1924. (Raceland Ch.: Bapt. Bk., v.5, p.104)
DUGAS, Louisabelle (Octave & Marie GUEDRY) b. 3 Sept. 1896 (Raceland Ch.: v.5, p.29)
DUGAS, Marguerite Lelia (Alphonse & Myrtilia BOUDREAUX) b. 30 Sept. 1899 (Montegut Ch.: v.6, p.93)
DUGAS, Marie Laeta (Philippe & Malvina ROUNDTREE) b. 19 April 1899 (Thib. Ch.: v.7, p.600)
DUGAS, Marie Mildred (Alphonse & Myrtilia BOUDREAUX) b. 30 March 1898 (Montegut Ch.: v.6, p.69)
DUGAS, Marigus Elie (Augustin & Bobby BELANGER) d. 15 May 1899 at age 1 yr. (Montegut Ch.: v.2, p.25)
DUGAS, Marigus Elie (Augustin & Bobry BELLANGER) b. 26 May 1898 (Montegut Ch.: v.6, p.72)
DUGAS, Maurice Harris (Augustin & Bobery BELANGER) b. 25 Dec. 1899 (Montegut Ch.: v.6, p.98)
DUGAS, Olivia Marianne (Octave Augustin & Bobery Marie BELANGER) b. 20 July 1896 (Montegut Ch.: v.6, p.43)
DUGAS, Olympe Marguerite (Symphorien & Evelia MALBROUGH) b. 22 Dec. 1896 (Thib. Ch.: v.7, p.431)
DUGAS, Paul Harry (Syphorien & Marie NAQUIN) b. 11 April 1899 (Thib. Ch.: v.7, p.545)
DUGAS, Philippe (Emile & Mary CONINGHAM) m. 16 Jan. 1899 Malvina ROUNDTREE (Thib. Ct. Hse.: Mar. v.38, #15)
DUGAS, Philippe (Emile & Mary CONINGHAM) m. 16 Jan. 1899 Malvina ROUNDTREE (Thib. Ch.: v.14, p.238)
DUGAS, Rosalie Marie m. Achille BREAUX d. 18 March 1896 at age 88 yrs. (Thib. Ch.: v.3, p.180)
DUGAS, Symphorien d. 12 May 1898 at age 36 yrs. (Thib. Ch.: v.3, p.214)
DUMAS, Alfred m. 21 Sept. 1899 Bettie M. RIDLEY (Houma Ct. Hse.: Mar. v.31 & 32, #138")
DUMAS, Alfred of Terrebonne Parish m. 21 Sept. 1899 Betta M. RIDLEY (Houma Ch.: v.6-B, p.4)
DUMAS, Frances m. 1 Feb. 1897 Robert SEARS (Houma Ct. Hse.: Mar. v.29 & 30, #271)

DUMAS, John L. m. 15 June 1896 Fannie LEWIS (Houma Ct. Hse.: Mar. v.29 & 30, #93)
DUMESNIL, Benjamin m. 22 Dec. 1898 Mary BOUDELOCHE (Houma Ct. Hse.: Mar. v.30 & 31, #158)
DUMESNIL, Benjamin (Benjamin & Cleonise TRAHAN) m. 29 Dec. 1898 Marie BOUDELOCHE (Houma Ch.: v.6-a, p.261)

DUMONT (Sometimes: DUMOND)
DUMONT, Jean Maurice (Jean Pierre & Marguerite FANGUY) b. 9 July 1897 (Theriot Ch.: v.2, p.10)
DUMOULIN, Cathrine of France m. Joseph PENISSON d. 24 June 1899 at age 70 yrs. (Chacahoula Ch.: Gibson Ch.: v.2, p.182)
DUNAWAY, Katie m. 16 Feb. 1898 John JENKINS (Houma Ct. Hse.: Mar. v.30 & 31, #297)
DUNBY, Ruberda m. 22 Nov. 1899 Adam CEASAR (Thib. Ct. Hse.: Mar. v.39, #266)
DUNCAN, Adeline m. 17 March 1898 Henry WHEELER (Thib. Ct. Hse.: Mar. v.37, #129)
DUON, Clay d. 20 July 1898 at age 35 yrs. (Lockport Ch.: v.1, #15)
DUPIED, Philomene m. Omer BERTRAND d. 10 Dec. 1899 at age 22 yrs. (Thib. Ch.: v.3, p.245)

DUPIN (Sometimes: DUPIS)

DUPLANTIS (Sometimes: DUPLANTE, DUPLANTI, DUPLANTY)
DUPLANTIS, Anastasie M. b. 17 May 1894; d. 8 May 1899 (Houma Ch.: Funeral Bk., v.3, p.22)
DUPLANTIS, Bussy (Joseph C. & Suzanne JOLET) m. 5 April 1897 Julie DUPLANTIS (Houma Ct. Hse.: Mar. v.29 & 30, #375)
DUPLANTIS, Clarisse Emelie (Olivat & Eloise GUIDRY) b. 3 March 1896 (Montegut Ch.: v.6, p.36)
DUPLANTIS, Cynthia (Henry Clay & Evelida DASPIT) m. 6 Oct. 1898 Omer DUPLANTIS (Houma Ch.: v.6-a, p.255)
DUPLANTIS, Cynthia m. 26 Sept. 1898 Omer DUPLANTIS (Houma Ct. Hse.: Mar. v.30 & 31, #105)
DUPLANTIS, Daisy (Philip & Eugenie LASSAGNE) m. 28 Aug. 1899 Stephen GRIFFIN (Houma Ct. Hse.: Mar. v.31 & 32, #111)
DUPLANTIS, Daisy (Philip & Eugenie LASSAGNE) m. 5 Sept. 1899 Stephen GRIFFIN (Theriot Ch.: v.1-B, p.7)
DUPLANTIS, Elie V. (Lezin & Amelia GAIDRY) m. 2 Sept. 1899 Marie Victoria DUPLANTIS (Houma Ct. Hse.: Mar. v.31 & 32, #113)
DUPLANTIS, Elie Valmore (Lezin & Amelia GUIDRY) m. 21 Sept. 1899 Marie Victoria DUPLANTIS (Montegut Ch.: v.4, p.269)
DUPLANTIS, Elmire (Justin & Alida GUIDRY) m. 11 March 1899 Louis CHAUVIN (Houma Ct. Hse.: Mar. v.31 & 32, #363)
DUPLANTIS, Elmire (Justin & Alida GUIDRY) m. 3 April 1899 Louis CHAUVIN (Montegut Ch.: v.4, p.259)

DUPLANTIS, Emelia m. 11 Feb. 1899 Caliste CALLAHAN (Houma Ct. Hse.: Mar. v.31 & 32, #332)

DUPLANTIS, Emelia (Elysse & Emelie AUTHEMENT) m. 13 Feb. 1899 Coliste CALLAHAN (Houma C.: v.6-a, p.287)

DUPLANTIS, Emma (Trasimond & Eliska DUGAS) m. 26 Jan. 1898 Sydney LIRETTE (Montegut Ch.: v.4, p.233)

DUPLANTIS, Emma (Trasimond & Eliska DUGAS) m. 4 Jan. 1898 Sidney LIRETTE (Houma Ct. Hse.: Mar. v.30 & 31, #174)

DUPLANTIS, Ernest (Eusebe & Eliza PARR) m. 12 Oct. 1897 Louise DUPLANTIS (Montegut Ch.: v.4, p.225)

DUPLANTIS, Ernest (Eusebe & Eliza PARR) m. 2 Oct. 1897 Louisa DUPLANTIS (Houma Ct. Hse.: Mar. v.29 & 30, #104)

DUPLANTIS, Etienne Isaie (Israel & Josephine ROBICHAUX) b. 30 March 1897 (Montegut Ch.: v.6, p.53)

DUPLANTIS, Evelina m. Thomas ELLENDER d. 1 Feb. 1897 at age 41 yrs. (Montegut Ch.: v.2, p.9)

DUPLANTIS, Felicie m. Auristile PELEGRIN d. 17 Dec. 1899 at age 32 yrs. (Montegut Ch.: v.2, p.32)

DUPLANTIS, Francois Normand (Clodomy & Octavie PARR) b. 3 May 1896; m. Louise Dragon BROWN on 16 July 1961. (Houma Ch.: Bapt. Bk., v.5, p.152)

DUPLANTIS, Francois Xavier (Victor Terence & Euselia GUIDRY) b. 26 Jan. 1899 (Houma Ch.: v.5, p.238)

DUPLANTIS, Georges Lucius (Theophile & Julienne MARCEL) b. 1 Aug. 1899 (Montegut Ch.: v.6, p.92)

DUPLANTIS, Isaac m. 19 June 1897 Georgie BARRAS (Houma Ct. Hse.: Mar. v.29 & 30, #34)

DUPLANTIS, Isaac (Felicien & Emelia PICOU) m. 8 July 1897 Georgiana BARRAS (Houma Ch.: v.6-a, p.209)

DUPLANTIS, John (---- & Angelique DUPLANTIS) b. 11 Sept. 1897 (Houma Ch.: v.5, p.190)

DUPLANTIS, John d. 1 June 1898 at age 4 yrs. & 8 mths. (Montegut Ch.: v.2, p.17)

DUPLANTIS, John (Elize & Emelie ARCEMENT) m. 10 Jan. 1896 Alice HENRI (Houma Ch.: v.6-a, p.168)

DUPLANTIS, Joseph d. 8 Jan. 1897 at age 82 yrs. (Montegut Ch.: v.2, p.9)

DUPLANTIS, Joseph (Trasimond & Elisca DUGAS) b. 16 Dec. 1896 (Montegut Ch.: v.6, p.48)

DUPLANTIS, Joseph Bussy (Joseph & d.Suzanne JOLET) m. 29 April 1897 Julie DUPLANTIS (Montegut Ch.: v.4, p.221)

DUPLANTIS, Joseph Harris (Therance & Uselia GUIDRY) b. 19 Oct. 1896 (Montegut Ch.: v.6, p.47)

DUPLANTIS, Joseph Houston (Isaac & Georgy BARRON) b. 16 Oct. 1898 (Houma Ch.: v.5, p.221)

DUPLANTIS, Joseph Laurence (Telesphore & Marguerite BELANGER) d. 30 Dec. 1899 at age 7 mths. (Montegut Ch.: v.2, p.32)

DUPLANTIS, Joseph Laurens (Telesphore & Marguerite BELLANGER) b. 2 June 1899 (Houma Ch.: v.5, p.249)

DUPLANTIS, Joseph O. m. d.Marie Susanne JOLET Children listed: Joseph Bussy; Israel; Georgiana m. Theophile

DUPLANTIS; Meloe; Joseph Auguste. Donation of land: 17 Dec. 1897. (Houma Ct. Hse.: Book of Donations: v.A, p.149)
DUPLANTIS, Josephine (Narcisse & Lucie STEWART) b. 18 Feb. 1899 (Montegut Ch.: v.6, p.84)
DUPLANTIS, Julia Lucretia (John & Alice HENRI) b. 15 Oct. 1896 (Houma Ch.: v.5, p.159)
DUPLANTIS, Julie (Lezin & Emelia GUIDRY) m. 5 April 1897 Bussy DUPLANTIS (Houma Ct. Hse.: Mar. v.29 & 30, #375)
DUPLANTIS, Julie (Lezin & Emelie GUIDRY) m. 29 April 1897 Joseph Bussy DUPLANTIS (Montegut Ch.: v.4, p.221)
DUPLANTIS, Louis m. 7 Jan. 1898 Laura GUIDRY (Houma Ct. Hse.: Mar. v.30 & 31, #185)
DUPLANTIS, Louis (Perrin & Euphrasie CHAUVIN) m. 19 Jan. 1898 Laura GUIDRY (Montegut Ch.: v.4, p.230)
DUPLANTIS, Louis (Phil. & Eugenie LASAGNE) m. 4 Sept. 1899 Felicite GRIFFIN (Theriot Ch.: v.1-B, p.6)
DUPLANTIS, Louis (Philipe & Eugenie LASSAIGNE) m. 12 June 1899 Felicite GRIFFIN (Houma Ct. Hse.: Mar. v.31 & 32, #22)
DUPLANTIS, Louisa (Alexis & Rosella ROBICHAUX) m. 2 Oct. 1897 Ernest DUPLANTIS (Houma Ct. Hse.: Mar. v.29 & 30, #104)
DUPLANTIS, Louise (Alexis & d.Rosella ROBICHAUX) m. 12 Oct. 1897 Ernest DUPLANTIS (Montegut Ch.: v.4, p.225)
DUPLANTIS, Luc (Joseph & d.Lucette TOUPS) m. 7 Aug. 1899 Eva CHAUVIN (Montegut Ch.: v.4, p.268)
DUPLANTIS, Luke (Joseph & Lucette TOUPS) m. 22 July 1899 Eva CHAUVIN (Houma Ct. Hse.: Mar. v.31 & 32, #96)
DUPLANTIS, Marguerite (Alexis & d.Rosella ROBICHAUX) m. 1 March 1897 William HEBERT (Montégut Ch.: v.4, p.219)
DUPLANTIS, Marguerite (Alexis & Rosella ROBICHAUX) m. 25 Feb. 1897 William HEBERT (Houma Ct. Hse.: Mar. v.29 & 30, #328)
DUPLANTIS, Marguerite Nora (Ernest & Anaiste LIRETTE) b. 20 July 1897 (Theriot Ch.: v.2, p.9)
DUPLANTIS, Marguerite Santie (Olivat & Eloise GUIDRY) b. 7 April 1898 (Montegut Ch.: v.6, p.70)
DUPLANTIS, Marie (Joseph & Louise CARET) b. 21 Nov. 1897 (Theriot Ch.: v.2, p.15)
DUPLANTIS, Marie Azelie (Israel & Josephine ROBICHAUX) b. 10 Sept. 1898 (Montegut Ch.: v.6, p.77)
DUPLANTIS, Marie Julienne (Octave & Lorenza BILLOT) b. 27 Dec. 1897 (Montegut Ch.: v.6, p.75)
DUPLANTIS, Marie Lily (Lewis & Laura GUIDRY) b. 1 Aug. 1899 (Montegut Ch.: v.6, p.93)
DUPLANTIS, Marie Nennie (Joseph & Bussy & Julie Elizabeth DUPLANTIS) b. 17 Dec. 1898 (Montegut Ch.: v.6, p.80)
DUPLANTIS, Marie Nesia (Alcee & Marie LEBOEUF) b. 23 Dec. 1899 (Houma Ch.: v.5, p.270)
DUPLANTIS, Marie Nesia (Alcee & Marie LEBOEUF) b. 23 Dec. 1899 (Houma Ch.: v.6, p.5)

DUPLANTIS, Marie Victoire Waltring (Narcisse & Lucie STUART) b. 15 April 1897 (Montegut Ch.: v.6, p.56)

DUPLANTIS, Marie Victoria (Terrance & Euzelia GUIDRY) m. 2 Sept. 1899 Elie V. DUPLANTIS (Houma Ct. Hse.: Mar. v.31 & 32, #113)

DUPLANTIS, Marie Victoria (Therance & Euselia GUIDRY) m. 21 Sept. 1899 Elie Valmore DUPLANTIS (Montegut Ch.: v.4, p.269)

DUPLANTIS, Marie Victoria Velida (Derbigny & Adolphine TERREBONNE) b. 20 Aug. 1896 (Montegut Ch.: v.6, p.51)

DUPLANTIS, Mary Alder (John & Alice HENRY) b. 25 Sept. 1897 (Houma Ch.: v.5, p.189)

DUPLANTIS, Noemie Josephine (Joseph & Louise CARRIERE) b. 10 Oct. 1899 (Montegut Ch.: v.6, p.95)

DUPLANTIS, Oliver Holden (Clodmire & Octavie PARR) b. 19 Feb. 1899 (Houma Ch.: v.5, p.239)

DUPLANTIS, Omer m. 26 Sept. 1898 Cynthia DUPLANTIS (Houma Ct. Hse.: Mar. v.30 & 31, #105)

DUPLANTIS, Omer (Elzee & Emilie ARCEMENT) m. 6 Oct. 1898 Cynthia DUPLANTIS (Houma Ch.: v.6-a, p.255)

DUPLANTIS, Toussaint Eustis (Theophile & Julienne MARCEL) b. 1 Nov. 1897 (Montegut Ch.: v.6, p.21)

DUPLANTIS, Unes Agnes (Telesphore & Greni BOUDREAU) b. 19 Feb. 1899 (Theriot Ch.: v.2, p.34)

DUPLANTIS, Valerie (Joseph & Lusette TOUPS) m. 30 Dec. 1899 Victor LEBOEUF (Houma Ct. Hse.: Mar. v.31 & 32, #221)

DUPLANTIS, Willy m. 3 Feb. 1898 Mary ALECK (Thib. Ct. Hse.: Mar. v.37, #79)

DUPLANTIS, Zulema m. 15 Feb. 1896 Cestive CHAUVIN, Jr. (Houma Ct. Hse.: Mar. v.28, #460)

DUPLANTIS, Zulema (Jean & Amelia ESHTE) m. 15 Feb. 1896 Cestive CHAUVIN (Houma Ch.: v.6-a, p.170)

DUPLESSIS, Malvina (Maximilien & Rosalie CLEMENT) b. 23 June 1898 (Larose Ch.: v.3, p.24)

DUPONT, Adeline Celina (Willie & Margarite RILINDA) b. 6 Oct. 1896 (Chacahoula Ch.: v.4, p.7)

DUPONT, Eugene Celestin (Albert & Alice HENSON) b. 3 Nov. 1897 (Houma Ch.: v.5, p.196)

DUPONT, Hanson (Albert M. & Alice HANSON) b. 17 April 1896 (Houma Ch.: v.5, p.152)

DUPONT, Henry Clay (Ernest A. & Anastasie DUPLANTIS) b. 6 Jan. 1896; m. Cornelia NEUBIG on May 1922 (Houma Ch.: Bapt. Bk., v.5, p.142)

DUPONT, Hilda Addie (Willie & Marguerite LACKET) b. 5 Dec. 1897; bt. 19 Dec. 1897 (Chacahoula Ch.: v.4, p.26)

DUPONT, Lydie Marie (Ernest & Anastasie DUPLANTY) b. 19 Feb. 1896 (Houma Ch.: v.5, p.174)

DUPONT, Paul D. m. 12 June 1896 Edna M. BONVILLAIN (Houma Ct. Hse.: Mar. v.29 & 30, #87)

DUPONT, Paul J. (Jean Marie & Lydie M. TASSET) m. 16 June 1896 Edna M. BONVILLAIN (Houma Ch.: v.6-a, p.176)

DUPONT, Paul Nold Earl (Paul & Edna BONVILLAIN) b. 13 April 1896 (Houma Ch.: v.5, p.179)
DUPONT, Robert Adolphe (A. M. & Alice HANSON) b. 20 Sept. 1899 (Houma Ch.: v.5, p.259)

DUPRE (Sometimes: DUPRES)
DUPRE, Ada (Claverie & Elizabeth BELANGER) m. 26 Aug. 1899 Augustave DUPRE (Houma Ct. Hse.: Mar. v.31 & 32, #109)
DUPRE, Agnes Florance (Thomas & Victoria PORTIER) b. 6 Oct. 1899; m. Marie May BREAUD on 19 May 1920. (Houma Ch.: Bapt. Bk., v.5, p.257)
DUPRE, Alfred Paul (Germain & Louise THIBODAUX) b. 4 July 1898 (Montegut Ch.: v.6, p.75)
DUPRE, Alzina (Eugene & Marie DUGAS) m. 17 Jan. 1898 Marcelle Pierre BLANCHARD (Houma Ct. Hse.: Mar. v.30 & 31, #215)
DUPRE, Amedee (Ulysse & Doriska BOURG) m. 14 Jan. 1899 Victoria RODRIGUES (Houma Ct. Hse.: Mar. v.30 & 31, #234)
DUPRE, Amedee (Ulysse & Doriska BOURG) m. 2 Feb. 1899 Victoria RODRIGUE (Montegut Ch.: v.4, p.254)
DUPRE, Artelien (Simeon & Melina BOURG) m. 12 Jan. 1898 Maggie LEBOEUF (Houma Ct. Hse.: Mar. v.30 & 31, #198)
DUPRE, Arthur (Albert & Aimee LEBLANC) b. 23 Oct. 1898 (Thib. Ch.: v.7, p.533)
DUPRE, Artilien (Simeon & Melina BOURG) m. 31 Jan. 1898 Maggie LEBOEUF (Montegut Ch.: v.4, p.234)
DUPRE, Augustave (Treville & Evelia BOURG) m. 26 Aug. 1899 Ada DUPRE (Houma Ct. Hse.: Mar. v.31 & 32, #109)
DUPRE, Augustave (Treville & Evelia BOURG) m. 11 Sept. 1899 Eda DUPRE (Montegut Ch.: v.4, p.269)
DUPRE, Caliste Joseph (Moise & Ophelia LEBOEUF) b. 14 Oct. 1897 (Houma Ch.: v.5, p.192)
DUPRE, Catherine (Amedee & Elizabeth LIRETTE) m. 11 April 1898 John RODDY (Montegut Ch.: v.4, p.240)
DUPRE, Catherine (Amedee & Elizabeth LIRETTE) m. 25 March 1898 John RODDY (Houma Ct. Hse.: Mar. v.30 & 31, #353)
DUPRE, Christophe Wilsey (Germain & Louise THIBODAUX) b. 25 July 1896 (Montegut Ch.: v.6, p.43)
DUPRE, Clothilde (Claverie & Elizabeth BELANGER) m. 6 Feb. 1899 Felicien LEDET (Montegut Ch.: v.4, p.256)
DUPRE, Clotilde (Claverie & Elizabeth BELANGER) m. 21 Jan. 1899 Felicien LEDET (Houma Ct. Hse.: Mar. v.30 & 31, #275)
DUPRE, Domatile (Eugene & Marie DUGAS) m. 5 Oct. 1897 Benny DESTIVEAUX (Houma Ct. Hse.: Mar. v.29 & 30, #109)
DUPRE, Dorina Josephine (Frank & Eulodie DUPRE) b. 6 Feb. 1899 (Montegut Ch.: v.6, p.82)
DUPRE, Eda (Claverie & Elizabeth BELANGER) m. 11 Sept. 1899 Augustave DUPRE (Montegut Ch.: v.4, p.269)
DUPRE, Elles (Evariste & Azema DETREVAL) m. 2 April 1898 Ellen BERNARD (Houma Ch.: v.6-a, p.238)

DUPRE, Ellis m. 2 April 1898 Mrs. Ellen Bergeron BERNARD (Houma Ct. Hse.: Mar. v.30 & 31, #366)

DUPRE, Ellis William (Frank & Emeline NEIL) b. 7 May 1896 (Montegut Ch.: v.6, p.44)

DUPRE, Exelina Hamly (Deme & Brigitte LEDET) b. 29 Dec. 1897 (Montegut Ch.: v.6, p.64)

DUPRE, Fabiola (Claverie & Elizabeth BELANGER) m. 6 Sept. 1897 Henri NAQUIN (Montegut Ch.: v.4, p.224)

DUPRE, Fabiola (Claverie & Elizabeth BELANGER) m. 18 Aug. 1897 Henri NAQUIN (Houma Ct. Hse.: Mar. v.29 & 30, #80½)

DUPRE, Felicia Nesia (Joseph & Nezelia LEBOEUF) b. 5 March 1898 (Montegut Ch.: v.6, p.69)

DUPRE, Francois (Pelegrin & Henriette NAQUIN) m. 2 June 1898 Virginia TRAHAN (Montegut Ch.: v.4, p.245)

DUPRE, Francois (Pelegrin & Henriette NAQUIN) m. 17 May 1898 Virginia TRAHAN (Houma Ct. Hse.: Mar. v.30 & 31, #441)

DUPRE, Gilbert Joseph (Charly & Evela HEBERT) b. 28 Dec. 1899 (Houma Ch.: v.5, p.270)

DUPRE, Guilbert Joseph (Charly & Evella HEBERT) b. 28 Dec. 1899 (Houma Ch.: v.6, p.5)

DUPRE, Henry R. m. 3 Dec. 1898 Helene M. TAYLOR (Thib. Ct. Hse.: Mar. v.38, #314)

DUPRE, Jean (Leo & Eva BRUNET) b. 2 Jan. 1897 (Houma Ch.: v.5, p.176)

DUPRE, Joseph (Alfred & Marie RICHARD) m. 21 June 1897 Eugenie BABIN (Thib. Ch.: v.14, p.148)

DUPRE, Joseph (Alfred & Marie RICHARD) m. 21 June 1897 Eugenie BABIN (Thib. Ct. Hse.: Mar. v.36, #177)

DUPRE, Joseph Alcide (Clavery & Elizabeth BELANGER) b. 15 Feb. 1898 (Montegut Ch.: v.6, p.69)

DUPRE, Joseph Alexandre (Amedee & Elizabeth LIRETTE) b. 20 April 1897 (Montegut Ch.: v.6, p.56)

DUPRE, Joseph Elisee (Ulysse & Dolisca BOURG) b. 14 June 1898 (Montegut Ch.: v.6, p.76)

DUPRE, Laurence Marie (Albert & Emma LEBLANC) b. 8 Feb. 1896 (Houma Ch.: v.5, p.171)

DUPRE, Laurent Joseph (Albert & Emma LEBLANC) b. 8 Feb. 1896 (Houma Ch.: v.5, p.171)

DUPRE, Leo (Narcisse & Marie HENRI) m. 13 Jan. 1896 Eva BRUNET (Theriot Ch.: v.1, p.6)

DUPRE, Leopold (Leo & Justilia BRUNET) b. 28 Oct. 1899 (Theriot Ch.: v.2, p.54)

DUPRE, Marie m. 16 March 1897 Philip CLEMENT (Houma Ct. Hse.: Mar. v.29 & 30, #355)

DUPRE, Marie (Evariste & Azema DETRAVAE) m. 22 March 1897 Philip CLEMENT (Houma Ch.: v.6-a, p.197)

DUPRE, Marie Emma (Joseph & Lesilia LEBOEUF) b. 23 July 1896 (Montegut Ch.: v.6, p.43)

DUPRE, Marie Justilia (Francois & Virginie TRAHAN) b. 2 April 1899 (Montegut Ch.: v.6, p.90)

DUPRE, Marie Lucie (Ellett & Helene BERGERON) b. 20 Dec. 1898 (Houma Ch.: v.5, p.232)
DUPRE, Mary Henrie Ada (Thomas & Victoria PORTIER) b. 20 June 1896 (Houma Ch.: v.5, p.181)
DUPRE, May Marguerite d. 2 Sept. 1896 at age 4 mths. (Houma Ch.: v.3, p.9)
DUPRE, May Marguerite (Thomas & Victoria PORTIER) b. 8 May 1896 (Houma Ch.: v.5, p.150)
DUPRE, Octave (Eugene & Marie DUGAS) m. 12 Feb. 1898 Cezerie BERGERON (Montegut Ch.: v.4, p.235)
DUPRE, Paul Roger (Deme & Brigitte LEDET) b. 30 Dec. 1899 (Montegut Ch.: v.6, p.98)
DUPRE, Pierre (Charles & Evela HEBERT) b. 25 June 1896; m. Marie Justine RODRIGUE, on 1 June 1925 (Houma Ch.: Bapt. Bk., v.5, p.182)
DUPRE, Scholastique m. Euselien DESROCHES d. 9 April 1897 at age 76 yrs. (Montegut Ch.: v.2, p.10)
DUPRE, Victorine m. 13 Sept. 1897 Thomas J. GLYNN (Houma Ct. Hse.: Mar. v.29 & 30, #89)
DUPRE, Victorine (Sylvere & Orvilia LEBOEUF) m. 14 Sept. 1897 Thomas J. GLYNN (Houma Ch.: v.6-a, p.215)
DUPRE, Wilfrid Gustave (Martin & Roseline CHIASSON) b. 20 Dec. 1896 (Montegut Ch.: v.6, p.51)

DUPUIS (Sometimes: DUPUY)

DUPUIS, Henri Pierre (Robert & Ayma DISHER) b. 31 Jan. 1897 (Lockport Ch.: v.3-A, #12)
DUPUIS, Henri Pierre (Robert & Ayma DISHER) b. 31 Jan. 1897 (Lockport Ch.: v.3, #12)
DURDEN, Sarah Ann m. 16 Feb. 1898 Merryman COLLINS (Houma Ct. Hse.: Mar. v.30 & 31, #300)
DURDEN, Willis m. 4 Feb. 1897 Sarah WILSON (Houma Ct. Hse.: Mar. v.29 & 30, #283)
DURGAN, Fannie m. 10 Aug. 1898 Willie HOWARD (Thib. Ct. Hse.: Mar. v.38, #244)
DURNS, Francis m. 8 April 1897 Peter CAFFERY (Thib. Ct. Hse.: Mar. v.36, #109)

DUROCHER (Sometimes: DUROCHE)

DUROCHER, Albert (Azeme & Mary LANDRY) m. 3 April 1899 Louise ONCALE (Thib. Ct. Hse.: Mar. v.39, #120)
DUROCHER, Albert (Ozemee & Marie LANDRY) m. 3 April 1899 Marie Louise ONCAL (Chackbay Ch.: v.1, p.70)
DUROCHER, Clovis L. (Oscar & Pauline NAQUIN) m. 30 Aug. 1897 Louise Marie MORVAN (Thib. Ct. Hse.: Mar. v.37, #222)
DUROCHER, Clovis Louis (Oscar & Pauline NAQUIN) m. 30 Aug. 1897 Louise Marie MORVAN (Chackbay Ch.: v.1, p.48)
DUROCHER, Eva (Paulin & Mathilde JOLIBOIS) m. 17 Dec. 1896 Willie ADAM (Thib. Ch.: v.14, p.104)
DUROCHER, Joseph (Emile & Malvina CHIASSON) b. 6 Dec. 1898 (Chackbay Ch.: v.1, p.125)

DUROCHER, Sidney (Emile & Malvina CHIASSON) b. 4 Nov. 1896 (Chackbay Ch.: v.1, p.79)

DUROCHER, Sylvestre (Ozemee & Marie LANDRY) m. 23 Jan. 1899 Leontia CLEMENT (Thib. Ct. Hse.: Mar. v.38, #2)

DUROCHER, Sylvestre (Ozemee & Marie LANDRY) m. 23 Jan. 1899 Leontia CLEMENT (Thib. Ch.: v.14, p.244)

DURSAY, Percy Paul (Emile & Adele AYO) b. 9 Feb. 1896 (Thib. Ch.: v.7, p.397)

DUTHER, Victor d. 25 Nov. 1898 (Houma Ch.: Epis. Ch.: v.1, p.388)

DUTHU, Apoline Sedy (Lufroid & Avila DAIGLE) b. 10 Sept. 1896 (Houma Ch.: v.5, p.157)

DUTHU, Josephine Leonise (Lufroid & Avila DAIGLE) b. 9 Jan. 1899 (Houma Ch.: v.5, p.234)

DUTHU, Orelia (Joseph & Marguerite BILLIOT) m. 23 April 1898 Alfarez GREGOIRE (Houma Ct. Hse.: Mar. v.30 & 31, #416)

DUTREIL, Berthe Marie Louise d. 17 May 1898 at age 1 yr. & 16 days (Thib. Ch.: v.3, p.214)

DUTU, Leon d. 9 May 1898 at age 3 yrs. & 9 mths. (Houma Ch.: v.3, p.16)

DUVAL, Claiborne A. Jr. (Claiborne A. & Julia EASTON) m. 11 Dec. 1896 Leonora Bisland BRADFORD (Houma Ct. Hse.: Mar. v.29 & 30, #203)

DUVAL, Claiborne A. Jr. (Dr. E. A. & Julia EASTON) m. 17 Dec. 1896 Leonora B. BRADFORD (Houma Ch.: Epis. Ch.: v.1, p.340)

DUVAL, Claude Gordon (C. A., Jr. & Mrs. Bradford DUVAL) b. 29 March 1899 (Houma Ch.: Epis. Ch.: v.1, p.122)

DUVAL, Claude Gordon d. 30 April 1899 at age 1 mth. (Houma Ch.: Epis. Ch.: v.1, p.388)

DUVAL, Easten Willeam (Easton & Eugenie DODSON) b. 1 March 1896 (Houma Ch.: Epis. Ch.: v.1, p.118)

DUVAL, Leonora Bisland (Claiborne A., Jr. & Leonora BISLAND) b. 3 Nov. 1897 (Houma Ch.: Epis. Ch.: v.1, p.118)

DYE, Marie Angela (Joe & Lea DICKERSON) b. 10 June 1899 (Thib. Ch.: v.7, p.608)

DYER, David m. 23 Feb. 1898 Queen NIXON (Houma Ct. Hse.: Mar. v.30 & 31, #320)

DYER, Edna m. 27 Sept. 1899 John DILLARD (Houma Ct. Hse.: Mar. v.31 & 32, #146)

DYER, Joseph m. 13 Jan. 1897 Lea DICKERSON (Thib. Ct. Hse.: Mar. v.36, #26)

DYER, Margaret deceased; m. d.Robert COLLINS Children: John; Susan; Lea STEWART, of previous marriage. Petition for inventory: 4 Aug. 1896. (Houma Ct. Hse.: Succ. #867)

DYER, Nathan m.14 Jan. 1897 Louisa FURBIN (Thib. Ct. Hse.: Mar. v.36, #33)

DYER, Royal m. 24 March 1897 Mary LEE (Houma Ct. Hse.: Mar. v.29 & 30, #361)

DYER, Sarah d. 4 Dec. 1896; m. Thomas MILES Child listed: Lizzie m. Daniel PATTERSON. Petition to be placed in possession: 9 Feb. 1897. (Houma Ct. Hse.: Succ. #881)

DYER, Scipio S. Jr. m. 12 Aug. 1899 Maggie THOMAS (Houma Ct. Hse.: Mar. v.31 & 32, #95)

DYER, Walter m. 8 Sept. 1898 Eda PIERRE (Thib. Ct. Hse.: Mar. v.38, #274)

DYIAR, Sarah m. 26 Jan. 1899 Thomas WINSLOW (Houma Ct. Hse.: Mar. v.30 & 31, #283)

"E"

EASTON, Tristarie S. d. 7 Dec. 1897 at age 63 yrs. (Houma Ch.: Epis. Ch.: v.1, p.386)

ECHETE (See: CHETE)

EDMOND, Andrew (Willie & Annie MOSLEY) b. 15 Aug. 1899 (Thib. Ch.: v.7, p.567)
EDMOND, Joseph Witney (Willy & Anna MESLEY) b. 20 Sept. 1896 (Thib. Ch.: v.7, p.470)
EDMOND, Julia m. 24 Feb. 1897 Wilbert BAPTISTE (Thib. Ct. Hse.: Mar. v.36, #89)
EDMOND, Ophelia m. 26 Oct. 1896 George THOMPSON (Thib. Ct. Hse.: Mar. v.36, #159)
EDMOND, Willie m.27 Feb. 1897 Anna MOSEBY (Thib. Ct. Hse.: Mar. v.36, #93)
EDWARDS, Ella m. 6 Feb. 1896 Richard FAUCHEUX (Houma Ct. Hse.: Mar. v.28, #438)
EDWARDS, Ella (Charles D. & Evelina AYO) m. 17 Feb. 1896 Richard FAUCHEUX (Houma Ch.: v.6-a, p.171)
EDWARDS, Josephine m. 4 Jan. 1896 Benjamin BURNS (Houma Ct. Hse.: Mar. v.28, #373)
EDWARDS, Josephine m. 8 Jan. 1898 John N. BOOKER (Thib. Ct. Hse.: Mar. v.37, #11)
EDWARDS, William m. 10 Sept. 1898 Elizabeth JACKSON (Thib. Ct. Hse.: Mar. v.38, #277)

EGLOFF (Sometimes: EGLOFFE)
EGLOFF, Marie Daizie (Johnny & Eva BELANGER) b. 15 Aug. 1896; bt. 18 May 1901 (Montegut Ch.: v.7, p.22)
EHRHART, Thomas m. 3 May 1897 Armantine BOURGEOIS (Thib. Ct. Hse.: Mar. v.36, #136)
ELFER, Thomas m. 19 March 1896 Adeline HIMEL (Thib. Ct. Hse.: Mar. v.35, #53)
ELFERT, Charles (Octave & Louise SHAW) m. 29 April 1897 Elisabeth BERGERON (Thib. Ch.: v.14, p.142)
ELFERT, Charles (Octave & Louise SHAW) m. 29 April 1897 Elisabeth BERGERON (Thib. Ct. Hse.: Mar. v.36, #132)
ELFERT, Marie Annie (Charles & Elisabeth BERGERON) b. 15 May 1897 (Thib. Ch.: v.7, p.501)
ELFRET, Sarah of Terrebonne Parish m. 26 April 1899 Charles VERRET (Houma Ch.: v.6-B, p.3)
ELFRETH, Sarah m. 13 April 1899 Charles VERRET (Houma Ct. Hse.: Mar. v.31 & 32, #401)

ELIE (Sometimes: HELIE)
ELIE, Antoine Rameau (Cleophas & ----lic GALJOUR) b. 29 March 1896 (Larose Ch.: v.2, p.193)

ELIE, Lucie (Joseph & Emelie CHERAMI) b. 12 Feb. 1897 (Lockport Ch.: v.3-A, #24)
ELIE, Lucie Eulalie (Joseph & Emelie CHERAMI) b. 12 Feb. 1897 (Lockport Ch.: v.3, #24)
ELIE, Marie Clotilde (Francois & -----) b. 26 Sept. 1896 (Larose Ch.: v.2, p.184)
ELIE, Paul (Pierre & Azelie ALBAROND) m. 11 April 1896 Eugenie GIROIRE (Houma Ct. Hse.: Mar. v.29 & 30, #32)
ELIE, Seraphine (Cleopha & Rosalie GALJOUR) m. 23 April 1898 Orville FREMIN of Lafourche Parish (Larose Ch.: v.3, p.8)
ELIE, Seraphine (Cleopha & Rosalie GALJOUR) m. 23 April 1898 Orville FREMIN (Thib. Ct. Hse.: Mar. v.37, #150)
ELLENDER, Annie Marguerite (Joseph & Celemee DESROCHES) b. 13 April 1896 (Montegut Ch.: v.6, p.37)
ELLENDER, Elizabeth Walterine (Wallace & Victoria JARVEAU) b. 22 Sept. 1897 (Montegut Ch.: v.6, p.60)
ELLENDER, Jean Laurent (Dave & Emilie CHAUVIN) b. 10 Dec. 1898 (Montegut Ch.: v.6, p.79)
ELLENDER, Julia LeBlanc (Arthur & Marie CHAUVIN) m. 9 April 1898 John HEIDER (Houma Ct. Hse.: Mar. v.30 & 31, #390)
ELLENDER, Marie Evelia (Thomas & Evelia DUPLANTIS) b. 1 Feb. 1897 (Montegut Ch.: v.6, p.49)
ELLENDER, Paul Guy (Joseph & Celemee DESROCHES) b. 12 May 1898 (Montegut Ch.: v.6, p.72)
ELLENDER, Pierre Maurice (Joseph & Celemee DESROCHES) b. 12 May 1898 (Montegut Ch.: v.6, p.72)
ELLENDER, Ralph Lawrence (David & Emelie CHAUVIN) d. 13 Nov. 1896 at age 2 yrs. & 4 mths. (Montegut Ch.: v.2, p.7)

ELLINDER (Sometimes: ELINDA, ELLENDER, HELENDER)

ELLIOT (Sometimes: ELIOT, ELLIOTT)
ELLIOT, Armand (Joseph & Lize GUIDRY) m. 24 April 1897 Alice BERGERON (Lockport Ch.: v.2, p.161)
ELLIOT, Armand (Joseph & Lize GUIDRY) m. 24 April 1897 Alice BERGERON (Thib. Ct. Hse.: Mar. v.36, #110)
ELLIOT, Eliska (William & Felicie SAVOIE) m. 28 Jan. 1897 Pierre BREAUX (Thib. Ct. Hse.: Mar. v.36, #28)
ELLIOT, Eliska (Wuilliam & Felicie SAVOIE) m. 28 Jan. 1897 Felicien BREAUX (Lockport Ch.: v.2, p.158)
ELLIOT, Joseph Edouard (Charly & Felicia BRAUX) b. 3 March 1897 (Lockport Ch.: v.3-A, #32)
ELLIOT, Joseph Edouard (Charly & Felicia BREAUX) b. 3 March 1897 (Lockport Ch.: v.3, #32)
ELLIOT, Laura m. 1 Oct. 1897 Napoleon MARTINEZ (Thib. Ct. Hse.: Mar. v.37, #237)
ELLIOT, Rita Bernadette (Charly & Felicia BRAUX) b. 10 Oct. 1899 (Lockport Ch.: v.3-A, #9)
ELLIOT, Rita Bernadette (Charly & Felicia BRAUX) b. 10 Oct. 1899 (Lockport Ch.: v.3, #9)

ELLIOT, Zulema (Joseph & Elize GUIDRY) m. 16 Feb. 1896 Clay ORDOGNE (Lockport Ch.: v.2, p.150)
ELLIOT, Zulema (Joseph & Elize GUIDRY) m. 5 Feb. 1896 Clay ORDOGNE (Thib. Ct. Hse.: Mar. v.35, #21)

ELLIS (Sometimes: ELESSE, ELISS)
ELLIS, Jawsen d. 14 May 1896 at age 66 yrs. (Thib. Ch.: Epis. Ch.: v.1, p.394)
ELLS, George S. (D. Byron & Amelia D. SCHWING) m. 20 April 1898 Eva LANDRY (Houma Ct. Hse.: Mar. v.30 & 31, #410)
ENCALADE, Emanuel (Joseph & Noeda BILOT) b. 6 April 1899 (Larose Ch.: v.3, p.83)

ENGERON (Sometimes: ANGERAN, ENGERAN, ENGERAND, ENGERRON)
ENGERON, Alida (Theophile & d.Celeste LECOMPTE) m. 21 Feb. 1898 Nathaniel NETTLETON (Montegut Ch.: v.4, p.238)
ENGERON, Emma m. 16 May 1898 Henry MARIE (Houma Ct. Hse.: Mar. v.30 & 31, #443)
ENGERON, Emma (d.Alcee & Desire AYMARD) m. 6 June 1898 Henri MARIE (Montegut Ch.: v.4, p.246)
ENGERON, Eugene d. 25 Jan. 1898 at age 83 yrs. (Montegut Ch.: v.2, p.15)
ENGERON, Eugene m. 4 Jan. 1896 Brigitte RHODES (Houma Ct. Hse.: Mar. v.28, #374)
ENGERON, Eugene (Theophile & d.Celeste LECOMPTE) m. 18 Jan. 1896 Brigitte RHODES (Montegut Ch.: v.4, p.206)
ENGERON, Eva (Clodomire & Alfrida PELEGRIN) m. 18 May 1896 Toussaint THERIOT (Houma Ct. Hse.: Mar. v.29 & 30, #74)
ENGERON, Jean Maurice (Theophile & Regina MARIE) b. 16 May 1899 (Montegut Ch.: v.6, p.89)
ENGERON, Joseph Harry (Eugene & Brigitte RHODES) b. 25 March 1897 (Montegut Ch.: v.6, p.52)
ENGERON, Josephine (Theophile & Celeste LECOMPTE) m. 25 March 1899 Enos L. RHODES (Houma Ct. Hse.: Mar. v.31 & 32, #377)
ENGERON, Josephine (Theophile & d.Celeste LECOMPTE) m. 22 April 1899 Enos L. RHODES (Montegut Ch.: v.4, p.262)
ENGERON, Lelia (Theophile & Alfrida PELEGRIN) m. 6 Feb. 1899 Oliva LAPEROUSE (Houma Ct. Hse.: Mar. v.30 & 31, #312)
ENGERON, Marie Angelique m. Albert MARCEL d. 25 Jan. 1896 at age 40 yrs. (Montegut Ch.: v.2, p.3)
ENGERON, Marie Anne (Eugene & Brigitte RHODES) b. 8 June 1899 (Montegut Ch.: v.6, p.89)
ENGERON, Theophile m. 3 Jan. 1898 Regina MARY (Houma Ct. Hse.: Mar. v.30 & 31, #173)
ENGERON, Theophile (d.Alces & Desiree AYNARD) m. 24 Jan. 1898 Regina MARY (Montegut Ch.: v.4, p.231)
ENGERRAN, Alida (Theophile & Celeste LECOMPTE) m. 7 Feb. 1898 Nathaniel NETTLETON (Houma Ct. Hse.: Mar. v.30 & 31, #280)

ENGLAND, Benjamin m. 5 April 1898 Dora GAUTREAUX (Houma Ct. Hse.: Mar. v.30 & 31, #376)
ENGMAN, Ruth Edna (Edward & Zenobe ROBICHAUX) b. 2 Nov. 1897 (Houma Ch.: v.5, p.209)
ENGOALL, John m. 16 Dec. 1899 Lena BENOIT (Thib. Ct. Hse.: Mar. v.39, #286)
ERNEST, Elizabeth (Randoll G. & Louisiane P. DAVIS) m. 11 - 13 Feb. 1899 Henry V. DE LA BRETONNE (Houma Ch.: v.6-a, p.279)
ERNEST, Elizabeth C. m. 2 Feb. 1899 Henry O. DE LA BRETONNE (Houma Ct. Hse.: Mar. v.30 & 31, #298)
ERSKINE, Clementine m. Numa HEBERT d. 3 May 1897 at age 29 yrs. (Thib. Ch.: v.3, p.199)

ESCHETE (See: CHETE)

ESPONGE, Joachim Gustave (Policar & Eugenie CALET) b. 18 Aug. 1896 (Larose Ch.: v.2, p.186)
ESPONGE, Joseph (Thomas & Celima DANTIN) m. 15 July 1899 Julia LORRAINE (Larose Ch.: v.3, p.12)
ESPONGE, Joseph (Thomas & Celima DANTIN) m. 15 July 1899 Julia LAURRAINE (Larose Ch.: v.4, p.87)
ESPONGE, Marie Lucia (Esdras & Ernestine DANTIN) b. 2 July 1896 (Larose Ch.: v.2, p.194)
ESPONGE, Thomas m. 7 July 1899 Julia LORRAINE (Thib. Ct. Hse.: Mar. v.39, #194)
ESPONGE, Viola Andrea (Policar & Eugenie CALET) b. 4 Feb. 1899 (Larose Ch.: v.3, p.43)
ESPOSITO, ----- girl d. 22 Dec. 1896 at birth (Thib. Ch.: v.3, p.192)
ESPOSITO, Therese Berthilde (Victor & Victoria LUSIGNAN) b. 6 Nov. 1898 (Thib. Ch.: v.7, p.520)
ESTERE, Ozeme d. 11 Jan. 1899 at age 57 yrs. (Thib. Ch.: v.3, p.225)

ESTEVE (Sometimes: ESTIVE)

ESTEVE, Amedee (Lemet & Alida PONTIF) b. 4 Feb. 1897 (Thib. Ch.: v.7, p.447)
ESTEVE, Annette Celeste Pauline (Louis & Emma LEGENDRE) b. 6 May 1896 (Thib. Ch.: v.7, p.403)
ESTEVE, Aurelia Julienne (Aurelien & Marie GUILLOT) b. 6 Sept. 1898 (Thib. Ch.: v.7, p.564)
ESTEVE, Edouard Ulysse (Louis & Emma LEGENDRE) b. 17 Dec. 1899 (Thib. Ch.: v.8, p.21)
ESTEVE, Ella (Louis & Emma LEGENDRE) m. 16 Jan. 1899 Nicolas ADAM (Thib. Ct. Hse.: Mar. v.38, #8)
ESTEVE, Ella (Louis & Emma LEGENDRE) m. 16 Jan. 1899 Nicolas ADAM (Thib. Ch.: v.14, p.237)
ESTEVE, Elvine Georgette (Lemee & Alida PONTIFE) b. 22 April 1899 (Thib. Ch.: v.7, p.606)

ESTEVE, Ernest Etienne (Theophile & Leonide BOURGEOIS) b. 4 July 1898 (Thib. Ch.: v.7, p.510)
ESTEVE, Jean Eugene (Aurelien & Marie GUILLOTTE) b. 3 April 1896 (Thib. Ch.: v.7, p.398)
ESTEVE, Marie Augustine (Onesime & Angela GUILLOTTE) b. 7 July 1898 (Thib. Ch.: v.7, p.560)
ESTEVE, Paul Edy (Ozeme & Marie DUGAS) b. 25 Oct. 1896 (Thib. Ch.: v.7, p.423)
ESTEVE, Philippe Arthur (Louis & Aima LEGENDRE) b. 13 Nov. 1898 (Thib. Ch.: v.7, p.523)

ESTHE (Sometimes: CHETE)

ESTIVENNE (Sometimes: ESTEVAN, ESTIVAN, ESTIVENNES, STEPHEN)
ESTIVENNE, Adelain Irby Pierre (Charles & Noelie ROUNDTREE) b. 16 April 1899 (Thib. Ch.: v.7, p.603)
ESTIVENNE, Augustin d. 16 Oct. 1899 at age 10 minutes (Thib. Ch.: v.3, p.242)
ESTIVENNE, Augustine Menelba (Charles & Noeline LANDRY) b. 5 Sept. 1898 (Thib. Ch.: v.7, p.518)
ESTIVENNE, Celeste (William & Celina BERGERON) m. 9 Jan. 1899 Paulin DAIGLE (Thib. Ch.: v.14, p.234)
ESTIVENNE, Charles (Battie & Aimee ADAM) b. 13 Nov. 1899 (Thib. Ch.: v.8, p.17)
ESTIVENNE, Emile Charles (Willy & Louise LANDRY) b. 19 Feb. 1897 (Thib. Ch.: v.7, p.445)
ESTIVENNE, Eugenie Scholastique d. 21 July 1897 at age 22 yrs. (Thib. Ch.: v.3, p.203)
ESTIVENNE, Eve d. 13 July 1898 at age 24 yrs. (Thib. Ch.: v.3, p.216)
ESTIVENNE, Joseph (Joseph & Lucia RODRIGUE) b. 17 June 1899 (Thib. Ch.: v.7, p.608)
ESTIVENNE, Joseph Augustin (Olesime & Mirthe GUILLOT) b. 27 Oct. 1896 (Thib. Ch.: v.7, p.430)
ESTIVENNE, Liliane Scholastie (Alphonse & Veronique LUSIGNAN) b. 13 June 1897 (Thib. Ch.: v.7, p.452)
ESTIVENNE, Lovincia (Marcellin & Rosela TOUPS) m. 17 Sept. 1896 Lucius RODRIGUE (Thib. Ch.: v.14, p.99)
ESTIVENNE, Lovincia (Marcellin & Rosela TOUPS) m. 17 Sept. 1896 Lucien RODRIGUE (Thib. Ct. Hse.: Mar. v.36, #142)
ESTIVENNE, Lovincy m. 10 Feb. 1899 Alice BOUDREAUX (Thib. Ct. Hse.: Mar. v.39, #103)
ESTIVENNE, Lovincy (Marcelin & Rosela TOUPS) m. 13 Feb. 1899 Alice BOUDREAUX (Thib. Ch.: v.14, p.265)
ESTIVENNE, Lyla Philomene (Callixte & Celeste BABIN) b. 25 June 1897 (Thib. Ch.: v.7, p.454)
ESTIVENNE, Lylia d. 22 Jan. 1898 at age 6 mths. (Thib. Ch.: v.3, p.210)
ESTIVENNE, Lylienne d. 4 Oct. 1897 at age 4 mths. (Thib. Ch.: v.3, p.206)

ESTIVENNE, Marie Agnes (Betty & Aimee ADAM) b. 20 Aug. 1897 (Thib. Ch.: v.7, p.461)
ESTIVENNE, Marie Josephine (Joseph & Lucia RODRIGUE) b. 19 March 1898 (Thib. Ch.: v.7, p.491)
ESTIVENNE, Marie May Inez (Alphonse & Veronique LUSIGNAN) b. 19 Aug. 1898 (Thib. Ch.: v.7, p.509)
ESTIVENNE, Valerie Edna (Ernest & Anna BABIN) b. 7 Nov. 1897 (Thib. Ch.: v.7, p.478)
ESTIVENNE, Willie Ernest (Ernest & Aina BABIN) b. 9 March 1899 (Thib. Ch.: v.7, p.602)

ESTOUFFLET (See: STOUFFLET)

EUSTIS, Brigitte Nola (Joseph & Mathilde ADAM) b. 16 April 1896 (Lockport Ch.: v.2, p.328)
EUSTIS, Webre Denistan (Louis & Amanda ADAMS) b. 25 Nov. 1896 (Lockport Ch.: v.3, #21)

EVANS (Sometimes: EVENS, EVIVES)
EVANS, Evan J. m. 2 June 1897 Emma C. FLASH (Thib. Ch.: Epis. Ch.: v.1, p.331)
EVANS, Evan J. m. 2 June 1897 Emma FLASH (Thib. Ct. Hse.: Mar. v.36, #159)
EVANS, Floy (George W. & Mary V. BURNETTE) m. 14 Aug. 1899 Edgar BERGERON (Houma Ct. Hse: Mar. v.31 & 32, #98)
EVANS, Sarah m. 18 Jan. 1897 James TEMPLE (Thib. Ct. Hse.: Mar. v.36, #42)
EVANS, Sidney m. 21 Dec. 1898 Cora CROSIER (Houma Ct. Hse.: Mar. v.30 & 31, #156)
EVANS, Sue m. 11 Jan. 1897 Israel JENKINS (Houma Ct. Hse.: Mar. v.29 & 30, #232)
EWINGS, Bird m. 4 Feb. 1897 Carrie LEBLANC (Houma Ct. Hse.: Mar. v.29 & 30, #286)
EWINGS, William m. 2 Feb. 1898 Louisa SMITH (Houma Ct. Hse.: Mar. v.30 & 31, #266)

EXNICIOS (Sometimes: ENIXIOS)
EXNICIOS, John P. (John & Ellen FABIAN) m. 12 Jan. 1898 Edna BADEAUX (Lockport Ch.: v.2, p.178)
EXNICIOS, John P. (John & Ellen FABIAN) m. 12 Jan. 1898 Edna BADEAUX (Thib. Ct. Hse.: Mar. v.37, #5)
EXNICIOS, Joshua (Louis & Lorenza BOUDREAU) m. 17 Nov. 1898 Pauline BOUDREAU (Theriot Ch.: v.1-B, p.5)
EXNICIOS, Joshua (Louis & Lorenza BOUDREAUX) m. 5 Nov. 1898 Pauline BOUDREAUX (Houma Ct. Hse.: Mar. v.30 & 31, #128)
EXNICIOS, Marie Humius (Michel & Evelia BARROS) b. 2 April 1896 (Theriot Ch.: v.1-B, p.90)
EXNICIOS, Orlando F. m. Ella A. BOUDREAUX, d. 21 July 1897. Children listed: Edmire Franklina m. Forest SKIFF; Louis;

Noah; Franklin Clinton; Medora; Lillian Daisy; Mary Adita; Adrien. Tutorship: 6 March 1899. (Houma Ct. Hse.: Succ. #913)

EYMARD (Sometimes: AYMARD)

EYMARD, Emma of Lafourche Parish (Bienvenu & Florestine GASPARD) m. 16 April 1898 Alcee KEEFE, of Lafourche Parish (Larose Ch.: v.3, p.8)

EYMARD, Emma (Bienvenu & Florestine GASPARD) m. 16 April 1898 Alcee KEEFFE (Larose Ch.: v.4, p.8)

EYMARD, Emma (Bienvenu & Florestine GASPARD) m. 16 April 1898 Alcee KEEFFE (Thib. Ct. Hse.: Mar. v.37, #146)

EYMARD, Hypolite m. 1 July 1897 Matilde CHERAMI (Thib. Ct. Hse.: Mar. v.37, #188)

EYMARD, Hypolitte m. 17 July 1897 Mathilde CHERAMI (Larose Ch.: v.3, p.6)

EYMARD, Hyppolitte m. 17 July 1897 Mathilde CHERAMI (Larose Ch.: v.4, p.93-B)

EYMARD, Hyppolitte m. 17 July 1897 Mathilde CHERAMI (Larose Ch.: v.4, p.116)

"F"

FABIANI, Philippe of Smirne, Asia Minor (Baptiste & Angeline FABIANI) m. 18 Jan. 1896 Josephine DUFRENE (Thib. Ct. Hse.: Mar. v.35, #12)
FABIONI, Jean Baptiste (Philippe & Josephine DUFRENE) b. 4 Jan. 1896 (Lockport Ch.: v.3, #27)
FABIONI, Jean Baptiste (Philippe & Josephine DUFRENE) b. 4 Jan. 1896 (Lockport Ch.: v.3-A, #27)
FABIONI, Philippe (Baptiste & Angeline FABIONI) m. 18 Jan. 1896 Josephine DUFRENE (Lockport Ch.: v.2, p.149)

FABRE (Sometimes: FABER, FABERT)
FABRE, George Pierre (Honore & Edna MINNICH) b. 13 March 1896 (Larose Ch.: v.2, p.187)
FABRE, Jean Wilbert (Honore & Edna MINNICH) b. 18 Nov. 1897 (Larose Ch.: v.3, p.26)
FABREGIS, Marie Rose (Frank & Conception PUREZ) b. 30 Jan. 1896 (Houma Ch.: v.5, p.169)
FACQUET, H. (Octave & Domenia DUFOUR) d. 13 June 1896 (Thib. Ch.: v.3, p.183)
FALCON, Clarence Henri (Adam & Seraphine MAITREJEAN) b. 28 Oct. 1898 (Thib. Ch.: v.7, p.517)
FALCON, Faustine Jeanne (Adam & Seraphine Marhe JEAN) b. 1 Feb. 1897 (Thib. Ch.: v.7, p.439)
FALCON, Francis (Domingue & Augestine IDARGO) m. 14 Feb. 1898 Amelia DUGAS (Thib. Ch.: v.14, p.185)
FALCON, Francis (Domingue & Augustine IDARGO) m. 14 Feb. 1898 Aurelia DUGAS (Thib. Ct. Hse.: Mar. v.37, #96)
FALCON, Henri d. 18 April 1899 at age 6 mths. (Thib. Ch.: v.3, p.232)
FALCON, Joseph Edouard (Francis & Aurelia DUGAS) b. 21 May 1899 (Thib. Ch.: v.7, p.549)

FALGOUT (Sometimes: FALGOAT, FALGOU, FALGOUET)
FALGOUT, Albertine m. 14 July 1899 Remy or Reme ROUSSEL (Thib. Ct. Hse.: Mar. v.39, #199)
FALGOUT, Albertine (Onesime & Antoinette OTIN) m. 17 July 1899 Remy ROUSSELL (Raceland Ch.: v.2, p.101)
FALGOUT, Alidor (Arsene & Odilia SAVOIE) m. 23 Jan. 1899 Brigitte LECOMPTE (Montegut Ch.: v.4, p.251)
FALGOUT, Alidore m. 14 Jan. 1899 Brigitte LECOMPTE (Houma Ct. Hse.: Mar. v.30 & 31, #230)
FALGOUT, Aline (Emile & Charlotte CHAMPAGNE) m. 1 March 1897 Charles Watkins CAMPBELL (Thib. Ch.: v.14, p.133)
FALGOUT, Andre Clay (Clay & Melina MATERN) b. 13 June 1897 (Larose Ch.: v.3, p.11)
FALGOUT, Anitha Emelie (Wilfrid & Ezelia POINCON) b. 20 Aug. 1897 (Theriot Ch.: v.2, p.10)
FALGOUT, Anne Mabel (Myrtil & Helene DETIVEAU) b. 10 Oct. 1898 (Montegut Ch.: v.6, p.77)

FALGOUT, Becca (Arcene & Odilia SAVOIE) m. 7 Jan. 1899 Loetitia ADAM (Thib. Ct. Hse.: Mar. v.38, #7)

FALGOUT, Becca (Arcine & Odilia SAVOIE) m. 7 Jan. 1899 Loetitia ADAM (Lockport Ch.: v.2, p.198)

FALGOUT, Bernadette Euphrosie (Armand & Aimee DANTIN) b. 22 March 1899 (Raceland Ch.: v.5, p.93)

FALGOUT, Charles (Felix & Lovinia WURTHNEY) m. 18 Jan. 1896 Augusta BRAUX (Lockport Ch.: v.2, p.149)

FALGOUT, Charles (Felix & Lovinia WURTHNEY) m. 18 Jan. 1896 Augusta BRAUX (Thib. Ct. Hse.: Mar. v.35, #191)

FALGOUT, Charles Sidney (Felicien & Amy SAMANIE) b. 28 Jan. 1896 (Houma Ch.: v.5, p.168)

FALGOUT, Dorothee Odilia (Ferjus & Felicia ELLIOT) b. 17 Dec. 1896 (Lockport Ch.: v.3, #8)

FALGOUT, Dorothee Odilia (Ferjus & Felicia ELLIOT) b. 17 Dec. 1896 (Lockport Ch.: v.3-A, #8)

FALGOUT, Elmire Marie (Charles & Augusta BREAUX) b. 23 Dec. 1896 (Lockport Ch.: v.3, #14)

FALGOUT, Elmire Marie (Charles & Augusta BRAUX) b. 23 Dec. 1896 (Lockport Ch.: v.3-A, #14)

FALGOUT, Eusebe (Blodmire & Helose MARTIN) m. 15 Aug. 1899 Rosa RODRIGUE (Thib. Ch.: v.14, p.290)

FALGOUT, Eusebe (Blodomire & Helise MARTIN) m. 15 Aug. 1899 Rosa RODRIGUEZ (Thib. Ct. Hse.: Mar. v.39, #206)

FALGOUT, Francois V. d. 31 May 1899 at age 61 yrs. (Larose Ch.: v.1, p.52)

FALGOUT, Georges (Emile & Charlotte CHAMPAGNE) m. 29 April 1896 Marie NAQUIN (Thib. Ch.: v.14, p.86)

FALGOUT, Georges (Emile & Charlotte CHAMPAGNE) m. 29 April 1896 Marie NAQUIN (Thib. Ct. Hse.: Mar. v.35, #70)

FALGOUT, Hebert Joseph (Felicien & Anny SAMONI) b. 20 Feb. 1897 (Houma Ch.: v.5, p.202)

FALGOUT, Helene Blanche (Wilfred & Emilia POINCEAU) b. 18 Aug. 1899 (Theriot Ch.: v.2, p.47)

FALGOUT, Henriette m. 1 Feb. 1899 Joseph A. BOUDREAUX (Thib. Ct. Hse.: Mar. v.38, #82)

FALGOUT, Henriette m. 13 Feb. 1899 Joseph A. BOUDREAUX (Larose Ch.: v.4, p.37)

FALGOUT, Henriette m. 13 Feb. 1899 Joseph A. BOUDREAUX (Larose Ch.: v.3, p.11)

FALGOUT, Idie Joseph (Joseph & Elvire GRABERT) b. 6 June 1898 (Thib. Ch.: v.7, p.500)

FALGOUT, J. Frank d. 2 June 1895; m. Hermina BERGERON. Children listed: Franklin, 14; Frederick, 13; Fernand, 12; Charles, 11; Mary, 10; Guy, 8; Joseph, 6; Lena, 4; Anna, 2. Petition for appointment: 16 Feb. 1897. (Houma Ct. Hse.: Succ. #882)

FALGOUT, Jean Andua (Taylor & Octavie COLON) b. 28 Feb. 1896 (Theriot Ch.: v.1-B, p.94)

FALGOUT, Joseph Felicien m. 16 May 1896 Annie SAMANI (Houma Ct. Hse.: Mar. v.29 & 30, #73)

FALGOUT, Joseph Felicien (Felicien & Amai SAMANI) b. 10 Oct. 1899 (Houma Ch.: v.5, p.260)
FALGOUT, Joseph Felicien (Marcelin & Mathilde BELANGER) m. 18 May 1896 Annie SAMANIE (Houma Ch.: v.6-a, p.175)
FALGOUT, Joseph Oleus (Joseph & Elvire GRABERT) b. 8 Jan. 1896 (Raceland Ch.: v.5, p.17)
FALGOUT, Joseph Pierre Harry (Homere & Malvina ROBICHAUX) b. 26 Nov. 1897 (Raceland Ch.: v.5, p.59)
FALGOUT, Josephine (Marcellin & Matile BELANGER) m. 23 Dec. 1899 Tilden Peter BASCLE (Houma Ct. Hse.: Mar. v.31 & 32, #189)
FALGOUT, Julia m. Francois LECOMPTE d. 29 May 1898 at age 41 yrs. (Montegut Ch.: v.2, p.16)
FALGOUT, Lina Thomassine (Wuillie & Cecilia CHONES) b. 29 Dec. 1899 (Lockport Ch.: v.3-A, #4)
FALGOUT, Lucia Thomassine (Wuillie & Cecilia CHONES) b. 29 Dec. 1899 (Lockport Ch.: v.3, #4)
FALGOUT, Marcel d. 1898 Children listed: Peter; Taylor; Wilfred; Marcel; Aime m. Michel BRIEN; Frank; Azema; Sarah m. (2) T. C. BERGERON; Olinda m. Alfred NAQUIN; Seraphine or Celestine m. Ursin CARLIN, Sr. Inventory: 11 Aug. 1898. (Houma Ct. Hse.: Succ. #903)
FALGOUT, Marcelle d. 14 May 1898 at age 80 yrs. (Theriot Ch.: v.1, p.1)
FALGOUT, Marcellin d. 29 July 1898 at age 78 yrs. (Montegut Ch.: v.2, p.19)
FALGOUT, Marie Elise (Armand & Aimee DANTIN) b. 18 July 1897 (Raceland Ch.: v.5, p.52)
FALGOUT, Marie Glorina (Edouard & Clara SAVOIE) b. 23 Feb. 1897 (Lockport Ch.: v.3, #45)
FALGOUT, Marie Glorina (Edouard & Clara SAVOIE) b. 23 Feb. 1897 (Lockport Ch.: v.3-A, #46)
FALGOUT, Marie Gratieuse (Leon & Celina BOUTERIE) b. 28 Nov. 1896 (Lockport Ch.: v.3-A, #4)
FALGOUT, Marie Gratieuse (Leon & Celine BOUTERIE) b. 29 Nov. 1896 (Lockport Ch.: v.3, #4)
FALGOUT, Marie Jula (Myrtilde & Helene DETIVEAU) b. 27 Jan. 1897 (Montegut Ch.: v.6, p.50)
FALGOUT, Marie Leona (Leonard & Argentine FAUCHEUX) b. 3 May 1898 (Raceland Ch.: v.5, p.70)
FALGOUT, Melanie m. 27 Sept. 1897 Wilson CHOUESSE (Thib. Ct. Hse.: Mar. v.37, #230)
FALGOUT, Melanie m. 27 Sept. 1897 Wilson CHOUESSE (Lockport Ch.: v.2, p.176)
FALGOUT, Rene Joseph (Joseph & Angeline SAVOIE) b. 19 Feb. 1897 (Lockport Ch.: v.3, #46)
FALGOUT, Rene Joseph (Joseph & Angeline SAVOIE) b. 19 Feb. 1897 (Lockport Ch.: v.3-A, #46)
FALGOUT, Sophia Rita (John T. & Octavie COLOMB) b. 4 Feb. 1898 (Houma Ch.: v.5, p.205)

FALGOUT, William (Felix & Louisiane WHITNEY) m. 9 Aug. 1897 Cecilia CHOISTRE (Thib. Ct. Hse.: Mar. v.37, #198)
FALGOUT, William (Felix & Louisiane WHITNEY) m. 16 Aug. 1897 Cecilia CHOUESSE (Lockport Ch.: v.2, p.164)
FALIZE, Pasquale (Pasquale &Santa CANINO) b. 9 Feb. 1899 (Thib. Ch.: v.8, p.19)
FANDAL, Joseph (Fritz & Mary SMITH) m. 23 June 1898 Theres FAUCHEUX (Houma Ct. Hse.: Mar. v.30 & 31, #23)
FANDAL, Mary m. 10 June 1897 John Howard BUFORD (Houma Ct. Hse.: Mar. v.29 & 30, #19)
FANDAL, Peter m. 20 July 1898 Agnes Alice PICOU (Houma Ct. Hse.: Mar. v.30 & 31, #64)
FANDALL, Catherine (F. & Marie Anna SCHMIDT) m. 15 April 1896 James D. BUFORD (Houma Ct. Hse.: Mar. v.29 & 30, #11)

FANGUY (Sometimes: FANGUI, FANGUIT)
FANGUY, Alceste Vincent (Theophile & Zoe BEAUDOIN) b. 24 April 1898 (Theriot Ch.: v.2, p.23)
FANGUY, Alice Zoe (Theogene & Angelique DUPRE) b. 28 June 1899 (Theriot Ch.: v.2, p.47)
FANGUY, Alton Joseph (Lafayette & Briget PARRE) b. 26 Nov. 1897 (Houma Ch.: v.5, p.195)
FANGUY, Bernadette (Edgar & Leonide PICOU) m. 8 Oct. 1896 Adam CHARPENTIER (Montegut Ch.: v.4, p.214)
FANGUY, Bernadette (Edgar & Leonide PICOU) m. 25 Sept. 1896 Abel CHARPENTIER (Houma Ct. Hse.: Mar. v.29 & 30, #153)
FANGUY, Felicia (Charles & Aimee CAMMEL) m. 12 Jan. 1899 Philip CHAMPAGNE (Houma Ct. Hse.: Mar. v.30 & 31, #223)
FANGUY, Felicia (Charley & Aimie CAMMEL) m. 23 Jan. 1899 Philippe CHAMPAGNE (Theriot Ch.: v.1-B, p.5)
FANGUY, Joseph Clarance (Jules & Meloe MARTIN) b. 14 June 1898 (Montegut Ch.: v.6, p.73)
FANGUY, Joseph Elie (William & Alice BELANGER) b. 8 Dec. 1898 (Theriot Ch.: v.2, p.17)
FANGUY, Leonce m. 25 Jan. 1899 Orfise ST. MARTIN (Houma Ct. Hse.: Mar. v.30 & 31, #281)
FANGUY, Leonce (Charli & Hunie CAMPBELL) m. Jan. - Feb. 1899 Defise ST. MARTIN (Theriot Ch.: v.1-B, p.6)
FANGUY, Lucien Gustave (William & Alice BELANGER) b. 5 March 1899 (Theriot Ch.: v.2, p.38)
FANGUY, Moise Edmond (Jules & Meloe MARTIN) b. 13 Aug. 1896 (Montegut Ch.: v.6, p.43)
FANGUY, Pierre Jacques (Volcar & Justilia MARTIN) b. 20 April 1899 (Montegut Ch.: v.6, p.86)
FANGUY, Regina Ursule (Volcan & Justilia MARTIN) b. 21 Sept. 1896 (Montegut Ch.: v.6, p.44)
FANGUY, Sandy Cynthe (William & Alice BELANGER) b. 5 June 1896 (Theriot Ch.: v.1-B, p.100)
FANIEL, Mary m. 14 Oct. 1899 Charley ROCKWOOD (Houma Ct. Hse.: Mar. v.31 & 32, #150)

FANSECOT (See: FONSECA)

FARACIE, Cuggittina (Giuseppe & Guiseppina GLORIUSO) b. 29 Nov. 1898 (Thib. Ch.: v.7, p.577)
FARINO, Cattarino (Henry & Joseph POMEGLIO) m. 21 Jan. 1899 Marione MILONI (Thib. Ch.: v.14, p.242)

FARRELL (Sometimes: FARALL, FARELL)

FASIN, Augustine d. 29 July 1899 at age 6 days (Raceland Ch.: v.1, p.26)
FASIN, Gustave (Gustave & Angelique ROUMAGE) m. 3 Sept. 1899 Victoria KERNER (Raceland Ch.: v.2, p.103)

FAUCHEUX (Sometimes: FAUCHE, FAUCHUX, FOCHEUX)
FAUCHEUX, Henri Lucien (Joseph & Marie GUITROZ) d. 22 Oct. 1897 at age 2 mths. (Lockport Ch.: v.1, #21)
FAUCHEUX, Lucille Celeste (Joseph & Marie GUITROZ) d. 12 Nov. 1897 (Lockport Ch.: v.1, #27)
FAUCHEUX, Richard m. 6 Feb. 1896 Ella EDWARDS (Houma Ct. Hse.: Mar. v.28, #438)
FAUCHEUX, Richard (Evalture & Josephine WALKER) m. 17 Feb. 1896 Ella EDWARDS (Houma Ch.: v.6-a, p.171)
FAUCHEUX, Rodney George (Richard & Ella EDWARDS) b. 13 July 1899 (Chacahoula Ch.: v.4, p.29)
FAUCHEUX, Theresa (Evarture & Josephine WALKER) m. 23 June 1898 Joseph FANDAL (Houma Ct. Hse.: Mar. v.30 & 31, #23)
FAULS, Victoria m. 21 Oct. 1898 Mose VAUGHN (Thib. Ct. Hse.: Mar. v.38, #299)
FAVROT, William Raynauld (Henry Mortimer & Celestine DUBROCA) m. 29 Dec 1897 Elise WILLIAMS (Houma Ct. Hse.: Mar. v.29 & 30, #161)
FAZENDE, Willie Paul (Paul & Marie BRAUD) b. 30 Sept. 1896 (Thib. Ch.: v.7, p.419)
FAZISCA, Franlisca d. 2 Jan. 1897 at age 39 yrs. (Houma Ch.: v.3, p.10)
FAZZIO, Vincent (Gaetano & Maria Gratia PERARO) b. 28 May 1898 (Houma Ch.: v.5, p.212)
FEDERINE, Antoine (Andre & Josephine THOMASSIE) m. 16 Dec. 1899 Alice DUFFY (Thib. Ct. Hse.: Mar. v.39, #287)
FEDERINE, Antoine (Andre & Josephine THOMASSEE) m. 18 Dec. 1899 Alice DUFFY (Thib. Ch.: v.14, p.311)
FEDERINI, Antoinette Anita (Joseph & Margueritte BYCHURCH) b. 4 Oct. 1898 (Larose Ch.: v.3, p.29)
FEDERINI, Clement Charles (Joseph & Marguerite BYCHURCH) b. 23 Nov. 1896 (Larose Ch.: v.3, p.1)
FEDERINI, Louie Clotilde (Andre & Josephine TOMASI) b. 3 Dec. 1897 (Thib. Ch.: v.7, p.474)
FELISE, Maria Anna (Guiseppe & Lucia PINTA) b. 23 April 1899 (Raceland Ch.: v.5, p.96)

FELIX, George m. 4 Jan. 1898 Fanchonette JACKSON (Thib. Ct. Hse.: Mar. v.37, #4)

FELIX, Lucinda m. 20 Jan. 1897 William BUTLER (Thib. Ct. Hse.: Mar. v.36, #44)

FELIX, Susanna widow of Wilson KING m. 22 Feb. 1898 Joshua FREEMAN (Thib. Ct. Hse.: Mar. v.37, #112)

FELLOK, Angela d. 29 June 1899 at age 34 yrs. (Houma Ch.: v.3, p.23)

FELLS, Bella Marie (John) d. 27 May 1896 at age 2 yrs. & 6 mths. (Lockport Ch.: v.1, #12)

FELLS, Joseph Paul (Manuel & Mary WATSON) b. 28 Nov. 1896; bt. 10 April 1898 (Chacahoula Ch.: Gibson Ch.: v.2, p.127)

FELLS, Joseph Paul (Manuel & Mary WATSON) b. 28 Nov. 1896 (Chacahoula Ch.: Gibson Records: Mar. Bk., v.1, #43)

FERADES, Fernand m. 15 Dec. 1898 Malvina CALLAIS (Thib. Ct. Hse.: Mar. v.38, #318)

FERAGOOD, Marie Rimer (Cornelius & Laura LEBLANC) b. 5 March 1898 (Thib. Ch.: v.7, p.545)

FERANTELLE, Liborio (Cosimo & Lucia YANNSOT) m. 16 June 1898 Caterina MONDELLO (Thib. Ch.: v.14, p.208)

FERDINAND, Manuel m. 21 Feb. 1898 Ella REED (Thib. Ct. Hse.: Mar. v.37, #110)

FERGUSON, James Walter m. 29 March 1899 Rachel MAGRUDER (Houma Ct. Hse.: Mar. v.31 & 32, #381)

FERIGOUT, Mary Anna (Cornelius & Laura LEBLANC) b. 15 Feb. 1898 (Thib. Ch.: v.7, p.490)

FERIGOUT, Maurice Emile (Emile & Mathilde JOLIBOIS) bt. 7 Feb. 1898 (Thib. Ch.: v.7, p.484)

FERINA, Katharine (Vincenzo & Joseppa POMEGLIA) m. 21 Jan. 1899 Marione MILONI (Thib. Ct. Hse.: Mar. v.38, #14)

FERNANDEZ, Bernard Theophile (Gustave of Assumption Parish & Idea FREDERIC of Assumption Parish) b. 25 Feb. 1898 (Theriot Ch.: v.2, p.21)

FERNANDEZ, Gustave m. 27 July 1896 Ida FREDERICK (Houma Ct. Hse.: Mar. v.29 & 30, #118)

FERNANDEZ, Gustave (Theophile & Virginie JUDICE) m. 10 Aug. 1896 Ida FREDERICK (Theriot Ch.: v.1, p.4)

FERRANTELLE, Liborio (Cosimo & Lucia YAMOT) m. 13 June 1898 Caterina MONDELLA (Thib. Ct. Hse.: Mar. v.38, #186)

FERRANTELLE, Marguerita (Cosimo & Lugia SAMOZA) m. 30 July 1898 Guiseppe CAMPO (Thib. Ct. Hse.: Mar. v.38, #220)

FERRANTELLE, Marguerite (Cosimo & Lugia IANAZA) m. 30 July 1898 Guiseppe CAMPO (Thib. Ch.: v.14, p.212)

FERRARO, Maria (Mark & Maria Chenzer FERRARO) b. 24 Aug. 1899 (Houma Ch.: v.5, p.254)

FEY, Charles Ines (Peter & Cela BARKER) b. 29 July 1896 (Lockport Ch.: v.2, p.333)

FEY, Emile (Joseph & Elizabeth BOURGEOIS) b. 21 April 1897 (Lockport Ch.: v.3-A, #49)

FIELD, Joseph Laubet (Edouard & Mathilde LEBLANC) b. 8 Feb. 1898 (Thib. Ch.: v.7, p.540)

FIELDS (Sometimes: FEILDS, FIELD)
FIELDS, Ada (Deine & Elmire CHAUVIN) m. 13 Feb. 1899 Ovide SEVIN (Montegut Ch.: v.4, p.258)
FIELDS, Ada (Deme & Elmire CHAUVIN) m. 4 Feb. 1899 Ovide SEVIN (Houma Ct. Hse.: Mar. v.30 & 31, #310)
FIELDS, Eugene Sandoz (Marius & Adrienne GUILBAULT) b. 4 Oct. 1899 (Montegut Ch.: v.6, p.94)
FIELDS, Henri Hudson (John & Agnes FORET) b. 6 March 1897 (Raceland Ch.: v.5, p.42)
FIELDS, Henry (Justilien & Catherine PICOU) m. 26 Dec. 1899 Edna SAVOIE (Houma Ct. Hse.: Mar. v.31 & 32, #193)
FIELDS, John m. 19 Jan. 1899 Odelia MELTON (Houma Ct. Hse.: Mar. v.30 & 31, #255)
FIELDS, Joseph Justilien (Justilien & Catherine PICOU) b. 23 June 1899 (Montegut Ch.: v.6, p.90)
FIELDS, Joseph Preston (William & Eglantine LEBLANC) b. 27 Oct. 1897 (Thib. Ch.: v.7, p.471)
FIELDS, Justine m. Ozeme TRAHAN d. 26 Aug. 1896 at age 59 yrs. (Houma Ch.: v.3, p.9)
FIELDS, Loubry Cecile` (Arthur & Josephine ROGER) b. 5 June 1899 (Montegut Ch.: v.6, p.88)
FIELDS, Marie (Demetrius & Elmire CHAUVIN) m. 30 April 1896 Leopold CROCHET (Montegut Ch.: v.4, p.210)
FIELDS, Marie Adele (Justilien & Catherine PICOU) b. 25 Jan. 1897 (Montegut Ch.: v.6, p.49)
FIELDS, Marie Elina (Neidde & Mathilde LEBLANC) b. 28 Aug. 1897 (Thib. Ch.: v.7, p.463)
FIELDS, Marie Emma (Justilien & Catherine PICOU) b. 27 Feb. 1898 (Montegut Ch.: v.6, p.67)
FIELDS, Marie Eugene m. Onesippe ARCEMENT d. 13 Sept. 1899 at age 45 days (Montegut Ch.: v.2, p.29)
FIELDS, Mary m. 4 April 1896 Leopold CROCHET (Houma Ct. Hse.: Mar. v.29 & 30, #29)
FIELDS, Myrthile Joseph (Joseph & Myrthee DAIGLE) b. 24 Aug. 1897 (Larose Ch.: v.3, p.6)
FIELDS, Richard John (John & Agnes FORET) b. 30 Nov. 1898 (Raceland Ch.: v.5, p.83)
FIELDS, Sylvestre Harold (Ellis & Felicia FOURNIER) b. 31 Dec. 1897 (Montegut Ch.: v.6, p.64)
FIELDS, Sylvestre Harold (Ellis & Felicia FOURNIER) d. 13 Feb. 1898 (Montegut Ch.: v.2, p.15)
FIELDS, William (Hudson & Clementine GUITREAU) m. 3 June 1896 Eglantine LEBLANC (Thib. Ch.: v.14, p.90)
FIELDS, Williams (Hudson & Clementine GUITREAU) m. 3 June 1896 Eglantine LEBLANC (Thib. Ct. Hse.: Mar. v.35, #98)
FIGHT, Emile d. 14 Feb. 1899 at age 2 yrs. (Raceland Ch.: v.1, p.23)

FIGHT, Louise m. Adolphe BOUDREAUX d. 20 Jan. 1898 at age 26 yrs. (Thib. Ch.: v.3, p.209)
FIGHT, Rose (Clerville & Eve FOLSE) b. 8 Jan. 1898 (Raceland Ch.: v.5, p.64)
FILER, Judith Eulalie (Clerville & Eve FOLSE) b. 23 March 1896 (Raceland Ch.: v.5, p.22)
FILINICH, Lucie Olivia (Jacomo & Rosalie LEE) b. 23 Feb. 1896 (Larose Ch.: v.2, p.195)
FILSE, Marie Eunice (John & Mira MIRE) b. 3 March 1897 (Chacahoula Ch.: v.4, p.17)
FINLEY, Jefferson (John & Josephine FINLEY) m. 16 Jan. 1899 Lea BERGERON (Houma Ct. Hse.: Mar. v.30 & 31, #242)
FINLEY, Lilly (John & Josephine FINLEY) m. 16 Jan. 1899 Joseph LEBLANC (Houma Ct. Hse.: Mar. v.30 & 31, #236)
FINNIGS, Mary m. 25 March 1898 Ozemie BANKS (Thib. Ct. Hse.: Mar. v.37, #133)
FIRANDELLA, Cosimo (Liboric & Catherina MONTELLA) b. 9 Dec. 1899 (Thib. Ch.: v.7, p.578)
FISHER, Elizabeth m. 16 March 1896 Oscar GOODMAN (Thib. Ct. Hse.: Mar. v.35, #51)
FISHER, Lilly m. 6 April 1899 George JONES (Thib. Ct. Hse.: Mar. v.39, #136)
FITCH, Edouard Davis (Lucien & Suzanne ROBERT) b. 16 Sept. 1898 (Montegut Ch.: v.6, p.81)
FITCH, Joseph Henry (Lucien & Josephine CAILLON) b. 26 Feb. 1897 (Theriot Ch.: v.2, p.5)
FITCH, Joseph Jacques (Francisco & Marie DION) b. 22 Dec. 1897 (Theriot Ch.: v.2, p.22)
FITCH, Louise m. Auguste BERTRAND d. 2 Nov. 1897 at age 77 yrs. (Montegut Ch.: v.2, p.12)
FITCH, Lucien m. 11 April 1896 Josephine SAULET (Houma Ct. Hse.: Mar. v.29 & 30, #34)
FITCH, Lucien (Francois) m. 7 Oct. 1897 Josephine SAULE (Theriot Ch.: v.1-B, p.1)
FITCH, Marie Elnora (Marcel & Genevieve HEBERT) b. 7 Aug. 1897 (Montegut Ch.: v.6, p.59)
FITCH, Victorine m. Napoleon GUIDRY d. 8 Jan. 1899 at age 70 yrs. (Montegut Ch.: v.2, p.23)
FLASH, Emma m. 2 June 1897 Evan J. EVANS (Thib. Ct. Hse.: Mar. v.36, #159)
FLASH, Emma C. m. 2 June 1897 Evan J. EVANS (Thib. Ch.: Epis. Ch.: v.1, p.331)
FLEETWOOD, John Norbert d. 28 May 1898 at age 39 yrs. (Thib. Ch.: v.3, p.215)
FLEMING, Joseph m. 27 Oct. 1898 Emma JOHNSON (Thib. Ct. Hse.: Mar. v.38, #306)
FLETCHER, Ethel m. 9 Feb. 1898 Sam COULON (Thib. Ct. Hse.: Mar. v.37, #95)
FLINICH, Lisa Euphemie (Jacomo & Rosalie LEE) b. 30 Oct. 1898 (Larose Ch.: v.3, p.42)

FLUENCE, Oscar m. 6 March 1897 Ophelia DAVIS (Houma Ct. Hse.: Mar. v.29 & 30, #338)

FLUENCE, Willie m. 25 March 1896 Mary PARKER (Houma Ct. Hse.: Mar. v.29 & 30, #15)

FLUNCE, Charlie m. 1 July 1899 Anna ROBERTSON (Houma Ct. Hse.: Mar. v.31 & 32, #64)

FOLD, Pierre Jacques (Jacques & Henriette TOUPS) b. 16 May 1899 (Thib. Ch.: v.7, p.549)

FOLKES, James A. (Edmond J. & Eliza FIELDS) m. 25 Oct. 1897 Ida BOUDREAUX (Houma Ct. Hse.: Mar. v.29 & 30, #128)

FOLKES, John Edmund (John Edgar & Helena WISE) b. 4 Dec. 1897 (Houma Ch.: Epis. Ch.: v.1, p.116)

FOLSE, Adolphe Adam (Antoine & Isabella FORET) b. 7 July 1896 (Raceland Ch.: v.3, p.24)

FOLSE, Alice d. 25 Dec. 1896 at age 16 yrs. (Raceland Ch.: v.1, p.11)

FOLSE, Alidor d. 19 Feb. 1899 at age 74 yrs. (Raceland Ch.: v.1, p.23)

FOLSE, Antoinette m. 21 Jan. 1897 Joseph FRANCE (Thib. Ct. Hse.: Mar. v.36, #46)

FOLSE, Antoinette (Numa & Melasie BOURGEOIS) m. 8 Feb. 1897 Joseph FRANCE (Raceland Ch.: v.2, p.31)

FOLSE, Benjamin d. 21 July 1895; m.(1) d.Virginie BECNEL Children listed: d.Clairville; Antoine; Sylvestre. m.(2) Rosalie MOLAISON Children listed: Rosela m. d.Oscar LEPINE; John; Drausin; Justine m. Prosper TOUPS. Petition for administration & inventory: 26 March 1896. (Thib. Ct. Hse.: Succ. #1486)

FOLSE, Camille Marcel (Arthur & Veronique LEDET) b. 16 Jan. 1896 (Thib. Ch.: v.7, p.390)

FOLSE, Celina minor, over 18, emancipated by marriage. (Oscar P. & Ophelia FOLSE) m. Leonce TROSCLAIR. Emancipation: 7 March 1898. (Thib. Ct. Hse.: Succ. #1528)

FOLSE, Celina (Oscar & Ophelia TEMPLET) m. 7 July 1897 Leonce TROSCLAIR (Thib. Ct. Hse.: Mar. v.37, #185)

FOLSE, Clothilde d. 29 July 1897 at age 43 yrs. (Raceland Ch.: v.1, p.14)

FOLSE, Emilie Edna (Abel & Cecilia TOUPS) b. 18 May 1898 (Thib. Ch.: v.7, p.498)

FOLSE, Florestine m. 6 Oct. 1897 Felix DESLATTES (Thib. Ct. Hse.: Mar. v.37, #243)

FOLSE, Helene Elda (Homere & Josephine GUEDRY) b. 16 April 1898 (Raceland Ch.: v.5, p.69)

FOLSE, Homere (Antoine & Theolene NICOLAS) m. 31 May 1897 Josephine GUEDRY (Raceland Ch.: v.2, p.40)

FOLSE, Joseph m. 25 April 1899 Notesia WAGESPACK (Thib. Ct. Hse.: Mar. v.39, #152)

FOLSE, Joseph (Octave & Theodorine WALKER) m. 22 April 1899 Notesia WAGESPACK (Raceland Ch.: v.2, p.95)

FOLSE, Joseph Columbus (Homere & Josephine GUEDRY) b. 14 Dec. 1899 (Raceland Ch.: v.5, p.109)

FOLSE, Joseph Numa (Joseph & Emelie LUQUETTE) b. 21 Jan. 1899 (Raceland Ch.: v.5, p.89)
FOLSE, Joseph Uselien (Pierre & Alice AUTIN) b. 12 June 1897 (Raceland Ch.: v.5, p.50)
FOLSE, Joseph Yvonne (Leandre & Adolphine MATERNE) b. 23 March 1898 (Raceland Ch.: v.5, p.68)
FOLSE, Lilian Agathe (Abel & Cecilia TOUPS) b. 5 Feb. 1896 (Raceland Ch.: v.5, p.19)
FOLSE, Marie Adele (Antoine & Iabella FORET) b. 3 Aug. 1898 (Raceland Ch.: v.5, p.75)
FOLSE, Marie Josephine (Joseph & Ernestine BRAUD) b. 20 Feb. 1898 (Raceland Ch.: v.5, p.66)
FOLSE, Marie Philomene (Eugene & Marie BOUVIER) b. 5 Feb. 1897 (Raceland Ch.: v.5, p.40)
FOLSE, Mary m. 7 Jan. 1897 E. E. FRAZIER (Thib. Ct. Hse.: Mar. v.36, #13)
FOLSE, Nelson m. 10 Feb. 1898 Clemence ZERINGUE (Thib. Ct. Hse.: Mar. v.37, #86)
FOLSE, Nelson (Octave & Theodorine WALKER) m. 10 Feb. 1898 Clemence ZERINGUE (Raceland Ch.: v.2, p.67)
FOLSE, Numa Jr., Dr. (Numa, Sr. & Oville TREXILLO) m. 27 April 1898 Marie MORVAN (Thib. Ch.: v.14, p.196)
FOLSE, Octavie m. 17 Jan. 1899 Clement ZERINGUE (Thib. Ct. Hse.: Mar. v.38, #26)
FOLSE, Octavie (Octave & Theodorine WALKER) m. 24 Jan. 1899 Clement ZERINGUE (Raceland Ch.: v.2, p.85)
FOLSE, Omer m. 24 May 1897 Josephine GUIDRY (Thib. Ct. Hse.: Mar. v.36, #146)
FOLSE, Philippe Edwin (William & Azelie BRAUD) b. 29 Feb. 1896 (Raceland Ch.: v.5, p.20)
FOLSE, Pierre m. 13 Aug. 1896 Alice AUTIN (Thib. Ct. Hse.: Mar. v.36, #135)
FOLSE, Pierre (Lovinski & Odilia DANTIN) m. 8 Aug. 1896 Alice AUTIN (Raceland Ch.: v.2, p.20)
FOLSE, Pierre Lovinski (Pierre & Alice AUTIN) b. 11 Jan. 1899 (Raceland Ch.: v.5, p.87)
FOLSE, Rosalie m. 14 Jan. 1897 Simon HARRISON (Thib. Ct. Hse.: Mar. v.36, #29)
FOLSE, Taylor m. 2 Sept. 1897 Ida CHAMPAGNE (Thib. Ct. Hse.: Mar. v.37, #219)
FOLSE, Taylor (Octave & Theodorine WALKER) m. 2 Sept. 1897 Ida CHAMPAGNE (Raceland Ch.: v.2, p.49)
FOLSE, Valerie Corinne (Arthur & Veronique LEDET) b. 19 Feb. 1898 (Thib. Ch.: v.7, p.488)
FOLSE, Villier Jean (Nelson & Clemence ZERINGUE) b. 10 March 1899 (Raceland Ch.: v.5, p.93)
FOLSE, Zoe m. 30 Aug. 1897 Arthur E. HOFFMAN (Thib. Ct. Hse.: Mar. v.37, #225)
FONS, Agnes Adeline (Arthur & Julienne DUET) b. 26 Sept. 1899 (Chackbay Ch.: v.1, p.146)

FONS, John Zimms (Arthur & Julienne DUET) b. 4 Dec. 1897 (Chackbay Ch.: v.1, p.104)

FONSECA (Sometimes: FANSECOT, FONSECOT)

FONSECA, Alidor m. 31 Dec. 1898 Armantine PLAISANCE (Thib. Ct. Hse.: Mar. v.38, #329)

FONSECA, Elisabeth (Jean & Lydia ELLIOT) d. 4 July 1897 at age 4 mths. (Lockport Ch.: v.1, #24)

FONSECA, Joseph d. 5 Feb. 1897 at age 19 yrs. (Lockport Ch.: v.1, #4)

FONSECA, Lucile Lyna (Jean & Lydia ELLIOT) b. 31 Oct. 1899 (Lockport Ch.: v.3-A, #12)

FONSECA, Lucile Lyna (Jean & Lydia ELLIOT) b. 30 Oct. 1899 (Lockport Ch.: v.3, #12)

FONSECA, Olidor (Hippolyte & Meonce DOMINIQUE) m. 20 July 1899 Armantine PLAISANCE (Lockport Ch.: v.2, p.209)

FORD (Sometimes: FORDE)

FORD, Albert (William & -----) m. 17 July 1899 Mary Anne KIRK (Montegut Ch.: v.4, p.267)

FORD, Alexandre Ambroise (Joseph & Aima ROME) b. 18 Feb. 1898 (Thib. Ch.: v.7, p.489)

FORD, Edouard Williams (James & Henriette TOUPS) b. 4 Aug. 1897 (Thib. Ch.: v.7, p.459)

FORD, Eve (Adolphe & Laura DUHE) m. 7 Feb. 1899 Klebert BOUDREAUX (Thib. Ct. Hse.: Mar. v.38, #57)

FORD, Eve (Adolphe & Laura DUHE) m. 7 Feb. 1899 Klebert BOUDREAUX (Thib. Ch.: v.14, p.257)

FORD, Jacques Nelson (Joseph & Emma ROME) b. 21 April 1899 (Thib. Ch.: v.7, p.601)

FORD, Joseph Clarence (Seraphin & Osea HEBERT) b. 19 March 1898 (Thib. Ch.: v.7, p.492)

FORD, Joseph N. (Joseph & Emma ROM) b. 5 Nov. 1896 (Thib. Ch.: v.7, p.424)

FORD, Joseph Patrick (James & Henriette TOUPS) b. 3 March 1896 (Thib. Ch.: v.7, p.394)

FORD, Louis (Hilaire & Ophelia NAQUIN) m. 14 Oct. 1897 Adele BENOIT (Thib. Ct. Hse.: Mar. v.37, #239)

FORD, Louis (Hilaire & Ophelia NAQUIN) m. 14 Oct. 1897 Adele BENOIT (Thib. Ch.: v.14, p.164)

FORD, Luc Junius (Paul & Rebecca ROGER) b. 29 Oct. 1899 (Thib. Ch.: v.8, p.18)

FORD, Victora m. 20 Feb. 1899 Johna COLEMAN, Jr. (Thib. Ct. Hse.: Mar. v.39, #109)

FORD, Victorin d. 28 Jan. 1897 at age 3 mths. (Thib. Ch.: v.3, p.195)

FORD, Victorin Norbert (Joseph & Emma ROM) b. 5 Nov. 1896 (Thib. Ch.: v.7, p.425)

FOREST, Blanche m. 22 April 1896 Julien A. BOURGEOIS (Thib. Ct. Hse.: Mar. v.35, #61)

FORET (Sometimes: FAURET, FOREST)

FORET, Adolphine (Felix & Batistile HOTARD) m. 4 Feb. 1899 Ferjus BRAUX (Lockport Ch.: v.2, p.200)

FORET, Adolphine (Felix & Batistile HOTARD) m. 4 Feb. 1899 Ferjus BRAUX (Thib. Ct. Hse.: Mar. v.38, #71)

FORET, Adoptele d. 16 Dec. 1899 at age 85 yrs. (Raceland Ch.: v.1, p.29)

FORET, Albert m. 22 June 1899 Elecia THERIOT (Thib. Ct. Hse.: Mar. v.39, #182)

FORET, Albert (Alfred & Louise PICHOFF) m. 8 Feb. 1898 Eleonore BOURGEOIS (Thib. Ct. Hse.: Mar. v.37, #45)

FORET, Albert (Alfred & Louise PICHOFF) m. 5 Feb. 1898 Eleonore BOURGEOIS (Lockport Ch.: v.2, p.184)

FORET, Albert (Francois & Hirma OTIN) m. 22 June 1899 Elecia THERIOT (Raceland Ch.: v.2, p.100)

FORET, Albert Joseph (Theodule & Aimee DUPRE) m. 26 Dec. 1899 Cinthia CHAUVIN (Houma Ct. Hse.: Mar. v.31 & 32, #195)

FORET, Alceste m. 22 Jan. 1898 Azema ARCEMENT (Thib. Ct. Hse.: Mar. v.37, #3)

FORET, Alceste (Felicien & Uzeline FORET) m. 22 Jan. 1898 Azema ARCEMENT (Raceland Ch.: v.2, p.58)

FORET, Anne Izelle (Ernest & Marie FORET) b. 3 Oct. 1898 (Raceland Ch.: v.5, p.79)

FORET, Antoine Albert (Alphonse & Laura DUGAS) b. 13 June 1896 (Lockport Ch.: v.2, p.331)

FORET, Antoine E. (Arthur & Bernadette CHAUVIN) b. 22 April 1897 (Lockport Ch.: v.3-A, #48)

FORET, Antoine Eucide (Arthur & Bernadette CHAUVIN) b. 22 April 1897 (Lockport Ch.: v.3, #48)

FORET, Aurelien (Leo & Augustine DANOS) b. 19 Oct. 1898 (Raceland Ch.: v.5, p.80)

FORET, Azema m. 10 May 1898 Odressy ROBICHAUX (Thib. Ct. Hse.: Mar. v.38, #180)

FORET, Azema (Osemee & Eugenie LINGUIN) m. 21 May 1898 Odressie ROBICHAUX (Raceland Ch.: v.2, p.74)

FORET, Bessie Helene (Lee Joseph & Sara BARKER) b. 22 Dec. 1898 (Thib. Ch.: v.7, p.527)

FORET, Blanche (Onesippe & Philomene BARILLAU) m. 22 April 1896 Julien A. BOURGEOIS (Raceland Ch.: v.2, p.15)

FORET, Camile (Joseph & Anna DOUCET) m. 7 July 1897 Olinda LUKE (Houma Ct. Hse.: Mar. v.29 & 30, #52)

FORET, Camilla (d.Joseph & d.Anna DOUCET) m. 1 Feb. 1897 Ernest CHIASSON (Montegut Ch.: v.4, p.217)

FORET, Camilla (Joseph & Anna DOUCET) m. 13 Jan. 1897 Ernest CHIASSON (Houma Ct. Hse.: Mar. v.29 & 30, #236)

FORET, Cecile d. 12 Feb. 1896 at age 5 yrs. (Raceland Ch.: v.1, p.7)

FORET, Celina m. Joseph BOUDREAUX Children listed: Eugenie; Viola; Regina; Bella. Commission for inventory: 2 Aug. 1899. (Thib. Ct. Hse.: Succ. #1584)

FORET, Celina m. Joseph BOUDREAUX d. 11 Oct. 1897 at age 38 yrs. (Lockport Ch.: v.1, #19)
FORET, David Joseph (David & Virginie TOUPS) b. 15 Nov. 1897 (Thib. Ch.: v.7, p.472)
FORET, Dorsena (d.Joseph & d.Anna DOUCY) m. 3 Oct. 1898 Ellis TOUPS (Montegut Ch.: v.4, p.249)
FORET, Dorsena (Joseph & Anna DOUCY) m. 19 Sept. 1898 Ellen TOUPS (Houma Ct. Hse.: Mar. v.30 & 31, #100-C)
FORET, Edgard Rolleur (Beauregard & Angele EUSTIS) b. 9 Aug. 1896 (Lockport Ch.: v.2, p.334)
FORET, Elizabeth Melodia (Robert & Melina PIERCE) b. 25 Jan. 1897 (Lockport Ch.: v.3-A, #13)
FORET, Elizabeth Melodia (Robert & Melina PIERCE) b. 25 Jan. 1897 (Lockport Ch.: v.3, #13)
FORET, Emelia d. 20 Jan. 1895; m. Alexander PERTUIT Children listed: Alexander, Jr., aged 21; Leopold, aged 19 yrs.; Alexanina, 15 yrs.; Amelina, 13 yrs.; Theodule, 17 yrs.; Odilia, 11 yrs.; Idelia, 9 yrs.; Emelia, 7 yrs.; Alcide, 3 yrs. Petition for inventory: 19 Jan. 1897. (Thib. Ct. Hse.: Succ. #1505)
FORET, Ernest m. 2 June 1897 Mary FORET (Thib. Ct. Hse.: Mar. v.36, #158)
FORET, Ernest (Adam & Ordalie FORET) m. 8 June 1897 Marie FORET (Raceland Ch.: v.2, p.41)
FORET, Eugene m. 6 Feb. 1897 Etolaine DIAS (Thib. Ct. Hse.: Mar. v.36, #72)
FORET, Eugene (Ozemee & Eugenie LAGUERRE) m. 8 Feb. 1897 Etolene DIEZ (Raceland Ch.: v.2, p.32)
FORET, Eugene Ernest (Theophile & Sarah BONNETT) b. 17 May 1898 (Montegut Ch.: v.6, p.74)
FORET, Felicia d. 2 Aug. 1899 at age 20 yrs. (Lockport Ch.: v.1, #31)
FORET, Felicien d. 7 Aug. 1898 at age 63 yrs. (Raceland Ch.: v.1, p.19)
FORET, Felix d. 16 Jan. 1896 at age 50 yrs. (Raceland Ch.: v.1, p.7)
FORET, Felix d. 16 Oct. 1897 at age 49 yrs. (Raceland Ch.: v.1, p.15)
FORET, Frank m. 9 Jan. 1899 Lucy PARFAIT (Houma Ct. Hse.: Mar. v.30 & 31, #194)
FORET, Frank (Francois & Marie L. DION) m. 14 Jan. 1899 Lucy PARFAIT (Houma Ch.: v.6-a, p.263)
FORET, Helena m. 7 Dec. 1897 Henri BERDON (Thib. Ct. Hse.: Mar. v.37, #216)
FORET, Helena (Fergus & Emelie AUTIN) b. 1 Oct. 1899 (Raceland Ch.: v.5, p.103)
FORET, Helena (Richard & Florence BARILLEAUX) m. 7 Dec. 1897 Henri BERDOU (Raceland Ch.: v.2, p.55)
FORET, Hyman (Ozemee & Alexina LEBOEUF) d. 7 Dec. 1897 at age 1 yr. & 3 mths. (Montegut Ch.: v.2, p.13)

FORET, Jean Baptiste (d.Francois & Marie Eulasie DION) m. 21 Feb. 1898 Celestine THIBODAUX (Montegut Ch.: v.4, p.237)
FORET, Jean Baptiste (Francois & Marie Eulazie DION) m. 10 Feb. 1898 Celestine THIBODAUX (Houma Ct. Hse.: Mar. v.30 & 31, #289)
FORET, Jean Baptiste Emile (Lusilien & Elisabeth FOLSE) b. 13 Dec. 1896 (Raceland Ch.: v.5, p.37)
FORET, Jean Helles (Thomas & Emelia TOUPS) b. 15 Feb. 1897 (Lockport Ch.: v.3, #18)
FORET, Jean Helles (Thomas & Emilia TOUPS) b. 15 Feb. 1897 (Lockport Ch.: v.3-A, #18)
FORET, Joseph m. 30 Sept. 1897 Lucile GUEDRY (Thib. Ct. Hse.: Mar. v.37, #235)
FORET, Joseph (Deterville & Louisa FALGOU) m. 31 Sept. 1897 Lucille GUEDRY (Raceland Ch.: v.2, p.51)
FORET, Joseph (Placide & Ophelia BABIN) b. 4 Dec. 1896 (Raceland Ch.: v.5, p.36)
FORET, Joseph Easton (Paul & Celestine THIBODAUX) b. 30 Nov. 1899 (Montegut Ch.: v.6, p.98)
FORET, Joseph Ignace (Georges & Emma MARTIN) b. 30 July 1898 (Raceland Ch.: v.5, p.75)
FORET, Joseph Simon (Oseme & Georgia LEBOEUF) b. 26 Sept. 1896 (Houma Ch.: v.5, p.159)
FORET, Joseph Zephirin (Pierre & Elda THERIOT) b. 13 Nov. 1897 (Raceland Ch.: v.5, p.57)
FORET, Lilian Philomene (Pierre Lesterville & Octavie MARTIN) b.14 Sept. 1896 (Raceland Ch.: v.5, p.30)
FORET, Livie (Prosper & Celine CANCIENNE) m. 3 Feb. 1897 Henry BERGERON (Thib. Ct. Hse.: Mar. v.36, #63)
FORET, Livie (Prosper & Celine CAUESIENNE) m. 3 Feb. 1897 Henry BERGERON (Thib. Ch.: v.14, p.119)
FORET, Louise (Nicles) d. 11 Dec. 1896 at age 18 yrs. (Lockport Ch.: v.1, #25)
FORET, Lucy (Justilien & Eliska BRAUD) Emancipation: 9 June 1899. (Thib. Ct. Hse.: Succ. #1579)
FORET, Lusilien d. 3 Jan. 1896 at age 8 days (Raceland Ch.: v.1, p.7)
FORET, Marcelline m. 14 Feb. 1898 Oscar GRABERT (Thib. Ct. Hse.: Mar. v.37, #100)
FORET, Marcelline (Justilien & Celina BLANCHARD) m. 14 Feb. 1898 Oscar GRABERT (Raceland Ch.: v.2, p.69)
FORET, Maria (Mark & Louise PARFAIT) b. 19 May 1898 (Houma Ch.: v.5, p.228)
FORET, Marie m. 2 June 1897 Ernest FORET (Thib. Ct. Hse.: Mar. v.36, #158)
FORET, Marie (Felicien & Justine BOURGEOIS) m. 8 June 1897 Ernest FORET (Raceland Ch.: v.2, p.41)
FORET, Marie Agnes (Ovile & Victorine ARCEMENT) b. 7 Sept. 1896 (Raceland Ch.: v.5, p.30)

FORET, Marie Alice (Paul & Arthemise DION) b. 3 April 1898 (Theriot Ch.: v.2, p.24)

FORET, Marie Aline (Arthur & Bernadette CHAUVIN) b. 27 April 1898 (Thib. Ch.: v.7, p.546)

FORET, Marie Anne (Ozemee & Alexina LEBOEUF) b. 15 Feb. 1898 (Montegut Ch.: v.6, p.65)

FORET, Marie Eugenie (Pierre & Elda THERIOT) b. 14 Oct. 1898 (Raceland Ch.: v.5, p.80)

FORET, Marie Idolia (Georges & Emma MARTIN) b. 15 March 1896 (Raceland Ch.: v.5, p.21)

FORET, Marie Laura (Theodule & Aimee DUPRE) b. 4 March 1898 (Montegut Ch.: v.6, p.68)

FORET, Marie Loetitia (Ferjus & Emelie AUTIN) b. 10 July 1897 (Raceland Ch.: v.5, p.52)

FORET, Marie Marguerite d. 23 Feb. 1899 at age 70 yrs. (Raceland Ch.: v.1, p.24)

FORET, Marie Nicia (Theophile & Sarah BONA----) b. 15 May 1896 (Montegut Ch.: v.6, p.41)

FORET, Marie Odilia (Pierre & Octavie MARTIN) b. 30 Oct. 1898 (Raceland Ch.: v.5, p.82)

FORET, Marie Severine m. Hamilton AYIO d. 12 Dec. 1897 at age 48 yrs. & 9 mths. (Lockport Ch.: v.1, #35)

FORET, Marie Zoe (Felicien & Celine FORET) b. 8 June 1898 (Raceland Ch.: v.5, p.72)

FORET, Mary Laura (Theodule & Aimee DUPRE) d. 20 May 1899 at age 1 yr. & 5 mths. (Montegut Ch.: v.2, p.25)

FORET, Meloe m. 16 Oct. 1897 Alceste AUTIN (Thib. Ct. Hse.: Mar. v.37, #242)

FORET, Michel Anatole (Augustin & Alice ARCEMENT) b. 28 Sept. 1897 (Raceland Ch.: v.5, p.55)

FORET, Moloe (Osemee & Eugenie LAGUERRE) m. 16 Oct. 1897 Alceste AUTIN (Raceland Ch.: v.2, p.52)

FORET, Noe Andre (Alceste & Azema ARCEMENT) b. 10 Nov. 1899 (Raceland Ch.: v.5, p.107)

FORET, Olesime b. 28 Dec. 1879. (d.Deterville) Petition & judgment: 4 March 1899. (Thib. Ct. Hse.: Succ. #1567)

FORET, Osemee Mercile (Eugene & Theolene DIEZ) b. 15 May 1898 (Raceland Ch.: v.5, p.71)

FORET, Philippe (Leo & Justine DANOS) b. 1 Sept. 1896 (Raceland Ch.: v.5, p.29)

FORET, Pierre m. 14 April 1897 Elda THERIOT (Thib. Ct. Hse.: Mar. v.36, #114)

FORET, Pierre (Felix & Marie Theoline AUTIN) m. 29 Aprl 1897 Elda THERIOT (Raceland Ch.: v.2, p.38)

FORET, Richard d. 24 May 1896 at age 50 yrs. (Lockport Ch.: v.1, #11)

FORET, Richard m. Florence BARRILLEAUX Children listed: Emile; Wiltz; Therese; Richard; Ida; Jeannette. Letters of tutrixship: 2 June 1898. (Thib. Ct. Hse.: Succ. #1492)

FORET, Robert d. 31 May 1897 at age 58 yrs. (Houma Ch.: v.3, p.13)
FORET, Telesse Joseph (Marcellin & Emelie FOLSE) b. 10 Dec. 1896 (Raceland Ch.: v.5, p.36)
FORET, Victorine m. 14 Jan. 1899 Joseph VERDAM (Houma Ch.: v.6-a, p.263)
FORET, Victorine (Francois & Melasie DION) m. 24 Jan. 1898 Joseph VERDIN (Houma Ct. Hse.: Mar. v.30 & 31, #247)
FORTIER, Juanita m. 19 March 1898 Frank MARSHALL (Thib. Ct. Hse.: Mar. v.37, #127)
FORTIER, Mary d. 30 May 1897 at age 20 yrs. (Lockport Ch.: v.1, #10)
FORTUNE, Jean Louis d. 30 April 1897 Petition for administration & inventory: 30 April 1897. (Thib. Ct. Hse.: Succ. #1513)
FOURNIER, Augustine Nora (Georges & Emelie CROCHET) b. 18 Feb. 1897 (Montegut Ch.: v.6, p.51)
FOURNIER, Elvire (Marcellin & Euphrosine PERTUIS) m. 31 Dec. 1898 Lee PIERCE (Thib. Ct. Hse.: Mar. v.38, #328)
FOURNIER, Elvire (Marcellin & Euphrosine PERTUIT) m. 31 Dec. 1898 Lee PIERCE (Lockport Ch.: v.2, p.197)
FOURNIER, Henri Wilfred (Georges & Emilie CROCHET) d. 24 April 1899 at age 1 mth. & 3 wks. (Montegut Ch.: v.2, p.25)
FOURNIER, Henri Wilfrid (Georges & Emelie CROCHET) b. 4 March 1899 (Montegut Ch.: v.6, p.84)
FRAGER, Marguerite d. 31 Jan. 1897 at age 40 yrs. (Raceland Ch.: v.1, p.13)
FRANCE, Joseph m. 21 Jan. 1897 Antoinette FOLSE (Thib. Ct. Hse.: Mar. v.36, #46)
FRANCE, Joseph (Anatole &Emelie MOUTET) m. 8 Feb. 1897 Antoinette FOLSE (Raceland Ch.: v.2, p.31)
FRANCIS, Cora m. 2 Aug. 1897 Timothy BROWN (Houma Ct. Hse.: Mar. v.29 & 30, #78)
FRANCIS, Henry m. 14 April 1898 Lizzie BARRET (Thib. Ct. Hse.: Mar. v.38, #153)
FRANCIS, Joseph Linesse (Pierre & Eva VERDIN) b. 25 Oct. 1898 (Theriot Ch.: v.2, p.40)
FRANCIS, Lizzie m. 5 June 1897 William REED (Houma Ct. Hse.: Mar. v.29 & 30, #3)
FRANCIS, Marguerite (Raymond & Rosalie BILLIOT) m. 19 Jan. 1899 Renade THIBODAUX (Houma Ct. Hse.: Mar. v.30 & 31, #261)
FRANCIS, Marie Louise (John & Elmire VERRET) b. 7 May 1898 (Theriot Ch.: v.2, p.38)
FRANCIS, Pierre (Raymond & Rosalie BILLIOT) m. 31 July 1897 Eva VERDIN (Houma Ct. Hse.: Mar. v.29 & 30, #72)
FRANCISCO, Jeff D. m. 25 May 1898 Joycie SPARKS (Houma Ct. Hse.: Mar. v.30 & 31, #451)
FRANCOIS, Noemie Fabiola (Andre & Hermina CHAUVIN) b. 27 June 1898 (Houma Ch.: v.5, p.217)
FRANCOISE, Juanita (Joseph & Alice DORVEY) b. 10 March 1898 (Houma Ch.: Epis. Ch.: v.1, p.116)

FRANK, James m. 14 April 1897 Sedonia ODUM (Thib. Ct. Hse.: Mar. v.36, #115)

FRANK, Leonie m. 27 Dec. 1899 Robert BENSON (Thib. Ct. Hse.: Mar. v.39, #300)

FRANKLIN, Bill m. 7 April 1898 Emma McGEE (Houma Ct. Hse.: Mar. v.30 & 31, #381)

FRAZIER, Bessie Gertrude (Thomas & Anne FRAZIER) b. 23 Nov. 1899 (Thib. Ch.: v.7, p.579)

FRAZIER, E. E. m. 7 Jan. 1897 Mary FOLSE (Thib. Ct. Hse.: Mar. v.36, #13)

FRAZIER, Emile (Edmond & Henriette DANTIN) b. 17 Sept. 1897 (Chacahoula Ch.: Gibson Ch.: Mar. Bk., v.1, #20)

FRAZIER, Thomas (Thomas & Cora NICHOLS) m. 3 June 1897 Annie JOHNSON (Thib. Ch.: v.14, p.146)

FRAZIER, Thomas (Thomas & Cora NICHOLS) m. 3 June 1897 Annie JOHNS (Thib. Ct. Hse.: Mar. v.36, #155)

FREDERICK (Sometimes: FREDERIC, FREDERIQUE)

FREDERICK, Adam m. 13 Feb. 1897 Eva LOVELL (Houma Ct. Hse.: Mar. v.29 & 30, #309)

FREDERICK, Adam (Charles & Magdeleine BILLIOT) m. 25 Feb. 1897 Eva LOVELL (Theriot Ch.: v.1, p.9)

FREDERICK, Chester (Agite & Louise FREDERIC) b. 23 Aug. 1897; bt. 10 April 1898 (Chacahoula Ch.: Gibson Ch.: v.2, p.120)

FREDERICK, Chester (Ayite & Louise FREDERIC) b. 23 Aug. 1897 (Chacahoula Ch.: Gibson Ch.: Mar. Bk., v.1, #26)

FREDERICK, Eve (Charles & Madelene BILLIOT) m. 11 Dec. 1899 Mark LOVELL (Theriot Ch.: v.1-B, p.7)

FREDERICK, Eve (Charles & Madeline BILLIOT) m. 2 Dec. 1899 Mack LOVELL (Houma Ct. Hse.: Mar. v.31 & 32, #170)

FREDERICK, Ida m. 27 July 1896 Gustave FERNANDEZ (Houma Ct. Hse.: Mar. v.29 & 30, #118)

FREDERICK, Ida (Charles & Madeleine BILLIOT) m. 10 Aug. 1896 Gustave FERNANDEZ (Theriot Ch.: v.1, p.4)

FREDERICK, Joseph Fernand (Adolphe & Eva LOVEL) b. 14 Nov. 1899 (Theriot Ch.: v.2, p.59)

FREDERICK, Lucie Eve (Adam & Eva LOBELL) b. 13 Dec. 1897 (Theriot Ch.: v.2, p.14)

FREDERICK, Norbert d. 11 July 1896 at age 19 yrs., 5 mths. (Theriot Ch.: v.1, p.101)

FREDERICK, Norbert d. 12 July 1896 at age 19 yrs. (Theriot Ch.: Mar. Bk., v.1, #3)

FREEMAN, Joseph Edville (Georges & Celina GUIDRY) b. 27 May 1897 (Montegut Ch.: v.6, p.76)

FREEMAN, Joshua m. 22 Feb. 1898 Susanna FELIX, widow of Wilson KING (Thib. Ct. Hse.: Mar. v.37, #112)

FREEMAN, Nancy m. 11 Aug. 1898 Silas ANDERSON (Thib. Ct. Hse.: Mar. v.38, #245)

FREEMAN, Rosa (Georges & Celina GUIDRY) m. 16 April 1898 George RHODES (Montegut Ch.: v.4, p.241)

FREEMAN, William d. 16 Feb. 1897 at age 20 yrs. (Thib. Ch.: v.3, p.197)
FREEMAN, Willie (Brooks & Suzanne ---) m. 11 Feb. 1897 Cecilia PELETIER (Thib. Ct. Hse.: Mar. v.36, #68)
FREEMAN, Willie (Brooks & Suzanne) m. 11 Feb. 1897 Cecilia PELLETIER (Thib. Ch.: v.14, p.123)
FREMIN, Joseph (Ernest & Tarzile BREAUX) m. 6 June 1898 Elfrida CHIASSON (Theriot Ch.: v.1-B, p.4)
FREMIN, Joseph (Ernest & Terzile BREAUX) m. 19 May 1898 Elfrida CHIASSON (Houma Ct. Hse.: Mar. v.30 & 31, #446)
FREMIN, Laurence Alexandre (Alexandre & Marie BREAUX) b. 28 Dec. 1899 (Thib. Ch.: v.7, p.581)
FREMIN, Lezima m.20 Jan. 1896 Albert GROS (Thib. Ct. Hse.: Mar. v.35, #30)
FREMIN, Orville of Lafourche Parish (Lester & Victorine BOUDREAU) m. 23 April 1898 Seraphine ELIE (Larose Ch.: v.3, p.8)
FREMIN, Orville (Lester & Victorine BOUDREAU) m. 23 April 1898 Seraphine ELIE or LEE (Larose Ch.: v.4, p.11)
FREMIN, Orville (Lester & Victorine BOUDREAU) m. 23 April 1898 Seraphine ELIE (Thib. Ct. Hse.: Mar. v.37, #150)
FREMIN, Rosa (George & Celina GUIDRY) m. 19 March 1898 George RHODES (Houma Ct. Hse.: Mar. v.30 & 31, #346)
FREMIN, Selima m. 1 April 1899 Sabin LANDRY (Thib. Ct. Hse.: Mar. v.39, #127)
FREMIN, Sophie Edna (Alexandre & Marie BRAUD) b. 1 Nov. 1896 (Thib. Ch.: v.7, p.426)
FREN, Victoria m. 4 Nov. 1899 Xavier SHERMAN (Thib. Ct. Hse.: Mar. v.39, #258)
FREY, Emile (Joseph & Elizabeth BOURGEOIS) b. 21 April 1897 (Lockport Ch.: v.3, #49)
FROMENTHAL, Mathilde Narcissia (Louis & Mary SIMMONS) b. 9 Jan. 1898 (Chacahoula Ch.: Gibson Ch.: v.2, p.120)
FROSSIER, Emile Francis (Edmond & Henriette DANTON) b. 17 Sept. 1897; bt. 14 March 1898 (Chacahoula Ch.: Gibson Ch.: v.2, p.118)
FROST, Anrie Lilian (Richmond & Esther AUBERT) b. 10 Nov. 1897 (Thib. Ch.: Epis. Ch.: v.1, p.42)
FROST, Henri d. 22 Dec. 1899 at age 21 yrs. (Thib. Ch.: v.3, p.247)
FROST, John d. 15 - 23 March 1897 at age 21 yrs. (Thib. Ch.: v.3, p.198)
FRY, Rebecca m. 9 Feb. 1899 William OWENS (Thib. Ct. Hse.: Mar. v.38, #99)
FUNK, Eugene (John & Marie HUNT) b. 7 Jan. 1898 (Thib. Ch.: v.7, p.485)
FURBIN, Louisa m. 14 Jan. 1897 Nathan DYER (Thib. Ct. Hse.: Mar. v.36, #33)
FURLONG, George Dewey (James P. & Mary Agnes POCHE) b. 6 May 1898 (Chacahoula Ch.: Gibson Records: Mar. Bk., v.1, #47)

FURLONG, George Dewey (James P. & Mary Agnes POCHE) b. 6 May 1898 (Chacahoula Ch.: Gibson Ch.: v.2, p.128)
FUSANDO, Carme Varaco m. 13 May 1899 Caterina VIVONA (Houma Ct. Hse.: Mar. v.31 & 32, #4)

"G"

GABBIO, Salvatore (Calogers & Maxiainne SOIANNE) m. 27 Feb. 1897 Benna GEMORA (Houma Ch.: v.6-a, p.194)
GABRIEL, Celeste Dereber (Philipp & Maggie CROZIER) b. 6 June 1899 (Thib. Ch.: v.7, p.609)
GABRIEL, Lou m. 24 June 1898 Willie THOMAS (Thib. Ct. Hse.: Mar. v.38, #211)
GABRIEL, Philippe (Auguste & Celeste GILES) m. 10 July 1899 Maggie CROSIER (Thib. Ch.: v.14, p.288)
GAGE, John m. 8 March 1897 Martha A. WILLIAMS (Thib. Ct. Hse.: Mar. v.36, #96)
GAGLIANELLO, Emmanuel (Emmanuel & Gioseppina RUSSO) b. 26 Dec. 1897 (Chacahoula Ch.: Gibson Ch.: Mar. Bk., v.1, #11)
GAGLIANELLO, Emmanuel (Emmanuel & Josephine RUSSO) b. 26 Dec. 1897; bt. 19 Feb. 1898 (Chacahoula Ch.: Gibson Ch.: v.2, p.117)

GAGNE (Sometimes: GOGNE)
GAGNE, H. Mr. d. 25 Oct. 1899 (Houma Ch.: v.3, p.25)
GAGNE, Henry Sidney d. 24 Oct. 1899; m. Mary Alice NAQUIN Child listed: Nolan Frank, aged 5. Petition for tutorship: 17 Nov. 1899. (Houma Ct. Hse.: Succ. #928)
GAGNE, Sophy A. m. 27 April 1897 David F. GRAY (Houma Ct. Hse.: Mar. v.29 & 30, #394)

GAGNOUX (Sometimes: GAGNAUX, GAGNEAUX)
GAGNOUX, Emile Robert (Wash & Selasie HEBERT) b. 7 June 1899 (Chacahoula Ch.: v.4, p.27)

GAIDRY (See perhaps: GUIDRY)
GAIDRY, Harold Langdon (Wilson Jos. & Clara Catherine SLATTER) b.27 May 1898 (Houma Ch.: Epis. Ch.: v.1, p.120)
GAIDRY, Lowell R. (Adolphe & Agale CADIERE) m. 31 July 1896 Bernice Daisy Pearl HANAGRIFF (Houma Ct. Hse.: Mar. v.29 & 30, #119)
GAIENNE, Louis Raphael (Florestan & Alice FARENDE) m. 22 Jan. 1896 Juanita ALBERTI, widow of Pierre LORIO (Thib. Ct. Hse.: Mar. v.35, #26)
GAIENNIE, Cecile Alex (Raphael & Joanna ALBERT) b. 30 May 1897 (Thib. Ch.: v.7, p.501)
GAIENNIE, Louis Raphael (Florestan & Alice FAZENDE) m. 22 Jan. 1896 Juanita ALBERT (Thib. Ch.: v.14, p.68)
GAIENNIE, Marie Lucile (FLorestan & Jeanne CURIEZ) b. 8 May 1896 (Thib. Ch.: v.7, p.404)
GAITA, Antonina (Paola & Vincenza NAVARRA) b. 22 March 1899 (Thib. Ch.: v.7, p.598)
GAITANO, Saleme m. 26 March 1898 Maria ZABBIO (Houma Ct. Hse.: Mar. v.30 & 31, #357)

GALAIS (Sometimes: GALLEE)

GALAIS, Roselia (Oscar & Eveline DUPRE) m. 24 Jan. 1898 Octave CHIASSON (Houma Ct. Hse.: Mar. v.30 & 31, #245)

GALIANO (Sometimes: GALLIANO)

GALIANO, Antoine m. 14 July 1896 Myrthe GUIDRY (Thib. Ct. Hse.: Mar. v.36, #124)

GALIANO, Antoinette 15 yrs. old (Ernest & Honriete GUEDRY) m. 11 July 1896 Etienne ROUX, 26 yrs. old (Thib. Ct. Hse.: Mar. v.36, #122)

GALIANO, Appollina Melodia (Andre & Marie CHOUESSE) b. 9 Feb. 1897 (Raceland Ch.: v.5, p.42)

GALIANO, Carla (Joseph & Carla PALAZA) b. 5 Sept. 1898 (Thib. Ch.: v.7, p.566)

GALIANO, Julie m. 15 July 1898 Taylor GALLIANO (Thib. Ct. Hse.: Mar. v.38, #226)

GALIANO, Leonie Edissie (Andre & Eve CHOUESTRE) b. 22 April 1898 (Thib. Ch.: v.7, p.545)

GALIANO, Raphael m. 27 April 1899 Louisa ROUSSE (Thib. Ct. Hse.: Mar. v.39, #158)

GALIANO, Sylvain m. 14 June 1898 Emilia BERNARD (Thib. Ct. Hse.: Mar. v.38, #207)

GALIANO, Taylor m. 15 July 1898 Julie GALLIANO (Thib. Ct. Hse.: Mar. v.38, #226)

GALJOUR, Angele of Lafourche Parish (Andre & Josephine PIERCE) m. 21 July 1898 Jackson PETIT, of Lafourche Parish (Larose Ch.: v.3, p.10)

GALJOUR, Angele (Andre & Josephine PIERCE) m. 21 July 1898 Jackson PETIT (Thib. Ct. Hse.: Mar. v.38, #230)

GALJOUR, Angele (Andre & Josephine PIERCE) m. 21 July 1898 Jackson PETIT (Larose Ch.: v.4, p.23)

GALJOUR, Camile Gaston (Joseph & Emilia ADAM) b. 7 Aug. 1896 (Larose Ch.: v.2, p.182)

GALJOUR, Eleonore m. 14 Feb. 1899 Felix PARA (Thib. Ct. Hse.: Mar. v.39, #107)

GALJOUR, Eleonore (Andre & Josephine PIERCE) m. 18 Feb. 1899 Felix PARRA (Larose Ch.: v.4, p.39)

GALJOUR, Eleonore (Andre & Josephine PIERCE) m. 18 Feb. 1899 Felix PARRA (Larose Ch.: v.3, p.11)

GALJOUR, Jean Jackson (Andre & Josephine PIERCE) b. 27 Feb. 1896 (Larose Ch.: v.2, p.188)

GALJOUR, Jeanne Antoinette (Jean & Blanche LEFORT) b. 13 March 1898 (Larose Ch.: v.3, p.18)

GALJOUR, Jeanne Etiennette (Oscar & Pauline CRETINI) b. 27 Dec. 1897 (Larose Ch.: v.3, p.15)

GALJOUR, Julie m. 25 April 1896 Felicien GUIDROZ (Lockport Ch.: v.4, p.122)

GALJOUR, Julie m. 25 April 1896 Felicien GUIDROZ (Larose Ch.: v.3, p.3)

GALJOUR, Julie m. 25 April 1896 Felicien GUIDROZ (Thib. Ct Hse.: Mar. v.35, #78)

GALJOUR, Luc Francois (Andre & Josephine PIERCE) b. 29 Jan. 1898 (Larose Ch.: v.3, p.17)
GALLADO, Sam Joseph (Vincent & Cecilia BOURG) b. 11 March 1897; bt. 28 May 1898 (Chacahoula Ch.: Gibson Ch.: v.2, p.128)
GALLADO, Samee Joseph (Vincent & Cecilia BOURG) b. 11 March 1897 (Chacahoula Ch.: Gibson Ch.: Mar. Bk., v.1, #44)

GALLEE (See: GALAIS)

GALLET, Roselia (Oscar & Eveline DUPRE) m. 21 Feb. 1898 Octave CHIASSON (Montegut Ch.: v.4, p.237)
GALLIANO, ----- m. James BOULANGER d. 6 Aug. 1898 (Larose Ch.: v.1, p.44)
GAMBARAL, Marie Marguerite (Eugene & Elisabeth AUTIN) b. 20 Nov. 1897 (Larose Ch.: v.3, p.29)
GAROFALE, Horazia (Salvatore & Angela MAGALUSA) b. 17 Aug. 1898 (Thib. Ch.: v.7, p.512)
GAROFERO, Ignazio (Salvatore & Angelie MACALUZZO) b. 30 Oct. 1899 (Thib. Ch.: v.8, p.16)
GARRET, Birdie m. 23 Feb. 1898 Andrew THOMAS (Houma Ct. Hse.: Mar. v.30 & 31, #309-A)
GARRIBOTTE, Antoinette (Antoine & Mary WHITE) m. 26 July 1898 Onesippe SEVIN (Houma Ct. Hse.: Mar. v.30 & 31, #67)
GARIBOTTE, Antoinette (Antoine & Mary WHITE) m. 16 Aug. 1898 Onesippe SEVIN (Montegut Ch.: v.4, p.248)
GASCON, Joseph Nickles (Valery & Josephine HEBERT) b. 18 Jan. 1898 (Montegut Ch.: v.6, p.67)

GASPARD (Sometimes: GASPAR)
GASPARD, Clotile (Nelson & Marie SMITH) m. 31 Jan. 1899 Baptiste BLANCHARD (Houma Ct. Hse.: Mar. v.30 & 31, #294)
GASPARD, Ernest d. 20 Jan. 1897 at age 40 yrs. (Larose Ch.: v.1, p.39)
GASPARD, Genevieve Theresa (Augustin & Roselia VIZIER) b. 4 Jan. 1897 (Larose Ch.: v.3, p.12)
GASPARD, Oscar Joachim (Ernest & Marie Louise CHABERT) b. 17 Aug. 1896 (Larose Ch.: v.2, p.186)
GASPARD, Prosper d. 11 Dec. 1898 at age 95 yrs. (Thib. Ch.: v.3, p.223)
GASTON, Anatole (d.Jean Baptiste & d.Azema BELANGER) m. 2 June 1897 Emma ROBICHAUX (Montegut Ch.: v.4, p.222)
GASTON, Anatole (Jean Baptiste & Azema BELANGER) m. 4 May 1897 Emma ROBICHAUX (Houma Ct. Hse.: Mar. v.29 & 30, #399)
GASTON, Jean Israel (Anatole & Emma ROBICHAUX) b. 13 March 1898 (Montegut Ch.: v.6, p.68)
GASTON, William (Jean Baptiste & Eveline BERGERON) b. 1 May 1896 (Houma Ch.: v.5, p.153)
GATERS, Henry m. 22 Aug. 1898 Mary WALKER (Thib. Ct. Hse.: Mar. v.38, #260)

GATES, Sarah m. 12 May 1896 James VERGEN (Houma Ct. Hse.: Mar. v.29 & 30, #62)
GATEWOOD, Carrie S. (Frank U. & Cornelia RABY) m. 3 Feb. 1897 Frank D. PENDAS (Houma Ct. Hse.: Mar. v.29 & 30, #278)
GATTEN, Dennis m. 27 Nov. 1897 Mary Jane TOUSSAINT (Thib. Ct. Hse.: Mar. v.37, #258)

GAUBERT (Sometimes: GAUBER, GOBERT)
GAUBERT, Agnes Valerie (Justilien & Josephine LEVRON) b. 24 Dec. 1897 (Thib. Ch.: v.7, p.477)
GAUBERT, Anne Marie (Theophile & Augusta BRAUD) b. 30 Nov. 1899 (Thib. Ch.: v.8, p.19)
GAUBERT, Auguste (Arsene & Liza BRAUD) m. 13 Jan. 1896 Eveline ORDOGNE (Thib. Ct. Hse.: Mar. v.35, #196)
GAUBERT, Auguste (Arsene & Liza BRAUD) m. 13 Jan. 1896 Eveline ORDOGNE (Chackbay Ch.: v.1, p.25)
GAUBERT, Christophe Maurice (Leon & Eugenie BERGERON) b. 19 Nov. 1896 (Thib. Ch.: v.7, p.473)
GAUBERT, Emeline (Emile & Ayladie GUILLOT) m. 15 Feb. 1897 Joseph RICHARD (Thib. Ct. Hse.: Mar. v.36, #75)
GAUBERT, Emeline (Emile & Sylvaide GUILLOT) m. 15 Feb. 1897 Joseph RICHARD (Thib. Ch.: v.14, p.125)
GAUBERT, Joseph (Auguste & Helena PANVELLE) m. 13 Nov. 1899 Aimee ORDOGNE (Chackbay Ch.: v.1, p.76)
GAUBERT, Joseph Auguste (Auguste & Eveline ORDOGNE) b. 27 April 1899 (Chackbay Ch.: v.1, p.135)
GAUBERT, Joseph Harris (Joseph & Angelie GUILLOT) b. 5 June 1899 (Thib. Ch.: v.7, p.605)
GAUBERT, Lea (Augustin & Augustine TOUPS) b. 4 March 1896 (Thib. Ch.: v.7, p.394)
GAUBERT, Marie Elisa (Auguste & Eveline ORDOGNE) b. 10 Oct. 1897 (Chackbay Ch.: v.1, p.98)
GAUBERT, Marie Meandre (Theophile & Augusta BREAUX) b. 17 March 1899 (Thib. Ch.: v.7, p.543)
GAUBERT, Oleus (Ernest & Bertine BARRAS) m. 20 June 1899 Celeste LENAIN (Thib. Ct. Hse.: Mar. v.39, #183)
GAUBERT, Oleus (Ernest & Bertine BARRAS) m. 20 June 1899 Celeste LENAIN (Thib. Ch.: v.14, p.286)
GAUBERT, Pierre Odon (Augustin & Augustine TOUPS) b. 29 April 1898 (Thib. Ch.: v.7, p.546)
GAUBERT, Theophile (Emile & Agladee GUILLOTE) m. 16 Feb. 1898 Augusta BREAUX (Thib. Ch.: v.14, p.191)
GAUBERT, Theophile (Emile & Agladie GUILLOTE) m. 16 Feb. 1898 Augusta BREAUX (Thib. Ct. Hse.: Mar. v.37, #81)

GAUDE (Sometimes: GAUDET)
GAUDE, Agathe (Ferdinand & Mathilde GAUDET) m. 12 Feb. 1898 Armand ROBICHAUX (Raceland Ch.: v.2, p.68)
GAUDE, Alceste (Alphonse & Leontine AUCOIN) m. 5 Sept. 1898 Etiennette LEBLANC (Thib. Ct. Hse.: Mar. v.38, #262)

GAUDE, Alceste (Alphonse & Leontine AUCOIN) m. 5 Sept. 1898 Etiennette LEBLANC (Lockport Ch.: v.2, p.194)

GAUDE, Alice (Leon & Marie Louisa GAUDE) m. 6 Nov. 1899 Arthur TOUPS (Thib. Ct. Hse.: Mar. v.39, #257)

GAUDE, Alice (Leon & Marie Louisa GAUDE) m. 6 Nov. 1899 Arthur TOUPS (Thib. Ch.: v.14, p.307)

GAUDE, Celeste m. 31 May 1899 Jules PLAISANCE (Thib. Ct. Hse.: Mar. v.39, #173)

GAUDE, Celeste (Joseph & Justine LASEIGNE) m. 24 June 1899 Jules PLAISANCE (Larose Ch.: v.4, p.86)

GAUDE, Celeste (Joseph & Justine LASSEIGNE) m. 24 June 1899 Jules PLAISANCE (Larose Ch.: v.3, p.12)

GAUDE, Charles d. 20 Dec. 1896 at age 78 yrs. (Thib. Ch.: v.3, p.192)

GAUDE, Charles Arthur (Louis & Clemance FALGOUT) m. 12 Sept. 1899 Mrs. Marie Oceana DANTIN (Thib. Ch.: v.14, p.293)

GAUDE, Charles Arthur (Louis & Clemence FALGOUT) m. 12 Sept. 1899 Marie Oceana DANTIN (Thib. Ct. Hse.: Mar. v.39, #227)

GAUDE, Charles Dr. d. 19 Dec. 1896; m. Emelie FALGOUT Children listed: Louisa m. L. F. GAUDET; Charles; Jules; Marie m. GAUDET; Arthur; Josephine m. --- LEBLANC. [These are children of a previous marriage, wife not named.] Inventory: 31 Dec. 1896. (Houma Ct. Hse.: Succ. #876)

GAUDE, Clara Marie (Tom & Clara GUEDRY) b. 12 Oct. 1899 (Raceland Ch.: v.5, p.104)

GAUDE, Eve Emelie (Fernand & Leotia ARCEMENT) b. 16 May 1898 (Raceland Ch.: v.5, p.71)

GAUDE, Felix J. (Charles Arthur & Marie GAUDE) m. 10 Aug. 1898 Helene Josephine BABIN (Thib. Ch.: v.14, p.289)

GAUDE, Felix J. (Charles Arthur & Marie GAUDE) m. 3 Aug. 1899 Helene Josephine BABIN (Thib. Ct. Hse.: Mar. v.39, #205)

GAUDE, Fernand m. 30 Jan. 1896 Leotia ARSEMENT (Thib. Ct. Hse.: Mar. v.35, #32)

GAUDE, Fernand (Augustin & Mathilde Emelie GAUDET) m. 30 Jan. 1896 Leotia ARCEMENT (Raceland Ch.: v.2, p.11)

GAUDE, Gracieuse Elisabeth (Edouard & Regina ROBICHAUX) b. 18 Feb. 1896 (Raceland Ch.: v.5, p.21)

GAUDE, Henry (Leon Raphael & Louisa GAUDE) m. 23 April 1896 Celestine GERVAIS (Lockport Ch.: v.2, p.151)

GAUDE, Henry (Leon Raphael & Louisa GAUDE) m. 23 April 1896 Celestine GERVAIS (Thib. Ct. Hse.: Mar. v.35, #66)

GAUDE, Jean Sylvestre (Arthur & Adelaide Louise CONTRAIRE) b. 26 Dec. 1896 (Thib. Ch.: v.7, p.433)

GAUDE, Joseph d. 29 March 1898 at age 73 yrs. (Houma Ch.: v.3, p.16)

GAUDE, Joseph (Jules & Alice LANDRY) b. 1 Dec. 1896 (Raceland Ch.: v.5, p.34)

GAUDE, Joseph Abel d. 22 Sept. 1896 at age 4 yrs. & 6 mths. (Thib. Ch.: v.3, p.187)

GAUDE, Joseph Harrisson (Fernand & Leotia ARCEMENT) b. 31 April 1897 (Raceland Ch.: v.5, p.47)
GAUDE, Joseph Henri (Louis Emile & Louisa BRAUX) b. 18 Oct. 1896 (Thib. Ch.: v.7, p.423)
GAUDE, Joseph Olivier (Thomas & Clara GUEDRY) b. 17 Aug. 1896 (Raceland Ch.: v.5, p.30)
GAUDE, Laurence Espenan (Louis Philippe & Jeanne Josephine ESPENAN) b. 20 Sept. 1898 (Thib. Ch.: v.7, p.572)
GAUDE, Louise of Lafourche Parish (Raphael & Marie CALLAHAN) m. 2 July 1898 Martial LEFORT, of Lafourche Parish (Larose Ch.: v.3, p.9)
GAUDE, Louise (Raphael & Marie CALLAHAN) m. 2 July 1898 Martial LEFORT (Thib. Ct. Hse.: Mar. v.38, #216)
GAUDE, Louise (Raphael & Marie CALLAHAN) m. 2 July 1898 Martial LEFORT (Larose Ch.: v.4, p.20)
GAUDE, Lucie d. 28 Sept. 1896 at age 16 mths. (Thib. Ch.: v.3, p.188)
GAUDE, Lucile Berthe d. 21 Oct. 1896 at age 19 yrs. & 3 mths. (Thib. Ch.: v.3, p.189)
GAUDE, Lucille Langtry (Wade & Celestine BARILLEAUX) b. 28 April 1898 (Chacahoula Ch.: v.4, p.9)
GAUDE, Marcel d. 1 Dec. 1897 at age 71 yrs. (Thib. Ch.: v.3, p.208)
GAUDE, Marie m. Arthur GAUDE d. 7 Nov. 1898 at age 46 yrs. (Thib. Ch.: v.3, p.221)
GAUDE, Marie (Jules & Alice LANDRY) b. 1 Dec. 1896 (Raceland Ch.: v.5, p.34)
GAUDE, Marie Aline (Henry & Celestine GERVAIS) b. 15 Aug. 1899 (Raceland Ch.: v.5, p.101)
GAUDE, Marie Judith (Henri & Celestine GERVAIS) b. 21 Oct. 1897 (Raceland Ch.: v.5, p.56)
GAUDE, Marie Lolanre (Felix & Therese GAUDE) b. 29 Aug. 1896 (Thib. Ch.: v.7, p.415)
GAUDE, Marie Nelly (Albert & Louise FALGOUT) b. 14 May 1898 (Thib. Ch.: v.7, p.550)
GAUDE, Paul Arthur (Arthur & Louise CANTRELLE) b. 14 June 1899 (Thib. Ch.: v.7, p.552)
GAUDE, Therese J. d. 16 July 1897; m. 15 Oct 1895 to Felix J. GAUDE. Child listed: Solenge M. Petition for inventory: 7 Dec. 1897. (Thib. Ct. Hse.: Succ. #1524)
GAUDE, Therese Josephine d. 17 July 1897 at age 59 yrs. (Thib. Ch.: v.3, p.203)
GAUDE, Thomas (Thomas & Clara GUEDRY) b. 8 Jan. 1898 (Raceland Ch.: v.5, p.65)
GAUDEZ, Agathe m. 12 Feb. 1898 Armand ROBICHAUX (Thib. Ct. Hse.: Mar. v.37, #64)
GAUNNIE, Armand Florestan Thomas (Raphael & Juanita ALBERTI) b. 14 Oct. 1899 (Thib. Ch.: v.7, p.571)

GAUTHIER (Sometimes: GAUTIER)

GAUTHIER, Ida Faustine (Pierre & Marie THERIOT) b. 27 Aug. 1897 (Houma Ch.: v.5, p.191)

GAUTHIER, J. Eda d. 29 Oct. 1898 at age 14 mths. (Houma Ch.: v.3, p.19)
GAUTHIER, Joseph d. 17 Nov. 1897 at age 19 yrs. (Houma Ch.: v.3, p.14)

GAUTREAUX (Sometimes: GAUTERAU, GAUTHREAUX, GAUTRAUX, GAUTREAU, GOTREAU, GOUDRAUX)

GAUTREAUX, Albert (Simon & Josephine BABIN) m. 9 Feb. 1898 Josephine LEBLANC (Thib. Ct. Hse.: Mar. v.37, #59)
GAUTREAUX, Albert (Simon & Josephine BABIN) m. 9 Feb. 1898 Josephine LEBLANC (Lockport Ch.: v.2, p.185)
GAUTREAUX, Angela Lelande (Henri & Jane BALLAD) b. 17 Aug. 1898 (Thib. Ch.: v.7, p.562)
GAUTREAUX, Angelina m. d.Alexandre LIRETTE d. 22 Jan. 1898 at age 77 yrs. (Houma Ch.: v.3, p.15)
GAUTREAUX, Annita Aline (Felix & Lodie CROCHET) b. 25 Jan. 1896 (Houma Ch.: v.5, p.145)
GAUTREAUX, Antoine Noe (Oleus & Manuela PONCHE) b. 13 June 1896 (Lockport Ch.: v.2, p.331)
GAUTREAUX, Augusta Evela (Treville & Anita BERGERON) b. 3 Jan. 1899 (Montegut Ch.: v.6, p.81)
GAUTREAUX, Cleophas Norbert (Clement & Victoria ADAM) b. 7 June 1896 (Larose Ch.: v.2, p.193)
GAUTREAUX, Dora m. 5 April 1898 Benjamin ENGLAND (Houma Ct. Hse.: Mar. v.30 & 31, #376)
GAUTREAUX, Elcee d. 5 Dec. 1897 at age 28 yrs. (Montegut Ch.: v.2, p.13)
GAUTREAUX, Elina d. 9 May 1897 at age 29 yrs. (Thib. Ch.: v.3, p.200)
GAUTREAUX, Elisa (Vasseur & Anaise BOUDREAUX) m. 10 Feb. 1898 Ernest ORGERON (Thib. Ct. Hse.: Mar. v.37, #58)
GAUTREAUX, Elisa (Vasseur & Anaise BOUDREAUX) m. 10 Feb. 1898 Ernest ORGERON (Lockport Ch.: v.2, p.186)
GAUTREAUX, Felix d. 27 Jan. 1898 (Houma Ch.: v.3, p.15)
GAUTREAUX, Joseph (Justilien) d. 8 Sept. 1899 at age 2 mths. (Lockport Ch.: v.1, #35)
GAUTREAUX, Joseph Loles Toussaint (Alcee & Celina AUTUN) b. 31 Nov. 1896 (Montegut Ch.: v.6, p.51)
GAUTREAUX, Joseph Michel (Joseph & Zolida LAMBERT) b. 2 May 1897 (Montegut Ch.: v.6, p.57)
GAUTREAUX, Joseph Wales (Charlesonne & Roselia CREPEL) b. 30 Nov. 1896 (Larose Ch.: v.2, p.190 & p.210, #83)
GAUTREAUX, Joseph Wilson (Alcee & Marie AUTIN) b. 15 March 1898 (Montegut Ch.: v.6, p.73)
GAUTREAUX, Josephine d. 21 Nov. 1899 at age 20 yrs. (Houma Ch.: v.3, p.26)
GAUTREAUX, Josephine (Vasseur & Anaise BOUDREAUX) m. 15 June 1898 Arthur LEBLANC (Lockport Ch.: v.2, p.190)
GAUTREAUX, Josephine (Vasseur & Anaise BOUDREAUX) m. 15 June 1898 Arthur LEBLANC (Thib. Ct. Hse.: Mar. v.38, #195)

GAUTREAUX, Laura m. 15 July 1898 Georges DIONNE (Houma Ct. Hse.: Mar. v.30 & 31, #60)
GAUTREAUX, Lillie M. (Alexander & Sarah HICKS) m. 4 Feb. 1896 Randolph BLANCHARD (Houma Ct. Hse.: Mar. v.28, #435)
GAUTREAUX, Lillie M. (Alexandre & Sarah HICKS) m. 4 Feb. 1896 Randolphe BLANCHARD (Thib. Ch.: v.14, p.72)
GAUTREAUX, Louis m. 14 March 1896 Ernestine HEBERT (Houma Ct. Hse.: Mar. v.29 & 30, #9)
GAUTREAUX, Louis (Felix & Elodie COLWART) m. 9 April 1896 Ernestine HEBERT (Houma Ch.: v.6-a, p.173)
GAUTREAUX, Lucie Marie (Serafin & Amanda CANTRELLE) b. 5 April 1899 (Chacahoula Ch.: v.4, p.20)
GAUTREAUX, Marguerite Jeanne (Henri & Marie BALAD) b. 14 Dec. 1896 (Thib. Ch.: v.7, p.430)
GAUTREAUX, Marie m. 16 Oct. 1899 Homere BILLOT (Thib. Ct. Hse.: Mar. v.39, #237)
GAUTREAUX, Marie Daisy (Joseph & Zolida LAMBERT) b. 26 Oct. 1899 (Montegut Ch.: v.6, p.96)
GAUTREAUX, Marie Daisy Bernicia (Ecee & Felicie NAVARRE) b. 29 July 1897 (Montegut Ch.: v.6, p.60)
GAUTREAUX, Marie Ella (Treville & Anita BERGERON) b. 11 Sept. 1896 (Montegut Ch.: v.6, p.49)
GAUTREAUX, Marie Helena (Emile & Felicia PLAISANCE) b. 7 Oct. 1897 (Larose Ch.: v.3, p.6)
GAUTREAUX, Marie Justilia (Emile & Felicia PLAISANCE) b. 29 Sept. 1899 (Larose Ch.: v.3, p.45)
GAUTREAUX, Marie Unisse (Louis & Ernestine HEBERT) b. 11 Oct. 1899 (Houma Ch.: v.5, p.260)
GAUTREAUX, Olive (Simon & Josephine BABIN) m. 11 Feb. 1899 Volzim TOURELLE (Lockport Ch.: v.2, p.204)
GAUTREAUX, Olive (Simon & Josephine BABIN) m. 11 Feb. 1899 Valzime TOURRELL (Thib. Ct. Hse.: Mar. v.38, #65)
GAUTREAUX, Ophelia (Simon & Josephine BABIN) m. 8 Feb. 1899 Fedles HIMEL (Lockport Ch.: v.2, p.202)
GAUTREAUX, Ophelia (Simon & Josephine BABIN) m. 8 Feb. 1899 Fedless HIMEL (Thib. Ct. Hse.: Mar. v.38, #66)
GAUTREAUX, Pierre Furcy d. 2 Dec. 1898 at age 83 yrs. (Montegut Ch.: v.2, p.22)
GAUTREAUX, Robert (Pierre & Jemy WHITE) b. 4 Jan. 1897 (Houma Ch.: v.5, p.166)
GAUTREAUX, Serafin (Trasimond & Eulalie BOUDREAUX) m. 3 June 1898 Amanda CANTRELLE (Chacahoula Ch.: v.1, p.62)
GAUTREAUX, Seraphin m. 15 June 1898 Amanda CANTRELLE (Houma Ct. Hse.: Mar. v.30 & 31, #18)
GAZZARDO, Giuseppa (Dieco & Theresa PUCCIA) b. 9 May 1898 (Houma Ch.: v.5, p.208)
GAZZO, John (John & Lizzie YOUNGS) b. 7 Feb. 1898 (Raceland Ch.: v.5, p.67)
GEBBIA, Guiseppe (Carmela & Domenica LOMONTE) b. 12 Nov. 1897 (Thib. Ch.: v.7, p.473)

GENDRON (See: JEANDRON)

GENNARA, Hypolite of Houma m. 12 Dec. 1899 Angela CACCATORA (Houma Ch.: v.6-B, p.5)
GENNARD, Hypolite m. 6 Nov. 1899 Angela CAECATORA (Houma Ct. Hse.: Mar. v.31 & 32, #165)
GENNORA, Benna m. 3 Feb. 1897 Salvatore ZABBIO (Houma Ct. Hse.: Mar. v.29 & 30, #277)
GEMORA, Benna (Gioseppe & Maria --IPOMA?) m. 27 Feb. 1897 Salvatore GABBIO (Houma Ch.: v.6-a, p.194)
GEORGE, Ellis (Steven & Martha NOCU) b. 4 Sept. 1899 (Houma Ch.: v.5, p.254)
GEORGE, Willie m. 27 Oct. 1898 Nancy JOSEPH (Thib. Ct. Hse.: Mar. v.38, #305)
GERVAIS, Albert (Florestan & Mary LEPINE) m. 11 Feb. 1899 Augustine BRAUX (Lockport Ch.: v.2, p.203)
GERVAIS, Albert F. (Florestan & Mary LEPINE) m. 11 Feb. 1899 Augustine BRAUX (Thib. Ct. Hse.: Mar. v.38, #72)
GERVAIS, Armand (Florestan & Mary LEPINE) m. 5 Nov. 1898 Myrthilia CHAUVIN (Thib. Ct. Hse.: Mar. v.38, #301)
GERVAIS, Armand (Florestan & Mary LEPINE) m. 5 Nov. 1898 Myrthilia CHAUVIN (Lockport Ch.: v.2, p.196)
GERVAIS, Benjamin d. 15 Feb. 1899 at age 8 mths. (Raceland Ch.: v.1, p.23)
GERVAIS, Celestine (Onezippe & Octavie THERIOT) m. 23 April 1896 Henry GAUDE (Thib. Ct. Hse.: Mar. v.35, #66)
GERVAIS, Celestine (Onezyppe & Octavie THERIOT) m. 23 April 1896 Henry GAUDE (Lockport Ch.: v.2, p.151)
GERVAIS, Florestine (Onesippe & Octavie THERIOT) m. 28 Jan. 1899 Clovis GUIDRY (Thib. Ct. Hse.: Mar. v.38, #25)
GERVAIS, Florestine (Onesippe & Octavie THERIOT) m. 28 Jan. 1899 Clovis GUIDRY (Lockport Ch.: v.2, p.199)
GERVAIS, Joseph (Amedee & Clemance THERIOT) m. 25 Jan. 1896 Odilia ARABIE (Thib. Ct. Hse.: Mar. v.35, #14)
GERVAIS, Joseph (Amedee & Clemence THERIOT) m. 25 Jan. 1896 Odilia ARABIE (Lockport Ch.: v.2, p.144)
GERVAIS, Judith Lilian (Edgard & Clemence BRAUD) b. 16 May 1897 (Raceland Ch.: v.5, p.49)
GERVAIS, Lawrence James (Florestan & Marie LEPINE) b. 7 June 1897 (Raceland Ch.: v.5, p.50)
GERVAIS, Louis Ede (Florestan & Mary LEPINE) b. 27 July 1899 (Raceland Ch.: v.5, p.100)
GERVAIS, Lovincy (Amede & Clemence THERIOT) m. 20 Aug. 1898 Elmire BREAUX (Lockport Ch.: v.2, p.193)
GERVAIS, Lovincy (Amedee & Clemance THERIOT) m. 20 Aug. 1898 Elmire BRAUX (Thib. Ct. Hse.: Mar. v.38, #235)
GERVAIS, Olympe m. 18 Sept. 1897 Joseph BEAUDOIN (Thib. Ct. Hse.: Mar. v.37, #229)
GERVAIS, Olympe m. 18 Spt. 1897 Joseph BEAUDOIN (Lockport Ch.: v.2, p.174)

GERVAIS, Oscar (Amede & Clemence THERIOT) m. 25 April 1896 Clotilde BRAUX (Thib. Ct. Hse.: Mar. v.35, #72)

GERVAIS, Oscar (Florestan & Mary LEPINE) m. 20 Aug. 1898 Mary DUFRENE (Thib. Ct. Hse.: Mar. v.38, #247)

GERVAIS, Oscar (Florestan & Mary LEPINE) m. 20 Aug. 1898 Mary DUFRENE (Lockport Ch.: v.2, p.193)

GERVAIS, Oscar Maurice (Oscar & Marie DUFRENE) b. 23 Sept. 1899 (Lockport Ch.: v.3-A, #6)

GERVAIS, Oscar Maurice (Oscar & Marie DUFRENE) b. 23 Sept. 1899 (Lockport Ch.: v.3, #6)

GERVAIS, Pierre (Oscar & Clotilde BRAUX) b. 14 Jan. 1897 (Lockport Ch.: v.3-A, #23)

GERVAIS, Pierre (Oscar & Clotilde BRAUX) b. 14 Jan. 1897 (Lockport Ch.: v.3, #23)

GERVAIS, Pierre Sidney (Onesippe & Octavie THERIOT) b. 16 July 1896 (Raceland Ch.: v.5, p.25)

GETRIDGE, John m. 4 Aug. 1898 Sophie YOUNG (Thib. Ct. Hse.: Mar. v.38, #238)

GHIRARDY (Sometimes: GHIRARDI)

GHIRARDY, Etienne d. 27 June 1899 (Houma Ch.: Epis. Ch.: v.1, p.388)

GHIRARDY, Etienne d. 27 June 1899; m. Lorena CHAUVIN Children listed: Peter B.; Joseph Stephen; Florence Elmina; Isabella; Laura m. Philip YOST; Louisa, 19; Clara, 17; Sadie, 14; Mary, 8. Petition for inventory: 5 July 1899. (Houma Ct. Hse.: Succ. #922)

GIACOMO, Maria Nita (Guiseppe & Concetta DICHIAZA) b. April 1898; bt. 16 Oct. 1898 (Raceland Ch.: v.5, p.80)

GIANCOLA, Chiara m. 20 May 1899 Martino ANZALONE (Houma Ct. Hse.: Mar. v.31 & 32, #9)

GIANCOLA, Chiara of Terrebonne Parish m. 15 July 1899 Martino ANZALONE (Houma Ch.: v.6-B, p.4, #11 & p.3, #9)

GIBSON, Sarah Mrs. m. d.Joseph A. HUMPHREYS Donation of land: 20 May 1898. (Houma Ct. Hse.: Book of Donations: v.A, p.157)

GIEBBE, Camello d. 22 May 1898 at age 45 yrs. (Thib. Ch.: v.3, p.214)

GIGLIO, Bernardo (Giovanai & Santa REINA) b. 16 July 1896 (Thib. Ch.: v.7, p.408)

GIGLIO, Maria Rita (Benedetto & Lena ZEBIA) b. 24 Sept. 1899 (Raceland Ch.: v.5, p.103)

GIGLIO, Vincenzo d. 3 Oct. 1896 at age 2½ mths. (Thib. Ch.: v.3, p.188)

GIGLIO, Vincenzo (Giovanai & Santa REINA) b. 16 July 1896 (Thib. Ch.: v.7, p.408)

GILBERT, ----- infant (Joseph & Felicien BOURG) d. 29 April 1899 at age 1½ mth. (Montegut Ch.: v.2, p.25)

GILES, Clay m. 14 Dec. 1897 Ella HILL (Thib. Ct. Hse.: Mar. v.37, #262)

GILES, Ernestine m. 8 March 1898 Thomas JEFFERSON (Thib. Ct. Hse.: Mar. v.37, #122)

GILES, John m. 20 Dec. 1898 Clothilde TABOR (Thib. Ct. Hse.: Mar. v.38, #320)

GILES, John m. 7 Feb. 1899 Clotilde TABOR (Thib. Ch.: v.14, p.258)

GILES, Louis m. 26 May 1898 Virginia Agnes ANDERSON (Thib. Ct. Hse.: Mar. v.38, #191)

GILES, Lucy Insanity: 2 June 1899. (Thib. Ct Hse.: Succ. #1577)

GILTON, John m. 11 June 1896 Maggie MANUEL (Thib. Ct. Hse.: Mar. v.35, #104)

GIMARVO, Antonino (Joachime & Joanina LOVERDE) m. 12 Jan. 1899 Maria BONFIGLIA (Thib. Ch.: v.14, p.236)

GIMARVO, Antonino (Joachimo & Joanina LOVERDE) m. 12 Jan. 1898 Maria BOUFIGLIO (Thib. Ct. Hse.: Mar. v.38, #316)

GINSMORE, Margaret m. 23 Sept. 1899 John BELASON (Houma Ct. Hse.: Mar. v.31 & 32, #142)

GIOLMALVA, Joanina (Antonino & Maria BONFILIA) b. 7 Dec. 1899 (Thib. Ch.: v.7, p.582)

GIOVANI, Guiseppa Castro (Guiseppe & Pietro SINAGRA) b. 24 May 1897 (Thib. Ch.: v.7, p.451)

GIOVENCO, Joseph (Salvatore & Maria LOPIPARA) b. 19 June 1896 (Thib. Ch.: v.7, p.406)

GIOVINCO, Guiseppe (Salvatore & Maria LAPIPARA) d. 28 June 1896 at age 9 days (Thib. Ch.: v.3, p.184)

GIOVINCO, Paolo (Salvadore & Maria SOPIPARONE) b. 8 Oct. 1899 (Thib. Ch.: v.7, p.571)

GIOVINGO, Guiseppe (Salvatore & Maria LOPPIPADA) b. 13 July 1897 (Thib. Ch.: v.7, p.456)

GIROIR (Sometimes: GIROIRE, GIROUARD)

GIROIR, Adam (Felix & Victoire BOUDELOCHE) b. 18 Sept. 1898 (Houma Ch.: v.5, p.232)

GIROIR, Antoine Duglass (Edgar & Celestine OLLIVIER) b. 26 Feb. 1896 (Houma Ch.: v.5, p.174)

GIROIR, Claud (Mascele & Mathilde BONVILLAIN) b. 17 Feb. 1896 (Houma Ch.: v.5, p.146)

GIROIR, Ernest Camille (Maxille & Mathilde BONVILLAIN) b. 17 July 1896 (Houma Ch.: v.5, p.183)

GIROIR, Eugenie (Jean Baptiste & Clementine GREAN) m. 11 April 1896 Paul ELIE (Houma Ct. Hse.: Mar. v.29 & 30, #32)

GIROIR, Ida Marguerite (Edgar & Celestine OLIVIER) b. ----; bt. 26 Feb. 1899 (Houma Ch.: v.5, p.235)

GIROIR, Josephine (Jean Baptiste & Euranie BONVILLAIN) m. 7 Nov. 1899 Wilfred ANTILL (Houma Ct. Hse.: Mar. v.31 & 32, #160)

GIROIR, Marguerite Josephine (Louis Banon & Corine Adelaide GUIDRY) b. 20 Feb. 1896 (Houma Ch.: v.5, p.172)

GIROIR, Paul Firmain (Maxile & Mathilde BEN) b. 3 Nov. 1899 (Houma Ch.: v.5, p.262)

GIROIR, Robert Joseph (Valsain & Marie LEBOEUF) b. 8 Jan. 1899 (Chacahoula Ch.: v.4, p.16)

GIROIR, Stelite m. 31 Jan. 1896 Corinne ROSS (Houma Ct. Hse.: Mar. v.28, #428)
GIROIR, Telisia m. Ulysse PENISSON d. 31 Dec. 1897 at age 38 yrs. (Chacahoula Ch.: Gibson Ch.: v.2, p.181)
GIROIR, Theophile m. 1 Feb. 1899 Antoinette LANCON (Houma Ct. Hse.: Mar. v.30 & 31, #297)
GIROIR, Theophile m. 13 Feb. 1899 Antoinette LANCON (Houma Ch.: v.6-a, p.288)

GISCLAR (Sometimes: GISCLA, GISCLAIR)
GISCLAR, Abraham m. 10 July 1897 Ovilia HEBERT (Larose Ch.: v.3, p.6)
GISCLAR, Abraham m. 10 July 1897 Ovilia HEBERT (Thib. Ct. Hse.: Mar. v.37, #181)
GISCLAR, Abraham m. 10 July 1897 Ovilia HEBERT (Larose Ch.: v.4, p.93-A)
GISCLAR, Adele m. d.Francois LECOMPTE d. 6 July 1897 at age 85 yrs. (Montegut Ch.: v.2, p.11)
GISCLAR, Augustine Uranie (Valsin & Marie CHAMPAGNE) b. 11 Dec. 1898 (Larose Ch.: v.3, p.35)
GISCLAR, Camilla of Lafourche Parish (Emilien GISCLAIR) m. 2 July 1898 Lovency TOUPS, of Lafourche Parish (Larose Ch.: v.3, p.10)
GISCLAR, Camilla (Emilien & -----) m. 2 July 1898 Lovency TOUPS (Larose Ch.: v.4, p.21)
GISCLAR, Camilla (Emilien & ----) m. 2 July 1898 Lovencie TOUPS (Thib. Ct. Hse.: Mar. v.38, #215)
GISCLAR, Clefedge Joseph (Oscar & Alzina PITRE) b. 28 March 1899 (Larose Ch.: v.3, p.39)
GISCLAR, Dominique (Emilien & Augustine PITRE) m. 4 Feb. 1899 Camilla TOUPS (Thib. Ct. Hse.: Mar. v.38, #39)
GISCLAR, Dominique (Emilien & Augustine PITRE) m. 4 Feb. 1899 Camilla TOUPS (Larose Ch.: v.4, p.35)
GISCLAR, Dominique (Emilien & Augustine PITRE) m. 4 Feb. 1899 Camilla TOUPS (Larose Ch.: v.3, p.11)
GISCLAR, Jean Wolf (Jean & Olivia GISCLAR) b. 16 Dec. 1897 (Larose Ch.: v.3, p.32)
GISCLAR, Joseph Francois (Francois & Melasie DUET) b. 19 May 1896 (Larose Ch.: v.2, p.184)
GISCLAR, Joseph Lazare (Alidore & Marie Vitalie LEDET) b. 10 July 1896 (Larose Ch.: v.2, p.186)
GISCLAR, Joseph Octave (---- & Victoria TOUPS) b. 2 Feb. 1899 (Larose Ch.: v.3, p.39)
GISCLAR, Josephine Celima (Francois & Melasie DUAY) b. 1 Jan. 1898 (Larose Ch.: v.3, p.25)
GISCLAR, Leon (Francois & Celima PITRE) m. 30 June 1898 Laurenza VEGAS (Thib. Ct. Hse.: Mar. v.38, #202)
GISCLAR, Louis Maurice (Francois & Melasie DUET) b. 11 Oct. 1899 (Larose Ch.: v.3, p.48)
GISCLAR, Louise of Lafourche Parish (Theophile & Melanie PITRE) m. 2 July 1898 Charles CALAIS, of Lafourche Parish (Larose Ch.: v.3, p.10)

GISCLAR, Louise (Theophile & Melanie PITRE) m. 2 July 1898 Charles CALLAIS (Thib. Ct. Hse.: Mar. v.38, #201)
GISCLAR, Louise (Theophile & Melanie PITRE) m. 2 July 1898 Charles CALAIS (Larose Ch.: v.4, p.22)
GISCLAR, Marie (---- & Marie Rose GISCLAR) b. 22 Feb. 1899 (Larose Ch.: v.3, p.37)
GISCLAR, Marie Edna (Dominique & Camilia TOUPS) b. 5 Sept. 1898 (Larose Ch.: v.3, p.46)
GISCLAR, Melina m. 7 July 1896 Albert DANOS (Larose Ch.: v.4, p.71)
GISCLAR, Melina m. 7 July 1896 Albert DANOS (Larose Ch.: v.3, p.3)
GISCLAR, Noe Rene (Oscar & Alzina PITRE) b. 6 Sept. 1896 (Larose Ch.: v.2, p.197)
GISCLAR, Valorie Louisa (Jean & Ovilia GISCLA) b. 28 Aug. 1899 (Larose Ch.: v.3, p.45)
GLALIONI, Marie Aline (Jules & Anaise GUIDROZ) b. 28 July 1896 (Lockport Ch.: v.2, p.333)

GLEAN (Sometimes: GLEAM, GLEEM, GLENN, GLIND, GLINN)

GLOIONI, Giuseppe d. 28 Dec. 1898 at age 1 day (Thib. Ch.: v.3, p.224)
GLORIASO, Rosario (Guiseppe & Rosa GUIDRY) m. 28 Aug. 1899 Francesca CITRANO (Thib. Ch.: v.14, p.292)
GLORISO, Rosario (Guiseppe & Rosa GIORDINA) m. 28 Aug. 1898 Francisca CITRANO (Thib. Ct. Hse.: Mar. v.38, #285)
GLOSE, Ida m. Sylvere BERGERON d. 27 Sept. 1899 at age 38 yrs. (Montegut Ch.: v.2, p.29)
GLYNN, Amy Agnes (James & Mary PICHOP) b. 15 Feb. 1896 (Houma Ch.: v.5, p.158)
GLYNN, Clara Mabel (James & Mary PICHON) b. 26 Oct. 1899 (Theriot Ch.: v.2, p.59)
GLYNN, Louis (Thomas & Victorine DUPRE) b. 24 Dec. 1898 (Houma Ch.: v.5, p.234)
GLYNN, Thomas J. m. 13 Sept. 1897 Victorine DUPRE (Houma Ct. Hse.: Mar. v.29 & 30, #89)
GLYNN, Thomas J. (James & Mary PICHOF) m. 14 Sept. 1897 Victorine DUPRE (Houma Ch.: v.6-a, p.215)

GODET (See: GAUDE)

GODFREY, Melinda m. 5 Jan. 1899 Collins MACKLIN (Houma Ct. Hse.: Mar. v.30 & 31, #180)
GOFF, Ida m. 20 Feb. 1897 Richard HYDE (Thib. Ct. Hse.: Mar. v.36, #84)
GOGONO, Antonina m. 11 April 1899 Vita CICIA (Houma Ct. Hse.: Mar. v.31 & 32, #394)
GOLDEN, J. T. m. 8 Nov. 1899 Sara MORRIS (Thib. Ct. Hse.: Mar. v.39, #260)

GOLDEN, Willis m. 8 Oct. 1896 Anna WILLIAMS (Houma Ct. Hse.: Mar. v.29 & 30, #163)

GOLLEE, Pauline d. 5 March 1899 at age 36 yrs. (Houma Ch.: v.3, p.21)

GONARDE, Labris (Michaele & Maria DIAMICO) b. 5 June 1898 (Houma Ch.: v.5, p.212)

GONZALES (Sometimes: GONSALES, GONSALEZ)

GONZALES, Celestin (Celestin & Marie UZE) b. 15 Feb. 1898 (Thib. Ch.: v.7, p.538)

GONZALES, Clairfait (Adam & Natilie UZE) m. 27 Dec. 1899 Elizabeth PREJEAN (Thib. Ch.: v.14, p.317)

GONZALES, Clerfy m. 9 Dec. 1899 Elizabeth PREJEANT (Thib. Ct. Hse.: Mar. v.39, #278)

GONZALES, Edgar (Celestin & Marie USE) m. 11 June 1896 Amelia BENOIT (Thib. Ct. Hse.: Mar. v.35, #99)

GONZALES, Edgar (Celestin & Marie USE) m. 11 June 1896 Amelie BENOIT (Thib. Ch.: v.14, p.92)

GONZALES, Ernest Joseph (Antoine & Marie JOACIN) b. 19 July 1897 (Thib. Ch.: v.7, p.460)

GONZALES, Faustine (Celestin & Marie UZE) m. 4 Oct. 1897 Odressy BENOIT (Thib. Ct. Hse.: Mar. v.37, #241)

GONZALES, Faustine (Celestin & Marie UZE) m. 4 Oct. 1897 Odressy BENOIT (Thib. Ch.: v.14, p.161)

GONZALES, Francisca (Francis & Rose GROS) m. 23 Jan. 1896 Paulin NAQUIN (Thib. Ch.: v.14, p.69)

GONZALES, Francisca (Francis & Rose GROS) m. 23 Jan. 1896 Paulin NAQUIN (Thib. Ct. Hse.: Mar. v.35, #18)

GONZALES, Jean (Celestin & Marie UZE) m. 24 Feb. 1898 Cecilia KELLER (Thib. Ch.: v.14, p.173)

GONZALES, Jean (Celestin & Marie UZE) m. 24 Jan. 1898 Cecilia KEELER (Thib. Ct. Hse.: Mar. v.37, #53)

GONZALES, Joseph (Joseph & Julie GONSALEZ) b. 26 March 1898 (Raceland Ch.: v.5, p.68)

GONZALES, Joseph Francois (Francisque & Rosa MALBROUGH) b. 2 Dec. 1896 (Thib. Ch.: v.7, p.433)

GONZALES, Joseph Oliver (Edgard & Amelia BENOIT) b. 10 June 1897 (Thib. Ch.: v.7, p.452)

GONZALES, Louis Harry (Jean & Cecilia KELLER) b. 10 Feb. 1899 (Thib. Ch.: v.7, p.537)

GONZALES, Morgan m. 1 March 1897 Emma HEBERT (Larose Ch.: v.3, p.5)

GONZALES, Morgan m. 1 March 1897 Emma HEBERT (Larose Ch.: v.4, p.100)

GONZALES, Morgan m. 19 Feb. 1897 Emma HEBERT (Thib. Ct. Hse.: Mar. v.36, #83)

GONZALES, Roy Antoine (Antoine & Marie JOACHIM) b. 25 Oct. 1899 (Raceland Ch.: v.5, p.107)

GONZALES, Samuel (Edgard & Emelia BENOIT) b. 19 July 1898 (Thib. Ch.: v.7, p.556)

GONZALES, Velma (Adam & Notilia UZEE) m. 6 April 1897 Valcour BERNARD (Thib. Ct. Hse.: Mar. v.36, #107)

GOODE (Sometimes: GOUDE)

GOODE, Felix m. 24 Feb. 1897 Mary WARD (Thib. Ct. Hse.: Mar. v.36, #90)

GOODMAN, Alces (Fritz & Julienne MARS) m. 24 April 1897 Pauline BENOIT (Chackbay Ch.: v.1, p.43)

GOODMAN, Alies (Fritz & Julienne MARS) m. 24 April 1897 Pauline BENOIT (Thib. Ct. Hse.: Mar. v.36, #113)

GOODMAN, Henriette (Alice & Pauline BENOIT) b. 24 Jan. 1898 (Chackbay Ch.: v.1, p.105)

GOODMAN, Joseph m. 26 Sept. 1898 Josephine WHITE (Thib. Ct. Hse.: Mar. v.38, #283)

GOODMAN, Mathilde (Fritz & Julienne MARS) b. 17 April 1897 (Chackbay Ch.: v.1, p.88)

GOODMAN, Numa m. 23 Nov. 1898 Lily DUCKER (Thib. Ct. Hse.: Mar. v.38, #312)

GOODMAN, Oscar m. 16 March 1896 Elizabeth FISHER (Thib. Ct. Hse.: Mar. v.35, #51)

GOODMAN, Victoria (Joseph & Rosa BREMA) b. 15 Oct. 1899 (Larose Ch.: v.3, p.59)

GOODNESS, Florence (Isaac & Julie JOACHIM) b. 4 Oct. 1897; bt. 6 April 1899 (Larose Ch.: v.3, p.43)

GOODNEY, Joseph (Joseph & Rosa BROWN) b. 7 May 1898 (Larose Ch.: v.3, p.24)

GOODNEY, Zacharie (Joseph & Rosa BROWN) b. 7 May 1898 (Larose Ch.: v.3, p.24)

GOODS, Reuben m. 8 Jan. 1896 Ollie LILLY (Thib. Ct. Hse.: Mar. v.35, #15)

GOODWIN, Joseph m. 3 March 1898 Rosa BROWN (Houma Ct. Hse.: Mar. v.30 & 31, #323)

GORDON, John A. Jr. m. 2 Jan. 1896 Elizabeth KING (Houma Ct. Hse.: Mar. v.28, #366)

GORE, Virginia widow of Bannister BRICKLEY m. 14 Sept. 1899 Sam WORDON (Thib. Ct. Hse.: Mar. v.39, #230)

GOSSENT, Henry d. 28 Jan. 1897 at age 45 yrs. (Thib. Ch.: v.3, p.195)

GOUAUX (Sometimes: GAUX)

GOUAUX, Emma M. m. 28 Oct. 1896 Camille M. ST. MARTIN (Houma Ct. Hse.: Mar. v.29 & 30, #181)

GOUAUX, Emma M. (Francois & Cecile FOLSE) m. 4 Nov. 1896 Camille ST. MARTIN (Houma Ch.: v.6-a, p.184)

GOUAUX, Jean Roger (Charles & Henriette DANSEREAU) b. 10 June 1896 (Thib. Ch.: v.7, p.453)

GOUAUX, Paul Henri (Charles & Henriette DANSEREAUX) b. 8 Sept. 1899 (Thib. Ch.: v.7, p.579)

GOULOTTA, Maria Odentia (Francisco & Rosa GIGLIN) b. 23 Sept. 1899 (Houma Ch.: v.5, p.256)

GOVERNA, Ebraggio d. 15 July 1898 at age 49 yrs. (Thib. Ch.: v.3, p.217)

GRABERT (Sometimes: GRABER, GRABERE)

GRABERT, Anne Dora (Felicien & Viola MATER) b. 22 July 1899 (Raceland Ch.: v.5, p.99)

GRABERT, Emilie m. Sylvere LEDET d. 28 May 1897 at age 62 yrs. (Thib. Ch.: v.3, p.200)

GRABERT, Ernest m. 7 May 1897 Alexina PERTUIT (Thib. Ct. Hse.: Mar. v.36, #140)

GRABERT, Ernest (Leon & Marie RIVET) m. 15 May 1897 Alexina PERTUIS (Raceland Ch.: v.2, p.39)

GRABERT, Helene m. 7 Sept. 1898 Allain DUFRESNE (Thib. Ct. Hse.: Mar. v.38, #273)

GRABERT, Helene (Evariste & Marcelline BABIN) m. 14 Sept. 1898 Alain DUFRESNE (Raceland Ch.: v.2, p.81)

GRABERT, Jean (Justilien & Domitilde CORTEZ) b. 19 Jan. 1898 (Chackbay Ch.: v.1, p.107)

GRABERT, Jean Homere (Alfred & Estelina RICHARD) b. 5 Jan. 1896 (Raceland Ch.: v.5, p.17)

GRABERT, Joseph d. 4 Sept. 1897 (Raceland Ch.: v.1, p.15)

GRABERT, Justilien (d.Justin & Marguerite FOLSE) m. 2 Sept. 1899 Virginie CORTES (Chackbay Ch.: v.1, p.72)

GRABERT, Justilien (Justin & Maggie FOLSE) m. 2 Sept. 1899 Virginie CORTES (Thib. Ct. Hse.: Mar. v.39, #214)

GRABERT, Marie Canelia (Felicien & Viola MATERNE) b. 30 Aug. 1897 (Raceland Ch.: v.5, p.54)

GRABERT, Marie Flocee (Albert & Adovida GUIDRY) b. 9 Nov. 1896 (Lockport Ch.: v.3, #15)

GRABERT, Marie Flocee (Albert & Adovida GUIDRY) b. 9 Nov. 1896 (Lockport Ch.: v.3-A, #15)

GRABERT, Marie Rivet d. 25 Nov. 1896 at age 70 yrs. (Raceland Ch.: v.1, p.10)

GRABERT, Marie Winnie (Felicien & Eviola MATERNE) b. 26 Feb. 1896 (Raceland Ch.: v.5, p.20)

GRABERT, Olga d. 14 May 1897 at age 7 yrs. (Raceland Ch.: v.1, p.13)

GRABERT, Oscar m. 14 Feb. 1898 Marcelline FORET (Thib. Ct. Hse.: Mar. v.37, #100)

GRABERT, Oscar (Evariste & Marcelline BABIN) m. 14 Feb. 1898 Marcelline FORET (Raceland Ch.: v.2, p.69)

GRABERT, Rene d. 17 April 1899 at age 21 yrs. (Lockport Ch.: v.1, #15)

GRABERT, Wilkenson Paul (Felix & Elisabeth DANTIN) b. 20 Nov. 1897 (Raceland Ch.: v.5, p.58)

GRABERT, Wilson Joseph (Felix & Elisabeth DANTIN) b. 20 Nov. 1897 (Raceland Ch.: v.5, p.58)

GRABERT, Winnie d. 9 Oct. 1896 at age 8 mths. (Raceland Ch.: v.1, p.10)

GRAFIA, Grazia m. 4 Feb. 1899 Salvatore LAPESA (Houma Ch.: v.6-a, p.274)

GRAMER, Marie Lea (Emilien & Marie THIBAULT) b. 11 Jan. 1897 (Chackbay Ch.: v.1, p.82)

GRANATA, Joseph (Giuseppe & Maria RUSSO) b. 31 Jan. 1898 (Chacahoula Ch.: Gibson Records: Mar. Bk., v.1, #35)

GRANATA, Joseph (Joseph & Maria RUSSO) b. 31 Jan. 1898 (Chacahoula Ch.: Gibson Ch.: v.2, p.122)

GRANGER, Anthony m. Ophelia HOLLINS. Petition for inventory & administration: 14 April 1897. (Thib. Ct. Hse.: Succ. #1512)

GRANGER, Georges (Georges & Philomene BALTHAZAR) b. -- Oct. 1896; bt. 19 Nov. 1897 (Thib. Ch.: v.7, p.472)

GRANIER, Jean Theophile (Emilien & Marie THIBAUD) b. 14 April 1899 (Chackbay Ch.: v.1, p.132)

GRANIER, Theodore (Emilien & Marie THIBAUD) b. 14 April 1899 (Chackbay Ch.: v.1, p.132)

GRASSO, Salvatore (Antonio & Maria Gratia CATARISSA) b. 18 Nov. 1898 (Houma Ch.: v.5, p.238)

GRAVIRE, Theodore d. 3 Oct. 1899 at age 2 yrs. (Thib. Ch.: v.3, p.241)

GRAVOIS, Elisabeth Sidonia (Alexandre & Suzanne AUGUSTIN) b. 26 Jan. 1897 (Raceland Ch.: v.5, p.40)

GRAVOIS, Jean Armand (Rodolphe & Denise EUSKING) b. 3 Oct. 1898 (Thib. Ch.: v.7, p.568)

GRAVOIS, Joseph Seraphin (Rodolphe & Denise EARSKINE) b. 22 Jan. 1898 (Thib. Ch.: v.7, p.483)

GRAVOIS, Louis Theodore (Charles & Mirthe SEVIN) b. 7 Nov. 1897 (Thib. Ch.: v.7, p.475)

GRAVOIS, Sydney Alcindor (Alexandre & Suzanne AUGUSTIN) b. 27 June 1899 (Thib. Ch.: v.7, p.612)

GRAVOY, Armand Gabriel (Albert & Prsilia AUTIN) b. 2 Dec. 1897 (Thib. Ch.: v.7, p.474)

GRAY, David F. m. 27 April 1897 Sophy A. GAGNE (Houma Ct. Hse.: Mar. v.29 & 30, #394)

GRAY, Henry m. 13 May 1897 Annie SMITH (Thib. Ct. Hse.: Mar. v.36, #142)

GRAY, James m. 27 April 1899 Junella GRIFFIN (Houma Ct. Hse.: Mar. v.31 & 32, #427)

GRAY, James Andrew (Augustin & Constance VERDUN) b. 30 Nov. 1896; bt. 27 Nov. 1897 (Montegut Ch.: v.6, p.62)

GRAY, Marie Perlie Lovelland (John & Eveline GRIFFIN) b. 2 May 1898 (Montegut Ch.: v.6, p.74)

GRAY, Nancy m. 17 April 1897 Louis E. WRIGHT (Thib. Ct. Hse.: Mar. v.36, #118)

GRAY, Philip m. 4 Jan. 1899 Annie BROWN (Thib. Ct. Hse.: Mar. v.38, #4)

GRAY, Tadeus d. 14 Aug. 1899 at age 4 yrs. (Houma Ch.: v.3, p.24)

GRAY, Waltrene m. 22 Aug. 1899 Samuel Butler CASTON (Houma Ct. Hse.: Mar. v.31 & 32, #105)

GRAY, Waltrene S. (Walker J. & Mary Ann HANNAGRIFF) m. 23 Aug. 1899 Samuel Butler CASTON (Houma Ch.: Epis. Ch.: v.1, p.344)

GRECO, Rosalia m. 18 June 1898 Nicolas SPICOLA (Houma Ct. Hse.: Mar. v.30 & 31, #19)
GRECO, Rosalia (Vencenizo & Caroline TOBBATO) m. 2 July 1898 Nicola SPICALA (Houma Ch.: v.6-a, p.244)
GREEN, Andrew m. 31 Ma 1897 Sarah ALLEN (Houma Ct. Hse.: Mar. v.29 & 30, #434)
GREEN, David m. 20 Sept. 1897 Annie TOUPS (Houma Ct. Hse.: Mar. v.29 & 30, #95)
GREEN, Elbia m. Isaac TALBERT Children listed: Victoria; Leonora; Albert; Fanny; Nobiana. Oath of under-tutorship: 15 Oct. 1896. (Thib. Ct. Hse.: Succ. #1498)
GREEN, Ida m. 25 Feb. 1897 Gilbert VERRET (Houma Ct. Hse.: Mar. v.29 & 30, #334)
GREEN, Jerry m. 5 Jan. 1897 Clarissa MOORE (Houma Ct. Hse.: Mar. v.29 & 30, #220)
GREEN, Jesse m. 28 Sept. 1897 Gracie WILLIS (Houma Ct. Hse.: Mar. v.29 & 30, #102)
GREEN, Joseph m. 16 Sept. 1899 Louisiana SHELBY (Thib. Ct. Hse.: Mar. v.39, #232)
GREEN, Joseph m. 20 Jan. 1898 Rebecca DAVIS (Thib. Ct. Hse.: Mar. v.37, #46)
GREEN, Lorenzo S. S. d. 1 July 1898 at age 86 yrs. (Thib. Ch.: Epis. Ch.: v.1, p.394)
GREEN, Louise O. (Reuben E. & Rosanna E. RIPPEIN) m. 18 Aug. 1897 Lure BEHR (Houma Ch.: Epis. Ch.: v.1, p.342)
GREEN, Mary m. 17 Aug. 1899 Oscar RILEY (Houma Ct. Hse.: Mar. v.31 & 32, #103)
GREEN, Rosalie E. m.(1) Albert C. KOHMANN Children of 1st marriage: Albert C.; William L.; Blondina m. Fred B. HEIDENRICH of Miss. m.(2) Reuben E. GREEN, who d. 25 Dec. 1898. Children of 2nd marriage: Louise m. Leon BEHR; Reuben E., aged 17 of Miss. (Houma Ct. Hse.: Succ. #912)
GREEN, Rosanna Emma d. 25 Dec. 1898 at age 67 yrs. (Houma Ch.: Epis. Ch.: v.1, p.388)
GREEN, Sophie m. 21 Dec. 1899 John WILLIAMS (Thib. Ct. Hse.: Mar. v.39, #293)
GREEN, Wilson m. 11 Sept. 1899 Adeline MOORE (Houma Ct. Hse.: Mar. v.31 & 32, #124)
GREGOIRE, Alfarez (Faustin & Octavia THIBODAUX) m. 23 April 1898 Orelia DUTHU (Houma Ct. Hse.: Mar. v.30 & 31, #416)
GREGOIRE, Marie Elvina (Leopold & Madeleine DION) b. 2 Sept. 1897 (Theriot Ch.: v.2, p.15)
GREGOIRE, Theophile (Pierre & Elisabeth LINA) b. 12 Aug. 1897 (Theriot Ch.: v.2, p.10)
GRENIER, Marie Lisca (Paul & Victoria PELEGRIN) b. 1 Jan. 1898 (Montegut Ch.: v.6, p.67)

GRIFFIN (Sometimes: GRIFFEN)
GRIFFIN, Abraham (William & Marie E. GREY) m. 15 Dec. 1899 Marallitte GUIDRY (Larose Ch.: v.4, p.30)

GRIFFIN, Abraham (William & Marie E. GREY) m. 15 Dec. 1899 Marcelitte GUIDRY (Larose Ch.: v.3, p.13)
GRIFFIN, Alexandre (Wuach & Eulalie SAVOIE) b. 3 March 1897 (Lockport Ch.: v.3-A, #37)
GRIFFIN, Alexandre (Wuach & Eulalie SAVOIE) b. 3 March 1897 (Lockport Ch.: v.3, #37)
GRIFFIN, Amanda Jane m. 11 May 1896 Joseph T. HINGLE (Thib. Ct. Hse.: Mar. v.35, #83)
GRIFFIN, Bruce d. 2 July 1899 at age 50 yrs. (Lockport Ch.: v.1, #25)
GRIFFIN, Clifton (Joseph & Felicite ROBESSON) b. 10 Aug. 1898 (Chackbay Ch.: v.1, p.117)
GRIFFIN, Edna Julie (Nathaniel & Clementine CHIASSON) b. 1 Feb. 1896 (Lockport Ch.: v.2, p.321)
GRIFFIN, Emma m. 21 April 1898 Andre CROSBY (Thib. Ct. Hse.: Mar. v.38, #162)
GRIFFIN, Felicite (Stephen & Mary Ann ERIS) m. 4 Sept. 1899 Louis DUPLANTIS (Theriot Ch.: v.1-B, p.6)
GRIFFIN, Felicite (Steven H. & Mary Ann ARIO) m. 12 June 1899 Louis DUPLANTIS (Houma Ct. Hse.: Mar. v.31 & 32, #22)
GRIFFIN, Felonise Constance (Washington & Eulalie SAVOIE) b. 10 Feb. 1899 (Larose Ch.: v.3, p.38)
GRIFFIN, Franck Mathurin of Lafourche Parish (Frank Joseph & Virginie COLET) m. 13 June 1898 Eve ORGERON of Lafourche Parish (Larose Ch.: v.3, p.9)
GRIFFIN, Frank Mathurin (Frank Joseph & Virginie CALET) m. 13 June 1898 Eve ORGERON (Larose Ch.: v.4, p.17)
GRIFFIN, George m. 19 Jan. 1899 Georgianna BISLAND (Houma Ct. Hse.: Mar. v.30 & 31, #254)
GRIFFIN, Isaac m. 22 March 1897 Louisa SPENCER (Houma Ct. Hse.: Mar. v.29 & 30, #358)
GRIFFIN, Jackson Erin (T---- & Laura GROSBY) b. 26 Sept. 1897 (Larose Ch.: v.3, p.22)
GRIFFIN, Joseph Voorhies (Abraham & Marcelite GUIDRY) b. 3 July 1898 (Larose Ch.: v.3, p.31)
GRIFFIN, Junella m. 27 April 1899 James GRAY (Houma Ct. Hse.: Mar. v.31 & 32, #427)
GRIFFIN, Justilien Simon (Frank & Eve ORGERON) b. 28 Oct. 1897 (Larose Ch.: v.3, p.9)
GRIFFIN, Louisa m. Valsin ARCENAUX d. 1 March 1897 at age 44 yrs. (Thib. Ch.: v.3, p.197)
GRIFFIN, Lucien (Frank & Eve ORGERON) d. 4 Nov. 1897 at age 2 yrs. & 3 mths. (Larose Ch.: v.1, p.41)
GRIFFIN, Paul Leonce (Samuel & Emma CROSBY) b. 19 Aug. 1897 (Larose Ch.: v.3, p.10)
GRIFFIN, Pauline Celina (Sam & Rosana ORGERON) b. 11 June 1896 (Lockport Ch.: v.2, p.331)
GRIFFIN, Sarah m. 23 June 1898 Nathan MACK (Houma Ct. Hse.: Mar. v.30 & 31, #33)
GRIFFIN, Silas Adam (Abraham & Marcelite GUIDRY) b. 3 Feb. 1896 (Larose Ch.: v.2, p.189)

GRIFFIN, Stephen (Stephen & Mary Ann ERIS) m. 28 Aug. 1899 Daisy DUPLANTIS (Houma Ct. Hse.: Mar. v.31 & 32, #111)
GRIFFIN, Stephen (Stephen H. & Mary Ann ERIS) m. 5 Sept. 1899 Daisy DUPLANTIS (Theriot Ch.: v.1-, p.7)
GRIFFIN, Thomas m. 18 Nov. 1899 Clemence GUIDRY (Thib. Ct. Hse.: Mar. v.39, #256)

GRIMARD (Sometimes: GRIMAN, GRIMAR, GRIMOND, GRINARD)

GRIMMALVA, Josephine (Lodovico & Aurelia ROSATA) b. 17 Jan. 1899 (Raceland Ch.: v.5, p.88)

GRINAGE (Sometimes: GRENAGE)
GRINAGE, Bessy Josephine (Jos. A. & Amanda MARCEL) b. 18 Jan. 1896; m. Joseph A. THIBODEAUX on 30 June 1925. (Houma Ch.: Bapt. Bk., v.5, p.146)
GRISAMORE, Silas T. d. 24 July 1897 at age 72 yrs. (Thib. Ch.: Epis. Ch.: v.1, p.394)
GRIZZOF, Angello (Leoluca & Venzenza RUSSA) b. 8 Jan. 1898 (Chacahoula Ch.: Gibson Ch.: v.2, p.115)
GRIZZOFF, Angelo (Leoluca & Vinzenza RUSSA) b. 8 Jan. 1898 (Chacahoula Ch.: Gibson Record: Mar. Bk., v.1, #3)

GROS (Sometimes: GRAUX, GROSS)
GROS, Abel (Numa & Philomene HEBERT) m. 5 Sept. 1898 Dolphine BENOIT (Thib. Ct. Hse.: Mar. v.38, #259)
GROS, Abel (Numa & Philomene HEBERT) m. 5 Sept. 1898 Dolphine BENOIT (Thib. Ch.: v.14, p.219)
GROS, Adelina (Sylvere & Eulalia AYO) m. 31 Jan. 1898 Texon VICKNAIR (Thib. Ct. Hse.: Mar. v.37, #20)
GROS, Adeline m. 30 March 1898 Taylor PORTIER (Thib. Ct. Hse.: Mar. v.37, #137)
GROS, Agnes Odilia (Cleophas & Mathilde HEBERT) b. 29 Aug. 1896 (Thib. Ch.: v.7, p.420)
GROS, Albert m. 20 Jan. 1896 Lezima FREMIN (Thib. Ct. Hse.: Mar. v.35, #30)
GROS, Aline m. 18 Jan. 1897 Henry AUCOIN (Thib. Ct. Hse.: Mar. v.36, #41)
GROS, Avis d. 12 June 1897 at age 3 yrs. (Thib. Ch.: v.3, p.201)
GROS, Celema m. 4 March 1897 Eugene CADIERE (Thib. Ct. Hse.: Mar. v.36, #94)
GROS, Celema (Jean Baptiste & Severine MARCEL) m. 11 March 1897 Eugene CADIERE (Houma Ct. Hse.: Mar. v.30 & 31, #291)
GROS, Celema (Jean Baptiste & Severine MARCEL) m. 11 March 1897 Eugene CADIERE (Thib. Ch.: v.14, p.131)
GROS, Celeste (Trasimond & Evelina BOUDREAUX) m. 30 April 1896 Rosemond WAGESPACK (Thib. Ch.: v.14, p.87)
GROS, Celeste (Trasimond & Evelina BOUDREAUX) m. 30 April 1896 Rosemond WAGESPACK (Thib. Ct. Hse.: Mar. v.35, #75)

GROS, Clara (Jean Baptiste & Severine MARCEL) m. 24 Aug. 1899 Ernest HOTARD (Thib. Ch.: v.14, p.291)

GROS, Clara (Jean Baptiste & Severine MARCEL) m. 24 Aug. 1899 Ernest HOTARD (Thib. Ct. Hse.: Mar. v.39, #210)

GROS, Exulta d. 24 Feb. 1898 at age 3 mths. (Lockport Ch.: v.1, #5)

GROS, Joseph d. 16 July 1897 at age 77 yrs. (Lockport Ch.: v.1, #14)

GROS, Joseph Aida (Numa & Philomene HEBERT) b. 21 Feb. 1897 (Thib. Ch.: v.7, p.440)

GROS, Joseph Anidas (Joseph & Ophelia PICOU) b. 15 Feb. 1898 (Larose Ch.: v.3, p.16)

GROS, Joseph Avit (Albert & Adolphine BENOIT) b. 9 July 1898 (Thib. Ch.: v.7, p.554)

GROS, Joseph Eno Cleandre (Oscar & Mathilde NAQUIN) b. 10 Nov. 1898 (Chackbay Ch.: v.1, p.123)

GROS, Joseph Lovencie (Berthille & Celina PUNCH) b. 16 Aug. 1897 (Larose Ch.: v.3, p.6)

GROS, Josephine Armelise (Berthel & Celina PUNCH) b. 14 July 1898 (Larose Ch.: v.3, p.23)

GROS, Jules (Oleus & Marie BOUDREAUX) m. 13 Feb. 1897 Elmire LERILLE (Thib. Ct. Hse.: Mar. v.36, #62)

GROS, Justilien Joel (Edgard & Julia ARCEMENT) b. 21 Oct. 1896 (Thib. Ch.: v.7, p.422)

GROS, Laura (Trasimond & Azelie BOUDREAU) m. 23 Jan. 1899 Volzi BORNE (Thib. Ct. Hse.: Mar. v.38, #1)

GROS, Laura (Trasimond & Azelie BOUDREAU) m. 23 Jan. 1899 Volzi BORNE (Chackbay Ch.: v.1, p.67)

GROS, Louis Laura (Leon & Marie RICHARD) b. 11 Nov. 1897 (Thib. Ch.: v.7, p.475)

GROS, Lucien d. 2 Oct. 1896 at age 20 days (Thib. Ch.: v.3, p.188)

GROS, Lucien Pierre (Leon & Marie RICHARD) b. 12 Sept. 1896 (Thib. Ch.: v.7, p.418)

GROS, Marie Adela (Joseph & Ophelia PICOU) b. 2 March 1896 (Larose Ch.: v.2, p.181)

GROS, Marie Alfrida (Joseph & Ida CLEMENT) b. 13 Feb. 1899 (Chackbay Ch.: v.1, p.126)

GROS, Marie Olivia (Denise & Dolphine BADEAUX) b. 3 April 1898 (Larose Ch.: v.3, p.18)

GROS, Marie Zulma (Oscar & Mathilde NAQUIN) b. 28 Nov. 1897 (Chackbay Ch.: v.1, p.101)

GROS, Omer Eddy (Leonce & Merentia MELANCON) b. 25 March 1899 (Thib. Ch.: v.7, p.596)

GROS, Philippe Aurelien (Joseph & Ida CLEMENT) b. 15 July 1896 (Chackbay Ch.: v.1, p.71)

GROS, Seraphine (Alcide & Cordilia DUPRE) b. 5 April 1896 (Lockport Ch.: v.2, p.329)

GROS, Thomas Eusebe (Leony & Philomene MELANCON) b. 8 April 1898 (Thib. Ch.: v.7, p.495)

GROSBY, Julie Louise (Julien & Virginie HENRY) b. 31 Dec. 1897 (Larose Ch.: v.3, p.22)
GRUBOURGIA???????, Guiseppe (Guiseppe & Rosie BATTE) m. 16 June 1898 Catherine SCANNIA (Thib. Ch.: v.14, p.207)

GUENO (Sometimes: GUENAUD, GUENOT)
GUENO, Claiborne H. m. 21 June 1899 Ellen VERRET (Houma Ct. Hse.: Mar. v.31 & 32, #49)
GUENO, Normand Frances (A. O. & Marie Josephine ZARINGER) b. 3 March 1898 (Houma Ch.: v.5, p.208)
GUERIN, Angelique also known as Rev. Mother St. Bernard. She was Superior General of the Mont Carmel nuns. d. 1 Feb. 1897 at age 78 yrs. & 8 mths. (Thib. Ch.: v.3, p.196)
GUGANHEIM, ----- boy (Ziegman) d. 18 - 24 Dec. 1899 at age 6 days (Thib. Ch.: v.3, p.247)
GUGGARDO, Michale (Aspan & Laurina GURREVA) m. 13 Feb. 1897 Maria DIMECO (Houma Ch.: v.6-a, p.192)
GUGGARDO, Michele m. 11 Feb. 1897 Maria DIMICO (Houma Ct. Hse.: Mar. v.29 & 30, #301)
GUGGENHEIMER, Sig. m. 4 Feb. 1899 Lillie WHATLEY (Thib. Ct. Hse.: Mar. v.38, #92)
GUGGINO, Joseph (Salvatore & Marie CASTELLANO) b. 12 Sept. 1896 (Thib. Ch.: v.7, p.420)
GUICEPPA, Cologero Catalonello (Di & Rosaria CIACCIO) b. 12 Oct. 1899 (Houma Ch.: v.5, p.259)

GUICHE (Sometimes: GUICHET)

GUICHET, Jean Philippe (Philibert & Louisa VERRETTE) b. 22 Dec. 1896 (Raceland Ch.: v.5, p.38)
GUICHET, Jeanne Philomene (Philibert & Louisa VERRET) b. 20 Sept. 1898 (Raceland Ch.: v.5, p.78)
GUICHET, Louis Raymond (Jean & Letitia MARTIN) bt. 6 March 1898 (Thib. Ch.: v.7, p.489)
GUICHET, Marie Claudine (Jean & Leotitia MARTIN) b. 24 July 1896 (Thib. Ch.: v.7, p.413)

GUIDROZ (Sometimes: GUIDRAUX, GUIDREAU, GUIDREAUX, GUIDROS, GUITRAU, GUITRAUX, GUITREAUX, GUITROS, GUITROZ)
GUIDROZ, ----- m. Pierre UZE d. 10 April 1898 at age 30 yrs. (Lockport Ch.: v.1, #9)
GUIDROZ, Agnes (Etienne & Emelia GRIFFIN) b. 21 Jan. 1897 (Lockport Ch.: v.3-A, #6)
GUIDROZ, Agnes Amelia (Etienne & Emelia GREFFIN) b. 21 Jan. 1897 (Lockport Ch.: v.3, #6)
GUIDROZ, Augustin m. 16 Oct. 1897 Augusta SAPIA (Thib. Ct. Hse.: Mar. v.37, #249)
GUIDROZ, Augustin (Gustave & Amelie BOURGEOIS) m. 16 Oct. 1897 Augusta SAPIER (Raceland Ch.: v.2, p.53)

GUIDROZ, Berthe Gabriel (Saulet & Louisa CHAUVIN) b. 9 March 1896 (Lockport Ch.: v.2, p.325)
GUIDROZ, Cecile d. 28 Nov. 1899 at age 27 yrs. (Lockport Ch.: v.1, #46)
GUIDROZ, Clarens Fortune (Emery & Mamie LAROZE) b. 31 May 1896 (Lockport Ch.: v.2, p.330)
GUIDROZ, Clifford d. 3 April 1898 at age 1 yr. (Raceland Ch.: v.1, p.18)
GUIDROZ, Coralie (Sole & Emelina CANTRELLE) m. 6 Nov. 1899 Emile CANTRELLE (Thib. Ct. Hse.: Mar. v.39, #259)
GUIDROZ, Coralie (Sole & Emelina CANTRELLE) m. 6 Nov. 1899 Emile CANTRELLE (Lockport Ch.: v.2, p.210)
GUIDROZ, Edith Veronique (Marcellin & Mathilde DUPUIS) b. 13 Oct. 1896 (Larose Ch.: v.2, p.183)
GUIDROZ, Ernestine m. 13 April 1898 Ovide TRICHE (Thib. Ct. Hse.: Mar. v.38, #151)
GUIDROZ, Eugene Clifford (Emile & Georges BOUTERIE) b. 3 April 1897 (Raceland Ch.: v.5, p.47)
GUIDROZ, Felicien m. 25 April 1896 Julie GALJOUR (Lockport Ch.: v.4, p.122)
GUIDROZ, Felicien m. 25 April 1896 Julie GALJOUR (Larose Ch.: v.3, p.3)
GUIDROZ, Felicien m. 25 April 1896 Julie GALJOUR (Thib. Ct. Hse.: Mar. v.35, #78)
GUIDROZ, Firmin of Lafourche Parish (Ernest & Augusta BOURGEOIS) m. 27 Jan. 1898 Bernadette ARCENEAUX of Lafourche Parish (Larose Ch.: v.3, p.7)
GUIDROZ, Firmin (Ernest & Augusta BOURGEOIS) m. 27 Jan. 1898 Bernadette ARCENAUX (Larose Ch.: v.4, p.1)
GUIDROZ, Firmin (Ernest & Augusta BOURGEOIS) m. 27 Jan. 1898 Bernadette ARCENEAUX (Thib. Ct. Hse.: Mar. v.37, #39)
GUIDROZ, Georgina Gertrude (Emile & Georgina BOUTERIE) b. 26 Feb. 1896 (Raceland Ch.: v.5, p.21)
GUIDROZ, Hortence Justine (Henri & Clemance TOUPS) b. 30 March 1896 (Lockport Ch.: v.2, p.327)
GUIDROZ, Jean Emile (Felicien & Julie GALJOUR) b. 6 April 1898 (Larose Ch.: v.3, p.18)
GUIDROZ, Jean Norbert (Felicien & Julie GALJOUR) b. 28 Dec. 1899 (Larose Ch.: v.3, p.50)
GUIDROZ, Joseph Howard Walter (Joseph & Movilia AUCOIN) b. 8 March 1896 (Montegut Ch.: v.6, p.35)
GUIDROZ, Joseph Sidney (Joseph & Ovilia AUCOIN) b. 13 July 1898 (Montegut Ch.: v.6, p.75)
GUIDROZ, Lewis Harris (Firmin & Bernadette ARCENEAUX) b. 3 Jan. 1899 (Larose Ch.: v.3, p.34)
GUIDROZ, Marie Elvire (Felicien & Julie GALJOUR) b. 7 Dec. 1896 (Larose Ch.: v.3, p.1)
GUIDROZ, Marie Elvire (Felicien & Julie GALJOUR) b. 7 Dec. 1896 (Larose Ch.: v.3, p.2)
GUIDROZ, Marie Germaine (Paul & Auguste CLAUDET) b. 28 Nov. 1899 (Raceland Ch.: v.5, p.107)

GUIDROZ, Marthe Marie (Paul & Augusta CLAUDET) b. 29 Feb. 1896 (Raceland Ch.: v.5, p.20)
GUIDROZ, Paul Clifford Winfield (Emile & Georgina BOUTERIE) b. 22 April 1899 (Raceland Ch.: v.5, p.97)
GUIDROZ, Paul Emmanuel (Thomas & Josephine CANTRELLE) b. 20 July 1896 (Lockport Ch.: v.2, p.332)
GUIDROZ, Tema m. 7 Oct. 1897 Willie BARTLEY (Thib. Ct. Hse.: Mar. v.37, #245)
GUIDROZ, Thomas (Marcellus) d. 1 Dec. 1897 at age 15 yrs. (Lockport Ch.: v.1, #31)
GUIDROZ, Virginie Ayda (Louis & Aurelia HOTARD) b. 22 Feb. 1896 (Lockport Ch.: v.2, p.323)

GUIDRY (Sometimes: GAIDRY, GUEDRY)
GUIDRY, Adelaide m. 25 May 1897 Andre PLAISANCE (Thib. Ct. Hse.: Mar. v.36, #148)
GUIDRY, Adelaide m. 5 June 1897 Andre PLAISANCE (Larose Ch.: v.3, p.5)
GUIDRY, Adelaide m. 5 June 1897 Andre PLAISANCE (Larose Ch.: v.4, p.73)
GUIDRY, Adele m. 3 July 1896 Numa ALLEMAN (Thib. Ct. Hse.: Mar. v.36, #116)
GUIDRY, Adele m. 8 July 1896 Numa ALLEMAND (Larose Ch.: v.4, p.89)
GUIDRY, Adele m. 8 July 1896 Numa ALLEMAND (Larose Ch.: v.3, p.3)
GUIDRY, Adele m. 8 July 1896 Numa ALLEMAND (Larose Ch.: v.4, p.41)
GUIDRY, Adelina m. 22 Dec. 1896 Francois L. DOUCET (Thib. Ct. Hse.: Mar. v.36, #168)
GUIDRY, Adelina (Felicien & Eugenie GASPARD) m. 10 Jan. 1898 Francois DOUCET (Larose Ch.: v.3, p.6)
GUIDRY, Adelina (Felicien & Eugenie GASPAR) m. 10 Jan. 1898 Francois DOUCET (Larose Ch.: v.4, p.109)
GUIDRY, Adolphe m. 1 Sept. 1896 Zilda DOUCET (Thib. Ct. Hse.: Mar. v.36, #139)
GUIDRY, Adolphine m. 16 April 1898 Anatole TERREBONNE (Thib. Ct. Hse.: Mar. v.37, #148)
GUIDRY, Adrien Valfroid (Orgeron & Adele GUIDRY) b. 28 May 1899 (Larose Ch.: v.3, p.40)
GUIDRY, Agnes Emelie (Aristile & Leontine THERIOT) b. 27 Dec. 1898 (Raceland Ch.: v.5, p.86)
GUIDRY, Alexandre (Clairville & Marie J. RHODES) m. 17 July 1899 Julia SONGE (Montegut Ch.: v.4, p.267)
GUIDRY, Alexandre (Clerville & Marie Key RHODES) m. 24 June 1899 Julia SONGE (Houma Ct. Hse.: Mar. v.31 & 32, #55)
GUIDRY, Alida m. Joseph LECOMPTE d. 19 June 1899 at age 65 yrs. (Montegut Ch.: v.2, p.27)
GUIDRY, Amelie Louise (Belonie & Camila BOURC) b. 3 Oct. 1899 (Larose Ch.: v.3, p.50)

GUIDRY, Andre Joseph (Marcellin & Josephine RAYMOND) b. 30 Nov. 1898 (Larose Ch.: v.3, p.34)
GUIDRY, Anne Sidonia (Ernest & Sidonia THERIOT) b. 24 July 1897; m. Joseph Willis TROSCLAIR on 1 May 1943. (Raceland Ch.: Bapt. Bk., v.5, p.52)
GUIDRY, Armance m. 24 Feb. 1899 John LAFONT (Thib. Ct. Hse.: Mar. v.39, #113)
GUIDRY, Armand J. m. 19 March 1898 Rosine A. LEE (Thib. Ct. Hse.: Mar. v.37, #114)
GUIDRY, Azelie Angelina (Armond & R. Caroline LEE) b. 5 Dec. 1898 (Larose Ch.: v.3, p.32)
GUIDRY, Belel d. 30 Nov. 1899 at age 10 mths. (Raceland Ch.: v.1, p.29)
GUIDRY, Berthilde Geneva (Albert & Solema BOURK) b. 4 Jan. 1898 (Theriot Ch.: v.2, p.16)
GUIDRY, Blaise Manuel (William & Felicia BABIN) b. 3 Feb. 1899 (Raceland Ch.: v.5, p.92)
GUIDRY, Brigitte Suzanne (Aristile & Leontine THERIOT) b. 11 Aug. 1896 (Raceland Ch.: v.5, p.27)
GUIDRY, Carles Thomas (Klebert & Marcellin BREAUX) b. 11 Feb. 1899 (Thib. Ch.: v.7, p.537)
GUIDRY, Cecilia Laly (William & Felicia BABIN) b. 19 Feb. 1897 (Raceland Ch.: v.5, p.44)
GUIDRY, Cedonia (Francois & Marie GUIDRY) m. 1 June 1898 Joseph Neuville AUTHEMENT (Theriot Ch.: v.1-B, p.3)
GUIDRY, Cedonia (Francois & Marie GUIDRY) m. 16 May 1898 Joseph Neuville AUTHEMENT (Houma Ct. Hse.: Mar. v.30 & 31, #444)
GUIDRY, Celia Ida (Frosin & Alida BABIN) b. 9 Sept. 1896 (Raceland Ch.: v.5, p.29)
GUIDRY, Celina m. 24 July 1897 Joseph THERIOT (Lockport Ch.: v.2, p.164)
GUIDRY, Celma (Valfroid & Marcelitte BERNARD) m. 24 July 1897 Joseph THERIOT (Thib. Ct. Hse.: Mar. v.35, #189)
GUIDRY, Charles (Adam & Aimee TOUPS) m. 20 Sept. 1898 Marie PITRE (Thib. Ch.: v.14, p.224)
GUIDRY, Charles (Adrien & Aimee TOUPS) m. 29 Sept. 1898 Marie PITRE (Thib. Ct. Hse.: Mar. v.38, #269)
GUIDRY, Charles Eugene (Charles & Mary PITRE) b. 4 Sept. 1898 (Thib. Ch.: v.7, p.561)
GUIDRY, Charles Narcisse (Arthur & Octavie HEBERT) d. 23 Sept. 1896 at age 11 mths. (Montegut Ch.: v.2, p.6)
GUIDRY, Charles Noe (Klebert & Marceline BRAU) b. 23 March 1897 (Thib. Ch.: v.7, p.446)
GUIDRY, Clemence m. 18 Nov. 1899 Thomas GRIFFIN (Thib. Ct. Hse.: Mar. v.39, #256)
GUIDRY, Clemence m. 6 May 1897 Joseph LAFONT (Thib. Ct. Hse.: Mar. v.36, #139)
GUIDRY, Clorinda (Calliste & Ozite GUIDRY) m. 29 June 1896 Pierre CHERAMIE (Thib. Ct. Hse.: Mar. v.36, #113)

GUIDRY, Clovis (Felicien & Elmire MOLAISON) m. 28 Jan. 1899 Florestine GERVAIS (Thib. Ct. Hse.: Mar. v.38, #25)
GUIDRY, Clovis (Felicien & Elmire MOLAISON) m. 28 Jan. 1899 Florestine GERVAIS (Lockport Ch.: v.2, p.199)
GUIDRY, Edgard Bonaventure (Lovencie & Azelie AUTIN) b. 14 July 1897 (Larose Ch.: v.3, p.9)
GUIDRY, Elidia Melanie (Raphael & Argentine DANOS) b. 29 Oct. ----; bt. 14 Oct. 1896 (Larose Ch.: v.2, p.197)
GUIDRY, Elima (Donat & Mathilde BELANGER) m. 27 April 1896 Frank RHODES (Montegut Ch.: v.4, p.208)
GUIDRY, Ella Evelida (Orestille & Odillia BEAUDOIN) b. 24 March 1899 (Larose Ch.: v.3, p.39)
GUIDRY, Elles Celestin (Toussaint & Pauline RAYMOND) b. 28 Sept. 1897 (Larose Ch.: v.3, p.13)
GUIDRY, Elles Eugene (Raphael & Argentine DANOS) b. 6 Aug. 1898 (Larose Ch.: v.3, p.28)
GUIDRY, Elson Jean (Joseph & Celestine CHOUESS) b. 8 Feb. 1898 (Larose Ch.: v.3, p.19)
GUIDRY, Emelia (Valfroid & Marcelite BERNARD) m. 29 Jan. 1898 Augustave TOURRIL (Thib. Ct. Hse.: Mar. v.37, #41)
GUIDRY, Emelia (Valfroid & Marcelite BERNARD) m. 29 Jan. 1898 Augustave TOURREL (Lockport Ch.: v.2, p.182)
GUIDRY, Emelie (Alidor & d.Octavie BLANCHARD) m. 9 Oct. 1899 Marshall THERIOT (Montegut Ch.: v.4, p.271)
GUIDRY, Emelie (Charles G. & Celeste Emelia LEONVAL) m. 16 June 1897 Abel DONNAUD (Thib. Ch.: v.14, p.147)
GUIDRY, Emelie Celestine (Joseph & Celestine CHOUESS) b. 17 Feb. 1896 (Larose Ch.: v.2, p.187)
GUIDRY, Emilie Alcida (Gabriel & Euphelia AUTIN) b. 3 May 1897 (Raceland Ch.: v.5, p.48)
GUIDRY, Emily (Alidor & Octavie BLANCHARD) m. 16 Sept. 1899 Marshall THERIOT (Houma Ct. Hse.: Mar. v.31 & 32, #132)
GUIDRY, Emily (Charles & Celeste Emelia LEONVAL) m. 16 June 1897 Abel S. DAUNAUD (Thib. Ct. Hse.: Mar. v.36, #164)
GUIDRY, Enezile Marie (Joseph & Louisiane Marie PITRE) b. 31 Jan. 1897 (Thib. Ch.: v.7, p.488)
GUIDRY, Eugenie Jeanne (Moise & Lydia MORRIS) b. 21 Aug. 1896 (Raceland Ch.: v.5, p.28)
GUIDRY, Eve (Orgeron) d. 16 June 1898 at age 11 mths. (Lockport Ch.: v.1, #13)
GUIDRY, Farguard P. (Ernest & Lucie CHAMPAGNE) m. 12 Oct. 1897 Grace CHAUVIN (Montegut Ch.: v.4, p.226)
GUIDRY, Farquard P. (Ernest & Lucie CHAMPAGNE) m. 25 Sept. 1897 Grace CHAUVIN (Houma Ct. Hse.: Mar. v.29 & 30, #96)
GUIDRY, Florestal m. 23 April 1896 Uzeline CHARPENTIER (Thib. Ct. Hse.: Mar. v.35, #77)
GUIDRY, Frank d. 31 March 1898 at age 53 yrs. (Thib. Ch.: v.3, p.212)

GUIDRY, Gustave (Jean & Alexina PITRE) b. 24 Jan. 1898 (Larose Ch.: v.3, p.17)
GUIDRY, Henriette Bernadette (Moise & Josephine ELLIOT) b. 9 Oct. 1898 (Raceland Ch.: v.5, p.79)
GUIDRY, Iba (Jho) d. 28 May 1899 at age 5 mths. (Lockport Ch.: v.1, #21)
GUIDRY, Irma m. 7 July 1899 Paul CALAIS (Thib. Ct. Hse.: Mar. v.39, #196)
GUIDRY, Irma (Pierre & Elisa TERREBONNE) m. 8 July 1899 Paul CALAIS (Larose Ch.: v.3, p.12)
GUIDRY, Irma (Pierre & Elisa TERREBONNE) m. 8 July 1899 Paul CALAIS (Larose Ch.: v.4, p.95)
GUIDRY, Jean Eddie (Volcar & Marcellin MARTIN) b. 14 Nov. 1899 (Montegut Ch.: v.6, p.97)
GUIDRY, Jean Stanley (Noe & Cecile RODRIGUE) b. 5 Dec. 1896 (Thib. Ch.: v.7, p.429)
GUIDRY, John (Alidor N. & Onezile ROBICHAUX) m. 3 April 1899 Ludovia LIRETTE (Montegut Ch.: v.4, p.260)
GUIDRY, John J. (Alidore N. & Onezile ROBICHAUX) m. 22 March 1899 Ludovia LIRETTE (Houma Ct. Hse.: Mar. v.31 & 32, #371)
GUIDRY, John L. (Ernest & Marie Odelia CHAMPAGNE) m. 6 Jan. 1899 Mary Magnolty HOTARD (Houma Ct Hse.: Mar. v.30 & 31, #189)
GUIDRY, John Louis (Ernest & Marie Odelia CHAMPAGNE) m. 26 Jan. 1899 Marie Magnolty HOTARD (Montegut Ch.: v.4, p.252)
GUIDRY, Joseph d. 7 April 1897 at age 77 yrs. (Houma Ch.: v.3, p.12)
GUIDRY, Joseph m. 16 Jan. 1896 Louise TOMASSIE (Larose Ch.: v.3, p.1)
GUIDRY, Joseph m. 2 Jan. 1896 Louise TOMASSI (Thib. Ct. Hse.: Mar. v.35, #1)
GUIDRY, Joseph (Lagarde & Emeline ---) m. 1 Feb. 1896 Emelina CHAUVIN (Lockport Ch.: v.2, p.145 & 146)
GUIDRY, Joseph (Lagarde & Marie ORGERON) m. 1 Feb. 1896 Emelina CHAUVIN (Thib. Ct. Hse.: Mar. v.35, #23)
GUIDRY, Joseph (Theophile & Marguerite DOUCET) m. 16 Jan. 1896 Louise TOMASI (Larose Ch.: v.2, p.187)
GUIDRY, Joseph Allie (Volcar & Marcellin MARTIN) b. 3 June 1897 (Montegut Ch.: v.6, p.57)
GUIDRY, Joseph Aris Harris (Willie & Elidia FOLSE) b. 25 May 1896 (Theriot Ch.: v.1-B, p.96)
GUIDRY, Joseph Arthur (Lezin & Malvina GUIDRY) b. 5 March 1897 (Larose Ch.: v.3, p.13)
GUIDRY, Joseph Claude (Johnny & Philomene ROUEN) b. 15 June 1897 (Montegut Ch.: v.6, p.58)
GUIDRY, Joseph Edouard (Arthur & Octavie HEBERT) b. 26 April 1897 (Montegut Ch.: v.6, p.54)
GUIDRY, Joseph Francis (Orestille & Odillia BEAUDOIN) b. 29 Jan. 1897 (Larose Ch.: v.3, p.4)

GUIDRY, Joseph Harris (Joseph & Louise TOMASSIE) b. 7 Jan. 1897 (Larose Ch.: v.3, p.1)
GUIDRY, Joseph Iba (Joseph & Melina CHAUVIN) b. 20 Jan. 1899 (Larose Ch.: v.3, p.35)
GUIDRY, Joseph Ines (Lovincy & Berthe CHIASSON) b. 23 Nov. 1897 (Montegut Ch.: v.6, p.64)
GUIDRY, Joseph Luby (Facquhard & Grace CHAUVIN) b. 8 July 1899 (Montegut Ch.: v.6, p.90)
GUIDRY, Joseph Nelson (Nelson & Eugenie BOURGEOIS) b. 7 July 1896 (Raceland Ch.: v.3, p.25)
GUIDRY, Joseph Richard (Arthur & Octavie HEBERT) d. 5 May 1899 at age 19 days (Montegut Ch.: v.2, p.25)
GUIDRY, Joseph Simpson (Wilfrid & Elmire FANLSE) b. 10 Aug. 1898 (Theriot Ch.: v.2, p.28)
GUIDRY, Joseph Vorhies (Leonce & Carmelite CHOUESSE) b. 18 Nov. 1898 (Larose Ch.: v.3, p.37)
GUIDRY, Josephine m. 24 May 1897 Omer FOLSE (Thib. Ct. Hse.: Mar. v.36, #146)
GUIDRY, Josephine (Charles Joseph & Leontine GAUDET) m. 8 Feb. 1899 Louis Alphonse SCOTT (Thib. Ct. Hse.: Mar. v.38, #60)
GUIDRY, Josephine (Charles Joseph & Leontine GAUDET) m. 8 Feb. 1899 Louis A. SCOTT (Thib. Ch.: v.14, p.260)
GUIDRY, Josephine (Onesippe & Sarah KNIGHT) m. 31 May 1897 Homere FOLSE (Raceland Ch.: v.2, p.40)
GUIDRY, Julienne Marie (Alidor & Anezile ROBICHAUX) m. 25 Oct. 1897 Lineas J. LAPEROUSE (Montegut Ch.: v.4, p.226)
GUIDRY, Julienne Mary (Alidor & Anezile ROBICHAUX) m. 11 Oct. 1897 Leanus J. LAPEROUSE (Houma Ct. Hse.: Mar. v.29 & 30, #119)
GUIDRY, Laura m. 7 Jan. 1898 Louis DUPLANTIS (Houma Ct. Hse.: Mar. v.30 & 31, #185)
GUIDRY, Laura (Aristile & Emilie DUPLANTIS) m. 19 Jan. 1898 Louis DUPLANTIS (Montegut Ch.: v.4, p.230)
GUIDRY, Leonce m. 3 March 1898 Carmelite CHOUEST (Larose Ch.: v.3, p.8)
GUIDRY, Leonce m. 3 March 1898 Charmelitte CHOUESSE (Larose Ch.: v.4, p.79)
GUIDRY, Lola Sybil (Lowell & Pearl Bernice HANAGRIFF) b. 5? Aug. 1897 (Houma Ch.: Epis. Ch.: v.1, p.116)
GUIDRY, Louise (Jean & Alexina PITRE) m. 18 April 1898 Felicien DUET (Thib. Ct. Hse.: Mar. v.38, #160)
GUIDRY, Lovincy m. 30 June 1899 Marie ACHEE (Thib. Ct. Hse.: Mar. v.39, #191)
GUIDRY, Lucile m. 30 Sept. 1897 Joseph FORET (Thib. Ct. Hse.: Mar. v.37, #235)
GUIDRY, Lucile (Celestin & Emelie BABIN) m. 31 Sept. 1897 Joseph FORET (Raceland Ch.: v.2, p.51)
GUIDRY, Lucile (Emile & Adele BABIN) b. 28 Jan. 1897 (Raceland Ch.: v.5, p.40)

GUIDRY, Marcalitte (Adrien & Eugenie ORGERON) m. 15 Dec. 1899 Abraham GRIFFIN (Larose Ch.: v.4, p.30)

GUIDRY, Marcelitte (Adrien & Eugenie ORGERON) m. 15 Dec. 1899 Abraham GRIFFIN (Larose Ch.: v.3, p.13)

GUIDRY, Marguerite Edna (Theophile & Adeline CAMPEAU) b. 18 Jan. 1898 (Larose Ch.: v.3, p.15)

GUIDRY, Marie m. 15 Jan. 1897 Elie Teadore TOUPS (Larose Ch.: v.4, p.119-A)

GUIDRY, Marie m. 15 Jan. 1897 Elie Teodore TOUPS (Larose Ch.: v.3, p.5)

GUIDRY, Marie Edith (Clairville & Dolphine FOLSE) b. 5 Jan. 1899 (Raceland Ch.: v.5, p.87)

GUIDRY, Marie Elodie (Belonie & Camilla BOURG) b. 27 Jan. 1897 (Larose Ch.: v.3, p.8)

GUIDRY, Marie Estelle (Leopold & Arthemise CUROL) b. 14 Jan. 1899 (Larose Ch.: v.3, p.35)

GUIDRY, Marie Henriette (Paul & Armantine RIVET) b. 7 Nov. 1898 (Raceland Ch.: v.5, p.92)

GUIDRY, Marie Josephine (Felix & Alice GERVAIS) b. 16 June 1896 (Lockport Ch.: v.2, p.331)

GUIDRY, Marie Lilia (Willy & Ldia FANLSE) b. 7 Aug. 1898 (Theriot Ch.: v.2, p.28)

GUIDRY, Marie Louisianne (Jean Baptiste & Marie CUNNINGHAM) b. 24 May 1897 (Montegut Ch.: v.6, p.70)

GUIDRY, Marie Lydia (Louis & Francois DOUCET) b. 4 March 1899 (Larose Ch.: v.3, p.41)

GUIDRY, Marie Marguerite (Alfred & Evelina GEDRY) b. 10 Oct. 1896; m. Harry Joseph CHAISSON on 26 July 1952 (Houma Ch.: Bapt. Bk., v.5, p.167)

GUIDRY, Marie Phillis (Johnny & Dairy HOTARD) b. 10 Nov. 1899 (Montegut Ch.: v.6, p.95)

GUIDRY, Marie Rose m. 25 Jan. 1896 Isidore TOUPS (Thib. Ct. Hse.: Mar. v.35, #31)

GUIDRY, Mary of Lafourche Parish (Joseph & Emilie BRUCE) m. 6 March 1898 Robert CHOUESS, of Lafourche Parish (Larose Ch.: v.3, p.8)

GUIDRY, Mary (Joseph & Emilie BRUCE) m. 6 March 1898 Robert CHOUESS (Larose Ch.: v.4, p.7)

GUIDRY, Meldof d. 28 Nov. 1898 at age 31½ yrs. (Theriot Ch.: v.1, p.1)

GUIDRY, Myrthe m. 14 July 1896 Antoine GALIANO (Thib. Ct. Hse.: Mar. v.36, #124)

GUIDRY, Odile Bayola (Raymond & Eve UZE) b. 19 Feb. 1897 (Lockport Ch.: v.3-A, #26)

GUIDRY, Odile Bayola (Raymond & Eve UZE) b. 19 Feb. 1897 (Lockport Ch.: v.3, #26)

GUIDRY, Pauline Pocecaille d. 21 Aug. 1898 at age 23 yrs. (Montegut Ch.: v.2, p.20)

GUIDRY, Philip m. 8 July 1899 Maggie CROSIER (Thib. Ct. Hse.: Mar. v.39, #197)

GUIDRY, Pierre Noe (Moise & Lylia MORRIS) b. 18 Jan. 1899 (Raceland Ch.: v.5, p.88)
GUIDRY, Pierre Odom (Oscar & Victoria GLOVER) b. 21 March 1899 (Larose Ch.: v.3, p.38)
GUIDRY, Pierre Vincent (Denis & Elmire BOURGEOIS) b. 20 Oct. 1899 (Larose Ch.: v.3, p.46)
GUIDRY, Raymond m. 12 May 1896 Eve UZE (Thib. Ct. Hse.: Mar. v.35, #88)
GUIDRY, Raymond m. 23 Jan. 1899 Eve UZE (Lockport Ch.: v.2, p.199)
GUIDRY, Raymond Paul (Marcellin & Josephine RAYMOND) b. 13 May 1896 (Larose Ch.: v.3, p.12)
GUIDRY, Samson Jerome (Nelson & Eugenie BOURGEOIS) b. 8 Nov. 1898 (Raceland Ch.: v.5, p.82)
GUIDRY, Selema (Donat & Mathilde BELANGER) m. 11 April 1896 Frank RHODES (Houma Ct. Hse.: Mar. v.29 & 30, #30)
GUIDRY, Solomon (Trasimond & Madeleine THEVE) d. 9 Sept. 1896 at age 41 yrs. (Montegut Ch.: v.2, p.6)
GUIDRY, Theophile (Ovide & Catherine DUPRE) m. 3 Jan. 1899 Eugenie NETTLETON (Houma Ct. Hse.: Mar. v.30 & 31, #174)
GUIDRY, Theophile (Ovide & Catherine DUPRE) m. 4 Feb. 1899 Eugenie NETTLETON (Montegut Ch.: v.4, p.255)
GUIDRY, Trasimond d. 9 Sept. 1896 at age 41 yrs. (Montegut Ch.: v.2, p.6)
GUIDRY, Valfroi d. 22 Nov. 1899 at age 6 mths. (Lockport Ch.: v.1, #47)
GUIDRY, Wilfred Zenon (Paul & Cecilia BEAUDOIN) b. 12 April 1897 (Larose Ch.: v.3, p.8)

GUILBEAU (Sometimes: GUILBO)

GUILBEAU, Marie m. 18 April 1896 Jimmy J. PITRE (Thib. Ct. Hse.: Mar. v.35, #57)
GUILBEAU, Pierre Davey (Frank & Leocadie BOURG) b. 30 June 1898 (Larose Ch.: v.3, p.33)
GUILBERT, Freddy (Adam & Augustine GIROUARD) b. 4 Feb. 1896 (Houma Ch.: v.5, p.171)

GUILLIANO (See: GALIANO)

GUILLOT (Sometimes: GUILLOTE, GUILLOTTE, GUYOT)

GUILLOT, Adam Joseph d. 16 Nov. 1896 at age 8 days (Thib. Ch.: v.3, p.190)
GUILLOT, Adam Joseph (Jean & Mathilde HOHENSEE) b. 8 Nov. 1896 (Thib. Ch.: v.7, p.425)
GUILLOT, Adela (Jean Baptiste & Leontine RICHARD) m. 30 Aug. 1897 Arthur BREAUX (Thib. Ct. Hse.: Mar. v.37, #223)
GUILLOT, Adela (Jean Baptiste & Leontine RICHARD) m. 30 Aug. 1897 Arthur BREAUX (Thib. Ch.: v.14, p.159)
GUILLOT, Agnes (Thomas & Justilia BERNARD) m. 26 Sept. 1899 Camille NAQUIN (Thib. Ch.: v.14, p.298)

GUILLOT, Agnes (Thomas & Justilia BERNARD) m. 26 Sept. 1899 Camille J. NAQUIN (Thib. Ct. Hse.: Mar. v.39, #235)
GUILLOT, Agnes Marie (Adam & Pauline LADOUCEUR) b. 1 Aug. 1898 (Thib. Ch.: v.7, p.507)
GUILLOT, Alfred (Odressy & Marie GUILLOTTE) m. 27 April 1898 Camille RICHARD (Thib. Ct. Hse.: Mar. v.38, #159)
GUILLOT, Alfred (Ordressy & Marie GUILLOTE) m. 27 April 1898 Camille RICHARD (Thib. Ch.: v.14, p.197)
GUILLOT, Alice Henriette (Orvile & Lea BOUDREAUX) b. 25 Aug. 1898 (Thib. Ch.: v.7, p.512)
GUILLOT, Altee Annette (Edgard & Cecilia PONTIFE) b. 8 June 1899 (Thib. Ch.: v.7, p.608)
GUILLOT, Alvin Lionel Clayton (Albert & Florida TORPOLIN) b. 23 Jan. 1899 (Thib. Ch.: v.7, p.592)
GUILLOT, Angeline (Eugene & Honorene THIBODAUX) m. 24 Jan. 1898 Nelson THIBODAUX (Thib. Ch.: v.14, p.172)
GUILLOT, Angeline (Eugene & Honorine THIBODAUX) m. 24 Jan. 1898 Nelson THIBODAUX (Thib. Ct. Hse.: Mar. v.37, #15)
GUILLOT, Anidas m. 2 Sept. 1899 Berthe BOUDREAUX (Thib. Ct. Hse.: Mar. v.39, #240)
GUILLOT, Arthur (Evariste & H. THIBODAUX) m. 18 April 1898 Elizabeth AUCOIN (Thib. Ch.: v.14, p.194)
GUILLOT, Arthur (Evariste & Honorine AUCOIN) m. 18 April 1898 Elizabeth AUCOIN (Thib. Ct. Hse.: Mar. v.37, #140)
GUILLOT, Augusta Eve Melanie (Edgar & Julie MIRE) b. 2 Nov. 1899 (Thib. Ch.: v.7, p.573)
GUILLOT, Aurelie m. 15 Sept. 1896 Jean BOUDREAUX (Thib. Ct. Hse.: Mar. v.36, #143)
GUILLOT, Aurelien Leonel (Edgar & Julie MIRE) b. 23 Oct. 1898 (Thib. Ch.: v.7, p.524)
GUILLOT, Cecile Helvine (Clovis & Odilia CALAHAN) b. 6 Nov. 1898 (Thib. Ch.: v.7, p.522)
GUILLOT, Clemantina (Leonard & Josephine THIBODAUX) m. 18 June 1896 Fernand ROGER (Thib. Ct. Hse.: Mar. v.35, #97)
GUILLOT, Clementine (Leonard & Josephine THIBODAUX) m. 18 June 1896 Fernand ROGER (Lockport Ch.: v.2, p.151)
GUILLOT, David d. 16 April 1899 at age 5 wks. (Thib. Ch.: v.3, p.231)
GUILLOT, David (Louis & Marie GUILLOT) b. 11 March 1899 (Thib. Ch.: v.7, p.542)
GUILLOT, Denys Henri (Felicien & Emilienne BRAUD) b. 8 April 1897 (Thib. Ch.: v.7, p.447)
GUILLOT, Edgar m. 20 Jan. 1898 Emma LEONARD (Houma Ct. Hse.: Mar. v.30 & 31, #239)
GUILLOT, Edgar (Emile & Oleander BERGERON) m. 3 Jan. 1898 Emma LEONARD (Houma Ch.: v.6-a, p.228)
GUILLOT, Edgard (Clodomire & Lulina ALBERT) m. 24 Jan. 1898 Cecile PONTIFF (Thib. Ct. Hse.: Mar. v.37, #14)
GUILLOT, Edgard (Clodomire & Zulina ALBERT) m. 24 Jan. 1898 Cecile PONTIFF (Thib. Ch.: v.14, p.174)

GUILLOT, Elisabeth m. Elivaudais DANTIN d. 13 Feb. 1896 at age 58 yrs. & 6 mths. (Thib. Ch.: v.3, p.179)
GUILLOT, Ella Linda (Felicien & Emilienne BREAUX) b. 26 Aug. 1898 (Thib. Ch.: v.7, p.562)
GUILLOT, Emelie (J. Emile & Josephine AYCOCK) m. 18 Sept. 1896 Charles BOURG (Chacahoula Ch.: v.1, p.54)
GUILLOT, Emile (Aurelien & Alouisa MIRE) m. 18 May 1899 Judith RICHARD (Thib. Ch.: v.14, p.282)
GUILLOT, Emile (Emile & Dolestine GRAUS or GROS) m. 19 Feb. 1898 Malvina CLEMENT (Chackbay Ch.: v.1, p.57)
GUILLOT, Emile (Emile & Dolestine GRAUS) m. 19 Feb. 1898 Malvina CLEMENT (Thib. Ct. Hse.: Mar. v.37, #80)
GUILLOT, Enee Alcida (Anidas & Alcida THIBODAUX) b. 26 July 1897 (Thib. Ch.: v.7, p.459)
GUILLOT, Evariste d. 1 March 1896 at age 80 yrs. (Thib. Ch.: v.3, p.180)
GUILLOT, Eve Katy (Franklin & Victoria PITT) b. 4 May 1897 (Thib. Ch.: v.7, p.450)
GUILLOT, Evelie (Emile & Dolestine GRAUS or GROS) m. 17 Feb. 1898 Leo LANDRY (Chackbay Ch.: v.1, p.56)
GUILLOT, Evelie (Emile & Dolestine GRAUS) m. 17 Feb. 1898 Leo LANDRY (Thib. Ct. Hse.: Mar. v.37, #62)
GUILLOT, Felicia (Odressy & Marie GUILLOTE) m. 25 Jan. 1897 Henri ROGER (Thib. Ct. Hse.: Mar. v.36, #25)
GUILLOT, Felicie (Odressy & Marie GUILLOT) m. 25 Jan. 1897 Henri ROGER (Thib. Ch.: v.14, p.117)
GUILLOT, Flavia (Omer & Marie BERGERON) m. 7 Dec. 1899 Joseph BERGERON (Houma Ct. Hse.: Mar. v.31 & 32, #174)
GUILLOT, Flavie of Terrebonne Parish m. 7 Dec. 1899 Joseph BERGERON (Houma Ch.: v.6-B, p.5)
GUILLOT, Franklin (Adam & Pauline LADOMER) m. 25 June 1896 Victoria PITRE (Thib. Ch.: v.14, p.94)
GUILLOT, Franklin (Adam & Pauline LADOUCEUR) m. 25 June 1896 Victoria PITRE (Thib. Ct. Hse.: Mar. v.35, #103)
GUILLOT, Georgina Augustine (Marcelien & Angeline BOUDREAUX) b. 28 July 1899 (Thib. Ch.: v.8, p.4)
GUILLOT, Guilbert Luc (Edgar & Berthe BOUDREAU) b. 12 Feb. 1898 (Chacahoula Ch.: v.4, p.2)
GUILLOT, Henri Webre (Arthur & Adelaide GAUBERT) b. 3 Dec. 1899 (Thib. Ch.: v.7, p.577)
GUILLOT, Howard Joseph (Edgard & Ema LEONARD) b. 9 Dec. 1898 (Houma Ch.: v.5, p.233)
GUILLOT, Jean Joseph Florian (Louis & Marie GUILLOT) b. 20 March 1899 (Thib. Ch.: v.7, p.598)
GUILLOT, Jean Lionel Thomas (Jean Lionel & Mathilde HOHENSIE) b. 16 Oct. 1897 (Thib. Ch.: v.7, p.468)
GUILLOT, Joachim (Arthur & Adelaide GAUBERT) b. 3 March 1898 (Thib. Ch.: v.7, p.489)
GUILLOT, John (Charles & Josephine CARPENTIER) m. 23 Sept. 1897 Mathilde HOHENSEE (Thib. Ch.: v.14, p.160)

GUILLOT, Joseph d. 24 Oct. 1896 at age 22 yrs. & 9 mths. (Thib. Ch.: v.3, p.189)

GUILLOT, Joseph (Felicien) d. 9 Feb. 1896 at age 7 yrs. (Montegut Ch.: v.2, p.3)

GUILLOT, Joseph Anicet (Arthur & Adelaine GAUBERT) b. 25 July 1896 (Thib. Ch.: v.7, p.409)

GUILLOT, Joseph Helene (Theophile & Celeste GAUBERT) b. 2 July 1898 (Thib. Ch.: v.7, p.503)

GUILLOT, Joseph Henri Philibert (Emile & Malvina CLEMENT) b. 25 Sept. 1899 (Chackbay Ch.: v.1, p.142)

GUILLOT, Joseph Ozilien (Marcilien & Angeline BOUDREAUX) b. 25 March 1899 (Thib. Ch.: v.7, p.546)

GUILLOT, Josephine (Jean Baptiste & Leontine RICHARD) m. 8 Feb. 1899 Joseph LEGENDRE (Thib. Ct. Hse.: Mar. v.38, #77)

GUILLOT, Josephine (Jean Baptiste & Leontine RICHARD) m. 8 Feb. 1899 Joseph LEGENDRE (Thib. Ch.: v.14, p.259)

GUILLOT, Julia (Louis & Philomene THIBODAUX) m. 14 July 1898 James D. MILLER (Thib. Ch.: v.14, p.209)

GUILLOT, Julia (Louis & Philonise THIBODAUX) m. 14 July 1898 James D. MILLER (Thib. Ct. Hse.: Mar. v.38, #218)

GUILLOT, Julien Victor (Arthur & Elisabet AUCOIN) b. 22 Feb. 1898 (Thib. Ch.: v.7, p.539)

GUILLOT, Juliette Edna (Theophile & Armantine MARONGE) b. 1 July 1898 (Thib. Ch.: v.7, p.553)

GUILLOT, Leandre Celestin (Edgard & Julie MIRE) b. 4 July 1896 (Thib. Ch.: v.7, p.408)

GUILLOT, Lionel d. 1 Jan. 1899 at age 2 mths. (Thib. Ch.: v.3, p.224)

GUILLOT, Lydia Aline (Theophile & Armantine MARONGE) b. 31 Dec. 1896 (Thib. Ch.: v.7, p.438)

GUILLOT, Marcel d. 1 March 1897 at age 82 yrs. (Thib. Ch.: v.3, p.197)

GUILLOT, Maria (Pietra & Calozera AMODEA) m. 5 Feb. 1898 Philippe HAMMANO (Houma Ch.: v.6-a, p.230)

GUILLOT, Marie Agnes (Theophile & Celeste GAUBERT) b. 4 Nov. 1896 (Thib. Ch.: v.7, p.424)

GUILLOT, Marie Berthe Elizabeth (Jean & Myrtile HOHENSEE) b. 20 March 1899 (Thib. Ch.: v.7, p.598)

GUILLOT, Marie Judith (Louis & Marie GUILLOTE) b. 29 Dec. 1896 (Thib. Ch.: v.7, p.433)

GUILLOT, Marie Lorenza d. 13 Dec. 1897 at age 53 yrs. (Thib. Ch.: v.3, p.208)

GUILLOT, Martial d. 2 Feb. 1899 at age 57 yrs. (Thib. Ch.: v.3, p.227)

GUILLOT, Paul Ophele (Edgar & Cecile PONTIF) b. 17 Nov. 1898 (Thib. Ch.: v.7, p.523)

GUILLOT, Philibert (Silvere & Josephine GUILLOT) b. 5 Nov. 1899 (Thib. Ch.: v.8, p.19)

GUILLOT, Philomene (Aurelien & Alouisia MIRE) m. 1 Feb. 1897 Peter MIRE (Thib. Ct. Hse.: Mar. v.36, #53)

GUILLOT, Philomene (Aurelien & Olanisia MIRE) m. 1 Feb. 1897 Pierre MIRE (Thib. Ch.: v.14, p.118)

GUILLOT, Sylvain (Emile & Adolestine GRAUS) m. 8 Feb. 1899 Myrthee THIBODAUX (Thib. Ct. Hse.: Mar. v.38, #32)

GUILLOT, Sylvain (Emile & Adolestine GROS) m. 8 Feb. 1899 Myrte THIBODAUX (Chackbay Ch.: v.1, p.68)

GUITANO, Salome (Conneo & Lornino LIOSEPPO) m. 23 April 1898 Maria ZABIA (Houma Ch.: v.6-a, p.240)

GUITRIAGE, Drauzin m. 14 Jan. 1897 Lily SMITH (Thib. Ct. Hse.: Mar. v.36, #34)

GULOTTA, Maria m. 22 Jan. 1898 Philip LAMMANO (Houma Ct. Hse.: Mar. v.30 & 31, #244)

GULOTTA, Nina (Sebastiona & Maria UTOUIALLULE) b. 26 Dec. 1897 (Houma Ch.: v.5, p.198)

GUSPERA, Jaquina (Frank & Josephine PURCELL) b. 22 April 1898 (Thib. Ch.: v.7, p.551)

GUTHRIDGE, Sallie m. 31 Oct. 1898 John PHILLIP (Thib. Ct. Hse.: Mar. v.38, #307)

GUTHRIE, Albert Augustin (Sheldron & Marcelline CREPEL) b. 7 March 1898 (Larose Ch.: v.3, p.25)

GYLES, Joseph Louis (Louis & Virginie ANDERSON) b. 17 Dec. 1898 (Thib. Ch.: v.7, p.536)

"H"

HACHE (Sometimes: ACHE, ACHEZ)

HACHE, Andre Philippe Antoine (Andre Sylvia & Aimee HEBERT) b. 16 Dec. 1898 (Thib. Ch.: v.7, p.538)

HACHE, Davis aged 17 & William HACHE, aged 14 (Pierson & Mathilde RICHOUX) Tutorship: 26 Aug. 1899. (Thib. Ct. Hse.: Succ. #1585)

HACHE, Jeanne Marie (Samuel & Julie DELONDE) b. 12 June 1896 (Thib. Ch.: v.7, p.405)

HACHE, Lovely Marie Antoinette (Elphege & Angela GILLY) b. 4 Feb. 1899 (Thib. Ch.: v.7, p.597)

HACHE, Marie m. 30 June 1899 Lovincy GUIDRY (Thib. Ct. Hse.: Mar. v.39, #191)

HACHE, Marie Noemi Annette (Samuel & Julie DELAUNE) b. 2 July 1898 (Thib. Ch.: v.7, p.502)

HACHE, Pierre Theand (Andre & Aimee HEBERT) b. 10 Aug. 1897 (Thib. Ch.: v.7, p.460)

HACHE, William aged 14 & Davis HACHE, aged 17 (Pierson & Mathilde RICHOUX) Tutorship: 26 Aug. 1899. (Thib. Ct. Hse.: Succ. #1585)

HACQ, Jeanne Beie (Raoul & Justilia LEBLANC) b. 19 July 1897 (Thib. Ch.: v.7, p.462)

HACQ, Marie Ida (Luca & Ida ESTIVEN) b. 20 May 1898 (Thib. Ch.: v.7, p.504)

HADDAD, Alexander m.28 March 1896 Anna SCHROEDER (Houma Ct. Hse.: Mar. v.29 & 30, #22)

HADDAD, Alexander P. m. 11 April 1896 Anna SCHROEDER (Thib. Ch.: Epis. Ch.: v.1, p.331)

HAEG, Anonyme d. 1 Aug. 1896 at age a few hours old (Thib. Ch.: v.3, p.185)

HAINS (Sometimes: HAYNES, HAYNS)

HAKEL, Sidny (Abraham & Eva SIMON) b. 27 Oct. 1897 (Houma Ch.: v.5, p.191)

HAKEL, Sydney Michel d. 25 Jan. 1898 at age 3 mths., 1 day old (Houma Ch.: v.3, p.15)

HALL, Alina (Olver & Cora TABOR) b. 19 Oct. 1899 (Thib. Ch.: v.7, p.586)

HALL, Allen m. 4 Feb. 1897 Joanna PIERRE (Thib. Ct. Hse.: Mar. v.38, #66)

HALL, James (Olivier & Emely TABOR) b. 1 Dec. 1897 (Thib. Ch.: v.7, p.484)

HALL, Oliver m. 22 April 1897 Cora TABOR (Thib. Ct. Hse.: Mar. v.36, #130)

HALL, Tommy m. 12 March 1896 Henrietta WILLIAMS (Houma Ct. Hse.: Mar. v.29 & 30, #8-A)

HAMMANO, Philippe (Biaggio & Maria ADA) m. 5 Feb. 1898 Maria GUILLOTTE (Houma Ch.: v.6-a, p.230)

HAMMOND, Lee m. 20 Jan. 1898 Dora THOMPSON (Houma Ct. Hse.: Mar. v.30 & 31, #234)
HAMMOND, Paul m. 29 Dec. 1898 Elouise MORGAN (Thib. Ct. Hse.: Mar. v.38, #327)
HAMMOND, Richard m. 25 Aug. 1898 Laura M. BANKS (Thib. Ct. Hse.: Mar. v.38, #265)
HAMPTON, Adelina m. 7 Sept. 1899 Nathaniel TONEY (Thib. Ct. Hse.: Mar. v.39, #223)
HAMPTON, Harriet m. 23 March 1899 Thomas TONEY (Thib. Ct. Hse.: Mar. v.39, #122)

HANAGRIFFE (Sometimes: HANAGRIF, HENNEGREFF)
HANAGRIFFE, Bernice Daisy Pearl (Elisha W. & Ruth J. HARLAN) m. 31 July 1896 Lowell R. GAIDRY (Houma Ct. Hse.: Mar. v.29 & 30, #119)
HANAGRIFFE, Charles Alexandre (Charles & Marie A. DRUILHET) b. 15 Jan. 1896 (Houma Ch.: v.5, p.144)
HANAGRIFFE, Robertha Lee widow of C. F. CELESTIN (Matthew L. & Virginia WATKINS) m. 19 Dec. 1898 Stewart A. WILKINS, of Lafayette Parish (Houma Ct. Hse.: Mar. v.30 & 31, #151)
HANCEY, Ellen m. 19 Jan. 1899 Peter JONES (Houma Ct. Hse.: Mar. v.30 & 31, #201)
HANG, William Leandre (Theophile & Mande GRIFFIN) b. 24 Sept. 1898 (Larose Ch.: v.3, p.29)
HANK, Lawton Joseph (Gordon & Cecile PERTUIT) b. 25 Oct. 1899 (Raceland Ch.: v.5, p.118)
HANLEY, George H. m. 2 March 1899 Agnes LEBLANC (Houma Ct. Hse.: Mar. v.31 & 32, #351)
HANLEY, George H. (Patrick & Mary AVERY) m. 26 April 1899 Agnes LEBLANC (Houma Ct. Hse.: Mar. v.31 & 32, #1)
HANLEY, George H. (Patrick & Mary AVERY) m. 26 Aprl 1899 Agnes LEBLANC (Thib. Ch.: v.14, p.276)
HARANG, Labadie Louis (Theophile & Zoemie LABADIE) m. 9 Feb. 1898 Sidonie LEBLANC (Thib. Ct. Hse.: Mar. v.37, #74)
HARANG, Labadie Louis (Theophile & Zoemie LABADIE) m. 9 Feb. 1898 Sidonie LEBLANC (Lockport Ch.: v.2, p.184)
HARANG, Louis Alexandre d. 26 July 1898 (Larose Ch.: v.1, p.43)
HARDEN, Joseph m. 17 Feb. 1897 Louise CHAMPAGNE (Houma Ct. Hse.: Mar. v.29 & 30, #317)
HARDIN, Leafy m.4 May 1898 James PREVOST (Houma Ct. Hse.: Mar. v.30 & 31, #430)
HARDONO, Elma Anne (Theophile & Lydia KELLER) b. 18 Jan. 1898 (Thib. Ch.: v.7, p.539)
HARDY, L. Amelia m. 21 Oct. 1899 Willie VERRET (Houma Ct. Hse.: Mar. v.31 & 32, #152)

HARGIS (Sometimes: HARGUS)
HARGIS, Maurice Clamy (Clamy & Rosa FORET) b. 25 Jan. 1896 (Lockport Ch.: v.2, p.320)

HARLAN (Sometimes: HARLAND)

HARRIET, Ana m. 1 June 1899 Primas BROYL (Houma Ct. Hse.: Mar. v.31 & 32, #65)

HARRIS (Sometimes: HARIS)

HARRIS, Bertha m. 13 Jan. 1896 Isaac SMITH (Houma Ct. Hse.: Mar. v.28, #385-C)

HARRIS, Bertha m. 9 March 1899 William VICTOR (Thib. Ct. Hse.: Mar. v.39, #117)

HARRIS, Cora m. 8 Dec. 1897 Scott T. SMITH, Jr. (Houma Ct. Hse.: Mar. v.29 & 30, #141)

HARRIS, Eddie m. 9 July 1898 Maria McGEE (Houma Ct. Hse.: Mar. v.30 & 31, #52)

HARRIS, George m. 3 Dec. 1897 Bertha ALDRIDGE (Houma Ct. Hse.: Mar. v.29 & 30, #140)

HARRIS, James William (Marquis de Lafayette & Julia WILLIAMS) b. 22 April 1896 (Thib. Ch.: v.7, p.445)

HARRIS, Jennie m. 2 Dec. 1897 Frank MANSFIELD (Thib. Ct. Hse.: Mar. v.37, #259)

HARRIS, Lettie m. 22 July 1897 Walton HUBBARD (Houma Ct. Hse.: Mar. v.29 & 30, #68)

HARRIS, Marcus Andrew C. (Marcus L. & Julia WILLIAMS) b. 14 May 1898 (Thib. Ch.: v.8, p.50)

HARRIS, Martha Jane born near Louisville, Kentucky. Received in Presbyterian Church: 21 Dec. 1897. (Houma Ch.: First Presbyt. Ch.: v.1, p.1)

HARRIS, Mollie m. 24 Dec. 1898 Daniel JEFFERSON (Thib. Ct. Hse.: Mar. v.38, #323)

HARRIS, Pinkey m. 29 April 1896 Abraham BROOKS (Houma Ct. Hse.: Mar. v.29 & 30, #46)

HARRIS, Roden m. 14 May 1896 Eveline DOUGLAS (Houma Ct. Hse.: Mar. v.29 & 30, #68)

HARRIS, Virginia A. m. 11 May 1899 John A. JACKSON (Thib. Ct. Hse: Mar. v.39, #164)

HARRIS, Wallis d. 27 March 1897 (Archie) m. Molly RICE Petition for probate of will & decree: 10 April 1897. (Thib. Ct. Hse.: Succ. #1511)

HARRISON (Sometimes: HARISSON, HARRISSON)

HARRISON, Joseph (Maximilien & Josephine LEDET) b. 26 Feb. 1896 (Lockport Ch.: v.3-A, #44)

HARRISON, Sarah m. 15 Oct. 1896 Alfred DICKSON (Thib. Ct. Hse.: Mar. v.36, #155)

HARRISON, Simon m. 14 Jan. 1897 Rosalie FOLSE (Thib. Ct. Hse.: Mar. v.36, #29)

HARTMAN, Augustine (Wuillie & Augustine ROGER) m. 29 April 1899 Ulysse DUFRENE (Thib. Ct. Hse.: Mar. v.39, #130)

HARTMAN, Augustine (Wuillie & Augustine ROGER) m. 29 April 1899 Ulysse DUFRENE (Lockport Ch.: v.2, p.207)

HARTMAN, Edwin Wales (William & Augustine ROGERS) b. 17 Oct. 1896 (Larose Ch.: v.2, p.190)

HARTMAN, Henry m. 19 Feb. 1896 Virginia BONNER (Houma Ct. Hse.: Mar. v.28, #463)

HARTY, Agnes (Michel & Wilhemina FLOCHORZY) m. 7 July 1898 Robt. Boner BUTLER (Houma Ch.: Epis. Ch.: v.1, p.342)

HARVARD, Plado m. 23 April 1898 Sidney Ann WOODER (Houma Ct. Hse.: Mar. v.30 & 31, #419)

HATCH, Henry Nicholson (W. Scott & Anzeline HAINS) b. 16 Feb. 1897 (Houma Ch.: Epis. Ch.: v.1, p.114)

HATCH, Melvin Allen d. 13 Feb. 1899 at age 8 yrs. (Houma Ch.: Epis. Ch.: v.1, p.388)

HATCH, Winslow (Lewellyn & Florence SMALL) m. 14 June 1897 Geneva THERIOT (Theriot Ch.: v.1, p.10)

HATCH, Winslow G. (Llewellyn & Florence SMALL) m. 5 June 1897 Geneva THERIOT (Houma Ct. Hse.: Mar. v.29 & 30, #8)

HATCHET, Robert Antoine (Alfred & Emilie) bt. 23 May 1897 (Thib. Ch.: v.7, p.451)

HATCHISSON (See: HUTCHINSON)

HATTON, Davy d. 3 Dec. 1896 at age 85 yrs. (Thib. Ch.: v.3, p.191)

HAUTEMENT (See: AUTHEMENT)

HAUTIN (See: AUTIN)

HAWK, Joseph Willie (Willie & Angele BERGERON) b. 5 Sept. 1899 (Thib. Ch.: v.7, p.570)

HAWKINS, Augustus m. 9 Sept. 1897 Isabella AUGUSTIN (Houma Ct. Hse.: Mar. v.29 & 30, #88)

HAWKINS, Elias Commission for sale: 17 Jan. 1898. (Thib. Ct. Hse.: Succ. #1522)

HAWKINS, Elys d. 21 Nov. 1896 at age 56 mths. (Thib. Ch.: v.3, p.190)

HAWKINS, Peyton m. 10 July 1897 Gracie ROSS (Houma Ct. Hse.: Mar. v.29 & 30, #64)

HAWKINS, Phil m. 25 Sept. 1896 Alice LOPEZ (Thib. Ct. Hse.: Mar. v.36, #148)

HAWTHORN, Arthur E. m. 21 Dec. 1897 Amelia CHINN (Thib. Ct. Hse.: Mar. v.37, #264)

HAYDEL (Sometimes: AYDELL)

HAYDEL, Angele Mrs. d. 13 Oct. 1897 at age 62 yrs. (Houma Ch.: v.3, p.14)

HAYDEL, Dexan of St. James Parish (Valcour & Julienne BEAUDOIN) m. 10 Sept. 1898 Magdelaine KRAEMER (Thib. Ct. Hse.: Mar. v.38, #272)

HAYDEL, Dexen (Valcour & Julienne BEAUDOUIN) m. 10 Sept. 1898 Magdeleine KRAEMER (Chackbay Ch.: v.1, p.64)

HAYDEL, Elma Juliette (Sebastien & Modeste DIONNE) b. 2 July 1896 (Thib. Ch.: v.7, p.409)
HAYDEL, Marie Edna (Sebastien & Modeste DIONNE) b. 2 Oct. 1898 (Thib. Ch.: v.7, p.517)
HAYDEL, Marie Evelina m. Gabriel Antoine BRIANT d. 4 Jan. 1896 at age 72 yrs. (Thib. Ch.: v.3, p.193)

HAYES (Sometimes: HAYS)

HAYES, Ida m. 3 Feb. 1897 Vincent DAVIS (Houma Ct. Hse.: Mar. v.29 & 30, #276)
HAYGOOD, Anna Ruth (James Wilmer & Caso D. KELLY) b. 16 June 1898 (Houma Ch.: Epis. Ch.: v.1, p.118)
HAYGOOD, John Edwin (James Wilmer & Caroline Dungan KELLEY) b. 6 Oct. 1899 (Houma Ch.: Epis. Ch.: v.1, p.122)

HAYWARD (Sometimes: HAIWARD)

HEAD, Lewis Joseph (Clay & Marguerite DARDAR) b. 24 March 1899 (Larose Ch.: v.3, p.39)
HEARD, Almeady m. 31 May 1897 William CARY (Thib. Ct. Hse.: Mar. v.36, #157)

HEBERT (Sometimes: EBER, HEBER, HEBERRE)

HEBERT, ----- boy d. 24 Jan. 1899 at age 3 hrs. (Thib. Ch.: v.3, p.226)
HEBERT, Adam (Emile & Mercedes ALEMAND) b. 4 April 1896 (Larose Ch.: v.2, p.188)
HEBERT, Agatha (Rene & Josephine BONVILLAIN) m. 14 Feb. 1898 Clay Peter DASPIT (Houma Ch.: v.6-a, p.232)
HEBERT, Agathe m. 31 Jan. 1898 Clay Peter DASPIT (Houma Ct. Hse.: Mar. v.30 & 31, #262)
HEBERT, Aimee Cecile (Richard & Evelia GROS) b. 9 Sept. 1899 (Thib. Ch.: v.7, p.565)
HEBERT, Alain Aristildes (Allan & Marie THEBE) b. 15 Dec. 1898 (Chackbay Ch.: v.1, p.129)
HEBERT, Albert d. 3 April 1897 at age 18 yrs. (Thib. Ch.: v.3, p.198)
HEBERT, Albert m. 5 April 1899 Odilia AUTHEMENT (Thib. Ct. Hse.: Mar. v.39, #131)
HEBERT, Albert (Vasseur & Zulema WUAGESPACK) m. 22 April 1899 Odilia AUTHEMENT (Lockport Ch.: v.2, p.206)
HEBERT, Albert Henri (Aubert P. & Elisa RICHARD) b. 23 March 1896 (Thib. Ch.: v.7, p.397)
HEBERT, Alcide m. 23 Jan. 1896 Ulicia TRAHAN (Houma Ct. Hse.: Mar. v.28, #404)
HEBERT, Alcide (Rene & Josephine BONVILLAIN) m. 12 Feb. 1896 Ulicia TRAHAN (Houma Ch.: v.6-a, p.169)
HEBERT, Alcide Denis Paul (Amedee & Henriette PITRE) b. 25 Aug. 1898 (Thib. Ch.: v.7, p.561)
HEBERT, Alcide Marie (Amede & Tarzil BOUDELOCHE) b. 10 May 1898 (Houma Ch.: v.5, p.211)

HEBERT, Alens Guillaume (Emile & Mercedes ALEMAN) b. 10 Jan. 1899 (Larose Ch.: v.3, p.35)
HEBERT, Alexandre (Jean Baptiste & Zulema CEVIN) m. 24 June 1897 Alice BALLARD (Thib. Ch.: v.14, p.149)
HEBERT, Alexandre (Jean Baptiste Francois & Zulema CEVIN) m. 24 June 1897 Alice BALLARD (Thib. Ct. Hse.: Mar. v.36, #160)
HEBERT, Alexis m. 17 Jan. 1898 Celestine LEONARD (Houma Ct. Hse.: Mar. v.30 & 31, #221)
HEBERT, Alexis (Clay & Severine GUIDRY) m. 27 Jan. 1898 Celestine LEONARD (Houma Ch.: v.6-a, p.225)
HEBERT, Alice (James & Ademise TOUPS) m. 3 June 1896 Thomas MARTIN (Montegut Ch.: v.4, p.210)
HEBERT, Alice (James & Adenise TOUPS) m. 14 May 1896 Thomas MARTIN (Houma Ct. Hse.: Mar. v.29 & 30, #69)
HEBERT, Amanda Josephine (Alcide & Alicia TRAHAN) b. 15 Jan. 1897 (Houma Ch.: v.5, p.202)
HEBERT, Anatole m. ---- 1899 Laura LEE (Larose Ch.: v.4, p.131)
HEBERT, Anatole m. 15 Jan. 1898 Laura LEE (Thib. Ct. Hse.: Mar. v.37, #1)
HEBERT, Anatole of Lafourche Parish m. 19 - 30 Dec. 1899 Laura LEE (Larose Ch.: v.3, p.13)
HEBERT, Andre Cleophat (Ceresie & Elvire LECOMPTE) b. 10 Nov. 1899 (Montegut Ch.: v.6, p.101)
HEBERT, Angela m. 13 Dec. 1897 Leonie KELLER (Thib. Ct. Hse.: Mar. v.37, #260)
HEBERT, Angela (Emile & Ovilia ANDRA) m. 29 Dec. 1897 Leon KELLER (Thib. Ch.: v.14, p.168)
HEBERT, Angelina (Joachim & Adelina BOUDREAU) m. 21 Jan. 1897 Henri LIRETTE (Chackbay Ch.: v.1, p.36)
HEBERT, Angelina (Joachim & Adelina BOUDREAU) m. 21 Jan. 1897 Henry LIRETTE (Thib. Ct. Hse.: Mar. v.36, #16)
HEBERT, Armand (Felicien & Georgina RODRIGUE) b. 8 June 1898 (Chackbay Ch.: v.1, p.114)
HEBERT, Arthur (Edmond & Helena BOUDELOCHE) m. 24 Jan. 1896 Marie BOUDELOCHE (Houma Ct. Hse.: Mar. v.28, #409)
HEBERT, Arthur Nicolas (Nicolas & Anasie BESSON) b. 29 March 1899 (Thib. Ch.: v.7, p.544)
HEBERT, Augustin m. 26 Aug. 1898 Alice CLULEE (Thib. Ct. Hse.: Mar. v.38, #267)
HEBERT, Augustin (Jules & Emelie GERVAIS) m. 3 Sept. 1898 Alice CLULEY (Raceland Ch.: v.2, p.79)
HEBERT, Bertha (Jean Baptiste & Clothilde DUGAS) m. 18 March 1899 Albert DOMINIQUE (Houma Ct. Hse.: Mar. v.31 & 32, #368)
HEBERT, Bertha (Jean Baptiste & Clothilde DUGAS) m. 10 April 1899 Albert DOMINGUE (Montegut Ch.: v.4, p.261)
HEBERT, Berthilde (Olezime & Rosa TRAHAN) m. 24 June 1899 Michel BREZILLAC (Houma Ct. Hse.: Mar. v.31 & 32, #50-A)

HEBERT, Body Benjamin (Drozin & Estelina CHIASSON) b. 1 Aug. 1898 (Chackbay Ch.: v.1, p.120)
HEBERT, Boyda d. 3 Aug. 1898 at age 12 yrs. (Thib. Ch.: v.3, p.218)
HEBERT, Cecile Marie (Jules & Alice PAR) b. 20 Nov. 1896 (Thib. Ch.: v.7, p.429)
HEBERT, Charles R. (Cleophas & Helen DE LABRETONNE) m. 29 Nov. 1899 Emolyn HEPLER (Houma Ct. Hse.: Mar. v.31 & 32, #168)
HEBERT, Clara (Amedee & Rosalie TRAHAN) m. 11 June 1898 Marcel VEYRE (Houma Ct. Hse.: Mar. v.30 & 31, #16)
HEBERT, Corinne d. 21 Nov. 1897 at age 20 yrs. (Raceland Ch.: v.2, p.15)
HEBERT, Dalcina (Emile & Mercedes ALEMAN) m. 10 Feb. 1898 Alcibiade BADEAU (Larose Ch.: v.4, p.5)
HEBERT, Dennis m. 14 Jan. 1899 Alice THERIOT (Houma Ct. Hse.: Mar. v.30 & 31, #229)
HEBERT, Dennis (Clay & Emelie BABIN) m. 31 Jan. 1899 Alice THERIOT (Houma Ch.: v.6-a, p.272)
HEBERT, Dolcina (Emile & Mercedes ALEMAN) m. 10 Feb. 1898 Alcibiade BADEAUX (Thib. Ct. Hse.: Mar. v.37, #82)
HEBERT, Doleina of Lafourche Parish (Emile & Mercedes ALEMAN) m. 10 Feb. 1898 Alcibiade BADEAU, of Lafourche Parish (Larose Ch.: v.3, p.7)
HEBERT, Douglas d. 10 Dec. 1898; m. Mathilde DUPLANTIS Children: Marguerite, 7; Higman 1½. Tutorship: 21 Jan. 1899. (Houma Ct. Hse.: Succ. #911)
HEBERT, Eda Clementine (James & Isabelle LEDET) b. 27 Dec. 1897 (Montegut Ch.: v.6, p.64)
HEBERT, Edgard (A---- & Leontine WEBRE) m. 31 Jan. 1899 Cecilia BREAUX (Thib. Ch.: v.14, p.250)
HEBERT, Edgard (Aubert & Leontia WEBB) m. 31 Jan. 1899 Cecilia BREAUX (Thib. Ct. Hse.: Mar. v.38, #30)
HEBERT, Elie Aline (William & Marguerite DUPLANTIS) b. 5 Dec. 1898 (Montegut Ch.: v.6, p.80)
HEBERT, Elizabeth m. Henry RODDAY d. 20 June 1898 at age 81 yrs. (Montegut Ch.: v.2, p.17)
HEBERT, Ellida d. 23 July 1897 at age 17 yrs. (Houma Ch.: v.3, p.13)
HEBERT, Elmire Robert (Numa & Regina PITRE) b. 12 Nov. 1899 (Thib. Ch.: v.7, p.574)
HEBERT, Elvire m. 25 March 1899 Alfred CROCHET (Houma Ct. Hse.: Mar. v.31 & 32, #374)
HEBERT, Elvire of Terrebonne Parish m. 6 April 1899 Alfred CROCHET (Houma Ch.: v.6-B, p.3)
HEBERT, Emile d. 28 Feb. 1898 at age 28 yrs. (Thib. Ch.: v.3, p.211)
HEBERT, Emilie (Emile & Louisiane UZE) m. 9 April 1896 Louis LADOUCEUR (Thib. Ch.: v.14, p.83)
HEBERT, Emilie (Emile & Louisiane UZE) m. 9 April 1896 Louis LADOUCEUR (Thib. Ct. Hse.: Mar. v.35, #59)

HEBERT, Emilie (Emile & Ovilia ANDRA) m. 9 Feb. 1899 Arthur RODRIGUE (Thib. Ct. Hse.: Mar. v.38, #51)
HEBERT, Emilie (Emile & Ovilia ANDRA) m. 9 Feb. 1899 Arthur RODRIGUE (Thib. Ch.: v.14, p.263)
HEBERT, Emma m. 1 March 1897 Morgan GONZALES (Larose Ch.: v.3, p.5)
HEBERT, Emma m. 1 March 1897 Morgan GONZALES (Larose Ch.: v.4, p.100)
HEBERT, Emma m. 15 Dec. 1899 Sylvain HEBERT (Thib. Ct. Hse.: Mar. v.39, #285)
HEBERT, Emma m. 19 Feb. 1897 Morgan GONZALES (Thib. Ct. Hse.: Mar. v.36, #83)
HEBERT, Emma (Emile & Orville ANDRAS) m. 20 Dec. 1899 Sylvain HEBERT (Thib. Ch.: v.14, p.313)
HEBERT, Ernest (Clay & Severine GUIDRY) m. 1 June 1896 Clemence CLEMENT (Thib. Ch.: v.14, p.89)
HEBERT, Ernest (Clay & Severine GUIDRY) m. 1 June 1896 Clemence CLEMENT (Thib. Ct. Hse.: Mar. v.35, #90)
HEBERT, Ernestine m. 14 March 1896 Louis GAUTREAUX (Houma Ct. Hse.: Mar. v.29 & 30, #9)
HEBERT, Ernestine (Clay & Severine GUIDRY) m. 9 April 1896 Louis GAUTREAUX (Houma Ch.: v.6-a, p.173)
HEBERT, Esilda d. 2 June 1898 at age 28 yrs. (Raceland Ch.: v.1, p.18)
HEBERT, Etienne m. 5 Feb. 1898 Eselima CROSSBY (Thib. Ct. Hse.: Mar. v.37, #66)
HEBERT, Etienne (Osemee & Odile SANCHEZ) m. 5 Feb. 1898 Eselima CROSBY (Raceland Ch.: v.2, p.65)
HEBERT, Eugene d. 10 July 1898 at age 75 yrs. (Larose Ch.: v.1, p.43)
HEBERT, Eugene d. 9 July 1897; m. Amelia DUET Children listed: Emma m. Jules PLAISANCE; Alzise m. Raphael ORGERON; Clemence m. Emile BARBIER; Carmelite m. Clement LACROIX; Emile; Lovincy; Eugene; Damiens; Paul; George. Petition for inventory: 19 Aug. 1898. (Thib. Ct. Hse.: Succ. #1547)
HEBERT, Eugene Ernest (Durald & Eve MALBROUGH) b. 9 July 1896 (Thib. Ch.: v.7, p.454)
HEBERT, Eulalie Octavie (Theogene & Georgina LIRETTE) b. 19 Oct. 1898 (Thib. Ch.: v.7, p.572)
HEBERT, Eva Marie (Albert & Odile TROSCLAIR) b. 6 Aug. 1897 (Theriot Ch.: v.2, p.9)
HEBERT, Eve Mabel (Desire & Emma LADOUCEUR) b. 11 April 1896 (Thib. Ch.: v.7, p.399)
HEBERT, Felix Antoine (Felix & Anna LOVY) b. 17 Nov. 1899 (Theriot Ch.: v.2, p.67)
HEBERT, Firmin Serius (Obon & Emma GIROUARD) b. 13 May 1896 (Houma Ch.: v.5, p.181)
HEBERT, Frances Brigitte (Emile & Louisiane EUSE) b. 15 Feb. 1896 (Thib. Ch.: v.7, p.392)

HEBERT, Franck Junia (Philippe & Ilda PITT) b. 2 Feb. 1898 (Thib. Ch.: v.7, p.485)
HEBERT, Gaston Adam (Neuville & Philomene CLEMENT) b. 7 Aug. 1898 (Thib. Ch.: v.7, p.559)
HEBERT, George (Clovis & Julienne SEVIN) m. 18 Sept. 1899 Alice ADAM (Thib. Ch.: v.14, p.296)
HEBERT, George (Clovis & Zulima SEVIN) m. 18 Sept. 1899 Alice ADAMS (Thib. Ct. Hse.: Mar. v.39, #217)
HEBERT, Harry d. 7 June 1897 at age 7 yrs. (Thib. Ch.: v.3, p.201)
HEBERT, Harry Raymond (Amedee & Rosalie TRAHAN) b. 26 March 1899 (Chacahoula Ch.: v.4, p.20)
HEBERT, Helene Edna (Joseph & Mathilde ACOSTE) b. 25 April 1897 (Raceland Ch.: v.5, p.47)
HEBERT, Helene Therese (Ernest & Leontine LEGENDRE) b. 7 Sept. 1896 (Thib. Ch.: v.7, p.417)
HEBERT, Henri (Scaller & Clara LEBLANC) m. 14 Feb. 1898 Camille BERNARD (Thib. Ct. Hse.: Mar. v.37, #102)
HEBERT, Henri (Scalles & Clara LEBLANC) m. 14 Feb. 1898 Camille BERNARD (Thib. Ch.: v.14, p.184)
HEBERT, Irene d. 10 March 1897 at age 50 yrs. (Houma Ch.: v.3, p.12)
HEBERT, James Charles (Emile & Ovilia ANDRA) b. 8 Oct. 1896 (Thib. Ch.: v.7, p.428)
HEBERT, James Teurling (James & Ademise TOUPS) b. 23 Dec. 1898 (Montegut Ch.: v.6, p.79)
HEBERT, Jean Alce (Lovincie & Mathilde SANCHEZ) b. 17 July 1899 (Chackbay Ch.: v.1, p.139)
HEBERT, Jeanne Adele (Emile & Eugelia GAUBERT) b. 29 June 1896 (Thib. Ch.: v.7, p.453)
HEBERT, Joan Marie m. ---- THIBODAUX d. 30 March 1896 at age 82 yrs. (Thib. Ch.: v.3, p.181)
HEBERT, John Joseph (Amedee & Henriette PITT) b. 19 March 1897 (Thib. Ch.: v.7, p.446)
HEBERT, Joseph d. 13 July 1898 at age 5 mths. (Raceland Ch.: v.1, p.19)
HEBERT, Joseph m. 2 Jan. 1896 Mathilde ACOSTA (Thib. Ct. Hse.: Mar. v.35, #4)
HEBERT, Joseph m. 25 Jan. 1896 Louisa BABIN (Houma Ct. Hse.: Mar. v.28, #420)
HEBERT, Joseph m. 9 Jan. 1896 Mathilda ACOSTA (Larose Ch.: v.4, p.76)
HEBERT, Joseph m. 9 Jan. 1896 Mathilda ACOSTA (Larose Ch.: v.3, p.2)
HEBERT, Joseph (d.Jean Louis & d.Fleurine BABIN) m. 10 Jan. 1898 Eva LAPEROUSE (Montegut Ch.: v.4, p.228)
HEBERT, Joseph (Jean Louis & Irene BABIN) m. 16 Dec. 1897 Eva LAPEROUSE (Houma Ct. Hse.: Mar. v.29 & 30, #146)
HEBERT, Joseph (Jules & Eugenie HEBERT) b. 29 Jan. 1898 (Raceland Ch.: v.5, p.65)

HEBERT, Joseph (Ozeme & Odile SANCHES) m. 9 Jan. 1896 Mathilde ACOSTA (Larose Ch.: v.2, p.185)
HEBERT, Joseph (Volcar & Victoria BUQUET) m. 13 Feb. 1896 Louisa BABIN (Houma Ch.: v.6-a, p.169)
HEBERT, Joseph Abbie (Leo & Eveline DUPLANTIS) b. 28 Aug. 1897 (Montegut Ch.: v.6, p.60)
HEBERT, Joseph Alexandre (Alexandre & Alice BALLARD) b. 17 May 1898 (Thib. Ch.: v.7, p.499)
HEBERT, Joseph Alphonse (Evariste & Pomela LEBOEUF) b. 20 Jan. 1897 (Houma Ch.: v.5, p.200)
HEBERT, Joseph Andre (Felix & Rebecca THIBODAUX) b. 20 June 1899 (Thib. Ch.: v.7, p.552)
HEBERT, Joseph Aris (Alcide & Alicia TRAHAN) b. 13 Nov. 1899 (Theriot Ch.: v.2, p.55)
HEBERT, Joseph Arseme (Cleo & Angele LEBOEUF) b. 30 Oct. 1898 (Houma Ch.: v.5, p.223)
HEBERT, Joseph Clement (Lucas & Zeolide ARLANDEGER) b. 27 Sept. 1896 (Thib. Ch.: v.7, p.421)
HEBERT, Joseph Edmond (Robert Douglas & Mathilde DUPLANTIS) b. 11 July 1897 (Montegut Ch.: v.6, p.58)
HEBERT, Joseph Every (Lovinci & Eva DUPLANTY) b. 22 Nov. 1896 (Houma Ch.: v.5, p.166)
HEBERT, Joseph Felix (Felicien & Georgina LANDRIGUE) bt. 23 July 1896 (Chackbay Ch.: v.1, p.70)
HEBERT, Joseph Hector (Felix & Josephine THIBODAUX) b. 28 Feb. 1897 (Thib. Ch.: v.7, p.441)
HEBERT, Joseph Hombard (Evine & Josephine CHAUVIN) b. 8 Jan. 1896 (Houma Ch.: v.5, p.145)
HEBERT, Joseph Ines (Joseph & Eva LAPEROUSE) b. 3 Nov. 1898 (Montegut Ch.: v.6, p.82)
HEBERT, Joseph Ivel (Aurelie & Augustine NAQUIN) b. 6 Oct. 1898 (Houma Ch.: v.5, p.219)
HEBERT, Joseph Joseph (Alphonse & Evelia BERGERON) b. 8 May 1897 (Houma Ch.: v.5, p.177)
HEBERT, Joseph Julius (Joseph & Marie BOUDREAUX) b. 13 Feb. 1896 (Thib. Ch.: v.7, p.393)
HEBERT, Joseph Magnes (Emile & Laura DUPLANTIS) b. 29 March 1898 (Montegut Ch.: v.6, p.76)
HEBERT, Joseph Myrtile (Jules & Alice PAR) b. 10 Aug. 1898 (Thib. Ch.: v.7, p.510)
HEBERT, Joseph Walter (Jean Baptiste & Clothilde DUGAS) b. 9 Sept. 1897 (Montegut Ch.: v.6, p.60)
HEBERT, Josephine d. 29 June 1898 at age 5 mths. (Raceland Ch.: v.1, p.19)
HEBERT, Jules m. 12 Jan. 1899 Anastasia BABIN (Thib. Ct. Hse.: Mar. v.38, #18)
HEBERT, Jules (Jules & Emelie GERVAIS) m. 28 Jan. 1899 Anastasie BABIN (Raceland Ch.: v.2, p.84)
HEBERT, Jules Pierre (Jules & Uranie GRABERT) b. 3 Jan. 1898 (Chackbay Ch.: v.1, p.111)

HEBERT, Klebert m. 15 Jan. 1897 Lidia SAPIA (Thib. Ct. Hse.: Mar. v.36, #36)
HEBERT, Klebert (Vasseur & Zulema WAGUESPACK) m. 27 Jan. 1897 Lydia SAPIER (Raceland Ch.: v.2, p.29)
HEBERT, Leo m. 3 July 1897 Laura OLIVIER (Houma Ct. Hse.: Mar. v.29 & 30, #47)
HEBERT, Leo (Rene & Josephine BONVILLAIN) m. 13 July 1897 Laura OLIVIER (Houma Ch.: v.6-a, p.211)
HEBERT, Leocadie m. Cordelius CLEMENT d. 15 Aug. 1898 (Thib. Ch.: v.3, p.219)
HEBERT, Leontine Irma (Ernest & Leontine LEGENDRE) b. 17 Dec. 1898 (Thib. Ch.: v.7, p.527)
HEBERT, Lily (Clovis & Zulema CEVIN) m. 9 Feb. 1899 Wallace BAYE (Thib. Ct. Hse.: Mar. v.38, #79)
HEBERT, Lily (Clovis & Zulema CEVIN) m. 9 Feb. 1899 Wallace BAYE (Thib. Ch.: v.14, p.262)
HEBERT, Louis d. 29 April 1896 at age 82 yrs. (Thib. Ch.: v.3, p.182)
HEBERT, Louis Adam (Adam & Lydia BOUDREAU) b. 21 Jan. 1896 (Thib. Ch.: v.7, p.390)
HEBERT, Louis Edgard (Edgard & Cecilia BRAUD) b. 25 Oct. 1899 (Thib. Ch.: v.7, p.571)
HEBERT, Louis Mrs. d. 23 Dec. 1898 at age 75 yrs. (Thib. Ch.: v.3, p.223)
HEBERT, Louis William (Abel & Adele NORMAND) b. 21 Dec. 1897 (Thib. Ch.: v.7, p.476)
HEBERT, Louise Aula (Felix & Anna LONG) b. 25 Sept. 1897 (Houma Ch.: v.5, p.202)
HEBERT, Louise Lily (Eulice & Lucette CLEMENT) b. 26 Jan. 1899 (Montegut Ch.: v.6, p.85)
HEBERT, Lowel Joseph (Ovide & Melanie GISCLAIR) b. 13 Feb. 1897 (Larose Ch.: v.3, p.8)
HEBERT, Lucile m.27 Jan. 1897 Dassas BROUSSARD (Thib. Ct. Hse.: Mar. v.36, #57)
HEBERT, Lucile Aline (Felix & Anna LONG) b. 25 Sept. 1897 (Houma Ch.: v.5, p.202)
HEBERT, Lucile Angelina (Joe & Elizabeth DUMING) b. 15 July 1897; bt. 29 Aug. 1897 (Chacahoula Ch.: Gibson Ch.: v.2, p.114)
HEBERT, Lucille Agathe (Clay & Clara ROUSSEL) b. 29 July 1897 (Lockport Ch.: v.3, #52-A)
HEBERT, Lucille Agathe (Clay & Clara ROUSSEL) b. 29 July 1897 (Lockport Ch.: v.3-A, #52-A)
HEBERT, Lucille Angelina (Joe & Elizabeth DUMING) b. 15 July 1897; bt. 29 Aug. 1897; m. Otis LOUVIERE on 10 July 1920 (Chacahoula Ch.: Gibson Ch.: Baptism Bk., v.2, p.129)
HEBERT, Lutecia (Klebert & Emelie BABIN) m. 26 Dec. 1896 Edgar LEBLANC (Houma Ct. Hse.: Mar. v.29 & 30, #211)
HEBERT, Lydia (Drauzin & Aurelia STEVEN) m. 13 Feb. 1899 Onezime BERGERON (Thib. Ch.: v.14, p.264-a)

HEBERT, Lylia d. 9 Oct. 1898 at age 1 yr. (Thib. Ch.: v.3, p.220)
HEBERT, Malvina m. Telesphore BOURG d. 23 March 1897 at age 41 yrs. (Montegut Ch.: v.2, p.10)
HEBERT, Marguerite Addee (Emile & Laura DUPLANTIS) b. 29 April 1896 (Montegut Ch.: v.6, p.41)
HEBERT, Marguerite Josephine (Octave & Mathilde COLWART) b. 2 May 1896 (Montegut Ch.: v.6, p.39)
HEBERT, Marguerite Marie (Berton & Evelia BERGERON) b. 25 Oct. 1899 (Houma Ch.: v.5, p.264)
HEBERT, Maria Angele (Desiree & Aima LADOUCEUR) b. 14 April 1897 (Thib. Ch.: v.7, p.447)
HEBERT, Marie m. Froisin HOTARD d. 2 Nov. 1897 at age 58 yrs. (Thib. Ch.: v.3, p.207)
HEBERT, Marie (Amedee & Rosalie TRAHAN) m. 18 May 1897 Joseph LAJAUNIE (Chacahoula Ch.: v.1, p.60)
HEBERT, Marie (Amedee & Rosalie TRAHAN) m. 18 May 1897 Joseph LAJAUNIE (Houma Ct. Hse.: Mar. v.29 & 30, #395)
HEBERT, Marie Abraham (Philippe & Elda PITRE) b. 27 Oct. 1896 (Thib. Ch.: v.7, p.424)
HEBERT, Marie Adela (Joseph & Mathilde ACOSTA) b. 21 May 1899 (Raceland Ch.: v.5, p.96)
HEBERT, Marie Adele (Myrtil & Emma CLEMENT) b. 20 Feb. 1898 (Montegut Ch.: v.6, p.73)
HEBERT, Marie Agnes (Lovincy & Laurenza HUCLE) b. 18 Aug. 1896 (Chacahoula Ch.: v.4, p.3)
HEBERT, Marie Anciana (Allan & Marie THEBE) b. 22 July 1897 (Chackbay Ch.: v.1, p.94)
HEBERT, Marie Bulla (Lovincie & Ulalie ORGERON) b. 27 Dec. 1899 (Larose Ch.: v.3, p.50)
HEBERT, Marie Camille (Auban & Anastasie NAVARRE) b. 30 March 1899 (Chacahoula Ch.: v.4, p.27)
HEBERT, Marie Celian (Amedee & Aimee DETIVEAU) b. 19 May 1898 (Montegut Ch.: v.6, p.73)
HEBERT, Marie Darisse (Leo & Eveline DUPLANTIS) b. 23 Dec. 1899 (Houma Ch.: v.6, p.4)
HEBERT, Marie Ella (Ulysse & Lucette CLEMENT) b. 24 Aug. 1896 (Montegut Ch.: v.6, p.44)
HEBERT, Marie Eloncia (Alence & Marie THABOR) b. 10 Feb. 1896 (Chackbay Ch.: v.1, p.65)
HEBERT, Marie Emilie (Felix & Josephine THIBODAUX) b. 20 April1898 (Thib. Ch.: v.7, p.495)
HEBERT, Marie Josephine (Jules & Eugenie HEBERT) b. 29 Jan. 1898 (Raceland Ch.: v.5, p.64)
HEBERT, Marie Mabel (Georges & Felicie BUQUET) b. 6 June 1899 (Montegut Ch.: v.6, p.89)
HEBERT, Marie Mable (Albert & Clemence GUITRY) b. 28 March 1898 (Chacahoula Ch.: v.4, p.9)
HEBERT, Marie Rubie (Auguste & Francoise BELANGER) b. 8 Sept. 1899 (Montegut Ch.: v.6, p.92)

HEBERT, Marie Victorine (Alexis & Marcelline STOUFFLET) b. 18 April 1897 (Montegut Ch.: v.6, p.57)
HEBERT, Martial d. 12 Feb. 1896 at age 72 yrs. (Montegut Ch.: v.2, p.3)
HEBERT, Martin d. 7 Aug. 1897 Children: Edmond; Achille of Iberai, La.; Emelie m. Ulysse BOUDREAUX of Rayne, La.; Odelia m. John P. SANDERS of Jeannerette; Ozea m. Laclair HEBERT of Iberia, La.; Trasimond. Petition for inventory: 11 Aug. 1897. (Houma Ct. Hse.: Succ. #887)
HEBERT, Martin d. 9 Aug. 1897 at age 75 yrs. (Houma Ch.: v.3, p.13)
HEBERT, Mary m. 26 Dec. 1896 Wallace LIRETTE (Houma Ct. Hse.: Mar. v.29 & 30, #214)
HEBERT, Mary (Volcar & Victoria BUQUET) m. 4 Jan. 1897 Wallace LIRETTE (Houma Ch.: v.6-a, p.188)
HEBERT, Mary Amanda (Denis & Alice THERIOT) b. 2 Nov. 1899 (Houma Ch.: v.5, p.263)
HEBERT, Mary Dorisse (Leo & Eveline DUPLANTIS) b. 23 Dec. 1899 (Houma Ch.: v.5, p.269)
HEBERT, Mary Ruby d. 16 May 1899 at age 13 mths. (Raceland Ch.: v.1, p.25)
HEBERT, Mary Ruby (Alphonse & Lu CUNNINGHAM) b. 19 April 1898 (Raceland Ch.: v.5, p.71)
HEBERT, Moise Alve (Lovinski & Mathilde SINDGEOK) b. 5 July 1896 (Raceland Ch.:v.5, p.28)
HEBERT, Nelson minor over 18 (Manuel & Zoe PICOU) Emancipation: 26 April 1898. (Thib. Ct. Hse.: Succ. #1532)
HEBERT, Nerola d. 8 March 1898 at age 3 mths. (Raceland Ch.: v.1, p.17)
HEBERT, Nore (Leo & Laura OLIVIER) b. 27 Aug. 1898 (Houma Ch.: v.5, p.220)
HEBERT, Numa (Evariste & Justilien UZET) m. 19 Aug. 1897 Regina PITRE (Thib. Ct. Hse.: Mar. v.37, #214)
HEBERT, Numa (Evariste & Justilien UZET) m. 19 Aug. 1897 Regina PITRE (Thib. Ch.: v.14, p.158)
HEBERT, Octave Ovide (Joseph & Malvina CHAUVIN) b. 3 Nov. 1897 (Montegut Ch.: v.6, p.62)
HEBERT, Odalie (Joseph & Elea DUPUIS) m. 12 April 1899 Augustin ROGERE (Lockport Ch.: v.2, p.205)
HEBERT, Odalie (Joseph & Elia DUPUIS) m. 12 April 1899 Augustin ROGERE (Thib. Ct. Hse.: Mar. v.39, #124)
HEBERT, Odressia d. 15 March 1897 at age 14 yrs. (Thib. Ch.: v.3, p.198)
HEBERT, Onezime d. 28 Nov. 1896 at age 65 yrs. (Chacahoula Ch.: v.2, p.23)
HEBERT, Ophelia d. 29 Aug. 1899 at age 50 yrs. (Chacahoula Ch.: Gibson Ch.: v.2, p.183)
HEBERT, Orphelia Nelly Lilia (Neuvelle & Philomene CLEMENT) b. 14 Oct. 1897 (Chackbay Ch.: v.1, p.96)

HEBERT, Ovilia m. 10 July 1897 Abraham GISCLAIR (Larose Ch.: v.3, p.6)
HEBERT, Ovilia m. 10 July 1897 Abraham GISCLAR (Thib. Ct. Hse.: Mar. v.37, #181)
HEBERT, Ovilia m. 10 July 1897 Abraham GISCLAR (Larose Ch.: v.4, p.93-A)
HEBERT, Paul d. 25 Dec. 1899 at age 2 mths. (Thib. Ch.: v.3, p.247)
HEBERT, Paul (Madeo & Elmina BEAUFORD) b. 27 Oct. 1896 (Houma Ch.: v.5, p.163)
HEBERT, Paul Emile (Madere & Josephine HEBERT) b. 11 Jan. 1899 (Thib. Ch.: v.7, p.592)
HEBERT, Paul F. (Loventie & Mathilde SANCHEZ) b. 13 April 1898 (Chackbay Ch.: v.1, p.111)
HEBERT, Paul Jean (Adam & Lydia BOUDREAU) b. 7 Jan. 1897 (Thib. Ch.: v.7, p.480)
HEBERT, Paul Octave (Theogene & Georgina LIRETTE) b. 19 Oct. 1898 (Thib. Ch.: v.7, p.572)
HEBERT, Pierre Gaston (Pierre & Camillia GUIDROZ) b. 6 Aug. 1896 (Lockport Ch.: v.2, p.334)
HEBERT, Pierre Ives (Serisie & Elvire LECOMPTE) b. 24 Feb. 1897 (Montegut Ch.: v.6, p.53)
HEBERT, Pierre Lucius (Alexis & Marcelline STOUFFLET) b. 23 Feb. 1899 (Montegut Ch.: v.6, p.83)
HEBERT, Pierre Onesime (Anatole & Laura LEE) b. 7 Aug. 1899 (Larose Ch.: v.3, p.46)
HEBERT, Placide (Edmond & Dalida LANCON) m.21 Feb. 1899 Louise CLEMENT (Houma Ct. Hse.: Mar. v.31 & 32, #345)
HEBERT, Rene m. 21 July 1899 Emelienne TRAHAN (Houma Ct. Hse.: Mar. v.31 & 32, #80½)
HEBERT, Rene of Terrebonne Parish m. 26 July 1899 Emilienne TRAHAN, of Terrebonne Parish (Houma Ch.: v.6-B, p.4)
HEBERT, Robert Douglas d. 11 Dec. 1898 at age 37 yrs. (Montegut Ch.: v.2, p.22)
HEBERT, Stanwood (Ernest & Clemence CLEMENT) b. 24 April 1897 (Houma Ch.: v.5, p.179)
HEBERT, Sydney Joseph (Amede & Rose TRAHAN) b. 23 Feb. 1898 (Chacahoula Ch.: v.4, p.3)
HEBERT, Sylvain m. 15 Dec. 1899 Emma HEBERT (Thib. Ct. Hse.: Mar. v.39, #285)
HEBERT, Sylvain (Ursin & Marie BENOIT) m. 20 Dec. 1899 Emma HEBERT (Thib. Ch.: v.14, p.313)
HEBERT, Therese Era (Pierre & Celanie GRABERT) b. 16 March 1896 (Raceland Ch.: v.5, p.26)
HEBERT, Thomas (Martial, d. 1896 & Margaret CLARK, d. 1896) m. Mary BELANGER Child: Edward, aged 5. Tutorship: 5 Feb. 1897. (Houma Ct. Hse.: Succ. #886)
HEBERT, Ursule Evelina (Richard & Cecilia GROS) b. 4 Oct. 1897 (Thib. Ch.: v.7, p.468)
HEBERT, Victoire (Drauzin & Tina CHIASSON) m. 7 June 1897 Otimen CORTEZ (Thib. Ct. Hse.: Mar. v.36, #161)

HEBERT, Victoria m. 25 Jan. 1896 Winifield BOYER (Houma Ct. Hse.: Mar. v.28, #419)
HEBERT, Victoria (Drauzin & Sera CHIASSON) m. 28 June 1897 Ottimen CORTEZ (Chackbay Ch.: v.1, p.45)
HEBERT, Victoria (Louis & Octavie TOUPS) m. 13 Feb. 1896 Wilfrid BOYER (Houma Ch.: v.6-a, p.170)
HEBERT, Violet Valerie (Ulgere & Constance DUPONT) b. 25 Sept. 1897 (Chacahoula Ch.: v.4, p.25)
HEBERT, Weyler Samy (Madere & Josephine HEBERT) b. 25 Sept. 1898 (Thib. Ch.: v.7, p.514)
HEBERT, Wilfrid (Adam & Augustine GIROIR) b. 20 Aug. 1898 (Houma Ch.: v.5, p.220)
HEBERT, William (Dural & Eve MALBROUGH) m. 4 Aug. 1898 Cecile PITRE (Thib. Ct. Hse.: Mar. v.38, #231)
HEBERT, William (Dural & Eve MALBROUGH) m. 4 Aug. 1898 Cecile PITRE (Thib. Ch.: v.14, p.213)
HEBERT, William (Louis & d.Octavie TOUPS) m. 1 March 1897 Marguerite DUPLANTIS (Montegut Ch.: v.4, p.219)
HEBERT, William (Louis & Octavie TOUPS) m. 25 Feb. 1897 Marguerite DUPLANTIS (Houma Ct. Hse.: Mar. v.29 & 30, #328)
HEBERT, William Elie (Wallis & Emma SEVIN) b. 27 Dec. 1897 (Montegut Ch.: v.6, p.66)
HEBERT, Willie Martial (Georges & Felicie BUQUET) b. 23 June 1897 (Montegut Ch.: v.6, p.57)
HEBERT, Xavier Thomas (Numa & Regina PITT) b. 15 Oct. 1898 (Thib. Ch.: v.7, p.517)
HEIDER, John from city of St. Louis (John & Brbara LOBINE) m. 12 April 1898 Mrs. Julia LEBLANC, widow of Willie ELLENDER (Montegut Ch.: v.4, p.241)
HEIDER, John (John & Barbara LOBLINE) m. 9 April 1898 Julia Leblanc ELLENDER (Houma Ct. Hse.: Mar. v.30 & 31, #390)

HELI (See: LEE)

HELLIER, Florence Elizabeth (James & Josephine PREVOST) m. 22 June 1897 George Howard MOAT (Houma Ch.: Epis. Ch.: v.1, p.342)
HELLIER, Florence Elizabeth (James & Josephine PREVOST) m. 3 June 1897 George Howard MOATE (Houma Ct. Hse.: Mar. v.29 & 30, #435)
HELLIER, Lillian (James & Josephine PREVOST) m. 20 Jan. 1898 Alonyo C. KISSE (Houma Ch.: Epis. Ch.: v.1, p.342)
HELLIER, Lillian (James & Josephine PREVOST) m. 20 Jan. 1898 Alonzo C. KISSEE (Houma Ct. Hse.: Mar. v.30 & 31, #237)
HENDERSON, Coraline m. 26 Feb. 1898 Harrison SMITH (Thib. Ct. Hse.: Mar. v.37, #117)
HENDERSON, Fillis m. 7 March 1898 Lorenza COLEMAN (Houma Ct. Hse.: Mar. v.30 & 31, #330)
HENDERSON, Kitty m. 28 April 1898 Reuben BLUE (Houma Ct. Hse.: Mar. v.30 & 31, #423)

HENDERSON, Louis d. 26 Dec. 1897 m. Henriette ANDERSON Children listed: Ophelia. Petition to be placed in possession: 2 March 1897. (Thib. Ct. Hse.: Succ. #1508)
HENDERSON, Luminica m. 16 April 1896 Charley BENDON (Thib. Ct. Hse.: Mar. v.35, #73)
HENDERSON, Mary m.11 May 1898 John MELVEY (Houma Ct. Hse.: Mar. v.30 & 31, #440)
HENDERSON, Mary Jane m. 1 July 1897 Edgar MILLIARD (Houma Ct. Hse.: Mar. v.29 & 30, #46-B)
HENDERSON, Thomas m. 8 April 1899 Julia BARKER (Thib. Ct. Hse.: Mar. v.39, #138)
HENDERSON, Viola m. 12 Jan. 1899 Thomas WIGS (Thib. Ct. Hse.: Mar. v.38, #20)
HENDERSON, Vrginia m. 23 Nov. 1899 Perry JONES (Houma Ct. Hse.: Mar. v.31 & 32, #167)
HENNERY, Joseph d. 20 July 1896 at age 6 mths. (Thib. Ch.: v.3, p.185)

HENRI (Sometimes: HENRY)

HENRI, Adam d. 21 Nov. 1899 at age 31 yrs. & 7 mths. (Houma Ch.: v.3, p.26)
HENRI, Adam m. 4 Sept. 1896 Marie BELANGER (Houma Ct. Hse.: Mar. v.29 & 30, #143)
HENRI, Adam (Leandre & Elise BERGERON) m. 5 Sept. 1896 Mary BELANGER (Houma Ch.: v.6-a, p.180)
HENRI, Adam Joseph (Adam & Marie BELANGER) b. 30 Jan. 1897 (Houma Ch.: v.5, p.198)
HENRI, Alice (Trasimond & Julie BOUDREAU) m. 10 Jan. 1896 John DUPLANTIS (Houma Ch.: v.6-a, p.168)
HENRI, Charles m. 20 Feb. 1897 Anna SCOTT (Thib. Ct. Hse.: Mar. v.36, #87)
HENRI, Emelie (Jules & Louise VERRET) m. 20 May 1896 Joachim BROWN (Houma Ct. Hse.: Mar. v.29 & 30, #76)
HENRI, Emelie (Jules & Louise VERRET) m. 8 June 1896 Joachim BROWN (Montegut Ch.: v.4, p.211)
HENRI, Ennis (Etienne & Lorenza PELEGRIN) m. 21 Feb. 1898 Euphrasie MARCEL (Montegut Ch.: v.4, p.239)
HENRI, Ennis (Etienne & Lorenza PELEGRIN) m. 8 Feb. 1898 Euphrasie MARCEL (Houma Ct. Hse.: Mar. v.30 & 31, #285)
HENRI, Felicia (Urbain & Marie DOMINGUE) m. 11 Feb. 1899 Henry AUTIN (Montegut Ch.: v.4, p.257)
HENRI, Felicie (Urbain & Marie DOMINGUE) m. 29 Dec. 1898 Henry AUTIN (Houma Ct. Hse: Mar. v.30 & 31, #163)
HENRI, John m. 16 Sept. 1899 Fanny DAVIS (Thib. Ct. Hse.: Mar. v.39, #231)
HENRI, John Hampton (John & Carmelite G. HENRY) b. 3 Oct. 1897 (Thib. Ch.: First Presbyt. Ch.: v.1, p.176)
HENRI, Joseph (Luc & Ernestine PELEGRIN) b. 20 Sept. 1899 (Theriot Ch.: v.2, p.52)
HENRI, Joseph Lignesse (Joseph & Victoria LAPEROUSSE) b. 18 Feb. 1898 (Theriot Ch.: v.2, p.38)

HENRI, Julienne (Leon & Elise BERGERON) m. 10 Jan. 1896 Serville ORGERON (Houma Ch.: v.6-a, p.168)

HENRI, Loda m. 29 July 1899 Joseph A. BOUDREAUX (Houma Ct. Hse.: Mar. v.31 & 32, #87)

HENRI, Lodo (Ovide & Melazie MYRE) m. 9 Aug. 1899 Joseph BOUDREAUX (Chacahoula Ch.: v.1, p.72 [92])

HENRI, Ludovic m. 4 Oct. 1897 Octavie TROSCLAIR (Houma Ct. Hse.: Mar. v.29 & 30, #106)

HENRI, Ludovic (Leandre & Elise BERGERON) m. 14 Oct. 1897 Octavie TROSCLAIR (Houma Ch.: v.6-a, p.219)

HENRI, Marie d. 14 July 1898 at age 3 days (Houma Ch.: v.3, p.17)

HENRI, Marie Adonis (Luc & Ernestine PELEGRIN) b. 23 Sept. 1897 (Theriot Ch.: v.2, p.12)

HENRI, Marie Felicia (Etienne & Lorenza PELEGRIN) b. 23 Feb. 1898 (Montegut Ch.: v.6, p.71)

HENRI, Marie Julienne (Etienne & Lorenza) b. 17 March 1896 (Montegut Ch.: v.6, p.36)

HENRI, Marie Luly (Augustin & Azora TOUPS) b. 28 Oct. 1898 (Theriot Ch.: v.2, p.31)

HENRI, Marie Sidonia (Ernest & Euphrasie MARCEL) b. 23 Jan. 1899 (Montegut Ch.: v.6, p.89)

HENRI, Mary Lily (Simon & Mary RODAY) b. 15 March 1899 (Montegut Ch.: v.6, p.84)

HENRI, Mathilda m. 5 May 1897 John BAPTISTE (Thib. Ct. Hse.: Mar. v.36, #137)

HENRI, Niclis Joseph (Willie & Ella LOUVIERE) b. 5 Sept. 1899 (Houma Ch.: v.5, p.257)

HENRI, Robert Ruffin Barrow sister of Theodosia Jane Stevenson HENRI. Donation of land: 30 Dec. 1896. (Houma Ct. Hse.: Book of Donations: v.A, p.156)

HENRI, Seymour (Marcellus & Eliza BOUDREAUX) m. 25 May 1898 Mary RODDY (Houma Ct. Hse.: Mar. v.30 & 31, #454)

HENRI, Simon of Bayou de large after Texas (d.Marcellus & d.Eliza BOUDREAUX) m. 15 June 1898 Mary RODDY (Montegut Ch.: v.4, p.247)

HENRI, Sydney Augustin (Augustin & Azora TOUPS) b. 13 Aug. 1896 (Houma Ch.: v.5, p.155)

HENRI, Trasimon (Leandre & Lesce BERGERON) m. 29 Feb. 1896 Marie BABIN (Houma Ct. Hse.: Mar. v.6-a, p.172)

HENRI, Trasimond m.29 Feb. 1896 Marie BABIN (Houma Ct. Hse.: Mar. v.28, #470)

HENRI, Virginia (Etienne & Lorenza PELEGRIN) m. 31 May 1899 Julien LIRETTE (Houma Ct. Hse.: Mar. v.31 & 32, #20)

HENRI, Virginia (Etienne & Lorenza PELEGRIN) m. 19 June 1899 Aurelien LIRETTE (Montegut Ch.: v.4, p.265)

HENRI, Willie m. 6 June 1896 Ella LOUVIERE (Houma Ct. Hse.: Mar. v.29 & 30, #86)

HENRI, Willie (Oville & Melazie MUIR) m. 25 June 1896 Ella LOUVIERE (Houma Ch.: v.6-a, p.177)

HENRIETTE, Rosalie (Cora THIBODAUX) b. 15 Dec. 1898 (Montegut Ch.: v.6, p.87)
HEPLER, Bertha (Earnest & Eloise HOTARD) m. 24 Feb. 1899 Roscoe C. PALMER (Houma Ch.: Epis. Ch.: v.1, p.344)
HEPLER, Bertha (Ernest H. & Eloise HOTARD) m. 24 Feb. 1899 Roscoe C. PALMER (Houma Ct. Hse.: Mar. v.31 & 32, #349)
HEPLER, Emolyn (Ernest A. & Eloise HOTARD) m. 29 Nov. 1899 Charles R. HEBERT (Houma Ct. Hse.: Mar. v.31 & 32, #168)
HERNANDEZ, Aime d. 5 Dec. 1896 at age 4 mths. (Thib. Ch.: v.3, p.191)
HERNANDEZ, Augusta m. 8 Jan. 1897 Elles DANTIN (Thib. Ct Hse.: Mar. v.36, #17)
HERNANDEZ, Augusta (Augustin & Marie BOURGEOIS) m. 16 Jan. 1897 Ellis DANTIN (Raceland Ch.: v.2, p.27)
HERNANDEZ, Eusebe Augustin (Pierre & Marceline BABIN) b. 20 Oct. 1897 (Thib. Ch.: v.7, p.469)
HERNANDEZ, Felicie (Augustin & Maria BOURGEOIS) m. 10 Feb. 1896 Thomas LAJAUNIE (Raceland Ch.: v.2, p.12)
HERNANDEZ, Horace m. 22 June 1896 Lise SAVOIE (Thib. Ct. Hse.: Mar. v.35, #93)
HERNANDEZ, Horace m. 22 June 1896 Lise SAVOIE (Larose Ch.: v.4, p.96)
HERNANDEZ, Horace m. 22 June 1896 Lise SAVOIE (Larose Ch.: v.3, p.3)
HERNANDEZ, Joseph Voorhies (Joseph & Victoria LERILLE) b. 12 July 1896 (Lockport Ch.: v.2, p.332)
HERNANDEZ, Marie Beatrice (Augustin & Maria BOURGEOIS) b. 17 Oct. 1896 (Raceland Ch.: v.5, p.35)
HERNANDEZ, Marie Bella (Augustin & Maria BOURGEOIS) b. 17 Oct. 1896; m. Pierre Moise CHAMPAGNE on 20 Jan. 1923. (Raceland Ch.: Bapt. Bk., v.5, p.35)
HERNANDEZ, Zeolide m. Lucas HEBERT d. 6 Oct. 1896 at age 20 yrs. (Thib. Ch.: v.3, p.189)
HESSE, Simon d. 28 Jan. 1899 Petition for curatorship: 28 Jan. 1899. (Thib. Ct. Hse.: Succ. #1562)
HESSE, Simon d. 28 Jan. 1899 at age 80 yrs. (Thib. Ch.: v.3, p.226)
HESSE, Simon m. 30 Aug. 1898 Marie Elisa CAMUS (Thib. Ch.: v.14, p.214-a)
HICKMAN, Anna m. 6 June 1899 Henry BISLAND (Houma Ct. Hse.: Mar. v.31 & 32, #35)
HICKMAN, Henry d. 21 Jan. 1897 at age 99 yrs. & 3 mths. (Thib. Ch.: v.3, p.194)

HIDALGO (Sometimes IDALGO)

HIDALGO, Joseph Homer (Franck & Philomene GAUTREAUX) b. 27 Feb. 1898 (Thib. Ch.: v.7, p.491)
HIGGANZA, Andrew d. 3 March 1896 at age 52 yrs. (Raceland Ch.: v.1, p.8)

HIGGINBOTHAM, Joseph Walter Marion (Mathieu & Emma BERGERON) b. 6 Sept. 1896 (Thib. Ch.: v.7, p.417)
HIGGINS, Ignatius m. 15 June 1898 Ida LANDRY (Thib. Ct. Hse.: Mar. v.38, #208)
HIGGINS, Ignatius (Andrew & Helena WOUELSH) m. 25 June 1898 Ida LANDRY (Raceland Ch.: v.2, p.76)
HIGGINS, Thomas Andrus (Ignatius & Ida LANDRY) b. 12 June 1899 (Raceland Ch.: v.5, p.98)
HILAIRE, Henri d. 9 Aug. 1896 (Theriot Ch.: Mar. Bk., v.1, #5)
HILAIRE, Mine Henri d. 8 Aug. 1896 (Theriot Ch.: v.1, p.101)
HILL, Abner m. 21 March 1898 Liddy CALDWELL (Thib. Ct. Hse.: Mar. v.37, #130)
HILL, Elizabeth m. 3 March 1898 Nelson RAYMOND (Thib. Ct. Hse.: Mar. v.37, #116)
HILL, Ella m. 14 Dec. 1897 Clay GILES (Thib. Ct. Hse.: Mar. v.37, #262)
HILL, Marie Philomene d. 21 April 1897 at age 46 yrs. (Thib. Ch.: v.3, p.199)
HILL, Marie Theresa (Alfred & Pauline DUNN) b. 19 Jan. 1898 (Thib. Ch.: v.7, p.548)
HILL, Priscilla m. 14 April 1898 William WALLACE, Jr. (Thib. Ct. Hse.: Mar. v.38, #157)
HILLS, Abe m. 25 July 1898 Belle PARKER (Thib. Ct. Hse.: Mar. v.38, #232)
HILLS, Alice m. 5 April 1899 William SHY (Thib. Ct. Hse.: Mar. v.39, #129)
HILLS, Louisiana m. 2 Jan. 1896 Alex HOOPER (Thib. Ct. Hse.: Mar. v.35, #3)
HILLS, Phoebae m. 9 Jan. 1896 Joseph ROBINSON (Thib. Ct. Hse.: Mar. v.35, #16)
HILLS, Phoebe m. 19 March 1896 Joseph WHITING (Thib. Ct. Hse.: Mar. v.35, #52)
HILLS, Rebecca m. 27 May 1899 Mathew WALLACE (Thib. Ct. Hse.: Mar. v.39, #170)
HILLS, Thomas m. 11 Feb. 1897 Rosella COLEMAN (Thib. Ct. Hse.: Mar. v.36, #77)

HIMEL (Sometimes: HYMEL)

HIMEL, ----- boy (Jean Baptiste) d. 4 Feb. 1897 (Thib. Ch.: v.3, p.196)
HIMEL, Adeline m. 19 March 1896 Thomas ELFER (Thib. Ct. Hse.: Mar. v.35, #53)
HIMEL, Augustin d. 29 Aug. 1898 at age 65 yrs. (Thib. Ch.: v.3, p.219)
HIMEL, Cecile d. 19 May 1899 at age 28 yrs. (Raceland Ch.: v.1, p.25)
HIMEL, Cleore Elis (Edouard & Eugenie RODRIGUE) b. 1 Sept. 1899 (Chackbay Ch.: v.1, p.140)
HIMEL, Edgar Joseph (Prosper & Rosela HEBERT) b. 7 May 1899 (Thib. Ch.: v.7, p.604)

HIMEL, Edward Earle (Charles & Pearle MILER) b. 6 June 1897 (Thib. Ch.: v.7, p.452)
HIMEL, Ernest d. 16 July 1896 at age 48 yrs. (Thib. Ch.: v.3, p.185)
HIMEL, Fedles (Valery & Laurenza BRAUX) m. 8 Feb. 1899 Ophelia GAUTREAUX (Lockport Ch.: v.2, p.202)
HIMEL, Fedless (Valery & Laurenza BRAUX) m. 8 Feb. 1899 Ophelia GAUTHREAUX (Thib. Ct. Hse.: Mar. v.38, #66)
HIMEL, Felix Davis (Zephyrin & Eve TOUPS) b. 18 May 1897 (Thib. Ch.: v.7, p.451)
HIMEL, Henry Louis (Dennis & Alida GAGNOU) b. 19 July 1899 (Chacahoula Ch.: v.4, p.28)
HIMEL, Isidore Joseph (Ida HYMEL) b. 30 Aug. 1899 (Thib. Ch.: v.8, p.12)
HIMEL, Jean Baptiste (Jean Baptiste & Marie Aspasie SAUSSIER) b. 3 Feb. 1897 (Thib. Ch.: v.7, p.439)
HIMEL, Joseph Laurens (Merthil & Aurore BAYEUX) b. 26 Dec. 1896 (Larose Ch.: v.3, p.1)
HIMEL, Joseph Odphee Edgard (Joseph & Marie GUILLOT) b. 7 April 1897 (Thib. Ch.: v.7, p.446)
HIMEL, Joseph Sampson (Prosper & Rosela HEBERT) b. 14 March 1897 (Thib. Ch.: v.7, p.447)
HIMEL, Marguerite Easle (Denis & Alida GAGNOUX) b. 8 Nov. 1896 (Chacahoula Ch.: v.4, p.9)
HIMEL, Marie Clara (Allan & Alfrida DUPLANTIS) b. 7 Dec. 1899 (Montegut Ch.: v.6, p.100)
HIMEL, Mary Bessie (Allan & Alfrida DUPLANTIS) b. 29 June 1897 (Montegut Ch.: v.6, p.59)
HIMEL, Nicholas m. 26 Dec. 1899 Eliska BOUDREAUX (Houma Ct. Hse.: Mar. v.31 & 32, #197)
HIMEL, Rodolphe Jean Baptiste d. 14 Sept. 1896 at age 16 yrs. & 1 mth. (Thib. Ch.: v.3, p.187)
HIMEN, Clarence Augustin (Joseph & Justilia GUILLOT) b. 9 Feb. 1899 (Thib. Ch.: v.7, p.535)
HIMERE, Marie Cecile (Thideles & Ophelia GAUTREAUX) b. 13 Nov. 1899 (Larose Ch.: v.3, p.48)
HINGLE, Joseph T. m. 11 May 1896 Amanda Jane GRIFFIN (Thib. Ct. Hse.: Mar. v.35, #83)
HIRIARD, Cecile m. 7 June 1897 Oscar SOIGNET (Thib. Ct. Hse.: Mar. v.36, #162)
HITE, Eliza m. 3 Oct. 1898 Anatole LEWIS (Houma Ct. Hse.: Mar. v.30 & 31, #115)
HITE, Moses m. 11 Feb. 1897 Nancy Elizabeth COLEMAN (Houma Ct. Hse.: Mar. v.29 & 30, #304)
HITE, Rufus m. 13 March 1899 Roberta WILSON (Thib. Ct. Hse.: Mar. v.39, #118)

HOBERT (See: AUBERT)

HOCK (Sometimes: HOC)

HOCK, Adam Royl (Raoul & Justilia LEBLANC) b. 28 Dec. 1899 (Thib. Ch.: v.7, p.592)

HOCK, Lula Josephine (Romain & Olympia ROGER) m. 1 March 1899 Gaston BOUDREAUX (Thib. Ch.: v.14, p.267)

HOCK, Lula Josephine (Roman & Olympia ROGER) m. 1 March 1899 Gaston BOUDREAUX (Thib. Ct. Hse.: Mar. v.39, #114)

HOCK, Odette Beatrix (Edouard & Josephine DOMINGUE) b. 1 Sept. 1899 (Thib. Ch.: v.8, p.13)

HOCK, Roman d. Sept. 1896; m. Letitia ROGER Children listed: Lucas; Willie; Lula m. Gaston BOUDREAUX; Nannie, 17 yrs. old; Daisy, 15 yrs.; Harry, 12 yrs. Petition for tutorship: 1 June 1899. (Thib. Ct. Hse.: Succ. #1575)

HOFFMAN (Sometimes: HOFFMANN)

HOFFMAN, Alfred Reginald (Frank & Augustine PHILIPPEAU) b. 9 Feb. 1896 (Thib. Ch.: v.7, p.449)

HOFFMAN, Arthur E. m. 30 Aug. 1897 Zoe FOLSE (Thib. Ct. Hse.: Mar. v.37, #225)

HOFFMAN, Earl Honore (Frank & Augustine PHILIPPE) b. 28 Feb. 1899 (Thib. Ch.: v.7, p.602)

HOFFMAN, Harold Andrew (Arthur H. & Zoe FOLSE) b. 11 July 1898 (Thib. Ch.: v.7, p.504)

HOFFMAN, Julia Hazel (Jules & Jeanne FAQUET) b. 27 Jan. 1897 (Thib. Ch.: v.7, p.485)

HOFFMAN, Louise Josephine m. Edgard RIVIERE d. 4 June 1896 at age 33 yrs. & 3 mths. (Thib. Ch.: v.3, p.183)

HOGAN, Dan m. 23 Sept. 1896 Adeline COLLINS (Houma Ct. Hse.: Mar. v.29 & 30, #151)

HOGAN, Mary (Patrick & Mary DALY) m. 17 Feb. 1897 William McCORMICK (Thib. Ch.: v.14, p.127)

HOGAN, Mary (Patrick & Mary DALY) m. 17 Feb. 1897 William McCORMICK (Thib. Ct. Hse.: Mar. v.36, #81)

HOGAN, Nadine Marie (J. & Arthemise DUFRESNE) b. 16 April 1899 (Larose Ch.: v.3, p.40)

HOHENSEE, Mathilde (Gottieb & Elisabeth SUAREZ) m. 23 Sept. 1897 John GUILLOT (Thib. Ch.: v.14, p.160)

HOLDEN, John m. 11 July 1897 Sidonia YOUNG (Thib. Ct. Hse.: Mar. v.37, #191)

HOLEMAN, Francois (William) d. 19 July 1898 at age 15 yrs. (Chacahoula Ch.: v.2, p.28)

HOLLINS, Daniel m. 9 Sept. 1897 Jeannetta MARSHALL, widow of Amos GRIMS (Thib. Ct. Hse.: Mar. v.37, #231)

HOLLOWAY, James m. 17 May 1897 Kate McDUFFY (Thib. Ct. Hse.: Mar. v.36, #145)

HOLMES, Louisa m. 29 June 1899 Sidney BURREL (Thib. Ct. Hse.: Mar. v.39, #189)

HOMENE, Georges (Alexandre & Pauline BEANDITON) b. 26 June 1897 (Theriot Ch.: v.2, p.6)

HOMER, Marie Esta (Nicolas & Amelisa ARABIE) b. 21 April 1899 (Raceland Ch.: v.5, p.96)

HONORINE, Marguerite (Agnes BELANGER) b. 16 Feb. 1896 (Montegut Ch.: v.6, p.41)

HOOPER, Alex m. 2 Jan. 1896 Louisiana HILLS (Thib. Ct. Hse.: Mar. v.35, #3)

HOTARD (Sometimes: AUTARD, AUTORD, HAUTAR, HAUTARD, HOTTARD, OTAR, OTTARD)

HOTARD, Adeline Armantine (Charley & Josephine BILLOT) b. 26 Dec. 1896 (Montegut Ch.: v.6, p.49)

HOTARD, Adeline Armantine (Charley & Josephine BILLOT) d. 20 Feb. 1897 at age 2 mths. (Montegut Ch.: v.2, p.9)

HOTARD, Albert Clovis (Emile & Angelina THEVE) b. 24 Oct. 1896 (Montegut Ch.: v.6, p.54)

HOTARD, Alexina (Joseph & Marie PARR) m. 10 Nov. 1896 Ernest ADAM (Lockport Ch.: v.2, p.155 & 156)

HOTARD, Alexina (Joseph & Marie PARR) m. 16 Nov. 1896 Ernest ADAM (Thib. Ct. Hse.: Mar. v.36, #160)

HOTARD, Anne Thelma (Noel & Jaetine MARTIN) b. 29 April 1898 (Montegut Ch.: v.6, p.73)

HOTARD, Arthur m. 15 Jan. 1897 Valerie LABIT (Houma Ct. Hse.: Mar. v.29 & 30, #239)

HOTARD, Arthur (L. Demetrius & Justilia FIELDS) m. 16 Jan. 1897 Valerie LABIT (Houma Ch.: v.6-a, p.189)

HOTARD, Drosin d. 15 Sept. 1896 at age 55 yrs. (Montegut Ch.: v.2, p.6)

HOTARD, Edna Marie (Joe & Ulalie PITRE) b. 25 Oct. 1898 (Thib. Ch.: v.7, p.572)

HOTARD, Emelie (Joseph & Marie PAQUES) m. 6 Feb. 1897 Alceste ADAM (Lockport Ch.: v.2, p.159)

HOTARD, Emelie (Joseph & Marie PAYNES) m. 6 Feb. 1897 Alceste ADAM (Thib. Ct. Hse.: Mar. v.36, #45)

HOTARD, Ernest (Demetrius & Justilia FIELDS) m. 24 Aug. 1899 Clara GROS (Thib. Ch.: v.14, p.291)

HOTARD, Ernest (Demetrius & Justilia FIELDS) m. 24 Aug. 1899 Clara GROS (Thib. Ct. Hse.: Mar. v.39, #210)

HOTARD, Florentin m. 17 April 1899 Victoria THIBODAUX (Houma Ct. Hse.: Mar. v.31 & 32, #405)

HOTARD, Heloise (Euphrosin, Sr. & Marie Celine MARS) m. Ernest A. HEPLER. Petition for interdiction: 11 Jan. 1896. (Houma Ct. Hse.: Succ. #866)

HOTARD, Inezeda (Demetrius & Justilia FIELDS) m. 30 Jan. 1899 Eugene CARRO (Houma Ch.: v.6-a, p.270)

HOTARD, Inezida m. 12 Jan. 1899 Eugene CARRO (Houma Ct. Hse.: Mar. v.30 & 31, #222)

HOTARD, Jemy Ethna (Adam & Marguerite LOMBAS) b. 19 Aug. 1896 (Lockport Ch.: v.2, p.334)

HOTARD, Joseph m. 14 Sept. 1897 Eulalie PITRE (Thib. Ct. Hse.: Mar. v.37, #233)

HOTARD, Joseph (Froizin & Marie HEBERT) m. 16 Dec. 1898 Eulalie PITRE (Thib. Ct. Hse.: Mar. v.14, #232)

HOTARD, Josephine Isabelle (Arthur & Valerie LABIE) b. 22 Oct. 1897; m. David WALLER on 10 Aug. 1924. (Houma Ch.: Bapt. Bk., v.5, p.192)

HOTARD, Josephine Laiza (Joseph & Ozea BOURG) b. 26 March 1896 (Lockport Ch.: v.2, p.327)

HOTARD, Jules m. 27 Dec. 1897 Lorinza ADAM (Thib. Ct. Hse.: Mar. v.37, #267)
HOTARD, Julie Marcelline (Joseph & Louise DUPRE) b. 1 Sept. 1897 (Montegut Ch.: v.6, p.60)
HOTARD, Lilian (J. Noel & Gugtine MARTIN) m. 21 April 1897 Augustin JAVAUX (Montegut Ch.: v.4, p.220)
HOTARD, Lillian (J. Noel & Guytine MARTIN) m. 5 April 1897 Augustin JAVAUX (Houma Ct. Hse.: Mar. v.29 & 30, #374)
HOTARD, Marguerite Irene (Johnny & Similia SAVOIE) b. 22 Sept. 1899 (Montegut Ch.: v.6, p.93)
HOTARD, Marguerite Rositte (Johnny & Similia SAVOIE) b. 21 Aug. 1897 (Montegut Ch.: v.6, p.59)
HOTARD, Maria Hazel (Gaetine & Noel HOTARD) b. 30 March 1896 (Montegut Ch.: v.6, p.38)
HOTARD, Marie Cora (Arthur & Valerie LABIT) b. 3 Sept. 1899; m. Willie C. SHEPHERD on 25 July 1940. (Houma Ch.: Bapt. Bk., v.5, p.256)
HOTARD, Marie Eveline m. Fillmore CHAUVIN d. 25 Dec. 1899 at age 45 yrs. (Montegut Ch.: v.2, p.32)
HOTARD, Marie Lucie (Duncan & Lucie FALGOUST) b. 28 Oct. 1897 (Thib. Ch.: v.7, p.471)
HOTARD, Marie Magnolty (Noel & Guytine MARTIN) m. 26 Jan. 1899 John Louis GUIDRY (Montegut Ch.: v.4, p.252)
HOTARD, Mary Magnolty (Newell & Guytine MARTIN) m. 6 Jan. 1899 John L. GUIDRY (Houma Ct. Hse.: Mar. v.30 & 31, #189)
HOTARD, Oneil Gaston (James & Emma LASSEIGNE) d. 17 Aug. 1898 at age 4 yrs. & 1 day (Montegut Ch.: v.2, p.19)
HOTARD, Pierre m. 24 May 1899 Carrie BELANGER (Houma Ct. Hse.: Mar. v.31 & 32, #14)
HOTARD, Pierre of Terrebonne Parish m. 19 June 1899 Carrie BELANGER (Houma Ch.: v.6-B, p.3)
HOTARD, Pierre (John & Simelia SAVOIE) d. 3 May 1896 at age 2 days (Montegut Ch.: v.2, p.4)
HOUSSET, Jennie m. Clotane BERNARD; d. 17 July 1896 at age 30 yrs. (Thib. Ch.: v.3, p.185)
HOUSSETTE, Marie d. 2 Oct. 1897 at age 2 mths. (Thib. Ch.: v.3, p.206)
HOUSSETTE, Marie Eugenie (Josephine) b. 1 July 1896 (Thib. Ch.: v.7, p.466)
HOWARD, Cornelius m. 26 Jan. 1899 Dora SHELDON (Thib. Ct. Hse.: Mar. v.38, #62)
HOWARD, Josephine m. 14 Oct. 1897 James SELBY (Thib. Ct. Hse.: Mar. v.37, #244)
HOWARD, Melvin m. 10 March 1898 Charlotte WILLIAMS (Thib. Ct. Hse.: Mar. v.37, #124)
HOWARD, Reuben m. 16 July 1896 Emily BOSEMAN (Houma Ct. Hse.: Mar. v.29 & 30, #114)
HOWARD, Richard m. 7 Sept. 1899 Della YOUNG (Thib. Ct. Hse.: Mar. v.39, #225)

HOWARD, William m. 27 Feb. 1896 Henrietta PERKINS (Houma Ct. Hse.: Mar. v.28, #469)
HOWARD, Willie m. 10 Aug. 1898 Fannie DURGAN (Thib. Ct. Hse.: Mar. v.38, #244)
HOWELL, John M. d. 16 June 1896 at age 75 yrs. (Thib. Ch.: Epis. Ch.: v.1, p.394)
HOWELL, John Moses d. 7 Sept. 1897 at age 4 mths. (Thib. Ch.: Epis. Ch.: v.1, p.394)
HOWELL, John Moses (William E. & Florence PERKINS) b. 6 May 1897 on Waverly Plantation (Thib. Ch.: Epis. Ch.: v.1, p.42)
HUBBARD, Walton m. 22 July 1897 Lettie HARRIS (Houma Ct. Hse.: Mar. v.29 & 30, #68)
HUBBS, John m. 8 Feb. 1899 Peggie MILTON (Thib. Ct. Hse.: Mar. v.38, #96)
HUGEL, Euseline (Duane & Therese TOMASSIE) b. 29 July 1896 (Larose Ch.: v.2, p.182)
HUGHS, Henry m. 26 Jan. 1899 Edna WILSON (Thib. Ct. Hse.: Mar. v.38, #68)
HULIN, Alcide (Adam & Velida DIEZ) m. 28 Sept. 1899 Matilde PRICE (Raceland Ch.: v.2, p.104)
HULING, Thomas m. 26 Jan. 1899 Rosa DAVIS (Thib. Ct. Hse.: Mar. v.38, #64)
HUMPHREY, Ernest (Victor & Victoire RICHARD) m. 15 Feb. 1898 Therese TOUSSAINT (Thib. Ch.: v.14, p.188)
HUMPHREY, Ernest (Victor & Victoire RICHARD) m. 15 Feb. 1898 Therese TOUSSAINT (Thib. Ct. Hse.: Mar. v.37, #85)
HUMPHREYS, Edna m. 12 Dec. 1899 Monroe VERRET (Houma Ct. Hse.: Mar. v.31 & 32, #182)
HUMPHREYS, Medard (Victor & Victoire RICHARD) m. 17 Jan. 1899 Lena LAGARDE (Thib. Ct. Hse.: Mar. v.38, #9)
HUMPHREYS, Medard (Victor & Victorine RICHARD) m. 17 Jan. 1899 Lena LAGARDE (Thib. Ch.: v.14, p.239)
HUNSHBAY, Marie Aline (James & Madeleine NAQUIN) b. 25 April 1896 (Montegut Ch.: v.6, p.42)
HUNT, E. Mrs. d. 2 Nov. 1898 at age 65 yrs. (Thib. Ch.: v.3, p.221)
HUNTER, Henri Jonas d. 9 March 1899 at age 13 mths. (Larose Ch.: v.1, p.51)
HUNTER, Henry Jones (Robert & Marie BAYEUX) b. 2 Feb. 1898 (Larose Ch.: v.3, p.16)
HUNTER, Robert Joseph (Robert & Marie BAYEUX) b. 24 Jan. 1896 (Larose Ch.: v.2, p.180)
HUSBAND, Henry August (Redmond & Florestine LEBLANC) b. 26 March 1898 (Chacahoula Ch.: Gibson Ch.: v.2, p.122)
HUSBANDS, Henry August (Redmond & Florestine LEBLANC) b. 26 March 1898 (Chacahoula Ch.: Gibson Records: Mar. Bk., v.1, #37)
HUTCHINSON, Joseph Harvey (William & Lisca RHODES) b. 18 Aug. 1898 (Montegut Ch.: v.6, p.77)

HUTCHINSON, Joseph Harvey (William & Lisca RHODES) d. 16 Nov. 1899 at age 1 yr. & 3 mths. (Montegut Ch.: v.2, p.30)
HUTCHINSON, Louise (Felix & Anastasie HEBERT) m. 23 April 1898 Augustave LEDET (Montegut Ch.: v.4, p.243)
HUTCHINSON, Louise (Felix & Anastasie HEBERT) m. 4 April 1898 Augustave LEDET (Houma Ct. Hse.: Mar. v.30 & 31, #370)
HUTCHINSON, Paul Wiley (William & Lisca RHODES) b. 18 Aug. 1898 (Montegut Ch.: v.6, p.77)
HYDE, Richard m. 20 Feb. 1897 Ida GOFF (Thib. Ct. Hse.: Mar. v.36, #84)

HYMEL (See: HIMEL)

"I"

INAISE, Beatrix Viola (Charles & Louisiane LABATHE) b. 16 Aug. 1896 (Houma Ch.: v.5, p.156)

INCALADE (See: ENCALADE)

INCLADE, Jacques (Joseph & Noida RIBAULT) b. 12 Oct. 1897 (Larose Ch.: v.3, p.26)

INGHAM, Martha m. 17 June 1896 Henry WILLIAMS (Thib. Ct. Hse.: Mar. v.35, #107)

INGLAND (See Perhaps: ENGLAND)

INGLAND, Katie m.18 June 1899 Samuel JOSEPH (Houma Ct. Hse.: Mar. v.31 & 32, #47)

INGNAFFIA, Rozia (Luciano & Francesca AUZELMA) m. 12 Jan. 1899 Salvatore CASPISA, Jr. (Houma Ch.: v.6-a, p.262)

INGNAPFIA, Razia m. 4 Jan. 1899 Salvatore LASPISA, Jr. (Houma Ct. Hse.: Mar. v.30 & 31, #176)

INZINGA, Carmelo (Antonino & Guiseppa BELLOVIA) m. 3 Feb. 1898 Maria CASTROGIOVANNI (Thib. Ch.: v.14, p.179)

INZINGA, Carmelo (Antonino & Guiseppa BELLAVIA) m. 3 Feb. 1898 Maria CASTROGIOVANNI (Thib. Ct. Hse.: Mar. v.37, #54)

INZINGA, Guiseppe d. 19 Nov. 1899 at age 39 yrs. (Thib. Ch.: v.3, p.243)

INZINGA, Guiseppe d. 20 Nov. 1899 at age 39 yrs. (Thib. Ch.: v.3, p.244)

IPPOLITO, Santa (Guiseppe & Angela CASTELLANO) b. 6 Aug. 1897 (Houma Ch.: v.5, p.186)

IVERY, William m. 2 Feb. 1899 Clarissa MILLER (Thib. Ct. Hse.: Mar. v.38, #85)

IVES, Paul H. m. 6 April 1899 Hattie LAWLESS (Thib. Ct. Hse.: Mar. v.39, #133)

"J"

JABEAU, Ada m. Drauzin BERGERON d. 13 Feb. 1899 at age 45 yrs. (Thib. Ch.: v.3, p.227)
JACKS, James B. m. 14 Sept. 1899 Lina WHITE (Houma Ct. Hse.: Mar. v.31 & 32, #131)
JACKSON, Albert (Tilman & Eve NEUVILLE) b. 19 April 1899 (Thib. Ch.: v.7, p.604)
JACKSON, Allen m. 20 Jan. 1897 Louisa TONEY (Houma Ct. Hse.: Mar. v.29 & 30, #241)
JACKSON, Donella June b. 5 June 1896 (Gibson Ch.: Epis. Ch.: v.1, p.104)
JACKSON, Donnilla (Geo. Andrew & Lula May CHAUVIN) b. 15 June 1896 (Houma Ch.: Epis. Ch.: v.1, p.114)
JACKSON, Edward m. 11 Nov. 1897 Bertha BARKUS (Houma Ct. Hse.: Mar. v.39 & 30, #136)
JACKSON, Elizabeth m. 10 Sept. 1898 William EDWARDS (Thib. Ct. Hse.: Mar. v.38, #277)
JACKSON, Emma m. 22 Feb. 1899 George WALKER (Thib. Ct. Hse.: Mar. v.39, #111)
JACKSON, Fanchonette m. 4 Jan. 1898 George FELIX (Thib. Ct. Hse.: Mar. v.37, #4)
JACKSON, Frank m. 5 Dec. 1898 Clara BROWN (Thib. Ct. Hse.: Mar. v.38, #315)
JACKSON, Jessie m. 23 March 1896 Nancy MOORE (Thib. Ct. Hse.: Mar. v.35, #55)
JACKSON, John d. 18 Oct. 1897 Children: d.Francis m. Edmond HUDSON. Petition to put heirs in possession: 27 Oct. 1897. (Houma Ct. Hse.: Succ. #889)
JACKSON, John A. m. 11 May 1899 Virginia A. HARRIS (Thib. Ct. Hse.: Mar. v.39, #164)
JACKSON, Joseph Moise (Moise & Victoria RICHARD) b. 9 Jan. 1899 (Thib. Ch.: v.7, p.586)
JACKSON, Lena m. 27 Oct. 1898 Shelton ROOKS (Thib. Ct. Hse.: Mar. v.38, #304)
JACKSON, Louisa m. 24 Jan. 1898 Arty or Arthur ROUNDS (Thib. Ct. Hse.: Mar. v.37, #52)
JACKSON, Lucinda m. 20 Feb. 1899 Thomas B. DAVIS (Houma Ct. Hse.: Mar. v.31 & 32, #344)
JACKSON, Marie Aurelia (Mose & Victoria RICHARD) b. 1 Jan. 1898 (Thib. Ch.: v.7, p.482)
JACKSON, Marie Bessie (Joseph & Philomene ROBERTSON) b. 26 Sept. 1899 (Thib. Ch.: v.8, p.15)
JACKSON, Mary m. 26 Jan. 1899 Lemuel BROWN (Houma Ct. Hse.: Mar. v.30 & 31, #286)
JACKSON, Mary m. 26 March 1896 Marcellin MEYERS (Thib. Ct. Hse.: Mar. v.35, #56)
JACKSON, Mary Myrthe (George Andrew & Loula May CHAUVIN) b. 19 Dec. 1897 (Houma Ch.: Epis. Ch.: v.1, p.120)
JACKSON, Mary Myrtle b. 19 Dec. 1897 (Gibson Ch.: Epis. Ch.: v.1, p.104)

JACKSON, Odelia m. 5 Feb. 1896 Clay THIBODAUX (Houma Ct. Hse.: Mar. v.28, #437)
JACKSON, Patience m. 29 Dec. 1898 James CITIZEN (Houma Ct. Hse.: Mar. v.30 & 31, #165)
JACKSON, Paul m. 28 May 1897 Sarah WASHINGTON (Houma Ct. Hse.: Mar. v.29 & 30, #431)
JACKSON, Polly m. 7 Jan. 1896 Trooty BLUE (Houma Ct. Hse.: Mar. v.28, #377)
JACKSON, Rebecca m. 22 July 1899 Eddie WILLIAMS (Houma Ct. Hse.: Mar. v.31 & 32, #84)
JACKSON, Robert (Robert & Emerante DAUTEVILLE) m. 10 Feb. 1896 Josephine PARR (Lockport Ch.: v.2, p.150)
JACKSON, Salomon m. 3 Feb. 1898 Malley WALKER (Thib. Ct. Hse.: Mar. v.37, #78)
JACKSON, Tillman (Edward & Martha DIXON) m. 27 April 1898 Eva NEUVILLE (Thib. Ct. Hse.: Mar. v.38, #170)
JACKSON, Tillman (Edward & Martha DIXON) m. 27 April 1898 Eva NEUVILLE (Thib. Ch.: v.14, p.200)
JACKSON, William m. Mary Child listed: Ella. Insanity of: 25 Jan. 1899. (Thib. Ct. Hse.: Succ. #1561)
JACKSON, William m. 12 May 1897 Emily WARREN (Houma Ct. Hse.: Mar. v.29 & 30, #418)
JACONA, Antonino (Joseph & Rosalia ANELLO) b. 7 March 1898 (Houma Ch.: v.5, p.207)
JAGOMAS, Nicholas (Nicholas & Salvatore CHIRNIJA) b. 5 June 1899 (Houma Ch.: v.5, p.246)
JAMARO, Carola (Sabatho & Jeosepa ZABIA) b. 25 Oct. 1896 (Houma Ch.: v.5, p.159)
JAMBON, Alcide Neutilis (Joseph & Valentine CHICHIZOLA) b. 8 Sept. 1896 (Larose Ch.: v.3, p.12)
JAMBON, Antoine Abel (Etienne & Ernestine LANDRY) b. 17 Jan. 1898 (Larose Ch.: v.3, p.27)
JAMBON, Pauline Aimee (Achille & Louisiane PITRE) b. 15 Jan. 1898 (Larose Ch.: v.3, p.27)
JAMES, Benjamin m. 23 Nov. 1899 Mary BAPTISTE (Thib. Ct. Hse.: Mar. v.39, #269)
JAMES, Joseph m. 18 Jan. 1899 Elizabeth LEWIS (Thib. Ct. Hse.: Mar. v.38, #31)
JAMES, Williams Joseph (Prosper & Victorine JULES) b. 2 Aug. 1897 (Thib. Ch.: v.7, p.463)

JANDRON (See: JEANDRON)

JANFRAU, John m. 1 Feb. 1897 Marie CALLAIS (Thib. Ct. Hse.: Mar. v.36, #60)
JASPER, Joshua m. 21 June 1898 Rebecca JONES (Houma Ct. Hse.: Mar. v.30 & 31, #25)
JASPER, Mary Louisa m. 1 Aug. 1898 Malachi or Melciah NIXON (Houma Ct. Hse.: Mar. v.30 & 31, #70)
JAVAUX, Augustin (Auguste & Elodie GUIDRY) m. 5 April 1897 Lillian HOTARD (Houma Ct. Hse.: Mar. v.29 & 30, #374)

JAVAUX, Augustin (d.Auguste & d.Eulodie GUIDRY) m. 21 April 1897 Lilian HOTARD (Montegut Ch.: v.4, p.220)
JAVAUX, Marguerite Effie (Augustin & Lilianne HOTARD) b. 3 March 1899 (Montegut Ch.: v.6, p.83)
JAVEAU, Marguerite Ephie (Augustin & Lilianne HOTARD) d. 11 Dec. 1899 at age 9 mths. & 8 days (Montegut Ch.: v.2, p.31)

JEANDRON (Sometimes: JANDRON)
JEANDRON, Elles (Jean Baptiste & Estelle LAPEYROUSE) m. 25 July 1899 Regina PICOU (Larose Ch.: v.3, p.12)
JEANDRON, Elles (Jean Baptiste & Estelle LAPEYROUSE) m. 25 July 1899 Regina PICOU (Larose Ch.: v.4, p.94)
JEANDRON, Ellis m.15 July 1899 Regina PICOU (Thib. Ct. Hse.: Mar. v.39, #201)
JEANDRON, Joseph Dorsen (Jean Baptiste & Cecile LEDET) b. 22 Sept. 1897 (Larose Ch.: v.3, p.11)
JEANDRON, Maurice Michel (Numa & Marie ARGUS) b. 13 Dec. 1896 (Lockport Ch.: v.3, #32)
JEANDRON, Maurice Michel (Numa & Marie ARGUS) b. 17 Dec. 1896 (Lockport Ch.: v.3-A, #32)
JEANDRON, May Adela (Ernest & Josephine MELANCON) b. 11 June 1899 (Thib. Ch.: v.7, p.551)
JEANDRON, Toussaint Sidney (Ernest & Josephine MELANCON) b. 1 Nov. 1896 (Larose Ch.: v.2, p.196)
JEANFRAU, James Albert (Louis & Marie KIGGER) b. 17 Jan. 1899 (Larose Ch.: v.3, p.41)
JEANFRAU, Josephine (John & Marie CALLET) b. 23 Nov. 1899 (Larose Ch.: v.3, p.59)
JEANMARD, Leonel Jules Beauvais (Raoul & Elizabeth BEAUVAIS) b. 15 June 1898 (Thib. Ch.: v.7, p.501)
JEANMARD, Raoul (Jules & Blanche BROWN) m. 28 April 1897 Elisabeth BEAUVAIS (Thib. Ch.: v.14, p.140)
JEANMARD, Raoul (Jules & Blanche BROWN) m. 28 April 1897 Elizabeth BEAUVAIS (Thib. Ct. Hse.: Mar. v.36, #127)

JEANSON (See JOHNSON)

JEBANGILISTA, Aguinaldo (Lucas & Elizabeth BILLAMOUR) b. 19 Oct. 1899 (Theriot Ch.: v.2, p.50)
JEFF, John m. 7 April 1898 Lucinda THOMPSON (Houma Ct. Hse.: Mar. v.30 & 31, #378)
JEFFERS, Mary Elmo (George & Mary CHAMPAGNE) b. 29 May 1897 (Thib. Ch.: v.7, p.452)
JEFFERSON, Daniel m. 24 Dec. 1898 Mollie HARRIS (Thib. Ct. Hse.: Mar. v.38, #323)
JEFFERSON, Elizabeth m. 28 March 1896 Sidney VERRET (Houma Ct. Hse.: Mar. v.29 & 30, #25)
JEFFERSON, Josephine (Thomas & Ernestine CHILDS) b. 6 Feb. 1899 (Thib. Ch.: v.7, p.601)

JEFFERSON, Mary Gertrude (Thomas & Ernestine) b. 29 Aug. 1897 (Thib. Ch.: v.7, p.514)
JEFFERSON, Philip m. 10 Feb. 1898 Lizzie WASHINGTON (Houma Ct. Hse.: Mar. v.30 & 31, #288)
JEFFERSON, Rebecca d. 16 Oct. 1897 at age 52 yrs. (Thib. Ch.: v.3, p.206)
JEFFERSON, Thomas m. 8 March 1898 Ernestine GILES (Thib. Ct. Hse.: Mar. v.37, #122)
JEFFERSON, Thomas O'Neil (Edouard & Lylia JACKSON) b. 27 April 1896 (Thib. Ch.: v.8, p.25)
JEFFRIES, Corinne Aimee (Georges & Marie CHAMPAGNE) b. 10 Oct. 1898 (Thib. Ch.: v.7, p.519)
JEFFRIES, Joseph Georges (Georges & Marie CHAMPAGNE) d. 29 May 1896 at birth (Thib. Ch.: v.3, p.183)
JENKINS, Ann m. 6 Feb. 1897 Louis TURNER (Houma Ct. Hse.: Mar. v.29 & 30, #295)
JENKINS, Israel m. 11 Jan. 1897 Sue EVANS (Houma Ct. Hse.: Mar. v.29 & 30, #232)
JENKINS, John m. 16 Feb. 1898 Katie DUNAWAY (Houma Ct. Hse.: Mar. v.30 & 31, #297)
JENKINS, Margaret m. 2 Feb. 1899 James SCRUBB (Houma Ct. Hse.: Mar. v.30 & 31, #303)
JENKINS, Philip m. 14 Oct. 1899 Mary REED (Houma Ct. Hse.: Mar. v.31 & 32, #149)
JENKINS, Sarah m. 5 Jan. 1899 James E. RHODES (Thib. Ct. Hse.: Mar. v.38, #5)
JENKINS, Thomas m. 9 Nov. 1897 Lorena JONES (Houma Ct. Hse.: Mar. v.29 & 30, #133)
JOANNY, Felicia (George & Galogera CACIOPA) b. 9 Jan. 1899 (Houma Ch.: v.5, p.235)
JOANNY, Sarah Argentine (Mathias & Marie AUTHEMENT) b. 8 Sept. 1896 (Houma Ch.: v.5, p.160)
JOBARD, Rev. Father Gustave d. 20 June 1898 at age 45 yrs. in Labadieville, Louisiana. (Lockport Ch.: v.1, #14)
JOHN (--- & Angelique DUPLANTIS) b. 11 Sept. 1897 (Houma Ch.: v.5, p.190)
JOHN, Rosalie (Henri & Ales JOHN) b. 5 April 1898 (Thib. Ch.: v.7, p.544)
JOHNFRAU, Jean Felicien (John & Marie CALET) b. 15 Dec. 1897 (Larose Ch.: v.3, p.21)
JOHNS, Annie (Eunice & Rosa PARR) m. 3 June 1897 Thomas FRAZIER (Thib. Ct. Hse.: Mar. v.36, #155)

JOHNSON (Sometines JEANSON)

JOHNSON, Aaron m. 1 July 1896 Anna DAVIS (Houma Ct. Hse.: Mar. v.29 & 30, #100)
JOHNSON, Abraham m. 18 June 1896 Joephine REGIS (Thib. Ct Hse.: Mar. v.35, #109)
JOHNSON, Adeline m. 14 Sept. 1896 Robert JOHNSON, Jr. (Houma Ct. Hse.: Mar. v.29 & 30, #148)

JOHNSON, Aleck m. 4 Jan. 1897 Malvina RAINEY (Thib. Ct. Hse.: Mar. v.36, #6)
JOHNSON, Alice m. 16 Feb. 1899 Douglas WRIGHT (Thib. Ct. Hse.: Mar. v.39, #108)
JOHNSON, Anie (Eunice & Rosa PAN) m. 3 June 1897 Thomas FRAZIER (Thib. Ch.: v.14, p.146)
JOHNSON, Bertha m. 2 Feb. 1899 George J. WASHINGTON, Jr. (Thib. Ct. Hse.: Mar. v.38, #86)
JOHNSON, Charlie m. 2 Jan. 1896 Carline ANDERSON (Thib. Ct. Hse.: Mar. v.35, #7)
JOHNSON, Christina m. 10 Sept. 1898 Fulton MOSES (Houma Ct. Hse.: Mar. v.30 & 31, #93)
JOHNSON, Christophe Columbus (Adam & Eliza STEWART) m. 3 May 1897 Lilly E. TAYLOR (Thib. Ct. Hse.: Mar. v.36, #135)
JOHNSON, Cristopher Columbus (Adam & Eliza STEWART) m. 3 May 1897 Lily TAYLOR (Thib. Ch.: v.14, p.143)
JOHNSON, Edward m. 27 April 1898 Marguerite BELL (Thib. Ct. Hse.: Mar. v.38, #171)
JOHNSON, Emma m. 27 Oct. 1898 Joseph FLEMING (Thib. Ct. Hse.: Mar. v.38, #306)
JOHNSON, Fanny m. 6 Jan. 1898 William SMITH (Houma Ct. Hse.: Mar. v.30 & 31, #183)
JOHNSON, Francis Elisabeth (Christopher Columbus & Elisabeth Lily TAYLOR) b. 14 Sept. 1899 (Thib. Ch.: v.7, p.567)
JOHNSON, Godfrey Raphael (Christopher Columbus & Lily TAYLOR) b. 26 Nov. 1896 (Thib. Ch.: v.7, p.475)
JOHNSON, Harry m. 16 Feb. 1897 Leana SANDERS (Thib. Ct. Hse.: Mar. v.36, #80)
JOHNSON, Isaac m. 2 Oct. 1897 Creacy DAVIS (Thib. Ct. Hse.: Mar. v.37, #238)
JOHNSON, James m. 26 Feb. 1896 Ella ZINKINS (Houma Ct. Hse.: Mar. v.28, #466)
JOHNSON, James H. m. 14 Dec. 1899 Nettie COLLINS (Houma Ct. Hse.: Mar. v.31 & 32, #184)
JOHNSON, Johnny m. 3 April 1899 Selma ROBINSON (Houma Ct. Hse.: Mar. v.31 & 32, #384)
JOHNSON, Joseph m. 12 Feb. 1897 Dora SPEED (Houma Ct. Hse.: Mar. v.29 & 30, #308)
JOHNSON, Joseph m. 5 April 1898 Francis SOUTH (Houma Ct. Hse.: Mar. v.30 & 31, #377)
JOHNSON, Julia m. 2 Feb. 1898 Peyton DABNEY (Thib. Ct. Hse.: Mar. v.37, #67)
JOHNSON, Lelia m. 2 Jan. 1899 Noah WEBB (Houma Ct. Hse.: Mar. v.30 & 31, #172)
JOHNSON, Lithia m. 25 May 1899 Joseph M. YOUNG (Thib. Ct. Hse.: Mar. v.39, #168)
JOHNSON, Margaret d. 20 March 1884 m. Michel THIBODAUX; Child: Eriphile m. Adam GUIDRY. Affidavit: 11 March 1898. (Houma Ct. Hse.: Succ. #896)

JOHNSON, Marie Florence (Victorin & Octavie LAGUERRE) b. 23 April 1897 (Raceland Ch.: v.5, p.48)
JOHNSON, Mingo m. 20 April 1899 Sarah VALENTIN (Houma Ct. Hse.: Mar. v.31 & 32, #410)
JOHNSON, Nellie m. 13 Aug. 1896 Robert CAMPBELL (Houma Ct. Hse.: Mar. v.29 & 30, #130)
JOHNSON, Philson m. 30 June 1898 Sophy KING (Houma Ct. Hse.: Mar. v.30 & 31, #37)
JOHNSON, Richard m. 4 April 1898 Mary SHANKLING (Thib. Ct. Hse.: Mar. v.37, #142)
JOHNSON, Robert Jr. m. 14 Sept. 1896 Adeline JOHNSON (Houma Ct. Hse.: Mar. v.29 & 30, #148)
JOHNSON, Rose m. 19 April 1897 Warren MARSHALL (Houma Ct. Hse.: Mar. v.29 & 30, #387)
JOHNSON, Seely Insanity: 5 July 1899. (Thib. Ct. Hse.: Succ. #1583)
JOHNSON, Shelton m. 19 June 1897 Prescilla JONES (Houma Ct. Hse.: Mar. v.29 & 30, #30)
JOHNSON, Smith m. 8 Feb. 1899 Louisa YOUNG (Thib. Ct. Hse.: Mar. v.38, #95)
JOHNSON, Spencer m. 21 Feb. 1899 Mary D. SMITH (Houma Ct. Hse.: Mar. v.31 & 32, #347)
JOHNSON, Stella m. 21 Sept. 1898 William ANDREWS, Jr. (Thib. Ct. Hse.: Mar. v.38, #281)
JOHNSON, Stella B. m. 16 April 1896 James M. TAYLOR (Thib. Ct. Hse.: Mar. v.35, #74)

JOLET (Sometimes: JAULLET, JOLOT)
JOLET, Agnes (Joseph & Elvina ROBICHAUX) d. 9 Dec. 1896 at age 4 yrs., 4 mths. (Houma Ch.: v.3, p.10)
JOLET, Irene Alexina (Henry Clay & Marceline DAIGLE) b. 20 Sept. 1896 (Houma Ch.: v.5, p.170)
JOLET, Lucille Elvire (Auguste & Heloise DUPLANTIS) b. 25 Jan. 1896; m. Joseph VICKNAIR on 29 Jan. 1914. (Houma Ch.: Bapt. Bk., v.5, p.152)
JOLLET, Marie Josehine (Joseph & Malvina ROBICHAUX) b. 14 Jan. 1898 (Houma Ch.: v.5, p.198)
JOMEN, Joseph Benoit d. 10 April 1899 at age 33 yrs. (Thib. Ch.: v.3, p.231)
JONCLAS, Robert (Albert & Georgina BALLADE) b. 27 Jan. 1896 (Houma Ch.: v.5, p.146)
JONES, Adam m. 2 Feb. 1899 Irene SANTEE (Houma Ct. Hse.: Mar. v.30 & 31, #299)
JONES, Adelaide m. 25 Nov. 1896 Joseph MITCHELL (Thib. Ct. Hse.: Mar. v.36, #163)
JONES, Adelaide (Henry & Merenthe CHARLES) m. 26 Nov. 1896 Joseph MITCHEL (Thib. Ch.: v.14, p.102)
JONES, Alfred m. 24 Jan. 1896 Alice BABIN (Houma Ct. Hse.: Mar. v.28, #414)
JONES, Andre Frederic (Anthony & Lucretia CHAUVIN) b. 6 July 1899 (Montegut Ch.: v.6, p.89)

JONES, Anna m. 13 April 1898 Alexander WALKER (Houma Ct. Hse.: Mar. v.30 & 31, #399)
JONES, Antoine Gilmer (Anthony & Lucretia CHAUVIN) b. 4 Jan. 1898 (Montegut Ch.: v.6, p.63)
JONES, Dan m. 3 June 1899 Hester CLARK (Houma Ct. Hse.: Mar. v.31 & 32, #27)
JONES, Emma m. 11 Jan. 1899 Ellick WILSON (Houma Ct. Hse.: Mar. v.30 & 31, #208)
JONES, George m. 6 April 1899 Lilly FISHER (Thib. Ct. Hse.: Mar. v.39, #136)
JONES, Harriet m. 5 Aug. 1899 James COLEMAN (Thib. Ct. Hse.: Mar. v.39, #204)
JONES, Horace m. 21 Dec. 1898 Clementine BAPTISTE (Thib. Ct. Hse.: Mar. v.38, #321)
JONES, James m. 23 April 1898 Rebecca JONES (Thib. Ct. Hse.: Mar. v.38, #165)
JONES, James (John W. & Alice BONVILLAIN) b. 30 July 1897 (Houma Ch.: v.5, p.185)
JONES, Jane m. 6 Feb. 1897 William BELLMAN (Houma Ct. Hse.: Mar. v.29 & 30, #298)
JONES, Joseph m. 8 June 1898 Lily BETTIS (Houma Ct. Hse.: Mar. v.30 & 31, #6)
JONES, Lea Phanelie Anne (Anthony & Lucricia CHAUVIN) b. 16 July 1896 (Montegut Ch.: v.6, p.42)
JONES, Lorena m. 9 Nov. 1897 Thomas JENKINS (Houma Ct. Hse.: Mar. v.29 & 30, #133)
JONES, Margerie Fleming (Dr. R. Fleming & Elise Heaton GILL) b. 26 Jan. 1897 (Houma Ch.: Epis. Ch.: v.1, p.114)
JONES, Marie Eve (Joseph & Celestin LEBLANC) b. 4 June 1897 (Houma Ch.: v.5, p.179)
JONES, Marie Ista (Oniel & Emma JONES) b. 22 July 1897 (Larose Ch.: v.3, p.11)
JONES, Martha m. 19 Feb. 1898 Harry MOSES (Houma Ct. Hse.: Mar. v.30 & 31, #310)
JONES, Mary Anne d. 21 Aug. 1899 at age 75 yrs. (Thib. Ch.: v.3, p.239)
JONES, Mary Loulie (John M. & Heloise V. BASCLE) m. 23 Jan. 1897 John Charles BRIANT (Houma Ct. Hse.: Mar. v.29 & 30, #253)
JONES, Pauline Anna Eve Mitchel (Mary) b. 9 March 1896 (Thib. Ch.: v.7, p.400)
JONES, Perry m. 23 Nov. 1899 Virginia HENDERSON (Houma Ct. Hse.: Mar. v.31 & 32, #167)
JONES, Peter m. 19 Jan. 1899 Ellen HANCEY (Houma Ct. Hse.: Mar. v.30 & 31, #201)
JONES, Prescilla m. 19 June 1897 Shelton JOHNSON (Houma Ct. Hse.: Mar. v.29 & 30, #30)
JONES, Rebecca m. 21 June 1898 Joshua JASPER (Houma Ct. Hse.: Mar. v.30 & 31, #25)
JONES, Rebecca m.23 April 1898 James JONES (Thib. Ct. Hse.: Mar. v.38, #165)

JONES, Robert m. 7 May 1896 Cairie MOSEBY (Thib. Ct. Hse.: Mar. v.35, #85)
JONES, Susanna m. 29 June 1899 Thomas COMMODORE (Houma Ct. Hse.: Mar. v.31 & 32, #59)
JONES, Thomas m. 17 Aug. 1899 Lizzie or Elizabeth LEE (Thib. Ct. Hse.: Mar. v.39, #212)
JONES, William m. 10 Aug. 1897 Margaret WALKER, widow of William REED (Thib. Ct Hse.: Mar. v.37, #210)
JORDAN, Sylvester m. 18 Feb. 1897 Betsey MOORE (Houma Ct. Hse.: Mar. v.29 & 30, #322)
JORDAN, Sylvester of Wake County, North Carolina m. 26 April 1899 Ellen WILSON, of Virginia (Thib. Ct. Hse.: Mar. v.39, #147)
JORDAN, Walter m. 11 March 1897 Emma MOORE (Houma Ct. Hse.: Mar. v.29 & 30, #348)
JOSEPH WALLIS (Mace BAPTISTE) b. 1 April 1896 (Thib. Ch.: v.8, p.15)
JOSEPH, Anna m. 16 Dec. 1897 Henderson WHITE (Thib. Ct. Hse.: Mar. v.37, #263)
JOSEPH, Cecilia m. 21 March 1898 Mervin J. TAYLOR (Thib. Ct. Hse.: Mar. v.37, #131)
JOSEPH, Emely (Thomas & Marie THOMAS) b. 26 Sept. 1899 (Houma Ch.: v.5, p.256)
JOSEPH, Falgout Mercedes Marguerite (Falgout & Savoie MARGUERITE) b. 1 Feb. 1896 (Lockport Ch.: v.2, p.324)
JOSEPH, James (Hand & Angelina JOSEPH) b. 28 Oct. 1897 (Thib. Ch.: v.7, p.471)
JOSEPH, Leontine m. 28 Dec. 1899 Fulman URSENE (Thib. Ct. Hse.: Mar. v.39, #303)
JOSEPH, Louise d. 13 May 1899 at age 67 yrs. (Thib. Ch.: v.3, p.233)
JOSEPH, Lucy m. 27 April 1899 Joseph DOTTRY or DOBERTY (Thib. Ct. Hse.: Mar. v.39, #157)
JOSEPH, Mary (Thomas & Anny THOMAS) b. 4 Sept. 1897 (Houma Ch.: v.5, p.187)
JOSEPH, Mathilda m. 12 March 1898 Henry ALLEN (Thib. Ct. Hse.: Mar. v.37, #126)
JOSEPH, Nancy m. 27 Oct. 1898 Willie GEORGE (Thib. Ct. Hse.: Mar. v.38, #305)
JOSEPH, Samuel m. 18 June 1899 Katie INGLAND (Houma Ct. Hse.: Mar. v.31 & 32, #47)
JOST, Della Emmolyn (Phillip & Laura J. GIRARDIE) b. 22 Sept. 1896 (Houma Ch.: Epis. Ch.: v.1, p.112-B)
JOUCLOS, Ernest d. 18 Nov. 1896 at age 28 yrs. (Thib. Ch.: v.3, p.190)
JOUGLAS, Ernest d. 17 Nov. 1896; m. Octavie MALBROUGH Petition for administration, inventory: 28 Dec. 1898. (Thib. Ct. Hse.: Succ. #1555)
JULES, Benoit (Jean & Annie HILL) b. 8 Dec. 1899 (Thib. Ch.: v.7, p.590)

JULES, Henry Junius (Henry & Emelia ROBICHAUX) b. 30 June 1897 (Thib. Ch.: v.7, p.460)
JULES, Jean Baptiste d. 9 April 1898 at age 62 yrs. (Thib. Ch.: v.3, p.213)
JULES, Joseph Junius (Johnny & Anna HILLS) b. 14 July 1897 (Thib. Ch.: v.7, p.468)

JUNEAU (Sometimes: JUNOT)
JUNEAU, Jean Baptiste (Clifton & Adele DELORETTE) b. 8 Sept. 1897 (Thib. Ch.: v.7, p.464)
JUNIFORD, Ella m. 18 Jan. 1899 William MARTIN (Houma Ct. Hse.: Mar. v.30 & 31, #246)
JUNO, Agnes Beatrix (Cletus & Adele DE LORETTE) b. 10 July 1899 (Thib. Ch.: v.7, p.556)
JUSTILIEN, Elie Rosalius (Constant & Anita PALKET) b. 28 Oct. 1897 (Chacahoula Ch.: Gibson Ch.: Mar. Bk., v.1, #81)
JUSTILIEN, Elie Rosalius (Constant & Anita PALKET) b. 28 Oct. 1897 (Chacahoula Ch.: Gibson Ch.: v.2, p.114)

"K"

KAHN, Leon m. 29 Oct. 1899 Tillie C. LOEB (Thib. Ct. Hse.: Mar. v.39, #254)

KAIN, Marie Gertrude Marguerite (Thomas & Camilla LEBLANC) b. 26 Oct. 1899 (Chacahoula Ch.: v.4, p.32)

KANE, Adam m. 15 Jan. 1896 Lavinia CARTER (Houma Ct. Hse.: Mar. v.28, #391)

KANE, Louisa m. 29 Sept. 1898 William WESTLEY (Houma Ct. Hse.: Mar. v.30 & 31, #113)

KANE, Mary d. 2 Dec. 1896 at age 60 yrs. (Raceland Ch.: v.1, p.11)

KASCINSKO, Joseph Condon (S. B. Staples & Dasey B. HYMES) b. 1 Dec. 1899 (Houma Ch.: v.6, p.3)

KEEFE (See: KIFF)

KEELER, Cecilia (Sosthene & Esilda NAQUIN) m. 24 Jan. 1898 Jean GONZALES (Thib. Ct. Hse.: Mar. v.37, #53)

KELLER, Agnes Eugenie (Emmanuel & Alice BRAUD) b. 2 Aug. 1899 (Thib. Ch.: v.7, p.557)

KELLER, Alcide Edouard (Sylvestre & Corine TROSCLAIR) b. 29 Oct. 1897 (Thib. Ch.: v.7, p.474)

KELLER, Aline Velma (Emmanuel & Alice BROU) b. 6 Dec. 1896 (Thib. Ch.: v.7, p.429)

KELLER, Cecilia (Sosthene & Eselda NAQUIN) m. 24 Feb. 1898 Jean GONZALES (Thib. Ch.: v.14, p.173)

KELLER, Claude (Ignace & Ella RICHARD) b. 7 Sept. 1898 (Thib. Ch.: v.7, p.563)

KELLER, Clotilde (Ignace & Ella RICHARD) b. 7 Sept. 1898 (Thib. Ch.: v.7, p.563)

KELLER, Clotine d. 21 Nov. 1899 at age 2 mths. & 15 days (Thib. Ch.: v.3, p.244)

KELLER, Edgard (Alcide & Mirza TREGUE) m. 22 March 1897 Euphrosine CHIASSON (Thib. Ch.: v.14, p.135)

KELLER, Edgard (Alcide & Mirza TREIGUE) m. 22 March 1897 Euphrosine CHIASSON (Thib. Ct. Hse.: Mar. v.36, #98)

KELLER, Emelie (Sosthene & Esilda NAQUIN) m. 3 Jan. 1897 Pierre TREGRE (Thib. Ch.: v.14, p.120)

KELLER, Emelie (Sosthene & Esilda NAQUIN) m. 3 Jan. 1897 Pierre TREGLE (Thib. Ct. Hse.: Mar. v.36, #40)

KELLER, Flavie (Theodule & Mathilde TROSCLAIR) b. 11 Feb. 1897 (Thib. Ch.: v.7, p.441)

KELLER, Harry Odressy (Cyprien & Eulalia NAQUIN) b. 5 Oct. 1899 (Chacahoula Ch.: v.4, p.30)

KELLER, John m. 12 Jan. 1898 Creecy DONALDSON (Houma Ct. Hse.: Mar. v.30 & 31, #195)

KELLER, Leon (Gustave & Amelia MORVAN) m. 29 Dec. 1897 Angela HEBERT (Thib. Ch.: v.14, p.168)

KELLER, Leonie m. 13 Dec. 1897 Angela HEBERT (Thib. Ct. Hse.: Mar. v.37, #260)

KELLER, Louis Frederic (Sylvestre & Corinne TROSCLAIR) b. 2 July 1898 (Thib. Ch.: v.7, p.555)
KELLER, Louisa Elmira (Sylvestre & Corinne TROSCLAIR) b. 14 Feb. 1896 (Thib. Ch.: v.7, p.394)
KELLER, Maria Melodia Celine (Theodule & Mathilde TROSCLAIR) b. 27 Oct. 1897 (Thib. Ch.: v.7, p.522)
KELLER, Marie (Alcide & Mirza TREGRE) m. 17 Sept. 1896 Clairfait AYO (Thib. Ch.: v.14, p.98)
KELLER, Marie Lucie Anastasie (Maximilien & Elomina LAJAUNIE) b. 22 Jan. 1897 (Chacahoula Ch.: v.4, p.16)
KELLER, Mary (Alcide & Mirza TREGRE) m. 17 Sept. 1896 Clerfe AYO (Thib. Ct. Hse.: Mar. v.36, #138)
KELLER, Ovilia Armance (Leonie & Angela HEBERT) b. 1 Dec. 1899 (Thib. Ch.: v.7, p.578)
KELLER, Raymond Sydney (Cyprien & Eulalie NAQUIN) b. 31 Aug. 1897; bt. 15 Sept. 1897 (Chacahoula Ch.: v.4, p.24)
KELLER, Valerie Amelia (Leony & Angele HEBERT) b. 7 Nov. 1898 (Thib. Ch.: v.7, p.521)
KELLEY, Henry D. m. 13 June 1896 Felicie CALLAIS (Thib. Ct. Hse.: Mar. v.35, #94)
KELLOWA, Ella d. 4 Feb. 1898 at age 2 yrs. & 6 mths. (Thib. Ch.: v.3, p.210)
KELLY, Edward Ernest (Ernest & Aspasie DUPLAULEY) b. 3 April 1896 (Houma Ch.: Epis. Ch.: v.1, p.112)
KELLY, Georges m. 28 May 1896 Mathilda CALLAIS (Thib. Ct. Hse.: Mar. v.35, #89)
KELLY, Ida Selene (N. Viztor & Ida Louise HARLAU) b. 30 Jan. 1896 (Houma Ch.: Epis. Ch.: v.1, p.112)
KELLY, John m. 12 Jan. 1898 Creecy DONALDSON (Houma Ct. Hse.: Mar. v.30 & 31, #195)
KELLY, Laura (Victor & Ida Holland KELLY) b. 8 March 1899 (Houma Ch.: Epis. Ch.: v.1, p.124)
KELLY, Loretta (Victor & Ida Holland KELLY) b. 8 March 1899 (Houma Ch.: Epis. Ch.: v.1, p.124)
KELLY, Melville Ray d. 15 July 1896 at age 3 yrs. (Houma Ch.: Epis. Ch.: v.1, p.386)
KELLY, Teresa Myrtle (James & Mary EAGAN) b. 9 Jan. 1898 (Chacahoula Ch.: Gibson Records: Mar. Bk., v.1, #7)
KELLY, William m. 11 Jan. 1897 Francine LEDET (Larose Ch.: v.3, p.4)
KELLY, William m. 11? Jan. 1897 Francine LEDET (Lockport Ch.: v.4, p.121)
KELLY, William m. 2 Jan. 1897 Francine LEDET (Thib. Ct. Hse.: Mar. v.36, #2)
KELLY, William m. 4 Dec. 1899 Susan LATHROP (Thib. Ct. Hse.: Mar. v.39, #275)
KELLY, William over 18 yrs. Emancipation: 28 July 1896. (Thib. Ct. Hse.: Succ. #1496)
KENT, Thomas D. m. 8 June 1897 Earline CARVER (Thib. Ch.: Epis. Ch.: v.1, p.331)

KENT, Thomas D. m. 8 June 1897 Earline CARVER (Thib. Ct. Hse.: Mar. v.36, #163)

KERN, Camille of St. Mary Parish (Desire & Julie LAGRANGE) m. 31 Jan. 1899 Lydia PONTIFE (Thib. Ct. Hse.: Mar. v.38, #54)

KERN, Camille (Desire & Julie LAGRANGE) m. 31 Jan. 1899 Lydia PONTIFE (Thib. Ch.: v.14, p.249)

KERN, Cyprien d. 5 Jan. 1897 at age 74 yrs. (Thib. Ch.: v.3, p.192)

KERNE (Sometimes: KIERNE)

KERNE, Emile (Desire & Julie LAGRANGE) m. 30 April 1896 Daisy PONTIFF (Thib. Ch.: v.14, p.88)

KERNE, Emile (Desire & Julie LAGRANGE) m. 30 April 1896 Daisy Marie PONTIFE (Thib. Ct. Hse.: Mar. v.35, #81)

KERNER, Victoria (Victor & Idamee PISANI) m. 3 Sept. 1899 Gustave FASIN (Raceland Ch.: v.2, p.103)

KETTERINGHAM, William Watson (Georges W. & Modeste GENVIE) b. 29 Sept. 1899 (Houma Ch.: v.5, p.263)

KIFF (Sometimes: KEEFF, KEITH, KIFE)

KIFF, Alcee of Lafourche Parish (Joseph & Celina BROUSSARD) m. 16 April 1898 Emma AYMARD of Lafourche Parish (Larose Ch.: v.3, p.8)

KIFF, Alcee (Joseph & Celina BROUSSARD) m. 16 April 1898 Emma AYMARD (Larose Ch.: v.4, p.8)

KIFF, Alcee (Joseph & Celina BROUSSARD) m. 16 April 1898 Emma AYMARD (Thib. Ct. Hse.: Mar. v.37, #146)

KIFF, Antoine Clement (Euphemond & Julie LEDET) b. 2 Feb. 1899 (Larose Ch.: v.3, p.35)

KIFF, Carie (Edmond & Agatha THIBODEAUX) m. 5 May 1898 Octave COULON, Jr. of Jefferson Parish (Larose Ch.: v.3, p.9)

KIFF, Carie (Edmond & Agathe THIBODEAUX) m. 5 May 1898 Octave COULON, Jr. Both residents of Jefferson Parish. (Larose Ch.: v.4, p.14)

KIFF, Edmond Joseph (Forest & Elmire EXNECIAS) b. 15 Oct. 1897 (Theriot Ch.: v.2, p.24)

KIFF, Jean Abdon (Anatole & Aimee ENGERRAN) b. 31 July 1899 (Montegut Ch.: v.6, p.94)

KIFF, Joseph Alcee (Anatole & Aimee ENGERRAN) b. 1 April 1897 (Montegut Ch.: v.6, p.55)

KIFF, Joseph Davidson (Beauregard & Clemence LECOMPTE) b. 23 Jan. 1898 (Montegut Ch.: v.6, p.69)

KIFF, Lucie of Lafourche Parish (Nicholas & Limina PLESSALA) m. 25 April 1898 Washington SMITH of Lafourche Parish (Larose Ch.: v.3, p.9)

KIFF, Lucie (Nicolas & Limina PLESSALA) m. 25 April 1898 Washington SMITH (Thib. Ct. Hse.: Mar. v.38, #163)

KIFF, Lucie (Nicolas & Limino PLESSALA) m. 25 April 1898 Washington SMITH (Larose Ch.: v.4, p.40)

KIFF, Maria Louise (Euphemond & Julie LEDET) b. 26 Aug. 1896 (Larose Ch.: v.2, p.186)

KIFF, Maria Viola (Euphemond & Julie LEDET) b. 26 Aug. 1896 (Larose Ch.: v.2, p.186)

KIMELE, Juanne (Francisco & Carmela SPERRE) b. 7 July 1897 (Thib. Ch.: v.7, p.455)

KING, Aaron Vernael (William H. & Rosa P. GAUTIER) b. 28 Oct. 1896 (Houma Ch.: Epis. Ch.: v.1, p.112-B)

KING, Bertha m. 19 Dec. 1898 John McELROY (Houma Ct. Hse.: Mar. v.30 & 31, #150)

KING, Bertha (Aleck & Octavie COMAUX) m. 21 Dec. 1898 John McELROY (Houma Ch.: v.6-a, p.259)

KING, Elizabeth m. 2 Jan. 1896 John A. GORDON, Jr. (Houma Ct. Hse.: Mar. v.28, #366)

KING, Ella m. 5 July 1899 Walter SPORT (Thib. Ct. Hse.: Mar. v.39, #192)

KING, Eloise A. (Richard & Mary STRINGER) m. 29 June 1896 Edeoin ROSS (Houma Ch.: Epis. Ch.: v.1, p.340)

KING, Eloise A. (Richard & Mary STRINGER) m. 29 June 1896 Edwin ROSS, 22 yrs. old (Gibson Ch.: Epis. Ch.: v.1, p.134)

KING, General m. 6 March 1899 Eliza WELSH (Houma Ct. Hse.: Mar. v.31 & 32, #354)

KING, Henry J. (Richard & Mary A. STRINGER) m. 27 July 1897 Mary LANCON (Houma Ct. Hse.: Mar. v.29 & 30, #69)

KING, Henry J. (Richard & Nancy STRINGER) m. 27 July 1897 Mary LANCON (Houma Ch.: Epis. Ch.: v.1, p.342)

KING, Inez m. 22 April 1899 Hugh McELROY (Houma Ct. Hse.: Mar. v.31 & 32, #415)

KING, Inez (William & Rosa GAUTIER) m. -- April 1899 Hugh McELROY (Houma Ch.: Epis. Ch.: v.1, p.344)

KING, Jean Joseph Albert (Thomas & Camila LEBLANC) b. 29 May 1896 (Houma Ch.: v.5, p.182)

KING, John m. 8 May 1897 Dora BRAUGHS (Houma Ct. Hse.: Mar. v.29 & 30, #407)

KING, John (Thomas & Sarah ROBERTSON) m. 20 May 1897 Dora BRAUGHS (Houma Ch.: v.6-a, p.202)

KING, Josephine Jessee (Wilfrid & Emma PYE) b. 15 Dec. 1898 (Houma Ch.: v.5, p.231)

KING, Lily d. 21 Aug. 1896 (Houma Ch.: Epis. Ch.: v.1, p.386)

KING, Louisa (Richard & Mary SPRINGER) m. 26 June 1896 Edwin ROSS (Houma Ct. Hse.: Mar. v.29 & 30, #97)

KING, Nolton Joseph d. 7 Feb. 1899 at age 7 days (Houma Ch.: Epis. Ch.: v.1, p.388)

KING, Nolton Joseph (William & Rosa Gautier KING) b. 31 Jan. 1899 (Houma Ch.: Epis. Ch.: v.1, p.122)

KING, Richard d. 14 Sept. 1899 (Houma Ch.: Epis. Ch.: v.1, p.388)

KING, Robert d. 21 March 1899 at age 28 yrs. (Houma Ch.: v.3, p.22)

KING, Sophy m. 30 June 1898 Philson JOHNSON (Houma Ct. Hse.: Mar. v.30 & 31, #37)
KING, Thomas d. 20 Jan. 1896 at age 71 yrs. (Houma Ch.: v.3, p.6)
KING, Wilfred m. 26 Jan. 1898 Emma PYE (Houma Ct. Hse.: Mar. v.30 & 31, #251)
KING, Wilfred (Thomas & Sarah ROBINSON) m. 27 Jan. 1898 Emma PYE (Houma Ch.: v.6-a, p.226)
KIRK, Mary Anne (Michael & Anne GOWAN) m. 17 July 1899 Albert FORD (Montegut Ch.: v.4, p.267)
KISSE, Alonyo C. (John R. & Marie DICKERSON) m. 20 Jan. 1898 Lillian HELLIER (Houma Ch.: Epis. Ch.: v.1, p.342)
KISSEE, Alonzo C. (John R. & Marie DICKERSON) m. 20 Jan. 1898 Lillian HELLIER (Houma Ct. Hse.: Mar. v.30 & 31, #237)
KIT, Mary d. 14 Jan. 1897 at age 70 yrs. (Lockport Ch.: v.1, #2)
KLING, Amelia minor over 18 (David & Mathilda KAHN) Emancipation: 26 March 1898. (Thib. Ct. Hse.: Succ. #1531)
KLING, Lillian minor over 18 (David & Mathilda KAHN) Emancipation: 26 March 1898. (Thib. Ct. Hse.: Succ. #1530)
KLINGMAN, Annie Lucie (Frank & Aida CROCHET) b. 15 Oct. 1896 (Montegut Ch.: v.6, p.47)
KLINGMAN, Edouard d. 13 Feb. 1897 (Montegut Ch.: v.2, p.9)
KLINGMAN, Joseph C. d. 2 May 1899 at age 7 days (Houma Ch.: v.3, p.22)
KLINGMAN, Laura Pauline m. 31 Aug. 1896 Thomas McCULLA (Houma Ct. Hse.: Mar. v.29 & 30, #142)
KLINGMAN, Laura Pauline (John & Emelia DUTHU) m. 2 Sept. 1896 Thomas McCULLA (Houma Ch.: v.6-a, p.179)
KLINGMAN, Louis Camille (Henry & Regine DARDEAU) b. 6 Feb. 1897 (Montegut Ch.: v.6, p.49)
KLINGMAN, Maria Rebecca (Frank & Edda CROCHET) b. 27 Feb. 1899 (Houma Ch.: v.5, p.236)
KLINGMAN, Marie Regina (Henry & Regina DARDEAU) b. 10 Jan. 1899; m. Daniel Joseph MURPHY on 8 Nov. 1922. (Houma Ch.: Bapt. Bk., v.5, p.238)

KNIGHT (Sometimes: KGNIGHT, NAIT, NIGHT)

KNIGHT, Alcide (Timothy & d.Eliska SAVOIE) m. 28 Jan. 1897 Marie MATHERNE (Montegut Ch.: v.4, p.216)
KNIGHT, Alcide (Timothy & Eliska SAVOIE) m. 20 Jan. 1897 Marie MATHERNE (Houma Ct. Hse.: Mar. v.29 & 30, #242)
KNIGHT, Annie E. d. 28 Feb. 1898 (Houma Ch.: Epis. Ch.: v.1, p.388)
KNIGHT, Annie E. of Kentucky d. 28 Feb. 1898 (Gibson Ch.: Epis. Ch.: v.1, p.114)
KNIGHT, Beula Rebecca (Peter A. & Eliza KING) b. 16 Jan. 1897 (Houma Ch.: Epis. Ch.: v.1, p.114)
KNIGHT, Della Elizabeth (George & Rosa ROGER) b. 29 Nov. 1896 (Lockport Ch.: v.3-A, #3)

KNIGHT, Della Elizabeth (Georges & Rosa ROGER) b. 29 Nov. 1896 (Lockport Ch.: v.3, #3)
KNIGHT, Edna Toutsey (Joseph & Olympe LABATTE) b. 14 April 1897 (Raceland Ch.: v.5, p.46)
KNIGHT, Edwin Hamilton d. 13 June 1897 (Gibson Ch.: Epis. Ch.: v.1, p.114)
KNIGHT, Edwin Hamilton d. 13 June 1897 (Houma Ch.: Epis. Ch.: v.1, p.386)
KNIGHT, Ida Eletia (Joseph & Olympe LABATTE) b. 3 Dec. 1899 (Raceland Ch.: v.5, p.108)
KNIGHT, Josephine d. 14 Sept. 1897 at age 13 yrs. (Raceland Ch.: v.1, p.15)
KNIGHT, Marceline m. Odea DELAUNE d. 17 July 1899 at age 26 yrs. (Lockport Ch.: v.1, #26)
KNIGHT, Nanny Zelia (Peter Armand & Anna Eliza KING) bt. 2 Sept. 1899 (Houma Ch.: Epis. Ch.: v.1, p.122)
KNIGHT, Rosanna E. (J. McClelland & Ann Eliza JARVIS) m. William WALTHER. Commission to sell property: 13 June 1898. (Houma Ct. Hse.: Succ. #899)
KNIGHT, Rosemond (Benjamin & Josephine CHIASSON) d. 2 Nov. 1899 at age 8 days (Lockport Ch.: v.1, #41)
KNIGHT, William Jr. m. 9 June 1898 Pricilla CALLAWAY (Houma Ct. Hse.: Mar. v.30 & 31, #1)
KNOBASS, Joseph Albert (John & Marie BABIN) b. 1 Nov. 1897 (Houma Ch.: v.5, p.193)

KNOBLOCK (Sometimes: KNOBLOC, KNOBLOCH)

KNOBLOCK, Anicet (Ernest & Odelia HEBERT) m. 31 Jan. 1899 Octavie LEDET (Thib. Ch.: v.14, p.251)
KNOBLOCK, Anicet (Ernest & Odilia HEBERT) m. 30 Jan. 1899 Octavie LEDET (Thib. Ct. Hse.: Mar. v.38, #56)
KNOBLOCK, Clarence Joseph (Oscar & Victoria DE QUIZE) b. 20 April 1898 (Thib. Ch.: v.7, p.544)
KNOBLOCK, Edith m. 5 Feb. 1897 Walter THIBODAUX (Thib. Ct. Hse.: Mar. v.36, #69)
KNOBLOCK, Edith (Ernest & Odilia HEBERT) m. 10 Feb. 1897 Walter THIBODAUX (Raceland Ch.: v.2, p.33)
KNOBLOCK, Elvire m. Theophile GISCLARD In the matter of insanity of: 11 July 1898. (Thib. Ct. Hse.: Succ. #1543)
KNOBLOCK, Jimmy Mile (Gustave & Elma ARCEMENT) b. 19 April 1898 (Raceland Ch.: v.5, p.69)
KNOBLOCK, John Guile (Gustave & Elma ARCEMENT) b. 19 April 1898 (Raceland Ch.: v.5, p.69)
KNOBLOCK, Joseph Elmer Roger (Tuile & Velma ROGER) b. 19 Nov. 1897 (Thib. Ch.: v.7, p.472)
KNOBLOCK, Marie Ethel (Gustave & Elma ARCEMENT) b. 16 March 1896 (Raceland Ch.: v.5, p.21)
KNOBLOCK, Maude Odette m. ----- BENSBERG d. 29 Dec. 1899 (Thib. Ch.: v.3, p.247)
KNOBLOCK, Maude Odette (Clay Henry & Flavia KNIGHT) m. 19 Jan. 1897 Robert BENSBERG, of New Orleans (Thib. Ch.: v.14, p.111)

KNOBLOCK, Olympe (Voltaire & Ophelia BAUDOIN) m. 9 Aug. 1897 Stanisle WAGUESPACK (Raceland Ch.: v.2, p.48)
KNOBLOCK, Paul Cyrus (Thomas & Seraphine THIBODAUX) b. 5 Aug. 1898 (Raceland Ch.: v.5, p.76)
KNOBLOCK, Rosalie Unez (Ernest & Lucia BOURGEOIS) b. 4 Sept. 1897 (Raceland Ch.: v.5, p.54)
KOGAN, Elizabeth d. 23 Feb. 1898 at age 81 yrs. (Thib. Ch.: v.3, p.211)
KOHMANN, Charles (Albert & Emma BOURE) b. 4 May 1896 (Theriot Ch.: v.1-B, p.98)
KOHMANN, Wade Joseph (Albert & Emma BOWIE) b. 4 May 1898 (Houma Ch.: v.5, p.210)
KOHMANN, William L. (Albert & Rosanna E. RIPPIEN) m. 23 March 1898 Gertrude M. DILL (Houma Ch.: Epis. Ch.: v.1, p.342)
KOHMANN, William L. (Albert & Rosanna E. RIPPIEN) m. 23 March 1898 Gertrude DILL (Houma Ct. Hse.: Mar. v.30 & 31, #348)
KORA, Marie Michel (Michel Simon & Anna SAMAHA) b. 19 March 1899 (Thib. Ch.: v.7, p.599)

KRAMER (Sometimes: CRAMER, CRANMER, CREMER, KREMMER)
KRAMER, Anderson Paschal (Cyriac & Victoria MARTINEZ) b. 24 Feb. 1899 (Chackbay Ch.: v.1, p.132)
KRAMER, Antoine (Antoine & Rosalie TORES) m. 30 July 1898 Antonia TRAIGLE (Chackbay Ch.: v.1, p.63)
KRAMER, Antoine (Antoine & Rosalie TORES) m. 30 July 1898 Antonia TREGLE (Thib. Ct. Hse.: Mar. v.38, #227)
KRAMER, Charles (Cyriac & Victoria MARTINEZ) b. 9 Jan. 1897 (Chackbay Ch.: v.1, p.83)
KRAMER, Jean (Faragus & Aurelie TROSCLAIR) b. 9 Oct. 1898 (Chackbay Ch.: v.1, p.120)
KRAMER, Jean (Joseph & Antoinette BORNE) b. 14 July 1897 (Chackbay Ch.: v.1, p.91)
KRAMER, John (d.Erath & Marguerite GOMLICK) m. 17 Feb. 1896 Aurelie TROSCLAIR (Chackbay Ch.: v.1, p.26)
KRAMER, John Flaragus (Erasth & Marguerite GOMLICK) m. 17 Feb. 1896 Aurelie TROSCLAIR (Thib. Ct. Hse.: Mar. v.35, #37)
KRAMER, Joseph Charles (Howard & Marie Philomene KRAEMER) bt. 13 June 1896 (Chackbay Ch.: v.1, p.68)
KRAMER, Julia (Louis & Eve MAURICE) b. 11 Sept. 1899 (Thib. Ch.: v.7, p.566)
KRAMER, Laura (Furgus & Amelie TROSCLAIR) b. 24 July 1897 (Chackbay Ch.: v.1, p.91)
KRAMER, Louis (Isidore & Marguerite DEMPSTER) m. 24 Jan. 1898 Eve MORRIS (Chackbay Ch.: v.1, p.52)
KRAMER, Louis (Isidore & Marguerite DEMPTER) m. 25 Jan. 1898 Eve MORRIS (Thib. Ct. Hse.: Mar. v.37, #10)
KRAMER, Magdelaine (Howard & Philomene GRANIER) m. 10 Sept. 1898 Dexan HAYDEL, of St. James Parish (Thib. Ct. Hse.: Mar. v.38, #272)

KRAMER, Magdeleine (Howard & Philomene KRAMER) m. 10 Sept. 1898 Dexen HAYDELL (Chackbay Ch.: v.1, p.64)
KRAMER, Marie Alice (Joseph & Antoinette BONAMOUR) b. 13 July 1899 (Chackbay Ch.: v.1, p.138)
KRAMER, Marie Edith (Antoine & Antoinette TRAIGLE) b. 1 May 1899 (Chackbay Ch.: v.1, p.133)
KRAMER, Marie Josephine (Sylvestre & Marguerite BOUDREAU) b. 3 June 1898 (Chackbay Ch.: v.1, p.113)
KRAMER, Marie Rosalie (Antoine & Rosalie TORES) b. 14 July 1897 (Chackbay Ch.: v.1, p.92)
KRAMER, Octavie (Laurent & d.Josephine MARTINEZ) m. 19 Jan. 1898 John BERNARD (Chackbay Ch.: v.1, p.51)
KRAMER, Octavie (Laurent & Josephine MARTINEZ) m. 16 Jan. 1898 John BERNARD (Thib. Ct. Hse.: Mar. v.37, #2)
KRAMER, Rose Marguerite (Louis & Enezilda ROUSSEL) b. 27 March 1898 (Chackbay Ch.: v.1, p.110)
KRAMER, Sylvestre (Laurent & d.Josephine MARTINEZ) m. 28 April 1896 Marguerite BOUDREAUX (Chackbay Ch.: v.1, p.27)
KRAMER, Sylvestre (Laurent & Josephine MARTINEZ) m. 28 April 1896 Maggie BOUDREAUX (Thib. Ct. Hse.: Mar. v.35, #80)
KUHN, John of Germany Child: Freida Emma, living in Germany. Inventory: 19 Oct. 1897. (Houma Ct. Hse.: Succ. #888)
KURTZ, Charles Walter Claude (Charles & Felicia BERTIN) b. 5 Nov. 1899 (Thib. Ch.: v.7, p.573)
KYLE, Volney Howard (Volhe H. & Mary S. KYLE) b. 6 Nov. 1899 (Houma Ch.: Epis. Ch.: v.1, p.126)

"L"

LABAIE, Clement Josephine (Jean Marie & Marie SAVOIE) b. 18 Sept. 1897 (Houma Ch.: v.5, p.189)
LABARBERA, Francesco (Francesco & Guiseppa LEVARCRE) b. 8 Jan. 1899 (Thib. Ch.: v.7, p.531)
LABARBERA, Laurita (Francisco & Guiseppa LIVACCARI) b. 4 May 1896 (Thib. Ch.: v.7, p.452)

LABAT (Sometimes: LABATTE, LABET, LABOT)
LABAT, Georgina (Georges & Armantine FORET) m. 20 Sept. 1898 Emile ARCENEAUX (Thib. Ct. Hse.: Mar. v.38, #278)
LABAT, Georgina (Georges & Armantine FORET) m. 20 Sept. 1898 Emile ARCENAUX (Lockport Ch.: v.2, p.195)
LABAT, Josephine Ida (Celestin & Alexina PRICE) b. 19 March 1899 (Raceland Ch.: v.5, p.93)
LABAT, Lucina m. 29 Jan. 1898 Telesse MATHERNE (Houma Ct. Hse.: Mar. v.30 & 31, #192)
LABAT, Lucina (Georges & Armantine FORET) m. 29 Jan. 1898 Telesse MATERNE (Raceland Ch.: v.2, p.60)
LABAT, Marie d. 9 Dec. 1897 at age 5 mths. (Raceland Ch.: v.1, p.15)
LABAT, Marie Anne d. 29 April 1896 at age 64 yrs. (Houma Ch.: v.3, p.7)
LABAT, Marie Lilia (Celestin & Alexina PRICE) b. 17 June 1897 (Raceland Ch.: v.5, p.51)
LABAT, Marie Mirtilia (Georges & Armantine FORET) b. 3 April 1897 (Raceland Ch.: v.5, p.44)
LABAT, Mercilia d. 17 Jan. 189 at age 9 mths. (Raceland Ch.: v.1, p.17)
LABICHE, Theodore (d.Gustave & d.Celeste FREMIN) m. 17 April 1899 Emma PICOU (Montegut Ch.: v.4, p.261)
LABICHE, Theodore (Gustave & Celeste FREMIN) m. 10 April 1899 Emma PICOU (Houma Ct. Hse.: Mar. v.31 & 32, #392)

LABIT (Sometimes: LABIS, LABY, LHABIT)
LABIT, Beatrice Bella (Seraphin & Justilia ROBICHAUX) b. 5 Aug. 1899 (Houma Ch.: v.5, p.253)
LABIT, Dorothee Herman (Charles & Anna MERMON) b. 25 Sept. 1899 (Houma Ch.: v.5, p.259)
LABIT, Exelina Leona (Victor & Angelique PELEGRIN) b. 11 April 1898 (Houma Ch.: v.5, p.210)
LABIT, Ida (Dacisse & Aspasie Madora BURKETT) m. 23 Jan. 1897 John PICOU (Houma Ct. Hse.: Mar. v.29 & 30, #251)
LABIT, Leona d. 22 Feb. 1899 at age 10 mths. (Houma Ch.: v.3, p.21)
LABIT, Marie Valerie (Emile & Josephine BOUDREAU) b. 12 April 1897 (Houma Ch.: v.5, p.207)
LABIT, Millard Filmore (J. C. & Amy WEARMAN) b. 17 Jan. 1897 (Houma Ch.: v.5, p.198)

LABIT, Onezime Sidny (Victor & Angelique PELEGRIN) b. 21 Sept. 1896 (Houma Ch.: v.5, p.159)
LABIT, Pauline Zoe (Charles & Clothilde ROSSIGNOL) b. 9 Oct. 1899 (Thib. Ch.: v.7, p.568)
LABIT, Therese d. 5 Dec. 1899 at age 2 mths. (Thib. Ch.: v.3, p.245)
LABIT, Therese Marie (Charles & Clotilde ROSSIGNOL) b. 9 Oct. 1899 (Thib. Ch.: v.7, p.568)
LABIT, Valerie m. 15 Jan. 1897 Arthur HOTARD (Houma Ct. Hse.: Mar. v.29 & 30, #239)
LABIT, Valerie (Henry & Clementine CROCHET) m. 16 Jan. 1897 Arthur HOTARD (Houma Ch.: v.6-a, p.189)
LABIT, Victoire d. 22 Aug. 1899 at age 7 yrs. (Houma Ch.: v.3, p.24)
LABIT, Viles Randolphe (Seraphin & Justilia ROBICHAUX) b. 26 Feb. 1897 (Houma Ch.: v.5, p.177)
LABORBEZ, Marie (Dominique PRESSEG & Nathala LABORBEZ) b. 10 April 1899 (Chackbay Ch.: Bapt. Bk., v.1, p.13)
LABOVE, Callagero (Angelo & Paola PLEPCHER) b. 14 Feb. 1898 (Raceland Ch.: v.5, p.66)
LABRUCCHI, Riattata Cleria m. 22 May 1899 Tony PALAZZO (Thib. Ct. Hse.: Mar. v.39, #166)

LABRUYERE (Sometimes: LABRUIGERE, LABRUIERE, LABRVIRE)

LACASSAGNE, Laurent d. 3 Jan. 1896 at New Orleans; m. Sophie TIMMERMAN, d. 14 Feb. 1895. Children: Laurent Auguste, 17; Fernand Charles, 15. Tutorship: 11 March 1896. (Houma Ct. Hse.: Succ. #868)
LACOMBONE, Joseph Siano (Siano & Justilia CARRERE) b. 23 Sept. 1898 (Montegut Ch.: v.6, p.85)
LACOMBONE, Julienne Priscilia (Siano & Justilia CARRERE) b. 23 Sept. 1898 (Montegut Ch.: v.6, p.85)
LACOSTE, Gracieuse m. 10 Feb. 1899 Onesippe ARCENEAUX (Thib. Ct. Hse.: Mar. v.39, #102)
LACOSTE, Gracieuse (Julien & Melina BERNARD) m. 13 Feb. 1899 Onesippe ARCEMENT (Raceland Ch.: v.2, p.91)
LACOUBAQUE, William Justinian (Ciano & Justilia CARERE) b. 22 Feb. 1896 (Theriot Ch.: v.1-B, p.94)
LACROIX, Berthe Emilie d. 28 June 1896 at age 5 mths. & 15 days (Thib. Ch.: v.3, p.184)
LACROIX, Berthe Marguerite Emelie (Emile & Berthe BOURGEOIS) b. 9 Jan. 1896 (Lockport Ch.: v.2, p.320)

LADOUCEUR (Sometimes: LADONEUR)
LADOUCEUR, Adam Joseph (Octave & Estelle LEBLANC) b. 12 April 1898 (Thib. Ch.: v.7, p.497)
LADOUCEUR, Joseph Wallace (Louis & Emelie HEBERT) b. 8 Jan. 1897 (Thib. Ch.: v.7, p.436)
LADOUCEUR, Laihe Joseph (Octave & Estelle LEBLANC) b. 20 May 1897 (Thib. Ch.: v.7, p.455)

LADOUCEUR, Louis (Martin & Marie HEBERT) m. 9 April 1896 Emilie HEBERT (Thib. Ch.: v.14, p.83)
LADOUCEUR, Louis (Martin & Marie HEBERT) m. 9 April 1896 Emilie HEBERT (Thib. Ct. Hse.: Mar. v.35, #59)
LADOUCEUR, Lush d. 24 Oct. 1897 at age 5 mths. (Houma Ch.: v.3, p.14)
LADOUCEUR, Marie Lily (Louis & Emilie HEBERT) b. 13 Aug. 1898 (Thib. Ch.: v.7, p.510)
LADOUCEUR, Octave m. 1 July 1897 Estelle LEBLANC (Houma Ch.: v.6-a, p.208)
LADOUCEUR, Octave (Martin & Marie HEBERT) m. 1 June 1896 Estelle LEBLANC (Houma Ct. Hse.: Mar. v.29 & 30, #83)

LAFONT (Sometimes: LAFOND)
LAFONT, Cledomire (d.Charles & Melina TERREBONNE) m. 9 Dec. 1899 Adolsine CHERAMIE (Larose Ch.: v.4, p.130)
LAFONT, Cledoniere (Charles & Melina TERREBONNE) m. 9 Dec. 1899 Adolsine CHERAMIE (Larose Ch.: v.3, p.13)
LAFONT, Cleodomire (Charles & Melina TERREBONNE) m. 28 Nov. 1899 Adolsine CHERAMIE (Thib. Ct. Hse.: Mar. v.39, #271)
LAFONT, Doise Victoria (Theogene & Myra TERREBONNE) b. 21 July 1898 (Larose Ch.: v.3, p.42)
LAFONT, Ernest m. Elise LABAUVE, alias Catherine. Inventory: 4 March 1899. (Thib. Ct. Hse.: Succ. #1565)
LAFONT, Ernest m. 17 July 1896 Ophelia PITRE (Thib. Ct. Hse.: Mar. v.36, #126)
LAFONT, Ernest m. 25 July 1896 Ophelia PITRE (Larose Ch.: v.4, p.78)
LAFONT, Ernest m. 25 July 1896 Ophelia PITRE (Larose Ch.: v.4, p.42)
LAFONT, Ernest m. 25 July 1896 Ophelia PITRE (Larose Ch.: v.3, p.4)
LAFONT, Etienne Loveless (Ernest & Ophelia PITRE) b. 2 Aug. 1897 (Larose Ch.: v.3, p.10)
LAFONT, Eusevie Camillia (Joseph & Clemence GUIDRY) b. 18 July 1897 (Larose Ch.: v.3, p.9)
LAFONT, Gertrude m. 1 May 1899 Amadeo TERREBONNE (Thib. Ct. Hse.: Mar. v.39, #160)
LAFONT, Gertrude m. 20 May 1899 Amadeo TERREBONNE (Larose Ch.: v.3, p.12)
LAFONT, Gertrude m. 20 May 1899 Amedeo TERREBONNE (Larose Ch.: v.4, p.102)
LAFONT, John m. 24 Feb. 1899 Armance GUEDRY (Thib. Ct. Hse.: Mar. v.39, #113)
LAFONT, Joseph m. 6 May 1897 Clemence GUIDRY (Thib. Ct. Hse.: Mar. v.36, #139)
LAFONT, Joseph Eustache (Joseph & Clemance GUIDRY) b. 4 June 1899 (Larose Ch.: v.3, p.47)
LAFOREST, Aimie Esta (Steven & Amelia NAVARRE) b. 5 Sept. 1899 (Chackbay Ch.: v.1, p.140)

LAFOREST, Aline Annie (Stephen & Amelia NAVARE) b. 5 Feb. 1898 (Chackbay Ch.: v.1, p.104)
LAFOREST, Helen (James & Marie BARIAU) m. 1 March 1897 Ambroise BERTEAU (Thib. Ct. Hse.: Mar. v.36, #88)
LAFOREST, Helene (James & Marie BARIAU) m. 1 March 1897 Ambroise BERTEAU (Chackbay Ch.: v.1, p.40)
LAFOREST, Stephen m. 29 April 1897 Amelia NAVARRE (Thib. Ct. Hse.: Mar. v.36, #134)
LAFOREST, Stephen (James & Marie BARIAU) m. 10 May 1897 Amelia NAVARRE (Chackbay Ch.: v.1, p.44)

LAGARDE (Sometimes: DE LAGARDE, LAGARD, LEGARDE)
LAGARDE, Annette m. 14 Nov. 1899 Thomas A. RIVIERE (Thib. Ct Hse.: Mar. v.39, #265)
LAGARDE, Elisabeth (Joachim & Clara CAILLOUET) m. 9 Jan. 1896 Alexandre LEDET (Thib. Ct. Hse.: Mar. v.35, #2)
LAGARDE, Elizabeth (Joachim & Clara CAILLOUET) m. 9 Jan. 1896 Alexandre LEDET (Thib. Ch.: v.13, p.90)
LAGARDE, Ernest m. 24 March 1897 Cecile PIERRE (Houma Ct. Hse.: Mar. v.29 & 30, #364)
LAGARDE, Harris (Joseph & Camelia TOUPS) b. 30 July 1897 (Thib. Ch.: v.7, p.459)
LAGARDE, Henri d. 9 Feb. 1897 at age 6 yrs. & 3 mths. (Thib. Ch.: v.3, p.196)
LAGARDE, Jean Andre (Joseph & Camelie TOUPS) b. 1 July 1898 (Thib. Ch.: v.7, p.553)
LAGARDE, Jules d. 20 March 1896 at age 28 yrs. (Thib. Ch.: v.3, p.180)
LAGARDE, Jules Pierre (Klebert & Elisabeth LEDET) b. 27 Nov. 1897 (Thib. Ch.: v.7, p.527)
LAGARDE, Lena (Perrian & Laura GREENE) m. 17 Jan. 1899 Medard HUMPHREYS (Thib. Ch.: v.14, p.239)
LAGARDE, Lena (Perrin & Laura GREENE) m. 17 Jan. 1899 Medard HUMPHREYS (Thib. Ct. Hse.: Mar. v.38, #9)
LAGARDE, Marie Josephine (Klebert & Elizabeth LEDET) b. 23 March 1897 (Thib. Ch.: v.7, p.444)
LAGARDE, Mary Hazel (G. P. & Odalie POCHET) b. 3 Nov. 1897 (Thib. Ch.: v.7, p.470)
LAGRANGE, Camilia (Amos & Josephine BOUDELOCHE) m. 21 Feb. 1898 Emilien BOUDREAUX (Houma Ct. Hse.: Mar. v.30 & 31, #305)

LAGREZE (Sometimes: (LAGRAIZE)
LAGREZE, Louis d. 1 June 1899 Children listed: Desire; Eliska m. Frank BERGERON. Petition for probate of will: 7 June 1899. (Thib. Ct. Hse.: Succ. #1578)
LAGREZE, Louis d. June 1899 at age 74 yrs. (Thib. Ch.: v.3, p.237)
LAGREZE, Marie d. 24 June 1897 at age 3 mths. (Thib. Ch.: v.3, p.201)

LAGREZE, Marie Celeste (Desire & Alice BERGERON) b. 23 March 1897 (Thib. Ch.: v.7, p.444)

LAGREZE, Odette Marie (Desiree & Alice BERGERON) b. 13 June 1898 (Thib. Ch.: v.7, p.501)

LAGREZE, Paul Olivier (Desire & Alice Marie BERGERON) b. 8 Aug. 1899 (Thib. Ch.: v.7, p.558)

LAGUERRE, Edgar Webster (Louise) b. 9 Feb. 1897 (Raceland Ch.: v.5, p.44)

LAGUERRE, Marie Marguerite (Oscar & Alphonsine JONES) b. 26 Aug. 1896 (Lockport Ch.: v.2, p.335)

LAINE (Sometimes: LAINES, LAISNE)

LAINE, Auguste Anatole (Claiborne & Caroline BURY) m. 27 Dec. 1897 Laura TOUPS (Thib. Ch.: v.14, p.167)

LAINE, Auguste Anatole (Claiborne & Caroline BEERY) m. 27 Dec. 1897 Laura TOUPS (Thib. Ct. Hse.: Mar. v.37, #265)

LAINE, Clay (Leon & Louisa BOURGEOIS) m. 25 April 1899 Clotilde SUREAU (Thib. Ch.: v.14, p.274)

LAINE, Clay (Leon & Louise BOURGEOIS) m. 15 April 1899 Clotilde SUREAU (Thib. Ct. Hse.: Mar. v.39, #150)

LAJAUNIE (Sometimes: LAJANNE, LAJANNIS, LAJAUNI)

LAJAUNIE, Adolphe m. Carmelite BARRILLEAUX Child listed: Adolphe Antoine. Donation of land: 20 May 1897. (Houma Ct. Hse.: Book of Donations: v.A, p.148)

LAJAUNIE, Charles (Meldoff & Josephine ADONE) m. 14 April 1898 Celeste BERGERON (Chacaoula Ch.: v.1, p.61)

LAJAUNIE, Charles (Meldoff & Josephine ADONE) m. 14 April 1898 Celeste BERGERON (Chacahoula Ch.: v.1, p.66 [86])

LAJAUNIE, Charles (Meldoff & Josephine ADOUE) m. 25 March 1898 Celeste BERGERON (Houma Ct. Hse.: Mar. v.30 & 31, #352)

LAJAUNIE, Emilie d. 26 Feb. 1898 at age 72 yrs. (Theriot Ch.: v.1, p.1)

LAJAUNIE, Eunice Joseph (Laurence & Emma FALGOUT) b. 19 Oct. 1897 (Chacahoula Ch.: v.4, p.25)

LAJAUNIE, Henry Joseph (Joseph & Marie HEBERT) b. 23 April 1898 (Chacahoula Ch.: v.4, p.7)

LAJAUNIE, Hubert d. 15 April 1898 at age 42 yrs. (Chacahoula Ch.: v.2, p.28)

LAJAUNIE, Joseph (Edgar & Rosa AUCOIN) m. 18 May 1897 Marie HEBERT (Chacahoula Ch.: v.1, p.60)

LAJAUNIE, Joseph (Edgar & Rosa AUCOIN) m. 18 May 1897 Marie HEBERT (Houma Ct. Hse.: Mar. v.29 & 30, #395)

LAJAUNIE, Joseph Meldof Loyds (Charles & Celeste BERGERON) b. 7 Feb. 1899 (Chacahoula Ch.: v.4, p.19)

LAJAUNIE, Lidie Pearl (Amedee & Philomene BRIANT) b. 27 March 1896 (Houma Ch.: v.5, p.178)

LAJAUNIE, Linda Adele Maria (Thomas & Felicia HERNANDEZ) b. 14 May 1899 (Chacahoula Ch.: v.4, p.27)

LAJAUNIE, Maria Josephine Marguerite (Adolphe & Zulma KELLER) b. 23 Jan. 1898 (Chacahoula Ch.: v.4, p.4)

LAJAUNIE, Marie Clara Agnes (Adolphe & Zulma KELLER) b. 25 July 1896 (Chacahoula Ch.: v.4, p.2)
LAJAUNIE, Marie Sophie (Adolphe & Zulma KELLER) b. 28 Sept. 1899 (Chacahoula Ch.: v.4, p.31)
LAJAUNIE, Paul Sidney (Joseph & Marie HEBERT) b. 3 Oct. 1899 (Chacahoula Ch.: v.4, p.30)
LAJAUNIE, Thomas (Lucien & Adele BOUDELOCHE) m. 10 Feb. 1896 Felicie HERNANDEZ (Raceland Ch.: v.2, p.12)
LAJURA, Antonino (Gasparo & Vincenza MARCHELLA) b. 27 Nov. 1899 (Thib. Ch.: v.8, p.22)
LAKUE, Louise Celina (Henry & Louise DUPONT) b. 2 Oct. 1897 (Chacahoula Ch.: v.4, p.26)
LALLASPIT, Agnes Cecile (Joseph & Lydia HEBERT) b. 11 Dec. 1896 (Thib. Ch.: v.7, p.430)
LAMBERT, Marie Sevie (Mack & Amanda HENRI) b. 10 Sept. 1899 (Theriot Ch.: v.2, p.53)
LAMBERT, Velada (Leufroy & Zeolide BLANCHARD) m. 11 April 1898 Mitchell ROBICHAUX (Houma Ct. Hse.: Mar. v.30 & 31, #394)
LAMBERT, Veleda (Lufroi & Zeolide BLANCHARD) m. 23 April 1898 Michel ROBICHAUX (Montegut Ch.: v.4, p.243)
LAMIAN, Edwin d. 4 Oct. 1899 at age 10 mths. (Thib. Ch.: v.3, p.241)
LAMMANO, Philip m. 22 Jan. 1898 Maria GULOTTA (Houma Ct. Hse.: Mar. v.30 & 31, #244)
LAMONTE, Salvatore (Giovanni & Anna COLITTA) b. 24 July 1899 (Raceland Ch.: v.5, p.100)

LAMOUREAUX (Sometimes: LAMOUREAU, LAMOUREUX)

LAMOUREAUX, Anne Eugenie (Ladupreux & Laurina RODDY) b. 3 March 1899 (Houma Ch.: v.5, p.249)
LAMOUREAUX, Marie Louise (Saint Preux & Laura Laurina RODDY) b. 3 Nov. 1896 (Houma Ch.: v.5, p.160)
LAMOUREAUX, St. Preux (Jean Edouard & Antoinette Alida FOLSE) m. 7 Jan. 1896 Laura Lorena RODDY (Houma Ch.: v.6-a, p.167)
LANAUX, Oneida H. m. Dr. Pierre DAUSEREAUX d. 4 April 1896 at age 61 yrs. (Thib. Ch.: v.3, p.181)
LANCON, Antoinette m. 1 Feb. 1899 Theophile GIROIR (Houma Ct. Hse.: Mar. v.30 & 31, #297)
LANCON, Antoinette m. 13 Feb. 1899 Theophile GIROIR (Houma Ch.: v.6-a, p.288)
LANCON, Clothilde (Fortune & Marie LEGRANDE) m. 3 Feb. 1898 Adam BOURGEOIS (Houma Ct. Hse.: Mar. v.30 & 31, #259)
LANCON, Elvire m. 9 Jan. 1899 Odressy REMOIN (Houma Ct. Hse.: Mar. v.30 & 31, #195)
LANCON, Lawrence (Marcelin & Denise LEBLANC) b. 29 July 1896 (Houma Ch.: v.5, p.184)
LANCON, Marcelin Antoine (Marcelin & Denise LEZOLAUS) b. 11 Nov. 1899 (Houma Ch.: v.5, p.265)

LANCON, Maria Anita Telisia (Lucien & Angele BOUDREAUX) b. 23 Oct. 1897 (Chacahoula Ch.: Gibson Ch.: v.1, #8)

LANCON, Maria Anita Telisia (Lucien & Angelle BOUDREAUX) b. 23 Oct. 1897 (Chacahoula Ch.: Gibson Ch.: v.2, p.116)

LANCON, Mary (Entiene & Mary LAGRANGE) m. 27 July 1897 Henry J. KING (Houma Ch.: Epis. Ch.: v.1, p.342)

LANCON, Mary (Fortune & Mary LAGRANGE) m. 27 July 1897 Henry J. KING (Houma Ct. Hse.: Mar. v.29 & 30, #69)

LANDOR, Phillis m. 16 April 1898 Samuel WILLIAMS (Houma Ct. Hse.: Mar. v.30 & 31, #402)

LANDRY, Adam Donat (Valcar & Vctorine RODRIGUE) b. 2 Oct. 1899 (Chackbay Ch.: v.1, p.141)

LANDRY, Albert (Clay & Josephine LEGENDRE) b. 27 May 1899 (Chackbay Ch.: v.1, p.136)

LANDRY, Albert (Clay & Josephine LEGENDRE) b. 27 May 1899 (Chackbay Ch.: v.1, p.136)

LANDRY, Amelia (Drozin & Liza TROSCLAIR) bt. 14 March 1896 (Chackbay Ch.: v.1, p.62)

LANDRY, Aristide Sylvin (Volse & Marceline CHIASSON) b. 18 Nov. 1898 (Thib. Ch.: v.7, p.530)

LANDRY, Augustin (Viliers & Eulalie CHIASSON) m. 26 Jan. 1899 Marie SANDRAS (Thib. Ct. Hse.: Mar. v.38, #6)

LANDRY, Augustin (Viliers & Eulalie CHIASSON) m. 26 Jan. 1899 Marie SANDRAS (Thib. Ch.: v.14, p.246)

LANDRY, Azema (Joseph & Celima ARCENEAUX) m. 10 Jan. 1898 Sidney VICKNAIR (Thib. Ct. Hse.: Mar. v.37, #266)

LANDRY, Claudia (Louis & Augusta LEROY) d. 12 Nov. 1899 (Montegut Ch.: v.2, p.30)

LANDRY, Clementine Florentine (Villier & Ulalie CHIASSON) b. 14 Jan. 1899 (Chackbay Ch.: v.1, p.128)

LANDRY, Clet (Arsene & Marie PELLETIER) m. 7 Feb. 1898 Josephine LEGENDRE (Thib. Ct. Hse.: Mar. v.37, #51)

LANDRY, Clet (d.Arsene & Marie PELLETIER) m. 7 Feb. 1898 Josephine LEGENDRE (Chackbay Ch.: v.1, p.55)

LANDRY, Clothilde (d.Edgar & Celestine SOURDELIER) m. 3 Feb. 1898 Ernest CROCHET (Montegut Ch.: v.4, p.234)

LANDRY, Clothilde (Edgar & Celestine SOURDELIER) m. 15 Jan. 1898 Ernest CROCHET (Houma Ct. Hse.: Mar. v.30 & 31, #205)

LANDRY, Elus (Jules & Cecile LENGENDRE) b. 25 Sept. 1896 (Chackbay Ch.: v.1, p.77)

LANDRY, Ernestine d. 7 Sept. 1896 at age 59 yrs. (Raceland Ch.: v.1, p.9)

LANDRY, Eudoxie Lilia (Andressie & Eveline GRAUS) b. 10 June 1899 (Chackbay Ch.: v.1, p.136)

LANDRY, Eva (Lucien & Azema AUCOIN) m. 20 April 1898 George S. ELLS (Houma Ct. Hse.: Mar. v.30 & 31, #410)

LANDRY, Flavie m. Clarance CUNNINGHAM d. 20 Nov. 1899 at age 19 yrs. (Montegut Ch.: v.2, p.31)

LANDRY, Flavie (d.Oscar & Celestine SOURDELIER) m. 1 March 1897 Clarence CUNNINGHAM (Montegut Ch.: v.4, p.219)

LANDRY, Flavie (Edgar & Celestine SOURDELIER) m. 20 Feb. 1897 Clarence CUNNINGHAM (Houma Ct. Hse.: Mar. v.29 & 30, #323)
LANDRY, Frosin (Frosin & Lisa TROSCLAIR) b. 10 June 1899 (Chackbay Ch.: v.1, p.138)
LANDRY, Helene May (Mc & Marie GUILLOTE) b. 18 Aug. 1899 (Thib. Ch.: v.8, p.6)
LANDRY, Ida m. 15 June 1898 Ignatius HIGGINS (Thib. Ct. Hse.: Mar. v.38, #208)
LANDRY, Ida (Onesippe & Josephine LAGUINZE) m. 25 June 1898 Ignatius HIGGINS (Raceland Ch.: v.2, p.76)
LANDRY, Joseph (Froisin & Liza TROSCLAIR) b. 18 March 1897 (Chackbay Ch.: v.1, p.85)
LANDRY, Joseph (Theophile & Angele CLEMENT) b. 29 July 1896 (Chackbay Ch.: v.1, p.71)
LANDRY, Joseph Alcide (Arthur & Alice CHIASSON) b. 27 Dec. 1897 (Chackbay Ch.: v.1, p.103)
LANDRY, Leo (Paul & d.Ursule SEVAIN) m. 17 Feb. 1898 Evelie GUYOT (Chackbay Ch.: v.1, p.56)
LANDRY, Leo (Paul & Ursule SEVAIN) m. 17 Feb. 1898 Evelie GUYOT (Thib. Ct. Hse.: Mar. v.37, #62)
LANDRY, Leonida Ursule (Leo & Evelie GUYOT) b. 5 Dec. 1898 (Chackbay Ch.: v.1, p.124)
LANDRY, Louis (Odressy & Eveline GRAUS) b. 28 Dec. 1896 (Chackbay Ch.: v.1, p.81)
LANDRY, Louis Drozilien (Taylor & Marie PERCLE) b. 10 Jan. 1898 (Chackbay Ch.: v.1, p.103)
LANDRY, Louis Joseph (McDuffy & Marie GUILLOTE) b. 2 Oct. 1897 (Thib. Ch.: v.7, p.469)
LANDRY, Marceline (Arsene & Marie PELLETIER) m. 25 Jan. 1898 Justine ROBESSON (Thib. Ct. Hse.: Mar. v.37, #33)
LANDRY, Marcellin (d.Arsene & Marie PELLETIER) m. 25 Jan. 1898 Gustine ROBESSON (Chackbay Ch.: v.1, p.53)
LANDRY, Maria (Arthur & Alice CHIASSON) bt. 13 Jan. 1896 (Chackbay Ch.: v.1, p.59)
LANDRY, Marie Anita (Villiers & Augustine BOURGEOIS) b. 31 Oct. 1899 (Chacahoula Ch.: v.4, p.33)
LANDRY, Marie Viola (Oscar & Cecilia DIEZ) b. 12 Feb. 1899 (Raceland Ch.: v.5, p.89)
LANDRY, Marie Zoe (Marcellin & Augustine ROBERTSON) b. 2 Nov. 1899 (Chackbay Ch.: v.1, p.144)
LANDRY, Mary m. 29 March 1897 Benny BROWN (Thib. Ct. Hse.: Mar. v.36, #103)
LANDRY, Nestor d. 1 Nov. 1899 at age 24 yrs. (Chacahoula Ch.: Gibson Ch.: v.2, p.183)
LANDRY, Oscar m. 23 April 1898 Cecilia DIEZ (Thib. Ct. Hse.: Mar. v.37, #149)
LANDRY, Oscar (Onesippe & Josephine LAGUERRE) m. 23 April 1898 Cecilia DIEZ (Raceland Ch.: v.2, p.73)
LANDRY, Regina Valerie (Willie & Victorine RODRIGUE) b. 19 Feb. 1897 (Chackbay Ch.: v.1, p.86)

LANDRY, Rita Delvida (Augustin & Marie SANDRAS) b. 9 Nov. 1899 (Chackbay Ch.: v.1, p.144)
LANDRY, Rose (Oscar & Amelia RODRIGUE) b. 14 Dec. 1896 (Chackbay Ch.: v.1, p.80)
LANDRY, Rose Laisy (Willy & Leonard GUIDRY) b. 30 Aug. 1898 (Thib. Ch.: v.7, p.565)
LANDRY, Sabin m. 1 April 1899 Selima FREMIN (Thib. Ct. Hse.: Mar. v.39, #127)
LANDRY, Simeon (Lovincy & Aurelia DAIGRE) m.6 April 1899 Margueritte LEBLANC (Thib. Ct. Hse.: Mar. v.39, #132)
LANDRY, Simon (Lovincy & Orelia DAIGRE) m. 24 April 1899 Marguerite LEBLANC (Lockport Ch.: v.2, p.207)
LANDRY, Thomas (d.Aristide & Rosa GROS) m. 13 Feb. 1899 Marie BOUDREAU (Chackbay Ch.: v.1, p.69)
LANDRY, Thomassi (Aristide & Rosa GRAUS) m. 13 Feb. 1899 Marie BOUDREAU (Thib. Ct. Hse.: Mar. v.38, #40)
LANDRY, Ulysse (Jules & Cecile LEGENDRE) b. 28 Oct. 1898 (Chackbay Ch.: v.1, p.128)
LANDRY, Valerie (Bazile & Marceline CHIASSON) b. 28 July 1896 (Chackbay Ch.: v.1, p.71)
LANDRY, Valerie Letitia (William & Leonarde GUETRY) b. 20 Nov. 1896 (Thib. Ch.: v.7, p.430)
LANDRY, Volcar (Oscar & Amelia RODRIGUE) b. 12 Oct. 1898 (Chackbay Ch.: v.1, p.131)
LANDRY, Wallace m. 26 Jan. 1899 Alcida AUTIN (Thib. Ct. Hse.: Mar. v.38, #63)
LANDRY, Wallace (Onesippe & Josephine LAQUIN) m. 2 Feb. 1899 Alcida AUTIN (Raceland Ch.: v.2, p.90)
LANGE, Laura (Robert & Marie RICHARD) b. 12 March 1898 (Theriot Ch.: v.2, p.25)
LANTERMAN, Louis d. 28 Jan. 1897 at age 90 yrs. (Thib. Ch.: v.3, p.195)
LAORO, Accurcio (Laurenzo & Vicenza SALLADINA) b. 1 March 1898 (Thib. Ch.: v.7, p.493)

LAPEROUSE (Sometimes: LAPEREUSE, LAPERUSE, LAPERUZE)

LAPEROUSE, Amanda (Dorado & Celema MOLAISON) m. 26 Jan. 1899 Francois THIBODAUX (Montegut Ch.: v.4, p.252)
LAPEROUSE, Amanda (Dorado & Selema MOLAISON) m. 7 Jan. 1899 Frank THIBODAUX (Houma Ct. Hse.: Mar. v.30 & 31, #191)
LAPEROUSE, Caliste (Edmond & Louise ROBICHAUX) m. 21 Jan. 1899 Felicia PICOU (Houma Ct. Hse.: Mar. v.30 & 31, #210)
LAPEROUSE, Doudou d. 2 Dec. 1899 at age 59 yrs. (Montegut Ch.: v.2, p.31)
LAPEROUSE, Eva (Zephiran & Louisiane BENOIT) m. 16 Dec. 1897 Joseph HEBERT (Houma Ct. Hse.: Mar. v.29 & 30, #146)
LAPEROUSE, Eva (Zephirin & Philomene CALLOUATRE) m. 10 Jan. 1898 Joseph HEBERT (Montegut Ch.: v.4, p.228)
LAPEROUSE, Exzelina m. 6 Feb. 1897 Augustin LEBLANC (Houma Ct. Hse.: Mar. v.29 & 30, #293)

LAPEROUSE, Jean Pierre Junius (Lygnes & Julienne GUIDRY) b. 24 Nov. 1899 (Montegut Ch.: v.6, p.97)
LAPEROUSE, Joseph Edmond (Lygnes & Julienne GUIDRY) b. 14 Aug. 1898 (Montegut Ch.: v.6, p.76)
LAPEROUSE, Joseph Inez (Joseph & Emma DUPLANTIS) b. 30 Oct. 1896 (Montegut Ch.: v.6, p.48)
LAPEROUSE, Joseph Junius (Ludovic & Elisabeth MARCEL) b. 26 Feb. 1896 (Thib. Ch.: v.7, p.397)
LAPEROUSE, Joseph Narcisse (Ernest & Celestine ROBICHAUX) b. 24 March 1896 (Montegut Ch.: v.6, p.37)
LAPEROUSE, Julia Euphrasie (Davis & Marie BOURGEOIS) b. 19 Feb. 1896 (Thib. Ch.: v.7, p.392)
LAPEROUSE, Julien (Zephirin & Louisiana BENOIT) m. 11 Dec. 1899 Lydia LAPEROUSE (Houma Ct. Hse.: Mar. v.31 & 32, #179)
LAPEROUSE, Leanus J. (Edmond & Louisa ROBICHAUX) m. 11 Oct. 1897 Julienne Mary GUIDRY (Houma Ct. Hse.: Mar. v.29 & 30, #119)
LAPEROUSE, Leo (Octave & Malvina HENRI) d. 12 July 1898 at age 21 yrs. (Montegut Ch.: v.2, p.18)
LAPEROUSE, Lineas J. (Edmond & Louisa ROBICHAUX) m. 25 Oct. 1897 Julienne Marie GUIDRY (Montegut Ch.: v.4, p.226)
LAPEROUSE, Louise (Octave & Malvina HENRI) d. 24 Aug. 1899 at age 12 yrs. (Montegut Ch.: v.2, p.28)
LAPEROUSE, Lucide Marguerite (Zephirin & Louisiana BENOIT) b. 28 April 1897 (Montegut Ch.: v.6, p.55)
LAPEROUSE, Ludger Lawrence (Davis & Marie BOURGEOIS) b. 6 Dec. 1898 (Thib. Ch.: v.7, p.522)
LAPEROUSE, Lydia (Douradon & Celema MOLAISON) m. 11 Dec. 1899 Julien LAPEROUSE (Houma Ct. Hse.: Mar. v.31 & 32, #179)
LAPEROUSE, Marie Alzina (Ernest & Celestine ROBICHAUX) b. 4 Dec. 1897 (Montegut Ch.: v.6, p.67)
LAPEROUSE, Marie Emelie (Ernest & Celestine ROBICHAUX) b. 23 April 1899 (Montegut Ch.: v.6, p.90)
LAPEROUSE, Marie Eunice (Ellis & Eveline RHODES) b. 23 Sept. 1899 (Montegut Ch.: v.6, p.94)
LAPEROUSE, Marie Julie (Octave & Malvina HENRI) b. 5 April 1896 (Montegut Ch.: v.6, p.37)
LAPEROUSE, Martha Olivia (Emile & Lilia DAUNIS) b. 9 Jan. 1896 (Thib. Ch.: v.7, p.399)
LAPEROUSE, Maurice Wallice (Ludovic & Elizabeth MARCEL) b. 8 Dec. 1897 (Thib. Ch.: v.7, p.481)
LAPEROUSE, Oliva (Douradou & Celima MOLAISON) m. 6 Feb. 1899 Lelia ENGERON (Houma Ct. Hse.: Mar. v.30 & 31, #312)
LAPEROUSE, Rosa (Emile & Rosa LEJEUNE) m. 12 Feb. 1896 Alfred BOURGEOIS (Thib. Ch.: v.14, p.76)
LAPEROUSE, Rosa (Emile & Rosa LEJEUNE) m. 12 Feb. 1896 Alfred BOURGEOIS (Houma Ct. Hse.: Mar. v.28, #433)
LAPEROUSE, Rose Odette (Emile & Lelia DAUNIS) b. 10 Sept. 1898 (Thib. Ch.: v.7, p.530)

LAPEROUSE, Walter d. 29 Sept. 1897 at age 3 yrs. (Thib. Ch.: v.3, p.206)
LAPESA, Salvatore m. 4 Feb. 1899 Grazia GRAFIA (Houma Ch.: v.6-a, p.274)
LAPUMA, Gacoma (Chichala & Dominica SPARACHINA) m. 11 Jan. 1896 Paolo CACIEPPO (Houma Ch.: v.6-a, p.164)
LARKIN, Charlotte Earla Mathilde (Charly & Henriette ROCKAWAY) b. 4 Sept. 1896 (Larose Ch.: v.3, p.77)
LARKIN, Edward Charles (Charly & Henriette ROCKAWAY) b. 6 Feb. 1899 (Larose Ch.: v.3, p.77)
LARKIN, John Lockaway (Charley & Henriette ROCKAWAY) b. 24 Nov. 1897; bt. 28 April 1901 (Larose Ch.: v.3, p.77)

LAROSE (Sometimes: LAROSSE, LAROUSSE, LAROUX, LAROZE)

LAROSE, Amede m. 19 Oct. 1896 Olympe BOURG (Thib. Ct. Hse.: Mar. v.36, #157)
LAROSE, Catherine Ozalie (John & Eve GUIDRY) b. 22 July 1898 (Montegut Ch.: v.6, p.81)
LAROSE, Helene m. Theodore VEIGES d. 28 May 1899 at age 22 yrs. (Lockport Ch.: v.1, #22)
LAROSE, Helene m. 22 June 1896 Theodore BERGER (Thib. Ct. Hse.: Mar. v.35, #110)
LAROSE, Helene (Lucien & Almira CHAUVIN) m. 22 June 1896 Theodore BERGER (Raceland Ch.: v.2, p.17)
LAROSE, Joseph Edde (Theophile & Josephine LEDET) b. 17 Sept. 1899 (Thib. Ch.: v.7, p.565)
LAROSE, Mare Eva Conchide (Johnny & Eva GUIDRY) b. 3 June 1896 (Montegut Ch.: v.6, p.43)
LAROSE, Marie Annie (Seraphin & Cecilia FOLSE) b. 8 Dec. 1896 (Raceland Ch.: v.5, p.37)
LAROSE, Melodia Philomene (Seraphin & Cecilia FOLSE) b. 13 Nov. 1898 (Raceland Ch.: v.5, p.83)
LAROSE, Theophile (Theogene & Armantine -----) m. 6 Oct. 1898 Josephine LEDET (Thib. Ch.: v.14, p.226)
LAROSE, Theophile (Theogene & Armantine LEVRON) m. 6 Oct. 1898 Josephine LEDET (Thib. Ct. Hse.: Mar. v.38, #279)
LAROUSE, Victor d. 13 Nov. 1899 at age 70 yrs. (Lockport Ch.: v.1, #42)
LAROUSSE, Joseph d. 19 Jan. 1896 at age 27 yrs. (Lockport Ch.: v.1, #2)
LAROUSSE, Theresa Noemie (Arthur & Mercedes LOMBAS) b. 13 May 1896 (Lockport Ch.: v.2, p.329)

LARPENTEUR (Sometimes: LARPANTEUR, LARPENTER)

LARPENTEUR, Mary (Auguste & Euphrosine TOUPS) m. 29 May 1896 Arthur CROCHET (Houma Ct. Hse.: Mar. v.29 & 30, #80)
LARRE, Adeline Louise (Eugene & Lydia DUGAS) b. 17 Aug. 1899 (Thib. Ch.: v.7, p.567)
LASCARO, Tony d. 13 Nov. 1898 at age 4 yrs. (Raceland Ch.: v.1, p.20)

LASCIATE, Philippe (Nicolas & Anna PERRARA) b. 15 March 1898 (Raceland Ch.: v.5, p.68)
LASHBROOKE, Peter Gresham d. 12 Sept. 1896 (Houma Ch.: Epis. Ch.: v.1, p.386)
LASHBROOKE, Peter Greshaw (Edward L. & May PIERCE) b. 7 July 1896 (Houma Ch.: Epis. Ch.: v.1, p.112-B)
LASPISA, Salvatore Jr. m. 4 Jan. 1899 Razia INGNAPFIA (Houma Ct. Hse.: Mar. v.30 & 31, #176)

LASSEIGNE (Sometimes: LASSAEGNIER, LASSAIGNE, LASSEIGN, LASSIGNE)
LASSEIGNE, Alice Georgina (Justin & Augustine GISCLAIR) b. 22 Jan. 1897 (Larose Ch.: v.3, p.12)
LASSEIGNE, Amelie (Theophile & Philomene FREMIN) m. 29 June 1897 Adam BARRIOS (Thib. Ct. Hse.: Mar. v.37, #184)
LASSEIGNE, Arcene Albert (Augustin & Augustine GISCLAR) b. 27 Jan. 1899 (Larose Ch.: v.3, p.36)
LASSEIGNE, Blanche Claurette (Albert & Blanche CONRAD) b. 16 Feb. 1896 (Raceland Ch.: v.5, p.23)
LASSEIGNE, Cecile Agnes (Albert & Blanche CONRAD) b. 25 Feb. 1897 (Raceland Ch.: v.5, p.45)
LASSEIGNE, Eleonore Rita Eve (Alfred & Aurore HEBERT) b. 8 Aug. 1896 (Thib. Ch.: v.7, p.412)
LASSEIGNE, Everule d. 11 June 1899 at age 7 mths. (Thib. Ch.: v.3, p.235)
LASSEIGNE, Ida (Abel & Doliska KELLER) m. 24 Feb. 1897 Leonidas SEVIN (Thib. Ch.: v.14, p.129)
LASSEIGNE, Ida (Abel & Doliska KELLER) m. 24 Feb. 1897 Anidas SEVIN (Thib. Ct. Hse.: Mar. v.36, #79)
LASSEIGNE, Irene Anastasie Marie (Alfred & Aurore HEBERT) b. 22 Jan. 1897 (Thib. Ch.: v.7, p.483)
LASSEIGNE, Joseph Alfred Fernand (Alfred & Laure HEBERT) b. 17 Oct. 1899 (Thib. Ch.: v.7, p.570)
LASSEIGNE, Joseph Emile (Theodore & Lea BOUDREAUX) b. 21 Jan. 1898 (Thib. Ch.: v.7, p.482)
LASSEIGNE, Josephine m. 13 Jan. 1897 George PIERCE (Thib. Ct. Hse.: Mar. v.36, #24)
LASSEIGNE, Lilia Marie (Theodore & Lea BOUDREAUX) b. 31 July 1896 (Thib. Ch.: v.7, p.410)
LASSEIGNE, Marie Joseph (Theodore & Lea BOUDRAUX) b. 19 Jan. 1898 (Thib. Ch.: v.7, p.538)
LASSEIGNE, Naura d. 6 Feb. 1899 at age 2 mths. & 1 day (Thib. Ch.: v.3, p.227)
LASSEIGNE, Zenaide Judith (Charles & Cecile LEONARD) b. 17 Sept. 1897 (Thib. Ch.: v.7, p.464)
LATHROP, Clifton m. 6 June 1896 Jessi SANDERS (Thib. Ch.: Epis. Ch.: v.1, p.331)
LATHROP, Clifton m.6 June 1896 Jessie SANDERS (Thib. Ct. Hse.: Mar. v.35, #102)
LATHROP, Louis Clifton (Clifton & Jesse SANDERS) b. -----; bt. 9 Jan. 1898 (Larose Ch.: v.3, p.15)

LATHROP, Susan m. 4 Dec. 1899 William KELLEY (Thib. Ct. Hse.: Mar. v.39, #275)

LAURO, Calozziera (Francesco & Vitta RAUSSO) b. 15 Nov. 1898 (Thib. Ch.: v.7, p.532)

LAWLESS, Hattie m. 6 April 1899 Paul H. IVES (Thib. Ct. Hse.: Mar. v.39, #133)

LAWRENCE, John m. 3 May 1898 Eliza SHERMAN (Thib. Ct. Hse.: Mar. v.38, #176)

LAWSON, Jean Baptiste (Joseph Frement & Alfrida CHIASSON) b. 13 Aug. 1899 (Theriot Ch.: v.2, p.49)

LAWTON, Jordan m. 28 Oct. 1897 Rosaline BRANSON (Thib. Ct. Hse.: Mar. v.37, #254)

LAZIGNAU (See: LUZIGNAN)

LEBAUVE, Hattie d. 5 May 1896 at age 48 yrs. (Thib. Ch.: Epis. Ch.: v.1, p.394)

LEBERTTE, Touride (Leonard & Francisca ODDO) b. 19 Aug. 1896 (Thib. Ch.: v.7, p.413)

LEBLANC, Adam Joseph Robert (Neuville & Zoe LAMBERT) b. 28 Dec. 1896 (Montegut Ch.: v.6, p.50)

LEBLANC, Adele Odilia (Alcide & Malvina HENRY) b. 25 Feb. 1898 (Chacahoula Ch.: v.4, p.6)

LEBLANC, Agathe (Paul & Philomene DAUNIS) m. 17 Feb. 1896 Arthur LEDET (Thib. Ch.: v.14, p.80)

LEBLANC, Agathe (Paul & Thelomene DAUNIS) m. 12 Feb. 1896 Arthur LEDET (Thib. Ct. Hse.: Mar. v.35, #36)

LEBLANC, Agnes m. 2 March 1899 George H. HANLEY (Houma Ct. Hse.: Mar. v.31 & 32, #351)

LEBLANC, Agnes (Prosper & Elfodia GAUTREAUX) m. 26 April 1899 George H. HANLEY (Houma Ct. Hse.: Mar. v.31 & 32, #1)

LEBLANC, Agnes (Prosper & Elfoitia GAUTRAUX) m. 26 April 1899 George H. HANLEY (Thib. Ch.: v.14, p.276)

LEBLANC, Aida d. 21 Nov. 1897 at age 6 yrs. (Thib. Ch.: v.3, p.207)

LEBLANC, Albert Nollen (Odressie & Octavie MARCEL) b. 22 June 1898 (Thib. Ch.: v.7, p.505)

LEBLANC, Alice Cora (Augustin & Cecilia PELTIER) b. 26 Sept. 1899 (Thib. Ch.: v.8, p.16)

LEBLANC, Alvin George (Constant & Corine LOGAN) b. 12 Oct. 1898 (Thib. Ch.: v.7, p.521)

LEBLANC, Armande Brigitte (Augustin & Cecile PELTIER) b. 13 Jan. 1898 (Thib. Ch.: v.7, p.532)

LEBLANC, Arthur (Camille & Amanda LEBLANC) m. 15 June 1898 Josephine GAUTREAUX (Lockport Ch.: v.2, p.190)

LEBLANC, Arthur (Camille & Amanda LEBLANC) m. 15 June 1898 Josephine GAUTREAUX (Thib. Ct. Hse.: Mar. v.38, #195)

LEBLANC, Arthur Antoine (Edouard & Eugenie ALLEMAND) b. 14 Jan. 1896 (Lockport Ch.: v.2, p.319)

LEBLANC, Augustin d. 19 Jan. 1892; m. Melazie LABIT, d. 17 Sept. 1893. Children: John; Marie; Henry. Tutorship: 20 Jan. 1896 (Houma Ct. Hse.: Succ. #869)
LEBLANC, Augustin d. 3 June 1898 at age 20 yrs., 3 mths. (Thib. Ch.: v.3, p.215)
LEBLANC, Augustin m. 6 Feb. 1897 Exzelina LAPEROUSE (Houma Ct. Hse.: Mar. v.29 & 30, #293)
LEBLANC, Augustine d. 10 Sept. 1899 at age 28 yrs., 8 mths. (Thib. Ch.: v.3, p.240)
LEBLANC, Blanche m. 25 Oct. 1897 Joseph LEBLANC (Lockport Ch.: v.2, p.177)
LEBLANC, Blanche (Ozeme & Rose BARILLEAU) m. 25 Oct. 1897 Joseph E. LEBLANC (Thib. Ct. Hse.: Mar. v.37, #253)
LEBLANC, Carrie m. 4 Feb. 1897 Bird EWINGS (Houma Ct. Hse.: Mar. v.29 & 30, #286)
LEBLANC, Cedee Marguerite (Ernest & Celestine PICOU) b. 20 Aug. 1896 (Montegut Ch.: v.6, p.43)
LEBLANC, Charles m. 14 Jan. 1897 Virginia AUGUSTIN (Thib. Ct. Hse.: Mar. v.36, #31)
LEBLANC, Clara (Arthur & Augusta LEBLANC) m. 25 July 1898 Ernest LEBLANC (Thib. Ct. Hse.: Mar. v.38, #223)
LEBLANC, Clara (Arthur & Augusta LEBLANC) m. 25 July 1898 Ernest LEBLANC (Thib. Ch.: v.14, p.211)
LEBLANC, Clarence Severin (Emile & Regina THIBODEAUX) b. 23 Oct. 1899 (Thib. Ch.: v.8, p.16)
LEBLANC, Clothilde Theresia (Neuville & Genevieve BOUDREAU) b. 25 July 1897 (Theriot Ch.: v.2, p.12)
LEBLANC, Corinne m. 11 April 1896 James WALKER (Houma Ct. Hse.: Mar. v.29 & 30, #35)
LEBLANC, Cynthia (Francois & Azema LOUVIERE) m. 20 Jan. 1898 Edward ROBICHAUX (Thib. Ch.: v.14, p.170)
LEBLANC, Cynthia (Francois & Azema LOUVIERE) m. 20 Jan. 1898 Edouard robichaux (Houma Ct. Hse.: Mar. Vols.29 & 30, #156)
LEBLANC, Eddy Adam (Joseph & Augustine BADEAU) b. 21 Nov. 1897 (Thib. Ch.: v.7, p.475)
LEBLANC, Edgar (Jean Marie & Aglae BOUDREAUX) m. 26 Dec. 1896 Lutecia HEBERT (Houma Ct. Hse.: Mar. v.29 & 30, #211)
LEBLANC, Effie (Simonet & Amelia BERTHELOTTE) m. 10 May 1899 Herbert ROUSSEL (Chacahoula Ch.: v.1, p.70 [90])
LEBLANC, Effie (Simonet & Amelia BERTHELOTTE) m. 21 Jan. 1899 Herbert ROUSSELL (Houma Ct. Hse.: Mar. v.30 & 31, #264)
LEBLANC, Eglantine (Rosemond & Aglae THIBODAUX) m. 3 June 1896 Williams FIELDS (Thib. Ct. Hse.: Mar. v.35, #98)
LEBLANC, Eglantine (Rosemond & Aglae THIBODAUX) m. 3 June 1896 William FIELDS (Thib. Ch.: v.14, p.90)
LEBLANC, Elisa Nitia (Joseph & Elisa GAUDET) b. 29 Aug. 1897 (Larose Ch.: v.3, p.5)

LEBLANC, Elphege Augustin (Auguste & Azelina LAPEROUSE) b. 12 March 1898 (Montegut Ch.: v.6, p.71)

LEBLANC, Ernest (Allison & Zulma MOLAISON) m. 13 May 1897 Marthe NEWELL (Thib. Ch.: v.14, p.144)

LEBLANC, Ernest (Allison & Zulma MOLAISON) m. 13 May 1897 Lelia or Merthe NEWELL (Thib. Ct. Hse.: Mar. v.36, #143)

LEBLANC, Ernest (Edmond & Lesine RICHARD) m. 12 Jan. 1899 Nelsana PICOU (Montegut Ch.: v.4, p.251)

LEBLANC, Ernest (Edmond & Lezine RICHARD) m. 24 Aug. - 26 Dec. 1898 Nelsona PICOU (Montegut Ch.: v.4, p.250)

LEBLANC, Ernest (Leo & Marie BELLANGER) m. 25 July 1898 Clara LEBLANC (Thib. Ct. Hse.: Mar. v.38, #223)

LEBLANC, Ernest (Leo & Marie BELLANGER) m. 25 July 1898 Clara LEBLANC (Thib. Ch.: v.14, p.211)

LEBLANC, Ernest M. (Edmond & Lezine RICHARD) m. 18 Oct. 1898 Nelsana PICOU (Houma Ct. Hse.: Mar. v.30 & 31, #125)

LEBLANC, Estel d. 13 March 1899 at age 34 yrs. (Houma Ch.: v.3, p.28)

LEBLANC, Estelle m. 1 July 1897 Octave LADOUCEUR (Houma Ch.: v.6-a, p.208)

LEBLANC, Estelle (Jean Marie & Aglae BOUDREAUX) m. 1 June 1896 Octave LADOUCEUR (Houma Ct. Hse.: Mar. v.29 & 30, #83)

LEBLANC, Etienette (Jho. & Celestine TOUPS) m. 5 Sept. 1898 Alceste GAUDE (Thib. Ct. Hse.: Mar. v.38, #262)

LEBLANC, Etienne Mrs. d. 12 March 1899 at age 60 yrs. (Lockport Ch.: v.1, #13)

LEBLANC, Etiennette (Jho & Celestine TOUPS) m. 5 Sept. 1898 Alceste GAUDE (Lockport Ch.: v.2, p.194)

LEBLANC, Eugene (Edouard & Eugene ALLEMAND) m. 19 July 1899 Celestine BOURGEOIS (Lockport Ch.: v.2, p.209)

LEBLANC, Eugene (Edouard & Eugenie ALLEMAND) m. 19 July 1899 Celestine BOURGEOIS (Thib. Ct. Hse.: Mar. v.39, #198)

LEBLANC, Eugene Joseph (Beauregard & Marie FOREST) b. 7 Sept. 1897 (Thib. Ch.: v.7, p.463)

LEBLANC, Eve Madeleine (Joseph & Alice CAILLONET) b. 29 Dec. 1898 (Thib. Ch.: v.7, p.533)

LEBLANC, Evelia (Omer & Rosa AUTHEMENT) m. 8 March 1897 Philogene PELEGRIN (Houma Ct. Hse.: Mar. v.29 & 30, #340)

LEBLANC, Exelina d. 10 Feb. 1898 at age 56 yrs. (Houma Ch.: v.3, p.15)

LEBLANC, Francois Augustin (Beauregard & Marie FOREST) b. 16 Oct. 1897 (Thib. Ch.: v.7, p.518)

LEBLANC, Frederick (David & Julenne PORCHE) m. 28 June 1897 Minerva COOK (Houma Ch.: Epis. Ch.: v.1, p.342)

LEBLANC, Frederick (David & Zulema PORCHE) m. 22 June 1897 Minerva COOK (Houma Ct. Hse.: Mar. v.29 & 30, #38)

LEBLANC, Georges Joseph (Joseph Louis & Aline OLMICHEN) b. 27 Nov. 1897 (Thib. Ch.: v.7, p.508)

LEBLANC, Gustin (Desire & Clementine NEUVILLE) m. 11 May 1899 Cecile PELTIER (Thib. Ch.: v.14, p.281)
LEBLANC, Hampton d. 30 April 1896 at age 42 yrs. & 6 mths. (Thib. Ch.: v.3, p.182)
LEBLANC, Henriette Genessy (Calixte & Helene HACQ) b. 27 Dec. 1896 (Thib. Ch.: v.7, p.444)
LEBLANC, Hermance Monique (Frank & Zulma FALGOUT) b. 4 May 1896 (Thib. Ch.: v.7, p.403)
LEBLANC, Ida (Adrien & Aglae PELLEGRIN) m. 28 Nov. 1898 Ulfred SMITH (Thib. Ch.: v.14, p.231)
LEBLANC, Ida (Adrien & Aglae PELLEGRIN) m. 28 Nov. 1898 Alfred SMITH (Thib. Ct. Hse.: Mar. v.38, #311)
LEBLANC, Idea d. 25 Aug. 1899 at age 3 mths. (Thib. Ch.: v.3, p.239)
LEBLANC, Irene Marie (Calice & Helene HOCQ) b. 16 May 1898 (Thib. Ch.: v.7, p.553)
LEBLANC, Irma m. 26 Jan. 1899 Sidney J. BOYER (Houma Ct. Hse.: Mar. v.30 & 31, #287)
LEBLANC, Irma (Mitchel & Agladie LOUVIERE) m. 13 Feb. 1899 Sidney J. BOYER (Houma Ch.: v.6-a, p.280)
LEBLANC, Jean m. 20 July 1897 Leah LIRETTE (Houma Ct. Hse.: Mar. v.29 & 30, #65)
LEBLANC, Jean (Augustin & Melanie LABIT) m. 20 July 1897 Leah LIRETTE (Houma Ch.: v.6-a, p.212)
LEBLANC, Jean C. (Adernas & Sisca AUTEMENT) b. 13 March 1897 (Houma Ch.: v.5, p.171)
LEBLANC, Jean Marie m. 6 Feb. 1899 Aglae BOUDREAUX (Houma Ch.: v.6-a, p.276)
LEBLANC, Jean Marie Jr. m. 23 Jan. 1899 Julienne SMITH (Houma Ct. Hse.: Mar. v.30 & 31, #279)
LEBLANC, Jean Pierre Etienne (Joseph & Marie HEBERT) b. 2 Sept. 1898 (Chacahoula Ch.: v.4, p.13)
LEBLANC, Jeanne Agnes (Ernest & Mathilde BOUDREAUX) b. 7 March 1897 (Lockport Ch.: v.3-A, #30)
LEBLANC, Jeanne Agnes (Ernest & Mathilde BOUDREAUX) b. 7 March 1897 (Lockport Ch.: v.3, #30)
LEBLANC, John Edouard (Wilfrid & Alida SONICA) b. 23 April 1896 (Houma Ch.: v.5, p.179)
LEBLANC, Joseph d. 24 July 1899 at age 3 days (Houma Ch.: v.3, p.24)
LEBLANC, Joseph m. 10 March 1897 Josephine ALLEMAND (Larose Ch.: v.4, p.103)
LEBLANC, Joseph m. 15 Feb. 1897 Josephine ALLEMAND (Larose Ch.: v.3, p.5)
LEBLANC, Joseph m. 2 Feb. 1897 Josephine ALLEMAND (Thib. Ct. Hse.: Mar. v.36, #64)
LEBLANC, Joseph m. 25 Oct. 1897 Blanche LEBLANC (Lockport Ch.: v.2, p.177)
LEBLANC, Joseph (Felix & Mary BADEAU) b. 21 Nov. 1896 (Thib. Ch.: v.7, p.436)

LEBLANC, Joseph (Leonce & Berthilde CANTRELLE) m. 12 Jan. 1899 Felicia BOURG (Houma Ct. Hse.: Mar. v.30 & 31, #213)
LEBLANC, Joseph (Leonce & Berthilde CANTRELLE) m. 5 Feb. 1899 Felicia BOURG (Montegut Ch.: v.4, p.255)
LEBLANC, Joseph (Varris & Eva DIGGS) m. 16 Jan. 1899 Lilly FINLEY (Houma Ct. Hse.: Mar. v.30 & 31, #236)
LEBLANC, Joseph Allan (Ernest & Celestine PICOU) b. 7 July 1898 (Montegut Ch.: v.6, p.74)
LEBLANC, Joseph Allan (Ernest & Celestine PICOU) d. 6 Dec. 1898 at age 6 mths. (Montegut Ch.: v.2, p.22)
LEBLANC, Joseph Ally (Arthe & Marie RICHARD) b. 30 Aug. 1897 (Theriot Ch.: v.2, p.11)
LEBLANC, Joseph Antoine (Jean Evariste & Bridget Emma PORCHE) b. 1 April 1898 (Houma Ch.: v.5, p.205)
LEBLANC, Joseph Bryan (Clement & Marie STOUT) b. 27 Aug. 1899 (Houma Ch.: v.5, p.252)
LEBLANC, Joseph Clarence (Klebert & Marceline Julia GAUDET) b. 12 Dec. 1896 (Raceland Ch.: v.5, p.38)
LEBLANC, Joseph Dinas (Sylvin & Ernestine FORET) b. 3 Nov. 1897 (Thib. Ch.: v.7, p.476)
LEBLANC, Joseph E. (Edward & Eugenia ALEMAN) m. 25 Oct. 1897 Blanche LEBLANC (Thib. Ct. Hse.: Mar. v.37, #253)
LEBLANC, Joseph Elie (Numa & Josephine LEBLANC) b. 30 March 1896 (Lockport Ch.: v.2, p.327)
LEBLANC, Joseph Freddy (Albert & Zulema THIBODAUX) b. 16 Aug. 1898 (Thib. Ch.: v.7, p.517)
LEBLANC, Joseph Freddy (Felicien & Celestine PONTIFF) b. 27 Jan. 1897 (Thib. Ch.: v.7, p.443)
LEBLANC, Joseph Herve (Wallace & Leontine DOMINIQUE) b. 16 Oct. 1898 (Thib. Ch.: v.7, p.578)
LEBLANC, Joseph Leo (Elma & Elea BUQUET) b. 6 Jan. 1898 (Montegut Ch.: v.6, p.63)
LEBLANC, Joseph Noldan (Jean & Lea LIRETTE) b. 16 Jan. 1899 (Houma Ch.: v.5, p.237)
LEBLANC, Joseph Wily (Ernest & Martha NEWELL) b. 24 Feb. 1898 (Thib. Ch.: v.7, p.488)
LEBLANC, Josephine (Camille & Amanda LEBLANC) m. 9 Feb. 1898 Albert GAUTREAUX (Thib. Ct. Hse.: Mar. v.37, #59)
LEBLANC, Josephine (Camille & Amanda LEBLANC) m. 9 Feb. 1898 Albert GAUTREAUX (Lockport Ch.: v.2, p.185)
LEBLANC, Julia Mrs. widow of Willie ELLENDER (Arthur & Marie CHAUVIN) m. 12 April 1898 John HEIDER, from city of St. Louis (Montegut Ch.: v.4, p.241)
LEBLANC, Julie (Gustave & Louisiane BRAUX) m. 27 Jan. 1898 Albert BUQUET (Thib. Ct. Hse.: Mar. v.37, #48)
LEBLANC, Julie (Gustave & Louisiane BREAUX) m. 27 Jan. 1898 Albert BUQUET (Thib. Ch.: v.14, p.177)
LEBLANC, Julie (Theodule & Marie MOLAISON) m. 21 Feb. 1898 Francis LIRETTE (Montegut Ch.: v.4, p.238)

LEBLANC, Julie (Theodule & Marie MOLAISON) m. 12 Feb. 1898 Francis LIRETTE (Houma Ct. Hse.: Mar. v.30 & 31, #292)
LEBLANC, Justin or Gustin m. 21 Feb. 1898 Cecilia PELTIER, widow of FREEMAN (Thib. Ct. Hse.: Mar. v.37, #111)
LEBLANC, Laura m. 12 May 1897 Cornelius PHARAGUTT (Thib. Ct. Hse.: Mar. v.36, #141)
LEBLANC, Lelia (Gustave & Louisiane BREAUX) m. 13 Feb. 1896 Felix DARCE (Thib. Ch.: v.14, p.77)
LEBLANC, Lelia (Gustave & Louisiane BREAUX) m. 13 Feb. 1896 Felix DARCE (Thib. Ct. Hse.: Mar. v.35, #38)
LEBLANC, Lemuel Eugene Pierre Gaston (Albert & Zulema THIBODAUX) b. 10 Jan. 1896 (Thib. Ch.: v.7, p.438)
LEBLANC, Leo d. 5 Dec. 1898 at age 51 yrs. (Thib. Ch.: v.3, p.222)
LEBLANC, Leon (Leo & Mary BELLANGER) m. 23 Aug. 1898 Mary TUITE (Thib. Ct. Hse.: Mar. v.38, #254)
LEBLANC, Leon (Leo & Mary BELLANGER) m. 23 Aug. 1898 Mary TUITE (Lockport Ch.: v.2, p.193 & 194)
LEBLANC, Leon Milton (Jean Baptiste & Alcida LEJEUNE) b. 22 April 1898 (Houma Ch.: v.5, p.208)
LEBLANC, Leona Laura (Edgar & Septime HEBERT) b. 12 Feb. 1898 (Chacahoula Ch.: v.4, p.5)
LEBLANC, Louis Bertrand (Calixte & Helene HOCK) b. 25 June 1899 (Thib. Ch.: v.7, p.610)
LEBLANC, Louis Eugene (Camille & Olympe BARRIOS) b. 20 Dec. 1898 (Chacahoula Ch.: v.4, p.16)
LEBLANC, Ludovic (Villiers & Ophelia GIROUARD) m. 13 Feb. 1896 Felicia PELTIER (Houma Ct. Hse.: Mar. v.28, #405)
LEBLANC, Malvina m. Alfred CROCHET d. 16 Jan. 1899 at age 21 yrs. (Montegut Ch.: v.2, p.24)
LEBLANC, Marguerite (Leo & Mary BELANGER) m. 24 April 1899 Simon LANDRY (Lockport Ch.: v.2, p.207)
LEBLANC, Marguerite Louise (Justin & Rosanna CHAUVIN) b. 18 July 1896 (Montegut Ch.: v.6, p.42)
LEBLANC, Margueritte (Leo & Mary BELANGER) m. 6 April 1899 Simeon LANDRY (Thib. Ct. Hse.: Mar. v.39, #132)
LEBLANC, Marie d. 8 Jan. 1898 at age 11 days (Thib. Ch.: v.3, p.209)
LEBLANC, Marie m. 15 Sept. 1899 Emile RICHARD (Houma Ct. Hse.: Mar. v.31 & 32, #135)
LEBLANC, Marie Aline (Odreci & Octavie MASSEL) b. 26 Oct. 1899 (Thib. Ch.: v.8, p.16)
LEBLANC, Marie Diola (Ernest & Claire LEBLANC) b. 20 Sept. 1899 (Thib. Ch.: v.8, p.15)
LEBLANC, Marie Esther (Emile & Marie NEWELL) b. 28 July 1896 (Thib. Ch.: v.7, p.410)
LEBLANC, Marie Irene (Klebert & Julia GAUDE) b. 22 June 1898 (Thib. Ch.: v.7, p.502)
LEBLANC, Marie Laura (J. O. & Albertine STOUT) b. 4 Jan. 1899 (Raceland Ch.: v.5, p.87)

LEBLANC, Marie Loulie (Justin & Rosanna CHAUVIN) b. 6 March 1898 (Montegut Ch.: v.6, p.66)
LEBLANC, Marie Lucille d. 21 Aug. 1896 at age 35 yrs. (Thib. Ch.: v.3, p.186)
LEBLANC, Marie Minnie (Edgar & Emma DOMINGUE) b. 11 Nov. 1899 (Montegut Ch.: v.6, p.95)
LEBLANC, Marie Odette Cedey (Wallace & Leontine DOMINIGUE) b. 7 Aug. 1897 (Thib. Ch.: v.7, p.465)
LEBLANC, Martial d. 24 Dec. 1898 at age 25 yrs. (Thib. Ch.: v.3, p.224)
LEBLANC, Mary m. 19 Feb. 1898 Buddy DAIGLE (Houma Ct. Hse.: Mar. v.30 & 31, #313)
LEBLANC, Mary m. 20 Dec. 1898 Herman CANTRELLE (Thib. Ct. Hse.: Mar. v.38, #319)
LEBLANC, Mary (Augustin & Melazie LABIT) m. 21 Feb. 1898 Buddy DAIGLE (Houma Ch.: v.6-a, p.236)
LEBLANC, Mary Bertha (Marchal & Clementine NAQUIN) b. 29 Aug. 1897 (Thib. Ch.: v.7, p.466)
LEBLANC, Mary Eurline (Augustin & Louise ALLAIS) b. 19 Sept. 1897 (Thib. Ch.: v.7, p.471)
LEBLANC, Maud Natalie (Arthur & Olympe HEBERT) b. 1 Jan. 1898 (Chacahoula Ch.: v.4, p.5)
LEBLANC, Maurice d. 1 Jan. 1898 at age 2 mths. (Thib. Ch.: v.3, p.209)
LEBLANC, Maurice Guilbert (Edgar & Septime AUBERT) b. 24 Oct. 1899 (Chacahoula Ch.: v.4, p.31)
LEBLANC, Nicolas (Joseph & Celina BARRIOS) m. 9 Feb. 1899 Noemie LEBLANC (Thib. Ct. Hse.: Mar. v.38, #75)
LEBLANC, Nicolas (Joseph & Celina BARRIOS) m. 9 Feb. 1899 Noemie LEBLANC (Lockport Ch.: v.2, p.203)
LEBLANC, Noe m. 17 Feb. 1896 Melinas LEBEUF (Thib. Ct. Hse.: Mar. v.35, #40)
LEBLANC, Noemie (Camille & Amanda LEBLANC) m. 9 Feb. 1899 Nicolas LEBLANC (Thib. Ct. Hse.: Mar. v.38, #75)
LEBLANC, Noemie (Camille & Amanda LEBLANC) m. 9 Feb. 1899 Nicolas LEBLANC (Lockport Ch.: v.2, p.203)
LEBLANC, Norah Margueritte (Cleopha & Rosalie GUIDRY) b. 8 July 1898 (Larose Ch.: v.3, p.22)
LEBLANC, Numa d. 16 Oct. 1896 at age 67 yrs. (Lockport Ch.: v.1, #19)
LEBLANC, Palmyre (Etienne & Audolie LEBLANC) m. 24 Jan. 1898 Alceste MAYET (Thib. Ct. Hse.: Mar. v.37, #27)
LEBLANC, Palmyre (Etienne & Oudolie LEBLANC) m. 24 Jan. 1898 Alceste MAYET (Lockport Ch.: v.2, p.180)
LEBLANC, Paul d. 17 May 1899 at age 59 yrs., 10 mths., 15 days (Thib. Ch.: v.3, p.234)
LEBLANC, Paul d. 29 June 1896 at age 79 yrs. (Thib. Ch.: v.3, p.184)
LEBLANC, Paul (Ozeme & Rose BARRILLEAUX) m. 20 Oct. 1898 Josephine UZE (Thib. Ct. Hse.: Mar. v.38, #295)

LEBLANC, Paul (Ozeme & Rosi BARRILLEAUX) m. 20 Oct. 1898 Josephine UZE (Lockport Ch.: v.2, p.195)
LEBLANC, Philippe Adam (Jean & Lotitia OTIN) b. 15 May 1896 (Lockport Ch.: v.2, p.330)
LEBLANC, Philomene Mayble (Camille & Olinda BARRIOS) b. 21 July 1897 (Chacahoula Ch.: v.4, p.22)
LEBLANC, Regina Zoe (Edgar & Emma DOMINGUE) b. 20 May 1897 (Montegut Ch.: v.6, p.56)
LEBLANC, Robert Edouard (Andress & Octavie MARCEL) b. 8 Aug. 1896 (Thib. Ch.: v.7, p.416)
LEBLANC, Roger Vincent (Jean Marie & Julienne SMITH) b. 30 Dec. 1899 (Houma Ch.: v.6, p.4)
LEBLANC, Rogere Vincent (Jean Marie & Julienne SMITH) b. 30 Dec. 1899 (Houma Ch.: v.5, p.269)
LEBLANC, Sidonie (Marcellus & Marcelline BRAUX) m. 9 Feb. 1898 Labadie Louis HARANG (Thib. Ct. Hse.: Mar. v.37, #74)
LEBLANC, Sidonie (Marcellus & Marcelline BRAUX) m. 9 Feb. 1898 Labadie Louis HARANG (Lockport Ch.: v.2, p.184)
LEBLANC, Simonet d. 14 Aug. 1898 (Chacahoula Ch.: v.2, p.28)
LEBLANC, Sydney (Cyprien) d. 11 Sept. 1899 at age 3½ yrs. (Lockport Ch.: v.1, #36)
LEBLANC, Thomas Pierre (Felix & Marie BADEAUX) b. 6 June 1898 (Thib. Ch.: v.7, p.554)
LEBLANC, Victoria m. 6 Oct. 1898 George AUGUSTIN (Thib. Ct. Hse.: Mar. v.38, #288)
LEBLANC, Victoria (Edouard & Eugenie ALLEMAND) m. 2 Feb. 1898 Arthur UZE (Thib. Ct. Hse.: Mar. v.37, #60)
LEBLANC, Victorine (Edouard & Eugenie ALLEMAND) m. 2 Feb. 1898 Arthur UZE (Lockport Ch.: v.2, p.182 & 183)
LEBLANC, Victorine Adaline (Cleophas & Rose GUIDRY) b. 5 July 1896 (Larose Ch.: v.2, p.193)
LEBLANC, Wallace (Theodule & Ernestine TOUPS) m. 29 July 1896 Leontine DOMINGUE (Thib. Ch.: v.14, p.95)
LEBLANC, Wallace (Theodule & Ernestine TOUPS) m. 24 June 1896 Leontine DOMINGUE (Thib. Ct. Hse.: Mar. v.36, #111)
LEBLANC, Waren Abdon (Joseph & Rosa THOMASSI) b. 31 Jan. 1896 (Lockport Ch.: v.3, #17)
LEBLANC, Waren Abdon (Joseph & Rosa THOMASSI) b. 31 Jan. 1896 (Lockport Ch.: v.3-A, #17)
LEBLANC, Warren Joseph (Beauregard & Mary FORET) b. 6 Oct. 1899 (Thib. Ch.: v.7, p.569)
LEBLANC, William Edward m. 17 Oct. 1898 Adele AUTHEMENT (Houma Ct. Hse.: Mar. v.30 & 31, #123)
LEBLANC, William Edward (John Adolphe & widow Marie C. PERRET) m. 20 Oct. 1898 Adele AUTHEMENT (Houma Ch.: v.6-a, p.256)
LEBLANC, Wilson Louis (Wilfrid & Alida SOIGNIER) b. 14 Jan. 1899 (Thib. Ch.: v.7, p.590)
LEBLANC, Zulma (David & Zulma POCHE) m. 7 Feb. 1896 Onezippe ADAM (Thib. Ch.: v.14, p.75)

LEBOEUF (Sometimes: LEBEUF, LEBOEUFF, LEBOUF, LEBOVE)

LEBOEUF, ----- (Ovile & Ophelia PARKS) m. 2 May 1898 Alida BOURG (Montegut Ch.: v.4, p.244)

LEBOEUF, Abel Joseph (Alexis & Augusta DESLATTES) b. 3 May 1899 (Chacahoula Ch.: v.4, p.26)

LEBOEUF, Alexina m. 23 June 1897 Evans RHODES (Houma Ct. Hse.: Mar. v.29 & 30, #40)

LEBOEUF, Alexina (d.Cleophat & Victorine DOMINGUE) m. 12 July 1897 Evans RHODES (Montegut Ch.: v.4, p.223)

LEBOEUF, Alfred Gerin (Joseph & Marie GOTREAUX) b. 15 Nov. 1897 (Montegut Ch.: v.6, p.63)

LEBOEUF, Alice (Eleste & Oliva COLLIN) b. 16 April 1897 (Theriot Ch.: v.2, p.1)

LEBOEUF, Andre Octave (Gabriel & Licia BOURG) b. 30 Nov. 1897 (Montegut Ch.: v.6, p.63)

LEBOEUF, Arthur (Charles & Marie HEBERT) m. 9 Jan. 1899 Cleontine BUTCHER (Houma Ct Hse.: Mar. v.30 & 31, #177)

LEBOEUF, Arthur (Charles & Marie HEBERT) m. 9 Jan. 1899 Cleontine BUTCHER (Thib. Ch.: v.14, p.235)

LEBOEUF, Aubert m. Eve Emelie BOURGEOIS Donation of land: 17 March 1898. (Houma Ct. Hse.: Book of Donations: v.A, p.154)

LEBOEUF, Aubin Medar (Nolatheus & Josephine DAIGLE) b. 8 June 1898 (Houma Ch.: v.5, p.211)

LEBOEUF, Augustin m. 29 May 1897 Mrs. Felecite MARCEL (Houma Ch.: v.6-a, p.204)

LEBOEUF, Augustin Columbus d. 16 Dec. 1896 at age 8 mths. (Montegut Ch.: v.2, p.8)

LEBOEUF, Augustin Columbus (Felicien & Alexina BRUNET) b. 14 April 1896 (Montegut Ch.: v.6, p.37)

LEBOEUF, Bernard Wilfred (Oscar & Augustin BILLOT) b. 1 June 1896 (Montegut Ch.: v.6, p.43)

LEBOEUF, Bernard Wilfred (Oscar & Augustine BILLOT) b. 1 June 1896 (Montegut Ch.: v.6, p.43)

LEBOEUF, Cathrine Marie (Eugene & Ernestine BOUDREAUX) b. 7 Dec. 1898 (Chacahoula Ch.: v.4, p.16)

LEBOEUF, Cecilia Aida (Mack & Odilia MOLAISON) b. 22 Nov. 1899 (Chacahoula Ch.: v.4, p.31)

LEBOEUF, Clovis (Cleophas & Victorine DOMINGUE) m. 19 Aug. 1898 Nolia PICOU (Houma Ct. Hse.: Mar. v.30 & 31, #82)

LEBOEUF, Clovis (d.Cleophat & Victorine DOMINGUE) m. 24 Aug. 1898 Nolia PICOU (Montegut Ch.: v.4, p.249)

LEBOEUF, Dominique Maurice (Placide & Eugenie DUPRE) b. 4 Aug. 1896 (Montegut Ch.: v.6, p.44)

LEBOEUF, Edouard Paul (Beattie & Olympe HEBERT) b. 14 March 1898 (Montegut Ch.: v.6, p.68)

LEBOEUF, Elvire Marie (Frank & Henriette LEBLANC) b. 27 Oct. 1898 (Houma Ch.: v.5, p.226)

LEBOEUF, Etienne (Oville & Ophelia PARK) m. 9 April 1898 Alida BOURG (Houma Ct. Hse.: Mar. v.30 & 31, #386)

LEBOEUF, Evariste Henry (Placide & Eugenie DUPRE) b. 15 July 1898 (Montegut Ch.: v.6, p.76)
LEBOEUF, Felicia Eve (Augustin & Felicite MARCEL) b. 22 Feb. 1898 (Thib. Ch.: v.7, p.493)
LEBOEUF, Felton Joannes (Ellis & Oliva COLLINS) b. 17 Dec. 1898 (Theriot Ch.: v.2, p.37)
LEBOEUF, Francois Marcelin (Ovile & Philomene LEBLANC) b. 7 July 1896 (Houma Ch.: v.5, p.184)
LEBOEUF, Henriette Felicia (Felicien & Alexina BRUNET) b. 25 March 1898 (Montegut Ch.: v.6, p.69)
LEBOEUF, Ida d. 17 Dec. 1896 at age 1 yr. 6 days (Houma Ch.: v.3, p.10)
LEBOEUF, Jean Julien (Alexis & Marie PELEGRIN) b. 14 Jan. 1899 (Montegut Ch.: v.6, p.84)
LEBOEUF, Jean Louis (Joseph & Valerie BABIN) b. 6 Oct. 1899 (Raceland Ch.: v.5, p.103)
LEBOEUF, Jean Marie d. 29 April 1896 at age 86 yrs. (Houma Ch.: v.3, p.7)
LEBOEUF, Jean Marie Joseph (Nelson & Josephine DAIGLE) b. 23 Sept. 1896 (Houma Ch.: v.5, p.158)
LEBOEUF, Joseph d. 27 March 1896 at age 68 yrs. (Montegut Ch.: v.2, p.4)
LEBOEUF, Joseph m. 13 Oct. 1898 Valerie BABIN (Thib. Ct. Hse.: Mar. v.38, #294)
LEBOEUF, Joseph (Jean & Marie COSLEY) m. 22 Oct. 1898 Valerie BABIN (Raceland Ch.: v.2, p.82)
LEBOEUF, Joseph (John & Eva DUPLANTIS) b. 26 Oct. 1897 (Montegut Ch.: v.6, p.62)
LEBOEUF, Joseph Emilien (Marcellus & Aurelia HEBERT) b. 15 Nov. 1896 (Montegut Ch.: v.6, p.54)
LEBOEUF, Joseph Herman (Arthur & Clementine BUTCHER) b. 3 Oct. 1899; m. Marie Corinne THIBODAUX (Houma Ch.: Bapt. Bk., v.5, p.259)
LEBOEUF, Joseph Hubert (Urbin & Marguerite BUQUET) b. 7 July 1898 (Houma Ch.: v.5, p.214)
LEBOEUF, Joseph Joachim (Eugene & Armentine BOUDREAUX) b. 8 Oct. 1896 (Chacahoula Ch.: v.4, p.4)
LEBOEUF, Joseph Merthil (Frank & Josephine PONCECAIL) b. 30 April 1896 (Houma Ch.: v.5, p.180)
LEBOEUF, Joseph Nicles (Calixte & Euseline LEDAY) b. 11 Oct. 1897 (Montegut Ch.: v.6, p.61)
LEBOEUF, Joseph Olivier (John & Eva DUPLANTIS) b. 30 Oct. 1899 (Montegut Ch.: v.6, p.95)
LEBOEUF, Josephine (Orvile & Ophelia PARQUE) m. 13 Feb. 1899 Frederic LEVRON (Montegut Ch.: v.4, p.259)
LEBOEUF, Josephine (Orville & Ophelia PARQUE) m. 18 Jan. 1899 Frederick LEVRON (Houma Ct. Hse.: Mar. v.30 & 31, #249)
LEBOEUF, Josephine Olivia (Eugene & Josephine LEDET) b. 7 Jan. 1897 (Montegut Ch.: v.6, p.50)
LEBOEUF, Julien Paul (Etienne & Elizabeth GUIDRY) b. 4 Oct. 1897 (Montegut Ch.: v.6, p.70)

LEBOEUF, Julienne (Theles & Rosine CARRERE) b. 18 Feb. 1897 (Montegut Ch.: v.6, p.54)

LEBOEUF, Laura (Charles & Marie HEBERT) m. 26 Dec. 1899 Wallace SAMANIE (Houma Ct. Hse.: Mar. v.31 & 32, #201)

LEBOEUF, Lidia Esthel (Joachim & Josephine LEVRON) b. 5 Oct. 1898 (Houma Ch.: v.5, p.220)

LEBOEUF, Lisca (Gabriel & Lucia BOURG) buried: 19 Dec. 1897 at age 19 yrs. (Montegut Ch.: v.2, p.13)

LEBOEUF, Mack (Eugene & Zoe LEBLANC) m. 24 April 1899 Odelia MOLAISON (Houma Ct. Hse.: Mar. v.31 & 32, #416)

LEBOEUF, Maggie (d.Theophile & Philomene COULLATRE) m. 31 Jan. 1898 Artilien DUPRE (Montegut Ch.: v.4, p.234)

LEBOEUF, Maggie (Theophile & Philomene COULLATRE) m. 12 Jan. 1898 Artelien DUPRE (Houma Ct. Hse.: Mar. v.30 & 31, #198)

LEBOEUF, Marcellin (Desire & Lily SAMANIA) b. 9 Jan. 1898 (Houma Ch.: v.5, p.197)

LEBOEUF, Marcelline Adeline (Victor & A. BUQUET) b. 14 March 1899 (Houma Ch.: v.5, p.242)

LEBOEUF, Marie (Joseph & Odelia GAUTREAU) m. 22 April 1899 Theodore BRUNET (Houma Ct. Hse.: Mar. v.31 & 32, #412)

LEBOEUF, Marie (Joseph & Odelia GAUTREAUX) m. 15 May 1899 Theodore BRUNET (Montegut Ch.: v.4, p.263)

LEBOEUF, Marie Aimee Esthel (Beattie & Olympe HEBERT) b. 3 May 1896 (Montegut Ch.: v.6, p.38)

LEBOEUF, Marie Ambroisine (Frank & Josephine POSSEQUAR) b. 8 Jan. 1896 (Montegut Ch.: v.4, p.36)

LEBOEUF, Marie Attie (Joseph & Odilia GAUTREAUX) d. 20 Dec. 1898 at age 3½ yrs. (Montegut Ch.: v.2, p.22)

LEBOEUF, Marie Carrie (Faustin & Odile DUPRE) b. 8 Dec. 1897 (Montegut Ch.: v.6, p.63)

LEBOEUF, Marie Eveline (Clovis & Nolia PICOU) b. 12 Aug. 1899 (Montegut Ch.: v.6, p.94)

LEBOEUF, Marie Lonelia (Etienne & Alida BOURG) b. 21 Feb. 1899 (Montegut Ch.: v.6, p.84)

LEBOEUF, Mary Virginie (Desire & Lalia SAMANIE) b. 13 Sept. 1899 (Houma Ch.: v.5, p.254)

LEBOEUF, Melinas m. 17 Feb. 1896 Noe LEBLANC (Thib. Ct. Hse.: Mar. v.35, #40)

LEBOEUF, Olivain Onesippe (U. & Emma DAIGLE) b. 6 Sept. 1898 (Thib. Ch.: v.7, p.571)

LEBOEUF, Olivia (Eugene & Zoe LEBLANC) m. 3 Nov. 1896 Joanie VEYRE (Chacahoula Ch.: v.1, p.59)

LEBOEUF, Olivia (Eugene & Zoe LEBLANC) m. 3 Nov. 1896 Joani VEYRE (Houma Ct. Hse.: Mar. v.29 & 30, #171)

LEBOEUF, Oscar d. 8 Oct. 1898 at age 54 yrs. (Montegut Ch.: v.2, p.21)

LEBOEUF, Ovilia m.(1) Sylvere DUPRE, d. 15 April 1892; m.(2) Ernest DARCE, 23 June 1898. Children: Albert; Alphonse; Exelina m. Simon LEBLANC; Octave; Victorine;

Joseph; Jean Marie; Frances. Tutorship: 1 June 1897. (Houma Ct. Hse.: Succ. #885)

LEBOEUF, Ovilia (Jean & Rosalie DUPRE) m. 23 June 1898 Ernest DARCE (Houma Ct. Hse.: Mar. v.30 & 31, #29)

LEBOEUF, Philippe Joseph (Willy & Emma DAIGLE) b. 14 April 1896 (Houma Ch.: v.5, p.179)

LEBOEUF, Pierre Emile (Frank & Josehine POSECAILLE) b. 18 Jan. 1899 (Montegut Ch.: v.6, p.89)

LEBOEUF, Theles Domingue (Theles & Flosine CARRIE) b. 15 Jan. 1899 (Theriot Ch.: v.2, p.39)

LEBOEUF, Theogene m. 11 May 1897 Marie MOLAISON (Houma Ct. Hse.: Mar. v.29 & 30, #412)

LEBOEUF, Theogene (Eugene & Zoe LEBLANC) m. 3 June 1897 Marie MOLAISON (Chacahoula Ch.: v.1, p.63)

LEBOEUF, Victor (Joseph & Elmire DUPRE) m. 30 Dec. 1899 Valerie DUPLANTIS (Houma Ct. Hse.: Mar. v.31 & 32, #221)

LEBOEUF, Victor Ignace (Alexis & Augusta DELOTTE) b. 17 Jan. 1897 (Chacahoula Ch.: v.4, p.12)

LEBRUN, Octave (Leon & Octavie VICKNER) m. 12 April 1899 Anna BARRIOS (Lockport Ch.: v.2, p.205)

LEBRUN, Octave V. (Leon & Octavie VICKNER) m. 12 April 1899 Anna BARRIOS (Thib. Ct. Hse.: Mar. v.39, #137)

LECCO, Felix Francis (Gaudio & Victorine BOURG) b. 17 Feb. 1899 (Montegut Ch.: v.6, p.87)

LECHE, Celeste (Ernest & Josephine LEONARD) m. 24 Fb. 1897 Philippe BOURGEOIS (Thib. Ch.: v.14, p.130)

LECHE, Celeste (Ernest & Josephine LEONARD) m. 24 Feb. 1897 Philippe BOURGEOIS (Thib. Ct. Hse.: Mar. v.36, #78)

LECHE, Chester Adam (James & Adoska HEBERT) b. 6 June 1898 (Thib. Ch.: v.7, p.501)

LECHE, Lea (Ernest & Josephine LEONARD) m. 27 Jan. 1897 Victor PORTIER (Thib. Ct. Hse.: Mar. v.36, #39)

LECHE, Mina (Ernest & Josephine LEONARD) m. 9 July 1896 William WEST (Thib. Ch.: v.14, p.96)

LECHE, Mina (Ernest & Josephine LEONARD) m. 9 July 1896 William WEST, of East Baton Rouge (Thib. Ct. Hse.: Mar. v.36, #121)

LECOMPTE (Sometimes: LECOMTE)

LECOMPTE, Adele Rebecca (Frank & Sclisie BRUNET) b. 27 Oct. 1898 (Theriot Ch.: v.2, p.33)

LECOMPTE, Aline Josephine (Lucien & Selima HENRI) b. 15 Dec. 1898 (Houma Ch.: v.5, p.231)

LECOMPTE, Allan Romain (Eugene & Elidia GOODCH) b. 28 Feb. 1899 (Montegut Ch.: v.6, p.87)

LECOMPTE, Aubin (Joseph & Alida GUIDRY) m. 18 May 1899 Johanna CUNIO (Houma Ct. Hse.: Mar. v.31 & 32, #7)

LECOMPTE, Aubin (Joseph & Alida GUIDRY) m. 10 June 1899 Johanna CUNEO (Montegut Ch.: v.4, p.265)

LECOMPTE, Augustin Cleophat (Joseph & Emelie BETHANCOURT) b. 26 June 1896 (Montegut Ch.: v.6, p.42)
LECOMPTE, Brigitte m. 14 Jan. 1899 Alidore FALGOUT (Houma Ct. Hse.: Mar. v.30 & 31, #230)
LECOMPTE, Brigitte (Francois & Julia FALGOUT) m. 23 Jan. 1899 Alidor FALGOUT (Montegut Ch.: v.4, p.251)
LECOMPTE, Charles Joseph (Charles & Eve DUPRE) b. 25 Nov. 1897 (Montegut Ch.: v.6, p.64)
LECOMPTE, Charles Ruffin (Nieles & Leodile CHAUVIN) b. 10 June 1897 (Montegut Ch.: v.6, p.58)
LECOMPTE, Claude Isidor (Colombus & Emma FORET) b. 4 April 1897 (Montegut Ch.: v.6, p.53)
LECOMPTE, Elise (Pierre & Adeline CUNNINGHAM) m. 22 Feb. 1897 Arthur LIRETTE (Montegut Ch.: v.4, p.218)
LECOMPTE, Elise (Pierre & Adeline CUNNINGHAM) m. 10 Feb. 1897 Arthur LIRETTE (Houma Ct. Hse.: Mar. v.29 & 30, #299)
LECOMPTE, Emilie Poela (Clay & Alida ROBICHAUX) b. 26 Jan. 1899 (Montegut Ch.: v.6, p.82)
LECOMPTE, Eva Aglae (Celestine LECOMPTE) b. 20 Nov. 1897 (Theriot Ch.: v.2, p.17)
LECOMPTE, Isabelle Therese (Olaus & Josephine RODAY) b. 17 March 1897 (Montegut Ch.: v.6, p.56)
LECOMPTE, Jean Gratien (Jean Clay & Alida ROBICHAUX) b. 15 Jan. 1897 (Montegut Ch.: v.6, p.50)
LECOMPTE, Joseph (Francois) d. 7 June 1898 at age 8 days (Montegut Ch.: v.2, p.17)
LECOMPTE, Joseph Bailey (Joseph & Emelie BETHANCOURT) b. 13 March 1898 (Montegut Ch.: v.6, p.68)
LECOMPTE, Joseph Elcee (Freeman & Julienne BERGERON) d. 21 May 1896 at age 5 mths., & 18 days (Montegut Ch.: v.2, p.5)
LECOMPTE, Joseph Eliee (Freeman & Julienne BERGERON) b. 3 Jan. 1896 (Montegut Ch.: v.6, p.33)
LECOMPTE, Joseph F. X. (Ernestine LECOMPTE) bt. 13 April 1896 (Theriot Ch.: v.1-B, p.90)
LECOMPTE, Joseph Felix (Will & Rosalia LEBLANC) b. 30 Dec. 1897 (Theriot Ch.: v.2, p.18)
LECOMPTE, Joseph Leonce (Justin & Laura ARTIGUE) b. 6 Nov. 1896 (Montegut Ch.: v.6, p.48)
LECOMPTE, Joseph Luly (Freeman & Julienne BERGERON) b. 19 March 1897 (Houma Ch.: v.5, p.204)
LECOMPTE, Josephine Laurine (Frank & Laura PITRE) b. 11 Dec. 1896 (Montegut Ch.: v.6, p.48)
LECOMPTE, Louis Even (Frank & Celesie BRUNET) b. 22 March 1896 (Theriot Ch.: v.1-B, p.90)
LECOMPTE, Maggie (Francois & d.Julia FALGOUT) m. 6 Feb. 1899 Michel PROSPERI (Montegut Ch.: v.4, p.256)
LECOMPTE, Maggie (Francois & Julia FALGOUT) m. 14 Jan. 1899 Michel PROSPER (Houma Ct. Hse.: Mar. v.30 & 31, #231)
LECOMPTE, Marguerite Eugenie (Nickles & Leodile CHAUVIN) b. 1 Feb. 1899 (Montegut Ch.: v.6, p.89)

LECOMPTE, Marie Augustine (Frank & Laura PITRE) b. 21 Jan. 1898 (Montegut Ch.: v.6, p.65)
LECOMPTE, Marie Berthilde Vayola (Francois & Julia FALGOUT) b. 22 July 1896 (Montegut Ch.: v.6, p.43)
LECOMPTE, Martha Marie (Oleus & Josephine RODDY) b. 14 Dec. 1898 (Houma Ch.: v.5, p.234)
LECOMPTE, Nickless m. 28 March 1896 Leodile CHAUVIN (Houma Ct. Hse.: Mar. v.29 & 30, #26)
LECOMPTE, Nickless (Joseph & Alida GUIDRY) m. 30 April 1896 Leodile CHAUVIN (Montegut Ch.: v.4, p.209)
LECOMPTE, Paul (Roger & Celina Madeleine BRAULT) d. 23 July 1897 at age 1 yr. & 15 days (Montegut Ch.: v.2, p.11)
LECOMPTE, Paul Maurice (Eugene & Eulodia GOOCK) b. 22 Jan. 1898 (Montegut Ch.: v.6, p.71)
LECOMPTE, Paul Zenon (Roger & Celina BRAULT) b. 9 July 1896 (Montegut Ch.: v.6, p.42)
LECOMPTE, Pierre Sylvestre (Colomb & Emma FORET) d. 19 Sept. 1899 at age 6 mths. & 7 days (Montegut Ch.: v.2, p.29)
LECOMPTE, Pierre Sylvestre (Colomb & Emma FORET) b. 13 March 1899 (Montegut Ch.: v.6, p.85)
LECOMPTE, Virginie m. d.Michel BELANGER d. 21 Aug. 1899 at age 84 yrs. (Montegut Ch.: v.2, p.28)
LECOMPTE, Wilfrid Sidney (Roger & Celina BREAULT) b. 11 Oct. 1897 (Montegut Ch.: v.6, p.61)
LECOMPTE, William Euslache (William & Rosalie LEBLANC) b. 16 March 1896 (Theriot Ch.: v.1-B, p.90)

LEDET (Sometimes: LEDE, LEDEE, LEDAY)
LEDET, Agustave (Joseph & Marie VETO) m. 23 April 1898 Louise HUTCHISON (Montegut Ch.: v.4, p.243)
LEDET, Alexandre (Prosper & Celema BREAUX) m. 9 Jan. 1896 Elisabeth LAGARDE (Thib. Ct. Hse.: Mar. v.35, #2)
LEDET, Alexandre (Prosper & Celima BREAUX) m. 9 Jan. 1896 Elizabeth LAGARDE (Thib. Ch.: v.13, p.90)
LEDET, Alfred Thomas (Emile & Angelina MALBROUGH) b. 7 March 1896 (Montegut Ch.: v.6, p.34)
LEDET, Alida Marie (Emile & Angelina MARLBOROUGH) b. 6 Jan. 1899 (Montegut Ch.: v.6, p.81)
LEDET, Amanda (Josep & Marie VETO) m. 19 Jan. 1898 Leopold SCOTT (Houma Ct. Hse.: Mar. v.30 & 31, #232)
LEDET, Amanda (Joseph & Marie --ITEAU) m. 3 Feb. 1898 Loepold SCOTT (Montegut Ch.: v.4, p.235)
LEDET, Anette Ondine (Leon & Helene TOUPS) b. 29 Nov. 1896 (Thib. Ch.: v.7, p.428)
LEDET, Antoine Alcee (Oscar & Celina KEEF) b. 24 Oct. 1896 (Larose Ch.: v.2, p.185)
LEDET, Arthur (Ulysse & Henriette GAUTREAU) m. 17 Feb. 1896 Agathe LEBLANC (Thib. Ch.: v.14, p.80)
LEDET, Arthur (Ulysse & Henriette GUITREAU) m. 12 Feb. 1896 Agathe LEBLANC (Thib. Ct. Hse.: Mar. v.35, #36)

LEDET, Augustave (Joseph & Marie VETO) m. 4 April 1898 Louise HUTCHINSON (Houma Ct. Hse.: Mar. v.30 & 31, #370)

LEDET, Augustin Boyd (Frank & Melicie DUPRE) b. 29 Feb. 1896 (Montegut Ch.: v.6, p.36)

LEDET, Beatrice Marguerite (Azemee & Louise DIAS) b. 26 May 1899 (Thib. Ch.: v.7, p.606)

LEDET, Berthe Suzanne d. 26 Jan. 1896 at age 17 yrs. & 5 mths. (Thib. Ch.: v.3, p.178)

LEDET, Blanche Marguerite (Leo & Irma ESTIVEN) b. 31 March 1898 (Thib. Ch.: v.7, p.494)

LEDET, Camila (Hyman & Celemie BAILLE) m. 8 Jan. 1896 Albert LEJEUNE (Thib. Ch.: v.13, p.91)

LEDET, Camilla (Ilman & Celemie BAILLE) m. 8 Jan. 1896 Albert LEJEUNE (Thib. Ct. Hse.: Mar. v.35, #194)

LEDET, Camille Ambroise (Arthur & Georgina TOUPS) b. 7 Jan. 1896 (Thib. Ch.: v.7, p.389)

LEDET, Cecile (Leo & Caroline TOUPS) m. 3 Feb. 1897 Walter BERGERON (Thib. Ch.: v.14, p.121)

LEDET, Cecile (Leo & Caroline TOUPS) m. 3 Feb. 1897 Walter BERGERON (Thib. Ct. Hse.: Mar. v.36, #59)

LEDET, Cecilia (Paulin & Lydia BOURGEOIS) b. 4 May 1897 (Thib. Ch.: v.7, p.449)

LEDET, Claire Aline (Ernest & Angelina ERLNIDEZ) b. 12 Dec. 1897 (Thib. Ch.: v.7, p.475)

LEDET, Danis d. 4 Nov. 1897 at age 4 wks. (Houma Ch.: v.3, p.14)

LEDET, Denis Colombus (Joseph &Elise DUPRE) b. 12 Oct. 1899 (Montegut Ch.: v.6, p.94)

LEDET, Edgard Augustin (Gustave & Merthilia ORGERON) b. 14 Jan. 1899 (Larose Ch.: v.3, p.34)

LEDET, Edouard Leo (Leo & Caroline TOUPS) b. 22 Aug. 1898 (Thib. Ch.: v.7, p.560)

LEDET, Elizabeth m. Kleber LAGARDE d. 12 Nov. 1899 at age 23 yrs. & 2 mths. (Thib. Ch.: v.3, p.243)

LEDET, Elles (Ulysse & Henriette GUIDROZ) m. 20 Oct. 1896 Angele BREAUX (Thib. Ct. Hse.: Mar. v.36, #154)

LEDET, Elma Rita (Alexandre & Elizabeth LAGARDE) b. 15 July 1898 (Thib. Ch.: v.7, p.506)

LEDET, Emilie (Gustave & Justillia ORGERON) d. 14 March 1898 at age 11 mths. (Larose Ch.: v.1, p.42)

LEDET, Euclide d. 20 Sept. 1899 at age 10 mths. (Thib. Ch.: v.3, p.240)

LEDET, Evela Emilie (Gustave & Mertillia ORGERON) b. 15 March 1897 (Larose Ch.: v.3, p.13)

LEDET, Felicien (Livoday & Marie MARLBOROUGH) m. 6 Feb. 1899 Clothilde DUPRE (Montegut Ch.: v.4, p.256)

LEDET, Felicien (Livode & Marie MALBROUGH) m. 21 Jan. 1899 Clotilde DUPRE (Houma Ct. Hse.: Mar. v.30 & 31, #275)

LEDET, Felix (Armand & Mathilde BABIN) m. 20 April 1899 Julia MANZEROLLES (Thib. Ct. Hse.: Mar. v.39, #126)

LEDET, Felix (Armand & Mathilde BABIN) m. 20 April 1899 Julia MONZEROLLES (Thib. Ch.: v.14, p.272)

LEDET, Francine m. 11 Jan. 1897 William KELLY (Larose Ch.: v.3, p.4)

LEDET, Francine m. 11? Jan. 1897 William KELLY (Lockport Ch.: v.4, p.121)

LEDET, Francine m. 2 Jan. 1897 William KELLY (Thib. Ct. Hse.: Mar. v.36, #2)

LEDET, Francois Robert (Auguste & Marie GRIFFIN) b. 20 Dec. 1898 (Larose Ch.: v.3, p.43)

LEDET, Franklin Henri (Marcel & Laura CANTRELLE) b. 15 March 1896 (Lockport Ch.: v.2, p.326)

LEDET, George d. 22 May 1897 at age 9 yrs. (Thib. Ch.: v.3, p.200)

LEDET, Harry Joseph (Joseph & Denisia KALAHAN) b. 19 Sept. 1899 (Larose Ch.: v.3, p.45)

LEDET, Helene (Ulysse & Josephine GAUBERT) m. 25 Feb. 1897 Leon LEGENDRE (Thib. Ch.: v.14, p.131)

LEDET, Helene (Ulysses & Josephine GAUBERT) m. 25 Feb. 1897 Leon LEGENDRE (Thib. Ct. Hse.: Mar. v.36, #73)

LEDET, Jean Julien (Olaus & Esther BOQUET) b. 5 Dec. 1896 (Montegut Ch.: v.6, p.51)

LEDET, Jeanne (Sim & Silvie DORSEY) b. 8 June 1899 (Houma Ch.: v.5, p.248)

LEDET, Jeanne Annette (Arthur & Georgine TOUPS) b. 24 Nov. 1896 (Thib. Ch.: v.7, p.477)

LEDET, Joseph Antoine (Marcel & Laura CANTRELLE) b. 1 Sept. 1899 (Larose Ch.: v.3, p.44)

LEDET, Joseph Arnold (Marcellin & Madeleine RICHOUX) b. 1 May 1898 (Larose Ch.: v.3, p.18)

LEDET, Joseph Arsene (Arthur & Malvina BAYE) b. 14 May 1897 (Thib. Ch.: v.7, p.451)

LEDET, Joseph Bagley (Felicien & Clothilde DUPRE) b. 30 Dec. 1899 (Montegut Ch.: v.6, p.98)

LEDET, Joseph Elfege (Jules & Helene MELANCON) b. 20 April 1898 (Thib. Ch.: v.7, p.494)

LEDET, Joseph Emilien (Augustin & Clothilde DUPRE) b. 4 Dec. 1899 (Montegut Ch.: v.6, p.96)

LEDET, Joseph Enard (Augustin & Odile BABIN) b. 27 April 1898 (Thib. Ch.: v.7, p.546)

LEDET, Joseph Fortune (Denis & Margueritte RICHOUX) b. 1 March 1898 (Larose Ch.: v.3, p.16)

LEDET, Joseph Nickles (Joseph & Elise DUPRE) b. 18 Oct. 1896 (Montegut Ch.: v.6, p.46)

LEDET, Joseph Raoul (Antoine & Angelina GISCLAR) b. 10 Feb. 1899 (Larose Ch.: v.3, p.37)

LEDET, Joseph Wiley (Lygnes & Veronie PITRE) b. 30 Aug. 1899 (Montegut Ch.: v.6, p.92)

LEDET, Josephine (Ulysse & Josephine GAUBERT) m. 6 Oct. 1898 Theophile LAROSE (Thib. Ct. Hse.: Mar. v.38, #279)

LEDET, Josephine (Ulysse & Josephine GAUBERT) m. 6 Oct. 1898 Theophile LAROSE (Thib. Ch.: v.14, p.226)
LEDET, Jules Claude (Philippe & Clara LAGARDE) b. 10 April 1897 (Thib. Ch.: v.7, p.445)
LEDET, Justilien (Louis & Olinda GUIDRY) m. 20 Jan. 1898 Julia RODAY (Montegut Ch.: v.4, p.230)
LEDET, Justilien (Louis & Olinda GUIDRY) m. 7 Jan. 1898 Julia RODDY (Houma Ct. Hse.: Mar. v.30 & 31, #186)
LEDET, Leola Marie (Leo & Anna ESTIVEN) b. 24 Sept. 1899 (Thib. Ch.: v.7, p.569)
LEDET, Leonard d. 25 July 1896 at age 24 yrs. & 8 mths. (Thib. Ch.: v.3, p.185)
LEDET, Leonard Abel (Arthur & Georgina TOUPS) b. 15 Dec. 1899 (Thib. Ch.: v.7, p.579)
LEDET, Livaudais m. 18 Jan. 1898 Angelique TROSCLAIR (Larose Ch.: v.3, p.7)
LEDET, Livaudais m. 18 Jan. 1898 Angelique TROSCLAIR (Larose Ch.: v.4, p.111)
LEDET, Livaudais m. 18 Jan. 1898 Angelique TROXLAIR (Thib. Ct. Hse.: Mar. v.37, #23)
LEDET, Louis Leonard (Alexandre & Elisabeth LAGARDE) b. 12 Nov. 1896 (Thib. Ch.: v.7, p.426)
LEDET, Louise Rita (Philippe & Clara LAGARDE) b. 23 March 1899 (Thib. Ch.: v.7, p.541)
LEDET, Luc (Louis & Eveline GUIDRY) m. 18 April 1898 Laurencia SCOTT (Montegut Ch.: v.4, p.242)
LEDET, Luke (Louis & Eveline GUIDRY) m. 5 April 1898 Laurencia SCOTT (Houma Ct. Hse.:Mar. v.30 & 31, #374)
LEDET, Mabel Rita (Laurent & Clara GUILLOTE) b. 30 Jan. 1898 (Thib. Ch.: v.7, p.491)
LEDET, Marcelle Jerome (Prosper & Eloise BAUVAIS) b. 18 Jan. 1898 (Thib. Ch.: v.7, p.536)
LEDET, Marguerite Isabella (Leo & Irma STEVEN) b. 14 Nov. 1896 (Thib. Ch.: v.7, p.429)
LEDET, Marie Annette (Ernest & Amelia GAUBERT) b. 2 Aug. 1898 (Thib. Ch.: v.7, p.506)
LEDET, Marie Annette (Ozemee & Louise DIAZ) b. 6 April 1897 (Raceland Ch.: v.5, p.46)
LEDET, Marie Edith (Prosper & Eloise BEAUVAIS) b. 30 Oct. 1896 (Thib. Ch.: v.7, p.426)
LEDET, Marie Elise (Livaudais & Angelique TROXLAIR) b. 3 Jan. 1899 (Larose Ch.: v.3, p.34)
LEDET, Marie Emilienne (Emile & Angelina MALBOROUGH) b. 24 Aug. 1897 (Montegut Ch.: v.6, p.60)
LEDET, Marie Helene (Leon & Helene TOUPS) b. 26 March 1898 (Thib. Ch.: v.7, p.492)
LEDET, Marie Josephine (Luc & Laurentia SCOTT) d. 14 June 1899 at age 5 mths. (Montegut Ch.: v.2, p.26)
LEDET, Marie Josephine (Luc & Laurentine SCOTT) b. 16 Jan. 1899 (Montegut Ch.: v.6, p.80)

LEDET, Marie Josephine (Olaus & Esther BOQUET) b. 20 June 1898 (Montegut Ch.: v.6, p.73)
LEDET, Marie Lea (Paulin & Lydie BOURGEOIS) b. 23 March 1898 (Thib. Ch.: v.7, p.543)
LEDET, Marie Leola (Augustin & Clotilde DUPRE) b. 15 June 1897 (Montegut Ch.: v.6, p.57)
LEDET, Marie Lilia (Joseph & Denisia CALLAHEIN) b. 13 Dec. 1896 (Larose Ch.: v.2, p.190)
LEDET, Marie Lorenza (Augustin & Lilianne HOTARD) b. 3 March 1899 (Montegut Ch.: v.6, p.83)
LEDET, Marie Odille (Oscar & Camillia RODRIGUE) b. 8 April 1898 (Larose Ch.: v.3, p.18)
LEDET, Marie Ulyssia (Joseph & Louisiane BABIN) b. 25 Sept. 1897 (Thib. Ch.: v.7, p.523)
LEDET, Marie Voyola (Justilien & Julia RODAY) b. 3 Nov. 1898 (Montegut Ch.: v.6, p.78)
LEDET, Octavie (Prosper & Celina BREAUX) m. 30 Jan. 1899 Anicet KNOBLOCH (Thib. Ct. Hse.: Mar. v.38, #56)
LEDET, Octavie (Prosper & Celina BREAUX) m. 31 Jan. 1899 Anicet KNOBLOCK (Thib. Ch.: v.14, p.251)
LEDET, Odilia Ursule (Ernest & Amelia GAUBERT) b. 4 Sept. 1896 (Thib. Ch.: v.7, p.415)
LEDET, Oscar (Jules & -----) m. 29 April 1897 Camillia RODRIGUEZ (Thib. Ct. Hse.: Mar. v.36, #129)
LEDET, Paul Abbey (Augustave & Eloise HUTCHISON) b. 29 May 1899 (Montegut Ch.: v.6, p.89)
LEDET, Pauline Eloise (Lygnes & Veronique PITRE) b. 12 March 1896 (Montegut Ch.: v.6, p.35)
LEDET, Philomene Julia (Jules & Helene MELANCON) b. 17 Sept. 1896 (Thib. Ch.: v.7, p.419)
LEDET, Pierre Eldon (Oscar & Celima KEEF) b. 30 May 1899 (Larose Ch.: v.3, p.40)
LEDET, Rene Ucride (Ozemee & Louise DIAZ) b. 12 Nov. 1897 (Thib. Ch.: v.7, p.525)
LEDET, Sim m. 13 Feb. 1896 Sylvia DARCE (Houma Ct. Hse: Mar. v.28, #457)
LEDET, Simms (Adam & Sidonise TRAHAN) m. 18 Feb. 1896 Sylvia DARCE (Houma Ch.: v.6-a, p.172)
LEDET, Sylvain Marcel (Marcel & Laura CANTRELLE) b. 17 Feb. 1898 (Larose Ch.: v.3, p.16)
LEDET, Sylvestre Alick (Augustin & Odile BABIN) b. 2 Oct. 1896 (Thib. Ch.: v.7, p.421)
LEDET, Theophile (Prosper & Celima BRAUD) m. 7 June 1899 Hilda BOURGEOIS (Thib. Ct. Hse.: Mar. v.39, #172)
LEDET, Theophile (Prospere & Celima BRAUD) m. 7 June 1899 Elda BOURGEOIS (Thib. Ch.: v.14, p.284)
LEDET, Valerie Emelie (Leon & Helene TOUPS) b. 21 Dec. 1898 (Thib. Ch.: v.7, p.579)

LEE (Sometimes: HELI)

LEE, Elizabeth or Lizzie m. 17 Aug. 1899 Thomas JONES (Thib. Ct. Hse.: Mar. v.39, #212)

LEE, Emilie Elisabeth (---- & Marguerite -----) b. 1 Aug. 1898 (Larose Ch.: v.3, p.23)
LEE, Jean d. 31 Dec. 1898 at age 21 yrs. (Larose Ch.: v.1, p.45)
LEE, Joseph Richard (Francois & Emma SAVOIE) b. 22 Oct. 1898 (Larose Ch.: v.3, p.29)
LEE, Julia Letitia (Andre & Azalie Clementine CROSBY) m. 14 Dec. 1896 Martial Felicien CALLAIS (Thib. Ct. Hse.: Mar. v.36, #167)
LEE, Laura m. ---- 1899 Anatole HEBERT (Larose Ch.: v.4, p.131)
LEE, Laura m. 15 Jan. 1898 Anatole HEBERT (Thib. Ct. Hse.: Mar. v.37, #1)
LEE, Laura m. 19 - 30 Dec. 1899 Anatole HEBERT Both of Lafourche Parish. (Larose Ch.: v.3, p.13)
LEE, Lilly m. 12 Feb. 1896 Thomas COLLINS (Houma Ct. Hse.: Mar. v.28, #453)
LEE, Marcillia Isabella (Pierre Achille & Delphine CALET) b. 19 Nov. 1896 (Larose Ch.: v.3, p.4)
LEE, Marie Virginie d. 10 Nov. 1898 at age 41 yrs. (Thib. Ch.: v.3, p.221)
LEE, Mary m. 24 March 1897 Royal DYER (Houma Ct. Hse.: Mar. v.29 & 30, #361)
LEE, Paul Benoit (Cleopha & Rosalie GALJOUR) b. 12 Feb. 1898 (Larose Ch.: v.3, p.27)
LEE, Pierre Hennesy (Pierre & Dolphine CALET) b. 13 Dec. 1898 (Larose Ch.: v.3, p.42)
LEE, Richard m. 26 April 1899 Delia WALLIS (Houma Ct. Hse.: Mar. v.31 & 32, #424)
LEE, Rosine A. m. 19 March 1898 Armand J. GUIDRY (Thib. Ct. Hse.: Mar. v.37, #114)
LEE, Seraphine (Cleopha & Rosalie GAGOUR) m. 23 April 1898 Orville FREMIN (Larose Ch.: v.4, p.11)
LEE, Sophie (Robert & Ophelia KLING) b. 20 July 1897 (Thib. Ch.: v.7, p.514)
LEE, Victor m. 10 Feb. 1897 Ida SHERMAN (Thib. Ct. Hse.: Mar. v.36, #76)

LEFORT (Sometimes: LEFOUR)
LEFORT, Alexis m. 27 April 1899 Anna PIERCE (Thib. Ct. Hse.: Mar. v.39, #159)
LEFORT, Alexis m. 6 May 1899 Anna PIERCE (Larose Ch.: v.3, p.11)
LEFORT, Alexis m. 6 May 1899 Anne PIERCE (Larose Ch.: v.4, p.106)
LEFORT, Allain Hyppolite (Hyppolite & Alice GAUDE) b. 15 Oct. 1898 (Larose Ch.: v.3, p.29)
LEFORT, Aurore (Noel & Jeanne JAMBON) m. 28 May 1898 Edmond MARTIN (Thib. Ct. Hse.: Mar. v.38, #177)
LEFORT, Edgard Antoine (Martial & Louise GAUDE) b. 11 May 1899 (Larose Ch.: v.3, p.41)

LEFORT, Emilienne (Adrien & Elisa PITRE) b. 18 March 1897 (Larose Ch.: v.3, p.7)

LEFORT, Fernand Joseph (Emile P. & Adeline TETREAU) b. 23 Jan. 1896 (Thib. Ch.: v.7, p.390)

LEFORT, Joseph Donat (Emilien & Elmire HENRY) b. 19 Jan. 1899 (Larose Ch.: v.3, p.36)

LEFORT, Josephine m. 22 June 1897 Joseph PICCIOLA (Thib. Ct. Hse.: Mar. v.36, #180)

LEFORT, Josephine m. 26 June 1897 Joseph PICCIOLA (Larose Ch.: v.4, p.64)

LEFORT, Josephine m. 26 June 1897 Joseph PICCIOLA (Larose Ch.: v.3, p.6)

LEFORT, Lilianne Marie (Paul & Emilie RAYMOND) b. 17 Aug. 1898 (Larose Ch.: v.3, p.31)

LEFORT, Louise Mabel (Pierre Wallis & Louise TUCKER) b. 15 March 1898 (Thib. Ch.: v.7, p.490)

LEFORT, Marie Edia (Deoda & Euphemie LEBLANC) b. 13 March 1897 (Lockport Ch.: v.3, #34)

LEFORT, Martial of Lafourche Parish (Felicien & Marcelline PITRE) m. 2 July 1898 Louis GAUDET, of Lafourche Parish (Larose Ch.: v.3, p.9)

LEFORT, Martial (Felicien & Marcelline PITRE) m. 2 July 1898 Louise GAUDET (Thib. Ct. Hse.: Mar. v.38, #216)

LEFORT, Martial (Felicien & Marcelline PITRE) m. 2 July 1898 Louise GAUDET (Larose Ch.: v.4, p.20)

LEFORT, Paul m. 11 June 1897 Emilie RAYMOND (Larose Ch.: v.3, p.6)

LEFORT, Paul m. 11 June 1897 Emilie RAYMOND (Larose Ch.: v.4, p.77)

LEFORT, Paul m. 29 May 1897 Emelie RAYMOND (Thib. Ct. Hse.: Mar. v.36, #152)

LEFORT, Philippe Jean Hercule (Emile & Adeline TETREAU) b. 24 June 1899 (Thib. Ch.: v.7, p.553)

LEGAULT, Benitta (Gorio & Victorine BOURK) b. 21 March 1897 (Theriot Ch.: v.2, p.2)

LEGENDRE, ----- boy d. 13 Sept. 1898 at birth (Thib. Ch.: v.3, p.220)

LEGENDRE, Aimee Marie (Joseph & Felicia GAUBERT) b. 18 Jan. 1899 (Thib. Ch.: v.7, p.531)

LEGENDRE, Albert d. 8 Aug. 1899 at age 24 days (Raceland Ch.: v.1, p.26)

LEGENDRE, Anna (Adrien & Adolphina THEBE) b. 18 June 1898 (Chackbay Ch.: v.1, p.115)

LEGENDRE, Armel Klebert (Klebert & Olynda Marie MALBROUGH) b. 4 Jan. 1898 (Thib. Ch.: v.7, p.479)

LEGENDRE, Augustave minor over 18 (Augustave LEGENDRE) Emancipation: 16 May 1898. (Thib. Ct. Hse.: Succ. #1534)

LEGENDRE, Augustin (Victor & Adelaide GOBERT) m. 11 April 1898 Tibicia RODRIGUE (Thib. Ct. Hse.: Mar. v.37, #135)

LEGENDRE, Augustin (Victor & d.Adelaide GOBERT) m. 11 April 1898 Tilicia RODRIGUE (Chackbay Ch.: v.1, p.59)

LEGENDRE, Ben d. 19 July 1897 at age 7 mths. (Raceland Ch.: v.1, p.14)
LEGENDRE, Celestine (Joseph & Azilie RODRIGUE) b. 3 March 1896 (Chackbay Ch.: v.1, p.64)
LEGENDRE, Charles Benet (Arthur & Eloise LEPINE) b. 3 Jan. 1897 (Raceland Ch.: v.5, p.41)
LEGENDRE, Denis Emile d. 15 May 1896 at age 15 mths. & 9 days (Thib. Ch.: v.3, p.182)
LEGENDRE, Ella Dora (Leonard & Marie ELULEE) b. 20 Jan. 1899 (Raceland Ch.: v.5, p.90)
LEGENDRE, Eugene (Joseph & Felicia GAUBERT) m. 5 April 1899 Alice BOUDREAUX (Thib. Ct. Hse.: Mar. v.39, #123)
LEGENDRE, Eugene (Joseph & Felicia GAUBERT) m. 5 April 1899 Alice BOUDREAUX (Thib. Ch.: v.14, p.269)
LEGENDRE, Georges Paulin (Klebert & Marie MALBROUGH) b. 23 Jan. 1899 (Thib. Ch.: v.7, p.585)
LEGENDRE, Irene Brigitte (Camille & Helene LEGENDRE) b. 9 Oct. 1898 (Thib. Ch.: v.7, p.515)
LEGENDRE, James Norbert (Oscar & Marie BONVILAIN) b. 25 Sept. 1897 (Thib. Ch.: v.7, p.466)
LEGENDRE, Joseph (Antoine & Adele GAUBERT) m. 8 Feb. 1899 Josephine GUILLOT (Thib. Ct. Hse.: Mar. v.38, #77)
LEGENDRE, Joseph (Antoine & Adele GAUBERT) m. 8 Feb. 1899 Josephine GUILLOT (Thib. Ch.: v.14, p.259)
LEGENDRE, Joseph Armand (Felix & Henriette TOUPS) b. 21 Sept. 1896 (Lockport Ch.: v.2, p.337)
LEGENDRE, Joseph Claude (Leonce & Adolphine TROSCLAIR) b. 4 June 1896 (Chackbay Ch.: v.1, p.69)
LEGENDRE, Joseph Jem (Adrien & Dosina THEBE) bt. 14 March 1896 (Chackbay Ch.: v.1, p.62)
LEGENDRE, Joseph Leopold (Camille & Helene LEGENDRE) b. 28 Aug. 1896 (Thib. Ch.: v.7, p.415)
LEGENDRE, Josephine (Jules & Merante RODRIGUE) m. 7 Feb. 1898 Clet LANDRY (Chackbay Ch.: v.1, p.55)
LEGENDRE, Josephine (Jules & Merante RODRIGUE) m. 7 Feb. 1898 Clet LANDRY (Thib. Ct. Hse.: Mar. v.37, #51)
LEGENDRE, Leo (Jules & Merante RODRIGUE) m. 21 Oct. 1899 Clotilde MARS (Chackbay Ch.: v.1, p.75)
LEGENDRE, Leo (Jules & Merante RODRIGUE) m. 21 Oct. 1899 Clotilde MARS (Thib. Ct. Hse.: Mar. v.39, #246)
LEGENDRE, Leon d. 1 Nov. 1897 at birth (Thib. Ch.: v.3, p.207)
LEGENDRE, Leon (Antoine & Odile GAUBERT) m. 25 Feb. 1897 Helene LEDET (Thib. Ch.: v.14, p.131)
LEGENDRE, Leon (Antoine & Odile GAUBERT) m. 25 Feb. 1897 Helene LEDET (Thib. Ct. Hse.: Mar. v.36, #73)
LEGENDRE, Louis Edey (Leonard & Marie CLAULEY) b. 4 April 1897 (Raceland Ch.: v.5, p.46)
LEGENDRE, Louis Eugene (Emile & Sidonia TOUPS) b. 27 June 1898 (Thib. Ch.: v.7, p.502)

LEGENDRE, Lucette (Victorin & Angelique RODRIGUE) b. 29 June 1898 (Chackbay Ch.: v.1, p.116)
LEGENDRE, Lucia (Placide & Loventia RODRIGUE) b. 16 March 1898 (Chackbay Ch.: v.1, p.109)
LEGENDRE, Lydia Felicie (Joseph A. & Felicia GAUBERT) b. 14 April 1896 (Thib. Ch.: v.7, p.398)
LEGENDRE, Marie Adela (Leon & Ellen LEDET) b. 25 Oct. 1899 (Thib. Ch.: v.7, p.571)
LEGENDRE, Marie Augustilia (Augustin & Tibucia RODRIGUE) b. 9 March 1899 (Chackbay Ch.: v.1, p.129)
LEGENDRE, Marie Cecilia (Walter & Presela PARCK) b. 3 May 1898 (Raceland Ch.: v.5, p.70)
LEGENDRE, Marie Edna (Eugene & Alice BOUDREAUX) b. 12 Jan. 1899 (Thib. Ch.: v.7, p.583)
LEGENDRE, Marie Elise (Oscar & Marie BONVILAIN) b. 27 Aug. 1899 (Thib. Ch.: v.7, p.567)
LEGENDRE, Marie Julia (Abedon & Estellina RICHARD) b. 30 July 1897 (Thib. Ch.: v.7, p.459)
LEGENDRE, Marie Julie d. 19 Aug. 1897 at age 3 wks. (Thib. Ch.: v.3, p.204)
LEGENDRE, Marie Marguerite (Walter & Albertine DUFRESNEY) b. 28 Nov. 1899 (Raceland Ch.: v.5, p.108)
LEGENDRE, Norbert (Joseph & Azelie RODRIGUE) b. 31 Jan. 1898 (Chackbay Ch.: v.1, p.108)
LEGENDRE, Norman Francois Philippe (Philippe Francois & Carmelite ROSSIGNOL) b. 16 March 1897 (Thib. Ch.: v.7, p.443)
LEGENDRE, Placide (Victor & Agathe TROSCLAIR) m. 19 April 1897 Lovencia RODRIGUE (Chackbay Ch.: v.1, p.42)
LEGENDRE, Placidre (Victor & Agathe TROSCLAIR) m. 19 April 1897 Lovencia RODRIGUE (Thib. Ct. Hse.: Mar. v.36, #105)
LEGENDRE, Priscilla d. 10 Aug. 1899 at age 22 yrs. (Raceland Ch.: v.1, p.27)
LEGENDRE, Suzane (Leonce & Adolphine TROSCLAIR) b. 1 April 1898 (Chackbay Ch.: v.1, p.110)
LEGENDRE, Ulysses d. 23 Jan. 1899 at age 64 yrs. (Thib. Ch.: v.3, p.226)
LEGENDRE, Victor d. 22 July 1898 at age 85 yrs. (Thib. Ch.: v.3, p.217)
LEGENDRE, Villiers Pierre (Emile & Sidonia TOUPS) b. 19 Oct. 1896 (Thib. Ch.: v.7, p.422)
LEGENDRE, Wallace (Arthur & Louise LEPINE) m. 28 Jan. 1899 Albertine DUFRENE (Thib. Ct. Hse.: Mar. v.38, #34)
LEGENDRE, Wallace (Arthur & Louise LEPINE) m. 28 Jan. 1899 Albertine DUFRENE (Lockport Ch.: v.2, p.198)
LEGENDRE, Walter m. 9 June 1897 Priscilla PARKS (Thib. Ct. Hse.: Mar. v.36, #166)
LEGENDRE, Walter (Arthur & Louise LEPINE) m. 14 June 1897 Presela PARK (Raceland Ch.: v.2, p.43)
LEGENDRE, Willy d. 4 Nov. 1898 at age 2 mths. (Thib. Ch.: v.3, p.221)

LEGENDRE, Willy Adolphe (Abdon & Estellina RICHARD) b. 21 Aug. 1898 (Thib. Ch.: v.7, p.509)

LEJEUNE, Albert (Joseph & Marguerite MARTIN) m. 8 Jan. 1896 Camila LEDET (Thib. Ch.: v.13, p.91)

LEJEUNE, Albert (Joseph & Marguerite MARTIN) m. 8 Jan. 1896 Camilla LEDET (Thib. Ct. Hse.: Mar. v.35, #194)

LEJEUNE, Amadeo m. Velida LEPINE Insanity: 4 June 1896. (Thib. Ct. Hse.: Succ. #1491)

LEJEUNE, Charles m. 18 Nov. 1899 Laura LOLAND Both of Raceland. (Thib. Ct. Hse.: Mar. v.39, #263)

LEJEUNE, Charles (Amadeo & Eveleda LEPINE) m. 18 Nov. 1899 Laura LOLAND (Raceland Ch.: v.2, p.106)

LEJEUNE, Eugenie of Lafourche Parish (Ovide & Eugenie HUNTER) m. 1 Aug. 1898 Luc BREAUX, of Lafourche Parish (Larose Ch.: v.3, p.10)

LEJEUNE, Eugenie (Ovide & Eugenie HUNTER) m. 1 Aug. 1898 Luke BRAUD (Thib. Ct. Hse.: Mar. v.38, #229)

LEJEUNE, Eugenie (Ovide & Eugenie HUNTER) m. 1 Aug. 1898 Luc BREAUX (Larose Ch.: v.4, p.27)

LEJEUNE, Joseph (Marie) b. 17 Sept. 1896 (Thib. Ch.: v.7, p.423)

LEJEUNE, Louis Casimir (Albert & Camilla LEDET) b. 4 March 1897 (Thib. Ch.: v.7, p.443)

LEJEUNE, Marie Lylienne (Albert & Camilla LEDET) b. 13 July 1898 (Thib. Ch.: v.7, p.505)

LEJEUNE, Nita Marie Christine (Henry & Alice DOUCET) b. 3 Oct. 1897 (Thib. Ch.: v.7, p.467)

LEJEUNE, Noema (Ovile & Cecilia BERNARD) m. 21 Dec. 1897 Abel TOUPS (Thib. Ch.: v.14, p.166)

LEJEUNE, Noema (Ovile & Cecilia BERNARD) m. 21 Dec. 1897 Albert or Abel TOUPS (Thib. Ct. Hse.: Mar. v.37, #261)

LEJEUNE, Noemie (Ovide & Cecilia BERNARD) m. 21 Dec. 1896 Aristide TOUPS (Thib. Ch.: v.14, p.105)

LEJEUNE, Noemie (Ovide & Cecilia BERNARD) m. 21 Dec. 1896 Orestide TOUPS (Thib. Ct. Hse.: Mar. v.36, #164)

LEJEUNE, Norma m. Abel TOUPS Emancipation: 10 April 1899 (Thib. Ct. Hse.: Succ. #1573)

LEJEUNE, Valentin Allain (Allain & Louisa MELANCON) b. 14 Feb. 1898 (Thib. Ch.: v.7, p.488)

LELORIC, Wallace (Jean Baptiste & Emilie BERGERON) m. 8 Feb. 1899 Zulma SAVOIE (Thib. Ct. Hse.: Mar. v.38, #28)

LELORIC, Wallace (Jean Baptiste & Emilie BERGERON) m. 8 Feb. 1899 Zulma SAVOIE (Thib. Ch.: v.14, p.261)

LENAIN, Celeste (Jean Baptiste & Marguerite LEGENDRE) m. 20 June 1899 Oleus GAUBERT (Thib. Ct. Hse.: Mar. v.39, #183)

LENAIN, Celeste (Jean Baptiste & Marguerite LEGENDRE) m. 20 June 1899 Oleus GAUBERT (Thib. Ch.: v.14, p.286)

LEO, Magdalena (Carmelo & Biagia DI FURCE) b. 5 Feb. 1896 (Thib. Ch.: v.7, p.394)

LEONARD, Adele (Joseph & Florencia VICNAIRE) m. 18 April 1898 Valmon LEVRON (Thib. Ct. Hse.: Mar. v.37, #138)
LEONARD, Adele (Joseph & Florentia VITENACIE) m. 18 April 1898 Valmon LEVRON (Chackbay Ch.: v.1, p.59)
LEONARD, Agnes Olivia (Aurelian & Franklina BABIN) b. 17 March 1899 (Houma Ch.: v.5, p.242)
LEONARD, Albert (Oleus & Azelie KERN) m. 5 July 1897 Clara DAIGRE (Thib. Ch.: v.14, p.151)
LEONARD, Albert (Oleus & Azelie KERN) m. 5 July 1897 Clara DAIGLE (Thib. Ct. Hse.: Mar. v.36, #176)
LEONARD, Alida m. 17 March 1896 Alcide OLIVIER (Houma Ct. Hse.: Mar. v.29 & 30, #10)
LEONARD, Alida (Adam & Lezida BOUDREAUX) m. 6 April 1896 Alcide OLIVIER (Houma Ch.: v.6-a, p.173)
LEONARD, Amanda Evela (Aureli & Marie CROCHET) b. 26 Feb. 1896 (Houma Ch.: v.5, p.148)
LEONARD, Amede (Ernest & Evelina BOUDREAUX) m. 5 Sept. 1898 Terzile BONVILLAIN (Houma Ch.: v.6-a, p.252)
LEONARD, Amedee m. 20 Aug. 1898 Terzile BONVILLAIN (Houma Ct. Hse.: Mar. v.30 & 31, #84)
LEONARD, Andre Camil (Edmond & Jacqline BABIN) b. 13 April 1898 (Houma Ch.: v.5, p.211)
LEONARD, Antoine Arthur (Aurelie & Marie CROCHET) b. 5 Sept. 1897 (Houma Ch.: v.5, p.188)
LEONARD, Arthur (Leon & Donatile BOURG) m. 7 July 1896 Oceanie ARCEMENT (Thib. Ct. Hse.: Mar. v.36, #114)
LEONARD, Augustin m. 22 Sept. 1896 Felicite MARCEL (Thib. Ct. Hse.: Mar. v.36, #145)
LEONARD, Celestine m.17 Jan. 1898 Alexis HEBERT (Houma Ct. Hse.: Mar. v.30 & 31, #221)
LEONARD, Celestine (Ernest & Evelina BOUDREAUX) m. 27 Jan. 1898 Alexis HEBERT (Houma Ch.: v.6-a, p.225)
LEONARD, Clarence Joseph (Arthur & Oceana ARCEMENT) b. 19 Aug. 1899 (Thib. Ch.: v.8, p.3)
LEONARD, Edmond Henri (Thomas & Antonia LORIO) b. 5 May 1897 (Thib. Ch.: v.7, p.450)
LEONARD, Eduard (Charles & Alcida KELLER) b. 14 July 1898 (Thib. Ch.: v.7, p.555)
LEONARD, Elie (Joseph & d.Julienne DUE) m. 3 June 1899 Uranie NEAL (Montegut Ch.: v.4, p.264)
LEONARD, Elie (Joseph & Julienne USE) m. 16 May 1899 Uranie NEAL (Houma Ct. Hse.: Mar. v.31 & 32, #5)
LEONARD, Elie Roselius (Louis & Eulalie BOUDREAUX) b. 4 Sept. 1897 (Larose Ch.: v.3, p.27)
LEONARD, Emma m. 20 Jan. 1898 Edgar GUILLOT (Houma Ct. Hse.: Mar. v.30 & 31, #239)
LEONARD, Emma (Ernest & Eveline BOUDREAU) m. 3 Jan. 1898 Edgar GUILLOT (Houma Ch.: v.6-a, p.228)
LEONARD, Flavie Buthie (Aurelien & Franchlina BABIN) b. 5 Nov. 1896 (Houma Ch.: v.5, p.165)

LEONARD, Ines Maria (Charles & Alcida KELLER) b. 25 Nov. 1899 (Thib. Ch.: v.8, p.20)

LEONARD, Jacques Clarence Joseph (Albert & Clara DAIGLE) b. 25 July 1897 (Thib. Ch.: v.7, p.507)

LEONARD, Jean Baptiste (Volcar & Eve CHERAMI) b. 21 May 1896 (Larose Ch.: v.2, p.193)

LEONARD, Jean Cecile Mabel (Arthur & Oceana ARSENAT) b. 15 Dec. 1898 (Thib. Ch.: v.7, p.528)

LEONARD, Jenney Claud (Aurelie & Marie CROCHET) b. 16 Sept. 1899 (Theriot Ch.: v.2, p.50)

LEONARD, Joseph Irby (Pete & Elmire POLASKY) b. 8 March 1898 (Chacahoula Ch.: Gibson Ch.: v.2, p.127)

LEONARD, Joseph Irby (Peter & Elmyre POLASKY) b. 8 March 1898 (Chacahoula Ch.: Gibson Records: Mar. Bk., v.1, #39)

LEONARD, Josephine Marie (Alcide & Valerie OLIVIER) b. 25 July 1898 (Houma Ch.: v.5, p.215)

LEONARD, Laura (Edmond & Jacelinat BABIN) b. 25 Feb. 1896 (Houma Ch.: v.5, p.147)

LEONARD, Louise Olenda (Alcide & Valerie OLIVIER) b. 25 Feb. 1897 (Houma Ch.: v.5, p.175)

LEONARD, Lucile Marie Alice (Thomas & Antonia LORIOT) b. 26 June 1899 (Thib. Ch.: v.7, p.609)

LEONARD, Marie Alida (Adam & Lesida BOUDREAU) b. 11 Feb. 1896 (Houma Ch.: v.5, p.147)

LEONARD, Marie Neltie (Ernest & Evelina BOUDREAUX) b. 22 March 1896 (Houma Ch.: v.5, p.175)

LEONARD, Mathilda Mrs. m. d.Nicholas RANDALL Donation of land: 12 Aug. 1896. (Houma Ct. Hse.: Book of Donations: v.A, p.145)

LEONARD, Octave Ignace (Charles & Alcida KELLER) b. 30 July 1896 (Thib. Ch.: v.7, p.412)

LEONARD, Octavie Leonard (Charles & Marie KELLER) b. 28 Feb. 1897 (Thib. Ch.: v.7, p.490)

LEONARD, Theophile Henri (Arthur & Otiana ARSEMA) b. 9 May 1897 (Thib. Ch.: v.7, p.450)

LEONE, Biaggio (Carmelo & Biaggia DIFIORA) b. 5 Nov. 1899 (Thib. Ch.: v.8, p.19)

LEPINE, Earling Gertrude (Felix Alexandre & Marie Gertrude BERTRAND) b. 29 Oct. 1899 (Raceland Ch.: v.5, p.106)

LEPINE, Emma m. 24 Jan. 1898 Denis SEVIN (Thib. Ct. Hse.: Mar. v.37, #44)

LEPINE, Emma (Homere & Marie GUEDRY) m. 24 Jan. 1898 Denis SEVIN (Raceland Ch.: v.2, p.59)

LEPINE, Felix Alexandre (Oscar & Rosela FOLSE) m. 5 May 1898 Marie BERTRAND (Thib. Ct. Hse.: Mar. v.38, #168)

LEPINE, Felix Alexandre (Oscar & Rosela FOLSE) m. 5 May 1898 Marie BERTRAND (Thib. Ch.: v.14, p.203)

LEPINE, Ines Heloise (Wilson & Heloise BERTRAND) b. 12 June 1897 (Thib. Ch.: v.7, p.506)

LEPINE, Maud Antoinette (Wilson & Eloise BERTRAND) b. 12 March 1899 (Thib. Ch.: v.7, p.603)

LEPINE, Phelie (Homere & Marie GUIDRY) m. 28 July 1897 Charles BERGER (Raceland Ch.: v.2, p.46)

LEPINE, Phoebie of St. Mary m. 28 July 1897 Charles BERGER of Franklin (Thib. Ct. Hse.: Mar. v.37, #200)

LERICHE, L. A. A. m. Marie Louisa LERICHE Petition for inventory: 29 March 1899. (Thib. Ct. Hse.: Succ. #1571)

LERILLE, Azema (Julien & Sage BARRIOS) m. 24 June 1897 Eugene ALLEMAN (Lockport Ch.: v.2, p.173)

LERILLE, Azema (Julien & Sages BARRIOS) m. 24 June 1897 Eugene ALLEMAN (Thib. Ct. Hse.: Mar. v.36, #167)

LERILLE, Edgard (Julien & Enagece BARRIOS) m. 13 Feb. 1899 Ernestine ORGERON (Thib. Ct. Hse.: Mar. v.38, #67)

LERILLE, Edgard (Julien & Exagus BARRIOS) m. 13 Feb. 1899 Ernestine ORGERON (Lockport Ch.: v.2, p.204)

LERILLE, Elmire (Julien & Carmelite BARRIOS) m. 13 Feb. 1897 Jules GROS (Thib. Ct. Hse.: Mar. v.36, #62)

LERILLE, Elmire (Louis & Victorine DELAUNE) m. 6 Feb. 1899 Octave John SOMMERS (Thib. Ct. Hse.: Mar. v.38, #55)

LERILLE, Elmire (Louis & Victorine DELAUNE) m. 6 Feb. 1899 Octave John SOMMERS (Lockport C.: v.2, p.201)

LEROY (Sometimes: LERAY)

LEROY, Kleber d. 24 Feb. 1896 at age 5 yrs. (Thib. Ch.: v.3, p.179)

LES, Josephine (Jho & Alice PLAISANCE) b. 19 Jan. 1896 (Lockport Ch.: v.2, p.319 & 320)

LESAGE, Jean Robertson (Emile & Elda GROS) b. 14 Feb. 1898 (Thib. Ch.: v.7, p.492)

LESAGE, Philogene Paul (Emile & Ada GROS) b. 2 May 1899 (Thib. Ch.: v.7, p.607)

LESTER, Florence Cecilia (Harris & Mary WHITNEY) b. 6 March 1899; m. Arthur James BARRY on 8 Sept. 1926. (Houma Ch.: Bapt. Bk., v.5, p.240)

LESTER, George A. m. 15 July 1898 Evela BABIN (Houma Ct. Hse.: Mar. v.30 & 31, #59)

LESTER, George A. (William & Rosa PITRE) m. 1 Aug. 1898 Evela BABIN (Houma Ch.: v.6-a, p.250)

LESTER, Harris Joseph (Andre & Luly LACASSE) b. 12 Jan. 1897 (Houma Ch.: v.5, p.165)

LESTER, Joseph Albert (Thomas & Camila BERGERON) b. 3 March 1896 (Houma Ch.: v.5, p.146)

LESTER, Joseph Nolden (Harris & Marie WHITNEY) b. 1 July 1896 (Houma Ch.: v.5, p.183)

LESTER, Joseph Williams (Oscar & Lovely LACASSE) b. 4 Nov. 1899 (Houma Ch.: v.5, p.262)

LESTER, Josephine m. 1 Aug. 1898 Albert BABIN (Houma Ch.: v.6-a, p.250)

LESTER, Josephine (Thomas & Camilla BERGERON) m. 21 June 1897 Albert BABIN (Houma Ct. Hse.: Mar. v.29 & 30, #36)

LESTER, Marie Eugenie (Nathalie) b. 12 July 1897 (Houma Ch.: v.5, p.185)
LESTER, Mary Bursesse (George & Evela BABIN) b. 13 Sept. 1899 (Houma Ch.: v.5, p.255)
LESTER, Mattie bt. 6 Dec. 1896 as an adult (Houma Ch.: Epis. Ch.: v.1, p.112-B)
LESTER, Nathalie (William F. & Rosa PITRE) m. 21 Dec. 1898 James ATES (Houma Ct. Hse.: Mar. v.30 & 31, #154)
LESTER, Voltha Joseph d. 4 Sept. 1897 at age 2 mths. (Houma Ch.: v.3, p.14)
LETILLEUX, Judith A. (Charles & Laisa FORET) b. 20 Feb. 1897 (Lockport Ch.: v.3, #25)
LETILLEUX, Judith A. (Charles & Loise FORET) b. 20 Feb. 1897 (Lockport Ch.: v.3-A, #25)
LETLET, Waltrim Mary (Sim & Silvia DARSEE) b. 14 Dec. 1896 (Houma Ch.: v.5, p.164)
LEVEL, Ellick m. 30 Jan. 1899 Sidonia PINKNEY (Houma Ct. Hse.: Mar. v.30 & 31, #290)

LEVERT (Sometimes: LEVERTE)
LEVERT, Eloi d. 18 Nov. 1897 at age 72 yrs. (Thib. Ch.: v.3, p.207)
LEVERT, Lucille Agnes d. 18 Aug. 1896 at age 1 yr. & 1 mth. (Thib. Ch.: v.3, p.185)
LEVERT, Marie Ella (Deoda & Euphemie LEBLANC) b. 13 March 1897 (Lockport Ch.: v.3-A, #34)
LEVERT, Philippe d.12 June 1898 at age 7 mths. (Thib. Ch.: v.3, p.215)
LEVERT, Philippe Edouard (Marcelin & Alida GUILLOT) b. 16 Nov. 1897 (Thib. Ch.: v.7, p.473)
LEVERT, Veronique (Vileor & Victorine SANCHEZ) m. 27 Sept. 1899 Whitney WEBRE (Thib. Ch.: v.14, p.301)
LEVERT, Veronique (Vileor & Victorine SANCHEZ) m. 27 Sept. 1899 Whitney WEBRE (Thib. Ct. Hse.: Mar. v.39, #236)

LEVRON (Sometimes: LEGRANO, LEUVRON, LEVRANT, LEVROND, LEVRONT)
LEVRON, Angelina m. 7 July 1896 Nicolas MALBROUGH (Thib. Ct. Hse.: Mar. v.36, #118)
LEVRON, Angelina (Joseph & Clauthilde HEBERT) m. 14 Nov. 1896 Nicolas MALBROUGH (Thib. Ch.: v.14, p.104)
LEVRON, Camila m. 14 Aug. 1897 J. Schuyler PORCHE (Houma Ct. Hse.: Mar. v.29 & 30, #79)
LEVRON, Camilia (Marcel & Victorine DAIGLE) m. 14 Aug. 1897 James Schuyler PORCHE, Jr. (Houma Ch.: v.6-a, p.213)
LEVRON, Cecile (Evariste & Pamela LANDRY) m. 31 Jan. 1898 Joseph RODRIGUE (Chackbay Ch.: v.1, p.54)
LEVRON, Cecile (Evariste & Pamela LANDRY) m. 31 Jan. 1898 Joseph RODRIGUE (Thib. Ct. Hse.: Mar. v.37, #36)
LEVRON, Frederic (d.Joseph & d.Melina NAQUIN) m. 13 Feb. 1899 Josephine LEBOEUF (Montegut Ch.: v.4, p.259)

LEVRON, Frederick (Joseph & Melina NAQUIN) m. 18 Jan. 1899 Josephine LEBOEUF (Houma Ct. Hse.: Mar. v.30 & 31, #249)
LEVRON, Gertrude m. 26 May 1897 Oliver BROWN (Thib. Ct. Hse.: Mar. v.36, #150)
LEVRON, Gladys May (James S. & Mary Olympe MISTROT) b. 1 Aug. 1896 (Thib. Ch.: v.7, p.411)
LEVRON, Jean Gaiden (Augustin & Clely PONTIFF) b. 3 Aug. 1899 (Houma Ch.: v.5, p.256)
LEVRON, Jean Paul (Ernest & Augustin LEDET) b. 22 Jan. 1898 (Montegut Ch.: v.6, p.65)
LEVRON, Jean Rubby (Washington & Alfrida CAREAU) b. 8 Feb. 1896 (Houma Ch.: v.5, p.173)
LEVRON, Joseph d. 13 May 1899 at age 1 yr. & 9 mths. (Thib. Ch.: v.3, p.233)
LEVRON, Jules Abraham (W. & Alf. CAREAU) b. 2 March 1899 (Houma Ch.: v.5, p.242)
LEVRON, Julien Joseph (Justilien & Lorenza BERGERON) b. 4 July 1897 (Thib. Ch.: v.7, p.458)
LEVRON, Julienne d. 28 Jan. 1896 at age 3 yrs. (Thib. Ch.: v.3, p.178)
LEVRON, Laurance Paul (Marcelin & Marie BONVILLAIN) b. 21 Sept. 1898; bt. 15 Jan. 1899; confirmed here on 1 May 1945; m. Camille BERGERON on 4 Feb. 1929. (Houma Ch.: Bapt. Bk., v.5, p.230)
LEVRON, Laurentia Marie (Valmont & Adele LEONARD) b. 27 July 1899 (Thib. Ch.: v.8, p.2)
LEVRON, Louise m. 8 April 1899 Leufroid V. DAUNIS (Thib. Ct. Hse.: Mar. v.39, #139)
LEVRON, Louise of Terrebonne Parish m. 19 April 1899 Lufroid DAUNIO (Houma Ch.: v.6-B, p.3)
LEVRON, Marie Agnes (Ellis & Celina BRUNET) b. 21 Jan. 1896 (Montegut Ch.: v.6, p.34)
LEVRON, Marie Cecile (Oscar & Octavie BOURG) d. 16 July 1898 at age 6 mths. (Montegut Ch.: v.2, p.18)
LEVRON, Marie Cecile (Oscar & Octavie BOURG) b. 30 Jan. 1898 (Houma Ch.: v.5, p.201)
LEVRON, Marie Melina (Ellis & Celina BRUNET) b. 24 March 1898 (Montegut Ch.: v.6, p.70)
LEVRON, Oscar (d.Victor & d.Cecile DUPRE) m. 25 Jan. 1897 Octavie BOURG (Montegut Ch.: v.4, p.216)
LEVRON, Oscar (Victor & Cecile DUPRE) m. 9 Jan. 1897 Octavie BOURG (Houma Ct. Hse.: Mar. v.29 & 30, #226)
LEVRON, Paul Wilson (Augustin & Clelie PONTIFF) b. 10 Feb. 1896; m. Adole ESCHETE on 9 March 1920 (Houma Ch.: Bapt. Bk., v.5, p.172)
LEVRON, Unisse (Marcelin & Marie BONVILAIN) b. 22 Oct. 1896; Theophile MARCEL on 19 Sept. 1919 (Houma Ch.: Bapt. Bk., v.5, p.169)
LEVRON, Valmon (Evariste & Pamela LANDRY) m. 18 April 1898 Adele LEONARD (Chackbay Ch.: v.1, p.59)

LEVRON, Valmon (Evariste & Pamela LANDRY) m. 18 April 1898 Adele LEONARD (Thib. Ct. Hse.: Mar. v.37, #138)
LEVRON, Victoria m. 18 Jan. 1898 George PORCHE (Houma Ct. Hse.: Mar. v.30 & 31, #227)
LEVRON, Victoria (Marcel & Victorine LEVRON) m. 19 Jan. 1898 George PORCHE (Houma Ch.: v.6-a, p.223)
LEVY, Irma m. 23 Jan. 1897 Leon BLUM (Thib. Ct. Hse.: Mar. v.36, #50)
LEVY, Michael m. 22 April 1896 Wilia ORGERON (Larose Ch.: v.3, p.2)
LEVY, Michael m. 22 April 1896 Willia ORGERON (Larose Ch.: v.4, p.50)
LEVY, Mike m. 6 April 1896 Milia ORGERON (Thib. Ct. Hse.: Mar. v.35, #64)
LEWIS, Anatole m. 3 Oct. 1898 Eliza HITE (Houma Ct. Hse.: Mar. v.30 & 31, #115)
LEWIS, Bertha m. 16 Sept. 1899 Hampton RAYMOND (Thib. Ct. Hse.: Mar. v.39, #226)
LEWIS, Carter m. 7 Feb. 1899 Ella PINCKNEY (Houma Ct. Hse.: Mar. v.31 & 32, #322)
LEWIS, Elizabeth m. 18 Jan. 1899 Joseph JAMES (Thib. Ct. Hse.: Mar. v.38, #31)
LEWIS, Fannie m. 15 June 1896 John L. DUMAS (Houma Ct. Hse.: Mar. v.29 & 30, #93)
LEWIS, Jacob m. 23 Dec. 1897 Cora SPENCER (Houma Ct. Hse.: Mar. v.29 & 30, #152)
LEWIS, John m. 10 Feb. 1898 Victoria SMITH (Thib. Ct. Hse.: Mar. v.37, #94)
LEWIS, Lizzie m. 11 Jan. 1899 Joseph PIERRE (Houma Ct. Hse.: Mar. v.30 & 31, #204)
LEWIS, Mary L. (Simon & Missouri WADE) m. 16 June 1898 Thomas J. WILLIAMS (Houma Ct. Hse.: Mar. v.30 & 31, #10)
LEWIS, Matilda m. 15 Oct. 1898 Peter MOORE (Houma Ct. Hse.: Mar. v.30 & 31, #121)
LEWIS, Robert m. 13 July 1898 Mamie UNIFORTS (Thib. Ct. Hse.: Mar. v.38, #224)
LEWIS, Rose m. 12 Feb. 1896 Florida MICHENS (Houma Ct. Hse.: Mar. v.28, #447)
LEWIS, William m. 12 Dec. 1898 Edmonia THOMAS (Houma Ct. Hse.: Mar. v.30 & 31, #142)
LIBERTA, Gilorma (Leonard & Francesca ODDA) m. 8 Jan. 1897 Rosario CARENZO (Thib. Ch.: v.14, p.122)
LIBERTA, Gilorma (Leonard & Francesca ODDA) m. 8 Feb. 1897 Rosario CARENZO (Thib. Ct. Hse.: Mar. v.36, #71)
LIBERTA, Marietta (Leonardo & Francisca VOLTA) b. 25 May 1898 (Thib. Ch.: v.7, p.501)
LIBERTO, Antonino (Vincenzo & Carmela COCO) b. 18 Sept. 1898 (Thib. Ch.: v.7, p.515)
LICATA, Joseph (Rosario & Antonina FURENZA) b. 11 Jan. 1899 (Raceland Ch.: v.5, p.88)

LILLY, Ollie m. 8 Jan. 1896 Reuben GOODS (Thib. Ct. Hse.: Mar. v.35, #15)
LINA, Jean Daniel d. 2 Nov. 1897 at age 6 mths. (Theriot Ch.: v.1, p.1)
LINA, Laura d. 8 Nov. 1898 at age 20 yrs. (Theriot Ch.: v.1, p.1)
LINA, Laura (Philippe & Virginie DARDARE) m. 6 Nov. 1898 Thelesphore BILLIOT (Theriot Ch.: v.1-B, p.5)
LINE, Arthur Jefson (Jefson & Marie VERRET) b. 23 Aug. 1897 (Theriot Ch.: v.2, p.33)

LINER (Sometimes: LYNER)
LINER, Cecile Maud (Pleasant & Mary McCULLER) b. 20 May 1899 (Theriot Ch.: v.2, p.44)
LINER, Evela (Jefferson & Felonise VERRET) b. 31 July 1899 (Theriot Ch.: v.2, p.56)
LINER, Jean Daniel (Plaisant & Mary McCOLLAN) b. 28 May 1897 (Theriot Ch.: v.2, p.7)
LINER, Jos Ludovic (Louis & Marie CARAIRE) b. 26 Feb. 1898 (Theriot Ch.: v.2, p.27)
LINER, Louis m. 12 Aug. 1899 Henriette DEHART (Houma Ct. Hse.: Mar. v.31 & 32, #93)
LINER, Louis (John & Marguerite HENRY) m. 12 April 1897 Marie CARRERE (Houma Ct. Hse.: Mar. v.29 & 30, #381)
LINER, Marie Elise (John & Octavie SCOTT) b. 13 Sept. 1899 (Theriot Ch.: v.2, p.109)
LINER, Wickline Olliver (Henri & Aufeleque THIBODEAUX) b. 25 Nov. 1896 (Theriot Ch.: v.1-B, p.106)

LIRETTE (Sometimes: LIRETE, LYRETT)
LIRETTE, Angelina Myrtil (Edgard & Marie THIBODEAU) b. 10 Jan. 1898 (Houma Ch.: v.5, p.197)
LIRETTE, Angelina Nesta (Ernest & Emelina BELANGER) b. 26 Feb. 1897 (Houma Ch.: v.5, p.175)
LIRETTE, Angelique Clemence (Henri & Angelina HEBERT) b. 27 Nov. 1897 (Chackbay Ch.: v.1, p.101)
LIRETTE, Angelique Dora (Jean & Lutitia HENRI) b. 24 Nov. 1896 (Houma Ch.: v.5, p.168)
LIRETTE, Anthony Clifford (Berony & Mary McELROY) b. 11 Jan. 1896 (Thib. Ch.: v.7, p.454)
LIRETTE, Arthur (Leo & Celestine LOUVIERE) m. 22 Feb. 1897 Elise LECOMPTE (Montegut Ch.: v.4, p.218)
LIRETTE, Arthur (Leo & Celestine LOUVIERE) m. 10 Feb. 1897 Elise LECOMPTE (Houma Ct. Hse.: Mar. v.29 & 30, #299)
LIRETTE, Aurelien (Henri & Victorine TRAHAN) m. 19 June 1899 Virginia HENRI (Montegut Ch.: v.4, p.265)
LIRETTE, Camille Joannes (Emile & Marie Louise Benoit THIBODEAUX) b. 31 Dec. 1899 (Montegut Ch.: v.6, p.97)
LIRETTE, Catherine (Arthur & Elise LECOMPTE) d. 1 Dec. 1897 at age 5 days (Montegut Ch.: v.2, p.13)

LIRETTE, Corine Valerie Marie (Joseph & Elizabeth LADOUCEUR) b. 13 Sept. 1898 (Thib. Ch.: v.7, p.515)
LIRETTE, Desire Henri (Henri & Celestine SUAREZ) b. 10 Oct. 1898 (Thib. Ch.: v.7, p.515)
LIRETTE, Ernest (Franklin & Philomise LAMARIE) m. 30 April 1896 Emeline BELANGER (Houma Ch.: v.6-a, p.174)
LIRETTE, Ernest P. m. 18 April 1896 Emeline E. BELLANGER (Houma Ct. Hse.: Mar. v.29 & 30, #42)
LIRETTE, Evelina (Joseph & Elisabeth LADOUCEUR) b. 10 March 1896 (Thib. Ch.: v.7, p.395)
LIRETTE, Francis (James & Feralie THIBODAUX) m. 21 Feb. 1898 Julie LEBLANC (Montegut Ch.: v.4, p.238)
LIRETTE, Francis (James & Feralie THIBODAUX) m. 12 Feb. 1898 Julie LEBLANC (Houma Ct. Hse.: Mar. v.30 & 31, #292)
LIRETTE, Frederic Joseph (Joseph & Elisabeth LADOUCEUR) b. 15 Sept. 1896 (Thib. Ch.: v.7, p.461)
LIRETTE, Henri (Guillaume & Anastasie RICHARD) m. 21 Jan. 1897 Angelina HEBERT (Chackbay Ch.: v.1, p.36)
LIRETTE, Henri (Guillaume & Anastasie RICHARD) m. 21 Jan. 1897 Angelina HEBERT (Chackbay Ch.: v.1, p.36)
LIRETTE, Henry (Guillaume & Anastasie RICHARD) m. 21 Jan. 1897 Angelina HEBERT (Thib. Ct. Hse.: Mar. v.36, #16)
LIRETTE, James Paul (Jean & Luthitia HENRI) b. 12 Oct. 1899 (Houma Ch.: v.5, p.262)
LIRETTE, Joseph (Emile & Euphroisine SMITH) m. 13 Dec. 1897 Eva PELEGRIN (Houma Ct. Hse.: Mar. v.29 & 30, #142)
LIRETTE, Joseph (Emile & Euphrosine SMITH) m. 10 Jan. 1898 Eva PELEGRIN (Montegut Ch.: v.4, p.228)
LIRETTE, Joseph (Oscar & Amanda THIBODEAUX) b. 3 Jan. 1899 (Houma Ch.: v.5, p.235)
LIRETTE, Joseph Marcel (Camille & Ernestine BRAUD) b. 13 July 1897 (Thib. Ch.: v.7, p.459)
LIRETTE, Joseph Moise Sylvain (Ludovic & Osea HENRI) b. 25 Aug. 1897 (Montegut Ch.: v.6, p.61)
LIRETTE, Joseph Randolphe (Dave & Emelia BERGERON) b. 23 Sept. 1896 (Montegut Ch.: v.6, p.50)
LIRETTE, Josephine (Guillaume & Amelia LEDET) m. 21 Oct. 1897 Maurice PITRE (Thib. Ch.: v.14, p.165)
LIRETTE, Josephine (Guillaume & Amelia LEDET) m. 21 Oct. 1897 Maurice PITRE (Thib. Ct. Hse.: Mar. v.37, #248)
LIRETTE, Josephine Stella (Arthur & Elise LECOMPTE) b. 19 Aug. 1899 (Montegut Ch.: v.6, p.91)
LIRETTE, Julien (Henri & Victorine TRAHAN) m. 31 May 1899 Virginia HENRI (Houma Ct. Hse.: Mar. v.31 & 32, #20)
LIRETTE, Leah m. 20 July 1897 Jean LEBLANC (Houma Ct. Hse.: Mar. v.29 & 30, #65)
LIRETTE, Leah (Homer D. & Elvire BABIN) m. 20 July 1897 Jean LEBLANC (Houma Ch.: v.6-a, p.212)
LIRETTE, Leo Pierre (Joseph & Elisabeth LADOUCEUR) b. 26 Feb. 1899 (Thib. Ch.: v.7, p.592)

LIRETTE, Lorida Agladie (Francis & Julie LEBLANC) b. 14 Feb. 1899 (Montegut Ch.: v.6, p.87)
LIRETTE, Ludovia (Volcar & Angele PORCHE) m. 22 March 1899 John J. GUIDRY (Houma Ct. Hse.: Mar. v.31 & 32, #371)
LIRETTE, Ludovia (Volcar & Angele PORCHE) m. 3 April 1899 John GUIDRY (Montegut Ch.: v.4, p.260)
LIRETTE, Ludovic M. (Franklin J. & Felonise SAMANIE) m. 27 Dec. 1899 Henrietta PYE (Houma Ct. Hse.: Mar. v.31 & 32, #219)
LIRETTE, Ludovie M. of Houma m. 28 Dec. 1899 Henrietta PYE (Houma Ch.: v.6-B, p.5)
LIRETTE, Marie Bernadette (Anody & Adelina BERGERON) b. 2 Sept. 1898 (Montegut Ch.: v.6, p.77)
LIRETTE, Marie Berthe (Walas & Mary HEBERT) b. 19 Jan. 1897 (Houma Ch.: v.5, p.200)
LIRETTE, Marie Emilie (Emile & Ophelia GUIDRY) b. 1 April 1897 (Thib. Ch.: v.7, p.446)
LIRETTE, Marie Emma Philomene (Henri & Celestine LUAREZ) b. 6 Sept. 1896 (Thib. Ch.: v.7, p.416)
LIRETTE, Marie Evela (Joseph & Eva PELEGRIN) b. 13 Oct. 1898 (Montegut Ch.: v.6, p.81)
LIRETTE, Marie Felicienne (Emile & Marie Louise BENOIT) b. 5 April 1897 (Montegut Ch.: v.6, p.55)
LIRETTE, Marie Lucretia (Sidney & Emma DUPLANTIS) b. 2 Dec. 1898 (Montegut Ch.: v.6, p.79)
LIRETTE, Nicholas m. 25 Sept. 1899 Elise DAIGLE (Houma Ct. Hse.: Mar. v.31 & 32, #143)
LIRETTE, Nicholas of Terrebonne Parish m. 25 Sept. 1899 Elise DAIGLE (Houma Ch.: v.6-B, p.4)
LIRETTE, Ophelia Desilia (Caliste & Francoise VERRETTE) b. 17 March 1898 (Houma Ch.: v.5, p.204)
LIRETTE, Paul Ernest (Ernest Paul & Emeline BELANGER) b. 14 Sept. 1899 (Houma Ch.: v.5, p.260)
LIRETTE, Pierre (Taylor & Latitia DEGRAIZE) b. 14 Oct. 1898 (Thib. Ch.: v.7, p.520)
LIRETTE, Sarah (Henri & Victorine TRAHAN) m. 13 April 1896 Dumreis PRICE (Houma Ct. Hse.: Mar. v.29 & 30, #36)
LIRETTE, Sarah (Henri & Victorine TRAHAN) m. 29 April 1896 Dunreis PRICE (Montegut Ch.: v.4, p.209)
LIRETTE, Sidney (Volcar & Angele PORCHE) m. 26 Jan. 1898 Emma DUPLANTIS (Montegut Ch.: v.4, p.233)
LIRETTE, Sidney (Volcar & Angele PORCHE) m. 4 Jan. 1898 Emma DUPLANTIS (Houma Ct. Hse.: Mar. v.30 & 31, #174)
LIRETTE, Sidonie Louise (Louis & Moloway WOLF) b. 23 Aug. 1899 (Thib. Ch.: v.7, p.561)
LIRETTE, Victoria Maria (David & Evelia BERGERON) b. 5 Aug. 1898 (Montegut Ch.: v.6, p.78)
LIRETTE, Wallace m. 26 Dec. 1896 Mary HEBERT (Houma Ct. Hse.: Mar. v.29 & 30, #214)
LIRETTE, Wallace (Franklin & Felonise SAMANIE) m. 4 Jan. 1897 Mary HEBERT (Houma Ch.: v.6-a, p.188)

LIVANIA, Jocalino (Louisiana & Tantilla GRATIA) b. 15 July 1898 (Houma Ch.: v.5, p.213)
LIVAS, Anthony m. 30 March 1897 Susanna SAULSBURY (Houma Ct. Hse.: Mar. v.29 & 30, #369)
LOCATTA, Nic (Francesco & Guiseppa SALERNO) b. 13 Oct. 1896 (Thib. Ch.: v.7, p.433)
LOCKWOOD, Abella m. 31 March 1898 William WILLIAMS (Houma Ct. Hse.: Mar. v.30 & 31, #360)
LOCKWOOD, Cora m. 28 Jan. 1897 Leonard TONEY (Houma Ct. Hse.: Mar. v.29 & 30, #264)
LOEB, Tillie C. m. 29 Oct. 1899 Leon KAHN (Thib. Ct. Hse.: Mar. v.39, #254)
LOKE, Henry Thomas (Elles & Elda MARCEL) b. 27 July 1897 (Houma Ch.: v.5, p.185)
LOLAND, Laura m. 18 Nov. 1899 Charles LEJEUNE Both of Raceland. (Thib. Ct. Hse.: Mar. v.39, #263)
LOLAND, Laura (Edouard & Laure LANDRY) m. 18 Nov. 1899 Charles LEJEUNE (Raceland Ch.: v.2, p.106)

LOMBAS (Sometimes: LOMBARD, LOMBASSE)
LOMBAS, Francois Barthelemise (Mac & Amanda HENRI) b. 11 Sept. 1896 (Theriot Ch.: v.1-B, p.98)
LOMBAS, Marguerite Laetitia (Marck & Manda HENRI) b. 21 Jan. 1898 (Theriot Ch.: v.2, p.24)
LOMBAS, Ozea (Theophile & Meleina RI) b. 10 April 1896 (Larose Ch.: v.2, p.194)
LONDON, Adam m. 27 July 1898 Edna NICHOL (Thib. Ct. Hse.: Mar. v.38, #234)
LONG, Rachel m. 26 Feb. 1896 Ezekiel NOBLE (Thib. Ct. Hse.: Mar. v.35, #48)
LONGBAS, Marie Amelie (George & Mary BABIN) b. 15 Oct. 1899 (Houma Ch.: v.5, p.263)
LONGO, Salvatore (Steven & Anna VITRANA) b. 28 April 1898 (Thib. Ch.: v.7, p.535)
LONGUEPIE, Celima (Theodore & Odilia LEVRON) m. 18 June 1896 Wallace TROSCLAIR (Thib. Ct. Hse.: Mar. v.35, #101)
LONGUEPIE, Celima (Theodore & Odilia LEVRON) m. 18 June 1896 Wallace TROSCLAIR (Thib. Ch.: v.14, p.93)
LONIBOS, Oneil Jean (Jean Marie & Celima PIERCE) b. 3 May 1897 (Larose Ch.: v.3, p.3)

LOOK (See: LUKE)

LOPEZ (Sometimes: LOPE)
LOPEZ, Alice m. 25 Sept. 1896 Phil HAWKINS (Thib. Ct. Hse.: Mar. v.36, #148)
LOPEZ, Fred. m. 19 Jan. 1898 Laura THOMAS (Houma Ct. Hse.: Mar. v.30 & 31, #230)
LOPEZ, Oscar m. 7 Jan. 1897 Frances WILLIAMS (Houma Ct. Hse.: Mar. v.29 & 30, #225)

LORAINE, Philomeine m. 5 June 1897 Ulysse TERREBONNE (Larose Ch.: v.4, p.72)

LORIO (Sometimes: LORIOT)

LORIO, Agnes (Edouard & Emilie BERTHELOTTE) b. 24 Jan. 1896 (Thib. Ch.: v.7, p.440)

LORIO, Lucien (J. B. N. & Laura HAYDEL) m. 9 Feb. 1899 Felicie BECNEL (Houma Ct. Hse.: Mar. v.30 & 31, #239)

LORIO, Roland Etienne (Lucien & Felicie BECKNEL) b. 26 Dec. 1899 (Thib. Ch.: v.7, p.581)

LORIOT, Edouard Hardway (Edouard & Elmire BERTELOTTE) b. 25 Nov. 1898 (Thib. Ch.: v.7, p.530)

LORRAINE, Eliza of Lafourche Parish (William & Melina BRUCE) m. 11 June 1898 Adrien PITRE, of Lafourche Parish (Larose Ch.: v.3, p.9)

LORRAINE, Eliza (William & Melina BRUCE) m. 11 June 1898 Adrien PITRE (Thib. Ct. Hse.: Mar. v.38, #197)

LORRAINE, Eliza (William & Melina BRUCE) m. 11 June 1898 Adrien PITRE (Larose Ch.: v.4, p.16)

LORRAINE, Joseph Elie (William & Melina BRUCE) b. 15 Dec. 1897 (Larose Ch.: v.3, p.31)

LORRAINE, Julia m. 7 July 1899 Thomas ESPONGE (Thib. Ct. Hse.: Mar. v.39, #194)

LORRAINE, Julia (William & Melina BRUCE) m. 15 July 1899 Joseph ESPONGE (Larose Ch.: v.4, p.87)

LORRAINE, Julia (Williame & Melina BRUCE) m. 15 July 1899 Joseph ESPONGE (Larose Ch.: v.3, p.12)

LORRAINE, Philomene m. 25 May 1897 Ulysse TERREBONNE (Thib. Ct. Hse.: Mar. v.36, #147)

LORRAINE, Philomene m. 5 June 1897 Ulysse TERREBONNE (Larose Ch.: v.3, p.5)

LORTON, Frances J. of Dublin, Ireland (Henry & Elizabeth SEIVE) m. 4 March 1899 James P. RATCLIFF, of Sumit, Mississippi (Thib. Ch.: v.14, p.266-a)

LORTON, Frances J. (Henry & Elizabeth SEIVE) m. 4 March 1899 James P. RATLIFF (Thib. Ct. Hse.: Mar. v.39, #115)

LOTTINGER (Sometimes: LOTTINGUE)

LOTTINGER, Francois Marc (Victor J. & Lucille THERIOT) b. 9 Nov. 1899 (Theriot Ch.: v.2, p.53)

LOTTINGER, Jean d. 25 Dec. 1897 at age 19 yrs (Thib. Ch.: v.3, p.209)

LOTTINGER, Lucius Victor (Julien Victor & Matilde Lucille THERIOT) b. 19 Sept. 1896 (Theriot Ch.: v.1-B, p.100)

LOTTINGER, Oreste Joseph (Frank & Elvire TROSCLAIR) b. 19 July 1898 (Theriot Ch.: v.2, p.28)

LOTTINGER, Pierre Elie (----- & Marguerite ROGER) b. 11 Feb. 1898 (Theriot Ch.: v.2, p.19)

LOUIS, Rosa m. 8 June 1899 John RANDOLPH (Thib. Ct. Hse.: Mar. v.39, #176)

LOUISA, Catarina (Rosario & Salvatora MARANTA) b. 21 April 1898 (Thib. Ch.: v.7, p.548)
LOUISA, Teresina (Rosario & Salvatora MARANTA) b. 21 April 1898 (Thib. Ch.: v.7, p.548)

LOUPE (Sometimes: LOOPE, LOUP, LOUPES)
LOUPE, Jean (Adam & Lina DEMPSTER) b. 9 Nov. 1896 (Chackbay Ch.: v.1, p.78)
LOUPE, Jean Lionel (Paul & Desiree CORTEZ) b. 27 Oct. 1899; m. Marie Louise BERTHELOTTE on 20 Feb. 1928. (Chackbay Ch.: Bapt. Bk., v.1, p.143)
LOUPE, Joseph (Bienaime & Marcelline BARRIOS) m. 6 July 1896 Bernadette ORGERON (Thib. Ct. Hse.: Mar. v.35, #106)
LOUPE, Joseph (Bienaime & Marcelline BARRIOS) m. 6 July 1896 Bernadette ORGERON (Lockport Ch.: v.2, p.152)
LOUPE, Joseph (Joseph & Nestle CORTEZ) b. 19 March 1898 (Chackbay Ch.: v.1, p.110)
LOUPE, Joseph (Seraphin & Octavie BORNE) m. 22 July 1899 Azelienia CORTEZ (Chackbay Ch.: v.1, p.71)
LOUPE, Joseph (Seraphin & Octavie BORNE) m. 15 July 1899 Azelima CORTEZ (Thib. Ct. Hse.: Mar. v.39, #200)
LOUPE, Josephine (Bienaime & Marcelline BARRIOS) m. 22 June 1896 Joseph ORGERON (Thib. Ct. Hse.: Mar. v.35, #105)
LOUPE, Leopold (Paul & Desiree CORTES) b. 19 July 1898 (Chackbay Ch.: v.1, p.116)
LOUPE, Lydia d. 15 Nov. 1899 at age 22 yrs. (Lockport Ch.: v.1, #44)
LOUPE, Maria (Joseph & Nezilia CORTEZ) b. 28 Jan. 1896 (Chackbay Ch.: v.1, p.61)
LOUPE, Marie (Bienaime & Marcelline BARRIOS) m. 1 Sept. 1897 Felicien BRAUX (Lockport Ch.: v.2, p.167)
LOUPE, Marie (Bienaime LOUPE) m. 28 Aug. 1897 Felicien BREAUX (Thib. Ct. Hse.: Mar. v.37, #221)
LOUPE, Marie (Louis & Julia CORTEZ) b. 7 Jan. 1897 (Chackbay Ch.: v.1, p.83)
LOUPE, Marie Alfrida (Octave & Josephine CORTES) b. 6 Dec. 1898 (Chackbay Ch.: v.1, p.126)
LOUPE, Ozeme m. 27 June 1896 Selima RODRIGUE (Thib. Ct. Hse.: Mar. v.35, #108)
LOUPE, Ozeme m. 27 June 1896 Selima RODRIGUE (Larose Ch.: v.4, p.91)
LOUPE, Ozeme m. 27 June 1896 Selima RODRIGUE (Larose Ch.: v.3, p.3)
LOUPE, Paul (Seraphin & Octavie BORNE) m. 18 Sept. 1897 Desiree CORTEZ (Chackbay Ch.: v.1, p.49)
LOUPE, Paul (Seraphin & Octavie BORNE) m. 18 Sept. 1897 Desiree CORTEZ (Thib. Ct. Hse.: Mar. v.37, #228)
LOUPE, Pierre (Edouard & Leonise BRAUX) b. 21 Nov. 1896 (Lockport Ch.: v.3, #23)
LOUPE, Pierre (Edouard & Leonise BRAUX) b. 26 Nov. 1896 (Lockport Ch.: v.3-A, #23)

LOUVIERE (Sometimes: LOUVIER)

LOUVIERE, Ella m. 6 June 1896 Willie HENRY (Houma Ct. Hse.: Mar. v.29 & 30, #86)

LOUVIERE, Ella (Leonie & Mary COLLINS) m. 25 June 1896 Willie HENRY (Houma Ch.: v.6-a, p.177)

LOUVIERE, Ernest E. m. 17 Sept. 1898 Leona LOUVIERE (Houma Ct. Hse.: Mar. v.30 & 31, #100-B)

LOUVIERE, Ernest E. (Henry & Marie WHITNEY) m. 5 Oct. 1898 Leona LOUVIERE (Houma Ch.: v.6-a, p.254)

LOUVIERE, Evariste d. 8 July 1897 at age 93 yrs. (Thib. Ch.: v.3, p.202)

LOUVIERE, Florestine d. 14 Oct. 1897 at age 38 yrs. (Houma Ch.: v.3, p.14)

LOUVIERE, Henry Joseph (Finne) b. 18 Oct. 1897 (Houma Ch.: v.5, p.213)

LOUVIERE, John Otis (Henri & Lucia MICHEL) b. 6 Sept. 1898 (Chacahoula Ch.: v.4, p.13)

LOUVIERE, Julie Laura (Leoni & Mary COLLONS) b. 20 July 1899 (Houma Ch.: v.5, p.255)

LOUVIERE, Leona m. 17 Sept. 1898 Ernest E. LOUVIERE (Houma Ct. Hse.: Mar. v.30 & 31, #100-B)

LOUVIERE, Leona (Leonie & Mary COLLINS) m. 5 Oct. 1898 Ernest E. LOUVIERE (Houma Ch.: v.6-a, p.254)

LOUVIERE, Lilia (Henri & Lucia MICHEL) b. 13 March 1896 (Houma Ch.: v.5, p.150)

LOUVIERE, Luger d. 30 Nov. 1897 at age 48 yrs. (Thib. Ch.: v.3, p.208)

LOUVIERE, Marie Mable (Alexandre & Domitille GUILLOT) b. 7 Oct. 1896 (Houma Ch.: v.5, p.162)

LOUVIERE, Mary Acklen (Alex & Domitile GUILLOT) b. 26 Sept. 1898 (Houma Ch.: v.5, p.222)

LOUVIERE, Winney Madeleine (Leoni & Masie COLLINS) b. 25 June 1896 (Houma Ch.: v.5, p.182)

LOVE, Alice m. 10 Nov. 1897 Henry SMITH (Thib. Ct. Hse.: Mar. v.37, #256)

LOVEJOY, Alfred m. 8 Nov. 1899 Louise BABIN (Thib. Ct. Hse.: Mar. v.39, #261)

LOVEJOY, Alfred (Charley & Maria KURNEY) m. 18 Nov. 1899 Louise BABIN (Raceland Ch.: v.2, p.105)

LOVELESS, Paul (Josephine CROCHET) b. 13 April 1898 (Montegut Ch.: v.6, p.68)

LOVELL, Ceoa (Dominique & Victorine DARDARE) b. 29 Jan. 1899 (Theriot Ch.: v.2, p.68)

LOVELL, Eva m. 13 Feb. 1897 Adam FREDERICK (Houma Ct. Hse.: Mar. v.29 & 30, #309)

LOVELL, Eva (Neuville & Josephine BILLIOT) m. 25 Feb. 1897 Adam FREDERIC (Theriot Ch.: v.1, p.9)

LOVELL, Evelina (Lawrence & Rosa BILLIOT) b. 27 Nov. 1898 (Theriot Ch.: v.2, p.52)

LOVELL, Johnnie (Laurence & Rosa BILLIOT) b. 17 Dec. 1896 (Theriot Ch.: v.2, p.52)

LOVELL, Mack (Walker & Marie NAQUIN) m. 2 Dec. 1899 Eve FREDERICK (Houma Ct. Hse.: Mar. v.31 & 32, #170)

LOVELL, Madeline Alice (Augustin & Asea FREDERIC) b. 22 Dec. 1899 (Theriot Ch.: v.2, p.60)

LOVELL, Marie Agnes (Augustin & Ozea FREDERIC) b. 7 Feb. 1898 (Theriot Ch.: v.2, p.20)

LOVELL, Marie Madeleine (Domingue & Victorine DARDARE) b. 7 Sept. 1897 (Theriot Ch.: v.2, p.26)

LOVELL, Mark (Walker & Marie NAQUIN) m. 11 Dec. 1899 Eve FREDERICK (Theriot Ch.: v.1-B, p.7)

LOVELL, Neville (Eugene & Marie VERRET) b. 13 March 1896 (Theriot Ch.: v.2, p.58)

LOVELL, Paul (Augustin & Ozea FREDERIC) b. 15 Nov. 1896 (Theriot Ch.: v.1-B, p.102)

LOVELL, Pearly Salina (Walden & Bertha L. ADAMS) b. 6 Jan. 1898 (Houma Ch.: Epis. Ch.: v.1, p.116)

LOVELL, Walker (Perry & Juliet RATLIF) bt. 21 May 1898 as an adult (Houma Ch.: Epis. Ch.: v.1, p.116)

LOVELL, Walker (Perry & Juliet RATTLER) m. 15 June 1896 Bertha Lucinda ADAMS (Houma Ct. Hse.: Mar. v.29 & 30, #89)

LOVELL, Willie (Lawrence) d. 5 Nov. 1899 at age 13 yrs. (Theriot Ch.: v.1, p.2)

LOYER, Elizabeth m. 28 Sept. 1896 Alexandre BUTLER (Houma Ct. Hse.: Mar. v.29 & 30, #160)

LOYSON, Agnes Menela (Alice) b. 11 Sept. 1898 (Houma Ch.: v.5, p.219)

LOZZARDI, Laveri d. 6 Dec. 1899 at age 18 mths. (Houma Ch.: v.3, p.26)

LUBIN, Louise d. 11 May 1898 at age 19 yrs. (Raceland Ch.: v.1, p.18)

LUCAS, Elizabeth m. 25 Jan. 1899 Willie MORTON (Thib. Ct. Hse.: Mar. v.38, #59)

LUCITA, Rosalia (Salvatore & Cattarina MOLE) m. 18 Feb. 1899 Badassano MAGIO (Thib. Ct. Hse.: Mar. v.38, #94)

LUCITO, Rosalia (d.Salvatore & Catharine MOLE) m. 18 Feb. 1899 Badassano MAGIO (Thib. Ch.: v.14, p.266)

LUCK, Laurence (Elice & Alice TROSCLAIR) b. 5 June 1896 (Houma Ch.: v.5, p.159)

LUCKETT, Samuel (Harry & Prescilla LUCKETT) m. 15 Jan. 1896 Ellen PAYNE (Houma Ct. Hse.: Mar. v.28, #392)

LUCY MARY d. 20 April 1896 at age 2 mths. (Thib. Ch.: v.3, p.182)

LUKE (Sometimes: LUCK, LUCKE, LUK)

LUKE, Brigitte (Alcide & Josephine HENRI) b. 4 April 1897 (Theriot Ch.: v.2, p.3)

LUKE, Clara (Frank & Eva LEBLANC) b. 17 Aug. 1899 (Theriot Ch.: v.2, p.49)

LUKE, Dosia Valerie (Gilbert & Louisiane TROSCLAIR) b. 6 July 1898 (Theriot Ch.: v.2, p.28)

LUKE, Florence (Gilbert & Louisiane TROSCLAIR) m. 7 Feb. 1898 Jonas THIBEAUDEAU (Theriot Ch.: v.1-B, p.2)
LUKE, Florence (Gilbert & Louisiane TROSCLAIR) m. 19 Jan. 1898 Jonas THIBODAUX (Houma Ct. Hse.: Mar. v.30 & 31, #228)
LUKE, Joseph Thadeus (Ellis & Elda MARCELLE) b. 9 Aug. 1899 (Theriot Ch.: v.2, p.49)
LUKE, Olinda (Gilbert & Louisiane TROSCLAIR) m. 7 July 1897 Camile FOREST (Houma Ct. Hse.: Mar. v.29 & 30, #52)
LUKE, Ophelia (Frank & Eva LEBLANC) b. 29 May 1897 (Theriot Ch.: v.2, p.6)
LUM, Laura (Robert & Mary VERDIN) b. 20 Feb. 1898 (Houma Ch.: v.5, p.241)
LUPO, Angello (Georgio & Stabbile -----) m. 24 April 1897 Ignazia MORIONE (Thib. Ct. Hse.: Mar. v.36, #101)
LUPO, Angelo (Georgio & Stabbile ANTONIO) m. 24 April 1897 Ignatia MORIONE (Thib. Ch.: v.14, p.138)
LUPO, Antonina (Angelo & Niacci Ignacia MARIONI) b. 3 Oct. 1899 (Thib. Ch.: v.7, p.570)
LUPO, Dominica (Tomaso & Guiseppa BORROMEA) b. 16 March 1898 (Thib. Ch.: v.7, p.492)

LUQUET (Sometimes: LIQUET, LUQUETTE)

LUQUET, Gratien (Georges & Antoinette DOMINIQUE) m. 5 Feb. 189 Celeste BABIN (Lockport Ch.: v.2, p.183)
LUQUET, Gratien (Georges & Antoinette DOMINIQUE) m. 5 Feb. 1898 Celeste BABIN (Thib. Ct. Hse.: Mar. v.37, #25)
LUQUET, Joseph Aurelien (Felicien & Felitia FORET) b. 16 Nov. 1897 (Raceland Ch.: v.5, p.58)
LUQUET, Joseph George (Felicien & Felicia FORET) b. 17 Sept. 1899; m. Marie Aline ORGERON on 18 June 1930. (Raceland Ch.: Bapt. Bk., v.5, p.102)
LUQUET, Marie m. 8 June 1898 Desire BOURGEOIS (Thib. Ct. Hse.: Mar. v.38, #200)
LUQUET, Marie Celestine (Felicien & Felicia FORET) b. 14 Sept. 1896 (Raceland Ch.: v.5, p.31)

LUZIGNAN (Sometimes: LAZIGNAU, LASIGNON, LUZIGNAN)

LUZIGNAN, Beatrice Melgride (Baptiste & Octavie BENOIT) b. 11 Jan. 1897 (Thib. Ch.: v.7, p.436)
LUZIGNAN, Junius Severin (Jean Baptiste & Octavie BENOIT) b. 11 Feb. 1899 (Thib. Ch.: v.7, p.535)
LUZIGNAN, Laurina d. 11 Sept. 1896 at age 10 mths. (Thib. Ch.: v.3, p.186)
LUZIGNAN, Louis Jules (Clovis & Josephine ESTIVEN) b. 11 Feb. 1897 (Thib. Ch.: v.7, p.438)
LUZIGNAN, Marie d. 8 Sept. 1897 at age 77 yrs. (Thib. Ch.: v.3, p.205)
LUZIGNAN, Marie Louise May (Clovis & Mirthilia ESTIVEN) b. 27 June 1898 (Thib. Ch.: v.7, p.502)
LUZIGNAN, May d. 10 Aug. 1899 at age 9 mths. 9 days (Thib. Ch.: v.3, p.238)

LUZIGNAN, Veronique m. Alphonse ESTIVEN d. 5 Sept. 1898 at age 25 yrs. (Thib. Ch.: v.3, p.219)

LYALL, Ayda Jeannette (John & Euphrasie MELANCON) b. 14 Feb. 1896 (Lockport Ch.: v.2, p.332)

LYNOR (See: LINER)

LYNUS, Hill Jr. d. 1884 (d.Lynus, Sr. & d.Martha HILL) Inventory: 5 Aug. 1898. (Thib. Ct. Hse.: Succ. #1545)

LYON, Carrie Maria (John F. & Emelie LA BRUGERE) d. 14 Aug. 1898 at age 21 yrs. (Montegut Ch.: v.2, p.19)

LYONS, Augustin Vanus (Johnny & Emelie LABRUYERE) b. 15 Aug. 1899 (Montegut Ch.: v.6, p.92)

LYONS, Belden m. 7 Jan. 1896 Clara COLLINS (Houma Ct. Hse.: Mar. v.28, #378)

LYONS, Carrie Florence Marie (Johnny & Emelie LABRUYERE) b. 16 Nov. 1896 (Montegut Ch.: v.6, p.48)

LYONS, George Dewey (Joseph & Letitia DUPLANTIS) b. 6 Nov. 1898 (Houma Ch.: v.5, p.223)

LYONS, James (d.Lucius C. & d.Caroline WHIPPLE) m. 7 June 1897 Marcellite MARBOROUGH (Montegut Ch.: v.4, p.222)

LYONS, James (Lucius C. P. & Caroline WHIPPLE) m. 12 May 1897 Marcelite MALBROUX (Houma Ct. Hse.: Mar. v.29 & 30, #419)

LYONS, Jane (Drew & Louisa LYONS) m. 16 July 1898 Taffy CHIASSON (Houma Ct. Hse.: Mar. v.30 & 31, #61)

LYONS, Marie Lina (Jimmy & Marcellite MALBOROUGH) b. 19 April 1898 (Montegut Ch.: v.6, p.71)

LYONS, Sarah m. 1 July 1899 William BURKS (Houma Ct. Hse.: Mar. v.31 & 32, #70)

LYONS, Thelma Julia (Paul & Rosa GILROY) b. 18 Feb. 1898 (Chacahoula Ch.: Gibson Records: Mar. Bk., v.1, #21)

LYONS, Thelma Julia (Paul & Rosa GILROY) b. 18 Feb. 1898 (Chacahoula Ch.: Gibson Ch.: v.2, p.119)

"M"

MACALOSA, Francisca (Salvatore & Maria CHIERAMA) m. 24 April 1899 Francesco MAGLIA (Raceland Ch.: v.2, p.94)
MACALUSA, Domenica (Salvatore & Maria CIRANIE) m. 10 June 1899 Guiseppe CONIGLIO (Raceland Ch.: v.2, p.98)
MACALUSA, Maria Guiseppa (Vincenza & Maria DURSA) m. -- March 1898 Guiseppe DORSA (Thib. Ch.: v.14, p.193)
MACALUSA, Marie Giuseppa (Vincenzo & Maria DARSA) m. 19 March 1898 Giuseppe DORSA (Thib. Ct. Hse.: Mar. v.37, #120)
MACK, Emma m. 9 Feb. 1899 James REDDMAN (Thib. Ct. Hse.: Mar. v.39, #100)
MACK, Nathan m. 23 June 1898 Sarah GRIFFIN (Houma Ct. Hse.: Mar. v.30 & 31, #33)
MACKLIN, Collins m. 5 Jan. 1899 Melinda GODFREY (Houma Ct. Hse.: Mar. v.30 & 31, #180)
MACORO, Antonino (Francesco & Maria Patello ANTONINA) b. 2 March 1896 (Thib. Ch.: v.7, p.397)
MADISON, James m. 9 March 1896 Matilda ANDERSON (Houma Ct. Hse.: Mar. v.29 & 30, #8)
MADISON, Mandy m. 11 Oct. 1897 Anderson MITCHELL (Houma Ct. Hse.: Mar. v.29 & 30, #118)
MADISON, Margaret m. 17 Jan. 1898 Wesley ROOKS (Houma Ct. Hse.: Mar. v.30 & 31, #218)
MADISON, Sam m. 18 June 1896 Rebecca SHELTER (Houma Ct. Hse.: Mar. v.29 & 30, #96)
MADONIA, Crucifissa (Vincenzo & Anna MAZZOLA) b. 6 Jan. 1899 (Thib. Ch.: v.7, p.594)
MAGAREGINA, Catharine (Nicholas & Rosa CAICHOPA) b. 3 Oct. 1898 (Houma Ch.: v.5, p.220)
MAGGIO, Antonino (Guesseppe & Francisca CATALANELLA) b. 23 Jan. 1899 (Houma Ch.: v.6, p.4)
MAGGIO, Biagio John (Stephano & Johanna MANTOGIO) b. 21 Aug. 1899 (Houma Ch.: v.5, p.252)
MAGIO, Badassano (d.George & Rosa CARCGNA) m. 18 Feb. 1899 Rosalia LUCITO (Thib. Ch.: v.14, p.266)
MAGIO, Badassano (George & Rosa CAREAGNA) m. 18 Feb. 1899 Rosalia LUCITA (Thib. Ct. Hse.: Mar. v.38, #94)
MAGIOR, Georges m. 7 May 1896 Susan CARTER (Thib. Ct. Hse.: Mar. v.35, #84)
MAGLIA, Francesco m. 11 April 1899 Francesca PAULA (Thib. Ct. Hse.: Mar. v.39, #140)
MAGLIA, Francesco (Tobia & Natalo NICARA) m. 24 April 1899 Francisca MACALOSA (Raceland Ch.: v.2, p.94)
MAGOTA, Maria (Salvatore & Catharina CACHIOPA) b. 29 Nov. 1899 (Houma Ch.: v.5, p.265)
MAGRUDER, Rachel m. 29 March 1899 James Walter FERGUSON (Houma Ct. Hse.: Mar. v.31 & 32, #381)
MAHONEY, Bertha m. 4 May 1897 Joseph BOYKINS (Houma Ct. Hse.: Mar. v.29 & 30, #403)

MAILLET, Edith Joseph (Alcide & Marie GRIFFEN) b. 18 Nov. 1896 (Larose Ch.: v.2, p.190)
MAILLET, Hector Liberal (Alcide & Marie GRIFFIN) b. 9 Sept. 1898 (Larose Ch.: v.3, p.28)
MAILLET, Marie Rose d. 4 Jan. 1897 at age 72 yrs. (Thib. Ch.: v.3, p.193)

MALBROUGH (Sometimes: MALBOROUGH, MALBRAU, MALBROU, MALBROUX)
MALBROUGH, Angela (Nicolas & Angelina LEVRON) b. 30 Aug. 1899 (Thib. Ch.: v.8, p.6)
MALBROUGH, Arthur Menville (Frejus & Eve USE) b. 25 Feb. 1896 (Houma Ch.: v.5, p.170)
MALBROUGH, Arthur Mrs. d. 24 June - 4 July 1899 at age 35 yrs. (Thib. Ch.: v.3, p.236)
MALBROUGH, Augustin Mrs. d. 15 July 1898 at age 69 yrs. (Houma Ch.: v.3, p.17)
MALBROUGH, Catherine (William & Lea AUZIO) b. 9 Aug. 1897 (Thib. Ch.: v.7, p.514)
MALBROUGH, Cecile Pauline Helene (Arthur & Louise RICHARD) b. 23 May 1898 (Thib. Ch.: v.7, p.499)
MALBROUGH, Clervil Mrs. d. 5 April 1897 at age 84 yrs. (Houma Ch.: v.3, p.12)
MALBROUGH, Delphine m. 2 Dec. 1898 Theodore ADAM (Larose Ch.: v.3, p.10)
MALBROUGH, Delphine m. 2 Dec. 1898 Theodore ADAM (Larose Ch.: v.4, p.108)
MALBROUGH, Elise Marie (Olesiphore & Henriette LABIT) b. 26 Dec. 1898 (Houma Ch.: v.5, p.233)
MALBROUGH, Elvire m. Felicien ROBICHAUX d. 1 Nov. 1899 at age 39 yrs. (Montegut Ch.: v.2, p.30)
MALBROUGH, Francis Ernest (Petro Surand & Maria FANGUY) b. 21 Feb. 1899 (Theriot Ch.: v.2, p.34)
MALBROUGH, Harris Joseph (Harris & Dolisca SOURDELIER) b. 20 Sept. 1898 (Houma Ch.: v.5, p.219)
MALBROUGH, Helene d. 12 July 1899 at age 1 yr. & 6 mths. (Thib. Ch.: v.3, p.237)
MALBROUGH, Joseph Veday (Nickles & Emma BERGERON) b. 30 Jan. 1899 (Montegut Ch.: v.6, p.82)
MALBROUGH, Josephina Rosa (Joseph & Maria BOURQUE) b. 20 Dec. 1898 (Theriot Ch.: v.2, p.35)
MALBROUGH, Leon d. 8 April 1897 at age 2 days (Thib. Ch.: v.3, p.198)
MALBROUGH, Linies d. 12 Jan. 1898 at age 17 yrs. (Theriot Ch.: v.1, p.1)
MALBROUGH, Marcelite (Emile & Allida ESHTE) m. 12 May 1897 James LYONS (Houma Ct. Hse.: Mar. v.29 & 30, #419)
MALBROUGH, Marcellite (Emile & Alida ESCHETE) m. 7 June 1897 James LYON (Montegut Ch.: v.4, p.222)
MALBROUGH, Marie Olinda (Frejus & Eve USE) b. 24 Nov. 1898 (Houma Ch.: v.5, p.222)

MALBROUGH, Marie Therese (Onesiphore & Henriette LABIE) b. 20 Feb. 1896 (Houma Ch.: v.5, p.173)
MALBROUGH, Mary d. 9 April 1896 at age 28 yrs. (Houma Ch.: v.3, p.7)
MALBROUGH, Mary Cezec (Arisse & Dorisca SOURDELIER) b. 14 Jan. 1896 (Houma Ch.: v.5, p.143)
MALBROUGH, Maud Ella (Joseph & Valerie ROUNDTREE) b. 14 Jan. 1897 (Thib. Ch.: v.7, p.438)
MALBROUGH, Nana m. Lother ROBICHAUX d. 4 May 1899 at age 41 yrs. (Montegut Ch.: v.2, p.25)
MALBROUGH, Nicholas (Emile & Alida ESCHETE) m. 28 Dec. 1897 Emma BERGERON (Houma Ct. Hse.: Mar. v.29 & 30, #163)
MALBROUGH, Nickles (Emile & Alida ESCHTE) m. 15 Jan. 1898 Emma BERGERON (Montegut Ch.: v.4, p.229)
MALBROUGH, Nickles (Emile & d.Alida ESCHTE) d. 16 Aug. 1899 at age 22 yrs. (Montegut Ch.: v.2, p.27)
MALBROUGH, Nicolas m. 7 July 1896 Angelina LEVRON (Thib. Ct. Hse.: Mar. v.36, #118)
MALBROUGH, Nicolas (Thuriane & Pomela MARTIN) m. 14 Nov. 1896 Angelina LEVRON (Thib. Ch.: v.14, p.104)
MALBROUGH, Octavie (John & Leonide MARTIN) m. 9 Oct. 1899 Fernand BAYE (Thib. Ch.: v.14, p.302)
MALBROUGH, Octavie (John & Leonide MARTIN) m. 9 Oct. 1899 Fernand BAYE (Thib. Ct. Hse.: Mar. v.39, #243)
MALBROUGH, Odelia (Henry & Odelia WATKINS) m. 1 July 1897 Arthur ESCHETE (Houma Ct. Hse.: Mar. v.29 & 30, #45)
MALBROUGH, Paul Auguste (Harris & Victoria BOUDRAUX) b. 29 Aug. 1897 (Thib. Ch.: v.7, p.462)
MALBROUGH, Pauline Anna (Benoit & Marie LIRETTE) b. 23 March 1898 (Thib. Ch.: v.7, p.495)
MALBROUGH, Saddie d. 18 Aug. 1899 at age 3 yrs. (Houma Ch.: v.3, p.24)
MALBROUGH, Usilia d. 11 Jan. 1897 at age 59 yrs. (Houma Ch.: v.3, p.11)
MALBROUGH, Volkar d. 13 Jan. 1896 at age 37 yrs. (Thib. Ch.: v.3, p.178)
MALBROUGH, Winfield Columbus (Joseph & Marie BOURQUE) b. 4 Sept. 1896 (Theriot Ch.: v.1-B, p.100)
MALCOMBE, Ida Felicie (Pitre & Lea DUET) b. 9 Jan. 1899 (Larose Ch.: v.3, p.37)
MALCOMBE, Marie Francois (Francois & Lea DUET) b. 23 July 1896 (Larose Ch.: v.2, p.184)
MALCOMBE, Peet m. 7 June 1896 Lea DUET (Larose Ch.: v.4, p.99)
MALCOMBE, Pete m. 7 May 1896 Lea DUET (Thib. Ct. Hse.: Mar. v.35, #82)
MALCOMBE, Pitre m. 7 May 1896 Lea DUET (Larose Ch.: v.3, p.3)
MALGORME, Xavier m. 6 Aug. 1898 Josephine DANTIN (Thib. Ct. Hse.: Mar. v.38, #239)

MALLET, Alfred m. 18 Feb. 1898 Viney RUFFINS (Houma Ct. Hse.: Mar. v.30 & 31, #307)
MALONE, Vincenzo (Mariano & Catarina FARINA) b. 7 Nov. 1899 (Thib. Ch.: v.7, p.574)
MANCUSO, Bernardo m. 1 April 1899 Maria BARRILLE (Houma Ct. Hse.: Mar. v.31 & 32, #382)
MANCUSO, Bernardo of Terrebonne Parish m. 29 April 1899 Maria BARRILE (Houma Ch.: v.6-B, p.3)
MANDIBOURG, Gaston Paul (Henry Martin & Noemie COULON) b. 30 June 1896 (Larose Ch.: v.2, p.187)
MANGIANICINA, George (Nicolas & Rosa KATCIOPA) b. -- Sept. 1896; bt. 10 Oct. 1896 (Houma Ch.: v.5, p.158)
MANGIARACINA, Antonino (George & Antonina LUCITA) m. 2 July 1898 Nunzia CIACCIO (Houma Ct. Hse.: Mar. v.30 & 31, #48)
MANGIRACINO, Antonino (George & Antonina LUCITA) m. 30 July 1898 Nuzia CIACCIO (Houma Ch.: v.6-A, p.249)
MANGO, Biofio (Stephano & Johanna MAUGROGE) b. 21 June 1898 (Houma Ch.: v.5, p.210)
MANGONIA, Giovanni (Guiseppe & Rosaria LESCIANNA) b. 30 Sept. 1898 (Chacahoula Ch.: v.4, p.15)
MANINA, Katarina (Louis & Francesca MAZARA) b. 6 Sept. 1899 (Thib. Ch.: v.7, p.565)
MANINA, Lucie (Antonino & Manella SARVATRICE) b. 6 March 1898 (Thib. Ch.: v.7, p.498)
MANINO, Guiseppa (Petre & Francesca COLETTA) m. 3 Sept. 1898 Dominico BRUNO (Thib. Ch.: v.14, p.217)
MANINO, Guiseppa (Petro & Francesca COLETTA) m. 3 Sept. 1898 Domenico BRUNO (Thib. Ct. Hse.: Mar. v.38, #242)
MANISCALCO, Caloggiera (Gaspare & Perrone ANNA) b. 17 April 1898 (Thib. Ch.: v.7, p.502)
MANLEY, Arthur m. 25 Jan. 1896 Lena MOORE (Houma Ct. Hse.: Mar. v.28, #423)
MANN, William m. 25 Oct. 1899 Rosella VERRET (Houma Ct. Hse.: Mar. v.31 & 32, #154)
MANNO, Vito (Francesco & Rosalia ZOLAMARTA) b. 23 Jan. 1898 (Thib. Ch.: v.7, p.534)
MANPARACINA, Antonino (Antonino & Munzia CIACIA) b. 2 Sept. 1899 (Houma Ch.: v.5, p.252)
MANSFIELD, Frank m. 2 Dec. 1897 Jennie HARRIS (Thib. Ct. Hse.: Mar. v.37, #259)
MANUEL, Maggie m. 11 June 1896 John GILTON (Thib. Ct. Hse.: Mar. v.35, #104)
MANUEL, Robertha m. 18 June 1898 John SINGLETON (Houma Ct. Hse.: Mar. v.30 & 31, #21)
MANZEROLLES, Julia (Etienne & Aima ESTIVEN) m. 20 April 1899 Felix LEDET (Thib. Ct. Hse.: Mar. v.39, #126)
MAORELLO, Odensio (Caloggio & Catharina MORTELLARO) b. 6 Feb. 1899 (Houma Ch.: v.5, p.240)
MARANTO, Maria (Salvatore & Dorothia MESSINA) b. 23 Jan. 1898 (Thib. Ch.: v.7, p.534)

MARANTO, Maria Christina d. 30 May 1897 at age 6 mths. (Houma Ch.: v.3, p.13)
MARANTO, Maria Christina (Pasquale & Francisca DAZIA) b. 8 Dec. 1896 (Houma Ch.: v.5, p.161)
MARASSA, Francesco (Michaele & Louisa SOTERO) m. 11 Aug. 1896 Carolina PALAZZO (Thib. Ct. Hse.:Mar. v.36, #132)

MARCANTE (Sometimes: MAXCIANTO)

MARCEL (Sometimes: MARCELL, MARCELLE)
MARCEL, Adam Uzilien (Ulysse & Roselia BABIN) b. 26 Sept. 1897 (Thib. Ch.: v.7, p.471)
MARCEL, Albert (Theogene & Servelia CHIASSON) m. 28 Sept. 1898 Mrs. Clemance AUTHEMENT, widow of Miguel EXPOSITO (Houma Ct. Hse.: Mar. v.30 & 31, #108)
MARCEL, Augustin Steve (George & Cecile DERCE) b. 13 Feb. 1898 (Thib. Ch.: v.7, p.542)
MARCEL, Brigitte m.7 April 1898 Albert BABIN (Houma Ct. Hse.: Mar. v.30 & 31, #385)
MARCEL, Brigitte (Theodule & Adelaide BERGERON) m. 20 April 1898 Albert BABIN (Houma Ch.: v.6-a, p.239)
MARCEL, Ceal d. 28 March 1896 at age 57 yrs. (Houma Ch.: v.3, p.7)
MARCEL, Celestine (Albert & Emelie BOUDREAUX) m. 6 June 1899 John ESHTE (Houma Ct. Hse.: Mar. v.31 & 32, #29)
MARCEL, Claud Philippe (Edgar & Julia LEBLANC) b. 26 Oct. 1899 (Houma Ch.: v.5, p.260)
MARCEL, Clotilde (Ceade & Elizabeth BERGERON) m. 11 May 1899 Augustin MOLAISON (Thib. Ct. Hse.: Mar. v.39, #154)
MARCEL, Clotilde (Ceade & Elizabeth BERGERON) m. 11 May 1899 Augustin MOLAISON (Thib. Ch.: v.14, p.280)
MARCEL, Clovis Joseph (Cead & Marie BERNARD) b. 18 June 1897 (Thib. Ch.: v.7, p.507)
MARCEL, Euphrasie (Albert & Angelique ANGERRAN) m. 8 Feb. 1898 Ennis HENRI (Houma Ct. Hse.: Mar. v.30 & 31, #285)
MARCEL, Euphrasie (Albert & Angelique ENGERRAN) m. 21 Feb. 1898 Ennis HENRI (Montegut Ch.: v.4, p.239)
MARCEL, Eve Lea (Milton & Augustilia LEBLANC) b. 5 Dec. 1898 (Houma Ch.: v.5, p.233)
MARCEL, Felecite Mrs. m. 29 May 1897 Augustin LEBOEUF (Houma Ch.: v.6-a, p.204)
MARCEL, Felicite m. 22 Sept. 1896 Augustin LEONARD (Thib. Ct. Hse.: Mar. v.36, #145)
MARCEL, George (Cead & Elise BERGERON) m. 14 April 1896 Cecile DARCE (Thib. Ch.: v.14, p.84)
MARCEL, George (Cead & Elise BERGERON) m. 17 April 1896 Cecile DARCE (Thib. Ct. Hse.: Mar. v.35, #69)
MARCEL, Jeannette Bernadette (D. & Adelaide BERGERON) b. 20 Feb. 1899 (Houma Ch.: v.5, p.243)
MARCEL, Joseph Davis (Edgard & Julia LEBLANC) b. 2 July 1897 (Thib. Ch.: v.7, p.457)

MARCEL, Joseph Theophile (Albert & d.Cisse ENGERRAN) d. 20 Oct. 1898 at age 25 yrs. (Montegut Ch.: v.2, p.21)

MARCEL, Leonard (Robert & Emilie BOUDREAUX) m. 3 Feb. 1898 Alice BERGERON (Houma Ct. Hse.: Mar. v.30 & 31, #271)

MARCEL, Lucie Gracieuse (Theodule & Adelaide BERGERON) b. 27 March 1896 (Houma Ch.: v.5, p.178)

MARCEL, Mable Valerie (Oseme & Marie BOUDREAU) b. 6 July 1898 (Houma Ch.: v.5, p.216)

MARCEL, Marie Agnes Louisianne (Felicien & Josehine LAPEYROUSE) b. 21 Nov. 1896 (Montegut Ch.: v.6, p.49)

MARCEL, Ozemee m. 6 Feb. 1897 Marie BOUDREAUX (Houma Ct. Hse.: Mar. v.29 & 30, #294)

MARCEL, Ozemee (Emile & Aimee BERGERON) m. 25 Feb. 1897 Marie BOUDREAUX (Houma Ch.: v.6-a, p.193)

MARCEL, Paul Louis (Eulice & Josephine LAPEROUSE) b. 11 March 1898 (Montegut Ch.: v.6, p.68)

MARCEL, Saul (Octave & Mary PORTIER) b. 23 Nov. 1898; m. Louisa A. MOLAISON on 11 June 1923. (Houma Ch.: Bapt. Bk., v.5, p.227)

MARCEL, Theodule d. 9 June 1898 at age 65 yrs. (Houma Ch.: v.3, p.17)

MARCOMBE, Joseph Sylvain (Auguste & Elisa PITRE) b. 17 Feb. 1897 (Larose Ch.: v.3, p.6)

MARCOMBE, Paul (Auguste & Elisa PITRE) b. 26 Jan. 1899 (Larose Ch.: v.3, p.36)

MARESCO, Marguerite Philomene (Francis & Josephine ORGERON) b. 21 Dec. 1896 (Larose Ch.: v.2, p.190)

MARGIOTTE, Cologgere (Guiseppe & Maria ERNE) b. 1 Jan. 1899 (Houma Ch.: v.5, p.229)

MARIA d. 22 Feb. 1899 at age 1 day (Houma Ch.: v.3, p.21)

MARIE, Bernadette Gertrude (Henry & Emma ENGERRAN) b. 30 July 1899 (Montegut Ch.: v.6, p.94)

MARIE, Henri (Gustave & Catherine GARIBOTTE) m. 6 June 1898 Emma ENGERRAN (Montegut Ch.: v.4, p.246)

MARIE, Henri (Joseph & Cecilia DOMINGUE) d. 18 Oct. 1899 (Montegut Ch.: v.2, p.30)

MARIE, Henry m. 16 May 1898 Emma ENGERRAN (Houma Ct. Hse.: Mar. v.30 & 31, #443)

MARINO, Guiseppe (Pedro & Maria AZZARE) b. 13 March 1897 (Thib. Ch.: v.7, p.443)

MARINO, Ignatio (Petro & Marie ADZALE) b. 1 Aug. 1898 (Thib. Ch.: v.7, p.558)

MARIONE, Guiseppe (Guiseppe & Calaggiera MANESCACA) b. 27 Dec. 1898 (Thib. Ch.: v.7, p.529)

MARMANDE (Sometimes: MARMAN, MARMONDE)

MARONGE, Adam Joseph (Volcar & Marie LEBOEUF) b. 28 May 1898 (Thib. Ch.: v.7, p.505)

MARONGE, Ismee d. 28 March 1899 at age 10 mths. (Houma Ch.: v.3, p.22)

MARONGE, James Maurice (Philippe & Nelly McCOLLOM) b. 11 Dec. 1897 (Thib. Ch.: v.7, p.476)
MARONGE, Josephine Isme (Adam & Alida PITT) b. 14 May 1898 (Thib. Ch.: v.7, p.505)
MARONGE, Louis Sabon (Emile & Marie LEVRON) b. 11 July 1899 (Thib. Ch.: v.8, p.5)
MARONGE, Magnolia d. 13 July 1899 at age 4½ mths. (Thib. Ch.: v.3, p.237)
MARONGE, Marianne Magnolia Mabel (Philippe & Nelly McCOLLUM) b. 26 Feb. 1899 (Thib. Ch.: v.7, p.545)
MARONGE, Marie d. 21 May 1899 at age 2 mths. (Thib. Ch.: v.3, p.234)
MARONGE, Marie Neuve Darcet (Andreze & Camille DARCET) b. 6 Nov. 1896 (Thib. Ch.: v.7, p.436)
MARONGE, Philippe (Andre & Marie Anne THIBODAUX) m. 10 June 1896 Nellie McCOLLUM (Thib. Ch.: v.14, p.91)
MARONGE, Philippe (Andrew & Mary Ann THIBODAUX) m. 10 June 1896 Nellie McCOLLUM (Thib. Ct. Hse.: Mar. v.35, #100)
MARONGE, Zulma Virginie (Theophile & Marguerite DAIGLE) b. 30 March 1898 (Thib. Ch.: v.7, p.497)
MARONI, Guiseppe (Guiseppe & Vincenza MIRABLE) b. 2 Jan. 1899 (Chacahoula Ch.: v.4, p.17)
MAROSSA, Francesco (Michoule & Louisa SOTERS) m. 11 Aug. 1896 Carolina PALAZZO (Thib. Ch.: v.14, p.97)
MAROUSSE, Valerie Marie (Emile & Marie LEVRON) b. 14 March 1899 (Houma Ch.: v.5, p.244)
MARS, Clotilde (Trasimond & Eveline LEGENDRE) m. 21 Oct. 1899 Leo LEGENDRE (Chackbay Ch.: v.1, p.75)
MARS, Clotilde (Trasimond & Eveline LEGENDRE) m. 21 Oct. 1899 Leo LEGENDRE (Thib. Ct. Hse.: Mar. v.39, #246)
MARS, Domitille d. 15 Aug. 1899 at age 70 yrs. (Thib. Ch.: v.3, p.239)
MARS, Josephine (Alcide & Ernestine ROUSSEL) b. 2 June 1897 (Chackbay Ch.: v.1, p.90)
MARS, Marie (Trasimond & Melina LEGENDRE) b. 28 Aug. 1898 (Chackbay Ch.: v.1, p.118)
MARS, Marie Laura (Alcide & Ernestine ROUSSEL) b. 2 Oct. 1899 (Chackbay Ch.: v.1, p.142)
MARSHALL, Frank m. 19 March 1898 Juanita FORTIER (Thib. Ct. Hse.: Mar. v.37, #127)
MARSHALL, Jeannetta widow of Amos GRIMS m. 9 Sept. 1897 Daniel HOLLINS (Thib. Ct. Hse.: Mar v.37, #231)
MARSHALL, Warren m. 19 April 1897 Rose JOHNSON (Houma Ct. Hse.: Mar. v.29 & 30, #387)
MARTEL, Rose m. 18 Feb. 1897 Willis REID (Houma Ct. Hse.: Mar. v.29 & 30, #320)
MARTIN, Aglae (Justin & Aglae DUPLANTIS) m. 12 Sept. 1899 Clay CHAUVIN (Houma Ct. Hse.: Mar. v.31 & 32, #126)
MARTIN, Aglaee (Justin & Aglaee DUPLANTIS) m. 5 Oct. 1899 Clay CHAUVIN (Montegut Ch.: v.4, p.271)

MARTIN, Aimee Valerie (Willie & Alice ANDRAS) b. 7 Feb. 1899 (Chackbay Ch.: v.1, p.129)
MARTIN, Anaise d. 4 Sept. 1897 at age 67 yrs. (Raceland Ch.: v.1, p.15)
MARTIN, Augustin (Joseph & Evelina AUTIN) m. 19 Feb. 1898 Lovincia MATHERNE (Thib. Ct. Hse.: Mar. v.37, #93)
MARTIN, Augustin (Joseph & Evelina AUTIN) m. 19 Feb. 1898 Lovinia MATHERNE (Lockport Ch.: v.2, p.186 & 187)
MARTIN, Azelie m. 6 May 1897 John VALENCE (Thib. Ct. Hse.: Mar. v.36, #138)
MARTIN, Cinthia m. 6 Jan. 1898 Ernest NAQUIN (Houma Ct. Hse.: Mar. v.30 & 31, #181)
MARTIN, Cynthia (Joseph & Anaise MATHERNE) m. 24 Jan. 1898 Ernest NAQUIN (Montegut Ch.: v.4, p.231)
MARTIN, Edmond (Robert & Octavie DANTIN) m. 28 May 1898 Aurore LEFORT (Thib. Ct. Hse.: Mar. v.38, #177)
MARTIN, Edmond Davidson (Louis & Virginie CHAUVIN) b. 12 Oct. 1896 (Montegut Ch.: v.6, p.46)
MARTIN, Elesia Marie (Joseph & Marie TERREBONNE) b. 5 Feb. 1897 (Larose Ch.: v.3, p.4)
MARTIN, Elvira Angella (William & Alice ANDRA) b. 21 Jan. 1896 (Thib. Ch.: v.7, p.437)
MARTIN, Eugene m. 6 Aug. 1898 Odile COLIN (Thib. Ct. Hse.: Mar. v.38, #241)
MARTIN, Froselie d. 3 March 1897 at age 52 yrs. (Houma Ch.: v.3, p.12)
MARTIN, Gustave d. 4 March 1899 at age 45 yrs. (Raceland Ch.: v.1, p.24)
MARTIN, Hecton Silas (Laurent & Mathilde VIZIER) b. 1 Feb. 1898 (Larose Ch.: v.3, p.20)
MARTIN, Helene Eulalie (Edouard & Eda GAUTHREAUX) b. 14 April 1898 (Chacahoula Ch.: v.4, p.8)
MARTIN, Isaac (Justilien & Aglae DUPLANTIS) m. 21 April 1898 Dorina ROGER (Montegut Ch.: v.4, p.242)
MARTIN, Isaac (Justin & Aglae DUPLANTIS) m. 28 March 1898 Dorina ROGER (Houma Ct. Hse.: Mar. v.30 & 31, #358)
MARTIN, James (Justin & Aglaee DUPLANTIS) d. 21 Jan. 1898 at age 21 yrs. (Montegut Ch.: v.2, p.15)
MARTIN, Jean Alebat (Robert & Octavie MATHERNE) b. 10 Sept. 1896 (Montegut Ch.: v.6, p.47)
MARTIN, Jean Edmond (Edmond & Aurore LEFORT) b. 5 May 1899 (Larose Ch.: v.3, p.41)
MARTIN, Joachim Wilbur (Theles & Elizabeth DOMINGUE) b. 13 Sept. 1896 (Montegut Ch.: v.6, p.45)
MARTIN, Joseh Cleophard (Alphrey & Rebecca LECOMPTE) b. 16 July 1898 (Montegut Ch.: v.6, p.75)
MARTIN, Joseph m. 29 April 1898 Azemia TERREBONNE (Thib. Ct. Hse.: Mar. v.38, #173)
MARTIN, Joseph (Laurent & Mathilde VIZIER) b. 25 March 1896 (Larose Ch.: v.2, p.195)

MARTIN, Joseph Beny (Clovis & Felicia FOLSE) b. 1 June 1896 (Raceland Ch.: v.5, p.24)
MARTIN, Joseph Claude (Gerard & Josephine DUPLANTIS) b. 20 April 1898 (Montegut Ch.: v.6, p.70)
MARTIN, Joseph Lawless (Justilien & Emelie GUEDRY) b. 14 Feb. 1897 (Raceland Ch.: v.5, p.41)
MARTIN, Joseph Loveless (Justinien & Emilie GUYDRI) b. 8 Aug. 1898 (Raceland Ch.: v.5, p.76)
MARTIN, Joseph Magnor (Elfrid & Rebecca LECOMPTE) b. 21 Sept. 1896 (Montegut Ch.: v.6, p.45)
MARTIN, Joseph Maurice (Welly & Melia REDMOND) b. 27 Jan. 1898 (Montegut Ch.: v.6, p.65)
MARTIN, Joseph Maurice (Welly & Melia REDMOND) d. 4 Jan. 1899 at age 11 mths. & 23 days (Montegut Ch.: v.2, p.23)
MARTIN, Joseph Natalie (Jean & Odile COLIN) b. 25 Aug. 1899 (Larose Ch.: v.3, p.47)
MARTIN, Joseph O'Neil (Theodule & Elitia FORET) b. 24 Dec. 1897 (Raceland Ch.: v.5, p.61)
MARTIN, Joseph Preston (Isaac & Dorina ROGER) b. 4 April 1899 (Montegut Ch.: v.6, p.86)
MARTIN, Josephine Marie (Robert & Octavie DANTIN) b. 26 Aug. 1898 (Larose Ch.: v.3, p.31)
MARTIN, Laurent Noe (Edouard & Ada GAUTHREAUX) b. 10 Aug. 1899 (Chacahoula Ch.: v.4, p.29)
MARTIN, Lawrence Manton (Thomas & Alice HEBERT) b. 23 June 1897 (Montegut Ch.: v.6, p.57)
MARTIN, Lezin d. 30 Oct. 1899 at age 56 yrs. (Raceland Ch.: v.1, p.28)
MARTIN, Lovinia m. 23 Jan. 1899 Charles BERGERON (Thib. Ct. Hse.: Mar. v.38, #53)
MARTIN, Lovinia (Louis & Armance BOURGEOIS) m. 2 Feb. 1899 Auguste BERGERON (Raceland Ch.: v.2, p.88)
MARTIN, Luc Sylvestre (Manuel Francois & Celestine HEBERT) b. 31 Dec. 1897 (Larose Ch.: v.3, p.10)
MARTIN, Mariana Nora (Louis & Virginie CHAUVIN) b. 20 Feb. 1899 (Montegut Ch.: v.6, p.86)
MARTIN, Marie Clarance (Thomas & Alice HEBERT) b. 2 March 1899 (Montegut Ch.: v.6, p.82)
MARTIN, Marie Leonise (Theles & Elizabeth DOMINGUE) b. 30 Sept. 1898 (Montegut Ch.: v.6, p.78)
MARTIN, Marie Reda (Augustin & Lovintia MATERNE) b. 24 Nov. 1899 (Raceland Ch.: v.5, p.107)
MARTIN, Melodia Marie (Theodule & Elecia FORET) b. 23 July 1899 (Raceland Ch.: v.5, p.99)
MARTIN, Ovide (Francois & Naise HEBERT) m. 13 April 1899 Alice PANVELLE (Chackbay Ch.: v.1, p.70)
MARTIN, Ovide (Frs. or Francois & Naise HEBERT) m. 13 April 1899 Alice PANVELLE (Thib. Ct. Hse.: Mar. v.39, #125)
MARTIN, Phroselie m. d.Lafayette WATKINS d. 2 March 1897 (Montegut Ch.: v.2, p.10)

MARTIN, Rita (Clofar & Armantine ROBICHAUX) b. 2 July 1899 (Raceland Ch.: v.5, p.98)

MARTIN, Robert Baptiste (Robert & Octavie DANTIN) b. 13 Feb. 1896 (Larose Ch.: v.2, p.191)

MARTIN, Rose Georgia (Thomas Joseph & Emelina DEVILIA) b. 13 Oct. 1897 (Chacahoula Ch.: Gibson Ch.: Mar. Bk. 1, #78)

MARTIN, Rose Georgio (Thomas Joseph & Augusta Emelina DEVILIA) b. 13 Oct. 1897 (Chacahoula Ch.: Gibson Ch.: v.2, p.113)

MARTIN, Sylvestre Joseph (Edouard & Eda GAUTREAUX) b. 3 March 1897 (Chacahoula Ch.: v.4, p.16)

MARTIN, Thomas (Justin & Aglae DUPLANTIS) m. 14 May 1896 Alice HEBERT (Houma Ct. Hse.: Mar v.29 & 30, #69)

MARTIN, Thomas (Justin & Aglae DUPLANTIS) m. 3 June 1896 Alice HEBERT (Montegut Ch.: v.4, p.210)

MARTIN, Thornton m. 27 Dec. 1899 Lucinda POWELL (Houma Ct. Hse.: Mar. v.31 & 32, #210)

MARTIN, Ulysse (Theodule & Letia FORET) b. 11 Feb. 1896 (Raceland Ch.: v.5, p.19)

MARTIN, Vileor Fridolin (Joseph & Ozeme TERREBONNE) b. 6 March 1899 (Larose Ch.: v.3, p.42)

MARTIN, William m. 18 Jan. 1899 Ella JUNIFORD (Houma Ct. Hse.: Mar. v.30 & 31, #246)

MARTINEZ, Alidore (Joseph & Eliza HOTARD) m. 24 Sept. 1898 Leontine DELATTE (Chackbay Ch.: v.1, p.65)

MARTINEZ, Alidore (Joseph & Eliza HOTARD) m. 24 Sept. 1898 Leontine DELATTE (Thib. Ct. Hse.: Mar. v.38, #271)

MARTINEZ, Cecile (Frank) d. 16 Dec. 1896 at age 2 mths. (Lockport Ch.: v.1, #26)

MARTINEZ, Ferdinand Olide (Joseph & Carmelite CAILLOUET) b. 22 March 1899 (Chackbay Ch.: v.1, p.130)

MARTINEZ, Jean Dewey (Sylvestre & Anna SCHAUBUTT) b. 1 Feb. 1899 (Chackbay Ch.: v.1, p.128)

MARTINEZ, Joseph m. 19 April 1896 Octavie BORNE (Chackbay Ch.: v.1, p.27)

MARTINEZ, Joseph (d.Joseph & d.Eliza HOTARD) m. 21 Nov. 1896 Carmelite CAILLOUET (Chackbay Ch.: v.1, p.33)

MARTINEZ, Joseph Eddy (Victor & Magdeleine Anna KRAEMER) b. 21 Oct. 1897 (Chackbay Ch.: v.1, p.102)

MARTINEZ, Joseph Jr. (Joseph & Eliza HOTARD) m. 21 Nov. 1896 Carmelite CAILLOUET (Thib. Ct. Hse.: Mar. v.36, #161)

MARTINEZ, Josephine d. 5 March 1896; m. Lawrence KRAEMER Children listed: Sylvestre, aged 21 yrs.; Octavie, 18 yrs.; Eliza, 17 yrs.; Wilfrid, 15 yrs.; Emilia, 13 yrs.; Isabelle, 11 yrs.; Arthur, 9 yrs.; Elisa, 7 yrs.; Edna, 4 yrs.; Malvina, 1 yr. Petition for inventory: 13 July 1896. (Thib. Ct. Hse.: Succ. #1495)

MARTINEZ, Marie (Albert & Alexina SIMON) b. 26 July 1896 (Chackbay Ch.: v.1, p.75)

MARTINEZ, Marie (Sylvestre & Anna SCHAUBUTT) b. 31 Jan. 1897 (Chackbay Ch.: v.1, p.83 & 84)

MARTINEZ, Marie Melanie (Albert & Aexina CIMON) b. 29 Jan. 1898 (Chackbay Ch.: v.1, p.107)
MARTINEZ, Napoleon m. 1 Oct. 1897 Laura ELLIOT (Thib. Ct. Hse.: Mar. v.37, #237)
MARY, Joseph (Gustave & Catherine GARIBOTTE) m. 10 Aug. 1898 Cecilia DOMINGUE (Houma Ct. Hse.: Mar. v.30 & 31, #75)
MARY, Joseph (Gustave & Catherine GARIBOTTE) m. 24 Aug. 1898 Cecilia DOMINGUE (Montegut Ch.: v.4, p.248)
MARY, Regina m. 3 Jan. 1898 Theophile ENGERRAN (Houma Ct. Hse.: Mar. v.30 & 31, #173)
MARY, Regina (Gustave & Catherine GUILLOTE) m. 24 Jan. 1898 Theophile ENGERRAN (Montegut Ch.: v.4, p.231)
MASON, Lulilia m. 10 Oct. 1898 Leon CARTER (Thib. Ct. Hse.: Mar. v.38, #290)
MASON, Richard Robert (Joseph & Albany FOOLKES) b. 21 Jan. 1897 (Houma Ch.: v.5, p.206)
MASSINO, Gaeton d. 26 Sept. 1899 at age 10 mths. (Thib. Ch.: v.3, p.240)
MASSON, Augustin Jacques of Niort, France (Jacques & Augustine PERON) m. 16 Nov. 1896 Antonia Rowena SAMSON of Point Coupee Parish (Larose Ch.: v.3, p.4)
MASSON, Augustin Jacques (d.Jacques & d.Augustine PERON) native of Niort France m. 16 Nov. 1896 Antonia Rowena SAMSON (Larose Ch.: v.4, p.90)
MASSON, Constant (Joseph & Anne PIOTE) m. 14 April 1898 Julia PACKS (Lockport Ch.: v.2, p.187)
MASSON, Constant (Joseph & Anne PROTE) m. 14 April 1898 Julia PARR (Thib. Ct. Hse.: Mar. v.37, #103)
MATANE, Joseph Winsay (Onesip & Eloisa MARCEL) b. 21 Nov. 1899 (Theriot Ch.: v.2, p.35)
MATHERINE, Lovincia (Cyprien & Lauvenia CHAMPAGNE) m. 19 Feb. 1898 Augustin MARTIN (Thib. Ct. Hse.: Mar. v.37, #93)

MATHERNE (Sometimes: MATERNE, MATTERNE)

MATHERNE, Ada (Jacques & Emelie MATHERNE) m. 11 Aug. 1896 Nelson CUNNINGHAM (Houma Ct. Hse.: Mar. v.29 & 30, #127)
MATHERNE, Adelina m. Noel Dalmas DUFRESNE d. 27 Jan. 1899 at age 40 yrs. (Lockport Ch.: v.1, #3)
MATHERNE, Aimee Marie (Alphonse & Emma ARCEMENT) b. 23 April 1897 (Raceland Ch.: v.5, p.47)
MATHERNE, Aimee Mathilde (Alceste & Emelina MATHERNE) b. 14 March 1896 (Montegut Ch.: v.6, p.38)
MATHERNE, Alcide m. 15 June 1897 Aime BOSSUET (Thib. Ct. Hse.: Mar. v.36, #173)
MATHERNE, Alcide (Alcide & Evelida RIVET) m. 10 July 1897 Aimee BOUSSOT (Raceland Ch.: v.2, p.45)
MATHERNE, Alice (Paul & Palmiere BLANCHARD) m. 15 Aug. 1898 Oscar BREAUX (Houma Ct. Hse.: Mar. v.30 & 31, #78)

MATHERNE, Alice Victoria (Victor & Julia ROBICHAUX) b. 2 Nov. 1898 (Raceland Ch.: v.5, p.81)

MATHERNE, Aline d. 29 March 1896 at age 4 mths. (Raceland Ch.: v.1, p.8)

MATHERNE, Alphonse m. 7 July 1896 Emma ARCEMENT (Thib. Ct. Hse.: Mar. v.36, #119)

MATHERNE, Alphonse (Alfred & Aimee VERRET) m. 23 July 1896 Emma ARCEMENT (Raceland Ch.: v.2, p.18)

MATHERNE, Antoine Felicie (John & Emma DOMINIQUE) b. 9 June 1897 (Larose Ch.: v.3, p.3)

MATHERNE, Bertrand (Celestin & Adelaide OURSEAU) b. 10 June 1896 (Raceland Ch.: v.5, p.32)

MATHERNE, Camillia m. 20 Jan. 1897 Robert T. BEARD (Thib. Ct. Hse.: Mar. v.36, #43)

MATHERNE, Celestine m. Ulysse BRUNET d. 26 Dec. 1899 at age 27 yrs. (Montegut Ch.: v.2, p.32)

MATHERNE, Cesaire m. Jean ARCENEAUX d. 20 Jan. 1899 at age 71 yrs. (Lockport Ch.: v.1, #1)

MATHERNE, Davis Paul (Davis & Olivia FOLSE) b. 18 Oct. 1896 (Raceland Ch.: v.5, p.34)

MATHERNE, Elvina m. 30 Jan. 1899 Richard BABIN (Thib. Ct. Hse.: Mar. v.38, #80)

MATHERNE, Elvina (Alfred & Emelie VERRET) m. 14 Feb. 1899 Richard BABIN (Raceland Ch.: v.2, p.92)

MATHERNE, J. Marcellin d. 16 Feb. 1897 at age 6 mths. (Lockport Ch.: v.1, #7)

MATHERNE, Jeanne Flassy (Philippe & Celimie HEBERT) b. 10 Oct. 1898 (Raceland Ch.: v.5, p.80)

MATHERNE, Jeanne Flosie (Leopold & Ellis CALLAHAN) b. 22 Aug. 1896 (Houma Ch.: v.5, p.162)

MATHERNE, Joseph Alfred (Anatole & Mathilde BRAUD) b. 24 Oct. 1896 (Raceland Ch.: v.5, p.33)

MATHERNE, Joseph Nestor (Alain & Elisa DUHET) b. 22 Aug. 1897 (Raceland Ch.: v.5, p.53)

MATHERNE, Josephine m. 9 Jan. 1899 Marcel BOUDELOCHE (Houma Ct. Hse.: Mar. v.30 & 31, #200)

MATHERNE, Josephine (Jacque & Emelie MATHERNE) m. 19 Jan. 1899 Marcel BOUDELOCHE (Houma Ch.: v.6-a, p.266)

MATHERNE, Laure Corinne (Davis & Olivia FOLSE) b. 4 Oct. 1898 (Thib. Ch.: v.7, p.516)

MATHERNE, Lovinia (Cyprien & Luvinia CHAMPAGNE) m. 19 Feb. 1898 Augustin MARTIN (Lockport Ch.: v.2, p.186 & 187)

MATHERNE, Lucie m. 7 Jan. 1899 Charles CARLOS (Houma Ct. Hse.: Mar. v.30 & 31, #193)

MATHERNE, Lucie (Onesipe & Louise MARCEL) m. 23 Jan. 1899 Charles CARLOS (Houma Ch.: v.6-a, p.268)

MATHERNE, Marguerite Anness (Leopol & Alice CALAHAN) b. 29 Sept. 1897 (Houma Ch.: v.5, p.202)

MATHERNE, Marie (Alces & Melina MATHERNE) m. 28 Jan. 1897 Alcide KNIGHT (Montegut Ch.: v.4, p.216)

MATHERNE, Marie (Alces & Melina MATHERNE) m. 20 Jan. 1897 Alcide KNIGHT (Houma Ct. Hse.: Mar. v.29 & 30, #242)
MATHERNE, Marie Constance Alice (Justin & Celestine BARRIOS) b. 12 Dec. 1896 (Lockport Ch.: v.3, #35)
MATHERNE, Marie Constance Alice (Justin & Celestine BARRIOS) b. 12 Dec. 1896 (Lockport Ch.: v.3-A, #35)
MATHERNE, Marie Eve d. 9 March 1899 at age 3 wks. (Raceland Ch.: v.1, p.24)
MATHERNE, Marie Eve (Victorin & Eva LADRET) b. 20 Aug. 1897 (Raceland Ch.: v.5, p.53)
MATHERNE, Marie Lucile (Victor & Julia ROBICHAUX) b. 23 Jan. 1896 (Raceland Ch.: v.5, p.18)
MATHERNE, Marie Margueritte Agale (Augustin & Celestine BARRIOS) b. 11 Jan. 1898 (Larose Ch.: v.3, p.16)
MATHERNE, Marie Margueritte Aglae (Augustin & Celestine BARRIOS) b. 11 Jan. 1898 (Larose Ch.: v.3, p.20)
MATHERNE, Marie Menble (Philippe & Celene HEBERT) b. 25 March 1896 (Lockport Ch.: v.2, p.327)
MATHERNE, Marie Ociana (Joseph & Augustine PONTIFF) b. 20 Jan. 1896 (Montegut Ch.: v.6, p.33)
MATHERNE, Mary m. 11 Aug. 1897 Leo BREAUX (Lockport Ch.: v.2, p.165)
MATHERNE, Mary m. 11 Sept. 1897 Leo BREAUX (Thib. Ct. Hse.: Mar. v.37, #217)
MATHERNE, Mary Eunice (Leopal & Alice CALAHAN) b. 29 Sept. 1897 (Houma Ch.: v.5, p.201)
MATHERNE, Melia (John & Ayma DOMINIQUE) m. 29 Jan. 1898 Elles BREAUX (Lockport Ch.: v.2, p.181)
MATHERNE, Melia (John & Ayma DOMINIQUE) m. 27 Jan. 1898 Ellis BREAUX (Thib. Ct. Hse.: Mar. v.37, #37)
MATHERNE, Octavie Therese (William & Octavie DANIELS) b. 17 Sept. 1899 (Thib. Ch.: v.7, p.568)
MATHERNE, Seleme m. 25 Jan. 1899 Wilfred DANTIN (Thib. Ct. Hse.: Mar. v.38, #58)
MATHERNE, Semelie (William & Octavie DANER) m. 2 Feb. 1899 Wilfrid DANTIN (Raceland Ch.: v.2, p.89)
MATHERNE, Telesse m. 29 Jan. 1898 Lucina LABATTE (Houma Ct. Hse.: Mar. v.30 & 31, #192)
MATHERNE, Telesse (Joseph & Azelina SAVOIE) m. 29 Jan. 1898 Lucina LABATTE (Raceland Ch.: v.2, p.60)
MATHERNE, Victorin d. 13 Aug. 1896 at age 8 days (Raceland Ch.: v.1, p.9)
MATHEWS, George m. 25 March 1898 Octavie THOMAS (Thib. Ct. Hse.: Mar. v.37, #134)
MATHEY, Sylvia m. 4 Feb. 1897 John SIMMONS (Thib. Ct. Hse.: Mar. v.36, #67)
MATTEATO, Ignatio d. 7 Jan. 1899 at age 23 yrs. (Thib. Ch.: v.3, p.225)
MATTHEWS, Evelina m. 2 July 1898 Charles McCRAY (Houma Ct. Hse.: Mar. v.30 & 31, #47)

MATTHEWS, Rose m. 15 April 1897 Willie RUFFIN (Houma Ct. Hse.: Mar. v.29 & 30, #383)
MATTHEWS, Sarah m. 12 Oct. 1899 Milton VERRET (Houma Ct. Hse.: Mar. v.31 & 32, #147)
MAUFFRAY, Alice V. m. 28 Jan. 1899 Amadeo E. AUCOIN (Thib. Ct. Hse.: Mar. v.38, #78)
MAURICE, Cabrol d. 26 Oct. 1899 at age 6 mths. (Thib. Ch.: v.3, p.242)
MAURICE, Francesco m. 28 Jan. 1899 Anna RAIA (Houma Ct. Hse.: Mar. v.30 & 31, #289)
MAURICE, Francesco (Antonino & Felicia CAMPELL) m. 11 Feb. 1899 Anna RAIA (Houma Ch.: v.6-a, p.277)
MAURICE, Jean Maurice Corat (Johnny & Pauline NAQUIN) b. 9 April 1899 (Chackbay Ch.: v.1, p.133)
MAURICE, Vivienne Annette (Jean & Pauline NAQUIN) b. 22 March 1899 (Thib. Ch.: v.7, p.601)
MAURICHA, Antonio (Antonio & Felicia CAMBECHE) m. 29 Oct. 1898 Rosalie CAMBECHE (Houma Ch.: v.6-a, p.257)
MAUTERER, Mary Pearl (Victor & Mary Catherine Eliza BERET) b. 17 Oct. 1898 (Houma Ch.: Epis. Ch.: v.1, p.120)
MAVRICHA, Antonio m. 18 Oct. 1898 Rosalie CAMBECHE (Houma Ct. Hse.: Mar. v.30 & 31, #124)

MAXCIANTO (See: MARCANTE)

MAY, Joseph Nelson Aide (Aurelien & Odille GUILLOT) b. 21 Jan. 1897 (Thib. Ch.: v.7, p.440)
MAY, Joseph Vilier (Justilien & Marie GUILLOTTE) b. 4 April 1896 (Thib. Ch.: v.7, p.398)

MAYER (Sometimes: MEYER)

MAYET, Alceste (Andre & Angelique LERROY) m. 24 Jan. 1898 Palmyre LEBLANC (Lockport Ch.: v.2, p.180)
MAYET, Alceste (Andre & Angelique LERROY) m. 24 Jan. 1898 Palmyre LEBLANC (Thib. Ct. Hse.: Mar. v.37, #27)
MAYET, Clarence (Ernest & Angella CRETIONI) b. 18 July 1897 (Thib. Ch.: v.7, p.457)
MAYFIELD, Antoinette widow of Beverly JUDAH m. 18 July 1898 Henry PRICE (Thib. Ct. Hse.: Mar. v.38, #228)
MAYO, ----- child d. 22 June 1898 at age 1 day (Houma Ch.: v.3, p.17)
MAYOTTA, Callogero d. 15 Aug. 1899 (Houma Ch.: v.3, p.24)
MAYS, Abraham m. 12 June 1899 Louisa PARKER (Houma Ct. Hse.: Mar. v.31 & 32, #44)
MAZARACK, Joseph d. 12 Feb. 1897 at age 15 minutes (Houma Ch.: v.3, p.11)
MAZARIN, Elsei m. 21 Feb. 1898 Cecilia THERIOT (Houma Ch.: v.6-a, p.235)
MAZERAC, Alsie (Philip & Armance MAZERAC) m. 25 Feb. 1897 Cecilia THERIOT (Houma Ct. Hse.: Mar. v.29 & 30, #330)

MAZERIN, Mary (Alcide & Cecilia THERRIAULT) b. 22 Jan. 1898 (Houma Ch.: v.5, p.199)
McBRIDE, Ada d. 25 Jan. 1899 at age 55 yrs. (Thib. Ch.: Epis. Ch.: v.1, p.394)
McBRIDE, Malcolm Duane (Jos. M. & Mary A. McBRIDE) b. 9 Sept. 1896 (Houma Ch.: First Presbyt. Ch.: v.1, p.262)
McBRIDE, Olive over 18 yrs. (d.Robert R. & Ada THIBODAUX) Emancipation: 20 Aug. 1897. (Thib. Ct. Hse.: Succ. #1519)
McBRIDE, Robert Edwin (Robert Rankin & Emile Ada THIBODEAUX) m. 12 May 1898 Genevieve Edmondson WILLIAMS (Houma Ct. Hse.: Mar. v.30 & 31, #434)
McCLENNAN, Denis m. 29 Jan. 1897 Sarah COLLINS (Houma Ct. Hse.: Mar. v.29 & 30, #267)
McCODUM, Mildred Lee d. 4 Nov. 1899 at age 6½ mths. (Thib. Ch.: Epis. Ch.: v.1, p.394)

McCOLLUM (Sometimes: McCOLLA, McCOLLAM, McCOLLON, McCOLUN, McCULLA)

McCOLLUM, Elizabeth Jeanne (Nehemiah & Marie SCALLIN) b. 9 Feb. 1896 (Lockport Ch.: v.2, p.321)
McCOLLUM, Francis d. 29 Aug. 1899 at age 2 mths., 28 days (Thib. Ch.: v.3, p.239)
McCOLLUM, Nellie (Jno. & Louisiana LUSIGNAN) m. 10 June 1896 Philippe MARONGE (Thib. Ct. Hse.: Mar. v.35, #100)
McCOLLUM, Nellie (John & Louisiane LUSIGNAN) m. 10 June 1896 Philippe MARONGE (Thib. Ch.: v.14, p.91)
McCOMACHIE, John m. 6 Feb. 1899 Ellen K. PUGH (Thib. Ct. Hse.: Mar. v.38, #93)
McCORMACHIE, John m. 7 Feb. 1899 Ellen K. PUGH (Thib. Ch.: Epis. Ch.: v.1, p.331)
McCORMICK, Mary Lucy (William & Mollie HOGAN) b. 7 Jan. 1898 (Thib. Ch.: v.7, p.483)
McCORMICK, William (James & Mary McGUIRE) m. 17 Feb. 1897 Mary HOGAN (Thib. Ch.: v.14, p.127)
McCORMICK, William (James & Mary McGUIRE) m. 17 Feb. 1897 Mary HOGAN (Thib. Ct. Hse.: Mar. v.36, #81)
McCRAY, Charles m. 2 July 1898 Evelina MATTHEWS (Houma Ct. Hse.: Mar. v.30 & 31, #47)
McCULLA, Francis Joseph (Frank & Victorine ESTEVE) b. 2 June 1898 (Thib. Ch.: v.7, p.551)
McCULLA, Henriette Muriel (John & Louise MICHELOT) b. 22 Nov. 1899 (Thib. Ch.: v.8, p.18)
McCULLA, Joseph (John & Jane MULLON) m. 22 Nov. 1898 Emilie RIVIERE (Thib. Ct. Hse.: Mar. v.38, #309)
McCULLA, Joseph (John & Jane MULLON) m. 22 Nov. 1898 Emilie RIVIERE (Thib. Ch.: v.14, p.230)
McCULLA, Thomas m. 31 Aug. 1896 Laura Pauline KLINGMAN (Houma Ct. Hse.: Mar. v.29 & 30, #142)
McCULLA, Thomas (John & Jane MULLON) m. 2 Sept. 1896 Laura Pauline KLINGMAN (Houma Ch.: v.6-a, p.179)

McCULLOM, Francisque m. Emile BENOIT d. 18 Jan. 1896 at age 25 yrs. & 5 mths. (Thib. Ch.: v.3, p.178)
McCULLOM, John Clarence (Frank & Victorine ESTEVE) b. 9 Oct. 1896 (Thib. Ch.: v.7, p.421)
McCULLOM, Rosa d. 15 Nov. 1898 at age 4 yrs. (Thib. Ch.: v.3, p.222)
McDERMOTT, Joseph Albert Thomas (Thomas & Mary Ann TAYLOR) b. 16 Feb. 1897 (Thib. Ch.: v.7, p.439)

McDONALD (Sometimes: McDONELD)
McDONALD, Andre (John & Felicie HEBERT) m. 28 Jan. 1896 Alexina SAPIER (Raceland Ch.: v.2, p.30)
McDONALD, Andrew m. 14 Jan. 1897 Alexina SAPIER (Thib. Ct. Hse.: Mar. v.36, #30)
McDONALD, John (John & Felicie HEBERT) m. 29 Nov. 1897 Lucinda SAPIER (Raceland Ch.: v.2, p.54)
McDONALD, John Jr. m. 29 Nov. 1897 Lucinda SAPIER (Thib. Ct. Hse.: Mar. v.37, #257)
McDONALD, William D. (James B. & Elizabeth NICHOLS) m. 7 July 1897 Emily CHAPPUIS (Thib. Ch.: v.14, p.152)
McDONALD, William D. (James B. & Elizabeth NICHOLS) m. 7 July 1897 Emilie CHAPPUIS (Thib. Ct. Hse.: Mar. v.37, #186)
McDUFFY, Kate m. 17 May 1897 James HOLLOWAY (Thib. Ct. Hse.: Mar. v.36, #145)
McELROY, Daniel d. 19 Jan. 1897 at age 68 yrs. (Houma Ch.: v.3, p.11)
McELROY, Himond James (John & Roberta KING) b. 15 Sept. 1899 (Houma Ch.: v.5, p.253)
McELROY, Hugh m. 22 April 1899 Inez KING (Houma Ct. Hse.: Mar. v.31 & 32, #415)
McELROY, Hugh (Daniel & Celeste GAUTIER) m. -- April 1899 Inez KING (Houma Ch.: Epis. Ch.: v.1, p.344)
McELROY, John m. 19 Dec. 1898 Bertha KING (Houma Ct. Hse.: Mar. v.30 & 31, #150)
McELROY, John (Daniel & Celeste GAUTHIER) m. 21 Dec. 1898 Bertha KING (Houma Ch.: v.6-a, p.259)

McEVERS (Sometimes: MAC EVERS, McENESS)
McEVERS, Emma (Ghim & Josephine BOUDREAUX) m. 21 April 1898 Adam ALLEMAND (Thib. Ct. Hse.: Mar. v.38, #158)
McEVIST, Emma (Ghim & Josephine BOUDREAUX) m. 21 April 1898 Adam ALLEMAND (Lockport Ch.: v.2, p.188)
McGEE, Emma m. 7 April 1898 Bill FRANKLIN (Houma Ct. Hse.: Mar. v.30 & 31, #381)
McGEE, Maria m. 9 July 1898 Eddie HARRIS (Houma Ct. Hse.: Mar. v.30 & 31, #52)
McGEE, Thomas m. 30 June 1898 Eliza WILLIAMS (Houma Ct. Hse.: Mar. v.30 & 31, #40)
McGEE, Virginia m. 27 Dec. 1897 Eugene BAPTISTE (Houma Ct. Hse.: Mar. v.29 & 30, #160)

McHUGHES, Sylvestre Joseph (John & Elmire BERNARD) b. 8 Jan. 1899 (Larose Ch.: v.3, p.34)
McKILLARD, Albert Oscar (Daniel & Marie J. LECOMTE) b. 18 Feb. 1898 (Houma Ch.: v.5, p.205)
McKINNEY, Charles m. 7 July 1896 Vina WAGNER (Houma Ct. Hse.: Mar. v.29 & 30, #106)
McKROL, Marie Edith (Robert & Laetitia BOUDREAU) b. 12 Dec. 1897 (Houma Ch.: v.5, p.197)
McMAHON, Henri Owens (Richard & Mathilde DANSEREAU) b. 3 Sept. 1896 (Thib. Ch.: v.7, p.419)
McMANUS, Elisabeth (Patrick & Catherine BARRY) m. 16 April 1896 Numa NAQUIN (Thib. Ct. Hse.: Mar. v.35, #58)
McNEAL, Joseph m. 2 June 1896 Mary SANTEE (Houma Ct. Hse.: Mar. v.29 & 30, #85)
McROY, Pierre Alidor (Pierre & Justine LECOMPTE) b. 6 March 1896 (Theriot Ch.: v.1-B, p.90)
McZELAND, Joseph m. 19 Jan. 1899 Rosela MOORE (Thib. Ct. Hse.: Mar. v.38, #43)
MEAD, Ella m. 25 Aug. 1898 William NELSON (Thib. Ct. Hse.: Mar. v.38, #264)
MEAD, Joseph Arthur m. 25 Jan. 1897 Georgina WILLIAMS (Thib. Ct. Hse.: Mar. v.36, #55)
MEAD, Layar B. m. 5 Dec. 1899 Willie WILLIAMS (Thib. Ct. Hse.: Mar. v.39, #277)
MEADE, Electa Hannah d. 14 May 1897 at age 39 yrs. (Thib. Ch.: Epis. Ch.: v.1, p.394)
MEADOWS, Epsie m. 13 Feb. 1896 Simuel DIRDEN (Houma Ct. Hse.: Mar. v.28, #455)
MEDAL, Elmire m. Oleus ROUSSEAU d. 10 June 1898 at age 38 yrs. (Houma Ch.: v.3, p.17)

MELANCON (See Perhaps: LANCON)

MELANCON (Sometimes: LANCON, MELANSON)
MELANCON , Laura Josephine (Emile & Alfida ADAM) b. 12 July 1899 (Thib. Ch.: v.7, p.555)
MELANCON, Adam Edmond (Edgar & Marguerite GONSALES) b. 21 May 1896 (Larose Ch.: v.2, p.192)
MELANCON, Anastasie Marie (Jules & Laura PLAISANCE) b. 16 Sept. 1899 (Larose Ch.: v.3, p.45)
MELANCON, Charles Harris (Orestille & Argentine LEE) b. 26 Dec. 1897 (Larose Ch.: v.3, p.11)
MELANCON, Christophe Gilbert (Austin & Eglantine MARTIN) b. 24 July 1899 (Raceland Ch.: v.5, p.101)
MELANCON, Clay (Ozeme & Augustine LANDRY) m. 25 Jan. 1897 Marie BARBIER (Thib. Ct. Hse.: Mar. v.36, #27)
MELANCON, Clay (Ozeme & Augustine SANDROZ) m. 25 Jan. 1897 Marie BARBIER (Lockport Ch.: v.2, p.158)
MELANCON, Dovida (Alfred & Lize ALENA) m. 24 April 1899 Adam UZE (Thib. Ct. Hse.: Mar. v.39, #156)

MELANCON, Dovida (Alfred & Lize ALENA) m. 3 May 1899 Adam UZE (Lockport Ch.: v.2, p.208)
MELANCON, Felecine m. Franklin PIERCE Inventory: 4 April 1899. (Thib. Ct. Hse.: Succ. #1557)
MELANCON, Fliys d. 2 Feb. 1899 at age 67 yrs. (Lockport Ch.: v.1, #4)
MELANCON, Gustave d. 22 Dec. 1898 at age 4 yrs. (Larose Ch.: v.1, p.45)
MELANCON, Henri d. 25 Feb. 1899 at age 1 mth. (Thib. Ch.: v.3, p.229)
MELANCON, Henri Jean (Ozeme & Eugenie DAIGLE) b. 28 Jan. 1898 (Thib. Ch.: v.7, p.534)
MELANCON, Louis Harris (Alexandre & Francine TOUPS) b. 30 Nov. 1897 (Thib. Ch.: v.7, p.524)
MELANCON, Louis Ozemee (Ozeme & Eugenie DAIGLE) b. 1 Jan. 1899 (Thib. Ch.: v.7, p.580)
MELANCON, Louis Thomas (Clet & Olympe TOUPS) b. 10 Jan. 1897 (Thib. Ch.: v.7, p.435)
MELANCON, Louise Marie (Leo & Camilla BOURGEOIS) b. 17 Aug. 1899 (Raceland Ch.: v.5, p.101)
MELANCON, Maria Anita (Clay & Olimpe TOUPS) b. 12 Feb. 1898 (Thib. Ch.: v.7, p.535)
MELANCON, Octave Apolinaire (Jules & Laura PLAISANCE) b. 23 July 1897 (Larose Ch.: v.3, p.2)
MELANCON, Olivier Moise (Alexandre & Marie TOUPS) b. 1 Nov. 1896; m. Marie Elisa GAUBERT on 26 April 1923. (Raceland Ch.: Bapt. Bk., v.5, p.35)
MELANCON, Paul Fernand (Emile & Olfida ADAM) b. 13 July 1896 (Thib. Ch.: v.7, p.461)
MELANCON, Philomene d. 4 Jan. 1897; m. Francis FALCON Children: Frank, 19 yrs.; Lezin, 9 yrs. Petition for inventory: 28 Aug. 1897. (Thib. Ct. Hse.: Succ. #1520)
MELANCON, Samson m. 19 March 1898 Eugenie BERNARD (Thib. Ct. Hse.: Mar. v.37, #128)
MELANCON, Theodule (Gilbert & Edna CHAUVIN) d. 13 Sept. 1896 at age 65 yrs. (Thib. Ch.: v.3, p.187)
MELANCON, Thomas m. 5 Feb. 1898 Indiana BROOKS (Thib. Ct. Hse.: Mar. v.37, #75)
MELANCON, V. Mrs. d. 22 July 1897 (Larose Ch.: v.1, p.41)
MELANCON, Victor (Alfred & Lisee LAINEN) m. 9 Dec. 1899 Amelia RICHOUX (Larose Ch.: v.4, p.129)
MELANCON, Victor Jr. (Alfred & Lisee LAINEN) m. 9 Dec. 1899 Amelia RICHOUX (Larose Ch.: v.3, p.13)
MELANCON, Victore Jr. (Alfred & Lisee LAINER) m. 29 Nov. 1899 Amelia RICHOUX (Thib. Ct. Hse.: Mar. v.39, #273)
MELANCON, Victorine Olive (Ozeme & Eugenie DAIGUE) b. 22 Dec. 1896 (Thib. Ch.: v.7, p.430)
MELANCON, William Sampson (Edgard & Marguerite GONSALES) b. 26 July 1899 (Larose Ch.: v.3, p.43)
MELTON, Odelia m. 19 Jan. 1899 John FIELDS (Houma Ct. Hse.: Mar. v.30 & 31, #255)

MELVEY, John m. 11 May 1898 Mary HENDERSON (Houma Ct. Hse.: Mar. v.30 & 31, #440)
MENARD, Rev. Charles M. d. 7 Jan. 1896 Petition to raise the seals and for inventory: 21 Jan. 1896. (Thib. Ct. Hse.: Succ. #1477)
MENARD, Rev. Father Charles d. 9 Jan. 1896. He was Pastor in this parish for 54 yrs. (Thib. Ch.: v.3, p.177)
MENVILLE, Louis Paul (Louis J. & Victoire GOUAUX) b. 29 June 1898; m. Annette Jane DOUCET on 17 April 1920. (Houma Ch.: Bapt. Bk., v.5, p.215)
MERANTE, Guisto (Francisco & Paola GUSTANZA) m. 9 Oct. 1897 Maria Concietta CALI (Thib. Ch.: v.14, p.162)

MERCANDE (Sometimes: MERCANT)
MERCANDE, Francisca (Ignacio & Crucifixa LOMBARDA) b. 10 March 1897 (Thib. Ch.: v.7, p.443)
MERCANDE, Philippe d. 3 Sept. 1897 at age 9 yrs. (Thib. Ch.: v.3, p.205)
MERCANTE, Andrea (Ignagio & Crocifissa LOMBARDA) b. 19 July 1899 (Raceland Ch.: v.5, p.99)
MERCANTE, Antonina d. 4 Nov. 1899 at age 3 mths. (Raceland Ch.: v.1, p.28)
MERCANTE, Antonina (Ignagio & Crocifissa LOMBARDA) b. 19 July 1899 (Raceland Ch.: v.5, p.99)
MERCANTE, Francisca Chichina (Ignacio & Dominica LABARBERA) b. 28 July 1896 (Thib. Ch.: v.7, p.453)
MERCANTE, Francisco (Justo & Concietta CALI) b. 16 Aug. 1898 (Thib. Ch.: v.7, p.511)
MERCANTE, Guisto (Francisco & Paola GUSTANZA) m. 9 Oct. 1897 Marie Concietta CALI (Thib. Ct. Hse.: Mar. v.37, #232)
MERCANTE, Salvatore (Ignazio & Domenica LABARBERA) b. 28 Jan. 1899 (Thib. Ch.: v.7, p.586)
MERLO, Francesca m. 31 Jan. 1898 Biaggio ROIA (Houma Ct. Hse.: Mar. v.30 & 31, #263)
MERLO, Guisappa (Frangisco & Maria ROSOLA) m. 12 Feb. 1898 Biaggio ROIA (Houma Ch.: v.6-a, p.231)
MERONE, Francois d. 8 Aug. 1896 at age 72 yrs. (Larose Ch.: v.1, p.37)
MERRITT, Ellick m. 11 June 1898 Ellen TILLMAN (Houma Ct. Hse.: Mar. v.30 & 31, #13)
MERZULLO, Semi (Castreuge & Angela SAUZONA) b. 6 Oct. 1899 (Houma Ch.: v.5, p.257)
MESSINA, Josue (Dominique & Paula COURTO) b. 16 April 1899 (Thib. Ch.: v.7, p.600)

MEYER (See: MAYER)
MEYER, Alma (Leon & Delphine MORVAN) b. 16 March 1899 (Chackbay Ch.: v.1, p.131)
MEYER, Antoinette (Joseph & Eveline MORVANT) b. 27 Dec. 1896 (Chackbay Ch.: v.1, p.81)

MEYER, Charles Claude (Joseph & Eveline MORVAN) b. 29 Nov. 1899 (Chackbay Ch.: v.1, p.145)
MEYER, Clara (d.Salomon & Flore BERIAULT) bt. 24 Aug. 1896 (Chackbay Ch.: v.1, p.72)
MEYER, Clara (d.Solomon & Flora BARIAU) m. 3 Sept. 1896 Felix CLEMENT (Chackbay Ch.: v.1, p.30 & 31)
MEYER, Clara (Solomon & Flore BERIAN) m. 3 Sept. 1896 Felix CLEMENT (Thib. Ct. Hse.: Mar. v.36, #136)
MEYER, Lehman m. d.Henrietta LEVY Child listed: Julius. Account of administration: 24 Sept. 1896. (Thib. Ct. Hse.: Succ. #1489)
MEYER, Leon (d.Salomon & Flore PERILLO) m. 15 June 1898 Delphine MORVAN (Chackbay Ch.: v.1, p.62)
MEYER, Lloyd Louis (Albert J. & Brigitte BRAUD) b. 12 Feb. 1899 (Thib. Ch.: v.7, p.537)
MEYER, Louis J. d. 2 Aug. 1897 at age 72 yrs. & 11 mths. (Thib. Ch.: v.3, p.204)
MEYER, Marcellin m. 26 March 1896 Mary JACKSON (Thib. Ct. Hse.: Mar. v.35, #56)
MEYER, Marie Lucille (Albert & Brigitte BRAUD) b. 22 Oct. 1899 (Thib. Ch.: v.8, p.14)
MEYER, Thomas Emmett (Albert & Brigitte BRAUD) b. 19 Sept. 1896 (Thib. Ch.: v.7, p.419)
MICCELE, Domenico (Pascuale & Francesca SCCORTINO) b. 26 March 1899 (Thib. Ch.: v.7, p.543)
MICHANEL, Agnes Julienne (Faustin & Heloise CROCHET) b. 23 Aug. 1897; m. Miller Joseph DUPLANTIS on 12 Feb. 1922. (Houma Ch.: Bapt. Bk., v.5, p.186)

MICHEL (Sometimes: MICHAEL, MICHELS)
MICHEL, Delphine (Elphege & Aspasie PREVOST) m. 5 May 1896 Albert SENAC (Houma Ct. Hse.: Mar. v.29 & 30, #51)
MICHEL, Henry (Pasquale & Francisca SCIORTINA) b. 6 May 1896 (Thib. Ch.: v.7, p.448)
MICHEL, Marie Oniffe Bibienne (Lucien & Theodilia MIRRE) b. 12 June 1898 (Houma Ch.: v.5, p.216)
MICHEL, Michel Eulaide d. 9 April 1897 at age 27 yrs. (Thib. Ch.: v.3, p.198)
MICHEL, Ophelia m. 26 June 1896 Duncan BOUDREAUX (Houma Ct. Hse.: Mar. v.29 & 30, #99)
MICHEL, Ophelia (Elphege & Aspalie PREVOST) m. 14 June 1898 Henry NEAL (Montegut Ch.: v.4, p.246)
MICHEL, Ophelia (Elphege & Aspolie PREVOST) m. 31 May 1898 Henry NEAL (Houma Ct. Hse.: Mar. v.30 & 31, #458)
MICHEL, Philomene Elizabeth (Joseph & Adelaide MITCHEL) b. 24 Feb. 1897 (Thib. Ch.: v.7, p.441)
MICHEL, Walter Alvin (Jean & Louisiana LESBSTROY) b. 24 Sept. 1899 (Larose Ch.: v.3, p.56)
MICHELET, Marie Ada (Albert & Celeste LEBLANC) b. 7 Dec. 1898 (Thib. Ch.: v.7, p.525)

MICHENS, Florida m. 12 Feb. 1896 Rose LEWIS (Houma Ct. Hse.: Mar. v.28, #447)

MIDDLETON or MILTON, Mathilde m. 7 Oct. 1897 Frank DAIGLE (Thib. Ct. Hse.: Mar. v.37, #246)

MIDDLETON, Henry m. 23 Dec. 1899 Sarah RANKINS (Thib. Ct. Hse.: Mar. v.39, #297)

MILES, Henry m. 24 Oct. 1896 Martha SPENCER (Houma Ct. Hse.: Mar. v.29 & 30, #175)

MILES, Ida m. 3 June 1898 Warren WOODS (Thib. Ct. Hse.: Mar. v.38, #193)

MILLARD, Modeste Agnes (Alfred & Mary HENNAGRIFF) b. 21 March 1897 (Houma Ch.: v.5, p.190)

MILLER, Blanche Leonise (John & Uranie MARTIN) b. 11 March 1898 (Larose Ch.: v.3, p.21)

MILLER, Charles Blanchard (John & Uranie MARTIN) b. 11 March 1898 (Larose Ch.: v.3, p.21)

MILLER, Clarissa m. 2 Feb. 1899 William IVERY (Thib. Ct. Hse.: Mar. v.38, #85)

MILLER, Evelyn May (James S. & Elvina J. SCHEFFLER) b. 14 Feb. 1898 (Houma Ch.: Epis. Ch.: v.1, p.120)

MILLER, Grace Esther (Jos. S. & Evelina J. SCHEFFLER) b. 23 Jan. 1896 (Houma Ch.: Epis. Ch.: v.1, p.112)

MILLER, James D. (Walter & Marie Jane BESSON) m. 14 July 1898 Julia GUILLOT (Thib. Ct. Hse.: Mar. v.38, #218)

MILLER, James D. (Walter & Mary Jane BESSAIN) m. 14 July 1898 Julia GUILLOT (Thib. Ch.: v.14, p.209)

MILLER, Martha m. 13 April 1898 George PATTERSON (Houma Ct. Hse.: Mar. v.30 & 31, #396)

MILLER, Melissaire Josephine d. 14 March 1899 at age 86 yrs. (Lockport Ch.: v.1, #14)

MILLER, Peter m. 28 May 1896 Betsy DAVIS (Thib. Ct. Hse.: Mar. v.35, #92)

MILLER, William m. 3 Sept. 1898 Josephine MOORE (Houma Ct. Hse.: Mar. v.30 & 31, #90)

MILLET, Pierre Noel (John & Josephine TERREBONNE) b. 21 Jan. 1897 (Larose Ch.: v.3, p.7)

MILLIARD, Edgar m. 1 July 1897 Mary Jane HENDERSON (Houma Ct. Hse.: Mar. v.29 & 30, #46-B)

MILONI, Marione (Vincenzo & Vincenza CAESAMINA) m. 21 Jan. 1899 Katharine FERINA (Thib. Ct. Hse.: Mar. v.38, #14)

MILONI, Marione (Vincenzo & Vincenza CENSAMINO) m. 21 Jan. 1899 Cattarino FARINO (Thib. Ch.: v.14, p.242)

MILTON or MIDDLETON, Mathilde m. 7 Oct. 1897 Frank DAIGLE (Thib. Ct. Hse.: Mar. v.37, #246)

MILTON, Peggie m. 8 Feb. 1899 John HUBBS (Thib. Ct. Hse.: Mar. v.38, #96)

MINNICH, Louise (Adam & Myrthe RIGAULT) b. 11 July 1898 (Larose Ch.: v.3, p.33)

MINOR, Henry C. d. 13 March 1898 m. Annie L. BUTLER Children: John Duncan, 21; Margaret, 14; Mary, 11. Tutorship: 25 March 1898. (Houma Ct. Hse.: Succ. #901)

MINOR, Henry Choland d. 13 March 1898 at age 56 yrs. (Houma Ch.: Epis. Ch.: v.1, p.388)
MINOR, Rebecca G. m. 16 Dec. 1897 James COLOMB (Houma Ct. Hse.: Mar. v.29 & 30, #145)
MIRABELLE, Marie Germaine Madame d. 11 Jan. 1896. She was Rev. Father Menard's servant for 35 yrs. (Thib. Ch.: v.3, p.178)

MIRE (Sometimes: MIER, MIRRE, MYRE)
MIRE, Agathe Natty (Oscar & Lea MIRE) b. 10 Nov. 1897 (Thib. Ch.: v.7, p.524)
MIRE, Alida (Evariste & Aurelie GUILLOT) m. 3 Feb. 1896 Joseph AUCOIN (Thib. Ch.: v.14, p.71)
MIRE, Augustin (Numa & Amelia MIRE) m. 25 April 1899 Leontia ROGER (Thib. Ct. Hse.: Mar. v.39, #145)
MIRE, Augustin (Numa & Amelia MIRE) m. 25 April 1899 Leontia ROGER (Thib. Ch.: v.14, p.273)
MIRE, Bertha d. 22 Nov. 1899 at age 9 mths. (Thib. Ch.: v.3, p.244)
MIRE, Effie Beatrice (Alcide & Marie MIRE) b. 3 Jan. 1898 (Thib. Ch.: v.7, p.482)
MIRE, Eliva m. Colville BERNARD d. 3 Dec. 1899 at age 33 yrs. (Thib. Ch.: v.3, p.245)
MIRE, Ellis m. 10 June 1899 Faustine BOUDREAUX (Thib. Ct. Hse.: Mar. v.39, #178)
MIRE, Emma m. 2 June 1899 Elphege J. CLEMENT (Thib. Ct. Hse.: Mar. v.39, #175)
MIRE, Emma (Justilien & Villia GUILLOT) m. 6 June 1899 Elfege J. CLEMENT (Thib. Ch.: v.14, p.283)
MIRE, Gabriel d. 18 Feb. 1898 at age 3 mths. (Thib. Ch.: v.3, p.211)
MIRE, Gertrude (Comere & Georgina BINA) b. 31 July 1896 (Thib. Ch.: v.7, p.460)
MIRE, Gustave d. 18 April 1894 m. Adeline BERNARD Children listed: Omer; Oscar; Ellis; Lubin; Odelia; John; Ida; Therese. Petition for inventory: 28 May 1898. (Thib. Ct. Hse.: Succ. #1536)
MIRE, Harry Gabriel (Justilien & Marie GUILLOT) b. 9 Sept. 1897 (Thib. Ch.: v.7, p.465)
MIRE, Jean (Dorville & Lezida BERNARD) m. 26 Feb. 1897 Lilia ADAM (Thib. Ch.: v.14, p.132)
MIRE, Jeanne m. 15 April 1899 Bernard CLEMENT (Thib. Ct. Hse.: Mar. v.39, #144)
MIRE, Jeanne (Numa & Amelia MIRE) m. 19 April 1899 Bernard CLEMENT (Thib. Ch.: v.14, p.271)
MIRE, John m. 26 Feb. 1897 Lilia ADAM (Thib. Ct. Hse.: Mar. v.36, #92)
MIRE, Joseph (Justilien & Evia GUILLOT) b. 6 April 1896 (Thib. Ch.: v.7, p.400)
MIRE, Lea (Justilien & Hervilie GUILLOTE) m. 27 April 1897 Oscar MIRE (Thib. Ch.: v.14, p.139)

MIRE, Lea (Justilien & Hervilien GUILLOTTE) m. 17 April 1897 Oscar MIRE (Thib. Ct. Hse.: Mar. v.36, #131)
MIRE, Leonarde Azilie (Pierre & Philomene GUILLOT) b. 7 March 1899 (Thib. Ch.: v.7, p.541)
MIRE, Lucie Althea (Paul & Georgina CLEMENT) b. 22 Feb. 1896 (Thib. Ch.: v.7, p.393)
MIRE, Marie Laure (Paul & Georgina CLEMENT) b. 6 Jan. 1898 (Thib. Ch.: v.7, p.531)
MIRE, Oscar (Gustave & Adelia BERNARD) m. 27 April 1897 Lea MIRE (Thib. Ch.: v.14, p.139)
MIRE, Oscar (Gustave & Adelia BERNARD) m. 17 April 1897 Lea MIRE (Thib. Ct. Hse.: Mar. v.36, #131)
MIRE, Peter (Dorville & Lesida BERNARD) m. 1 Feb. 1897 Philomene GUILLOTTE (Thib. Ct. Hse.: Mar. v.36, #53)
MIRE, Pierre (Dorville & Lesidie BERNARD) m. 1 Feb. 1897 Philomene GUILLOTE (Thib. Ch.: v.14, p.118)
MIRE, Thomas Frederique (Oscar & Lea MIRE) b. 24 Jan. 1899 (Thib. Ch.: v.7, p.588)
MIRE, Valery Bertha (Homer & Georgina BINER) b. 13 Feb. 1899 (Thib. Ch.: v.7, p.539)
MIRE, Viola Carmelita Marguerite (Alcide & Marie MIRE) b. 24 Feb. 1896 (Thib. Ch.: v.7, p.393)
MISERAGO, Frank (Vincenzo & Veradia CARDINALE) b. 5 Jan. 1898 (Raceland Ch.: v.5, p.64)
MISSE, Aitana (Dominico & Paola LACURTA) b. 26 April 1898 (Thib. Ch.: v.7, p.499)
MISSURACA, Antonina (Francisco & Maria Gracia VANDALSO) b. 6 Feb. 1897 (Raceland Ch.: v.5, p.41)
MISURACA, Angelina (Francisco & Maria Gracia RANGAZZA) b. 26 Jan. 1899 (Raceland Ch.: v.5, p.91)
MISURACA, Salvatore (Vincenza & Doratia CARDINALE) b. 22 Sept. 1899 (Raceland Ch.: v.5, p.103)
MITCHEL, Anne d. 24 March 1896 at age 15 days (Thib. Ch.: v.3, p.180)
MITCHEL, Joseph m. 25 Nov. 1896 Adelaide JONES (Thib. Ct. Hse.: Mar. v.36, #163)
MITCHEL, Joseph (Hentmare & Eveline ADAM) m. 26 Nov. 1896 Adelaide JONES (Thib. Ch.: v.14, p.102)
MITCHELL, Anderson m. 11 Oct. 1897 Mandy MADISON (Houma Ct. Hse.: Mar. v.29 & 30, #118)
MITCHELL, Easter m. 4 July 1898 Willie COLEMAN (Thib. Ct. Hse.: Mar. v.38, #219)
MITCHELL, Jake m. 9 July 1896 Mary BOLDEN (Houma Ct. Hse.: Mar. v.29 & 30, #111-C)
MITCHELL, Lawrence Charley (Charley MITCHELL) d. 23 Oct. 1899 at age 2 yrs. 6 mths. (Theriot Ch.: v.1, p.2)
MITCHELL, William m. 28 Dec. 1899 Beatrice TARDY (Thib. Ct. Hse.: Mar. v.39, #302)
MOAT, George Howard (Fred & Annie McKINNON) m. 22 June 1897 Florence Elizabeth HELLIER (Houma Ch.: Epis. Ch.: v.1, p.342)

MOATE, George Howard (Frederick & Annie McKINNON) m. 3 June 1897 Florence Elizabeth HELLIER (Houma Ct. Hse.: Mar. v.29 & 30, #435)

MOBLEY, Aimee Edna (Thomas & Henriette CANTRELLE) b. 16 May 1896 (Larose Ch.: v.2, p.191)

MOBLEY, Henry (Thomas & Henriette CANTRELLE) b. 25 March 1898 (Larose Ch.: v.3, p.25)

MOHANNA, Josephine (S. & L. ONARDITI) b. 15 Sept. 1899; m. Ferris SAADI on 16 Nov. 1925. (Houma Ch.: Bapt. Bk., v.5, p.254)

MOHANNA, Victoria (Stephen & Rosa SPATH) b. 15 May 1896 (Houma Ch.: v.5, p.180)

MOISE, Leonard Mrs. d. 5 April 1898 at age 5 hrs. (Houma Ch.: v.3, p.16)

MOISE, Thomas Garland (H. C. & Regina MOUTON) b. 6 Feb. 1896 (Houma Ch.: v.5, p.143)

MOLAIRE, Bernadette (Octave & Lavigna LAJAUNIE) m. 12 Jan. 1898 Clay BOUDREAUX (Houma Ct. Hse.: Mar. v.29 & 30, #148)

MOLAIRE, Bernadette (Octave & Luvigna LAJAUNIE) m. 12 Ja. 1898 Clay BOUDREAUX (Chacahoula Ch.:v.1, p.64 [84])

MOLAISON (Sometimes: MOLESON, MOLOISON)

MOLAISON, ----- boy d. 17 Feb. 1897 (Thib. Ch.: v.3, p.197)

MOLAISON, Agnes Carmelite (Justin & Leontine GRABERT) b. 6 Sept. 1896 (Lockport Ch.: v.2, p.336)

MOLAISON, Augustin (Augustin & Louisa HEBERT) m. 11 May 1899 Clotilde MARCEL (Thib. Ct. Hse.: Mar. v.39, #154)

MOLAISON, Augustin (Augustin & Louisa HEBERT) m. 11 May 1899 Clotilde MARCEL (Thib. Ch.: v.14, p.280)

MOLAISON, Celina d. 16 Aug. 1897 at age 75 yrs. (Thib. Ch.: v.3, p.204)

MOLAISON, Danvil (Prosper & Melie BABIN) b. 3 March 1898 (Thib. Ch.: v.7, p.547)

MOLAISON, Ernest (Peter & Rosema HEBERT) m. 23 May 1898 Emilie NAVARE (Thib. Ct. Hse.: Mar. v.38, #178)

MOLAISON, Ernest (Pierre & Rose Emma HEBERT) m. 23 May 1898 Emelie NAVARRE (Chackbay Ch.: v.1, p.61)

MOLAISON, Eudolia (Justin & Leontine GRABERT) m. 29 Jan. 1898 Alceste ARABIE (Thib. Ct. Hse.: Mar. v.37, #19)

MOLAISON, Joseph (Lovincy & Aurelia ADAM) m. 3 Feb. 1896 Celeste BOUDREAUX (Chacahoula Ch.: v.1, p.56)

MOLAISON, Joseph (Lovincy & Aurelia ADAM) m. 3 Feb. 1896 Celeste BOUDREAUX (Houma Ct. Hse.: Mar. v.28, #431)

MOLAISON, Joseph Pierre (Pierre & Celestine HEBERT) b. 4 April 1896 (Thib. Ch.: v.7, p.400)

MOLAISON, Joseph Sylvestre (Augustin & Louisa HEBERT) b. 24 Nov. 1897 (Thib. Ch.: v.7, p.481)

MOLAISON, Leo Frost d. 29 Oct. 1897 at age 18 mths. (Thib. Ch.: v.3, p.207)

MOLAISON, Leo Frost (Leo & Virginia FROST) b. 21 June 1896 (Thib. Ch.: v.7, p.406)

MOLAISON, Louisiane (Pierre & Rosanna HEBERT) m. 1 Feb. 1897 Joseph SANCHEZ (Thib. Ct. Hse.: Mar. v.36, #38)
MOLAISON, Louisiane (Pierre & Rosarina HEBERT) m. 1 Feb. 1897 Joseph SANCHEZ (Chackbay Ch.: v.1, p.38)
MOLAISON, Lucie Eleonore (Pierre & Celeste HEBERT) b. 1 Sept. 1898 (Thib. Ch.: v.7, p.512)
MOLAISON, Marie m. 11 May 1897 Theogene LEBOEUF (Houma Ct. Hse.: Mar. v.29 & 30, #412)
MOLAISON, Marie (Lovincy & Aurelia ADAM) m. 3 June 1897 Theogene LEBOEUF (Chacahoula Ch.: v.1, p.63)
MOLAISON, Mathilde (Justin & Leontine GRABERT) m. 6 June 1898 Ernest PLAISANCE (Thib. Ct. Hse.: Mar. v.38, #194)
MOLAISON, Mathilde (Justin & Leontine GRABERT) m. 6 June 1898 Ernest PLAISANCE (Lockport Ch.: v.2, p.189)
MOLAISON, Michel (Justin & Leontine GRABERT) m. 4 Feb. 1897 Ernestine AUTHEMENT (Thib. Ct. Hse.: Mar. v.36, #48)
MOLAISON, Michel (Justin & Leontine GRABERT) m. 4 Feb. 1897 Ernestine AUTHEMENT (Lockport Ch.: v.2, p.159)
MOLAISON, Odelia (Lovency & Amelia ADAM) m. 24 April 1899 Mack LEBOEUF (Houma Ct. Hse.: Mar. v.31 & 32, #416)
MOLAISON, Oscar Joseph (Joseph & Celeste BOUDREAUX) b. 14 April 1897 (Chacahoula Ch.: v.4, p.19)
MOLAISON, Philomene (Justin & Leontine GRABERT) m. 29 Jan. 1898 Alceste ARABIE (Lockport Ch.: v.2, p.181)
MOLAISON, Philomore d. 28 Jan. 1898 at age 50 yrs. (Thib. Ch.: v.3, p.210)
MOLE, Calogero (Antoinino & Larita PIAZZA) b. 6 Feb. 1897 (Houma Ch.: v.5, p.165)
MOLHER, Azelia (Botley & Philomene SANCHEZ) m. 7 Oct. 1899 Joseph PEREZ (Thib. Ct. He.: Mar. v.39, #239)
MOLHER, Azelia (Botly & Philomene SANCHEZ) m. 7 Oct. 1899 Joseph PEREZ (Chackbay Ch.: v.1, p.74)

MOLINAIRE (Sometimes: MOLINERE)
MOLINAIRE, Emma Eulalie (Omer & Marie CHIASSON) b. 12 Feb. 1897 (Montegut Ch.: v.6, p.52)
MOLINAIRE, Lives Andre (Omer & Marie CHIASSON) b. 15 Dec. 1898 (Montegut Ch.: v.6, p.80)
MOLLA, Elisabeth (Antonio & Antonina GOULOTTE) b. 16 Dec. 1897 (Houma Ch.: v.5, p.196)
MOLLE, Caterina (Viarzo & Pefania RISASSE) m. 13 April 1899 Guiseppe COSENZA (Thib. Ch.: v.14, p.270)
MOLLE, Caterina (Vincenzo & Pefania RISASSE) m. 13 April 1899 Guiseppe COSENZA (Thib. Ct. Hse.: Mar v.39, #141)
MOLLET, Epiphania (Antony & Antonia BOULLOT) b. 13 June 1899 (Houma Ch.: v.5, p.247)
MOLLET, Guisepe (Antonino & Laurita PIAZZA) b. 16 Dec. 1898 (Houma Ch.: v.5, p.227)
MOLLEUR, Alidore (Bartholemi & Philomene SANCHEZ) b. 3 May 1896 (Chackbay Ch.: v.1, p.70)

MOLTON, Sam m. 10 Feb. 1898 Josephine CARTER (Thib. Ct. Hse.: Mar. v.37, #97)
MONDELLA, Caterina (Luco & -----) m. 13 June 1898 Liborio FERRANTELLE (Thib. Ct. Hse.: Mar. v.38, #186)
MONDELLO, Caterina (Luca) m. 16 June 1898 Liborio FERANTELLE (Thib. Ch.: v.14, p.208)
MONIER, Jules d. 9 May 1899 at age 49 yrs. (Raceland Ch.: v.1, p.25)
MONIER, Marie Agnes (Ernest & Amelie CHAMPAGNE) b. 17 Sept. 1897 (Raceland Ch.: v.5, p.55)
MONROE, Ella m. 27 March 1897 Walter VERNA (Thib. Ct. Hse.: Mar. v.36, #102)
MONTAGUS, Antonio d. 17 Dec. 1899 at age 27 yrs. (Larose Ch.: v.1, p.54)
MONTICCIOLO, Maria Antonina (Gaetano & Maria LORIO) b. 8 March 1896 (Thib. Ch.: v.7, p.395)
MONZEROLLES, Julia (Etienne & Anna ESTIVEN) m. 20 April 1899 Felix LEDET (Thib. Ch.: v.14, p.272)
MOODEY, Hilda Christine (John B. & Elizabeth CARLIN) b. 10 Oct. 1897 (Houma Ch.: Epis. Ch.: v.1, p.116)
MOODY, Ada (John B. & Elizabeth CARLIN) b. 10 July 1896 (Gibson Ch.: Epis. Ch.: v.1, p.62)
MOODY, Ada (John B. & Elizabeth CARLIN) b. 10 July 1896 (Houma Ch.: Epis. Ch.: v.1, p.110)
MOODY, Ada Menge d. 20 July 1896 (Gibson Ch.: Epis. Ch.: v.1, p.114)
MOODY, Ada Minge d. 20 July 1896 (Houma Ch.: Epis. Ch.: v.1, p.386)
MOODY, Hilda Christine b. 10 Oct. 1897 (Gibson Ch.: Epis. Ch.: v.1, p.106)
MOODY, Hilda Christine (John B. & Elizabeth CARLIN) b. 10 Oct. 1897 (Gibson Ch.: Epis. Ch.: v.1, p.64)
MOODY, Shady listed on bond as MILLER m. 19 Jan. 1899 Robert WALKER (Houma Ct. Hse: Mar. v.30 & 31, #267)
MOODY, Susan m. 10 June 1897 Moses NEWTON (Houma Ct. Hse.: Mar. v.29 & 30, #24)

MOORE (Sometimes: MORE)

MOORE, Adeline m. 11 Sept. 1899 Wilson GREEN (Houma Ct. Hse.: Mar. v.31 & 32, #124)
MOORE, Betsey m. 18 Feb. 1897 Sylvester JORDAN (Houma Ct. Hse.: Mar. v.29 & 30, #322)
MOORE, Charles m. 18 Sept. 1899 Nettie CROCHET (Houma Ct. Hse.: Mar. v.31 & 32, #138)
MOORE, Charles m. 18 Sept. 1899 Nettie CROCHET (Houma Ch.: v.6-B, p.4)
MOORE, Clara (William & Anna THIBODAUX) m. 14 July 1898 Lum DARCE (Houma Ct. Hse.: Mar. v.30 & 31, #55)
MOORE, Clarissa m. 5 Jan. 1897 Jerry GREEN (Houma Ct. Hse.: Mar. v.29 & 30, #220)
MOORE, Curomin Joseph (Thomas & Eva CROCHET) b. 26 May 1898 (Houma Ch.: v.5, p.212)

MOORE, Elmira m. 28 Jan. 1899 Leonard SPARKS (Thib. Ct. Hse.: Mar. v.38, #76)
MOORE, Emma m. 11 March 1897 Walter JORDAN (Houma Ct. Hse.: Mar. v.29 & 30, #348)
MOORE, Felicia m. 21 June 1896 Harvey SHY (Houma Ct. Hse.: Mar. v.26, #229)
MOORE, Henry m. 6 May 1897 John WASHINGTON (Houma Ct. Hse.: Mar. v.29 & 30, #406)
MOORE, Joseph Thomas (Thomas & Eva CROCHET) b. 22 Oct. 1898; bt. 6 Oct. 1899; m. Josephine Henrietta LIRETTE, on 28 April 1962. (Houma Ch.: Bapt. Bk., v.5, p.255)
MOORE, Josephine m. 3 Sept. 1898 William MILLER (Houma Ct. Hse.: Mar. v.30 & 31, #90)
MOORE, Lena m. 25 Jan. 1896 Arthur MANLEY (Houma Ct. Hse.: Mar. v.28, #423)
MOORE, Louis (Shedrick & Josephine SAVOIE) b. 25 Dec. 1897 (Houma Ch.: v.5, p.203)
MOORE, Marie Anna d. 25 Feb. 1897 at age 3 mths. (Houma Ch.: v.3, p.12)
MOORE, Marie Anna (Frederic & Josephine SAVOIE) b. 24 Nov. 1896 (Houma Ch.: v.5, p.163)
MOORE, Marie Nora (Clay & Eve LADOUCEUR) b. 15 Aug. 1898 (Houma Ch.: v.5, p.222)
MOORE, Mary m. 26 June 1897 Godfrey DAVIS (Houma Ct. Hse.: Mar. v.29 & 30, #43)
MOORE, Mirian Corinne (Hamlet & Haydee SITGES) b. 22 Jan. 1899 (Thib. Ch.: v.7, p.582)
MOORE, Nancy m. 23 March 1896 Jessie JACKSON (Thib. Ct. Hse.: Mar. v.35, #55)
MOORE, Peter m. 15 Oct. 1898 Matilda LEWIS (Houma Ct. Hse.: Mar. v.30 & 31, #121)
MOORE, Richard m. 3 March 1898 Louisa BROWN (Houma Ct. Hse.: Mar. v.30 & 31, #327)
MOORE, Rosela m. 19 Jan. 1899 Joseph McZELAND (Thib. Ct. Hse.: Mar. v.38, #43)
MOORE, Sam m. 16 Feb. 1899 Henrietta TURNER (Houma Ct. Hse.: Mar. v.31 & 32, #341)
MOORE, Thomas m. 14 June 1897 Eva CROCHET (Houma Ch.: v.6-a, p.207)
MOORE, Thomas m. 5 June 1897 Eva CROCHET (Houma Ct. Hse.: Mar. v.29 & 30, #4)
MOORE, Thomas Edward Jr. d. 13 Jan. 1898 (Houma Ch.: Epis. Ch.: v.1, p.386)
MOORE, Violet m. 24 Feb. 1896 Samuel ANDERSON (Thib. Ct. Hse.: Mar. v.35, #49)

MORANGE (See: MARONGE)

MORBLEY, Ellen m. 9 March 1899 Nick COLLINS (Houma Ct. Hse.: Mar. v.31 & 32, #360)

MOREONE, Marguerite (Guiseppe & Calagiera MANESCALCHA) b. 16 Nov. 1897 (Thib. Ch.: v.7, p.478)

MORESCO, Johannine m. 22 Jan. 1898 Jean RICHOUX (Larose Ch.: v.4, p.112)

MORESCO, Johannine m. 22 Jan. 1898 Jean RICHOUX (Larose Ch.: v.3, p.7)

MORESCO, Johannine m. 22 Jan. 1898 Jean RICHOUX (Thib. Ct. Hse.: Mar. v.37, #24)

MORGAN, Alice m. 25 April 1899 Charles TAYLOR (Houma Ct. Hse.: Mar. v.31 & 32, #421)

MORGAN, Elouise m. 29 May 1898 Paul HAMMOND (Thib. Ct. Hse.: Mar. v.38, #327)

MORGAN, Geneva m. 10 March 1898 Elijah YOUNG (Thib. Ct. Hse.: Mar. v.37, #125)

MORGAN, Jacob m. 31 July 1897 Rina ROOSHA (Houma Ct. Hse.: Mar. v.29 & 30, #76)

MORGAN, Joseph Hebert (Gonzague & Hirma HEBERT) b. 5 Aug. 1899 (Raceland Ch.: v.5, p.99)

MORGAN, Mary m. 18 March 1897 Elas YOUNG (Thib. Ct. Hse.: Mar. v.36, #99)

MORGAN, Primrose m. 24 Feb. 1898 Bertha YOUNG (Thib. Ct. Hse.: Mar. v.37, #115)

MORILLON, Theodore d. 27 July 1899 at age 76 yrs. (Thib. Ch.: v.3, p.238)

MORILLON, William L. (Theodule & Letitia COCES) m. 31 Aug. 1898 Elizabeth BOURGEOIS (Thib. Ct. Hse.: Mar. v.38, #263)

MORILLON, Wuilly (Theodule & Loetitia COCES) m. 31 Aug. 1898 Elizabeth BOURGEOIS (Lockport Ch.: v.2, p.193)

MORIONE, Ignatia (Giuseppe & Vincenza VINTIVENIA) m. 24 April 1897 Angelo LUPO (Thib. Ch.: v.14, p.138)

MORIONE, Ignazia (Guiseppe & Vincenza VINTIVENIA) m. 24 April 1897 Angello LUPO (Thib. Ct. Hse.: Mar. v.36, #101)

MORRIONE, Giovanina (Guiseppe & Calogiera MANIOCALCO) b. 7 March 1896 (Thib. Ch.: v.7, p.395)

MORRIS, Calvin m. 12 Feb. 1896 Mima PARKER (Houma Ct. Hse.: Mar. v.28, #444)

MORRIS, Eve (John & Pauline NAQUIN) m. 24 Jan. 1898 Louis KRAMER (Chackbay Ch.: v.1, p.52)

MORRIS, Eve (John & Pauline NAQUIN) m. 25 Jan. 1898 Louis KRAEMER (Thib. Ct. Hse.: Mar. v.37, #10)

MORRIS, Fannie m. 24 Aug. 1899 Robert C. WILLIAMS (Houma Ct. Hse.: Mar. v.31 & 32, #108)

MORRIS, Florestine Clementine (John A. & Pauline NAQUIN) b. 26 March 1897 (Thib. Ch.: v.7, p.448)

MORRIS, Sara m. 8 Nov. 1899 J. T. GOLDEN (Thib. Ct. Hse.: Mar. v.39, #260)

MORRIS, Willie E. m. 3 Feb. 1898 Cora SMITH (Thib. Ct. Hse.: Mar. v.37, #77)

MORTON, Willie m. 25 Jan. 1899 Elizabeth LUCAS (Thib. Ct. Hse.: Mar. v.38, #59)

MORVANT (Sometimes: MORVAN)

MORVANT, ----- d. 8 April 1899 at age 6 mths. (Thib. Ch.: v.3, p.231)

MORVANT, Angelina (Jimmy & Adolphine GRAUS) b. 1 Aug. 1897 (Chackbay Ch.: v.1, p.93)

MORVANT, Carl Alvin (Domingue & Bertha SINGLETON) b. 31 Aug. 1899 (Houma Ch.: Epis. Ch.: v.1, p.122)

MORVANT, Cecile (Claybert & Lucia BENOIT) b. 19 Feb. 1897 (Chackbay Ch.: v.1, p.82 & 83)

MORVANT, Cecile (Ulysse & Corinne BREAUX) b. 26 Sept. 1897 (Thib. Ch.: v.7, p.465)

MORVANT, Delfine (Gustave & Marie DESROCHERS) m. 15 June 1898 Leon BRUCE (Thib. Ct. Hse.: Mar. v.38, #199)

MORVANT, Delphine d. 8 Aug. 1898 at age 5 yrs. (Thib. Ch.: v.3, p.218)

MORVANT, Delphine (Gustave & Marie DESROCHES) m. 15 June 1898 Leon MAYER (Chackbay Ch.: v.1, p.62)

MORVANT, Dominique (---- & Cecilia GROS) m. 26 Jan. 1898 Bertha SINGLETON (Houma Ch.: Epis. Ch.: v.1, p.342)

MORVANT, Dominique (Furci & Cecilia GROS) m. 21 Jan. 1898 Bertha SINGLETON (Houma Ct. Hse.: Mar. v.30 & 31, #240)

MORVANT, Eveline (Odressy & Philomene DURANTE) m. 14 Jan. 1897 Theobert DUHE (Thib. Ch.: v.14, p.110)

MORVANT, Eveline (Odressy & Philomene DUROCHER) m. 14 Jan. 1897 Robert DUHE (Thib. Ct. Hse.: Mar. v.36, #4)

MORVANT, Genevieve (Ulysse & Corinne BRAUD) b. 26 Sept. 1896 (Thib. Ch.: v.7, p.420)

MORVANT, Genevieve Lydna (Ulysse & Corinne BRAUD) b. 26 Sept. 1896 (Thib. Ch.: v.7, p.427)

MORVANT, Henri (Jules & Adelina CLEMENT) bt. 27 Jan. 1896 (Chackbay Ch.: v.1, p.60)

MORVANT, Joseph d. 2 June 1896 at age 3 days (Thib. Ch.: v.3, p.183)

MORVANT, Joseph Haede (Robert & Georgina MARTIN) b. 23 May 1898 (Thib. Ch.: v.7, p.556)

MORVANT, Joseph Wilnes (Claybert & Lucia BENOIT) b. 22 Oct. 1899 (Chackbay Ch.: v.1, p.144)

MORVANT, Louis (Amedee & Celanie BREAUX) b. 28 Sept. 1897 (Thib. Ch.: v.7, p.516)

MORVANT, Louis Victor (Victor & Helene DIONNE) b. 11 May 1897 (Thib. Ch.: v.7, p.500)

MORVANT, Louise (Gustave & Olympe WEBB) m. 19 April 1897 Charles BERGERON (Thib. Ch.: v.14, p.136)

MORVANT, Louise (Gustave & Olympe WEBB) m. 19 April 1897 Charles A. BERGERON (Thib. Ct. Hse.: Mar. v.36, #119)

MORVANT, Louise Marie (Eugene & Euphemie BENOIT) m. 30 Aug. 1897 Clovis Louis DUROCHER (Chackbay Ch.: v.1, p.48)

MORVANT, Louise Marie (Eugene & Euphemie BENOIT) m. 30 Aug. 1897 Clovis L. DUROCHER (Thib. Ct. Hse.: Mar. v.37, #222)

MORVANT, Mabel Marie (Hector & Emma WILTON) b. 23 July 1896 (Raceland Ch.: v.5, p.25)
MORVANT, Marie (Emile & Emilie WEBRE) m. 27 April 1898 Dr. Numa FOLSE, Jr. (Thib. Ch.: v.14, p.196)
MORVANT, Marie (Eugene & Euphemie BENOIT) m. 24 Jan. 1898 Henri BOUDREAUX (Chackbay Ch.: v.1, p.52)
MORVANT, Marie Boil (Albert & Myrtilia MIRE) b. 21 April 1897 (Thib. Ch.: v.7, p.495)
MORVANT, Marie Germaine (Joseph Paul & Adele NORMAND) m. 27 Oct. 1898 Robert BOURGEOIS (Thib. Ct. Hse.: Mar. v.38, #303)
MORVANT, Marie Germaine (Joseph Paul & Adelle NORMAND) m. 27 Oct. 1898 Robert BOURGEOIS (Thib. Ch.: v.14, p.229)
MORVANT, Martha Lylia (Victor & Helene GUILLOTTE) b. 17 Nov. 1896 (Thib. Ch.: v.7, p.434)
MORVANT, Mary (Eugene & Euphemie BENOIT) m. 24 Jan. 1898 Henri BOUDREAUX (Thib. Ct. Hse.: Mar. v.37, #22)
MORVANT, May Louise (Victor & Helene DION) b. 9 May 1899 (Thib. Ch.: v.7, p.604)
MORVANT, Robert Mrs. d. 26 July 1898 at age 3 mths. (Thib. Ch.: v.3, p.217)
MORVANT, Thomas Benjamin (Amede & Celanise BRAUD) b. 29 Oct. 1898 (Thib. Ch.: v.7, p.573)
MORVANT, Thomas Donies (Albert & Metilia MIRE) b. 29 Dec. 1899 (Thib. Ch.: v.7, p.581)
MORVANT, Ulysse d. 1 June 1899 at age 6 hours (Thib. Ch.: v.3, p.235)
MORVANT, Wallice (Jules & Adelina CLEMENT) b. 25 April 1898 (Chackbay Ch.: v.1, p.111)
MOSEBY, Anna m. 27 Feb. 1897 Willie EDMOND (Thib. Ct. Hse.: Mar. v.36, #93)
MOSEBY, Cairie m. 7 May 1896 Robert JONES (Thib. Ct. Hse.: Mar. v.35, #85)
MOSELY, Thomas m. 6 Oct. 1898 Ella BRADLEY (Thib. Ct. Hse.: Mar. v.38, #289)
MOSEMAN, Janie Jones (Jacob Edward & Agnes Atkinson HOBSON) b. 23 July 1896 (Thib. Ch.: Epis. Ch.: v.1, p.42)
MOSES, Fulton m. 10 Sept. 1898 Christina JOHNSON (Houma Ct. Hse.: Mar. v.30 & 31, #93)
MOSES, Harry m. 19 Feb. 1898 Martha JONES (Houma Ct. Hse.: Mar. v.30 & 31, #310)

MOUTARDIER (Sometimes: MONTARDIER)

MOYSE, Joseph Agenant (Oscar & Louisiana CHIASSON) b. 18 March 1897 (Lockport Ch.: v.3, #38)
MOYSE, Joseph Agenant (Oscar & Louisiane CHIASSON) b. 18 March 1897 (Lockport Ch.: v.3-A, #38)
MULE, Nicola (Guiseppa & Antonina RINARDA) b. 12 Feb. 1899 (Chacahoula Ch.: v.4, p.18)

MULLEN, Jane m. John McCULLA d. 5 Jan. 1899 at age 62 yrs. (Thib. Ch.: v.3, p.225)

MUNCH, Joseph Leopold Rene (Rene & Emilia BARBERIN) b. 16 Feb. 1897 (Thib. Ch.: v.7, p.441)

MUNCH, Maria Adele (Rene J. & Emilia BARBARIN) b. 16 July 1899 (Thib. Ch.: v.7, p.569)

MUNSON (Sometimes: MANSON, MONSON)

MUNSON, Alice m. 29 March 1897 Frank TRAHAN (Houma Ct. Hse.: Mar. v.29 & 30, #366)

MUNSON, Alice (Asa & Emma LEBOEUF) m. 1 April 1897 Frank TRAHAN (Houma Ch.: v.6-a, p.198)

MURPHY, Henry Auguste (Harry & Valentine CREPEL) b. 15 July 1896 (Larose Ch.: v.3, p.12)

"N"

NACCARI, Amendee Octave (Ottillia & Octavie COULON) b. 11 Oct. 1897 (Larose Ch.: v.3, p.24)
NACCARI, Herman m. 8 Sept. 1896 Cecile COULON (Larose Ch.: v.4, p.49)
NACCARI, Herman m. 8 Sept. 1896 Cecile COULON (Larose Ch.: v.3, p.4)
NANZ, Caroline Dorothy d. 7 Dec. 1897 (Houma Ch.: Epis. Ch.: v.1, p.386)

NAQUIN (Sometimes: NACQUIN, NAKIN, NANQUIN)
NAQUIN, Ada (Maxi & Josephine NAQUIN) m. 6 April 1896 Rodolphe CROCHET (Houma Ct. Hse.: Mar. v.29 & 30, #1)
NAQUIN, Albano Joseph (Octave & Marie GRATIANO) b. 21 April 1899 (Thib. Ch.: v.7, p.603)
NAQUIN, Albert m. 10 Jan. 1896 Emilienne BERNARD (Thib. Ct. Hse.: Mar. v.35, #17)
NAQUIN, Alice Victoria (Desiree & Elisabet DARDAR) b. 15 Jan. 1899; bt. 10 March 1903 (Larose Ch.: v.4, p.28)
NAQUIN, Alma Annie (Joseph & Alma AZEMA) b. 9 Jan. 1899 (Thib. Ch.: v.7, p.529)
NAQUIN, Ambroise Children listed: Paul; Emilie m. d.L. L. AUCOIN; Eveline m. d.Valsin PREJEAN; Lovinsky; Eugene; Odresky. Petition for inventory: 2 March 1897. (Thib. Ct. Hse.: Succ. #1509)
NAQUIN, Anna Fabiola (Maximin & Josephine SONGE) b. 1 Sept. 1898 (Chacahoula Ch.: v.4, p.12)
NAQUIN, Antoine Martin (Clement & Rosemee NAQUIN) b. 31 Jan. 1896 (Montegut Ch.: v.6, p.39)
NAQUIN, Arthemise who married Joseph VERRET d. 3 Oct. 1899 at age 68 yrs. (Theriot Ch.: v.1, p.2)
NAQUIN, Augustin (Audressey & Angele VISE) m. 3 Feb. 1898 Eliska TROXLER (Thib. Ct. Hse.: Mar. v.37, #69)
NAQUIN, Aurelie Ravanelle (Bernard & Mathilde BILLOT) b. 1 Dec. 1898 (Montegut Ch.: v.6, p.88)
NAQUIN, Bertha b. Dec. 1878. (Ozeme) Emancipation: 7 Jan. 1899. (Thib. Ct. Hse.: Succ. #1556)
NAQUIN, Bertha m. 30 June 1899 Avila PEDEAUX (Thib. Ct. Hse.: Mar. v.39, #190)
NAQUIN, Camille (Paulin & Azema DANTIN) m. 26 Sept. 1899 Agnes GUILLOT (Thib. Ch.: v.14, p.298)
NAQUIN, Camille J. (Paulin & Azema DANTIN) m. 26 Sept. 1899 Agnes GUILLOT (Thib. Ct. Hse.: Mar. v.39, #235)
NAQUIN, Cecile m. 21 Oct. 1899 Lenus STANSBURY (Thib. Ct. Hse.: Mar. v.39, #251)
NAQUIN, Cecile Julie (Jules & Louise NAVARRE) b. 6 July 1898 (Thib. Ch.: v.7, p.504)
NAQUIN, Charles (Marcelin & Alida AUCOIN) m. 12 Jan. 1897 Alice AUCOIN (Thib. Ct. Hse.: Mar. v.36, #22)

NAQUIN, Charles (Marcelin & Alida AUCOIN) m. 12 Jan. 1897 Alice AUCOIN (Thib. Ch.: v.14, p.107)
NAQUIN, Charles Olivier (Leonie & Alice MIRE) b. 13 Dec. 1896 (Thib. Ch.: v.7, p.431)
NAQUIN, Clarence (Emile & Amanda MIRE) b. 20 March 1898 (Thib. Ch.: v.7, p.492)
NAQUIN, Constance Alida (Charles & Alice AUCOIN) b. 23 Jan. 1898 (Thib. Ch.: v.7, p.485)
NAQUIN, Elmire m. 13 Feb. 1897 Denis THIBODAUX (Houma Ct. Hse.: Mar. v.29 & 30, #310)
NAQUIN, Elmire (Aristide & Elfrida THERIOT) m. 7 Feb. 1897 Denis THIBODAUX (Theriot Ch.: v.1, p.9)
NAQUIN, Elmire (Felicien & Mathilde LEBEUF) m. 4 Jan. 1897 Frank RHODES (Houma Ct. Hse.: Mar. v.29 & 30, #221)
NAQUIN, Elmire (Felicien & Mathilde LEBOEUF) m. 30 Jan. 1897 Frank RHODES (Montegut Ch.: v.4, p.217)
NAQUIN, Emelie Marie (Emile & Evelina BERGERON) b. 14 Sept. 1899 (Houma Ch.: v.6, p.13)
NAQUIN, Emma Velina (Elie & Mathilde BERGERON) b. 1 Nov. 1898 (Montegut Ch.: v.6, p.79)
NAQUIN, Ernest m. 6 Jan. 1898 Cinthia MARTIN (Houma Ct. Hse.: Mar. v.30 & 31, #181)
NAQUIN, Ernest (Emile & Aimee DUPRE) m. 24 Jan. 1898 Cynthia MARTIN (Montegut Ch.: v.4, p.231)
NAQUIN, Ernestine m. 24 Aug. 1898 Emile Joseph TOUPS (Houma Ct. Hse.: Mar. v.30 & 31, #85)
NAQUIN, Ernestine (Neuville & Malvina CHAUVIN) m. 25 Aug. 1898 Emile Joseph TOUPS (Houma Ch.: v.6-a, p.251)
NAQUIN, Euzelia (Ernest & Victorine NAQUIN) b. 4 Jan. 1898 (Montegut Ch.: v.6, p.74)
NAQUIN, Exelina (James & Josephine BERGERON) d. 14 Oct. 1897 at age 3 yrs. (Montegut Ch.: v.2, p.12)
NAQUIN, Felician Joseph (Clovis & Marguerite NAQUIN) b. 26 May 1898 (Theriot Ch.: v.2, p.36)
NAQUIN, Francois Adam (Adolphe & Ellephile BILLOT) b. 17 Sept. 1897 (Montegut Ch.: v.6, p.61)
NAQUIN, Frederic Nelson (Henry & Pauline BREAUX) b. 21 Nov. 1899 (Thib. Ch.: v.7, p.576)
NAQUIN, Gabriel Arthur (Leon & Alice MIRE) b. 29 June 1898 (Thib. Ch.: v.7, p.503)
NAQUIN, Henri (Edouard & Augustine DUPRE) m. 6 Sept. 1897 Fabiola DUPRE (Montegut Ch.: v.4, p.224)
NAQUIN, Henri (Edward & Augustine DUPRE) m. 18 Aug. 1897 Fabiola DUPRE (Houma Ct. Hse.: Mar. v.29 & 30, #80½)
NAQUIN, Henri (Justilien & Marie GUILLOTE) m. 1 Feb. 1899 Pauline BREAUX (Thib. Ct. Hse.: Mar. v.38, #50)
NAQUIN, Henri (Justilien & Marie GUILLOTE) m. 1 Feb. 1899 Pauline BREAUX (Thib. Ch.: v.14, p.253)
NAQUIN, Ida (Maxi. & Josephine NAQUIN) m. 6 April 1896 Rodolphe CROCHET (Chacahoula Ch.: v.1, p.57)

NAQUIN, J. Clay (J. Emile & Azema BOUDREAUX) m. Louise BERGERON Children listed: Edward; Philip. Petition for inventory: 27 April 1898. (Thib. Ct. Hse.: Succ. #1533)
NAQUIN, Jean Sylvestre (Paulin & Francisca GONZALEZ) b. 3 April 1898 (Thib. Ch.: v.7, p.545)
NAQUIN, Joseph (Edouard & Augustine DUPRE) d. 25 Jan. 1898 (Montegut Ch.: v.2, p.15)
NAQUIN, Joseph (Leonie & Vilca MORVAN) b. 23 July 1898 (Chackbay Ch.: v.1, p.117)
NAQUIN, Joseph A. (Ozemee & Amelia NAQUIN) m. 7 Jan. 1896 Alma AZEMA (Thib. Ct. Hse.: Mar. v.35, #11)
NAQUIN, Joseph Buddy (Victor & Marie DARDAR) b. 20 Dec. 1897 (Montegut Ch.: v.6, p.74)
NAQUIN, Joseph Claudon (James & Josephine BERGERON) b. 26 Dec. 1896 (Montegut Ch.: v.6, p.49)
NAQUIN, Joseph Denis (Henry & Fabiola DUPRE) b. 8 Sept. 1898 (Montegut Ch.: v.6, p.77)
NAQUIN, Joseph Gilbert (Ulysse & Aglaee LEBOEUF) b. 21 Nov. 1896 (Montegut Ch.: v.6, p.48)
NAQUIN, Joseph Harry (Felicien & Mathilde LEBOEUF) b. 7 May 1896 (Montegut Ch.: v.6, p.39)
NAQUIN, Joseph Maurice (Bernard & Mathilde BILLOT) b. 15 April 1897 (Montegut Ch.: v.6, p.61)
NAQUIN, Joseph O. (Ozemee & Amelia NAQUIN) m. 7 Jan. 1896 Alma AZEMA (Thib. Ch.: v.13, p.93)
NAQUIN, Joseph Olaus (Adolphe & Marie BILLOT) b. 22 Aug. 1899 (Montegut Ch.: v.6, p.92)
NAQUIN, Joseph Willis (Theogene & Azellia THIBODEAU) b. 30 Jan. 1896 (Theriot Ch.: v.1-B, p.88)
NAQUIN, Josephine (Marcellin & Armelise DARDAR) m. 26 Aug. 1896 Sylvere A. BOURG (Montegut Ch.: v.4, p.213)
NAQUIN, Jules (Cleophas & Marie ONCALE) m. 13 Jan. 1896 Louise NAVARRE (Thib. Ch.: v.13, p.89)
NAQUIN, Jules (Cleophas & Marie ONCALE) m. 13 Jan. 1896 Louise NAVARRE (Thib. Ct. Hse.: Mar. v.35, #197)
NAQUIN, Julia Elvire (Ernest & Santie MARTIN) b. 17 Oct. 1898 (Montegut Ch.: v.6, p.78)
NAQUIN, Labon Etienne (Albert & Justile POINCEAUX) b. 6 May 1896 (Thib. Ch.: v.7, p.450)
NAQUIN, Lelia m. 1 June 1897 Elvie COMAUX (Houma Ch.: v.6-a, p.205)
NAQUIN, Lelia m. 31 May 1897 Elsie COMEAUX (Thib. Ct. Hse.: Mar. v.36, #156)
NAQUIN, Lelia (J. Emile & Azema BOUDREAUX) m. Elsie COMEAUX. Petition for family meeting: 17 May 1898. (Houma Ct. Hse.: Succ. #902)
NAQUIN, Leo (Ulger & Azelie ONCALE) m. 14 Jan. 1897 Ulyssia BENOIT (Thib. Ch.: v.14, p.108)
NAQUIN, Leo (Ulger & Ozelie ONCALE) m. 14 Jan. 1897 Ulyssia BENOIT (Thib. Ct. Hse.: Mar. v.36, #3)

NAQUIN, Lothair m. 12 Jan. 1899 Mary THIBODAUX (Houma Ct. Hse.: Mar. v.30 & 31, #215)
NAQUIN, Lothere (Edouard & Gustine DUPRE) m. 30 Jan. 1899 Mary THIBODAUX (Montegut Ch.: v.4, p.253)
NAQUIN, Louis Edde Allen (Charles & Alice AUCOIN) b. 25 Aug. 1898 (Thib. Ch.: v.7, p.563)
NAQUIN, Louis Noley (Leo & Ulyssia BENOIT) b. 14 Oct. 1897 (Thib. Ch.: v.7, p.469)
NAQUIN, Louis Placide (Cyprien & Louise DARDAR) b. 1 Dec. 1897; bt. 10 March 1903 (Larose Ch.: v.4, p.27)
NAQUIN, Louisa Agnes (Cyprien & Louise DARDAR) b. 24 Dec. 1899; bt. 10 March 1903 (Larose Ch.: v.4, p.27)
NAQUIN, Lucie Edna (Lothere & Marie THIBODAUX) b. 13 Dec. 1899 (Montegut Ch.: v.6, p.96)
NAQUIN, Marie m. Taylor LAGARDE d. 23 Feb. 1897 at age 50 yrs. (Thib. Ch.: v.3, p.197)
NAQUIN, Marie m. 10 June 1899 Ulysse AYO (Thib. Ct. Hse.: Mar. v.39, #177)
NAQUIN, Marie (Myrtile & Emeline JOLIBOIS) m. 29 April 1896 Georges FALGOUT (Thib. Ch.: v.14, p.86)
NAQUIN, Marie (Myrtile & Emeline JOLIBOIS) m. 29 April 1896 Georges FALGOUT (Thib. Ct. Hse.: Mar. v.35, #70)
NAQUIN, Marie Amelie (Albert & Justilia POINCEAUX) b. 31 Aug. 1898 (Thib. Ch.: v.7, p.563)
NAQUIN, Marie Augustine (Desire & Elisabeth DARDAR) b. 17 June 1897; bt. 10 March 1903 (Larose Ch.: v.4, p.27)
NAQUIN, Marie Brigitte (Leo & Ulyssia BENOIT) b. 4 Nov. 1898 (Thib. Ch.: v.7, p.577)
NAQUIN, Marie Celeste (Joseph & Alma Gertrude AZEMA) b. 15 Nov. 1896 (Thib. Ch.: v.7, p.426)
NAQUIN, Marie Cleotilde (Edouard & Justine DUPRE) b. 10 April 1896 (Montegut Ch.: v.6, p.39)
NAQUIN, Marie Felicia (Felicien & Mathilde LEBOEUF) m. 31 Jan. 1898 Alexandre Forest THIBODAUX (Montegut Ch.: v.4, p.233)
NAQUIN, Marie Felicia (Felicien & Mathilde LEBOEUF) m. 13 Jan. 1898 Alexandre Forest THIBODAUX (Houma Ct. Hse.: Mar. v.30 & 31, #200)
NAQUIN, Marie Florence (Lener & Heleda CHAUVIN) b. 4 March 1898 (Theriot Ch.: v.2, p.17)
NAQUIN, Marie Josephine (James & Josephine BERGERON) b. 15 Aug. 1899 (Montegut Ch.: v.6, p.91)
NAQUIN, Marie Lorinne (Narcisse & Marguerite VERDUN) m. 12 July 1898 Drosin DARDAR (Montegut Ch.: v.4, p.247)
NAQUIN, Marie Lorinne (Narcisse & Marguerite VERDUN) m. 8 July 1898 Drozin DARDAR (Houma Ct. Hse.: Mar. v.30 & 31, #50)
NAQUIN, Marie Lucie (Maxime & Josephine SONG) b. 20 Feb. 1897; bt. 21 March 1897 (Chacahoula Ch.: v.4, p.18)
NAQUIN, Nellie Pauline (Edgar & Josephine CROCHET) b. 24 Feb. 1898; m. Joseph Albert OLIVIER on 29 Aug. 1918. (Chacahoula Ch.: Bapt. Bk., v.4, p.7)

NAQUIN, Numa (Lovency & Anais PREJEAN) m. 16 April 1896 Elisabeth McMANUS (Thib. Ct. Hse.: Mar. v.35, #58)
NAQUIN, Odilia Adesie (Clovis & Marguerite NAQUIN) b. 17 Feb. 1896 (Theriot Ch.: v.1-B, p.96)
NAQUIN, Paul Franc (Paulin & Francisca GONZALES) b. 29 Nov. 1896 (Thib. Ch.: v.7, p.428)
NAQUIN, Paul George (Emile & Emelia AIZAIN) b. 23 April 1898 (Thib. Ch.: v.7, p.549)
NAQUIN, Paul Wilson (Emile & Aimee DUPRE) b. 8 Sept. 1896 (Montegut Ch.: v.6, p.47)
NAQUIN, Paulin (Ulger & Azelie ONCALE) m. 23 Jan. 1896 Francisca GONZALES (Thib. Ch.: v.14, p.69)
NAQUIN, Paulin (Ulger & Azelie ONCALE) m. 23 Jan. 1896 Francisca GONZALES (Thib. Ct. Hse.: Mar. v.35, #18)
NAQUIN, Philomene (Marcelin & Marie DARDAR) m. 29 June 1899 Gabrielle BOURG (Houma Ct. Hs.: Mar. v.31 & 32, #60)
NAQUIN, Philomene (Marcellin & Marie DARDAR) m. 17 July 1899 Gabriel BOURG (Montegut Ch.: v.4, p.268)
NAQUIN, Philomene Palmyre (Gustave & Gratiena ADAM) b. 29 July 1898 (Thib. Ch.: v.7, p.508)
NAQUIN, Rosaire Clovis (Louis & Marie PITRE) b. 12 Feb. 1899 (Montegut Ch.: v.6, p.82)
NAQUIN, Severin Francis (Clement & Rozemee NAQUIN) b. 11 Feb. 1898 (Montegut Ch.: v.6, p.74)
NAQUIN, Talcide (Skelina NAVARRE) m. 10 June 1898 Adolphe BOUDREAUX (Thib. Ch.: v.14, p.205)
NAQUIN, Telcide (----- & Thelma NAVARRE) m. 6 June 1898 Adolphe BOUDREAUX (Thib. Ct. Hse.: Mar. v.38, #184)
NAQUIN, Thadeus Coralice (Clotilde) b. 5 Dec. 1899 (Thib. Ch.: v.7, p.577)
NAQUIN, Therese d. 13 Oct. 1896 at age 3 wks. (Thib. Ch.: v.3, p.189)
NAQUIN, Thomas (Paulin & Azema DANTIN) m. 27 Dec. 1899 Louise BELTEAU (Thib. Ch.: v.14, p.316)
NAQUIN, Thomas J. m. 22 Dec. 1899 Louise BELTEAU (Thib. Ct. Hse.: Mar. v.39, #295)
NAQUIN, Victor Philippe (Leonie & Alice MIRE) b. 24 April 1899 (Thib. Ch.: v.7, p.601)
NAQUIN, Wilfrid Adam (Victor & Marie DARDARD) b. 25 Jan. 1896 (Montegut Ch.: v.6, p.44)
NAQUIN, Xavier (Celovis NAQUIN) d. 6 Nov. 1899 at age 8 yrs. (Theriot Ch.: v.1, p.2)
NAQUIN, Zulema (Cleophas & Dozelia THIBODAUX) m. 25 Nov. 1896 Charles CUNNINGHAM (Houma Ct. Hse.: Mar. v.29 & 30, #195)
NARCISSE, Joseph Chester (Desire & Anastasie PIERRE) b. 24 Oct. 1897 (Chacahoula Ch.: Gibson Ch.: Mar. Bk., v.1, #14)
NARCISSE, Joseph Chester (Desire & Anastasie PIERRE) b. 24 Oct. 1897 bt. 27 Feb. 1898 (Chacahoula Ch.: Gibson Ch.: v.2, p.117)

NASH, Henry m. 26 May 1899 Fanny DENNIS (Houma Ct. Hse.: Mar. v.31 & 32, #19)

NAVARRE (Sometimes: NAVAR, NAVARE, NAVOR)

NAVARRE, Amelia m. 29 April 1897 Stephen LAFOREST (Thib. Ct. Hse.: Mar. v.36, #134)

NAVARRE, Amelia (Anatole & Aimee CHIASSON) m. 10 May 1897 Stephen LAFOREST (Chackbay Ch.: v.1, p.44)

NAVARRE, Annie Marie (Ulysse & Georgina MARTIN) b. 10 Oct. 1898 (Thib. Ch.: v.7, p.573)

NAVARRE, Aurelia (Joseph & Mary CHIASSON) m. 5 Oct. 1896 Laurentie CHIASSON (Thib. Ct. Hse.: Mar. v.36, #144)

NAVARRE, Cecelia (Orelien & Rebecca LASSEIGNE) m. 15 April 1899 Evariste NAVARRE (Houma Ct. Hse.: Mar. v.31 & 32, #402)

NAVARRE, Cecilia m. 3 May 1899 Evariste NAVARRE (Chacahoula Ch.: v.1, p.69 [89])

NAVARRE, Clincy Joseph (Shelly & Julie NAVARRE) b. 15 Oct. 1898 (Chacahoula Ch.: v.4, p.17)

NAVARRE, Daisy Evelina (Henri & Ella BEAUFORD) b. 14 Jan. 1897; m. William Joseph HUGHES on 8 April 1934. (Houma Ch.: Bapt. Bk., v.5, p.206)

NAVARRE, Domatile (Marcellin & Julia BLANCHARD) m. 8 Dec. 1899 Leo DOMINGUE, Jr. (Houma Ct. Hse.: Mar. v.31 & 32, #176)

NAVARRE, Elvela (Ulysse & Estherina MARTIN) d. 27 Aug. 1896 at age 5 days (Thib. Ch.: v.3, p.186)

NAVARRE, Emelie (Anatole & Aimee CHIASSON) m. 23 May 1898 Ernest MOLAISON (Chackbay Ch.: v.1, p.61)

NAVARRE, Emile (d.Evariste & Marie MIGUEZ) m. 6 June 1898 Emilia RINK (Chackbay Ch.: v.1, p.62)

NAVARRE, Emile (Evariste & Mary MINGUEZ) m. 6 June 1898 Emelia RINK (Thib. Ct. Hse.: Mar. v.38, #189)

NAVARRE, Emilie (Anatole & Aimee CHIASSON) m. 23 May 1898 Ernest MOLAISON (Thib. Ct. Hse.: Mar. v.38, #178)

NAVARRE, Evariste d. 23 Dec. 1899 Children listed: Joseph C.; Emile; Felix; Henry; Shelley. Petition to put heirs in possession: 29 Dec. 1899. (Houma Ct. Hse.: Succ. #931)

NAVARRE, Evariste d. 24 Dec. 1899 at age 64 yrs. (Chacahoula Ch.: v.2, p.30)

NAVARRE, Evariste m. 3 May 1899 Cecilia NAVARRE (Chacahoula Ch.: v.1, p.69 [89])

NAVARRE, Evariste (Jean C. & Carmelite BENOIT) m. 15 April 1899 Cecelia NAVARRE (Houma Ct. Hse.: Mar. v.31 & 32, #402)

NAVARRE, Evelie (Ernest & Eveline LANDRY) m. 27 Jan. 1898 Kelly PREJEAN (Thib. Ch.: v.14, p.178)

NAVARRE, Evelie (Ernest & Eveline LANDRY) m. 27 Jan. 1898 Kelly PREJEAN (Thib. Ct. Hse.: Mar. v.37, #16)

NAVARRE, Inola Marie Louise (Ulysse & Angela FYTHE) b. 26 Sept. 1896 (Chackbay Ch.: v.1, p.76)
NAVARRE, Joseph Anthony (Valcour & Cecile BERNARD) b. 12 Sept. 1899 (Thib. Ch.: v.7, p.578)
NAVARRE, Julia (Aurelien & Rebecca LASSEIGNE) m. 24 Feb. 1897 Elmer BERGERON (Thib. Ch.: v.14, p.128)
NAVARRE, Julia (Aurelien & Rebecca LASSEIGNE) m. 24 Feb. 1897 Elmer BERGERON (Houma Ct. Hse.: Mar. v.29 & 30, #257)
NAVARRE, Julie (Aurelien & Rebecca LASSAIGNE) m. 27 Jan. 1898 Shelly NAVARRE (Chacahoula Ch.: v.1, p.65 [85])
NAVARRE, Julie (Aurelien & Rebecca LASSEIGNE) m. 27 Jan. 1898 Shelly NAVARRE (Houma Ct. Hse.: Mar. v.30 & 31, #190)
NAVARRE, Louise (Auguste & Sarah MORVAN) m. 13 Jan. 1896 Jules NAQUIN (Thib. Ct. Hse.: Mar. v.35, #197)
NAVARRE, Louise (Auguste & Sarah MORVANT) m. 13 Jan. 1896 Jules NAQUIN (Thib. Ch.: v.13, p.89)
NAVARRE, Marie Evella (Ulysse & Georgina MARTIN) b. 14 March 1896 (Thib. Ch.: v.7, p.396)
NAVARRE, Marie Honore d. 24 Dec. 1899 at age 3 mths. (Thib. Ch.: v.3, p.247)
NAVARRE, Noe Olesy (Ulysse & Angela FYTE) b. 13 Feb. 1898 (Chackbay Ch.: v.1, p.106)
NAVARRE, Paul Gaston (Adam & Myrthee HEBERT) b. 2 May 1896 (Chacahoula Ch.: v.4, p.1)
NAVARRE, Paulin d. 12 Jan. 1898 at age 56 yrs. (Chacahoula Ch.: v.2, p.25)
NAVARRE, Philomene m. 13 July 1899 Willis CHIASSON (Houma Ct. Hse.: Mar. v.31 & 32, #74)
NAVARRE, Philomene of Terrebonne Parish m. 25 July 1899 Willie CHIASSON, of Terrebonne Parish (Houma Ch.: v.6-B, p.4)
NAVARRE, Shelly (Evariste & Eveline DAIGLE) m. 27 Jan. 1898 Julie NAVARRE (Chacahoula Ch.: v.1, p.65 [85])
NAVARRE, Shelly (Evariste & Eveline DAIGLE) m. 27 Jan. 1898 Julie NAVARRE (Houma Ct. Hse.: Mar. v.30 & 31, #190)
NAVARRE, Thomas Albert (Ulysse & Georgina MARTIN) b. 4 April 1897 (Thib. Ch.: v.7, p.445)
NAVARRE, Valcour (Auguste & Sarah MORVAN) m. 13 Feb. 1899 Cecile BERNARD (Thib. Ct. Hse.: Mar. v.38, #89)
NAVARRE, Valcour (Auguste & Sarah MORVAN) m. 13 Feb. 1899 Cecile BERNARD (Thib. Ch.: v.14, p.264)

NEAL (Sometimes: NEEL, NIEL)

NEAL, Arthur Henri (Henry & Ophelia MICHEL) b. 15 Sept. 1899 (Montegut Ch.: v.6, p.97)
NEAL, Henry (Edouard & Azema GROS) m. 14 June 1898 Ophelia MICHEL (Montegut Ch.: v.4, p.246)
NEAL, Henry (Edward & Azema GROS) m. 31 May 1898 Ophelia MICHEL (Houma Ct. Hse.: Mar. v.30 & 31, #458)
NEAL, Jerry m. 12 Feb. 1896 Katie SHORT (Houma Ct. Hse.: Mar. v.28, #448)

NEAL, Mare Evelia Clemeia (Michel & Julia ROCH) b. 13 Sept. 1898 (Montegut Ch.: v.6, p.79)
NEAL, Marie Justilia (Michel & Julia ROCK) b. 11 Sept. 1896 (Montegut Ch.: v.6, p.44)
NEAL, Uranie (Edouard & Azema GROS) m. 3 June 1899 Elic LEONARD (Montegut Ch.: v.4, p.264)
NEAL, Uranie (Edward & Azema GROS) m. 16 May 1899 Elie LEONARD (Houma Ct. Hse.: Mar. v.31 & 32, #5)
NEGUE, Alexina m. 27 April 1896 Marcel DANOS (Larose Ch.: v.3, p.3)
NELSON, Edward m. 28 April 1896 Isabella WRIGHT (Houma Ct. Hse.: Mar. v.29 & 30, #45)
NELSON, Leefie m. 12 May 1897 Joseph TONEY (Houma Ct. Hse.: Mar. v.29 & 30, #415)
NELSON, William m. 25 Aug. 1898 Ella MEAD (Thib. Ct. Hse.: Mar. v.38, #264)
NELTON, Marie Armelise (Daniel & Delia PRICE) b. 18 Nov. 1896 (Montegut Ch.: v.6, p.54)
NELTON, Marie Julie (Daniel & Dilia PRIZE) b. 8 Oct. 1898; m. Dominique RIBARDI on 8 April 1920. (Houma Ch.: Bapt. Bk., v.5, p.238)
NETTLETON, Eugenie (Ozias & Severine DOMINGUE) m. 3 Jan. 1899 Theophile GUIDRY (Houma Ct. Hse.: Mar. v.30 & 31, #174)
NETTLETON, Eugenie (Ozias & Severine DOMINGUE) m. 4 Feb. 1899 Theophile GUIDRY (Montegut Ch.: v.4, p.255)
NETTLETON, Joseph Wilson (Lasseigneuil & Alida ENGERRAN) b. 5 Jan. 1899 (Montegut Ch.: v.6, p.82)
NETTLETON, Marie Rosana (Ozias & Severina DOMINGUE) b. 5 Dec. 1897 (Montegut Ch.: v.6, p.75)
NETTLETON, Nathaniel (Olias & Severine DOMINGUE) m. 21 Feb. 1898 Alida ENGERRAN (Montegut Ch.: v.4, p.238)
NETTLETON, Nathaniel (Ozias & Severine DOMINGUE) m. 7 Feb. 1898 Alida ENGERRAN (Houma Ct. Hse.: Mar. v.30 & 31, #280)
NEUVILLE, Cliften (Lewis & Florence NEUVILLE) b. 14 Sept. 1896 (Thib. Ch.: v.7, p.423)
NEUVILLE, Eva (Louizan & Laurence DWYER) m. 27 April 1898 Tillman JACKSON (Thib. Ch.: v.14, p.200)
NEUVILLE, Eva (Louzian & Lawrence DWYER) m. 27 April 1898 Tillman JACKSON (Thib. Ct. Hse.: Mar. v.38, #170)
NEUVILLE, Henri d. 14 Sept. 1896 at age 1 yr. & 2 mths. (Thib. Ch.: v.3, p.187)
NEVERS, Lucy m. 11 Jan. 1897 James SMITH (Houma Ct. Hse.: Mar. v.29 & 30, #229)
NEVILLE, Ignation Florence (Lusignan & Florence Elisabeth NEVILLE) b. 15 Nov. 1897 (Thib. Ch.: v.7, p.526)
NEWELL, Evariste d. 12 April 1896 at age 69 yrs. (Thib. Ch.: v.3, p.181)
NEWELL, Jean Joseph d. 22 Feb. 1896 at age 2 days (Thib. Ch.: v.3, p.179)

NEWELL, Lelia or Merthe (Evariste & Victorine BRAUD) m. 13 May 1897 Ernest LEBLANC (Thib. Ct. Hse.: Mar. v.36, #143)
NEWELL, Marie Aline (Joseph & Octavie LEBLANC) b. 6 Feb. 1897 (Thib. Ch.: v.7, p.437)
NEWELL, Marthe (Evariste & Victorine BRAUD) m. 13 May 1897 Ernest LEBLANC (Thib. Ch.: v.14, p.144)
NEWELL, May Maggy Therese (Neil Joseph & Octavie LEBLANC) b. 19 June 1899 (Thib. Ch.: v.7, p.552)
NEWTON, Moses m. 10 June 1897 Susan MOODY (Houma Ct. Hse.: Mar. v.29 & 30, #24)
NICHOLSON, Maria Elizabeth m. d.Samuel HORNSBY d. 11 June 1896 at age 77 yrs. (Montegut Ch.: v.2, p.5)
NICOLA, Spicala (Rosario & Greces NICOLINA) m. 2 July 1898 Rosalia GRECO (Houma Ch.: v.6-a, p.244)

NICOLAS (Sometimes: NICHOLAS, NICHOLLS, NICHOLS)
NICOLAS, Aime Elisca d. 14 Aug. 1899 at age 37 yrs. (Raceland Ch.: v.1, p.27)
NICOLAS, Corinne (Elocio & Rosalie MARTINEZ) b. 27 Nov. 1898 (Chackbay Ch.: v.1, p.125)
NICOLAS, Edna m. 27 July 1898 Adam LONDON (Thib. Ct. Hse.: Mar. v.38, #234)
NICOLAS, Jeanne (Ulicio & Rosa MARTINEZ) b. 2 Feb. 1897 (Chackbay Ch.: v.1, p.83)
NICOLAS, Joseph (Homere & Emelisa ARABI) b. 17 Sept. 1896 (Raceland Ch.: v.5, p.32)
NICOLAS, Justilien (Sims & Virginie KRAEMER) b. 15 Aug. 1897 (Chackbay Ch.: v.1, p.93)
NICOLAS, Lucie F. Mrs. d. 22 Sept. 1899 at age 20 yrs. (Thib. Ch.: v.3, p.240)
NICOLAS, Marie Esta d. 21 July 1899 at age 3 mths. (Raceland Ch.: v.1, p.26)
NICOLO, Felippe d. 8 Sept. 1898 at age 5 mths. (Raceland Ch.: v.1, p.20)
NICOLOSI, Jimie (Frank & Madalia LINACIA) m. 25 April 1898 Lucile VINET (Thib. Ct. Hse.: Mar. v.38, #156)
NICOLOSI, Junie (Frank & Madalia SINACIA) m. 25 April 1898 Lucile VINET (Thib. Ch.: v.14, p.195)
NICOLOSO, Lucien (Frank & Lucie VINET) b. 21 Sept. 1899 (Thib. Ch.: v.7, p.564)
NILE, Melonie Eva (Edward & Asema BREAUX) b. 10 Nov. 1897 (Houma Ch.: v.5, p.200)
NIPLITT, Timothy m. 5 Jan. 1899 Mrs. Ellen BALLARD (Houma Ct. Hse.: Mar. v.30 & 31, #187)
NIXON, Malachi or Melciah m. 1 Aug. 1898 Mary Louisa JASPER (Houma Ct. Hse: Mar. v.30 & 31, #70)
NIXON, Queen m. 23 Feb. 1898 David DYER (Houma Ct. Hse.: Mar. v.30 & 31, #320)
NIXON, Susie m. 6 Feb. 1899 William BONVILLAIN (Houma Ct. Hse.: Mar. v.31 & 32, #319)

NOBLE, Ezekiel m. 26 Feb. 1896 Rachel LONGS (Thib. Ct. Hse.: Mar. v.35, #48)

NOBLE, Susan m. 18 April 1899 Henry ALLEN (Thib. Ct. Hse.: Mar. v.39, #148)

NODDA, Jesse (Frank & Maranna LORELLO) b. 2 Oct. 1899 (Houma Ch.: v.5, p.257)

NODDA, Josse d. 28 Nov. 1899 at age 1 mth. & 1 day (Houma Ch.: v.3, p.26)

NOLAS, Loulie m. 21 Feb. 1898 William BROWN (Houma Ct. Hse.: Mar. v.30 & 31, #317)

NOTO, Vincenza d. 16 Dec. 1899 at age 19 yrs. & 6 mths. (Thib. Ch.: v.3, p.246)

NUCIA, Rosa (Vincinca & Francesca PRIORA) b. 18 Oct. 1899 (Houma Ch.: v.5, p.258)

"O"

O'NEAL, Joseph Neal (John & Emma HARRISSON) b. 11 Sept. 1899 (Larose Ch.: v.3, p.45)
O'NOARED, Marie Alzira (Charley & Manola PREHOE) b. 13 Sept. 1899 (Raceland Ch.: v.5, p.106)
OCHONER, Barbara d. 20 Dec. 1899 at age 42½ yrs. (Thib. Ch.: Epis. Ch.: v.1, p.394)
ODDO, Congetta (Francisca & Francisca FARINA) b. 20 Feb. 1897 (Thib. Ch.: v.7, p.444)
ODDO, Guiseppe (Francesco & Ciccia FARINA) b. 16 March 1899 (Thib. Ch.: v.7, p.543)
ODDO, Salvatore (Francesco & Francesca FARINA) b. 1 Dec. 1899 (Thib. Ch.: v.8, p.19)
ODUM, Sedonia m. 14 April 1897 James FRANK (Thib. Ct. Hse.: Mar. v.36, #115)

OGERON (Sometimes: AUGERON)

OLIVEA, Mariana m. 23 Oct. 1899 Andrea DIVARCA (Thib. Ct. Hse.: Mar. v.39, #253)
OLIVEA, Marianne (Guiseppe & Maria BRANATA) m. 16 Dec. 1899 Andrea DIVARCA (Thib. Ch.: v.14, p.310)
OLIVER, Joseph (Vincenzo & Maria HENRIETTA) b. 17 Dec. 1898 (Thib. Ch.: v.7, p.534)

OLIVIER (Sometimes: OLLIVIER)

OLIVIER, Agnes (Bobby & Ozelia BREAUX) b. 15 July 1899 (Theriot Ch.: v.2, p.46)
OLIVIER, Albert (Alcide & Eleda LEONARD) b. 16 March 1899 (Houma Ch.: v.5, p.247)
OLIVIER, Alcide m. 17 March 1896 Alida LEONARD (Houma Ct. Hse.: Mar. v.29 & 30, #10)
OLIVIER, Alcide (Gustave & Orelia HEBERT) m. 6 April 1896 Alida LEONARD (Houma Ch.: v.6-a, p.173)
OLIVIER, Dollina Gladis (Levie & Maria BONVILLAIN) b. 10 Jan. 1899 (Houma Ch.: v.5, p.236)
OLIVIER, Edna Lucia (Eleda & Alcide OLIVIER) b. 1 Jan. 1897 (Houma Ch.: v.5, p.164)
OLIVIER, J. Mortimer m. 18 April 1899 Agnes SHINN (Houma Ct. Hse.: Mar. v.31 & 32, #406)
OLIVIER, J. Mortinet of Terrebonne Parish m. 26 April 1899 Agnes SHIN (Houma Ch.: v.6-B, p.3)
OLIVIER, Joseph Albert (Augustin & Eve LEBLANC) b. 26 Feb. 1898; m. Nellie NAQUIN on 29 Aug. 1918. (Chacahoula Ch.: Bapt. Bk., v.4, p.6)
OLIVIER, Laura m. 3 July 1897 Leo HEBERT (Houma Ct. Hse.: Mar. v.29 & 30, #47)
OLIVIER, Laura (Treville & Clemance HEBERT) m. 13 July 1897 Leo HEBERT (Houma Ch.: v.6-a, p.211)

OLIVIER, Listen (Body & Ozelia BREAULT) b. 1 Sept. 1897 (Houma Ch.: v.5, p.189)

OLIVIER, Louise (Alcide & Heleda LEONARD) b. 25 Dec. 1897 (Houma Ch.: v.5, p.199)

OLIVIER, Marie Lina (Augustave & Eve LEBLANC) b. 5 June 1896; bt. 18 July 1896 (Chacahoula Ch.: v.4, p.1)

OMIN, Joseph Lawrence (Alexandre & Pauline PONTITON) b. 11 Oct. 1899 (Theriot Ch.: v.2, p.60)

ONCALE (Sometimes: OCALE, ONCAL,ONCALL,ONCALLE,ONCOLE, ONKAL)

ONCALE, Bernard (Victorin & Victorine NAVARRE) m. 21 April 1898 Alida DARDEN (Chackbay Ch.: v.1, p.60)

ONCALE, Bernard (Victorin & Victorine NAVARE) m. 21 April 1898 Alida DARDEN (Thib. Ct. Hse.: Mar. v.37, #147)

ONCALE, Edwina (John & Mathilde MORVAN) b. 9 Jan. 1897 (Chackbay Ch.: v.1, p.80)

ONCALE, Emma m. 6 April 1896 Willy CHIASSON (Thib. Ct. Hse.: Mar. v.35, #62)

ONCALE, Ferdinand Urgele (Ernest & Sidonia ONCALE) b. 19 July 1899 (Chackbay Ch.: v.1, p.139)

ONCALE, Joseph (Davis & Ophylia DUROCHER) b. 13 Feb. 1897 (Chackbay Ch.: v.1, p.85)

ONCALE, Joseph Jean (John & Mathilde MORVAN) b. 3 Jan. 1899 (Chackbay Ch.: v.1, p.124)

ONCALE, Joseph Paul (Olivier & Emilia LANDRY) b. 18 Feb. 1898 (Chackbay Ch.: v.1, p.108)

ONCALE, Louis Silvain (Octave & Annee BENOIT) b. 24 Oct. 1897 (Chackbay Ch.: v.1, p.97)

ONCALE, Louise (Louis & Gustine PANVELLE) m. 3 April 1899 Albert DUROCHER (Thib. Ct. Hse.: Mar. v.39, #120)

ONCALE, Marie Lina (Alces & Virginie TRICHE) b. 7 March 1896 (Thib. Ch.: v.7, p.394)

ONCALE, Marie Louise (Louis & Justine PANVELLE) m. 3 April 1899 Albert DUROCHER (Chackbay Ch.: v.1, p.70)

ONCALE, Marie Olivia Modeste (Octave & Aimee BENOIT) b. 11 May 1899 (Chackbay Ch.: v.1, p.134)

ONCALE, Marie Ursule (Olivaire & Melia LANDRY) b. 10 July 1896 (Chackbay Ch.: v.1, p.70)

ONCALE, Octave (Louis & Augustine PANVELLE) m. 18 Jan. 1897 Aimee BENOIT (Chackbay Ch.: v.1, p.35)

ONCALE, Octave (Louis & Augustine PANVELLE) m. 18 Jan. 1897 Aimee BENOIT (Thib. Ct. Hse.: Mar. v.36, #12)

ONCALE, Olivia (Joseph & Artemise CLEMENT) b. 27 Jan. 1898 (Chackbay Ch.: v.1, p.104)

ONCALE, Zephire (Oscar & Seraphine GRAUS) m. 2 Feb. 1899 Sydonia BOUDREAUX (Thib. Ct. Hse.: Mar. v.38, #27)

ONEAL, Zephyr (Oscar & Seraphine GROS) m. 2 Feb. 1899 Sydonia BOUDREAUX (Chackbay Ch.: v.1, p.67 & 68)

OPICOT, Etienne Hermand (Ulysse & Helina BOURGEOIS) b. 26 Dec. 1896 (Thib. Ch.: v.7, p.432)

ORDOGNE, Adam Joseph (Pierre & Mathilde THIBODEAUX) b. 22 Feb. 1898 (Thib. Ch.: v.7, p.544)
ORDOGNE, Aimee (Augustin & Mathilde ANDRAS) m. 13 Nov. 1899 Joseph GOBERT (Chackbay Ch.: v.1, p.76)
ORDOGNE, Alice Henriette (Adonis & Eve ANDRAS) b. 23 July 1899 (Thib. Ch.: v.8, p.2)
ORDOGNE, Ambroise Beauregard (Daunis & Eve ANDRAS) b. 27 July 1898 (Thib. Ch.: v.7, p.508)
ORDOGNE, Anna (Augustin & Mathilde DANOS) m. 1 Oct. 1896 Bernard RICK (Thib. Ct. Hse.: Mar. v.36, #141)
ORDOGNE, Arthur (Louis & Cecile FORD) m. 13 Feb. 1899 Adeline THIBODAUX (Thib. Ct. Hse.: Mar. v.38, #73)
ORDOGNE, Arthur (Louis & Cecile FORD) m. 13 Feb. 1899 Adeline THIBODAUX (Thib. Ch.: v.14, p.264-B)
ORDOGNE, Beauregard d. 13 Oct. 1898 at age 2 yrs. (Thib. Ch.: v.3, p.220)
ORDOGNE, Clay (Emile & Mathilde DUE) m. 16 Feb. 1896 Zulema ELLIOT (Lockport Ch.: v.2, p.150)
ORDOGNE, Clay (Emile & Mathilde DUE) m. 5 Feb. 1896 Zulema ELLIOT (Thib. Ct. Hse.: Mar. v.35, #21)
ORDOGNE, Danice (Augustin & Marie THEBE) m. 20 April 1897 Eve ANDRAS (Thib. Ct. Hse.: Mar. v.36, #111)
ORDOGNE, Danice (d.Augustin & Marie THEBE) m. 20 April 1897 Eve ANDRAS (Chackbay Ch.: v.1, p.43)
ORDOGNE, Dorcina (Joseph & Josephine CHIASSON) b. 14 Dec. 1898 (Chackbay Ch.: v.1, p.128)
ORDOGNE, Elie Paul (Lovincie & Josephine ORDOGNE) b. 15 Jan. 1899 (Thib. Ch.: v.7, p.588)
ORDOGNE, Eloncia (Oleus & Marcelite THIBODAUX) b. 5 June 1898 (Chackbay Ch.: v.1, p.112)
ORDOGNE, Emeline (Arthur & Uranie RODRIGUE) b.8 Sept. 1898 (Chackbay Ch.: v.1, p.127)
ORDOGNE, Euphrasine (Therence & Emelina HEBERT) b. 17 Dec. 1897 (Thib. Ch.: v.7, p.484)
ORDOGNE, Eveline (Bazile & Liza HEBERT) m. 13 Jan. 1896 Auguste GOBERT (Thib. Ct. Hse.: Mar. v.35, #196)
ORDOGNE, Eveline (Bazile & Liza HEBERT) m. 13 Jan. 1896 Auguste GOBERT (Chackbay Ch.: v.1, p.25)
ORDOGNE, Francois (Olesie & Emma ANDRAS) b. 1 Oct. 1898 (Chackbay Ch.: v.1, p.127)
ORDOGNE, Frozin Joachim (Terance & Emilina HEBERT) b. 26 Jan. 1896 (Chackbay Ch.: v.1, p.61)
ORDOGNE, Frozin Odelia (Joachim & Eugenie PNAVELLE) b. 22 March 1896 (Chackbay Ch.: v.1, p.64)
ORDOGNE, Helene Philomene (Arthur & Uranie RODRIGUE) b. 14 Sept. 1896 (Chackbay Ch.: v.1, p.76)
ORDOGNE, Joseph Adam Beauregard (Pierre & Mathilde THIBODAUX) b. 5 Dec. 1896 (Thib. Ch.: v.7, p.437)
ORDOGNE, Josephine (Bazile & Liza HEBERT) m. 21 Feb. 1898 Hypolite THIBODAUX (Chackbay Ch.: v.1, p.58)

ORDOGNE, Josephine (Bazile & Liza HEBERT) m. 21 Feb. 1898 Hypolite THIBODAUX (Thib. Ct. Hse.: Mar. v.37, #72)
ORDOGNE, Josephine (Jules & Leontine LAINE) m. 8 Feb. 1898 Lovincy ORDOGNE (Thib. Ch.: v.14, p.181)
ORDOGNE, Josephine (Jules & Leontine LAINE) m. 8 Feb. 1898 Lovincy ORDOGNE (Thib. Ct. Hse.: Mar. v.37, #47)
ORDOGNE, Lea (Oleus & Marcelite THIBODEAUX) b. 31 Jan. 1896 (Chackbay Ch.: v.1, p.63)
ORDOGNE, Louise Angelina (Lucien & Romela HEBERT) b. 19 March 1898 (Chackbay Ch.: v.1, p.112)
ORDOGNE, Lovincy (Louis & Cecile FORD) m. 8 Feb. 1898 Josephine ORDOGNE (Thib. Ch.: v.14, p.181)
ORDOGNE, Lovincy (Louis & Cecile FORET) m. 8 Feb. 1898 Josephine ORDOGNE (Thib. Ct. Hse.: Mar. v.37, #47)
ORDOGNE, Lydia Alice (Jules & Leontine LAINE) b. 22 Jan. 1898 (Thib. Ch.: v.7, p.484)
ORDOGNE, Marie d. 22 Feb. 1898 at age 23 yrs. (Thib. Ch.: v.3, p.211)
ORDOGNE, Marie Aline (Bazile & Elisa HEBERT) b. 18 April 1897 (Chackbay Ch.: v.1, p.88)
ORDOGNE, Marie Annette (Joseph & Josephine CHIASSON) b. 10 May 1896 (Chackbay Ch.: v.1, p.66)
ORDOGNE, Marie Eve (Onesie & Emma ANDRA) b. 27 Feb. 1896 (Chackbay Ch.: v.1, p.67)
ORDOGNE, Olivain (Julien & Eugenie TABOR) m. 9 Feb. 1899 Delphine BOUDREAUX (Thib. Ct. Hse.: Mar. v.38, #74)
ORDOGNE, Olivain (Julien & Eugenie TABOR) m. 9 Feb. 1899 Delphine BOUDREAUX (Thib. Ch.: v.14 p.262-a)
ORDOGNE, Wallace Joseph (Albert & Louisa ANDRA) b. 12 March 1898 (Thib. Ch.: v.7, p.493)

ORDONNAUX (Sometimes: ORDENAUX, ORDONAUX, ORDONNEAU, ORDONNEAU)

ORDONNAUX, Alfred (Felix & Alvina BERGERON) b. 8 Sept. 1898 (Thib. Ch.: v.7, p.563)
ORDONNAUX, Aline (Theophile & Lydia KELLER) b. 20 June 1897 (Thib. Ch.: v.7, p.453)
ORDONNAUX, Felix (Alfred & Lea UZE) m. 2 Jan. 1898 Hermina BERGERON (Thib. Ct. Hse.: Mar. v.38, #325)
ORDONNAUX, Felix (Alfred & Lea UZE) m. 2 Jan. 1899 Hermina BERGERON (Thib. Ch.: v.14, p.233)

ORDOYNE (Sometimes: ORDOGNE, ORDONNE, ORDOUIN)

ORGERON, ----- child (John) d. 20 Aug. 1899 at age 3 yrs. (Larose Ch.: v.1, p.53)
ORGERON, Adam Clement (Alidore & Eve PREJEAN) b. 19 Jan. 1897 (Larose Ch.: v.2, p.190)
ORGERON, Adolph Gaetan (Orville & Camillia GUIDRY) b. 7 April 1898 (Larose Ch.: v.3, p.24)

ORGERON, Albert Fortune (Justillien & Manda BOUVIER) b. 19 March 1896 (Larose Ch.: v.2, p.181)
ORGERON, Alfreda (Oleus) d. 15 Aug. 1896 at age 4 yrs. (Lockport Ch.: v.1, #14)
ORGERON, Augustin Fortune (Alidor & Eve PREJEAN) b. 17 Dec. 1899 (Larose Ch.: v.3, p.49)
ORGERON, Azelie (Leo & Josephine ALLEMAND) b. 4 Feb. 1897 (Lockport Ch.: v.3-A, #15-a)
ORGERON, Azelie (Leo & Josephine ALLEMAND) b. 4 Feb. 1897 (Lockport Ch.: v.3, #16)
ORGERON, Bernadette (Oleus & Adele BADEAUX) m. 6 July 1896 Joseph LOUP (Thib. Ct. Hse.: Mar. v.35, #106)
ORGERON, Bernadette (Oleus & Adele BADEAUX) m. 6 July 1896 Joseph LOUP (Lockport Ch.: v.2, p.152)
ORGERON, Camille Joseph (Antoni & Azelida ARCENEAUX) b. 1 Jan. 1899 (Larose Ch.: v.3, p.34)
ORGERON, Celima Marie (Ernest & Lisa GAUTREAUX) b. 2 Jan. 1899 (Larose Ch.: v.3, p.34)
ORGERON, Claudia Anita (John & Augustine CANTRELLE) b. 21 Jan. 1897 (Larose Ch.: v.3, p.15)
ORGERON, Elmire m. 2 Jan. 1897 Pierre BAILLE (Thib. Ct. Hse.: Mar. v.36, #5)
ORGERON, Elmire m. 4 Jan. 1897 Pierre BAYE (Larose Ch.: v.3, p.4)
ORGERON, Elmire m. 4 Jan. 1897 Pierre BAYE (Larose Ch.: v.4, p.67)
ORGERON, Elmire m. 4? Jan. 1897 Pierre BAILLE (Larose Ch.: v.4, p.120)
ORGERON, Elson Joseph (Anthony & Azelida ARCENEAUX) b. 4 May 1896 (Larose Ch.: v.2, p.185)
ORGERON, Ernest (Adolphe & Marcelline PLAISANCE) m. 10 Feb. 1898 Elisa GAUTREAUX (Thib. Ct. Hse.: Mar. v.37, #58)
ORGERON, Ernest (Adolphe & Marcelline PLAISANCE) m. 10 Feb. 1898 Elisa GAUTREAUX (Lockport Ch.: v.2, p.186)
ORGERON, Ernestine (Adolphe & Marceline PLAISANCE) m. 13 Feb. 1899 Edgard LERILLE (Lockport Ch.: v.2, p.204)
ORGERON, Ernestine (Adolphe & Marcelline PLAISANCE) m. 13 Feb. 1899 Edgard LERILLE (Thib. Ct. Hse.: Mar. v.38, #67)
ORGERON, Estella Rita (Oleus & Adele BADEAUX) b. 15 March 1896 (Lockport Ch.: v.2, p.325)
ORGERON, Ethna Virginie (John & Augustine CANTRELLE) b. 2 Dec. 1896 (Larose Ch.: v.2, p.180)
ORGERON, Eve (Francois & Celestine BERNARD) m. 13 June 1898 Frank Mathurin GRIFFIN (Larose Ch.: v.4, p.17)
ORGERON, Eve of Lafourche Parish (Francois & Celestine BERNARD) m. 13 June 1898 Franck Mathurin GRIFFIN of Lafourche Parish (Larose Ch.: v.3, p.9)
ORGERON, Francois d. 14 June 1899 (Larose Ch.: v.1, p.53)
ORGERON, Joseph m. 22 June 1896 Josephine TOUPS (Lockport Ch.: v.2, p.155)

ORGERON, Joseph (Oleus & Adele BADEAUX) m. 22 June 1896 Josephine LOUP (Thib. Ct. Hse.: Mar. v.35, #105)
ORGERON, Josephine Sylvanie (Adolphe & Marcelline PLAISANCE) b. 23 Nov. 1896 (Larose Ch.: v.2, p.195)
ORGERON, Julia (Justilien & ---- BOUVIER) d. 30 Aug. 1897 (Larose Ch.: v.1, p.41)
ORGERON, Julien Roland (Justillien & Amanda BOUVIER) b. 14 July 1898 (Larose Ch.: v.3, p.23)
ORGERON, Leontine (Adam & Marcelline PLAISANCE) m. 2 Feb. 1899 Lineus PLAISANCE (Thib. Ct. Hse.: Mar. v.38, #44)
ORGERON, Leontine (Adam & Marcelline PLAISANCE) m. 2 Feb. 1899 Simon PLAISANCE (Lockport Ch.: v.2, p.200)
ORGERON, Marcelline (Hypolite & Zulema GUIDRY) m. 3 Sept. 1896 Colomb CHIASSON (Thib. Ct. Hse.: Mar. v.36, #133)
ORGERON, Marcelline (Hypolithe & Zulema GUIDRY) m. 3 Sept. 1896 Colomb CHIASSON (Lockport Ch.: v.2, p.153)
ORGERON, Marie Ella (Seraphin & Cecilia GAUTREAUX) b. 26 Nov. 1896 (Larose Ch.: v.2, p.195)
ORGERON, Marie Linda (Anatole & Celestine PLAISANCE) b. 5 Dec. 1898 (Larose Ch.: v.3, p.30)
ORGERON, Marie Sidonie Cecilia (Seraphin & Cecilia GAUTREAUX) b. 23 Aug. 1898 (Larose Ch.: v.3, p.28)
ORGERON, Melia m. 1 June 1896 Leon ROGER, Jr. (Thib. Ct. Hse.: Mar. v.35, #91)
ORGERON, Milia m. 6 April 1896 Mike LEVY (Thib. Ct. Hse.: Mar. v.35, #64)
ORGERON, Odeo (Oleus & Adele BADEAU) m. 26 June 1897 Ella RICHARD (Thib. Ct. Hse.: Mar. v.36, #169)
ORGERON, Odeo (Oleus & Adele BADEAUX) m. 26 June 1897 Ella RICHARD (Lockport Ch.: v.2, p.168)
ORGERON, Odillia m. Clebert SAVOIE d. 4 May 1897 at age 76 yrs. (Lockport Ch.: v.1, #9)
ORGERON, Ovile d. 6 March 1899 at age 40 yrs. (Lockport Ch.: v.1, #10)
ORGERON, Pierre Hypolithe (Louis & Marie GRIFFIN) b. 19 Aug. 1896 (Lockport Ch.: v.2, p.334)
ORGERON, Regina Mathilde (Andre & Helene GRIFFIN) b. 17 April 1896 (Larose Ch.: v.2, p.192)
ORGERON, Regina Mathilde (Andre & Olem GRIFFIN) d. 15 June 1896 at age 18 days (Lockport Ch.: v.1, #13)
ORGERON, Richard (Samuel & Laura GUITROZ) m. 30 Dec. 1899 Unetia DUBOIS (Thib. Ct. Hse.: Mar. v.39, #308)
ORGERON, Rosemond d. May 1897 (Lockport Ch.: v.1, #22)
ORGERON, Rosemond Mrs. d. 7 Oct. 1899 at age 73 yrs. (Lockport Ch.: v.1, #38)
ORGERON, Serville (Martial & Emma DUPLANTIS) m. 10 Jan. 1896 Julienne HENRI (Houma Ch.: v.6-a, p.168)
ORGERON, Sidney Alphonse (Davis & Adelina TERREBONNE) b. 26 Dec. 1896 (Larose Ch.: v.3, p.8)
ORGERON, Sidonia Marie (Wilfrid & Cordilia ADAM) b. 26 Dec. 1896 (Larose Ch.: v.3, p.1)

ORGERON, Victor Henri (Andre & Helene GRIFFIN) b. 28 July 1897 (Larose Ch.: v.3, p.2)
ORGERON, Wilia m. 22 April 1896 Michael LEVY (Larose Ch.: v.3, p.2)
ORGERON, Willia m. 22 April 1896 Michel LEVY (Larose Ch.: v.4, p.50)
ORGOGNE, Anna (Augustin & Mathilde ANDRAS) m. 1 Oct. 1896 Bernard RICK (Chackbay Ch.: v.1, p.31)

ORILLAN (Sometimes: ORELION, ORILLON, ORRILLOU)
ORILLAN, Lucie Rita (Albert & Justilia BRAUD) b. 23 July 1899 (Thib. Ch.: v.7, p.557)
ORILLAN, Octave Norbert (Albert & Justilia BREAUX) b. 8 Jan. 1897 (Thib. Ch.: v.7, p.437)
OSHWALD, Bertha m. 10 Dec. 1896 Thomas PIERSON (Thib. Ct. Hse.: Mar. v.36, #165)
OSHWALD, Bertha (Georges & Mary SUTHERLITTER) m. 14 Nov. 1896 Thomas H. PIERSON (Thib. Ch.: v.14, p.103)
OSHWALD, Emile m. 20 Oct. 1896 Mary E. THIBODAUX (Thib. Ct. Hse.: Mar. v.36, #158)
OSHWALD, Emile m. 21 Oct. 1896 Mary E. THIBODAUX (Thib. Ch.: Epis. Ch.: v.1, p.331)
OSHWALD, George Henry (George & Clara PIERSON) b. 29 Oct. 1896 (Thib. Ch.: v.7, p.428)
OSHWALD, James Frost (Joseph & Ida Josephine FROST) b. 2 Oct. 1896 (Thib. Ch.: v.7, p.421)
OSHWALD, Joseph Benedict (Emile & Mary E. THIBODEAUX) b. 24 Oct. 1897 (Thib. Ch.: Epis. Ch.: v.1, p.44)
OSHWALD, Joseph Clarence (George & Clara PIERSON) b. 25 Oct. 1898 (Thib. Ch.: v.7, p.521)
OSHWALD, Rosa Cecilia (Joseph & Aida FROST) b. 13 Dec. 1898 (Thib. Ch.: v.7, p.528)

OTIN (See: AUTIN)

OTTEMAN (See: AUTHEMENT)

OURSEAU, Louis (Joseph & Philomene THEBE) bt. 6 Aug. 1898 (Chackbay Ch.: v.1, p.117)
OURSO, Charles (Joseph & Philomene THEBE) b. 29 Aug. 1896 (Chackbay Ch.: v.1, p.75)
OUTLEY, Lily m. 19 June 1897 John WILLIAMS (Houma Ct. Hse.: Mar. v.29 & 30, #33)
OWENS, Mariah m. 31 Aug. 1896 Frank CALLAWAY (Houma Ct. Hse.: Mar. v.29 & 30, #141)
OWENS, William m. 9 Feb. 1899 Rebecca FRY (Thib. Ct. Hse.: Mar. v.38, #99)
OZIO, Loula (Joseph & Leila GATEWOOD) m. 6 Nov. 1899 Lawrence CARLOS (Houma Ct. Hse.: Mar. v.31 & 32, #162)
OZIO, Lulu (Jos. & Leila GATEWOOD) m. 20 Nov. 1899 Lawrence CARLOS (Theriot Ch.: v.1-B, p.7)

"P"

PACKS (See: PARKS)

PAETT, Edouard Willy (Willy & Octavie PONTIFE) b. 15 Jan. 1899 (Houma Ch.: v.5, p.235)
PAGE, Joseph Napoleon (Albert & Lisca GILES) b. 2 Sept. 1898 (Thib. Ch.: v.7, p.566)
PAGLINGHI, Rosa Isola (Pietro & Teresa CUNEL) b. 1 Sept. 1896 (Lockport Ch.: v.2, p.335)
PALADINO, Antonio Augusto (Philipo & Vincenza PEDONE) b. 13 Jan. 1898 (Chacahoula Ch.: Gibson Records: Mar. Bk., v.1, #4)
PALADINO, Antonio Augusto (Philipo & Vincenza PEDRONE) b. 13 Jan. 1898 (Chacahoula Ch.: Gibson Ch.: v.2, p.115)
PALAZZO, Carolina (Pracito & Francisca TISSITORE) m. 11 Aug. 1896 Francesco MAROSSA (Thib. Ch.: v.14, p.97)
PALAZZO, Carolina (Pracito & Francisca TISSITORE) m. 11 Aug. 1896 Francesco MARASSA (Thib. Ct. Hse.: Mar. v.36, #132)
PALAZZO, Theresa (Antonino & Cosina TERRITA) b. 20 Feb. 1897 (Thib. Ch.: v.7, p.489)
PALAZZO, Tony m. 22 May 1899 Riattata Cleria LABRUCCHI (Thib. Ct. Hse.: Mar. v.39, #166)
PALMER, Roscoe C. (William W. & Lydia M. -----) m. 24 Feb. 1899 Bertha HEPLER (Houma Ch.: Epis. Ch.: v.1, p.344)
PALMER, Roscoe C. (Wm. W. & Lydia M. PALMER) m. 24 Feb. 1899 Bertha HEPLER (Houma Ct. Hse.: Mar. v.31 & 32, #349)
PALMERI, Ignazio (Joseph & Calogera TOUGALE) b. 10 April 1898 (Chacahoula Ch.: Gibson Ch.: v.2, p.121)
PALMIERI, Rosa Evelyn m. 16 Sept. 1899 Louis Theodore PELLERIN (Houma Ct. Hse.: Mar. v.31 & 32, #134)
PALMIRE, Palmire d. 11 Dec. 1898 at age 68 yrs. (Houma Ch.: v.3, p.19)
PALMIRIE, Rosa E. of Terrebonne Parish m. 3 Oct. 1899 Louis J. PELLERIN (Houma Ch.: v.6-B, p.5)
PANCICA, Vincenza d. 23 Dec. 1898 at age 4 yrs. (Thib. Ch.: v.3, p.223)
PANDANO, Maria (Salvatore & Giuseppa LAPLAQUE) m. 3 Sept. 1898 Carmela DEFIGLIO (Thib. Ch.: v.14, p.218)
PANI, Rosina Mangia (Vincenzio Mangia & Ninfa PENACHIO) b. 8 Aug. 1898 (Thib. Ch.: v.7, p.509)
PANTANO, Maria (Salvatore & Guiseppe LAPLAQUE) m. 3 Sept. 1898 Carmelo DEFIGLIO (Thib. Ct. Hse.: Mar. v.38, #248)

PANVEL (Sometimes: PANDEVEL, PANDEVELLE, PANEL, PANELLE, PANEVEL, PANVELLE, PANNEL)

PANVEL, Alice (Eli & Louise ADAM) m. 13 April 1899 Ovide MARTIN (Chackbay Ch.: v.1, p.70)

PANVEL, Alice (Elie & Louise ADAM) m. 13 April 1899 Ovide MARTIN (Thib. Ct. Hse.: Mar. v.39, #125)
PANVEL, Alve Guilbert (Joseph & Josephine CHIASSON) b. 30 Dec. 1896 (Chackbay Ch.: v.1, p.80)
PANVEL, Cecile (Elie & Louise ADAM) m. 27 Jan. 1898 James THABOR (Chackbay Ch.: v.1, p.54)
PANVEL, Cecile (Elie & Louise ADAMS) m. 27 Jan. 1898 James THABOR (Thib. Ct. Hse.: Mar. v.37, #21)
PANVEL, Cleophee (Eli & Louise ADAM) bt. 20 April 1896 (Chackbay Ch.: v.1, p.64)
PANVEL, Eddy (Joachim & Justilia USEE) b. 18 April 1896 (Chackbay Ch.: v.1, p.65)
PANVEL, Joseph Lueday (Eli & Louise ADAM) b. 24 July 1898 (Chackbay Ch.: v.1, p.116)
PANVEL, Joseph Volcare (Gustave & Helene MORVAN) b. 4 Oct. 1897 (Chackbay Ch.: v.1, p.98)
PANVEL, Marie d. 30 April 1899 at age 14 days (Thib. Ch.: v.3, p.233)
PANVEL, Marie Magnolia (Joseph & Josephine CHIASSON) b. 27 Oct. 1899 (Chackbay Ch.: v.1, p.144)
PANVEL, Octavie (Hilaire & Louisa THAUZIN) b. 4 Aug. 1897 (Chackbay Ch.: v.1, p.93)
PANZICA, Vincenzo (Leonardo & Domenica BARTHOLOTO) b. 12 Nov. 1897 (Thib. Ch.: v.7, p.525)
PAOLO, Rosina (Francisco & Guiseppa SALERMA) b. 16 Feb. 1899 (Raceland Ch.: v.5, p.93)
PAPANIA, Josepina (Luca & Conjetta GENOVEYA) b. 12 Nov. 1897 (Raceland Ch.: v.5, p.63)
PAPANIO, Giovanna (Luca & Concetta GENOVESA) b. 2 July 1896 (Thib. Ch.: v.7, p.407)
PAPASSIA, Leonardo (Luca & Concetta ZENUISA) b. 15 April 1899 (Raceland Ch.: v.5, p.96)
PAQUES, ----- child (Thomas) d. 22 Aug. 1896 at age 4 yrs. (Lockport Ch.: v.1, #16)
PAQUES, Lucille (Thomas & Nesile HOTARD) m. 4 Feb. 1899 Cleopha BOURGEOIS (Thib. Ct. Hse.: Mar. v.38, #70)
PARA, Felix m. 14 Feb. 1899 Eleonore GALJOUR (Thib. Ct. Hse.: Mar. v.39, #107)
PARFAIT, Adelaide (Jean Baptiste & Rosalie BILLIOT) b. 6 Dec. 1898 (Theriot Ch.: v.2, p.43)
PARFAIT, Emile Esly (Emile of Grand Caillou & Mende LOOK of Grand Caillou) b. 11 March 1896 (Theriot Ch.: v.2, p.1)
PARFAIT, Eugene Frederic (Jean Marie & Marie BILLOT) b. 1898; bt. 29 April 1899 (Houma Ch.: v.5, p.242)
PARFAIT, Henry Lessie (Emile & Amanda LOUK) d. 3 Dec. 1899 at age 2 mths. (Montegut Ch.: v.2, p.31)
PARFAIT, Henry Lessie (Emile & Amanda LOUKE) b. 10 Oct. 1899 (Montegut Ch.: v.6, p.95)
PARFAIT, Louis Ernest (Jean Baptiste & Ozalie BILLIOT) b. 17 July 1896 (Theriot Ch.: v.1-B, p.106)

PARFAIT, Lucy m. 9 Jan. 1899 Frank FOREST (Houma Ct. Hse.: Mar. v.30 & 31, #194)
PARFAIT, Lucy (Emile & Mandy LUKE) m. 14 Jan. 1899 Frank FOREST (Houma Ch.: v.6-a, p.263)
PARFAIT, Marie Octavie (Octave & Rosalie Clemence GALLET) m. 17 Feb. 1896 Joseph Edwin BILLOT (Montegut Ch.: v.4, p.206)
PARFAIT, Marie Octavie (Octave & Rosalie Clemence GALLET) m. 13 Feb. 1896 Joseph Edwin BILLOT (Houma Ct. Hse.: Mar. v.28, #458)
PARKER, Aaron m. 8 June 1898 Julian THORNSBURY (Houma Ct. Hse.: Mar. v.30 & 31, #3)
PARKER, Belle m. 25 July 1898 Abe HILLS (Thib. Ct. Hse.: Mar. v.38, #232)
PARKER, Charles m. 7 April 1898 Olivia BRYAN (Thib. Ct. Hse.: Mar. v.37, #144)
PARKER, Dave m. 9 June 1897 Emilie CARTER, widow of WELTON (Thib. Ct. Hse.: Mar. v.36, #165)
PARKER, Elvira m. 4 Jan. 1899 Ben WILLIAMS (Thib. Ct. Hse.: Mar. v.38, #3)
PARKER, Louisa m. 12 June 1899 Abraham MAYS (Houma Ct. Hse.: Mar. v.31 & 32, #44)
PARKER, Mary m. 25 March 1896 Willie FLUENCE (Houma Ct. Hse.: Mar. v.29 & 30, #15)
PARKER, Mima m. 12 Feb. 1896 Calvin MORRIS (Houma Ct. Hse.: Mar. v.28, #444)

PARKS (Sometimes: PARK, PAKS)
PARKS, Ella m. 12 June 1897 Odressie CHAUVIN (Thib. Ct. Hse.: Mar. v.36, #168)
PARKS, Ernest Robert (Joseph & Ernestine BOURGEOIS) b. 1 Sept. 1897 (Raceland Ch.: v.5, p.54)
PARKS, Julia (Thomas & Oresile HOTARD) m. 14 April 1898 Constant MASSON (Lockport Ch.: v.2, p.187)
PARKS, Lucille (Thomas & Nesile HOTARD) m. 4 Feb. 1899 Cleopha BOURGEOIS (Lockport Ch.: v.2, p.201)
PARKS, Mathilde m. Arthee CHAUVIN d. 7 Nov. 1897 at age 18 yrs. (Lockport Ch.: v.1, #25)
PARKS, Presela (Tom & Nesile OTAR) m. 14 June 1897 Walter LEGENDRE (Raceland Ch.: v.2, p.43)
PARKS, Priscilla m. 9 June 1897 Walter LEGENDRE (Thib. Ct. Hse.: Mar. v.36, #166)
PARMERI, Ignazio (Joseph & Cologera TOUGALE) b. 10 April 1898 (Chacahoula Ch.: Gibson Records: Mar. Bk., v.1, #32)

PARR (Sometimes: PAR)
PARR, Armand (Marcellin & Mathilde ROBICHAUX) m. 29 Nov. 1899 Felicia RICHARD (Thib. Ct. Hse.: Mar. v.39, #268)
PARR, Armand (Marcellin & Mathilde ROBICHAUX) m. 29 Nov. 1899 Felicia RICHARD (Lockport Ch.: v.2, p.211)

PARR, Augusta m. Paul BREAUX d. 27 Sept. 1899 at age 31 yrs. (Lockport Ch.: v.1, #37)
PARR, Cecile (Euphrozin & Mary BOURG) m. 31 Oct. 1899 Volcar TRAHAN (Theriot Ch.: v.1-B, p.11)
PARR, Cecile (Euphrozin & Mary BOURQUE) m. 27 Oct. 1899 Volcar TRAHAN (Houma Ct. Hse.: Mar. v.31 & 32, #155)
PARR, Celestine Alexandrine (Ernest & Malvina PUNCH) b. 6 April 1896 (Larose Ch.: v.2, p.191)
PARR, John m. 14 July 1898 Aline COMEAUX (Houma Ct. Hse.: Mar. v.30 & 31, #58)
PARR, Joseph (Onesipe & Amelia MOLAISON) m. 14 July 1898 Aline COMEAUX (Houma Ch.: v.6-a, p.246)
PARR, Josephine (Joseph & Marie ERNANDEZ) m. 10 Feb. 1896 Robert JACKSON (Lockport Ch.: v.2, p.150)
PARR, Josephine (Marcellin & Mathilde ROBICHAUX) m. 12 July 1899 Felix RICHARD (Thib. Ct. Hse.: Mar. v.39, #187)
PARR, Josephine (Marcellin & Mathilde ROBICHAUX) m. 12 July 1899 Felix RICHARD (Lockport Ch.: v.2, p.209)
PARR, Julia (Thomas & Onezile HOTARD) m. 14 April 1898 Constant MASSON (Thib. Ct. Hse.: Mar. v.37, #103)
PARR, Laura (Marcellin & Mathilde ROBICHAUX) m. 20 Jan. 1897 Evariste RICHARD (Thib. Ct. Hse.: Mar. v.36, #19)
PARR, Laura (Marcellin & Matilde ROBICHAUX) m. 20 Jan. 1897 Evariste RICHARD (Lockport Ch.: v.2, p.157)
PARR, Marceline Lidia (Octave & Melasie LEBLANC) b. 4 Oct. 1899 (Houma Ch.: v.5, p.261)
PARR, Marguerite Mary Elvire (J. J. & Aline Clara COMEAU) b. 22 Aug. 1899 (Houma Ch.: v.5, p.251)
PARR, Marie d. 16 July 1898 at age 4 days (Houma Ch.: v.3, p.17)
PARR, Marie Ariana Francoise (Octave & Elvire RODRIGUE) b. 29 Jan. 1896 (Lockport Ch.: v.2, p.321)
PARR, Marie Bella (Georges & Zoe BOURGEOIS) b. 19 April 1896 (Lockport Ch.: v.2, p.329)
PARR, Marie M. (Lovincy & Adele BOURGEOIS) b. 27 Sept. 1896 (Lockport Ch.: v.3, #6)
PARR, Marie Messi (Lovincy & Adele BOURGEOIS) b. 27 Sept. 1896 (Lockport Ch.: v.3-A, #6)
PARR, Purcy Louis (Alexandre & Lucia HENRY) b. 16 Nov. 1898; m. Lillie SAVOIE on 21 June 1922. (Houma Ch.: Bapt. Bk., v.5, p.227)
PARR, Vilia (Alexandre & Lucia HENRY) b. 6 Aug. 1896; m. Hervin Paul MARONGE on 5 Aug. 1922. (Houma Ch.: Bapt. Bk., v.5, p.156)
PARR, Virginie m. Alcy POLESKY d. 17 Nov. 1899 at age 23 yrs. (Lockport Ch.: v.1, #45)
PARRA, Felix (Frank & Josephine SANCHEZ) m. 18 Feb. 1899 Eleonore GALJOUR (Larose Ch.: v.4, p.39)
PARRA, Felix (Frank & Josephine SANCHEZ) m. 18 Feb. 1899 Eleonore GALJOUR (Larose Ch.: v.3, p.11)

PARRAZZO, Gaetano d. 26 Nov. 1896 at age 44 yrs. (Raceland Ch.: v.1, p.11)
PARRO, Dolph m. 1 April 1899 Ida RODRIGUE (Thib. Ct. Hse.: Mar. v.39, #128)
PARRO, Dolph (Joseph & Dylia BOISVIN) m. 15 April 1899 Ida RODRIGUE (Raceland Ch.: v.2, p.93)
PARSON, Daisy m. 10 Jan. 1899 Alfred BOFFINGER (Thib. Ct. Hse.: Mar. v.38, #13)
PARSONS, Betty m. 16 Feb. 1898 James SMITH (Thib. Ct. Hse.: Mar. v.37, #99)
PART, Francis Joseph (Felicien & Eva LIRETTE) b. 12 Nov. 1897 (Houma Ch.: v.5, p.192)

PASCAILLE (See: POUSSECAILLE)

PATTE, Caloggere (Jacomo & Loretta BAVADA) b. 5 March 1898 (Thib. Ch.: v.7, p.490)
PATTERSON, George m. 13 April 1898 Martha MILLER (Houma Ct. Hse.: Mar. v.30 & 31, #396)
PATTI, Angela (Giacomo & Loreta BAVIDA) m. 18 Jan. 1896 Carmelo BELLAVIA (Thib. Ct. Hse.: Mar. v.35, #10)
PATTI, Calogero (Giacomo & Loretta BAVIDA) d. 1 Sept. 1896 at age 15 days (Thib. Ch.: v.3, p.186)
PATTI, Calogiero (Giacomo & Loretta BOVIDAS) b. 17 Aug. 1896 (Thib. Ch.: v.7, p.415)
PAUCH, Emma (Amedee & Severine DAIGLE) m. 1 March 1897 Oscar BOURGEOIS (Raceland Ch.: v.2, p.36)
PAULA, Francesca m. 11 April 1899 Francesco MAGLIA (Thib. Ct. Hse.: Mar. v.39, #140)
PAULESANTA, Santa (Martino & Darda PASCALA) b. 2 May 1899 (Houma Ch.: v.5, p.246)
PAULIN, Emma Henri d. 18 Feb. 1896 at age 19 yrs. (Montegut Ch.: v.2, p.3)
PAUSARET, Anna m. 14 Oct. 1896 John B. RIDER (Houma Ct. Hse.: Mar. v.29 & 30, #167)
PAYNE, Ellen (Spencer & ----) m. 15 Jan. 1896 Samuel LUCKETT (Houma Ct. Hse.: Mar. v.28, #392)
PAYNE, Rena m. 31 March 1898 Edward WATKINS (Houma Ct. Hse.: Mar. v.30 & 31, #363)
PEDEAUX, Avila m. 30 June 1899 Bertha NAQUIN (Thib. Ct. Hse.: Mar. v.39, #190)
PEET, Victor Marquez (Didier & Julia PEET) b. 24 Feb. 1896 (Larose Ch.: v.2, p.181)

PELEGRIN (Sometimes: PELLEGRIN)

PELEGRIN, Aimee d. 27 Sept. 1898 at age 12 yrs. (Montegut Ch.: v.2, p.20)
PELEGRIN, Andre Telemaque (Gustave & Ophelia MARCEL) b. 4 Feb. 1897 (Montegut Ch.: v.6, p.53)
PELEGRIN, Arthur (Numa & Dorisca KELLY) m. 21 Dec. 1899 Josephine PERTUIT (Houma Ch.: Epis. Ch.: v.1, p.344)

PELEGRIN, Arthur (Numa & Dorisca KELLY) m. 18 Dec. 1899 Josephine PERTUIT (Houma Ct.Hse.: Mar. v.31 & 32, #186)
PELEGRIN, Brigitte (Prosper & Louisa DULOT) b. 2 April 1897 (Montegut Ch.: v.6, p.56)
PELEGRIN, Domingue Joseph (Lovincy & Clothilde LABRUYERE) b. 16 Feb. 1898 (Montegut Ch.: v.6, p.68)
PELEGRIN, Dominique Loel (Louis & Julienne LEBLANC) b. 20 Dec. 1898 (Montegut Ch.: v.6, p.81)
PELEGRIN, Elder Elda Louise (Sylvan & Marguerite PELEGRIN) b. 23 Jan. 1898 (Houma Ch.: Epis. Ch.: v.1, p.116)
PELEGRIN, Elie Philogene (Philogene & Evelia LEBLANC) b. 13 Aug. 1897 (Theriot Ch.: v.2, p.25)
PELEGRIN, Elmire Suzanne m. Ernest BOUDREAUX, lived on the Hope Farm Plantation. d. 29 Sept. 1896 at age 35 yrs. & 2 mths. (Montegut Ch.: v.2, p.7)
PELEGRIN, Eva (Theobald & Ernestine HENRY) m. 13 Dec. 1897 Joseph LIRETTE (Houma Ct. Hse.: Mar. v.29 & 30, #142)
PELEGRIN, Eva (Theobald & Ernestine HENRY) m. 10 Jan. 1898 Joseph LIRETTE (Montegut Ch.: v.4, p.228)
PELEGRIN, Eva Wilda (Theodore & Nesia DASETTE) b. 6 Dec. 1897 (Theriot Ch.: v.2, p.18)
PELEGRIN, Felix Adam (Theobald & Ernestine HENRI) b. 25 Feb. 1896 (Montegut Ch.: v.6, p.34)
PELEGRIN, Gilles m. 2 Oct. 1897 Alice BABIN (Houma Ct. Hse.: Mar. v.29 & 30, #103)
PELEGRIN, Gillis (Wilfrid & Rosalie BERGERON) m. 7 Oct. 1897 Alice BABIN (Houma Ch.: v.6-a, p.218)
PELEGRIN, Irvin Connely (Silvan & Marguerite PELEGRIN) b. 23 May 1899 (Houma Ch.: Epis. Ch.: v.1, p.122)
PELEGRIN, Jean Baptiste Theophile (Idone & Virginie DEROCHE) b. 27 March 1897 (Theriot Ch.: v.2, p.6)
PELEGRIN, Joseph Calisius Eustin (Calixte & Myrtee PICOU) b. 9 Sept. 1896 (Montegut Ch.: v.6, p.48)
PELEGRIN, Joseph Cives (Theobald & Ernestine HENRI) b. 13 May 1897 (Montegut Ch.: v.6, p.57)
PELEGRIN, Joseph Osee (Jean Baptiste & Celestia CHAUVIN) b. 8 Sept. 1896 (Montegut Ch.: v.6, p.45)
PELEGRIN, Josephine d. 17 Jan. 1899 at age 8 yrs. (Houma Ch.: v.3, p.20)
PELEGRIN, Justin (Francois & Melasie NAQUIN) m. 24 Jan. 1898 Eva BOURG (Montegut Ch.: v.4, p.232)
PELEGRIN, Justin (Francois & Melasie NAQUIN) m. 15 Jan. 1898 Eva BOURG (Houma Ct. Hse.: Mar. v.30 & 31, #207)
PELEGRIN, Laurent Gilles (Calixte & Myrtee PICOU) b. 12 March 1899 (Montegut Ch.: v.6, p.90)
PELEGRIN, Louise (Prosper & Louisa DULEAU) m. 7 Feb. 1898 Jules CHAUVIN (Theriot Ch.: v.1-B, p.2)
PELEGRIN, Louise (Prosper & Louisa DULEAU) m. 17 Jan. 1898 Jules CHAUVIN (Houma Ct. Hse.: Mar. v.30 & 31, #222)
PELEGRIN, Louise Theodosia (Theophile & Elene RICHOUX) b. 17 Feb. 1899 (Larose Ch.: v.3, p.36)

PELEGRIN, Louise Veniola (Felicien & Jeanne DAZET) b. 4 Feb. 1897 (Houma Ch.: v.5, p.196)
PELEGRIN, Marie Albana (Vital & Lilia BERGERON) b. 6 April 1898 (Houma Ch.: v.5, p.208)
PELEGRIN, Marie Anne (Theobald & Ernestine HENRI) b. 4 Nov. 1899 (Montegut Ch.: v.6, p.95)
PELEGRIN, Marie Floree (Jean Baptiste & Cistilia CHAUVIN) b. 30 Aug. 1898 (Montegut Ch.: v.6, p.77)
PELEGRIN, Marie Josephine (Guilles & Alice BABIN) b. 3 July 1898 (Houma Ch.: v.5, p.214)
PELEGRIN, Neuville Joseph (Theophile & Helene RICHOUX) b. 27 Sept. 1896 (Larose Ch.: v.2, p.196)
PELEGRIN, Noe Justin (Philogene & Emelia LEBLANC) b. 14 April 1899 (Theriot Ch.: v.2, p.45)
PELEGRIN, Oliva (Theobald & Ernestine HENRY) m. 12 Jan. 1899 Euzalia BERGERON (Houma Ct. Hse.:Mar. v.30 & 31, #216)
PELEGRIN, Oliva (Theobald & Ernestine HENRY) m. 31 Jan. 1899 Euselia BERGERON (Montegut Ch.: v.4, p.253)
PELEGRIN, Orestile (Dannis & Elvire THERIOT) m. 26 Dec. 1899 Emma CHAUVIN (Houma Ct. Hse.: Mar. v.31 & 32, #204)
PELEGRIN, Paul Denis (Lovincy & Clotilde LABRUYERE) b. 18 July 1896 (Montegut Ch.: v.6, p.45)
PELEGRIN, Paul Oris (Justilien & Emma BOURG) b. 22 March 1899 (Montegut Ch.: v.6, p.85)
PELEGRIN, Philogene (Elie & Madeleine FANGUY) m. 8 March 1897 Evelia LEBLANC (Houma Ct. Hse.: Mar. v.29 & 30, #340)
PELEGRIN, Rose Celestin (Sylvan & Marguerite PELEGRIN) b. 2 March 1896 (Houma Ch.: Epis. Ch.: v.1, p.112)
PELEGRIN, Victoria (Prosper & Leouisa LETAMP) m. 21 Nov. 1896 Paul BRUNET (Houma Ct. Hse.: Mar. v.29 & 30, #189)
PELEGRIN, Vital m. 25 Jan. 1897 Lelia BERGERON (Houma Ct. Hse.: Mar. v.29 & 30, #249-A)
PELEGRIN, Vital (Wilfrid & Rosalie BERGERON) m. 25 Jan. 1897 Lelia BERGERON (Houma Ch.: v.6-a, p.190)
PELLERIN, Louis J. of Houma m. 3 Oct. 1899 Rosa E. PALMIRIE (Houma Ch.: v.6-B, p.5)
PELLERIN, Louis Theodore m. 16 Sept. 1899 Rosa Evelyn PALMIERI (Houma Ct. Hse.: Mar. v.31 & 32, #134)

PELTIER (Sometimes: PELLETIER, PELTHIER)

PELTIER, Andrew Harvey (Ozemee & Eloise CONSCIERS) b. 20 Oct. 1899 (Thib. Ch.: v.7, p.570)
PELTIER, Cecile (Joseph & Angeline DANIEL) m. 11 May 1899 Gustin LEBLANC (Thib. Ch.: v.14, p.281)
PELTIER, Cecilia widow of FREEMAN m. 21 Feb. 1898 Justin or Gustin LEBLANC (Thib. Ct. Hse.: Mar. v.37, #111)
PELTIER, Cecilia (Joseph & Angelina DANIEL) m. 11 Feb. 1897 Willie FREEMAN (Thib. Ch.: v.14, p.123)
PELTIER, Cecilia (Joseph & Angelina DANIEL) m. 11 Feb. 1897 Willie FREEMAN (Thib. Ct. Hse.: Mar. v.36, #68)

PELTIER, Felicia (Etienne & Philomene BOUDREAUX) m. 13 Feb. 1896 Ludovic LEBLANC (Houma Ct. Hse.: Mar. v.28, #405)
PELTIER, Flore Marie (Adolphe & Marie BENOIT) b. 20 Feb. 1898 (Chackbay Ch.: v.1, p.108)
PELTIER, Joseph Robert (Alfred & Scholastique RODRIGUE) b. 21 Aug. 1897 (Chackbay Ch.: v.1, p.95)
PELTIER, Lilia Lucie (Ozemee Uzelien & Heloise CANCIENNE) b. 7 Jan. 1898 (Thib. Ch.: v.7, p.479)
PELTIER, Mande Rose d. 29 April 1899 at age 4 mths. (Thib. Ch.: v.3, p.233)
PELTIER, Marie Clarisse (Alfred & Scholastique RODRIGUE) b. 12 Aug. 1899 (Chackbay Ch.: v.1, p.141)
PELTIER, Maud Rose (Louis & Marguerite LEBLANC) b. 2 Dec. 1898 (Thib. Ch.: v.7, p.524)
PELTIER, Valerie (Arsene & Alida BENOIT) b. 11 Aug. 1898 (Chackbay Ch.: v.1, p.118)
PELTIER, Valerie (Arsene & Alida BENOIT) b. 24 May 1896 (Chackbay Ch.: v.1, p.68)
PELTIER, Valerie Hattie (Ozemee & Heloise CANCIENNE) b. 9 May 1896 (Thib. Ch.: v.7, p.402)
PENDAS, Frank D. (Santiego & Mathilde GUTHERIEZ) m. 3 Feb. 1897 Carrie S. GATEWOOD (Houma Ct. Hse.: Mar. v.29 & 30, #278)
PENDOS, Clarence Santiago (Francisco & Carry GATEWOOD) b. 15 March 1898 (Theriot Ch.: v.2, p.23)

PENISSON (Sometimes: PENESON)
PENISSON, Adam Thomas (Emile & Corinne BOURGEOIS) b. 29 Dec. 1899 (Chacahoula Ch.: v.4, p.33)
PENISSON, Aline Therese (Clovis & Helene CANCIENNE) b. 22 March 1896 (Thib. Ch.: v.7, p.396)
PENISSON, Marianne d. 15 Jan. 1899 at age 52 yrs. (Chacahoula Ch.: Gibson Ch.: v.2, p.183)
PENISSON, Marie Elizabeth (Emile & Corinne BOUDREAUX) b. 9 May 1898 (Chacahoula Ch.: v.4, p.10)
PENISSON, Mary A. m. 12 Sept. 1896 Peter E. BURKE (Houma Ct. Hse.: Mar. v.29 & 30, #144)
PENISSON, Theophile m. Ophelia BOUDREAUX, d.1882. (Charles M., d.1885 & Marcelite OZELET, d.1885) Child: Marcelite. Tutorship: 8 Dec. 1896. (Houma Ct. Hse.: Succ. #893)
PENZENI, Guiseppe m. 15 April 1896 Margerita BILA (Houma Ct Hse.: Mar. v.29 & 30, #41)
PERCLE, Armance (Jean Baptiste & Ursanie LANDRY) b. 20 Jan. 1899 (Chackbay Ch.: v.1, p.126)
PERCLE, Arthur (Ernest & Esilda TROSCLAIR) b. 7 Dec. 1897 (Chackbay Ch.: v.1, p.101)
PERCLE, Eve Juliette (Ernest & Zilda TROSCLAIR) b. 7 July 1899 (Chackbay Ch.:v.1, p.137)
PERCLE, Henriette Edna (Omer & Laurentia ROUSSEAU) b. 20 Jan. 1897 (Chackbay Ch.: v.1, p.84)

PERCLE, Jean Baptiste (Aubin & Angela TROSCLAIR) b. 28 Aug. 1897 (Chackbay Ch.: v.1, p.95)
PERCLE, Julia Lorina (Wilfrid & Justilia ROUSSEAU) b. 15 March 1899 (Chackbay Ch.: v.1, p.131)
PERCLE, Juliette (Aubin & Angele TROSCLAIR) m. 5 July 1897 Armand RODRIGUE (Chackbay Ch.: v.1, p.45)
PERCLE, Juliette (Aubin & Angele TROSCLAIR) m. 15 June 1897 Armand RODRIGUE (Thib. Ct. Hse.: Mar. v.36, #172)
PERCLE, Marie Julia (Ėmile & Loetitia LANDRY) b. 13 Feb. 1898 (Chackbay Ch.: v.1, p.109)
PERCLE, Marie Zulmee (Ernest & Marie TROSCLAIR) bt. 7 Sept. 1896 (Chackbay Ch.: v.1, p.74)
PERCLE, Orphe (Aubin & Angela TROSCLAIR) b. 4 June 1899 (Chackbay Ch.: v.1, p.136)
PERCLE, Rita Philomene (Omer & Laurentia ROUSSEAU) b. 20 Oct. 1898 (Chackbay Ch.: v.1, p.122)
PERCLE, Villier Rene Dosilien (Jean Baptiste & Ursenie LANDRY) b. 23 Aug. 1896 (Chackbay Ch.: v.1, p.74)
PERE, Agnes Bernadette (Jean & Josephine BOURGEOIS) b. 23 Oct. 1898 (Larose Ch.: v.3, p.30)
PERE, Charles Joseph (Henry & Anastasie LEBLANC) b. 13 March 1897 (Chacahoula Ch.: v.4, p.20)
PERE, Henri Guillaume (Henri & Anastasie LEBLANC) b. 7 April 1899 (Chacahoula Ch.: v.4, p.26)
PEREZ, Antoine Bernadette (Antoine & Julia ADAM) b. 5 Feb. 1899 (Chackbay Ch.: v.1, p.133)
PEREZ, Benjamin Baptiste (Antoine & Julia ADAM) b. 23 Feb. 1897 (Chackbay Ch.: v.1, p.85)
PEREZ, Joseph (Antoine & Julia ADAM) m. 7 Oct. 1899 Azelia MOLHER (Chackbay Ch.: v.1, p.74)
PEREZ, Joseph (Antoine & Julia ADAM) m. 7 Oct. 1899 Azelia MOLHER (Thib. Ct. Hse.: Mar. v.39, #239)
PERILLOUX, Annette d. 26 April 1897 at age 9 mths. (Thib. Ch.: v.3, p.199)
PERILLOUX, Bruno Sylvere (Joseph & Lydia HEBERT) b. 6 Oct. 1899 (Thib. Ch.: v.8, p.13)
PERILLOUX, Ella Sallonge (Joseph & Lydia HEBERT) b. 8 Dec. 1898 (Thib. Ch.: v.7, p.532)
PERILLOUX, Octave Andre (Joseph & Lydia HEBERT) b. 11 Nov. 1897 (Thib. Ch.: v.7, p.476)
PERINGUE, Paul Charles (Ernest & Ernestine KOSHNER) b. 10 Sept. 1899 (Raceland Ch.: v.5, p.108)
PERJERON, Jean Alga (Francois & Elisa LARGRESE) b. 23 May 1898 (Thib. Ch.: v.7, p.549)
PERKINS, Angelina Aida (John & Angelina LEGENDRE) b. 25 Dec. 1898 (Thib. Ch.: v.7, p.527)
PERKINS, Henrietta m. 27 Feb. 1896 William HOWARD (Houma Ct. Hse.: Mar. v.28, #469)
PERKINS, Joseph Walter (William & Evelia GUEDRY) b. 12 Oct. 1896 (Raceland Ch.: v.5, p.32)

PERKINS, Marie (William & Evelia GUEDRY) b. 25 Aug. 1898 (Raceland Ch.: v.5, p.77)
PERKINS, Robert J. d. 23 April 1896 at age 62 yrs. (Thib. Ch.: Epis. Ch.: v.1, p.394)
PERKINS, Thomas m. 26 Dec. 1899 Hannah BROWN (Houma Ct. Hse.: Mar. v.31 & 32, #200)
PERONE, Antonino (Filicie & Theresa CAGIOPA) b. 24 June 1898 (Houma Ch.: v.5, p.213)
PERQUIT, ----- d. 12 Oct. 1899 at age 8 yrs., 5 mths. (Houma Ch.: v.3, p.25)
PERRES, Octavie m. 14 Feb. 1899 Arthee CHAUVIN (Thib. Ct. Hse.: Mar. v.39, #106)
PERREY, Marie Antoinette (Jean & Josephine BOURGEOIS) b. 7 March 1896 (Larose Ch.: v.2, p.188)
PERRIN, Arthemise Josephine (Etienne & Josephine BOUDREAUX) b. 3 May 1896 (Larose Ch.: v.2, p.194)
PERRIN, Dulcina (Etienne & Josephine BOUDREAUX) b. 1 Nov. 1897 (Larose Ch.: v.3, p.32)
PERRIN, Etienne (Etienne & Eva MELANCON) m. 1 June 1897 Josephine BOUDREAU (Larose Ch.: v.3, p.5)
PERRIN, Etienne (Etienne & Eva MELANCON) m. 1 June 1897 Josephine BOUDREAU (Larose Ch.: v.4, p.97)
PERRIN, Marie Thertille (Etienne & Josephine BOUDREAU) b. 13 June 1899 (Larose Ch.: v.3, p.47)
PERRO, Alphonse m. 19 Jan. 1899 Rudder BERNO (Houma Ct. Hse.: Mar. v.30 & 31, #257)
PERRONA, Salvatore (Antonino & Maria CARNORA) m. 2 May 1898 Francesca TRANTACOSTE (Thib. Ct. Hse.: Mar. v.38, #175)

PERROT (Sometimes: PIERROT)

PERROUE, Salvatore (Antonino & Maria CARNOVA) m. 2 May 1898 Nophia TRANTACOSTE (Thib. Ch.: v.14, p.201)

PERTUIT (Sometimes: PERTUI, PERTUIS)

PERTUIT, Aimee (Joseph & Anastasie GRABERT) b. 24 March 1899 (Raceland Ch.: v.5, p.95)
PERTUIT, Alexandre m. 23 Jan. 1897 Eleonore CHAUVIN, widow of Robert TASTET (Thib. Ct. Hse.: Mar. v.36, #51)
PERTUIT, Alexandre (Alexandre & Emelia FORET) m. 8 Aug. 1896 Adele AUTIN (Raceland Ch.: v.2, p.19)
PERTUIT, Alexandre (Leopold & Irma NICOLAS) m. 25 Jan. 1897 Eleonore CHAUVIN (Raceland Ch.: v.2, p.28)
PERTUIT, Alexandre P. m. 25 July 1896 Adele AUTIN (Thib. Ct. Hse.: Mar. v.36, #128)
PERTUIT, Alexina m. 7 May 1897 Ernest GRABERT (Thib. Ct. Hse.: Mar. v.36, #140)
PERTUIT, Alexina (Alexandre & Melia FORET) m. 15 May 1897 Ernest GRABERT (Raceland Ch.: v.2, p.39)

PERTUIT, Anastasie Ida (Elesse & Clorine MARTIN) b. 2 June 1897 (Raceland Ch.: v.5, p.50)
PERTUIT, Edmond (Alexandre & Leonarda CHAUVIN) b. 28 Aug. 1899 (Raceland Ch.: v.5, p.101)
PERTUIT, Hector Valcourt (Valcourt & Lucia DUPUIS) b. 17 Nov. 1898 (Raceland Ch.: v.5, p.83)
PERTUIT, Helena m. 20 Feb. 1897 Louis VERRET (Thib. Ct. Hse.: Mar. v.36, #86)
PERTUIT, Helena (Leopold & Irma NICOLAS) m. -- Feb. 1896 Louis VERRET (Raceland Ch.: v.2, p.35)
PERTUIT, Joseph Benson (Elesse & Clorene MARTIN) b. 15 March 1899 (Raceland Ch.: v.5, p.94)
PERTUIT, Josephine (Theodule & Eufora WOLFF) m. 21 Dec. 1899 Arthur PELEGRIN (Houma Ch.: Epis. Ch.: v.1, p.344)
PERTUIT, Josephine (Theodule & Eufora WOLFF) m. 18 Dec. 1899 Arthur PELEGRIN (Houma Ct. Hse.: Mar. v.31 & 32, #186)
PERTUIT, Louis Joseph (Theodule & Zephor WOLF) b. 27 Jan. 1898 (Montegut Ch.: v.6, p.66)
PERTUIT, Noe (Alexandre & Adele AUTIN) b. 19 Dec. 1897 (Raceland Ch.: v.5, p.63)
PERTUIT, Therese Hortense (Valcourt & Letitia DUPUIT) b. 10 Dec. 1896 (Raceland Ch.: v.5, p.50)
PERTUIT, Valcourt d. 5 Feb. 1899 at age 30 yrs. (Raceland Ch.: v.1, p.23)
PETER, Louis Price (Alidor & Elevele DANTIN) b. 4 Sept. 1899 (Larose Ch.: v.3, p.46)
PETIT, Emelienne Mercedes (Jackson & Angele GALJOUR) b. 29 May 1899 (Larose Ch.: v.3, p.40)
PETIT, Felonise Evelina (Emile & Eva SANDERS) b. 23 Oct. 1898 (Larose Ch.: v.3, p.31)
PETIT, Jackson of Lafourche Parish (Armand & Alice LEFORT) m. 21 July 1898 Angele GALJOUR, of Lafourche Parish (Larose Ch.: v.3, p.10)
PETIT, Jackson (Armand & Alice LEFORT) m. 21 July 1898 Angele GALJOUR (Thib. Ct. Hse.: Mar. v.38, #230)
PETIT, Jackson (Armand & Alice LEFORT) m. 21 July 1898 Angele GALJOUR (Larose Ch.: v.4, p.23)
PHARAGUTT, Cornelius m. 12 May 1897 Laura LEBLANC (Thib. Ct. Hse.: Mar. v.36, #141)
PHARR, Melvia m. 13 Sept. 1898 Romey SIMS (Houma Ct. Hse.: Mar. v.30 & 31, #96)
PHILLIP, John m. 31 Oct. 1898 Sallie GITRIDGE (Thib. Ct. Hse.: Mar. v.38, #307)
PHILTZ, Joseph Columbus (Johnnie & Myra MIRE) b. 18 Sept. 1898 (Chacahoula Ch.: v.4, p.14)
PICCIOLA, Joseph m. 22 June 1897 Josephine LEFORT (Thib. Ct. Hse.: Mar. v.36, #180)
PICCIOLA, Joseph m. 26 June 1897 Josephine LEFORT (Larose Ch.: v.3, p.6)
PICCIOLA, Joseph m. 26 June 1897 Josephine LEFORT (Larose Ch.: v.4, p.64)

PICCIOLA, Marco Jean (Joseph & Josephine LEFORT) b. 24 June 1898 (Larose Ch.: v.3, p.33)
PICCO, Guiseppe (Ignazio & Caterina LALOMIA) b. 20 April 1898 (Thib. Ch.: v.7, p.498)

PICHOFF (Sometimes: PICCHOFF, PICHAUF, PICHOF, PICHOPH)
PICHOFF, Bernadette m. 3 Jan. 1898 Edgar BREAUX (Thib. Ct. Hse.: Mar. v.37, #270)
PICHOFF, Joseph Warmesth (Adam & Alice HEBERT) b. 24 Oct. 1897; m. Mary Rosa Dell HEBERT on 2 March 1967. (Houma Ch.: Bapt. Bk., v.5, p.196)
PICHOFF, Josephine m. 22 June 1897 Paul DUFRESNE (Thib. Ct. Hse.: Mar. v.36, #179)
PICHOFF, Louis Earl (Adam & Alice HEBERT) b. 31 Oct. 1899; m. Blanche M. BLANCHARD on 15 Feb. 1926. (Houma Ch.: Bapt. Bk., v.5, p.262)
PICHOFF, Marie Josephine (Bernadette) b. 24 Feb. 1896 (Lockport Ch.: v.2, p.324)
PICHOT, Ema Anne (Louis & --- SCANLINGL) b. 23 Sept. 1896 (Lockport Ch.: v.3-A, #2)
PICONE, Marie Louise (Joseph & Louise BUFORD) b. 17 June 1899 (Houma Ch.: v.5, p.248)
PICONI, Agnes Irmeni (John & Eva DUPLANTI) b. 24 Dec. 1897 (Houma Ch.: v.5, p.196)
PICONI, Joseph Theodore (Joseph & Louisa BUFORD) b. 18 Aug. 1896 (Houma Ch.: v.5, p.157)

PICOU (Sometimes: PICOUT)
PICOU, Agnes Alice m. 20 July 1898 Peter FANDAL (Houma Ct. Hse.: Mar. v.30 & 31, #64)
PICOU, Aline Brunette (Charles T. & Victoria ESTIVEN) b. 27 July 1898 (Thib. Ch.: v.7, p.506)
PICOU, Celestina m. Ernest LEBLANC d. 27 July 1898 at age 33 yrs. (Montegut Ch.: v.2, p.18)
PICOU, Celine Camille (Charles T. & Victoria ESTIVEN) b. 27 July 1898 (Thib. Ch.: v.7, p.506)
PICOU, Effie (Eusebe & d.Mathilde LEBLANC) m. 12 Feb. 1898 Augustin DOMINGUE (Montegut Ch.: v.4, p.236)
PICOU, Effie (Euzebe & Mathilde LEBLANC) m. 25 Ja. 1898 Augustin DOMINGUE (Houma Ct. Hse.: Mar. v.30 & 31, #252)
PICOU, Eliska d. 14 Feb. 1894; m. Justilien MARTIN Child listed: Augustin. Petition for inventory & tutorship: 21 Oct. 1898. (Thib. Ct. Hse.: Succ. #1552)
PICOU, Emile Marcellin (Emile & Dolisca HENRI) b. 22 Nov. 1896 (Montegut Ch.: v.6, p.49)
PICOU, Emma (Ellis & Victorine LEBLANC) m. 10 April 1899 Theodore LABICHE (Houma Ct. Hse.: Mar. v.31 & 32, #392)
PICOU, Emma (Ellis & Victorine LEBLANC) m. 17 April 1899 Theodore LABICHE (Montegut Ch.: v.4, p.261)
PICOU, Emma Catherine m. 25 July 1899 Joseph Gabriel ROBERTS (Houma Ct. Hse.: Mar. v.31 & 32, #85)

PICOU, Estelle Isabelle (Willis & Evela CROCHET) b. 23 Feb. 1897 (Houma Ch.: v.5, p.205)
PICOU, Evelina (Elphege & Lea MICHAEL) b. 10 April 1899 (Theriot Ch.: v.2, p.46)
PICOU, Felicia (Marcillien & Mezelie LAPEROUSE) m. 21 Jan. 1899 Caliste LAPEROUSE (Houma Ct. Hse.: Mar. v.30 & 31, #210)
PICOU, Frank d. 25 Aug. 1898 at age 59 yrs. (Houma Ch.: v.3, p.18)
PICOU, Frank deceased; m. Harriet LESTER. Petition putting heirs in poss.: 30 Dec. 1898. (Houma Ct. Hse.: Succ. #910)
PICOU, George Washington (Charles & Victoria ESTIVEN) b. 22 Feb. 1897 (Thib. Ch.: v.7, p.440)
PICOU, Jean Wilsey (Wallis & Marie ENGERRAN) b. 28 Jan. 1898 (Montegut Ch.: v.6, p.70)
PICOU, John (Louis & Evelina MALBROUX) m. 23 Jan. 1897 Ida LABIT (Houma Ct. Hse.: Mar. v.29 & 30, #251)
PICOU, Joseph Philippe (Howard & Eda FORET) b. 9 Nov. 1897 (Montegut Ch.: v.6, p.63)
PICOU, Marguerite m. d.Hypolite CHAUVIN d. 13 June 1896 at age 58 yrs. (Montegut Ch.: v.2, p.5)
PICOU, Marguerite Lucile (Emile & Dorisca HENRI) b. 16 June 1899 (Theriot Ch.: v.2, p.45)
PICOU, Marie Anaise m. Robert Alfred BOURGEOIS d. 6 June 1896 at age 32 yrs. (Thib. Ch.: v.3, p.183)
PICOU, Marie Beatrix (Camille & Loetitia BOUVIER) b. 15 March 1898 (Larose Ch.: v.3, p.25)
PICOU, Nelsana (Urbain & Mary GUILLOU) m. 12 Jan. 1899 Ernest LEBLANC (Montegut Ch.: v.4, p.251)
PICOU, Nelsana (Urbin & Mary GUILLOU) m. 18 Oct. 1898 Ernest M. LEBLANC (Houma Ct. Hse.: Mar. v.30 & 31, #125)
PICOU, Nelsona (Urbain & Mary GUILLOU) m. 24 Aug.- 26 Dec. 1898 Ernest LEBLANC (Montegut Ch.: v.4, p.250)
PICOU, Nolia (Elphege & Azema LEBLANC) m. 19 Aug. 1898 Clovis LEBOEUF (Houma Ct. Hse.: Mar. v.30 & 31, #82)
PICOU, Nolia (Elphege & Azema LEBLANC) m. 24 Aug. 1898 Clovis LEBOEUF (Montegut Ch.: v.4, p.249)
PICOU, Paul Earl (Eusebe & Amanda CHAUVIN) b. 5 Oct. 1896 (Montegut Ch.: v.6, p.46)
PICOU, Regina m. 15 July 1899 Ellis JEANDRON (Thib. Ct. Hse.: Mar. v.39, #201)
PICOU, Regina (Leon & Anais BOUVIER) m. 25 July 1899 Elles JEANDRON (Larose Ch.: v.3, p.12)
PICOU, Regina (Leon & Anais BOUVIER) m. 25 July 1899 Elles JEANDRON (Larose Ch.: v.4, p.94)
PICOU, Saintete m. Ozeme BRAUD d. 3 May 1899 at age 30 yrs. (Lockport Ch.: v.1, #17)
PICOU, Sante of Terrebonne m. 2 Jan. 1896 Ozeme BRAUX (Lockport Ch.: v.2, p.143 & 144)

PICOU, Sante or Semte m. 22 Jan. 1896 Ozeme BRAUX (Thib. Ct. Hse.: Mar. v.35, #27)
PICOU, Sylvestre (Elphege & Lea MICHEL) b. 30 Dec. 1897 (Montegut Ch.: v.6, p.67)
PICOU, Theodule d. 8 March 1899 at age 73 yrs. (Thib. Ch.: v.3, p.229)
PIEDRA, Paulina m. 20 May 1898 Charles PORTER, Jr. (Houma Ct. Hse.: Mar. v.30 & 31, #450)
PIEDRO, Paulina (Manuel & Mathilde ARMENGOL) m. 26 May 1898 Charles PORTER, Jr. (Houma Ch.: v.6-a, p.241)

PIERCE (Sometimes: PIERS)
PIERCE, ----- child (Edgard) d. 25 Aug. 1899 at age 20 days (Larose Ch.: v.1, p.53)
PIERCE, Anna m. 27 April 1899 Alexis LEFORT (Thib. Ct. Hse.: Mar. v.39, #159)
PIERCE, Anna m. 6 May 1899 Alexis LEFORT (Larose Ch.: v.3, p.11)
PIERCE, Anne m. 6 May 1899 Alexis LEFORT (Larose Ch.: v.4, p.106)
PIERCE, Annette Clarrisse (Edwin & Ida DANOS) b. 23 Nov. 1896 (Larose Ch.: v.2, p.189)
PIERCE, Antoine (Georges & Josehine LASSEIGNE) b. 31 Oct. 1898 (Larose Ch.: v.3, p.31)
PIERCE, Camillia Anna (Henri & Aimee LEFORT) b. 4 Nov. 1898 (Larose Ch.: v.3, p.30)
PIERCE, Ceres Clement (Ines & Sidonie PITRE) b. 23 Nov. 1897 (Larose Ch.: v.3, p.15)
PIERCE, Elina (Hines & Sidonia PIERCE) d. 17 Nov. 1899 at age 8 yrs. (Larose Ch.: v.1, p.54)
PIERCE, Ella m. 24 May 1899 Augustin PITRE (Thib. Ct. Hse.: Mar. v.39, #167)
PIERCE, Ella m. 27 May 1899 Augustin PITRE (Larose Ch.: v.3, p.12)
PIERCE, Ella m. 27 May 1899 Augustin PITRE (Larose Ch.: v.4, p.84)
PIERCE, Ella m. 27 May 1899 Augustin PITRE (Larose Ch.: v.4, p.101)
PIERCE, Elodia (Wuilliam & Estelina BABIN) m. 27 Jan. 1898 Elias ADAM (Lockport Ch.: v.2, p.180)
PIERCE, Elodia (Wuilliam & Esthel BABIN) m. 27 Jan. 1898 Elias ADAM (Thib. Ct. Hse.: Mar. v.37, #31)
PIERCE, Emile (William & Tina BABIN) m. 24 April 1897 Lea SAMPE (Thib. Ct. Hse.: Mar. v.36, #100)
PIERCE, Emile (Wuilliam & Tina BABIN) m. 24 April 1897 Lea SAMPE (Lockport Ch.: v.2, p.161)
PIERCE, Felicie m. Eugene DUCY d. 25 Aug. 1897 (Larose Ch.: v.1, p.40)
PIERCE, Fielden (Franklin & Felicie MELANCON) m. 25 June 1898 Dora ADAM (Thib. Ct. Hse.: Mar. v.38, #212)

PIERCE, Fielden (Franklin & Felicie MELANCON) m. 25 June 1898 Dora ADAM (Lockport Ch.: v.2, p.191)

PIERCE, George m. 13 Jan. 1897 Josephine LASSEIGNE (Thib. Ct. Hse.: Mar. v.36, #24)

PIERCE, Ivonne Antonia (Jacques & Margueritte LEFORT) b. 6 Nov. 1897 (Larose Ch.: v.3, p.11)

PIERCE, Jean Erman (Henri & Merantia LEFORT) b. 10 Jan. 1897 (Larose Ch.: v.3, p.2)

PIERCE, Jeanne Eulalie (Volgie & Myrta BOURGEOIS) b. 27 Dec. 1899 (Larose Ch.: v.3, p.50)

PIERCE, Lee (Franklin & Felicia MELANCON) m. 31 Dec. 1898 Elvire FOURNIER (Lockport Ch.: v.2, p.197)

PIERCE, Lee (Franklin & Felicien MELANCON) m. 31 Dec. 1898 Elvire FOURNIER (Thib. Ct. Hse.: Mar. v.38, #328)

PIERCE, Marie (William & Estellina BABIN) m. 15 July 1897 Georges ROCK (Lockport Ch.: v.2, p.163)

PIERCE, Marie Ela (Edgard & Olphida BRUCE) b. 28 July 1897 (Larose Ch.: v.3, p.3)

PIERCE, Marie Nora (Nunley & Celestine THIBODAUX) b. 30 Jan. 1896 (Larose Ch.: v.2, p.180)

PIERCE, Mary (William & Estellina BABIN) m. 15 Jan. 1897 George ROCK (Thib. Ct. Hse.: Mar. v.37, #193)

PIERCE, Mary Elizabeth (Wesley & Mathilde DUPRE) b. 6 Oct. 1897 (Chacahoula Ch.: Gibson Ch.: Mar. Bk., v.1, #2)

PIERCE, Mary Elysabeth (Ursley & Mathilde DUPRE) b. 6 Oct. 1897; bt. 21 Jan. 1898 (Chacahoula Ch.: Gibson Ch.: v.2, p.115)

PIERCE, Nolsey m. 8 Feb. 1899 Myrthe BOURGEOIS (Thib. Ct. Hse.: Mar. v.38, #97)

PIERCE, Olympe Onesile (Enes & Sidonia PITRE) b. 31 March 1896 (Larose Ch.: v.2, p.191)

PIERCE, Pauline Rita (Jackson & Marguerite LEFORT) b. 24 June 1896 (Larose Ch.: v.2, p.193)

PIERCE, Valsey (Wales & Celestine THIBODEAUX) m. 11 Feb. 1899 Myrthe BOURGEOIS (Larose Ch.: v.4, p.36)

PIERCE, Victoire Angelique (Wales & Celestine THIBODAUX) b. 27 April 1897 (Larose Ch.: v.3, p.7)

PIERCE, Volsey (Wales & Celestine THIBODAUX) m. 11 Feb. 1899 Myrthe BOURGEOIS (Larose Ch.: v.3, p.11)

PIERCE, Volsey (Wales & Celestine THIBODEAUX) m. 11 Feb. 1899 Myrthe BOURGEOIS (Larose Ch.: v.4, p.123)

PIERO, Pete m. 15 Jan. 1898 Coralie AVERY (Thib. Ct. Hse.: Mar. v.37, #40)

PIERON, Louis Elie (Louis Elie & Virginie FABRE) b. 18 March 1896 (Larose Ch.: v.2, p.183 & p.218, #108)

PIERRE, Caroline m. 16 Jan. 1896 Charles TURNER (Thib. Ct. Hse.: Mar. v.35, #24)

PIERRE, Cecile m. 24 March 1897 Ernest LAGARDE (Houma Ct. Hse.: Mar. v.29 & 30, #364)

PIERRE, Eda m. 8 Sept. 1898 Walter DYER (Thib. Ct. Hse.: Mar. v.38, #274)

PIERRE, Florence Caroline (Felix & Alice SMITH) b. 22 April 1898 (Thib. Ch.: v.7, p.499)
PIERRE, Joanna m. 4 Feb. 1897 Allen HALL (Thib. Ct. Hse.: Mar. v.38, #66)
PIERRE, Joseph m. 11 Jan. 1899 Lizzie LEWIS (Houma Ct. Hse.: Mar. v.30 & 31, #204)
PIERRE, Joseph Albert Velles (Joseph & Olenda SOULE) b. 3 March 1899 (Theriot Ch.: v.2, p.43)
PIERRE, Joseph Remy (Frank & Armantine FERRAND) b. 26 March 1896 (Lockport Ch.: v.2, p.326)
PIERRE, Joseph Silvestre (Joseph & Olenda SAULE) b. 15 April 1896 (Theriot Ch.: v.1-B, p.102)
PIERRE, Mandy m. 24 Dec. 1896 Henry BOSMAN (Thib. Ct. Hse.: Mar. v.36, #169)
PIERRE, Mary Magnolia (Felix & Alice SMITH) b. 31 Jan. 1897 (Thib. Ch.: v.7, p.438)
PIERRON, Louis Elie (Louis Elie & Virginie FABRE) b. 18 March 1896 (Larose Ch.: v.2, p.189 & p.200, #44)
PIERRON, Lucie (Constant & Selemee HENRI) m. 27 March 1896 Adam TROSCLAIR (Houma Ct. Hse.: Mar. v.29 & 30, #16)
PIERSON, Thomas m. 10 Dec. 1896 Bertha OSCHWALD (Thib. Ct. Hse.: Mar. v.36, #165)
PIERSON, Thomas H. (Henry & Mary SANCHEZ) m. 14 Nov. 1896 Bertha OSCHWALD (Thib. Ch.: v.14, p.103)
PIKE, Fletcher d. 28 March 1899 at age 11 yrs. & 8 mths. (Thib. Ch.: v.3, p.230)
PILAUNE, Esner d. 12 March 1898 at age 14 yrs. at college of St. Stainslas, Bay St. Louis, Mississippi. (Lockport Ch.: v.1, #7)
PINCKNEY, Ella m. 7 Feb. 1899 Carter LEWIS (Houma Ct. Hse.: Mar. v.31 & 32, #322)
PINCKNEY, John m. 11 Feb. 1897 Rosa BELL (Houma Ct. Hse.: Mar. v.29 & 30, #305)
PINEA, Joseph Augustin (Ozeme & Victoria DUBOIS) b. 1 July 1897 (Houma Ch.: v.5, p.187)

PINELLE (Sometimes: PINEL, PYNEL)
PINELLE, Jean Neuville (Onesime & Victoria DUBOIS) b. 6 Feb. 1899 (Theriot Ch.: v.2, p.42)
PINKNEY, Elias m. 2 April 1898 Mary RAINEY (Houma Ct. Hse.: Mar. v.30 & 31, #367)
PINKNEY, Sidonia m. 30 Jan. 1899 Ellick LEVEL (Houma Ct. Hse.: Mar. v.30 & 31, #290)
PINSANO, Josephina (Guisepe & Margarithe BELA) b. 14 Dec. 1898 (Houma Ch.: v.5, p.227)
PINTO, Andrea (Joseph & Lucia RISSA) m. 21 Aug. 1899 Anna CALCAGNA (Raceland Ch.: v.2, p.102)
PINTO, Joseph Benjamin (Jhon & Clara MARTINEZ) b. 30 Jan. 1896 (Lockport Ch.: v.3, #20)
PINTO, Joseph Benjamin (Jhon & Clara MARTINEZ) b. 30 Jan. 1896 (Lockport Ch.: v.3-A, #20)

PINZINI, Madelena (Giuseppe & Margarita BILA) b. 15 Jan. 1896 (Houma Ch.: v.5, p.165)
PIRON, Julienne Pauline (Louis & Virginie FABRE) b. 18 April 1898 (Larose Ch.: v.3, p.24)

PITRE (Sometimes: PETRE, PITE, PITTRE)
PITRE, ----- child (Louis) d. 22 July 1897 (Larose Ch.: v.1, p.41)
PITRE, Adam Joseph (Harris & Madeleine PONTIFF) b. 10 Dec. 1899 (Houma Ch.: v.6, p.4)
PITRE, Adam Joseph (Harris & Magdeleine PONTIFF) b. 10 Dec. 1899 (Houma Ch.: v.5, p.269)
PITRE, Adrien of Lafourche Parish (Adrien & Elizabeth ORTIS) m. 11 June 1898 Eliza LORRAINE of Lafourche Parish (Larose Ch.: v.3, p.9)
PITRE, Adrien (Adrien & Elisabeth ORTIS) m. 11 June 1898 Eliza LORRAINE (Thib. Ct. Hse.: Mar. v.38, #197)
PITRE, Adrien (Adrien & Elizabeth ORTIS) m. 11 June 1898 Eliza LORRAINE (Larose Ch.: v.4, p.16)
PITRE, Agathe (Leufroy & Paulina BOUTERY) m. 31 Aug. 1898 Arthur PITRE (Thib. Ch.: v.14, p.216)
PITRE, Agathe (Leufroy &Paulina BOUTERY) m. 31 Aug. 1898 Arthur PITRE (Thib. Ct. Hse.: Mar. v.38, #250)
PITRE, Agnes Carrie (Henri & Lea AYO) b. 26 March 1896 (Thib. Ch.: v.7, p.454)
PITRE, Aliska m. 16 Sept. 1897 Adam Albert BABIN (Houma Ct. Hse.: Mar. v.29 & 30, #92)
PITRE, Aliska (Jean & Camila DARCE) m. 4 Oct. 1897 Adam Albert BABIN (Houma Ch.: v.6-a, p.217)
PITRE, Alzina (Theodule & d.Emelia GUIDRY) m. 5 May 1898 Clay BELLANGER (Montegut Ch.: v.4, p.244)
PITRE, Alzina (Theodule & Emelia GUIDRY) m. 9 April 1898 Clay BELANGER (Houma Ct. Hse.: Mar. v.30 & 31, #392)
PITRE, Arfelia m. 5 June 1897 Laurent BERGERON (Houma Ch.: v.6-a, p.206)
PITRE, Arnold Joseph (Pierre & Adolphine HEBERT) b. 23 Dec. 1899 (Larose Ch.: v.3, p.37)
PITRE, Artelia (Joseph & Emelie HEBERT) m. 1 Aug. 1896 Laurent BERGERON (Houma Ct. Hse.: Mar. v.29 & 30, #122)
PITRE, Arthur (John & Rosa PITRE) m. 31 Aug. 1898 Agathe PITRE (Thib. Ct. Hse.: Mar. v.38, #250)
PITRE, Arthur (John & Rosa PITRE) m. 31 Aug. 1898 Agatha PITRE (Thib. Ch.: v.14, p.216)
PITRE, Auguste Joseph Romuald (Henri & Eugenie CRETINI) b. 1 Feb. 1899 (Larose Ch.: v.3, p.38)
PITRE, Augustin m. 24 May 1899 Ella PIERCE (Thib. Ct. Hse.: Mar. v.39, #167)
PITRE, Augustin m. 27 May 1899 Ella PIERCE (Larose Ch.: v.3, p.12)
PITRE, Augustin m. 27 May 1899 Ella PIERCE (Larose Ch.: v.4, p.84)

PITRE, Augustin m. 27 May 1899 Ella PIERCE (Larose Ch.: v.4, p.101)
PITRE, Blanche (William & Ema DUET) m. 2 July 1896 Olucien CHERAMIE (Thib. Ct. Hse.: Mar. v.36, #115)
PITRE, Blanche (William & Emma DUET) m. 16 April 1898 Olucien CHERAMI (Larose Ch.: v.3, p.8)
PITRE, Blanche (William & Emma DUET) m. 16 April 1898 Olucien CHERAMI (Larose Ch.: v.4, p.80)
PITRE, Cecile (Henri & Victoria GLARDON) m. 4 Aug. 1898 William HEBERT (Thib. Ct. Hse.: Mar. v.38, #231)
PITRE, Cecile (Henri & Victoria GLARDON) m. 4 Aug. 1898 William HEBERT (Thib. Ch.: v.14, p.213)
PITRE, Charles m. 18 May 1898 Julia DANTIN (Thib. Ct. Hse.: Mar. v.38, #183)
PITRE, Charles Pitt (Charles & Julia DANTIN) b. 5 April 1899 (Raceland Ch.: v.5, p.94)
PITRE, Cheritia Marie (William & Emma DUAY) b. 8 Dec. 1897 (Larose Ch.: v.3, p.22)
PITRE, Corinne Nativite (Gilles & Ernestine HEBERT) b. 3 Aug. 1896 (Thib. Ch.: v.7, p.411)
PITRE, David m. 17 Dec. 1898 Liza ADAM (Thib. Ct. Hse.: Mar. v.38, #317)
PITRE, David m. 17 Dec. 1899 Liza ADAM (Larose Ch.: v.4, p.31)
PITRE, David m. 19 Dec. 1899 Liza ADAM (Larose Ch.: v.3, p.13)
PITRE, Elfere Joseph (Eugene & Emma GISCLAR) b. 1 Dec. 1898 (Larose Ch.: v.3, p.37)
PITRE, Elie d. 19 April 1898 at age 56 yrs. (Montegut Ch.: v.2, p.16)
PITRE, Elie Joseph (Johnny & Frances AUTUN) b. 8 Feb. 1898 (Montegut Ch.: v.6, p.86)
PITRE, Ernestine m. Leonce PITRE d. 2 Nov. 1898 at age 30 yrs. (Larose Ch.: v.1, p.45)
PITRE, Ernestine (Marcellus & Clemance GUIDRY) m. 17 Jan. 1898 Sidney Albert BELANGER (Houma Ct. Hse.: Mar. v.30 & 31, #224)
PITRE, Ernestine (Marcellus & Clemence GUIDRY) m. 14 Feb. 1898 Sidney Albert BELLANGER (Montegut Ch.: v.4, p.236)
PITRE, Estelle Josephine (Victor & Alphonsine TERREBONNE) b. 9 April 1899 (Larose Ch.: v.3, p.41)
PITRE, Estellina m. d.Theophile RAYMOND d. 20 Nov. 1896 at age 28 yrs. (Larose Ch.: v.1, p.38)
PITRE, Eugene Norbert (Philippe & Marie PICOU) b. 31 May 1898 (Thib. Ch.: v.7, p.551)
PITRE, Eulalie m. 14 Sept. 1897 Joseph HOTARD (Thib. Ct. Hse.: Mar. v.37, #233)
PITRE, Eulalie (Henri & Victoria GLARDON) m. 16 Dec. 1898 Joseph HOTARD (Thib. Ct. Hse.: Mar. v.14, p.232)
PITRE, Euphemie m. Amedee LEDET d. 19 Oct. 1899 at age 72 yrs. & 22 days (Thib. Ch.: v.3, p.242)

PITRE, Felix of Lafourche Parish (Gratien & Marguerite LANDRY) m. 8 June 1898 Aglonie BRUCE of Lafourche Parish (Larose Ch.: v.3, p.9)

PITRE, Felix (Gratien & Marguerite LANDRY) m. 8 June 1898 Aglonie BRUCE (Thib. Ct. Hse.: Mar. v.38, #198)

PITRE, Felix (Gratien & Margueritte LANDRY) m. 8 June 1898 Aglonie BRUCE (Larose Ch.: v.4, p.15)

PITRE, Ferdinand Jr. d. 9 May 1899; m. Louise BERTHAU Child listed: Evelina, about 7 mths. Petition for inventory: 15 May 1899. (Thib. Ct. Hse.: Succ. #1574)

PITRE, Guilles Elma Benoit (Guillace & Ernestine HEBERT) b. 1 Sept. 1898 (Thib. Ch.: v.7, p.510)

PITRE, Gustave m. 31 Dec. 1898 Justilia BLANCHARD (Houma Ct. Hse.: Mar. v.30 & 31, #168)

PITRE, Gustave (Zephirin & Bazelise DUPRE) m. 16 Jan. 1899 Justilia BLANCHARD (Houma Ch.: v.6-a, p.264)

PITRE, Gustave Fernand (Philippe & Marie PICOU) b. 1 Jan. 1897 (Thib. Ch.: v.7, p.434)

PITRE, Harry (Leufroy) d. 16 Nov. 1899 at age 2 yrs., 1 mth. & 15 days (Thib. Ch.: v.3, p.243)

PITRE, Henri d. 4 July 1899 at age 68 yrs. (Thib. Ch.: v.3, p.236)

PITRE, Henri m. 23 April 1898 Eugenie CRETINI (Larose Ch.: v.4, p.12)

PITRE, Henri of Lafourche Parish m. 23 April 1898 Eugenie CRETINI of Lafourche Parish (Larose Ch.: v.3, p.9)

PITRE, Henri Joachim (James & Arthelise GUILBERT) b. 15 July 1897 (Larose Ch.: v.3, p.9)

PITRE, Henri Joachim (James & Arthilise GUILBERT) b. 15 July 1897 (Larose Ch.: v.3, p.9)

PITRE, Henry (Alexis & Romela DUET) m. 23 April 1898 Eugenie CRETINI (Thib. Ct. Hse.: Mar. v.38, #154)

PITRE, Herbert (Simeon & Mary L. BROUSSARD) m. 8 Nov. 1898 Mary BABIN (Houma Ct. Hse.: Mar. v.30 & 31, #130)

PITRE, Ignace Wallace (Ignace & Nora ROUSSEL) b. 7 Dec. 1897 (Thib. Ch.: v.7, p.482)

PITRE, Isah m. 6 Sept. 1896 Mrs. Dorcina DANTIN, widow (Larose Ch.: v.4, p.68)

PITRE, Isah m. 6 Sept. 1896 Dorcina DANTIN, widow of DANDRAS (Larose Ch.: v.3, p.4)

PITRE, Jacob Joseph Mrs. d. 27 Sept. 1899 at age 20 days (Larose Ch.: v.1, p.54)

PITRE, Jean Leo (Didier & Julia PITRE) b. 8 Feb. 1898 (Larose Ch.: v.3, p.16)

PITRE, Jimmy J. m. 18 April 1896 Marie GILLEBAUX (Thib. Ct. Hse.: Mar. v.35, #57)

PITRE, John (Elie & Cornelia WHITE) m. 5 May 1896 Frances AUTIN (Houma Ct. Hse.: Mar. v.29 & 30, #54)

PITRE, Joseph m. Philomene GUIDRY d. 10 Nov. 1897 at age 46 yrs. (Larose Ch.: v.1, p.41)

PITRE, Joseph Clarence (Maurice & Josephine LIRETTE) b. 30 July 1898 (Thib. Ch.: v.7, p.558)
PITRE, Joseph Evins (Frank & Mary DUPRE) b. 25 Sept. 1898; m. Marie Alcea BOURGEOIS on 7 April 1959. (Houma Ch.: Bapt. Bk., v.5, p.221)
PITRE, Joseph Howard (Johnny & Frances AUTIN) b. 29 Nov. 1899 (Montegut Ch.: v.7, p.2)
PITRE, Joseph James (Harris & Laura BERGERON) b. 28 Nov. 1896 (Houma Ch.: v.5, p.162)
PITRE, Joseph Murphy (Alidore & Hermilia BABIN) b. 29 Aug. 1899 (Houma Ch.: v.5, p.255)
PITRE, Josephine m. William PRICE d. 5 May 1897 at age 72 yrs. (Thib. Ch.: v.3, p.199)
PITRE, Josephine Evangeline (L. M. & Josephine ST. AMAND) b. 27 Aug. 1899 (Raceland Ch.: v.5, p.109)
PITRE, Julien (Sylvain & Marie LIRETTE) m. 15 June 1899 Camila UZE (Thib. Ch.: v.14, p.285)
PITRE, Julien (Sylvain & Marie LIRETTE) m. 15 June 1899 Camila UZE (Thib. Ct. Hse: Mar. v.39, #169)
PITRE, Junius (Louise PITRE) b. 30 Nov. 1899 (Thib. Ch.: v.8, p.19)
PITRE, Lee (d.Elie & Carnelia WHITE) m. 27 April 1899 Julienne RHODES (Montegut Ch.: v.4, p.262)
PITRE, Lee (Elie & Cornelia WHITE) m. 8 April 1899 Julienne RHODES (Houma Ct. Hse.: Mar. v.31 & 32, #390)
PITRE, Leopold (Alidor & d.Laurenza CHERAMIE) m. 17 Feb. 1899 Julie AUTIN (Thib. Ct. Hse.: Mar. v.39, #291)
PITRE, Livaudais d. 11 July 1898 at age 37 yrs. (Larose Ch.: v.1, p.43)
PITRE, Louis Rameau (Louis & Eve CHERAMI) b. 3 April 1898 (Larose Ch.: v.3, p.22)
PITRE, Louise Rose (Pierre & Adolphine HEBERT) b. 8 Dec. 1896 (Larose Ch.: v.3, p.4)
PITRE, Marguerite Gentillote (Julien & Camille UZE) b. 5 Nov. 1899 (Thib. Ch.: v.8, p.18)
PITRE, Marguerite Laura (Gustave & Annie MARTIN) b. 7 Aug. 1899 (Montegut Ch.: v.6, p.91)
PITRE, Margueritte (Leonce & Augustine PITRE) d. 24 Sept. 1897 at age 5 days (Larose Ch.: v.1, p.40)
PITRE, Marie (Ferdinand & Enesile MELANCON) m. 29 Sept. 1898 Charles GUIDRY (Thib. Ct. Hse.: Mar. v.38, #269)
PITRE, Marie (Ferdinand & Eusila MELANCON) m. 20 Sept. 1898 Charles GUIDRY (Thib. Ch.: v.14, p.224)
PITRE, Marie Agnes (Louis & Angelique CARRERE) b. 25 Nov. 1897 (Montegut Ch.: v.6, p.66)
PITRE, Marie Anne Eve (Ariste & Madelane PONTIFF) b. 20 Oct. 1897 (Houma Ch.: v.5, p.191)
PITRE, Marie Annesia (Gilbert & Marie BABIN) b. 22 Aug. 1899 (Houma Ch.: v.5, p.254)
PITRE, Marie Aurore Ortilia (Lucien & Julie FODE) b. 1 Feb. 1897 (Chackbay Ch.: v.1, p.81)

PITRE, Marie Evelina (Ferdinand & Louise BERTHAUD) b. 25 Sept. 1898 (Thib. Ch.: v.7, p.513)
PITRE, Marie Ida (Gustave & Annie MARTIN) b. 18 Dec. 1896 (Montegut Ch.: v.6, p.48)
PITRE, Marie Josephine m. William Trenton PRICE Final account & administration: 15 Oct. 1897. (Thib. Ct. Hse.: Succ. #1515)
PITRE, Marie Lilly (Willy & Octavie PONTIFF) b. 22 March 1896 (Houma Ch.: v.5, p.175)
PITRE, Marie Sereza (David & Lezida SCOTT) b. 31 Jan. 1896 (Larose Ch.: v.2, p.186)
PITRE, Marie Therese (Willie & Josephine HEBERT) b. 25 March 1896 (Thib. Ch.: v.7, p.400)
PITRE, Marie Variola (Olaus & Lea DERIS) b. 12 Dec. 1899 (Montegut Ch.: v.6, p.98)
PITRE, Marie Westilia (Johnny & Marie Francis AUTIN) b. 3 Jan. 1897 (Montegut Ch.: v.6, p.54)
PITRE, Mary Agnes (Arris & Laura BERGERON) b. 21 Oct. 1899 (Houma Ch.: v.5, p.263)
PITRE, Maurice (Victorin & Marie MOLAISON) m. 21 Oct. 1897 Josephine LIRETTE (Thib. Ch.: v.14, p.165)
PITRE, Maurice (Victorin & Marie MOLAISON) m. 21 Oct. 1897 Josephine LIRETTE (Thib. Ct. Hse.: Mar. v.37, #248)
PITRE, Mildred Doris (Oleneus & Nora ROUSSEL) b. 21 Dec. 1899 (Thib. Ch.: v.7, p.580)
PITRE, Milride d. 13 July 1899 at age 42 yrs., 3 mths. & 4 days (Thib. Ch.: v.3, p.237)
PITRE, Ophelia m. 25 July 1896 Ernest LAFOND (Larose Ch.: v.4, p.78)
PITRE, Ophelia m. 25 July 1896 Ernest LAFOND (Larose Ch.: v.4, p.42)
PITRE, Ophelia m. 25 July 1896 Ernest LAFOND (Larose Ch.: v.3, p.4)
PITRE, Ophelia (Alexis, Sr. & Romela DUET) m. 17 July 1896 Ernest LAFONT (Thib. Ct. Hse.: Mar. v.36, #126)
PITRE, Paul Laurent (Marcell & Clemilia DETIVEAU) b. 15 March 1898 (Montegut Ch.: v.6, p.67)
PITRE, Raoul (Victorin & Marie MOLAISON) m. 31 Jan. 1899 Annette SOIGNIER (Thib. Ct. Hse.: Mar. v.38, #19)
PITRE, Raoul (Victorin & Marie MOLAISON) m. 31 Jan. 1899 Annette SOIGNIER (Thib. Ch.: v.14, p.252)
PITRE, Regina (Lufroy & Pauline BOUTTARY) m. 19 Aug. 1897 Numa HEBERT (Thib. Ct. Hse.: Mar. v.37, #214)
PITRE, Regina (Lufroy & Pauline BOUTTARY) m. 19 Aug. 1897 Numa HEBERT (Thib. Ch.: v.14, p.158)
PITRE, Rose m. 18 May 1898 Emanuel CHERAMIE (Thib. Ct. Hse.: Mar. v.38, #181)
PITRE, Severin Wilson (Julien & Camillia GUIDRY) b. 10 Feb. 1898 (Larose Ch.: v.3, p.16)
PITRE, Vene Jacob Joseph (Adrien & Louisa LORAIN) b. 8 Sept. 1899 (Larose Ch.: v.3, p.45)

PITRE, Victoria (Dasral & Josephine PITRE) m. 4 Nov. 1899 Dupre TERREBONNE (Larose Ch.: v.4, p.125)
PITRE, Victoria (David & Josephine PITRE) m. 4 Nov. 1899 Duprey TERREBONNE (Thib. Ct. Hse.: Mar. v.39, #245)
PITRE, Victoria (David & Josephine PITRE) m. 4 Nov. 1899 Dupre TERREBONNE (Larose Ch.: v.3, p.12)
PITRE, Victoria (Henri & Victoria GLORDA) m. 25 June 1896 Franklin GUILLOTTE (Thib. Ct. Hse.: Mar. v.35, #103)
PITRE, Victoria (Henri & Victoria GLORDON) m. 25 June 1896 Franklin GUILLOTTE (Thib. Ch.: v.14, p.94)
PITRE, Vina m. 7 July 1899 Ernest CANTRELLE (Thib. Ct. Hse.: Mar. v.39, #193)
PITRE, Voltaire m. 7 June 1899 Laura TOUPS (Thib. Ct. Hse.: Mar. v.39, #195)
PITT, Alice (Cevola & Pauline BOUTTARY) b. 30 Sept. 1897 (Thib. Ch.: v.7, p.468)
PITT, Antoine d. 10 July 1897 at birth (Thib. Ch.: v.3, p.202)
PITT, Charles (Ferdinand & Nesile MELANCON) m. 14 June 1898 Julia DANTIN (Raceland Ch.: v.2, p.75)
PITT, Claude Joseph (Willie & Josephine HEBERT) b. 25 March 1899 (Thib. Ch.: v.7, p.610)
PITT, Cyrus Allet (Louise & Angelique CARRERE) b. 24 Sept. 1896 (Theriot Ch.: v.1-B, p.92)
PITT, Eulalie Georgina (Ignace & Nora ROUSSEL) b. 7 Oct. 1896 (Thib. Ch.: v.7, p.431)
PITT, Ferdinand Jr. d. 10 May 1899 at age 38 yrs. (Thib. Ch.: v.3, p.233)
PITT, Freddy Clifford (Arthur & Agathe PITT) b. 15 June 1899 (Thib. Ch.: v.7, p.552)
PITT, Joseph d. 10 July 1897 at birth (Thib. Ch.: v.3, p.202)
PITT, Joseph Alcee (Willy & Josephine HEBERT) b. 19 April 1898 (Thib. Ch.: v.7, p.496)
PITT, Joseph Bernard (Marcel & Clemelia DETIVEAU) b. 17 April 1896 (Montegut Ch.: v.6, p.38)
PITT, Pelonia Sidonia (Lucien & Julie FODE) b. 29 Nov. 1899 (Chackbay Ch.: v.1, p.145)
PITTMAN, Charles Nolan (Jean & Ernestine KNOBLOCK) b. 30 May 1899 (Raceland Ch.: v.5, p.97)
PITTMAN, Philippe Lawrence (John F. & Ernestine KNOBLOCK) b. 14 Nov. 1896 (Raceland Ch.: v.5, p.34)
PITZOLATO, Pauline (Vincenzo & Antoinica GIORDANA) b. 18 May 1899 (Thib. Ch.: v.7, p.606)

PIZANI (Sometimes: PESANI, PISANI)

PLAISANCE (Sometimes: PLAZENCIA, PLESENCE)
PLAISANCE, ----- child (Jules & Minice HEBERT) d. 28 July 1896 at age 1 day (Larose Ch.: v.1, p.37)
PLAISANCE, Abel (Napoleon & Marcelline ALLEMAND) b. 1 Dec. 1896 (Lockport Ch.: v.3, #29)

PLAISANCE, Abel Horace (Napoleon & Marcelline ALLEMAND) b. 1 Dec. 1896 (Lockport Ch.: v.3-A, #29)

PLAISANCE, Alexina (Baptiste & Marie DAIGLE) m. 30 Jan. 1899 Francois ROGER (Larose Ch.: v.3, p.11)

PLAISANCE, Alexine (Baptiste & Marie DAIGLE) m. 30 Jan. 1899 Francois ROGERE (Thib. Ct. Hse.: Mar. v.38, #35)

PLAISANCE, Aline Therese (Eugene & Everina BADEAUX) b. 27 Sept. 1896 (Larose Ch.: v.2, p.184)

PLAISANCE, Anatole Joseph (Melien & Manuela BERNARD) b. 31 July 1897 (Raceland Ch.: v.5, p.52)

PLAISANCE, Andre m. 25 May 1897 Adelaide GUIDRY (Thib. Ct. Hse.: Mar. v.36, #148)

PLAISANCE, Andre m. 5 June 1897 Adelaide GUIDRY (Larose Ch.: v.3, p.5)

PLAISANCE, Andre m. 5 June 1897 Adelaide GUIDRY (Larose Ch.: v.4, p.73)

PLAISANCE, Armantine m. 31 Dec. 1898 Alidor FONSECA (Thib. Ct. Hse.: Mar. v.38, #329)

PLAISANCE, Armantine (Joseph & Marie RICHOU) m. 20 July 1899 Olidor FONSECA (Lockport Ch.: v.2, p.209)

PLAISANCE, Aurore Philomene (Alexis & Alice SAVOIE) b. 6 June 1898 (Larose Ch.: v.3, p.20)

PLAISANCE, Camillia Felecite (Philippe & Alcina DANOS) b. 10 July 1896 (Larose Ch.: v.2, p.184)

PLAISANCE, Charles m. 26 Oct. 1897 Ernestine BOURGEOIS (Lockport Ch.: v.2, p.177)

PLAISANCE, Charles (Philippe & Zeolite DANTIN) m. 26 Oct. 1897 Ernestine BOURGEOIS (Thib. Ct. Hse.: Mar. v.37, #252)

PLAISANCE, Clementine m. Andre ALEMAN d. 11 March 1899 at age 88 yrs. (Larose Ch.: v.1, p.52)

PLAISANCE, Emilien m. 12 Oct. 1896 Manuella BERNARD (Larose Ch.: v.4, p.47)

PLAISANCE, Emilien m. 12 Oct. 1896 Manuella BERNARD (Larose Ch.: v.3, p.4)

PLAISANCE, Ernest (Eusebe & Anastasie BOURGEOIS) m. 6 June 1898 Mathilde MOLAISON (Thib. Ct. Hse.: Mar. v.38, #194)

PLAISANCE, Ernest (Eusebe & Anastasie BOURGEOIS) m. 6 June 1898 Mathilde MOLAISON (Lockport Ch.: v.2, p.189)

PLAISANCE, Eunice Guillaume (Jules & Emma HEBERT) b. 17 Aug. 1899 (Larose Ch.: v.3, p.44)

PLAISANCE, Francois Horace (Olivier & Cecilia BOUVIER) b. 3 Dec. 1898 (Larose Ch.: v.3, p.30)

PLAISANCE, Gustave (Baptiste & Marie DAIGLE) m. 23 Jan. 1899 Eugenie BERNARD (Thib. Ct. Hse.: Mar. v.38, #36)

PLAISANCE, Gustave (Baptiste & Marie DAIGLE) m. 23 Jan. 1899 Eugenie BERNARD (Larose Ch.: v.4, p.32)

PLAISANCE, Gustave (Baptiste & Marie DAIGLE) m. 23 Jan. 1899 Eugenie BERNARD (Larose Ch.: v.3, p.11)

PLAISANCE, Hayes Marie (Lignes & Leontine ORGERON) b. 29 Oct. 1899 (Larose Ch.: v.3, p.46)

PLAISANCE, Helene m. 10 July 1897 Joseph DUFRESNE (Thib. Ct. Hse.: Mar. v.37, #183)
PLAISANCE, Helene m. 10 July 1897 Joseph DUFRENE (Lockport Ch.: v.2, p.169)
PLAISANCE, Henri (Andre & Adelaide GUIDRY) b. 15 May 1898 (Larose Ch.: v.3, p.26)
PLAISANCE, Ives Jean (Philippe & Alzina DANOS) b. 18 Dec. 1899 (Larose Ch.: v.3, p.51)
PLAISANCE, Joseph m. 10 June 1897 Daisy ALLEMAN (Larose Ch.: v.3, p.6)
PLAISANCE, Joseph m. 10 June 1897 Daisy ALLEMAN (Larose Ch.: v.4, p.72-A)
PLAISANCE, Joseph m. 15 May 1897 Daisy ALLEMAND (Thib. Ct. Hse.: Mar. v.36, #144)
PLAISANCE, Joseph Isidore (Isidore & Jeannette HERNANDEZ) b. 4 Dec. 1897 (Thib. Ch.: v.7, p.475)
PLAISANCE, Joseph Laurens (Joseph & Josephine CANTRELLE) b. 10 April 1896 (Lockport Ch.: v.2, p.327)
PLAISANCE, Joseph Loule (Raymond & Berthe TEMPLE) b. 13 April 1896 (Lockport Ch.: v.2, p.328)
PLAISANCE, Joseph Noe (Emilien & Manuela BERNARD) b. 24 July 1899 (Larose Ch.: v.3, p.43)
PLAISANCE, Jules m. 31 May 1899 Celeste GAUDE (Thib. Ct. Hse.: Mar. v.39, #173)
PLAISANCE, Jules (Jules & Mathilde DANOS) m. 24 June 1899 Celeste GAUDE (Larose Ch.: v.3, p.12)
PLAISANCE, Jules (Philippe & Mathilde DANOS) m. 24 June 1899 Celeste GAUDE (Larose Ch.: v.4, p.86)
PLAISANCE, Julia m. 19 June 1897 Lovincie CHERAMIE (Larose Ch.: v.3, p.6)
PLAISANCE, Julia m. 19 June 1897 Lovincie CHERAMIE (Larose Ch.: v.4, p.66)
PLAISANCE, Julia m. 29 May 1897 Lovincie CHERAMIE (Thib. Ct. Hse.: Mar. v.36, #153)
PLAISANCE, Julien (Jules & Ema HEBERT) m. 14 July 1898 Emelie ROBINSON (Thib. Ct. Hse.: Mar. v.38, #221)
PLAISANCE, Julien (Jules & Emma HEBERT) m. 14 July 1898 Emilie ROBERTSON (Lockport Ch.: v.2, p.192)
PLAISANCE, Leonce Lernard (Gustave & Eugenie BERNARD) b. 6 Nov. 1899 (Larose Ch.: v.3, p.48)
PLAISANCE, Levy Joseph (Philippe & Alzina DANOS) b. 12 Feb. 1898 (Larose Ch.: v.3, p.18)
PLAISANCE, Lineus (Arthur & Ordasie THERIOT) m. 2 Feb. 1899 Leontine ORGERON (Thb. Ct. Hse.: Mar. v.38, #44)
PLAISANCE, Marie Regina (Joseph & Daisie ALEMAN) b. 28 Nov. 1898 (Larose Ch.: v.3, p.30)
PLAISANCE, Milien m. 7 Oct. 1896 Manuella BERNARD (Thib. Ct. Hse.: Mar. v.36, #151)
PLAISANCE, Numa Josephine (Jules & Myrthee DUGAS) b. 17 May 1897 (Lockport Ch.: v.3-A, #52)

PLAISANCE, Numa Josephine (Jules & Myrthee DUGAS) b. 23 May 1897 (Lockport Ch.: v.3, #52)
PLAISANCE, Sidney Fidelus (Ernest & Mathilde MOLESON) b. 24 April 1899 (Raceland Ch.: v.5, p.96)
PLAISANCE, Simon (Arthur & Ordasie THERIOT) m. 2 Feb. 1899 Leontine ORGERON (Lockport Ch.: v.2, p.200)
PLAISANCE, Warren Evariste (Napoleon & Marcelline NAPOLEON) b. 15 Nov. 1899 (Lockport Ch.: v.3, #13)
PLAISANCE, Wuares Evariste (Napoleon & Marcelline ALLEMAND) b. 15 Nov. 1899 (Lockport Ch.: v.3-A, #13)

PLASENCIA (See also: PLAISANCE)
PLASENCIA, Angela (Joseph M. & Mannella PIEDRA) m. 27 Dec. 1899 Arthur Ronald TRIST (Houma Ct. Hse.: Mar. v.31 & 32, #206)
PLASENCIA, Angela (Joseph M.) m. 28 Dec. 1899 Arthur Ronald TRIST (Houma Ch.: Epis. Ch.: v.1, p.344)
PLASENCIA, Mary J. m. 29 Oct. 1898 Andrew J. DANA (Houma Ct. Hse.: Mar. v.30 & 31, #127)
PLASENCIA, Mary J. (Joseph M. & Manuda PIADRA) m. 30 Oct. 1898 Andrew J. DANA (Houma Ch.: v.6-a, p.258)
PLESSALA, Eddy Ulyssia (Augusta & Baptistine EGLE) b. 12 Feb. 1896 (Larose Ch.: v.2, p.189)
PLONGIOSSI, Guiesseppe m. 10 May 1898 Francesca CIACCIO (Houma Ct. Hse.: Mar. v.30 & 31, #433)

POCHE (See also: PORCHE)
POCHE, Joseph (Alcee & Victoria THIBODAUX) b. 28 May 1899 (Raceland Ch.: v.5, p.98)
POCHE, Joseph Lucien (Felix & Eugenie ZERIN) b. 2 Jan. 1898 (Thib. Ch.: v.7, p.479)
POCHE, Julie Edna (Nicolas & Alice BOURGEOIS) b. 11 Sept. 1896 (Thib. Ch.: v.7, p.416)
POICHENS, Wallace d. 28 Sept. 1899 at age 33 yrs. (Raceland Ch.: v.1, p.27)
POINCOT, Augustin Avis (Aurelie & Eva CHIASSON) b. 29 Aug. 1897 (Theriot Ch.: v.2, p.11)
POINDEXTER, Northern m. 10 June 1897 Sarah WHITAKER (Houma Ct. Hse.: Mar. v.29 & 30, #27)

POINSON (Sometimes: POINCON, POINCEAU)
POINSON, Jean Inez (Aurelia & Eva CHIASSON) b. 17 Aug. 1899 (Theriot Ch.: v.2, p.48)
POINSON, Joseph Davis (Ben & Laura MARCEL) b. 16 June 1898 (Thib. Ch.: v.7, p.505)
POINSON, Toussaint Armand (Benois & Laura MARCEL) b. 1 Nov. 1899 (Thib. Ch.: v.8, p.20)
POLASKI, Adolphe Lovelace (Adolphe & Olda VERRET) b. 2 May 1898 (Chacahoula Ch.: Gibson Records: Mar. Bk., v.1, #46)

POLASKI, Adolphe Loveless (Adolphe & Olda VERRET) b. 2 May 1898 (Chacahoula Ch.: Gibson Ch.: v.2, p.128)

POLASKI, Nattie Mary (James & Alice MORGAN) b. 19 Aug. 1897 (Chacahoula Ch.: Gibson Ch.: v.2, p.114)

POLATZA, Theresa d. 1 Dec. 1899 at age 1 yr. & 9 mths. (Thib. Ch.: v.3, p.245)

POLLARA, Sarilla (Antonino & Carmela PANZICA) b. 1 Jan. 1899 (Thib. Ch.: v.7, p.529)

POLLARD, Nellie m. 9 March 1896 George WASHINGTON (Houma Ct. Hse.: Mar. v.29 & 30, #5)

PONCE (Sometimes: PONCHE, PONS, PONSE, PONTIO, PORTIO)

PONTIFF (Sometimes: PONTIF, PONTIFE, PONTIFFE)

PONTIFF, Alexis d. 9 April 1898 at age 59 yrs. (Thib. Ch.: v.3, p.213)

PONTIFF, Alice (Valery & Celina ROBICHAUX) m. 7 Jan. 1896 Amedee ROBICHAUX (Houma Ch.: v.6-a, p.167)

PONTIFF, Aline Valerie (Neuville & A. LEBLANC) b. 20 July 1896 (Thib. Ch.: v.7, p.409)

PONTIFF, Brigitte Jean Baptiste Henri (Adam & Marie BERGERON) b. 7 Aug. 1898 (Thib. Ch.: v.7, p.530)

PONTIFF, Cecile (Joachim & Marie ESTEVE) m. 24 Jan. 1898 Edgard GUILLOTE (Thib. Ch.: v.14, p.174)

PONTIFF, Cecile (Joachim & Marie ESTEVE) m. 24 Jan. 1898 Edgard GUILLOTE (Thib. Ct. Hse.: Mar. v.37, #14)

PONTIFF, Daisy (Lubin & Emilie ADAM) m. 30 April 1896 Emile KERNE (Thib. Ch.: v.14, p.88)

PONTIFF, Daisy Marie (Lubin & Emilie ADAM) m. 30 April 1896 Emile KERNE (Thib. Ct. Hse.: Mar. v.35, #81)

PONTIFF, Elvire (Julien & Virginie NAQUIN) m. 16 Feb. 1897 Ernest BERGERON (Thib. Ch.: v.14, p.126)

PONTIFF, Elvire (Julien & Virginie NAQUIN) m. 16 Feb. 1897 Ernest BERGERON (Houma Ct. Hse.: Mar. v.29 & 30, #255)

PONTIFF, Felicia (Joachim & Marie ESTIVE) m.27 April 1899 Leonie RICHARD (Thib. Ch.: v.14, p.279)

PONTIFF, Felicie (Joachim & Marie ESTEVE) m. 27 April 1899 Leonie RICHARD (Thib. Ct. Hse.: Mar. v.39, #146)

PONTIFF, Felix d. Sept. 1897; m. Odille SCHEXNYDER Children listed: Zoe; Denis; Sidney; Jeannie. Application for letters of administration: 13 Jan. 1898. (Thib. Ct. Hse.: Succ. #1527)

PONTIFF, Felix d. 27 Aug. 1897 at age 36 yrs. (Thib. Ch.: v.3, p.205)

PONTIFF, Jean Lawrence (Augustin & Marie GUIDRY) b. 13 Oct. 1897; m. Neuville BERGERON on 5 May 1928. (Houma Ch.: Bapt. Bk., v.5, p.196)

PONTIFF, Joseph (Alexis & Eulalie HEBERT) m. 9 Oct. 1898 Leontia BERNARD (Thib. Ct. Hse.: Mar. v.38, #286)

PONTIFF, Joseph (Alexis & Eulalie HEBERT) m. 9 Oct. 1898 Leontia BERNARD (Thib. Ch.: v.14, p.227)

PONTIFF, Joseph Aeris (Augustin & Marie GUIDRY) b. 18 July 1896 (Houma Ch.: v.5, p.157)
PONTIFF, Joseph Edouard (Augustin & Laura GASSIE) b. 14 Oct. 1896 (Houma Ch.: v.5, p.163)
PONTIFF, Joseph Sylvestre (Valere & Marie COMEAU) b. 13 Jan. 1896; m. Lucy THIBODEAUX on 27 April 1922 (Houma Ch.: Bapt. Bk., v.5, p.167)
PONTIFF, Joseph Victor (Osea & Alice CASTAGNE) b. 19 June 1896 (Thib. Ch.: v.7, p.406)
PONTIFF, Josephine d. 13 Feb. 1898 at age 75 yrs. (Thib. Ch.: v.3, p.210)
PONTIFF, Josephine (Augustin & Marie GUIDRY) b. 11 June 1899 (Montegut Ch.: v.6, p.90)
PONTIFF, Josephine Barthelia (Adam & Marie BERGERON) b. 10 April 1896 (Chackbay Ch.: v.1, p.65)
PONTIFF, Lydia (Lubin & Emilie ADAM) m. 31 Jan. 1899 Camille KERN, of St. Mary Parish (Thib. Ct. Hse.: Mar. v.38, #54)
PONTIFF, Lydia (Lubin & Emilie ADAM) m. 31 Jan. 1899 Camille KERN (Thib. Ch.: v.14, p.249)
PONTIFF, Marie Mabel (Augustin & Laura GAGNIER) bt. 5 Nov. 1899 (Thib. Ch.: v.7, p.572)
PONTIFF, Marie Zoe (Felix & Odile SHEXNAYDER) b. 6 Sept. 1897 (Thib. Ch.: v.7, p.464)
PONTIFF, Mary Lelia (Augustin & Laura SAVOIE) b. 17 Feb. 1896 (Houma Ch.: v.5, p.149)
PONTIFF, Octavie d. 7 Feb. 1899 at age 26 yrs. (Houma Ch.: v.3, p.21)
PONTIFF, Odile Ophelia (Martial & Odile MARLBOUROUGH) b. 8 July 1896 (Thib. Ch.: v.7, p.418)
PONTIFF, Pierre Nicholas (Joseph & Eugenie CARRO) b. 22 Jan. 1899 (Houma Ch.: v.5, p.237)
PONTIFF, Valerie Merilia (Adam & Mary BERGERON) b. 11 Sept. 1898 (Thib. Ch.: v.7, p.566)
PONTIFF, Wilfred (Auguste & Maria ORDONNEAUX) m. 17 March 1898 Clara CHATAGNIER (Houma Ct. Hse.: Mar. v.30 & 31, #344)
PONTIFF, Wilson Laurence Joseph (Neuville & Zilda LEBLANC) b. 23 Jan. 1898 (Thib. Ch.: v.7, p.541)

PORCHE (Sometimes: POCHE, POCHET)

PORCHE, Adele Francis d. 1 Aug. 1899 at age 19 yrs. (Houma Ch.: v.3, p.24)
PORCHE, Albert Hypolitte (Baptiste & Cecilia PLAISANCE) b. 13 Aug. 1896 (Larose Ch.: v.2, p.195)
PORCHE, Auguste (Alfred & Louisa GAUDE) m. 15 Nov. 1899 Eleonore AUCOIN (Thib. Ch.: v.14, p.308)
PORCHE, Auguste E. C. (Alfred & Louisa GAUDE) m. 15 Nov. 1899 Eleonore AUCOIN (Thib. Ct. Hse.: Mar. v.39, #262)
PORCHE, Augustin Emile (Emile & Elfrida GUIDRY) b. 28 Aug. 1898 (Theriot Ch.: v.2, p.29)

PORCHE, Carol Paul (George & Victoria LEVRON) b. 24 Sept. 1898 (Houma Ch.: v.5, p.217)

PORCHE, Celeste Emelie (Franklin & Lora TOUPS) b. 16 Sept. 1899 (Theriot Ch.: v.2, p.50)

PORCHE, Domitilde m. Valcour RODRIGUE d. 17 May 1899 at age 63 yrs. (Lockport Ch.: v.1, #20)

PORCHE, Elisha Shelby d. 12 Sept. 1898 at age 2 yrs. (Houma Ch.: Epis. Ch.: v.1, p.388)

PORCHE, Emma m. 12 Jan. 1897 William WHITE (Houma Ct. Hse.: Mar. v.29 & 30, #235)

PORCHE, Felix Augustin (Guilles & Nobee DAIGLE) b. 23 Jan. 1898 (Houma Ch.: v.5, p.199)

PORCHE, George m. 18 Jan. 1898 Victoria LEVRON (Houma Ct. Hse.: Mar. v.30 & 31, #227)

PORCHE, George (J. Schuyler & Octavie BONVILLAIN) m. 19 Jan. 1898 Victoria LEVRON (Houma Ch.: v.6-a, p.223)

PORCHE, Hortense Justile (Guilles & Nobletia DAIGLE) b. 11 Jan. 1899 (Thib. Ch.: v.7, p.592)

PORCHE, J. Schuyler m. 14 Aug. 1897 Camila LEVRON (Houma Ct. Hse.: Mar. v.29 & 30, #79)

PORCHE, James Schuyler Jr. (J. Schuyler & Octavie BONVILLAIN) m. 14 Aug. 1897 Camilia LEVRON (Houma Ch.: v.6-a, p.213)

PORCHE, Jos Roland (Henri & Emelie LEGRAND) bt. 4 Oct. 1896 (Theriot Ch.: v.1-B, p.100)

PORCHE, Joseph m. 9 March 1899 Victoria WARDNER (Houma Ct. Hse.: Mar. v.31 & 32, #362)

PORCHE, Joseph (Henry Clay & Sophie BONVILLAIN) m. 20 Jan. 1896 Josephine VICE (Theriot Ch.: v.1, p.7)

PORCHE, Joseph Curry (Edouard & Estelle LEGRAND) b. 30 Nov. 1896 (Houma Ch.: v.5, p.165)

PORCHE, Joseph E. (Henry Clay & Sophie BONVILLAIN) m. 1 Aug. 1896 Josephine E. VICE (Houma Ct. Hse.: Mar. v.29 & 30, #125)

PORCHE, Joseph Luban (Willy & Agnes BOUDREAU) b. 5 Aug. 1896 (Thib. Ch.: v.7, p.414)

PORCHE, Mable (Franklin & Sara TOUPS) b. 26 Dec. 1896 (Theriot Ch.: v.1-B, p.104)

PORCHE, Marie Alice (Gilles & Noblicia DAIGLE) b. 16 Jan. 1896 (Thib. Ch.: v.7, p.393)

PORCHE, Marie Iola (Henry & Emelie LEGRAND) b. 11 Dec. 1898 (Houma Ch.: v.5, p.230)

PORCHE, Marie Lydia (Alce & Victoria THIBODAUX) b. 24 Feb. 1897 (Raceland Ch.: v.5, p.42)

PORCHE, Marie Madge (William & Spencine GENTI) b. 18 July 1899 (Houma Ch.: v.5, p.250)

PORCHE, Mary Adeline (Joseph & Eveline BERGERON) b. 8 June 1896 (Houma Ch.: v.5, p.154)

PORCHE, Mary Amy (Justilien & Eva LIRETTE) b. 19 Nov. 1896; m. John Joseph BELLANGER on 8 Aug. 1939. (Houma Ch.: Bapt. Bk., v.5, p.164)

PORCHE, Nicolas Wallace (Theodore & Olivia CARO) b. 29 Nov. 1897 (Thib. Ch.: v.7, p.481)
PORCHE, Onezia Marie (Frank & Louisa THIBODAUX) b. 15 Sept. 1898 (Thib. Ch.: v.7, p.542)
PORCHE, Paul (Emile Andrien & Elphidu GUIDRY) b. 9 Aug. 1896 (Theriot Ch.: v.1-B, p.98)
PORCHE, Philippe (Octave & Eugenie BOURGEOIS) m. 25 Oct. 1899 Olympe BORNE (Thib. Ct. Hse.: Mar. v.39, #252)
PORCHE, Philippe (Octave & Eugenie BOURGEOIS) m. 25 Oct. 1899 Olympe BORNE (Thib. Ch.: v.14, p.304)
PORCHE, Thomas (Taylor & Olivia CARO) m. 18 Sept. 1899 Lydia THIBODEAUX (Thib. Ch.: v.14, p.295)
PORCHE, Thomas (Taylor & Olivia CARO) m. 18 Sept. 1899 Lydia THIBODEAUX (Thib. Ct. Hse.: Mar. v.39, #218)
PORCHE, Velma Marie (Nicolas & Alice BOURGEOIS) b. 31 March 1898 (Thib. Ch.: v.7, p.543)
PORTER, Charles Emanuel (Charley & Paola PIETRA) b. 12 Feb. 1899 (Houma Ch.: v.5, p.241)
PORTER, Charles Jr. m. 20 May 1898 Paulina PIEDRA (Houma Ct. Hse.: Mar. v.30 & 31, #450)
PORTER, Charles Jr. (Charles & Mary BRODY) m. 26 May 1898 Paulina PIEDRO (Houma Ch.: v.6-a, p.241)
PORTER, Gladys Ruth (Charles & Cecile GOTREAU) b. 24 Dec. 1897 (Houma Ch.: v.5, p.194)
PORTER, Willy Walter (Willy & Victoria KELY) b. 10 April 1899 (Houma Ch.: v.5, p.243)

PORTIER (Sometimes: PORTER, POTIER)
PORTIER, Agnes m. Firmin BLANCHARD d. 13 Sept. 1898 at age 18 yrs. (Montegut Ch.: v.2, p.20)
PORTIER, Agnes (Cyrille & Odelia ARCEMENT) m. 15 June 1896 Firmin BLANCHARD (Montegut Ch.: v.4, p.212)
PORTIER, Agnes (Cyrille & Odelia ARCEMENT) m. 15 May 1896 Firmin BLANCHARD (Houma Ct. Hse.: Mar. v.29 & 30, #71)
PORTIER, Bessie Marguerite (William & Victory KELLY) b. 28 Nov. 1897 (Houma Ch.: v.5, p.194)
PORTIER, Beulah Mariane (Charles & Cecile GAUTREAU) b. 11 May 1896 (Houma Ch.: v.5, p.151)
PORTIER, Edgar m. 16 April 1897 Elve BOUDREAUX (Thib. Ct. Hse.: Mar. v.36, #117)
PORTIER, Joseph Servile (Cyrille & Odilia ARCEMENT) b. 3 March 1898 (Montegut Ch.: v.6, p.69)
PORTIER, Lea (Victor & Vela AYO) m. 18 Jan. 1897 Rodolphe AISENE (Thib. Ct. Hse.: Mar. v.36, #8)
PORTIER, Mary widow of A. ESCASUT (Trasimond & Elizabeth OLIVER) m. 5 April 1897 Henry BOYCE (Houma Ct. Hse.: Mar. v.29 & 30, #377)
PORTIER, Taylor m. 30 March 1898 Adeline GROS (Thib. Ct. Hse.: Mar. v.37, #137)
PORTIER, Victor (Albert & Evela AYO) m. 27 Jan. 1897 Lea LECHE (Thib. Ct. Hse.: Mar. v.36, #39)

POTTMAN, William (Dora) b. 17 Oct. 1897 (Thib. Ch.: v.7, p.469)
POUSARET, Anna (Jacques & Rosaline THIBODEAU) m. 14 Oct. 1896 John B. RIDER (Houma Ch.: v.6-a, p.182)

POUSSECAILLE (Sometimes: POCECAILLE)
POUSSECAILLE, Marie Lorina (Louis & Josephine RHODES) b. 13 Nov. 1897 (Montegut Ch.: v.6, p.66)
POUSSECAILLE, Paul Ivory (Louis & Josephine RHODES) b. 29 Dec. 1899 (Montegut Ch.: v.6, p.101)
POWELL, Irma m. 7 Jan. 1896 Wesley WILLIAMS (Houma Ct. Hse.: Mar. v.28, #379)
POWELL, Joseph Dewey (Ernest & Flavia BURNS) b. 26 Feb. 1898 (Thib. Ch.: v.7, p.546)
POWELL, Lucinda m. 27 Dec. 1899 Thornton MARTIN (Houma Ct. Hse.: Mar. v.31 & 32, #210)
PRATT, ----- Mrs. d. 29 Dec. 1898 at age 35 yrs. (Raceland Ch.: v.1, p.21)

PREJEAN (Sometimes: PREGEANT, PREGENT, PREJAN)
PREJEAN, Abel L. (Victor & Marie Clara KELLER) m. 17 Feb. 1896 Ida DAUNIS (Thib. Ch.: v.14, p.78)
PREJEAN, Abel S. m. 31 Jan. 1896 Ida DAUNIS (Houma Ct. Hse.: Mar. v.28, #430)
PREJEAN, Alice Atee (Joseph & Emly DARDEN) b. 15 Oct. 1898 (Chackbay Ch.: v.1, p.121)
PREJEAN, Auguste d. 6 Jan. 1897 at age 72 yrs. (Thib. Ch.: v.3, p.194)
PREJEAN, Augustin Blaise (Joseph & Emelie DALDEN) b. 9 Sept. 1897 (Thib. Ch.: v.7, p.464)
PREJEAN, Bernadette Eve (Adam & Celima ORGERON) b. 18 Feb. 1896 (Larose Ch.: v.2, p.180)
PREJEAN, Blaise d. 23 Sept. 1897 at age 2 wks. (Thib. Ch.: v.3, p.206)
PREJEAN, Cecile (Auguste & Ursanie BOUDREAUX) m. 7 Feb. 1898 Aramis BOURGEOIS (Thib. Ch.: v.14, p.180)
PREJEAN, Cecile (Auguste & Ursanie BOUDREAUX) m. 7 Feb. 1898 Aramis BOURGEOIS (Thib. Ct. Hse.: Mar. v.37, #89)
PREJEAN, Elizabeth m. 9 Dec. 1899 Clerfy GONZALES (Thib. Ct. Hse.: Mar. v.39, #278)
PREJEAN, Elizabeth (Auguste & Marie BOUDREAUX) m. 27 Dec. 1899 Clairfait GONZALES (Thib. Ch.: v.14, p.317)
PREJEAN, Ellen (Eugene V. & Ida C. PREJEANT) b. 8 Aug. 1898 (Thib. Ch.: First Presbyt. Ch.: v.1, p.174)
PREJEAN, Eugene Philippe (Adam & Celima ORGERON) b. 30 June 1897 (Larose Ch.: v.3, p.20)
PREJEAN, Eugene Victor (Eugene Victor & Ida C. PREJEANT) b. 31 March 1897 (Thib. Ch.: First Presbyt. Ch.: v.1, p.174)
PREJEAN, Henry m. 2 Sept. 1898 Louise DAUNIS (Houma Ct. Hse.: Mar. v.30 & 31, #86)

PREJEAN, Henry (Victor & Clara KELLY) m. 12 Sept. 1898 Louise DAUNIS (Houma Ch.: v.6-a, p.253)
PREJEAN, Jeanne Flavia (Pierre & Louisianne GUILLOT) b. 5 May 1899 (Thib. Ch.: v.7, p.606)
PREJEAN, Kelly (Eugene & Marie KELLY) m. 27 Jan. 1898 Evelie NAVARRE (Thib. Ch.: v.14, p.178)
PREJEAN, Kelly (Eugene & Marie KELLY) m. 27 Ja. 1898 Evelie NAVARRE (Thib. Ct. Hse.: Mar. v.37, #16)
PREJEAN, Laurence d. 1 June 1897 at age 6 mths. (Thib. Ch.: v.3, p.200)
PREJEAN, Laurence Roye (Abel & Aida DAUNIS) b. 7 Dec. 1896 (Thib. Ch.: v.7, p.442)
PREJEAN, Marie Aline (Kelly & Evelie NAVARRE) b. 5 Oct. 1898 (Thib. Ch.: v.7, p.516)
PREJEAN, Martha Pearl (Abel & Ida DANNIS) b. 16 Dec. 1897 (Houma Ch.: v.5, p.204)
PREJEAN, Paul Nolen (Pierre & Louisiane GUILLOTE) b. 24 Jan. 1896 (Thib. Ch.: v.7, p.442)
PREJEAN, Philomene Andrea Elvire (Alfred & Cordelia GUILLOTE) b. 25 Dec. 1896 (Thib. Ch.: v.7, p.434)
PREJEAN, Therese d. 13 July 1899 at age 23 yrs. (Thib. Ch.: v.3, p.237)
PRESSEG, Marie Laborbez (Dominique & Nathala LABORBEZ) b. 10 April 1899 (Chackbay Ch.: Bapt. Bk., v.1, p.13)
PRESTENBACH, Louisa m. Baptiste BARRILLEAUX Children: Aubin; Paul; Lizzie. Petition for new inventory & appraisement: 31 May 1897. (Thib. Ct. Hse.: Succ. #1363)
PRESTENBACK, Jean (Louis & Marie Aurelie CONSTANT) b. 6 March 1897 (Chackbay Ch.: v.1, p.87)
PRESTON, Lizzie m. 5 March 1896 Charles THIBODAUX (Thib. Ct. Hse.: Mar. v.35, #50)
PRESTONBACK, Clarence (Gustave & Emma GAUTREAUX) b. 31 Jan. 1898 (Raceland Ch.: v.5, p.68)
PRESTONBACK, Dora (Louis & Amelie CONSTANT) m. 6 Sept. 1899 Ben THEBE (Chackbay Ch.: v.1, p.72)
PRESTONBACK, Dora (Louis & Aurelie CONSTANT) m. 6 Sept. 1899 Ben TABOR (Thib. Ct. Hse.: Mar. v.39, #221)
PRESTONBACK, John Cleveland (William & Felicia SHAUBUTT) b. 10 Oct. 1898 (Chackbay Ch.: v.1, p.132)
PRESTONBACK, Maria Clara (Is. & Amelie CONSTANT) b. 5 Sept. 1899 (Chackbay Ch.: v.1, p.143)
PRESTONBACK, Mary Rose m. 4 Feb. 1899 Thomas CONNER (Thib. Ct. Hse.: Mar. v.38, #90)
PREUZENI, Guiseppe (Marian & Madalena PREGOLA) m. 15 April 1896 Margarita BIBA (Houma Ch.: v.6-a, p.174)
PREVOST, Frank m. 24 March 1897 Rose THIBODAUX (Houma Ct. Hse.: Mar. v.29 & 30, #365)
PREVOST, James m. 4 May 1898 Leafy HARDIN (Houma Ct. Hse.: Mar. v.30 & 31, #430)
PREVOST, Mary m. 14 April 1898 Mitchell ALEXANDRE (Thib. Ct. Hse.: Mar. v.37, #118)

PREVOST, Thomas A. (Leufroy & Sarah Ann DEHART) m. 28 Sept. 1897 Eleonore TROSCLAIR (Houma Ct. Hse.: Mar. v.29 & 30, #98)
PREZELIN, Agathe minor over 18 yrs. (d.Pierre & Azema BOUTERIE) Emancipation: 22 March 1897. (Thib. Ct. Hse.: Succ. #1510)
PRICE, Albertine m. 23 Jan. 1896 Arthur BERGERON (Thib. Ct. Hse.: Mar. v.35, #5)
PRICE, Albertine (Abdon & Azelina BLANCHARD) m. 23 Jan. 1896 Arthur BERGERON (Raceland Ch.: v.2, p.10)
PRICE, Anne Lottie (William & Zenobia COLLIN) b. 24 Sept. 1899 (Thib. Ch.: v.7, p.566)
PRICE, Dumreis (Oscar & Victoria DUPRE) m. 13 April 1896 Sarah LIRETTE (Houma Ct. Hse.: Mar. v.29 & 30, #36)
PRICE, Dunreis (Oscar & d.Victoria DUPRE) m. 29 April 1896 Sarah LIRETTE (Montegut Ch.: v.4, p.209)
PRICE, Henry m. 18 July 1898 Antoinette MAYFIELD, widow of Beverly JUDAH (Thib. Ct. Hse.: Mar. v.38, #228)
PRICE, Joseph (Adam & Azelie THIBEAUDEAU) b. 3 Aug. 1897 (Theriot Ch.: v.2, p.19)
PRICE, Louis Esto (Abdon & Azelina BLANCHARD) b. 15 May 1896 (Lockport Ch.: v.2, p.330)
PRICE, Louisa m. 15 Feb. 1898 Willie SEMORE (Thib. Ct. Hse.: Mar. v.37, #104)
PRICE, Marie Eda (Walter & Odile PONTIFE) b. 8 Aug. 1898 (Montegut Ch.: v.6, p.86)
PRICE, Marie Georgina (Georges & Ernestine RHODES) b. 2 Feb. 1897 (Montegut Ch.: v.6, p.52)
PRICE, Marie Rosina (Danis & Sara LIRETTE) b. 2 Oct. 1898 (Montegut Ch.: v.6, p.87)
PRICE, Matilde m. 8 Sept. 1899 Alcide AUTIN (Thib. Ct. Hse.: Mar. v.39, #228)
PRICE, Matilde (Leo & Velida GRABERT) m. 28 Sept. 1899 Alcide HULIN (Raceland Ch.: v.2, p.104)
PRICE, Pierre Arcide (Leo & Josephine LAGUERRE) b. 8 April 1896 (Raceland Ch.: v.5, p.22)
PRICE, Warner m. 12 Aug. 1897 Katie REED (Thib. Ct. Hse.: Mar. v.37, #213)
PRICE, William Trenton m. Marie Josephine PITRE Petition for putting in possession: 20 July 1897. (Thib. Ct. Hse.: Succ. #1516)
PROLASKI, Nattie Mary (James & Alice MORGAN) b. 19 Aug. 1897 (Chacahoula Ch.: Gibson Ch.: Mar. Bk., v.1, #80)
PROPHETA, Biajea d. 22 Feb. 1896 at age 8 mths. (Thib. Ch.: v.3, p.179)
PROSPER, Dominique (Etienne & Zelida ORTIS) m. 25 Jan. 1898 Marie BABIN (Montegut Ch.: v.4, p.232)
PROSPER, Dominique (Etienne & Zelida ORTIS) m. 5 Jan. 1898 Mary BABIN (Houma Ct. Hse.: Mar. v.30 & 31, #176)
PROSPER, Eugenie Agnes (Louis & Augustine PONTIFE) b. 6 Feb. 1898 (Montegut Ch.: v.6, p.71)

PROSPER, Lavery m. 19 May 1898 Caldonia DICKSON (Thib. Ct. Hse.: Mar. v.38, #185)
PROSPER, Marie Camelia (Louis & Augustin PONTIFE) b. 26 Jan. 1896 (Montegut Ch.: v.6, p.38)
PROSPER, Marie Hazel (Savery & Cora DONIA) b. 7 Sept. 1898 (Thib. Ch.: v.7, p.564)
PROSPER, Marie Rosalie (Domingue & Marie BABIN) b. 23 Feb. 1899 (Montegut Ch.: v.6, p.84)
PROSPER, Mary Agnes d. 6 Sept. 1896 at age 1 yr. & 11 mths. (Thib. Ch.: v.3, p.186)
PROSPER, Michel (Etienne & Zelida ORTIS) m. 14 Jan. 1899 Maggie LECOMPTE (Houma Ct. Hse.: Mar. v.30 & 31, #231)
PROSPER, Nickles Noel (Victor & Emma CHIASSON) b. 25 Dec. 1898 (Montegut Ch.: v.6, p.87)
PROSPER, Victor Laurent (Victor & Emma CHIASSON) b. 13 Sept. 1896 (Montegut Ch.: v.6, p.48)
PROSPERI, Angelique m. Jim RHODE d. 17 Nov. 1896 at age 42 yrs. (Montegut Ch.: v.2, p.7)
PROSPERI, Michel (Etienne & Zelida ORTIS) m. 6 Feb. 1899 Maggie LECOMPTE (Montegut Ch.: v.4, p.256)
PROVENZANO, Guiseppe (Nunzio & Leonorda DI MICELI) m. 3 July 1897 Francisca Pasla COLORA (Thib. Ch.: v.14, p.150)
PROVENZANO, Guiseppe (Nunzio Leonardo & Leonarda DE MICHELI) m. 3 July 1897 Francisca Paolà COLORA (Thib. Ct. Hse.: Mar. v.36, #175)
PROVENZANO, Leonarda (Guiseppe & Francesca PAOLA) b. 26 Dec. 1898 (Thib. Ch.: v.7, p.526)
PROVOST, Marie Rosaline (Leufroy & Elizabeth OZARE) b. 28 Sept. 1897 (Theriot Ch.: v.2, p.20)
PROVOST, Sara Vivienne (Thomas & Eleonore TROSCLAIR) b. 14 Aug. 1898 (Theriot Ch.: v.2, p.29)
PROVOST, Thomas Albert (Lufroy PROVOST) m. 7 Oct. 1897 Eleonore TROSCLAIR (Theriot Ch.: v.1-B, p.1)
PRUDEN, Zora m. 29 July 1897 George ANDERSON (Thib. Ct. Hse.: Mar. v.37, #202)
PUGH, Ellen K. m. 6 Feb. 1899 John McCOMACHIE (Thib. Ct. Hse.: Mar. v.38, #93)
PUGH, Ellen K. m. 7 Feb. 1899 John McCORMACHIE (Thib. Ch.: Epis. Ch.: v.1, p.331)
PUGH, Nathan m. 24 Nov. 1899 Elizabeth ZEAL (Thib. Ct. Hse.: Mar. v.39, #270)
PUGH, Polly m. 30 June 1896 Felix REED (Thib. Ct. Hse.: Mar. v.35, #34)
PUJOS, Reginald Albert (Joseph A. & Emma CARTER) b. 22 Dec. 1896 (Thib. Ch.: v.7, p.435)
PUJOS, Reynold Albert d. 13 Feb. 1897 at age 1 mth. & 3 wks. (Thib. Ch.: v.3, p.196)
PULLEN, Joseph Avery (Joseph H. & Eloise L. PULLEN) bt. 5 April 1898 (Houma Ch.: First Presbyt. Ch.: v.1, p.262)
PULLEN, Viola Virginia (Joseph H. & Eloise L. PULLEN) bt. 5 April 1898 (Houma Ch.: First Presbyt. Ch.: v.1, p.262)

PUNCH, Adam Lucien (Maxim & Dora USAY) b. 30 March 1898 (Larose Ch.: v.3, p.18)
PUNCH, Camile Ludger (Baptiste & Cecilia PLAISANCE) b. 26 March 1898 (Larose Ch.: v.3, p.27)
PUNCH, Emma m. 26 Feb. 1897 Oscar BOURGEOIS (Thib. Ct. Hse.: Mar. v.36, #91)
PYE, Emma m. 26 Jan. 1898 Wilfred KING (Houma Ct. Hse.: Mar. v.30 & 31, #251)
PYE, Emma (William & Rosa SAVOIE) m. 27 Jan. 1898 Wilfred KING (Houma Ch.: v.6-a, p.226)
PYE, Henrietta of Terrebonne Parish m. 28 Dec. 1899 Ludovie M. LIRETTE (Houma Ch.: v.6-B, p.5)
PYE, Henrietta (William & Rose SAVOIE) m. 27 Dec. 1899 Ludovic M. LIRETTE (Houma Ct. Hse.: Mar. v.31 & 32, #219)
PYE, Marie Burnice (Robert & Evelia MARLBROUGH) b. 30 July 1896 (Houma Ch.: v.5, p.184)
PYE, Marie Jennie Eva (Georges & Julia EXNICIOS) b. 24 Dec. 1896 (Houma Ch.: v.5, p.171)
PYE, Marie Laurenza (Georges & Julia EXNICIOS) b. 11 Dec. 1897 (Houma Ch.: v.5, p.203)

"Q"

QUEEN, Rosa m. 16 Feb. 1898 Charles WHITE (Thib. Ct. Hse.: Mar. v.37, #107)

QUICK, Agnes Mable Mary (Edmund & Marie Therese LEBOEUF) b. 16 Sept. 1898 (Houma Ch.: v.5, p.219)

QUICK, Albert S. (William & Virginia BUFORD) m. 9 April 1898 Lydia Bernadette ROBICHAUX (Houma Ct. Hse.: Mar. v.30 & 31, #388)

QUICK, Albert S. (William & Virginie BEAUFORT) m. 25 April 1898 Lydia Bernadette ROBICHAUX (Theriot Ch.: v.1-B, p.3)

QUICK, Annie Elizabeth (William A., Sr. & Virginia BUFORD) m. 17 Aug. 1898 Henry Clay BOUDREAUX (Houma Ct. Hse.: Mar. v.30 & 31, #80)

QUICK, Annie Virginie (William & Virginie BEAUFORT) m. 5 Sept. 1898 Henry Clay BOUDREAU (Theriot Ch.: v.1-B, p.5)

QUICK, Loretta M. m. 4 Jan. 1899 Adam TROSCLAIR (Houma Ct. Hse.: Mar. v.30 & 31, #179)

QUICK, Loretta M. (William & Virginia BUFORD) m. 23 Jan. 1899 Adam TROSCLAIR (Houma Ch.: v.6-a, p.267)

QUILLER, Peter m. 8 July 1897 Bessie CLAYTON (Houma Ct. Hse.: Mar. v.29 & 30, #62)

"R"

RAGAN, Clarence Elli Joseph (James & Georgina BESSON) b. 16 Nov. 1898 (Thib. Ch.: v.7, p.531)
RAGAN, Elmira Elizabeth (William F. & Josephine CRABB) b. 11 Oct. 1896 (Thib. Ch.: Epis. Ch.: v.1, p.42)
RAGAN, Mary Jane (William H. & Josephine CRABB) b. 16 Oct. 1898 (Thib. Ch.: Epis. Ch.: v.1, p.44)
RAIA, Anna m. 28 Jan. 1899 Francesco MAUERICE (Houma Ct. Hse.: Mar. v.30 & 31, #289)
RAIA, Anna (Francesca & Andrea MAIA) m. 11 Feb. 1899 Francesco MAURICE (Houma Ch.: v.6-a, p.277)
RAIA, Antonino (Antonino & Calogera TROUCALE) b. 4 Feb. 1897 (Houma Ch.: v.5, p.170)
RAIA, Giovanni (Francisca & Morandenzia MAIA?) m. 19 Feb. 1898 Antonina CIACCIO (Houma Ch.: v.6-a, p.234)
RAIA, Salvatore (Mateo & Calogero POMILE) b. 12 Oct. 1899 (Thib. Ch.: v.8, p.13)
RAINEY, Geneva m. 10 March 1898 Edmund BROWN (Houma Ct. Hse.: Mar. v.30 & 31, #333)
RAINEY, Malvina m. 4 Jan. 1897 Aleck JOHNSON (Thib. Ct. Hse.: Mar. v.36, #6)
RAINEY, Mary m. 2 April 1898 Elias PINKNEY (Houma Ct. Hse.: Mar. v.30 & 31, #367)
RAIO, Batasson (Beaggio & Josephina MERLE) b. 22 Dec. 1898 (Houma Ch.: v.5, p.231)
RALPH, Wilfrid d. 29 May 1899 at age 1 yr, 11 mths., 14 days (Houma Ch.: v.3, p.23)

RANDALL (Sometimes: RANDAL)

RANDALL, Annie m. 8 Feb. 1899 Howard CARROLL (Thib. Ct. Hse.: Mar. v.38, #98)
RANDAZZO, Vicenzo (Guiseppe & Antonina CENTANE) m. 16 July 1898 Maria DINARCA (Thib. Ch.: v.14, p.210)
RANDAZZO, Vincenzo (Guiseppe & Antonino CENTANE) m. 16 July 1898 Maria DIMARCO (Thib. Ct. Hse.: Mar. v.38, #196)
RANDOLPH, John m. 8 June 1899 Rosa LOUIS (Thib. Ct. Hse.: Mar. v.39, #176)
RANDOLPH, Mary m. 28 March 1898 Louis DELAUNE (Thib. Ct. Hse: Mar. v.37, #136)
RANEIRI, Bastiano d. 7 April 1899 (Thib. Ch.: v.7, p.544)
RANKINS, Frank Joseph (Walter & Julia TELLMANN) b. 14 Dec. 1896 (Thib. Ch.: v.7, p.447)
RANKINS, Sarah m. 23 Dec. 1899 Henry MIDDLETON (Thib. Ct Hse.: Mar. v.39, #297)
RAOUSSA, Pippina (Salvatore & Rosa PIZOLATTO) b. 26 May 1899 (Thib. Ch.: v.7, p.551)
RAPELET, Maxime Wilford (Rene & Evelina TERREBONNE) b. 14 May 1897 (Larose Ch.: v.3, p.26)

RAPP (Sometimes: RAPE)

RATCLIFF, James P. of Sumit, Mississippi (Walton & Seyra AVANTE) m. 4 March 1899 Frances J. LORTON of Dublin, Ireland (Thib. Ch.: v.14, p.266-a)
RATCLIFF, James P. (Walton & Sera AVANTE) m. 4 March 1899 Frances J. LORTON (Thib. Ct. Hse.: Mar. v.39, #115)
RAY, Philip m. 9 Feb. 1898 Margaret SINGLETON (Houma Ct. Hse.: Mar. v.30 & 31, #287)

RAYMOND (Sometimes: RAYMONT, REMOND, REMONT)
RAYMOND, Emelie m. 29 May 1897 Paul LEFORT (Thib. Ct. Hse.: Mar. v.36, #152)
RAYMOND, Emilie m. 11 June 1897 Paul LEFORT (Larose Ch.: v.3, p.6)
RAYMOND, Emilie m. 11 June 1897 Paul LEFORT (Larose Ch.: v.4, p.77)
RAYMOND, Esther m. 13 Jan. 1898 Mack SEAY (Thib. Ct. Hse.: Mar. v.37, #30)
RAYMOND, Hampton m. 16 Sept. 1899 Bertha LEWIS (Thib. Ct. Hse.: Mar. v.39, #226)
RAYMOND, Nelson m. 3 March 1898 Elizabeth HILL (Thib. Ct. Hse.: Mar. v.37, #116)
RAYMOND, Theophile Victor (Joseph & Angela MELANCON) b. 29 July 1898 (Larose Ch.: v.3, p.28)
REAGENS, Rachael m. 23 Feb. 1899 Kellogg WALKER (Thib. Ct. Hse.: Mar. v.39, #112)
REDDICK, Mills Insanity: 28 Aug. 1899. (Thib. Ct. Hse.: Succ. #1586)
REDDMAN, James m. 9 Feb. 1899 Emma MACK (Thib. Ct. Hse.: Mar. v.39, #100)
REDLY, ----- d. 5 April 1897 at age 14 yrs. (Houma Ch.: v.3, p.12)
REDMOND, Josephine Clara (James & Suzanne HEBERT) b. 3 Feb. 1898 (Montegut Ch.: v.6, p.65)
REDMOND, Marie Agnes (Jimmy & Suzanne HEBERT) b. 6 March 1896 (Montegut Ch.: v.6, p.37)
REED, Bernadette Celima (Georges & Victoria BOUDREAUX) b. 10 June 1897 (Larose Ch.: v.3, p.11)
REED, Charlton m. 2 Feb. 1898 Bertha VERRET (Thib. Ct. Hse.: Mar. v.37, #76)
REED, Daniel m. 24 June 1896 Lieza RITTMAN (Thib. Ct. Hse.: Mar. v.36, #112)
REED, Elias m. 10 Jan. 1899 Sallie ROBINSON (Thib. Ct. Hse.: Mar. v.38, #12)
REED, Ella m. 21 Feb. 1898 Manuel FERDINAND (Thib. Ct. Hse.: Mar. v.37, #110)
REED, Felix m. 30 Jan. 1896 Polly PUGH (Thib. Ct. Hse.: Mar. v.35, #34)
REED, Jack d. 1893; m. Louisa REED, d. June 1898. Children listed: Amy m. Jake HOLLOWAY; John; Joe. Petition

for inventory adm.: 21 Feb. 1899. (Thib. Ct. Hse.: Succ. #1564)

REED, Jane d. 24 June 1899 at age 110 yrs. (Thib. Ch.: v.3, p.236)

REED, Janey m. 12 Jan. 1899 Harry TAYLOR (Thib. Ct. Hse.: Mar. v.38, #16)

REED, John m. 24 Aug. 1899 Louisa TAYLOR (Thib. Ct. Hse.: Mar. v.39, #213)

REED, Joseph W. m. 26 Dec. 1898 Susie WALTON (Houma Ct. Hse.: Mar. v.30 & 31, #161)

REED, Katie m. 12 Aug. 1897 Warner PRICE (Thib. Ct. Hse.: Mar. v.37, #213)

REED, Mary m. 14 Oct. 1899 Philip JENKINS (Houma Ct. Hse.: Mar. v.31 & 32, #149)

REED, Mary m. 18 Feb. 1897 Charles BLACKLEDGE (Thib. Ct. Hse.: Mar. v.36, #82)

REED, Mary Agnes m. 11 Jan. 1897 John SMITH (Thib. Ct. Hse.: Mar. v.36, #21)

REED, Munford (Jhony & Augustine ARSENEAUX) m. 17 Feb. 1898 Ernestine BUTLER (Lockport Ch.: v.2, p.186)

REED, Munford or Melford of Lafourche crossing (Jheney & Augustine ARSENEAUX) m. 17 Feb. 1898 Ernestine BUTLER of Lockport (Thib. Ct. Hse.: Mar. v.37, #84)

REED, William m. 5 June 1897 Lizzie FRANCIS (Houma Ct. Hse.: Mar. v.29 & 30, #3)

REED, Willis m. 18 Feb. 1897 Rose MARTEL (Houma Ct. Hse.: Mar. v.29 & 30, #320)

REEM, Joseph Elphege d. 20 July 1899 at age 4 wks. (Thib. Ch.: v.3, p.237)

REGIS, Josephine m. 18 June 1896 Abraham JOHNSON (Thib. Ct. Hse.: Mar. v.35, #109)

RELESSO, Francesco d. 21 Nov. 1896 at age 55 yrs. (Raceland Ch.: v.1, p.10)

REMOIN, Odressy m. 9 Jan. 1899 Elvire LANCON (Houma Ct. Hse.: Mar. v.30 & 31, #195)

REMONT, Theophile m. d.Estelina PITRE Children listed: Alice, aged 12; George, aged 10; Leonce, aged 8; Julienne, aged 5 yrs. Petition for family meeting: 13 Dec. 1897. (Thib. Ct. Hse.: Succ. #1526)

RENEN, Marie Clophine (Paul & Eugenie BADEAU) b. 14 Jan. 1897 (Larose Ch.: v.3, p.2)

REPSTOCK, Jefferson Joseph (Camille & Rema TERREBONNE) b. 13 March 1898 (Larose Ch.: v.3, p.21)

RERIS, Lorenzo m. 30 March 1897 Rosalia CALANDRO (Thib. Ct. Hse.: Mar. v.36, #106)

RERIS, Lorenzo (Frank & Joseppa GRAZIANO) m. 19 April 1897 Rosalia CALANDRO (Raceland Ch.: v.2, p.37)

RERISI, Guiseppa (Lorenzo & Rosalia GALANTRA) b. 29 Aug. 1899 (Raceland Ch.: v.5, p.102)

RESNAYS, Pierre m. 2 Oct. 1897 Marguerite SERRES (Thib. Ct. Hse.: Mar. v.37, #236)

RESNEY, Reine Noemie (Pierre & Marguerite ROUBION) b. 17 Aug. 1898 (Raceland Ch.: v.5, p.78)
RESTIVO, Rosario (Mariano & Congietta TORANELLA) b. 23 July 1898 (Thib. Ch.: v.7, p.514)
RHODEN, Amelia m. 21 April 1897 W. H. YOUNG (Thib. Ct. Hse.: Mar. v.36, #123)

RHODES (See perhaps: RODDY)
RHODES, Antoine Harry (Henry & Irma SONGE) b. 2 June 1899 (Chacahoula Ch.: v.4, p.28)
RHODES, Bernard Alma (Sydny & Angella ECHTE) b. 7 Aug. 1899 (Houma Ch.: v.5, p.253)
RHODES, Brigitte m. 4 Jan. 1896 Eugene ENGERRAN (Houma Ct. Hse.: Mar. v.28, #374)
RHODES, Brigitte (Anatole & Leontine BABIN) m. 18 Jan. 1896 Eugene ENGERRAN (Montegut Ch.: v.4, p.206)
RHODES, Columbus Sidney m. 7 June 1897 Angela ESCHETE (Houma Ch.: v.6-a, p.206)
RHODES, Columbus Sidney m. 7 June 1897 Angela ESHTE (Houma Ct. Hse.: Mar. v.29 & 30, #11)
RHODES, Enos L. (Leon & Victoria PRICE) m. 25 March 1899 Josephine ENGERRAN (Houma Ct. Hse.: Mar. v.31 & 32, #377)
RHODES, Enos L. (Leon & Victoria PRICE) m. 22 April 1899 Josephine ENGERRAN (Montegut Ch.: v.4, p.262)
RHODES, Eria Joseph (Nicolas & Louise RODDY) b. 24 Feb. 1896 (Houma Ch.: v.5, p.169)
RHODES, Estive (Anatole & Leontine BABIN) m. 23 Dec. 1899 Emma DOMINGUE (Houma Ct. Hse.: Mar. v.31 & 32, #191)
RHODES, Evans m. 23 June 1897 Alexina LEBOEUF (Houma Ct. Hse.: Mar. v.29 & 30, #40)
RHODES, Evans (Anatole & Leontine BABIN) m. 12 July 1897 Alexina LEBOEUF (Montegut Ch.: v.4, p.223)
RHODES, Frank (Anatole & Leontine BABIN) m. 4 Jan. 1897 Elmire NAQUIN (Houma Ct. Hse.: Mar. v.29 & 30, #221)
RHODES, Frank (Frank & Leontine BABIN) m. 30 Jan. 1897 Elmire NAQUIN (Montegut Ch.: v.4, p.217)
RHODES, Frank (Thomas & Victorine USE) m. 11 April 1896 Selema GUIDRY (Houma Ct. Hse.: Mar. v.29 & 30, #30)
RHODES, Frank (Thomas & Victorine USEE) m. 27 April 1896 Elima GUIDRY (Montegut Ch.: v.4, p.208)
RHODES, George (Thomas & Victorine USE) m. 19 March 1898 Rosa FREMIN (Houma Ct. Hse.: Mar. v.30 & 31, #346)
RHODES, George (Thomas & Victorine USEE) m. 16 April 1898 Rosa FREMAN (Montegut Ch.: v.4, p.241)
RHODES, Georges Loveless (William & Alice FOREST) b. 8 Feb. 1899 (Montegut Ch.: v.6, p.83)
RHODES, James E. m. 5 Jan. 1899 Sarah JENKINS (Thib. Ct. Hse.: Mar. v.38, #5)
RHODES, John (d.Georges & Rosalie PELEGRIN) m. 11 April 1898 Catherine DUPRE (Montegut Ch.: v.4, p.240)

RHODES, John (George & Rosalie PELEGRIN) m. 25 March 1898 Catherine DUPRE (Houma Ct. Hse.: Mar. v.30 & 31, #353)
RHODES, Joseph m. 15 Aug. 1896 Nettie TOUPS (Houma Ct. Hse.: Mar. v.29 & 30, #131)
RHODES, Joseph (William & Franklina PIERCE) m. 18 Aug. 1896 Nettie TOUPS (Houma Ch.: v.6-a, p.178)
RHODES, Joseph Bagley (Calixte & Lisca NETTLETON) b. 8 April 1899 (Montegut Ch.: v.6, p.89)
RHODES, Joseph Dewey (Ernest & Argentine POCECAILLE) b. 4 Nov. 1899 (Montegut Ch.: v.7, p.1)
RHODES, Joseph Elvince (Elcee & Felonise HENRI) b. 4 Dec. 1897 (Montegut Ch.: v.6, p.71)
RHODES, Joseph Howard (Maximin & Marie POSECAILLE) b. 3 July 1897 (Montegut Ch.: v.6, p.61)
RHODES, Joseph Laurent (Ernest & Argentine POSSEQUAYLE) b. 29 April 1896 (Montegut Ch.: v.6, p.42)
RHODES, Joseph Nolan (Frank & Celima GUIDRY) b. 17 Sept. 1898 (Montegut Ch.: v.6, p.87)
RHODES, Joseph O'Neill (Elcee & Felonise HENRI) b. 3 June 1896 (Montegut Ch.: v.6, p.43)
RHODES, Joseph Sidney (William & Alice FOREST) b. 14 May 1896 (Montegut Ch.: v.6, p.41)
RHODES, Joseph William (Americus & Netty TOUPS) b. 28 Oct. 1897 (Houma Ch.: v.5, p.190)
RHODES, Josephine Agnes (Calixte & Lisca NELTON) b. 21 Jan. 1897 (Montegut Ch.: v.6, p.53)
RHODES, Julia (George & Rosalie PELEGRIN) m. 7 Jan. 1898 Justilien LEDET (Houma Ct. Hse.: Mar. v.30 & 31, #186)
RHODES, Julienne (Robert & Zulma ROBICHAUX) m. 27 April 1899 Lee PITRE (Montegut Ch.: v.4, p.262)
RHODES, Julienne (Robert & Zulma ROBICHAUX) m. 8 April 1899 Lee PITRE (Houma Ct. Hse: Mar. v.31 & 32, #390)
RHODES, Laura Lorena (Taylor & Melina ANGULARE) m. 7 Jan. 1896 St. Preux LAMOUREUX (Houma Ch.: v.6-a, p.167)
RHODES, Leonie (William & Edmire GUIDRY) m. 7 April 1899 Justine WALKER (Houma Ct. Hse.: Mar. v.31 & 32, #385)
RHODES, Leonie (William & Elmire GUIDRY) m. 29 April 1899 Justine WALKER (Montegut Ch.: v.4, p.263)
RHODES, Louis J. m. 22 June 1898 Mary DARCE (Houma Ct. Hse.: Mar. v.30 & 31, #28)
RHODES, Louis J. (William & Frankline PICOU) m. 22 June 1898 Mary DARCE (Houma Ch.: v.6-a, p.243)
RHODES, Louis Joseph (Henry & Irma LANG) b. 3 Aug. 1896 (Chacahoula Ch.: v.4, p.3)
RHODES, Louisa (William & Franklina PICOU) m. 1 April 1896 Nickless RHODES (Houma Ct. Hse.: Mar. v.29 & 30, #27)
RHODES, Louisa (William & Franklina PICOU) m. 6 April 1896 Nickless RHODES (Montegut Ch.: v.4, p.208)
RHODES, Marie Angelique (James & Angelique PROSPERI) b. 17 Dec. 1896 (Montegut Ch.: v.6, p.50)

RHODES, Marie Ella (Evans & Alexina LEBOEUF) b. 2 Feb. 1899 (Montegut Ch.: v.6, p.84)
RHODES, Marie Ephee (Frank & Celima GUIDRY) b. 27 Feb. 1897 (Montegut Ch.: v.6, p.52)
RHODES, Marie Ida (Gilbert & Julia GUIDRY) b. 3 Oct. 1898 (Montegut Ch.: v.6, p.79)
RHODES, Marie Maudie (Maximin & Marie POCECAILLE) b. 5 June 1899 (Montegut Ch.: v.6, p.91)
RHODES, Marie Victorine (Ernest & Argentine POCECAILLE) b. 22 Sept. 1897 (Montegut Ch.: v.6, p.73)
RHODES, Mary (d.Georges & Rosalie PELEGRIN) m. 15 June 1898 Simon HENRI (Montegut Ch.: v.4, p.247)
RHODES, Mary (Georges & Rosalie PELEGRIN) m. 25 May 1898 Seymour HENRY (Houma Ct. Hse.: Mar. v.30 & 31, #454)
RHODES, Mary Victoria Amanda (Leon & Victoria PRICE) b. 13 Feb. 1897 (Houma Ch.: v.5, p.203)
RHODES, Mathilde Rosie (Frank & Celina GUIDRY) b. 29 Dec. 1899 (Montegut Ch.: v.7, p.3)
RHODES, Nickless (James & Angelique PROSPER) m. 1 April 1896 Louisa RODDY (Houma Ct. Hse.: Mar. v.29 & 30, #27)
RHODES, Nickless (James & Angelique PROSPER) m. 6 April 1896 Louisa RODDY (Montegut Ch.: v.4, p.208)
RHODES, Paul Joseph (Joseph & Nellie TOUPS) b. 17 Aug. 1898 (Houma Ch.: v.5, p.253)
RHODES, Willie m. 16 March 1898 Celestine DOMINGUE (Houma Ct. Hse.: Mar. v.30 & 31, #339)
RHODES, Willie (Anatole & Leontine BABIN) m. 11 April 1898 Celestine DOMINGUE (Montegut Ch.: v.4, p.239)
RIBAORA, Francisca (Guiseppe & Rosalia CONSTANZA) b. 24 Feb. 1898 (Thib. Ch.: v.7, p.488)
RIBARDY, Helena (Dominique & Pomella WESS) b. 19 Dec. 1897 (Chacahoula Ch.: Gibson Ch.: Mar. Bk., v.1, #42)
RIBAULT, Nathalie of Jefferson Parish (Charles & Roseline TERREBONNE) m. 28 July 1898 Leonce SANTINI, of Jefferson Parish (Larose Ch.: v.3, p.10)
RIBAULT, Nathalie of Jefferson Parish (Charles & Roseline TERREBONNE) m. 28 July 1898 Leonce SANTINI (Larose Ch.: v.4, p.25)

RICHARD (Sometimes: RICHARDS)

RICHARD, ----- boy d. 7 March 1898 at birth (Thib. Ch.: v.3, p.212)
RICHARD, ----- m. Pierre BOURGEOIS d. 22 June 1896 at age 45 yrs. (Thib. Ch.: v.3, p.184)
RICHARD, Agnes Marguerite (Aristide & Helene BOURGEOIS) b. 23 March 1897 (Thib. Ch.: v.7, p.444)
RICHARD, Aimee Anne (Leonce & Felicia PONTIFE) b. 31 March 1899 (Thib. Ch.: v.7, p.598)
RICHARD, Aline Berthe d. 22 Feb. 1896 at age 1 mth. (Thib. Ch.: v.3, p.179)

RICHARD, Antoine Casmir (Arthur & Julia BOURGEOIS) b. 27 March 1896 (Houma Ch.: v.5, p.178)
RICHARD, Arthur m. 31 Aug. 1897 Ernestine CHIASSON (Thib. Ct. Hse.: Mar. v.37, #218)
RICHARD, Arthur (Leon & Angelina MORILLON) m. 31 Aug. 1897 Ernestine CHIASSON (Lockport Ch.: v.2, p.172)
RICHARD, Arthur (Thelesphore & Dellia LIRETTE) m. 21 May 1897 Julia BOURGEOIS (Houma Ch.: v.6-a, p.203)
RICHARD, Augusta Eiline Clotilde (Allain & Ophelie MIRE) b. 30 Aug. 1898 (Thib. Ch.: v.7, p.564)
RICHARD, Aurelien Raphael (Frank & Josephine TOUPS) b. 19 Feb. 1898 (Thib. Ch.: v.7, p.487)
RICHARD, Berthe Aline (Aurestile & Helene BOURGEOIS) b. 13 Jan. 1896 (Thib. Ch.: v.7, p.389)
RICHARD, Camille (Allain & Ophelia MIRE) m. 27 April 1898 Alfred GUILLOTTE (Thib. Ct. Hse.: Mar. v.38, #159)
RICHARD, Camille (Allain & Ophelia MIRE) m. 27 April 1898 Alfred GUILLOTE (Thib. Ch.: v.14, p.197)
RICHARD, Clarence Enos (Albert & Eugenie LEBRUN) b. 21 Feb. 1898 (Thib. Ch.: v.7, p.487)
RICHARD, Claude Antoine (Arthur & Julia BOURGEOIS) b. 25 Nov. 1899 (Thib. Ch.: v.7, p.580)
RICHARD, Edgard d. 18 Dec. 1898 at age 23 yrs. (Lockport Ch.: v.1, #23)
RICHARD, Edgard m. 9 Sept. 1897 Philomene DUBOIS (Thib. Ct. Hse.: Mar. v.37, #227)
RICHARD, Edgard m. 9 Sept. 1897 Philomene DUBOIS (Lockport Ch.: v.2, p.175)
RICHARD, Elisabeth (Joseph & Emilie GUIDRY) m. 17 May 1898 Charles BOURGEOIS (Thib. Ct. Hse.: Mar. v.38, #179)
RICHARD, Elisabeth (Joseph & Emilie GUIDRY) m. 17 May 1898 Charles BOURGEOIS (Thib. Ch.: v.14, p.204)
RICHARD, Elisabeth (Prosper & Odressia ESTIVEN) m. 16 Aug. 1897 Willie BOURGEOIS (Thib. Ct. Hse.: Mar. v.37, #207)
RICHARD, Elisabeth (Prosper & Odressia ESTIVEN) m. 16 Aug. 1897 Willie BOURGEOIS (Thib. Ch.: v.14, p.157)
RICHARD, Ella (Jules & Philomene ARCENEAUX) m. 26 June 1897 Odeo ORGERON (Lockport Ch.: v.2, p.168)
RICHARD, Ella (Jules & Philomene ARCENEAUX) m. 26 June 1897 Odeo ORGERON (Thib. Ct. Hse.: Mar. v.36, #169)
RICHARD, Emile m. 15 Sept. 1899 Marie LEBLANC (Houma Ct. Hse.: Mar. v.31 & 32, #135)
RICHARD, Evariste (Oleus & Alexina RODRIGUE) m. 20 Jan. 1897 Laura PARR (Thib. Ct. Hse.: Mar. v.36, #19)
RICHARD, Evariste (Oleus & Alexina RODRIGUE) m. 20 Jan. 1897 Laura PARR (Lockport Ch.: v.2, p.157)
RICHARD, Faralie Therese (Theophile & Aime LIRETTE) b. 1 July 1897 (Theriot Ch.: v.2, p.8)
RICHARD, Felicia (Oleus & Alexina RODRIGUE) m. 29 Nov. 1899 Armand PARR (Thib. Ct. Hse.: Mar. v.39, #268)

RICHARD, Felicia (Oleus & Alexina RODRIGUE) m. 29 Nov. 1899 Armand PARR (Lockport Ch.: v.2, p.211)
RICHARD, Felix (Oleus & Alexina RODRIGUE) m. 12 July 1899 Josephine PARR (Thib. Ct. Hse.: Mar. v.39, #187)
RICHARD, Felix (Oleus & Alexina RODRIGUE) m. 12 July 1899 Josephine PARR (Lockport Ch.: v.2, p.209)
RICHARD, Felix Moise (Adam & Maria ADAM) b. 13 Nov. 1898 (Thib. Ch.: v.7, p.579)
RICHARD, Frank (Aurelien & Odelia HEBERT) m. 17 Feb. 1896 Josephine TOUPS (Thib. Ch.: v.14, p.79)
RICHARD, Frank (Aurelien & Odelia HEBERT) m. 17 Feb. 1896 Josephine TOUPS (Thib. Ct. Hse.: Mar. v.35, #44)
RICHARD, Ignace (Onesime & Celima LAINE) m. 25 Nov. 1896 Marie Olivia RODRIGUE (Thib. Ch.: v.14, p.101)
RICHARD, Ignace (Onesime & Celima LAINE) m. 25 Nov. 1896 Marie Olivia RODRIGUE (Thib. Ct. Hse.: Mar. v.36, #162)
RICHARD, Joseph (Leo & Azelia THERIOT) m. 12 Oct. 1899 Justine BOURGEOIS (Thib. Ch.: v.14, p.303)
RICHARD, Joseph (Leo & Azelia THERIOT) m. 12 Oct. 1899 Justine BOURGEOIS (Thib. Ct. Hse.: Mar. v.39, #244)
RICHARD, Joseph (Marcelin & Emelie HEBERT) m. 15 Feb. 1897 Emeline GAUBERT (Thib. Ch.: v.14, p.125)
RICHARD, Joseph (Marcelin & Emelie HEBERT) m. 15 Feb. 1897 Emeline GAUBERT (Thib. Ct. Hse.: Mar. v.36, #75)
RICHARD, Joseph Albert (Edgar & Julie BOUDREAUX) b. 3 July 1897 (Chacahoula Ch.: v.4, p.21)
RICHARD, Joseph Arnold (Joseph Arthur & Emilie GAUBERT) b. 27 Feb. 1898 (Thib. Ch.: v.7, p.538)
RICHARD, Joseph Camille d. 26 May 1897 (Houma Ch.: v.3, p.13)
RICHARD, Joseph Camille (Arthur & Julia BOURGEOIS) b. 29 March 1896 (Houma Ch.: v.5, p.178)
RICHARD, Josephine (Joseph & Emilie GUIDRY) m. 22 Jan. 1896 Nicolas BOUDREAUX (Thib. Ch.: v.14, p.67)
RICHARD, Josephine (Joseph & Emilie GUIDRY) m. 22 Jan. 1896 Nicolas BOUDREAUX (Thib. Ct. Hse.: Mar. v.35, #19)
RICHARD, Judith (Allain & Ophelia MIRE) m. 18 May 1899 Emile GUILLOTE (Thib. Ch.: v.14, p.282)
RICHARD, Julien d. 10 June 1899 at age 5 yrs. (Thib. Ch.: v.3, p.235)
RICHARD, Leonie (Taylor & Philomene BERNARD) m. 27 April 1899 Felicia PONTIFE (Thib. Ch.: v.14, p.279)
RICHARD, Leonie (Taylor & Pilomene BERNARD) m. 27 April 1899 Felicie PONTIFE (Thib. Ct. Hse.: Mar. v.39, #146)
RICHARD, Lillie Anna (Prosper & Odressia ESTIVEN) b. 22 March 1898 (Thib. Ch.: v.7, p.491)
RICHARD, Louis Joseph (Lucien & Mathilde TOUSSAINT) b. 5 April 1898 (Thib. Ch.: v.7, p.506)
RICHARD, Lucien (Noel & Julienne BOUDREAUX) m. 29 April 1897 Mathilde TOUSSAINT (Thib. Ch.: v.14, p.141)
RICHARD, Lucien (Noel & Julienne BOUDREAUX) m. 29 April 1897 Mathilde TOUSSAINT (Thib. Ct. Hse.: Mar. v.36, #120)

RICHARD, Marie m. Louis BOURGEOIS d. 25 Sept. 1898 (Thib. Ch.: v.3, p.220)
RICHARD, Marie (Jules & Philomene ARCENEAUX) m. 14 June 1897 Emile CHIASSON (Thib. Ct. Hse.: Mar. v.36, #170)
RICHARD, Marie Alexina (Evariste & Laura PARR) b. 30 Oct. 1897 (Larose Ch.: v.3, p.13)
RICHARD, Marie Beatrice (Ignace & Marie Olivia RODRIGUE) b. 4 Jan. 1899 (Thib. Ch.: v.7, p.528)
RICHARD, Marie Clemence d. 6 Dec. 1895; m. J. Severin FORET Children listed: Onesippe; Richard; Marcellin; Trasimond; Severine m. Hamilton AYO; Marie m. S. C. BOURGEOIS; d.Valfroid; d.Zephirin m. Louisiane BABIN; d.Elles m. Louise LEBLANC. Inventory: 1 May 1896. (Thib. Ct. Hse.: Succ. #1488)
RICHARD, Marie Levie (Arthur & Julie BOURGEOIS) b. 28 Aug. 1898 (Houma Ch.: v.5, p.217)
RICHARD, Marie Olivia (Adam & Marie ADAM) b. 26 April 1896 (Thib. Ch.: v.7, p.449)
RICHARD, Marie Victoria (Augustin & Marie TRAHAN) b. 5 May 1897 (Montegut Ch.: v.6, p.55)
RICHARD, Mary d. 29 Nov. 1898 at age 23 yrs. (Thib. Ch.: v.3, p.222)
RICHARD, Noeli Marguerite (Frank & Josephine TOUPS) b. 9 Jan. 1897 (Thib. Ch.: v.7, p.434)
RICHARD, Oleus d. 3 Feb. 1898 at age 44 yrs. (Lockport Ch.: v.1, #3)
RICHARD, Oleus m. Alexina RODRIGUE Children listed: Felix; Felicia; Lucy; Ada; Felicien; Philip; Olide m. Narcise LEBOEUF. Family meeting: 12 July 1898. (Thib. Ct. Hse.: Succ. #1539)
RICHARD, Ordressy d. 14 Nov. 1899 at age 21 yrs. (Lockport Ch.: v.1, #43)
RICHARD, Philippe Jerome (Ignace & Olivia RODRIGUE) b. 30 Sept. 1896 (Thib. Ch.: v.7, p.467)
RICHARD, Sidonia m. 3 March 1898 Willis SAMUEL (Houma Ct. Hse.: Mar. v.30 & 31, #324)
RICHARD, Sophie G. d. 18 July 1897 (Houma Ch.: Epis. Ch.: v.1, p.386)
RICHARD, Valerie (Oscar & Justilia BABIN) b. 27 April 1898 (Thib. Ch.: v.7, p.496)
RICHARDELL, Carmelitte (Pierre & Catherine VINET) b. 17 Oct. 1899 (Larose Ch.: v.3, p.35)
RICHAUD, Sophie G. d. 18 July 1897 (Gibson Ch.: Epis. Ch.: v.1, p.114)
RICHE, Edward A. m. 23 Feb. 1899 Logan ROGERS (Thib. Ct. Hse.: Mar. v.39, #101)
RICHET, Nelson Gaston Logan (Adrien & Josephine RICHARD) b. 21 April 1899 (Thib. Ch.: v.7, p.601)

RICHOUX (Sometimes: RICHAUX)

RICHOUX, Amelia (Arsene & Melasie PRICE) m. 9 Dec. 1899 Victor MELANCON (Larose Ch.: v.4, p.129)

RICHOUX, Amelia (Arsene & Melasie PRICE) m. 29 Nov. 1899 Victore MELANCON, Jr. (Thib. Ct. Hse.: Mar. v.39, #273)
RICHOUX, Amelia (Arsene & Melasie PRICE) m. 9 Dec. 1899 Victor MELANCON, Jr. (Larose Ch.: v.3, p.13)
RICHOUX, Clovis Michel (Amedee & Marcelite LOUP) b. 14 March 1897 (Lockport Ch.: v.3-A, #36)
RICHOUX, Clovis Michel (Amedee & Marcelite LOUP) b. 14 March 1897 (Lockport Ch.: v.3, #36)
RICHOUX, Estelle Marie (Felix & ---- BEAUDOIN) b. 10 July 1896 (Larose Ch.: v.2, p.194)
RICHOUX, Jean m. 22 Jan. 1898 Johannine MORESCO (Larose Ch.: v.4, p.112)
RICHOUX, Jean m. 22 Jan. 1898 Johannine MORESCO (Larose Ch.: v.3, p.7)
RICHOUX, Jean m. 22 Jan. 1898 Johannine MORESCO (Thib. Ct. Hse.: Mar. v.37, #24)
RICHOUX, Jean Louis d. 31 Aug. 1898 at age 78 yrs. (Larose Ch.: v.1, p.44)
RICHOUX, Joseph Eddy (Nicolas & Clemence CHERAMI) b. 13 Feb. 1896 (Lockport Ch.: v.2, p.322)
RICHOUX, Joseph Lucan (Farin & Elmire PLAISANCE) b. 8 Jan. 1896 (Larose Ch.: v.2, p.179)
RICHOUX, Julia Felecite (Felix & Zulma BEAUDOIN) b. 4 Sept. 1898 (Larose Ch.: v.3, p.28)
RICHOUX, Maria m. 24? Jan. 1896 Clebert ROGERS (Larose Ch.: v.2, p.188)
RICHOUX, Marie m. 25 Jan. 1896 Clebert ROGERS (Larose Ch.: v.3, p.2)
RICHOUX, Marie m. 25 Jan. 1896 Clebert ROGERS (Thib. Ct. Hse.: Mar. v.35, #25)
RICHOUX, Marie Lydia (Fazende & Elmire PLAISANCE) b. 27 Oct. 1898 (Larose Ch.: v.3, p.29)
RICHOUX, Michel d. 5 Nov. 1898 at age 86 yrs. (Lockport Ch.: v.1, #19)
RICHOUX, Odille m. 26 Oct. 1898 Urbain BARRIOS (Thib. Ct. Hse.: Mar. v.38, #302)
RICHOUX, Odille of Lafourche Parish (Hyacinthe) m. 29 Oct. 1898 Urbain BARRIOS, of Lafourche Parish (Larose Ch.: v.3, p.10)
RICHOUX, Paul Albert (Hyacinthe & Clara SAVOIE) b. 19 Jan. 1896 (Larose Ch.: v.2, p.180)
RICHOUX, Sidonie m. 11 April 1896 Ethen BOURGEOIS (Larose Ch.: v.4, p.45)
RICHOUX, Sidonie m. 11 April 1896 Ethen BOURGEOIS (Thib. Ct. Hse.: Mar. v.35, #67)
RICHOUX, Sidonie m. 11 April 1896 Etienne BOURGEOIS (Larose Ch.: v.3, p.2)
RICK, Bernard (Baptiste & Ophelia MARS) m. 1 Oct. 1896 Anna ORDOGNE (Thib. Ct. Hse.: Mar. v.36, #141)
RICK, Bernard (Baptiste & Ophelia MARS) m. 1 Oct. 1896 Anna ORDOGNE (Chackbay Ch.: v.1, p.31)

RIDEAU, J. E. d. 25 Sept. 1899 at age 6 yrs. & 6 mths. (Houma Ch.: v.3, p.25)

RIDER, John B. m. 14 Oct. 1896 Anna PAUSARET (Houma Ct. Hse.: Mar. v.29 & 30, #167)

RIDER, John B. (John & Mary CLARK) m. 14 Oct. 1896 Anna POUSARET (Houma Ch.: v.6-a, p.182)

RIDER, Mary Diana (John & Mary Anna PASERETTE) b. 1 May 1897 (Houma Ch.: v.5, p.177)

RIDER, Rosa Mabel (John & Anna POSARAY) b. 2 Nov. 1898 (Montegut Ch.: v.6, p.81)

RIDLEY, Betta M. of Terrebonne Parish m. 21 Sept. 1899 Alfred DUMAS (Houma Ch.: v.6-B, p.4)

RIDLEY, Bettie M. m. 21 Sept. 1899 Alfred DUMAS (Houma Ct. Hse.: Mar. v.31 & 32, #138")

RIDLEY, Cora Mrs. d. 20 Oct. 1897 at age 43 yrs. & 10 mths. (Houma Ch.: v.3, p.14)

RIGAULT, Felix Leonce (Edgard & Jeanne JAMBON) b. 29 May 1897 (Larose Ch.: v.3, p.26)

RIGAULT, Ophelia of Jefferson Parish (Joseph & Therese RIBAULT) m. 6 Feb. 1898 Victor BOUDREAUX, of Jefferson Parish (Larose Ch.: v.3, p.7)

RIGAULT, Ophelia (Joseph & Therese RIBAUD) m. 6 Feb. 1898 Victor BOUDREAUX (Larose Ch.: v.4, p.3)

RIGAULT, Theresa m. 8 Sept. 1896 Onesiphore COULON (Larose Ch.: v.4, p.81)

RIGAULT, Theresa m. 8 Sept. 1896 Onesiphore COULON (Larose Ch.: v.3, p.4)

RIGGINS, Priscilla m. 5 Aug. 1897 Thomas CEASAR (Thib. Ct. Hse.: Mar. v.37, #205)

RIGGS, Marguerite m. Valery BREAUX d. 19 May 1898 at age 98 yrs. (Lockport Ch.: v.1, #11)

RILEY, Anderson m. 29 April 1897 Florestine CAILLOUET (Thib. Ct. Hse.: Mar. v.36, #133)

RILEY, Duncan m. 28 Jan. 1897 Lucy CLARK (Houma Ct. Hse.: Mar. v.29 & 30, #261)

RILEY, Hannah m. 27 Dec. 1897 Edward STEWART (Houma Ct. Hse.: Mar. v.29 & 30, #155)

RILEY, Oscar m. 17 Aug. 1899 Mary GREEN (Houma Ct. Hse.: Mar. v.31 & 32, #103)

RINGGOLD, Bertha m.27 Jan. 1898 Willie WILLIAMS (Houma Ct. Hse.: Mar. v.30 & 31, #225)

RINGGOLD, Cato m. 6 July 1896 Carrie SMITH (Houma Ct. Hse.: Mar. v.29 & 30, #103)

RINGGOLD, Charles m. 8 Oct. 1896 Harriet SPENCER (Houma Ct. Hse.: Mar. v.29 & 30, #166)

RINGGOLD, Osborne Jr. m. 23 July 1896 Arthemise CELESTIN (Houma Ct. Hse.: Mar. v.29 & 30, #117)

RINI, Leonardo (Gioseppa & Vita IAUTELLO) b. 10 Nov. 1899 (Houma Ch.: v.5, p.264)

RINK, Emelia (Jean Baptiste & Ophelia MARS) m. 6 June 1898 Emile NAVARRE (Thib. Ct. Hse.: Mar. v.38, #189)

RINK, Emilia (Jean Baptiste & Ophelia MARS) m. 6 June 1898 Emile NAVARRE (Chackbay Ch.: v.1, p.62)
RINK, Marie Mathilde (Bernard & Anna ORDOGNE) b. 20 July 1899 (Chackbay Ch.: v.1, p.140)
RIPP, Martin Joseph (Frank G. & Mary WENDLING) b. 5 Feb. 1899 (Thib. Ch.: v.7, p.591)
RIPSTOCK, Jackson Fernand (John & Rose PETIT) b. 22 July 1897 (Larose Ch.: v.3, p.27)
RITTER, Bernard d. 5 April 1896 Application for administration: 23 May 1896. (Houma Ct. Hse.: Succ. #878)
RITTMAN, Lieza m. 24 June 1896 Daniel REED (Thib. Ct. Hse.: Mar. v.36, #112)
RIVET, Anita (Joseph & Louisiana CHONES) b. 24 Sept. 1899 (Lockport Ch.: v.3-A, #7)
RIVET, Anita (Joseph & Louisiane CHONES) b. 24 Sept. 1899 (Lockport Ch.: v.3, #7)
RIVET, Elibert d. 9 May 1899 at age 10 mths. (Lockport Ch.: v.1, #18)
RIVET, Messine d. 15 Jan. 1897 at age 27 yrs. (Raceland Ch.: v.1, p.13)
RIVET, Pierre m. 23 Oct. 1897 Euphrasie DUFRESNE (Lockport Ch.: v.2, p.176)
RIVET, Pierre Jr. (Pierre & Philomene MATHERNE) m. 23 Oct. 1897 Euphrasie DUFRESNE (Thib. Ct. Hse.: Mar. v.37, #251)
RIVET, Silvere m. 4 Dec. 1899 Mathilde DUFRENE (Thib. Ct. Hse.: Mar. v.39, #276)
RIVET, Sylvere (Pierre & Philomene MATHERNE) m. 16 Dec. 1899 Mathilde DUFRENE (Lockport Ch.: v.2, p.212)
RIVIERE, Aline Marie (Leonie & Octavie BOURGEOIS) b. 16 Feb. 1897 (Thib. Ch.: v.7, p.438)
RIVIERE, Denys Oneil (Leonie & Octavie BOURGEOIS) b. 27 Nov. 1898 (Thib. Ch.: v.7, p.523)
RIVIERE, Edgard F. (Francois & Eulalie LEGENDRE) m. 17 Dec. 1899 Louise ROBICHAUX (Thib. Ct. Hse.: Mar. v.39, #284)
RIVIERE, Edgard F. (Francois & Eulalie LEGENDRE) m. 17 Dec. 1899 Louise ROBICHAUX (Thib. Ch.: v.14, p.312)
RIVIERE, Emilie (Lange & Lucile PHILIPPEAU) m. 22 Nov. 1898 Joseph McCULLA (Thib. Ct. Hse.: Mar. v.38, #309)
RIVIERE, Emilie (Lange & Lucile PHILIPPEAUX) m. 22 Nov. 1898 Joseph McCULLA (Thib. Ch.: v.14, p.230)
RIVIERE, Hilda Eulalie (Numa Joseph & Hilda Madeleine RICHARD) b. 11 July 1897 (Thib. Ch.: v.7, p.455)
RIVIERE, Numa d. 5 Aug. 1897 at age 33 yrs. (Thib. Ch.: v.3, p.204)
RIVIERE, Odette Eulalie (Louis & Marie Elda PIERSON) b. 22 Dec. 1897 (Thib. Ch.: v.7, p.476)
RIVIERE, Thelma Anna (Louis & Elda Marie PIERSON) b. 16 Feb. 1899 (Thib. Ch.: v.7, p.591)
RIVIERE, Thomas A. m. 14 Nov. 1899 Annette LAGARDE (Thib. Ct. Hse.: Mar. v.39, #265)

RIZAN (Sometimes: RISAN)

RIZZO, Joseph d. 14 Dec. 1896 at age 48 yrs. (Thib. Ch.: v.3, p.192)
ROBERT, Augusta (Constantin & Octavie ROUSSEL) m. 23 July 1898 Emile TROSCLAIR (Raceland Ch.: v.2, p.77)
ROBERT, Clarine Cecilia (Anatole & Augustine Anastasie DARDA) b. 12 Aug. 1899 (Larose Ch.: v.3, p.58)
ROBERT, Lovinia m. 22 April 1899 Joseph DARDARD (Thib. Ct. Hse.: Mar. v.39, #155)
ROBERT, Robert Victor (William & Emelie BOUDREAU) b. 11 Oct. 1898 (Houma Ch.: v.5, p.221)
ROBERTS, David d. 25 Dec. 1899 at age 12½ yrs. (Thib. Ch.: v.3, p.247)
ROBERTS, Joseph Gabriel m. 25 July 1899 Emma Catherine PICOU (Houma Ct. Hse.: Mar. v.31 & 32, #85)

ROBERTSON (Sometimes: ROBERSON, ROBESON)

ROBERTSON, Agnes Lilian (Charles & Palmyra CHARLES) b. 28 May 1898 (Thib. Ch.: v.7, p.550)
ROBERTSON, Anna m. 1 July 1899 Charlie FLUNCE (Houma Ct. Hse.: Mar. v.31 & 32, #64)
ROBERTSON, Corine (Marie ROBERTSON) b. 3 Oct. 1897 (Larose Ch.: v.3, p.6)
ROBERTSON, Eleanore m. 26 May 1898 Moses COOK (Thib. Ct. Hse.: Mar. v.38, #190)
ROBERTSON, Elmire (Trasimond & Ulalie HIMEL) m. 18 Sept. 1899 Aurelien TROSCLAIR (Chackbay Ch.: v.1, p.73)
ROBERTSON, Elmire (Trasimond & Ulalie HIMEL) m. 5 Sept. 1899 Aurelien TROSCLAIR (Thib. Ct. Hse.: Mar. v.39, #220)
ROBERTSON, Emilie (Ozeme & Mary LEBLANC) m. 14 July 1898 Julien PLAISANCE (Lockport Ch.: v.2, p.192)
ROBERTSON, Freddy Charles (Willis & Florence ROBICHAUX) b. 25 Aug. 1899 (Thib. Ch.: v.7, p.567)
ROBERTSON, Gustine (Trasimond & Ulalie HIMEL) m. 25 Jan. 1898 Marcellin LANDRY (Chackbay Ch.: v.1, p.53)
ROBERTSON, Joseph d. 5 April 1898 at age 40 days (Thib. Ch.: v.3, p.212)
ROBERTSON, Joseph Charles (Charles & Palmyra CHARLES) b. 22 Feb. 1898 (Thib. Ch.: v.7, p.487)
ROBERTSON, Justine (Trasimond & Ulalie HIMEL) m. 25 Jan. 1898 Marceline LANDRY (Thib. Ct. Hse.: Mar. v.37, #33)
ROBERTSON, Marie Adette (John & Severine BERGERON) b. 2 March 1897 (Houma Ch.: v.5, p.207)
ROBERTSON, Marie Mamie (Ulysseo & Lilie NAQUIN) b. 23 June 1899 (Thib. Ch.: v.7, p.609)
ROBERTSON, Paul Chester (Helece & Luly NAQUIN) b. 25 Feb. 1897 (Thib. Ch.: v.7, p.450)
ROBERTSON, Sam m. 12 Oct. 1898 Emma SANDERS (Thib. Ct. Hse.: Mar. v.38, #292)

ROBICHAUX (Sometimes: ROBICHAU, ROBICHAUD, ROBICHAUT, ROBICHEAU, ROBICHEAUX, ROBICHOUX)

ROBICHAUX, Adele (Felicien & Elvire MARLBOROUGH) d. 22 Sept. 1899 at age 3 yrs. (Montegut Ch.: v.2, p.29)

ROBICHAUX, Adele Marcellite (Felicien & Elvire MARLBOROUGH) b. 4 May 1897 (Montegut Ch.: v.6, p.56)

ROBICHAUX, Aimee Justine (Odressie & Azema FORET) b. 22 April 1899; m. Gillis ARCENEAUX on 8 April 1931. (Raceland Ch.: Bapt. Bk., v.5, p.95)

ROBICHAUX, Alfred (J. R. C. & Bazelise DUPRE) m. 27 Jan. 1896 Gracieuse ARCENAUX (Theriot Ch.: v.1, p.3)

ROBICHAUX, Alfred (Jean Baptiste & Bazelise DUPRE) m. 13 Jan. 1896 Gracieuse ARCENAUX (Houma Ct. Hse.: Mar. v.28, #384)

ROBICHAUX, Alida m. 17 Aug. 1898 Onesippe DUFRESNE (Thib. Ct. Hse.: Mar. v.38, #256)

ROBICHAUX, Alida (Alidor & Justine ARCEMENT) m. 29 Aug. 1898 Onesippe DUFRESNE (Raceland Ch.: v.2, p.78)

ROBICHAUX, Alidor Child listed: Melance. In the matter of insanity of: 12 July 1898. (Thib. Ct. Hse.: Succ. #1541)

ROBICHAUX, Amedee (Amedee & Emma LEBOEUF) m. 7 Jan. 1896 Alice PONTIFF (Houma Ch.: v.6-a, p.167)

ROBICHAUX, Amelia Iberie (Edouard & Aimee GRABERT) b. 23 Feb. 1896 (Raceland Ch.: v.5, p.20)

ROBICHAUX, Anna d. 1 Aug. 1899 at age 6 mths. (Thib. Ch.: v.3, p.238)

ROBICHAUX, Anna Philomene (Alidor & Justine ARCEMENT) b. 18 Jan. 1899 (Raceland Ch.: v.5, p.87)

ROBICHAUX, Anne m. 12 Jan. 1899 Hermogene ROBICHAUX (Thib. Ct. Hse.: Mar. v.38, #17)

ROBICHAUX, Anne (Justilien & Marie SEVIN) m. 19 Jan. 1899 Hermogene ROBICHAUX (Raceland Ch.: v.2, p.83)

ROBICHAUX, Anne Sidonia (Adam & Lea LECOMPTE) b. 28 Sept. 1896 (Montegut Ch.: v.6, p.45)

ROBICHAUX, Antoine Jean (Albert & Louisa THERIOT) b. 17 Jan. 1899 (Raceland Ch.: v.5, p.90)

ROBICHAUX, Armand m. 12 Feb. 1898 Agathe GAUDEZ (Thib. Ct. Hse.: Mar. v.37, #64)

ROBICHAUX, Armand (Felix & Marie FORET) m. 12 Feb. 1898 Agathe GAUDET (Raceland Ch.: v.2, p.68)

ROBICHAUX, Arthur J. d. 17 Oct. 1898 at age 28 yrs. (Houma Ch.: Epis. Ch.: v.1, p.388)

ROBICHAUX, Aurelie Martin (Emile & Josephine CHIASSON) b. 30 Jan. 1896 (Montegut Ch.: v.6, p.33)

ROBICHAUX, Clarance Joseph (Amede & Alice PONTIFF) b. 23 Nov. 1899 (Houma Ch.: v.5, p.267)

ROBICHAUX, Clarance Joseph (Amedee & Alice PONTIFF) b. 23 Nov. 1899 (Houma Ch.: v.3, p.3)

ROBICHAUX, Clementine m. 3 Feb. 1898 Justilien VEDROSE (Thib. Ct. Hse.: Mar. v.37, #57)

ROBICHAUX, Clementine (Homere & Marie SEVIN) m. 3 Feb. 1898 Justilien VEDROSE (Raceland Ch.: v.2, p.62)
ROBICHAUX, Edna Nathalie (Felicien & Elvire MALBOROUGH) b. 27 July 1899 (Montegut Ch.: v.6, p.91)
ROBICHAUX, Edouard (Willy) d. 17 Sept. 1897 at age 1 yr. & 8 mths. (Montegut Ch.: v.2, p.11)
ROBICHAUX, Edward (Neville & Aimee GUIDRY) m. 20 Jan. 1898 Cynthia LEBLANC (Thib. Ch.: v.14, p.170)
ROBICAHAUX, Edward (Neuville & Aimee GUIDRY) m. 20 Jan. 1898 Cynthia LEBLANC (Houma Ct. Hse.: vols.29-30, #156)
ROBICHAUX, Ellis (d.Onesippe & Florentine HOTARD) m. 18 Feb. 1897 Justilia ROBICHAUX (Montegut Ch.: v.4, p.218)
ROBICHAUX, Ellis (Onesipe & Florentine HOTARD) m. 30 Jan. 1897 Justilia ROBICHAUX (Houma Ct. Hse.: Mar. v.29 & 30, #268)
ROBICHAUX, Emilie Florance (Michel & Veleda LAMBERT) b. 25 April 1899 (Montegut Ch.: v.6, p.88)
ROBICHAUX, Emma (Narcisse & Emelie BELANGER) m. 4 May 1897 Anatole GASTON (Houma Ct. Hse.: Mar. v.29 & 30, #399)
ROBICHAUX, Emma (Narcisse & Emilie BELANGER) m. 2 June 1897 Anatole GASTON (Montegut Ch.: v.4, p.222)
ROBICHAUX, Esther (Leo & Odilia STOUFFLET) d. 12 Oct. 1898 at age 8 mths. (Montegut Ch.: v.2, p.21)
ROBICHAUX, Etienne d. 16 March 1896 at age 54 yrs., 6 mths. & 4 days (Montegut Ch.: v.2, p.3)
ROBICHAUX, Etienne P. d. 16 March 1895 (d.J. Narcisse ROBICHAUX) m. Camillia HEBERT, d. 23 Sept. 1898. Children listed: Joseph A.; Alfred L.; Lee N.; Josephine N. m. Israel DUPLANTIS; Ada M., about 16. Petition for inventory: 7 Nov. 1898. (Houma Ct. Hse.: Succ. #923)
ROBICHAUX, Eugene Alphonse (Jean Baptiste & Mary LEBLANC) b. 2 Oct. 1896 (Larose Ch.: v.2, p.184)
ROBICHAUX, Eugene G. m. 12 Aug. 1897 Brigitte THIBODAUX (Thib. Ct. Hse.: Mar. v.37, #204)
ROBICHAUX, Eve Nola (Adam & Elda FOLSE) b. 24 Feb. 1898 (Raceland Ch.: v.5, p.67)
ROBICHAUX, Fabiola Madeleine (Welly & Marcelline SEVIN) d. 12 April 1899 at age 14 mths. (Montegut Ch.: v.2, p.24)
ROBICHAUX, Felicia m. 6 June 1896 Paul THERIOT (Thib. Ct. Hse.: Mar. v.35, #96)
ROBICHAUX, Felicia (Felix & Marie FORET) m. 6 June 1896 Paul THERIOT (Raceland Ch.: v.2, p.16)
ROBICHAUX, Francois Edmond (Oborn & Ernestine LANDRY) b. 5 Feb. 1898 (Houma Ch.: v.5, p.198)
ROBICHAUX, Frank (Theophile & Elmire ESTOUFFLET) m. 14 July 1896 Palmiere CHARPENTIER (Houma Ct. Hse.: Mar. v.29 & 30, #112)
ROBICHAUX, Frank (Theophile & Elmire ESTOUFFLET) m. 6 Aug. 1896 Palmiree CHARPENTIER (Montegut Ch.: v.4, p.213)
ROBICHAUX, Harry Adam (Frank & Amanda MARTIN) b. 8 Nov. 1898 (Raceland Ch.: v.5, p.82)

ROBICHAUX, Hermogene m. 12 Jan. 1899 Anne ROBICHAUX (Thib. Ct. Hse.: Mar. v.38, #17)
ROBICHAUX, Hermogene (Octave & Palmyre DIEZ) m. 19 Jan. 1899 Anne ROBICHAUX (Raceland Ch.: v.2, p.83)
ROBICHAUX, Isaac Dewey (Gustin & Amanda HEBERT) b. 28 Aug. 1898 (Montegut Ch.: v.6, p.77)
ROBICHAUX, J. Narcisse d. 23 Sept. 1898; m. Marie Ursule ROBICHAUX Children listed: William T.; Marie Clemence m. Desire BREAUX; d.Etienne P.; Michael Onezippe. Petition placing heirs in possession: 24 Feb. 1899. (Houma Ct. Hse.: Succ. #916)
ROBICHAUX, James Paul (Emile & Josephine CHIASSON) b. 8 July 1898 (Montegut Ch.: v.6, p.75)
ROBICHAUX, James Paul (Emile & Josephine CHIASSON) d. 24 Oct. 1898 at age 3 mths. & 17 days (Montegut Ch.: v.2, p.21)
ROBICHAUX, Jean Baptiste (Ellis & Justilia ROBICHAUX) d. 14 April 1899 at age 3 hrs. (Montegut Ch.: v.2, p.24)
ROBICHAUX, Jean Edouard (Welly & Marcelline SEVIN) b. 8 Feb. 1896 (Montegut Ch.: v.6, p.35)
ROBICHAUX, Jean Harry (Frank & Palmyre CHARPENTIER) b. 12 July 1897 (Montegut Ch.: v.6, p.58)
ROBICHAUX, Joseph m. 26 Aug. 1898 Ernestine THERIOT (Thib. Ct. Hse.: Mar. v.38, #266)
ROBICHAUX, Joseph (Ellis & Justilia ROBICHAUX) d. 3 Nov. 1897 at age 5 days (Montegut Ch.: v.2, p.12)
ROBICHAUX, Joseph (Joseph & Celima DUFRESNE) m. 10 Sept. 1898 Ernestine THERIOT (Raceland Ch.: v.2, p.80)
ROBICHAUX, Joseph Eclan (Narcisse & Eda LEBLANC) b. 11 July 1896 (Montegut Ch.: v.6, p.42)
ROBICHAUX, Joseph Noel Wickles (Adam & Lea LECOMPTE) b. 25 Dec. 1898 (Montegut Ch.: v.6, p.80)
ROBICHAUX, Joseph O'Neill (Frank & Amanda MARTIN) b. 23 July 1896 (Raceland Ch.: v.5, p.26)
ROBICHAUX, Joseph Onesippe (Frank & Lucie DOMINGUE) b. 19 Aug. 1897 (Montegut Ch.: v.6, p.60)
ROBICHAUX, Joseph Samson (Armand & Agathe GAUDEY) b. 8 Nov. 1898 (Raceland Ch.: v.5, p.81)
ROBICHAUX, Joseph Sidney (Oscar & Euphemie BABIN) b. 1 Oct. 1898 (Raceland Ch.: v.5, p.79)
ROBICHAUX, Joseph Unez (Edouard & Aimee GRABERT) b. 15 Jan. 1899 (Raceland Ch.: v.5, p.90)
ROBICHAUX, Joseph Wilfrid (Narcisse & Eda LEBLANC) d. 21 Aug. 1896 at age 3 yrs. (Montegut Ch.: v.2, p.6)
ROBICHAUX, Joseph Xavier (Lothere & Ophelia MARLBOROUGH) d. 5 June 1899 at age 2 mths. (Montegut Ch.: v.2, p.26)
ROBICHAUX, Justilia (Justilien & Marie CHIASSON) m. 18 Feb. 1897 Ellis ROBICHAUX (Montegut Ch.: v.4, p.218)
ROBICHAUX, Justilia (Justilien & Marie CHIASSON) m. 30 Jan. 1897 Ellis ROBICHAUX (Houma Ct. Hse.: Mar. v.29 & 30, #268)

ROBICHAUX, Leon Xavier (Lothere & Ophelia MALBOROUGH) b. 11 April 1899 (Montegut Ch.: v.6, p.85)
ROBICHAUX, Leufroy d. 29 Oct. 1897 at age 89 yrs. (Raceland Ch.: v.1, p.15)
ROBICHAUX, Louise (Theodule & Josephine NAQUIN) m. 17 Dec. 1899 Edgard F. RIVIERE (Thib. Ct. Hse.: Mar. v.39, #284)
ROBICHAUX, Louise (Theodule & Josephine NAQUIN) m. 17 Dec. 1899 Edgard F. RIVIERE (Thib. Ch.: v.14, p.312)
ROBICHAUX, Louise Lina (Adam & Marie DUPLANTIS) b. 17 Oct. 1899 (Montegut Ch.: v.6, p.95)
ROBICHAUX, Lucia Bernadette (Edwin & Victoria ROBICHAUX) b. 12 Sept. 1898 (Raceland Ch.: v.5, p.78)
ROBICHAUX, Lufroy d. 1 April 1898 at age 84 yrs. (Raceland Ch.: v.1, p.17)
ROBICHAUX, Lydia Bernadette (Alfred & Telesia MICHEL) m. 25 April 1898 Albert S. QUICK (Theriot Ch.: v.1-B, p.3)
ROBICHAUX, Lydia Bernadette (Alfred & Telesia MICHEL) m. 9 April 1898 Albert S. QUICK (Houma Ct. Hse.: Mar. v.30 & 31, #388)
ROBICHAUX, Madeleine Fabiola (Wellie & Marcellin SEVIN) b. 11 Feb. 1898 (Montegut Ch.: v.6, p.67)
ROBICHAUX, Marceline m. Aubert HEBERT d. 28 July 1899 at age 67 yrs. (Thib. Ch.: v.3, p.238)
ROBICHAUX, Marguerite Olivia (Adam & Marie DUPLANTIS) b. 3 Feb. 1897 (Montegut Ch.: v.6, p.51)
ROBICHAUX, Marie Adelina (Felicien & Aydi HEBERT) b. 13 Sept. 1896 (Lockport Ch.: v.3, #1)
ROBICHAUX, Marie Adelina (Felicien & Aydi HEBERT) b. 13 Sept. 1896 (Lockport Ch.: v.3-A, #1)
ROBICHAUX, Marie Aline (Albert & Louisa THERIOT) b. 19 Aug. 1897; m. Charley ROGERS on 12 Jan. 1924. (Raceland Ch.: Bapt. Bk., v.5, p.53)
ROBICHAUX, Marie Clevia (Adam & Marie DUPLANTIS) b. 3 Feb. 1897 (Montegut Ch.: v.6, p.51)
ROBICHAUX, Marie Josephine (Joseph & Marie LATOUR) b. 18 Jan. 1898 (Thib. Ch.: v.7, p.482)
ROBICHAUX, Marie Nobie Camilia (Alfred & Adeline FOURNIER) b. 17 Jan. 1898 (Montegut Ch.: v.6, p.65)
ROBICHAUX, Marie Philomene (Amedee & Alice PONTIFF) b. 1 Feb. 1897 (Houma Ch.: v.5, p.202)
ROBICHAUX, Mary Esther (Leo N. & Odilia STOUFFLET) b. 23 Feb. 1898 (Montegut Ch.: v.6, p.67)
ROBICHAUX, Michel (Narcisse & Emelie BELANGER) m. 23 April 1898 Veleda LAMBERT (Montegut Ch.: v.4, p.243)
ROBICHAUX, Mitchell (Narcisse & Emelie BELANGER) m. 11 April 1898 Velada LAMBERT (Houma Ct. Hse.: Mar. v.30 & 31, #394)
ROBICHAUX, Narcisse d. 23 Sept. 1898 at age 78 yrs. (Montegut Ch.: v.2, p.20)
ROBICHAUX, Obane d. 11 Feb. 1898 at age 35 yrs. (Houma Ch.: v.3, p.15)

ROBICHAUX, Odressie (Alidor & Justine ARCEMENT) m. 21 May 1898 Azema FORET (Raceland Ch.: v.2, p.74)
ROBICHAUX, Odressy m. 10 May 1898 Azema FORET (Thib. Ct. Hse.: Mar. v.38, #180)
ROBICHAUX, Oscar m. 29 July 1897 Euphemie BABIN (Thib. Ct. Hse.: Mar. v.37, #199)
ROBICHAUX, Oscar (Amede & Irma ARABIE) m. 29 July 1897 Euphemie BABIN (Raceland Ch.: v.2, p.47)
ROBICHAUX, Ozea m. 22 June 1897 Charles BARANCO (Thib. Ct. Hse.: Mar. v.37, #182)
ROBICHAUX, Pierre m. 27 April 1899 Valerie BABIN (Thib. Ct. Hse.: Mar. v.39, #149)
ROBICHAUX, Pierre (Homere & Marie SEVIN) m. 27 April 1899 Valerie BABIN (Raceland Ch.: v.2, p.96)
ROBICHAUX, Pierre W. d. 23 Aug. 1897 at age 1 yr. (Raceland Ch.: v.1, p.14)
ROBICHAUX, Seraphin Sidney (Narcisse & Eda LEBLANC) b. 12 Sept. 1899 (Montegut Ch.: v.6, p.92)
ROBICHAUX, Therese Odilia (Adam & Elda FOLSE) b. 28 April 1899 (Raceland Ch.: v.5, p.95)
ROBICHAUX, Ursule m. Narcisse ROBICHAUX d. 25 Nov. 1897 at age 76 yrs. (Montegut Ch.: v.2, p.13)
ROBICHAUX, Viola Eliza (Augustin & Amanda HEBERT) b. 3 Sept. 1896 (Montegut Ch.: v.6, p.44)
ROBICHAUX, Wilson Pierre (Edwin & Victoria ROBICHAUX) b. 25 Aug. 1896 (Raceland Ch.: v.5, p.29)
ROBIN, Agnes Therese (Vincent & Stephanie TOMASSI) b. 13 Feb. 1896 (Larose Ch.: v.2, p.181)
ROBIN, Arthur (Vincent & Stephanie THOMMASSI) b. 19 Feb. 1898 (Larose Ch.: v.3, p.17)
ROBINSON, Andrew m. 27 May 1897 Bertha DOUGLASS (Houma Ct. Hse.: Mar. v.29 & 30, #428)
ROBINSON, Cordelia m. 22 Dec. 1898 John ROSE (Thib. Ct. Hse.: Mar. v.38, #322)
ROBINSON, Emelie (Ozeme & Mary LEBLANC) m. 14 July 1898 Julien PLAISANCE (Thib. Ct. Hse.: Mar. v.38, #221)
ROBINSON, Joseph m. 9 Jan. 1896 Phoebae HILLS (Thib. Ct. Hse.: Mar. v.35, #16)
ROBINSON, Louisa m. 13 Jan. 1898 Dave CASTLE (Houma Ct. Hse.: Mar. v.30 & 31, #202)
ROBINSON, Louisa m. 25 March 1898 Anatole BAPTISTE (Thib. Ct. Hse.: Mar. v.37, #132)
ROBINSON, Sallie m. 10 Jan. 1899 Elias REED (Thib. Ct. Hse.: Mar. v.38, #12)
ROBINSON, Sarah m. 22 June 1899 Thomas WILLIAMS (Thib. Ct. Hse.: Mar. v.39, #185)
ROBINSON, Selma m. 3 April 1899 Johnny JOHNSON (Houma Ct. Hse.: Mar. v.31 & 32, #384)
ROCK, George (Arthur & Celima PICHOFF) m. 15 Jan. 1897 Mary PIERCE (Thib. Ct. Hse.: Mar. v.37, #193)

ROCK, Georges (Arthur & Celina PICHOF) m. 15 July 1897 Marie PIERCE (Lockport Ch.: v.2, p.163)
ROCKWOOD, Charley m. 14 Oct. 1899 Mary FANIEL (Houma Ct. Hse.: Mar. v.31 & 32, #150)
RODAY, Julia (d.George & Rosalie PELEGRIN) m. 20 Jan. 1898 Justilien LEDET (Montegut Ch.: v.4, p.230)

RODDY (Sometimes: RHODE, RHODES, RHODEZ, RODES, RODY)

RODRIGUE (Sometimes: RODDERICK, RODRI, RODRIGUES, RODRIGUEZ, RODRY)
RODRIGUE, Adela Clotilde (Florestin & Angela ARCENAUX) b. 1 June 1898 (Thib. Ch.: v.7, p.499)
RODRIGUE, Adrien Noe (Leopol & Octavie PARR) b. 5 March 1896 (Lockport Ch.: v.3-A, #33)
RODRIGUE, Adrien Noe (Leopol & Octavie PARR) b. 5 March 1897 (Lockport Ch.: v.3, #33)
RODRIGUE, Aimee m. 29 Jan. 1898 Lami RODRIGUE (Thib. Ct. Hse.: Mar. v.37, #35)
RODRIGUE, Albert (Laurentie & Emelia LEGENDRE) m. 4 Aug. 1896 Louisiane BOUDREAU (Chackbay Ch.: v.1, p.28)
RODRIGUE, Albert (Laurentie & Emilia LEGENDRE) m. 4 Aug. 1896 Louisiane BOUDREAU (Thib. Ct. Hse.: Mar. v.36, #125)
RODRIGUE, Alice m. 20 Jan. 1898 Clemile BOURGEOIS (Thib. Ct. Hse.: Mar. v.37, #12)
RODRIGUE, Alice (Antoine & Palmyre MARTIN) m. 20 Jan. 1898 Clemile BOURGEOIS (Raceland Ch.: v.2, p.57)
RODRIGUE, Alice Angele (Faragus & Angelina BENOIT) b. 4 Feb. 1899 (Larose Ch.: v.3, p.36)
RODRIGUE, Alve (Augustin & Marie THEBE) b. 22 March 1897 (Chackbay Ch.: v.1, p.86)
RODRIGUE, Armand (Lester & Victoria LEGENDRE) m. 5 July 1897 Juliette PERCLE (Chackbay Ch.: v.1, p.45)
RODRIGUE, Armand (Lesteur & Victoria LEGENDRE) m. 15 June 1897 Juliette PERCLE (Thib. Ct. Hse.: Mar. v.36, #172)
RODRIGUE, Armand (Louis & Marie MARS) m. 11 Nov. 1899 Desiree CHIASSON (Thib. Ct. Hse.: Mar. v.39, #255)
RODRIGUE, Armand (Louis & Marie MARS) m. 11 Nov. 1899 Desiree CHIASSON (Chackbay Ch.: v.1, p.76)
RODRIGUE, Arthur (Hermogene & Ophelia CHIASSON) m. 9 Feb. 1899 Emilie HEBERT (Thib. Ct. Hse.: Mar. v.38, #51)
RODRIGUE, Arthur (Hermogene & Ophelia CHIASSON) m. 9 Feb. 1899 Emilie HEBERT (Thib. Ch.: v.14, p.263)
RODRIGUE, Arthur (Lesteur & Victoria LEGENDRE) m. 15 Feb. 1898 Marie BENOIT (Chackbay Ch.: v.1, p.56)
RODRIGUE, Arthur (Lesteur & Victoria LEGENDRE) m. 15 Feb. 1898 Mary BENOIT (Thib. Ct. Hse.: Mar. v.37, #68)
RODRIGUE, Augustin (Augustin & Marie THEBE) b. 23 Oct. 1898 (Chackbay Ch.: v.1, p.129)
RODRIGUE, Augustin Haustin (Symphore & Marie LOUPE) b. 29 Jan. 1899 (Chackbay Ch.: v.1, p.129)

RODRIGUE, Augustine d. 18 Dec. 1899 at age 13 yrs. (Thib. Ch.: v.3, p.246)
RODRIGUE, Camillia m. 29 April 1897 Oscar LEDET (Thib. Ct. Hse.: Mar. v.36, #129)
RODRIGUE, Claude Fernand (Ernest & Octavie BOUDREAUX) b. 26 July 1897 (Thib. Ch.: v.7, p.509)
RODRIGUE, Clay (Armogene & Orphelia CHIASSON) m. 2 Feb. 1897 Berthe CAILLOUET (Thib. Ct. Hse.: Mar. v.36, #52)
RODRIGUE, Clay (d.Hermogene & Ophelia CHIASSON) m. 2 Feb. 1897 Berthe CAILLOUET (Chackbay Ch.: v.1, p.38)
RODRIGUE, Clinse (Georges & Onilia LANDRY) b. 7 June 1898 (Chackbay Ch.: v.1, p.115)
RODRIGUE, Edmond Gabriel (Celestin & Marie CUROL) b. 27 Sept. 1896 (Larose Ch.: v.2, p.196)
RODRIGUE, Edna Rose (Oscar & Emma BREAUX) b. 21 Feb. 1896 (Houma Ch.: v.5, p.174)
RODRIGUE, Elesse Thomacile (Joseph & Josephine RODRIGUE) b. 9 April 1897 (Chackbay Ch.: v.1, p.86)
RODRIGUE, Eliane (Ursain & Marie LANDRY) b. 31 Aug. 1898 (Chackbay Ch.: v.1, p.118)
RODRIGUE, Ernestine Uzelia (Ferdinand & Louise SAVOIE) b. 11 Jan. 1897 (Lockport Ch.: v.3-A, #21)
RODRIGUE, Ernestine Uzelia (Ferdinand & Louise SAVOIE) b. 11 Jan. 1897 (Lockport Ch.: v.3, #21)
RODRIGUE, Florestan m. 28 Aug. 1897 Angea ARSENEAUX (Thib. Ct. Hse.: Mar. v.37, #224)
RODRIGUE, Florestan m. 30 Aug. 1897 Angela ARCENEAUX (Larose Ch.: v.3, p.6)
RODRIGUE, Florestan m. 30 Aug. 1897 Angela ARCENEAUX (Larose Ch.: v.4, p.53)
RODRIGUE, Francois Eugene (Felicien & Emelia LOQUET) b. 17 Sept. 1897; m. Mary R. HERNANDEZ on 17 June 1939. (Raceland Ch.: Bapt. Bk., v.5, p.54)
RODRIGUE, Francois Valentin (Symphore & Marie LOUPE) bt. 22 Feb. 1896 (Chackbay Ch.: v.1, p.60)
RODRIGUE, Horace Theophile (Faragus & Angelina BENOIT) b. 10 Feb. 1896 (Lockport Ch.: v.2, p.322)
RODRIGUE, Ida m. 1 April 1899 Dolph PARRO (Thib. Ct. Hse.: Mar. v.39, #128)
RODRIGUE, Ida (Celestin & Victoria MARTIN) m. 15 April 1899 Dolph PARRO (Raceland Ch.: v.2, p.93)
RODRIGUE, Jean Adelard (Joseph & Armantine RODRIGUE) b. 24 June 1898 (Chackbay Ch.: v.1, p.115)
RODRIGUE, Jean Louis (William & Dovelia PONTIF) b. 5 May 1898 (Theriot Ch.: v.2, p.25)
RODRIGUE, Jean Zephyr (Jean & Marie Delvina KRAEMER) b. 26 Aug. 1899 (Chackbay Ch.: v.1, p.142)
RODRIGUE, Jeanne Victoire (Louis & Euliska BOURG) b. 29 Dec. 1897 (Montegut Ch.: v.6, p.65)
RODRIGUE, Joseph m. 19 Feb. 1898 Evelina CROSSBY (Thib. Ct Hse.: Mar. v.37, #91)

RODRIGUE, Joseph (Celestin & Victorine MATERNE) m. 19 Feb. 1898 Evelina CROSSBY (Raceland Ch.: v.2, p.71)

RODRIGUE, Joseph (Symphore & Marie LOUP) m. 31 Jan. 1898 Cecile LEVRON (Chackbay Ch.: v.1, p.54)

RODRIGUE, Joseph (Symphore & Mary LOUPE) m. 31 Jan. 1898 Cecile LEVRON (Thib. Ct. Hse.: Mar. v.37, #36)

RODRIGUE, Joseph Allan (Aurelien & Eugenie RODRIGUE) b. 8 Sept. 1897 (Chackbay Ch.: v.1, p.94)

RODRIGUE, Joseph Bernard (Ozeme & Angele ARCENEAUX) b. 25 Sept. 1897 (Larose Ch.: v.3, p.6)

RODRIGUE, Joseph Bernard (Ozeme & Angele ARCENAUX) b. 25 Sept. 1897 (Larose Ch.: v.3, p.6)

RODRIGUE, Joseph Douglas (Sylvestre & Josephine TROSCLAIR) b. 13 Feb. 1899 (Chackbay Ch.: v.1, p.130)

RODRIGUE, Joseph Felicien (Lucien & Melite BENOIT) b. 16 Aug. 1898 (Chackbay Ch.: v.1, p.119)

RODRIGUE, Joseph Harison (Maximilien & Josephine LEDET) b. 26 Feb. 1896 (Lockport Ch.: v.3, #44)

RODRIGUE, Joseph Harry (Lucienne) b. 20 May 1899 (Lockport Ch.: v.3-A, #18) & v. 3, #19

RODRIGUE, Joseph Maurice (Eusebe & Arsene LEDET) b. 28 Sept. 1899 (Montegut Ch.: v.6, p.92)

RODRIGUE, Joseph Raymond (Eugene & Josephine RODRIGUE) b. 15 June 1897 (Chackbay Ch.: v.1, p.89)

RODRIGUE, Joseph Sureis (Lamy Archange & Aimee RODRIGUE) b. 3 Jan. 1899 (Chackbay Ch.: v.1, p.147)

RODRIGUE, Joseph Ursain (Albert & Odile HEBERT) b. 20 Dec. 1898 (Chackbay Ch.: v.1, p.126)

RODRIGUE, Josephine m. 10 July 1897 Haywood WILLIAMS (Thib. Ct. Hse.: Mar. v.37, #192)

RODRIGUE, Josephine Bernadette (Ozeme & Angele ARCENEAUX) b. 25 Sept. 1897 (Larose Ch.: v.3, p.6)

RODRIGUE, Lami m. 29 Jan. 1898 Aimee RODRIGUE (Thib. Ct. Hse.: Mar. v.37, #35)

RODRIGUE, Lea (Theophile & Louise THAUZIN) m. 26 June 1899 Albert ADAM (Thib. Ct. Hse.: Mar. v.39, #179)

RODRIGUE, Lea (Theophile & Louise THAUZIN) m. 26 June 1899 Albert ADAM (Chackbay Ch.: v.1, p.71)

RODRIGUE, Lise d. 2 Feb. 1897 at age 62 yrs. (Raceland Ch.: v.1, p.13)

RODRIGUE, Louisa (George & Devilia LANDRY) b. 25 Aug. 1896 (Chackbay Ch.: v.1, p.74)

RODRIGUE, Lovencia (Loventia & Amelia LEGENDRE) m. 19 April 1897 Placide LEGENDRE (Chackbay Ch.: v.1, p.42)

RODRIGUE, Lovencia (Lovincie & Amelia LEGENDRE) m. 19 April 1897 Placidre LEGENDRE (Thib. Ct. Hse.: Mar. v.36, #105)

RODRIGUE, Lucien (Celestin & Victorine MATHERNE) m. 17 Sept. 1896 Lovincia ESTIVAN (Thib. Ct. Hse.: Mar. v.36, #142)

RODRIGUE, Lucien (Elphege & Cecilia LEGENDRE) b. 17 Oct. 1897 (Chackbay Ch.: v.1, p.102)

RODRIGUE, Lucius (Celestin & Victorine MATHERNE) m. 17 Sept. 1896 Lovincia ESTIVANS (Thib. Ch.: v.14, p.99)
RODRIGUE, Malvina (Armogene & Ophelia CHIASSON) m. 22 Feb. 1897 Joachim BENOIT (Thib. Ct. Hse.: Mar. v.36, #85)
RODRIGUE, Malvina (d.Armogene & Ophelia CHIASSON) m. 22 Feb. 1897 Joachim BENOIT (Chackbay Ch.: v.1, p.40)
RODRIGUE, Marie Aimee (Abraham & Valentine LANDRY) b. 24 March 1898 (Chackbay Ch.: v.1, p.109)
RODRIGUE, Marie Anna (Adam & Eve TROSCLAIR) b. 6 Feb. 1898 (Chackbay Ch.: v.1, p.107)
RODRIGUE, Marie Elodia (Albert & Louisiane BOUDREAUX) b. 20 April 1897 (Chackbay Ch.: v.1, p.88)
RODRIGUE, Marie Eve (Eugene & Julia LANDRY) b. 13 Oct. 1899 (Chackbay Ch.: v.1, p.146)
RODRIGUE, Marie Julie (Euzebe & Arsene LEDET) b. 22 May 1897 (Montegut Ch.: v.6, p.56)
RODRIGUE, Marie Lena (William & Dovelia PONTIFF) b. 30 July 1896 (Theriot Ch.: v.1-B, p.104)
RODRIGUE, Marie Lydia (Michael & Josephine LEDET) b. 12 Aug. 1899 (Larose Ch.: v.3, p.44)
RODRIGUE, Marie Olivia (Florestan & Felicie RODRIGUE) m. 25 Nov. 1896 Ignace RICHARD (Thib. Ch.: v.14, p.101)
RODRIGUE, Marie Olivia (Florestan & Felicie RODRIGUE) m. 25 Nov. 1896 Ignace RICHARD (Thib. Ct. Hse.: Mar. v.36, #162)
RODRIGUE, Mathilde Eliza Francqise (Delphin & Nancy SAVOIE) b. 4 Oct. 1899 (Lockport Ch.: v.3-A, #5)
RODRIGUE, Mathilde Eliza Francoise (Delphin & Nancy SAVOIE) b. 4 Oct. 1899 (Lockport Ch.: v.3, #5)
RODRIGUE, Melodia (Telesphore & Louisa THAUZIN) m. 4 Oct. 1898 Louis ADAM (Chackbay Ch.: v.1, p.66)
RODRIGUE, Melodia (Telesphore & Louisa THAUZIN) m. 4 Oct. 1898 Louis ADAM (Thib. Ct. Hse.: Mar. v.38, #280)
RODRIGUE, Nora Zulma (Clay & Berthe CAILLOUET) b. 20 Nov. 1897 (Chackbay Ch.: v.1, p.99)
RODRIGUE, Notilia (Albert & Louisiane BOUDREAU) b. 1 Sept. 1898 (Chackbay Ch.: v.1, p.118)
RODRIGUE, O'Neil Callixte (Julien & Anastasie PARR) b. 25 April 1897 (Lockport Ch.: v.3, #50)
RODRIGUE, O'Neil Callixte (Julien & Anastasie PARR) b. 25 April 1897 (Lockport Ch.: v.3-A, #50)
RODRIGUE, Rene Felix (Armand & Juliette PERCLE) b. 30 May 1898 (Chackbay Ch.: v.1, p.114)
RODRIGUE, Rosa (Louis & Eulalie ESTEVE) m. 15 Aug. 1899 Eusebe FALGOUT (Thib. Ch.: v.14, p.290)
RODRIGUE, Rose (Eugenie & Julia LANDRY) b. 9 Oct. 1897 (Chackbay Ch.: v.1, p.100)
RODRIGUE, Selima m. 27 June 1896 Ozeme LOUP (Thib. Ct. Hse.: Mar. v.35, #108)
RODRIGUE, Selima m. 27 June 1896 Ozeme LOUP (Larose Ch.: v.3, p.3)

RODRIGUE, Selima m. 27 June 1896 Ozeme LOUP (Larose Ch.: v.4, p.91)
RODRIGUE, Tibicia (Eudore & Marie TROSCLAIR) m. 11 April 1898 Augustin LEGENDRE (Thib. Ct. Hse.: Mar. v.37, #135)
RODRIGUE, Tilicia (Isidore & Marie TROSCLAIR) m. 11 April 1898 Augustin LEGENDRE (Chackbay Ch.: v.1, p.59)
RODRIGUE, Victoria (Eusebe & Rosema LEDET) m. 2 Feb. 1899 Amedee DUPRE (Montegut Ch.: v.4, p.254)
RODRIGUE, William Eward (Josephine) b. 18 April 1897 (Raceland Ch.: v.5, p.48)
RODRIGUE, Zoe m. 6 Sept. 1897 Leo TRAHAN (Houma Ct. Hse.: Mar. v.29 & 30, #87)
RODRIGUE, Zoe (Antoine & Palimire MARTIN) m. 23 Sept. 1897 Leo TRAHAN (Houma Ch.: v.6-a, p.216)
RODRIGUE, Zoe (Jean & Marie Delma KRAEMER) b. 6 July 1897 (Chackbay Ch.: v.1, p.91)
RODRIGUES, Victoria (Eusebe & Arsenna LEDET) m. 14 Jan. 1899 Amedee DUPRE (Houma Ct. Hse.: Mar. v.30 & 31, #234)
RODRIGUEZ, Rosa (Louis & Eulalie ESTEVE) m. 15 Aug. 1899 Eusebe FALGOUT (Thib. Ct. Hse.: Mar. v.39, #206)
ROFFA, Rosa d. 8 Feb. 1899 at age 34 yrs. (Houma Ch.: v.3, p.21)

ROGER (Sometimes: ROGERE, ROGERS, ROGET)

ROGER, ----- boy d. 23 March 1897 at age 6 hrs. (Thi. Ch.: v.3, p.198)
ROGER, ----- child (Leon & Melia ORGERON) d. 18 Dec. 1898 at age 3 mths. (Larose Ch.: v.1, p.45)
ROGER, Adam Joseph (Leon & Emilia ORGERON) b. 21 Nov. 1899 (Larose Ch.: v.3, p.48)
ROGER, Adelia Elisabeth (Clebert & Marie RICHOUX) b. 20 Nov. 1898 (Larose Ch.: v.3, p.30)
ROGER, Ambroise Joseph (Felicien & Alphida NAQUIN) b. 8 July 1897 (Thib. Ch.: v.7, p.456)
ROGER, Augustin (Joseph & Alice ARCENAUX) m. 12 April 1899 Odalie HEBERT (Thib. Ct Hse.: Mar. v.39, #124)
ROGER, Augustin (Joseph & Alice ARCENAUX) m. 12 April 1899 Odalie HEBERT (Lockport Ch.: v.2, p.205)
ROGER, Azema Odile (Henri & Felicia GUILLOT) b. 13 July 1898 (Thib. Ch.: v.7, p.555)
ROGER, Bernadette (Leon & Melia ORGERON) d. 12 May 1898 at age 18 mths. (Larose Ch.: v.1, p.43)
ROGER, Bernadette Malvina (Leon & Melia ORGERON) b. 27 Sept. 1896 (Larose Ch.: v.2, p.186)
ROGER, Brigitte (Francois & Aiglomier MOUTARDIER) m. 28 Dec. 1899 Joseph Albert BOUDREAUX (Houma Ct. Hse.: Mar. v.31 & 32, #211)
ROGER, Catherine Eleonore (Thomas H. & Verna KNOBLOCH) b. 25 Nov. 1897 (Thib. Ch.: v.7, p.526)
ROGER, Cecilia Aline d. 29 Oct. 1896 at age 13 mths. (Thib. Ch.: v.3, p.190)

ROGER, Clebert m. 24? Jan. 1896 Maria RICHOUX (Larose Ch.: v.2, p.188)
ROGER, Clebert m. 25 Jan. 1896 Marie RICHOUX (Larose Ch.: v.3, p.2)
ROGER, Clebert m. 25 Jan. 1896 Marie RICHOUX (Thib. Ct. Hse.: Mar. v.35, #25)
ROGER, Clemile Eugene (Desire & Laurenza ECHETE) b. 27 June 1897 (Larose Ch.: v.3, p.11)
ROGER, Cletus d. 23 Jan. 1896 at age 4 yrs. (Lockport Ch.: v.1, #3)
ROGER, Davis Joseph (Joseph & Odillia BOURGEOIS) b. 18 Jan. 1899 (Larose Ch.: v.3, p.36)
ROGER, Denis (Francois & Marie BOURGEOIS) m. 15 July 1897 Ida TOUPS (Lockport Ch.: v.2, p.163)
ROGER, Denis (Francois & Mary BOURGEOIS) m. 15 July 1897 Ida TOUPS (Thib. Ct. Hse.: Mar. v.37, #190)
ROGER, Dorina (Alex & Elvina TRAHAN) m. 28 March 1898 Isaac MARTIN (Houma Ct. Hse: Mar. v.30 & 31, #358)
ROGER, Dorina (Alexandre & Eloina TRAHAN) m. 21 April 1898 Isaac MARTIN (Montegut Ch.: v.4, p.242)
ROGER, Elda Bernadette (Albert & Louise ARCENAUX) b. 21 Feb. 1896 (Lockport Ch.: v.2, p.324)
ROGER, Elisca (Joseph & Odellia BOURGEOIS) d. 27 Feb. 1899 at age 3 yrs. (Larose Ch.: v.1, p.51)
ROGER, Eulalie d. March 1894 (Jean Baptiste) m. Adam MALBROUGH Children listed: Emilie, aged 9; Virginia, aged 7; Wilson, aged 6. Inventory: 1 Aug. 1898. (Thib. Ct. Hse.: Succ. #1542)
ROGER, Faustin Maurice (Adam & Nathalie ORGERON) b. 15 Feb. 1896 (Larose Ch.: v.2, p.181)
ROGER, Fernand (Joseph & Alice ARCENAUX) m. 18 June 1896 Clementine GUILLOT (Lockport Ch.: v.2, p.151)
ROGER, Fernand (Joseph & Alice ARCENAUX) m. 18 June 1896 Clementina GUILLOT (Thib. Ct. Hse.: Mar. v.35, #97)
ROGER, Francois (Joachim & Eulalie LEE) m. 30 Jan. 1899 Alexine PLAISANCE (Thib. Ct. Hse.: Mar. v.38, #35)
ROGER, Francois (Joachim & Eulalie LEE) m. 30 Jan. 1899 Alexina PLAISANCE (Larose Ch.: v.4, p.34)
ROGER, Francois (Joachim & Eulalie LEE) m. 30 Jan. 1899 Alexina PLAISANCE (Larose Ch.: v.3, p.11)
ROGER, Gratia d. 29 June 1898 at age 1 yr. & 1 mth. (Thib. Ch.: v.3, p.216)
ROGER, Henri (Jean Baptiste & Azema BOURQUE) m. 25 Jan. 1897 Felicia GUILLOTE (Thib. Ct. Hse.: Mar. v.36, #25)
ROGER, Henri (Jean Baptiste & Azema BOURQUE) m. 25 Jan. 1897 Felicie GUILLOTE (Thib. Ch.: v.14, p.117)
ROGER, Idoline (Joseph & Estellina GUILLOT) b. 21 June 1898 (Thib. Ch.: v.7, p.554)
ROGER, Joseph Onesime Danimas (Francois & Alexina PLAISANCE) b. 19 Oct. 1899 (Larose Ch.: v.3, p.46)

ROGER, Joseph Alfred (Henri & Felicia GUILLOT) b. 22 Oct. 1897 (Thib. Ch.: v.7, p.470)
ROGER, Juliette (Joseph & Stellina GUILLOT) b. 18 Dec. 1896 (Thib. Ch.: v.7, p.431)
ROGER, Laura (Adrien & Octavie BRAUX) m. 26 Sept. 1898 Raoul BAYE (Thib. Ct. Hse.: Mar. v.38, #282)
ROGER, Laura (Adrien & Octavie BRAUX) m. 26 Sept. 1898 Raoul BAYE (Thib. Ch.: v.14, p.225)
ROGER, Leon Jr. m. 1 June 1896 Melia ORGERON (Thib. Ct. Hse.: Mar. v.35, #91)
ROGER, Leontia (Xavier & Nina CLEMENT) m. 25 April 1899 Augustin MIRE (Thib. Ch.: v.14, p.273)
ROGER, Leontia (Xavier & Ninia CLEMENT) m. 25 April 1899 Augustin MIRE (Thib. Ct. Hse.: Mar. v.39, #145)
ROGER, Lina Marie (Klebert & Marie RICHOU) b. 29 Nov. 1896 (Lockport Ch.: v.3, #1)
ROGER, Lina Marie (Klebert & Marie RICHOU) b. 29 Nov. 1896 (Lockport Ch.: v.3-A, #1)
ROGER, Logan m. 23 Feb. 1899 Edward A. RICHE (Thib. Ct. Hse.: Mar. v.39, #101)
ROGER, Louise Elisca (Joseph & Odillia BOURGEOIS) b. 4 April 1896 (Larose Ch.: v.2, p.191)
ROGER, Marie (Jean Baptiste & Azema BOURQUE) m. 16 Aug. 1898 Marcilien BOUDREAUX (Thib. Ct. Hse.: Mar. v.38, #249)
ROGER, Marie (Jean Baptiste & Azema BOURQUE) m. 16 Aug. 1898 Marcelien BOUDREAU (Thib. Ch.: v.14, p.214)
ROGER, Marie Anne Dalmas d. 15 Feb. 1899 at age 1 yr. (Thib. Ch.: v.3, p.228)
ROGER, Mary Verna (Thomas Henry & Verna Flavie KNOBLOCH) b. 12 Dec. 1899 (Thib. Ch.: v.7, p.584)
ROGER, Maurice Henri (Albert & Augustine DONALD) b. 14 March 1896 (Thib. Ch.: v.7, p.396)
ROGER, Phelonise (Francois & Marie BOURGEOIS) m. 4 July 1898 Michael BARRIOS (Thib. Ct. Hse.: Mar. v.38, #217)
ROGER, Phelonize (Francois & Marie BOURGEOIS) m. 4 July 1898 Michel BARRIOS (Lockport Ch.: v.2, p.191 & 192)
ROGER, Pierre Louis (Theophile & Amanda BRAUX) b. 6 March 1899 (Thib. Ch.: v.7, p.540)
ROGER, Regina Virginie (Adam & Nathalie ORGERON) b. 8 July 1898 (Larose Ch.: v.3, p.23)
ROGGERO, Maria (Simon & Guiseppa LAMONICA) b. 6 March 1897 (Thib. Ch.: v.7, p.443)
ROGIERE, Grazzia (Guiseppe & Rosa TERENALA) b. 11 Feb. 1899 (Thib. Ch.: v.7, p.595)
ROGIERE, Maria Rita (Ciro & Gelorina DIVARCO) b. 2 May 1899 (Thib. Ch.: v.7, p.603)
ROIA, Biaggio m. 31 Jan. 1898 Francesca MERLO (Houma Ct. Hse.: Mar. v.30 & 31, #263)
ROIA, Biaggio (Bardasse & Margarita GOLATA) m. 12 Feb. 1898 Guisappa MERLO (Houma Ch.: v.6-a, p.231)

ROIA, Giovanne m. 3 Feb. 1898 Antonia CIACCIO (Houma Ct. Hse.: Mar. v.30 & 31, #273)
ROIA, J. d. 31 Oct. 1898 at age 4 days (Houma Ch.: v.3, p.19)
ROLLINS, Minty m. 12 June 1899 Henry WILBERT (Houma Ct. Hse.: Mar. v.31 & 32, #41)
ROLLINS, Willie m. 6 Feb. 1899 Isham WILLIAMS (Houma Ct. Hse.: Mar. v.31 & 32, #316)

ROMAGOSA (Sometimes: RAMAGOS, RAMAGOSSA, RAMOGOSSA, ROMAGOSE)

ROMAGOSA, Mabel Gertrude (Fernand & Lucia RICHARD) b. 16 Nov. 1899 (Thib. Ch.: v.8, p.18)
ROMAGOSA, Pauline Lucie (Fernand & Lucia RICHARD) b. 8 Feb. 1898 (Thib. Ch.: v.7, p.484)
ROMAIN, John Sidney (Peter & Emma LANDRY) b. 10 April 1898 (Chacahoula Ch.: Gibson Records: Mar. Bk., v.1, #45)
ROMAIN, John Sidney (Peter & Emma LANDRY) b. 10 April 1898 (Chacahoula Ch.: Gibson Ch.: v.2, p.128)
ROMAN, Nora Anastasie (Augustin & Eugenie DUPLANTIS) b. 29 Sept. 1897 (Houma Ch.: v.5, p.191)
ROMANA, Antonia (Pietro & Vincenza MANGIARASINA) b. 6 Feb. 1899 (Houma Ch.: v.5, p.240)

ROME (Sometimes: RHOME, RHUM, ROM)

ROME, Alcide Joseph (Henri & Virginie UZET) b. 27 July 1897 (Thib. Ch.: v.7, p.462)
ROME, Clarence Abel (Cleophas & Euphemie FOLSE) b. 17 Feb. 1899 (Raceland Ch.: v.5, p.91)
ROME, Henry (Victorin & Louisa CAN or CARR) m. 20 Aug. 1896 Virginie USE (Thib. Ct. Hse.: Mar. v.36, #129)
ROME, Henry (Victorin & Louisa PARR) m. 20 Aug. 1896 Virginie USEE (Chackbay Ch.: v.1, p.29)
ROME, Lucile (Cleophas & Euphemie FOLSE) b. 1 Nov. 1896 (Raceland Ch.: v.5, p.33)
ROME, Marie Sedae Utopia (Gustave & Martha BOURGEOIS) b. 10 Jan. 1897 (Raceland Ch.: v.5, p.44)
RONQUILLE, Hamilcar Augustin (Joseph & Rosella DUBOIS) b. 26 Sept. 1896 (Chacahoula Ch.: v.4, p.5)
RONQUILLE, Leon Euchere (Joseph & Rosella DUBOIS) b. 16 Nov. 1898 (Chacahoula Ch.: v.4, p.14)
RONQUILLE, Leonard Euchere (Joseph & Rosella DUBOIS) b. 16 Nov. 1898 (Chacahoula Ch.: v.4, p.14)
ROODS, Shelton m. 27 Oct. 1898 Lena JACKSON (Thib. Ct. Hse.: Mar. v.38, #304)
ROOKS, Wesley m.17 Jan. 1898 Margaret MADISON (Houma Ct. Hse.: Mar. v.30 & 31, #218)
ROOSHA, Rina m. 31 July 1897 Jacob MORGAN (Houma Ct. Hse.: Mar. v.29 & 30, #76)
ROPER, Marguerite m. Valery BREAUX Children listed: Eliska m. Justilien FORET; Mathilde m. Marcellin FORET;

Marguerite m. Theodule BOUDREAUX; Marcelline m. Manouche LEBLANC; Donatte; Scholastique; Frank. Inventory: 8 July 1898. (Thib. Ct. Hse.: Succ. #1540)

ROPOLO, Santo (Isidore & Angela NAPOLI) b. 12 Aug. 1898 (Thib. Ch.: v.7, p.508)

ROQUES, Emile m. 15 Aug. 1899 Claire Louise BENSON (Thib. Ct. Hse.: Mar. v.39, #211)

ROSALIA, Scimeca (Nicaccio & Antonina LUZZIA) m. 28 Oct. 1899 Ange SALVATORE (Thib. Ct. Hse.: Mar. v.39, #247)

ROSE, Helene Melanie (Philippe & Philomene BARIAUX) b. 22 Oct. 1896 (Chackbay Ch.: v.1, p.77)

ROSE, John m. 22 Dec. 1898 Cordelia ROBINSON (Thib. Ct. Hse.: Mar. v.38, #322)

ROSE, Joseph Jr. m. 19 Jan. 1899 Alice SANTEE (Houma Ct. Hse.: Mar. v.30 & 31, #258)

ROSS (Sometimes: ROOS, ROSSET)

ROSS, Corinne m. 31 Jan. 1896 Stelite GIROIR (Houma Ct. Hse.: Mar. v.28, #428)

ROSS, Edeoin (Alford & Eunice BUFORD) m. 29 June 1896 Eloise A. KING (Houma Ch.: Epis. Ch.: v.1, p.340)

ROSS, Edwin (Alfred & Eunice BUFORD) m. 26 June 1896 Louisa KING (Houma Ct. Hse.: Mar. v.29 & 30, #97)

ROSS, Edwin 22 yrs. old (Alfred & Eunice BUFORD) m. 29 June 1896 Eloise A. KING (Gibson Ch.: Epis. Ch.: v.1, p.134)

ROSS, Edwine Joseph Murphey (Edwin & Eloise KING) b. 5 July 1897 (Houma Ch.: Epis. Ch.: v.1, p.114)

ROSS, Gracie m. 10 July 1897 Peyton HAWKINS (Houma Ct. Hse.: Mar. v.29 & 30, #64)

ROSS, Joseph m. 12 Jan. 1899 Eliza WILSON (Houma Ct. Hse.: Mar. v.30 & 31, #218)

ROSS, Juanita Rebecca (Edwin & Louisa Annie King ROSS) b. 10 Nov. 1898 (Houma Ch.: Epis. Ch.: v.1, p.122)

ROSS, Martha m.15 Jan. 1896 Frank CLENNON (Houma Ct. Hse.: Mar. v.28, #388)

ROSS, Polly d. 24 Sept. 1899; m. d.Randall ALLEN Child listed: Clara. Petition for administration: 27 Sept. 1899. (Thib. Ct. Hse.: Succ. #1588)

ROSSI, Albert m. 8 Sept. 1897 Celeste SAVOIE (Larose Ch.: v.3, p.4)

ROSSI, Albert m. 8 Sept. 1897 Celeste SAVOIE (Larose Ch.: v.4, p.54)

ROSSI, Albert Michel m. 26 Dec. 1896 Celeste SAVOIE, 21 yrs. (Thib. Ct. Hse.: Mar. v.36, #170)

ROSSI, Paul Rita (Robert & Cecilia BREAUX) b. 6 Aug. 1896 (Lockport Ch.: v.2, p.334)

ROSSIGNOL, Alice Rita (Joseph & Athenaise BARILLEAUX) b. 19 Oct. 1896 (Lockport Ch.: v.3, #9)

ROSSIGNOL, Alice Zita (Joseph & Athenaise BARILLEAUX) b. 19 Oct. 1896 (Lockport Ch.: v.3-A, #9)

ROSSO, Cristina d. 27 Sept. 1899 at age 52 yrs. (Chacahoula Ch.: Gibson Ch.: v.2, p.183)
ROSYN, Mathilde Camelia (John & Camelia LAMOUREUX) b. 3 Aug. 1897 (Thib. Ch.: v.7, p.513)
ROTOLOES, Guiseppe Ropolo (Salvatore & Maria TONNAZZO) b. 18 Jan. 1898 (Thib. Ch.: v.7, p.482)
ROUBION, Clement d. 25 June 1899 at age 5 yrs. (Raceland Ch.: v.1, p.25)
ROUEN, Joseph Nolan (Augustin & Eugenie DUPLANTIS) b. 20 Jan. 1899 (Montegut Ch.: v.6, p.83)
ROUEN, Nora (Loulou & Eugenie DUPLANTIS) d. 9 May 1898 at age 8 mths. (Montegut Ch.: v.2, p.16)
ROUGER, Marie Anne Beatrice (Damase & Sidney JHON) b. 15 Jan. 1899 (Thib. Ch.: v.7, p.530)
ROUGERON, Joseph (Sergure & Julianne HENRY) b. 28 Oct. 1897; m. Noemi Abadie on 22 Feb. 1922. (Houma Ch.: Bapt. Bk., v.5, p.192)
ROUNDS, Arty or Arthur m. 24 Jan. 1898 Louisa JACKSON (Thib. Ct. Hse.: Mar. v.37, #52)

ROUSSEAU (Sometimes: ROUSSAU, ROUSSEAUX)

ROUSSEAU, Lucia Armelise (Joseph & Marie GUYET) b. 22 July 1899 (Chackbay Ch.: v.1, p.139)
ROUSSEAU, Marie Agnies (Joseph & Marie GUYOL) b. 29 Aug. 1896 (Chackbay Ch.: v.1, p.87)
ROUSSEAU, Marie Francoise Claire (Ozemee & Marie Odile DARDEN) b. 8 Aug. 1897 (Thib. Ch.: v.7, p.462)

ROUSSEL (Sometimes: ROUSEL, ROUSSELL)

ROUSSEL, Albert (Arthur & Justine GRABERT) m. 27 Jan. 1899 Bernadette BAUDOUIN (Lockport Ch.: v.2, p.213)
ROUSSEL, Annie (Romuald & Marie GAUTHREAUX) b. 10 Jan. 1899 (Chacahoula Ch.: v.4, p.19)
ROUSSEL, Augustin Harry (Augustin & Eletia BAUDOUIN) b. 20 Dec. 1897 (Raceland Ch.: v.5, p.60)
ROUSSEL, Celestine Aline (Augustin & Elecia BEAUDOUIN) b. 11 June 1899 (Raceland Ch.: v.5, p.98)
ROUSSEL, Earl Joseph (Alfred & Corinne BOUDREAUX) b. 27 July 1897 (Chacahoula Ch.: v.4, p.23)
ROUSSEL, Elvire (Arthur & Justine GRABERT) m. 29 Jan. 1898 Edouard ST. PIERRE (Thib. Ct. Hse.: Mar. v.37, #83)
ROUSSEL, Elvire (Arthur & Justine GRABERT) m. 29 Jan. 1898 Edouard ST. PIERRE (Lockport Ch.: v.2, p.181 & 182)
ROUSSEL, Florantine (Arthur & Justine GRABERT) m. 1 Feb. 1896 Gustave SAINT PE (Thib. Ct. Hse.: Mar. v.35, #8)
ROUSSEL, Florentine (Arthur & Justine GRABERT) m. 1 Feb. 1896 Gustave SAMPE (Lockport Ch.: v.2, p.145)
ROUSSEL, Herbert (Romuald & Mary GAUTHREAUX) m. 10 May 1899 Effie LEBLANC (Chacahoula Ch.: v.1, p.70 [90])
ROUSSEL, Herbert (Roumald & Mary GAUTREAUX) m. 21 Jan. 1899 Effie LEBLANC (Houma Ct. Hse.: Mar. v.30 & 31, #264)

ROUSSEL, Lilian m. 3 Feb. 1898 Paul Emile SCOTT (Thib. Ct. Hse.: Mar. v.37, #70)
ROUSSEL, Lilian (Louis & Georgina GRIMAS) m. 3 Feb. 1898 Paul Emile SCOTT (Raceland Ch.: v.2, p.64)
ROUSSEL, May Carry (Leopold & Zurma LEONARD) b. 11 Aug. 1896 (Thib. Ch.: v.7, p.412)
ROUSSEL, Remy (William & Marie TROXCLAIR) m. 17 July 1899 Albertine FALGOUT (Raceland Ch.: v.2, p.101)
ROUSSEL, Remy or Reme m. 14 July 1899 Albertine FALGOUT (Thib. Ct. Hse.: Mar. v.39, #199)
ROUSSEL, Victor Laurence (Adrien & Irma GAUTHREAUX) b. 23 Dec. 1898 (Chacahoula Ch.: v.4, p.17)
ROUSSEL, Victorine Mabel (John & Louise LEVERT) b. 8 Jan. 1897 (Thib. Ch.: v.7, p.439)
ROUVERA, Marie m. 16 Aug. 1898 Ben THOMPSON (Thib. Ct. Hse.: Mar v.38, #255)
ROUVERT, Julia m. ----- BREEN d. 9 March 1898 at age 61 yrs. (Thib. Ch.: v.3, p.212)

ROUX (Sometimes: ROUSSE)
ROUX, Etienne 26 yrs. old m. 11 July 1896 Antoinette GALIANO, 15 yrs. (Thib. Ct. Hse.: Mar. v.36, #122)
ROUX, Louisa m. 27 April 1899 Raphael GALLIANO (Thib. Ct. Hse.: Mar. v.39, #158)
ROUX, Marcelitte Leonise (Oleus & Olympe BOURG) b. 13 Jan. 1897 (Larose Ch.: v.3, p.10)
ROUX, Paul Theodule (Oleus & Olympe BOURG) b. 2 Nov. 1899 (Larose Ch.: v.3, p.56)
ROUX, Thomas Onesime (Louis & Adolphine CHERAMIE) b. 15 Aug. 1896 (Larose Ch.: v.2, p.196)
ROVERT, Julia d. 8 March 1898; m. Thomas BREEN Notice to heirs of probate of will: 14 March 1898. (Thib. Ct. Hse.: Succ. #1529)

ROWNTREE (Sometimes: ROUNDTREE)
ROWNTREE, Gertrude Odile (Valmont & Marie ONCALE) b. 27 June 1897 (Thib. Ch.: v.7, p.455)
ROWNTREE, Joseph Noe (Willy & Ernestine BREAUX) b. 20 March 1898 (Thib. Ch.: v.7, p.491)
ROWNTREE, Lydia widow of William CALLOWAY m. 14 Nov. 1898 Alfred DAIGLE (Thib. Ct. Hse.: Mar. v.38, #308)
ROWNTREE, Lydia (Joseph & Velina BOUDRAUX) m. 24 Nov. 1898 Alfred DAIGLE (Thib. Ch.: v.14, p.230)
ROWNTREE, Magnolia Marie m. Albert MARONGE d. 2 Dec. 1897 at age 25 yrs. & 9 mths. (Thib. Ch.: v.3, p.208)
ROWNTREE, Malvina (Thomas & Marie ESTIVEN) m. 16 Jan. 1899 Philippe DUGAS (Thib. Ct. Hse.: Mar. v.38, #15)
ROWNTREE, Malvina (Thomas & Marie ESTIVEN) m. 16 Jan. 1899 Philippe DUGAS (Thib. Ch.: v.14, p.238)
ROWNTREE, Marie d. 29 July 1898 at age 7 days (Thib. Ch.: v.3, p.218)

ROWNTREE, Marie (Thomas & Lucilia ESTIVEN) m. 31 Jan. 1899 James DAIGLE (Thib. Ct. Hse.: Mar. v.38, #23)
ROWNTREE, Marie (Thomas & Lucilia ESTIVEN) m. 31 Jan. 1899 James DAIGLE (Thib. Ch.: v.14, p.248)
ROWNTREE, Willie m. 28 July 1897 Ernestine BREAUX (Thib. Ct. Hse.: Mar. v.37, #201)
ROWNTREE, Willie (Sam & Mathilde BERGERON) m. 6 Aug. 1897 Ernestine BREAUX (Thib. Ch.: v.14, p.156)
ROY, Edmond John (Francois & Cleopatre PASI) b. 30 Oct. 1899 (Thib. Ch.: v.8, p.46)
RUDLEY, Katy m. 25 June 1898 John TAYLOR (Houma Ct. Hse.: Mar. v.30 & 31, #35)
RUFFIN, Willie m. 15 April 1897 Rose MATTHEWS (Houma Ct. Hse.: Mar. v.29 & 30, #383)
RUFFINS, Viney m. 18 Feb. 1898 Alfred MALLET (Houma Ct. Hse.: Mar. v.30 & 31, #307)
RUGERRA, Guiseppe (Gerome & Guiseppa LAMORICA) b. 3 Oct. 1899 (Thib. Ch.: v.7, p.568)
RUSSELL, Frank (Frank & Francisca RESLA) m. 20 May 1899 Osciana BERGERON (Raceland Ch.: v.2, p.97)
RUSSELL, Joseph m. 13 June 1898 Leonide WILLIAMS (Houma Ct. Hse.: Mar. v.30 & 31, #17)
RUTHERFORD, Alicia m. 6 April 1899 Samuel SARGEANT (Thib. Ct. Hse.: Mar. v.39, #135)
RYAN, Walter Edouard (Walter & Kate FOSTER) b. 31 July 1898 (Raceland Ch.: v.5., p.77)

"S"

SABATIER, Joseph d. 29 Jan. 1899 at age 68 yrs. (Thib. Ch.: v.3, p.226)

SAGONA, Antonino (Antoinno & Vitta CICIA) b. 12 July 1899 (Houma Ch.: v.5, p.250)

SAIK, Abraham Joseph (Ayoub & Bhaggy SAIK) b. 5 Feb. 1898 (Chacahoula Ch.: Gibson Records: Mar. Bk., v.1, #36)

SAIK, Abraham Joseph (Ayoub & Bhagy SAIK) b. 5 Feb. 1898 (Chacahoula Ch.: Gibson Ch.: v.2, p.122)

SAINT AMAND, Genevieve (Oscar & Genevieve ADAM) b. 14 March 1897 (Raceland Ch.: v.5, p.49)

SAINT BERNARD, Rev. Mother also known as Angelique GUERIN. She was the Superior General of the Mont Carmel nuns. d. 1 Feb. 1897 at age 78 yrs. & 8 mths. (Thib. Ch.: v.3, p.196)

SAINT CLAIR (Sometimes: SAINT CLAIRE)

SAINT MARTIN, Camille (Armand & Louise TERRIOT) m. 4 Nov. 1896 Emma M. GOUAUX (Houma Ch.: v.6-a, p.184)

SAINT MARTIN, Camille M. m. 28 Oct. 1896 Emma M. GOUAUX (Houma Ct. Hse.: Mar. v.29 & 30, #181)

SAINT MARTIN, Defise (Armand & Louisa THERIOT) m. Jan. - Feb. 1899 Leonce FANGUY (Theriot Ch.: v.1-B, p.6)

SAINT MARTIN, Jean Xavier m. 26 Jan. 189 Eleonore THERIOT (Theriot Ch.: v.1-B, p.3-A)

SAINT MARTIN, Lucille Marie Aline (Camil & Emma GOUAUX) b. 24 Oct. 1899; m. Alston McNEILL on 22 March 1930. (Houma Ch.: Bapt. Bk., v.5, p.260)

SAINT MARTIN, Marie Inez (Xavier & Elenore THERIOT) b. 17 Aug. 1899 (Theriot Ch.: v.2, p.47)

SAINT MARTIN, Orfise m. 25 Jan. 1899 Leonce FANGUY (Houma Ct. Hse.: Mar. v.30 & 31, #281)

SAINT MARTIN, Palmyra m. Victor RICHARD d. 11 Feb. 1896 at age 68 yrs. (Thib. Ch.: v.3, p.178)

SAINT MARTIN, Xavier (d.A. & Louisa THERIOT) m. 20 Feb. 1898 Eleonore THERIOT (Theriot Ch.: v.1-B, p.2)

SAINT MARTIN, Xavier H. (Amand & Louisa THERIOT) m. 18 Feb. 1898 Eleanora THERIOT (Houma Ct. Hse.: Mar. v.30 & 31, #308)

SAINT MARTIN, Yvette Louise (Camel & Emma GOUAUX) b. 6 April 1898 (Houma Ch.: v.5, p.205)

SAINT PE (Sometimes: SAINPEE, SAINTPEE)

SAINT PE, Gustave (Gustave & Julienne BOURGEOIS) m. 1 Feb. 1896 Florantine ROUSSEL (Thib. Ct. Hse.: Mar. v.35, #8)

SAINT PE, Lea (Frank & Laura DUFRENE) m. 24 April 1897 Emile PIERCE (Thib. Ct. Hse.: Mar. v.36, #100)

SAINT PE, Leo (Frank & Laura DUFRENE) m. 28 Jan. 1899 Ernestine THERIOT (Thib. Ct. Hse.: Mar. v.38, #24)

SAINT PE, Leo (Frank & Laura DUFRENE) m. 28 Jan. 1899 Ernestine THERIOT (Lockport Ch.: v.2, p.199)
SAINT PIERRE, Edouard d. 17 Feb. 1899 at age 3 mths. (Lockport Ch.: v.1, #6)
SAINT PIERRE, Edouard (Jean & Eulalie SAMPE) m. 29 Jan. 1898 Elvire ROUSSEL (Thib. Ct. Hse.: Mar. v.37, #83)
SAINT PIERRE, Edouard (Jean & Eulalie SAMPE) m. 29 Jan. 1898 Elvire ROUSSEL (Lockport Ch.: v.2, p.181 & 182)
SAINT PIERRE, Edward (Menonce & Marguerite CHOUESS) m. 12 Feb. 1898 Ernestine THERIOT (Thib. Ct. Hse.: Mar. v.37, #32)
SAINT PIERRE, Elisa Marie (Wilfred & Sara WILLIAM) b. 25 July 1896 (Larose Ch.: v.2, p.196)
SAINT PIERRE, Elmire William (Etienne & Mary WILLIAM) b. 15 Oct. 1897 (Larose Ch.: v.3, p.7)
SAINT PIERRE, Felix (Wuilly) d. 28 March 1898 at age 3 mths. (Lockport Ch.: v.1, #8)
SAINT PIERRE, Joseph Higues (Paul & Louise PLAISANCE) b. 20 March 1896 (Lockport Ch.: v.2, p.326)
SAINT PIERRE, Josephine (Melance & Marguerite CHONES) m. 1 Feb. 1896 Wuilliam DUFRENE (Lockport Ch.: v.2, p.145)
SAINT PIERRE, Josephine (Melance & Marguerite CHOUES) m. 1 Feb. 1896 Wuilliam DUFRENE (Thib. Ct. Hse.: Mar. v.35, #22)
SAINT PIERRE, Leon (Joseph) d. 29 Jan. 1898 at age 3 yrs. (Lockport Ch.: v.1, #1)
SAINT PIERRE, Marie Evigilia (Alfred & Sara WILLIAM) b. 19 Dec. 1899 (Larose Ch.: v.3, p.50)
SAINT PIERRE, Marie Julie (Paul & Louise PLAISANCE) b. 30 Aug. 1898 (Lockport Ch.: v.3-A, #2)
SAINT PIERRE, Marie Julie (Paul & Louise PLAISANCE) b. 30 Aug. 1898 (Lockport Ch.: v.3, #2)
SAINT PIERRE, Victoria Delphine (E. & Delphine OLIVIER) b. 19 Feb. 1899 (Lockport Ch.: v.3, #11)
SAINT PIERRE, Victoria Delphine (Eo & Delphine OLIVIER) b. 19 Feb. 1899 (Lockport Ch.: v.3-A, #11)
SAINT PIERRE, Wuilfred (Joseph) d. 19 Aug. 1896 at age 5 mths. (Lockport Ch.: v.1, #15)
SALARDINO, Pipino (Tana & Antonina CARONA) b. 21 Aug. 1899 (Houma Ch.: v.5, p.253)
SALEM, Cecile m. Florence BEAUDOIN d. 18 March 1898 at age 75 yrs. (Larose Ch.: v.1, p.43)
SALEMINE, Josephina (Cajetano & Maria ZABBIA) b. 23 Feb. 1899 (Houma Ch.: v.5, p.239)
SALLNORA, Maria (Pietero & Calogerot LABELLA) b. 6 Jan. 1898 (Houma Ch.: v.5, p.195)
SALOMON, Jenie Anjus (Roberts & Jane GRIER) b. 6 Jan. 1898 (Thib. Ch.:v.7, p.486)
SALVATORE, Ange (Vincenzo & Francisca SANZELLA) m. 28 Oct. 1899 Scimeca ROSALIA (Thib. Ct. Hse.: Mar. v.39, #247)

SALVATORE, Ange (Vincenzo & Francisca SANZELLA) m. 28 Oct. 1899 Rosalie SCIMECCA (Thib. Ch.: v.14, p.306)

SAMANI (Sometimes: LAMANI, SAMANIE, SAMANY, SEMAIN, SEMANI, ZAMANI)

SAMANI, Annie m. 16 May 1896 Joseph Felicien FALGOUT (Houma Ct. Hse.: Mar. v.29 & 30, #73)

SAMANI, Annie (Paul & Virginie CLARK) m. 18 May 1896 Joseph Felicien FALGOUT (Houma Ch.: v.6-a, p.175)

SAMANI, Cordilia Edna (Cordelius & Lesilia LADOUCEUR) b. 24 Sept. 1898 (Thib. Ch.: v.7, p.575)

SAMANI, Joseph Wilson (Jacson & Vitalie THIBODEAU) b. 29 March 1898 (Houma Ch.: v.5, p.206)

SAMANI, Maria (Philippo & Maria OLOTTE) b. 1 Dec. 1898 (Houma Ch.: v.5, p.229)

SAMANI, Wallace (Paul & Jennie CLARK) m. 26 Dec. 1899 Laura LEBOEUF (Houma Ct. Hse.: Mar. v.31 & 32, #201)

SAMPE (See also: SAINT PE)

SAMPE, ----- child (Gustave) d. 26 Aug. 1896 at age about 1 mth. (Lockport Ch.: v.1, #17)

SAMPE, Gustave (Gustave & Julienne BOURGEOIS) m. 1 Feb. 1896 Florentine ROUSSEL (Lockport Ch.: v.2, p.145)

SAMPE, Helene Vayna (Gustave & Julienne BOURGEOIS) b. 29 July 1896 (Lockport Ch.: v.2, p.333)

SAMPE, Lea (Frank & Laura DUFRENE) m. 24 April 1897 Emile PIERCE (Lockport Ch.: v.2, p.161)

SAMPE, Marie Ayna (Gustave & Julienne BOURGEOIS) b. 26 July 1896 (Lockport Ch.: v.2, p.333)

SAMSON, Antonia Rowena of Point Coupee Parish (Georges Clement & Philomene McDONALD) m. 16 Nov. 1896 Augustin Jacques MASSON, of Niort, France (Larose Ch.: v.3, p.4)

SAMSON, Antonia Rowena (d.George Clement & d.Philomene McDONALD) of Pointe Coupee m. 16 Nov. 1896 Augustin Jacques MASSON (Larose Ch.: v.4, p.90)

SAMUEL, Willis m. 3 March 1898 Sidonia RICHARD (Houma Ct. Hse.: Mar v.30 & 31, #324)

SANCAN, Francois d. 25 Jan. 1897. Order to affix seals: 28 Jan. 1897. (Thib. Ct. Hse.: Succ. #1506)

SANCAN, Francois d. 27 Jan. 1897 at age 70 yrs. (Thib. Ch.: v.3, p.195)

SANCHEZ (Sometimes: SANCHE, SANCHES, SANCTES, SANGES, SENCHE)

SANCHEZ, Alcida (Lawrence & Angele HEBERT) b. 19 Feb. 1898 (Chackbay Ch.: v.1, p.112)

SANCHEZ, Elie Walter (Justilien & Modeste SEVIN) b. 22 June 1898 (Montegut Ch.: v.6, p.76)

SANCHEZ, Joseph (Salvador & Marie THIBODEAUX) m. 1 Feb. 1897 Louisiane MOLAISON (Thib. Ct. Hse.: Mar. v.36, #38)

SANCHEZ, Joseph (Salvadore & Marie THIBODEAUX) m. 1 Feb. 1897 Louisiane MOLAISON (Chackbay Ch.: v.1, p.38)
SANCHEZ, Joseph Doyley (Salvadore & Marie THIBODAUX) b. 7 Feb. 1898 (Chackbay Ch.: v.1, p.105)
SANCHEZ, Joseph Thomas (Joseph & Louisiane MOLAISON) b. 1 Dec. 1897 (Chackbay Ch.: v.1, p.105)
SANCHEZ, Josephine Ernestine (Joseph & Louisiane MOLAISON) b. 19 Oct. 1899 (Chackbay Ch.: v.1, p.143)
SANCHEZ, Lea (Raphael & Marie WALKER) b. 13 June 1898 (Chackbay Ch.: v.1, p.119)
SANCHEZ, Marie Oseana (Raphael & Marie WALKER) b. 21 Aug. 1899 (Chackbay Ch.: v.1, p.141)
SANCHEZ, Raphael m. 29 Dec. 1896 Marie Anaise WALKER (Thib. Ct. Hse.: Mar. v.36, #174)
SANCHEZ, Raphael (Joseph & Mathilde HEBERT) m. 7 Jan. 1897 Anais WALKER (Raceland Ch.: v.2, p.25)
SANDBIG, Wern Allrik (Albert & Alma WATSON) b. 18 April 1898 (Thib. Ch.: Epis. Ch.: v.1, p.44)

SANDERS (Sometimes: SANDES, SANDEZ, SANDRA, SANDRAS, SANDRES, SAUNDERS)

SANDERS, Emma m. 12 Oct. 1898 Sam ROBERTSON (Thib. Ct. Hse.: Mar. v.38, #292)
SANDERS, Henry J. m. Belle W. SHAFFER Donation of Land: 13 Feb. 1897. (Houma Ct. Hse.: Book of Donations: v.A, p.147)
SANDERS, Inza Mary (Allen A. & Ella TRAHAN) b. 18 Aug. 1899 (Houma Ch.: Epis. Ch.: v.1, p.122)
SANDERS, Jessi m. 6 June 1896 Clifton LATHROP (Thib. Ch.: Epis. Ch.: v.1, p.331)
SANDERS, Jessie m. 6 June 1896 Clifton LATHROP (Thib. Ct. Hse.: Mar. v.35, #102)
SANDERS, Leana m. 16 Feb. 1897 Harry JOHNSON (Thib. Ct. Hse.: Mar. v.36, #80)
SANDERS, Leonard B. (James M. & Mary Jane MAY) m. 15 Dec. 1896 Luther WHITMORE (Houma Ct. Hse.: Mar. v.29 & 30, #200)
SANDERS, Lettie m. 1 June 1899 Bartley BROWN (Thib. Ct. Hse.: Mar. v.39, #174)
SANDERS, Lewis m. 9 March 1898 Melia STRIPLING (Thib. Ct. Hse.: Mar. v.37, #123)
SANDRAS, Marie (Augustin & Josephine PREJEAN) m. 26 Jan. 1899 Augustin LANDRY (Thib. Ct. Hse.: Mar. v.38, #6)
SANDRAS, Marie (Augustin & Josephine PREJEAN) m. 26 Jan. 1899 Augustin LANDRY (Thib. Ch.: v.14, p.246)

SANGE (See: SONGE)

SANGE, Eve m. Beauregard BARRIOS d. 17 Feb. 1896 (Lockport Ch.: v.1, #7)
SANGE, Marie Adele (Gustin & Ophelia GUIDRY) b. 12 Oct. 1896 (Montegut Ch.: v.6, p.47)

SANJEZ, Beneritte d. 14 Dec. 1898 at age 45 yrs. (Thib. Ch.: v.3, p.223)

SANSONI, Jean Aime (John & Marie VINET) b. 2 June 1896 (Larose Ch.: v.2, p.184)

SANTEE, Alice m. 19 Jan. 1899 Joseph ROSE, Jr. (Houma Ct. Hse.: Mar. v.30 & 31, #258)

SANTEE, Irene m. 2 Feb. 1899 Adam JONES (Houma Ct. Hse.: Mar. v.30 & 31, #299)

SANTEE, Mary m. 2 June 1896 Joseph McNEAL (Houma Ct. Hse.: Mar. v.29 & 30, #85)

SANTEE, Thomas m. 20 Feb. 1897 Ida ADAMS (Houma Ct. Hse.: Mar. v.29 & 30, #327)

SANTINI, Alice Anita (Giovani & Catherine VERDON) b. 30 Oct. 1897 (Larose Ch.: v.3, p.12)

SANTINI, Augustin Ovide (Ernest & Stella VERDAN) b. 10 March 1897 (Larose Ch.: v.3, p.7)

SANTINI, Clarisse Armantine (Giovani & Estellina VERDON) b. 25 Aug. 1899 (Larose Ch.: v.3, p.58)

SANTINI, Eugenie Olivia (Leon & Natalis RIBEAUX) b. 13 May 1899 (Larose Ch.: v.3, p.47)

SANTINI, Leonce of Jefferson Parsh (Thommassin & Armantine CYLE) m. 28 July 1898 Nathalie RIBAULT of Jefferson Parish (Larose Ch.: v.3, p.10)

SANTINI, Leonce (Thommassin & Armantine CYLE) of Jefferson Parish m. 28 July 1898 Nathalie RIBAULT, of Jefferson Parish (Larose Ch.: v.4, p.25)

SAOIE, Lema Santy (Aurilien & Evelia BABIN) b. 29 March 1899 (Houma Ch.: v.5, p.244)

SAONE, Francisco (Diego & Dominia MARINA) b. 11 Sept. 1898 (Houma Ch.: v.5, p.230)

SAONE, Joseph Guisepe (Gido & Rosalia ROCHEFORTE) b. 1 Jan. 1899 (Houma Ch.: v.5, p.229)

SAPIA, Alexina m. 14 Jan. 1897 Andrew McDONALD (Thib. Ct. Hse.: Mar. v.36, #30)

SAPIA, Alexina (Henri & Emelie KNIGHT) m. 28 Jan. 1896 Andre McDONALD (Raceland Ch.: v.2, p.30)

SAPIA, Augusta m. 16 Oct. 1897 Augustin GUITROZ (Thib. Ct. Hse.: Mar. v.37, #249)

SAPIA, Augusta (James & Louisa KNIGHT) m. 16 Oct. 1897 Augustin GUIDROZ (Raceland Ch.: v.2, p.53)

SAPIA, James Voorhies (Charley & Evelina PLAISANCE) b. 10 Dec. 1896 (Raceland Ch.: v.5, p.37)

SAPIA, Julia m. 7 Aug. 1896 Ernest BAUDOIN (Thib. Ct. Hse.: Mar. v.36, #130)

SAPIA, Julia (Louis & Liza KNIGHT) m. 22 Aug. 1896 Ernest BAUDOUIN (Raceland Ch.: v.2, p.21)

SAPIA, Lidia m. 15 Jan. 1897 Klebert HEBERT (Thib. Ct. Hse.: Mar. v.36, #36)

SAPIA, Lucinda m. 29 Nov. 1897 John McDONALD, Jr. (Thib. Ct. Hse.: Mar. v.37, #257)

SAPIA, Lucinda (Henri & Emelie KNIGHT) m. 29 Nov. 1897 John McDONALD (Raceland Ch.: v.2, p.54)
SAPIA, Lydia (Henri & Emelie KNIGHT) m. 27 Jan. 1897 Klebert HEBERT (Raceland Ch.: v.2, p.29)
SAPIA, Petronille m. 29 May 1897 Albert BROWN (Thib. Ct. Hse.: Mar. v.36, #151)
SAPIA, Petronille (James & Louisa KNIGHT) m. 12 June 1897 Albert BROWN (Raceland Ch.: v.2, p.42)
SAPIE, Antoine Mores (Charles & Evelina PLAISANCE) b. 23 July 1899 (Raceland Ch.: v.5, p.102)
SARGEANT, Margueritte m. 22 Feb. 1899 Andrew DESLATTE (Thib. Ct. Hse.: Mar. v.39, #110)
SARGEANT, Samuel m. 6 April 1899 Alicia RUTHERFORD (Thib. Ct. Hse.: Mar. v.39, #135)
SARMONEY, Hadney Paul (Cordelius & Lesilda LADOUCEUR) b. 3 May 1896 (Houma Ch.: v.5, p.154)
SASSONE, Marie Stella (John & Marie VINET) b. 3 May 1899 (Larose Ch.: v.3, p.40)
SAUBY, Mary d. 11 May 1896 at age 2 yrs. (Houma Ch.: v.3, p.7)
SAUCIDE, Joseph (Simeon & Julia SAVOIE) b. 7 Sept. 1896 (Houma Ch.: v.5, p.163)
SAUCIER, Ellen (Raymond & Ellen BOURGEOIS) b. 28 July 1898 (Thib. Ch.: v.7, p.559)
SAUCIER, Esilda Bernadette (Edmond & Estellina BOUDREAUX) b. 7 Nov. 1896 (Thib. Ch.: v.7, p.477)
SAUCIER, Jules m. 28 Aug. 1896 Letitia CHAMPAGNE (Thib. Ct. Hse.: Mar. v.36, #137)
SAUCIER, Jules (Victor & Amelia POULARD) m. 10 Sept. 1896 Loetitia CHAMPAGNE (Raceland Ch.: v.2, p.22)
SAUCIER, Raymond (Victor & Amelia POULARD) m. 14 Sept. 1898 Helene BOURGEOIS (Thib. Ct. Hse.: Mar. v.38, #270)
SAUCIER, Raymond (Victor & Amelia POULARD) m. 14 Sept. 1898 Helene BOURGEOIS (Thib. Ch.: v.14, p.223)
SAUCIER, Raymond Whitney (Raymond & Helene BOURGEOIS) b. 24 Aug. 1899 (Thib. Ch.: v.8, p.4)

SAULE (See: SOLE)

SAULE, Josephine d. 11 Oct. 1897 at age 19 yrs. (Theriot Ch.: v.1, p.1)

SAULNIER (Sometimes: SAUNIER, SOIGNE, SOIGNIER, SONNIER)

SAULNIER, Anne Jeanne (Rodolphe & Julia BERNARD) b. 25 July 1898 (Thib. Ch.: v.7, p.557)
SAULNIER, Annette (Clay & Elvire BAYE) m. 31 Jan. 1899 Raoul PITRE (Thib. Ct. Hse.: Mar. v.38, #19)
SAULNIER, Annette (Clay & Elvire BAYE) m. 31 Jan. 1899 Raoul PITRE (Thib. Ch.: v.14, p.252)
SAULNIER, Edgar d. 18 Dec. 1898 at age 24 yrs., 8 mths. & 21 days (Thib. Ch.: v.3, p.223)

SAULNIER, Edgar (Octafe & Celace ROUSSEL) m. 20 Jan. 1897 Sophie SMITH (Thib. Ct. Hse.: Mar. v.36, #20)
SAULNIER, Edgar (Octave & Celace ROUSSEL) m.20 Jan. 1897 Sophie SMITH (Thib. Ch.: v.14, p.112)
SAULNIER, Joseph Laurence (Egard & Josephine SMITH) b. 18 March 1897 (Thib. Ch.: v.7, p.492)
SAULNIER, Loretta Marie (Oscar & Cecile GRIARD) b. 9 July 1898 (Thib. Ch.: v.7, p.504)
SAULNIER, Octave d. 12 Feb. 1897 at age 48 yrs. (Thib. Ch.: v.3, p.196)
SAULNIER, Oscar m.7 June 1897 Cecile HIRIARD (Thib. Ct. Hse.: Mar. v.36, #162)
SAULNIER, Rodolphe (Octave & Celeste ROUSSEL) m. 4 Feb. 1896 Julia BERNARD (Thib. Ch.: v.14, p.73)
SAULNIER, Rodolphe (Octave & Celeste ROUSSEL) m. 4 Feb. 1896 Julia BERNARD (Thib. Ct. Hse.: Mar. v.35, #29)
SAULSBRY, H. C. m. 6 Oct. 1898 Josephine BUTLER (Houma Ct. Hse.: Mar. v.30 & 31, #118)
SAULSBURY, Susanna m. 30 March 1897 Anthony LIVAS (Houma Ct. Hse.: Mar. v.29 & 30, #369)
SAVAGE, Louisa m. 10 May 1899 Charles BARTLEY, Jr. (Thib. Ct. Hse.: Mar. v.39, #163)
SAVANO, Charles (Petro & Calojia ALLABALA) b. 25 May 1896 (Houma Ch.: v.5, p.152)

SAVOIE (Sometimes: SAVOI, SAVOIS, SAVOIT)

SAVOIE, ----- child (Klebert) d. 7 Feb. 1897 at age 2 yrs. (Lockport Ch.: v.1, #6)
SAVOIE, ----- child (Vindom & Mathilde UZE) d. 1 Aug. 1899 at age 11 days (Lockport Ch.: v.1, #30)
SAVOIE, Agnes Marie (William & Olivia BUQUET) b. 4 July 1897 (Thib. Ch.: v.7, p.456)
SAVOIE, Albert (Omer & Honorine GUIDRY) m. 16 April 1898 Arcade TOURELLE (Lockport Ch.: v.2, p.188)
SAVOIE, Albert (Omer & Honorine GUIDRY) m. 16 April 1898 Arcade TOURELLE (Thib. Ct. Hse.: Mar. v.37, #143)
SAVOIE, Albertine Catherine (Elien & Kate BESSON) b. 17 Oct. 1898 (Raceland Ch.: v.5, p.85)
SAVOIE, Aline Anita (Justillien & Lea LEBLANC) b. 3 May 1898 (Larose Ch.: v.3, p.19)
SAVOIE, Anna Stella (Edwin & Emma HOTARD) b. 4 Feb. 1898 (Montegut Ch.: v.6, p.67)
SAVOIE, Anne Lisemee (George & Emma CARREAU) b. 1 Nov. 1897 (Houma Ch.: v.5, p.193)
SAVOIE, Antoine Raoul (Beauregard & Aglaee ROGER) b. 4 April 1896 (Montegut Ch.: v.6, p.37)
SAVOIE, Augusta of Lafourche Parish (Auguste & Eveline PLAISANCE) m. 25 June 1898 Pierre BOUVIER, of Lafourche Parish (Larose Ch.: v.3, p.9)
SAVOIE, Augusta (Auguste & Eveline PLAISANCE) m. 25 June 1898 Pierre BOUVIER (Thib. Ct. Hse.: Mar. v.38, #204)

SAVOIE, Augusta (Auguste & Eveline PLAISANCE) m. 25 June 1898 Pierre BOUVIER (Larose Ch.: v.4, p.18)
SAVOIE, Celeste m. 8 Sept. 1897 Albert ROSSI (Larose Ch.: v.3, p.4)
SAVOIE, Celeste m. 8 Sept. 1897 Albert ROSSI (Larose Ch.: v.4, p.54)
SAVOIE, Celeste 21 yrs. old m. 26 Dec. 1896 Albert Michel ROSSI (Thib. Ct. Hse.: Mar. v.36, #170)
SAVOIE, Clement Albert (Mercedes SAVOIE) b. 1 Aug. 1897 (Larose Ch.: v.2, p.192)
SAVOIE, Desee Marie Anna (Hyacinthe & Leonarde THIBODAUX) bt. 29 Feb. 1896 (Lockport Ch.: v.2, p.324)
SAVOIE, Edmond m. 6 April 1899 Lena BOURGEOIS (Thib. Ct. Hse.: Mar. v.39, #134)
SAVOIE, Edmond (Estival & Marguerette DANOS) m. 12 March 1899 Lina BOURGEOIS (Larose Ch.: v.4, p.107)
SAVOIE, Edmond (Estival & Marguerite DANOS) m. 12 April 1899 Lina BOURGEOIS (Larose Ch.: v.3, p.11)
SAVOIE, Edmond (Estival & Margueritte DANOS) m. 12 April 1899 Lina BOURGEOIS (Larose Ch.: v.4, p.83)
SAVOIE, Edna (Felicien & Pamela PELEGRIN) m. 26 Dec. 1899 Henry FIELDS (Houma Ct. Hse.: Mar. v.31 & 32, #193)
SAVOIE, Edna Louise (Arsene & Odalie THERIOT) b. 7 Feb. 1899 (Larose Ch.: v.3, p.37)
SAVOIE, Elisa Maria (Jules & Marguerite DANOS) b. 9 Oct. 1897 (Larose Ch.: v.3, p.6)
SAVOIE, Elles m. 2 Feb. 1898 Ophelia BERNARD (Larose Ch.: v.4, p.115)
SAVOIE, Elles m. 2 Feb. 1898 Ophelia BERNARD (Larose Ch.: v.3, p.7)
SAVOIE, Elles (Theles & Adele ORGERON) m. 2 Feb. 1898 Ophelia BERNARD (Thib. Ct. Hse.: Mar. v.37, #56)
SAVOIE, Etienne Norbert (Leo & Annelie GUIDROZ) b. 7 April 1899 (Larose Ch.: v.3, p.38)
SAVOIE, Eugene of Lafourche Parish (Jourdain & Marie DUET) m. 18 April 1898 Alice AUTHEMENT of Lafourche Parish (Larose Ch.: v.3, p.8)
SAVOIE, Eugene (Joachim & Mary HOTARD) d. 27 Dec. 1897 at age 3½ yrs. (Montegut Ch.: v.2, p.14)
SAVOIE, Eugene (Jourdain & Marie DUAY) m. 18 April 1898 Alice AUTHEMENT (Larose Ch.: v.4, p.10)
SAVOIE, Eugene J. (Jourdain & Marie DUAY) m. 18 April 1898 Alice AUTHEMENT (Thib. Ct. Hse.: Mar. v.37, #139)
SAVOIE, Felix (Eugene & Ophelia CHERAMI) b. 4 Aug. 1899 (Larose Ch.: v.3, p.44)
SAVOIE, Gillis (Marcelin & Malvina BERGERON) m. 15 Feb. 1898 Helene BERGERON (Thib. Ch.: v.14, p.187)
SAVOIE, Gillis (Marcelin & Malvina BERGERON) m. 15 Feb. 1898 Helene BERGERON (Thib. Ct. Hse.: Mar. v.37, #88)
SAVOIE, Gustave (Ursin & Marie Lyse DUFRENE) m. 25 July 1896 Justilia DUFRENE (Thib. Ct. Hse.: Mar. v.36, #120)

SAVOIE, Harry (Joachim & Mary HOTARD) d. 26 Dec. 1897 at age 1 yr. & 5 mths. (Montegut Ch.: v.2, p.13)
SAVOIE, Henri (Joseph & Mary HOTARD) b. 24 Aug. 1896 (Lockport Ch.: v.2, p.335)
SAVOIE, Henry Cleophee (Cyprien & Bertha BERTRAND) b. 16 Dec. 1896 (Chacahoula Ch.: v.4, p.11)
SAVOIE, Honora Therese (Eugene & Selvie BOURGEOIS) b. 15 Oct. 1896 (Larose Ch.: v.2, p.189)
SAVOIE, Iuloh Marie Teldry (Eugene & Alice AUTEMENT) b. 27 Feb. 1899 (Larose Ch.: v.3, p.37)
SAVOIE, Jean Albert (Albert & Arcade THUREL) b. 27 Feb. 1899 (Larose Ch.: v.3, p.37)
SAVOIE, Jean Joseph (Scarfe & Emma CARRO) b. 5 Jan. 1896 (Houma Ch.: v.5, p.144)
SAVOIE, Joseph Elma (Guilette & Helene BERGERON) b. 16 Dec. 1898 (Thib. Ch.: v.7, p.528)
SAVOIE, Joseph Helia (Joseph Clay & Eda LEBLANC) b. 30 Feb. 1897 (Montegut Ch.: v.6, p.52)
SAVOIE, Joseph Henri (Bonval & Delphine PIERCE) b. 24 Sept. 1897 (Larose Ch.: v.3, p.5)
SAVOIE, Jules Paul (Odressie & Marguerite DUPLANTY) b. 20 Nov. 1897 (Raceland Ch.: v.5, p.58)
SAVOIE, Junetia Marie (Wales & Armantine MELANCON) b. 30 July 1899 (Larose Ch.: v.3, p.44)
SAVOIE, Laura (Theophile & Octavie CARO) b. 18 Jan. 1896 (Houma Ch.: v.5, p.145)
SAVOIE, Leonise m. Alex CHONES d. 11 May 1898 at age 75 yrs. (Lockport Ch.: v.1, #10)
SAVOIE, Libbie Agnes (Cyprien & Bertha BERTRAND) b. 11 Feb. 1899 (Chacahoula Ch.: v.4, p.18)
SAVOIE, Lise m. 22 June 1896 Horace HERNANDEZ (Thib. Ct. Hse.: Mar. v.35, #93)
SAVOIE, Lise m. 22 June 1896 Horace HERNANDEZ (Larose Ch.: v.4, p.96)
SAVOIE, Lise m. 22 June 1896 Horace HERNANDEZ (Larose Ch.: v.3, p.3)
SAVOIE, Lucia m. 27 Jan. 1898 Orestil CORTEZ (Thib. Ct. Hse.: Mar. v.37, #29)
SAVOIE, Lucia (Lucien & Lizzie DUPLANTIS) m. 27 Jan. 1898 Orestile CORTEZ (Raceland Ch.: v.2, p.61)
SAVOIE, Marguerite Laura (Joachim & Mary HOTARD) b 9 Aug. 1898 (Montegut Ch.: v.6, p.76)
SAVOIE, Marie (Orestile & Uranie FREMIN) m. 28 Sept. 1898 Manuel DOMINGUE (Houma Ct. Hse.: Mar. v.30 & 31, #109)
SAVOIE, Marie Anita (Eugene & Euseire BOURGEOIS) b. 2 Nov. 1898 (Larose Ch.: v.3, p.30)
SAVOIE, Marie Georgina (Arsene & Ordasie THERIOT) b. 23 Dec. 1896 (Larose Ch.: v.3, p.1)
SAVOIE, Marie Laudrius (Aurelien & Emelia BABIN) b. 22 Dec. 1896 (Houma Ch.: v.5, p.165)

SAVOIE, Marie Lelie (Adrecie & Marguerite DUPLANTIS) b. 2 Nov. 1899 (Theriot Ch.: v.2, p.61)
SAVOIE, Maurice (Justilien) d. 8 Jan. 1898 at age 2 yrs. (Lockport Ch.: v.1, #32)
SAVOIE, Maximin Sidney (Maximin & Elvina GAUTREAUX) b. 22 Sept. 1899 (Montegut Ch.: v.7, p.2)
SAVOIE, Melina (Jacques & Emma CAREAU) d. 13 July 1896 at age 2 yrs. (Houma Ch.: v.3, p.8)
SAVOIE, Noel Estival (Eugene & Ophelia CHERAMI) b. 25 Dec. 1896 (Larose Ch.: v.3, p.1)
SAVOIE, Norma Mathilde (Nindon & Mathilde UZE) b. 21 Aug. 1896 (Lockport Ch.: v.2, p.335)
SAVOIE, Onesipe Joannis (Onesipe & Emma CARRO) b. 3 Nov. 1899 (Houma Ch.: v.5, p.265)
SAVOIE, Paul Francois (Guillace & Helene BERGERON) b. 17 Sept. 1899 (Thib. Ch.: v.8, p.10)
SAVOIE, Pharelie m. Victor MELANCON d. 25 Sept. 1897 at age 76 yrs. (Larose Ch.: v.1, p.40)
SAVOIE, Philippe Corbet (Elias & Kate BELSON) b. 5 July 1896 (Raceland Ch.: v.5, p.31)
SAVOIE, Therese Effie (Beauregard & Aglaee ROGER) b. 14 March 1898 (Montegut Ch.: v.6, p.69)
SAVOIE, Widles Abel (Jules & Margueritte DANOS) b. 16 Aug. 1899 (Larose Ch.: v.3, p.44)
SAVOIE, Zoemie Mrs. d. 24 March 1899 at age 61 yrs. (Chacahoula Ch.: Gibson Ch.: v.2, p.182)
SAVOIE, Zulma (Theodore & Exelina ADAM) m. 8 Feb. 1899 Wallace LELORIC (Thib. Ct. Hse.: Mar. v.38, #28)
SAVOIE, Zulma (Theodore & Exelina ADAM) m. 8 Feb. 1899 Wallace LELORIC (Thib. Ch.: v.14, p.261)
SAVONA, Josephine (Atonino & Vita CHICHIA) b. 25 Jan. 1896; m. Salvatore LUSCA on 27 Dec. 1927. (Houma Ch.: Bapt. Bk., v.5, p.168)
SAVOUREAU, Marie Alida (Toussaint & Marie Evelina SEVIN) b. 1 June 1898 (Montegut Ch.: v.6, p.88)

SCALLY (Sometimes: SCALLEY)

SCANNIA, Catherine (Salvatore & Vincenza CARAVELLA) m. 16 June 1898 Guiseppe GRUBOURGIA? (Thib. Ch.: v.14, p.207)
SCARPOLLA, Carmela (Antonino & Carmela DIOGUARDI) b. 13 Sept. 1898 (Thib. Ch.: v.8, p.55)
SCHANYDER, Edouard (Numa & Eugenie LEVERT) m. 20 April 1897 Anastasie BREAUX (Thib. Ch.: v.14, p.137)

SCHETE (See: CHETE)

SCHEXNAIDER (Sometimes: SCHEKNAIDER, SCHENEIDER, SCHEXNEIDER, SHEXNIDER, SCHEXNIDES, SCHNEIDER, THEXNAIDER)

SCHEXNAIDER, Edouard (Numa & Eugenie LEVERT) m. 20 April 1897 Anastasie BREAUX (Thib. Ct. Hse.: Mar. v.36, #112)
SCHEXNAIDER, Ferjus m. Zoe HAYDEL Children listed: Odile m. d.Felix PONTIFFE; Imack; Elizabeth; Louis. Petition for inventory: 20 June 1899. (Thib. Ct. Hse.: Succ. #1580)
SCHEXNAIDER, George Felix (Klebert &Alice ORILLION) b. 6 Jan. 1898 (Thib. Ch.: v.7, p.479)
SCHEXNAIDER, John Joseph (Eugene & Marie JOURDAN) m. 22 June 1899 May BOURGEOIS (Raceland Ch.: v.2, p.99)
SCHEXNAIDER, Louis m. 6 Jan. 1896 Dora THOMAS (Thib. Ct. Hse.: Mar. v.35, #13)
SCHEXNAIDER, Marie Edna (Edouard & Anastasie BREAUX) b. 25 Nov. 1898 (Thib. Ch.: v.7, p.522)
SCHNEIDER, Charles (Peter & Catherine BLOU) m. 4 Sept. 1897 Anastasie THIBODAUX (Houma Ct. Hse.: Mar. v.29 & 30, #84)
SCHOONER, Henry U. m. 11 Feb. 1899 Violette THIBODAUX (Thib. Ct. Hse.: Mar. v.39, #104)
SCHOONOVER, Henry Ulysses of Nebraska (Hiram & Mary Jane) m. 14 Feb. 1898 Violette THIBODEAUX, of Lafourche Parish (Larose Ch.: v.3, p.8)
SCHOONOVER, Henry Ulysses (Hirman & Mary Jane of Nebraska) m. 14 Feb. 1898 Violette THIBODEAUX (Larose Ch.: v.4, p.38)
SCHREIBER, Mai Verna (Charles & Louise NACARI) b. 9 Dec. 1899 (Larose Ch.: v.3, p.59)
SCHROEDER, Anna m. 11 April 1896 Alexander P. HADDAD (Thib. Ch.: Epis. Ch.: v.1, p.331)
SCHROEDER, Anna m. 28 March 1896 Alexander HADDAD (Houma Ct. Hse.: Mar. v.29 & 30, #22)
SCHUBERT, Emily m. 8 March 1897 Ben WILLIAMS (Thib. Ct. Hse.: Mar. v.36, #97)
SCHWARTZ, Marie Louise (Martin & Leontia AUCOIN) b. 5 July 1898 (Thib. Ch.: v.7, p.559)
SCHWARTZ, Martin (Michel & Catherine MATERNE) m. 2 May 1898 Leontia AUCOIN (Thib. Ch.: v.14, p.202)
SCHWARTZ, Martin of New Orleans (Michel & Catherine MATERNE) m. 2 May 1898 Leontia AUCOIN (Thib. Ct. Hse.: Mar. v.38, #174)

SCHWEITZER (See: CHOISTRE)

SCIMECCA, Rosalie (Nicacio & Antonina LUZZIO) m. 28 Oct. 1899 Ange SALVATORE (Thib. Ch.: v.14, p.306)
SCIORTINA, Nora (Leonardo & Maria DISPENSA) b. 15 Feb. 1899 (Thib. Ch.: v.7, p.539)
SCIORTINO, Nicolo (Vincenzo & Maria Giuseppa BRAVATA) m. 3 April 1899 Maria DISPENSA (Thib. Ct. Hse.: Mar. v.39, #121)

SCIORTINO, Nicolo (Vincenzo & Maria Guiseppa BRAVATA) m. 3 April 1899 Maria DISPENSA (Thib. Ch.: v.14, p.268)
SCOOT, Paul Johnny or SCOTT (Remi & Valerine TRAHAN) b. 14 Jan. 1896 (Theriot Ch.: v.1-B, p.92)

SCOTT (Sometimes: SCOT)
SCOTT, Ann m. 12 May 1896 Washington SPEED (Houma Ct. Hse.: Mar. v.29 & 30, #65)
SCOTT, Anna m. 20 Feb. 1897 Charles HENRY (Thib. Ct. Hse.: Mar. v.36, #87)
SCOTT, Caroline m. 16 April 1896 Henry SHAFFER (Thib. Ct. Hse.: Mar. v.35, #68)
SCOTT, Charles Marie Inola (Paul Emile & Lilian Eda ROUSSEL) b. 16 Jan. 1899 (Thib. Ch.: v.7, p.531)
SCOTT, Gustave Sidney (Walter & Marguerite DOUCET) b. 29 Feb. 1896 (Larose Ch.: v.2, p.185)
SCOTT, John m. 23 April 1898 Volumnia BURKS (Houma Ct. Hse.: Mar. v.30 & 31, #413)
SCOTT, Joseph Jessie (Leopold & Amanda LEDET) d. 23 May 1899 at age 2 mths. & 7 days (Montegut Ch.: v.2, p.26)
SCOTT, Joseph Jessie (Leopold & Amanda LEDET) b. 17 March 1899 (Montegut Ch.: v.6, p.84)
SCOTT, Joseph Johnny Wheyly (Johnny & Mathilde TRAHAN) b. 4 Nov. 1897 (Theriot Ch.: v.2, p.51)
SCOTT, Laurencia (Paul & Ozea NAQUIN) m. 18 April 1898 Luc LEDET (Montegut Ch.: v.4, p.242)
SCOTT, Laurencia (Paul & Ozea NAQUIN) m. 5 April 1898 Luke LEDET (Houma Ct. Hse.: Mar. v.30 & 31, #374)
SCOTT, Leopold (Paul & Ozea NAQUIN) m. 19 Jan. 1898 Amanda LEDET (Houma Ct. Hse.: Mar. v.30 & 31, #232)
SCOTT, Leopold (Paul & Ozea NAQUIN) m. 3 Feb. 1898 Amanda LEDET (Montegut Ch.: v.4, p.235)
SCOTT, Lionel Anthony (Arthur Augustin & Mary Edilia LYALL) b. 22 June 1897 (Thib. Ch.: v.7, p.453)
SCOTT, Louis A. (Paul & Rosa HEBERT) m. 8 Feb. 1899 Josephine GUIDRY (Thib. Ch.: v.14, p.260)
SCOTT, Louis Alphonse (Paul & Rosa HEBERT) m. 8 Feb. 1899 Josephine GUIDRY (Thib. Ct Hse.: Mar. v.38, #60)
SCOTT, Marie Louvinia (Samuel & Ophelia INCLADE) b. 1 March 1897 (Larose Ch.: v.3, p.24)
SCOTT, Nellie m.17 Oct. 1898 Charles SMITH (Thib. Ct. Hse.: Mar. v.38, #298)
SCOTT, Paul (Joannis & Clementine TROSCLAIR) m. 11 April 1898 Clothilde TROSCLAIR (Theriot Ch.: v.1-B, p.3)
SCOTT, Paul (John & Clementine TROSCLAIR) m. 25 March 1898 Clothilde TROSCLAIR (Houma Ct. Hse.: Mar. v.30 & 31, #350)
SCOTT, Paul Emile m. 3 Feb. 1898 Lilian ROUSSEL (Thib. Ct. Hse.: Mar. v.37, #70)
SCOTT, Paul Emile (Paul & Rosa HEBERT) m. 3 Feb. 1898 Lilian ROUSSEL (Raceland Ch.: v.2, p.64)

SCOTT, Paul Johnny or SCOOT (Remi & Valerine TRAHAN) b. 14 Jan. 1896 (Theriot Ch.: v.1-B, p.92)
SCOTT, Samson Louis (Samuel & Ophelia INCALADE) b. 27 April 1899 (Larose Ch.: v.3, p.47)
SCOTT, Thomas d. 4 Jan. 1899 at age 17 yrs. (Raceland Ch.: v.1, p.23)
SCOTT, Thomas Lyall (Arthur Augustin & Marie Edilia LYALL) b. 9 Nov. 1899 (Thib. Ch.: v.8, p.18)
SCOTT, Wash m. 19 March 1896 Rebeca COACH (Thib. Ct. Hse.: Mar. v.35, #54)
SCOTT, Zachary Delaversary (Ezekiel & Joanna SCOTT) m. 26 Oct. 1896 Alice Marie CLARK (Houma Ct. Hse.: Mar. v.29 & 30, #179)
SCRUBB, Cecilia m. 3 Feb. 1898 Daniel BAPTISTE (Houma Ct. Hse.: Mar. v.30 & 31, #274)
SCRUBB, James m. 2 Feb. 1899 Margaret JENKINS (Houma Ct. Hse.: Mar. v.30 & 31, #303)
SCRUGGS, Richard m. 30 Dec. 1897 Sue BARRAS (Houma Ct. Hse.: Mar. v.29 & 30, #167)
SCURIA, Antonino (Salvatore & Guiseppa SCIMINNA) b. 16 Oct. 1899 (Thib. Ch.: v.8, p.16)
SCURIA, Isanni (Salvatore & Joseph CIMINA) b. 1 Nov. 1898 (Thib. Ch.: v.7, p.529)
SCURRI, Salvatore (Salvatore & Guiseppa CIMINA) b. 21 April 1897 (Thib. Ch.: v.7, p.449)
SCURRIA, Salvatore d. 23 March 1899 at age 2 yrs. & 1 mth. (Thib. Ch.: v.3, p.230)
SEALS, Richard m. 18 Jan. 1899 Louisa BUTLER (Houma Ct. Hse.: Mar. v.30 & 31, #251)
SEARS, Robert m. 1 Feb. 1897 Frances DUMAS (Houma Ct. Hse.: Mar. v.29 & 30, #271)
SEAY, Mack m. 13 Jan. 1898 Esther RAYMON (Thib. Ct. Hse.: Mar. v.37, #30)
SEBIA, Joseph d. 29 June 1898 at age 8 mths. (Thib. Ch.: v.3, p.215)
SEELY, Robert (John C. & Olympe WEBRE) m. 15 Sept. 1897 Victoire TROXLER (Thib. Ct. Hse.: Mar. v.37, #226)
SEELY, Thomas Watson d. 4 Nov. 1899 at age 30 yrs. (Thib. Ch.: v.3, p.242)
SEEMAN, Laura m. 24 Oct. 1898 Sidney BENSON (Thib. Ct. Hse.: Mar. v.38, #300)
SEEMAN, Laura E. m. 24 Oct. 1898 Sidney BENSON (Thib. Ch.: Epis. Ch.: v.1, p.331)
SELBEY, Joseph James (James & Josephine AURONET) b. 5 Aug. 1898; bt. 7 Sept. 1902 (Thib. Ch.: v.8, p.97)
SELBY, James m. 14 Oct. 1897 Joephine HOWARD (Thib. Ct. Hse.: Mar. v.37, #244)
SELBY, Joseph Georges (James & Josephine AURONET) b. 20 April 1899; bt. 7 Sept. 1902 (Thib. Ch.: v.8, p.97)

SEMANI (See: SAMANI)

SEMORE, Willie m. 15 Feb. 1898 Louisa PRICE (Thib. Ct. Hse.: Mar. v.37, #104)
SEMPER, Ede d. 6 Aug. 1899 at age 10 mths. (Raceland Ch.: v.1, p.26)

SENAC (Sometimes: CENAC)
SENAC, Albert (Pierre & Victorine FANGUY) m. 5 May 1896 Delphine MICHEL (Houma Ct. Hse.: Mar. v.29 & 30, #51)
SENAC, Alphonse (Albert & Josephine MICHEL) b. 3 March 1899 (Houma Ch.: v.5, p.243)
SENAC, Isaure Marie (Theophile & Sylvia BOURG) b. 5 Feb. 1898 (Chacahoula Ch.: Gibson Records: Mar. Bk., v.1, #25)
SENAC, Marie Isaure (Theophile & Sylvia BOURG) b. 3 Feb. 1898 (Chacahoula Ch.: Gibson Ch.: v.2, p.119)
SEPPATRE, Guiseppe Ferrara (Salvatore & Salvatora FERRARA) b. 11 Sept. 1898 (Raceland Ch.: v.5, p.78)
SERAPHINE, Leonarda (Salvatora & Domina MARINA) b. 20 July 1898 (Houma Ch.: v.5, p.214)
SERIGNE, Joseph Augustin (Christophe & Romanda LOMBAS) b. 19 March 1898 (Larose Ch.: v.3, p.26)
SERRACHINA, Dominique (Vincento & Philode BERGERON) b. 3 April 1898 (Thib. Ch.: v.7, p.554)
SERRE, Adam Foster (Antoine & Bernadette SERRE) b. 29 March 1899 (Raceland Ch.: v.5, p.102)
SERRES, Marguerite m. 2 Oct. 1897 Pierre RESNAYS (Thib. Ct. Hse.: Mar. v.37, #236)
SEVERE, Joseph d. 25 June 1897 at age 65 yrs. (Lockport Ch.: v.1, #12)
SEVERE, Mary (Joseph & Adeline BOUCHERAU) m. 17 Feb. 1896 Lawless BARTLEY (Thib. Ct. Hse.: Mar. v.35, #42)

SEVIN (Sometimes: CEVIN, SEVEN)
SEVIN, Agnes (Eloi) d. 30 Nov. 1897 at age 4 mths. (Lockport Ch.: v.1, #30)
SEVIN, Amelia (d.Prospere & Aglae CLEMENT) m. 8 Oct. 1896 Emile THAUZIN (Chackbay Ch.: v.1, p.32)
SEVIN, Anidas (Joseph & Azelie NAQUIN) m. 24 Feb. 1897 Ida LASSEIGNE (Thib. Ct. Hse.: Mar. v.36, #79)
SEVIN, Auguste d. 7 Oct. 1896 at age 78 yrs. (Raceland Ch.: v.1, p.10)
SEVIN, Aurelia (Prospere & Aglae CLEMENT) m. 8 Oct. 1896 Emile TAUZIN (Thib. Ct. Hse.: Mar. v.36, #146)
SEVIN, Daniel d. 22 Nov. 1899 at age 5 mths., & 10 days (Thib. Ch.: v.3, p.244)
SEVIN, Darise Catherine Marie (Leonidas & Ida LASSEIGNE) b. 16 April 1898 (Thib. Ch.: v.7, p.494)
SEVIN, Denis m. 24 Jan. 1898 Emma LEPINE (Thib. Ct. Hse.: Mar. v.37, #44)

SEVIN, Denis (Joseph & Adolphine LEJEUNE) m. 24 Jan. 1898 Emma LEPINE (Raceland Ch.: v.2, p.59)
SEVIN, Denise m. 11 Dec. 1896 Alfred CHAUVIN (Thib. Ct. Hse.: Mar. v.36, #166)
SEVIN, Denise (Joseph & Adolphine LEJEUNE) m. 16 Dec. 1896 Alfred CHAUVIN (Raceland Ch.: v.2, p.23)
SEVIN, Felicien Dolphis (Allen & Julienne LEBOEUF) b. 9 June 1896 (Montegut Ch.: v.6, p.44)
SEVIN, Hermenigilde Wuilfred (Charles & Eugenie RODRIGUE) b. 13 April 1896 (Lockport Ch.: v.2, p.329)
SEVIN, Ignes Aurellien (Aurelien & Emelie BOUDREAUX) b. 11 April 1897 (Lockport Ch.: v.3-A, #43)
SEVIN, Ignes Aurellien (Aurellien & Emelie BOUDREAUX) b. 11 April 1897 (Lockport Ch.: v.3, #43)
SEVIN, Joseph Abel (Auguste & Cecile ARCENAUX) b. 13 March 1897 (Raceland Ch.: v.5, p.43)
SEVIN, Joseph Denis (Denis & Emma LEPINE) b. 31 Dec. 1898 (Raceland Ch.: v.5, p.85)
SEVIN, Joseph Fernand (Auguste & Cecilia ARSENAUX) b. 23 June 1899 (Raceland Ch.: v.5, p.98)
SEVIN, Justilien Joseph (Henri & Melanie MELANCON) b. 1 Jan. 1898 (Larose Ch.: v.3, p.15)
SEVIN, Leonidas (Joseph & Azelie NAQUIN) m. 24 Feb. 1897 Ida LASSEIGNE (Thib. Ch.: v.14, p.129)
SEVIN, Marie Aline (Nicolas & Emma LUQUETTE) b. 12 May 1897 (Raceland Ch.: v.5, p.48)
SEVIN, Marie Ayda (Elie & Adelia BONNAMOUR) b. 3 Feb. 1896 (Lockport Ch.: v.2, p.321)
SEVIN, Marie Justilia (Valcour & Marie MELANCON) b. 17 Feb. 1896 (Lockport Ch.: v.2, p.323)
SEVIN, Marie Laura (Saturin & Elesia KNOBLOCK) b. 13 Jan. 1897 (Raceland Ch.: v.5, p.39)
SEVIN, Marie Louise (Victor & Zurelia HEBERT) b. 6 Nov. 1896 (Houma Ch.: v.5, p.167)
SEVIN, Marie Olinda (Onesippe & Antoinette GARIBOTTE) b. 12 June 1899 (Montegut Ch.: v.7, p.3)
SEVIN, Marie Sylvanie (Allan & Julienne LEBOEUF) b. 29 Oct. 1899 (Montegut Ch.: v.6, p.97)
SEVIN, Onesippe (d.Ferdinand & Euphrosine DUBOIS) m. 16 Aug. 1898 Antoinette GARIBOTTE (Montegut Ch.: v.4, p.248)
SEVIN, Onesippe (Ferdinand & Euphrosine DUBOIS) m. 26 July 1898 Antoinette GARRIBOTTE (Houma Ct. Hse.: Mar. v.30 & 31, #67)
SEVIN, Ovide (d.Edouard & Velada LASSEIGNE) m. 13 Feb. 1899 Ada FIELDS (Montegut Ch.: v.4, p.258)
SEVIN, Ovide (Edward & Velada LASEIGNE) m. 4 Feb. 1899 Ada FIELDS (Houma Ct. Hse.: Mar. v.30 & 31, #310)
SEVIN, Prosper Daniel (Nidas & Ida LASSEIGNE) b. 9 June 1899 (Thib. Ch.: v.7, p.551)
SEVIN, Richard Felix Joseph (Onesime Jules & Marie Leontine FALGOUT) b. 8 Jan. 1897 (Thib. Ch.: v.7, p.441)

SEVIN, Saturin d. 28 Aug. 1898 at age 32 yrs. (Raceland Ch.: v.1, p.20)
SEVIN, Wilfried (Charles) d. 20 Nov. 1897 at age 2 yrs. (Lockport Ch.: v.1, #29)
SHAFFER, Henry m. 16 April 1896 Caroline SCOTT (Thib. Ct. Hse.: Mar. v.35, #68)
SHAFFER, Marguerite Lee d. 10 May 1896 (Houma Ch.: Epis. Ch.: v.1, p.386)
SHAFFER, Mary Frances (John D. & Julia CUTLEFF) b. 19 Sept. 1896 (Houma Ch.: Epis. Ch.: v.1, p.114)
SHAFFLET, Marie Heaston (Daniel & Lucie THIBODAUX) b. 2 Feb. 1898 (Thib. Ch.: v.7, p.540)
SHANKLING, Mary m. 4 April 1898 Richard JOHNSON (Thib. Ct. Hse.: Mar. v.37, #142)
SHAUBAUT, Clarence (Potley & Marie URSEAU) b. 1 July 1899 (Chackbay Ch.: v.1, p.139)
SHAUBAUTH, Paul Andre (Bartholemie & Marie URSEAU) b. 22 Nov. 1897 (Chackbay Ch.: v.1, p.106)
SHAW, Antoine Robert (Jabez & Lea CHAUVIN) b. 16 Oct. 1896 (Montegut Ch.: v.6, p.46)
SHAW, Marie Lea (Jabas Alma & Marie Lea CHAUVIN) b. 12 March 1899 (Montegut Ch.: v.6, p.83)
SHAY, Harris Frank (John Harris & Ida BELLE) b. 23 June 1896 (Raceland Ch.: v.5, p.49)
SHEDRICK, Isiah m. 9 Aug. 1899 Mary BLUE (Houma Ct. Hse.: Mar. v.31 & 32, #90)
SHEDRICK, John m. 30 Oct. 1899 Florence TAYLOR (Houma Ct. Hse.: Mar. v.31 & 32, #158)
SHELBY, Louisiana m. 16 Sept. 1899 Joseph GREEN (Thib. Ct. Hse.: Mar. v.39, #232)
SHELDON, Dora m. 26 Jan. 1899 Cornelius HOWARD (Thib. Ct. Hse.: Mar. v.38, #62)
SHELTER, Rebecca m. 18 June 1896 Sam MADISON (Houma Ct. Hse.: Mar. v.29 & 30, #96)
SHELVEY, Adam d. 1 April 1896 at age 31 yrs. (Raceland Ch.: v.1, p.8)
SHEPHERD, Louis Clifton (Eugene & Selina BADEAUX) b. 14 Dec. 1899 (Chacahoula Ch.: v.4, p.32)
SHEPHERD, Robert Eugene (Eugene & Celina BADEAUX) b. 21 Nov. 1896 (Chacahoula Ch.: v.4, p.10)
SHEPHERD, William Alphonse (Joseph & Angelique SAMMEY) b. 19 Oct. 1899 (Raceland Ch.: v.5, p.108)
SHEPPARD, William Paul (Eugene & Selina BADEAUX) b. 26 Aug. 1898 (Chacahoula Ch.: v.4, p.12)
SHERMAN, Eliza m. 3 May 1898 John LAWRENCE (Thib. Ct. Hse.: Mar. v.38, #176)
SHERMAN, Ida m. 10 Feb. 1897 Victor LEE (Thib. Ct. Hse.: Mar. v.36, #76)
SHERMAN, Xavier m. 4 Nov. 1899 Victoria FREN (Thib. Ct. Hse.: Mar. v.39, #258)

SHIELD, Willie m. 14 Oct. 1897 Mary STRATTEN (Thib. Ct. Hse.: Mar. v.37, #250)

SHIELDS, Mary m. 1 Aug. 1898 Sam CALLAWAY (Thib. Ct. Hse.: Mar. v.38, #236)

SHIM, Elisabeth Bernice (Frank & Mary LANDRY) b. 16 Nov. 1898 (Houma Ch.: v.5, p.222)

SHIN, Agnes of Terrebonne Parish m. 26 April 1899 J. Mortinet OLIVIER (Houma Ch.: v.6-B, p.3)

SHIN, Franklin B. Marcelin (Frank & Marie LANDRY) b. 21 Dec. 1899 (Houma Ch.: v.6, p.3)

SHINN, Agnes m. 18 April 1899 J. Mortimer OLIVIER (Houma Ct. Hse.: Mar. v.31 & 32, #406)

SHORT, Katie m. 12 Feb. 1896 Jerry NEIL (Houma Ct. Hse.: Mar. v.28, #448)

SHULENBERG, Marie (Thomas & Louisa DELAUNE) m. 28 June 1898 John CLEMENT (Thib. Ct. Hse.: Mar. v.38, #213)

SHULENBERG, Marie (Thomas & Louise DELAUNE) m. 28 June 1898 John CLEMENT (Thib. Ch.: v.14, p.208)

SHY, Harvey m. 21 June 1896 Felicie MOORE (Houma Ct. Hse.: Mar. v.26, #229)

SHY, William m. 5 April 1899 Alice HILLS (Thib. Ct. Hse.: Mar. v.39, #129)

SICONET, Victor Angelo (Jiovanni & Dominica PEZIN) b. 21 June 1896 (Houma Ch.: v.5, p.182)

SILVE, Barbe Armentine (Augustin & Henriette INCLADE) m. 16 Feb. 1898 Antonio ALLIENDE (Larose Ch.: v.4, p.114)

SILVE, Barbe Armentine (Augustin & Henriette INCALADE) m. 2 Feb. 1898 Antonio ALLIENDE (Larose Ch.: v.3, p.7)

SIMMONS, Isabella m. 27 April 1898 Alfred ZILTON (Houma Ct. Hse.: Mar. v.30 & 31, #422)

SIMMONS, John m. 4 Feb. 1897 Sylvia MATHEY (Thib. Ct. Hse.: Mar. v.36, #67)

SIMMONS, Rodney m. 15 Sept. 1898 Hattie STEWART (Houma Ct. Hse.: Mar. v.30 & 31, #99)

SIMMS (Sometimes: SIMS)

SIMMS, Kitty m. 30 Dec. 1899 Henry WASHINGTON (Houma Ct. Hse.: Mar. v.31 & 32, #218)

SIMMS, Virginia m. 4 Sept. 1897 Baptiste BUSH (Houma Ct. Hse.: Mar. v.29 & 30, #83)

SIMPSON (Sometimes: SIMSON)

SIMS, Romey m. 13 Sept. 1898 Melvia PHARR (Houma Ct. Hse.: Mar. v.30 & 31, #96)

SINAGRO, Pietra m. Guiseppe CASTROGIOVANNI d. 16 March 1899 at age 33 yrs. (Thib. Ch.: v.3, p.230)

SINCLAIR, George d. 29 April 1899 at age 77 yrs. (Thib. Ch.: Epis. Ch.: v.1, p.394)

SINGLETON, Bertha (Thomas & Sarah BONNER) m. 21 Jan. 1898 Dominique MORVANT (Houma Ct. Hse.: Mar. v.30 & 31, #240)

SINGLETON, Bertha (Thomas W. & Sarah BONNER) m. 26 Jan. 1898 Dominique MORVANT (Houma Ch.: Epis. Ch.: v.1, p.342)
SINGLETON, Edison Winfield (G. Y. & Sarah J. SINGLETON) b. 31 Dec. 1896 (Houma Ch.: Epis. Ch.: v.1, p.124)
SINGLETON, Eunice Beula (G. J. & Sarah J. SINGLETON) b. 7 Feb. 1899 (Houma Ch.: Epis. Ch.: v.1, p.126)
SINGLETON, John m. 18 June 1898 Robertha MANUEL (Houma Ct. Hse.: Mar. v.30 & 31, #21)
SINGLETON, Margaret m. 9 Feb. 1898 Philip RAY (Houma Ct. Hse.: Mar. v.30 & 31, #287)
SKINNER, Clarisse d. 19 Feb. 1896 at age 74 yrs. (Thib. Ch.: v.3, p.179)
SKINNER, Ida m. 21 Jan. 1897 Frank P. SMITH (Houma Ct. Hse.: Mar. v.29 & 30, #247)
SMALL, Charles d. 15 Nov. 1898 at age 47 yrs. (Montegut Ch.: v.2, p.21)
SMALL, Mary Nellie (Charles Gomilia & Genevieve CHAUVIN) b. 4 April 1897 (Montegut Ch.: v.6, p.52)
SMITH, Alfred (Eugene & Laurentia VEBRE) m. 28 Nov. 1898 Ida LEBLANC (Thib. Ct. Hse.: Mar. v.38, #311)
SMITH, Andre Joseph (Washington & Lucie KEEF) b. 5 Feb. 1899 (Larose Ch.: v.3, p.38)
SMITH, Annie m. 13 May 1897 Henry GRAY (Thib. Ct. Hse.: Mar. v.36, #142)
SMITH, Carrie m. 6 July 1896 Cato RINGGOLD (Houma Ct. Hse.: Mar. v.29 & 30, #103)
SMITH, Carroll d. 1893; m. Fanny SMITH, d. 1893 Both died in 1893, within months of each other. Petition for inventory: 12 May 1896. (Thib. Ct. Hse.: Succ. #1490)
SMITH, Celina m. 2 Aug. 1899 Aploda BABIN (Houma Ch.: v.6-B, p.4)
SMITH, Celina Louviere m. 28 July 1899 Aploda BABIN (Houma Ct. Hse.: Mar. v.31 & 32, #86)
SMITH, Charles m. 17 Oct. 1898 Nellie SCOTT (Thib. Ct. Hse.: Mar. v.38, #298)
SMITH, Clara m. 6 July 1899 Benjamin STEWART (Houma Ct. Hse.: Mar. v.31 & 32, #73)
SMITH, Clara Mildren (C. P. & Clara DUPONT) b. 10 Oct. 1899 (Houma Ch.: v.5, p.259)
SMITH, Cora m. 3 Feb. 1898 Willie E. MORRIS (Thib. Ct. Hse.: Mar. v.37, #77)
SMITH, Daisy Belle (Beverly W. & Daisy WILLIAMS) b. 6 April 1899 (Thib. Ch.: Epis. Ch.: v.1, p.44)
SMITH, David Jr. m. 10 June 1897 Ida WHITE (Houma Ct. Hse.: Mar. v.29 & 30, #21)
SMITH, Felix d. 16 May 1896 at age 36 yrs. (Montegut Ch.: v.2, p.4)
SMITH, Frank (Felix & Elmire VETO) m. 29 Dec. 1899 Laura BONVILLAIN (Houma Ct. Hse.: Mar. v.31 & 32, #213)

SMITH, Frank P. (Samuel A. & Lucinda THRAILKILL) m. 21 Jan. 1897 Ida SKINNER (Houma Ct. Hse.: Mar. v.29 & 30, #247)
SMITH, Harrison m. 26 Feb. 1898 Coraline HENDERSON (Thib. Ct. Hse.: Mar. v.37, #117)
SMITH, Henry m. 10 Nov. 1897 Alice LOVE (Thib. Ct. Hse.: Mar. v.37, #256)
SMITH, Henry L. m. 7 Oct. 1897 Lilly WARD (Houma Ct. Hse.: Mar. v.29 & 30, #106-C)
SMITH, Isaac m. 13 Jan. 1896 Bertha HARRIS (Houma Ct. Hse.: Mar. v.28, #385-C)
SMITH, James m. 11 Jan. 1897 Lucy NEVERS (Houma Ct. Hse.: Mar. v.29 & 30, #229)
SMITH, James m. 16 Feb. 1898 Betty PARSONS (Thib. Ct. Hse.: Mar. v.37, #99)
SMITH, Jean Baptiste Sylvestre (John & Justilia NEIL) b. 11 Oct. 1898 (Montegut Ch.: v.6, p.80)
SMITH, Jessie m. 2 Nov. 1897 Macdella DORCEY (Thib. Ct. Hse.: Mar. v.37, #255)
SMITH, John d. 28 Sept. 1899 (John, Sr.) m. Elizabeth JOHNSON Inventory: 17 Feb. 1899. (Thib. Ct. Hse.: Succ. #1563)
SMITH, John m. 11 Jan. 1897 Mary Agnes REED (Thib. Ct. Hse.: Mar. v.36, #21)
SMITH, John M. m. 10 Aug. 1898 Cora DICKERSON (Thib. Ct. Hse.: Mar. v.38, #243)
SMITH, Jonas m.16 Feb. 1898 Victoire WATSON (Thib. Ct. Hse.: Mar. v.37, #106)
SMITH, Joseph Adam (Felicien & Marie Eve VERDUN) b. 23 March 1897 (Theriot Ch.: v.2, p.5)
SMITH, Julienne m. 23 Jan. 1899 Jean Marie LEBLANC, Jr. (Houma Ct. Hse.: Mar. v.30 & 31, #279)
SMITH, Laura m. 19 Jan. 1899 Alfred CROSIER (Thib. Ct. Hse.: Mar. v.38, #42)
SMITH, Laura Emma (Jean & Marie NAQUIN) b. 1 May 1897 (Montegut Ch.: v.6, p.58)
SMITH, Lily m. 14 Jan. 1897 Drauzin GUITRIAGE (Thib. Ct. Hse.: Mar. v.36, #34)
SMITH, Louisa m. 2 Feb. 1898 William EWINGS (Houma Ct. Hse.: Mar. v.30 & 31, #266)
SMITH, Louisa m. 20 Feb. 1896 Elijah WILSON (Thib. Ct. Hse.: Mar. v.35, #47)
SMITH, Luc Joseph (Luc & Victoria FOREST) b. 9 Oct. 1897 (Montegut Ch.: v.6, p.63)
SMITH, Marie Olympe (Onnesse & Agnes SCHETE) b. 5 Feb. 1898 (Houma Ch.: v.5, p.198)
SMITH, Mary D. m. 21 Feb. 1899 Spencer JOHNSON (Houma Ct. Hse.: Mar. v.31 & 32, #347)
SMITH, Paul Xavier (John & Marie NAQUIN) b. 18 March 1899 (Montegut Ch.: v.6, p.91)
SMITH, Scott T. Jr. m. 8 Dec. 1897 Cora HARRIS (Houma Ct. Hse.: Mar. v.29 & 30, #141)

SMITH, Sophie d. 1 Feb. 1897 at age 52 yrs. (Houma Ch.: v.3, p.11)
SMITH, Sophie (Eugene & Alome WEBB) m. 20 Jan. 1897 Edgar SOIGNET (Thib. Ct. Hse.: Mar. v.36, #20)
SMITH, Sophie (Eugene & Alonce WEBB) m. 20 Jan. 1897 Edgar SAULNIER (Thib. Ch.: v.14, p.112)
SMITH, Thomas d. 6 May 1899 Petition for administration: 14 Oct. 1899. (Houma Ct. Hse.: Succ. #924)
SMITH, Ulfred (Eugene & Laurentia VEHE) m. 28 Nov. 1898 Ida LEBLANC (Thib. Ch.: v.14, p.231)
SMITH, Uriah m. 8 Feb. 1898 Carrie ALDRIDGE (Houma Ct. Hse.: Mar. v.30 & 31, #282)
SMITH, Victoria m. 10 Feb. 1898 John LEWIS (Thib. Ct. Hse.: Mar. v.37, #94)
SMITH, Washington of Lafourche Parish (John & Lydia KEEFE) m. 25 April 1898 Lucie KEEFE, of Lafourche Parish (Larose Ch.: v.3, p.9)
SMITH, Washington (John & Lydia KEEFFE) m. 25 April 1898 Lucie KEEFFE (Larose Ch.: v.4, p.40)
SMITH, Washington (John & Lydia KEIFF) m. 25 April 1898 Lucie KEIFF (Thib. Ct. Hse.: Mar. v.38, #163)
SMITH, William m. 6 Jan. 1898 Fanny JOHNSON (Houma Ct. Hse.: Mar. v.30 & 31, #183)
SMOTH, Anna (Cesar & Mary JEFFERSON) b. 19 May 1897 (Thib. Ch.: v.7, p.455)
SOLAIZ, Joseph Leonel (Fortune & Louisa WHITE) b. 1 Nov. 1898 (Raceland Ch.: v.5, p.82)
SOLCO, Marcelin d. 16 May 1899 at age 57 yrs. (Houma Ch.: v.3, p.22)
SOLCO, Marcelin m. d.Elizabeth VERRET Children: Alfred & Sidney. Tutorship: 29 Dec. 1899. (Houma Ct. Hse.: Succ. #932)

SOLE (Sometimes: SOLET, SOULET)

SOLE, Antoine Dominique (Etienne & Marie BILLOT) b. 10 March 1896 (Larose Ch.: v.2, p.193)
SOLE, Eleste Joseph (Joseph & Marie VERRET) b. 4 Feb. 1897 (Theriot Ch.: v.2, p.7)
SOLE, Josephine m. 11 April 1896 Lucien FITCH (Houma Ct. Hse.: Mar. v.29 & 30, #34)
SOLE, Josephine (Valentin) m. 7 Oct. 1897 Lucien FITCH (Theriot Ch.: v.1-B, p.1)
SOLE, Marie Hollenda (Frederic & Josephine PIERRE) b. 22 Jan. 1897 (Theriot Ch.: v.2, p.5)
SOLE, Marie Irma (Charbonnier & Amelia BILLOT) b. 12 Sept. 1897 (Larose Ch.: v.3, p.19)
SOLEIF, Claude Erling (Fortune & Louise WHITE) b. 8 Dec. 1896 (Raceland Ch.: v.5, p.39)
SOLOMON, Numas (Oscar & Genevieve ADAM) b. 17 July 1899 (Raceland Ch.: v.5, p.100)

SOLOMON, Oscar (Oscar & Genevieve ADAM) b. 20 May 1898 (Raceland Ch.: v.5, p.76)
SOLOMONE, Josephine m. 11 Sept. 1899 Antonino CECALA (Houma Ct. Hse.: Mar. v.31 & 32, #125)
SOMANSON, ----- child (Antoine) d. 13 Aug. 1899 at age 10 mths. (Lockport Ch.: v.1, #33)
SOMME, Bernard Hector (Eugene & Marie Eulalie GONZALES) b. 29 June 1896 (Raceland Ch.: v.5, p.28)
SOMME, Theodore Max (Eugene & Eulalie GONZALES) b. 23 June 1898 (Raceland Ch.: v.5, p.77)
SOMMERS, Octave John (Jean Baptiste & Julie Magdeleine JOLIVEL) m. 6 Feb. 1899 Elmire LERILLE (Thib. Ct. Hse.: Mar. v.38, #55)
SOMMERS, Octave John (Jean Baptiste & Julia Magdeleine JOLIVET) m. 6 Feb. 1899 Elmire LERILLE (Lockport Ch.: v.2, p.201)
SON, Marie Julienne (Antoine & Rosilia DANTIN) b. 8 Aug. 1897 (Chacahoula Ch.: Gibson Ch.: Mar. Bk., v.1, #33)
SONBERG, Ella Alisc (Albert & Adma MATSON) b. 28 Feb. 1897 (Thib. Ch.: Epis. Ch.: v.1, p.42)
SONGE, Joseph Bernard d. 15 Jan. 1899 at age 71 yrs. (Montegut Ch.: v.2, p.23)
SONGE, Julia (Joseph & Eveline ROBICHAUX) m. 24 June 1899 Alexandre GUIDRY (Houma Ct. Hse.: Mar. v.31 & 32, #55)
SONGE, Julia (Joseph & Eveline ROBICHAUX) m. 17 July 1899 Alexandre GUIDRY (Montegut Ch.: v.4, p.267)
SONGE, Marie Ella (Augustin & Ophelia GUIDRY) b. 6 Jan. 1899 (Montegut Ch.: v.6, p.81)

SOURDELIER (Sometimes: SADILLER, SOURDELIER)
SOURDELIER, Louis (Louis & Elodie FOREST) m. 6 April 1899 Emma BLANCHARD (Houma Ct. Hse.: Mar. v.31 & 32, #387)
SOUSON, Marie Julienne (Antoine & Rosalie DANTIN) b. 8 Aug. 1897; bt. 2 May 1898 (Chacahoula Ch.: Gibson Ch.: v.2, p.121)
SOUTH, Francis m. 5 April 1898 Joseph JOHNSON (Houma Ct. Hse.: Mar. v.30 & 31, #377)
SOUTH, Marie Louise (Robert & Marie GUIDRY) b. 26 July 1899 (Larose Ch.: v.3, p.46)
SPARKS, Joycie m. 25 May 1898 Jeff D. FRANCISCO (Houma Ct. Hse.: Mar. v.30 & 31, #451)
SPARKS, Leonard m. 28 Jan. 1899 Elmira MOORE (Thib. Ct. Hse.: Mar. v.38, #76)
SPEED, Dora m. 12 Feb. 1897 Joseph JOHNSON (Houma Ct. Hse.: Mar. v.29 & 30, #308)
SPEED, Washington m. 12 May 1896 Ann SCOTT (Houma Ct. Hse.: Mar. v.29 & 30, #65)
SPENANA, Vinzenza d. 19 May 1896 at age 11 mths., 10 days (Houma Ch.: v.3, p.7)
SPENCER, Cora m. 23 Dec. 1897 Jacob LEWIS (Houma Ct. Hse.: Mar. v.29 & 30, #152)

SPENCER, Eliza m. 12 Jan. 1899 Willie ARTHUR (Houma Ct. Hse.: Mar. v.30 & 31, #219)
SPENCER, Harriet m. 8 Oct. 1896 Charles RINGGOLD (Houma Ct. Hse.: Mar. v.29 & 30, #166)
SPENCER, Louisa m. 22 March 1897 Isaac GRIFFIN (Houma Ct. Hse.: Mar. v.29 & 30, #358)
SPENCER, Martha m. 24 Oct. 1896 Henry MILES (Houma Ct. Hse.: Mar. v.29 & 30, #175)
SPENELLA, Lucas d. 15 Dec. 1898 at age 50 yrs. (Thib. Ch.: v.3, p.223)
SPENNALLA, Virginia (Bernardu & Lucia BRAKA) b. 3 Jan. 1897 (Houma Ch.: v.5, p.164)
SPENNELLA, Salvatorne (Bernardiste & Louisa BRACK) b. 22 April 1898 (Houma Ch.: v.5, p.209)
SPEYRER, Laura m. 30 Jan. 1899 Henry THIBODAUX (Thib. Ct. Hse.: Mar. v.38, #81)
SPEZIALE, Vito d. 14 May 1899 (Raceland Ch.: v.1, p.25)
SPICOLA, Nicola m. 18 June 1898 Rosalia GRECO (Houma Ct. Hse.: Mar. v.30 & 31, #19)
SPICALA, Nicola (Rosario & Greces NICOLINA) m. 2 July 1898 Rosalia GRECO (Houma Ch.: v.6-A, p.244)
SPICOLA, Rose (Nicolas & Lea GRECA) b. 7 July 1899 (Houma Ch.: v.5, p.249)
SPITALE, Antonino of Italy d. 3 Dec. 1898 at age 50 yrs. (Thib. Ch.: v.3, p.222)
SPORT, Walter m. 5 July 1899 Ella KING (Thib. Ct. Hse.: Mar. v.39, #192)
SPRINGER, Henrettie m. James M. SPRINGER Inventory: 7 Sept. 1898. (Thib. Ct. Hse.: Succ. #1548)
STAFFORD, Frances Clifton (Henry & Alice GABRIEL) bt. 30 Sept. 1897 (Thib. Ch.: v.7, p.465)
STAFFORD, George Clarence (Henri & Alix GABRIEL) b. 14 Sept. 1898 (Thib. Ch.: v.7, p.532)
STANSBURY, Kate A. m. 8 May 1899 Louis C. TABOR (Thib. Ct. Hse.: Mar. v.39, #162)
STANSBURY, Lenus m. 21 Oct. 1899 Cecile NAQUIN (Thib. Ct. Hse.: Mar. v.39, #251)
STAPLES, Georgiana m. 24 June 1899 Andrew THOMAS (Houma Ct. Hse.: Mar. v.31 & 32, #54)
STAPLES, Joseph Candon Koscinsko (S. B. & Dasy B. HYAMES) b. 1 Dec. 1899 (Houma Ch.: v.5, p.266)
STARK, Louise Marie (Thomas & Jeanne FOUSTON) b. 24 Oct. 1897 (Thib. Ch.: v.7, p.479)
STATEM, Mathews m. 12 Dec. 1899 Mabel BIRDSALL (Thib. Ct. Hse.: Mar. v.39, #281)
STEELONE, Giuseppa (d.Francesco & Guiseppa OLIVERE) m. 23 Jan. 1899 Caloggino BRIGANTE (Thib. Ch.: v.14, p.243)
STELLONE, Guiseppa (Francisco & Guiseppa OLIVERO) m. 23 Jan. 1899 Calaggiero BRIGANTE (Thib. Ct. Hse.: Mar. v.38, #29)

STEVEN, Celeste (William & Celina BERGERON) m. 10 Dec. 1898 Paulin DAIGLE (Houma Ct. Hse.: Mar. v.30 & 31, #138)
STEVEN, Jeanne Eve (Honore & Rebecca FOLSE) b. 13 Nov. 1897 (Raceland Ch.: v.5, p.59)
STEVEN, Margaret M. (Philip & Ophelia PONTIFF) m. 26 Oct. 1896 Marcellus H. DAUNIS (Houma Ct. Hse.: Mar. v.29 & 30, #177)
STEVEN, Maria Elona (Thomas & Osea SIMMONEAUX) b. 2 Jan. 1898 (Chacahoula Ch.: Gibson Ch.: v.2, p.116)
STEVEN, Maria Elona (Thomas & Ozea SIMMONEAU) b. 2 Jan. 1898 (Chacahoula Ch.: Gibson Record: Mar. Bk., v.1, #10)
STEVEN, Mary Rosa (Auleus & Aglay BABIN) b. 16 May 1896 (Houma Ch.: v.5, p.157)
STEVEN, Victoria (Louis & Amanda LEBLANC) m. 5 Dec. 1898 Arthur THIBODAUX (Houma Ct. Hse.: Mar. v.30 & 31, #135)
STEVENS, Gabriella m. Randolph FOWLER Will & Testament: 13 Nov. 1896. (Houma Ct. Hse.: Succ. #870)
STEVENSON, Melia m. 9 July 1896 George WASHINGTON (Houma Ct. Hse.: Mar. v.29 & 30, #111)
STEVENSON, Nannie m. 30 Jan. 1896 Grandison YOUNG (Houma Ct. Hse.: Mar. v.28, #426)

STEWART (Sometimes: STIVART, STUARD)
STEWART, Antoine m. 21 Sept. 1899 Rachel WILLIAMS (Houma Ct. Hse.: Mar. v.31 & 32, #139)
STEWART, Ben m. 16 Aug. 1898 Martha BURRELL (Thib. Ct. Hse.: Mar. v.38, #253)
STEWART, Benjamin m. 6 July 1899 Clara SMITH (Houma Ct. Hse.: Mar. v.31 & 32, #73)
STEWART, Edward m. 27 Dec. 1897 Hannah RILEY (Houma Ct. Hse.: Mar. v.29 & 30, #155)
STEWART, Gabe m. 8 May 1897 Rachel ANDERSON (Houma Ct. Hse.: Mar. v.29 & 30, #410)
STEWART, Hattie m. 15 Sept. 1898 Rodney SIMMONS (Houma Ct. Hse.: Mar. v.30 & 31, #99)
STEWART, Taylor m. 6 Jan. 1898 Sarah CHRISTIAN (Thib. Ct. Hse.: Mar. v.37, #8)
STIEFEL, Joseph Andrew (Adolphe & Josephine KLINGMAN) b. 27 March 1899 (Houma Ch.: v.5, p.246)
STIFEL, Francois Xavier (Adolphe & Josephine KLINGMAN) b. 21 Aug. 1897 (Houma Ch.: v.5, p.186)
STOBALL, Edward m. 2 Nov. 1896 Louisa TURNER (Houma Ct. Hse.: Mar. v.29 & 30, #184)
STONE, Helen E. m. 22 June 1897 Clarence R. BURTON (Thib. Ch.: Epis. Ch.: v.1, p.331)
STONE, Helene E. m. 21 June 1897 Clarence R. BURTON (Thib. Ct. Hse.: Mar. v.36, #178)

STOUFFLET (Sometimes: ESTOUFFLET)

STOUFFLET, Frederic d. 23 Aug. 1899 at age 3 yrs. & 6 mths. (Raceland Ch.: v.1, p.27)

STOUFFLET, Lucie d. 3 Aug. 1899 at age 2 yrs. & 2 mths. (Raceland Ch.: v.1, p.26)

STOUFFLET, Maggie Byner (William & Tersile DUPLANTIS) b. 11 Sept. 1896 (Montegut Ch.: v.6, p.46)

STOUFFLET, Marie Pearl (William & Eve DUPLANTIS) b. 6 Sept. 1898 (Montegut Ch.: v.6, p.68)

STRATTEN, Mary m. 14 Oct. 1897 Willie SHIELD (Thib. Ct. Hse.: Mar. v.37, #250)

STREAMS, Hattie m. 21 Sept. 1899 Samuel BIRD (Thib. Ct. Hse.: Mar. v.39, #234)

STRINGER, Agnes Fannie (Alexander & Valerie Marthe DUPLANTIS) b. 21 April 1899 (Montegut Ch.: v.6, p.86)

STRINGER, Marie Eazel (Alexander & Valerie DUPLANTIS) b. 29 Oct. 1897 (Montegut Ch.: v.6, p.61)

STRIPLING, Melia m. 9 March 1898 Lewis SANDERS (Thib. Ct. Hse.: Mar. v.37, #123)

STRIPLING, Viola m. 14 Oct. 1898 Harrison WILSON (Thib. Ct. Hse.: Mar. v.38, #296)

STUART (Sometimes: STUARD)

SUMLEN, Henry m. 5 June 1897 Catherine WHITE (Houma Ct. Hse.: Mar. v.29 & 30, #7)

SUREAU, Clotilde (Frank & Alida PONTIFE) m. 15 April 1899 Clay LAINE (Thib. Ct. Hse.: Mar. v.39, #150)

SUREAU, Clotilde (Frank & Alida PONTIFE) m. 25 April 1899 Clay LAINE (Thib. Ch.: v.14, p.274)

SUTHON, Lucius d. 22 April 1899 at age 78 yrs. (Thib. Ch.: Epis. Ch.: v.1, p.394)

SWEETWINE, Ella m. 4 Sept. 1899 Philip DAVE (Thib. Ct Hse.: Mar. v.39, #219)

SYLVESTRE (Sometimes: SYLVESTER)

SYLVESTRE, F. A. d. 6 March 1897 at age 51 yrs. (Houma Ch.: v.3, p.12)

SYLVESTRE, Felix A. d. 5 March 1897; m. (1) Helen BYRNES, d. 21 Sept. 1884; m.(2) Marie Ina Louise BOURG on 18 Nov. 1885; she died 9 Feb. 1892. Children listed: (1) marriage: Marie Louise m. Calvin H. WURZLOW; Felicie, 14; (2) marriage: Marie Laure Jeanne. Petition for family meeting: 9 March 1897. (Houma Ct. Hse.: Succ. #883)

SYLVESTRE, Mary Pearley (Charles & Virginia MEAD) b. 9 Nov. 1896 (Thib. Ch.: v.7, p.437)

"T"

TABOR (Sometimes: TAB, TABB, TABER, THABOR)

TABOR, Ben (Joseph & Julie BOUDREAUX) m. 6 Sept. 1899 Dora PRESTENBACK (Thib. Ct. Hse.: Mar. v.39, #221)

TABOR, Clothilde m. 20 Dec. 1898 John GILES (Thib. Ct. Hse.: Mar. v.38, #320)

TABOR, Clotilde m. 7 Feb. 1899 John GILES (Thib. Ch.: v.14, p.258)

TABOR, Cora m. 22 April 1897 Oliver HALL (Thib. Ct. Hse.: Mar. v.36, #130)

TABOR, Henri d. 16 Nov. 1898 at age 38 yrs. (Thib. Ch.: v.3, p.222)

TABOR, Hudsn W. Sr. d. 12 July 1898; m. Emelie M. BERNARD Children listed: Hudson W.; Charles M.; Robert J.; Laura M.; Louis; Ella P. Petition of heirs to be placed in possession: 22 Nov. 1898. (Thib. Ct. Hse: Succ. #1554)

TABOR, Hudson d. 13 July 1898 at age 11 yrs. & 5 mths. (Thib. Ch.: v.3, p.217)

TABOR, James (Gustave & Mandy MORVAN) m. 27 Jan. 1898 Cecile PANVELLE (Chackbay Ch.: v.1, p.54)

TABOR, James (Gustave & Mandy MORVAN) m.27 Jan. 1898 Cecile PANVELLE (Thib. Ct. Hse.: Mar. v.37, #21)

TABOR, Julia Helen m. Jean ABADIE d. 18 Dec. 1897 at age 74 yrs. & 11 mths. (Thib. Ch.: v.3, p.209)

TABOR, Laura m. Honore ROSS d. 25 Nov. 1896 at age 28 yrs. (Thib. Ch.: v.3, p.190)

TABOR, Louis C. m. 8 May 1899 Kate A. STANSBURY (Thib. Ct. Hse.: Mar. v.39, #162)

TABOR, Louis Dural (John & Zoemy BOUDEAUX) b. 16 Jan. 1897 (Thib. Ch.: v.7, p.446)

TABOR, Lucie (John & Zulima MOLAISON) m. 27 Aug. 1896 Arthur BENOIT (Thib. Ct. Hse.: Mar. v.36, #131)

TABOR, Marie Argentine or TEBE (Jimmy & Marie HEBERT) b. 10 April 1897 (Raceland Ch.: v.5, p.53)

TABOR, Marie Ava Rogers (Louis Clinton & Catherine Allen STANSBURY) b. 21 June 1899 (Thib. Ch.: v.7, p.609)

TAJAN, Claude Arthur (Felicien & Rosa BOURGEOIS) b. 1 Jan. 1897 (Chackbay Ch.: v.1, p.80)

TAJAN, Joseph Frank (Frank & Mary BOURGEOIS) b. 21 Nov. 1896 (Lockport Ch.: v.3, #2)

TAJAN, Joseph Frank (Frank & Mary BOURGEOIS) b. 21 Nov. 1896 (Lockport Ch.: v.3-A, #2)

TAJAN, Therese (Felicien & Rosa BOURGEOIS) b. 18 July 1898 (Chackbay Ch.: v.1, p.115)

TALBOT (Sometimes: TALBAT)

TALTAVUL, Therese Bernadine (Peter & Maggie DELANEY) b. 31 Dec. 1897; bt. 28 Feb. 1898 (Chacahoula Ch.: Gibson Ch.: v.2, p.117)

TALTAVULL, Teresa Bernadine (Peter & Maggie DELANEY) b. 31 Dec. 1897 (Chacahoula Ch.: Gibson Ch.: Mar. Bk., v.1, #15)

TANNER (Sometimes: TANAR, TANNEUR)

TANNER, Lemuel m. Celeste BELANGER Petition for administration: 17 Nov. 1899. (Houma Ct. Hse.: Succ. #929)

TANNY, Corinne (John & Ida BRAUD) b. 12 Jan. 1899; bt. 13 Oct. 1902 (Thib. Ch.: v.8, p.103)

TANNY, Ida (John & Ida BRAUD) b. 1 Feb. 1897; bt. 13 Oct. 1902 (Thib. Ch.: v.8, p.103)

TANTILLO, Antonino (Domenica & Marietta PICORALO) m. 3 April 1899 Francesca VARISCA (Thib. Ch.: v.14, p.268-a)

TANTILLO, Antonino (Domenico & Marietta PICORALO) m. 3 April 1899 Francesca VARISCO (Thib. Ct. Hse.: Mar. v.39, #105)

TANTILLO, Rosa (Domenico & Rosina PICORARA) m. 26 Dec. 1899 Guiseppe URSO (Thib. Ch.: v.14, p.315)

TARANELA, Philippa (Cosmo & Guiseppa MELARANGE) b. 13 May 1899 (Thib. Ch.: v.7, p.605)

TARDO, Catharina (Nicolas & Anica FARINA) b. 20 Dec. 1898 (Thib. Ch.: v.7, p.537)

TARDO, Domenico (Nictado & One FARNIA) b. 6 Dec. 1896 (Thib. Ch.: v.7, p.436)

TARDY, Beatrice m. 28 Dec. 1899 William MITCHELL (Thib. Ct. Hse.: Mar. v.39, #302)

TASSET, Lydia Marie d. 8 Oct. 1898 at age 69 yrs. (Houma Ch.: v.3, p.18)

TATROE, Amasa John (Frank & Josephine NEWELL) b. 18 Sept. 1897 (Chacahoula Ch.: Gibson Ch.: Mar. Bk., v.1, #5)

TATROE, Amassa John (Frank & Josephine NEWELL) b. 18 Sept. 1897; bt. 23 Jan. 1898 (Chacahoula Ch.: Gibson Ch.: v.2, p.115)

TAUTILLO, Rosie (Domenico & Rosina PICORARA) m. 11 Dec. 1899 Giuseppi URSSO (Thib. Ct. Hse.: Mar. v.39, #280)

TAUZIN (Sometimes: TAUSIN, TAUSSIN)

TAUZIN, Emile (d.Ulysse & Marie LANDRY) m. 8 Oct. 1896 Amelia SEVAIN (Chackbay Ch.: v.1, p.32)

TAUZIN, Emile (Ulysse & Mary LANDRY) m. 8 Oct. 1896 Aurelia SEVIN (Thib. Ct. Hse.: Mar. v.36, #146)

TAUZIN, Georgia (Louis & Georgina CHIASSON) b. 24 Feb. 1897 (Chackbay Ch.: v.1, p.82)

TAUZIN, Joseph Aurelien (Gustave & Aurelie SEVAIN) b. 12 Feb. 1899 (Chackbay Ch.: v.1, p.126)

TAUZIN, Joseph Louis (Gustave & Aurelie SEVAIN) bt. 29 Aug. 1896 (Chackbay Ch.: v.1, p.73)

TAUZIN, Leon d. Aug. 1896 m. Eugenie MEUDIER, d. 1863 or 1864 Children listed: Louise m. Telesphore RODRIGUES, Jr.; Numa, of St. Martin Parish; Aladin, of St. Martin Parish; Doliska m. Honore BENOIT; Doze m. Dorville BENOIT; Rositte m. John ADAM; Emma; d.Nicholas m.

Emelie SEVIN. Petition for inventory: 26 Feb. 1897. (Thib. Ct. Hse.: Succ. #1507)

TAUZIN, Marie (Ulysse & Marie LANDRY) m. 14 Dec. 1899 Jules G. BORNE (Thib. Ch.: v.14, p.309)

TAUZIN, Marie Aglae (Emile & Amelia SEVAIN) b. 3 Sept. 1897 (Chackbay Ch.: v.1, p.94)

TAUZIN, Mary (Ulysse & Marie LANDRY) m. 2 Dec. 1899 Jules G. BORNE (Thib. Ct. Hse.: Mar. v.39, #274)

TAUZIN, Pierre d. 14 Nov. 1897 (Thib. Ch.: v.3, p.207)

TAYLOR, Aloysius Nolen (John & Cecile BERGERON) b. 29 March 1897 (Thib. Ch.: v.7, p.445)

TAYLOR, Charles m. 25 April 1899 Alice MORGAN (Houma Ct. Hse.: Mar. v.31 & 32, #421)

TAYLOR, Florence m. 30 Oct. 1899 John SHEDRICK (Houma Ct. Hse.: Mar. v.31 & 32, #158)

TAYLOR, Harry m. 12 Jan. 1899 Janey REED (Thib. Ct. Hse.: Mar. v.38, #16)

TAYLOR, Helen M. m. 3 Dec. 1898 Henry R. DUPRE (Thib. Ct. Hse.: Mar. v.38, #314)

TAYLOR, James M. m. 16 April 1896 Stella B. JOHNSON (Thib. Ct. Hse.: Mar. v.35, #74)

TAYLOR, John m. 25 June 1898 Katy RUDLEY (Houma Ct. Hse.: Mar. v.30 & 31, #35)

TAYLOR, Lilly E. (Georges & Hannah HANLEY) m. 3 May 1897 Christophe Columbus JOHNSON (Thib. Ct. Hse.: Mar. v.36, #135)

TAYLOR, Lily (Georges S. & Hannah HANLEY) m. 3 May 1897 Christopher Columbus JOHNSON (Thib. Ch.: v.14, p.143)

TAYLOR, Louisa m. 24 Aug. 1899 John REED (Thib. Ct. Hse.: Mar. v.39, #213)

TAYLOR, Mary m. 29 Dec. 1898 Leroy COTTON (Thib. Ct. Hse.: Mar. v.38, #326)

TAYLOR, Mervin J. m. 21 March 1898 Cecilia JOSEPH (Thib. Ct. Hse.: Mar. v.37, #131)

TAYLOR, Myrthe Catherine (John B. & Cecile BERGERON) b. 13 Feb. 1899 (Thib. Ch.: v.7, p.536)

TAYLOR, Olivia m. 7 Oct. 1899 Barry VINCENT (Thib. Ct. Hse.: Mar. v.39, #241)

TEBE, Marie Argentine or TABOR (Jimmy & Marie HEBERT) b. 10 April 1897 (Raceland Ch.: v.5, p.53)

TEMPLE, James m. 18 Jan. 1897 Sarah EVANS (Thib. Ct. Hse.: Mar. v.36, #42)

TEMPLE, Marie Eleonore (Horace & Catherine HARRISON) m. 14 Feb. 1898 Thomas BOURGEOIS (Thib. Ch.: v.14, p.187)

TEMPLE, Marie Eleonore (Horace & Catherine HARRISON) m. 14 Feb. 1898 Thomas BOURGEOIS (Thib. Ct. Hse.: Mar. v.37, #98)

TEMPLET, Jean d. 5 Jan. 1899 at age 87 yrs. (Chacahoula Ch.: Gibson Ch.: v.2, p.182)

TEMPLET, Joseph Aurelien (Jules & Ophelia BAUDOUIN) b. 29 Jan. 1896 (Raceland Ch.: v.5, p.40)

TEMPLET, Lelia Bernadette (Eugene & Cecilia SOLAR) b. 4 March 1898 (Chacahoula Ch.: Gibson Records: Mar. Bk., v.1, #31)
TEMPLET, Lelia Bernadette (Eugene & Cecilia SOLAR) b. 4 March 1898 (Chacahoula Ch.: Gibson Ch.: v.2, p.121)
TEMPLET, Marie d. 19 Nov. 1899 at age 3 mths. (Raceland Ch.: v.1, p.29)
TEMPLET, Marie Eupheme (Alcee & Eufelia BAUDOUIN) b. 8 Sept. 1899 (Raceland Ch.: v.5, p.101)
TENNEY, Augusta (John L. & Ida BRAUD) b. 21 Oct. 1896 (Raceland Ch.: v.5, p.37)
TERENOLA, Attuzza (Giorgio & Carmela SPITALLA) b. 3 March 1899 (Thib. Ch.: v.7, p.595)
TERRACHIM, James m. 8 May 1896 Philodion BERGERON (Thib. Ct. Hse.: Mar. v.35, #87)
TERRACINA, Dominica (Vincent & Philodia BERGERON) b. 3 April 1899 (Thib. Ch.: v.7, p.545)
TERRANELLA, Lucia (Salvatore & Joseppa RANDAZZO) b. 17 Jan. 1898 (Thib. Ch.: v.7, p.533)
TERRANELLA, Mariano (Joseppe & Josepyne MODICA) b. 5 Jan. 1898 (Thib. Ch.: v.7, p.533)

TERREBONNE (Sometimes: TERREBONE)
TERREBONNE, Alice Marie (Arthur & America REEPSTOCK) b. 11 April 1898 (Larose Ch.: v.3, p.22)
TERREBONNE, Almina (Leoheme & Armimione TERREBONNE) m. 8 Nov. 1899 Paul CHERAMI Civil marriage on 19 June 1897. (Larose Ch.: v.4, p.126)
TERREBONNE, Alphonse Edward (Louis & Amanda ----CLAR) b. 16 Nov. 1896 (Larose Ch.: v.3, p.8)
TERREBONNE, Alphonse Eugene (Camille & Nancia FREYTT) b. 17 June 1897 (Larose Ch.: v.3, p.9)
TERREBONNE, Alvina of LaCheniere (Leonize & Arminioue TERREBONNE) m. 8 Nov. 1899 Paul CHERAMI (Larose Ch.: v.3, p.12)
TERREBONNE, Amadeo m. 1 May 1899 Gertrude LAFONT (Thib. Ct. Hse.: Mar. v.39, #160)
TERREBONNE, Amadeo m. 20 May 1899 Gertrude LAFONT (Larose Ch.: v.3, p.12)
TERREBONNE, Amedeo m. 20 May 1899 Gertrude LAFOND (Larose Ch.: v.4, p.102)
TERREBONNE, Anatole m. 16 April 1898 Adolphine GUIDRY (Thib. Ct. Hse.: Mar. v.37, #148)
TERREBONNE, Andre m. 19 Feb. 1898 Armance CHERAMI (Larose Ch.: v.3, p.8)
TERREBONNE, Andre m. 19 Feb. 1898 Armance CHERAMI (Larose Ch.: v.4, p.75)
TERREBONNE, Andre m. 29 Feb. 1898 Armance CHERAMIE (Thib. Ct. Hse.: Mar. v.37, #105)
TERREBONNE, Andre Lehes (Felix & Pauline CALET) b. 25 March 1898 (Larose Ch.: v.3, p.25)

TERREBONNE, Azemia m. 29 April 1898 Joseph MARTIN (Thib. Ct. Hse.: Mar. v.38, #173)
TERREBONNE, Dominique Eustache (Paul & Elisa JAMBON) b. 20 Sept. 1897 (Larose Ch.: v.3, p.26)
TERREBONNE, Duprey (Duprey & Leocadie TERREBONNE) m. 4 Nov. 1899 Victoria PITRE (Thib. Ct. Hse.: Mar. v.39, #245)
TERREBONNE, Duprey (Duprey & Leocadie TERREBONNE) m. 4 Nov. 1899 Victoria PITRE (Larose Ch.: v.3, p.12)
TERREBONNE, Duprey (William Duprey & Leocadie TERREBONNE) m. 4 Nov. 1899 Victoria PITRE (Larose Ch.: v.4, p.125)
TERREBONNE, Elocadie m. 24 June 1899 Pierre COLLIN (Thib. Ct. Hse.: Mar. v.39, #181)
TERREBONNE, Evariste Dominique (Louis & Rosema BOURG) b. 24 June 1898 (Larose Ch.: v.3, p.33)
TERREBONNE, Eve of Jefferson Parish (Azael & Donatille TERREBONNE) m. 28 July 1898 Edgard BOUZIGARD, of Jefferson Parish (Larose Ch.: v.3, p.10)
TERREBONNE, Eve (Azael & Donatille TERREBONNE) of Jefferson Parish m. 28 July 1898 Edgard BOUZIGARD, of Jefferson Parish (Larose Ch.: v.4, p.24)
TERREBONNE, Evelina Marguerite (Dupre & Elisa ARNAUDIN) b. 22 Aug. 1896 (Larose Ch.: v.2, p.186)
TERREBONNE, Felix Hebert (Louis & Rosema BOURG) b. 18 May 1896 (Larose Ch.: v.2, p.195)
TERREBONNE, Francois Joseph (Ulysse & Philomene LAURAINE) b. 4 May 1898 (Larose Ch.: v.3, p.19)
TERREBONNE, Genevieve Irma (Mark & Thelenie CHICHIZOLA) b. 15 June 1898 (Larose Ch.: v.3, p.24)
TERREBONNE, Harris Ambroise (Maurice & Odilia CAMARDEL) b. 7 Dec. 1896 (Lockport Ch.: v.3, #35)
TERREBONNE, Harris Ambroise (Maurice & Odilia CAMORDEL) b. 7 Dec. 1896 (Lockport Ch.: v.3-A, #35)
TERREBONNE, Idea Margaritte (Aymard & Ur--ry? LAFOND) b. 20 Jan. 1896 (Larose Ch.: v.2, p.194)
TERREBONNE, Jean Dupre (Dupre & Elisa ANORDIN) b. 18 April 1898 (Larose Ch.: v.3, p.21)
TERREBONNE, Jean Laurent (Anatole & Adolphine GUIDRY) b. 2 Feb. 1898 (Larose Ch.: v.3, p.21)
TERREBONNE, Joseph Alphonse (Joseph & Adele GUIDRY) b. 10 Sept. 1896 (Larose Ch.: v.2, p.196)
TERREBONNE, Josephine of Jefferson Parish (Etienne & Helene PALHEY) m. 30 July 1898 Gaston CHICHIZOLA, of Jefferson Parish (Larose Ch.: v.3, p.10)
TERREBONNE, Josephine of Jefferson Parish (Etienne & Helena PALKEY) m. 30 July 1898 Gaston CHICHIZOLA, of Jefferson Parish (Larose Ch.: v.4, p.26)
TERREBONNE, Mack of Jefferson Parish (Oscar & Emma TERREBONNE) m. 6 Feb 1898 Thelemie CHICHIZOLA, of Jefferson Parish (Larose Ch.: v.3, p.7)

TERREBONNE, Mack (Oscar & Emma TERREBONNE) m. 6 Feb. 1898 Thetenie CHICHIZOLA (Larose Ch.: v.4, p.4)
TERREBONNE, Marie Anneta (Adam & Olivia THIBODAUX) b. 27 Sept. 1897 (Houma Ch.: v.5, p.190)
TERREBONNE, Mezida of Lafourche Parish (Thele & Ulgerine CUROL) m. 21 Jan. 1898 Jules DANOS, of Lafourche Parish (Larose Ch.: v.3, p.7)
TERREBONNE, Mezida (Thele & Ulgerine CUROL) m. 21 Jan. 1898 Jules DANOS (Larose Ch.: v.4, p.2)
TERREBONNE, Mezida (Thele & Ulgerine CUROL) m. 21 Jan. 1899 Jules DANOS (Thib. Ct. Hse.: Mar. v.38, #37)
TERREBONNE, Oscar m. 1 May 1899 Motila DOUCET (Thib. Ct. Hse.: Mar. v.39, #161)
TERREBONNE, Oscar (Samjest & Constance SANDRAS) m. 13 May 1899 Notilia DOUCET (Larose Ch.: v.4, p.85)
TERREBONNE, Oscar (Samjest & Constance SANDRAS) m. 13 May 1899 Notilia DOUCET (Larose Ch.: v.4, p.105)
TERREBONNE, Oscar (Sanijest & Constance SANDRAS) m. 13 May 1899 Notilia DOUCET (Larose Ch.: v.3, p.12)
TERREBONNE, Paul Elles (Felix & Pauline CALET) b. 1 June 1896 (Larose Ch.: v.2, p.193)
TERREBONNE, Pierre (Theles & Ulgerine CUROL) m. 25 April 1898 Lolitte BRUCE (Thib. Ct. Hse.: Mar. v.38, #161)
TERREBONNE, Pierre (Theles & Ulgerine CUROL) m. 25 April 1898 Lolitte BRUCE (Larose Ch.: v.4, p.13)
TERREBONNE, Pierre of Lafourche Parish (Theles & Ulgerine CUROL) m. 25 April 1898 Lolitte BRUCE, of Lafourche Parish (Larose Ch.: v.3, p.9)
TERREBONNE, Rodolphe of Lafourche Parish (Rodolphe & Adelaide BOUDREAU) m. 25 June 1898 Felicie CHABERT, of Lafourche Parish (Larose Ch.: v.3, p.9)
TERREBONNE, Rodolphe (Rodolphe & Adelaide BOUDREAU) m. 25 June 1898 Felicie CHABERT (Thib. Ct. Hse.: Mar. v.38, #203)
TERREBONNE, Rodolphe (Rodolphe & Adelaide BOUDREAU) m. 25 June 1898 Felicie CHABERT (Larose Ch.: v.4, p.19)
TERREBONNE, Ulysse m. 25 May 1897 Philomene LORRAINE (Thib. Ct. Hse.: Mar. v.36, #147)
TERREBONNE, Ulysse m. 5 June 1897 Philomene LORRAINE (Larose Ch.: v.3, p.5)
TERREBONNE, Ulysse m. 5 June 1897 Philomeine LORAINE (Larose Ch.: v.4, p.72)
TERRECINA, Marie Rosalie (Vencenzo & Philodia Marie BERGERON) b. 10 April 1896 (Thib. Ch.: v.7, p.448)
TERRECINA, Vincenzo (Tony & Domenica CHULINA) m. 11 Jan. 1897 Philodia Marie BERGERON (Thib. Ch.: v.14, p.106)
TERRITA, Cosima d. 30 Jan. 1899 at age 22 yrs. (Thib. Ch.: v.3, p.226)
TERRY, Henry m. 17 Aug. 1899 Dolley ANDERSON (Thib. Ct. Hse.: Mar. v.39, #208)
TESSON, Jean d. 3 July 1897 (Houma Ch.: Epis. Ch.: v.1, p.386)

TESSON, Jean d. 3 July 1897; m. Ozea CLEMENT Petition to appoint administrator: 27 Nov. 1897. (Houma Ct. Hse.: Succ. #891)
TETREAU, Hercule d. 24 Feb. 1899 (Thib. Ch.: v.3, p.229)
THEBE, Alidore (Henri & Berthille ORDOGNE) b. 2 Aug. 1897 (Chackbay Ch.: v.1, p.92)
THEBE, Anna (John & Zoemile BOUDREAUX) b. 14 Aug. 1899 (Chackbay Ch.: v.1, p.140)
THEBE, Ben (Joseph & Julie BOUDREAU) m. 6 Sept. 1899 Dora PRESTENBACK (Chackbay Ch.: v.1, p.72)
THEBE, Edouard Foster (James & Cecile PANVELLE) b. 23 Oct. 1898; m. Lilliam VIDAL on 24 Feb. 1962. (Chackbay Ch.: Bapt. Bk., v.1, p.121)
THEBE, Josephine (John & Zulma MOLAISON) b. 12 March 1898 (Chackbay Ch.: v.1, p.113)
THEBE, Lucia (John & d.Zulma MOLAISON) m. 27 Aug. 1896 Arthur BENOIT (Chackbay Ch.: v.1, p.30)
THEBE, Marie Lilly (John & Zulma MOLAISON) b. 3 May 1899 (Chackbay Ch.: v.1, p.143)
THEBE, Walter (Henri & Bertille ORDOGNE) b. 2 Aug. 1897 (Chackbay Ch.: v.1, p.92)
THERAND, Louis (Adolphe & Alida LAMOUREUX) m. 20 Dec. 1899 Cecile CLEMENT (Thib. Ct. Hse.: Mar. v.39, #289)
THERAND, Louis (Adolphe & Alida LAMOUREUX) m. 20 Dec. 1899 Cecile CLEMENT (Chackbay Ch.: v.1, p.77)

THERIOT (Sometimes: TERIAUX, TERIOT, TERRIOT)

THERIOT, Adele d. 29 Oct. 1895 m. d.Joseph BARRILLEAUX Children listed: Francois L.; Philomene m. Onesippe FORET; Domithilde; Florence m. Richard FORET; Ferdinand; Rose m. Ozeme LEBLANC; Evelina m. Joseph LEBLANC. Petition for probate of will: 19 March 1896. (Thib. Ct. Hse.: Succ. #1485)
THERIOT, Adele Nelly (Levy & Nelly CHAMPAGNE) b. 9 Aug. 1898 (Theriot Ch.: v.2, p.30)
THERIOT, Agnes Junietta (Arthur & Celestinite MARCELLE) b. 5 Sept. 1897 (Theriot Ch.: v.2, p.11)
THERIOT, Alice m. 14 Jan. 1899 Dennis HEBERT (Houma Ct. Hse.: Mar. v.30 & 31, #229)
THERIOT, Alice (Dalmas & Dorphina HENRI) m. 31 Jan. 1899 Dennis HEBERT (Houma Ch.: v.6-a, p.272)
THERIOT, Amy Odette (Felicien A. & Jamy WRIGHT) b. 27 Sept. 1896 (Houma Ch.: v.5, p.159)
THERIOT, Angele (Edma & Eliscae CHAMPAGNE) m. 31 Jan. 1899 Ovide THERIOT (Theriot Ch.: v.1-B, p.6)
THERIOT, Angele (Edmee & Eliska CHAMPAGNE) m. 13 Jan. 1899 Ovide THERIOT (Houma Ct. Hse.: Mar. v.30 & 31, #227)
THERIOT, Anne Aglae (Florentin & Marie DUMONT) b. 24 Oct. 1898 (Theriot Ch.: v.2, p.32)
THERIOT, Anne Helene (Ludovico & Amanda FALGOUT) b. 19 Dec. 1897 (Theriot Ch.: v.2, p.14)

THERIOT, Augustave (Augustin & Alcee CHAUVIN) m. 21 Jan. 1896 Albertine CHAUVIN (Theriot Ch.: v.1, p.3)
THERIOT, Augustave (Augustin & Alice CHAUVIN) m. 4 Jan. 1896 Albertine CHAUVIN (Houma Ct. Hse.: Mar. v.28, #369)
THERIOT, Aurelie d. 7 Sept. 1885; m. Mary E. ROY Children listed: Ida m. A. G. GODARD; Lydia m. Odillon BLANCHET; Eleonore, 22; Honore, 21; Clotilde, 19; Martha, 17; Marie, 15; Clay, 13; Roy, 11. Tutorship: 28 June 1896. (Houma Ct. Hse.: Succ. #871)
THERIOT, Benoit Nede (Elie & Elia CHAMPAGNE) m. 27 Aug. 1899 (Theriot Ch.: v.2, p.56)
THERIOT, Cecilia m. 21 Feb. 1898 Elsei MAZARIN (Houma Ch.: v.6-a, p.235)
THERIOT, Cecilia (Ulysse & Estiliana LABIT) m. 25 Feb. 1897 Alsie MAZERAC (Houma Ct. Hse.: Mar. v.29 & 30, #330)
THERIOT, Claire Ceraline (Livag & Adele Heli CHAMPAGNE) b. 14 April 1896 (Theriot Ch.: v.1-B, p.94)
THERIOT, Claire Judith (Odressi & Celine GAUK) b. 6 Feb. 1898 (Houma Ch.: v.5, p.200)
THERIOT, Edouard d. 25 July 1898 at age 9 mths. (Houma Ch.: v.3, p.17)
THERIOT, Elda m. 14 April 1897 Pierre FORET (Thib. Ct. Hse.: Mar. v.36, #114)
THERIOT, Elda (Azael & Eugenie HEBERT) m. 29 April 1897 Pierre FORET (Raceland Ch.: v.2, p.38)
THERIOT, Eleanore (Aurelie & Editha ROY) m. 18 Feb. 1898 Xavier H. ST. MARTIN (Houma Ct. Hse.: Mar. v.30 & 31, #308)
THERIOT, Elecia m. 22 June 1899 Albert FORET (Thib. Ct. Hse.: Mar. v.39, #182)
THERIOT, Elecia (Israel & Eugenie HEBERT) m. 22 June 1899 Albert FORET (Raceland Ch.: v.2, p.100)
THERIOT, Eleonore m. 26 Jan. 1898 Jean Xavier ST. MARTIN (Theriot Ch.: v.1-B, p.3-A)
THERIOT, Eleonore (Aurelie & Laftae Edithae ROY) m. 20 Feb. 1898 Xavier ST. MARTIN (Theriot Ch.: v.1-B, p.2)
THERIOT, Elie m. 15 Jan. 1897 Elia CHAMPAGNE (Houma Ct. Hse.: Mar. v.29 & 30, #238)
THERIOT, Elie (Ulysse & Albertine THERIOT) m. 19 Jan. 1897 Elia CHAMPAGNE (Theriot Ch.: v.1, p.8)
THERIOT, Ernestine m. 26 Aug. 1898 Joseph ROBICHAUX (Thib. Ct. Hse.: Mar. v.38, #266)
THERIOT, Ernestine (Honore & Emilia MALBROUGH) m. 12 Feb. 1898 Edward ST. PIERRE (Thib. Ct. Hse.: Mar. v.37, #32)
THERIOT, Ernestine (Louis & Laura GUIDRY) m. 28 Jan. 1899 Leo SAINT PE (Thib. Ct. Hse.: Mar. v.38, #24)
THERIOT, Ernestine (Louis & Laura GUIDRY) m. 28 Jan. 1899 Leo ST. PE (Lockport Ch.: v.2, p.199)
THERIOT, Ernestine (Simjeste & Victorine LIVEZ) m. 10 Sept. 1898 Joseph ROBICHAUX (Raceland Ch.: v.2, p.80)
THERIOT, Geneva (G. Taylor & Florence WRIGHT) m. 14 June 1897 Winslow HATCH (Theriot Ch.: v.1, p.10)

THERIOT, Geneva (J. Taylor & Florence F. WRIGHT) m. 5 June 1897 Winslow G. HATCH (Houma Ct. Hse.: Mar. v.29 & 30, #8)

THERIOT, Gustave Joseph (Adressi & Celine GOUAUX) b. 9 Feb. 1896 (Houma Ch.: v.5, p.144)

THERIOT, Ida m. 16 March 1899 Walton THOMAS (Thib. Ct. Hse.: Mar. v.39, #119)

THERIOT, Ida m. 27 June 1898 J. A. BLOUIN (Thib. Ct. Hse.: Mar. v.38, #214)

THERIOT, Joseph m. 24 July 1897 Celina GUIDRY (Lockport Ch.: v.2, p.164)

THERIOT, Joseph (Honore & Marie BADEAU) m. 24 July 1897 Celma GUIDRY (Thib. Ct. Hse.: Mar. v.35, #189)

THERIOT, Joseph Addi (Damase & Eulalie BUQUET) b. 19 Nov. 1896 (Houma Ch.: v.5, p.160)

THERIOT, Joseph Augustin (Augustin & Alice CHAUVIN) b. 21 July 1896 (Theriot Ch.: v.1-B, p.98)

THERIOT, Joseph Edme (Edme & H. Elisca CHAMPAGNE) b. 1 June 1897 (Theriot Ch.: v.2, p.4)

THERIOT, Joseph Stanley (Ozese & Lucille CHAUVIN) b. 9 Oct. 1896 (Theriot Ch.: v.1-B, p.100)

THERIOT, Joseph Vare (Paul & Felicia ROBICHEAUX) b. 4 July 1896 (Raceland Ch.: v.5, p.51)

THERIOT, Julie (Wilfred & Marguerite BRUNET) m. 23 Aug. 1896 Valerie BOUDREAUX (Houma Ct. Hse.: Mar. v.29 & 30, #132)

THERIOT, Julie (Wilfrid & Marguerite BRUNET) m. 1 Sept. 1896 Valerie BOUDREAU (Theriot Ch.: v.1, p.7)

THERIOT, Lewis Edey (Joseph & Lea CHAMPAGNE) b. 11 Sept. 1897 (Raceland Ch.: v.5, p.55)

THERIOT, Louisa d. 9 Sept. 1898 at age 4 days (Theriot Ch.: v.1, p.1)

THERIOT, Louise Edna (Camille & Theodora ADAM) b. 31 Dec. 1897 (Larose Ch.: v.3, p.20)

THERIOT, Marie Azelia (Clement & Zolide MELANCON) b. 25 April 1897 (Raceland Ch.: v.5, p.49)

THERIOT, Marie Etiennette (Augustin & Alice CHAUVIN) b. 13 Nov. 1897 (Theriot Ch.: v.2, p.13)

THERIOT, Marie Louise (Ludovic & Amanda FALGOUT) b. 14 Jan. 1896 (Theriot Ch.: v.1-B, p.88)

THERIOT, Marshall (Ovide & Pauline BRUNET) m. 16 Sept. 1899 Emily GUIDRY (Houma Ct. Hse.: Mar. v.31 & 32, #132)

THERIOT, Marshall (Ovide & Pauline BRUNET) m. 9 Oct. 1899 Emelie GUIDRY (Montegut Ch.: v.4, p.271)

THERIOT, Masse of Houma m. 11 Dec. 1899 Ada CHIASSON (Houma Ch.: v.6-B, p.5)

THERIOT, Mathilde Elina (Louis & Marie Mathilde GAUDET) b. 21 April 1898 (Raceland Ch.: v.5, p.70)

THERIOT, Nicesse (Dalmas & Dolphina HENRI) m. 2 Dec. 1899 Ada CHIASSON (Houma Ct. Hse.: Mar. v.31 & 32, #172)

THERIOT, Oscar d. 3 Jan. 1899 at age 19 yrs. (Theriot Ch.: v.1, p.2)
THERIOT, Ovide (Ulysse & Albertine THERIOT) m. 13 Jan. 1899 Angele THERIOT (Houma Ct. Hse.: Mar. v.30 & 31, #227)
THERIOT, Ovide (Ulysses & Albertine THERIOT) m. 31 Jan. 1899 Angele THERIOT (Theriot Ch.: v.1-B, p.6)
THERIOT, Paul m. 6 June 1896 Felicia ROBICHAUD (Thib. Ct. Hse.: Mar. v.35, #96)
THERIOT, Paul (Paul & Celestine MOUTIE) m. 6 June 1896 Felicia ROBICHAUX (Raceland Ch.: v.2, p.16)
THERIOT, Paul Michel (Florestin & Marie DUMOUT) b. 15 Nov. 1896 (Theriot Ch.: v.1-B, p.102)
THERIOT, Pierre Elie (Pierre Elie & Bernadette DU PANTE) b. 6 May 1897 (Theriot Ch.: v.1-B, p.106)
THERIOT, Richard d. 8 Jan. 1897 at age 21 yrs. (Thib. Ch.: v.3, p.194)
THERIOT, Rodusta m. 31 Jan. 1899 Albert THIBODAUX (Houma Ct. Hse.: Mar. v.30 & 31, #293)
THERIOT, Rodusta (Frank & Ernestine THERIOT) m. 13 Feb. 1899 Albert THIBODEAU (Houma Ch.: v.6-a, p.280)
THERIOT, Simon Narcisse (Oscar & Rose GAUDET) b. 18 Feb. 1898 (Raceland Ch.: v.5, p.69)
THERIOT, Theodule (Clement & Zeolide MELANCON) b. 1 Dec. 1899 (Raceland Ch.: v.5, p.108)
THERIOT, Toussaint (Emilien & Arthemise Angelina MICHEL) m. 18 May 1896 Eva ENGERRAN (Houma Ct. Hse.: Mar. v.29 & 30, #74)
THERIOT, Ulysse J. m. 18 Dec. 1896 Helena BRYANT, formerly married to WATKINS (Houma Ct. Hse.: Mar. v.29 & 30, #205)
THERIOT, Ulysse J. (Zenon & Alexandrina LEBLANC) m. 20 Dec. 1896 Helena BUQUET, widow WATKINS (Houma Ch.: v.6-a, p.187)
THERIOT, Victoria m. 18 Jan. 1898 Valery BABIN (Houma Ct. Hse.: Mar. v.30 & 31, #226)
THERIOT, Victoria (Ulysse J. & Esteline LABIT) m. 19 Jan. 1898 Valery BABIN (Houma Ch.: v.6-a, p.222)
THIBAULT, Evelie (Florent & Emma GRAMIER) m. 21 Aug. 1897 Whine ZELAIRE (Chackbay Ch.: v.1, p.47)
THIBAULT, Evelie (Florent & Emma GRANIER) m. 21 Aug. 1897 Uhing or Ewing ZELAIRE (Thib. Ct. Hse.: Mar. v.37, #208)

THIBODAUX (Sometimes: THIBAUDAUX, THIBAUDEAUX, THIBODAUX, THIBODEAU, THIBODEAUX, TIBAUDAUX)

THIBODAUX, Adeline (Edouard & Adeline ANDRA) m. 13 Feb. 1899 Arthur ORDOGNE (Thib. Ct. Hse.: Mar. v.38, #73)
THIBODAUX, Adeline (Edouard & Adeline ANDRA) m. 13 Feb. 1899 Arthur ORDOGNE (Thib. Ch.: v.14, p.264-B)
THIBODAUX, Adeline (Ernest) d. 4 Nov. 1899 at age 1 mth. (Theriot Ch.: v.1, p.2)

THIBODAUX, Agathe Marie (Prosper & Mathilde TOUPS) b. 25 Dec. 1898 (Thib. Ch.: v.7, p.527)

THIBODAUX, Agnes Marie (Felicien & Emelie HEBERT) b. 27 Feb. 1896 (Thib. Ch.: v.7, p.440)

THIBODAUX, Albert d. 19 April 1897 at age 2 mths. (Thib. Ch.: v.3, p.199)

THIBODAUX, Albert m. 31 Jan. 1899 Rodusta THERIOT (Houma Ct. Hse.: Mar. v.30 & 31, #293)

THIBODAUX, Albert (Singleton & Rosalie HEBERT) m. 13 Feb. 1899 Rodusta THERIOT (Houma Ch.: v.6-a, p.280)

THIBODAUX, Alcida d. 4 Aug. 1897 at age 27 yrs. (Thib. Ch.: v.3, p.203)

THIBODAUX, Alcide Adam (Pierre & Victorine ROME) b. 2 Nov. 1896 (Thib. Ch.: v.7, p.435)

THIBODAUX, Alexandre Forest (Olivier & Evelina WATKINS) m. 31 Jan. 1898 Marie Feliia NAQUIN (Montegut Ch.: v.4, p.233)

THIBODAUX, Alexandre Forest (Olivier & Evelina WATKINS) m. 13 Jan. 1898 Marie Felicia NAQUIN (Houma Ct. Hse.:Mar. v.30 & 31, #200)

THIBODAUX, Amelia m. 20 July 1897 Clemille DHUE (Thib. Ct. Hse.: Mar. v.37, #197)

THIBODAUX, Amelia (Joseph & Denyse ADAM) m. 9 Aug. 1897 Camile DUET (Chackbay Ch.: v.1, p.46)

THIBODAUX, Anastasie (Olivier A. & Fedelie A. WATKINS) m. 4 Sept. 1897 Charles SCHNEIDER (Houma Ct. Hse.: Mar. v.29 & 30, #84)

THIBODAUX, Andrese d. 1 Sept. 1896 at age 3 yrs. (Thib. Ch.: v.3, p.188)

THIBODAUX, Anna Stella (Albert & Aulenda BERGERON) b. 26 July 1896 (Houma Ch.: v.5, p.184)

THIBODAUX, Annelie Adrienne (Adrien & Evelina LEBLANC) b. 16 April 1898 (Theriot Ch.: v.2, p.27)

THIBODAUX, Annita Modeste (---- & Anais THIBODAUX) b. 1 Nov. 1899 (Larose Ch.: v.3, p.49)

THIBODAUX, Arthur (Bennett & Eliska DUGAS) m. 5 Dec. 1898 Victoria STEVENS (Houma Ct. Hse.: Mar. v.30 & 31, #135)

THIBODAUX, Arthur Andre (Edmond & Angelina BOURGEOIS) b. 25 Dec. 1899 (Thib. Ch.: v.7, p.582)

THIBODAUX, Arthur Charles (Felicien & Emelie HEBERT) b. 5 March 1899 (Thib. Ch.: v.7, p.540)

THIBODAUX, Bernadette Jeanne (Maxime & Julie HEBERT) b. 25 April 1897 (Lockport Ch.: v.3, #51)

THIBODAUX, Bernadette Jeanne (Maxime & Julie HEBERT) b. 25 April 1897 (Lockport Ch.: v.3-A, #51)

THIBODAUX, Berthe Angelique (Marcellin & Aurelie ORDOGNE) b. 11 Dec. 1899 (Thib. Ch.: v.7, p.599)

THIBODAUX, Berthilde (Benjamin & Mathilde DESROCHES) m. 11 April 1898 Felicien BOURG (Montegut Ch.: v.4, p.240)

THIBODAUX, Bertille (Ben & Mathilde DEROCHE) m. 26 March 1898 Felicien BOURG (Houma Ct. Hse.: Mar. v.30 & 31, #355)

THIBODAUX, Bridget L. m. 20 July 1899 Charles Summer COLLINS (Houma Ct. Hse.: Mar. v.31 & 32, #80)
THIBODAUX, Brigitte m. 12 Aug. 1897 Eugene G. ROBICHAUX (Thib. Ct. Hse.: Mar. v.37, #204)
THIBODAUX, Cecilia m. 8 Oct. 1896 Thomas WALLER (Thib. Ct. Hse.: Mar. v.36, #152)
THIBODAUX, Celestine (Singleton & Rosalie HEBERT) m. 21 Feb. 1898 Jean Baptiste FOREST (Montegut Ch.: v.4, p.237)
THIBODAUX, Celestine (Singleton & Rosalie HEBERT) m. 10 Feb. 1898 Jean Baptiste FOREST (Houma Ct. Hse.:Mar. v.30 & 31, #289)
THIBODAUX, Cestive (Ernest & Octavie THERIOT) m. 21 Feb. 1898 Edna BLANCHARD (Theriot Ch.: v.1-B, p.2)
THIBODAUX, Cestive (Ernest & Octavie THERIOT) m. 1 Feb. 1898 Edna BLANCHARD (Houma Ct. Hse.: Mar. v.30 & 31, #264)
THIBODAUX, Charles m. 5 March 1896 Lizzie PRESTON (Thib. Ct. Hse.: Mar. v.35, #50)
THIBODAUX, Clay m. 5 Feb. 1896 Odelia JACKSON (Houma Ct. Hse.: Mar. v.28, #437)
THIBODAUX, Clifton Jeffry (Davis & Ida ROBERTSON) b. 6 July 1899 (Thib. Ch.: v.7, p.556)
THIBODAUX, Denis m. 13 Feb. 1897 Elmire NAQUIN (Houma Ct. Hse.: Mar. v.29 & 30, #310)
THIBODAUX, Denis (Telesmar & Azelina CHAUVIN) m. 7 Feb. 1897 Elmire NAQUIN (Theriot Ch.: v.1, p.9)
THIBODAUX, Eddy Henry (Pierre & Clara MILL) b. 20 Dec. 1899 (Houma Ch.: v.5, p.266)
THIBODAUX, Eddy Henry (Pierre & Clara NILE) b. 20 Dec. 1899 (Houma Ch.: v.6, p.3)
THIBODAUX, Ede Adam (Edouard & Adeline ANDRA) b. 2 Oct. 1898 (Thib. Ch.: v.7, p.533)
THIBODAUX, Edmond (Lemuel & Elizabeth DONNAUD) m. 20 July 1897 Angelina BOURGEOIS (Thib. Ct. Hse.: Mar. v.37, #194)
THIBODAUX, Edmond (Semuel & Elizabeth DONNAUD) m. 20 July 1897 Angelina BOURGEOIS (Thib. Ch.: v.14, p.153)
THIBODAUX, Elesia m. 17 Feb. 1896 Fergust BOURGEOIS (Thib. Ct. Hse.: Mar. v.35, #41)
THIBODAUX, Elitia (Cledmant & Mathilde FORET) m. 17 Feb. 1896 Fergus BOURGEOIS (Raceland Ch.: v.2, p.13)
THIBODAUX, Eloise Jeanne (Andrien & Eveline LEBLANC) b. 22 Jan. 1896 (Theriot Ch.: v.1-B, p.96)
THIBODAUX, Emelie Evelie (Theodule & Emelie ALBERT) b. 23 March 1896 (Thib. Ch.: v.7, p.445)
THIBODAUX, Engelie, (Duglio & Eugeie GROS) m. 26 July 1897 Joseph BENOIT (Thib. Ch.: v.14, p.154)
THIBODAUX, Eugelia (Douglas & Virginie GROS) m. 14 Jan. 1897 Wallace BENOIT (Thib. Ch.: v.14, p.100)
THIBODAUX, Eugelie (Duglis & Eugenie GROS) m. 26 July 1897 Joseph BENOIT (Thib. Ct. Hse.: Mar. v.37, #196)

THIBODAUX, Eugene (Alexandre & Victoria BOURGEOIS) m. 9 May 1899 Lucien HAUTIN (Lockport Ch.: v.2, p.209)
THIBODAUX, Eugenia (Douglas & Virginie GROS) m. 17 Jan. 1897 Wallace BENOIT (Thib. Ct. Hse.: Mar. v.36, #10)
THIBODAUX, Felicien d. June 1897; m. Celeste COURCIER Children listed: C. Melance; Anasthasie m. Alidor ROBICHAUX; Louisa m. Charles RHOME; Celina m. C. Alidor FOLSE; Felix of Assumption Parish; Joseph; Celestine m. Louis O. NICOLAS. Petition for inventory & appraisement: 5 July 1897. (Thib. Ct. Hse.: Succ. #1518)
THIBODAUX, Felicien d. 14 June 1897 at age 86 yrs. (Raceland Ch.: v.1, p.14)
THIBODAUX, Felix (Orville & Ozea LIRETTE) m. 28 Sept. 1896 Clementine CHIASSON (Houma Ct. Hse.: Mar. v.29 & 30, #155)
THIBODAUX, Felton m. 26 Jan. 1899 Myrthile BOUDREAUX (Houma Ct. Hse.: Mar. v.30 & 31, #282)
THIBODAUX, Felton (Alfred & Ermegilde ARCENAUX) m. 6 Feb. 1899 Myrtilde BOUDREAUX (Houma Ch.: v.6-a, p.275)
THIBODAUX, Francois (Cladomir & Urasie BLANCHARD) m. 26 Jan. 1899 Amanda LAPEROUSE (Montegut Ch.: v.4, p.252)
THIBODAUX, Francois Denis (Elise & Olenda MARCEL) b. 10 July 1896 (Theriot Ch.: v.1-B, p.98)
THIBODAUX, Frank (Clodomire & Urasie BLANCHARD) m. 7 Jan. 1899 Amanda LAPEROUSE (Houma Ct. Hse.: Mar. v.30 & 31, #191)
THIBODAUX, Henri Joseph (Henri & Virginia PITRE) b. 23 Dec. 1896 (Thib. Ch.: v.7, p.432)
THIBODAUX, Henriette m. Bannon BLAKE d. 2 March 1898 at age 21 yrs, 3 mths. (Thib. Ch.: v.3, p.212)
THIBODAUX, Henry m. 30 Jan. 1899 Laura SPEYERER (Thib. Ct. Hse.: Mar. v.38, #81)
THIBODAUX, Hypolite (Louis & Bernadette SANCHEZ) m. 21 Feb. 1898 Josephine ORDOGNE (Chackbay Ch.: v.1, p.58)
THIBODAUX, Hypolite (Louis & Bernadette SANCHEZ) m. 21 Feb. 1898 Josephine ORDOGNE (Thib. Ct. Hse.: Mar. v.37, #72)
THIBODAUX, Irma Justine (Banon & Bertha LEBLANC) b. 6 May 1899 (Thib. Ch.: v.7, p.611)
THIBODAUX, Jean (Denis & Elmir NAQUIN) b. 24 June 1899 (Theriot Ch.: v.2, p.44)
THIBODAUX, Jean Baptiste Livail (Ernest & Aurelia BERGERON) b. 11 Feb. 1897 (Houma Ch.: v.5, p.177)
THIBODAUX, Jean Edwin (Jean Wallon & Edith KNOBLOCK) b. 9 Nov. 1897 (Thib. Ch.: v.7, p.472)
THIBODAUX, Jean Lemuel d. 10 Dec. 1896 at age 44 yrs. & 6 mths. (Thib. Ch.: v.3, p.191)
THIBODAUX, Jesse Batey d. 18 April 1899 at age 54 yrs. (Thib. Ch.: v.3, p.232)
THIBODAUX, John Lemuel d. 17 Dec. 1896 m. Elizabeth DONNAUD Children listed: John W., 23 yrs.; Edmond, 19, emancipated; Henry, 18 yrs.; Charles; Marie Elizabeth, 14

yrs.; Louise Jessie, 12 yrs; Eudora, 10 yrs. Petition for inventory: 23 Dec. 1896. (Thib. Ct. Hse.: Succ. #1500)
THIBODAUX, Jonas (Alfred & Onesile ARSENAULT) m. 7 Feb. 1898 Florence LOOK (Theriot Ch.: v.1-B, p.2)
THIBODAUX, Jonas (Alfred & Onezile ARSENEAUX) m. 19 Jan. 1898 Florence LUKE (Houma Ct. Hse.: Mar. v.30 & 31, #228)
THIBODAUX, Joseh Aurilien (Francois & Cecilia BABIN) b. 26 July 1896 (Thib. Ch.: v.7, p.410)
THIBODAUX, Joseph d. 17 Sept. 1896 at age 60 yrs. (Raceland Ch.: v.1, p.9)
THIBODAUX, Joseph m. 18 Dec. 1899 Elda BENOIT (Thib. Ct. Hse.: Mar. v.39, #290)
THIBODAUX, Joseph (Alfred) d. 4 April 1897 at age 22 yrs. (Montegut Ch.: v.2, p.10)
THIBODAUX, Joseph Adam d. 7 Sept. 1898 at age 3 days (Thib. Ch.: v.3, p.220)
THIBODAUX, Joseph Adam (Hypolite & Josephine ORDOGNE) b. 4 Sept. 1898 (Thib. Ch.: v.7, p.510)
THIBODAUX, Joseph Alce (Marcelin & Aurelie ORDOGNE) b. 22 Aug. 1897 (Chackbay Ch.: v.1, p.97)
THIBODAUX, Joseph Alceste (Pierre & Victorine ROME) b. 2 Nov. 1896 (Thib. Ch.: v.7, p.435)
THIBODAUX, Joseph Ambroise (Auguste & Josephine THEBE) b. 14 July 1899 (Chackbay Ch.: v.1, p.140)
THIBODAUX, Joseph Bartholemie (Sylvain & Ulalie PERCLE) b. 26 Sept. 1899 (Chackbay Ch.: v.1, p.142)
THIBODAUX, Joseph Carol (Alfred & Emelina BERGERON) b. 28 Jan. 1899 (Theriot Ch.: v.2, p.34)
THIBODAUX, Joseph Denis (Antoine & Azema MOLAISON) b. 10 Oct. 1896 (Thib. Ch.: v.7, p.448)
THIBODAUX, Joseph Guillace (Melius & Julie ALBERT) b. 20 March 1899 (Thib. Ch.: v.7, p.542)
THIBODAUX, Joseph Guy Coleman (Leony & Fanny COLEMAN) b. 20 March 1897 (Thib. Ch.: v.7, p.448)
THIBODAUX, Joseph Harry (Joacin & Irma ROME) b. 7 Jan. 1899 (Thib. Ch.: v.7, p.534)
THIBODAUX, Joseph Julius Sampson (Emond & Angelina BOURGEOIS) b. 1 June 1898 (Thib. Ch.: v.7, p.500)
THIBODAUX, Joseph Numez (Ernest & Aurelia BERGERON) b. 20 July 1898 (Thib. Ch.: v.7, p.559)
THIBODAUX, Joseph Nunez (Ernest & Adele MARCEL) b. 2 June 1898 (Thib. Ch.: v.7, p.559)
THIBODAUX, Joseph William (Joseph William & Anette LEBLANC) b. 3 Aug. 1898 (Thib. Ch.: v.7, p.510)
THIBODAUX, Julia (Theophile & Julia BARRAS) m. 3 Aug. 1897 Alexandre CHENET (Thib. Ch.: v.14, p.155)
THIBODAUX, Julia (Theophile & Julia BARROS) m. 3 Aug. 1897 Alexandre CHENET (Thib. Ct. Hse.: Mar. v.37, #203)
THIBODAUX, Julie Egna (Camille & Ovilia LAPEYROUSE) b. 1 Nov. 1897 (Montegut Ch.: v.6, p.62)

THIBODAUX, Laurent Abbe (Alexandre & Olenda BERGERON) b. 1 Aug. 1899 (Houma Ch.: v.5, p.250)
THIBODAUX, Louis (Pierre & Victorine ROME) b. 19 Aug. 1899 (Chackbay Ch.: v.1, p.144)
THIBODAUX, Louis Hobson (Claiborne & Marie BERGERON) b. 21 June 1898 (Thib. Ch.: v.7, p.503)
THIBODAUX, Louis Jean (Marcelin & Aurelia ORDOGNE) b. 23 Sept. 1898 (Thib. Ch.: v.7, p.536)
THIBODAUX, Louisa Urenie (Joacin & Irma ROME) b. 3 Aug. 1897 (Thib. Ch.: v.7, p.478)
THIBODAUX, Louisiana (Clodomire & Eurazie BLANCHARD) m. 5 Feb. 1898 Joseph BENOIT (Houma Ct. Hse.: Mar. v.30 & 31, #278)
THIBODAUX, Lousdon d. 7 July 1899 at age 50 yrs. (Thib. Ch.: v.3, p.236)
THIBODAUX, Louvinia m. 4 Oct. 1898 Joseph BROWN (Thib. Ct. Hse.: Mar. v.38, #287)
THIBODAUX, Lydia (Ernest & Amelia BERGERON) m. 18 Sept. 1899 Thomas PORCHE (Thib. Ch.: v.14, p.295)
THIBODAUX, Lydia (Ernest & Amelia BERGERON) m. 18 Sept. 1899 Thomas PORCHE (Thib. Ct. Hse.: Mar. v.39, #218)
THIBODAUX, Marguerite Rosa (Ernest & Octavie THERIOT) b. 26 June 1897 (Theriot Ch.: v.2, p.8)
THIBODAUX, Marguerite Viviane (Walter & Edith KNOBLOCH) b. 10 March 1899 (Thib. Ch.: v.7, p.541)
THIBODAUX, Maria Emelia (Simon & Leuphrosia GUIDRY) b. 10 Nov. 1898 (Theriot Ch.: v.2, p.36)
THIBODAUX, Marie Adeline (Ernest & Octavie THERIOT) b. 18 Oct. 1899 (Theriot Ch.: v.2, p.51)
THIBODAUX, Marie Aglae (Camille & Ovilia LAPEYROUSE) b. 6 Feb. 1896 (Montegut Ch.: v.6, p.34)
THIBODAUX, Marie Agnes (Alcide & Armelise BENOIT) b. 6 Feb. 1897 (Thib. Ch.: v.7, p.439)
THIBODAUX, Marie Aureanna (Alfred & Eveline THIBODEAUX) b. 22 Feb. 1896 (Theriot Ch.: v.1-B, p.88)
THIBODAUX, Marie Clotilde (Auguste & Mathilde BRAUX) b. 9 Feb. 1899 (Thib. Ch.: v.7, p.535)
THIBODAUX, Marie Corinne (Claiborn & Marie BERGERON) b. 16 Jan. 1896 (Thib. Ch.: v.7, p.390)
THIBODAUX, Marie Felicia (Alexandre Foret & Marie Felicia NAQUIN) b.1 March 1899 (Montegut Ch.: v.6, p.85)
THIBODAUX, Marie Felicia (Enoch & Desiree BOUDREAUX) b. 24 Feb. 1898 (Thib. Ch.: v.7, p.493)
THIBODAUX, Marie Jeanne (Leo & Odile RICHARD) b. 9 Nov. 1896 (Thib. Ch.: v.7, p.473)
THIBODAUX, Marie Josephine (Pierre Amandes & Clara NEAR) b. 8 Sept. 1897 (Houma Ch.: v.5, p.187)
THIBODAUX, Marie Julia (Prosper & Mathilde TOUPS) b. 6 May 1896 (Thib. Ch.: v.7, p.402)
THIBODAUX, Marie Lylienne (Henri & Virginie PITT) b. 29 April 1897 (Thib. Ch.: v.7, p.457)

THIBODAUX, Marie Nathalie (Emile & Celisida BOURG) b. 13 Oct. 1898 (Montegut Ch.: v.6, p.80)
THIBODAUX, Marie Vajola (Sys. & Edna BLANCHARD) b. 29 March 1899 (Theriot Ch.: v.2, p.36)
THIBODAUX, Marie Vermin (Alcide & Armelie BENOIT) b. 15 June 1898 (Thib. Ch.: v.7, p.553)
THIBODAUX, Martha m. 21 Dec. 1899 Willie WALLER (Thib. Ct. Hse.: Mar. v.39, #294)
THIBODAUX, Mary m. 12 Jan. 1899 Lothair NAQUIN (Houma Ct. Hse.: Mar. v.30 & 31, #215)
THIBODAUX, Mary (Abel & Camelia BOURG) m. 30 Jan. 1899 Lothere NAQUIN (Montegut Ch.: v.4, p.253)
THIBODAUX, Mary E. m. 20 Oct. 1896 Emile ASCHWALD (Thib. Ct. Hse.: Mar. v.36, #158)
THIBODAUX, Mary E. m. 21 Oct. 1896 Emile OSCHWALD (Thib. Ch.: Epis. Ch.: v.1, p.331)
THIBODAUX, Mary V. (Walter & Edith KNOBLOCK) b. 31 May 1899 (Thib. Ch.: v.7, p.606)
THIBODAUX, Michel Aurelin d. 9 Feb. 1899; m. Adeline CHAUVIN, d. Feb. 1899. Children listed: Octavie m. Theogen THERIOT; Zulama m. Joseph CHAMPAGNE; Theolin m. Louis CHAMPAGNE; Aime m. Florestal CHAMPAGNE; Justine m. E. F. WATKINS; Adeline m. Arthur CHAUVIN living in Vermillion Par.; Olivier; Adrian; Amant, living in Vermillion Par.; Ernest; d.Coralie m. Joseph TOUPS, Jr. Petition for adm. & inv.: 17 Feb. 1899. (Houma Ct. Hse.: Succ. #915)
THIBODAUX, Myrte (Loventia & d.Emma BOUDREAUX) m. 8 Feb. 1899 Sylvain GUYOT (Chackbay Ch.: v.1, p.68)
THIBODAUX, Myrthee (Laurentie & Emma BOUDREAU) m. 8 Feb. 1899 Sylvain GUILLOT (Thib. Ct. Hse.: Mar. v.38, #32)
THIBODAUX, Nelson (Amedee & Celestine QUATREVINGT) m. 24 Jan. 1898 Angeline GUILLOT (Thib. Ch.: v.14, p.172)
THIBODAUX, Nelson (Amedee & Celestine QUATREVINGT) m. 24 Jan. 1898 Angeline GUILLOT (Thib. Ct. Hse.: Mar. v.37, #15)
THIBODAUX, Odile (Benjamin & Mathilde DESROCHES) m. 2 June 1898 Lawrence BOURG (Montegut Ch.: v.4, p.245)
THIBODAUX, Odile (Benjamin & Mathilde DESROCHES) m. 3 May 1898 Lawrence BOURG (Houma Ct. Hse.: Mar. v.30 & 31, #428)
THIBODAUX, Paul Beney (Clay & Cecilia FORET) b. 9 March 1897 (Raceland Ch.: v.5, p.44)
THIBODAUX, Paul J. Jr. d. 26 May 1898 at age 11 mths. & 20 days (Thib. Ch.: v.3, p.214)
THIBODAUX, Paul Joseph (Enoch & Desiree BOUDREAU) b. 2 April 1896 (Chackbay Ch.: v.1, p.66)
THIBODAUX, Renade (Singleton & Rosalie HEBERT) m. 19 Jan. 1899 Marguerite FRANCIS (Houma Ct. Hse.: Mar. v.30 & 31, #261)

THIBODAUX, Robert Evariste (Banon G. & Bertha C. LEBLANC) b. 16 Sept. 1897 (Thib. Ch.: v.7, p.494)
THIBODAUX, Rose m. 24 March 1897 Frank PREVOST (Houma Ct. Hse.: Mar. v.29 & 30, #365)
THIBODAUX, Sophie Marie (Henri & Virginie PITRE) b. 17 Oct. 1898 (Thib. Ch.: v.7, p.575)
THIBODAUX, Sylvestre d. 29 April 1896 at age 40 yrs. (Thib. Ch.: v.3, p.183)
THIBODAUX, Theodule m. 11 Feb. 1896 Emilia ALBERT (Thib. Ct. Hse.: Mar. v.35, #43)
THIBODAUX, Theresa (Sylvain & Ulalie PERCLE) b. 11 Feb. 1897 (Chackbay Ch.: v.1, p.84)
THIBODAUX, Thomas (Jules & Marie BOUTERIE) m. 25 Jan. 1898 Caroline BOURGEOIS (Thib. Ch.: v.14, p.175)
THIBODAUX, Thomas (Jules & Marie BOUTERIE) m. 25 Jan. 1898 Caroline BOURGEOIS (Thib. Ct. Hse.: Mar. v.37, #38)
THIBODAUX, Thomas Sylvestre (Antoine & Azema MOLEZON) b. 19 May 1898 (Thib. Ch.: v.7, p.559)
THIBODAUX, Uranie Marie (Marie) b. 20 Aug. 1899 (Thib. Ch.: v.7, p.568)
THIBODAUX, Victoria m. 17 April 1899 Florentin HOTARD (Houma Ct. Hse.: Mar. v.31 & 32, #405)
THIBODAUX, Violette m. 11 Feb. 1899 Henry U. SCHOONER (Thib. Ct. Hse.: Mar. v.39, #104)
THIBODAUX, Violette of Lafourche Parish (Pierre & Martha Rosanna LARKINS) m. 14 Feb. 1898 Henry Ulysses SCHOONOVER, of Nebraska (Larose Ch.: v.3, p.8)
THIBODAUX, Violette (Pierre & Martha Rosana LARKINS) m. 14 Feb. 1898 Henry Ulysses SCHOONOVER (Larose Ch.: v.4, p.38)
THIBODAUX, Vivienne Marguerite d. 28 April 1899 at age 6 wks. (Thib. Ch.: v.3, p.232)
THIBODAUX, Walter m. 5 Feb. 1897 Edith KNOBLOCK (Thib. Ct. Hse.: Mar. v.36, #69)
THIBODAUX, Walter (Samuel & Elisabeth DONNAUD) m. 10 Feb. 1897 Edith KNOBLOCK (Raceland Ch.: v.2, p.33)
THIBODAUX, Willie (Achille & Octavie HEBERT) m.17 Jan. 1898 Alida CROCHET (Houma Ct. Hse.: Mar. v.30 & 31, #212)
THIBODAUX, Willie Felicien (Camil & Ovilia LAPEROUSE) b. 8 Aug. 1899 (Houma Ch.: v.5, p.251)
THIBODAUX, Willie Jean (Joseph & Denysse ADAM) b. 27 March 1899 (Chackbay Ch.: v.1, p.130)
THIBODAUX, Zephire (Benett & Ulyska DUGAS) m. 27 April 1898 Luc BAYE (Thib. Ct. Hse.: Mar. v.38, #164)
THIBODAUX, Zephise (Benette & Ulyska DUGAS) m. 27 April 1898 Luc BAYE (Thib. Ch.: v.14, p.199)
THIVET, Maria Sarah (Marcelin & Menevia GRIFFIN) b. 6 Dec. 1897 (Chacahoula Ch.: Gibson Ch.: Mar. Bk., v.1, #23)
THIVET, Maria Sarah (Marcelin & Menevia GRIFFIN) b. 6 Dec. 1897; bt 24 March 1898 (Chacahoula Ch.: Gibson Ch.: v.2, p.119)

THOMAS, Andrew m. 23 Feb. 1898 Birdie GARRET (Houma Ct. Hse.: Mar. v.30 & 31, #309-A)
THOMAS, Andrew m. 24 June 1899 Georgiana STAPLES (Houma Ct. Hse.: Mar. v.31 & 32, #54)
THOMAS, Benjamin m. 17 Feb. 1898 Alice VERRET (Houma Ct. Hse.: Mar. v.30 & 31, #302)
THOMAS, Charles m. 27 March 1896 Lucinda ALEXANDER (Houma Ct. Hse.: Mar. v.29 & 30, #20)
THOMAS, Dora m. 6 Jan. 1896 Louis SCHEXNAYDER (Thib. Ct. Hse.: Mar. v.35, #13)
THOMAS, Edmonia m. 12 Dec. 1898 William LEWIS (Houma Ct. Hse.: Mar. v.30 & 31, #142)
THOMAS, George m. 4 April 1898 Lizzie WOLF (Houma Ct. Hse.: Mar. v.30 & 31, #372)
THOMAS, Laura m. 19 Jan. 1898 Fred. LOPEZ (Houma Ct. Hse.: Mar. v.30 & 31, #230)
THOMAS, Louisa m. 2 Feb. 1899 Andrew DAVIS (Thib. Ct. Hse.: Mar. v.38, #84)
THOMAS, Mack m. 20 Jan. 1898 Agnes WILLIAMS (Thib. Ct. Hse.: Mar. v.37, #50)
THOMAS, Maggie m. 12 Aug. 1899 Scipio S. DYER, Jr. (Houma Ct. Hse.: Mar. v.31 & 32, #95)
THOMAS, Octavie m. 25 March 1898 George MATHEWS (Thib. Ct. Hse.: Mar. v.37, #134)
THOMAS, Walton m. 16 March 199 Ida THERIOT (Thib. Ct. Hse.: Mar. v.39, #119)
THOMAS, Willie m. 24 June 1898 Lou GABRIEL (Thib. Ct. Hse.: Mar. v.38, #211)

THOMASSI (Sometimes: THOMASIE, THOMASSON, TOMASSI)

THOMASSI, Antoinette Eleonore (Leandre & Emelie BOURGEOIS) b. 1 Oct. 1896 (Larose Ch.: v.2, p.184)
THOMASSI, Bernadette Elmire (Toussaint & Marie GALJOUR) b. 16 Jan. 1897 (Larose Ch.: v.3, p.1)
THOMASSI, Lauretta Ida (Julien & Elisabeth GONSALEZ) b. 10 Dec. 1898 (Raceland Ch.: v.5, p.93)
THOMASSI, Leonce Alens (Ales & Loetitia ORGERON) b. 1 Aug. 1896 (Larose Ch.: v.2, p.195)
THOMASSI, Louise m. 16 Jan. 1896 Joseph GUEDRY (Larose Ch.: v.3, p.1)
THOMASSI, Louise m. 2 Jan. 1896 Joseph GUIDRY (Thib. Ct. Hse.: Mar. v.35, #1)
THOMASSI, Louise (Joseph & Louisa ORGERON) m. 16 Jan. 1896 Joseph GUIDRY (Larose Ch.: v.2, p.187)
THOMASSI, Marie Leona (Joseph & Olfida SAVOIE) b. 7 June 1898 (Larose Ch.: v.3, p.19)
THOMASSI, Octavie Marie (Joseph & Ophida SAVOIE) b. 12 April 1896 (Larose Ch.: v.2, p.191)
THOMPSON, Ben m. 16 Aug. 1898 Marie ROUVERA (Thib. Ct. Hse.: Mar. v.38, #255)

THOMPSON, Charles D. m. 24 Dec. 1898 Sophie Mary TOUJAN (Houma Ct. Hse.: Mar. v.30 & 31, #159)
THOMPSON, Charles D. (James F. & Eliza A. VORIS) m. 27 Dec. 1898 Sophie Maria TOUJAN (Houma Ch.: v.6-a, p.260)
THOMPSON, Dora m. 20 Jan. 1898 Lee HAMMOND (Houma Ct. Hse.: Mar. v.30 & 31, #234)
THOMPSON, Elias m. 12 Aug. 1897 Mary AUGUSTUS (Thib. Ct. Hse.: Mar. v.37, #212)
THOMPSON, George m. 26 Oct. 1896 Ophelia EDMOND (Thib. Ct. Hse.: Mar. v.36, #159)
THOMPSON, James (James & Emelie PELLETIER) b. 12 Aug. 1896 (Thib. Ch.: v.7, p.413)
THOMPSON, Laura m. 13 April 1899 Willie ANDERSON (Houma Ct. Hse.: Mar. v.31 & 32, #400)
THOMPSON, Lucinda m. 15 Feb. 1899 Alexander WOODS (Houma Ct. Hse.: Mar. v.31 & 32, #336)
THOMPSON, Lucinda m. 7 April 1898 John JEFF (Houma Ct. Hse.: Mar. v.30 & 31, #378)
THOMPSON, Marguerite Bertha (James & Emma PELLETIER) b. 18 Oct. 1898 (Thib. Ch.: v.7, p.518)
THOMPSON, Mary Eliza (Charles & Sophie TOUSANT) b. 28 Oct. 1899 (Houma Ch.: v.5, p.264)
THOMPSON, Monroe m. 27 Jan. 1898 Elizabeth TURNER (Thib. Ct. Hse.: Mar. v.37, #61)
THOMPSON, Virginia m. 2 Feb. 1899 Sam TURNER (Houma Ct. Hse.: Mar. v.30 & 31, #306)
THOMPSON, Walter m. 10 Sept. 1898 Louisa ALEXANDER (Thib. Ct. Hse.: Mar. v.38, #276)
THORNSBURY, Julian m. 8 June 1898 Aaron PARKER (Houma Ct. Hse.: Mar. v.30 & 31, #3)
THORNTON, Nellie m. 15 Jan. 1897 John DAVIS (Thib. Ct. Hse.: Mar. v.36, #35)
THRON, Willie m. 5 Aug. 1899 Lettie BROWN (Thib. Ct. Hse.: Mar. v.39, #188)
TILLMAN, Amanda m. 9 Aug. 1897 Wlliam BOWIE (Thib. Ct. Hse.: Mar. v.37, #209)
TILLMAN, Ellen m. 11 June 1898 Ellick MERRITT (Houma Ct. Hse.: Mar. v.30 & 31, #13)
TILLMAN, Rebecca m. 19 Feb. 1898 Jos. W. WOODS (Thib. Ct. Hse.: Mar. v.37, #109)
TINNEY, Laura Eunice (Stephen & Lilia VITTER) b. 12 March 1896 (Thib. Ch.: v.7, p.399)
TIRQUIT, Felix Marcellin (Felix & Alice JONES) b. 28 Oct. 1898 (Montegut Ch.: v.6, p.78)
TIVY, Delisca (Joacinlle Olivier & Eveline GRIFFIN) b. 16 June 1896 (Theriot Ch.: v.1-B, p.96)
TIVY, Marie Edna (Oleus & Marie ROMERO) b. 10 April 1896 (Theriot Ch.: v.2, p.27)
TOLIVER, Rosa m. 6 July 1896 Pat WELSH (Thib. Ct. Hse.: Mar. v.36, #117)

TONEY, Joseph m. 12 May 1897 Leefie NELSON (Houma Ct. Hse.: Mar. v.29 & 30, #415)
TONEY, Leonard m. 28 Jan. 1897 Cora LOCKWOOD (Houma Ct. Hse.: Mar. v.29 & 30, #264)
TONEY, Louisa m. 20 Jan. 1897 Allen JACKSON (Houma Ct. Hse.: Mar. v.29 & 30, #241)
TONEY, Nathaniel m. 7 Sept. 1899 Adelina HAMPTON (Thib. Ct. Hse.: Mar. v.39, #223)
TONEY, Thomas m. 23 March 1899 Harriet HAMPTON (Thib. Ct. Hse.: Mar. v.39, #122)
TORES, Clotilde (Antoine & Suzanne ATTENHOFER) b. 1 June 1898 (Chackbay Ch.: v.1, p.113)
TORNABENE, Rosalia (Francisco & Giovannina DISPENSA) b. 10 Oct. 1899 (Thib. Ch.: v.8, p.16)
TORRES, Antoine (Antoine & Suzanne ATTENHOFER) b. 26 Nov. 1896 (Chackbay Ch.: v.1, p.78)
TORRES, Eugenie Catherine (Gratien & Catherine HATTENFROF) b. 16 July 1899 (Chackbay Ch.: v.1, p.137)
TORRES, Marie Elisabet (Antoine & Elisca KRAEMER) b. 9 Nov. 1896 (Chackbay Ch.: v.1, p.82)
TORRES, Marie Isabelle (Albert & Elisa MARTINEZ) b. 5 Sept. 1898 (Chackbay Ch.: v.1, p.118)
TORTORICA, Rosalia m. 9 Sept. 1897 Cicio BALDASSARE (Houma Ct. Hse.: Mar. v.29 & 30, #63)
TORTORICH, Salvatore m. 21 March 1899 Katherina BARRILA (Houma Ct. Hse.: Mar. v.31 & 32, #370)
TORTORICHE, Salvatore of Terrebonne Parish m. 10 April 1899 Katharina BARRILE (Houma Ch.: v.6-B, p.3)
TORTORICI, Giovanni (Gaitano & Rosina CARDARUNA) m. 16 Sept. 1899 Giuseppa CANCILLA (Thib. Ct. Hse.: Mar. v.39, #207)
TORTORICI, Giovanni (Yaitana & Rosino CARDAREMA) m. 16 Sept. 1899 Guiseppa CANCILLA (Thib. Ch.: v.14, p.294)
TORTORICI, Rosalia (Calagro & Aviontonia CARUSA) m. 13 Sept. 1897 Cicio BALDASSARE (Houma Ch.: v.6-a, p.214)
TOUCHARD, Charles Lewis (---- & Catherine TOUCHARD) b. 6 Feb. 1897 (Larose Ch.: v.3, p.3)
TOUCHARD, Louis Avi (Jean & Felicia MATHERN) b. 17 June 1898 (Larose Ch.: v.3, p.23)
TOUJAN, Sophie Maria (Henry D. & Priscilla WILLIAM) m. 27 Dec. 1898 Charles D. THOMPSON (Houma Ch.: v.6-a, p.260)
TOUJAN, Sophie Mary m. 24 Dec. 1898 Charles D. THOMPSON (Houma Ct. Hse.: Mar. v.30 & 31, #159)

TOUPS (Sometimes: TOOPS, TOUPES)
TOUPS, Abel (Albert Telesiphore & Armance BOURGEOIS) m. 21 Dec. 1897 Noema LEJEUNE (Thib. Ch.: v.14, p.166)
TOUPS, Adele m. ----- BRUNET d. 12 Nov. 1897 at age 63 yrs. (Theriot Ch.: v.1, p.1)
TOUPS, Aime Zoe (Clovis & Josephine ROSSIGNOL) b. 13 Dec. 1897 (Thib. Ch.: v.7, p.478)

TOUPS, Aimee m. Adrien GUIDRY d. 18 May 1899 at age 80 yrs. (Thib. Ch.: v.3, p.234)
TOUPS, Albert m. 15 Feb. 1898 Mathilde TOUPS (Thib. Ct. Hse.: Mar. v.37, #87)
TOUPS, Albert (Felicien & Emelie HEBERT) m. 15 Feb. 1898 Mathilde TOUPS (Raceland Ch.: v.2, p.70)
TOUPS, Albert or Abel (Olesiphore & Armance BOURGEOIS) m. 21 Dec. 1897 Noema LEJEUNE (Thib. Ct. Hse.: Mar. v.37, #261)
TOUPS, Alcide Joseph (Alcide Joseph & Carmelite Marie CAILLOUETTE) b. 20 Jan. 1896 (Thib. Ch.: v.7, p.390)
TOUPS, Amelina m. 26 Jan. 1899 Firmin TOUPS (Thib. Ct. Hse.: Mar. v.38, #61)
TOUPS, Amelina (Felicien & Emelie HEBERT) m. 31 Jan. 1899 Firmin TOUPS (Raceland Ch.: v.2, p.87)
TOUPS, Anais Victorine (Elie Isidore & Marie GUIDRY) b. 26 Nov. 1896 (Larose Ch.: v.3, p.3)
TOUPS, Andre (Alcide & Carmelite CAILLOUET) m. 14 Oct. 1897 Augusta BRAUD (Thib. Ch.: v.14, p.163)
TOUPS, Andre (Alcide & Carmelite CAILLOUET) m. 14 Oct. 1897 Augusta BRAUD (Thib. Ct. Hse.: Mar. v.37, #247)
TOUPS, Anna Mable (Etienne & Josephine MICHEL) b. 17 Dec 1897 (Houma Ch.: v.5, p.203)
TOUPS, Anne Inez (Abel & Noema LEJEUNE) b. 17 Sept. 1897 (Thib. Ch.: v.7, p.513)
TOUPS, Annette Elvie (Joseph & Blandine SUREAU) b. 28 Jan. 1899 (Thib. Ch.: v.7, p.586)
TOUPS, Annie m. 20 Sept. 1897 David GREEN (Houma Ct. Hse.: Mar. v.29 & 30, #95)
TOUPS, Annie Laura (Clovis Prosper Auguste & Josephine ROSSIGNOL) b. 4 Dec. 1899 (Thib. Ch.: v.7, p.577)
TOUPS, Antoine Robert (Justin & Aimee WALSH) b. 1 Oct. 1898 (Thib. Ch.: v.7, p.567)
TOUPS, Aristide (Olezy & Armance BOURGEOIS) m. 21 Dec. 1896 Noemie LEJEUNE (Thib. Ch.: v.14, p.105)
TOUPS, Arthur (Oleus & Rosa TOUPS) m. 6 Nov. 1899 Alice GAUDE (Thb. Ct. Hs.: Mar. v.39, #257)
TOUPS, Arthur (Oleus & Rosa TOUPS) m. 6 Nov. 1899 Alice GAUDE (Thib. Ch.: v.14, p.307)
TOUPS, Azora d. 17 Aug. 1895; m. Victorin PONTIFF Petition for probate of will: 11 Jan. 1896. (Thib. Ct. Hse.: Succ. #1479)
TOUPS, Beulah Louise (Cleophas A. & Cecilia M. MEYER) b. 21 Jan. 1897 (Houma Ch.: v.5, p.164)
TOUPS, Camilla (Manuel & Celesida SCOTT) m. 4 Feb. 1899 Dominique GISCLAIR (Thib. Ct. Hse.: Mar. v.38, #39)
TOUPS, Camilla (Manuel & Celesida SCOTT) m. 4 Feb. 1899 Dominique GISCLAIR (Larose Ch.: v.3, p.11)
TOUPS, Camille Joseph (Octave & Alice TROUE) b. 11 June 1898 (Thib. Ch.: v.7, p.500)

TOUPS, Carmelite (Theodule & Marceline BOURGEOIS) m. 27 April 1898 Ernest DIAS (Thib. Ct. Hse.: Mar. v.38, #166)
TOUPS, Carmelite (Theodule & Marceline BOURGEOIS) m. 27 April 1898 Ernest DIAS (Thib. Ch.: v.14, p.198)
TOUPS, Caroline d. 18 March 1888; m. J. Paulin GUILLOT Children listed: Albert, aged 29; Ferducy, 27; Emilie, 24 m. Alphonse GUILLOT; Klebert, 21; Alice, 19; Joseph, 16; Sidney, 8. Petition for natural tutorship & for inventory: 12 Feb. 1896. (Thib. Ct. Hse.: Succ. #1484)
TOUPS, Celeste d. 30 Dec. 1896 at age 3 yrs. (Thib. Ch.: v.3, p.193)
TOUPS, Celestine (Oleus & Rosa TOUPS) m. 21 Dec. 1899 Volgie BENOIT (Thib. Ct. Hse.: Mar. v.39, #288)
TOUPS, Celestine (Oleus & Rosa TOUPS) m. 21 Dec. 1899 Volgie BENOIT (Thib. Ch.: v.14, p.314)
TOUPS, Charles Edouard (Zephirin & Marie Adele CHAUVIN) b. 7 Feb. 1899 (Thib. Ch.: v.7, p.537)
TOUPS, Charles Eugene (Charles & Maria FOREST) b. 4 Nov. 1899 (Thib. Ch.: v.8, p.17)
TOUPS, Charlotte Bioulet (Marie & Charlotte BOURGEOIS) b. 27 March 1897 (Thib. Ch.: v.7, p.446)
TOUPS, Claire Marie Elisabeth (Ambroise & Lydia WAGESPACK) b. 12 Aug. 1899 (Thib. Ch.: v.7, p.559)
TOUPS, Edgard (Emile & Victoria BOURGEOIS) m. 18 Jan. 1897 Alice BARRILLEAUX (Thib. Ct. Hse.: Mar. v.36, #37)
TOUPS, Edgard (Emile & Victoria BOURGEOIS) m. 18 Jan. 1897 Alice BARRILLEAUX (Lockport Ch.: v.2, p.156)
TOUPS, Edithe Agathe (Andre & Augusta BREAUX) b. 30 June 1898 (Thib. Ch.: v.7, p.503)
TOUPS, Edna Marguerite d. 1 June 1899 at age 17 yrs., 2 mths. & 29 days (Houma Ch.: v.3, p.23)
TOUPS, Edouard Ernest (Edouard & Octavie CANCIENNE) b. 4 March 1899 (Thib. Ch.: v.7, p.539)
TOUPS, Elie Teadore m. 15 Jan. 1897 Marie GUIDRY (Larose Ch.: v.4, p.119-A)
TOUPS, Elie Teodore m. 15 Jan. 1897 Marie GUIDRY (Larose Ch.: v.3, p.5)
TOUPS, Eliza (George & Felicie SAVOIE) m. 7 June 1897 Willie BERGERON (Houma Ct. Hse.: Mar. v.29 & 30, #13)
TOUPS, Elles (Ernest & Elodie ESHETE) m. 19 Sept. 1898 Dorsena FOREST (Houma Ct. Hse.: Mar. v.30 & 31, #100-C)
TOUPS, Ellis (Ernest & Eulodie ESCHETE) m. 3 Oct. 1898 Dorsena FOREST (Montegut Ch.: v.4, p.249)
TOUPS, Emile Joseph m. 24 Aug. 1898 Ernestine NAQUIN (Houma Ct. Hse.: Mar. v.30 & 31, #85)
TOUPS, Emile Joseph (Evins & Julia DASPIT) m. 25 Aug. 1898 Ernestine NAQUIN (Houma Ch.: v.6-a, p.251)
TOUPS, Etienne d. 6 Oct. 1898 at age 74 yrs. in Bayou Sale area. Body was moved on 13 June 1899 to Thibodeau area. (Thib. Ch.: v.3, p.235)

TOUPS, Etienne Onesil (Pierre & Marie CHIASSON) b. 23 July 1898 (Thib. Ch.: v.7, p.557)
TOUPS, Eva m. 5 May 1896 Joseph DOVER (Houma Ct. Hse.: Mar. v.29 & 30, #50)
TOUPS, Evelina m. Maximin NAQUIN d. 2 June 1898 at age 45 yrs. (Montegut Ch.: v.2, p.17)
TOUPS, Felicia (Auguste & Odilia BENOIT) m. 3 Feb. 1896 Leo TROSCLAIR (Thib. Ct. Hse.: Mar. v.35, #20)
TOUPS, Felicia (Auguste & Odilia BENOIT) m. 3 Feb. 1896 Leo TROSCLAIR (Chackbay Ch.: v.1, p.25)
TOUPS, Felicien d. 14 May 1897; m. Esilda GAUDE Children listed: Marie Angelina TOUPS m. William FIELDS; Edgar, b. 4 Dec. 1870; Charles B., b. 14 July 1872; Victorin, b. 5 Nov. 1876; Felicien H., b. 23 Oct. 1880; Olympe, b. 19 Oct. 1882; Julie, b. 28 Aug. 1885; Edith A., b. 26 Feb. 1892; Elisa, b. 18 March 1888. Application for inventory & tutorship: 20 May 1897. (Thib. Ct. Hse.: Succ. #1514)
TOUPS, Felicien d. 15 May 1897 at age 50 yrs. & 11 mths. (Thib. Ch.: v.3, p.200)
TOUPS, Fernand Pierre (Terence & Lydia MIRE) b. 27 June 1896 (Thib. Ch.: v.7, p.407)
TOUPS, Firmin m. 26 Jan. 1899 Amelina TOUPS (Thib. Ct. Hse.: Mar. v.38, #61)
TOUPS, Firmin (Pierre & Mathilde ZERINGUE) m. 31 Jan. 1899 Amelina TOUPS (Raceland Ch.: v.2, p.87)
TOUPS, Harold Joseph (Octave & Alice Marie TROUE) b. 28 March 1896 (Thib. Ch.: v.7, p.397)
TOUPS, Helene Inola (Felix & Philomene BOUDREAUX) b. 28 July 1898 (Thib. Ch.: v.7, p.507)
TOUPS, Ida (Ernest & Alexina MOULAISON) m. 15 July 1897 Denis ROGER (Thib. Ct. Hse.: Mar. v.37, #190)
TOUPS, Ida (Ernest & Alexina MOULAISON) m. 15 July 1897 Denis ROGER (Lockport Ch.: v.2, p.163)
TOUPS, Isidore m. 25 Jan. 1896 Marie Rose GUIDRY (Thib. Ct. Hse.: Mar. v.35, #31)
TOUPS, Jean Arthur d. 1 Jan. 1897 at age 4 yrs. (Thib. Ch.: v.3, p.193)
TOUPS, Jean Charles (Zephyrin & Marie Adele CHAUVIN) b. 28 Aug. 1897 (Thib. Ch.: v.7, p.462)
TOUPS, Jean Denys (Firmin & Therese ZERINGUE) b. 11 Jan. 1897 (Thib. Ch.: v.7, p.436)
TOUPS, Jean Emas (Albert & Mathilde TOUPS) b. 24 Feb. 1899 (Raceland Ch.: v.5, p.92)
TOUPS, Jean Fernand (Paulin & Louisa GAUDET) b. 27 Nov. 1897 (Thib. Ch.: v.7, p.522)
TOUPS, Jean Roy (Zephirin & Marie Adele CHAUVIN) b. 14 July 1896 (Thib. Ch.: v.7, p.409)
TOUPS, John Nolan (Noe & Eva ANGERAN) b. 1 July 1899 (Theriot Ch.: v.2, p.45)

TOUPS, Joseph Clement (Lesidor & Marie R. GUIDRY) b. 7 April 1899 (Larose Ch.: v.3, p.39)
TOUPS, Joseph Denis (Andre & Augusta BREAU) b. 13 Oct. 1899; m. Lorena DAIGLE on 26 June 1924. (Houma Ch.: Bapt. Bk., v.5, p.256)
TOUPS, Joseph Edouard (Albert & Cecile ONCALE) b. 20 Feb. 1898 (Thib. Ch.: v.7, p.487)
TOUPS or GISCLAR, Joseph Octave (-----& Victoria TOUPS) b. 2 Feb. 1899 (Larose Ch.: v.3, p.39)
TOUPS, Joseph O'Neil (Thomas & Helene FOLSE) b. 26 Dec. 1897 (Raceland Ch.: v.5, p.63)
TOUPS, Joseph Stanley (Felix & Philomene BOUDREAUX) b. 30 Oct. 1896 (Thib. Ch.: v.7, p.423)
TOUPS, Josephine m. 22 June 1896 Joseph ORGERON (Lockport Ch.: v.2, p.155)
TOUPS, Josephine m. 5 Feb. 1897 Dalmas CHAMPAGNE (Thib. Ct. Hse.: Mar. v.36, #70)
TOUPS, Josephine (Emile & Emilie BRAUD) m. 16 Feb. 1897 Delmas CHAMPAGNE (Raceland Ch.: v.2, p.34)
TOUPS, Josephine (Theodule & Marceline BOURGEOIS) m. 17 Feb. 1896 Frank RICHARD (Thib. Ct. Hse.: Mar. v.35 #44)
TOUPS, Josephine (Theodule & Marcelius BOURGEOIS) m. 17 Feb. 1896 Frank RICHARD (Thib. Ch.: v.14, p.79)
TOUPS, Julia Agnes (Evens & Julia DASPIT) b. 12 Dec. 1897 (Houma Ch.: v.5, p.194)
TOUPS, Juliette (Edouard & Lovinia BOURGEOIS) m. 15 Feb. 1898 Alcide BOURGEOIS (Thib. Ch.: v.14, p.189)
TOUPS, Juliette (Edouard & Lovinia BOURGEOIS) m. 15 Feb. 1898 Alcide BOURGEOIS (Thib. Ct. Hse.: Mar. v.37, #90)
TOUPS, Justin (Alcide & Carmelite CAILLOUET) m. 8 Sept. 1898 Annie WALSH (Thib. Ct. Hse.: Mar. v.38, #268)
TOUPS, Justin (Alcide & Carmelite CAILLOUET) m. 8 Sept. 1898 Annie WALSH (Thib. Ch.: v.14, p.221)
TOUPS, Laura d. 29 April 1899 at age 14 days (Thib. Ch.: v.3, p.233)
TOUPS, Laura m. 7 June 1899 Voltaire PITRE (Thib. Ct. Hse.: Mar. v.39, #195)
TOUPS, Laura (Onesime & Valentine BOUDREAUX) m. 27 Dec. 1897 Auguste Anatole LAINE (Thib. Ch.: v.14, p.167)
TOUPS, Laura (Onezie & Valentine BOUDREAUX) m. 27 Dec. 1897 Auguste Anatole LAINE (Thib. Ct. Hse.: Mar. v.37, #265)
TOUPS, Laura Odile (Joseph & Blandine SUREAU) b. 14 Dec. 1898 (Thib. Ch.: v.7, p.526)
TOUPS, Laura Velma (Edouard & Octavie CANCIENNE) b. 1 Dec. 1896 (Thib. Ch.: v.7, p.427)
TOUPS, Louis Birney (Lucien & Marie POCHE) b. 3 Sept. 1898 (Thib. Ch.: v.7, p.562)
TOUPS, Louis Felix (Desire & Josephine PARRE) b. 7 June 1896 (Houma Ch.: v.5, p.154)
TOUPS, Lovencie (Manuel & Celesaida SCOTT) m. 2 July 1898 Camilla GISCLAR (Thib. Ct. Hse.: Mar. v.38, #215)

TOUPS, Lovency of Lafourche Parish (Manuel & Celesida SCOTT) m. 2 July 1898 Camilla GISCLAIR of Lafourche Parish (Larose Ch.: v.3, p.10)

TOUPS, Lovency (Manuel & Celesida SCOTT) m. 2 July 1898 Camilla GISCLAR (Larose Ch.: v.4, p.21)

TOUPS, Lydia (Alcide & Carmelite CAILLOUET) m. 2 Feb. 1899 Charles BOURGEOIS (Thib. Ct. Hse.: Mar. v.38, #69)

TOUPS, Lydia (Alcide & Carmelite CAILLOUET) m. 2 Feb. 1899 Charles BOURGEOIS (Thib. Ch.: v.14, p.254)

TOUPS, Lydia (Drauzin & Aurelia STEVEN) m. 13 Feb. 1899 Onezime BERGERON (Thib. Ct. Hse.: Mar. v.38, #91)

TOUPS, Lyna (Joseph & Blandine SUROH) b. 14 April 1897 (Thib. Ch.: v.7, p.447)

TOUPS, Mabel Rosa (Volsey & Cecile BERGERON) b. 13 Oct. 1896 (Thib. Ch.: v.7, p.442)

TOUPS, Marguerite Marie (Joseph & Ophelia FOLSE) b. 18 Nov. 1896 (Raceland Ch.: v.5, p.35)

TOUPS, Marie Alley (Ellis & Adorsine FORET) b. 5 Sept. 1899 (Montegut Ch.: v.6, p.93)

TOUPS, Marie Anna (Aurelien & Evela CHAMPAGNE) b. 16 Sept. 1898 (Theriot Ch.: v.2, p.32)

TOUPS, Marie Anna (Firmin & Therese ZERINGUE) b. 1 March 1898 (Thib. Ch.: v.7, p.489)

TOUPS, Marie Azora (Clement & Julia HEBERT) b. 18 Sept. 1896 (Thib. Ch.: v.7, p.418)

TOUPS, Marie Brigitte (Joseph & Cecile LEBLANC) b. 9 July 1896 (Lockport Ch.: v.2, p.332)

TOUPS, Marie Bulia (Emile & Adele FOLSE) b. 15 March 1896 (Raceland Ch.: v.5, p.21)

TOUPS, Marie Lelia Cedee (John & Elizabeth BOURG) b. 5 Oct. 1898 (Montegut Ch.: v.6, p.77)

TOUPS, Marie Lovinia d. 2 Jan. 1897 at age 6½ yrs. (Thib. Ch.: v.3, p.193)

TOUPS, Marie Lucien (Charles & Maria FORET) b. 25 April 1899 (Thib. Ch.: v.7, p.546)

TOUPS, Marie Lucile (Charles & Maria FORET) b. 23 July 1897 (Thib. Ch.: v.7, p.458)

TOUPS, Marie Nolia (Ernest & Eulodie ESCHTE) b. 25 Dec. 1899 (Montegut Ch.: v.6, p.99)

TOUPS, Marie Pauline (Arthur & Marie CHIASSON) b. 5 Sept. 1897 (Thib. Ch.: v.7, p.464)

TOUPS, Marie Rosema (Louis & Julia CORTES) b. 22 July 1899 (Chackbay Ch.: v.1, p.138)

TOUPS, Marie Therese (Albert & Cecile ENCAL) b. 21 Oct. 1899 (Thib. Ch.: v.7, p.572)

TOUPS, Mary Ola (Lucien & Marie POCHE) b. 6 July 1897 (Thib. Ch.: v.7, p.458)

TOUPS, Mary Purline (Emile & Ernestine NAQUIN) b. 21 Sept. 1899 (Houma Ch.: v.5, p.258)

TOUPS, Mathilde m. 15 Feb. 1898 Albert TOUPS (Thib. Ct. Hse.: Mar. v.37, #87)

TOUPS, Mathilde (Emile & Emma BRAUD) m. 15 Feb. 1898 Albert TOUPS (Raceland Ch.: v.2, p.70)
TOUPS, May Agnes (Ambroise & Lydia WAGUESPACK) b. 11 Feb. 1898 (Thib. Ch.: v.7, p.486)
TOUPS, Meloe (Joseph & Evelina GAUBERT) m. 19 Jan. 1899 Ambroise J. BOURGEOIS (Thib. Ct. Hse.: Mar. v.38, #21)
TOUPS, Meloe (Joseph & Evelina GAUBERT) m. 19 Jan. 1899 Durand BOURGEOIS (Thib. Ch.: v.14, p.241)
TOUPS, Nettie m. 15 Aug. 1896 Joseph RODDY (Houma Ct. Hse.: Mar. v.29 & 30, #131)
TOUPS, Nettie (Evans & Julia DASPIT) m. 18 Aug. 1896 Joseph RHODES (Houma Ch.: v.6-a, p.178)
TOUPS, Olivier Joseph (Volzey & Cecile BERGERON) b. 2 April 1898 (Thib. Ch.: v.7, p.549)
TOUPS, Orestide (Olezy & Armande BOURGEOIS) m. 21 Dec. 1896 Noemie LEJEUNE (Thib. Ct. Hse.: Mar. v.36, #164)
TOUPS, Paul Samson (Emile & Adele FOLSE) b. 12 March 1897 (Raceland Ch.: v.5, p.43)
TOUPS, Philippe d.10 March 1899 at age 32 yrs. (Thib. Ch.: v.3, p.230)
TOUPS, Philippe (Ghim & Celina BOUDREAUX) m. 29 Nov. 1898 Elizabeth CHAUVIN (Thib. Ct. Hse.: Mar. v.38, #310)
TOUPS, Philippe (Ghim & Celina BOUDREAUX) m. 29 Nov. 1898 Elizabeth CHAUVIN (Lockport Ch.: v.2, p.197)
TOUPS, Pierre Edde (Thomas & Helene FOLSE) b. 17 Sept. 1898 (Thib. Ch.: v.7, p.571)
TOUPS, Pierre Julien (Pierre & Marie Eulalie CHIASSON) b. 20 July 1897 (Thib. Ch.: v.7, p.457)
TOUPS, Polycarpe Jean (Victoria Alexina) b. 24 Nov. 1896 (Larose Ch.: v.2, p.190)
TOUPS, Ray Nicholas (Cleophas & Cecilia M. MEYER) b. 17 July 1898 (Houma Ch.: v.5, p.213)
TOUPS, Rene Simon (Albert & Cecile ONCALE) bt. 24 April 1896 (Thib. Ch.: v.7, p.399)
TOUPS, Rodney Denis (Cleophas & Cecilia TOUPS) b. 2 Jan. 1896 (Houma Ch.: v.5, p.140)
TOUPS, Simon Rene d. 1 Jan. 1897 at age 8 mths. (Thib. Ch.: v.3, p.193)
TOUPS, Sydney d. 12 April 1899 at age 14 mths. (Thib. Ch.: v.3, p.231)
TOUPS, Sydney Klebert (Aristide & Noemie LEJEUNE) b. 26 Dec. 1897 (Thib. Ch.: v.7, p.479)
TOUPS, Sylvestre Willie (Emile & Adele FOLSE) b. 30 March 1898 (Raceland Ch.: v.5, p.67)
TOUPS, Therese Anny (Desire & Josephine PARR) b. 20 Feb. 1899 (Houma Ch.: v.5, p.238)
TOUPS, Unah Cecile (Thomas & Justine CANTIENNE) b. 5 Dec. 1896 (Raceland Ch.: v.5, p.36)
TOUPS, Valfroid M. (Emile & Victoria BOURGEOIS) m. 8 Feb. 1899 Julia CAILLOUET (Thib. Ct. Hse.: Mar. v.38, #88)

TOUPS, Valfroid M. (Emile & Victoria BOURGEOIS) m. 8 Feb. 1899 Julia CAILLOUET (Lockport Ch.: v.2, p.202)
TOUPS, Zurmie m. Florestin PITT d. 25 Jan. 1898 at age 78 yrs. (Lockport Ch.: v.1, #2)
TOURELLE, Arcade (Augustin & Emelia MARTIN) m. 16 April 1898 Albert SAVOIE (Lockport Ch.: v.2, p.188)
TOURELLE, Arcade (Augustin & Emelia MARTIN) m. 16 April 1898 Albert SAVOIE (Thib. Ct. Hse.: Mar. v.37, #143)
TOURELLE, Volzim (Augustin & Julia MARTIN) m. 11 Feb. 1899 Olive GAUTREAUX (Lockport Ch.: v.2, p.204)
TOURREL, Augustave (Augustin & Emelia MARTIN) m. 29 Jan. 1898 Emelia GUIDRY (Lockport Ch.: v.2, p.182)
TOURRELL, Valzime (Augustin & Julia MARTIN) m. 11 Feb. 1899 Olive GAUTREAUX (Thib. Ct. Hse.: Mar. v.38, #65)
TOURRIL, Augustave (Augustin & Emelia MARTIN) m. 29 Jan. 1898 Emelia GUIDRY (Thib. Ct. Hse.: Mar. v.37, #41)
TOUSSAINT, Joseph m. 22 April 1897 Alice ANDERSON (Thib. Ct. Hse.: Mar. v.36, #128)
TOUSSAINT, Mary Jane m. 27 Nov. 1897 Dennis GATTEN (Thib. Ct. Hse.: Mar. v.37, #258)
TOUSSAINT, Mathilde (Pierre & Noemie CARAMBAT) m. 29 April 1897 Lucien RICHARD (Thib. Ch.: v.14, p.141)
TOUSSAINT, Mathilde (Pierre & Noemie CARAMBAT) m. 29 April 1897 Lucien RICHARD (Thib. Ct. Hse.: Mar. v.36, #120)
TOUSSAINT, Therese (Pierre & Leonine CALABOSSE) m. 15 Feb. 1898 Ernest HUMPHREY (Thib. Ch.: v.14, p.188)
TOUSSAINT, Therese (Pierre & Leonine CALABASSE) m. 15 Feb. 1898 Ernest HUMPHREY (Thib. Ct. Hse.: Mar. v.37, #85)

TRAHAN (Sometimes: TRAHANT, TRAHEN, TRAHENT, TRAHON)

TRAHAN, ----- Mr. d. 7 Feb. 1896 (Houma Ch.: v.3, p.6)
TRAHAN, Abel Clifford (Onesime & Evela BREAUX) b. 19 April 1896; m. Leona C. NOLAN on 3 April 1893 (Houma Ch.: Bapt. Bk., v.5, p.180)
TRAHAN, Agnes Edna (Joseph & Aurelie GIROUARD) b. 5 March 1896 (Houma Ch.: v.5, p.174)
TRAHAN, Agnes Louise (Pierre & Adolia BREAU) b. 6 Aug. 1896 (Houma Ch.: v.5, p.156)
TRAHAN, Albert Adam (Justilien & Roselia AUTHEMENT) b. 24 Nov. 1899 (Montegut Ch.: v.6, p.99)
TRAHAN, Albert Henry (Auguste & Henilia BONVILLAIN) b. 22 Aug. 1899 (Theriot Ch.: v.2, p.48)
TRAHAN, Alfred Albert (Paul & Emma OLIVIER) b. 15 Aug. 1896 (Houma Ch.: v.5, p.156)
TRAHAN, Amy Mable (Augustin & Kenelie BONVILLAIN) b. 24 Oct. 1897 (Houma Ch.: v.5, p.190)
TRAHAN, Anna Ida (Veles & Marie HEBERT) b. 9 Feb. 1896 (Montegut Ch.: v.6, p.37)
TRAHAN, Cecimin Freddy (Frank & Alles MONSON) b. 19 Oct. 1899 (Theriot Ch.: v.2, p.53)

TRAHAN, Celanise d. 12 July 1897 at age 13 yrs. (Houma Ch.: v.3, p.13)
TRAHAN, Clifford Henry Harris (Joseph & Aledie GIROIN) b. 15 July 1899 (Theriot Ch.: v.2, p.48)
TRAHAN, Edna Leona (Oscar & Lalia OLIVIER) b. 4 Oct. 1899 (Theriot Ch.: v.2, p.51)
TRAHAN, Eglantine m. Eugene LEBOUF d. 30 Nov. 1899 at age 78 yrs. (Theriot Ch.: v.1, p.2)
TRAHAN, Elie Numa (Jean & Exelina AUTHEMENT) b. 2 April 1899 (Montegut Ch.: v.6, p.90)
TRAHAN, Elisabeth Annita (Joseph & Marie DOMINIQUE) b. 5 July 1899 (Houma Ch.: v.5, p.251)
TRAHAN, Emelienne m. 21 July 1899 Rene HEBERT (Houma Ct. Hse.: Mar. v.31 & 32, #80½)
TRAHAN, Emile Auguste (Pierre & Justlia LAPEYROUSE) b. 9 Feb. 1896 (Theriot Ch.: v.1-B, p.94)
TRAHAN, Emilienne of Terrebonne Parish m. 26 July 1899 Rene HEBERT, of Terrebonne Parish (Houma Ch.: v.6-B, p.4)
TRAHAN, Evelia (Eleutere & Evelia BREAUX) m. 7 June 1898 Norbert CHIASSON (Theriot Ch.: v.1-B, p.4)
TRAHAN, Evelia (Elotere & Evelia BREAUX) m. 19 May 1898 Norbert CHIASSON (Houma Ct. Hse.: Mar. v.30 & 31, #448)
TRAHAN, Frank m. 29 March 1897 Alice MUNSON (Houma Ct. Hse.: Mar. v.29 & 30, #366)
TRAHAN, Frank (Paul & Emma OLIVIER) m. 1 April 1897 Alice MUNSON (Houma Ch.: v.6-a, p.198)
TRAHAN, Frank William (Oscar & Fedora OLIVIER) b. 11 Oct. 1897 (Houma Ch.: v.5, p.189)
TRAHAN, Henry m. 5 July 1897 Eva BELANGER (Houma Ct. Hse.: Mar. v.29 & 30, #48)
TRAHAN, Henry (Wash & Julia PEAL) m. 13 July 1897 Eva BELANGER (Houma Ch.: v.6-a, p.210)
TRAHAN, Jean Baptiste (Justilien & Roselia AUTHEMENT) b. 9 April 1898 (Montegut Ch.: v.6, p.72)
TRAHAN, Jean Loles (Wallace & Marie HEBERT) b. 7 Feb. 1898 (Montegut Ch.: v.6, p.71)
TRAHAN, Joseph Adam Iveles (Wallace & Marie HEBERT) b. 14 Dec. 1899 (Montegut Ch.: v.7, p.24)
TRAHAN, Joseph Justilien (Justilien & Roselia AUTHEMENT) b. 8 June 1896 (Montegut Ch.: v.6, p.42)
TRAHAN, Josephine Hosanna (Pierre & Justilia LAPEROUSE) b. 7 Nov. 1897 (Montegut Ch.: v.6, p.62)
TRAHAN, Leo m. 6 Sept. 1897 Zoe RODRIGUE (Houma Ct. Hse.: Mar. v.29 & 30, #87)
TRAHAN, Leo (Pierre & Adolia BREAUX) m. 23 Sept. 1897 Zoe RODRIGUE (Houma Ch.: v.6-a, p.216)
TRAHAN, Lieme Eva (Joseph & Arcie GIROIR) b. 26 March 1898 (Houma Ch.: v.5, p.211)
TRAHAN, Lucile Leonice (Leo & Zoe LODRIGUE) b. 8 April 1899 (Theriot Ch.: v.2, p.39)

TRAHAN, Luma (Lovincy & Mary HUTCHINSON) m. 21 May 1897 Exzelina AUTHEMENT (Houma Ct. Hse.: Mar. v.29 & 30, #423)
TRAHAN, Mary Adelaide (Joseph & Marie DOMINGUE) b. 4 Feb. 1897 (Houma Ch.: v.5, p.175)
TRAHAN, Napoleon Joseph (Henry & Eva BELANGER) b. 27 March 1899 (Houma Ch.: v.5, p.243)
TRAHAN, Paul Wilbert (Petro & Adolia BREAUX) b. 21 May 1899 (Theriot Ch.: v.2, p.40)
TRAHAN, Ulicia m. 23 Jan. 1896 Alcide HEBERT (Houma Ct. Hse.: Mar. v.28, #404)
TRAHAN, Ulicia (Emile) m. 12 Feb. 1896 Alcide HEBERT (Houma Ch.: v.6-a, p.169)
TRAHAN, Virginia (Lovincy & Marie HUTCHINSON) m. 17 May 1898 Francois DUPRE (Houma Ct. Hse.: Mar. v.30 & 31, #441)
TRAHAN, Virginia (Lovincy & Marie HUTCHISON) m. 2 June 1898 Francois DUPRE (Montegut Ch.: v.4, p.245)
TRAHAN, Volcar (Cledomise & Azema BOUDREAUX) m. 31 Oct. 1899 Cecile PARR (Theriot Ch.: v.1-B, p.11)
TRAHAN, Volcar (Clodomise & Azema BOUDREAUX) m. 27 Oct. 1899 Cecile PARR (Houma Ct. Hse.: Mar. v.31 & 32, #155)

TRAIGLE (See: TREGLE)
TRANTACOSTE, Francesca (Francesco & Concietta SUGUI) m. 2 May 1898 Salvatore PERRONA (Thib. Ct. Hse.: Mar. v.38, #175)
TRANTACOSTE, Francisco (Petre & Francisca CANCIALUCE) b. 5 June 1898 (Thib. Ch.: v.7, p.553)
TRANTACOSTE, Nophia (Francesco & Conceitta GUGUI) m. 2 May 1898 Salvatore PERROUE (Thib. Ch.: v.14, p.201)

TREGLE (See TREGRE)
TREGLE, Antonia (Joseph & Antoinette -----) m. 30 July 1898 Antoine KRAMER (Chackbay Ch.: v.1, p.63)
TREGLE, Antonia (Joseph & Antoinette SERMETIT) m. 30 July 1898 Atoine KRAMER (Thib. Ct. Hse.: Mar. v.38, #227)
TREGLE, Clotilde Melodia (Leo & Mathilde BOUDREAU) b. 10 June 1899 (Chackbay Ch.: v.1, p.135)
TREGLE, Eugene (Pane & Emilie KELLER) b. 14 Sept. 1897 (Thib. Ch.: v.7, p.516)
TREGLE, Joseph Armand (Leo & Mathilde BOUDREAU) b. 11 Oct. 1897 (Chackbay Ch.: v.1, p.97)
TREGLE, Pierre (Roman & Elisa LEONARD) m. 3 Jan. 1897 Emelie KELLER (Thib. Ch.: v.14, p.120)
TREGLE, Pierre (Romon & Elisa LEONARD) m. 3 Jan. 1897 Emelie KELLER (Thib. Ct. Hse.: Mar. v.36, #40)
TREGLE, Theodule Francois (Jules & Adele SOMME) b. 16 July 1896; m. Lucie Alice BASS on 14 July 1927. (Raceland Ch.: Bapt. Bk., v.5, p.28)
TRICHE, Adele Anne (Joseph & Rosa GUIDROZ) b. 26 Feb. 1897 (Lockport Ch.: v.3-A, #29)

TRICHE, Adele Anne (Joseph & Rosa GUIDROZ) b. 26 Feb. 1897 (Lockport Ch.: v.3, #29)
TRICHE, Arthur Joseph (Joachim & Leontine MATHERNE) b. 1 Feb. 1896 (Lockport Ch.: v.2, p.320)
TRICHE, Jeanne Berthe (Joachim & Leontine MATHERNE) b. 4 April 1899 (Larose Ch.: v.3, p.38)
TRICHE, Marie Prescovia (Ovile & Ernestine GUITROZ) b. 2 May 1899 (Larose Ch.: v.3, p.39)
TRICHE, Ovide m. 13 April 1898 Ernestine GUIDROZ (Thib. Ct. Hse.: Mar. v.38, #151)
TRICHE, Rosalie m. Pierre HIMEL d. 27 April 1899 at age 52 yrs. (Lockport Ch.: v.1, #16)
TRICHE, Zulma m. 24 Feb. 1898 Joseph WASHINGTON (Thib. Ct. Hse.: Mar. v.37, #113)
TRISH, Josephine Ophelia (Nicles & Maria RUITA) b. 22 Sept. 1896 (Larose Ch.: v.2, p.196)
TRIST, Arthur Ronald (John & Mary A. TRIST) m. 27 Dec. 1899 Angela PLASENCIA (Houma Ct. Hse.: Mar. v.31 & 32, #206)
TRIST, Arthur Ronald (John & Mary A. TRIST) m. 28 Dec 1899 Angela PLASENCIA (Houma Ch.: Epis. Ch.: v.1, p.344)

TROSCLAIR (Sometimes: TROSCLAIRE, TROSCLER)

TROSCLAIR, Adam m. 4 Jan. 1899 Loretta M. QUICK (Houma Ct. Hse.: Mar. v.30 & 31, #179)
TROSCLAIR, Adam (Emile & Philmene TROSCLAIR) bt. 20 May 1896 (Chackbay Ch.: v.1, p.66)
TROSCLAIR, Adam (Laurent & Emilie HENRY) m. 23 Jan. 1899 Loretta M. QUICK (Houma Ch.: v.6-a, p.267)
TROSCLAIR, Adam (Rufin & Marie AUCOIN) m. 27 March 1896 Lucie PIERRON (Houma Ct. Hse.: Mar. v.29 & 30, #16)
TROSCLAIR, Albert (Emile & Zulmee RODRIGUE) m. 15 Feb. 1897 Elda TROSCLAIR (Chackbay Ch.: v.1, p.39)
TROSCLAIR, Albert (Emile & Zulmee RODRIGUE) m. 15 Feb. 1897 Elda TROSCLAIR (Thib. Ct. Hse.: Mar. v.36, #54)
TROSCLAIR, Alfred Nolan (Lesain & Dorelia THIBODEAUX) b. 31 April 1899 (Theriot Ch.: v.2, p.43)
TROSCLAIR, Alida (Adrien & Aurelia BENOIT) m. 9 Oct. 1899 Felicien ADAM (Thib. Ct. Hse.: Mar. v.39, #238)
TROSCLAIR, Alida (d.Adrien & Amelia BENOIT) m. 9 Oct. 1899 Felicien ADAM (Chackbay Ch.: v.1, p.74)
TROSCLAIR, Angelique m. 18 Jan. 1898 Livaudais LEDET (Larose Ch.: v.3, p.7)
TROSCLAIR, Angelique m. 18 Jan. 1898 Livaudais LEDET (Larose Ch.: v.4, p.111)
TROSCLAIR, Angelique m. 18 Jan. 1898 Livaudais LEDET (Thib. Ct. Hse.: Mar. v.37, #23)
TROSCLAIR, Aurelie (Joseph & Victoria GOBERT) m. 17 Feb. 1896 John Flaragus KRAMER (Thib. Ct. Hse.: Mar. v.35, #37)
TROSCLAIR, Aurelie (Joseph & Victoria GOBERT) m. 17 Feb. 1896 John KRAMER (Chackbay Ch.: v.1, p.26)

TROSCLAIR, Aurelien (Joseph & Victoria GOBERT) m. 18 Sept. 1899 Elmire ROBESSON (Chackbay Ch.: v.1, p.73)

TROSCLAIR, Aurelien (Joseph & Victoria GOBERT) m. 5 Sept. 1899 Elmire ROBERTSON (Thib. Ct. Hse.: Mar. v.39, #220)

TROSCLAIR, Azema Sylvina (Drozin & Noel Ida CLEMENT) b. 18 Dec. 1898 (Chackbay Ch.: v.1, p.121)

TROSCLAIR, Bernadett Viola (Ozeme & Angeline PELLEGRAZ) b. 13 Sept. 1899 (Thib. Ch.: v.8, p.8)

TROSCLAIR, Carrie Mary (Adam & Faustine DAIGLE) b. 3 Sept. 1896 (Thib. Ch.: v.7, p.417)

TROSCLAIR, Celina Zulmee (Dalferes & Josephine BERGERON) b. 13 May 1896 (Chackbay Ch.: v.1, p.67)

TROSCLAIR, Celine d. 17 Aug. 1898 at age 1 mth. (Thib. Ch.: v.3, p.219)

TROSCLAIR, Claude Joseph (Ulisse & Laura BERGERON) b. 19 May 1898 (Houma Ch.: v.5, p.215)

TROSCLAIR, Clothilde (Laurent & Aimee HENRI) m. 25 March 1898 Paul SCOTT (Houma Ct. Hse.: Mar. v.30 & 31, #350)

TROSCLAIR, Clothilde (Laurentis & Aimee HENRI) m. 11 April 1898 Paul SCOTT (Theriot Ch.: v.1-B, p.3)

TROSCLAIR, Constant Rufin (Adam & Lucie PIERRON) b. 17 March 1898 (Theriot Ch.: v.2, p.22)

TROSCLAIR, Edmond Hypolite (Leonidas & Octavie TRICHE) b. 13 Aug. 1896 (Thib. Ch.: v.7, p.413)

TROSCLAIR, Edouard Henri (Clebert & Celina LEBLANC) b. 14 July 1898 (Larose Ch.: v.3, p.23)

TROSCLAIR, Elda (Xavier & Augusta TOUPS) m. 15 Feb. 1897 Albert TROSCLAIR (Chackbay Ch.: v.1, p.39)

TROSCLAIR, Elda (Xavier & Augusta TOUPS) m. 15 Feb. 1897 Albert TROSCLAIR (Thib. Ct. Hse.: Mar. v.36, #54)

TROSCLAIR, Eleonore (Rufin & Marie AUCOIN) m. 28 Sept. 1897 Thomas A. PREVOST (Houma Ct. Hse.: Mar. v.29 & 30, #98)

TROSCLAIR, Eleonore (Rufin) m. 7 Oct. 1897 Thomas Albert PROVOST (Theriot Ch.: v.1-B, p.1)

TROSCLAIR, Eliska (Antoine & Eve GONZALES) m. 3 Feb. 1898 Augustin NAQUIN (Thib. Ct. Hse.: Mar. v.37, #69)

TROSCLAIR, Emile (Emile & Mathilde CHAMPAGNE) m. 23 July 1898 Augusta ROBERT (Raceland Ch.: v.2, p.77)

TROSCLAIR, Etienne Severe (Etienne & Otieana BERGERON) b. 24 Aug. 1896 (Larose Ch.: v.2, p.182)

TROSCLAIR, Felicia (Adrien & Aurelia BENOIT) m. 25 Aug. 1898 Felicien BENOIT (Thib. Ct. Hse.: Mar. v.38, #240)

TROSCLAIR, Felicia (Adrien & Durelia BENOIT) m. 25 Aug. 1898 Felicien BENOIT (Thib. Ch.: v.14, p.215)

TROSCLAIR, Felix (Ulysse & Azema LORIO) b. 28 Sept. 1899 (Thib. Ch.: v.7, p.567)

TROSCLAIR, Henri Didier (Ulysse & Laura BERGERON) b. 23 May 1896 (Chackbay Ch.: v.1, p.69)

TROSCLAIR, Jean (Emile & Philomene TROSCLAIR) b. 14 April 1898 (Chackbay Ch.: v.1, p.111)

TROSCLAIR, Jesse Elles (Wallace & Celima LONGUEPIT) b. 6 Sept. 1898 (Thib. Ch.: v.7, p.562)
TROSCLAIR, Joseph Luc (Drauzin & Nolida CLEMENT) bt. 13 April 1896 (Chackbay Ch.: v.1, p.64)
TROSCLAIR, Joseph Lynnwood (Adam & Lucille PIERRON) b. 3 Jan. 1897 (Theriot Ch.: v.1-B, p.104)
TROSCLAIR, Joseph Wilfred (Ozemee & Angelina PELEGRIN) b. 7 Dec. 1897 (Thib. Ch.: v.7, p.475)
TROSCLAIR, Josephine (Xavier & Augusta TOUPS) b. 27 Aug. 1898 (Chackbay Ch.: v.1, p.121)
TROSCLAIR, Josephine Ela Anita (Clebert & Celina LEBLANC) b. 31 Oct. 1896 (Larose Ch.: v.2, p.182)
TROSCLAIR, Lea (Xavier & Augusta TOUPS) m. 26 Jan. 1897 Sylvain BOUDREAUX (Chackbay Ch.: v.1, p.37)
TROSCLAIR, Lea (Xavier & Augusta TOUPS) m. 26 Jan. 1897 Sylvain BOUDREAUX (Thib. Ct. Hse.: Mar. v.36, #7)
TROSCLAIR, Leo (Emile & Zulmee RODRIGUE) m. 3 Feb. 1896 Felicia TOUPS (Thib. Ct. Hse.: Mar. v.35, #20)
TROSCLAIR, Leo (Emile & Zulmee RODRIGUE) m. 3 Feb. 1896 Felicia TOUPS (Chackbay Ch.: v.1, p.25)
TROSCLAIR, Leonce (Leonidas & Octavie TRICHE) m. 7 July 1897 Celina FOLSE (Thib. Ct. Hse.: Mar. v.37, #185)
TROSCLAIR, Levy Pierre (Ursain & Emma ROBESSON) b. 6 Oct. 1898 (Chackbay Ch.: v.1, p.123)
TROSCLAIR, Louis Noe (Adam & Austine DAIGLE) b. 2 Oct. 1899 (Chacahoula Ch.: v.4, p.30)
TROSCLAIR, Louisa (Ursain & Emma ROBENSON) b. 28 May 1896 (Chackbay Ch.: v.1, p.68)
TROSCLAIR, Marguerite Rosa (Dolpherese & Josephine BERGERON) b. 13 Sept. 1897 (Houma Ch.: v.5, p.188)
TROSCLAIR, Marie Augusta (Philibert & Emilie CALLAHAN) b. 9 Jan. 1898 (Larose Ch.: v.3, p.20)
TROSCLAIR, Marie Cecile (Elisee & Odile DESROCHES) b. 28 Feb. 1897 (Montegut Ch.: v.6, p.53)
TROSCLAIR, Marie Cecile (Elyree & Odilia DESROCHES) d. 4 May 1897 (Montegut Ch.: v.2, p.10)
TROSCLAIR, Marie Octavie (Albert & Elda TROSCLAIR) b. 19 Dec. 1897 (Thib. Ch.: v.7, p.485)
TROSCLAIR, Marie Olivia (Elisce & Odile DESROCHES) b. 28 July 1898 (Montegut Ch.: v.6, p.75)
TROSCLAIR, Marie Silvanie (Francois Xavier & Augusta TOUPS) b. 11 Sept. 1897 (Chackbay Ch.: v.1, p.95)
TROSCLAIR, Maurice Joseph Le (Drozin & Armide UZET) b. 3 Sept. 1898 (Thib. Ch.: v.7, p.514)
TROSCLAIR, Niclos Zacharie (Philibert & Emilie CALAHAN) b. 6 Oct. 1899 (Larose Ch.: v.3, p.46)
TROSCLAIR, Octavie m. 4 Oct. 1897 Ludovic HENRY (Houma Ct. Hse.: Mar. v.29 & 30, #106)
TROSCLAIR, Octavie (Rufin & Mary AUCOIN) m. 14 Oct. 1897 Ludovic HENRY (Houma Ch.: v.6-a, p.219)

TROSCLAIR, Olea (Drauzin & Marie DOUCET) m. 13 April 1896 Ulysse BENOIT (Thib. Ct. Hse.: Mar. v.35, #60)
TROSCLAIR, Olea (Drauzin & Marie DOUCET) m. 13 April 1896 Ulysse BENOIT (Chackbay Ch.: v.1, p.26)
TROSCLAIR, Philibert (Philibert & Emelie CALLAGHAN) b. 6 Jan. 1896 (Larose Ch.: v.2, p.179)
TROSCLAIR, Philodia Eve (Albert & Elda TROSCLAIR) b. 31 Oct. 1899 (Chackbay Ch.: v.1, p.145)
TROSCLAIR, Valerie m. 22 Feb. 1897 Theophile ADAM (Larose Ch.: v.3, p.5)
TROSCLAIR, Valerie m. 22 March 1897 Theophile ADAM (Larose Ch.: v.4, p.104)
TROSCLAIR, Valery m. 1 Feb. 1897 Theophile ADAM (Thib. Ct. Hse.: Mar. v.36, #61)
TROSCLAIR, Wallace (Adrien & Aurelia BENOIT) m. 18 June 1896 Celima LONGUEPIE (Thib. Ct. Hse.: Mar. v.35, #101)
TROSCLAIR, Wallace (Adrien & Aurelia BENOIT) m. 18 June 1896 Celima LONGUEPIE (Thib. Ch.: v.14, p.93)
TROXLER, Victoire (Antoine & Eve GONZALES) m. 15 Sept. 1897 Robert SEELY (Thib. Ct. Hse.: Mar. v.37, #226)
TUCKER, Antoine Alvis (Walter Joseph & Alice LORIOT) b. 12 Dec. 1897 (Thib. Ch.: v.7, p.476)
TUCKER, Edna J. m. 17 April 1897 Emile DAIGLE, Jr. (Houma Ct. Hse.: Mar. v.29 & 30, #384)
TUCKER, Edna J. (William P. & Amelia Z. THIBODEAUX) m. 20 April 1897 Emile DAIGLE, Jr. (Houma Ch.: v.6-a, p.199)
TUCKER, Henriette m. Alces BOURGEOIS d. 15 Oct. 1899 at age 60 yrs. & 2 mths. (Thib. Ch.: v.3, p.241)
TUCKER, Hortance Mildred (William P. & Amelia J. THIBODEAUX) b. 10 March 1896 (Houma Ch.: v.5, p.148)
TUCKER, Joseph d. 12 Nov. 1899 at age 64 yrs. (Thib. Ch.: v.3, p.243)
TUCKER, Mabel E. m. 30 Nov. 1896 Francis J. BOND (Houma Ct. Hse.: Mar. v.29 & 30, #196)
TUCKER, Mabel E. (William P. & Amelia THIBODAUX) m. 8 Dec. 1896 Francis J. BOND (Houma Ch.: v.6-a, p.186)
TUCKER, Maggie M. (Joseph P. & Brigette THIBODEAUX) m. 27 Sept. 1899 Henry E. BEAUVAIS (Thib. Ch.: v.14, p.299)
TUCKER, Maggie May (Joseph P. & Brigette THIBODEAUX) m. 27 Sept. 1899 Henry E. BEAUVAIS (Thib. Ct. Hse.: Mar. v.39, #222)
TUITE, Mary (James & Mary RYAN) m. 23 Aug. 1898 Leon LEBLANC (Thib. Ct. Hse.: Mar. v.38, #254)
TUITE, Mary (James & Mary RYAN) m. 23 Aug. 1898 Leon LEBLANC (Lockport Ch.: v.2, p.193 & 194)
TURNER, Charles m. 16 Jan. 1896 Caroline PIERRE (Thib. Ct. Hse.: Mar. v.35, #24)
TURNER, Daniel m. 17 Jan. 1898 Mary BOYNES (Houma Ct. Hse.: Mar. v.30 & 31, #210)
TURNER, Eddie m. 15 Dec. 1898 Rebecca BROOKS (Houma Ct. Hse.: Mar. v.30 & 31, #148)

TURNER, Elizabeth m. 27 Jan. 1898 Monroe THOMPSON (Thib. Ct. Hse.: Mar. v.37, #61)

TURNER, Henrietta m. 16 Feb. 1899 Sam MOORE (Houma Ct. Hse.: Mar. v.31 & 32, #341)

TURNER, Laura m. 6 July 1897 Fred BROOMFIELD, Jr. (Houma Ct. Hse.: Mar. v.29 & 30, #51)

TURNER, Louis m. 6 Feb. 1897 Ann JENKINS (Houma Ct. Hse.: Mar. v.29 & 30, #295)

TURNER, Louisa m. 2 Nov. 1896 Edward STOBALL (Houma Ct. Hse.: Mar. v.29 & 30, #184)

TURNER, Matilda m. d.John EUGENE. Petition for probate of will: 30 Aug. 1899. (Thib. Ct. Hse.: Succ. #1587)

TURNER, Sam m. 2 Feb. 1899 Virginia THOMPSON (Houma Ct. Hse.: Mar. v.30 & 31, #306)

"U"

UGGINA, Santa (Salvatore & Maria CASTELLANE) b. 1 Dec. 1898 (Houma Ch.: v.5, p.231)

UGUEL, Rodolphe (Johannes & Therese TOMMASSI) b. 18 Aug. 1898 (Larose Ch.: v.3, p.28)

UNIFORTS, Mamie m. 13 July 1898 Robert LEWIS (Thib. Ct. Hse.: Mar. v.38, #224)

URSENE, Fulman m. 28 Dec. 1899 Leontine JOSEPH (Thib. Ct. Hse.: Mar. v.39, #303)

URSIN, Joseph Irvin (Mertie & Morine TOUSSAINT) b. 13 Aug. 1898 (Thib. Ch.: v.7, p.561)

URSIN, Marie Lucilia (Metile & Valerie TOUSSAINT) b. 18 July 1896 (Thib. Ch.: v.7, p.411)

URSIN, Marie Modeste d. 27 March 1896 at age 64 yrs. (Thib. Ch.: v.3, p.181)

URSIN, Mirtilia (John & Marie MILLAN) m. 19 Jan. 1899 Dudley Joseph DANTIN (Thib. Ct. Hse.: Mar. v.38, #22)

URSIN, Mirtilia (John & Marie MILLAN) m. 19 Jan. 1899 Dudley Joseph DANTIN (Thib. Ch.: v.14, p.240)

URSO, Giuseppi (Salvatore & Giuseppa NUNCIA) m. 11 Dec. 1899 Rosie TAUTILLO (Thib. Ct. Hse.: Mar. v.39, #280)

URSO, Guiseppe (Salvatore & Guiseppa NUNCIA) m. 26 Dec. 1899 Rosa TANTILLO (Thib. Ch.: v.14, p.315)

USE (Sometimes: USEE, USEY, UZE)

USE, Adam (Carles & Odile GAUTREAUX) m. 3 May 1899 Dovida MELANCON (Lockport Ch.: v.2, p.208)

USE, Adam (Charles & Odile GAUTREAUX) m. 24 April 1899 Dovida MELANCON (Thib. Ct. Hse.: Mar. v.39, #156)

USE, Adele Odille (Adam & Dovida MELANCON) b. 2 Dec. 1898 (Larose Ch.: v.3, p.34)

USE, Alcide m. 2 Sept. 1899 Camillia BARTELLS (Houma Ct. Hse.: Mar. v.31 & 32, #115)

USE, Alcide m. 21 Sept. 1899 Amelia BARTELLO (Houma Ch.: v.6-B, p.4)

USE, Andre Raphael (Alceste & Emilie BERGERON) b. 24 Oct. 1897 (Thib. Ch.: v.7, p.470)

USE, Arthur (Arthur & Marie TRICHE) m. 2 Feb. 1898 Victoria LEBLANC (Thib. Ct. Hse.: Mar. v.37, #60)

USE, Arthur (Arthur & Marie TRICHE) m. 2 Feb. 1898 Victorine LEBLANC (Lockport Ch.: v.2, p.182 & 183)

USE, Arthur Mrs. d. -- May 1897 (Lockport Ch.: v.1, #11)

USE, Camila (Alfred & Alice HEBERT) m. 15 June 1899 Julien PITRE (Thib. Ch.: v.14, p.285)

USE, Camila (Alfred & Alice HEBERT) m. 15 June 1899 Julien PITRE (Thib. Ct. Hse.: Mar. v.39, #169)

USE, Charles Abel (Numa & Marguerite BERNARD) b. 10 Feb. 1897 (Lockport Ch.: v.3-A, #19)

USE, Charles Abel (Numa & Marguerite BERNARD) b. 10 Feb. 1897 (Lockport Ch.: v.3, #19)

USE, Charles Albert (Albert & Clauna PITT) b. 3 June 1899 (Thib. Ch.: v.7, p.551)
USE, Edward Olivier (Joseph & Clara BREAUX) b. 25 April 1899 (Thib. Ch.: v.7, p.601)
USE, Eugene William (Martial & Celina HEBERT) b. 17 March 1896 (Thib. Ch.: v.7, p.397)
USE, Eve m. 12 May 1896 Raymond GUIDRY (Thib. Ct. Hse.: Mar. v.35, #88)
USE, Eve m. 23 Jan. 1899 Raymond GUIDRY (Lockport Ch.: v.2, p.199)
USE, Francois (Francois & Emma ROME) b. 28 May 1896 (Chackbay Ch.: v.1, p.67)
USE, Joseph (Alfred & Alice HEBERT) m. 15 Feb. 1897 Clara BREAUX (Thib. Ch.: v.14, p.124)
USE, Joseph (Alfred & Alice HEBERT) m. 15 Feb. 1897 Clara BREAUX (Thib. Ct. Hse.: Mar. v.36, #58)
USE, Joseph Charles (Leo & Feliciane LACOSTE) b. 5 Feb. 1896 (Lockport Ch.: v.2, p.323)
USE, Josephine (Alfred & Alice HEBERT) m. 8 Feb. 1898 Volcar BERGERON (Thib. Ch.: v.14, p.182)
USE, Josephine (Alfred & Alice HEBERT) m. 8 Feb. 1898 Volcar BERGERON (Thib. Ct. Hse.: Mar. v.37, #42)
USE, Josephine (Arthur & Marie TRICHE) m. 20 Oct. 1898 Paul LEBLANC (Thib. Ct. Hse.: Mar. v.38, #295)
USE, Josephine (Arthur & Marie TRICHE) m. 20 Oct. 1898 Paul LEBLANC (Lockport Ch.: v.2, p.195)
USE, Lucien d. 11 Sept. 1897 at age 32 yrs. (Lockport Ch.: v.1, #23)
USE, Maria Curley (Leo & Julienne FIELDS) b. 29 Sept. 1896 (Montegut Ch.: v.6, p.45)
USE, Marie Agnes (Joseph & Lovina TOUPS) b. 7 May 1899 (Chackbay Ch.: v.1, p.136)
USE, Marie Eve Sophie (Leo & Julienne FIELDS) b. 27 Sept. 1899 (Montegut Ch.: v.6, p.94)
USE, Olivier Georges (Martial & Celina HEBERT) b. 14 Nov. 1898 (Thib. Ch.: v.7, p.521)
USE, Philomene Lucile (Joseph & Clara BRAUD) b. 24 Nov. 1897 (Thib. Ch.: v.7, p.474)
USE, Therese Marie (Alces & Emelie BERGERON) b. 19 Dec. 1899 (Thib. Ch.: v.7, p.579)
USE, Virginie (John & Justine DUET) m. 20 Aug. 1896 Henry ROME (Chackbay Ch.: v.1, p.29)
USE, Virginie (John & Justine DUTCH) m. 20 Aug. 1896 Henry ROME (Thib. Ct. Hse.: Mar. v.36, #129)
UTZA, Anita d. 14 Oct. 1897 at age 2 days (Thib. Ch.: v.3, p.206)
UTZA, Anitia (Ignatio & Carmela UTZA) b. 12 Oct. 1897 (Thib. Ch.: v.7, p.468)
UULLO, Salvatore (Luigi & Calogera PIAZZA) b. 24 Oct. 1898 (Houma Ch.: v.5, p.228)

UZZO, Francesco (Ignazio & Carmela UZZO) b. 22 Dec. 1898 (Thib. Ch.: v.7, p.529)

UZZO, Vincenza (Ignacio & Anna CARUNNA) m. 10 Sept. 1898 Giovanino BUFIGGERIO (Thib. Ct. Hse.: Mar. v.38, #257)

UZZO, Vincenza (Ignacio & Anna CAVANNA) m. 10 Sept. 1898 Giovanino BUFIGGERIO (Thib. Ch.: v.14, p.222)

"V"

VACARON, Arniqua (Nicholas & Apolonie CHACCIO) b. 27 June 1898 (Houma Ch.: v.5, p.213)
VALENCE, John m. 6 May 1897 Azelie MARTIN (Thib. Ct. Hse.: Mar. v.36, #138)
VALENS, Jacques (John & Azelie MARTIN) b. 25 Sept. 1897 (Larose Ch.: v.3, p.28)
VALENTE, Guiseppe (Guiseppe & Maria RIBAUDA) b. 15 June 1899 (Thib. Ch.: v.7, p.608)

VALENTIN (Sometimes: VALENTINE)
VALENTIN, Sarah m. 20 April 1899 Mingo JOHNSON (Houma Ct. Hse.: Mar. v.31 & 32, #410)
VALIN, Annine Helene (Joanni & Azalie MARTIN) b. 18 Aug. 1899 (Larose Ch.: v.3, p.47)
VANACORE, Andre Lovensie (Salvador & Azelie HAUTIN) b. 26 March 1896 (Larose Ch.: v.2, p.185)
VANACORE, Lucretia (Salvatore & Alzina SAVOIE) b. 5 April 1898 (Raceland Ch.: v.5, p.69)
VANACORE, Marie (Barthelemi & Alice SAVOIE) b. 5 Dec. 1898 (Raceland Ch.: v.5, p.85)
VANACORE, Marie (Salvadore & Alzina SAVOIE) b. 18 March 1897 (Raceland Ch.: v.5, p.45)
VANDACORE, Eveline (Bartelemi & Alice SAVOIE) b. 22 July 1896 (Raceland Ch.: v.5, p.26)
VARISCA, Francesca (Vincenzo & Rosalia LABONE) m. 3 April 1899 Antonino TANTILLO (Thib. Ch.: v.14, p.268-a)
VARISCO, Francesca (Vincenzo & Rosalia LABOUE) m. 3 April 1899 Antonino TANTILLO (Thib. Ct. Hse.: Mar. v.39, #105)
VARISCO, Rosalia (Salvador & Josephina GRAZIANO) b. 23 Sept. 1897 (Thib. Ch.: v.7, p.514)
VARNS, Philippe d. 18 May 1898 at age 21 yrs. (Thib. Ch.: v.3, p.214)
VAUGHN, Henry Thomas (Walter & Virginia HOFFMANN) b. 21 June 1898 (Montegut Ch.: v.6, p.73)
VAUGHN, Mose m. 21 Oct. 1898 Victoria FAULS (Thib. Ct. Hse.: Mar. v.38, #299)
VEDRAS, Joseph Onil (Paul & Ernestine BOUDREAUX) b. 13 Dec. 1896 (Lockport Ch.: v.3, #31)
VEDROS, Delphine (Gaetan & Elina BOURGEOIS) m. 10 Feb. 1898 Louis BLANCHARD (Thib. Ct. Hse.: Mar. v.37, #49)
VEDROS, Delphine (Gaetan & Elina BOURGEOIS) m. 10 Feb. 1898 Louis BLANCHARD (Lockport Ch.: v.2, p.185)
VEDROS, Joseph (Paul & Ernestine BOUDREAUX) b. 13 Dec. 1896 (Lockport Ch.: v.3-A, #31)
VEDROSE, Justilien m. 3 Feb. 1898 Clementine ROBICHAUX (Thib. Ct. Hse.: Mar. v.37, #57)
VEDROSE, Justilien (Gaetan & Celina BOURGEOIS) m. 3 Feb. 1898 Clementine ROBICHAUX (Raceland Ch.: v.2, p.62)

VEGA (Sometimes: VEGAS, VEGASSE, VEGUE, VEGUES, VESGAS, VIGUE)

VEGA or CHERAMI, Celeste Lucie (Raphael & Celestine HAUTIN) b. 10 April 1897 (Larose Ch.: v.3, p.8)

VEGA, ----- child d. 22 July 1897 (Larose Ch.: v.1, p.41)

VEGA, Alexina m. 27 April 1896 Marcel DANOS (Larose Ch.: v.4, p.92)

VEGA, Alexina m. 27 April 1896 Marcel DANOS (Thib. Ct. Hse.: Mar. v.35, #76)

VEGA, Donat d. 24 July 1897 at age 10 yrs. (Larose Ch.: v.1, p.40)

VEGA, Edward Joseph (Alfred & Florence HAUTIN) b. 25 April 1897 (Larose Ch.: v.3, p.7)

VEGA, Etienne Webber (Napoleon & Josephine LEFORT) b. 12 Oct. 1897 (Larose Ch.: v.3, p.6)

VEGA, Harris Gregoire (Raphael & Leontine GISCLAR) b. 17 Dec. 1898 (Larose Ch.: v.3, p.32)

VEGA, Laurenza (Perique & Josephine DANTIN) m. 30 June 1898 Leon GISCLAR (Thib. Ct. Hse.: Mar. v.38, #202)

VEGA, Marc (Antoine & Adorestine HUTIN) b. 28 April 1899 (Larose Ch.: v.3, p.40)

VEGA, Paul Napoleon (Napoleon & Josephine LEFORT) b. 27 Nov. 1899 (Larose Ch.: v.3, p.49)

VEGA, Pauline m. 13 Jan. 1897 Alexis DANOS (Thib. Ct. Hse.: Mar. v.36, #23)

VEGA, Pauline m. 25 Jan. 1897 Alexis DANOS (Larose Ch.: v.3, p.5)

VEGA, Pauline m. 25 Jan. 1897 Alexis DANOS (Larose Ch.: v.4, p.118)

VEGA, Raphael Raynault (Napoleon & Josephine LEFORT) b. 14 Feb. 1896 (Larose Ch.: v.2, p.181)

VEGA, Renault Raphael (Napoleon & Josephine LEFORT) b. 14 Feb. 1896 (Larose Ch.: v.2, p.183 & p.194, #25)

VEGA, Reno (Napoleon) d. 16 Jan. 1897 (Larose Ch.: v.1, p.39)

VEGA, Scott Enoche (Perrique & Myrthe GUEDRY) b. 6 July 1896 (Larose Ch.: v.2, p.184)

VEGA, Sidonia (Raphael & Leontine GISCLAR) b. 8 Jan. 1897 (Larose Ch.: v.3, p.4)

VEGA, Use d. 24 July 1897 at age 12 yrs. (Larose Ch.: v.1, p.40)

VENTRER, Clara (John & Cecile HOWARD) b. 17 Nov. 1897 (Raceland Ch.: v.5, p.67)

VERDAM, Joseph m. 14 Jan. 1899 Victorine FOREST (Houma Ch.: v.6-a, p.263)

VERDIN (Sometimes: VERDUN)

VERDIN, Cyriaque Augustin (Delmas & Honorine NAQUIN) b. 8 Aug. 1898; bt. 10 March 1903 (Larose Ch.: v.4, p.28)

VERDIN, Ernest Loveless (Theophile & Aspasie FRILEAN) b. 4 Sept. 1897; bt. 8 April 1899 (Houma Ch.: v.5, p.240)

VERDIN, Ernest Loveless (Theophile & Olivia SENEC) b. 19 May 1896; bt. 17 April 1899 (Houma Ch.: v.5, p.241)
VERDIN, Eva (Alexandre & Josephine TRAHAN) m. 31 July 1897 Pierre FRANCIS (Houma Ct. Hse.: Mar. v.29 & 30, #72)
VERDIN, Felicia Marie (Prospere & Olivia SENAC) b. 19 May 1896 (Houma Ch.: v.5, p.240)
VERDIN, Felicia Marie (Prospere & Olivia SENEC) b. 4 Sept. 1897; bt. 17 April 1899 (Houma Ch.: v.5, p.241)
VERDIN, Joseph (Alexander & Josephine TRAHAN) m. 24 Jan. 1898 Victorine FOREST (Houma Ct. Hse.: Mar. v.30 & 31, #247)
VERDIN, Joseph E. (Pierre & Marie PELEGRIN) b. 29 April 1898 (Houma Ch.: v.5, p.211)
VERDIN, Laine (Joseph & Victorine FOREST) b. 16 Oct. 1898 (Houma Ch.: v.5, p.229)
VERDIN, Lozema Louisa (Bernard & Rosalie BILLOT) b. 23 Jan. 1898 (Montegut Ch.: v.6, p.74)
VERDIN, Marcellite Angelina (George & Mathilde BILLOT) b. 22 Sept. 1897; bt. 3 Feb. 1900 (Larose Ch.: v.3, p.51)
VERDIN, Marie Agnes Albertine (Alexandre & Josephine TRAHAN) b. 15 Sept. 1898 (Houma Ch.: v.5, p.218)
VERDIN, Mary Louise (Pierre & Marie PELEGRIN) b. 4 March 1896 (Houma Ch.: v.5, p.150)
VERDIN, Nichol Bernard (Bernard & Rosalie BILLOT) b. 6 Dec. 1899; bt. 10 March 1903 (Larose Ch.: v.4, p.29)
VERDIN, Noe Ursin (Augustin & Constance VERDIN) b. 16 Dec. 1898 (Montegut Ch.: v.6, p.80)
VERDIN, Oleus Paul (Theodore & Valentine GUEDRY) b. 1 Feb. 1896 (Raceland Ch.: v.5, p.27)
VERDIN, Victor m. 9 Feb. 1899 Sidonia BILLOT (Houma Ct. Hse.: Mar. v.31 & 32, #331½)
VERDIN, Willy Simeon (Simeon & Augustine BILLOT) b. 11 March 1898; bt. 10 March 1903 (Larose Ch.: v.4, p.29)
VERGEN, James m. 12 May 1896 Sarah GATES (Houma Ct. Hse.: Mar. v.29 & 30, #62)
VERGNOLE, Julien m. Emma RIONDEL Child listed: Jeanne. Petition to administer: 18 Jan. 1896. (Thib. Ct. Hse.: Succ. #1504)
VERNA, Marie (John & Philomene ALEXIS) b. 10 June 1898 (Thib. Ch.: v.7, p.501)
VERNA, Walter m. 27 March 1897 Ella MONROE (Thib. Ct. Hse.: Mar. v.36, #102)
VERNACI, Francesco (Salvatore & Rosalie PALISI) b. 20 Jan. 1898 (Thib. Ch.: v.7, p.549)
VERNER, Arthur (Walter & Ella MONROE) b. 15 Feb. 1898 (Thib. Ch.: v.7, p.493)
VERNON, Emma m. 7 July 1898 Jake BROWN (Thib. Ct. Hse.: Mar. v.38, #222)
VERNON, John (Austin & Nina VERNON) m. 8 April 1896 Philomene ALEXIS (Thib. Ch.: v.14, p.82)
VERNON, John (Austin & Vina VERNON) m. 8 April 1896 Philomena ALEXIS (Thib. Ct. Hse.: Mar. v.35, #65)

VERNON, Mary Brigitt (John & Philomene ALEXIS) b. 1 Sept. 1896 (Thib. Ch.: v.7, p.440)

VERRET (Sometimes: VERRETTE)

VERRET, Alice m. 17 Feb. 1898 Benjamin THOMAS (Houma Ct. Hse.: Mar. v.30 & 31, #302)

VERRET, Bertha m. 2 Feb. 1898 Charlton REED (Thib. Ct. Hse.: Mar. v.37, #76)

VERRET, Charles m. 13 April 1899 Sarah ELFRETH (Houma Ct. Hse.: Mar. v.31 & 32, #401)

VERRET, Charles of Terrebonne Parish m.26 April 1899 Sarah ELFRET (Houma Ch.: v.6-B, p.3)

VERRET, Edward m. 9 Oct. 1897 Josephine BARKUS (Houma Ct. Hse.: Mar. v.29 & 30, #115)

VERRET, Ellen m. 21 June 1899 Claiborne H. GUENO (Houma Ct. Hse.: Mar. v.31 & 32, #49)

VERRET, Eloise of Terrebonne Parish who married Joseph NAQUIN d. 29 Oct. 1899 at age 64 yrs. (Theriot Ch.: v.1, p.2)

VERRET, Elvire (Ovide & Julie NAQUIN) b. 12 April 1896 (Theriot Ch.: v.1-B, p.100)

VERRET, Esther d. 13 May 1897 at age 6 mths. (Raceland Ch.: v.1, p.13)

VERRET, Gilbert m. 25 Feb. 1897 Ida GREEN (Houma Ct. Hse.: Mar. v.29 & 30, #334)

VERRET, Henri (Adam & Elisa GRAY) b. 12 Nov. 1897 (Theriot Ch.: v.2, p.21)

VERRET, Joseph d. 4 Nov. 1898 at age 10 days (Theriot Ch.: v.1, p.1)

VERRET, Joseph Ignesse (Willie & Albertine BILLIOT) b. 26 Oct. 1899 (Theriot Ch.: v.2, p.63)

VERRET, Louis m. 20 Feb. 1897 Helena PERTUIT (Thib. Ct. Hse.: Mar. v.36, #86)

VERRET, Louis (Pierre & Emetilde ROME) m. -- Feb. 1896 Helena PERTUIT (Raceland Ch.: v.2, p.35)

VERRET, Louis Walsie (Ernest & Lavanie VERDUN) b. 27 Feb. 1896 (Theriot Ch.: v.1-B, p.104)

VERRET, Marie Esther (Octave & Sara FALGOU) b. 20 Sept. 1896 (Raceland Ch.: v.5, p.30)

VERRET, Marie Eve (Jean & Eulalie NAQUIN) b. 14 Nov. 1897 (Theriot Ch.: v.2, p.17)

VERRET, Mary Genevieve (Albert & Evelina LEVRON) b. 11 Sept. 1899 (Houma Ch.: v.5, p.253)

VERRET, Meville Willie (Willie & Eveline NAQUIN) d. 25 Nov. 1896 at age 4 mths, 12 days (Theriot Ch.: v.1, p.101)

VERRET, Meville Willie (Willie & Exelina NAQUIN) d. 25 Nov. 1896 (Theriot Ch.: Mar. Bk., v.1, #5)

VERRET, Milton m. 12 Oct. 1899 Sarah MATHEWS (Houma Ct. Hse.: Mar. v.31 & 32, #147)

VERRET, Monroe m. 12 Dec. 1899 Edna HUMPHREYS (Houma Ct. Hse.: Mar. v.31 & 32, #182)

VERRET, Newell Willie (Willie & Evelinee NAQUIN) b. 11 July 1896 (Theriot Ch.: v.1-B, p.98)
VERRET, Olympe Venessa (Alfred & Leontine HARENG) b. 8 Jan. 1896 (Thib. Ch.: v.7, p.396)
VERRET, Pierre Noe d. 21 March 1899 at age 11 mths. (Raceland Ch.: v.1, p.24)
VERRET, Pierre Noe (Octave & Sara FALGOU) b. 27 April 1898 (Raceland Ch.: v.5, p.70)
VERRET, Rosella m. 25 Oct. 1899 William MANN (Houma Ct. Hse.: Mar. v.31 & 32, #154)
VERRET, Sidney m. 28 March 1896 Elizabeth JEFFERSON (Houma Ct. Hse.: Mar. v.29 & 30, #25)
VERRET, Valgrand Augustin d. 22 May 1899 at age 77 yrs. (Chacahoula Ch.: Gibson Ch.: v.2, p.182)
VERRET, Willie m. 21 Oct. 1899 L. Amelia HARDY (Houma Ct. Hse.: Mar. v.31 & 32, #152)
VERTE, Lucie Marie (Joannie & Olivia LEBOEUF) b. 29 Aug. 1898 (Chacahoula Ch.: v.4, p.12)
VEYRE, Anthony d. 2 Jan. 1896 at age 60 yrs. (Chacahoula Ch.: v.2, p.23)
VEYRE, Antoni d. 1 Jan. 1896; m. Eugenie BOUDREAUX, d. 1888 her parents: Charles M., d.1885 & Marcelite OZELET. Children listed: Joanie; Marcel; Willie. Petition for appointment of tutor: 8 Dec. 1896. (Houma Ct. Hse.: Succ. #892)
VEYRE, Joani (Anthony & Eugenie BOUDREAUX) m. 3 Nov. 1896 Olivia LEBOEUF (Houma Ct. Hse.: Mar. v.29 & 30, #171)
VEYRE, Joanie (Anthony & Eugenie BOUDREAUX) m. 3 Nov. 1896 Olivia LEBOEUF (Chacahoula Ch.: v.1, p.59)
VEYRE, Marcel (Anthony & Eugenie BOUDREAUX) m. 11 June 1898 Clara HEBERT (Houma Ct. Hse.: Mar. v.30 & 31, #16)
VEYRE, Maurice Joseph (Marcel & Clara HEBERT) b. 26 April 1899 (Chacahoula Ch.: v.4, p.21)
VEYRE, Willie d. 9 Sept. 1897 at age 13 yrs. (Chacahoula Ch.: v.2, p.24)
VICE, Joseph Loid (Essy & Alice GUIDRY) b. 4 Oct. 1898 (Theriot Ch.: v.2, p.29)
VICE, Josephine (Emile & Emelie PARR) m. 20 Jan. 1896 Joseph PORCHE (Theriot Ch.: v.1, p.7)
VICE, Josephine E. (Emile & Emelie PARR) m. 1 Aug. 1896 Joseph E. PORCHE (Houma Ct. Hse.: Mar. v.29 & 30, #125)

VICKNAIR (Sometimes: VICKNAIRE, VICKNER)

VICKNAIR, Edouard (Rodolphe & Cecile PREJEAN) b. 17 March 1896 (Chackbay Ch.: v.1, p.65)
VICKNAIR, Edwine (Horace & Angele ONCALE) b. 20 Jan. 1898 (Chackbay Ch.: v.1, p.103)
VICKNAIR, Etienne Mrs. d. 30 Set. 1899 at age 62 yrs., 2 mths., 22 days (Thib. Ch.: v.3, p.240)
VICKNAIR, Georges Albert (Maxi & Virginie JEWELL) b. 5 Dec. 1899 (Chackbay Ch.: v.1, p.146)

VICKNAIR, Joseph Calixte (Maxi & Virginie JOUELLE) b. 3 Nov. 1897 (Chackbay Ch.: v.1, p.98)
VICKNAIR, Marxy d. 17 Jan. 1897 at birth (Thib. Ch.: v.3, p.195)
VICKNAIR, Sidney (Leon & Delphine BERTHELOTE) m. 10 Jan. 1898 Azema LANDRY (Thib. Ct. Hse.: Mar. v.37, #266)
VICKNAIR, Texon (Adolphe & Josephine NAQUIN) m. 31 Jan. 1898 Adelina GROS (Thib. Ct. Hse.: Mar. v.37, #20)
VICTEAU, Delmas Valerie (Odrisee & Euselie PITRE) b. 11 Dec. 1899 (Montegut Ch.: v.6, p.96)
VICTEAU, Ludovic (Fortunat & Euselia PITRE) d. 30 Sept. 1898 at age 7 yrs. (Montegut Ch.: v.2, p.20)
VICTOR, William m. 9 March 1899 Bertha HARRIS (Thib. Ct. Hse.: Mar. v.39, #117)
VIDAL, Henry Joseph (John & Louise BERGERON) b. 31 Dec. 1898; m. Victoire BRUNET on 13 Dec. 1923. (Houma Ch.: Bapt. Bk., v.5, p.242)
VIDAL, John L. (Hidalgo & Celeste LEBLANC) m. 27 Aug. 1896 Mary Louise BERGERON (Houma Ct. Hse.: Mar. v.29 & 30, #138)
VIDAL, Loid Joseph (John & Louise BERGERON) b. 31 Aug. 1897; bt. 24 April 1899 (Houma Ch.: v.5, p.242)

VIGUERIE (Sometimes: VIGEURIE, VIRGUERI)
VIGUERIE, Albert R. m. 2 July 1898 Irene BASCLE (Houma Ct. Hse.: Mar. v.30 & 31, #46)
VIGUERIE, Albert R. (Francis & Georgiana METCALF) m. 12 July 1898 Irene BASCLE (Houma Ch.: v.6-a, p.245)
VIGUERIE, Emma d. 30 Dec. 1896 at age 21 yrs. (Houma Ch.: v.3, p.10)
VIGUERIE, Emma Agnes d. 27 Dec. 1896 at age 21½ yrs. (Montegut Ch.: v.2, p.8)
VIGUERIE, Francois in Kansas d. 25 May 1896 at age 67 yrs.; buried 28 May 1896. (Montegut Ch.: v.2, p.5)
VIGUERIE, Francois m. Georgianna METCALF. Children listed: Laura; Albert R.; Emma; Arthur; Clara. Inventory: 29 May 1896. (Houma Ct. Hse.: Succ. #865)
VINCENT, ----- twin girls (Sidney & Esmeralda Laura SUMAN) d. 10 May 1899 at age 3 wks. (Raceland Ch.: v.1, p.25)
VINCENT, Barry m. 7 Oct. 1899 Olivia TAYLOR (Thib. Ct. Hse.: Mar. v.39, #241)

VINENT (Sometimes: VINET, VINETTE)
VINENT, Pamela (Damien & Marie BARILLOS) m. 11 Jan. 1897 Vancenzo CABARIERE (Thib. Ch.: v.14, p.106)
VINET, Lucile (Damain & Marie BARILLO) m. 25 April 1898 Jimie NICOLOSI (Thib. Ct. Hse.: Mar. v.38, #156)
VINET, Lucile (Damain & Marie BARILLO) m. 25 April 1898 Junie NICOLOSI (Thib. Ch.: v.14, p.195)
VINET, Pamela (Damien & Marie BARILLOS) m. 11 Jan. 1897 Vincenzo CARBARIERE (Thib. Ct. Hse.: Mar. v.36, #18)

VIOLA, Giolormo (Cosmo & Miccela FACULA) b. 29 Nov. 1899 (Thib. Ch.: v.8, p.20)
VISSIER, Marie Marcelite (Eugene & Malvina GRIFFEN) b. 4 March 1896 (Larose Ch.: v.2, p.189)
VISSO, Lebbore d. 20 Nov. 1897 at age 55 yrs. (Thib. Ch.: v.3, p.207)
VITEAU, Justilia Olga (Jean Baptiste & Josephine SMITH) b. 3 Oct. 1899 (Montegut Ch.: v.7, p.97)
VITTO, Andre Frank (Jean Baptiste & Josephine SMITH) b. 3 March 1898 (Montegut Ch.: v.6, p.72)
VIVONA, Caterina m. 13 May 1899 Carme Varaco FUSANDO (Houma Ct. Hse.: Mar. v.31 & 32, #4)
VIZIER, Filogene m. 5 Aug. 1899 Maria DOUGHINE (Thib. Ct. Hse.: Mar. v.39, #203)
VIZIER, Julien (Julien & Useide LABAUVE) b. 13 Jan. 1899 (Larose Ch.: v.3, p.42)
VIZIER, Paul Felicien (Beauregard & ---- LEBAUVE) b. 9 June 1896 (Larose Ch.: v.2, p.194)
VIZIER, Samuel Ulger (Eugene & Malvina GRIFFIN) b. 22 June 1898 (Larose Ch.: v.3, p.33)
VIZIER, Silas d. 10 May 1898 (Larose Ch.: v.1, p.42)

VOISIN (Sometimes: VOINN, VOISSIN)
VOISIN, Helene (Joseph & Angelique BENOIT) b. 7 May 1899 (Theriot Ch.: v.2, p.42)
VOISIN, Joseph Leonard (Leonard & Aimee BOURG) b. 22 Nov. 1899 (Montegut Ch.: v.7, p.5)
VOISIN, Lawrence (Leonard & Celine SCOTT) m. 20 April 1899 Eve CARRERE (Houma Ct. Hse.: Mar. v.31 & 32, #407)
VOISIN, Leonard Jr. (Leonard, Sr. & Celine SCOTT) m. 1 Aug. 1898 Aimee BOURG (Houma Ct. Hse.: Mar. v.30 & 31, #72)
VOISIN, Paul (Joseph & Angelique BENOIT) b. 25 Nov. 1896 (Theriot Ch.: v.1-B, p.104)
VOISIN, Urbain (Leonce & Odile BENOIT) b. 25 May 1899 (Theriot Ch.: v.2, p.42)
VON NEINDORF, Boto d. 12 Jan. 1899; m. Gertrude BERGER, d. Aug. 1898. Children listed: Boto, 7; Felix, 5; Gertrude, 3. Tutorship: 11 March 1899. (Houma Ct. Hse.: Succ. #918)

"W"

WAGNER, Catherine Mrs. d. 19 Sept. 1896 at age 49 yrs., 9 mths. & 18 days (Houma Ch.: v.3, p.9)

WAGNER, Vina m. 7 July 1896 Charles McKINNEY (Houma Ct. Hse.: Mar. v.29 & 30, #106)

WAGUESPACK (Sometimes: VAVESPACH, WAGENSPACK, WAGESPACK, WAGGUESPACK, WAKESPACK)

WAGUESPACK, Amelie (Robert & Ernestine FORET) b. 25 April 1899 (Raceland Ch.: v.5, p.97)

WAGUESPACK, Amelina m. 20 Jan. 1899 Joseph ASHLEY (Thib. Ct. Hse.: Mar. v.38, #47)

WAGUESPACK, Angela d. 24 April 1899 at age 12 yrs. (Raceland Ch.: v.1, p.24)

WAGUESPACK, Anna Marie (Robert & Ernestine FORET) b. 7 March 1897 (Raceland Ch.: v.5, p.46)

WAGUESPACK, Antoine Augustin Elmire (Leonard & Augusta HEBERT) b. 7 Nov. 1898 (Thib. Ch.: v.7, p.521)

WAGUESPACK, Arthur d. 20 Nov. 1895; m. Mathilde FOUCHEUX Children listed: Felicie, 22 yrs. m. Sidney WAGGENSPACK; Addrienne, 20; Adele, 18; Lydia, 16; Eveline, 15; Martha, 11; Irene, 9; Rosney, 6; Rosine, 6; Yvonne, 4; John, 2. Inventory: 18 Aug. 1896. (Houma Ct. Hse.: Succ. #873)

WAGUESPACK, Clement Francois Xavier (Obiage & Nezilda WAGESPACK) b. 2 Jan. 1898 (Thib. Ch.: v.7, p.528)

WAGUESPACK, Duval (Valsin & Amelie SIMON) m. 6 Feb. 1896 Alice BOURGEOIS (Thib. Ch.: v.14, p.74)

WAGUESPACK, Duval (Valsin & Amelie SIMON) m. 6 Feb. 1896 Alice BOURGEOIS (Thib. Ct. Hse.: Mar. v.35, #33)

WAGUESPACK, Emelina (Raphael & Louise FALGOU) m. 25 Jan. 1899 Joseph ASHLEY (Raceland Ch.: v.2, p.86)

WAGUESPACK, Euphemie d. 6 April 1898 at age 13 yrs. (Raceland Ch.: v.1, p.18)

WAGUESPACK, Eve Agathe (Marcelin & Elda WAGESPACK) b. 3 Dec. 1898 (Thib. Ch.: v.7, p.522)

WAGUESPACK, Georges Denis (Raphael & Louise FALGOU) b. 9 Oct. 1897 (Raceland Ch.: v.5, p.57)

WAGUESPACK, Hilaire Rene (Lucien & Alice BOURGEOIS) b. 14 Jan. 1899 (Raceland Ch.: v.5, p.89)

WAGUESPACK, Horistine Henry Stanile (Stanile & Olimpe KNOBLOCK) b. 14 July 1899 (Raceland Ch.: v.5, p.99)

WAGUESPACK, Hubert d. 7 April 1896 at age 70 yrs. (Thib. Ch.: v.3, p.181)

WAGUESPACK, Jean Baptiste (Joseph & Marie WAGUESPACK) b. 19 Sept. 1899 (Thib. Ch.: v.7, p.565)

WAGUESPACK, Jean Francois Cyril (Sydney & Felicie WAGGENSPACK) b. 7 May 1898 (Houma Ch.: v.5, p.210)

WAGUESPACK, Jean Paul (Duval & Alice BOURGEOIS) b. 12 Nov. 1896 (Thib. Ch.: v.7, p.426)

WAGUESPACK, Jeanne Charlotte (Lucien & Alice BOURGEOIS) b. 23 Sept. 1896 (Raceland Ch.: v.5, p.31)
WAGUESPACK, John Sidney (Stanile & Olympe KNOBLOCK) b. 6 June 1898 (Raceland Ch.: v.5, p.72)
WAGUESPACK, Joseph Antoine (Sidney & Felicie WAGGENSPACK) b. 13 Aug. 1896 (Houma Ch.: v.5, p.157)
WAGUESPACK, Leonce Nicolas (Marcelin & Elda WAGUESPACK) b. 10 Dec. 1896 (Thib. Ch.: v.7, p.429)
WAGUESPACK, Leontine m. 8 Jan. 1897 Faustin CHAMPAGNE (Thib. Ct. Hse.: Mar. v.36, #14)
WAGUESPACK, Leontine (Francois & Mathilde FOLSE) m. 13 Jan. 1897 Faustin CHAMPAGNE (Raceland Ch.: v.2, p.26)
WAGUESPACK, Louisa Marie (Leonard & Eugenie MATHERNE) b. 20 June 1898 (Thib. Ch.: v.7, p.552)
WAGUESPACK, Maria Irma (Marcelin & Elda WAGUESPACK) b. 4 March 1899 (Thib. Ch.: v.7, p.593)
WAGUESPACK, Marie Adele (Duval & Alice BOURGEOIS) b. 28 March 1898 (Thib. Ch.: v.7, p.493)
WAGUESPACK, Notesia m. 25 April 1899 Joseph FOLSE (Thib. Ct. Hse.: Mar. v.39, #152)
WAGUESPACK, Notesia (Prudent & Odilia WAGESPACK) m. 22 April 1899 Joseph FOLSE (Raceland Ch.: v.2, p.95)
WAGUESPACK, Philomene Elicia (Rozemon & Celece GROS) b. 28 Feb. 1897 (Thib. Ch.: v.7, p.442)
WAGUESPACK, Roseline d. 12 May 1897 at age 72 yrs. (Raceland Ch.: v.1, p.13)
WAGUESPACK, Rosemond (Francois & Leonore WAGESPACK) m. 30 April 1896 Celeste GROS (Thib. Ch.: v.14, p.87)
WAGUESPACK, Rosemond (Francois & Leonore WAGESPACK) m. 30 April 1896 Celeste GROS (Thib. Ct. Hse.: Mar. v.35, #75)
WAGUESPACK, Stanisle (Amedee & Amelie FOLSE) m. 9 Aug. 1897 Olympe KNOBLOCK (Raceland Ch.: v.2, p.48)
WAGUESPACK, Sydney d. 23 March 1896 at age 11 yrs. (Raceland Ch.: v.1, p.8)
WAGUESPACK, Zulema d. 21 Dec. 1896 at age 37 yrs. (Raceland Ch.: v.1, p.11)
WALFERS, Bula Agnes (L. L. & Victoria TENDAL) b. 6 Dec. 1897 (Raceland Ch.: v.5, p.67)

WALKER (Sometimes: WAKER)

WALKER, Agne Jessey (James & Azema WALKER) b. 19 Sept. 1898 (Raceland Ch.: v.5, p.82)
WALKER, Alexander m. 13 April 1898 Anna JONES (Houma Ct. Hse.: Mar. v.30 & 31, #399)
WALKER, Anais (Honore & Marguerite FOLSE) m. 7 Jan. 1897 Raphael SANCHEZ (Raceland Ch.: v.2, p.25)
WALKER, Annette Philomene (Johnny & Celestine BABIN) b. 28 March 1898 (Montegut Ch.: v.6, p.69)
WALKER, Bertrand Wilson (Joseph & Marie COURTEAUX) b. 20 Sept. 1896 (Thib. Ch.: v.7, p.467)

WALKER, Edith (Edmond & Victoria DUFRESNE) b. 31 Oct. 1899 (Raceland Ch.: v.5, p.106)
WALKER, Elie Walter (Johnny & Celestine BABIN) b. 12 Aug. 1899 (Montegut Ch.: v.6, p.91)
WALKER, George m. 22 Feb. 1899 Emma JACKSON (Thib. Ct. Hse.: Mar. v.39, #111)
WALKER, Heloise m. Augustin BOUDREAUX d. 26 April 1899 at age 34 yrs. (Chacaoula Ch.: v.2, p.29)
WALKER, Henri Moise (Eugene & Domitille PERTUIT) b. 6 Jan. 1898 (Raceland Ch.: v.5, p.68)
WALKER, Iba m. 20 April 1896 Alfrida DANTIN (Thib. Ct. Hse.: Mar. v.35, #71)
WALKER, Iba (Honore & Bertile GUEDRY) m. 20 April 1896 Alfrida DANTIN (Raceland Ch.: v.2, p.14)
WALKER, James m. 11 April 1896 Corinne LEBLANC (Houma Ct. Hse.: Mar. v.29 & 30, #35)
WALKER, Jean William (Johnny & Celestine BABIN) d. 29 July 1896 (Montegut Ch.: v.2, p.6)
WALKER, Josephine m. 27 Sept. 1897 William DANTIN (Thib. Ct. Hse.: Mar. v.37, #234)
WALKER, Josephine (Honore & Marguerite FOLSE) m. 27 Sept. 1897 William DANTIN (Raceland Ch.: v.2, p.50)
WALKER, Josephine Annie (Iba & Alfrida DANTIN) b. 12 July 1899 (Chackbay Ch.: v.1, p.137)
WALKER, Justine (John & Celestine BABIN) m. 7 April 1899 Leonie RHODES (Houma Ct. Hse.: Mar. v.31 & 32, #385)
WALKER, Justine (John & Celestine BABIN) m. 29 April 1899 Leonie RHODES (Montegut Ch.: v.4, p.263)
WALKER, Kellogg m. 23 Feb. 1899 Rachael REAGENS (Thib. Ct. Hse.: Mar. v.39, #112)
WALKER, Malley m. 3 Feb. 1898 Salomon JACKSON (Thib. Ct. Hse.: Mar. v.37, #78)
WALKER, Marceline d. 28 March 1896 at age 55 yrs. (Raceland Ch.: v.1, p.8)
WALKER, Margaret widow of William REED m. 10 Aug. 1897 William JONES (Thib. Ct. Hse.: Mar. v.37, #210)
WALKER, Marie Alfrida (Iba & Alfrida DANTIN) b. 25 Feb. 1897 (Raceland Ch.: v.5, p.42)
WALKER, Marie Anaise (Honore & Marguerite FOLSE) m. 29 Dec. 1896 Raphael SANCHEZ (Thib. Ct. Hse.: Mar. v.36, #174)
WALKER, Mary m. 22 Aug. 1898 Henry GATERS (Thib. Ct. Hse.: Mar. v.38, #260)
WALKER, Odelia m. 25 March 1899 Prudent AYO (Houma Ct. Hse.: Mar. v.31 & 32, #373)
WALKER, Odilia (Jules & Mary FAULSE) m. 10 April 1899 Prudent AYO (Chacahoula Ch.: v.1, p.68 [88])
WALKER, Paul Alcee (Joseph & Justilia GRABERT) b. 7 Dec. 1897 (Raceland Ch.: v.7, p.60)
WALKER, Robert m. 19 Jan. 1899 Shady MOODY, listed on bond as MILLER (Houma Ct. Hse.: Mar. v.30 & 31, #267)

WALKER, Viola Anne (Johnny & Eda BLANCHARD) b. 22 April 1899 (Montegut Ch.: v.6, p.86)
WALKER, William J. (Theophile & Emela DUPRE) m. 25 March 1899 Jennie M. BELANGER (Houma Ct. Hse.: Mar. v.31 & 32, #375)
WALKER, William J. (Theophile & Emela DUPRE) m. 4 April 1899 Jennie M. BELANGER (Montegut Ch.: v.4, p.260)
WALL, Henry d. 21 Jan. 1899 at age 35 yrs. (Thib. Ch.: v.3, p.225)
WALLACE, Angele Juanita (Hugh U. & Sylvia Eugenie BRILLANT) b. 28 Dec. 1897 (Houma Ch.: v.5, p.194)
WALLACE, Mathew m. 27 May 1899 Rebecca HILLS (Thib. Ct. Hse.: Mar. v.39, #170)
WALLACE, William Jr. m. 14 April 1898 Priscilla HILL (Thib. Ct. Hse.: Mar. v.38, #157)
WALLER, Martha m. 15 June 1898 Louis CAILLOUET (Thib. Ct. Hse.: Mar. v.38, #209)
WALLER, Thomas m. 8 Oct. 1896 Cecilia THIBODAUX (Thib. Ct. Hse.: Mar. v.36, #152)
WALLER, Willie m. 21 Dec. 1899 Martha THIBODAUX (Thib. Ct. Hse.: Mar. v.39, #294)

WALLIS (Sometimes: WALLES)

WALLIS, Delia m. 26 April 1899 Richard LEE (Houma Ct. Hse.: Mar. v.31 & 32, #424)
WALLIS, Helen Gertrude m. 19 Nov. 1896 Theophile F. BAZET (Houma Ct. Hse.: Mar. v.29 & 30, #188)
WALLIS, Helen Gertrude (Hugh Maxwell & Mollie Highland PRICE) m. 26 Nov. 1896 Theophile F. BAZET (Houma Ch.: v.6-a, p.185)
WALLIS, John Dieux (John A. & Fannie SANDERS) b. 2 March 1896 (Houma Ch.: Epis. Ch.: v.1, p.112)
WALLIS, Justilia (Adam & Marie JOSEPH) b. 23 Feb. 1896 (Thib. Ch.: v.7, p.454)
WALLIS, Robert Maxwell (John A. & Fannie E. SANDERS) b. 17 Sept. 1898 (Houma Ch.: Epis. Ch.: v.1, p.120)
WALSES, Louis Norman (Gramble M. & Emely ALICE) b. 17 Jan. 1898 (Houma Ch.: v.5, p.209)

WALSH (See Also: WELSH)

WALSH (Sometimes: WALCH)

WALSH, Annie (Michel & Helene ALLAN) m. 8 Sept. 1898 Justin TOUPS (Thib. Ct. Hse.: Mar. v.38, #268)
WALSH, Annie (Michel & Helene ALLAN) m. 8 Sept. 1898 Justin TOUPS (Thib. Ch.: v.14, p.221)
WALSH, Claude Cyrus (Wallis & Julie VERRETT) b. 9 Feb. 1898 (Montegut Ch.: v.6, p.70)
WALSH, Gabriel Anthony (Richard & Marie FITCH) b. 1 Feb. 1898 (Montegut Ch.: v.6, p.70)

WALSH, Mary Carrie (Georges & Mary VERRETT) b. 30 Dec. 1896 (Montegut Ch.: v.6, p.55)
WALTER, Wasly Thomas (Thomas & Louise THOMAS) b. 29 Nov. 1898 (Thib. Ch.: v.7, p.541)
WALTHER, Curtis Clifford b. 27 July 1899 (Gibson Ch.: Epis. Ch.: v.1, p.106)
WALTHER, Curtis Clifford (Henry & Emma PRETT) b. 27 July 1899 (Thib. Ch.: Epis. Ch.: v.1, p.44)
WALTHER, Edith Lilian (Philipp & Jessie THIBODEAUX) b. 28 Aug. 1897 (Chacahoula Ch.: Gibson Ch.: Mar. Bk., v.1, #82)
WALTHER, Edith Lillian (Philip & Jessie THIBODEAUX) b. 28 Aug. 1897 (Chacahoula Ch.: Gibson Ch.: v.2, p.114)
WALTHER, John Earl d. 12 Nov. 1899 at age 8 yrs. (Gibson Ch.: Epis. Ch.: v.1, p.114)
WALTHER, John Earl d. 12 Nov. 1899 at age 8 yrs. (Houma Ch.: Epis. Ch.: v.1, p.388)
WALTHER, Laura Tucker b. 8 June 1896 (Gibson Ch.: Epis. Ch.: v.1, p.104)
WALTHER, Louise Gwendolin b. 19 Oct. 1897 (Gibson Ch.: Epis. Ch.: v.1, p.106)
WALTHER, Mande Agnes b. 3 Dec. 1897 (Gibson Ch.: Epis. Ch.: v.1, p.106)
WALTHER, Mary King b. 5 Dec. 1899 (Gibson Ch.: Epis. Ch.: v.1, p.106)
WALTHER, Maud Agnes (John & Laura THIBODAUX) b. 3 Dec. 1897 (Thib. Ch.: v.7, p.512)
WALTHER, Stanley Prosser b. 17 Aug. 1897 (Gibson Ch.: Epis. Ch.: v.1, p.106)
WALTHER, Stanley Prosser (Henry & Emma PRATT) b. 17 Aug. 1897 (Houma Ch.: Epis. Ch.: v.1, p.118)
WALTHER, Stanley Prosser (Henry & Emma PRATT) b. 17 Aug. 1897 (Gibson Ch.: Epis. Ch.: v.1, p.64)
WALTON, Susie m. 26 Dec. 1898 Joseph W. REED (Houma Ct. Hse.: Mar. v.30 & 31, #161)
WARD, Lilly m. 7 Oct. 1897 Henry L. SMITH (Houma Ct. Hse.: Mar. v.29 & 30, #106-C)
WARD, Mary m.24 Feb. 1897 Felix GOODE (Thib. Ct. Hse.: Mar. v.36, #90)
WARDNER, Victoria m. 9 March 1899 Joseph PORCHE (Houma Ct. Hse.: Mar. v.31 & 32, #362)
WARNER, Sarah m. 19 Jan. 1899 Joseph CRAWFORD (Thib. Ct. Hse.: Mar. v.38, #41)
WARREN, Emily m. 12 May 1897 William JACKSON (Houma Ct. Hse.: Mar. v.29 & 30, #418)

WASHINGTON (Sometimes: WASHANGTON, WASHINGTER)

WASHINGTON, George m. 9 July 1896 Melia STEVENSON (Houma Ct. Hse.: Mar. v.29 & 30, #111)
WASHINGTON, George m. 9 March 1896 Nellie POLLARD (Houma Ct. Hse.: Mar. v.29 & 30, #5)

WASHINGTON, George J. Jr. m. 2 Feb. 1899 Bertha JOHNSON (Thib. Ct. Hse.: Mar. v.38, #86)
WASHINGTON, Henry m. 30 Dec. 1899 Kitty SIMMS (Houma Ct. Hse.: Mar. v.31 & 32, #218)
WASHINGTON, Ida m. 9 Jan. 1899 Joseph E. WRIGHT (Thib. Ct. Hse.: Mar. v.38, #11)
WASHINGTON, Jack m. 14 Dec. 1899 Ella DARCEY (Thib. Ct. Hse.: Mar. v.39, #283)
WASHINGTON, John m. 6 May 1897 Henry MOORE (Houma Ct. Hse.: Mar. v.29 & 30, #406)
WASHINGTON, Joseph m. 24 Feb. 1898 Zulma TRICHE (Thib. Ct. Hse.: Mar. v.37, #113)
WASHINGTON, Lizzie m. 10 Feb. 1898 Philip JEFFERSON (Houma Ct. Hse.: Mar. v.30 & 31, #288)
WASHINGTON, Rebecca m. 7 Feb. 1898 Robert COLBERT (Thib. Ct. Hse.: Mar. v.37, #92)
WASHINGTON, Sarah m. 28 May 1897 Paul JACKSON (Houma Ct. Hse.: Mar. v.29 & 30, #431)

WATKINS (Sometimes: WATKIN, WATKING)
WATKINS, Anne H. (Luc & Lely KING) b. 16 Nov. 1896 (Houma Ch.: v.5, p.166)
WATKINS, Dewye Luke (G. Luke & Lelie KING) b. 19 May 1898 (Houma Ch.: v.5, p.212)
WATKINS, Edward m. 31 March 1898 Rena PAYNE (Houma Ct. Hse.: Mar. v.30 & 31, #363)
WATKINS, Evalina d. 2 Sept. 1897; m. Peter WELSH Appointment of adm.: 7 Sept. 1897. (Houma Ct. Hse.: Succ. #884)
WATKINS, George Washington (Edwin F. & Justine THIBODAUX) m. 20 April 1898 Catherine COOK (Houma Ct. Hse.: Mar. v.30 & 31, #408)
WATKINS, Georges Washington (Ed) d. 14 Sept. 1899 at age 28 yrs. (Theriot Ch.: v.1, p.2)
WATKINS, John d. 19 Dec. 1899 at age 7 wks. (Houma Ch.: v.3, p.27)
WATKINS, Joseph Louis (Joseph Washington & Sophie BONVILLAIN) b. 26 Nov. 1899 (Theriot Ch.: v.2, p.55)
WATKINS, Joseph W. m. 11 Feb. 1899 Sophie BONVILLAIN (Houma Ct. Hse.: Mar. v.31 & 32, #333)
WATKINS, Joseph W. (Lafayette & Rosalie MARTIN) m. 11 Feb. 1899 Sophie BONVILLAIN (Houma Ch.: v.6-a, p.278)
WATKINS, Josephine (d.Lafayette & d.Phioselie MARTIN) m. 18 March 1897 Joseph Oscar BOUDREAUX (Montegut Ch.: v.4, p.220)
WATKINS, Josephine (Lafayette & Frazilie MARTIN) m. 11 March 1897 Joseph Oscar BOUDREAUX (Houma Ct. Hse.: Mar. v.29 & 30, #344)
WATKINS, Louise Clara (Elemick & Elisa DASPIT) b. 23 Sept. 1897 (Theriot Ch.: v.2, p.15)
WATKINS, Maria m. 10 May 1898 Frederick BROOMFIELD (Houma Ct. Hse.: Mar. v.30 & 31, #436)

WATKINS, Mary (H. & P. DUPLANTIS) b. 16 Oct. 1899 (Houma Ch.: v.5, p.264)
WATKINS, Seles d. 27 Aug. 1899 at age 11 days (Houma Ch.: v.3, p.25)
WATKINS, Toussaint Isaac (Lowles & Elidia MARTEL) b. 1 Nov. 1897 (Theriot Ch.: v.2, p.15)
WATSON, Ann Insanity of: 25 Jan. 1899. (Thib. Ct. Hse.: Succ. #1560)
WATSON, Charles m. 21 Jan. 1897 Polly ALEXANDRE (Thib. Ct. Hse.: Mar. v.36, #47)
WATSON, Victoire m. 16 Feb. 1898 Jonas SMITH (Thib. Ct. Hse.: Mar. v.37, #106)
WEBB, Noah m. 2 Jan. 1899 Lelia JOHNSON (Houma Ct. Hse.: Mar. v.30 & 31, #172)

WEBRE (Sometimes: WEBB, WEBBRE, WEBER)
WEBRE, ----- boy d. 31 March 1898 at age 11 mths. (Thib. Ch.: v.3, p.212)
WEBRE, Eugenie m. Hermogene BERNARD d. 25 Oct. 1896 at age 76 yrs. (Thib. Ch.: v.3, p.189)
WEBRE, Wade d. 9 Aug. 1896 at age 28 yrs. (Thib. Ch.: v.3, p.185)
WEBRE, Whitney (Edmond & Federine ROGER) m. 27 Sept. 1899 Veronique LEVERT (Thib. Ch.: v.14, p.301)
WEBRE, Whitney (Edmond & Federine ROGER) m. 27 Sept. 1899 Veronique LEVERT (Thib. Ct. Hse.: Mar. v.39, #236)
WEBRE, Whitney Benedic (Whitney & Veronique LEVERT) b. 29 July 1899 (Thib. Ch.: v.8, p.2)
WEBRE, William W. m. 13 April 1899 Annette L. BOURG (Thib. Ct. Hse.: Mar. v.39, #143)
WEBRE, Willie (Joseph & Elda FLASH) m. 25 April 1899 Annette BOURG (Thib. Ch.: v.14, p.275)
WEIMER, Alice (Joseph & Mary WEIGLE) b. 12 Feb. 1897 in Chackbay (Thib. Ch.: Epis. Ch.: v.1, p.44)

WEISSENTHANNER (Sometimes: WEISSENTHAMER)

WELCOME, Albertha (John & Ignassia VERRET) b. 5 March 1899; bt. 17 Jan. 1903 (Houma Ch.: v.6, p.52)
WELLY, Bergeron d. 3 March 1899 at age 25 yrs. (Theriot Ch.: v.1, p.2)

WELSH (Sometimes: WALSH, WELCHE)
WELSH, Eliza m. 6 March 1899 General KING (Houma Ct. Hse.: Mar. v.31 & 32, #354)
WELSH, Lavinia m. 20 Dec. 1899 Wesly WILLIAMS (Houma Ct. Hse.: Mar. v.31 & 32, #188-B)
WELSH, Pat m. 6 July 1896 Rosa TOLIVER (Thib. Ct. Hse.: Mar. v.36, #117)
WELSH, Peter Mrs. d. 3 Sept. 1897 at age 85 yrs. (Houma Ch.: v.3, p.13)

WENGLOW, August d. 22 Sept. 1898 at age 78 yrs. (Houma Ch.: Epis. Ch.: v.1, p.388)

WEST, Alma Mary bt. 12 April 1898 as an adult (Thib. Ch.: Epis. Ch.: v.1, p.44)

WEST, Jesse m. 15 March 1899 Maria BENNETT (Houma Ct. Hse.: Mar. v.31 & 32, #367)

WEST, Marie Henriette (William & Mina LECHE) b. 14 March 1899 (Thib. Ch.: v.7, p.542)

WEST, William of East Baton Rouge (William & Rosalie MUSEAR) m. 9 July 1896 Mina LECHE (Thib. Ct. Hse.: Mar. v.36, #121)

WEST, William (William & Rosalie MASCAR) m. 9 July 1896 Mina LECHE (Thib. Ch.: v.14, p.96)

WESTLEY, William m. 29 Sept. 1898 Louisa KANE (Houma Ct. Hse.: Mar. v.30 & 31, #113)

WHATLEY, Lillie m. 4 Feb. 1899 Sig. GUGGENHEIMER (Thib. Ct. Hse.: Mar. v.38, #92)

WHEELER, Elizabeth m. 22 Jan. 1898 Luther BROWN (Thib. Ct. Hse.: Mar. v.37, #43)

WHEELER, Henry m. 17 March 1898 Adeline DUNCAN or DUNKINS (Thib. Ct. Hse.: Mar. v.37, #129)

WHIPPLE, Anne Wilhelmina (Walther & Ceraline FALGOUT) b. 22 March 1896 (Montegut Ch.: v.6, p.36)

WHIPPLE, George S. (Charles & Mary MARS) m. 22 Oct. 1897 Alice J. CHAUVIN (Houma Ct. Hse.: Mar. v.29 & 30, #125)

WHIPPLE, George S. (Charles & Mary MARS) m. 25 Oct. 1897 Alice J. CHAUVIN (Montegut Ch.: v.4, p.227)

WHIPPLE, Marie Therese (Georges & Alice CHAUVIN) b. 31 Oct. 1899 (Montegut Ch.: v.6, p.94)

WHIPPLE, Mary Ione Trilby (Georges & Alice CHAUVIN) b. 18 Nov. 1898 (Montegut Ch.: v.6, p.79)

WHITAKER, Sarah m. 10 June 1897 Northern POINDEXTER (Houma Ct. Hse.: Mar. v.29 & 30, #27)

WHITE, Catherine m. 5 June 1897 Henry SUMLEN (Houma Ct. Hse.: Mar. v.29 & 30, #7)

WHITE, Charles m. 16 Feb. 1898 Rosa QUEEN (Thib. Ct. Hse.: Mar. v.37, #107)

WHITE, Earle Abraham (Eliska & Anna RIDEAU) b. 16 Jan. 1896; m. Helen KORNMAN on 19 Dec. 1937. (Houma Ch.: Bapt. Bk., v.5, p.144)

WHITE, Frankie m. 11 Oct. 1897 William Henry BROWN (Houma Ct. Hse.: Mar. v.29 & 30, #121)

WHITE, Franklin m. 10 Aug. 1897 Lovinia CLARK (Thib. Ct. Hse.: Mar. v.37, #211)

WHITE, Georgiana m. 12 June 1899 Enos COOPER (Houma Ct. Hse.: Mar. v.31 & 32, #38)

WHITE, Henderson m. 16 Dec. 1897 Anna JOSEPH (Thib. Ct. Hse.: Mar. v.37, #263)

WHITE, Ida m. 10 June 1897 David SMITH, Jr. (Houma Ct. Hse.: Mar. v.29 & 30, #21)

WHITE, Joachim Clinsey (Joseph & Octavie LAPEROUSE) b. 18 May 1898 (Montegut Ch.: v.6, p.71)

WHITE, Josephine m. 26 Sept. 1898 Joseph GOODMAN (Thib. Ct. Hse.: Mar. v.38, #283)
WHITE, Josephine m. 28 Dec. 1899 Wallace CHAMPION (Thib. Ct. Hse.: Mar. v.39, #304)
WHITE, Lewis m. 8 Feb. 1899 Beatrice CREECY (Houma Ct. Hse.: Mar. v.31 & 32, #325)
WHITE, Lina m. 14 Sept. 1899 James B. JACKS (Houma Ct. Hse.: Mar. v.31 & 32, #131)
WHITE, Louis Gilbert (Daniel & Laura MARCEL) b. 30 Jan. 1897 (Montegut Ch.: v.6, p.51)
WHITE, Marie Mila (Joseph & Octavie LAPEYROUSE) b. 15 Jan. 1896 (Montegut Ch.: v.6, p.33)
WHITE, Rosella m. 21 Jan. 1897 Charles COOK (Houma Ct. Hse.: Mar. v.29 & 30, #246)
WHITE, William m. 12 Jan. 1897 Emma PORCHE (Houma Ct. Hse.: Mar. v.29 & 30, #235)
WHITE, William m. 4 Feb. 1897 Lucy WILSON (Houma Ct. Hse.: Mar. v.29 & 30, #292)
WHITEHEAD, Isadora Phoebe d. 6 July 1896 at age 65 yrs. (Thib. Ch.: Epis. Ch.: v.1, p.394)
WHITING, Joseph m. 19 March 1896 Phoebe HILLS (Thib. Ct. Hse.: Mar. v.35, #52)
WHITMORE, Luther (George L. & Rebecca A. USHER) m. 15 Dec. 1896 Leonard B. SANDERS (Houma Ct. Hse.: Mar. v.29 & 30, #200)

WHITNEY (Sometimes: WITNEY)
WHITNEY, Bentia (Washington & Millie HEMLEY) b. 30 May 1898 (Larose Ch.: v.3, p.33)
WHITNEY, Daisy Myrtle (Wash & Victoria BERNARD) b. 22 Feb. 1896 (Houma Ch.: v.5, p.148)
WHITNEY, Ilda Horace (Washington & Victoria BERNARD) b. 27 Aug. 1898 (Houma Ch.: v.5, p.219)
WHITNEY, Julia (Vand & Elvire PONTIFE) m. 8 Jan. 1896 Gustave ARCENAUX (Thib. Ch.: v.13, p.92)
WHITNEY, Julia (Vard & Elvire PONTIFE) m. 8 Jan. 1896 Gustave ARCENEAUX (Thib. Ct. Hse.: Mar. v.35, #195)
WHITNEY, Marie Birdie (Washington & Emil JONES) b. 12 Dec. 1898 (Larose Ch.: v.3, p.31)
WHITNEY, Mary Burnita (William & Josephine WILLEN) b. 13 Jan. 1896 (Houma Ch.: v.5, p.142)
WIGLE, William Paul (George & Alice WILLIAMS) b. 3 April 1897 (Thib. Ch.: v.7, p.450)
WIGS, Thomas m. 12 Jan. 1899 Viola HENDERSON (Thib. Ct. Hse.: Mar. v.38, #20)
WILBERT, Henry m. 12 June 1899 Minty ROLLINS (Houma Ct. Hse.: Mar. v.31 & 32, #41)
WILEY, Thomas m. 26 Sept. 1898 Maggie COLLINS (Thib. Ct. Hse.: Mar. v.38, #284)
WILKINS, Anderson m. 20 Sept. 1898 Lucy COLLINS (Houma Ct. Hse.: Mar. v.30 & 31, #103)

WILKINS, Stewart A. (John C. & Aminda GUIDRY) m. 19 Dec. 1898 Roberta Lee CELESTIN (Houma Ch.: Epis. Ch.: v.1, p.342)
WILKINS, Stewart A. of Lafayette Parish (John C. & Amande GUIDRY) m. 19 Dec. 1898 Robertha Lee HANAGRIFF, widow of C. F. CELESTIN (Houma Ct. Hse.: Mar. v.30 & 31, #151)

WILKINSON (Sometimes: WILKERSON, WILKISON)

WILLIAM, Isham m. 6 Feb. 1899 Willie ROLLINS (Houma Ct. Hse.: Mar. v.31 & 32, #316)

WILLIAMS (Sometimes: WILLIAM).
WILLIAMS, A. John m. 16 Jan. 1896 Bessie BROOKS (Houma Ct. Hse.: Mar. v.28, #398)
WILLIAMS, Agnes m. 20 Jan. 1898 Mack THOMAS (Thib. Ct. Hse.: Mar. v.37, #50)
WILLIAMS, Alexina Veronique (Alfred & Delphine BOURG) b. 24 Sept. 1899 (Larose Ch.: v.3, p.79)
WILLIAMS, Anderson m. 27 Jan. 1898 Ida WILLIAMS (Houma Ct. Hse.: Mar. v.30 & 31, #257)
WILLIAMS, Angelina Felicia (Wilfred & Delphine BOURG) b. 14 Sept. 1896 (Larose Ch.: v.3, p.12)
WILLIAMS, Anna m. 8 Oct. 1896 Willis GOLDEN (Houma Ct. Hse.: Mar. v.29 & 30, #163)
WILLIAMS, Antoine Joseph (Frank & Felicieanne CANTRELLE) b. 9 July 1899 (Larose Ch.: v.3, p.43)
WILLIAMS, Baptist m. 13 July 1898 Cora ARINGTON (Thib. Ct. Hse.: Mar. v.38, #225)
WILLIAMS, Bella m. 14 April 1898 Matthews BROWN (Thib. Ct. Hse.: Mar. v.38, #155)
WILLIAMS, Ben m. 4 Jan. 1899 Elvira PARKER (Thib. Ct. Hse.: Mar. v.38, #3)
WILLIAMS, Ben m. 8 March 1897 Emily SCHUBERT (Thib. Ct. Hse.: Mar. v.36, #97)
WILLIAMS, Carrie E. m. 23 Jan. 1899 William Henry BROWN (Houma Ct. Hse.: Mar. v.30 & 31, #280)
WILLIAMS, Charles d. 8 Feb. 1897 at age 12 yrs. & 7 mths. (Houma Ch.: v.3, p.11)
WILLIAMS, Charles m. 1 July 1899 Eliza DUET (Thb. Ct. Hse.: Mar. v.39, #184)
WILLIAMS, Charlotte m. 10 March 1898 Melvin HOWARD (Thib. Ct. Hse.: Mar. v.37, #124)
WILLIAMS, Coleman Jr. m. 9 June 1897 Julia DABNEY (Houma Ct. Hse.: Mar. v.29 & 30, #17)
WILLIAMS, Cornelius m. 13 March 1897 Laura CELESTIN (Houma Ct. Hse.: Mar. v.29 & 30, #354)
WILLIAMS, Eddie m. 22 July 1899 Rebecca JACKSON (Houma Ct. Hse.: Mar. v.31 & 32, #84)

WILLIAMS, Edgar (Evariste) d. 17 Dec. 1897 at age 35 yrs. (Lockport Ch.: v.1, #34)

WILLIAMS, Effie A. m. 13 April 1899 Joseph COX (Thib. Ct. Hse.: Mar. v.39, #142)

WILLIAMS, Elise (Nolan Stewart & Mary Kearis COOKE) m. 29 Dec. 1897 William Raynauld FAVROT (Houma Ct. Hse.: Mar. v.29 & 30, #161)

WILLIAMS, Eliza m. 30 June 1898 Thomas McGEE (Houma Ct. Hse.: Mar. v.30 & 31, #40)

WILLIAMS, Evariste Horace (Francois & Marie FICHT) b. 3 June 1897 (Larose Ch.: v.3, p.10)

WILLIAMS, Frances m. 7 Jan. 1897 Oscar LOPEZ (Houma Ct. Hse.: Mar. v.29 & 30, #225)

WILLIAMS, Francis In the matter of the insanity of: 22 July 1898. (Thib. Ct. Hse.: Succ. #1544)

WILLIAMS, Genevieve Edmondson (Nolan Stewart & Margaret Kearns COOKE) m. 12 May 1898 Robert Edwin McBRIDE (Houma Ct. Hse.: Mar. v.30 & 31, #434)

WILLIAMS, Georgina m. 25 Jan. 1897 Joseph Arthur MEAD (Thib. Ct Hse.: Mar. v.36, #55)

WILLIAMS, Haywood m. 10 July 1897 Josephine RODRIGUE (Thib. Ct. Hse.: Mar. v.37, #192)

WILLIAMS, Henrietta m. 12 March 1896 Tommy HALL (Houma Ct. Hse.: Mar. v.29 & 30, #8-A)

WILLIAMS, Henry m. 17 June 1896 Martha INGHAM (Thib. Ct. Hse.: Mar. v.35, #107)

WILLIAMS, Ida m. 27 Jan. 1898 Anderson WILLIAMS (Houma Ct. Hse.: Mar. v.30 & 31, #257)

WILLIAMS, James m. 4 Feb. 1897 Clara BALLS (Houma Ct. Hse.: Mar. v.29 & 30, #289)

WILLIAMS, James Paul d. 10 Nov. 1896 at age 74 yrs. (Thib. Ch.: v.3, p.191)

WILLIAMS, Jane m. 4 Sept. 1899 Henry CASEY (Houma Ct. Hse.: Mar. v.31 & 32, #118)

WILLIAMS, John m. 19 June 1897 Lily OUTLEY (Houma Ct. Hse.: Mar. v.29 & 30, #33)

WILLIAMS, John m. 21 Dec. 1899 Sophie GREEN (Thib. Ct. Hse.: Mar. v.39, #293)

WILLIAMS, Joseph (Nelson & Dora KING) b. 3 June 1897 (Thib. Ch.: v.7, p.457)

WILLIAMS, Joseph (William & Therese MILES) b. 20 Sept. 1896 (Thib. Ch.: v.7, p.442)

WILLIAMS, Joseph Clement (Francois & Marie FICH) b. 6 Sept. 1898 (Larose Ch.: v.3, p.38)

WILLIAMS, Joseph Neri (Franck & Alice BAPTISTE) b. 29 July 1898 (Thib. Ch.: v.7, p.509)

WILLIAMS, Joshua m. 13 May 1899 Eliza DAVIS (Thib. Ct. Hse.: Mar. v.39, #165)

WILLIAMS, Julienne Angela (Walter Scott & Margueritte DOUCET) b. 10 April 1898 (Larose Ch.: v.3, p.23)

WILLIAMS, Laura m. 14 April 1897 Sam WILLIAMS (Thib. Ct. Hse.: Mar. v.36, #116)
WILLIAMS, Leonide m. 13 June 1898 Joseph RUSSELL (Houma Ct. Hse.: Mar. v.30 & 31, #17)
WILLIAMS, Lily Helene (Eward & Josephine RODRIGUE) b. 18 Oct. 1899 (Raceland Ch.: v.5, p.105)
WILLIAMS, Louis m. 21 Jan. 1899 Sarah DAVIS (Thib. Ct. Hse.: Mar. v.38, #49)
WILLIAMS, Louisa m. 8 March 1899 Monroe COLLINS (Houma Ct. Hse.: Mar. v.31 & 32, #357)
WILLIAMS, Lucie Marie (Frank & Felicienne CANTRELLE) b. 18 March 1897 (Larose Ch.: v.3, p.13)
WILLIAMS, Martha A. m. 8 March 1897 John GAGE (Thib. Ct. Hse.: Mar. v.36, #96)
WILLIAMS, Mitchell m. 20 July 1899 Mary Eliza DAVIS (Thib. Ct. Hse.: Mar. v.39, #202)
WILLIAMS, Oville m. 21 Feb. 1898 Minerva BECKTON (Houma Ct. Hse.: Mar. v.30 & 31, #315)
WILLIAMS, Rachel m. 21 Sept. 1899 Antoine STEWART (Houma Ct. Hse.: Mar. v.31 & 32, #139)
WILLIAMS, Richard m. 21 Dec. 1898 Mathilde ABRIBAT (Larose Ch.: v.3, p.11)
WILLIAMS, Richard m. 29 Oct. 1898 Mathilde ABRIBAT, widow of Theophile DUCOS (Thib. Ct. Hse.: Mar. v.38, #293)
WILLIAMS, Robert C. m. 24 Aug. 1899 Fannie MORRIS (Houma Ct. Hse.: Mar. v.31 & 32, #108)
WILLIAMS, Roland Antony (George & Alice PREGENT) b. 19 April 1899 (Houma Ch.: v.5, p.246)
WILLIAMS, Rose m. 15 April 1896 William DANKS (Houma Ct. Hse.: Mar. v.29 & 30, #40)
WILLIAMS, Sam m. 14 April 1897 Laura WILLIAMS (Thib. Ct. Hse.: Mar. v.36, #116)
WILLIAMS, Samuel m. 16 April 1898 Phillis LANDOR (Houma Ct. Hse.: Mar. v.30 & 31, #402)
WILLIAMS, Shedrick m. 6 Nov. 1897 Sylvia WILLIAMS (Houma Ct. Hse.: Mar. v.29 & 30, #130)
WILLIAMS, Sylvia m. 6 Nov. 1897 Shedrick WILLIAMS (Houma Ct. Hse.: Mar. v.29 & 30, #130)
WILLIAMS, Thomas m. 22 June 1899 Sarah ROBINSON (Thib. Ct. Hse.: Mar. v.39, #185)
WILLIAMS, Thomas J. (West & Lucy SPAULDING) m. 16 June 1898 Mary L. LEWIS (Houma Ct. Hse.: Mar. v.30 & 31, #10)
WILLIAMS, Wesley m. 7 Jan. 1896 Irma POWELL (Houma Ct. Hse.: Mar. v.28, #379)
WILLIAMS, Wesly m. 20 Dec. 1899 Lavinia WELCH (Houma Ct. Hse.: Mar. v.31 & 32, #188-B)
WILLIAMS, Wilfred Ignace (Edgard & Virginie ROUBION) b. 1 Feb. 1896 (Lockport Ch.: v.2, p.320)
WILLIAMS, William m. 31 March 1898 Abella LOCKWOOD (Houma Ct. Hse.: Mar. v.30 & 31, #360)

WILLIAMS, William m. 5 April 1897 Ella COOK (Houma Ct. Hse.: Mar. v.29 & 30, #372)
WILLIAMS, Willie m. 11 March 1897 Emma CLARK (Houma Ct. Hse.: Mar. v.29 & 30, #351)
WILLIAMS, Willie m. 27 Jan. 1898 Bertha RINGGOLD (Houma Ct. Hse.: Mar. v.30 & 31, #225)
WILLIAMS, Willie m. 5 Dec. 1899 Layar B. MEAD (Thib. Ct. Hse.: Mar. v.39, #277)
WILLINSON, Anna m. 18 Feb. 1896 John ALLEN (Thib. Ct. Hse.: Mar. v.35, #46)
WILLIS, Gracie m. 28 Sept. 1897 Jesse GREEN (Houma Ct. Hse.: Mar. v.29 & 30, #102)
WILSON, Catherine Rose (H. L. & Minnie T. WILSON) b. 11 Nov. 1898 (Houma Ch.: First Presbyt. Ch.: v.1, p.262)
WILSON, Edna m. 26 Jan. 1899 Henry HUGHS (Thib. Ct. Hse.: Mar. v.38, #68)
WILSON, Elicia m. 2 June 1898 Handy DAVIS (Thib. Ct. Hse.: Mar. v.38, #192)
WILSON, Elijah m. 20 Feb. 1896 Louisa SMITH (Thib. Ct. Hse.: Mar. v.35, #47)
WILSON, Eliza m. 12 Jan. 1899 Joseph ROSS (Houma Ct. Hse.: Mar. v.30 & 31, #218)
WILSON, Ellen of Virginia m. 26 April 1899 Sylvester JORDAN, of Wake County, North Carolina (Thib. Ct. Hse.: Mar. v.39, #147)
WILSON, Ellick m. 11 Jan. 1899 Emma JONES (Houma Ct. Hse.: Mar. v.30 & 31, #208)
WILSON, Harrison m. 14 Oct. 1898 Viola STRIPLING (Thib. Ct. Hse.: Mar. v.38, #296)
WILSON, Jeannie Doris (James D. & Julia Florestine INGRAHAM) b. 27 Sept. 1896 (Montegut Ch.: v.6, p.53)
WILSON, Lucy m. 4 Feb. 1897 William WHITE (Houma Ct. Hse.: Mar. v.29 & 30, #292)
WILSON, Roberta m. 13 March 1899 Rufus HITE (Thib. Ct. Hse.: Mar. v.39, #118)
WILSON, Sarah m. 4 Feb. 1897 Willis DURDEN (Houma Ct. Hse.: Mar. v.29 & 30, #283)
WILTON, Joseph Damen (W. & Mary BOURG) bt. 27 Oct. 1896 (Lockport Ch.: v.3, #11)
WILTON, Webre Denistan (Louis & Amanda ADAM) b. 25 Nov. 1896 (Lockport Ch.: v.3-A, #21)
WINSLOW, Mary m. 15 Sept. 1897 Wash. BROWN (Houma Ct. Hse.: Mar. v.29 & 30, #91)
WINSLOW, Thomas m. 26 Jan. 1899 Sarah DYIAR (Houma Ct. Hse.: Mar. v.30 & 31, #283)
WISEMAN, Marie Anna (Thomas & Marie Caroline TOUCHARD) b. 18 Nov. 1898 (Larose Ch.: v.3, p.35)
WISEMAN, Marie Lina (Thomas & Marie Caroline TOUCHARD) b. 2 June 1896 (Larose Ch.: v.3, p.13)

WOLF (Sometimes: WOLFF, WOULFF)

WOLF, Lizzie m. 4 April 1898 George THOMAS (Houma Ct. Hse: Mar. v.30 & 31, #372)

WOLF, Mary Lester (Thomas & Camilla BERGERON) m. 12 June 1899 Albert BABIN (Houma Ct. Hse.: Mar. v.31 & 32, #25)

WOODER, Sidney Ann m. 23 April 1898 Plado HARVARD (Houma Ct. Hse.: Mar. v.30 & 31, #419)

WOODS, Alexander m. 15 Feb. 1899 Lucinda THOMPSON (Houma Ct. Hse.: Mar. v.31 & 32, #336)

WOODS, Jos. W. m. 19 Feb. 1898 Rebecca TILLMAN (Thib. Ct. Hse.: Mar. v.37, #109)

WOODS, Norman Tompkins (Richard Covington & Fannie W. PUGH) b. 5 July 1896 on Ducros Plantation (Thib. Ch.: Epis. Ch.: v.1, p.42)

WOODS, Susannah C. d. 13 July 1896 at age 68 yrs. (Houma Ch.: Epis. Ch.: v.1, p.386)

WOODS, Velonlia (Van & Augusta JOLET) m. 17 Feb. 1896 Amedee A. ABOUT (Houma Ch.: v.6-a, p.171)

WOODS, Venolia m. 10 Feb. 1896 Amedee A. ABOUT (Houma Ct. Hse.: Mar. v.28, #441)

WOODS, Warren m. 3 June 1898 Ida MILES (Thib. Ct. Hse.: Mar. v.38, #193)

WOOLSON, William (William & Marie BUJON) b. 8 April 1898 (Houma Ch.: v.5, p.226)

WORDON, Sam m. 14 Sept. 1899 Virginia GORE, widow of Bannister BRICKLEY (Thib. Ct. Hse.: Mar. v.39, #230)

WRIGHT, Camia Margarithe (Thomas & Livie DRIULHET) b. 26 Dec. 1898 (Houma Ch.: v.5, p.232)

WRIGHT, Douglas m. 16 Feb. 1899 Alice JOHNSON (Thib. Ct. Hse.: Mar. v.39, #108)

WRIGHT, Eldred Insanity: 20 Oct. 1896. (Thib. Ct. Hse.: Succ. #1499)

WRIGHT, Isabella m. 28 April 1896 Edward NELSON (Houma Ct. Hse.: Mar. v.29 & 30, #45)

WRIGHT, Joseph E. m. 9 Jan. 1899 Ida WASHINGTON (Thib. Ct. Hse.: Mar. v.38, #11)

WRIGHT, Livi Alva (Thomas E. & Livi Ella DRUILHET) b. 23 Jan. 1896; m. George Francis LAROSE on 18 Jan. 1923. (Houma Ch.: Bapt. Bk., v.5, p.146)

WRIGHT, Louis E. m. 17 April 1897 Nancy GRAY (Thib. Ct. Hse.: Mar. v.36, #118)

WRIGHT, Nancy d. 4 March 1898 at age 22 yrs. (Lockport Ch.: v.1, #6)

WRIGHT, Odelia Eunice (William & Annie KOHN) b. 29 Aug. 1897 (Houma Ch.: Epis. Ch.: v.1, p.116)

WRIGHT, Thomas Edouard (Thomas Edward & Livie E. DRUILHET) b. 18 May 1896 (Houma Ch.: v.5, p.182)

WRIGHT, Virginie Mildred (James N. & Cecilia TRICHE) b. 5 Nov. 1899 (Thib. Ch.: v.8, p.16)

WURZLOW, Elisabeth Aimee (Calvin & Louise SYLVESTRE) b. 18 Nov. 1898 (Houma Ch.: v.5, p.222)

WURZLOW, Helene Emilie (Calvin & Louise M. SYLVESTRE) b. 13 Oct. 1896 (Houma Ch.: v.5, p.159)
WURZLOW, Mary Agnes (August & Emeline BELANGER) m. 24 Sept. 1896 Ovid F. BAZET (Houma Ch.: v.6-a, p.181)
WURZLOW, Mary Agnes (August & Emeline BELANGER) m. 24 Sept. 1896 Ovid F. BAZET (Houma Ct. Hse.: Mar. v.29 & 30, #152)

"X"

XARSABA, Elville Vincent (Leopold & Delphine SOLE) b. 11 Feb. 1898 (Larose Ch.: v.3, p.21)

XNICE, Malvina (James & Louise JONES) b. 1 May 1898 (Thib. Ch.: v.7, p.503)

"Y"

YBANGELESTA, Lucas m. 23 April 1897 Elizabeth BILLIMORE (Houma Ct. Hse.: Mar. v.29 & 30, #391)
YOST, Richard Edmond (Philip & Laura GHIRARDI) b. 12 Aug. 1899 (Houma Ch.: Epis. Ch.: v.1, p.122)
YOUNG, Bertha m. 24 Feb. 1898 Primrose MORGAN (Thib. Ct. Hse.: Mar. v.37, #115)
YOUNG, Della m. 7 Sept. 1899 Richard HOWARD (Thib. Ct. Hse.: Mar. v.39, #225)
YOUNG, Elas m. 18 March 1897 Mary MORGAN (Thib. Ct. Hse.: Mar. v.36, #99)
YOUNG, Elijah m. 10 March 1898 Geneva MORGAN (Thib. Ct. Hse.: Mar. v.37, #125)
YOUNG, Grandison m. 30 Jan. 1896 Nannie STEVENSON (Houma Ct. Hse.: Mar. v.28, #426)
YOUNG, Henry Hamilet m. 29 April 1899 Secriana COLLINS (Houma Ct. Hse.: Mar. v.31 & 32, #428)
YOUNG, James Owen (Tolson Owen & Cecilia SERVILLE) b. 10 Feb. 1898 (Chacahoula Ch.: Gibson Records: Mar. Bk., v.1, #19)
YOUNG, James Owen (Tolson Owen & Cecilia SERVILLE) b. 10 Feb. 1898 (Chacahoula Ch.: Gibson Ch.: v.2, p.118)
YOUNG, Jesse M. m. 26 Nov. 1897 Eli J. CHAUVIN (Houma Ct. Hse.: Mar. v.29 & 30, #137)
YOUNG, Jessie M. (Samuel & Malie LESSLY) m. 28 Nov. 1897 Elie CHAUVIN (Houma Ch.: v.6-a, p.220)
YOUNG, Joseph m. 1 Aug. 1898 Martha BUTLER (Thib. Ct. Hse.: Mar. v.38, #237)
YOUNG, Joseph M. m. 25 May 1899 Lithia JOHNSON (Thib. Ct Hse.: Mar. v.39, #168)
YOUNG, Louisa m. 8 Feb. 1899 Smith JOHNSON (Thib. Ct. Hse.: Mar. v.38, #95)
YOUNG, Mary Luberta (Simon & Angelina DYER) b. 29 Sept. 1897 (Thib. Ch.: v.7, p.467).
YOUNG, Sidonia m. 11 July 1897 John HOLDEN (Thib. Ct. Hse.: Mar. v.37, #191)
YOUNG, Sophie m. 4 Aug. 1898 John GETRIDGE (Thib. Ct. Hse.: Mar. v.38, #238)
YOUNG, W. H. m. 21 April 1897 Amelia RHODEN (Thib. Ct. Hse.: Mar. v.36, #123)
YOUNGS, Joseph Streck Hicks (Louis & Marie ALMA) b. 26 Nov. 1897 (Raceland Ch.: v.5, p.59)
YOUNGS, Marie Hildegarde (H. Louis & Marie Alma STRECK) b. 8 Jan. 1899 (Raceland Ch.: v.5, p.88)
YOUNGS, Mary Olga (H. L. & Aimee STRECK) b. 11 Oct. 1896 (Raceland Ch.: v.5, p.33)

"Z"

ZABBIA, Anna (Salvatore & Bernarda GINNORA) b. 20 Jan. 1898 (Houma Ch.: v.5, p.199)
ZABBIO, Maria m. 26 March 1898 Saleme GAITANO (Houma Ct. Hse.: Mar. v.30 & 31, #357)
ZABBIO, Salvatore m. 3 Feb. 1897 Benna GENNORA (Houma Ct. Hse.: Mar. v.29 & 30, #277)
ZABIA, Maria (Calazero & Ane LEIANNA) m. 23 April 1898 Salome GUITANO (Houma Ch.: v.6-a, p.240)
ZAGONA, Antonia of Terrebonne Parish m. 24 April 1899 Vita CICIA (Houma Ch.: v.6-B, p.3)

ZAMANI (See: SAMANI)

ZEAL, Elizabeth m. 24 Nov. 1899 Nathan PUGH (Thib. Ct. Hse.: Mar. v.39, #270)
ZEBBIN, Antonino (Guiseppe & Grazia THURTINO) b. 2 Feb. 1899 (Thib. Ch.: v.7, p.537)
ZELAIRE, Ewing or Uhing (Cesar & Desiree LACENE) m. 21 Aug. 1897 Evelie THIBAULT (Thib. Ct. Hse.: Mar. v.37, #208)
ZELAIRE, Joseph Amedeus (Jules & Antonia LOUPE) b. 22 Nov. 1898 (Chackbay Ch.: v.1, p.125)
ZELAIRE, Marie Cleanne (Yinne & Evelie THIBAUD) b. 22 April 1899 (Chackbay Ch.: v.1, p.132)
ZELAIRE, Whine (Cesar & Desiree LACESSE) m. 21 Aug. 1897 Evelie THIBAULT (Chackbay Ch.: v.1, p.47)
ZELENKA, Randolph L. (Louis G. & Georgiana J. REDFORD) m. 1 March 1897 Eva BAZET (Houma Ch.: v.6-a, p.195)
ZELENKA, Rudolfe Louis (Rudolf N. & Eva BAZAT) b. 6 April 1899 (Houma Ch.: v.5, p.243)
ZELENKA, Rudolph L. m. 27 Feb. 1897 Eve BAZET (Houma Ct. Hse.: Mar. v.29 & 30, #335)
ZELENKA, Thelma Louise (Rudolphe & Eva BAZET) b. 28 Jan. 1898 (Houma Ch.: v.5, p.201)
ZELLA, Marie Alcide (Jules & Antonia LOUP) b. 3 Oct. 1896 (Chackbay Ch.: v.1, p.79)

ZERINGUE (Sometimes: ZERING, ZERINGER)

ZERINGUE, Andrew d. 27 July 1898; m. (1) Magdalena LIPPS who died in 1868 Children: Francis Xavier & Josephine m. A. Ovide GUENO. m.(2) Emma ARNOLD Children: Annie P.; George Adolph; Marie Louise; Clara Maude. Tutorship: 10 Feb. 1899. (Houma Ct. Hse.: Succ. #905)
ZERINGUE, Andrew d. 28 July 1898 at age 63 yrs. (Houma Ch.: v.3, p.18)
ZERINGUE, Clemence m. 10 Feb. 1898 Nelson FOLSE (Thib. Ct Hse.: Mar. v.37, #86)
ZERINGUE, Clemence (Anatole & Theolene MELANCON) m. 10 Feb. 1898 Nelson FOLSE (Raceland Ch.: v.2, p.67)

ZERINGUE, Clement m. 17 Jan. 1899 Octavie FOLSE (Thib. Ct. Hse.: Mar. v.38, #26)
ZERINGUE, Clement (Anatole & Teolene MELANCON) m. 24 Jan. 1899 Octavie FOLSE (Raceland Ch.: v.2, p.85)
ZERINGUE, Clementine Marie (Joseph & Celestine MELANCON) b. 31 Jan. 1896 (Thib. Ch.: v.7, p.393)
ZERINGUE, Corinne Agathe (Anatole & Theolene MELANCON) b. 5 Feb. 1899 (Raceland Ch.: v.5, p.92)
ZERINGUE, Eve Blanche (Desire & Armine DIAS) b. 22 March 1899 (Raceland Ch.: v.5, p.94)
ZERINGUE, Jean Oncell (Paulin & Josephine BREAUX) b. 30 Aug. 1897 (Thib. Ch.: v.7, p.513)
ZERINGUE, Josephine m. 21 Feb. 1898 Pierre J. BOURGEOIS (Thib. Ct. Hse.: Mar. v.37, #108)
ZERINGUE, Josephine (Joseph & Celestine MELANCON) m. 21 Feb. 1898 Pierre J. BOURGEOIS (Raceland Ch.: v.2, p.72)
ZERINGUE, Joseph Viltresse (Clement & Octavie FOLSE) b. 16 Dec. 1899 (Raceland Ch.: v.5, p.111)
ZERINGUE, Marie (Eugene & Pauline LEDET) m. 17 Jan. 1898 Thomas CHAMPAGNE (Lockport Ch.: v.2, p.179)
ZERINGUE, Marie (Eugene & Pauline LEDET) m. 17 Jan. 1898 Thomas CHAMPAGNE (Thib. Ct. Hse.: Mar. v.37, #18)
ZERINGUE, Marie Lylienne (Willy & Angele BOURGEOIS) b. 1 Sept. 1898 (Thib. Ch.: v.7, p.511)
ZERINGUE, Noe minor, over 18 yrs. old (P. Gabriel & d.Josephine CHAMPAGNE, her father is Florestan CHAMPAGNE, Sr.) Emancipation: 11 Dec. 1897. (Thib. Ct. Hse.: Succ. #1525)
ZERINGUE, Paul Hamson (Joseph & Florestine MELANCON) b. 5 June 1898 (Raceland Ch.: v.5, p.72)
ZERINGUE, Paul Jean (Anatole & Theoline MELANCON) b. 10 Feb. 1897 (Raceland Ch.: v.5, p.42)
ZERINGUE, Viva Josephine (Francis Havier & Lucy A. DAVIS) b. 3 Oct. 1897 (Houma Ch.: v.5, p.191)
ZILIO, Felice of New Orleans (Filippo & Maria BUONGIOVANI) m. 6 Feb. 1899 Cattarina CALI (Thib. Ct. Hse.: Mar. v.38, #45)
ZILIO, Telice Jr. (Telice Sr. & Maria BUORGIOVANI) m. 16 Feb. 1899 Catarina CALI (Thib. Ch.: v.14, p.255)
ZILTON, Alfred m.27 April 1898 Isabella SIMMONS (Houma Ct. Hse.: Mar. v.30 & 31, #422)
ZINKINS, Ella m. 26 Feb. 1896 James JOHNSON (Houma Ct. Hse.: Mar. v.28, #466)
ZITA, Cecilia m. 21 Jan. 1899 Leoluca CALLURA (Houma Ct. Hse.: Mar. v.30 & 31, #278)
ZITA, Corcilia (Salvatora & Catharine MARCELLE) m. 4 Feb. 1899 Leoluca CALLOVA (Houma Ch.: v.6-a, p.271)

www.ingramcontent.com/pod-product-compliance
Ingram Content Group UK Ltd.
Pitfield, Milton Keynes, MK11 3LW, UK
UKHW020223290926
15470UKWH00001B/340